ANNOTATED LEADING CASES OF

INTERNATIONAL CRIMINAL TRIBUNALS

VOLUME XXXIV:

THE INTERNATIONAL CRIMINAL TRIBUNAL
FOR THE FORMER YUGOSLAVIA
2007

ANNOTATED LEADING CASES OF

INTERNATIONAL CRIMINAL TRIBUNALS

VOLUME XXXIV:

THE INTERNATIONAL CRIMINAL TRIBUNAL
FOR THE FORMER YUGOSLAVIA
2007

André KLIP and Göran SLUITER (eds.)

intersentia

Cambridge – Antwerp – Portland

Intersentia Publishing Ltd.
Trinity House | Cambridge Business Park | Cowley Road
Cambridge | CB4 0WZ | United Kingdom
Tel.: +44 1223 393 753 | Email: mail@intersentia.co.uk

Distribution for the UK:
NBN International
Airport Business Centre, 10 Thornbury Road
Plymouth, PL6 7PP
United Kingdom
Tel.: +44 1752 202 301 | Fax: +44 1752 202 331
Email: orders@nbninternational.com

Distribution for the USA and Canada:
International Specialized Book Services
920 NE 58th Ave. Suite 300
Portland, OR 97213
USA
Tel.: +1 800 944 6190 (toll free)
Tel.: +1 503 287 3093
Email: info@isbs.com

Distribution for Austria:
Neuer Wissenschaftlicher Verlag
Argentinierstraße 42/6
1040 Wien
Austria
Tel.: +43 1 535 61 03 24
Email: office@nwv.at

Distribution for other countries:
Intersentia Publishing nv
Groenstraat 31
2640 Mortsel
Belgium
Tel.: +32 3 680 15 50
Email: mail@intersentia.be

Please cite as: ICTY, Decision on Preliminary Motions on the Indictment Pursuant to Rule 72 of the Rules, *Prosecutor v. Tolimir*, Case No. IT-05-88/2-PT, T. Ch. II, 14 December 2007, Klip/ Sluiter, ALC-XXXIV-29.

Annotated Leading Cases of International Criminal Tribunals
André Klip and Göran Sluiter (eds.)
Cover illustration: Hendrik E. Kluwer

ISBN 978-1-78068-098-9
D/2013/7849/97
NUR 828

British Library Cataloguing in Publication Data. A catalogue record for this book is available from the British Library.

TABLE OF CONTENTS

PREFACE

This is the thirty-fourth volume in the series "Annotated Leading Cases of International Criminal Tribunals" and contains the most important decisions of the International Criminal Tribunal for the former Yugoslavia (ICTY) from 4 April 2007 up to and including 14 December 2007. It is the seventeenth volume containing decisions of the ICTY.

The present volume is in its approach and structure similar to the previous volumes. Thus, the book contains the full text of all the decisions and judgements, including separate, concurring and dissenting opinions, as well as annexes to the decisions. As with the previous volumes, the editors have ensured that the decisions are fully identical to the *written* original text, as issued by the ICTY Press and Information Office and which bears the signatures of the judges. We are aware that more and more decisions are available on the internet. However, only the written decisions bearing the signatures of the judges can be considered as authoritative versions. In the course of our editorial work on this and previous volumes, we have discovered inconsistencies between the written original version of the decision and the internet version, if the latter is available at all. Much of our editorial efforts consist in making the texts in this series identical to the written original version.

We could only include the full text of the decisions in this volume by reducing their original format. Still, we wanted the reader to be able to identify the page number of the original text, which is throughout the text put in brackets [ ]. We are again very happy that a number of scholars in the field of international criminal law were prepared to write interesting and stimulating commentaries regarding the decisions.

A few words regarding the selection of decisions may give the user insight into our working method. In principle, we select all final judgements. In addition, we publish decisions taken at any stage of the procedure that are important for other reasons: because they deal with a specific legal question, because they are representative of a specific type of decision or because they enter new legal waters. Of course, we cannot publish all decisions. As a result, we may not publish decisions in which issues have been decided in a way similar or identical to a decision that has already been selected.

The decisions are presented in different parts and under different headings.

Part 1, "Preliminary matters", contains decisions regarding jurisdiction and the indictment, under headings 1 and 2.

Part 2 deals with procedural matters. Under heading 3, several decisions regarding counsel, self-representation and related issues are included. Heading 4 includes decisions regarding the investigation of equality of arms, effective defence investigations and bringing the accused to trial without undue delay. Decisions on issues regarding witnesses and the admissibility of evidence are included under heading 5. Heading 6 covers four decisions relating to judicial notice and the decisions under heading 7 relate to referral. Under heading 8, a decision regarding contempt of court is included.

Part 3, "Judgements", contains trial and appeal judgements (9) and sentencing judgements (10). As mentioned above, judgements are by definition included in this series, because of their importance, both from a factual and legal perspective.

Part 4 deals with issues regarding post-conviction and post-acquittal, and contains a decision on the request to re-open appeal proceedings (11).

We owe acknowledgements to many people without whom we could not have completed this thirty-fourth volume. These include the Press and Information Office of the ICTY, which offered generous assistance in obtaining all the hard copies of decisions. Our publisher Intersentia, in particular Hans Kluwer, Tom Scheirs and Isabelle van Dongen, facilitated our work. We also acknowledge the work of our student assistants, Anzinga Low (Maastricht), Mariam Pathan (Amsterdam) and Jeroen Gunning (Amsterdam), who assisted with the corrections of the text and without whom we would not be able to publish this series. The Netherlands School of Human Rights Research stimulated our work. Steven Freeland from the University of Western Sydney, Australia, offered tremendous help by correcting our English. Last but not least, we wish to thank the distinguished authors of for their commentaries on the decisions.

We hope that this volume will contribute to the further dissemination of the important work of the ICTY and that it will provide access to its decisions to practitioners, academics and students.

André Klip and Göran Sluiter

Maastricht/ Amsterdam, June 2013

UNITED NATIONS

International Tribunal for the Prosecution of Persons Responsible for Serious Violations of International Humanitarian Law Committed in the Territory of the Former Yugoslavia since 1991	Case No. IT-06-90-AR72.1 Date: 6 June 2007 Original: English

---

IN THE APPEALS CHAMBER

Before: **Judge Fausto Pocar, Presiding**
Judge Mehmet Güney
Judge Liu Daqun
Judge Andrésia Vaz
Judge Wolfgang Schomburg

Registrar: **Mr. Hans Holthuis**

Date : **6 June 2007**

PROSECUTOR

v.

ANTE GOTOVINA
IVAN ČERMAK
MLADEN MARKAČ

Public

DECISION ON ANTE GOTOVINA'S INTERLOCUTORY APPEAL AGAINST DECISION ON SEVERAL MOTIONS CHALLENGING JURISDICTION

The Office of the Prosecutor:
Mr. Alan Tieger
Ms. Laurie Sartorio

Counsel for the Accused:
Mr. Gregory Kehoe, Mr. Luka S. Mišetić and Mr. Payam Akhavan for Ante Gotovina
Mr. Čedo Prodanović and Ms. Jadranka Sloković for Ivan Čermak
Mr. Goran Mikuličić for Mladen Markač

[page 2] 1. **THE APPEALS CHAMBER** of the International Tribunal for the Prosecution of Persons Responsible for Serious Violations of International Humanitarian Law Committed in the Territory of the Former Yugoslavia Since 1991 ("Appeals Chamber" and "International Tribunal", respectively) is seized of an interlocutory appeal filed on 3 April 2007 by Ante Gotovina ("Interlocutory Appeal" and "Appellant", respectively) pursuant to Rule 72(B)(i) of the Rules of Procedure and Evidence of the International Tribunal ("Rules") against Trial Chamber I's "Decision on Several Motions Challenging Jurisdiction" rendered on 19 March 2007 ("Trial Chamber" and "Impugned Decision", respectively).[1] The Appeals Chamber is further seized of a motion filed by the Appellant requesting that he be allowed to bring oral arguments before the Chamber on his Interlocutory Appeal.[2]

I. BACKGROUND

2. On 17 July 2006, the Trial Chamber granted, in part, the Prosecution's motion to amend the indictment against the Appellant and the indictment against Ivan Čermak ("Čermak") and Mladen Markač ("Markač") and granted the Prosecution's request to join the Appellant's case[3] with that of Čermak and Markač[4] pursuant to Rule 48 of the Rules.[5] A joint indictment was subsequently filed by the Prosecution on 24 July 2006.[6] On 25 October 2006, the Appeals Chamber affirmed the Trial Chamber's Decision on Joinder.[7] On 6 March 2007, pursuant to Trial Chamber order,[8] the Prosecution filed a reduced version of the joint indictment pursuant to Rule 73*bis*(D) of the Rules ("Joint Indictment").[9] **[page 3]**

3. In the Joint Indictment, the Appellant is charged with persecutions on political, racial and religious grounds, deportation and forcible transfer, murder and inhumane acts as crimes against humanity under Article 5 of the Statute of the International Tribunal ("Statute") (Counts 1, 2, 3, 6, 8),[10] and plunder of public or private property, wanton destruction of cities, towns or villages, or devastation not justified by military necessity, murder and cruel treatment as violations of the laws or customs of war under Article 3 of the Statute (Counts 4, 5, 7, 9).[11] The crimes enumerated were allegedly committed in or on the territory of the former Yugoslavia and in particular in the Krajina region of the Republic of Croatia, from at least July 1995 to on or about 30 September 1995.[12]

4. The Appellant challenged the jurisdiction of the International Tribunal by way of two preliminary motions filed on 28 April 2006[13] and 18 January 2007[14] ("Preliminary Motions") against the First Joint Indictment, which were dismissed by the Trial Chamber in the Impugned Decision.

---

1 *Prosecutor v. Ante Gotovina et al.*, Case No. IT-06-90-PT, Decision on Several Motions Challenging Jurisdiction, 19 March 2007.

2 Defendant Ante Gotovina's Motion Requesting Oral Argument on the Interlocutory Appeal Challenging Jurisdiction, 20 April 2007 ("Motion for Oral Argument").

3 Case No. IT-01-45-PT.

4 Case No. IT-03-73-PT.

5 *Prosecutor v. Ivan Čermak and Mladen Markač*, Case No. IT-03-73-PT, and *Prosecutor v. Ante Gotovina*, Case No. IT-01-45-PT, Decision on Prosecution's Consolidated Motion to Amend the Indictment and for Joinder, 14 July 2006 ("Decision on Joinder").

6 *Prosecutor v. Ante Gotovina et al.*, Case No. IT-06-90-PT, Joinder Indictment, 24 July 2006 ("First Joint Indictment").

7 *Prosecutor v. Ante Gotovina*, Case No. IT-01-45-AR73.1, and *Prosecutor v. Ivan Čermak and Mladen Markač,* Case Nos. IT-03-73-AR73.1 and IT-03-73-AR73.2, Decision on Interlocutory Appeals against the Trial Chamber's Decision to Amend the Indictment and for Joinder, 25 October 2006.

8 *Prosecutor v. Ante Gotovina et al.*, Case No. IT-06-90-PT, Order Pursuant to Rule 73*bis*(D) to Reduce the Indictment, 21 February 2007, pp. 3–4.

9 *Prosecutor v. Ante Gotovina et al.*, Case No. IT-06-90-PT, Joinder Indictment, 6 March 2007. Although the Impugned Decision was made with respect to challenges to the First Joint Indictment, the Appeals Chamber will consider the most recent modified Joint Indictment when disposing of this Interlocutory Appeal in light of the fact that the provisions at issue are identical in both versions of the Indictment, unless otherwise noted. The Appeals Chamber notes that the Prosecution has filed a further proposed Amended Joinder Indictment before the Trial Chamber on 17 May 2007; however, as of the date of this decision, the proposed indictment is still pending before that Chamber.

10 The Appellant is charged with Article 7(1) and 7(3) responsibility for these crimes.

11 *Id.*

12 Joint Indictment, paras. 37, 55. The First Joint Indictment alleged from at least July 1995 to on or about 15 November 1995. *See* First Joint Indictment, para. 37.

13 *Prosecutor v. Ante Gotovina*, Case No. IT-01-45-PT, Defendant Ante Gotovina's Preliminary Motion to Dismiss the Proposed Joinder Indictment Pursuant to Rule 72 of the Rules of Procedure and Evidence on the basis of (1) Defects in the Form of the Indictment (Vagueness/Lack of Adequate Notice of Charges) and (2) Lack of Subject Matter Jurisdiction (*Ratione Materiae*), 28 April 2006.

14 *Prosecutor v. Ante Gotovina et al.*, Case No. IT-06-90-PT, Defendant Ante Gotovina's Preliminary Motion Challenging Jurisdiction Pursuant to Rule 72(A)(i) of the Rules of Procedure and Evidence, 18 January 2007.

5. In this Interlocutory Appeal, the Appellant raises four grounds of appeal pursuant to Rule 72(D) of the Rules to demonstrate that the Trial Chamber erred in law and in fact in the Impugned Decision. The Appellant submits that it would occasion a miscarriage of justice if the Appeals Chamber failed to reverse the Impugned Decision on these grounds[15] and requests the Appeals Chamber to strike portions of the Joint Indictment as appropriate.[16] The Prosecution responded on 13 April 2007, claiming that the appeal does not raise proper jurisdictional challenges and should therefore be dismissed.[17] The Prosecution further contests each of the four grounds raised by the Appellant.[18] The Appellant replied on 17 April 2007.[19] **[page 4]**

6. On 20 April 2007, the Appellant filed his Motion for Oral Argument with respect to this Interlocutory Appeal and on 24 April 2007, the Prosecution filed a response opposing the Motion.[20]

II. STANDARD OF REVIEW

7. When reviewing a Trial Chamber's decision on jurisdiction under Rule 72(B)(i) of the Rules, the Appeals Chamber will only reverse the decision "if the Trial Chamber committed a specific error of law or fact invalidating the decision or weighed relevant considerations or irrelevant considerations in an unreasonable manner."[21] In reaching its decision, it is incumbent upon a Trial Chamber "to provide a reasoned opinion that, among other things, indicates its view on all those relevant factors that a reasonable Trial Chamber would have been expected to take into account before coming to a decision."[22]

III. DISCUSSION

A. <u>Motion for Oral Hearing</u>

8. As a preliminary matter, the Appeals Chamber is not persuaded by the Appellant's submission in his Motion for Oral Hearing that oral argument on this Interlocutory Appeal "is exceptionally justified because of the far-reaching significance of the questions raised both for General Gotovina's defence as well as the jurisprudence of the Tribunal."[23] The Appeals Chamber has considered the parties' extensive submissions in the written pleadings and finds that they sufficiently appraise the Chamber of the issues to be disposed of in this Interlocutory Appeal such that oral argument is unnecessary for reaching its decision.

B. <u>Interlocutory Appeal</u>

9. Turning to the Interlocutory Appeal, the Appeals Chamber must first consider whether the Appellant raises proper jurisdictional challenges pursuant to Rule 72 of the Rules. The Appeals Chamber recalls that interlocutory appeals on jurisdiction lie as of right **[page 5]** under Rule 72(B)(i) only where they challenge an indictment on the ground that it does not relate to: (i) any of the persons indicated in Articles 1, 6, 7 and 9 of the Statute ("personal jurisdiction"); (ii) the territories indicated in Articles 1, 8 and 9 of the Statute ("territorial jurisdiction"); (iii) the period indicated in Articles 1, 8 and 9 of the Statute ("temporal jurisdiction"); or (iv) any of the violations indicated in Articles 2, 3, 4, 5 and 7 of the Statute ("subject-matter jurisdiction").[24]

---

15 Interlocutory Appeal, paras. 2–5.

16 *Id.*, para. 91.

17 Prosecution Response to Interlocutory Appeal Challenging Jurisdiction, 13 April 2007 ("Response"), paras. 2, 9–16.

18 *Id.*, paras. 3–8, 17–74.

19 Defendant Ante Gotovina's Reply to Prosecution Response to Interlocutory Appeal Challenging Jurisdiction, 17 April 2007 ("Reply").

20 Prosecution Response to Gotovina's Motion for Oral Hearing on Interlocutory Appeal Challenging Jurisdiction, 24 April 2007.

21 *Prosecutor v. Jadranko Prlić et. al*, Case No. IT-04-74-AR72.1, Decision on Petković's Interlocutory Appeal Against the Trial Chamber's Decision on Jurisdiction, 16 November 2005 ("*Prlić et al.* Interlocutory Appeal on Jurisdiction"), para. 11 quoting *Prosecutor v. Slobodan Milošević*, Case No. IT-02-54-AR73.7, Decision on Interlocutory Appeal of the Trial Chamber's Decision on the Assignment of Defense Counsel, 1 November 2004, para. 10.

22 *Prlić et al.* Interlocutory Appeal on Jurisdiction, para. 11, with reference to *Prosecutor v. Milan Milutinović*, Case No. IT-99-37-AR65.3, Decision Refusing Milutinović Leave to Appeal, 3 July 2003, para. 22.

23 Motion for Oral Argument, para. 4.

24 *See* Rule 72(D) of the Rules.

10. The Appellant claims that his four grounds of appeal appropriately challenge the jurisdiction of the International Tribunal because they demonstrate that the Joint Indictment "violates *nullem* [*sic*] *crimen sine lege* by expanding definitions of crimes beyond customary law, which is the basis for the Tribunal's jurisdiction *ratione materiae*."[25] The Prosecution responds by arguing that none of these grounds bring questions of jurisdiction as defined under Rule 72(D) of the International Tribunal's Rules. Rather, "while accepting that the Tribunal has jurisdiction over the violations charged in the Indictment, Gotovina seeks to modify the accepted legal definitions of these crimes, to challenge the sufficiency of the pleading in the Indictment and to attack the sufficiency of the evidence to be adduced at trial."[26] The Appeals Chamber turns to consider each of the Appellant's four grounds to determine whether they in fact qualify as jurisdictional challenges within the meaning of Rule 72(D) of the Rules.

C. First Ground of Appeal: Alleged Error of Law in Relation to Charges of Deportation and Forcible Transfer under Article 5(d) and (i) of the Statute

11. First, the Appellant submits that with respect to Counts 1-3 of the Joint Indictment, the Trial Chamber erred in law by expanding the *actus reus* of deportation and forcible transfer as crimes against humanity under Article 5 of the Statute when it failed to find that there is an "occupied territory" requirement pursuant to Article 49(1) of Geneva Convention IV and Article 17(1) of Protocol II to the Geneva Conventions for these crimes.[27] In his view, the Trial Chamber erred in failing to strike the Prosecution's definition of deportation and forcible transfer in the Joint Indictment to the extent that the charges "encompass alleged conduct of hostilities violations prior to actual control of the 'Krajina' by Croatian forces". He argues such a definition is contrary to customary law, violates the principle of *nullum* **[page 6]** *crimen sine lege* and falls outside of the International Tribunal's subject-matter jurisdiction within the meaning of Rule 72(D)(iv) of the Rules.[28]

12. In support of this ground, the Appellant states that the Trial Chamber erred by holding that in armed conflict, the *actus reus* for these crimes "differs when charged as war crimes rather than crimes against humanity"[29] and in concluding that "the laws of war do not generally form a *lex specialis* to the *actus reus* of crimes against humanity."[30] He argues that the Trial Chamber "disregards the close relationship between the laws of war and crimes against humanity in ICTY jurisprudence, as well as the fundamental customary law distinction between Geneva and Hague Law" and, in so doing, leaves open "the possibility that General Gotovina may prove his innocence under the laws of war but still be found guilty by reclassification of the same conduct as crimes against humanity."[31]

13. The Appellant further notes that under paragraphs 29 and 35 of the Joint Indictment, the allegations therein relate solely to ruses of war or to the conduct of hostilities prior to or during Operation Storm and not to deportation or forcible transfer of persons from territory under the authority of Croatian forces.[32] He argues that because of the "occupied territory requirement" under customary law for these crimes enumerated under Article 5 of the Statute, the Joint Indictment can only charge them "with respect to displacement of persons in 'Krajina' *after* it was placed under Croatian authority and not prior to or during Operation Storm as alleged."[33] The Appellant contends that, as a consequence of the Trial Chamber's "unprecedented view", he must now defend against deportation and forcible transfer charged in Counts 1–3 of the Joint Indictment "based on a novel legal standard that is wholly inconsistent with well—sestablished customary law, conflates Geneva and Hague Law, and leaves open the possibility of his conviction for crimes against humanity even if he can establish his compliance with the laws of war."[34] In addition, he claims that in the absence of a reasoned opinion by the Trial Chamber as to why the "occupied territory" requirement under Article 49(1) of Geneva

25 Reply, paras. 1, 4.
26 Response, para. 11.
27 Interlocutory Appeal, paras. 2, 21–30, 52–72.
28 *Id.*, para. 64.
29 *Id.*, para. 21.
30 *Id.*, para. 37.
31 *Id.*, paras. 21–22,
32 *Id.*, para. 25.
33 *Id.*, para. 28.
34 *Id.*, para. 29.

Convention IV and Article 17(1) of Protocol II to the Geneva Conventions is inapplicable, the Trial Chamber has committed an error of law invalidating its decision."[35] **[page 7]**

14. The Appeals Chamber notes that in the Impugned Decision, the Trial Chamber considered that the Appellant failed to cite any authority in support of his arguments with respect to the definitions of deportation and forcible transfer as crimes against humanity under Article 5 of the Statute.[36] Furthermore, the Trial Chamber noted, with reference to the definitions of the *actus reus* for the crimes of deportation and forcible transfer set out in the *Stakić* Appeals Judgement,[37] that there is nothing in the jurisprudence of the International Tribunal that supports the Appellant's contention that "occupation" is an element for these crimes.[38] On these bases, the Trial Chamber rejected this argument.

15. The Appeals Chamber finds that the Appellant fails to raise a proper jurisdictional challenge pursuant to Rule 72(D)(iv) of the Rules under his first ground of appeal or to demonstrate that the Trial Chamber erred in dismissing his argument as to "occupied territory" being a necessary requirement for the crimes of deportation and forcible transfer as crimes against humanity. Here, the Appellant is not contesting that the International Tribunal has jurisdiction over these crimes under Article 5 of the Statute, which are charged in the Joint Indictment according to their definitions and elements under customary international law as set out in the jurisprudence of the International Tribunal.[39] Rather, he argues that the interpretation of the definition for the *actus reus* of these crimes should be narrow and limited to displacement from occupied territory. As such, the Appellant may bring these arguments before the Trial Chamber to be considered on the merits at trial; however, they do not demonstrate the Tribunal's lack of subject-matter jurisdiction.[40] **[page 8]**

D. Second Ground of Appeal: Alleged Error of Law in Relation to Charges of Cruel Treatment and Inhumane Acts under Articles 3 and 5 of the Statute

16. Under his second ground of appeal, with reference to Counts 8 and 9 of the Joint Indictment, which allege inhumane acts as a crime against humanity under Article 5 of the Statute and cruel treatment as a violation of the laws or customs of war under Article 3 of the Statute respectively, the Appellant contends that the Trial Chamber erred in law in failing to find that for crimes based on Common Article 3 of the Geneva Conventions, there is a requirement that such acts be perpetrated against "persons in the power of a party to the conflict".[41] The Appellant notes that one of the fundamental requirements for grave breaches provisions under Article 2 of the Statute is that "protected persons" be "in the hands of" a party to the conflict.[42] He relies upon the Appeals Judgement in the *Čelebići* case[43] to claim that the element of "persons taking no active part in the hostilities" found in Common Article 3 "may be assimilated to persons in the hands of a party to the conflict who are not protected persons *stricto sensu*" under Article 4 of Geneva Convention IV because the "broader rules of international conflict in the Convention clearly exclude conduct of hostilities violations [and] it follows that the narrower scope of Common Article 3 cannot encompass Hague Law Violations."[44] In his view, the Appeals Chamber in *Čelebići* clearly indicated that "persons taking no active part in the hostilities

---

35 *Id.*, para. 22.

36 Impugned Decision, para. 54.

37 *Prosecutor v. Milomir Stakić*, Case No. IT-97-A, Judgement, 22 March 2006 ("*Stakić* Appeals Judgement").

38 Impugned Decision, para. 55 citing the *Stakić* Appeals Judgement, paras. 278, 317.

39 *See Stakić* Appeals Judgement, paras. 278–303, 317.

40 *See Prlić et al.* Decision on Jurisdiction, para. 13, which states:

> In his Appeal, the Appellant says that he accepts that the crimes charged and the modes of liability alleged in the Indictment do fall within the jurisdiction of the Tribunal but questions whether they 'nevertheless could be misdefined and misapplied in the particular Indictment and thus transform into some other crimes and/or forms of liability falling outside the Tribunal's jurisdiction'. The Appellant's complaint therefore is not whether the Tribunal has jurisdiction over the crimes and modes of liability alleged [...].

See also Prosecutor v. Delalić et al., Case No. IT-96-21-AR72.5, Decision on Application for Leave to Appeal by Hazim Delić (Defects in the Form of the Indictment), 6 December 1996 at para. 27 ("*Delalić et al.* Decision") (holding that "Articles 2, 3, 4 and 5 of the Statute are shorthand for the corresponding norms of international humanitarian law, and if there is any dispute as to those norms, that is a matter for trial not for pre-trial objections to the form of the Indictment.").

41 Interlocutory Appeal, paras. 73, 77.

42 *Id.*, para. 75.

43 *Prosecutor v. Zejnil Delalić et al.*, Case No. IT-96-21-A, Judgement, 20 February 2001 ("*Čelebići* Appeals Judgement").

44 Interlocutory Appeal, para. 75.

under Common Article 3 are the substantial equivalent of protected persons under Article 2."[45] Therefore, according to the Appellant, the Trial Chamber erroneously held that "Article 3 common to the 1949 Geneva Conventions in Counts 8-9 may encompass conduct of hostilities violations under Hague Law, in violation of customary law and the *nullum crimen sine lege* principle, and thus falling outside the Tribunal's jurisdiction *ratione materiae* under Rule 72(D)(iv)."[46]

17. In the Impugned Decision, the Trial Chamber noted that under established jurisprudence, for alleged cruel treatment based on Common Article 3 to the Geneva Conventions, "the only requirement concerning the status of the victims is that they were taking no active part in the hostilities at the time the crime was committed."[47] The Trial Chamber also noted that in the International Tribunal's jurisprudence on cumulative convictions found in the *Čelebići* Appeals Judgement, it was held that cruel treatment under **[page 9]** Article 3 of the Statute does not contain an element found in the Article 2 crimes of "wilfully causing great suffering or serious injury to body or health" and "inhuman treatment"—the protected persons status of the victim.[48] Finally, the Trial Chamber considered that in the jurisprudence of the International Tribunal, Article 3 violations have been applied to persons not in the hands of the perpetrators and, on these bases, rejected the Appellant's claim that violations charged under Common Article 3 of the Geneva Conventions apply only with respect to victims shown to have been in the power of a party to the conflict.[49]

18. The Appeals Chamber considers that the Appellant's second ground of appeal fails to raise a proper jurisdictional challenge under Rule 72(D)(iv) of the Rules. The Appellant does not dispute that the International Tribunal has jurisdiction over crimes charged under Articles 3 and 5 of the Statute as violations of Common Article 3 of the Geneva Conventions. Furthermore, he does not dispute that "committed against persons taking no active part in the hostilities" is a proper element of such crimes under customary international law. Rather, he contests the definition of that element and argues that the jurisprudence of the International Tribunal demonstrates that it should be interpreted narrowly to require that such persons be shown to be in the hands of a party to the conflict akin to the "protected person" element for crimes alleged to be grave breaches of the Geneva Conventions under Article 2 of the Statute. Such arguments are properly raised on the merits at trial[50] and do not demonstrate that the International Tribunal lacks subject-matter jurisdiction over the crimes and the elements of those crimes under Counts 8 and 9 of the Joint Indictment. Therefore, the Appellant's second ground of appeal is dismissed.

E. Third Ground of Appeal: Alleged Error of Fact in Failing to Hold that the Joint Indictment Pleads *Debellatio* on 7 August 1995

19. The Appellant's third ground of appeal alleges that the Trial Chamber erred by failing to weigh considerations in a reasonable manner when it declined to find that the facts as pleaded in the Indictment constitute *debellatio* or "the end of an armed conflict which results **[page 10]** in the occupation of the whole of the enemy's territory and the cessation of all hostilities" on 7 August 1995.[51] The Appellant submits that, as a consequence, the Trial Chamber erred in failing to hold that "all alleged conduct after that date falls outside the Tribunal's jurisdiction *ratione materiae*" within the meaning of Rule 72(D)(iv) of the Rules.[52]

20. In the Impugned Decision, the Trial Chamber noted that paragraph 28 of the Joint Indictment alleges that Operation Storm was "successfully completed" on 7 August 1995 with follow-up actions continuing

45 *Id.*, para. 76 (internal quote marks omitted).
46 *Id.*, para. 78.
47 Impugned Decision, para. 80.
48 *Id.*, para. 81.
49 *Id.*, paras. 82, 83.
50 *Cf. Delalić et al.* Decision at para. 27 (holding that "Articles 2, 3, 4 and 5 of the Statute are shorthand for the corresponding norms of international humanitarian law, and if there is any dispute as to those norms, that is a matter for trial not for pre-trial objections to the form of the Indictment."). *See e.g., Prosecutor v. Anto Furundžija,* Case No. IT-05-17/1-T, Judgement, 10 December 1998 at paras. 172–186 ("*Furundžija* Trial Judgement") (wherein the Trial Chamber further defines the elements of rape as a crime against humanity under Article 5(g) of the Statute as found in customary international law and broadens its definition*); Prosecutor v. Dragoljub Kunarac et al.*, Case Nos. IT-96-23-T & IT-96-23/1-T, Judgement, 22 February 2001 at paras. 436–460 (expanding upon the definition of the element "by coercion or force or threat of force against the victim or a third person" for rape as a crime against humanity under Article 5(g) of the Statute as established in the *Furundžija* Trial Judgement).
51 Interlocutory Appeal, paras. 79, 81, 84.
52 *Id.*, para. 84.

until 15 November 1995. It further noted that paragraph 33 of the Joint Indictment states that after "minimal" SVK resistance had been "overcome" an ethnic cleansing campaign was implemented.[53] The Trial Chamber declined to address the Appellant's contentions that these provisions are inconsistent with paragraph 56 of the Joint Indictment, which alleges that a state of armed conflict existed at all times with respect to the crimes alleged therein, and that the International Tribunal lacks jurisdiction over the acts allegedly committed after the end of Operation Storm.[54] Rather, the Trial Chamber rejected the Appellant's arguments on grounds that they go to the question of when the armed conflict ceased to exist, which is a factual issue to be determined at trial.[55]

21. The Appeals Chamber finds that the Appellant's third ground of appeal fails to raise a proper jurisdictional objection within the meaning of Rule 72(D)(iv) of the Rules and to demonstrate that the Trial Chamber erred in rejecting it. Clearly, the Joint Indictment provides that a state of armed conflict existed at all times with respect to the violations of international humanitarian law alleged therein. Whether an armed conflict actually existed post-Operation Storm is a factual determination to be made at trial. It was well within the discretion of the Trial Chamber to consider that determining this issue pre-trial is premature and can only be decided upon hearing and weighing all of the evidence.[56] To the extent that the Appellant claims that the provisions of the Joint Indictment on this issue are inconsistent or do "not plead any facts supporting the existence of an armed conflict after Operation **[page 11]** Storm",[57] these arguments may constitute allegations of defects in the form of the indictment, which may be challenged under Rule 72(A)(ii) of the Rules.[58] Therefore, on these bases, the Appellant's third ground of appeal is dismissed.

F. Fourth Ground of Appeal: Alleged Error of Law in Relation to the *Mens Rea* of Third Category Joint Criminal Enterprise

22. Finally, under his fourth ground of appeal, the Appellant claims that the Trial Chamber erred in law when it confirmed that the applicable *mens rea* for third category or the extended form of joint criminal enterprise ("JCE") liability is *dolus eventualis* but failed to strike references to "possible consequence" in paragraphs 12 and 43 of the Joint Indictment.[59] The Appellant contends that "[t]he Trial Chamber did not base its decision on a reasonable interpretation of *Tadić*" which does not incorporate the "possible consequence" threshold but rather requires that for crimes committed that were not within the purpose of the JCE, they must have been a "predictable consequence" of the JCE.[60] According to the Appellant, this "lower threshold substantively expands the scope of JCE in violation of the *nullem* [*sic*] *crimen sine lege* and *nullem* [*sic*] *crimen sine culpa* principles and thus falls outside the Tribunal's jurisdiction within the ambit of Rule 72(D)(i)."[61]

23. The Trial Chamber noted in the Impugned Decision that it is clearly established in the jurisprudence of the International Tribunal that JCE is a mode of liability over which the International Tribunal has jurisdiction.[62] It then considered that the phrase "this possible consequence" in paragraph 43 of the Joint Indictment, when read in the context of the paragraph as a whole, clearly referred to the "natural and foreseeable consequences" part of JCE liability and falls squarely within the definition of JCE as set out in *Tadić* and subsequent judgements.[63] It therefore concluded that, contrary to the Appellant's claim, the elements of JCE as set out in

---

53 Impugned Decision, para. 67.

54 *Id.*

55 *Id.*, para. 75 and fn. 117. *See also* paras. 29, 42.

56 *See Prosecutor v. Ljube Boškoski and Johan Tarčulovski,* Case No. IT-04-82-AR72.1, Decision on Interlocutory Appeal on Jurisdiction, 22 July 2005, paras. 11–13. *Cf. Prosecutor v. Rasim Delić*, Case No. IT-04-83-AR72, Decision on Interlocutory Appeal Challenging the Jurisdiction of the Tribunal, 8 December 2005, para. 11(holding that "[t]o the extent that the Appellant's argument concerns not the sufficiency of the indictment, but the sufficiency of the supporting evidence, the Appeals Chamber agrees with the Trial Chamber that this is an issue to be resolved at trial."); *Prosecutor v. Vojislav Šešelj,* Case No. IT-03-67-AR72.1, Decision on the Interlocutory Appeal Concerning Jurisdiction, 31 August 2004, para. 14 (holding that whether the Prosecution can establish a connection between alleged Article 5 crimes in Vojvodina and an armed conflict in Croatia and/or Bosnia and Herzegovina is a question of fact to be determined at trial).

57 Reply, para. 11.

58 *Cf. Prlić et al.* Decision on Jurisdiction, para. 13.

59 Interlocutory Appeal, para. 85.

60 *Id.*, para. 88.

61 *Id.*, para. 90.

62 Impugned Decision, para. 20 & fn. 19.

63 *Id.*, para. 22.

the Joint Indictment, including the subjective element for third category JCE, fall within the accepted ambit of Article 7(1) of the Statute as set out in the settled jurisprudence of the Tribunal.[64] Furthermore, the Trial Chamber held that the **[page 12]** Appellant's arguments with respect "to the contours of this mode of liability belong to the sphere of arguments on the merits and should be raised at that stage."[65]

24. The Appeals Chamber considers that the Appellant fails to demonstrate that his fourth ground of appeal raises a proper jurisdictional objection pursuant to Rule 72(D)(i) of the Rules. Here, the Appellant does not contest the International Tribunal's jurisdiction over JCE as a mode of liability under Article 7(1) of the Statute, which, as the Trial Chamber noted, is clearly established in the jurisprudence of the International Tribunal.[66] In the Joint Indictment, the Prosecution alleges JCE and its elements, as they are set out in the Tribunal's jurisprudence, and the Appellant merely challenges the definition and interpretation of a particular element as established in cases subsequent to the *Tadić* Appeals Judgement.[67] The Appeals Chamber agrees with the Trial Chamber that such a challenge is to be considered on the merits at trial.[68] To the extent that the Appellant submits that the Prosecution has failed to plead an element of this mode of liability properly, such an argument goes to pleading practice and the form of the indictment and is not a challenge to jurisdiction.[69] Accordingly, the Appellant's fourth ground of appeal is dismissed.

IV. DISPOSITION

25. On the basis of the foregoing, this Interlocutory Appeal and the Motion for Oral Hearing are **DISMISSED**.

[page 13] Done in English and French, the English text being authoritative.

Dated this 6th day of June 2007,
At The Hague,
The Netherlands.

Judge Fausto Pocar
Presiding Judge

[Seal of the International Tribunal]

64 *Id.*

65 *Id.*

66 *See* Impugned Decision, fn. 19.

67 *See Prosecutor v. Duško Tadić,* Case No. IT-94-1-A, Judgement, 15 July 1999 at para. 204 (using the phrase "predictable consequence"). *But see Prosecutor v. Mitar Vasiljević*, Case No. IT-98-32-A, Judgement, 25 February 2004 at para. 101 (using the phrases "might be" and "possible consequence"); *Prosecutor v. Tihomir Blaškić*, Case No. IT-95-14-A, Judgement, 29 July 2004 at para. 33 ("*Blaškić* Appeals Judgement") (referring to "possible consequence"); and *Prosecutor v. Milomir Stakić*, Case No. IT-97-24-A, Judgement, 22 March 2006 at paras. 65, 87 (referring to "might be perpetrated" and "possible consequence").

68 *See* Impugned Decision, para. 22 & fn. 25 citing to *Prosecutor v. Milan Milutinović et al.,* Case No. IT-05-87-PT, Decision on Ojdanić's Motion Challenging Jurisdiction: Indirect Co-Perpetration, 22 March 2006, para. 23 ("[l]ike challenges concerning the contours of a substantive crime, challenges concerning the contours of a form of responsibility are matters to be addressed at trial."). The Trial Chamber also cited to the *Blaškić* Appeals Judgement at paras. 34–42 wherein the Appeals Chamber considered whether the Trial Chamber's articulations of the definition for the mental element of "ordering" pursuant to Article 7(1) of the Statute were in error.

69 *See Prlić et al.* Decision on Jurisdiction, para. 13, which states:

> In his Appeal, the Appellant says that he accepts that the crimes charged and the modes of liability alleged in the Indictment do fall within the jurisdiction of the Tribunal but questions whether they 'nevertheless could be misdefined and misapplied in the particular Indictment and thus transform into some other crimes and/or forms of liability falling outside the Tribunal's jurisdiction'. The Appellant's complaint therefore is not whether the Tribunal has jurisdiction over the crimes and modes of liability alleged, but whether the Prosecution has pleaded those crimes and modes of liability properly. The Trial Chamber did not err in determining that this argument was addressed in its Decision on Defence Motions on the Form of the Indictment. Accordingly, the Trial Chamber was not required to address this argument in the Impugned Decision. (Footnotes omitted).

UNITED NATIONS

International Tribunal for the Prosecution of Persons Responsible for Serious Violations of International Humanitarian Law Committed in the Territory of Former Yugoslavia since 1991	Case No. IT-05-87/1-PT Date: 06 December 2007 Original: English

IN THE TRIAL CHAMBER

Before: **Judge Patrick Robinson, Presiding**
Judge Tsvetana Kamenova
Judge Frederik Harhoff, Pre-Trial Judge

Registrar: **Mr. Hans Holthuis**

Decision of: **6 December 2007**

THE PROSECUTOR

v.

VLASTIMIR ĐORĐEVIĆ

PUBLIC

DECISION ON VLASTIMIR ĐORĐEVIĆ'S PRELIMINARY MOTION ON JURISDICTION

Office of the Prosecutor
Mr. Thomas Hannis
Mr. Chester Stamp

Counsel for the Accused
Mr. Dragoljub Đorđević
Mr. Veljko Đurđić

[page 2] THIS TRIAL CHAMBER of the International Tribunal for the Prosecution of Persons Responsible for Serious Violations of International Humanitarian Law Committed in the Territory of the former Yugoslavia since 1991 ("Tribunal") is seised of "Vlastimir Đorđević's Preliminary Motion Challenging Jurisdiction", filed 19 October 2007 ("Motion"), and hereby issues this decision thereon.

A. Preliminary Motion

1. On 19 October 2007, the Defence filed its Motion challenging the Tribunal's territorial and temporal jurisdiction over the crimes alleged in the Indictment and requested that the Trial Chamber "dismiss the Indictment on the grounds that the ICTY lacks temporal and territorial jurisdiction to prosecute the Accused."[1]

2. With respect to the temporal jurisdiction of the Tribunal, *ratione temporis*, the Defence asserts that Security Council Resolution 827 established the temporal jurisdiction of the Tribunal from 1 January 1991 through a date to be determined by the Security Council upon the restoration of peace in the territory of the former Yugoslavia.[2] The Defence contends that the Dayton-Paris Agreement, signed 14 December 1995, marked the final establishment of peace.[3] Therefore, the Defence submits that the Dayton-Paris Agreement ended the competence of the Tribunal to prosecute persons responsible for serious violations of international humanitarian law committed on the territory of the former Yugoslavia since 1991, but not after 14 December 1995.[4] The Indictment charges the Accused with crimes beginning on or about 1 January 1999 and continuing until 20 June 1999.[5] Therefore, the Defence contends that the Indictment charges the Accused with crimes that occurred outside the scope of the Tribunal's temporal jurisdiction.[6]

3. The Defence also challenges the Tribunal's territorial jurisdiction, *ratione loci*, arguing that it ended with the termination of the existence of the former Socialist Federal Republic of Yugoslavia (SFRY) and the establishment of the successor states.[7] To reach this conclusion, the Defence argues that, by 1999, the former SFRY no longer existed, having been replaced by five new, internationally-recognised states, including the Federal Republic of Yugoslavia (FRY), within **[page 3]** which existed the Republic of Serbia and the province of Kosovo, and that these independent states are not subject to the Tribunal's jurisdiction.[8] The Defence claims that for the Tribunal to properly exercise jurisdiction over crimes committed on the territory of Kosovo in 1999, a new decision from the Security Council would have to be passed in order to amend the articles providing for the competence *ratione loci* of the Tribunal.[9] Accordingly, the Defence requests that the Trial Chamber dismiss the Indictment on the grounds that the Tribunal lacks temporal and territorial jurisdiction to prosecute the Accused.[10]

B. Prosecution's Response

4. On 1 November 2007, the Prosecution filed its response to the Motion, submitting that the Motion should be dismissed because "(a) the Appeals Chamber has confirmed the Tribunal's temporal jurisdiction for the Indictment period and its territorial jurisdiction over Kosovo; and (b) the Defence failed to establish that the Tribunal's temporal jurisdiction ended after the signing of the Dayton-Paris Agreement on 14 December 1995."[11]

5. Regarding temporal jurisdiction, the Prosecution asserts that the Tribunal's temporal jurisdiction for the Indictment Period is a matter of settled law.[12] The Prosecution first points to Article 8 (Territorial and Temporal Jurisdiction) of the Tribunal Statute, which provides that the temporal jurisdiction of the Tribunal begins in

---

1 Vlastimir Đorđević's Preliminary Motion Challenging Jurisdiction, 19 October 2007 ("Motion"), para. 20.
2 Motion, para. 7, citing Resolution 827 (1993) (adopted 25 May 1993), para. 2.
3 Motion, para. 8.
4 Motion, paras. 8–10.
5 Third Amended Joinder Indictment, IT-05-87/1, 21 June 2006, counts 1-5.
6 Motion, paras. 1, 10.
7 Motion, para. 15.
8 Motion, para. 13.
9 Motion, para. 18.
10 Motion, para. 20.
11 Prosecution's Response to Vlastimir Đorđević's Preliminary Motion Challenging Jurisdiction, 1 November 2007 ("Response"), para. 3.
12 Response, para. 6.

1991.[13] The Prosecution further notes that pursuant to Resolution 827, the Security Council is to determine the termination of the Tribunal's temporal jurisdiction.[14] Because the Security Council has not made this determination, the Prosecution asserts that the Indictment period clearly falls within the scope of the Tribunal Statute.[15]

6. In addition, the Prosecution contends that both Trial Chamber and Appeals Chamber decisions have affirmed the Tribunal's temporal jurisdiction for the Indictment Period.[16] The Prosecution notes that in the *Ojdanić* Jurisdiction Decision, the Trial Chamber held that Resolution 827 was both retroactive and prospective in that it related to crimes committed after 1991 and covered the **[page 4]** period before and after the adoption of the Statute establishing the Tribunal in 1993.[17] The Prosecution further cites the *Ojdanić* Jurisdiction Decision, in which the Trial Chamber noted that it would be odd if the Security Council's authority in 1991, 1992 and 1993 was lost in 1999 (when the alleged crimes in *Ojdanić* were committed), since the 1999 crimes were part of the same conflict with which the Council was dealing.[18] Similarly, in its decision joining the three indictments in *Slobodan Milošević*, the Appeals Chamber found that the acts alleged in the indictments were part of the same transaction, notwithstanding the fact that the transaction "was put into effect from time to time and over a period of time."[19] Finally, relying on the *Ojdanić* Jurisdiction Decision, the Prosecution submits that the temporal jurisdiction of the Tribunal was left open-ended because the Security Council foresaw the continuation of the conflict.[20]

7. In relation to territorial jurisdiction, the Prosecution asserts that both statutory authority and the Tribunal's jurisprudence support a finding of jurisdiction involving crimes committed in Kosovo.[21] Specifically, the Prosecution notes that the Appeals Chamber in the *Ojdanić* Jurisdiction Decision held that pursuant to Article I of the Tribunal Statute (Competence of the International Tribunal), Kosovo is and was at the relevant time, a part of the territory of the former SFRY.[22] Additionally, the Prosecution notes that the *Ojdanić* Trial Chamber relied upon on Article 8 of the Tribunal Statute (Territorial and Temporal Jurisdiction), in finding that the Tribunal's jurisdiction extended to the territory of the former SFRY.[23] Furthermore, the Prosecution points to several cases in which the Tribunal has conferred jurisdiction for crimes committed in the territory of Kosovo, including the *Slobodan Milošević*, *Milutinović*, *Limaj*, and *Haradinaj* cases.[24]

8. The Prosecution also argues that, contrary to the position of the Defence, peace was not established in Kosovo after the signing of the Dayton-Paris Agreement on 14 December 1995.[25] In support of this contention, the Prosecution relies upon Security Council Resolution 1199 (1998), which states that the situation in Kosovo represented an armed conflict within the terms of the **[page 5]** mandate of the Tribunal. In a February 2001 Report, the Secretary General states that decisions of the Security Council make it clear that it "does not consider peace to have been restored to the region".[26] The Prosecution further submits that the Trial Chamber in *Slobodan Milošević* found that the conflict in Kosovo occurred in the former SFRY well after the Dayton Peace Accords and the Trial Chamber in *Limaj* found that an armed conflict existed in Kosovo well after 1998.[27] Accordingly, the Prosecution contends that the Tribunal has both temporal and territorial jurisdiction to prosecute the Accused and requests that the Trial Chamber dismiss the Motion.[28]

---

13 Response, para. 6.
14 Response, para. 6.
15 Response, para. 6.
16 Response, para. 7.
17 Response, para. 7, citing *Prosecutor v. Milutinović, Šainović and Ojdanić*, Case IT-99-37-PT, Decision on Motion Challenging Jurisdiction, 6 May 2003 ("*Ojdanić* Jurisdiction Decision"), para. 46.
18 Response, para. 7, citing *Ojdanić* Jurisdiction Decision, para. 46.
19 Response, para. 7, citing *Prosecutor v. Slobodan Milošević*, Case No. IT-99-37-AR73, IT-01-50-AR73, IT-01-51-AR73, Reasons for Decision on Prosecution Interlocutory Appeal from Refusal to Order Joinder, 18 April 2002, para. 19–21.
20 Response, para. 7, citing *Ojdanić* Jurisdiction Decision, para. 61.
21 Response, para. 8.
22 Response, para. 8, citing *Prosecutor v. Milutinović, Šainović and Ojdanić*, Case No. IT-99-37-AR72.2, Reasons for Decision Dismissing Interlocutory Appeal Concerning Jurisdiction over the Territory of Kosovo ("*Ojdanić* Decision Dismissing the Jurisdictional Appeal"), 8 June 2004, page 4.
23 Response, para. 9, citing *Ojdanić* Jurisdiction Decision, para. 47.
24 Response, para. 10.
25 Response, paras. 12–15.
26 Response, para. 14.
27 Response, paras. 14–15.
28 Response, para. 17.

C. Deliberation

9. Article 1 of the Statute of the Tribunal ("Statute") provides that the Tribunal "shall have the power to prosecute persons responsible for serious violations of international humanitarian law committed on the territory of the former Yugoslavia since 1991". Article 8 states that "[t]he territorial jurisdiction of the ... Tribunal shall extend to the territory of the former [SFRY]" and that its "temporal jurisdiction ... shall extend to a period beginning on 1 January 1991". Article 8 is read consistently with Security Council Resolution 827, wherein the Security Council adopted the Statute of the Tribunal. Resolution 827 provides that the Security Council:

> Decides hereby to establish an international tribunal for the sole purpose of prosecuting persons responsible for serious violations of international humanitarian law committed in the territory of the former Yugoslavia between 1 January 1991 and a date to be determined by the Security Council upon the restoration of peace and to this end to adopt the Statute of the International Tribunal . . . .[29]

As the Statute and Resolution 827 make clear, an end-date for the Tribunal's jurisdiction has not yet been determined by the Security Council.

10. With respect to temporal jurisdiction, the Trial Chamber considers it settled jurisprudence that the jurisdiction of the Tribunal extends past 14 December 1995. In the past, Chambers confronted with this issue have construed the absence of a termination date determined by the Security Council to mean that the Tribunal's temporal jurisdiction is open-ended.[30] The Appeals Chamber in *Boškoski* affirmed that the Tribunal's temporal jurisdiction extended to allegations of serious violations of international law occurring as recently as after 2001.[31] The Trial Chamber in **[page 6]** *Ojdanić* remarked upon the unusual result that would occur if the Security Council's authority in 1991, 1992 and 1993 was somehow lost in 1999 – particularly where the later crimes were part of the same conflict with which the Council was dealing.[32] Accordingly, the Trial Chamber in *Ojdanić* observed that the Tribunal's temporal jurisdiction was left open-ended because the Security Council foresaw the continuation of the conflict."[33]

11. With respect to territorial jurisdiction, the Trial Chamber considers that the jurisprudence of the Tribunal unequivocally extends jurisdiction to the territory of Kosovo. In *Boškoski*, the Appeals Chamber held that the Statute "extends the Tribunal's jurisdiction to those entities that were a part of the former Yugoslavia prior to its dissolution".[34] More specifically, the Appeals Chamber has confirmed that Kosovo is, and was, at the relevant time, a part of the territory of the former Yugoslavia, and that, pursuant to the Article 1 of the Statute, the Tribunal has jurisdiction for crimes allegedly committed in the territory of Kosovo.[35] In the *Ojdanić* Jurisdiction Decision, the Trial Chamber found that the jurisdiction of the Tribunal is applicable to any country that was a part of the former SFRY, irrespective, *inter alia*, of its United Nations membership at the time of the commission of the crime.[36] In this same vein, this Trial Chamber rejects the notion that the existence of new, internationally-recognised states in 1995 would preclude the Tribunal from exercising jurisdiction over the territory that was formerly part of the SFRY.

12. Finally, the Chamber notes cases where the Tribunal has exercised jurisdiction for alleged crimes committed in Kosovo after 1995, such as *Limaj* and *Haradinaj*.[37] The Chamber further notes that while neither *Prosecutor v. Slobodan Milošević* nor *Prosecutor v. Milutinović et al.*, share the appellate disposition of *Limaj*, they do share identical temporal and territorial jurisdiction with the instant case. These facts

---

29 U.N. Doc. S/RES/827 (1993), para. 2 (emphasis in original).

30 *Prosecutor v. Boškoski*, Case No. IT-04-82-AR72.1, Decision on Interlocutory Appeal on Jurisdiction, 22 July 2005, para. 10; *Ojdanić* Jurisdiction Decision, para. 61.

31 *Prosecutor v. Boškoski*, Case No. IT-04-82-AR72.1, Decision on Interlocutory Appeal on Jurisdiction, 22 July 2005, para. 10.

32 *Ojdanić* Jurisdiction Decision, para. 61.

33 *Ojdanić* Jurisdiction Decision, para. 61.

34 *Prosecutor v. Boškoski*, Case No. IT-04-82-AR72.1, Decision on Interlocutory Appeal on Jurisdiction, 22 July 2005, para. 10.

35 *Prosecutor v. Milutinović, Šainović, and Ojdanić*, Case No. IT-99-37-AR72.2, Reasons for Decision Dismissing Interlocutory Appeal Concerning Jurisdiction over the Territory of Kosovo, 8 June 2004, p. 4.

36 *Ojdanić* Jurisdiction Decision, para. 62.

37 The Chamber considers that, in *Prosecutor v. Limaj et al.*, Case No. IT-03-66-T, and *Prosecutor v. Haradinaj et al.*, Case No. IT-03-66-T, the Tribunal has exercised jurisdiction for crimes committed in the territory of Kosovo in 1998.

and jurisprudence support the Trial Chamber's conclusion that the Tribunal possesses both temporal and territorial jurisdiction over the alleged crimes committed in Kosovo in 1999. **[page 7]**

D. Disposition

For the reasons stated above,

The Trial Chamber, pursuant to Articles 1 and 8 of the Statute and Rule 72 of the Rules of Procedure and Evidence of the Tribunal, **HEREBY DENIES** the Motion.

Done in English and French, the English text being authoritative.

Dated this sixth day of December 2007
At The Hague
The Netherlands

Judge Patrick Robinson
Presiding

[Seal of the Tribunal]

Commentary

1. Introduction

In both of the cases under discussion in this article,[1] the right of the ICTY to exercise its jurisdiction over the defendants was challenged. In the first, the debate is as to whether the legal basis of crimes against humanity has been sufficiently developed, and whether the charge can truly stand as separate and distinct from the law of war crimes. In the second case, the issue has more to do with direct statutory interpretation of the ICTY Statute – where and when can the temporal and territorial jurisdiction of the ICTY be definitively said to lie?

Both appeals were brought under Rule 72 of the International Criminal Tribunal for the former Yugoslavia (ICTY) Rules of Procedure and Evidence (RPE), by which any defendant has the right to challenge, by motion, the jurisdiction of the tribunal.[2] All challenges were dismissed.

2. The Gotovina decision of 6 June 2007[3]

The key question in the Gotovina decision is that of the distinction between crimes against humanity and war crimes. The regularity with which defence counsel queried this area of law suggests that it is one which even those who practice international criminal law find murky and unclear. The issue was raised throughout the appeal process: from initial submission through to final appeal.

The crux of the defence's argument is simply that one set of facts is cited in the indictment, and that these facts are then used as a basis for charges of both war crimes and crimes against humanity. The defence therefore states that it is unfair for the court to demand that the same set of facts be defended against on two levels: on the one hand as war crimes, and again entirely separately as crimes against humanity.[4] Throughout the case, defence counsel objects to what it describes as a conflation of Geneva Law, Hague Law, and international customary law[5]. The court's answer to this is relatively (perhaps overly) straightforward. The view expressed by the Trial Chamber (and later endorsed by the Appeal Chamber itself), is that the distinction is established by public international law,[6] and that as a matter of long precedent that court has the power to try these offences using the same fact pattern.[7]

What exactly are these precedents that the court calls upon? There are two which form the foundation of court's decision. On the one hand, we have an ICJ decision (dating from 1996,[8] three years after the ICTY's establishment), and on the other several case precedents, all of which rely strongly on the guidelines set out by the Tadić jurisdiction decision.[9] While cases such as Kordić[10] and Stakić[11] are strong proponents of the principle of double prosecution of offences as both war crimes and crime against humanity, where does this principle actually come from? And what precisely is the distinction?

In Tadić, the case for prosecuting crimes against humanity (as distinct from war crimes) was strongly

---

1 ICTY, Decision on Ante Gotovina's Interlocutory Appeal Against Decision on Several Motions Challenging Jurisdiction, *Prosecutor v. Gotovina et al.*, Case No. IT-06-90-AR72.1, A. Ch., 6 June 2007, in this volume, p. 11; ICTY, Decision of Vlastimir Đorđević's Preliminary Motion on Jurisdiction, *Prosecutor v. Đorđević*, Case No. IT-05-87/1-PT, T. Ch. III, 6 December 2007, in this volume, p. 19.

2 Rules of Procedure and Evidence of the International Criminal Tribunal for the former Yugoslavia.

3 Decision on Ante Gotovina's Interlocutory Appeal Against Decision on Several Motions Challenging Jurisdiction, *Prosecutor v. Gotovina et al.*, Case No. IT-06-90-AR72.1, A. Ch., *supra* note 1.

4 *Ibid.*, par.12.

5 *Ibid.*, par.12.

6 ICTY, Decision on the Defence Motion on Jurisdiction, *Prosecutor v. Tadić*, Case No. IT-94-1-T, T. Ch. II, 10 August 1995, Klip/ Sluiter, ALC-I-13, par. 24–28.

7 *Ibid.*, par. 26.

8 ICJ, Advisory Opinion on the legality of the threat of Nuclear Weapons, 8 July 1996, par. 25.

9 ICTY, Decision on the Defence Motion for Interlocutory Appeal on Jurisdiction, *Prosecutor v. Tadić*, Case No. IT-94-1-AR72, A. Ch., 2 October 1995, Klip/ Sluiter, ALC-I-33.

10 Judgement, *Prosecutor v. Kordić and Čerkez*, Case No. IT-95-14/2-A, A. Ch., 17 December 2004, Klip/ Sluiter, ALC-XXVI-19.

11 Judgement, *Prosecutor v. Stakić*, Case No. IT-97-24-A, A. Ch., 22 March 2006, Klip/ Sluiter, ALC-XXIX-213.

defended and upheld. To this case we owe the establishment of the precedent trail leading from the decisions of the International Military Tribunal,[12] via Eichmann[13] and Barbie,[14] and into the jurisdiction of the ICTY. Even with the best of intentions, these precedents can be regarded as a dangerously precarious basis for the prosecution of such a serious offence.

The template drawn up by the IMT, as is natural with a court established under the pressures of *vae victus*, is vague. Definitions were kept as flexible as possible, to ensure prosecution of a group of notorious criminals for previously unconsidered offences. As has been suggested elsewhere, legal analysis was not a predominant feature of its constitution.[15] To use this body as principle source of, and justification for, the prosecution of crimes against humanity, and moreover to regard its findings as firm proof of customary international law[16] (considering the relatively small number of countries involved in its development), is debatable in the extreme.

In the Eichmann case, the Israeli court muddied the water by classifying war crimes, genocide, and crimes against humanity as a single broad category: "Crimes against Humanity".[17] Again, it is difficult to describe this as a firm clarification of the state of customary international law.

In Barbie, the court again redefined the meaning of crimes against humanity, citing "inhumane acts" and "persecution" as the key features of the offence, when employed by a state practicing a policy of "ideological supremacy".[18]

By 1995, however, it was held that crimes against humanity had achieved the status of customary international law.[19] While it is not disputed that the offence had indeed been prosecuted in several national and international fora, the fact that no customary definition for the offence had been reached would seem to cast doubt upon its status in law.

Nevertheless, in spite of the "feebleness"[20] of the legal standing of the offence, the ICTY statute, under whose auspices the court in Tadić was established, laid out the first significant definitions.[21] In Article 5, it is stated that the factors are:

-That the offences are committed within the confines of an armed conflict; and

-That the crimes are committed against a civilian population.[22]

In the Tadić jurisdiction appeal, it is therefore regrettable that the chamber decided to remove the "armed conflict" section of the definition,[23] thus highlighting the general uncertainty surrounding the offence. The only remaining element therefore became that of the "civilian population". As this definition is also dissatisfyingly vague, the Tadić Trial Chamber was compelled to borrow the wording directly from Geneva Law,[24] something which can be regarded as partly responsible for the appeals launched in Gotovina, where the defendant claimed unfair conflation of Geneva Law, Hague Law, and international customary law.[25]

---

12 Charter of the International Military Tribunal (IMT), Article 6, paragraph c:

Crimes Against Humanity: namely, murder, extermination, enslavement, deportation, and other inhumane acts committed against any civilian population, before or during the war; or persecutions on political, racial or religious grounds in execution of or in connection with any crime within the jurisdiction of the Tribunal, whether or not in violation of the domestic law of the country where perpetrated.

13 Supreme Court of Israel, *Attorney General of Israel v. Eichmann*, 29 May 1962, 36 International Law Reports 1968, par. 287: "War Crimes, Genocide, and Crimes against Humanity are 'interdependent, and may [be] [...] group[ed] within the broad category of Crimes against Humanity."

14 Cour de Cassation, *Fédération nationale des déportés et internés résistants et al. v. Barbie*, 20 December 1985, 78 International Law Reports 1988, par. 125.

15 A. Zahar, G. Sluiter, International Criminal Law – A Critical Introduction, Oxford University Press, Oxford 2008, p. 200.

16 Decision on the Defence Motion for Interlocutory Appeal on Jurisdiction, *Prosecutor v. Tadić*, A. Ch., *supra* note 9, par. 141.

17 Supreme Court of Israel, *Attorney General of Israel v. Eichmann*, 29 May 1962, *supra* note 13, par. 287.

18 Cour de Cassation, *Fédération nationale des déportés et internés résistants et al. v. Barbie*, 20 December 1985, *supra* note 14, par. 137.

19 Decision on the Defence Motion for Interlocutory Appeal on Jurisdiction, *Prosecutor v. Tadić*, A. Ch., *supra* note 9, par. 141 and 142.

20 A. Zahar, G. Sluiter, International Criminal Law – A Critical Introduction, *supra* note 15, p. 203.

21 ICTY Statute.

22 ICTY Statute, Article 5.

23 Decision on the Defence Motion for Interlocutory Appeal on Jurisdiction, *Prosecutor v. Tadić*, A. Ch., *supra* note 9, par. 140.

24 ICTY, Opinion and Judgment, *Prosecutor v. Tadić*, Case No. IT-94-1-T, T. Ch. II, 7 May 1997, Klip/ Sluiter, ALC-I-287, par. 638; Article 50 of Protocol Additional to the Geneva Conventions of 12 August 1949, and relating to the Protection of Victims of International Armed Conflicts of 8 June 1977.

25 Decision on Ante Gotovina's Interlocutory Appeal Against Decision on Several Motions Challenging Jurisdiction, *Prosecutor v. Gotovina et al.*, A. Ch., *supra* note 1, par. 12.

From this early stage of ICTY development, it would seem apparent that even those given the task of meting out international criminal justice faced legal uncertainty. In fact, it can be argued that they went out of their way to ensure that the prosecution of crimes against humanity was left as open as possible, in much the same spirit as the IMT, to ensure that none of the accused could slip through the net. In this way, they can be suggested to be following the case law of Barbie,[26] where the Advocate General stated:

"I cannot accept that once such a stage is reached, that a legal choice should be made between different victims."[27]

In much the same spirit, the ICTY leaves the definition of crimes against humanity relatively vague, while also refusing to establish a firm definition of the class of people to whom the offence applies.[28]

This, then, is the shifting sand upon which the later decisions of the ICTY were based. Following on from this precedent, various cases took it upon themselves to refine the law. In Limaj, for example, it was held that an attack must be directed against a civilian population, must be widespread and systematic, and the acts indicted must have taken place as part of the attack.[29] Again, all definitions and distinctions were built upon those established by Tadić.

By way of comparison to the offence of crimes against humanity, the concurrent development of the war crimes regime offers some points of interest. Once again, Geneva Law is drawn upon to establish definitions of the categories of victims.[30] In addition, it is stated that a war crime can be defined as anything 'inhumane and inadmissible'.[31] (Note the definition of crimes against humanity quoted in Barbie, above). Article 3 of the ICTY statute, meanwhile, leaves the chargeable offences open, but states that the offence consists of anything "violating the laws or customs of war."[32] Naturally, this includes generalised attacks against civilian populations.

Bearing this in mind, to what extent can it be admitted that the defence counsel in Gotovina raises a legitimate point? Is it unfair for his client to have to defend himself on several levels against an indictment featuring what can potentially be described as a relatively arbitrary and, worse, fabricated distinction between two markedly similar sets of charges?

Considering the development of the two offences, the defendant's claim seems reasonable. It cannot but be argued that the development of the crimes in question has suffered an incestuous degree of inter-dependence. While it is in no way disputed that these offences are necessary cogs in the machine of international criminal justice, it is submitted that a significant re-write of the relevant law is necessary, at least in the context of the ICTY.

To be effective, the distinction between the two offences would have to be clearly and concretely established. With the law as it currently stands, I would agree with the defendant's claim that a dual charge for the same set of offences appears unwarranted.[33] In spite of the precedent supporting dual indictment for the same fact pattern,[34] I would argue that the need for such a system demonstrates the lack of distinction between the two offences. If the offences are sufficiently unclear and intermixed as to need explanation to counsel during the course of a trial, then the tribunal can easily be accused of lacking subject matter jurisdiction – it is surely a breach of the due process for the defendant to be held for offences which are essentially unclear?

---

26 Cour de Cassation, , *Fédération nationale des déportés et internés résistants et al. v. Barbie*, 20 December 1985, *supra* note 14, par. 137.

27 *Ibid.*, par. 146.

28 Decision on the Defence Motion on Jurisdiction, *Prosecutor v. Tadić*, T. Ch. II, *supra* note 6, par. 640.

29 ICTY, Judgement, *Prosecutor v. Limaj et al.*, Case No. IT-03-66, T. Ch. II, 30 November 2005, Klip/ Sluiter, ALC-XXVIII-189, par. 181.

30 Decision on the Defence Motion for Interlocutory Appeal on Jurisdiction, *Prosecutor v. Tadić*, A. Ch., *supra* note 9, par. 91 and 92.

31 *Ibid.*, par. 94.

32 ICTY statute, Article 3.

33 Decision on Ante Gotovina's Interlocutory Appeal Against Decision on Several Motions Challenging Jurisdiction, *Prosecutor v. Gotovina et al.*, A. Ch., *supra* note 1, par. 12.

34 See, for example, Judgement, *Prosecutor v. Kordić and Čerkez*, A. Ch., *supra* note 10 and Judgement, *Prosecutor v. Stakić*, A. Ch., *supra* note 11.

As it has always been clear that the law of war crimes is based upon agreed standards of conduct in war zones, namely Hague and Geneva Law, it is suggested that the most effective way to clearly split the offences of war crimes and crimes against humanity would be a UN resolution, with firm definitions and clear distinctions agreed upon. In this way, the courts would have a definite, internationally accepted base for their decisions, and a highly disconcerting, and potentially unjust area of legal uncertainty could be avoided.

3. The Đorđević decision of 6 December 2007[35]

In Đorđević, the issue under discussion was completely different. This appeal was with regard to the temporal and territorial jurisdiction of the tribunal.

The first ground of appeal states simply that, as the Dayton-Paris agreement was signed on 14 December 1995, the tribunal's jurisdiction ended with the declaration of peace.[36] This plea was based upon UN Security Resolution (UNSC) 827,[37] establishing the tribunal, which states that the tribunal shall have jurisdiction until a date to be determined by the Security Council on the restoration of peace.

The tribunal was unsurprisingly swift to quash this challenge. By reference first to Article 1 of the ICTY statute,[38] and the lack of a UNSC Resolution declaring the temporal boundaries of the tribunal's jurisdiction, the court declared that it continued to have jurisdiction for crimes committed after 14 December 1995. This argument was bolstered by reference to Boškoski,[39] where it was decided that the tribunal had jurisdiction over offences committed in 2001.

As a further spur to the debate, the defendant questioned the tribunal's territorial jurisdiction, stating that, as the offences charged occurred in 1999, when Yugoslavia was no longer in existence, , the tribunal lacked jurisdiction to prosecute.

Once again, the ICTY Statute was drawn into the debate, with the answer provided by Article 8:[40] as Kosovo makes up part of the territory of the former Yugoslavia, it falls under the territorial jurisdiction of the court. In addition, the case of Boškoski[41] once again provided verification of the territorial jurisdiction of the tribunal: all parts of the former Yugoslavia fall under ICTY jurisdiction. In the final section, Kosovo was expressly described as under the jurisdiction of the court, as a matter of long precedent.[42]

As with the case of Gotovina, both of these grounds of appeal appear at first simply optimistic, and then upon further examination mildly unsettling. The level of carte blanche granted to the ICTY by the UN seems surprisingly high, particularly given the (previously discussed) state of the international criminal justice system at the time of its creation. From the manner in which the appeal is interpreted, it appears clear that the tribunal is ready to assert its jurisdiction over almost any question which appears even tangentially connected to the events of the Yugoslav war.

With regard to the issue of territorial jurisdiction, at least, this seems relatively forgivable – at least an area of land is a concrete concept. The temporal issue, however, raises more questions. Given that the events in Kosovo could potentially be regarded as outwith the expectations of the UN in 1993, is it fair that events therein be prosecuted?

---

35 Decision of Vlastimir Đorđević's Preliminary Motion on Jurisdiction, *Prosecutor v. Đorđević*, T. Ch. III, *supra* note 1.

36 *Ibid.*, par. 2.

37 United Nations Security Council Resolution 827 on Establishing an International Tribunal for the Prosecution of Persons Responsible for Serious Violations of International Humanitarian Law Committed in the Territory of the Former Yugoslavia, S.C. res. 827, 48 U.N. SCOR, U.N. Doc. S/RES/827 (1992), 25 May 1993.

38 "The International Tribunal shall have the power to prosecute persons responsible for serious violations of international humanitarian law committed in the territory of the former Yugoslavia since 1991 in accordance with the provisions of the present Statute."

39 ICTY, Decision on interlocutory appeal on jurisdiction, *Prosecutor v. Boškoski et al*, Case No. IT-04-82-AR72.1, A. Ch., 22 July 2005, Klip/ Sluiter, ALC-XXVII-15, par. 10.

40 "The territorial jurisdiction of the International Tribunal shall extend to the territory of the former Socialist Federal Republic of Yugoslavia, including its land surface, airspace and territorial waters".

41 Decision on interlocutory appeal on jurisdiction, *Prosecutor v.Boškoski*, A. Ch., *supra* note 39, par. 10.

42 Decision of Vlastimir Đorđević's Preliminary Motion on Jurisdiction, *Prosecutor v. Đorđević*, T. Ch. III, *supra* note 1, par. 12.

While the Trial Chamber in Ojdanić considered that the UN foresaw the long term continuation of the conflict.[43] and thus left the temporal jurisdiction of the tribunal open- ended, I would argue that this development can be regarded as closer to serendipity than foresight. With the signing of a peace treaty, and the improving situation in most of the former Yugoslav territory, it would have seemed logical to assume that the conflict was at an end. While it is not disputed that the accused deserves to stand trial for the offences indicted, I would argue that the UN should have issued a further resolution following upon the heels of the Dayton – Paris agreement, reaffirming its commitment to the work of the ICTY, and specifically confirming its continuing jurisdiction. Not to have done so appears to contradict the settle principle of customary international law, which states that a conflict ends when the parties involved make an agreement to that effect.

4. Conclusion

Both of the cases under discussion raised important issues with regard to the jurisdiction of the ICTY: namely, what crimes can it prosecute, over what time period, and which territorial area. In all cases, the ICTY emerged as the clear winner, even though some of its arguments were based upon extremely fragile legal bases. What Đorđević made clear is that the territorial and temporal jurisdiction of the ICTY is, minus a UNSC Resolution to the contrary, beyond question, and under the complete control of those administering the justice process. The Gotovina decision, on the other hand, highlights some disturbingly underdeveloped areas of jurisdiction, and the decision itself seems merely to reinforce a legal system that was developed haphazardly and over-hastily. While it is just that the accused be tried for the offences that he has committed, it would seem in line with general legal practice for these crimes to be given a thorough review, and for the criminal code to finally brought to a state which can be considered as beyond repute.

David Bryden

43 ICTY, Decision on Motion Challenging Jurisdiction, *Prosecutor v. Milutinović, Ojdanić and Šainović*, Case No. IT-99-37-PT, T. Ch. III, 6 May 2003, Klip/ Sluiter, ALC-XIV-13, par. 61.

UNITED NATIONS

International Tribunal for the Prosecution of Persons Responsible for Serious Violations of International Humanitarian Law Committed in the Territory of the former Yugoslavia since 1991	Case No.	IT-05-88/2-PT
	Date:	14 December 2007
	Original:	English

IN TRIAL CHAMBER II

Before: **Judge Carmel Agius, Presiding**
Judge O-Gon Kwon
Judge Kimberly Prost, Pre-Trial Judge

Registrar: **Mr. Hans Holthuis**

Decision of: **14 December 2007**

PROSECUTOR

v.

ZDRAVKO TOLIMIR

PUBLIC

DECISION ON PRELIMINARY MOTIONS ON THE INDICTMENT PURSUANT TO RULE 72 OF THE RULES

Office of the Prosecutor
Mr. Peter McCloskey

The Accused
Zdravko Tolimir

[page 1] THIS TRIAL CHAMBER of the International Tribunal for the Prosecution of Persons Responsible for Serious Violations of International Humanitarian Law Committed in the Territory of the former Yugoslavia since 1991 ("Tribunal") is seised of the "Preliminary Motions on the Indictment in Accordance with Rule 72 of the Rules", submitted by the Accused Zdravko Tolimir on 30 October 2007 and filed in the English version on 7 November 2007 ("Preliminary Motions"), which includes the Accused's submissions on (1) the Tribunal's lack of jurisdiction ("Motion on Jurisdiction"), (2) the defects in the form of the Indictment ("Motion on the form of the Indictment"), and (3) the severance of counts ("Motion on severance of counts"), and hereby renders its decision thereon.

I. PROCEDURAL BACKGROUND

1. The Accused, originally charged with Radivoje Miletić and Milan Gvero in a single indictment[1] which was made public against him on 25 February 2005 ("original indictment"),[2] was transferred to the seat of the Tribunal on 1 June 2007.[3] On the same day, by order of the President of the Tribunal, the case against him ("*Tolimir* case") was assigned to Trial Chamber II,[4] and by order of the Presiding Judge of that Chamber, the Trial Chamber in the *Tolimir* case was composed of Judge Carmel Agius (Presiding), Judge O-Gon Kwon and Judge Kimberly Prost.[5] On 4 June 2007,[6] the initial appearance of the Accused took place before Judge Prost.[7] On that occasion, the Accused did not enter a plea on the counts in the original indictment.[8]

2. On 12 June 2007, the Prosecution sought leave to amend the indictment against Tolimir filed on 28 August 2006 ("amended indictment"),[9] requesting, as the only substantive change, that the reference to command responsibility under Article 7(3) of the Statute of the Tribunal ("Statute") be deleted from the last paragraph of the original indictment.[10] **[page 2]**

3. By order of 14 June 2007, the Presiding Judge of Trial Chamber II assigned Judge Prost as Pre-Trial Judge for this case.[11] The Pre-Trial Judge convened a further appearance on 3 July 2007. During this appearance, the Prosecution's request for leave to amend the indictment in the Prosecution's Submission of Amended Indictment was granted by the Pre-Trial Judge pursuant to Rule 50(A)(i)(c) of the Rules of the Procedure and Evidence ("Rules"), and the amended indictment became the operative indictment in the *Tolimir* case ("Indictment").[12] The Accused refused to enter a plea and, as provided for in Rule 62, the Pre-Trial Judge entered a plea of not guilty on each count of the Indictment on his behalf.[13]

4. On 20 July 2007, the Trial Chamber denied the Prosecution's motion for joinder of the *Tolimir* case with the case of *Prosecution v. Popović et. al.* filed on 6 June 2007.[14] On the same day, the Trial Chamber denied the Accused's motion to review the Registry's decision denying his request for the assignment of Mr. Nebojša Mrkić as Lead Counsel.[15] The Accused subsequently submitted that he wished to conduct his own defence in his case.[16]

---

1 *Prosecutor v. Tolimir, Miletić and Gvero*, Case No. IT-04-80-I, Indictment, 8 February 2005.

2 *Prosecutor v. Tolimir, Miletić and Gvero,* Case No. IT-04-80-I, Decision on Motion of the Prosecution to Further Vacate the Order for Non-disclosure, 25 February 2005.

3 *Prosecutor v. Tolimir*, Case No. IT-05-88-2/I, Order for Detention on Remand, 1 June 2007.

4 *Prosecutor v. Tolimir*, Case No. IT-05-88-2/I, Order Assigning a Case to a Trial Chamber, 1 June 2007.

5 *Prosecutor v. Tolimir*, Case No. IT-05-88-2/I, Order Regarding Composition of Trial Chamber, 1 June 2007.

6 On 4 June 2007, the Deputy Registrar "decided to assign Mr. Roger Sahota as counsel to represent the Accused at his initial appearance and in such other matters as may be necessary until a permanent counsel is assigned." *See Prosecutor v. Tolimir*, Case No. IT-05-88-2/I, Decision by the Deputy Registrar, 4 June 2007.

7 *Prosecutor v. Tolimir*, Case No. IT-05-88-2/I, Order Designating Judge for Initial Appearance, 1 June 2007.

8 Initial Appearance, T. 10 (4 June 2007).

9 *Prosecutor v. Tolimir*, Case No. IT-05-88-2/I, Prosecution's Submission of Amended Indictment with Attached Annexes A, B and C, 12 June 2007 ("Prosecution's Submission of Amended Indictment").

10 Prosecution's Submission of Amended Indictment, para. 3.

11 *Prosecutor v. Tolimir*, Case No. IT-05-88-2/I, Order Designating a Pre-Trial Judge, 15 June 2007.

12 Further Appearance, T. 24 (3 July 2007).

13 *Ibid.*, T. 31–38 (3 July 2007).

14 Decision on Motion for Joinder, 20 July 2007.

15 Decision on Motion by the Accused for Review of the Registrar's Decision of 29 June 2007, 20 July 2007.

16 *See* Motion of the Accused to be Allowed to Defend Himself Personally or to be Defended by Counsel of his own Choosing, 30 July 2007 (original version in BCS), 31 July 2007 (English translation); Submission by the Accused to the Registrar for Leave to Conduct his own Defence or to Appoint Counsel of his own Choosing Pursuant to Article 21.4(d), and Rule 45(F) and Amended Rule 62 (C) of the Rules, 6 August 2007 (original version in BCS), 10 October 2007 (English version).

On 27 August 2007, the Deputy Registrar notified the Trial Chamber and the parties of the Accused's election to conduct his own defence.[17]

5. On 14 September 2007, the first status conference took place. Having inquired about the Accused's understanding of his election of self-representation,[18] the Pre-Trial Judge set a deadline of 45 days starting from 17 September 2007 for him to file preliminary motions pursuant to Rule 72 (A), which motions include those challenging jurisdiction, alleging defects in the form of the indictment, and seeking the severance of counts joined in one indictment under Rule 49.[19]

6. On 25 September 2007, the Accused sought an extension of time for the filing of preliminary motions, which was denied by the Pre-Trial Judge on 18 October 2007.[20] The Accused filed the Preliminary Motions on 30 October 2007 within the time-limit prescribed by the Pre-Trial Judge. The Prosecution responded on 21 November 2007 ("Response"), requesting that the Motion **[page 3]** be dismissed in its entirety.[21] On 3 and 4 December 2007 the Prosecution filed a supplement to the Response and a corrigendum of the same ("Supplement").[22]

II. MOTION ON JURISDICTION

7. The Accused submits numerous challenges to the jurisdiction of the Tribunal. The Trial Chamber will address them in turn.

A. Legality of Arrest

(a) Submissions of the parties

(i) Motion

8. The Accused submits that the Tribunal has no jurisdiction to try abducted persons.[23] He claims that "the Tribunal has no jurisdiction to organise and conduct [an] abduction of the accused, effect and legalise a change of his legal identity and status, deny his acquired rights guaranteed by the [Serbian] Constitution and laws of an internationally recognised state whose citizen he is," and by other international human rights conventions.[24]

9. The Accused describes his alleged illegal arrest as follows:

(1) At 3.15 a.m. on 31 May 2007, the Accused was abducted from an apartment in Belgrade, Serbia. "The abduction was carried out by a well-equipped and organised group of 20 men" who introduced themselves as policemen. After having blown up the door of the apartment with explosives, the policemen put a sack over the Accused's head, put him in a van **[page 4]** accompanied by escort

[17] *See* Notification by the Deputy Registrar, 27 August 2007. The Deputy Registrar also acknowledged the termination of representation by duty counsel. *Ibid.*

[18] Status Conference, T. 54–59 (14 September 2007).

[19] *Ibid.*, T. 98–100 (14 September 2007).

[20] Decision on Motion for Suspension of Time Limit for Filing of Preliminary Motions, 18 October 2007.

[21] Prosecution Response to the Accused's Preliminary Motion on the Indictment, Public with Confidential Appendices, 21 November 2007.

[22] Supplement to Prosecution Response to the Accused's Preliminary Motion on the Indictment, confidential, 3 December 2007; *Supplement* to Prosecution Response to the Accused's Preliminary Motion on the Indictment – Correction, confidential, 4 December 2007. The supplement filed on 4 December 2007 contains all six documents mentioned in its Supplement filed on 3 December 2007, namely (i) a report from Republika Srpska, dated 4 June 2007 (in BSC with English translation) ("RS Report"), (ii) an ICTY investigator's report following arrest by Don King, dated 6 June 2007 ("Don King 6 June Report"), (iii) an ICTY investigator's debrief by Don King, dated 16 June 2007 ("Don King 16 June Report"), (iv) the formal request for information sent to the Serbian government on 17 September 2007, (v) the reminder sent on 6 November 2007 extending the deadline for the Serbian government to respond to the request for information until 4 December 2007, and (vi) an internal memorandum dated 23 November 2007. On 7 December 2007, the Prosecution filed a notice to change the status of the Response and the Supplement to public in its entirety. *See* Notice of Lifting Confidential Status of Three Prosecution Filings, 7 December 2007.

[23] Preliminary Motions, p. 2, para. 1.1.

[24] *Ibid.*, p. 2, para. 1.2. *See also ibid.*, pp. 2–3, paras. 1.3–1.4.

vehicles, and took him to a detention facility in Belgrade. All this was done without providing the Accused with an opportunity to be assisted by a lawyer.[25]

(2) At 8 a.m. on the same day, the Accused was taken from the detention facility to "the Pavlovića Ćuprija border crossing, near Bijeljina, on the border between Serbia and Republika Srpska ("RS")."[26] It is alleged that the fact that the Accused crossed the border without impediment indicates "the organisation, official relations, and links between the persons who abducted [him] and the state customs organs of Serbia and Bosnia and Herzegovina, which is responsible for the borders of [the RS]."[27]

(3) A patrol of the Ministry of the Interior of RS came to the border and told the Accused that they came to transfer him to Banja Luka "to speak with the Minister of Police about [his] surrender and a deal with the organs of [the RS] to carry out [his] extradition to The Hague from [the RS] with certain privileges."[28] The Accused refused the possibility of any deal to be transferred to The Hague from [the RS] and he insisted to be taken back to Serbia.[29]

(4) After a two-hour telephone conversation "conducted from Bijeljina with Belgrade and Banja Luka which were in contact with The Hague", the Accused's request to be brought back to Serbia was rejected. He was then told that "the international peacekeeping forces" would hand him over to the Tribunal.[30] The Accused was taken from Bijeljina to Bratunac where he "was kept for several hours in a vehicle which changed its location and was parked near military and police features used by the army and the police during the war."[31] According to his submission, "[s]ecret and public TV footage was continuously made in order to deceive the public that [he] had been arrested in the Bratunac area."[32]

(5) In the afternoon on the same day, the Accused was taken from Bratunac via Bijeljina to the Ministry of the Interior in Banja Luka where he was again "offered a deal to be extradited to The Hague as a citizen of [the RS]." He refused this offer and requested that he be taken back to Serbia, but his request was again rejected. Thereafter, he was handed over to **[page 5]** NATO.[33] The officers of NATO, in the presence of a representative of the Office of the Prosecutor from The Hague, put him in a helicopter at the airport in Banja Luka and brought him to the NATO base in Sarajevo. On the next day, 1 June 2007, the Accused was transferred to The Hague and placed under the jurisdiction of the Dutch police, who put him in the United Nations Detention Unit.[34]

10. The Accused also submits that his abduction was confirmed by public statements of the Serbian President, Prime Minister, Minister of the Interior, Minister of Justice, Minister for Local Administration, Minister of Labour and Social Policy, Director of the Serbian Police, and President of the National Council for Cooperation with The Hague.[35] These authorities stated, argues the Accused, that he "had not been arrested by legal organs of government of Serbia, thus confirming that [he] was abducted and that [his] abduction and transfer to [the RS] was carried out by illegal groups and individuals who unlawfully extradite [him] to a neighbouring state and to the [Tribunal]."[36] He further contends that his identity papers, files and documents which were found in the apartment in Belgrade were confiscated. The Accused submits that the whole process of his arrest and transfer to the RS and ultimately to the Tribunal constitutes "a violation of the Constitution and national laws of Serbia" and the Statute of the Tribunal as well as the Rules.[37]

---

25 *Ibid.*, p. 3, para. 1.5.
26 *Ibid.*, p. 3, para. 1.6.
27 *Ibid.*, p. 3, para. 1.7.
28 *Ibid.*, p. 3. para. 1.8.
29 *Ibid.*, p. 3, para. 1.9.
30 *Ibid.*, p. 3, para. 1.10.
31 *Ibid.*, p. 3, para. 1.11.
32 *Ibid.*, pp. 3–4, para. 1.11.
33 *Ibid.*, p. 4, para. 1.12.
34 *Ibid.*, p. 4, para. 1.13.
35 *Ibid.*, p. 4, para. 1.15.
36 *Ibid.* The Accused also states that "[t]he work of the Security Committee of the Serbian Assembly, and a parliamentary debate in the Serbian Assembly also confirmed [his abduction]." *Ibid.*
37 *Ibid.*, pp. 4–5, para. 1.17.

(ii) Response

11. The Prosecution response on this issue is premised on three grounds. First, it submits that it has no knowledge of, and had no involvement in, the alleged abduction and that there is "no reason to believe that any Tribunal personnel committed, or colluded with others in the commission of, any illegal activities."[38] The Prosecution states that it first became involved in the arrest of the Accused on 31 May 2007, when the RS Prime Minister contacted the Prosecution, and advised that the Accused was in the custody of the RS police.[39] In the evening of 31 May 2007, the Accused was "formally" arrested in Banja Luka by Mr. Don King, head investigator for the Office of the **[page 6]** Prosecutor's Sarajevo office and subsequently transferred to The Hague.[40] The Prosecution has filed two reports from Mr. King in support of its position.[41]

12. Second, the Prosecution contends that the Accused's claim that the Tribunal has denied his rights under the Serbian Constitution, the Statute of the Tribunal and other unspecified international human rights instruments is not substantiated.[42] The Prosecution stresses that it lawfully arrested and assisted in the transfer of the Accused to The Hague.[43]

13. Lastly, the Prosecution, referring to the case against Dragan Nikolić ("*Dragan Nikolić* case"),[44] submits that even if a violation of Serbia's sovereignty had occurred during his arrest, this merely would have resulted in the Accused being returned to Serbia, whereupon his extradition to The Hague would be required under Article 29(2) of the Federal Republic of Yugoslavia's law on cooperation with the ICTY.[45] Therefore, it is submitted that the Tribunal may validly exercise jurisdiction over the Accused.[46] Additionally, the Prosecution contends that the Accused does not raise any human rights violations that "are of such a serious nature that the Tribunal should decline to exercise jurisdiction."[47]

14. The two reports by Mr. King provide a substantially similar description of the events starting from the moment the Accused is in Banja Luka:

(1) During the afternoon of 31 May 2007, the Head of Mission of the Sarajevo Field Office informed Mr. King that the Accused had been detained and was being taken to Banja Luka prior to the handover to the Tribunal.[48] Mr. King went to the NATO office at the Butmir EUFOR Military Base in Sarajevo and was transported to the Banja Luka airport at 7:40 p.m. of the same day, together with a NATO legal adviser and other military staff. Shortly before 9 p.m. at the airport terminal building of the Banja Luka airport, Mr. King was **[page 7]** informed that it had been agreed that the handover and arrest procedure would take place by helicopter and that the arrival of the Accused was imminent.[49]

(2) Mr. King went to the helicopter and saw that two vehicles were parked nearby. He was informed that the Accused was in the rear of one of the vehicles. The Accused refused to leave the vehicle "because he believed that he was being filmed by a press photographer." The NATO legal advisor

---

38 Response, para. 6.
39 *Ibid.*, para. 5.
40 *Ibid.*
41 *See infra* para. 14.
42 Response, para. 8.
43 *Ibid.*
44 *See Prosecutor v. Dragan Nikolić*, Case No. IT-94-2-PT, Decision on Defence Motion Challenging the Exercise of Jurisdiction by the Tribunal, 9 October 2002 ("*Dragan Nikolić* Trial Decision"); *Prosecutor v. Dragan Nikolić*, Case No. IT-94-2-AR73, Decision on Interlocutory Appeal Concerning Legality of Arrest, 5 June 2003 ("*Dragan Nikolić* Appeal Decision").
45 Response, para. 14. The Prosecution notes that it has submitted to the Government of Serbia a formal request for information concerning the Accused's allegations about the manner of his arrest, seeking "all records of investigations into the alleged capture and transportation of [the] Accused Tolimir within the territory of Serbia prior to Tolimir's arrest in Republika Srpska on 31 May 2007, and any other information concerning these alleged events." The Prosecution states that it has not received a reply from the Government of Serbia. *Ibid.*, para. 9, fn. 5.
46 Response, para. 9.
47 *Ibid.*, para. 15.
48 Don King 6 June Report, p. 1. *See also* Don King 16 June Report.
49 Don King 6 June Report, p. 1.

explained to the Accused that a NATO officer was filming the operation for his safety and the security of all those involved, the role of which is known as "Combat Camera". The Accused declined to give his name.[50]

(3) The Accused remained uncooperative and refused to leave the vehicle "as he felt he had been kidnapped before being handed into the custody of the [RS] MUP officers." He also refused to enter the helicopter as he said he had not been arrested. Mr. King explained to him that he was believed to be Zdravko Tolimir, the subject of a Tribunal arrest warrant and that there was a procedure to be carried out on board.[51]

(4) At about 8:15 p.m., the Accused entered the helicopter. Two small bags of his personal property were also brought into the helicopter. The EUFOR security team searched him and offered a medical examination. The Accused initially declined the medical examination but, subsequently he agreed to it.[52]

(5) Following this, Mr. King went through the Tribunal's arrest procedure with the Accused, which was filmed by the Combat Camera. Throughout the procedure, the Accused did not confirm his identity, declined to reply to Mr. King's offer of a lawyer. He also refused a copy of the warrant for his arrest. Mr. King "formally" arrested the Accused and then they were flown back to the Butmir EUFOR Base. In this military base, the Accused was detained overnight to await air transfer to The Hague. During his detention, the Accused's property was listed and secured in his presence. He underwent further medical examinations. He refused to take any of the medication that was in his possession. He was given refreshments and slept in a bed in the security facility of the base.[53]

(6) On the morning of 1 June 2007, the Accused was transferred to The Netherlands and handed over to the Tribunal's Registry representatives at Rotterdam Airport. The Accused's **[page 8]** detention and transfers were filmed by the Combat Camera. Due to his health and physical condition he was not handcuffed at any time during his detention and transfers.[54]

15. The RS Report attached to the Supplement describes the events concerning the arrest of the Accused as follows:

(1) In the early hours of 31 May 2007, members of the Security and Information agency of the Republic of Serbia called the Criminal Police Administration in the RS, informing that they had intelligence information to the effect that in the course of the same day "some of the Hague indictees, most probably Ratko Mladić or someone close to him" would attempt to cross over from Serbia to the territory of the RS in Bosnia and Herzegovina ("BiH").[55] Based on this information, the deputy head and other members of the Criminal Police Administration went to the area of the Bijeljina Public Security Centre to blockade and control there. This coordinated action "both from the territory of Serbia and that of the [RS]" started around 2 p.m. on the same day.[56]

(2) At around 2:15 p.m., a mobile team of the Criminal Police Administration intercepted the movement of a person who was walking towards the settlement of Sopotnik. The man was stopped and an attempt to identify him was made. He stated that he had no identification papers and introduced himself as General Zdravko Tolimir, officer of the Army of the RS. He was asked where he came from, whether he was driven to the location, and where he was going but refused to respond. His clothes and two bags he was carrying were examined. Neither identification papers nor weapons were found. The man provided the following personal information: Zdravko Tolimir, son of Stanko

50 *Ibid.*
51 *Ibid.*
52 *Ibid.*, p. 2.
53 *Ibid.*
54 *Ibid.*
55 RS Report, p. 1. The RS Report states that the location was "between Zvornik and Ljubovija, most probably on the territory bordering with Ljubovija, to the municipality of Bratunac." *Ibid.*, pp. 1–2.
56 *Ibid.*, p. 2.

and Darinka, born on 27 November 1948 in Popovići, municipality of Glamoč in the BiH, residing in Belgrade, and a citizen of Serbia and of BiH.[57]

(3) The Accused was immediately put into a police vehicle and then transported to Banja Luka escorted by the entire team of the Criminal Police Administration. He was visibly nervous.[58]

(4) At around 6 p.m., the Accused was driven to the RS MUP official premises. At around 8:10 p.m., the Accused was taken from there to the Mahovljani airport near Banja Luka where **[page 9]** Mr. King officially apprehended him. The Accused was then put into a EUFOR helicopter with his personal belongings. At around 9 p.m., the helicopter flew him to Sarajevo.[59]

(b) <u>Discussion</u>

16. The Trial Chamber notes the jurisprudence of this Tribunal related to the question of jurisdiction in cases of alleged abductions.[60] In particular, in the *Dragan Nikolić* case the issue was examined in depth both by the Trial Chamber and by the Appeals Chamber.[61]

17. Applying that jurisprudence to the facts of this case, the Trial Chamber will consider whether the circumstances are such so as to require the Tribunal to decline to exercise its jurisdiction on the basis of a violation of State sovereignty or a violation of human rights.

(i) <u>Circumstances under which violation of State sovereignty require jurisdiction to be set aside</u>

18. The Appeals Chamber in the *Dragan Nikolić* case examined relevant national cases in order to determine State practice on whether irregularities in the manner in which an accused is brought before a court have an impact on the exercise of jurisdiction by the court itself.[62] The Appeals Chamber concluded that the following two principles seem to have support in State practice:

> First, in cases of crimes such as genocide, crimes against humanity and war crimes which are universally recognised and condemned as such ("Universally Condemned Offences"), courts seem to find in the special character of these offences and, arguably, in their seriousness, a good reason for not setting aside jurisdiction. Second, absent a complaint by the State whose sovereignty has been breached or in the event of a diplomatic resolution of the breach, it is easier for courts to assert their jurisdiction. The initial *iniuria* has in a way been cured and the risk of having to return the accused to the country of origin is no longer present.[63]

The Appeals Chamber further held: **[page 10]**

> Universally Condemned Offences are a matter of concern to the international community as a whole. There is a legitimate expectation that those accused of these crimes will be brought to justice swiftly. [...] This legitimate expectation needs to be weighed against the principle of State sovereignty and the fundamental human rights of the accused. [...] In the opinion of the Appeals Chamber, the damage caused to international justice by not

57 *Ibid.*, pp. 2–3.

58 *Ibid.*, p. 3.

59 *Ibid.*, p. 3. The Report also states that "the Minister of Interior of the RS was informed about the [Accused's] apprehension over the phone and he was aware of that the [Accused] was driven to Banja Luka because of a timely reaction regarding the representatives of the International Community and Hague Tribunal."

60 *See e.g., Prosecutor v. Mrksić, Radić, Šljivančanin, Dokmanović*, Case No. IT-95-13a-PT, "Decision on the Motion for Release by the Accused Slavko Dokmanović Trial Chamber I", 22 October 1997 ("*Dokmanović* Trial Decision"). Slavko Dokmanović was the first case before the Tribunal in which the accused raised the legality of his arrest. The Trial Chamber in that case found that the trickery used by the Prosecution to arrest Dokmanović did not amount to "a forcible abduction or kidnapping" and that such "luring" was consistent with principles of international law and the sovereignty of the FRY. Finally, the Trial Chamber held that "[g]iven that the Trial Chamber had found that the particular method used to arrest and detain Mr. Dokmanović was justified and *legal*, we need not decide at this time whether the International Tribunal has the authority to exercise jurisdiction over a defendant *illegally* obtained from abroad." *Dokmanović* Trial Decision, paras. 57, 78. *See also*, *Dragan Nikolić* Trial Decision and *Dragan Nikolić* Appeal Decision.

61 *See Dragan Nikolić* Trial Decision and *Dragan Nikolić* Appeal Decision.

62 *See* Dragan *Nikolić* Appeal Decision, paras. 21–23.

63 *Dragan Nikolić* Appeal Decision, para. 24.

apprehending fugitives accused of serious violations of international humanitarian law is comparatively higher than the injury, if any, caused to the sovereignty of a State by a limited intrusion in its territory, particularly when the intrusion occurs in default of the State's cooperation. Therefore, the Appeals Chamber does not consider that in cases of universally condemned offences, jurisdiction should be set aside on the ground that there was a violation of the sovereignty of a State, when the violation is brought about by the apprehension of fugitives from international justice, whatever the consequences for the international responsibility of the State or organisation involved. This is all the more so in cases [...] in which the State whose sovereignty has allegedly been breached has not lodged any complaint and thus has acquiesced in the International Tribunal's exercise of jurisdiction. *A fortiori*, and leaving aside for the moment human rights considerations, the exercise of jurisdiction should not be declined in cases of abductions carried out by private individuals whose actions, unless instigated, acknowledged or condoned by a State, or an international organisation, or other entity, do not necessarily in themselves violate State sovereignty.[64]

19. In the present case, the Accused is charged with genocide, crimes against humanity and war crimes. Assuming, without deciding, that a violation of state sovereignty occurred in the instant case, the Trial Chamber finds that given the serious crimes involved such a violation is not sufficient to justify the setting aside of jurisdiction by this Tribunal. Moreover, the Trial Chamber notes that Serbia did not lodge a complaint. Therefore, any alleged violation of state sovereignty is not a basis to decline jurisdiction in this instance.

(ii) Circumstances under which violation of human rights require jurisdiction to be set aside

20. In considering the question of the effect of alleged human rights violations, the Trial Chamber will also rely on the findings of the Appeals Chamber in the *Dragan Nikolić* case. The Appeals Chamber first endorsed the analysis of the Trial Chamber of that case, which found that the treatment of the Appellant was not of such an egregious nature so as to impede the exercise of jurisdiction, but did not exclude that jurisdiction should not be exercised in certain cases. The Trial Chamber held that:

[I]n a situation where an accused is very seriously mistreated, maybe even subject to inhuman, cruel or degrading treatment, or torture, before being handed over to the Tribunal, this may constitute a legal impediment to the exercise of jurisdiction over such an accused. This would certainly be the case where persons acting for SFOR or the Prosecution were involved in such very serious mistreatment.[65]

21. This approach was found by the Appeals Chamber as consistent with, among other cases, the approach taken by the Trial Chamber in the case against *Slavko Dokmanović* before this Tribunal, and the finding of the Appeals Chamber in the case against *Jean-Bosco Barayagwiza* **[page 11]** before the International Tribunal for Rwanda ("ICTR").[66] The ICTR Appeals Chamber held that a court may decline to exercise jurisdiction in cases "where to exercise that jurisdiction in light of serious and egregious violations of the accused's rights would prove detrimental to the court's integrity".[67]

22. The Appeals Chamber in the *Dragan Nikolić* case agreed with these views and stated that:

Although the assessment of the seriousness of the human rights violations depends on the circumstances of each case and cannot be made *in abstracto*, certain human rights violations are of such a serious nature that they require that the exercise of jurisdiction be declined. It would be inappropriate for a court of law to try the victims of these abuses. Apart from such exceptional cases, however, the remedy of setting aside jurisdiction

64 *Dragan Nikolić* Appeal Decision, paras. 25–26 (footnotes omitted).

65 *Dragan Nikolić* Trial Decision, para. 114.

66 *See Dragan Nikolić* Appeal Decision, para. 29, referring to *Dokmanović* Trial Decision, paras. 70–75.

67 *Jean-Bosco Barayagwiza v. Prosecutor*, Case No. ICTR-97-19-AR72, Decision, 3 November 1999, para. 74. The Appeals Chamber in *Barayagwiza* applied this principle in ordering the release of the accused, as he was found to be the subject of human rights violations, including an excessively long pre-trial detention and the failure to promptly inform the accused of the charges against him. At the request of the Prosecutor, the Appeals Chamber reviewed this decision. It in its decision of 31 March 2000, the Appeals Chamber reversed the remedy it had previously ordered on the basis of new facts put forward by the Prosecution. These new facts presented a different picture of the violations of rights suffered by the accused and of the omissions of the Prosecutor. Despite this, in the decision of March 2000, the Appeals Chamber "confirm[ed] its Decision of 3 November 1999 on the basis of the facts it was founded on." *Jean-Bosco Barayagwiza v. Prosecutor*, Case No. ICTR-97-19-AR72, Decision (Prosecutor's Request for Review or Reconsideration), 31 March 2000, para. 51.

> will, in the Appeals Chamber's view, usually be disproportionate. The correct balance must therefore be maintained between the fundamental rights of the accused and the essential interests of the international community in the prosecution of persons charged with serious violations of international humanitarian law.[68]

23. In the present case, the Accused alleges that he was forcibly abducted from his apartment in Belgrade by a group of 20 "policemen" and brought to the RS, where he was then surrendered to NATO forces. As confirmed by the Prosecution and the RS authorities, the Accused was handed over to a representative of the Office of the Prosecutor of the Tribunal and transferred to The Hague. The Accused submits that the manner in which his abduction, transfer to the RS and ultimately transfer to the Tribunal were conducted resulted in a violation of his rights. According to the Accused, the NATO forces and the representatives from the Prosecution involved in the abduction acted in collusion with his captors and therefore the unlawful conduct of his capture, detention and transfer to The Hague are imputable also to them.[69]

24. The Trial Chamber notes that the only information concerning the very initial phase of the Accused's arrest is the description of the events given by the Accused himself. Although there was a request by the Prosecution for information from the relevant authorities of Serbia, no response has been received regarding the Accused's capture in Belgrade and his transportation within the **[page 12]** territory of Serbia until his arrest in the RS on 31 May 2007.[70] Starting from the moment in which the Accused is in Banja Luka on 31 May 2007, the Prosecution and the RS authorities provide their description of the events, which substantially coincide with the one given by the Accused.

25. For the purpose of the present analysis only, the Trial Chamber is prepared to accept the factual allegations of the Accused related to the initial phase of his arrest. The Chamber has considered those facts, as well as the descriptions of the entire process of arrest as set out by the Accused and in the RS Report and the Prosecution's reports.[71] What is before the Trial Chamber—with reference to each phase of the arrest individually and cumulatively—does not amount to a human rights violation of such a serious nature so as to require that the exercise of jurisdiction be declined. In fact, the only irregular aspect of the arrest is the alleged circumstances surrounding the Accused's removal from his apartment in Belgrade. Assuming those allegations to be true, even that scenario however is not so egregious as to merit declining jurisdiction over this Accused in relation to the grave crimes charged against him.

26. Further, the Accused did not provide any evidence to show the involvement of either NATO or the Prosecution in the initial phase of his arrest. In addition, the Prosecution has provided evidence to the contrary, as the Investigator's report attached to the Prosecution's Response denies any such involvement. Once the Accused came into contact with NATO and the Prosecution his arrest was carried out in a lawful manner and without any violations of his rights. Thus, the Trial Chamber is satisfied that the circumstances of this case do not justify declining the exercise of jurisdiction by this Tribunal.

B. General submissions of lack of jurisdiction

(a) Submissions of the parties

(i) Motion

27. In support of his general argument that the Tribunal has no jurisdiction to try him, the Accused makes two broad submissions.[72] The Accused first contends that the Tribunal was not lawfully established.[73] In this

---

68 *See Dragan Nikolić* Appeal Decision, para. 30 (footnotes omitted).

69 *See supra* paras. 9–10.

70 *See* Supplement, the formal request for information sent to the Serbian government on 17 September 2007, the reminder sent on 6 November 2007 extending the deadline for the Serbian government to respond to the request for information until 4 December 2007, and an internal memorandum dated 23 November 2007.

71 Namely, Don King 6 June Report and Don King 16 June Report.

72 Preliminary Motions, pp. 5–9, para. 1.18.

73 *Ibid.*, pp. 5–7.

regard, he argues that the Security Council as a political organ of the United Nations exceeded its power in establishing the Tribunal, which, consequently, rendered it **[page 13]** unlawful and biased.[74] Second, the Accused asserts that the Tribunal is not set up in accordance with international human rights standards. He alleges that the Statute, the Rules and the practice before the Tribunal lead to violations of the accused's rights, as guaranteed by the International Covenant on Civil and Political Rights ("ICCPR") and the European Convention for the Protection of Human Rights and Fundamental Freedoms ("ECHR"). In particular, the Accused submits that the appellate system has not been set up properly "because Judges in the second-instance proceedings rotate between the fist-instance and appeals chambers, so they act as second-instance appeals chambers to one another";[75] the accused's right to be tried without undue delay is violated;[76] the length of sentences imposed contravenes international law and the general practice regarding prison sentences in the courts of the former Yugoslavia;[77] and the Tribunal does not guarantee "the principle of equality of the parties" by permitting the Prosecutor to be "in a privileged position."[78]

(ii) Response

28. The Prosecution responds that none of the Accused's 'general legal assertions' about the Tribunal's legal foundation,[79] appellate system,[80] detention policy,[81] sentencing guidelines[82] and the equality of arms between the parties before the Tribunal,[83] constitutes a valid challenge to the jurisdiction of the Tribunal.[84]

(b) Discussion

29 The jurisprudence of this Tribunal has clearly affirmed that the Tribunal was lawfully established. In particular, the Appeals Chamber in the *Tadić* case analysed the issue in depth,[85] and found that the Tribunal "has been lawfully established as a measure under Chapter VII of the Charter."[86] It further stated that the Tribunal was established in accordance with the principle of the rule of law. It held that: **[page 14]**

> For a tribunal such as this one to be established according to the rule of law, it must be established in accordance with the proper international standards; it must provide all the guarantees of fairness, justice and ever-handedness, in full conformity with internationally recognized human rights instruments.[87]

30. The provisions included in the Statute and the Rules demonstrate that the Tribunal has been established in accordance with the rule of law. Pursuant to Article 20(1), any Trial Chamber must ensure "that a trial is fair and expeditious and that proceedings are conducted in accordance with [the Rules], with full respect for the rights of the accused and due regard for the protection of victims and witnesses." The fair trial guarantees in Article 14 of the ICCPR have been adopted almost verbatim in Article 21.[88] Other fair trial guarantees

---

74 *Ibid.*, pp. 5–6. In this respect, the Accused also argues that the Tribunal has no jurisdiction over individuals because "no organ of the United Nations can ever have direct jurisdiction over them." *Ibid.*, pp. 8–9.

75 *Ibid.*, pp. 6–7.

76 *Ibid.*, p. 7.

77 *Ibid.*

78 *Ibid.*, pp. 7–9.

79 Response, para. 17.

80 *Ibid.*, para. 18.

81 *Ibid.*, para. 19.

82 *Ibid.*, para. 21.

83 *Ibid.*, paras. 22–24.

84 *Ibid.*, para. 16.

85 *Prosecutor v. Tadić*, Case No. IT-94-1-AR72, Decision on the Defence Motion for Interlocutory Appeal on Jurisdiction, 2 October 1995 ("*Tadić* Appeal Decision"), paras. 9–48.

86 *Tadić* Appeal Decision, para. 40.

87 *Ibid.*, para. 45.

88 Article 21 reads: "1. All persons shall be equal before the International Tribunal. 2. In the determination of charges against him, the accused shall be entitled to a fair and public hearing, subject to article 22 of the Statute ["Protection of victims and witnesses"]. 3. The accused shall be presumed innocent until proved guilty according to the provisions of the present Statute. 4. In the determination of any charge against the accused pursuant to the present Statute, the accused shall be entitled to the following minimum guarantees, in full equality: [...] (c) to be tried without undue delay; [...] (e) to examine, or have examined,

appear in the Statute and the Rules.[89] The Appeals Chamber in the *Tadić* case concluded that the Tribunal was "established in accordance with the appropriate procedures under the United Nations Charter and provides all the necessary safeguards of a fair trial. It is thus 'established by law'."[90]

31. In particular, both the Statute and Rules ensure that any decision rendered by a Trial Chamber may be subject to appeal.[91] The fact that permanent Judges may rotate on a regular basis between the Trial Chambers and the Appeals Chamber based on "the efficient disposal of case"[92] offers no basis for the Accused to claim that the appellate system of the Tribunal is flawed. Independence of judges is imperative before this Tribunal. Article 13 ensures the high moral character, impartiality, integrity and competence of the Judges of the Tribunal. **[page 15]**

32. Likewise, there is no basis for the Accused's assertion that "detention is a rule, and release to conduct one's defence is an exception, and trials are not held within a reasonable time."[93] The Rules provide for provisional release if conditions are met,[94] and there are numerous Rules and measures in place to ensure trials in a reasonable time.

33. The Trial Chamber further notes that it is well recognised in the jurisprudence of the Tribunal that although a Trial Chamber must consider the sentencing practices in the former Yugoslavia, it is not bound by such practice; rather, it should refer to this practice as an aid in determining an appropriate sentence.[95] Rule 101,[96] which, in accordance with Article 24,[97] grants the power to imprison for the remainder of a convicted person's life, is indicative of the fact that a Trial Chamber is not bound by a maximum sentence possible under a particular national legal system.[98]

34. Finally, the Trial Chamber does not find a basis for the Accused's general claim that the Tribunal violates the principle of equality of arms.[99] Quite to the contrary, Article 21, as referred to above, stipulates equal standing before the Tribunal, which is part of the guarantees of a fair trial provided by the Statute.[100]

---

the witness against him and to obtain the attendance and examination of witnesses on his behalf under the same conditions as witnesses against him [...]." *See also* Article 9(3) of the ICCPR which reads: "Anyone arrested or detained on a criminal charge shall be brought promptly before a judge or other officer authorized by law to exercise judicial power and shall be entitled to trial within a reasonable time or to release. It shall not be the general rule that persons awaiting trial shall be detained in custody, but release may be subject to guarantees to appear for trial, at any other stage of the judicial proceedings, and, should occasion arise, for execution of the judgement."; Article 14(3) of the ICCPR reads: "In the determination of any criminal charge against him, everyone shall be entitled to the following minimum guarantees, in full equality: [...] (c) To be tried without undue delay."

89 *See also*, *Tadić* Appeal Decision, para. 46.

90 *Ibid.*, para. 47.

91 Article 25 on "Appellate proceedings" reads: "1. The Appeals Chamber shall hear appeals from persons convicted by the Trial Chambers or from the Prosecutor on the following grounds: (a) an error on a question of law invalidating the decision; or (b) an error of fact which has occasioned a miscarriage of justice. 2. The Appeals Chamber may affirm, reverse or revise the decisions taken by the Trial Chambers." Part Seven of the Rules also contains provisions regarding the appellate proceedings (Rules 107– 110). *See* also Rule 72 (B) on interlocutory appeals in the pre-trial phase and Rule 73 (B) on interlocutory appeals in the trial phase.

92 Rule 27(A) ("Rotation").

93 Preliminary Motion, p. 7.

94 *See* Rule 65 on "Provisional Release".

95 *See Prosecutor v. Blagojević and Jokić*, Case No. IT-02-60-T, Judgement, 17 January 2005, para. 827, referring to, among others, *Prosecutor v. Tadić*, Judgement in Sentencing Appeal, 26 January 2000 ("*Tadić* Sentencing Appeal Judgement"), para. 20.

96 Rule 101 provides, *inter alia*, that: "(A) A convicted person may be sentenced to imprisonment for a term up to and including the remainder of the convicted person's life. (B) In determining the sentence, the Trial Chamber shall take into account the factors mentioned in Article 24, paragraph 2, of the Statute, as well as such factors as: (i) any aggravating circumstances; (ii) any mitigating circumstances including the substantial cooperation with the Prosecutor by the convicted person before or after conviction; (iii) the general practice regarding prison sentences in the courts of the former Yugoslavia; (iv) the extent to which any penalty imposed by a court of any State on the convicted person for the same act has already been served, as referred to in Article 10, paragraph 3, of the Statute."

97 Article 24 reads: "1. The penalty imposed by the Trial Chamber shall be limited to imprisonment. In determining the terms of imprisonment, the Trial Chambers shall have recourse to the general practice regarding prison sentences in the court of the former Yugoslavia. 2. In imposing the sentences, the Trial Chamber should take into account such factors as the gravity of the offence and the individual circumstances of the convicted person. [...]."

98 *See Tadić* Sentencing Appeal Judgement, para. 21.

99 Preliminary Motions, pp. 7–9, in which the Accused alleges violation of the "principle of equality of the parties".

100 *See Prosecutor v. Tadić*, Case No. IT'-94-1-A, Judgement, 15 July 1999 ("*Tadić* Appeal Judgement"), para. 44. *See also, Prosecutor v. Kordić and Čerkez*, Case No. IT-95-14/2-A, Decision on Application by Mario Čerkez for Extension of Time to file his Respondent's Brief, 11 September 2001, para. 5.

The principle of equality of arms has been applied in this Tribunal in many contexts.[101] Nothing in the Statute, the Rules, or the jurisprudence of the Tribunal violates **[page 16]** this principle. To the extent that the Accused argues that the Statute and the Rules violate this principle by, *inter alia*, allowing Trial Chambers to adopt measures aimed at protecting the rights of witnesses or information provided by States,[102] the Trial Chamber notes that in applying these measures, a balance is always struck between the rights of the accused and the other public interest considerations involved. Lastly, contrary to the Accused's argument, the independence of the Prosecutor acting as a separate organ of the Tribunal is guaranteed in the Statute.[103]

35. The provisions enshrined in the Statute and the Rules are indeed in full conformity with internationally recognized human rights instruments. For the reasons above, the Trial Chamber finds that the arguments set forth in the Motion on Jurisdiction do not demonstrate a lack of jurisdiction of the Tribunal over the Accused.

III. MOTION ON FORM OF THE INDICTMENT

A. Submissions of the parties

1. Motion

36. The Accused raises several arguments in challenging the form of the Indictment.[104] His main arguments can be summarised as follows.

37. First, the Accused submits that the Indictment "represents a ready-made form on which you can enter any of the hundreds of names of people from the Serbian state and political organs or military and political officers, and the contents of the [I]ndictment would remain literally the same."[105] **[page 17]**

38. The Accused claims that the Indictment does not provide information on the elements of the crimes charged, on how the crimes had allegedly been committed and how the Accused is held responsible for them.[106]

---

101 *See Prosecutor v. Kordić and Čerkez*, Case No. IT-95-14/2-A, Judgment, 17 December 2004, para. 176 ("the Appeals Chamber has already, prior to this appeal, had occasion to consider the principle and held that the 'principle of equality of arms is described as being only one feature of the wider concept of a fair trial.' Nevertheless, the right of an accused to have adequate time and facilities to prepare his or her defence does not imply that the Chambers are charged to ensure parity of resources between the Prosecutor and the Defence, such as the material equality of financial or personal resources. The right to equality arms is not a right to equality of relief." Footnotes omitted); *Tadić* Appeal Judgement, para. 52 ("This principle [of equality of arms] means that the Prosecution and the Defence must be equal before the Tribunal Chamber. It follows that the Chamber shall provide every practicable facility it is capable of granting under the Rules and [the] Statute when faced with a request by a party for assistance in presenting its case."). *See also*, *Prosecutor v. šešelj*, Case No. IT-03-67-PT, Decision on the Financing the Defence of the Accused, 30 July 2007, para. 52; *Prosecutor v. Krajišnik,* Case No. IT-00-39-A, Decision on Krajišnik Request and on Prosecution Motion, 11 September 2007, para. 41.

102 Preliminary Motions, pp. 7–9. The Accused argues that "[i]n accordance with Rule 66, paragraph (C), the Prosecutor may, pursuant to the approval by the Trial Chamber, deny the right to the defence to see evidence if it would be contrary to the public interest or affect the security interests of any State, and this is assessed by the Prosecutior. [...] Secretly concealing the identity of a witness (Rule 75), allowing a prosecution witness to decline to answer a question on grounds of confidentiality (Rule 70), compelling a witness to incriminate himself (Rule 90 E), and the possibility of withholding disclosure of evidence (Rule 70) put the Prosecutor in a privileged position and /allow/ the use of unequal and advantageous weapons in relation to the defence [...]. " *Ibid.*, p. 8.

103 Article 16 reads in part: "1. The Prosecutor shall be responsible for the investigation and prosecution of persons responsible for serious violations of international humanitarian law committed in the territory of the former Yugoslavia since 1 January 1991. 2. The Prosecutor shall act independently as a separate organ of the International Tribunal. He or she shall not seek or receive instructions from any Government or from any other source."

104 Preliminary Motions, pp. 9–13, paras. 2.1–2.18 Among the arguments, the Accused reiterates his claims concerning his illegal arrest (p. 9, para. 2.1) and his request to have the Indictment and the supporting material under Rule 66(A)(i) disclosed in the Cyrillic script (pp. 12–13, paras. 2.17–2.18).

105 *Ibid.*, p. 9, para. 2.2.

106 *Ibid.*, p. 10, para. 2.9. The Accused submits that "[t]he Indictment [...] contains no clear, unambiguous facts or factual information on the act and manner of commission of crimes, unlawfulness, causal link, objective and subjective elements necessary to identify the legal elements of a crime, or information indicating the likelihood that [he] committed the crimes with which [he is] charged [...]" and that "[c]onsidering that there are no elements of the crimes charged, [...] the International Tribunal has no jurisdiction to prosecute [him] for the counts of the Indictment." *Ibid.*

39. The Accused challenges a number of substantive allegations in the Indictment, claiming that some of them are not true, and others do not amount to criminal conduct or to any form of responsibility alleged in the Indictment.[107]

40. The Accused further challenges the joint criminal enterprise ("JCE"), arguing its lack of legal basis in the Statute[108] and the ambiguous way it is charged in the Indictment. In this last respect, the Accused submits that the Indictment (1) does not specify the causal link between the crimes charged and the Accused;[109] (ii) does not provide information on the creation of the common plan, its content and form;[110] and (iii) does not provide any basis for the existence of a joint criminal enterprise and for his alleged participation in it.[111] **[page 18]**

41. The Accused complains about the use of a document dated 1992 in support of the Indictment.[112] He also claims that the Prosecution has not provided facts relevant to the other forms of responsibility alleged in the Indictment.[113]

2. Response

42. The Prosecution avers that the Indictment is not defective because "the charges, specific crimes and nature of the Accused's involvement are clearly set out" and that the Indictment "details the nature and cause of the charges against the Accused in terms of these two JCEs", namely, his participation in the JCE to murder the able-bodied Muslim men from Srebrenica, and to forcibly transfer or deport the Bosnian Muslim population from Srebrenica and Žepa.[114] It also submits that the substantive allegations against the Accused that he seeks to address in the Indictment should be dealt with at trial.[115]

43. The Prosecution further submits the Accused's complaint about the reference to a document dated 1992 in support of the Indictment is ill-founded because "[t]here is no temporal limit on the evidence that may be used to prove any such crimes" as committed since 1991.[116]

B. General pleading principles

44. Article 18(4) and Rule 47(C) provide that an indictment shall contain a concise statement of the facts of the case and the crimes with which the accused is charged under the Statute. The provisions should be

---

107 The Accused alleges, *inter alia*, that "[t]he factual context of the Indictment and the description of [his] establishment duties and powers are incorrectly and imprecisely worded so that [he] can be imputed that [he] had any unit of the Army of Republika Srpska in the direct line of command or under [his] 'supervision', which is not true [...]" (*Ibid.*, pp. 9–10, para. 2.3) and that "[he is] charged in the Indictment with transmitting to General Krstić the order on the takeover of the Srebrenica enclave on 9 July 1995. This is neither a crime nor instigation [...]." (*Ibid.*, p. 11, para. 2.13); (iii) with regard to charges against him concerning Žepa, "[t]o conduct negotiations with soldiers and the population on the status of a demilitarised zone is not a war crime [...]." (*Ibid.*, p. 12, para. 2.15).

108 The Accused submits that "[w]hen adopting the Statute [...], the Security Council did not include conspiracy as a form or type of individual criminal responsibility. Insistence on [his] participation in joint criminal enterprises, against Article 7, paragraph 1 [...] constitutes a violation of the '*in dubio pro reo*' principle that suspicion is resolved in favour of the accused." *Ibid.*, p. 10, para. 2.6.

109 The Accused submits that "[his] alleged participation is used as a generally derived term for the commission or any form of co-perpetration, and there is a tendency to emphasize it or represent it outside any causal relationship. With this wording, the Indictment exceeds the prescribed and possible grounds of individual criminal responsibility and contravenes the provisions of Article 7 [...]." *Ibid.*, p. 10, para. 2.4.

110 The Accused submits that "[t]he Indictment does not specify at all who created the plan of a joint criminal enterprise, when the plan was made, what it contained, how it was worded orally or in writing, whether it was a public or secret document, etc". *Ibid.*, p. 10, para. 2.5.

111 The Accused submits that "[t]he wording 'participation in a joint criminal enterprise' in Article 7 [...] is groundless and represents an attempt at changing it and compensating for the lack of command responsibility and impossibility to prove the non-existent individual responsibility." (*Ibid.*, p. 10, para. 2.8) and that "[n]othing is provided to prove that such a 'joint enterprise' existed or how it could affect [his] criminal responsibility when [he] did not commit any of the crimes [charged] in the Indictment [...], nor [has he] ever or in any manner, consciously or unconsciously, took part and acted in any 'joint criminal enterprise'" (*Ibid.*, p. 11, para. 2.11).

112 The Accused submits that "[i]t is also unacceptable that 'Strategic Objectives of the Serbian People in Bosnia and Herzegovina', adopted on 12 May 1992 [...] are included in the Indictment as a preamble or pre-text for joint criminal enterprises, especially because the creator of the Statute did not criminalise them when it adopted the Statute a year later." *Ibid.*, p. 10, para. 2.7.

113 The Accused submits that "no crime which [he] personally planned and committed, or any specific crime by means of which [he] instigated, aided and abetted others has been listed. Nowhere does the Indictment cite my specific mutual relationship in the instigator-main perpetrator relation at the time the crime was committed." *Ibid.*, p. 11, para. 2.12.

114 Response, para. 25.

115 *Ibid.*, para. 26.

116 *Ibid.*, para. 27.

interpreted together with the rights of the accused set out in Article 21(2) and, in particular, Article 21(4)(a) and (b), which entitle the accused to be informed of the nature and cause of the charges against him in a language he understands, and to have adequate time and facilities for the preparation of his defence. These provisions translate into an obligation on the part of the Prosecution to plead the material facts underpinning the charges with enough detail to inform the accused clearly of the charges against him so that he may prepare his defence.[117] **[page 19]**

45. The materiality of a particular fact depends on the nature of the Prosecution case and the alleged criminal conduct with which the accused is charged. The materiality of facts such as the identity of the victims, the time and place of the events alleged in the indictment and the description of those events depends upon the proximity of the accused to those events and, therefore, the form of individual responsibility with which the accused is charged. It has been established in the jurisprudence of the Tribunal that the precise details to be pleaded as material facts are the acts of the accused himself, not the acts of those persons for whose acts he is alleged to be responsible.[118] Furthermore, where the scale of the crimes renders it impractical to require a high degree of specificity regarding, for example, the identity of the victims, the Prosecution does not need to identify every victim in the indictment in order to meet its obligation of specifying the material facts of the case.[119]

46. As to the pleading of different forms of liability under Article 7(1), it is required that the nature of the alleged individual responsibility of an accused be pleaded in an unambiguous way in the indictment.[120] The Prosecution is entitled to plead different forms of responsibility under Article 7(1). In such a case the Prosecution has to plead the material facts relevant to each of the modes of liability alleged in the indictment so that the accused may effectively prepare his defence.[121] Likewise, if the accused is charged with the "commission" of a crime, it should be made clear in the indictment whether he is charged with physical commission or participation in a JCE, or both.[122] An accused charged with participation in a JCE must be informed by the indictment of (i) the nature or purpose of the JCE; (ii) the period over which the enterprise is said to have existed; (iii) the identity of those engaged in the JCE, at least by reference to their category as a group; and (iv) the nature of participation of the accused in the JCE.[123] **[page 20]**

C. Discussion

47. As a preliminary matter, the Trial Chamber notes that the jurisdiction *ratione temporis* as defined in Article 1 of the Statute allows for the prosecution of crimes committed since 1991.[124] The Prosecution may use any evidence that it may deem relevant to support its case. There is no temporal limit on such evidence.

1. Challenges on the truth of allegations

48. Whether the allegations of the Indictment are true or not is not a matter to be considered at the pre-trial stage pursuant to Rule 72, but a matter of evidence to be proven during trial.[125] The Trial Chamber is not

117 *Prosecutor v. Blaškić*, Case No. IT-95-14-A, Judgement, 29 July 2004 ("*Blaškić* Appeal Judgement"), para. 209 citing *Prosecutor v. Kupreškić, Kupreškić, Kupreškić, Josipović, Šantić*, Case No. IT-95-16-A, Judgement, 23 October 2001 ("*Kupreškić et al.* Appeal Judgement"), para. 88). *See also, Prosecutor v. Popović, Beara, Nikolić, Borovčanin, Tolimir, Miletić, Gvero, Pandurević, Trbić*, Case No. IT-05-88-PT, Decision on Motions Challenging the Indictment pursuant to Rule 72 of the Rules, 31 May 2006 ("*Popović et al.* Decision Challenging Indictment"), para. 4.

118 *See e.g., Blaškić* Appeal Judgement, para. 210. *See also, Popović et al.* Decision Challenging Indictment, para. 5

119 *See e.g., Kupreškić et al.* Appeal Judgement, paras. 89–90. *See also, Popović et al.* Decision Challenging Indictment, para. 5.

120 *See e.g., Blaškić* Appeal Judgement, para. 226; *Krnojelac* Appeal Judgement, para. 138. *See also, Popović et al.* Decision Challenging Indictment, para. 25.

121 *See e.g., Prosecutor v. Kvočka, Radić, Žigić, Prcać*, Case No. IT-98-30/1-A, Judgement, 28 February 2005 ("*Kvočka* Appeal Judgement"), paras. 29, 41. *See also, Popović et al.* Decision Challenging Indictment, para. 25.

122 *See e.g., Prosecutor v. Krnojelac*, Case No. IT-97-25-A, Judgement, 17 September 2003 ("*Krnojelac* Appeal Judgement"), para. 138. *See also, Popović et al.* Decision Challenging Indictment, para. 25.

123 *See e.g., Prosecutor v. Brđanin,* Case No. IT-99-36-T, Judgement, 1 September 2004, para. 346; *Prosecutor v. Simić, Tadić, Zarić, Case* No. IT-95-9-T, Judgement, 17 October 2003, para. 145; *Prosecutor v. Krnojelac*, Case No. IT-97-25-PT, Decision on Form of Second Amended Indictment, 11 May 2000, para. 16; *Popović et al.* Decision Challenging Indictment, para. 44.

124 Article 1 of the Statute reads that the Tribunal "shall have the power to prosecute persons responsible for serious violations of international humanitarian law committed in the territory of the former Yugoslavia since 1991 [...]."

125 *See also, Popović et al.* Decision Challenging Indictment, para. 86.

required, at this stage in the proceedings, to determine whether there is sufficient evidence put forward by the Prosecution to support the allegations made against an accused in the indictment.[126] Accordingly, the Trial Chamber notes that any such submission of the Accused in his Motion on the form of the Indictment, including those in paragraphs 2.3, 2.14–2.15, relate to matters which do not concern the form of the Indictment, but to matters to be dealt with at trial.

2. Challenges to the pleading of material facts supporting crimes charged

49. The Accused is charged with two counts of genocide under Article 4, namely genocide and conspiracy to commit genocide;[127] five counts of crimes against humanity under Article 5, namely, extermination, murder, persecutions on political, racial and religious grounds, inhumane acts (forcible transfer) and deportation, and one count of violations of the laws or customs of war under Article 3, namely murder. The Indictment alleges that the Accused is individually responsible for the crimes charged against him pursuant to Article 7(1). The Indictment states that during the time **[page 21]** period relevant to the events described in the indictment, the Accused was the Assistant Commander for Intelligence and Security of the Main Staff of the VRS.[128]

50. The Prosecution has identified when and where the alleged crimes were committed. The Trial Chamber notes in particular that the Indictment pleads the alleged forcible separation of more than 1,000 Bosnian Muslim men and boys from their families in Potočari on 12 and 13 July 1995, and the removal of the entire Bosnian Muslim population from the area of Potočari by forced displacement of the women, children and elderly to Bosnian Muslim-controlled territory, and by forced displacement of the separated men and boys to different detention sites mentioned in the Indictment. The Indictment also pleads that, between 12 and about 19 July 1995, approximately 6,000 Bosnian men and boys, who were trying to escape the Srebrenica enclave, were captured or surrendered, and were together with the men who had been separated in Potočari detained in several detention sites and subsequently executed. Many of the detention and execution sites are listed and a detailed description of the alleged organised systematic murder of the Bosnian Muslim men provided in paragraphs 21.1 to 21.16 of the Indictment, as well of the alleged murder of the Bosnian Muslim men provided in paragraphs 22 to 22.4 of the Indictment. It further pleads in paragraphs 53–57 that on 14 July 1995 the Bosnian Serb Army ("VRS") started to attack the Žepa enclave by shelling civilian areas, that the women and children were transported out of the enclave from 25 July 1995 onwards, and that the men from the Žepa enclave were forced to flee to Serbia by, among other things, making life unbearable in the enclave.

51. The Trial Chamber is of the opinion that the Indictment contains a sufficient amount of information on the crimes charged, on their large-scale character, on the manner they were committed and on the fact they were committed with the alleged objectives to kill the able-bodied men of Srebrenica and to forcibly remove the Bosnian Muslim population from the Srebrenica and Žepa enclaves. The Trial Chamber is satisfied that this information provides the Accused with sufficient detail about the description of the events, including the victims of the alleged crimes.

3. Challenges on "joint criminal enterprise" and other forms of responsibility

52. In the present case, the Trial Chamber understands that the Accused's submissions on the JCE contain two allegations: (i) JCE is not a form of liability recognised in the Statute and (ii) the Indictment is ambiguous about the nature of the JCE and the role the Accused allegedly played in it. **[page 22]**

---

126 *See also, Prosecutor v. Pandurević and Trbić*, Case No. IT-05-86-AR73.1, Decision on Vinko Pandurević's Interlocutory Appeal Against the Trial Chamber's Decision on Joinder of Accused, 24 January 2006, para. 13.

127 The Indictment alleges that between 11 July 1995 and 1 November 1995, the Accused and others with intent to destroy a part of the Bosnian Muslim people as a national, ethnical, or religious group killed members of the group by summary execution, including both planned and opportunistic summary executions, and caused serious bodily or mental harm to both female and male members of the Bosnian Muslim population of Srebrenica and Žepa. The Indictment also alleges that the Accused and others entered into a conspiracy to commit genocide. According to the Indictment, the Accused and others agreed to kill the able-bodied Bosnian Muslim men from Srebrenica who were captured or surrendered after the fall of Srebrenica on 11 July 1995, and to remove the remaining Bosnian Muslim population of Srebrenica and Žepa from the RS, with the intent to destroy those Bosnian Muslims. *See* Indictment, paras. 10, 25.

128 *See* Indictment, para. 2.

53. The Appeals Chamber has on numerous occasions held that joint criminal enterprise is a mode of liability which is "firmly established in customary international law"[129] and is routinely applied in the Tribunal's jurisprudence.[130]

54. The Indictment charges the Accused with two JCEs, as it alleges that the Accused and others were members of and knowingly participated in a JCE, the common purpose of which was to summarily execute and bury the able-bodied Bosnian Muslim men from Srebrenica, and in another JCE, the common purpose of which was to force the Bosnian Muslim population out of the Srebrenica and Žepa enclaves to areas outside the control of the RS from about 8 March 1995 through the end of August 1995.[131] In this respect, the Trial Chamber notes that paragraphs 8 and 9 of the Indictment address both JCEs together, as they were closely interlinked. Paragraph 8 of the Indictment states that, following Radovan Karadžić's order of 8 March 1995 to remove the Bosnian Muslim population from the Srebrenica and Žepa enclaves, the Srebrenica enclave was taken over on 11 and 12 July 1995 and the plan to remove the Bosnian Muslim population from Srebrenica was implemented, along with the plan to murder all the able-bodied men of Srebrenica. Paragraph 9 of the Indictment alleges that, by 1 November 1995, the entire Bosnian Muslim population had either been removed or had fled from Srebrenica and Žepa, and that over 7,000 Muslim men and boys from Srebrenica had been murdered. The Trial Chamber further notes that the Indictment states that the time period during which the Accused is alleged to have committed genocide was between 11 July and 1 November 1995.[132] Moreover, the Trial Chamber notes that paragraph 18 alleges that, in the evening hours of 11 July and morning of 12 July—at the same time the plan to forcibly transport the Bosnian Muslim population from Potočari was developed—Ratko Mladić and members of his staff developed the plan to murder the hundreds of able-bodied men identified from the crowd of Muslims in Potočari. This paragraph further identifies the responsibilities of the Accused and others in relation to the execution of the plan to murder these men. In paragraph 19 the Prosecution alleges that on the afternoon of 12 July the plan to murder the able-bodied men of Srebrenica began to be carried out. **[page 23]**

55. In relation specifically to the JCE to kill the all the able-bodied Bosnian Muslim men, paragraph 27 explicitly deals with the Conspiracy and the JCE to murder the able-bodied Bosnian Muslim men from Srebrenica. It states that, on or about 12 July 1995, this JCE was implemented, and further specifies that the initial plan was to summarily execute around 1,000 Bosnian Muslim men who had been separated in Potočari on 12 and 13 July, but that in the same days this plan was broadened to include the summary execution of more than 6,000 men who were captured from the column of Bosnian Muslim men escaping the Srebrenica enclave. The plan is alleged to have extended in duration from 12 July through about 1 November 1995.

56. As to the JCE to forcibly remove the Bosnian Muslim population, paragraph 35 states that the Accused, together with other VRS and MUP (the Ministry of the Interior) officers and units and RS officials, were members of and knowingly participated in a JCE, the common purpose of which was to force the Bosnian Muslim population out of the Srebrenica and Žepa enclaves to areas outside the control of the RS, from about 8 March 1995 through the end of August 1995.

57. At paragraphs 71 and 72, the Prosecution identifies a number of officers within these JCEs, as well as various other individuals and military and police units who participated in the implementation of the two JCEs.

58. The Trial Chamber therefore considers that, with the above cited allegations in the Indictment, the Prosecution has pleaded with enough detail the purpose, the periods of the existence of the two JCEs, and the identification of their alleged members. Furthermore, the Trial Chamber observes that the paragraphs which

129 *Tadić* Appeal Judgement, para. 220.

130 *Prosecutor v. Stakić*, Case No. IT-97-24-A, Judgement, 22 March 2006, para. 62, referring to *Kvočka* Appeal Judgement, para. 79; *Prosecutor v. Vasiljević*, Case No. IT-98-32-A, Judgement, 25 February 2004, para. 95; *Prosecutor v. Krstić*, Case No. IT-98-33-A, Judgement, 19 April 2004, paras. 79–134; *Prosecutor v. Milutinović, Šainović, Ojdanić,* Case No. IT-99-37-AR72, Decision on *Dragoljub Ojdanić*'s Motion Challenging Jurisdiction – Joint Criminal Enterprise, 21 May 2003, paras. 20, 43; *Prosecutor v. Furundžija*, Case No. IT-95-17/1-A, Judgement, 21 July 2000, para. 119; *Krnojelac* Appeal Judgement paras. 29–32; *Prosecutor v. Delalić, Mucić, a.k.a. "Pavo", Delić, Landžo, a.k.a. "Zenga"*, Case No. IT-96-21-A, Judgement, 20 February 2001, para. 366; *Tadić* Appeal Judgement, para. 220, *Prosecutor v. Brđanin and Talić,* Case No: IT-99-36-PT, Decision on Form of Further Amended Indictment and Prosecution Application to Amend, 26 June 2001, para. 24; *Prosecutor v. Babić,* Case No. IT-03-72-A, Judgement on Sentencing Appeal, 18 July 2005, paras. 27, 38, 40. *See also, Popović et al.* Decision Challenging Indictment, para. 44.

131 *See* Indictment, para. 35.

132 *See* Indictment, para. 10.

describe the actions of the Accused in the two JCEs provide sufficient information as to when his actions took place.[133]

59. Finally, the Trial Chamber notes that paragraph 66 of the Indictment alleges that the Accused "committed, planned, instigated, ordered and otherwise aided and abetted in the planning, preparation, and execution of these charged crimes, as set out in detail in this indictment". It is further alleged that the term "committing" does include participation in a JCE. As mentioned above, the Trial Chamber is satisfied that the crimes charged have been pleaded with sufficient detail. Moreover, the acts and omissions ascribed to the Accused are described in the eight counts and in particular in paragraphs 29 and 60 of the Indictment.

60. In paragraph 29, the Prosecution alleges with regard to the JCE to kill the Bosnian Muslim men that the Accused committed acts in furtherance of the JCE and Conspiracy as described in paragraphs 25–28 and the following acts: (1) "[w]ith full knowledge of the plan to summarily **[page 24]** execute the able-bodied men from Srebrenica, he assisted in and facilitated the forcible transfer and deportation of the Muslim population of Srebrenica, as described in paragraphs 61 to 64 of this Indictment"; (2) "[o]n 13 July 1995, he assisted in the JCE to detain and execute the able-bodied men from Srebrenica by proposing to his commander Ratko Mladić that the hundreds of Muslim prisoners being detained along the Konjević Polje-Bratunac road be secreted from international forces by being placed in buildings so they could not be viewed from the air; (3) [h]e supervised the 10th Sabotage Detachment on 16 July 1995 when elements of this unit summarily executed more than 1,700 Muslim men and boys at the Branjevo Military Farm and the Pilica Cultural Centre; and (4) "[a]s Assistant Commander for Intelligence and Security of the Main Staff, and by virtue of the authority vested in him by his commander, Ratko Mladić, he had responsibility for the handling of all of the Bosnian Muslim prisoners taken after the fall of the Srebrenica enclave and to ensure their safety and welfare. He failed to do so".[134]

61. In paragraph 60, the Prosecution alleges, with regard to the Accused's role in the JCE to forcibly remove the Bosnian Muslims, that he committed acts in furtherance of the JCE as described in paragraphs 34–37 and as well as the following acts: (1) "[m]aking life unbearable for the inhabitants of the Žepa enclave: [...] in July 1995 he proposed to General Radivoje Miletić that the refugee columns comprised of the Muslim population from Žepa be attacked"; (2) "[d]efeating the Muslim forces militarily: [...] he communicated with the Drina Corps Forward Command Post and RS President Radovan Karadžić about combat operations around Srebrenica and the decision to take over Srebrenica; and [...] in July 1995 he proposed to General Radivoje Miletić to destroy the remaining Muslim army from Žepa by using chemical weapons"; (3) "[d]isabling the local UN forces militarily: [...] he assisted in disabling UNPROFOR in the attack on Srebrenica through his communications with UNPROFOR, specifically by lying to UNPROFOR, and coordinating lies with subordinate units"; (4) "[p]reventing and controlling outside international protection of the enclaves, including air strikes and international monitoring: [...] he organised and led the psychological and propaganda activities related to the operations in Žepa and Srebrenica"; and (5) "[c]ontrolling the movement of the Muslim population out of the enclaves: [...] he gave orders related to and coordinated the forcible transfer of men, including civilians, from the Srebrenica and Žepa enclaves; [...] he helped to coordinate the detention of prisoners from Srebrenica; [...] he took part in negotiations with Muslim representatives at Žepa and gave them the choice between "evacuation" or VRS "military action"; and, [...] he helped to organise and oversee the **[page 25]** transportation of the population of Žepa, including by assembling the buses and loading people onto the buses".[135]

62. The Trial Chamber notes that the Indictment must be considered as a whole, to the extent that the pleading of different forms of individual criminal liability in the alternative is substantiated by the allegations made throughout the entire Indictment.[136] The Trial Chamber is satisfied that the material facts to support each of those modes are adequately pleaded in the Indictment in order to allow the Accused to prepare his defence.

133 *See* Indictment, paras. 29, 60.
134 Indictment, para. 29.
135 Indictment, para. 60.
136 *See also, Popović et al.* Decision Challenging Indictment, para. 26.

IV. MOTION ON SEVERANCE OF COUNTS

A. Submissions of the parties

1. Motion

63. The Accused requests severance of the counts joined in the Indictment for Srebrenica and Žepa in accordance with "time and place", as this would facilitate his analysis of the numerous aspects of the Indictment.[137] He asserts that "it is unusual to join the counts of an indictment only because of the classification of crimes"[138] and that [p]revious practice at the Tribunal through the trials of the co-accused for Srebrenica and Žepa confirms the justification for the severance and the non-existence of the casual link which would necessitate a joinder, which opens up a possibility of making wrong conclusions, and presenting or failing to present evidence important for the fairness of the proceedings and establishment of the truth."[139] **[page 26]**

2. Response

64. The Prosecution submits that the request for severance of the joined count should be denied in light of Rule 49.[140] The charges clearly qualify, argues the Prosecution, "as forming the same transaction and may properly be joined in the Indictment" because they concern the events in Srebrenica and Žepa in Eastern Bosnia in 1995 and similar groups of persons participated in the two JCEs.[141]

B. Discussion

65. Rule 49 allows the joinder of two or more crimes in one indictment "if the series of acts committed together form the same transaction, and the said crimes were committed by the same accused." Rule 2(A) sets forth the definition of "transaction": "A number of acts or omissions whether occurring as one event or a number of events, at the same or different locations and being part of a common scheme, strategy or plan."

66. In the present case, the charges against the Accused are related to events that took place in Srebrenica and Žepa, which is part of Eastern Bosnia and in 1995. The crimes have therefore been allegedly committed in the same geographical area during substantially the same time period. Moreover, the Indictment alleges that similar groups belonging to the armed forces of the RS participated in the JCE to murder the able-bodied men from Srebrenica and the JCE to forcibly remove the Bosnian Muslim population from Srebrenica and Žepa. The Indictment alleges that the crimes committed in the two enclaves were part of a common scheme, strategy or plan. The Trial Chamber further notes that the Indictment in the *Popović et al.* case charges the seven accused in that case with the same events.

67. For the reasons above, the Trial Chamber finds that the fairness of the trial will not be affected by not severing the charges in the Indictment and that the Accused will not be prejudiced in the preparation of his defence. In fact, the Trial Chamber believes that it is in the interests of justice that the events related to crimes allegedly committed in Srebrenica and Žepa in July 1995 be considered in one single indictment. This Motion is therefore denied.

---

137 Preliminary Motions, p. 13, para. 3.1–3.2. The Accused numerates the following aspects: "the material truth of the existence of crimes; individual crimes charged; circumstances which led to the commission of crimes described; the formal evidence of my individual or conscious participation; the role of individual participations in a non-existent 'joint criminal enterprise'; the role of the instigator and main perpetrator; premeditation on the part of the instigator; elements, relationship and circumstances which confirm or deny criminal responsibility; the personal relationship between the perpetrator and victims; the difference in the degree of suspicion; the precise description of the crimes in respect of which the accused is charged with individual responsibility; avoidance of the possibility of the Prosecution's individualising the charges against [him] for alternative criminal responsibility; prevention and systematic application of international humanitarian law, or its violation; and a number of other elements of the substance of the crime charged for both locations, that is, both for Srebrenica and Žepa at the same time, but with different participants in the events." *Ibid.*, p. 13, para. 3.1.

138 *Ibid.*, p. 14, para. 3.2.

139 *Ibid.* The Accused however failed to refer to any case-law of the Tribunal.

140 Response, para. 29.

141 *Ibid.*

68. Lastly, the Trial Chamber notes that in the Preliminary Motions the Accused raises two other separate issues, namely, disclosure of the Indictment and the supporting material in the **[page 27]** Serbian language in the Cyrillic script,[142] and the appointment of hifs legal adviser and defence team.[143] The Trial Chamber notes that on 16 November 2007, the Accused submitted a separate motion on the very same issues.[144] During the second status conference held on 11 December 2007, the Pre-Trial Judge orally ruled on this motion.[145] Accordingly, the Trial Chamber will not address these matters in the present decision.

V. DISPOSITION

For these reasons, pursuant to Articles 20 and 21 of the Statute and Rules 49 and 72 of the Rules, the Trial Chamber hereby

(1) DENIES the Motion on Jurisdiction,

(2) DENIES the Motion on the form of the Indictment, and

(3) DENIES the Motion on severance of counts.

Done in English and French, the English text being authoritative.

Dated this fourteenth day of December 2007
At The Hague
The Netherlands

Carmel Agius
Presiding

[Seal of the Tribunal]

142 The Accused requests that the Indictment and the supporting material under Rule 66 (A)(ii) be disclosed in Serbian and in the Cyrillic script. Preliminary Motions, pp.12–13, paras. 2.16–2.18 and p. 14, paras. 4.3–4.4. The Prosecution responds that it is not obliged to provide documents to the Accused in the Cyrillic script and it has already set out its position in the "Prosecution's Response to Submission by the Accused dated 25 September 2007 with Appendix", filed on 10 October 2007. Response, para. 28. *See also ibid.*, para. 30.

143 Preliminary Motions, pp. 14–15 [4]. The Prosecution submits that it cannot comment on the arrangements for the Accused's representation as it is not aware of communications between the Accused and the Registry, but that "if the Accused is unwilling or unable to conduct his own defence in a competent manner, he should be assigned counsel." Response, para. 30.

144 Motion to the Pre-Trial Chamber and the Registrar Concerning Assistance in Appointing a Legal Advisor, Disclosure of Material in a Language the Accused Understands and Notification of Special Defence on the Charges in the Indictment, 16 November 2007 (BCS original), 20 November 2007 (English translation).

145 Status Conference, T. 112–117 (11 December 2007).

Commentary

1. Introduction

Challenges to the legality of arrests and transfer proceedings dramatically underscore the delicate balance that the judges at the ICTY and other international criminal tribunals must regularly maintain between the rights of the accused and the essential interests of the international community. Kidnapping and luring are the two most common forms of unlawful arrest. In such cases, the judges at the ICTY can issue remedies such as dismissing the case, declaring an abuse of process, deciding that they do not have jurisdiction to hear the case, reducing the sentence, or providing some monetary compensation to the accused in the case of acquittal. The position of the ICTY in these cases suggests its institutional divergence from national courts and the degree to which concerns about its integrity govern its regular operations.

In this case, the accused, Zdravko Tolimir, was arrested on the Serbia-Bosnia border on 31 May 2007 and taken by NATO to The Hague. At the preliminary hearing, the accused claimed that he had been abducted from his apartment and that the tribunal had no jurisdiction over him.[1] He further submitted that his arrest was illegal, violating the constitution and national laws of Serbia, the ICTY statute and RPE, and other international human rights instruments.[2] The prosecution responded by claiming that it had no knowledge or involvement in the alleged "illegal" arrest, and that there was no reason to believe that the arrest actually was conducted in an "illegal" manner.[3]

2. Past cases with claims of illegal arrest compared to Tolimir

This was not the first case in which the ICTY Trial Chambers heard an accused submit a similar claim. Thus, in order to decide this case, the court reexamined its previous jurisprudence on alleged illegal transnational arrests. In such cases, the court has generally framed the issue as a balancing test between the need to weigh the legitimate expectation that an individual accused of such grave crimes should be brought to justice against both the need to protect state sovereignty and the rights of the said accused. However, this equation is only partially applicable, since in cases where state sovereignty has been violated, chambers will usually not pursue the matter in the absence of a complaint lodged by the state.[4]

Regardless of this balancing test, the ICTY has never refused to exercise jurisdiction when deciding cases in which the accused claimed that he had been illegally abducted. The ICTR did find that the abuse of process had been so great in one case as to initially prohibit the court from exercising jurisdiction. In Barayagwiza, the Appeals Chamber found that a number of the rights of the accused had been violated before trial, including his right to be promptly charged, and to an initial appearance without undue delay. The judges invoked the abuse of process doctrine and dismissed the charges against the accused with prejudice.[5] However, in response, the Rwandan government refused to allow the ICTR to continue its activities. Shortly after, the Trial Chamber decision was overturned – suggesting the influence that States have on the functioning of the ICTY.[6]

The ICTY has frequently relied on European or Commonwealth jurisprudence when deciding difficult legal issues. More often than not, other international practices are taken as helpful guidance when making decisions at the ICTY.[7] Yet in the cases confronting the issue of illegal abduction, the ICTY has not followed European or Commonwealth practice. The ICTY's decisions in *Prosecutor v. Dokmanović, Prosecutor v. Todorović,*

---

1 ICTY, Decision on preliminary motions on the indictment pursuant to Rule 72 of the Rules, *Prosecutor v. Tolimir*, Case No. IT-05-88/2, T. Ch. II, 14 December 2007, in this volume, p. 29, par. 9.

2 *Ibid.*, par. 10.

3 *Ibid.*, par. 11.

4 *Ibid.*, par. 19.

5 ICTR, Decision, *Barayagwiza v. Prosecutor*, Case No. ICTR-97-19-AR72, A. Ch., 3 November 1999, Klip/ Sluiter, ALC-II-129, par.100, 101 and 108.

6 J. K. Cogan, International Criminal Courts and Fair Trials: Difficulties and Prospects, 27 Yale Journal of International Law 2002, p. 135.

7 See, for example, ICTY, Judgement, *Prosecutor v. Furundžija*, Case No. IT-95-17/1-T, T. Ch. II, 10 December 1998, Klip/ Sluiter, ALC-III-685, relying primarily on Austrian, French, Italian, Australian, and English cases.

Prosecutor v. Nikolić, and most recently in *Prosecutor v. Tolimir* suggest that it has adopted a limited reading of the circumstances under which a court may refuse to exercise jurisdiction over a defendant who has been abducted. The only possible grounds are a violation of state sovereignty or a violation of human rights—and neither have, thus far, been found. This decision not to follow European or Commonwealth practice on this issue points to a fundamental institutional difference between the ICTY and national courts.

Slavko Dokmanović was one of the first major war criminals brought before the ICTY. He had originally contacted the Office of the Prosecutor (OTP) to give evidence of atrocities committed by the Croats against the Serbs, but after luring him in, UNTAES handcuffed him and informed him of the charges against him.[8] The Trial Chamber decided that the defendant's rights had not been breached because the OTP had not participated in the arrest itself. Although the ICCPR's Human Rights Committee has found that forcible transnational abduction constitutes an arbitrary arrest under Article 9, paragraph 1 of the ICCPR (or a violation of the human rights of the accused), in this case it was held to be permissible luring.[9] The Trial Chamber also spent time assessing whether the Federal Republic of Yugoslavia's (FRY) sovereignty had been violated, but found that the arrest had not occurred in the FRY's territory, and that even if it had, there was a fundamental difference between the vertical relationship of the ICTY to States and the horizontal relationships of the States to each other.[10]

In Todorović, the ICTY again had to respond to a situation of alleged illegal abduction. Todorović was charged with crimes against humanity and war crimes, but claimed that he had been arrested through a forcible abduction, in which he was gagged and blindfolded, and then smuggled him out of Serbia into Bosnia where he was arrested by a NATO force.[11] However, shortly after Todorović presented this argument, he entered into a plea agreement and the circumstances of his arrest were not investigated further.[12]

Finally, the ICTY addressed the issue of an alleged transnational abduction in the *Prosecutor v. Nikolić* and once again sustained jurisdiction. Nikolić submitted that he had been kidnapped in Serbia and transferred to the hands of SFOR officers stationed in Bosnia and Herzegovina.[13] It was stipulated that he was taken against his will and that the alleged kidnapping was undertaken by officials with no ties to SFOR. In deciding to sustain jurisdiction, the Trial Chamber emphasized that once having received the accused, the SFOR was duty bound to turn him over to the ICTY; that the vertical relationship between the Tribunal and the state meant that no violation of state sovereignty had resulted; and that the accused's fundamental rights had not been violated.

This was affirmed by the Appeals Chamber, which following the *Attorney General of Israel v. Eichmann* and *Fédération Nationale des Déportés et Internés Résistants et Patriots v. Barbie*, held that in cases like genocide, crimes against humanity and war crimes, the special character of the offenses offered good reason for not setting aside jurisdiction.[14] Again, it emphasized the need to balance the principles of state sovereignty and the fundamental human rights of the accused against the expectation that individuals who commit these types of crimes should be brought to justice quickly.

In the present case, the accused, Tolimir, was charged with genocide, crimes against humanity, and war crimes. The Trial Chamber relied on its previous jurisprudence to find that the "serious crimes" charged in the case were too grave to warrant setting aside jurisdiction. Citing Nikolić, the court found that the treatment of the appellant was not so egregious as to impede the exercise of jurisdiction, and that only if the accused was seriously mistreated, subject to inhumane, cruel, degrading treatment or torture, if persons

---

8 ICTY, Decision on the Motion for Release by the Accused Slavko Dokmanović, *Prosecutor v. Mrkšić, Radić, Šljivančanin and Dokmanović*, Case No. IT-95-13a-PT, T. Ch. II, 22 October 1997, Klip/ Sluiter, ALC-III-127.

9 *Ibid.*, p. 136.

10 *Ibid.*, p. 138.

11 J. Sloan, Prosecutor v. Todorović: Illegal Capture as an Obstacle to the Exercise of International Criminal Jurisdiction, 16 Leiden Journal of International Law 2003, p. 85.

12 *Ibid.*, p. 85 and 92.

13 ICTY, Decision on Defence Motion Challenging the Exercise of Jurisdiction by the Tribunal, *Prosecutor v. Nikolić*, Case No. IT-94-2-PT, T. Ch. II, 9 October 2002, Klip/ Sluiter, ALC-XI-79, par. 85.

14 ICTY, Decision on Interlocutory Appeal Concerning Legality of Arrest, *Prosecutor v. Nikolić*, Case No. IT-94-2-AR73, A. Ch., 5 June 2003, Klip/ Sluiter, ALC-XIV-123, p. 24, 25 and 26 (interpreting Supreme Court of Israel, *Attorney General of Israel v. Eichmann*, 29 May 1962, 36 International Law Reports 1968, and Cour de Cassation, *Fédération nationale des déportés et internés résistants et al. v. Barbie*, 20 December 1985, 78 International Law Reports 1988).

acting for the SFOR or prosecutor were involved, or if exercising jurisdiction would prove detrimental to the court's integrity, would the court not exercise jurisdiction.[15] It found further that the remedy of setting aside jurisdiction would usually be disproportionate when balancing the rights of the accused against the essential interests of the international community.

The Trial Chamber held that even assuming that the accused rights were violated in such a manner, it was not grave enough to warrant his release and that there was no evidence that NATO or the prosecution was involved in the initial stage of his arrest.[16] The accused's argument that the tribunal itself was unlawful and biased and not in accordance with international standards and that the form of liability with which he was charged was not recognized by international law, were also similarly dismissed because, since Tadić, it has been established that the tribunal was lawfully established in accordance with international law and the ICTY has repeatedly applied the JCE form of liability.[17] None of his other general legal assertions about the sentencing guidelines, detention policy, or equality of arms, was found to constitute a valid challenge to the jurisdiction of the tribunal.[18] Thus, following in the established line of jurisprudence with regards to such cases, the court again framed the issue as a balancing test between the need to weigh the legitimate expectation that an individual accused of such grave crimes should be brought to justice against both the need to protect state sovereignty and the rights of the said accused. It found that there had not been such an egregious violation of the rights of the accused as to outweigh the other countervailing interests.

3. Insights gained from cases of transnational abduction

The position of the ICTY taken in these cases of alleged transnational abduction suggests first its differences from national courts, and second, the degree to which concerns about its institutional integrity govern its regular operations.

First, unlike national courts, the tribunal is a super-sovereign entity created by the Security Council, without a real executive arm. Its structure fundamentally affects the rights of the defendant. Whereas a national court may refuse to exercise jurisdiction because it feels that its territory has been illegally violated or because law enforcement has violated an extradition treaty,[19] neither of these are viable reasons not to exercise jurisdiction in the ICTY context. Legal scholars and ICTY judges agree that extradition treaties are inapplicable to the ICTY context.[20]

Second, the ICTY has both factually and legally resisted using the abuse of process doctrine. It has not linked any of the alleged illegal abductions to the responsibility of either the OTP or the SFOR and has declined to decide whether the OTP, SFOR, and tribunal, occupy the same relationship to one another as a national police office, prosecutor, and court.[21] The ICTY is necessarily handicapped in that it depends on states to be effective at all.[22] Because it has no means to execute arrests and relies heavily on the SFOR, it is unlikely to question the means by which defendants arrive at the tribunal. Technically, because of the ICTY's grounding in the Security Council's chapter VII powers, all states are obliged to cooperate with ICTY orders

---

15 *Ibid.*

16 Decision on preliminary motions on the indictment pursuant to Rule 72 of the Rules, *Prosecutor v. Tolimir*, T. Ch. II, *supra* note 1, par. 59–63.

17 ICTY, Decision on the Defence Motion for Interlocutory Appeal on Jurisdiction, *Prosecutor v. Tadić*, Case No. IT-94-1-AR72, A. Ch., 2 October 1995, Klip/ Sluiter, ALC-I-33, par. 9–48.

18 Decision on preliminary motions on the indictment pursuant to Rule 72 of the Rules, *Prosecutor v. Tolimir*, T. Ch. II, *supra* note 1, par. 28.

19 For example, see United States District Court Ohio, *In the Matter of the Extradition of John Demjanjuk*, 15 April 1985, 612 Federal Supplement 1985, p. 555, stating the treaty requirement; United States District Court New York, *In re the Extradition of Hermine Ryan* (*nee* Braunsteiner), a fugitive from the justice of the Federal Republic of Germany, 1 May 1973, 360 Federal Supplement 1973, p. 272 and 273, holding that if the two state parties are in conflict, any extradition treaty between them is suspended. Both decisions are important.

20 Decision on Defence Motion Challenging the Exercise of Jurisdiction by the Tribunal, *Prosecutor v. Nikolić*, T. Ch. II, *supra* note 13, par. 103; Decision on the Motion for Release by the Accused Slavko Dokmanović, *Prosecutor v. Mrkšić, Radić, Šljivančanin and Dokmanović*, Case No. IT-95-13a-PT, T. Ch. II, *supra* note 8, p. 136 and 137.

21 J. Sloan, Prosecutor v. Todorović: Illegal Capture as an Obstacle to the Exercise of International Criminal Jurisdiction, *supra* note 11, p. 104.

22 As seen with the Barayagwiza case at the ICTR.

and indictments. Further, because contrary domestic law does not excuse a violation of international law, even if the indictee were protected under domestic law, he could not argue that this protected him from the process of the ICTY.[23]

4. Conclusion

With the establishment of the ICC, the ICTY's jurisprudence on claims of illegal abduction has become particularly important. A *prima facie* standard has been used with regards to the ICTY, while it has been a reasonable basis test with the ICC, but the ICTY's case law is still formative. As the ICC has less state parties than the ICTY, which includes all U.N. Members, claims of illegal abductions are likely to be a continuing problem. The ICC will have to decide if it will follow the strict route of the ICTY governed by concerns of institutional integrity or model itself more after national jurisdictions.

Jocelyn Courtney

[23] See, for example, ICTY, Decision on Preliminary Motions, *Prosecutor v. Milošević*, Case No. IT-99-37-PT, T. Ch. III, 8 November 2001, Klip/ Sluiter, ALC-VIII-15, par. 47, for a rejection of this argument.

UNITED NATIONS

International Tribunal for the Prosecution of Persons Responsible for Serious Violations of International Humanitarian Law Committed in the Territory of Former Yugoslavia since 1991	Case No. IT-06-90-PT Date: 5 April 2007 Original: English

IN TRIAL CHAMBER I

Before:	**Judge Bakone Justice Moloto, Pre-Trial Judge** **Judge Alphons Orie** **Judge Christine Van den Wyngaert**
Registrar:	**Mr. Hans Holthuis**
Decision of:	**5 April 2007**

PROSECUTOR

v.

ANTE GOTOVINA

IVAN ČERMAK

MLADEN MARKAČ

DECISION ON CONFLICT OF INTEREST OF ATTORNEYS ČEDO PRODANOVIĆ AND JADRANKA SLOKOVIĆ

The Office of the Prosecutor:

Mr. Alan Tieger
Ms. Laurie Sartorio

Counsel for the Accused:

Mr. Luka S. Mišetić, Mr. Gregory Kehoe and Mr. Payam Akhavan for Ante Gotovina
Mr. Čedo Prodanović and Ms. Jadranka Sloković for Ivan Čermak
Mr. Miroslav Šeparović and Mr. Goran Mikuličić for Mladen Markač

[page 2] 1. In the present decision, the views expressed by the Judges of the Trial Chamber are held in common, unless otherwise indicated through reference to the "Majority". Judge Orie will file a Dissenting Opinion which discusses his reasons for disagreeing with the Majority.

2. The conflict of interest issue posed by Mr. Čedo Prodanović's ("Prodanović") and Ms. Jadranka Sloković's ("Sloković") (collectively "Prodanović/Sloković") dual representation of the Accused Ivan Čermak ("Čermak") in these proceedings and Rahim Ademi ("Ademi") in proceedings in Croatia pursuant to a Rule 11*bis* referral[1] was first raised in "Defendant Ante Gotovina's Response in Opposition to the Prosecution's Consolidated Motion to Amend the Indictment and for Joinder" of 4 April 2006 ("Gotovina Response to Joinder Motion"). Gotovina opposed the joinder of his case with that of Čermak's and the Accused Mladen Markač's ("Markač"). He argued, *inter alia,* that this potential conflict of interest would prejudice him.[2] On 25 October 2006, the Appeals Chamber, in its "Decision on Interlocutory Appeals against the Trial Chamber's Decision to Amend the Indictment and for Joinder" ("Decision of 25 October 2006"), confirmed Trial Chamber II's "Decision on Prosecution's Consolidated Motion to Amend the Indictment and for Joinder" of 14 July 2006 ("Decision of 14 July 2006"). The Decision of 14 July 2006 had held that any conflict of interest arising out of the Prodanović/Sloković representation was not such as to prevent the joinder of the cases of Markač, Čermak and Ante Gotovina ("Gotovina").[3]

3. The Trial Chamber notes the Advisory Opinion of the Disciplinary Council of the Association of Defence Counsel of the Tribunal of 17 January 2007, received on 18 January 2007[4] and the "Notice to the Trial Chamber concerning Undertakings provided by Ivan Čermak and Rahim Ademi" of 8 February 2007. Two undertakings, signed by the Accused Čermak ("Čermak Undertaking") and Rahim Ademi ("Ademi Undertaking") respectively (collectively "Čermak and Ademi Undertakings"), were attached. The Trial Chamber is seized of the "Submission to the Trial Chamber concerning the Alleged Conflict of Interest affecting Counsel Čedo Prodanović and Jadranka Sloković" of 14 February 2007 ("Prodanović/Sloković Submission") and the "Prosecution's Submission Regarding Potential Conflict of Interest of Defence Counsel" of 14 February 2007 ("Prosecution Submission"). It is also seized of Prodanović's and Sloković's further "Submission concerning the Prosecution's Submission regarding Potential Conflict of Interests of **[page 3]** Defence Counsel" which was filed confidentially on 15 February 2007 ("Prodanović/Sloković Further Submission").

4. The issue of conflict of interest arises out of Prodanović's and Sloković's dual representation of Čermak and Ademi. Gotovina contended that one of Čermak's defence strategies could be to argue that Gotovina, who was Čermak's commanding officer, was in fact responsible for certain alleged crimes.[5] According to Gotovina,

> During Operation Storm, General Ademi was General Gotovina's Chief of Staff and second-in-command to the Commander of the Split Military District. Given General Ademi's place in the chain of command as General Gotovina's immediate subordinate, the charges against General Gotovina in the proposed Joinder Indictment could be applied against General Ademi.[6]

Furthermore, Gotovina claims he will show that he was on honeymoon during the crucial time in which the charged crimes were allegedly committed and that during his leave of absence, General Ademi was Acting Commander of the Split Military District.[7] The Gotovina Defence has already indicated that it considers him a crucial witness[8] and it also raises the point that should Prodanović and Sloković cross-examine their client Ademi in the current proceedings, they may be privy to confidential information which could harm Ademi by challenging his credibility, if used, and which could harm Čermak, if not used.[9]

---

1 *Prosecutor v. Rahim Ademi et al*, "Decision for Referral to the Authorities of the Republic of Croatia pursuant to Rule 11*bis*", Case No. IT-04-78-PT, 14 September 2005.

2 Gotovina Response to Joinder Motion, paras 5–7, 54–62.

3 Decision of 14 July 2006, paras 63–64;71.

4 Advisory Opinion of the Disciplinary Council of the Association of Defence Counsel of the Tribunal, paras 3, 6, 11, 13, 16–17, 33–50, 53.

5 Gotovina Response to Joinder Motion, paras 54 and 61.

6 *Ibid.*, para. 55.

7 *Ibid.*, para. 56.

8 Gotovina Response to Joinder Motion, para. 55.

9 Gotovina Response to Joinder Motion, para. 60.

5. Prodanović and Sloković argue that conclusions as to the substance of Čermak's defence strategy are without merit. They have never mentioned such a defence as possible and they hold that the defences of all Accused can run in parallel.[10] Furthermore, Prodanović and Sloković argue that even if such a defence strategy was in Čermak's interest, it is highly unlikely in the context of the allegation of joint criminal enterprise with which all Accused are charged[11] that this would be a successful defence. Prodanović and Sloković state further that Ademi's chance to appear as a witness is very low. He will not be called as a witness for Čermak or for Markač, the possibility that he is called by the Trial Chamber is at best, at this time, remote and the Prosecution has not included him in its witness list. Prodanović and Sloković argue that since the underlying events material to the proceedings against Ademi in Croatia are unrelated to the events in the proceedings against Čermak, they would be able to cross-examine Ademi, even aggressively.[12] They state that **[page 4]** the Appeals Chamber, the Trial Chamber and the ADC Disciplinary Council agree that such a conflict might arise only if Ademi is called as a witness having *adverse* interests to Čermak *and* if there is a need to aggressively cross-examine him in favour of Čermak.[13] With regard to the possession and use of Ademi's confidential information, Prodanović and Sloković declare that Ademi revealed nothing in confidence to them which would be useful to Čermak.[14] Furthermore, they argue that a third counsel could be hired to handle the unlikely possibility that they may need to challenge Ademi's credibility should his cross-examination be necessary.[15]

6. In his Undertaking, Ademi confirms that he was informed by Prodanović and Sloković on the possibility of his being called as a witness in Čermak's case, and of their having to cross-examine him. Ademi states that he has openly and thoroughly discussed with his counsel the potential impact this could have on their ability to represent him.[16] Ademi confirms that he was Gotovina's Chief of Staff during the events which were the background of the alleged crimes for which Čermak is indicted,[17] that he will not testify voluntarily in the proceedings against Čermak[18] and he also states that he never discussed any event related to the Relevant Timeframe with his counsel and does not intend to do so since it is unrelated to the charges he is facing in Croatia.[19] On the other hand, Čermak confirms that his counsel have discussed the possibility that Ademi is called as a witness for one of the parties in the case, that they would have to cross-examine Ademi and the potential impact this could have on their ability to represent him. Čermak declares that he considers that his counsel's representation of Ademi would not affect their ability to cross-examine Ademi in his defence or to represent him effectively.[20]

7. The Prosecution holds that the Čermak and Ademi Undertakings should not be accepted and that Čermak's consent is not full and informed.[21] Furthermore, it notes that even if Prodanović and Sloković were to withdraw as counsel to Ademi in Croatia,

> [...] they would still need to obtain the assistance of an additional co-counsel to ensure that Mr. Ademi is not cross-examined using privileged information from a former client were he to be called **as a witness.**[22]

8. In its Decision of 25 October 2006, the Appeals Chamber affirmed Trial Chamber II's decision on the alleged conflict, and stated that **[page 5]**

> However, it is not certain at this stage in the proceedings that Prodanović's and Sloković's duty of loyalty to Čermak will be compromised because they will be unable to effectively cross-examine their other client,

10 Prodanović/Sloković Submission, para. 8.
11 *Ibid.*
12 Prodanović/Sloković Submission, para. 14.
13 Prodanović/Sloković Submission, para. 13.
14 Prodanović/Sloković Submission, paras 9–10.
15 Prodanović/Sloković Submission, para. 14.
16 Ademi Undertaking, p. 1, paras 2–4, 6.
17 Ademi Undertaking, p. 1, para. 5.
18 Ademi Undertaking, p. 2 (a). *See also* Prodanović/Sloković Submission, para. 13.
19 Ademi Undertaking, p. 1, para. 5.
20 Čermak Undertaking, p.1, paras 2–5; p. 2 (a) – (b).
21 Prosecution Submission, paras 14–16.
22 *Ibid.*, para. 17.

> Ademi, due to a desire to avoid causing Ademi to incriminate himself. As the Trial Chamber noted, they will be cross-examining Ademi with regard to events and crimes for which he has not been charged and which took place nearly two years after the incidents for which he is charged in Croatia. Nor is it clear that Prodanović and Sloković will be unable to effectively cross-examine Ademi in defence of Čermak without revealing privileged attorney-client communication arising out of representing Ademi in Croatia.[23]

The Appeals Chamber further noted that in the event that Prodanović and Sloković do find that their duty of loyalty to Ademi is compromised by their representation of Čermak, it would not necessarily lead to Čermak having to forego his right to counsel of choice. However, the Appeals Chamber also recalled that while the right to choose counsel is a fundamental right under Article 21(4) (b) and (d) of the Statute, this right is not without limits.[24]

9. Čermak and Ademi are charged with having committed, directly or indirectly, different alleged crimes at different times. Ademi is charged individually and as a superior with crimes against humanity and war crimes allegedly committed between 9 and 17 September 1993, in the vicinity of Gospić and in the Medak Pocket region, before, during and after the "Pocket 93" military operation took place.[25] On the other hand, in the indictment against him ("Indictment"), Čermak is charged, individually, as a superior and/or through participating in and furthering a joint criminal enterprise, with crimes against humanity and war crimes allegedly committed from at least July 1995 to 30 September 1995, in southern Republika Srpska Krajina, in the course of Operation Storm.[26]

10. In spite of the different underlying indictments, Ademi's position and possible activities at the time covered by the Indictment ("Relevant Timeframe") are relevant to these proceedings. Ademi confirms that he

> [...] held the position of Chief of Staff of General Ante Gotovina during the events for which proceedings have been instituted against Ivan Čermak and him [Gotovina] before the ICTY [...].[27]

The Trial Chamber notes that there appears to be a commander-subordinate relationship between Gotovina and Ademi, his second-in-command, on the one hand, and Čermak on the other. This situation and the representation of both Ademi and Čermak by Prodanović and Sloković raises a conflict of interest which falls under Article 14 (D)(i) of the Code of Professional Conduct for Counsel Appearing Before the International Tribunal ("Code") which states that: **[page 6]**

> (D) Counsel or his firm shall not represent a client with respect to a matter if:
>
> (i) such representation will be, or may reasonably be expected to be, adversely affected by representation of another client.

11. The Trial Chamber further recalls the Appeals Chamber's statement that

> [...] given Ademi's place in the chain of command as Gotovina's immediate subordinate, there is a substantial possibility that an important defence strategy in Čermak's interests will be to argue that "command responsibility for alleged wrongful acts lies with Ademi and Gotovina as Commanders of the Split Military District" and not with him. As such, Prodanović and Sloković will face a conflict of interests in representing Čermak vis-à-vis their duty of loyalty to Ademi whereby they may have to make arguments incriminating their client Ademi in order to defend Čermak whether or not Čermak's case is joined with Gotovina's.[28]

The Trial Chamber notes that Prodanović and Sloković have neither explicitly excluded nor adopted such potential line of defence for Čermak, though they said that

---

23 Decision of 25 October 2006, para 27.

24 *Ibid.*, para 30.

25 County State Prosecutor's Office in Zagreb, Croatia, Indictment against Rahim Ademi and Mirko Norac, Zagreb County Court, No. K-DO-349/05 of 22 November 2006, filed on 28 December 2006.

26 Reduced Joinder Indictment Pursuant to Rule 73*Bis* Order of 21 February 2007, 6 March 2007.

27 Ademi Undertaking, p. 1, para. 5.

28 Decision of 25 October 2006, para. 28.

Gotovina's Defence, the Appeals Chamber and the Disciplinary Council adopt a position that there is a substantial possibility that an important defence strategy in Čermak's interest will be to argue that responsibility for acts lies with Gotovina (implying Ademi) as a commander of the Split Military District although facts indicate otherwise.[29]

12. Furthermore, the Trial Chamber considers that there is a real possibility that Ademi will be called as a witness given his position as second-in-command to Gotovina at the Split Military District within the Relevant Timeframe, especially in the light of Gotovina's allegation that Ademi acted in his stead for some time during the Relevant Timeframe.[30] If Ademi is called as a witness, Prodanović and Sloković argue that they can cross-examine him, even aggressively, primarily because the underlying events giving rise to the two indictments with which their two clients, Čermak and Ademi, are charged are unrelated.[31] The Trial Chamber accepts that it is primarily for counsel to assess a conflict of interest issue because, being closest to the case, counsel is expected to be able to make the more informed judgement with regard to his/her client's interest.[32] The Trial Chamber notes with some concern, however, that Prodanović and Sloković have not addressed the allegation that Ademi, as Gotovina's Chief of Staff and his second-in-command, may have been in charge temporarily in Gotovina's absence, when certain alleged crimes with which Čermak is charged during the Relevant Timeframe were committed.[33] Just emphasizing the separate and distinct factual events underlying the two indictments of their respective clients does not reflect a complete analysis of the matter by counsel. **[page 7]**

13. The issue at stake is one of loyalty. The ability to aggressively cross-examine Ademi is not the main question but it may be an aspect of the duty of loyalty which Prodanović and Sloković owe to Ademi. The question is whether Prodanović's and Sloković's attitude to Ademi as a witness would be materially different if he were not their client. Even if the content of Ademi's evidence does not adversely affect Čermak, the fact that Prodanović's and Sloković's role changes from being Ademi's defence counsel to his cross-examiner, may inhibit Prodanović and Sloković when representing Čermak.[34]

14. The Trial Chamber reiterates that there is a real possibility that Ademi is called as a witness in the proceedings. However, it holds that the conflict of interest does not depend on whether Ademi is called as a witness in the proceedings or not, and recalls that the Appeals Chamber held that

> [...] if a conflict of interests does arise for Prodanović and Sloković with respect to their clients Čermak and Ademi, it will exist in the Čermak and Markač case whether or not they decide to call Ademi as a witness.[35]

15. Furthermore, the Trial Chamber holds that counsel's duty of loyalty to a client should be interpreted more widely than Prodanović's and Sloković's restrictive interpretation. The Trial Chamber holds that counsel's duty of loyalty to a client[36] affects both present and former clients. A client should trust in and feel comfortable with his/her attorney's conduct at any time, in any place. Indeed, the Appeals Chamber, in its Decision of 25 October 2006 held that

> [...] counsel's duty of loyalty to a client extends even to cases where a client is not a party to the litigation.[37]

16. The Trial Chamber also finds that Prodanović's and Sloković's argument that withdrawal from Čermak's defence because of the unlikely chance that one witness, meaning Ademi, could be called, when hundreds of witnesses are planned to testify, causing Čermak significant and unnecessary hardship, is misconstrued.[38] The

29 Prodanović/Sloković Submission, para. 8.
30 *See* para. 4 *supra.*
31 Prodanović/Sloković Submission, para. 14.
32 *Prosecutor v. Prlić*, "Decision on Requests for Appointment of Counsel", Case No.: IT-04-74-PT, 30 July 2004, para. 14.
33 *See* para. 4 *supra.*
34 The Trial Chamber is not persuaded that the Appeals Chamber, Trial Chamber II and the ADC Disciplinary Council found that such a conflict might only arise if Ademi is called as a witness having *adverse* interests to Čermak *and* if there is a *need to aggressively cross-examine* him in favour of Čermak as Prodanović and Sloković contend. *See* para. 5, *supra.*
35 Decision of 25 October 2006, para. 29, emphasis in original removed.
36 Article 14(A) of the Code.
37 Decision of 25 October 2006, para. 27.
38 Prodanović/Sloković Submission, para. 12.

value of a testimony is not a question of number but of its content and its implications. In Ademi's case, it may well be that his potential testimony is relevant for Čermak's defence and cannot be replaced by the testimony of other witnesses. **[page 8]**

17. With regard to the use or non-use of Ademi's confidential information which Prodanović and Sloković may possess,[39] the Trial Chamber notes that in his Undertaking, Ademi states that he never discussed any event related to the Relevant Timeframe with his counsel and does not intend to do so since it is unrelated to the charges he is facing in Croatia.[40] Furthermore, Prodanović and Sloković have confirmed that no confidential information was given to them by Ademi which would be useful to Čermak.[41] The Trial Chamber, recalling counsel's duty of loyalty and of candour to the Tribunal under Articles 14(A) and 23 respectively of the Code, is satisfied that no such confidential information is in Prodanović's and Sloković's possession.

18. The Trial Chamber holds that since Ademi appears to have been Čermak's superior during the Relevant Timeframe[42], there is a very real risk that Ademi will be implicated in the case, thus placing Prodanović and Sloković in the awkward position of defending Čermak while having to remain loyal to Ademi.

19. Furthermore, Prodanović and Sloković imply that they do not intend raising as a defence the fact that Gotovina (and therefore also Ademi) was Čermak's superior[43] The point, however, is not whether they will raise such a defence, but whether all potential defences remain available to Čermak. Unless all potential defences remain available to him, uncompromised by his counsel's duty of loyalty to Ademi, the administration of justice will be adversely impacted.

20. Faced with this situation, the Majority considers that Article 14 (E) of the Code is relevant here –

> Where a conflict of interest does arise, counsel shall:
>
> (i) promptly and fully inform each potentially affected present and former client of the nature and extent of the conflict; and
>
> (ii) either:
>
> (1) take all necessary steps to remove the conflict; or
>
> (2) obtain full and informed consent of all potentially affected present and former clients to continue the representation unless such consent is likely to irreversibly prejudice the administration of justice.

With regard to the requirement to fully inform each affected client of the conflict, the Majority considers that in his Undertaking, Ademi stated that he had not discussed his role in the events **[page 9]** underlying Čermak's case with Prodanović and Sloković. Ademi mentioned he had discussed the possibility of his being called as a witness in Čermak's case, his counsel's need to cross-examine him as Čermak's defence counsel in that eventuality and the potential impact this could have on their ability to represent him.[44] Ademi's Undertaking makes no reference to the details of Čermak's case and how he might be implicated as Gotovina's second-in-command during the Relevant Timeframe, and to that extent, the Majority considers it was made without him having complete information at hand. The Majority holds that Prodanović and Sloković were in fact duty-bound to discuss with Ademi the details of Čermak's case and how he might be implicated as Gotovina's second-in-command during the Relevant Timeframe.

21. Similarly, Čermak's Undertaking referred only to the possibility of Ademi being called as a witness to testify in his proceedings, to the fact that his counsel would need to cross-examine Ademi, whom they also represent and to the potential impact this could have on their ability to represent him.[45] Čermak's Undertaking did not refer to the potential defence which could be raised on his behalf in the light of information that

---

39 *See* para. 4 *supra.*
40 *See* para. 6 *supra.*
41 *See* para. 5 *supra.*
42 *See* paras 4, 6, 10 *supra.*
43 *See* para. 5 *supra.*
44 *See* para. 6 *supra.*
45 *Ibid.*

Ademi was Gotovina's Chief of Staff and second-in-command and was allegedly Acting Commander of the Split Military District in Gotovina's stead when the latter was temporarily absent. Again, the Majority holds that Prodanović and Sloković were in fact duty-bound to discuss this potential defence with Čermak,

22. For the foregoing reasons, the Majority contends that Čermak's and Ademi's Undertakings are not fully informed and holds that the conflict of interest posed by Prodanović's and Sloković's continued representation of both Čermak and Ademi is not in the interests of Čermak and Ademi and is likely to irreversibly prejudice the administration of justice.

23. Furthermore, the Majority holds that the suggestion by Prodanović and Sloković to employ a third counsel who would cross-examine Ademi if he were to be called as a witness[46] will not remedy the conflict arising from the duty of loyalty owed to both Ademi and Čermak. The uncompromised potential defence of shifting responsibility for certain alleged crimes onto Gotovina and Ademi would still remain unavailable to Čermak even if a third counsel is employed since such a third counsel would be on the same defence team as Prodanović and Sloković who are tainted with the conflict of interest. As stated above, Article 14(D) of the Code sets out that **[page 10]**

> Counsel or his *firm* shall not represent a client with respect to a matter [...].[47]

One can easily analogise the role of third counsel (and co-counsel) on a trial defence team with that of a co-member of a firm. The conflict which taints counsel also taints those whom counsel engage as co-counsel. Thus, the third counsel would by necessity be disqualified from representing Čermak .

24. Considering both Article 14(D)(i) and 14(E) of the Code and the fact that Ademi may be implicated in this case, the Majority finds that the dual representation must be terminated. The Majority notes that it has not been suggested that Čermak may be implicated in Ademi's case or be called as a witness in it. Indeed, it is submitted by Prodanović and Sloković that Čermak's and Ademi's cases are temporally and spatially separated.[48] It is therefore unnecessary for Prodanović and Sloković to withdraw as Ademi's counsel. Prodanović and Sloković must therefore withdraw from Čermak's representation.

25. Pursuant to Articles 20 and 21 of the Statute, Rule 54 of the Rules of Procedure and Evidence and Article 14 of the Code and the foregoing reasons, the Majority orders that Prodanović and Sloković withdraw as Čermak's counsel in this case, but stay on the case until such time as a new defence team is able to certify that it can take over Čermak's defence.

Done in English and French, the English version being authoritative.

Dated this fifth day of April 2007
At The Hague
The Netherlands

Judge Bakone Justice Moloto
Pre-Trial Judge

[Seal of the Tribunal]

46 *See* para, 5 *supra.*
47 Emphasis added.
48 Prodanović/Sloković Submission, para. 10.

[page 1] 1. As indicated in the "Decision on Conflict of Interest of Attorneys Čedo Prodanović and Jadranka Sloković" of 5 April 2007 ("Decision"), I respectfully disagree with the majority of the judges and set forth my reasons in this dissenting opinion.

2. The Decision notes that Rahim Ademi ("Ademi") and the Accused Ivan Čermak ("Čermak") are represented by counsel Čedo Prodanović ("Prodanović") and Jadranka Sloković ("Sloković") in separate proceedings which are unrelated and which concern different events occurring at different times.[1] Čermak has two co-accused, the Accused Ante Gotovina ("Gotovina") and Mladen Markač ("Markač").

3. It has never been suggested that Čermak could have an interest in the proceedings against Ademi. It is apparent, however, that Ademi was Gotovina's Chief of Staff and his second-in-command during the time covered by the indictment which charges Čermak, Gotovina and Markač with certain crimes ("Indictment").[2] Therefore, a real possibility exists for Ademi to be implicated in the case against the three Accused. He could be called as a witness or he could be the subject of an attempt by any of the Accused to shift responsibility for events referred to in the Indictment.

4. Under Article 14(A) of the Code of Professional Conduct for Counsel Appearing Before the International Tribunal ("Code"), a counsel owes a duty of loyalty to his or her clients. If in the course of representing a client a conflict arises between, on the one hand, this duty of loyalty owed to the client and, on the other hand, the counsel's own interests or the interests of another present or former client of counsel, then pursuant to Article 14 (D) of the Code such a conflict is presumed to adversely affect the representation of counsel on behalf of the client or clients involved. For this reason, counsel is duty-bound before representing a client to consider whether the representation would compromise, or reasonably be expected to compromise, his or her duty of loyalty towards any other client. If so, he or she should refuse such representation.

5. By way of background, Prodanović and Sloković have been providing legal services to Čermak since his second interview with the Office of the Prosecutor in 1999.[3] From the record, it appears that Prodanović (and later Sloković) has been representing Ademi since 2001, first in proceedings before this Tribunal and then in proceedings in Croatia following the referral of Ademi's case under Rule 11*bis*. The issue of a conflict of interest involving Prodanović and **[page 2]** Sloković representing Čermak and Ademi was first raised in April 2006 within the context of joining the Gotovina case with the Markač and Čermak case.

6. Whether the duty of loyalty could result in a conflict of interest when Prodanović and Sloković accepted to represent Ademi is not relevant to a determination of the ultimate matter before the Trial Chamber. Likewise, whether counsel from that time forward acted diligently, pursuant to Article 14(B) of the Code, to ensure that no conflict of interest would arise is not the essence of the matter. The Trial Chamber does not function primarily as a disciplinary court. It is the Trial Chamber's role to determine whether there are compelling reasons which would justify intervening in the attorney-client relationship to ensure that there is no prejudice to the administration of justice, and in particular to protect Čermak's right to a fair trial. In so doing, the Trial Chamber should weigh the interference with an accused's right to counsel of choice against the need to ensure the accused's right to a fair trial.

7. A compelling reason for the Trial Chamber to intervene in Čermak's choice of counsel would exist if divided loyalties would cause Prodanović's and Sloković's representation of Čermak to place his right to a fair trial in jeopardy. Although the right to be represented by counsel of choice is among the fundamental rights of an accused, there may be circumstances in which representation by counsel of choice, due to a conflict of interest, may irreversibly prejudice the administration of justice. It is especially in such cases that the Trial Chamber should intervene and ensure the fairness of trial by restoring the conditions for an effective defence.

8. Both the Appeals Chamber in its "Decision on Interlocutory Appeals Against the Trial Chamber's Decision to Amend the Indictment and for Joinder" of 25 October 2006 ("Appeals Chamber Decision")

---

1 Decision, para. 9.
2 Decision, para. 10.
3 "Submission to the Trial Chamber concerning the Alleged Conflict of Interest Affecting Counsel Čedo Prodanović and Jadranka Sloković", 14 February 2007, para. 22.

and the Disciplinary Council ("Disciplinary Council") of the Association of Defence Counsel's ("ADC") advisory opinion of 17 January 2007 ("Advisory Opinion") point to the substantial possibility of a conflict of interest arising in this case, but both also acknowledge that no conflict of interest existed at the time of the decision and advisory opinion. The Disciplinary Council of the ADC indicated certain factors which were unknown or uncertain at the time, such as,

- the case was not ready for trial
- no date for commencement of trial had been set
- whether the loyalty that Prodanović and Sloković owe to Čermak would be compromised by an inability to cross-examine Ademi aggressively
- whether the loyalty that Prodanović and Sloković owe to Ademi would be compromised if they were unable to cross-examine him without revealing confidential information he may have disclosed to them **[page 3]**
- the observation that it was at the time premature to conclude that Čermak did not intend to call Ademi as a witness because.[4]

9. With regard to these unknown or uncertain factors, I make the following observations:

- Whether or not there will be a need for Čermak's counsel to cross-examine Ademi, if he is called as a witness, will depend on the evidence he can be expected to give, which most likely, in turn, will depend on who calls him as a witness. There are therefore many variables. Čermak and his counsel appear determined to exclude the possibility of calling Ademi as a witness or to use him as a scapegoat in their defence strategy. One might consider it risky to exclude a defence strategy early in the proceedings and be so sure that the interests of Čermak and Ademi will not be adversely affected by counsel's continued representation of both. However, as the Decision, referring to the Appeals Chamber, has noted, it is primarily for counsel to assess a conflict of interest issue because, being closest to the case, counsel is expected to be able to make the most informed judgement with regard to his/her client's interest.[5] I therefore am hesitant to speculate, at this advanced stage of the proceedings, on whether any defence strategy could be developed, which may better serve Čermak but at the same time implicate Ademi.
- After the matter was considered by the Appeals Chamber and the Disciplinary Council of the ADC, both Ademi and his counsel have confirmed that there has been no disclosure of confidential information by Ademi which could be relevant to Čermak's defence.
- With regard to timing, we are now closer to the commencement of the trial than when the Appeals Chamber and Disciplinary Council of the ADC issued their Appeals Chamber Decision and Advisory Opinion respectively.

10. Concretely, a conflict of loyalty would materialize if counsel finds himself in a dilemma as to whether to use any information he has confidentially gained in his professional relationship with one or both of his clients. Such a dilemma would arise if, for example, the information favours client A but is detrimental to client B. If no such information is in counsel's hands, it may still be advisable (i) not to accept instructions from client B or (ii) to discontinue the represention of client B, in a case in which client A might be drawn in. Nevertheless, as long as client A has not provided information that would impair counsel's ability to conduct client B's case as any other **[page 4]** counsel might have done, I do not consider it mandatory *per se* for counsel to discontinue to represent client B.

11. Had Ademi shared confidential and relevant information with his counsel, the dilemma might be whether to use it and be disloyal to Ademi or not to use it and be disloyal to Čermak. In the absence of any shared information of a confidential character, I consider the duty of loyalty to both clients to be in jeopardy only in the abstract. The conflict of loyalty has not resulted in a concrete conflict of interest. In such circumstances, however, the other client may still experience unease that his counsel is in proceedings in which he might also become involved. I come back to this point in paragraph 13 below.

---

4 Disciplinary Council of the ADC's Advisory Opinion of 17 January 2007, para 36, quoting the Appeals Chamber Decision, paras 27–29.

5 Decision, para. 12, referring to *Prosecutor v. Prlić*, "Decision on Requests for Appointment of Counsel", Case No,: IT-04-74-PT, 30 July 2004, para. 14.

12. The Disciplinary Council of the ADC has expressed its opinion that the duty of loyalty to both Ademi and Čermak is incompatible with the continuation of representation of both clients.[6] I agree, although for me, like for the majority in the Decision, the possibility that Ademi is called as a witness is not the decisive factor.[7] Nor is it the possibility that Ademi may be implicated in the case.[8] A decisive factor for me to order that Prodanović and Sloković withdraw at this phase of the proceedings from Čermak's representation would have been that Ademi shared confidential information relevant to Čermak's defence with his counsel. As has clearly been explained by the ADC's Disciplinary Council in its Advisory Opinion, there are procedural uncertainties in this case to some extent beyond the control of counsel.[9] Another accused, the Office of the Prosecutor or the Trial Chamber may decide to call Ademi as a witness. The procedural developments in the twelve months prior to the Decision are such that counsel might further explore the circumstances around Ademi's position as Gotovina's Chief of Staff and his second-in-command at the time of the Indictment. Even if counsel currently firmly believe that in the exercise of their duties as defence counsel to Čermak, they have nothing to reveal which is unfavourable to Ademi, irrespective of its source, their role vis-á-vis Ademi would still be equivocal. In such an eventuality, there should be no shadow of doubt as to where counsel's loyalty lies. Counsel's role should be transparent to both Ademi and Čermak. Both have given Undertakings wherein they consent to Prodanović's and Sloković's continuing to represent them.[10] In view of the uncertainties, the possible need for further **[page 5]** inquiry concerning Ademi's position and the absolute need for transparency, representation of Ademi would be irreconcilable with the further representation of Čermak.

13. Discontinuation of dual representation requires a choice about whether to discontinue both relationships or one of them and which one. The issue for the Trial Chamber is whether to discontinue the representation of Čermak. Even in the present circumstances, where Ademi has shared no confidential information with counsel relevant to the Čermak defence, Ademi's consent for the continued representation by his counsel of Čermak is vital. Absent such consent, Ademi might interpret a situation wherein he is giving evidence in proceedings where his counsel is representing Čermak, as his counsel's failure of their duty of loyalty towards him. That possibility should in itself prohibit counsel from representing Čermak without Ademi's consent, even if Ademi's evidence would be unrelated to Ademi's own case. In other words, if a client experiences any dealings, direct or indirect, of his counsel, in the latter's capacity as counsel for another client, as a violation of the duty of loyalty which that counsel owes to him, the client's concerns should be respected and counsel should withdraw.

14. In the present situation, since Ademi has given his consent for his counsel to continue to represent Čermak, I find no compelling reason to prohibit counsel to continue the representation of Čermak under certain conditions.[11] The first condition would be that the dual representation ends which means that counsel would cease to further represent Ademi. While Ademi, being aware of the possibility that he may be called as a witness in this case and having confirmed that he has not shared any confidential information with his counsel, has consented to the continued representation of Čermak by Prodanović and Sloković, direct dealings with his, by then, former counsel should be avoided, since it might cloud Ademi's perception of the true relationship with his, by then, former counsel. Therefore the hiring of a third counsel on the Čermak defence with the specific task of performing any duties that are directly related to any involvement that Ademi may have in this case would be the second condition.

15. Should we anticipate the resolution of a conflict of interest under Article 14(E) of the Code if the conflict of interest does not yet exist?[12] In balancing the need for the Trial Chamber to **[page 6]** interfere

---

6 Advisory Opinion, paras 40–41.

7 Decision, para. 14.

8 Decision, para. 18.

9 Advisory Opinion, para. 40.

10 Undertakings filed in the "Notice to the Trial Chamber Concerning Undertakings Provided by Ivan Čermak and Rahim Ademi", 8 February 2007.

11 This is unlike the conflict of interest situations that arose with regard to Attorney Olujić in *Prosecutor v. Prlić et. al.* ("Decision on Requests for Appointment of Counsel", IT-04-74-PT, 30 July 2004) case and with regard to Attorney Šeparović in these proceedings ("Decision on Conflict of Interest of Attorney Miroslav Šeparović", 27 February 2007). In the former case, both clients represented by Mr. Olujić were charged with the same criminal acts and were allegedly linked by a close superior-subordinate relationship. In the latter case, the Trial Chamber found Mr, Šeparović had a personal interest in the case'.

12 Advisory Opinion, paras 42–44, discussing the applicability of Article 14(E) of the Code to a potential conflict of interest.

with the accused's right to be represented by counsel of choice and the need to avoid irreversible prejudice to the administration of justice, the potential nature of the conflict of interest at hand is relevant. It assists in assessing whether the withdrawal of Čermak's counsel from his representation is the appropriate remedy in the purely abstract conflict of loyalty that presently exists. In my opinion, the fact that it is still only a potential conflict of interest tilts the scales in favour of the view that further representation of Čermak by Prodanović and Sloković, under the conditions I mention in paragraph 14 above, is a sufficient remedy and will not result in irreversible prejudice to the administration of justice.

16. I have no reason to doubt that the consent given by both Čermak and Ademi are sufficiently informed.[13] The expression of consent does not have to set out in full detail all potential situations that might arise and that are covered by such consent. I further consider both Ademi and Čermak sufficiently competent so as not to be easily misled.

17. For the foregoing reasons, I would allow Prodanović and Sloković to continue representing Čermak in this case, subject to the conditions laid down in paragraph 14 above.

Done in English and French, the English text being authoritative.

Dated this eighteenth day of April 2007
At The Hague
The Netherlands

Judge Alphons Orie

[13] *See* fn 8 *supra*.

UNITED NATIONS

International Tribunal for the Prosecution of Persons Responsible for Serious Violations of International Humanitarian Law Committed in the Territory of Former Yugoslavia since 1991	Case No.	IT-04-79-PT
	Date:	24 April 2007
	Original:	English

IN TRIAL CHAMBER II

Before: **Judge Kevin Parker, Presiding**
Judge Christine Van Den Wyngaert
Judge Krister Thelin

Registrar: **Mr. Hans Holthuis**

Order of: **24 April 2007**

PROSECUTOR

v.

MIĆO STANIŠIĆ

DECISION ON REVIEW OF REGISTRAR'S DECISION RE CO-COUNSEL FOR MIĆO STANIŠIĆ

The Office of the Prosecutor:
Mr Alan Tieger
Ms Anna Richterova

Counsel for the Accused:
Mr Stevo Bezbradica

1. Background

[page 1] 1. This Trial Chamber of the International Tribunal for the Prosecution of Persons Responsible for Serious Violations of International Humanitarian Law in the Territory of the Former Yugoslavia since 1991 ("Tribunal") is seized of "Defence Counsel's Motion for Review of the Registrar's Refusal to Assign Mr. Slobodan Cvijetić as Co-Counsel" ("Motion") filed on 18 August 2006 by Stevo Bezbradica, Counsel for the Accused Mićo Stanišić ("Accused").

2. In a letter of 30 June 2006 to the Office of Legal Aid and Detention Matters ("OLAD") of the Registry of the Tribunal ("June 2006 letter"), Counsel for the Accused requested the assignment of Mr. Cvijetić as legal consultant and co-counsel.[1] On 12 July 2006 the Deputy Head of OLAD granted the request for the assignment of Mr. Cvijetić as legal consultant.[2] Subsequently in a communication of 6 August 2006 Counsel for the Accused confirmed the request for the assignment of Mr. Cvijetić as co-counsel.[3] In a letter of 11 August 2006 the Head of OLAD denied this request ("Impugned Decision"). The Head of OLAD stated that since the Registry understood that Mr. Cvijetić does not speak either of the Tribunal's two working languages, the question whether he can be assigned as co-counsel is governed by Article 16(D) of the Directive on the Assignment of Defence Counsel ("Directive"). The Head of OLAD concluded that the Registry was not satisfied that it would be justified to waive the language requirement pursuant to Article 16(D) of the Directive.[4] In the Motion the Accused submits that the Impugned Decision should be quashed on the grounds that the Registrar failed to comply with the legal requirements of the Directive, and procedural fairness has not been considered for the benefit of the Accused.[5] The Accused also submitted that the interests of justice test has not been applied in a proper way by the Registry and that Mr. Cvijetić should be assigned as co-counsel, because he can provide suitable assistance for the Accused's lead counsel.[6] On 24 August 2006 Counsel for the Accused filed the "Supplement to Defence Counsel's Motion for Review of the Registrar's Refusal to Assign Mr. Slobodan Cvijetić as Co-Counsel", which enclosed a letter from the Accused dated 16 August 2006 in which he strongly supported the assignment of Mr. Cvijetić as co-counsel. On 5 September 2006, the Registry filed its "Registry Rule 33(B) Submission on the Defence Motion for Review of the Registry Decision on the Assignment of Co-Counsel" ("Registry Submission") asserting that the Impugned Decision was reasonable and justified and therefore should be upheld. In its Submission, **[page 2]** the Registry submitted that it had complied with the standard for proper administrative decision-making in denying the request for the assignment of Mr. Cvijetić as co-counsel.[7]

2. Assignment of Counsel

3. By Article 21(4)(d) of the Statute of the Tribunal ("Statute") an Accused has the right to "defend himself in person or through legal assistance of his own choosing". Necessarily, the right of an Accused to choose his or her counsel is limited to counsel qualified to appear before the Tribunal. Rule 44 of the Rules of Procedure and Evidence ("Rules") sets out the required qualifications. They are extensive and deal in particular with the legal qualification, good standing and professional conduct of the counsel. There is a specific requirement that counsel has written and oral proficiency in one of the two working languages of the Tribunal, although it is also provided that, where the Registrar deems it to be in the interests of justice to waive this requirement, he may do so. In such an exceptional case, however, by Rule 44(D) the Registrar may impose conditions, *inter alia* regarding the costs of translation and interpretation, and requiring an undertaking from counsel not to seek any extension of time by virtue of his lack of proficiency in one of the working languages of the Tribunal.

4. The present is not such a case, however, as the Accused does not have the means to remunerate counsel of his choice. Instead, he sought the assignment of a counsel by the Registrar pursuant to the legal aid scheme

1 Motion, Annex 1.
2 Motion, Annex 2.
3 Motion, Annex 3.
4 Motion, Annex 4.
5 Motion, para. 7.
6 Motion, para. 8.
7 Submission, para. 13.

of the Tribunal. This is administered pursuant to Rule 45 and the Directive on Assignment of Defence Counsel ("Directive"): see Rules 44(C) and 45(A). For this purpose the Registrar maintains a list of counsel, who possess additional specific competence related to the jurisdiction of the Tribunal, have at least 7 years relevant experience, and have indicated their availability and willingness to be assigned to represent persons as counsel or co-counsel. Pursuant to Rule 45(A) and Article 16(C) of the Directive, a co-counsel may also be assigned at the request of lead counsel and where this is in the interests of justice.

3. Legal Basis for Review

5. By Rule 44(B) an Accused may seek a review by the President of a Decision of the Registrar to refuse to admit counsel of an accused's choice who has been retained by the Accused, but who does not meet the language requirement. In the case of the assignment of counsel to an Accused under the legal aid scheme (Rule 45), however, there is no provision for such a review by the President. **[page 3]**

6. As the jurisprudence of the Tribunal has recognised, however, it does not follow that the Registrar's decision to refuse a requested assignment of co-counsel is altogether final. In a number of decisions in this Tribunal it has been recognised that it is inherent in the judicial function of the Tribunal that a decision of the Registrar which affects, or is likely to affect, the right of an Accused to a fair and expeditious trial or the integrity of the proceedings, may as a jurisdictional matter be reviewed by the Trial Chamber before which the trial is to be held, or is being held.[8]

7. It has been made clear, that this jurisdiction is limited to cases which meet those jurisdictional conditions. Even then, it is not the role of the Trial Chamber to intervene in every complaint, recognising that the Registrar has, by his administrative decision-making, the primary responsibility in the matter of the assignment of counsel and co-counsel.[9] Indeed in the *Knežević* case, it was observed that a Chamber should only exercise its power relating to the assignment of counsel "in exceptional cases". [10]

8. In a case where a jurisdictional basis exists for a Trial Chamber to entertain a motion to review the refusal of the Registrar to assign a requested co-counsel, guidance as to the approach to a review of the merits by the Trial Chamber and the standard to be applied in determining whether to interfere with a decision of the Registrar may be found in the Appeals Chamber's decision in *Kvočka et al* where it was said:

> "The administrative decision will be quashed if the Registrar has failed to comply with the legal requirements of the Directive. This issue may in the particular case involve a consideration of the proper interpretation of the Directive. The administrative decision will also be quashed if the Registrar has failed to observe any basic rules of natural justice or to act with procedural fairness towards the person affected by the decision, or if he has taken into account irrelevant material or failed to take into account relevant material, or if he has reached a conclusion which no sensible person who has properly applied his mind to the issue could have reached (the "unreasonableness" test). These issues may in the particular case involve, at least in part, a consideration of the sufficiency of the material before the Registrar, but (in the absence of unreasonableness) there can be no interference with the margin of appreciation of the facts or merits of that case to which the maker of such an administrative decision is entitled." [11]

9. It is of relevance to the scope of the Chamber's judicial review that the Accused's preference as to co-counsel is to be taken into consideration. In this case, as has been indicated, the Accused has not the financial

---

8 *Prosecutor v. Mile Mrkšić et al.*, Case No.: IT-95-13/1-PT, Decision on Appointment of Co-Counsel for Mile Mrkšić, 7 October 2005 ("*Mrkšić* Decision"), para. 7; *Prosecutor v Enver Hadžihasanović et al,* Case No.: IT-01-47-PT, Decision on Prosecution's Motion for Review of the Decision of the Registrar to Assign Mr Rodney Dixon as Co-Counsel to the Accused Kubura, 26 March 2002 ("*Hadžihasanović* Decision"), paras 23–24. Note also Article 13(B) of the Directive which appears, however, to be directed to the case of a refusal to assign <u>any</u> counsel.

9 *Mrkšić* Decision, para. 8; *Prosecutor v Milan Martić,* Case No.: IT-95-11-PT, Decision on Appeal against Decision of Registry, 2 August 2002, p. 6; *Hadžihasanović* Decision, paras 23–24.

10 *Mrkšić* Decision para. 8; *Prosecutor* v *Duško Knežević,* Case No.: IT-95-4-PT and IT-95-8/1-PT, Decision on Accused's Request for Review of Registrar's Decision as to Assignment of Counsel, 6 September 2002, p. 4.

11 *Prosecutor v Miroslav Kvočka et al,* Case No.: IT-98-30/1-A, Decision on Review of Registrar's Decision to Withdraw Legal Aid from Zoran Žigić, 7 February 2003 ("*Kvočka* Decision"), para. 13.

means to retain his own counsel. Even so, the counsel he has selected to conduct his defence as lead counsel under the legal aid scheme at the Tribunal has been assigned **[page 4]** to him. In this respect, the Registrar took into account and, indeed, has fully respected, the expressed preference of the Accused by assigning Mr Bezbradica as counsel.[12]

10. In the *Šljivančanin* decision it was said by the President of the Tribunal:

> "19. Mr Šljivančanin claims that the Registrar's refusal to assign his preferred attorneys violates Mr Šljivančanin's right to counsel of his own choice, guaranteed by Article 21, paragraph 4 of the Statute. The claim may be quickly rejected.
>
> 20. This case concerns the assignment of counsel to be paid for by the Tribunal. Whatever may be the scope of the right to counsel of one's own choosing when a defendant hires his own counsel, the right to publicly paid counsel of one's own choice is limited. The ICTR Appeals Chamber and several ICTY Trial Chambers have repeatedly held that, while the Registrar should normally take a defendant's preferences into account, a defendant must accept any duly qualified counsel appointed from the list maintained by the Registrar. I fully concur in that view."[13]

Thus, while it is not a matter of legal right, well founded notions of fairness are reflected in the view expressed in the *Šljivančanin* decision, and also in the earlier *Martić* Trial Chamber decision.[14] It is to be noted that this concern for fairness appears to be in general keeping with the approach of the European Court of Human Rights, in respect of Article 6(3)(c) of the European Convention of Human Rights, as expressed in *Croissant v Germany,* where it was said

> "It is true that Article 6(3)(c) entitles 'everyone charged with a criminal offence' to be defended by counsel of his own choosing. Nevertheless, and notwithstanding the importance of a relationship of confidence between the lawyer and client, this right cannot be considered to be absolute. It is necessarily subject to certain limitations where free legal aid is concerned and also where, as in the present case, it is for the courts to decide whether the interests of justice require that the Accused be defended by counsel appointed by them. When appointing defence counsel the National Courts must certainly have regard to the defendant's wishes; indeed, German Law contemplates such course. However, they can override those wishes when there are relevant and sufficient grounds for holding that this is necessary in the interests of justice".[15]

11. It is to be emphasised, however, that the issue in this review of the Registrar's decision concerns the assignment of co-counsel. Under the terms of Article 16 of the Directive, it is the counsel, rather than the Accused, who seeks the appointment and assignment of a co-counsel. There is a different emphasis in the case of the assignment of co-counsel. The primary focus is on the needs of the Accused's lead counsel for suitable assistance by counsel chosen by the lead counsel, rather than on the preferences of the Accused. Indeed, it has been held by the Appeals Chamber in *Blagojević* that lead counsel may seek the appointment of a nominated co-counsel without the Accused's agreement to the choice of co-counsel. It was said by the Appeals Chamber: **[page 5]**

> "As already stated, the appointment of co-counsel is a decision to be made by Counsel pursuant to Article 16 of the Directive. In this respect, provided the Registrar is satisfied that the nominated person meets the requirements of Article 14 of the Directive, the propriety of Counsel seeking the appointment of a particular person does not turn upon the awareness of an Accused of the likelihood of such an appointment or upon the agreement of an Accused to that appointment."

It was further said

> "Further, while the selection of Co-counsel is a matter which falls to lead Counsel under Article 16 of the Directive, the selection of lead Counsel is a matter which falls to the Registrar under Article 14 of the Directive.

---

12 *Prosecutor v. Mićo Stanišić*, Case No.: IT-04-79-PT, Decision of the Deputy Registrar, 5 May 2006. *Cf. Mrkšić* Decision, para. 10.

13 *Prosecutor v Veselin Šljivančanin*, Case No.: IT-95-13/1-PT, Decision on Assignment of Defence Counsel, 20 August 2003, paras. 19–20 (footnotes omitted).

14 *Prosecutor v Milan Martić,* Case No.: IT-95-11-PT, Decision on Appeal against Decision of Registry, 2 August 2002, pp 5–6.

15 *Croissant v Germany,* EUR.CT.H.R. Judgement, 25 September 1992, Series A No. 237-B, para. 29.

> The Registrar may take into account an Accused's preferences, as he did in the appointment of lead counsel in this case, but it is within the Registrar's discretion to override that preference if he considers that it is in the interests of justice to do so."[16]

12. The apparent effect of these decisions is to confirm that the assignment of co-counsel is not a matter primarily involving the legal right of the Accused to be represented by counsel of his own choosing. Nevertheless, as they also indicate, considerations of fairness emphasise the desirability of the Registrar also taking into account any preference expressed by the Accused as to the co-counsel to be assigned. In a case such as the present, in which it appears that the lead counsel and the Accused each favour the assignment of Mr. Cvijetić, the Registrar would normally be expected to take into account the Accused's preference and would no doubt give effect to it unless, in the view of the Registrar, there was good reason for not doing so. This statement of the position is subject, however, to a further material consideration in a case in which, as in this case, the preferred co-counsel is not qualified to act as counsel before the Tribunal.[17]

4. Language of merits

13. In the present case, the assignment of co-counsel requested by Mr. Bezbradica and supported by the Accused is also most materially affected by the language qualification requirement of Rule 44(B) which is incorporated into the legal aid scheme by Rule 45(B). This is also reflected in Article 16(D) of the Directive. It is open to the Registrar under Rule 44(B) to admit a counsel who does not speak either of the two working languages of the Tribunal, but who speaks the native language of the Accused *and* where the interests of justice so *demand* (emphases added). Necessarily, the interests of justice must be viewed in light of the particular case.[18]

14. In this case, Mr Cvijetić is not proficient in either of the working languages of the Tribunal. He is proficient in the Accused's native language, as also is the assigned counsel, Mr Bezbradica. Thus, this is not a case in which, as at times has been the case, the assignment of a co-counsel who **[page 6]** speaks the native language of the Accused has the desirable advantage of facilitating adequate communication between the Accused and lead counsel.[19]

5. Discussion of merits

15. In support of the Motion, the Accused submits that Mr. Cvijetić has previous experience before the Tribunal, he is familiar with cases connected with the instant case and he has excellent advocacy skills and a detailed knowledge of the Statute and the Rules.[20] In the Impugned Decision the Head of OLAD states that the Registry does not consider that Mr. Cvijetić's advocacy skills constitute unique expertise and skills that are of significant importance to the Defence case,[21] and that the relevance of Mr. Cvijetić's prior experience at the Tribunal is reduced by his lack of trial experience.[22] In addition, the Registry submits that Mr. Cvijetić's knowledge of the Statute and the Rules is of less value than would be the case if the Accused were represented by a less experienced lead counsel.[23] The Chamber is aware that Mr. Cvijetić worked in *Prosecutor v. Miroslav Deronjić* as lead counsel.[24] Although the experience of Mr. Cvijetić in a sentencing case could be of some general use to the Defence of the Accused, it does not give him any specific advantage with respect to trial proceedings in this Tribunal for which he lacks experience. Also, the Chamber is persuaded that the Accused has not shown why Mr. Cvijetić's advocacy skills are of significant importance to the Defence case. Although

---

16 *Prosecutor v Vidoje Blagojević*, Case No.: IT-02-60-AR73.4, Public and Redacted Reasons for Decision on Appeal by Vidoje Blagojević to Replace his Defence Team, 7 November 2003, paras 21 and 22. This decision was made before the July 2004 amendments to Rules 44 and 45 but those amendments do not appear to affect these observations of the Appeals Chamber.

17 *Mrkšić* Decision, para. 15.

18 *Mrkšić* Decision, para. 16.

19 See *Mrkšić* Decision, para. 17.

20 June 2006 letter; Motion, para. 9.

21 *Cf.* Registry Submission, para. 25.

22 *Cf.* Registry Submission, para. 24.

23 *Cf.* Registry Submission, para. 24.

24 Motion, Annex 1.

the present case has certain broadly defined factual similarities with the *Deronjić* case,[25] the Trial Chamber does not accept that the considerations of the Accused in this respect are of major importance and it considers that it was well open to the Registry to conclude that these considerations do not justify an exception to the language qualification requirement.

16. The Accused submits that a further reason for the assignment of Mr. Cvijetić to the Accused is the expressed wish of the Accused that Mr. Cvijetić should be assigned on the grounds that there is a relationship of trust and confidence between the two of them;[26] and that the expressed wish of the Accused was not considered by the Registry in the Impugned Decision.[27] In the Registry Submission, the Registry states that it is not in a position to assess whether the relationship of trust and confidence exists or what weight should be given to it and that to the extent that the Accused has a preference for the assignment of Mr. Cvijetić, that preference cannot alone justify his **[page 7]** assignment because the Accused does not have a legal right to the choice of co-counsel.[28] The Trial Chamber concurs with the Registrar. For the reasons given in paragraph 11 above, lead counsel may seek the appointment of a nominated co-counsel even without the Accused's agreement to the choice of co-counsel. A relationship of trust and confidence is to be expected between every accused and his or her co-counsel. Therefore the existence of such a relationship already between the Accused and Mr. Cvijetić should be accorded little weight. The Trial Chamber is therefore of the view that neither the relationship of trust and confidence between them nor the expressed wish of the Accused are sufficient to justify a waiver of the language qualification requirement.

17. The Accused submits that the involvement of Mr. Cvijetić in the case is a further factor which counts in favour of his assignment as co-counsel. Specifically, Mr. Cvijetić is already involved in the case as a defence legal consultant; he has communicated with the Accused almost every day and he has participated in the preparation of his defence; and he is aware of all prospective defence and prosecution witnesses and would therefore be of great assistance to Counsel.[29] The Registry on the other hand submits that acceptance of the presence of Mr. Cvijetić on the Defence Team as a justification for his assignment as co-counsel would promote abuse of the exception set forth in Article 16(D) of the Directive. The Registry also observes that because Mr. Cvijetić will continue to act as a legal consultant on the Defence Team, Counsel for the Accused will not be deprived of the knowledge that Mr. Cvijetić has gained through that assignment.[30] The Trial Chamber accepts, for the reasons given by the Registry, that the consultant role of Mr. Cvijetić in the case should not be regarded as determinative in deciding whether his assignment as co-counsel is justified under Article 16(D) of the Directive. Clearly, if involvement in some capacity such as a consultant in a Defence Team were to be regarded as a significant consideration justifying assignment as a co-counsel under Article 16(D), the exceptional nature of the waiver of the language qualification requirement would be undermined. Moreover, no significant weight should be given to the existing contribution of Mr. Cvijetić to the defence of the Accused, since this contribution may continue if he is not assigned as co-counsel. Accordingly, in the view of the Chamber, it was reasonably open to the Registrar to conclude that the involvement of Mr. Cvijetić as a consultant in the case does not justify an exception being made to the language qualification requirement.

18. On this reasoning the Trial Chamber concludes that the Registrar has not failed to comply with the legal requirements of the Directive, nor has he failed to observe basic rules of natural justice or to act with procedural fairness towards the Accused. Further, in the Chamber's view, the **[page 8]** Registrar, in reaching his decision, has not taken into account irrelevant material or failed to take into account relevant material, nor has he reached a conclusion which is unreasonable, i.e. the application of the test set forth in the *Kvočka* Decision.[31] Thus, Mr. Stanišić has not established any basis on which the Chamber would be justified in finding that the Impugned Decision should be quashed.

---

25 Both concern events in Republika Srpska in 1992. *See* Prosecutor v. Miroslav Deronjić, Case No. IT-02-61-S, Sentencing Judgement, para. 2.

26 Motion, para. 11.

27 Motion, para. 11.

28 Registry Submission, para. 27.

29 Motion, para. 10.

30 Registry Submission, para. 26.

31 *Kvočka* Decision, para. 13.

6. Disposition

19. For these reasons the Chamber dismisses the Motion.

Done in English and French, the English version being authoritative.

Dated this 24th day of April 2007,
At The Hague,
The Netherlands

Kevin Parker
Presiding Judge

[Seal of the Tribunal]

UNITED
NATIONS

International Tribunal for the Prosecution of Persons Responsible for Serious Violations of International Humanitarian Law Committed in the Territory of the Former Yugoslavia since 1991	Case No.	IT-06-90-AR73.1
	Date:	4 May 2007
	Original:	English

IN THE APPEALS CHAMBER

Before: **Judge Liu Daqun, Presiding**
Judge Mohamed Shahabuddeen
Judge Andrésia Vaz
Judge Theodor Meron
Judge Wolfgang Schomburg

Registrar: **Mr. Hans Hothuis**

Decision: **4 May 2007**

PROSECUTOR

v.

ANTE GOTOVINA
IVAN ČERMAK
MLADEN MARKAČ

DECISION ON MIROSLAV ŠEPAROVIĆ'S INTERLOCUTORY APPEAL AGAINST TRIAL CHAMBER'S DECISIONS ON CONFLICT OF INTEREST AND FINDING OF MISCONDUCT

Office of the Prosecutor
Mr. Alan Tieger
Ms. Laurie Sartorio

Counsel for Ante Gotovina
Mr. Luka Mišetic
Mr. Gregory Kehoe
Mr. Payam Akhavan

Counsel for Mladen Markač
Mr. Miroslav Šeparović
Mr. Goran Mikuličić

Counsel for Ivan Čermak
Mr. Cedo Prodanović
Ms. Jadranka Sloković

[page 1] 1. The Appeals Chamber of the International Criminal Tribunal for the Prosecution of Persons Responsible for Serious Violations of International Humanitarian Law Committed in the Territory of the former Yugoslavia Since 1991 ("International Tribunal") is seized of "Appellant Miroslav Šeparović's Consolidated Interlocutory Appeal Against Trial Chamber's Decision on Conflict of Interest of Attorney Miroslav Šeparović and Against Trial Chamber's Decision on Finding of Misconduct of Attorney Miroslav Šeparović" filed on 20 March 2007 ("Appeal"), by Miroslav Šeparović ("Appellant").

I. PROCEDURAL BACKGROUND

2. On 20 February 2006 the Prosecution filed a consolidated motion to amend the Indictments against Mladen Markač, Ivan Čermak and Ante Gotovina and to jointly charge and try these three accused.[1] Gotovina objected to the proposed amendments and joinder of indictments arguing, *inter alia,* that a conflict of interest arises between himself and Markač because of his intention to call Markač's Counsel, the Appellant, as a "crucial witness" due to his previous capacity as Minister of Justice of the Republic of Croatia at the time of the alleged commission of the crimes in the Indictment.[2] He further submitted that the Appellant's testimony is expected to be "exculpatory", in that he has "vital information concerning several of the most serious allegations against Gotovina" together with knowledge of the functioning of the military and civilian systems of criminal justice throughout the Republic of Croatia.[3] Thus his right to fair trial and due process would be violated by the proposed joinder.[4]

3. On 17 July 2006, the Trial Chamber granted the Prosecution request to join the case against Markač and Čermak[5] with that of Gotovina[6] pursuant to Rule 48 of the Rules of Procedure and Evidence of the International Tribunal ("Rules"). With respect to a possible conflict of interest, the Trial Chamber reasoned that the matters to which the Appellant is expected to testify as regards the military courts in the Republic of Croatia being under the supervision of the Ministry of Justice rather than the Ministry of Defence appear to be of equal importance to Markač's defence and therefore held that "while a conflict of interest on the part of Mr. Šeparović may arise if the **[page 2]** assertions of the Gotovina Defence are true, this conflict would not be resolved" if joinder was denied.[7]

4. All three accused appealed the Trial Chamber Decision on Joinder.[8] On 25 October 2006, the Appeals Chamber dismissed these appeals.[9] With regard to the potential Gotovina-Separović conflict of interest pursuant to Article 26 of the Code of Professional Conduct for Counsel Appearing Before the International Tribunal ("Code of Professional Conduct"), the Appeals Chamber found that Gotovina failed to demonstrate that the Trial Chamber made a discernible error and that the Trial Chamber reasonably concluded that the conflict of interest caused by the assignment of the Appellant as Counsel to Markač would not be avoided

---

1 *Prosecutor v. Ivan Čermak and Mladen Markač*, Case No. IT-03-73-PT, Prosecution's Consolidated Motion to Amend the *Indictment* and for Joinder, 20 February 2006 ("Joinder Indictment"), para. 98.

2 *Prosecutor v. Ante Gotovina*, Case No. IT-01-45-PT, Defendant Ante Gotovina's Response in Opposition to the Prosecution's Consolidated Motion to Amend the Indictment and for Joinder, 4 April 2006 ("*Gotovina*'s Opposition to Joinder"), para. 8. *See* also *Gotovina*'s Opposition to Joinder, para. 63 ff.

3 *Gotovina*'s Opposition to Joinder, paras 8, 64–66.

4 *Gotovina's* Opposition to Joinder, para. 1.

5 IT-01-45-PT.

6 IT-03-73-PT.

7 *Prosecutor v. Ivan Čermak and Mladen Markač*, Case No. IT-03-73-PT, and *Prosecutor v. Ante Gotovina*, Case No. IT-01-45-PT, Decision on Prosecution's Consolidated Motion to Amend the Indictment and for Joinder, 14 July 2006 ("Trial Chamber Decision on Joinder"), para. 80. The Joinder Indictment was subsequently filed on 24 July 2006, and was further amended on 6 March 2007 in accordance with Order Pursuant to Rule 73bis(D) to Reduce the Indictment, 21 February 2007.

8 Appellant Mladen Markač's Interlocutory Appeal From the Trial Chamber's Decision on Prosecution's Consolidated Motion to Amend the Indictment and For Joinder, 21 August 2006; Appellant Ivan Čermak's Interlocutory Appeal Against the Trial Chamber's Decision on Prosecution's Consolidated Motion to Amend the Indictment and For Joinder, 23 August 2006; Brief of Interlocutory Appellant Ante Gotovina, 25 August 2006 ("Gotovina's Joinder Appeal"). On 14 August 2006, the Trial Chamber granted the Appellants' request for certification to appeal the Impugned Decision pursuant to Rule 73(B) (*Prosecutor v. Ante Gotovina*, Case No. IT-01-45-PT, *Prosecutor v. Ivan Čermak and Mladen Markač*, Case No. IT-03-73-PT, Decision on Defence Applications for Certification to Appeal Decision on Prosecution's Consolidated Motion to Amend the Indictment and for Joinder, 14 August 2006).

9 *Prosecutor v. Ante Gotovina,* Case No. IT-01-45-AR73.1, *Prosecutor v. Ivan Čermak and Mladen Markač*, Case Nos. IT-03-73-AR73.1 and IT-03-73-AR73.2, Decision on Interlocutory Appeal Against the Trial Chamber's Decision to Amend the Indictment and for Joinder, 25 October 2006 ("Appeals Chamber Decision on Joinder").

by ordering that the two cases be tried separately.[10] The Appeals Chamber further stated that "unless [the Appellant] can demonstrate that his withdrawal would cause a substantial hardship to Markač, the Appeals Chamber expects that he will withdraw".[11]

5. On 8 November 2006, Markač filed a request for clarification of the Appeals Chamber Decision on Joinder, specifically with regard to the above holding concerning the Appellant's withdrawal.[12] On 12 January 2007, the Appeals Chamber remitted to the Trial Chamber for further consideration consistent with its Clarification Decision and the Appeals Chamber Decision on Joinder, Markač's submissions relating to the question of whether the Appellant will in fact be a "necessary witness" in terms of Article 26 of the Code of Professional Conduct in this trial.[13] On 17 **[page 3]** January 2007, the Disciplinary Counsel of the ADC issued an advisory opinion that a conflict existed.[14]

6. At a Status Conference held on 9 February 2007, the Appellant indicated that he did not intend to withdraw from the case as he considers that there is no conflict of interest.[15] Pursuant to a request from the Trial Chamber,[16] written submissions were filed by the Appellant, the Prosecution and Čermak on 14 February 2007 to indicate their respective positions regarding the potential conflict of interest.[17]

7. The Trial Chamber rendered the First Impugned Decision on 27 February 2007. It held that a conflict of interest existed because : (1) the Appellant has a personal interest in this case which disqualifies him as counsel pursuant to Article 14(D)(iv)(2) of the Code of Professional Conduct and (2) due to his personal knowledge, he is likely to be called as a witness.[18] It warned the Appellant that by persisting in representing Markač in spite of the repeated notices given to him, he "has jeopardised his client's interests by not withdrawing earlier in the proceedings, and thus, in gross negligence, has failed to meet the standard of professional ethics required in the performance of his duties before this Tribunal".[19] The Trial Chamber further called upon the Appellant "to show cause why the Trial Chamber should not determine that this behaviour does not amount to misconduct under Rule 46 and why it should not proceed against him there under."[20] At a hearing held on 28 February 2007, the Appellant submitted that his conduct did not amount to misconduct in that he did not behave inappropriately in advocating his standpoint.[21]

8. On 5 March 2007, the Appellant submitted a request for certification to appeal the First Impugned Decision.[22] **[page 4]**

9. On 6 March 2007, the Trial Chamber rendered a decision in which it refused the Appellant audience before the Trial Chamber, found that he is no longer eligible to represent Markač in this case before the

---

10 *Appeals* Chamber Decision on Joinder, paras 24, 31–32.

11 *Ibid*., para. 34.

12 *Prosecutor v. Ante Gotovina, Ivan Čermak and Mladen Markač*, Case Nos. IT-01-45-AR73.1, IT-03-73-AR73.1 and IT-03-73-AR73.2, Appellant Mladen Markač's Motion for Clarification of the Appeals Chamber's Decision from 25 October 2006, 8 *November* 2006 ("Clarification Motion").

13 *Prosecutor v. Ante Gotovina, Ivan Čermak and Mladen Markač*, Case Nos. IT-01-45-AR73.1, IT-03-73-AR73.1 and IT-03-73-AR73.2, Decision on Appellant Mladen Markač's Motion for Clarification, 12 January 2007 ("Clarification Decision").

14 Response, para. 10. The Appeals Chamber has confirmed with the Registry that this advisory opinion was not filed.

15 Status Conference, 9 February 2007, T. 103–105.

16 Status Conference, 9 February 2007, T. 114.

17 *Prosecutor v. Ante Gotovina et al.*, Case No. IT-06-90-PT, Prosecution's Submission Regarding Potential Conflict of Interests of Defence Counsel, 14 February 2007 ("Prosecution's Conflict of Interest Submission"); *Prosecutor v. Ante Gotovinaet al.*, Case No. IT-06-90-PT, Submission to the Trial Chamber Concerning the Alleged Conflict of Interest Affecting Counsel Čedo Prodanović and Jadranka Sloković, 14 February 2007 ("Čermak's Conflict of Interest Submission"); *Prosecutor v. Ante Gotovina et al.,* Case No. IT-06-90-PT, Defence Counsel Miroslav Šeparović's Submission Re Conflict of Interests, 14 February 2007 ("Appellant's Conflict of Interest Submission").

18 *Prosecutor v. Ante Gotovina et al.*, Case No. IT-06-90-PT, Decision on Conflict of Interest of Attorney Miroslav Šeparović, 27 February 2007 ("First Impugned Decision"), p. 10.

19 First *Impugned* Decision, p. 10.

20 *Ibid.*

21 Motion Hearing, 28 February, 2007, T. 173–6.

22 *Prosecutor v. Ante Gotovina et al.*, Case No. IT-06-90-PT, Request for Certification to File Interlocutory Appeal against the Trial Chamber's Decision on Finding of Misconduct of Attorney Miroslav Šeparović, 12 March 2007 ("Request for Certification"). Čermak filed *Prosecutor v. Ante Gotovina et al.*, Case No. IT-06-90-PT, Ivan Čermak's Response to the Request for Certification to File Interlocutory Appeal against the Trial Chamber's Decision on Finding of Misconduct of Attorney Miroslav Šeparović, on 14 March 2007 ("Čermak's Response to Certification Request").

Trial Chamber pursuant to Rule 44 of the Rules, and ordered Markač to immediately engage new counsel ("Second Impugned Decision").[23] On 12 March 2007, the Appellant requested leave to appeal the Second Impugned Decision. Certification to appeal the First and Second Impugned Decisions was granted by the Trial Chamber on 13 March 2007.[24]

10. The Appellant filed his Appeal on 20 March 2007;[25] the Prosecution filed its response on 27 March 2007;[26] the Appellant did not file a reply. Additionally, the Appellant requested the Trial Chamber to suspend the procedural consequences of the First Impugned Decision.[27] This request was partly granted by the Trial Chamber which suspended measures ordered to be taken in the First Impugned Decision pending final resolution by the Appeals Chamber.[28]

II. STANDARD OF REVIEW

11. The Appeals Chamber recalls that an interlocutory appeal is not a *de novo* review of the Trial Chamber's decision.[29] Since decisions on matters relating to the calling of witnesses and assignment of counsel at trial fall squarely within the discretion of the Trial Chamber,[30] the question before the Appeals Chamber is not whether it "agrees with that decision" but "whether the Trial Chamber has correctly exercised its discretion in reaching that decision."[31] The party challenging a discretionary decision by the Trial Chamber must demonstrate that the Trial Chamber has **[page 5]** committed a "discernible error".[32] The Appeals Chamber will overturn a Trial Chamber's exercise of its discretion where it is found to be "(1) based on an incorrect interpretation of governing law; (2) based on a patently incorrect conclusion of fact; or (3) so unfair or unreasonable as to constitute an abuse of the Trial Chamber's discretion".[33]

III. PRELIMINARY ISSUE

12. As a preliminary matter, the Appeals Chamber notes that in support of his submissions on appeal, the Appellant filed 7 Annexes and a letter.[34] The Prosecution objects to their filing, submitting that the Appellant

---

23 *Prosecutor v. Ante Gotovina et al.*, Case No. IT-06-90-PT, Decision on Finding of Misconduct of Attorney Miroslav Šeparović, 6 March 2007 ("Second Impugned Decision"), pp. 2 and 7.

24 Prosecutor *v. Ante Gotovina et al.*, Case No. IT-06-90-PT, Decision on Request for Certification to File Interlocutory Appeal against the Trial Chamber's Decision on Conflict of Interest and on Request for Certification to File Interlocutory Appeal against the Trial Chamber's Decision on Finding of Misconduct of Attorney Miroslav Šeparović, 13 March 2007.

25 *Prosecutor v. Ante Gotovina, Ivan Čermak and Mladen Markač*, Case No. IT-06-90-AR73.1, Appellant Miroslav Šeparović's Consolidated Interlocutory Appeal Against Trial Chamber's Decision on Conflict of Interest of Attorney Miroslav Šeparović and Against Trial Chamber's Decision on Finding of Misconduct of Attorney Miroslav Šeparović, 20 March 2007. An Addendum was filed on 22 March 2007 (Appellant Miroslav Šeparović's Addendum to Consolidated Interlocutory Appeal Against Trial Chamber's Decision on Conflict of Interest of Attorney Miroslav Šeparović and Against Trial Chamber's Decision on Finding of Misconduct of Attorney Miroslav Šeparović).

26 Prosecution's Response Brief to Šeparović's consolidated Interlocutory Appeal, 27 March 2007 ("Response").

27 *Prosecutor v. Ante Gotovina et al.*, Case No. IT-06-90-PT, Attorney Miroslav Šeparović's Request for Suspending the Procedural Consequences from the Trial Chamber's Decision on Conflict of Interest and on Misconduct of Attorney Miroslav Šeparović, 20 March 2007.

28 *Prosecutor v. Ante Gotovina et al.*, Case No. IT-06-90-PT, Decision Suspending Execution of the Trial Chamber's Decision of 6 March 2007, 26 March 2007, p. 3.

29 *Prosecutor v. Milan Lukić and Sredoje Lukić,* Case No. IT-98-32/1-AR65.1, Decision on Defence Appeal Against Trial Chamber's Decision on Sredoje Lukić's Motion for Provisional Release, 16 April 2007 ("*Lukić* Provisional Release Decision"), para. 4; *Prosecutor v. Mico Stanišić,* Case No. IT-04-79-AR65.1, Decision on Prosecution's Interlocutory Appeal of Mićo Stanišić's Provisional Release, 17 October 2005 ("*Stanišić* Provisional Release Decision"), para. 6.

30 Clarification Decision, p. 4. *See* also, *Slobodan Milošević v. Prosecutor*, Case No. IT-02-54-AR73.7, Decision on Interlocutory Appeal of the Trial Chamber's Decision on the Assignment of Defense Counsel, 1 November 2004 ("*Milošević* Decision on Defence Counsel"), para. 9.

31 *Lukić* Provisional Release Decision, para. 4; *Stanišić* Provisional Release Decision, para. 6.

32 *Lukić* Provisional Release Decision, para. 5; *Stanišić* Provisional Release Decision, para. 6.

33 *Milošević* Decision on Defence Counsel, para. 10, *Prosecutor v. Vojislav Šešelj*, Case No. IT-03-67-AR73.4, Decision on Appeal Against the Trial Chamber's Decision (No.2) on Assignment of Counsel, 8 December 2006, para. 16.

34 The Annexes consist of two statements filed by the Appellant ("Annex 1"); two statements by Mladen Markač ("Annex 2"); a statement by former deputy President of the Court Martial in Split, Mr Zoran Matulović ("Annex 3"); a letter signed by the Deputy Attorney General of Croatia, Mr Lazo Pajić ("Annex 4"); a Decision of the House of Representatives of the Croatian Parliament and a State Bureau of Statistics Decree and a Directive on the Internal Structure of the Ministry of Justice

has improperly filed evidence for the first time on appeal without seeking leave of the Appeals Chamber to do so.[35] The Appeals Chamber notes that most of the Annexes, that is, except Annexes 2 and 3 in the addendum, are being introduced for the first time on appeal. In order for the said information to become part of the record, they have to be admitted as additional evidence pursuant to Rule 115 of the Rules.[36] Because the Appellant has failed to move for their admission pursuant to Rule 115, they will not be considered by the Appeals Chamber.

IV. SUBMISSIONS OF THE PARTIES AND DISCUSSION

13. The Appellant essentially raises five grounds of appeal. He argues that the Trial Chamber erred (1) in finding him to be a "necessary witness" pursuant to Article 26 of the Code of Professional Conduct; (2) in finding that he had a personal interest in the case; (3) in failing to find that his withdrawal would cause Markač substantial hardship; (4) in failing to find, in line with a decision in *Prosecutor v. Blagoje Simić*,[37] that his client's consent resolved any conflict of interest **[page 6]** and (5) in failing to weigh the overall interests of justice and the right of the Appellant to a fair trial.[38]

14. In addition, the Appellant requests an oral hearing for the purpose of advancing arguments relating to this ground of appeal.[39] In view of the extensive submissions made and filed by the parties before both the Trial Chamber and the Appeals Chamber[40] and the substantial discussion in the First and Second Impugned Decisions of the issues now under appeal, the Appeals Chamber does not consider it necessary to hold an oral hearing on the Appeal.

A. Alleged error in finding that the Appellant is a "necessary witness"

(a) Arguments of the Parties

15. The Appellant submits that other potential witnesses, such as the former President of the Split Military Court, Mr. Matulović, could provide the same evidence as he would provide in his anticipated testimony.[41] He also submits that "the alleged contested issue relating to the question of the authority over the civil and military court system and the organization of the Croatian judicial system *tempore criminis* is very clearly defined in the relevant Croatian legislation and the practice implementation."[42] Further, he argues that Čermak has affirmed that he is not a "necessary witness",[43] and that although Gotovina did not explicitly state his position in that respect, he repeatedly stressed that Markač has a fundamental right to counsel of his

("Annex 5"); a Decree on the Postings and Repeal of the War Postings of the Judges in court Martial in Split ("Annex 6"); a letter from the President of the Court Benko Velčić and a letter from the Assistant Minister of Justice, Ivan Lovrić ("Annex 7"). In addition, the Appellant filed a letter from Ms. Carla Del Ponte, see Appellant Miroslav Šeparović's Addendum to Consolidated Interlocutory Appeal Against Trial Chamber's Decision on Conflict of Interest of Attorney Miroslav Šeparović and against Trial Chamber's Decision on Finding of Misconduct of Attorney Miroslav Šeparović, 3 April 2007.

35 Response, para. 14.

36 *Prosecutor v. Radovan Stanković,* Case No. IT-96-23/2-AR11bis.1, Decision on Rule 11*bis* Referral, 1 September 2005, para. 37.

37 *Prosecutor v. Blagoje Simić et al.,* Case No. IT-95-9-PT, Decision on Prosecution Motion to Resolve Conflict of Interest Regarding Attorney Borislav Pisarević, 25 March 1999 ("*Simić* Case").

38 Appeal, paras 19 and 33.

39 Appeal, para. 30.

40 *See Supra* paras 1–9.

41 Appeal, paras 23–24.

42 Appeal, para. 23.

43 Appeal, para. 25, referring to Accused Ivan Čermak's Response to the Request for Certification to File Interlocutory Appeal Against Trial Chamber's Decision on Finding of Misconduct of Attorney Miroslav Šeparović, 14 March 2007, para. 2. The Appeals Chamber notes the Accused Ivan Čermak's submission therein that "Ivan Čermak further submits that he does not regard Miroslav Šeparović as a necessary witness as the facts needed for determination of his case can be obtained elsewhere. He also affirms that he does not intend to call Miroslav Šeparović as a witness as his testimony at this point does not seem either unobtainable elsewhere, relevant or material to establishing the defence for Ivan Čermak."

choice,[44] which in the Appellant's view implicitly means that he should not be disqualified from this case.[45] Regarding the Prosecution's position, the Appellant submits that it is significant that his name was never listed as a potential witness nor was any attempt to approach him made for the purpose of interviewing or obtaining some information from him concerning the indictment or its supporting material.[46] **[page 7]**

16. In response, the Prosecution points out that Gotovina considers the Appellant a crucial witness and has not abandoned his intention to call him to testify.[47] Further, the Prosecution argues that there is no showing that the proffered evidence and the proposed substitute witness, Mr. Matulović or anyone else at the same rank in the Croatian government, has the same knowledge as the Appellant. It submits that proposing a substitute does not circumvent the Trial Chamber's finding of the Appellant's level and knowledge.[48] As a result, it submits that the proposed substitute witness and evidence contained in the annexes do not establish that the Appellant is not likely to be a necessary witness.[49]

(b) Discussion

17. In its Decision on Joinder, the Appeals Chamber affirmed the Trial Chamber's finding with respect to the *possibility* of the Appellant being a necessary witness for the Gotovina case as well as the Čermak and Markač case.[50] After the question of whether the Appellant would in fact be a "necessary witness" was remitted to the Trial Chamber, pursuant to the Clarification Decision, the Trial Chamber found that it "reasonably foresees the *likelihood* that the Appellant will be called as a witness in this case because of his position as former Minister of Justice at the time of alleged crimes".[51]

18. The Appeals Chamber finds no error in this conclusion. Article 26 of the Code of Professional Conduct only envisages that "Counsel shall not act as an advocate in a proceeding in which counsel is *likely* to be a necessary witness".[52] The Appeals Chamber notes that because their trials have been joined, Gotovina, Cermak and Markač are in the same proceeding. Although the Prosecution did not envisage calling the Appellant as a witness, and Markač and Čermak appear to hold the view that their respective defence strategies will not involve calling the Appellant as a witness,[53] Gotovina has not ruled out the possibility of calling him as a witness.[54] Further, the Trial Chamber has not ruled out at this stage that it might choose to call him as a witness.[55] **[page 8]**

19. In addition, should the Appellant be called to testify, the Trial Chamber is not precluded from using his evidence in support of or against Čermak or Markač.[56] The Appeals Chamber recalls that the Trial Chamber found that the cases of the three accused are inherently connected because they took place in the same geographic area, in the same time period and in the course of the same military operation, and that they were allegedly committed pursuant to the same joint criminal enterprise of which all three accused are alleged to be members.[57] On the basis of this factual nexus some of the evidence, including that of the Appellant, may be the same.

20. The Appeals Chamber finds that the Appellant has failed to demonstrate that there was an error in the exercise of the Trial Chamber's discretion. This argument is accordingly dismissed.

---

44 Appeal, para. 25, referring to Defendant Ante Gotovina's Response to Request for Certification to File Interlocutory Appeal Against Trial Chamber's Decision on Finding of Misconduct of Attorney Miroslav Šeparović, 13 March 2007, paras 2, 8, 9.

45 Appeal, para. 25.

46 Appeal, para. 25.

47 Response, para. 13.

48 Response, para. 15.

49 Response, para. 15.

50 Appeals Chamber Decision on Joinder, paras 32–33; Clarification Decision, p. 2.

51 Impugned Decision, p. 8 (emphasis added).

52 Emphasis added.

53 *Čermak*'s Response to Certification Request, para. 2; Request for Certification, Annex 2, Statement of Mladen Markač, p. 1.

54 *Gotovina*'s Opposition to Joinder, para. 8; *Gotovina*'s Response to Certification Request, paras 8–9. The Appeals Chamber notes that in the Motion Hearing held on 28 February 2007, T. 172, Counsel for Gotovina asked the Trial Chamber, "I, of course, saw the Court's decision yesterday that was published, and my question to the Chamber is at this point would alter the Chamber's decision if General Gotovina decides not to call Mr. Separovic as a witness".

55 First Impugned Decision, p. 7.

56 See *Prosecutor v. Zdravko Tolimir et al.*, Case No. IT-04-80-AR73.1, Decision on Radivoje Miletić's Interlocutory Appeal Against the Trial Chamber's Decision on Joinder of the Accused, 27 January 2006, paras 14 and 15.

57 Appeals Chamber Decision on Joinder, para 20; Trial Chamber Decision on Joinder Decision, para. 59.

B. Alleged error in finding that the Appellant has a personal interest in the case

(a) Arguments of the Parties

21. The Appellant submits that the Trial Chamber erred in finding that he has a personal interest in this case which disqualifies him as counsel under Article 14(D)(iv)(2) of the Code of Professional Conduct.[58] In his view, this finding is not legally or factually correct because the Appellant's only and primary interest is that of his client, Markač.[59] Further, he submits that the Trial Chamber's finding is only based on unfounded speculation that he, as former Minister of Justice, "could decline his hypothetical responsibility and place it on the Ministry of Defence" whereas the question of the responsibility of the Croatian judicial system is not an issue in the Joinder Indictment and that because he has not been indicted or suspected of the alleged crimes, the fact that he was Minister of Justice does not disqualify him as Defence Counsel.[60] The Prosecution responds that the Trial Chamber acted within its discretion.[61]

(b) Discussion

22. The Appeals Chamber recalls that, in the First Impugned Decision, the Trial Chamber also addressed the issue as to whether the Appellant had a personal interest in the case and concluded in **[page 9]** this regard that it could not "accept [that] the professional judgement of Šeparović, lead counsel for the Accused Markač but also Minister of Justice at the time of the alleged crimes in this Indictment, may not reasonably be affected by his own personal interests".[62] In reaching this conclusion the Trial Chamber referred to the recent declarations made by the Appellant in connection with the issue of "whether the Ministry of Defence or the Ministry of Interior was responsible for the military police and whether the military justice system fell under the responsibility of the Ministry of Justice" and considered it to be relevant to its decision on the existence of a conflict of interest.[63] It further held that "it is obvious that one of the alternatives presented by the contested issue, whether it is the Ministry of Defence or Ministry of Justice who was responsible for the military courts, may affect the personal interests of the former Minister of Justice, Šeparović".[64]

23. Article 14(A) of the Code of Professional Conduct provides:

> Counsel owes a duty of loyalty to a client. Counsel also has a duty to the Tribunal to act with independence in the interests of justice and shall put those interests before his own interests or those of any other person, organisation or State.

The Appeals Chamber also recalls that a conflict of interest between an attorney and a client arises in any situation where, by reason of certain circumstances, representation by such an attorney prejudices, or could prejudice, the interests of the client and the wider interests of justice.[65]

24. As noted above, the Appellant has not denied personal knowledge of the relevant information which he has presented in his submissions that the Ministry of Justice was not responsible for the military courts.[66] In these circumstances, the Appeals Chamber agrees with the Trial Chamber that his denial at this early stage of proceedings that it was the Ministry of Justice that was responsible for the military courts, thereby eliminating

---

[58] Appeal, para. 27 and 29, referring to and quoting the *Simić* Case, p. 6, in which the Trial Chamber held, "A conflict of interest between an attorney and a client arises in any situation where, by reason of certain circumstances, representation by such an attorney prejudices, or could prejudice, the interest of the client and the wider interests of justice."

[59] Appeal, para. 27.

[60] Appeal, para. 27. *See* also, Appeal, para. 28.

[61] Response, para. 20.

[62] First Impugned Decision, p. 5.

[63] First Impugned Decision, p. 5.

[64] First Impugned Decision, p. 5.

[65] *Prosecutor v. Jadranko Prlić et al.*, Case No. IT-04-74-AR73.1, Decision on Appeal by Bruno Stojić Against Trial Chamber's Decision on Request for Appointment of Counsel, 24 November 2004 ("*Stojić* Decision"), para. 22; *Simić* Decision, p. 6.

[66] Misconduct Decision, p. 3. The Appeals Chamber further notes that in the Appellant's Conflict of Interest Submission, para. 13, the Appellant argued that he is "not the only one who can relevantly testify about the judicial system *tempore criminis*".

a defence strategy that was otherwise open to Markač, may be considered a significant indication of a conflict of interest. Therefore, the Appeals Chamber is of the view that the Appellant has failed to demonstrate that the Trial Chamber committed a discernible error in this respect.

25. This ground of appeal is accordingly dismissed. **[page 10]**

C. Alleged error in failing to consider that the Appellant's withdrawal would cause Markač "substantial hardship"

(a) Arguments of the Parties

26. The Appellant subm°its that Markač has already suffered substantial hardship which will be even greater if the Appeals Chamber upholds his withdrawal from this case.[67] He adds that this hardship is of a kind that undoubtedly affects the fairness of trial and equality of arms and thus places him at a substantial disadvantage in relation to his opponent.[68] He submits that he is Markač's attorney of his free choosing, has his confidence and trust, has already spent four years representing him from the time of his very first interview with Prosecution investigators and has spent numerous hours preparing for the trial.[69] Additionally, some important potential witnesses for the Defence promised to testify only if the Appellant was Markač's attorney.[70] He further submits that Markač has contacted some Croatian criminal lawyers, but was unable to get an agreement for representation.[71]

27. In response, the Prosecution submits that the Trial Chamber's decision to withdraw the Appellant as Counsel for Markač was based on "a full year of decisions and procedural history".[72] It points out that the conflict of interest was raised as early as 4 April 2006 by Gotovina, and further submits that had the Appellant withdrawn after the joinder motion had been granted, there would have been at least seven months for new counsel to prepare for the trial and that existing co-counsel is not prohibited from continuing to represent Markač.[73]

(b) Discussion

28. As noted by the Trial Chamber, due to the compelling circumstances of the Appellant's own personal interest in this case, the harm caused to Markač and the integrity of the proceedings if the Appellant were to continue as his counsel in the proceedings would clearly and demonstrably outweigh any hardship suffered by Markač as a result of the Appellant's withdrawal as his counsel.[74] Furthermore, the Appeals Chamber notes that the Markač is also represented by co-counsel who will likely continue to represent him in the absence of one of the exceptions under Article 9(B) of the Code of Professional Conduct. **[page 11]**

29. The Appeals Chamber further finds that, even though the Appellant's withdrawal will inevitably cause a delay in the proceedings, there could be greater hardship to Markač at a later stage of the proceedings, should the conflict of interest regarding the Appellant's representation of Markač not be resolved at the present stage. The Appeals Chamber notes in this respect that, for example, Gotovina's Defence has not waived his right to call the Appellant as a witness[75] and that therefore the Appellant could still face withdrawal pursuant to Article 26 of the Code of Professional Conduct. The Appeals Chamber is of the view that such situation is likely to irreversibly prejudice the administration of justice.

30. Accordingly, the Appeals Chamber finds that the Appellant has failed to demonstrate the existence of a discernible error in the Trial Chamber's Decision. This ground of appeal is dismissed.

---

67 Appeal, para. 26.
68 Appeal, para. 21.
69 Appeal, paras 19 and 26.
70 Appeal, para. 26.
71 Appeal, para. 26.
72 Response, para. 7.
73 Response, para. 8. *See* also *Supra* para.1.
74 Impugned Decision, pp. 7 and 8.
75 Defendant Gotovina's Response to Appellant Mladen Markač's Motion for Clarification of the Appeals Chamber's Decision from 25 October 2006, 22 November 2006.

D. Alledged failure to recognize the *Simić* case as a precedent with respect to curing the alleged conflict of interest

(a) Arguments of the Parties

31. The Appellant submits that a remedy for the alleged conflict of interest is already established in the jurisprudence of the tribunal[76] and that the First Impugned Decision erred in failing to consider it.[77] He refers to a decision in the *Simić* case, where the Trial Chamber found, when faced with a similar conflict, that the full and informed consent of a counsel's client was an appropriate remedy for continued representation.[78] The Appellant submits that the situation of counsel in the *Simić* case was much worse than his.[79] He argues that, although the current Article 14(E) of the Code of Professional Conduct has different wording from that of the former Article 9(5), the point in both is that consent of the accused must not generate further obstruction of justice.[80] He concludes that the Trial Chamber failed to take into account relevant precedent and in so doing failed to fulfil its statutory obligation to treat all people equally before the Tribunal.[81] The Prosecution responds that Article 14 of the Code of Professional Conduct does not allow for the possibility that client waiver may cure a conflict if "such consent is likely to irreversibly prejudice the administration of justice."[82] **[page 12]**

(b) Discussion

32. The Appeals Chamber agrees with the Trial Chamber that the giving of consent by Markač could not cure the conflict of interest between Markač and the Appellant in relation to his position as Minister of Justice *tempore criminis*.[83] Consent given by a potentially affected client to remove a conflict of interest with counsel is not conclusive of there being no conflict of interest.[84] Although the Trial Chamber resolved the conflict of interest in the *Simić* case by consent, the Trial Chamber in the present case was not bound to follow the *Simić* case.[85] In any event, the present case is distinguishable from that of *Simić*. First, the Appeals Chamber notes that the applicable provisions are different. At the time the decision in the *Simić* case was rendered, the Trial Chamber applied Article 9(5) of the Code of Professional Conduct which read:

> (5) Where a conflict of interest does arise, Counsel must-
>
> (a) promptly and fully inform each potentially affected Client of the nature and extent of the conflict; and
>
> (b) either:
>
> (i) take all steps necessary to remove the conflict; or
>
> (ii) obtain the full and informed consent of all potentially affected Clients to continue the representation, <u>so long as Counsel is able to fulfill all other obligations under this Code.</u>[86]

Article 9(5) of the Code of Professional Conduct has since been amended and currently provides, as Article 14(E) of the Code of Professional Conduct:

---

76 Appeal, para. 29.
77 Appeal, para. 21.
78 Appeal, paras 29 and 30.
79 Appeal, para. 30.
80 Appeal, para. 32.
81 Appeal, para. 32.
82 Response, para. 17.
83 Impugned Decision, p. 8.
84 *Stojić* Decision, para. 27.
85 *Prosecutor v. Zlatko Aleksovski*, Case No. IT-95-14/1-A, Judgement, 24 March 2004, para. 114 ("The Appeals Chamber considers that decisions of Trial Chambers, which are bodies with coordinate jurisdiction, have no binding force on each other, although a Trial Chamber is free to follow the decision of another Trial Chamber if it finds that decision persuasive.")
86 Emphasis added.

Where a conflict of interest does arise, counsel shall:

i. promptly and fully inform each potentially affected present and former client of the nature and extent of the conflict; and

ii. either:

1. take all steps necessary to remove the conflict; or
2. obtain the full and informed consent of all potentially affected present and former clients to continue the representation unless such consent is likely to irreversibly prejudice the administration of justice.[87] **[page 13]**

33. The Appeals Chamber has already found that the Appellant's further representation of Markač is likely to irreversibly prejudice the administration of justice.[88] In addition, whereas in the *Simić* case, all the co-accused stated that there was no conflict of interest between them and counsel, Gotovina, in the present case, has not waived his right to call the Appellant as a witness and has clearly indicated that there is, in his view, a conflict of interest.[89]

34. In light of the foregoing, the Appeals Chamber finds that the Appellant has failed to show that the Trial Chamber committed a discernible error by not considering consent by Markač a remedy to the conflict of interest. Accordingly, this ground of appeal is dismissed.

E. Error in weighing the overall interests of justice and the rights of the accused to consent to continued representation by the Appellant

(a) Arguments of the Parties

35. The Appellant submits that the fact that he, as former Minister of Justice was representing Markač in the "Operation Storm case" was very well known to the Tribunal's authorities for a long period of time.[90] He submits that no one ever raised the question of a possible conflict of interest, and no former motion was ever filed to disqualify him as counsel for Markač.[91] He points out that now he is facing disqualification from the case less than two months before the beginning of the trial[92] and argues that Markač's right to a fair trial is dangerously jeopardized.[93]

36. The Prosecution recalls that the Trial Chamber was particularly concerned that the Appellant has a personal interest in the issue of whether the Ministry of Justice or the Ministry of Defence controlled or administered the military courts.[94] It submits that this decision was founded on a concern for the integrity of the proceedings and the interests of justice[95] and that the Trial Chamber did not abuse its discretion.[96] **[page 14]**

(b) Discussion

37. As previously stated by the Appeals Chamber, in principle, the choice of any accused regarding his defence counsel in proceedings before the International Tribunals should be respected unless there are

---

87 Emphasis added.
88 *See supra*, para. 28.
89 *Gotovina*'s Opposition to Joinder, para. 8.
90 Appeal, para. 33.
91 Appeal, para. 33.
92 Appeal, para. 33.
93 Appeal, para. 33. Markač's further argument that "the proper administration of justice has been driven into a dead-end" by denying him equal treatment before the Tribunal and the right to counsel of his own choosing" is unsubstantiated and will not be discussed further.
94 Appeal, para.18.
95 Appeal, para. 20.
96 Appeal, para. 20.

sufficient grounds to override the accused's preference in the interests of justice.[97] When the fairness of the trial which is one of the fundamental rights of the accused also provided for in Article 21 of the Statute is at stake, as is suggested in the present case, the accused's choice might be overridden.[98] It is established jurisprudence that one of the limits to the accused's choice is the existence of a conflict of interest affecting his counsel.[99]

38. In the present case, the Appellant, as counsel, has been found to have a personal interest on account of his previous position as Minister of Justice.[100] Further, because he has personal knowledge directly relevant to the crimes allegedly committed by the three accused in the Indictment, he is likely to be called as a necessary witness for one of the accused. Such a conflict affects the essential fairness of the trial to all accused persons in this case. Cumulatively, these factors make his continued representation of Markač incompatible with the best interests of justice. Accordingly, this ground of appeal is dismissed.

V. DISPOSITION

On the basis of the foregoing, the Appeals Chamber,

DISMISSES the Appellant's appeal in its entirety.

Done in both English and French, the English text being authoritative.

Done this 4th day of May 2007
At The Hague,
The Netherlands.

Judge Liu Daqun
Presiding Judge

[Seal of the International Tribunal]

97 *Stojić* Decision, para. 19; Appeals Chamber Decision on Joinder, para. 30.
98 *Stojić* Decision, para. 19.
99 *Stojić* Decision, para. 19; *see* also *Prosecutor v. Željko Mejakić et al,* Case No. IT-02-65-AR73.1, Decision on Appeal by the Prosecution to Resolve Conflict of Interest Regarding Attorney Jovan Simić, 6 October 2004, para. 8.
100 First Impugned Decision, pp. 9, 10; *see* para. 24 *supra*.

UNITED NATIONS

International Tribunal for the Prosecution of Persons Responsible for Serious Violations of International Humanitarian Law Committed in the Territory of the Former Yugoslavia since 1991	Case No.	IT-00-39-A
	Date:	11 May 2007
	Original:	English

IN THE APPEALS CHAMBER

Before: **Judge Fausto Pocar, Presiding**
Judge Mohamed Shahabuddeen
Judge Andrésia Vaz
Judge Theodor Meron
Judge Wolfgang Schomburg

Registrar: **Mr. Hans Holthuis**

Decision of: **11 May 2007**

PROSECUTOR

v.

MOMČILO KRAJIŠNIK

DECISION ON MOMČILO KRAJIŠNIK'S REQUEST TO SELF-REPRESENT, ON COUNSEL'S MOTIONS IN RELATION TO APPOINTMENT OF *AMICUS CURIAE*, AND ON THE PROSECUTION MOTION OF 16 FEBRUARY 2007

The Office of the Prosecutor:
Mr. Peter Kremer
Ms. Christine Dahl

Previously Assigned Counsel for Mr. Krajišnik:
Mr. Colin Nicholls

The Appellant:
Momčilo Krajišnik

[page 1] 1. The Appeals Chamber of the International Tribunal for the Prosecution of Persons Responsible for Serious Violations of International Humanitarian Law Committed in the Territory of the Former Yugoslavia since 1991 ("Appeals Chamber" and "Tribunal", respectively) is seized of three motions filed by Assigned Counsel for Momčilo Krajišnik ("Assigned Counsel" and "Mr. Krajišnik", respectively). One motion, filed 27 December 2006, is the "Motion Seeking Review of the Decision of the Registry in Relation to Assignment of Counsel" ("First Motion"); the second one, filed 2 January 2007, is the "Motion Requesting Assignment as *Amicus Curiae*" ("Second Motion"); and the third one, filed 12 April 2007, is the "Motion Regarding Proposed Assignment as *Amicus*" ("Third Motion"). The Appeals Chamber is also seized of the "Prosecution Motion Regarding Filing of Notice of Appeal and Response by Momčilo Krajišnik" ("Prosecution Motion"), filed on 16 February 2007.

I. Preliminary Observations

2. The Appeals Chamber will not discuss the procedural history related to the First and Second Motions, as it has done so in its prior decision in the present case.[1] Indeed, the Appeals Chamber has already ruled as to some issues raised in the First Motion.[2]

3. With regard to this First Motion, the only issue still pending before the Appeals Chamber is Mr. Krajišnik's request to represent himself, which Mr. Krajišnik both wishes to do and believes he has a right to do. With regard to the Second Motion, the Appeals Chamber has before it a request by assigned counsel for Mr. Krajišnik that the Appeals Chamber appoint *amicus curiae* to "complement Mr. Krajišnik's self-representation on appeal."[3]

4. In the Third Motion, Assigned Counsel clarifies two points with regard to the Second Motion. First, Assigned Counsel specified that in requesting the appointment of *amicus curiae,* the Appeals Chamber "should not exclusively consider whether" Assigned Counsel himself "should be so appointed."[4] Second, Assigned Counsel stated that the Appeals Chamber should delineate the role that it envisions for *amicus curiae* prior to appointing a specific *amicus curiae,* so as to ensure **[page 2]** that the specific *amicus curiae* chosen is "aware beforehand of the role which he would be undertaking and ... agree[s] to fulfill that role."[5]

5. The Prosecution has not responded to the First, Second, or Third Motions. At the request of the Pre-Appeal Judge, however, the Prosecution filed "The Prosecution's Submissions in Relation to the Right to Self-Representation and the Role of *Amicus Curiae* in Appellate Proceedings" on 2 April 2007 and related submissions on the following day.[6] These filings detail the Prosecution's research regarding the right of self-representation on appeal and the role of *amici curiae* in criminal appeals. In addition, Assigned Counsel filed "Further Submissions Relating to Self-Representation on Appeal" ("Further Submissions") on 2 April 2007. In the Further Submissions, Assigned Counsel elaborates on his views regarding the right of self-representation, making reference to, among other things, some case law in England and Wales. Finally, two Status Conferences held in this case touched upon the pending issues in the First, Second, and Third Motions.[7] The Appeals Chamber has taken these filings and the transcripts of the Status Conferences into consideration.[8]

1 "Decision on 'Motion Seeking Review of the Decisions of the Registry in Relation to Assignment of Counsel'", 29 January 2007 ("29 January Decision"); *cf.* "Decision on Request for Review by the President of the Decisions of the Registry in Relation to Assignment of Counsel", 1 February 2007 ("President's Decision").

2 *See* generally 29 January Decision (declaring one issue moot and finding that power to review two other issues lay with the President of the Tribunal); *cf.* President's Decision, paras 12–13 (reviewing and resolving these two other issues).

3 Second Motion, para. 32.

4 Third Motion, para. 8.

5 Third Motion, para. 10. Assigned Counsel also clarified that he did not intend to file a Consolidated Notice of Appeal prior to a decision by the Appeals Chamber on the issue of self-representation raised in the First Motion. *Ibid.,* paras 11-14.

6 "Prosecution's Corrigendum Re Submissions", filed 3 April 2007 ("Prosecution's Corrigendum"); "Book of Authorities for the Prosecution Submission in Relation to the Right to Self-Representation and the Role of *Amicus Curiae* in Appellate Proceedings", 3 April 2007.

7 AT 21–70 (transcript of 26 March 2007 Status Conference); AT 71–98 (transcript of 5 April 2007 Status Conference).

8 The Appeals Chamber need not address "The Registrar's Submission on Counsel's Request for Review of the Registrar's Decisions on Assignment of Counsel", filed 16 January 2007, and Assigned Counsel's "Response to 'The Registrar's Submission on Counsel's Request for Review of the Registrar's Decisions on Assignment of Counsel'", filed 26 January 2007. These two

6. The Prosecution Motion relates to other filings in this case - namely, the Notice of Appeal and Response Brief filed personally by Mr. Krajišnik.[9] The Prosecution moved to strike these filings on the ground that Mr. Krajišnik had Assigned Counsel (who had also filed a Notice of Appeal and a Response Brief) and was thus not entitled to make his own filings.[10] Assigned Counsel filed a response to the Prosecution Motion, in which Assigned Counsel argued that, given the pending First Motion and the request for self-representation contained therein, Mr. Krajišnik's filings should be treated as validly filed.[11] The Prosecution filed a reply in which it reiterated its original arguments.[12] **[page 3]**

7. The Appeals Chamber now turns to discuss the substance and merits of the First Motion and, subsequently, of the Second and Third Motions. The Appeals Chamber addresses the Prosecution Motion in the course of discussing the First Motion.

II. The First Motion (Issue of Self-Representation on Appeal)

8. In the First Motion, Mr. Krajišnik claims that he is entitled to represent himself. He notes that the Appeals Chamber recognized a right to self-representation in the course of the *Slobodan Milošević* and *Vojislav Šešelj* trial proceedings.[13] He considers that "there is no inherent or compelling reason why the right to self-representation on appeal at the ICTY should be understood any differently from the right to self-representation during trial proceedings."[14] He recognizes that the right to self-representation is not unqualified and that, in case-by-case circumstances, a Chamber may impose counsel "in order to ensure that the conduct of a fair trial is not disrupted."[15] He considers, however, that no case-specific reasons here justify denial of the right of self-representation. He explains that he is a "literate and highly intelligent person who is certainly capable of defending himself in person"; that he "has made an informed waiver of professional legal assistance in full awareness of the possible consequences of waiving the opportunity of skilled legal representation"; and that he "has never engaged in any kind of obstructionist behavior during his lengthy pre-trial, trial, and now pre-appeal detention".[16]

9. The Appeals Chamber recalls its discussion of self-representation in the course of an interlocutory appeal in *Slobodan Milošević*.[17] There, the Appeals Chamber looked to the text of Article 21(4)(d) of the Statute of the Tribunal, which provides in relevant part that a defendant has the right "to defend himself in person or through legal assistance of his own choosing". The Appeals Chamber "s[aw] no reasonable way to interpret Article 21 except as a guarantee of the right of self-representation".[18] It considered that the "drafters of the Statute clearly viewed the right to self-representation as an indispensable cornerstone of justice, placing it on a structural par with defendants' right to remain silent, to confront the witnesses against them, to a speedy trial, and even to demand a court-appointed attorney if they cannot afford one themselves."[19] It concluded that "[d]efendants before this Tribunal, then, have the presumptive right to represent themselves notwithstanding a Trial Chamber's judgement that they would be better off if represented by **[page 4]** counsel."[20] The Appeals Chamber went on to note, however, that this right is a qualified one and "may be curtailed on the grounds that a defendant's self-representation is substantially and persistently obstructing the proper and expeditious conduct of his trial."[21]

---

filings deal either with issues that have since been resolved, *see generally* 29 January Decision; President's Decision, or with matters that the Appeals Chamber does not deem relevant to the core issues at hand.

9 "The Accused, Momčilo Krajišnik: Notice of Appeal", 20 February 2007; "Response to the Prosecution's Appeal Brief Against the Judgement of 27 September 2006 in the Case of Momčilo Krajišnik", 20 February 2007.

10 Prosecution Motion, para. 11.

11 "Response to 'Prosecution Motion Regarding Filing of Notice of Appeal and Response by Momčilo Krajišnik'", 22 February 2007, paras 20–30.

12 "Prosecution Reply Regarding Filing of Notice of Appeal and Response by Momčilo Krajišnik", 26 February 2007.

13 First Motion, para. 38 & fn. 18.

14 *Ibid.*, para. 42.

15 *Ibid.*, para. 38.

16 *Ibid.*, paras 43–44.

17 *Slobodan Milošević v. Prosecutor,* Case No. IT-02-54-AR73.7, Decision on Interlocutory Appeal of the Trial Chamber's Decision on the Assignment of Counsel, 1 November 2004 (*"Milošević* Decision of 1 November 2004").

18 *Ibid.*, para. 11.

19 *Ibid.*, para. 11 (footnotes omitted).

20 *Ibid.*, para. 11; *see also Prosecutor v. Vojislav Šešelj,* Case No. IT-03-67-AR73.3, Decision on Appeal Against the Trial Chamber's Decision on Assignment of Counsel, 20 October 2006 (*"Šešelj* Decision"), para. 8.

21 *Milošević* Decision of 1 November 2004, paras 12–13; *see also Šešelj* Decision, para. 8.

10. In the case at hand, the Appeals Chamber sees no case-specific reasons why any right to self-representation possessed by Mr. Krajišnik should be curtailed.[22] Rather, the core question before the Appeals Chamber is whether individuals possess a right to self-representation before this Tribunal during appeals from judgement. For the reasons that follow, the Appeals Chamber concludes that they do.

11. To begin with, Article 21(4)(d) of the Statute draws no distinctions between the trial stage and the appeal stage of a case. There is thus no textual basis for concluding that the guarantee to self-representation therein (as recognized in the *Milošević* Decision) evaporates with the issuance of the trial judgement.[23] Moreover, there is no obvious reason why self-representation at trial is so different in character from self-representation on appeal as to require an *a priori* distinction between the two. Self-representation on appeal may be a complex and tricky business, but on its face it is no more difficult (and indeed perhaps less difficult) than self-representation at trial. Both stages involve complicated factual and legal issues and require familiarity with a daunting set of procedural rules. It may never be in an individual's interests to represent himself, either at trial or at appeal, but he nonetheless has a "cornerstone" right to make his own case to the Tribunal.

12. Finally, a review of the case law of domestic jurisdictions does not support a distinction between the trial and appeal stages for purposes of self-representation. In the course of substantial research, as supplemented by the helpful submissions of the parties, the Appeals Chamber has come across only one jurisdiction – the United States–that finds a right to self-representation at trial but not on appeal.[24] Moreover, in concluding that the United States federal Constitution grants defendants a right to self-representation at trial but not on appeal, the United States Supreme Court relied heavily on the fact that the relevant constitutional provision "does not include any right to appeal" and thus that "[i]t necessarily follows that [this provision] does not provide any basis for **[page 5]** finding a right to self-representation on appeal."[25] Such reasoning has no force in the situation at hand, since Article 25 of the Statute of the Tribunal plainly provides a right of appeal. The Appeals Chamber thus declines to rely on the distinction drawn in United States jurisprudence. The Appeals Chamber further considers it noteworthy that no other jurisdiction appears to draw such a distinction.[26]

13. Accordingly, the Appeals Chamber concludes that Mr. Krajišnik has a right to represent himself on his appeal. As at trial, however, this right is not unqualified. Should Mr. Krajišnik's self-representation substantially and persistently obstruct the proper and expeditious conduct of his appeal, then counsel may be imposed upon him.

14. In light of the foregoing, the Appeals Chamber dismisses the Prosecution Motion and will treat Mr. Krajišnik's Notice of Appeal and his Response Brief as validly filed self-represented submissions.

15. The Appeals Chamber further considers it appropriate to specify time limits for Mr. Krajišnik's future filings. His Appeal Brief will be due within seventy-five days of the filing of the Trial Judgement translated into B/C/S. His Reply Brief will be due within fifteen days of the translation into B/C/S of the Prosecution Response to this Appeal Brief.

III. The Second and Third Motions (Issue of *Amicus Curiae)*

16. Having held that Mr. Krajišnik is currently entitled to represent himself on appeal, the Appeals Chamber now turns to the Second and Third Motions. In the Second Motion, Assigned Counsel observes that "[w]here an accused elects self-representation, the concerns about the fairness of the proceedings are, of

---

22 In this regard, the Appeals Chamber notes that Krajišnik's background and health present no case-specific barriers to self-representation; that he asserted his right to self-representation near the beginning of the appeal process; and that to date there has been no opportunity for obstruction to stem from his self-representation since, over his objections, he has not been representing himself but rather has had assigned counsel.

23 *See* Further Submissions, para. 4 (making this point).

24 *See Faretta v. California,* 422 U.S. 806 (1975) (finding a federal constitutional right to self-representation at trial); *Martinez v. Court of Appeal of California, Fourth Appellate District,* 528 U.S. 152 (2000) (finding no federal constitutional right to self-representation on appeal).

25 *Martinez,* 528 U.S., at 160.

26 Indeed, the Prosecution's extensive research led it to conclude affirmatively that common law systems which permit self-representation at trial also typically permit self-representation on appeal. Prosecution's Corrigendum, para. 39 ("Most common law systems studied allow self-representation on appeal").

course, heightened, and a Chamber must be particularly attentive to its duty of ensuring that the proceedings are fair."[27] Assigned counsel notes that in *Slobodan Milošević,* the Trial Chamber assigned *amici curiae* to assist in ensuring the fairness of the proceedings and suggests that the Appeals Chamber in this case should do likewise.[28] Assigned Counsel considers that this approach "will respect Mr. Krajišnik's right to self-representation while ensuring the Appeals Chamber is given all the legal assistance it requires."[29] **[page 6]**

17. The Appeals Chamber notes that, pursuant to Rule 74 of the Rules of Procedure and Evidence ("Rules"), the Appeals Chamber may, "if it considers it desirable for the proper determination of the case", invite submissions from an *amicus curiae* "on any issue specified by the Chamber". The Appeals Chamber further considers that, as was done in *Slobodan Milošević,* the Appeals Chamber can ask the *amicus curiae* to argue in favour of the interests of a particular party where this approach will serve the interests of justice.[30]

18. As part of the choice to self-represent, Mr. Krajišnik must "accept[] responsibility for the disadvantages this choice may bring."[31] He is not entitled to *amicus curiae.* Rather, the issue is whether, in being "particularly attentive to its duty of ensuring that the [appeal] be fair,"[32] the Appeals Chamber deems the appointment of *amicus curiae* to be warranted. The Appeals Chamber considers that in this case the answer is yes. The appointment of *amicus curiae* will not infringe on any rights of Mr. Krajišnik, such as the right to self-represent or the right to a speedy appeal. Moreover, such an appointment will help ensure that the appeal is a fair one. Of course, a fair appeal could well occur in the absence of *amicus curiae,* but this is an issue better judged with hindsight rather than with foresight. Since Mr. Krajišnik is the first defendant seeking to self-represent on appeal, the Appeals Chamber deems it prudent to appoint *amicus curiae* to keep an eye on his interests.

19. Accordingly, pursuant to Rule 74, the Appeals Chamber invites the participation of a particular *amicus curiae* to assist the Appeals Chamber by arguing in favour of Mr. Krajišnik's interests. *Amicus curiae* is not requested to conduct any new factual investigations. Rather, in light of the evidence at issue in the trial record, *amicus curiae* is to put forth grounds of appeal seeking reversal of convictions or reduction in sentence and to argue against grounds of appeal advanced by the Prosecution. *Amicus curiae* is to work independently from Mr. Krajišnik.

20. The Appeals Chamber emphasizes that *amicus curiae* is not a party to the proceedings.[33] The Appeals Chamber is therefore under no obligations to address all arguments raised by *amicus curiae.* Rather, the Appeals Chamber will look to the arguments raised by *amicus curiae* in **[page 7]** assessing whether the interest of justice requires the Appeals Chamber to consider, *proprio motu,* issues not raised in Mr. Krajišnik's appeal or in his responses to the Prosecution's appeal.

21. In the absence of other instructions from the Pre-Appeal Judge or the Appeals Chamber, *amicus curaie* is to make submissions to the Appeals Chamber similar to those which a party would make (including a notice of appeal, appeal brief, response brief, and reply brief) and pursuant to the requirements set out in the Rules and the relevant Practice Directions,[34] with one exception. This exception is that the word counts for *amicus curiae* are limited to two-thirds of those available to the parties under the Practice Direction on the Length of Briefs and Motions. *Amicus curiae* is to attend Status Conferences, either in person or via tele-conference, and to appear at the oral hearing of the appeal. *Amicus curiae* is also to have access to all *inter partes* confidential material in the case.

---

27 Second Motion, para. 24.

28 *Ibid.,* para. 25.

29 *Ibid.,* para. 29.

30 *See, e.g., Prosecutor v. Slobodan Milošević,* Case No. IT-99-37-PT, Order Inviting Designation of *Amicus Curiae,* 30 August 2001, pp. 2–3; *Prosecutor v. Slobodan Milošević,* Case No. IT-01-50-PT, Order Inviting Designation of *Amicus Curiae,* 30 October 2001, pp. 2–3; *Prosecutor v. Slobodan Milošević,* Case No. IT-99-37-PT, Order Concerning *Amici Curiae,* 11 January 2002; *Prosecutor v. Slobodan Milošević,* Case No. IT-02-54-T, Order of Further Instruction to the *Amici Curiae,* 6 October 2003, p. 2; *see also Dickerson v. United States,* 530 U.S. 428, 441–442 & n.7 (2000) (noting the appointment of the *amicus* "to assist our deliberations by arguing in support of the judgment below").

31 *Prosecutor v. Slobodan Milošević,* Case No. IT-02-54-AR73.6, Decision on the Interlocutory Appeal by the *Amici Curiae* Against the Trial Chamber Order Concerning the Presentation and Preparation of the Defence Case, 20 January 2004, para. 19.

32 *Ibid.,* para. 19.

33 *See ibid.,* para. 4.

34 Except as otherwise specified in this opinion, time limits for *amicus* will begin running from the date of *amicus*'s appointment.

22. The Prosecution is entitled to respond to *amicus curiae* in the same way that, pursuant to the Rules and the relevant Practice Directions, it is entitled to respond to the other party, save that the word counts for its responses are limited to two-thirds of those available to the parties under the Practice Direction on the Length of Briefs and Motions. The Appeals Chamber notes that the Prosecution may choose to respond separately to Mr. Krajišnik and to *amicus curiae* or instead choose to file consolidated responses and replies (with word counts for these consolidated filings equal to one and two-thirds those set forth in the the Practice Direction on the Length of Briefs and Motions). In oral proceedings, the Prosecution will similarly have a right of response with regard to *amicus curiae.*

23. As to the specific identity of *amicus curiae*, the Appeals Chamber agrees with Assigned Counsel's position in the Third Motion that no specific appointment should be made until after the issuance of this decision. This will enable the proposed *amicus curiae* to make an informed decision about whether to accept the assignment. The Appeals Chamber further agrees with Assigned Counsel's position in the Third Motion that the post of *amicus curiae* need not necessarily be filled by Colin Nicholls, QC, who has acted to date as Assigned Counsel. The Appeals Chamber nonetheless considers that Mr. Nicholls would be fit to fill the role of *amicus curiae* and wished to offer him the option of doing so. In particular, the Appeals Chamber notes both Mr. Nicholls' familiarity with the case and his impressive professional abilities. The Appeals Chamber therefore requests the Registry to consult with Mr. Nicholls as to his willingness to serve as *amicus curiae.* Should Mr. Nicholls accept this appointment, then the Notice of Appeal filed by Mr. Nicholls on **[page 8]** behalf of Mr. Krajišnik[35] will be deemed to be the Notice of Appeal of *amicus curiae* unless, within one week of this decision, Mr. Nicholls files a new Notice of Appeal as *amicus curiae.* Similarly, the Response Brief filed by Mr. Nicholls on behalf of Mr. Krajišnik[36] will be deemed to be the Response Brief of *amicus curiae* unless, within one week of this decision, Mr. Nicholls files a new Response Brief as *amicus curiae.*[37] Finally, Mr. Nicholls' Appeal Brief will be due within seventy-five days of the date of this decision. Should Mr. Nicholls decline the appointment as *amicus curiae,* then the Appeals Chamber will take other steps to identify a suitable *amicus curiae.*

IV. Disposition

24. For the foregoing reasons, the Appeals Chamber **GRANTS**, Judge Schomburg dissenting, the First Motion, as it relates to Mr. Krajišnik's request to represent himself; **GRANTS**, Judge Pocar and Judge Schomburg dissenting, the Second and Third Motions, according to the conditions set forth below; and **DISMISSES** the Prosecution's Motion.

25. The Appeals Chamber **REQUESTS** the Registry to take any necessary steps to implement the Appeals Chamber's decision as to the First Motion. With regard to the Second and Third Motions, the Appeals Chamber **REQUESTS** the Registry to consult with Mr. Nicholls to see whether he is willing to serve as *amicus curiae,* pursuant to the terms set out in paragraphs 19 and 21 above, and, if so, to make any necessary arrangements. Should Mr. Nicholls decline to serve as *amicus curiae,* the Appeals Chamber **REQUESTS** the Registry to consult further with the Appeals Chamber on the issue. The Appeals Chamber further **REQUESTS** the Registry to provide *amicus curiae,* once appointed, with access to all *inter partes* confidential information from the proceedings in this case.

26. The Appeals Chamber **ORDERS** Mr. Krajišnik to file his Appeal Brief within seventy-five days after the filing of the Trial Judgement translated into B/C/S, and to file his Reply Brief within 15 days of the translation of the Prosecution Response Brief into B/C/S.

27. The Appeals Chamber **ORDERS** *amicus curiae,* once appointed, to act pursuant to the terms set out in paragraphs 19 and 21 above. The Appeals Chamber further **STATES** that, should Mr. Nicholls accept the appointment as *amicus curiae,* the Notice of Appeal and Response Brief **[page 9]** filed by Mr. Nicholls on behalf of Mr. Krajišnik will be deemed to be the Notice of Appeal and Response Brief of *amicus curiae* unless,

---

35 "Counsel's Notice of Appeal", 12 February 2007 (filed confidentially, with a public and redacted version filed the same day).

36 "Counsel's Response to the Prosecution's Appeal Brief, 12 February 2007.

37 The Appeals Chamber notes that this existing filing satisfies the page limit requirements that an *amicus* would have to abide by pursuant to paragraph 21 of this decision. The Appeals Chamber also notes that the Prosecution's existing reply to this filing also satisfies the page limits set forth in paragraph 22 of this decision. *See* "The Prosecution's Reply Brief, 22 February 2007.

within one week of this decision, Mr. Nicholls files a new Notice of Appeal and/or Response Brief as *amicus curiae.* The Appeals Chamber further **STATES** that, should Mr. Nicholls accept the appointment as *amicus curiae,* his Appeal Brief will be due within seventy-five days of the date of this decision.

28. The Appeals Chamber **FURTHER ORDERS** that *amicus,* once appointed, and any employees who have been instructed or authorized by *amicus* to have access to the *inter partes* confidential material in this case shall not, without express leave of the Appeals Chamber:

(a) disclose to any third party information contained in this material in whole or in part, including the names of witnesses, their whereabouts, transcripts of witness testimonies, exhibits, written statements, prior testimony, any other information which would enable these witnesses to be identified and would breach the confidentiality of the protective measures already in place, documentary evidence, or other evidence; or

(b) contact any witness whose identity is subject to protective measures.

29. For the purposes of paragraph 28, third parties exclude: (i) Mr. Krajišnik; (ii) any employees who have been instructed or authorized by *amicus* to have access to confidential material; and (iii) personnel from the International Tribunal, including members of the Prosecution.

30. The Appeals Chamber **INFORMS** the Prosecution that it is entitled to respond to filings and oral submissions by *amicus,* as described in paragraph 22 above.

31. Judge Pocar dissents from this decision, Judge Shahabuddeen files a separate opinion and Judge Schomburg also dissents. The dissenting and separate opinions are attached.

Done in English and French, the English text being authoritative.

Dated this 11th day of May 2007,
At The Hague, The Netherlands.

Judge Fausto Pocar
Presiding Judge

[Seal of the Tribunal] [page 1]

DISSENTING OPINION OF JUDGE POCAR

1. I am unable to agree with the majority in this case. I disagree with the majority's view that any difficulties faced by Mr Krajišnik as a self-represented accused can be ameliorated by the appointment of *amicus curiae.*[38] Furthermore, I note that there is nothing in our Statute or Rules of Procedure and Evidence that allows for the appointment of *amicus curiae* to a trial or appeal proceeding to act as a *de facto* counsel.

Done in English and French, the English text being authoritative.

Dated this 11th day of May 2007,
At The Hague, The Netherlands.

Judge Fausto Pocar

[Seal of the International Tribunal] [page 1]

[38] Paras., 18 –20.

SEPARATE OPINION OF JUDGE SHAHABUDDEEEN

The issue

1. The issue, which is both important and one of first impression for the Appeals Chamber, is whether the appellant has a right to self-representation at his appeal from a conviction, or whether he only has a right to representation by counsel – in this case, by an assigned counsel, the appellant being indigent. Put another way, the question is whether the appellant has a right to do his appeal alone, or whether, without proven obstruction from him, the Appeals Chamber can force counsel on him, regarding counsel's words and actions as his, even if he makes it plain that he does not want counsel. Discounting early exchanges, it appears to me that the foregoing represents the present issue. Effectively, the instant appeal has not yet begun; when they do, the proceedings will be partly written and partly oral. In these circumstances, I respectfully agree with the preference of the Appeals Chamber for the view that the appellant has a right to self-representation, and give this separate opinion in support.

My primary position

2. Customary international law – the controlling body of law – requires that a trial shall be fair. There is indeed a question as to whether that is correct. In *Gbao,*[1] the Designated Judge of the Special Court for Sierra Leone, with seeming approval of the implied legal proposition, expressed "the considered view that it has not been established that the right of the Accused to a fair trial has become part of customary international law". I respect that view, but prefer to follow the Appeals Chamber of the Tribunal in *Aleksovski;* there it said: "The right to a fair trial is, of course, a requirement of customary international law".[2] Likewise there is the Trial Chamber's judgement in *Simić,*[3] stating that the right to a fair trial is encompassed in common article 3 of the Geneva Conventions of 1949, paragraph (d), which affords "all judicial guarantees, recognizable as indispensable by civilized peoples, an article which has reached international customary law status". Fair trial is represented by a situation which is the result of the application of a bundle of norms. The distinction between customary international law and general principles is not always easily drawn, but it may be noted that general principles know of important elements of that bundle of norms[4] which, when applied together, result in a trial being fair. Formally established international criminal tribunals did not exist earlier on, but that did not affect the development of **[page 2]** norms applicable to criminal situations, or the classification of such norms as part of customary international law.

3. If, as I therefore think, fairness is part of customary international law,[5] it applies to all proceedings in the Tribunal, inclusive of appeals to the Appeals Chamber from convictions. In thus applying, it answers possible argument that the reference in article 20(1) of the Statute of the Tribunal to the "Trial Chambers" confines the duty to be fair, as referred to in that provision, to those chambers. However, customary international law does not stipulate whether fairness at appeal is to be achieved through self-representation or through representation by counsel. The methods are each in fact used in relation to an appeal in one part of the world or another, but neither method has acquired the indicia entitling it to be regarded as customary international law. The Tribunal is not therefore bound by customary international law to apply one method or another. Customary international law may, however, be construed as giving the Tribunal a competence, or discretion, to select one method or the other, provided of course that the method selected is designed to achieve the objective of that law, namely, the dispensing of international criminal justice. But the Rules of Procedure and Evidence made by the judges of the Tribunal under article 15 of the Statute have not determined which method applies in the Tribunal. So the position may be understood as meaning that the matter has been left to the determination of the concerned judicial branch of the Tribunal, in this case, the Appeals Chamber.

---

1 SCSL-2003-09-PT, Decision on Prosecution Motion for Immediate Protective Measures for Witnesses and Victims and for Non-Public Disclosure, 10 October 2003, para. 41.

2 IT-95-14/1-A, 24 March 2000, Judgement, para 104.

3 IT-95-9-T, 17 October 2003, Judgement, para. 678.

4 Bin Cheng, *General Principles of Law* (Cambridge, 1987), cap. 13, referring to *nemo debet esse judex in propria sua causa, audiatur et altera pars,* judicial impartiality.

5 *See also Ohashi,* 5 LRTWC 25, 30 (1946); *Shinohara,* 5 LRTWC 32, 34 (1946); *Hisakasu,* 5 LRTWC 66, 73–77 (1946); *Altstötter,* 6 LRWTC 1, 96–104 (1947); and *Latza,* 14 LRTWC 49, 63, 67, 71, 77, 80, 81, 84 (1948).

4. The Appeals Chamber has determined the matter by now holding that there is a right to self-representation at appeal, having earlier held that there is a right to self-representation at trial.[6] The most that can be said in opposition to a holding that there is a right to self-representation at appeal is that some states consider that representation by counsel is better crafted to accomplish the objective of dispensing justice. But there are other states which do not share that view. The Appeals Chamber is not bound to exercise its competence by selecting what some states consider to be the better of the two methods. As noted above, neither method can now be regarded as customary international law which the Appeals Chamber is obliged to apply. Customary international law has at most given the Appeals Chamber a competence as to which of the two methods is to be selected. There is no basis for condemning the selection which the Appeals Chamber has made in the exercise of that competence. **[page 3]**

The basis of the opposite view

5. The foregoing represents my primary view. A secondary view derives from the fact that, as it seems to me, the jurisprudence relating to representation by counsel in other courts of appeal itself shows that in appeals from convictions to the Appeals Chamber there is a right to self-representation.

6. An inquiry might begin by noticing the position at trials. The Appeals Chamber has already established that article 21(4)(d) of the Statute is a "guarantee of the right to self-representation"[7] at trial. However, as is recognised, the right to self-representation at trial is not absolute. It is settled law that it can be restricted if an accused is guilty of misbehaviour which substantially and persistently obstructs the fairness and expeditiousness[8] of the trial. But, in the instant case, it is not said that the appellant, when an accused, misbehaved at trial – whether by boycotting the proceedings or otherwise. It is not suggested that he lacks intelligence; on the contrary, he was described by the Trial Chamber as "an intelligent and educated man".[9] The Trial Chamber also noted that he was "President of the Bosnian-Serb Assembly, a member of the SDS Main Board, a member of the SNB, and a member of the Presidency".[10] Nor is it suggested that, at trial, his health situation caused obstructive delays – intended or unintended. No reason has been given for fearing that any of these things will happen at appeal.

7. The inquiry might then pass on to consider the theoretical basis of the objection to the right to self-representation at appeal. The essence of the objection may be collected from the proposition that the "status of the accused defendant, who retains a presumption of innocence throughout the trial process, changes dramatically when a jury returns a guilty verdict".[11] Whereas he is presumed to be innocent during the trial, he does not enjoy that presumption during the appeal. But that is only the general position in common law countries; the general position in civil law countries is that **[page 4]** the presumption of innocence continues and comes to an end only when the conviction at trial is upheld on appeal. The objection lacks a sufficient measure of universality to be convincing.

8. I am likewise not persuaded by arguments based on the length, the size, the magnitude, the intricacies and the complexities of an appeal. An appeal may well have all of these qualities, but I am unable to assent

---

6 *Milosević,* IT-02-54-AR73.7, Decision on Interlocutory Appeal of the Trial Chamber's Decision on the Assignment of Counsel, 1 November 2004, para. 11.

7 Speaking of the reference in article 21(4)(d) of the Statute to the right of an accused "to defend himself in person or through legal assistance of his own choosing", the Appeals Chamber remarked that this "is a straightforward proposition. Given the text's binary opposition between representation žthrough legal assistance' and representation žin person', the Appeals Chamber sees no reasonable way to interpret Article 21 except as a guarantee of the right to self-representation". *See Milosević,* IT-02-54-AR73.7, Decision on Interlocutory Appeal of the Trial Chamber's Decision on Assignment of Counsel, 1 November 2004, para. 11. Since the provision is "straightforward", it does not appear to be necessary to refer to the interesting drafting history of model provisions.

8 A trial can be expeditious without being fair, but a trial cannot be fair unless it is also expeditious. See generally *Halilović,* IT-01-48-A, Decision on Defence Motion for Prompt Scheduling of Appeal Hearing, 27 October 2006, para. 17; *Kvočka,* IT-98-30/1-AR73.5, Decision on Interlocutory Appeal by the Accused Zoran Žigić Against the Decision of Trial Chamber I Dated 5 December 2000, 25 May 2001, para. 20; *Kovačević,* IT-97-24-AR73, Decision Stating the Reasons for the Appeal Chamber's Order of 29 May 1998, 2 July 1998, para. 30; *Karemera,* ICTR-98-44-AR73, Decision on Prosecutor's Interlocutory Appeal against Trial Chamber III Decision of 8 October 2003 Denying Leave to File an Amended Indictment, 19 December 2003, paras. 13 and 14.

9 Trial Judgement, para. 1160.

10 *Ibid.,* para. 1158.

11 *Martinez v. Court of Appeal of California, Fourth Appellate District,* 528 U.S. 152, 162 (2000).

to the suggestion which they convey that, *of necessity,* an appeal is technically and professionally more demanding than a trial. An appellant admittedly has a right to self-representation at trial, and is therefore to be presumed capable of managing on his own at trial. This being so, there is no reason to suppose that he cannot manage on his own at appeal. The factors mentioned may give rise to a need for a court of appeal to have the supplementary services of *amicus curiae,* but of themselves they cannot justify non-recognition of a right to self-representation at appeal.

9. In any event, it is hard to see how those factors (including those relating to the presumption of innocence) operate to deny an appellant's right to self-representation at an appeal to challenge a trial finding that he is guilty of having committed a crime – an appeal which the law of the Tribunal guarantees him. If a man is to suffer a loss of liberty, he has to be accorded a right to present a case in opposition – personally, if he wishes. Is there something in the Statute of the Tribunal to rebut that view?

The jurisprudence

10. There is much learning on the subject, both judicial and non-judicial. It is all helpful, and I am grateful for it. However, I do not propose to survey it *in extenso.* I shall limit myself to three cases. In various ways, they raise questions concerning representation by counsel, but, in my opinion, their underlying principles do not prohibit the right to self-representation by a convicted appellant in an appeal to the Appeals Chamber.

(i) The Martinez case

11. The first case is *Martinez v. Court of Appeal of California,*[12] decided in 2000 by the Supreme Court of the United States. This may seem to support mandatory representation by counsel at an appeal. But perhaps the case may be looked at again. The appellant claimed a right to self-representation under the constitution of the United States. The judgement of the Supreme Court of that country was based on the view that historically a man had a right to be sent for trial before a jury for a serious crime before he was punished for it; the constitution of the United States was concerned only with such trials. But, while the Supreme Court did not say that a right to appeal was **[page 5]** conferred by the constitution of the United States, it took the view that that constitution – a federal one – left each constituent State with a discretion, under its own constitution, to create a right to appeal and to determine the mode of exploitation of that right.

12. In his opinion concurring in the judgement of the Supreme Court, Justice Scalia summed up the position by stating "that there is no constitutional right to appeal."[13] Thus, the appellant could not rely on the constitution of the United States, as he had sought to do. Here, by contrast, there is something in the nature of a constitutional right to appeal: article 25 of the Statute – the organic instrument of the Tribunal – gives to a convicted appellant a right to appeal.

13. The local faculty is exercised on the basis that each State has an interest in ensuring that judicial proceedings are fair. This objective might be interfered with by the appellant's interest in self-representation, giving rise, as it might, to misunderstandings by the appellant of the law and the procedures of the court and to consequential delays and other difficulties. The Supreme Court balanced these two competing interests – a State's interest in ensuring the fairness and efficiency of the proceedings and the appellant's interest in self-representation – in holding that the "States are clearly within their discretion to conclude that the government's interests outweigh an invasion of the appellant's interest in self-representation".[14] Where a State has in its discretion so concluded, representation by counsel prevails over self-representation.

14. However, not every State is obliged so to conclude; its decision is to be made by the way it makes its own balance of those two competing interests. The Supreme Court made it clear that its holding against the right to self-representation at an appeal in California was "narrow" and did "not preclude the States [i.e., the other States of the Union] from recognizing such a right under their own constitutions".[15] I understand this to mean that the question whether an appellant was entitled to self-representation at an appeal depended on a study of

12 *Ibid.,* 152.
13 *Ibid.,* 165.
14 *Ibid.,* 163.
15 *Ibid.*

the California legal position; the legal position need not be the same in all States of the Union – although it might. Moreover, even where a State required representation by counsel, this did not remove the ordinary discretion of courts to see that justice was done, if necessary by ordering self-representation. In the words of the Supreme Court, "Courts, of course, may still exercise their discretion to allow a lay person to proceed *pro se*".[16] Courts continue to be entitled to exercise that discretion by virtue of their inherent and overriding responsibility to be fair. *Martinez* does not automatically ban self-representation at every appeal, but allows it in some cases. **[page 6]**

(ii) The Belziuk case

15. The second case is *Belziuk v. Poland,*[17] decided in 1998 by the European Court of Human Rights. That case stands for the proposition that the right of an accused to "defend himself in person" applies to any part of the proceedings – including appeal proceedings.[18] The court said:

> Criminal proceedings form an entity and the protection afforded by Article 6 does not cease with the decision at first instance. A State is required to ensure also before courts of appeal that persons amenable to the law shall enjoy before these courts the fundamental guarantees contained in this Article.[19]

However, in applying that right to appeal proceedings, the special features of the case have to be considered.[20] As the court also said:

> [T]he personal attendance of the defendant does not necessarily take on the same significance for an appeal hearing. Indeed, even where an appellate court has full jurisdiction to review the case on questions both of fact and law, Article 6 does not always entail rights to a public hearing and to be present in person. Regard must be had in assessing this question to, inter alia, the special features of the proceedings involved and the manner in which the defence's interests are presented and protected before the appellate court, particularly in the light of the issues to be decided by it and their importance for the appellant.[21]

The court indeed took the view that the differences between trial and appeal meant that an appellant does not have a right to be present at his appeal. However, in the view of the court, that prohibition is not absolute; it is conditional. The right to be present, indeed the associated right to self-representation, could be restored by the special features of the case. Observing that there was no counsel present at the appeal on behalf of the appellant, who himself was absent, the court said: "Had [the appellant] been present at the appeal hearing, he would have had an opportunity to challenge his convictions and the submissions of the public prosecutor and to present evidence in support of his appeal. ... [He] had the right in the circumstances to be present at his appeal and to defend himself in person".[22]

16. Belziuk could not present evidence – additional evidence – unless he had a previous opportunity to make the necessary arrangements. The case did not turn on the mere fact that it happened that on that specific occasion the appellant's counsel did not turn up. The reasoning was that the appellant had a continuing right to self-representation and could have used this right to fill **[page 7]** the breach caused by the absence of his counsel; the appellant himself could have adduced additional evidence. No doubt, the right could not be actively exercised while counsel was present, but in counsel's absence it could be – and indeed was expected to be. In this important sense, the right always existed. So, in certain circumstances, *Belziuk* allows self-representation at an appeal.

---

16 *Ibid.*

17 *Belziuk v. Poland,* ECtHR, App. No. 45/1997/829/1035, 25 March 1998.

18 See also *Delcourt v. Belgium,* ECtHR, App. No. 2689/65, 17 January 1970, paras. 23–26; *Kremzow v. Austria,* ECtHR, App. No. 12350/86, 21 September 1993, para. 58; and *Halilović,* IT-01-48-A, Decision on Defence Motion for Prompt Scheduling of Appeal Hearing, 27 October 2006, para. 17 (recognizing that the right of an "accused" to be tried without due delay under article 21(4)(c) of the Statute "applies to all stages of the proceedings, including an appeal").

19 *Belziuk v. Poland,* ECtHR, App. No. 45/1997/829/1035, 25 March 1998, para. 37(i) (citations omitted).

20 See also *Monnell and Morris v. The United Kingdom,* ECtHR, App. No. 9562/81, 9818/82, 2 March 1987, para. 56, and *Meftah v. France,* ECtHR, App. No. 32911/96, 35237/97 and 34595/97, 26 July 2002, para. 42 (citations omitted).

21 *Belziuk v. Poland,* ECtHR, App. No. 45/1997/829/1035, 25 March 1998, para. 37(ii).

22 *Ibid.,* para, 38. See likewise, on this point, *Kremzow v. Austria,* ECtHR, App. No. 12350/86, 21 September 1993, para. 67.

(iii) The Farhad case

17. The third case is *United States v. Farhad,*[23] decided in 1999 by the United States Court of Appeals for the Ninth Circuit. The accused in that case was allowed a right to self-representation at trial pursuant to *Faretta v. California,*[24] decided in 1975 by the United States Supreme Court. Through his lack of familiarity with the law, he made various mistakes; in particular, he made the egregious error of disclosing his previous crimes. On appeal, his counsel sought to argue that the fact that it was he [Farhad] who made the mistakes did not deprive him of the right to plead that the result of the mistakes was nevertheless a violation of his right to a fair trial. The argument was rejected on the ground that, having knowingly, intelligently and voluntarily waived his right to counsel, he had to bear the consequences of his ignorance. In the later words of the United States District Court for the District of Hawaii: "The U.S. Supreme Court has made it abundantly clear that once a defendant knowingly and voluntarily waives his right to representation, he cannot later complain that his own self representation was deficient".[25]

18. In his concurrence in *Farhad,* Judge Reinhardt thought that the circumstances showed a need to reconsider *Faretta,* which had upheld a right to self-representation at trial; he considered that the holding in that case should be reversed and a right to representation by counsel at trial substituted for a right to self-representation at trial. Thus, the concurrence was not concerned with self-representation at appeal. However, it becomes more difficult to argue for a right to self-representation at appeal if the right has been removed at trial. Should the Appeals Chamber, which is now considering the general subject of representation at appeal, depart from its previous holding on the grounds given by Judge Reinhardt?

19. Judge Reinhardt accepted the view that, though the mistakes were made by Farhad himself, they led to a violation of his fundamental right to a fair trial. A right to self-representation at trial, which could produce mistakes leading to such a violation, should therefore be nullified. It is trite that a court cannot validly hold a hearing which is unfair, and that an appellant has no competence to waive his right to a fair hearing. However, in *Farhad* there was no necessary clash with those **[page 8]** principles. Taking the disclosure of the previous crimes as an example of his mistakes, the law gave him a right not to have his previous crimes disclosed. But, if he himself wanted to disclose them, he was not violating any legal prohibition: all that happened was that he chose not to use an entitlement that the law gave him. The disclosed material came before the court which would assess it in accordance with the rules of evidence relating to admissibility and weight.

20. Thus understood, an accused has a right to disclose his previous crimes. It becomes difficult to accept that the exercise by him of that right is at the same time a violation of his right to a fair trial. If there is such a violation, any similar disclosure, even if made while the accused is represented by counsel, would be reversible error. All that the accused has to do to secure a quashing of his possible conviction is to make such a disclosure. True, the mistakes made by Farhad might not have been made had he a lawyer. But the desirability of avoiding those mistakes is a matter of policy for the lawgiver; it is not a reason why, absent appropriate legislation, a court of law should take the position that the trial was not fair.

21. Finally, it is to be noted that what Judge Reinhardt was suggesting was that there was need to reverse *Faretta* in so far as it granted a right of self-representation at trial. Before today, there has not been any judicial suggestion that the ICTY should reverse the previous holding by the Appeals Chamber[26] that there is such a right in the case of this Tribunal. I am of the respectful view that, like that of Judge Reinhardt, such a suggestion, made today, will not bear fruit.

22. In my opinion, the reasoning in *Martinez, Belziuk* and *Farhad* is not against the appellant's claim to a right to self-representation at appeal in this case.

---

23 190 F.3d 1097 (9th Cir. 1999).

24 422 U.S. 806, 834(1975).

25 See *United States v. Low,* 2006 U.S. Dist. LEXIS 90944, *22 (D. Haw. 15 December 2006). The United States jurisprudence shows some concern with the question whether the courts should inquire into the issue whether the accused had some minimum level of ability. *See Brooks v. McCaughtry,* 380 F.3d 1009 (7th Cir. 2004), and *Gomez v. Berge,* 2004 U.S. Dist. LEXIS 16360 (W.D. Wis., August 18, 2004).

26 *Milosević,* IT-02-54-AR73.7, Decision on Interlocutory Appeal of the Trial Chamber's Decision on the Assignment of Counsel, 1 November 2004, para. 11.

The special features in the case of appeals to the Appeals Chamber

23. Some countries tend to regard a criminal appeal as a technical matter to be determined by a court of appeal with the assistance of trained lawyers only. But even such countries seem to have a let-out permitting self-representation if the case, as in *Belziuk,* possesses special features justifying an exception. Are there any special features in this case? I believe the answer is in the affirmative. Some of the matters mentioned below may well occur in the case of other appellate judicial bodies, but, in the case of the Tribunal, they operate with special emphasis. I turn to them as follows: **[page 9]**

(i) The appellant has a right to be present at his appeal

24. Under the law of the Tribunal an appellant has a right, outside but not inconsistent with *Belziuk,* to be present at his appeal from a conviction. It does not follow that he has a right to self-representation at appeal; but the existence of the right to be present at least predisposes towards a holding that the right to self-representation at appeal exists.[27]

25. In support of the proposition that there is no right to be present at an appeal, it may be said that article 21(4) of the Statute[28] does not guarantee an appellant such a right. Assuming that this is so, it has to be recalled that the provision is only concerned to provide for certain "minimum guarantees"; nothing prevents the Appeals Chamber from, by practice, providing for a right to be present during the hearing of an appeal.[29] Has the Appeals Chamber done so?

26. The United Nations Detention Unit (UNDU), from where an appellant normally comes, is just a mile away from the Appeals Chamber, which is housed in the very building in which his trial took place. There are no travelling problems; all appellants at UNDU have an opportunity to come to the Appeals Chamber. Cases at the ICTY can involve an appellant who is not at UNDU, but, even in such cases, there is no dispute that the appellant has a right to be present at his appeal. The ICTR Appeals Chamber has likewise recognised the right of an appellant to be present during the hearing of his appeal – even when parts of the hearing are held in The Hague, thousands of miles away from the seat of that Appeals Chamber in Arusha.[30] It thus appears that the Appeals Chambers of both tribunals have a practice of allowing an appellant to be present at his appeal.

27. I have referred above to an assumption that article 21(4) of the Statute of the Tribunal does not guarantee an appellant a right to be present during the hearing of his appeal from conviction. The assumption is not founded. The provision gives to an "accused" a right "to defend himself in person". There is little of substance to say that the right "to defend himself in person" does not apply at the appeal stage. The opposite view is based on the fact that article 21(4) opens with the **[page 10]** words, "In the determination of any charge against the accused ...". It may be argued that this language (particularly but not exclusively the reference to "the accused") contemplates a limitation to the trial phase, since in relation to an appeal article 25 speaks of "persons convicted by the Trial Chambers". But a reasonable reading is that an appeal, where it is resorted to, is part of the overall proceedings for imposing punishment for the

---

27 Possibly because of its special features, there is generally no right to be present during the hearing of an interlocutory appeal. Special features may explain why in various jurisdictions the right of an accused to defend himself in person is qualified in cases involving crimes of a sexual nature. Such features may also explain why there is no right to personal appearance in an application for special leave to appeal. *See Milat v. R.,* 205 ALR 338 (2004) (High Court of Australia).

28 Article 21 (4) of the Statute provides: "In the determination of any charge against the accused pursuant to the present Statute, the accused shall be entitled to the following minimum guarantees, in full equality ... (d) to be tried in his presence, and to defend himself in person or through legal assistance of his own choosing; or to be informed, if he does not have legal assistance, of this right; and to have legal assistance assigned to him, in any case where the interests of justice so require, and without payment by him in any such case if he does not have sufficient means to pay for it".

29 *Martinez v. Court of Appeal of California* 528 U.S. 152, 158 (2000), recognises that, under controlling statutes, the position as regards the right to self-representation at appeal may be affected by rules of court. There is no reason why practice is not admissible.

30 In *Musema,* ICTR-96-13-A, Judgement, 16 November 2001, para. 5 of annex "A" to proceedings on appeal, additional evidence was taken in The Hague; the appellant was brought from Arusha to The Hague. The same thing happened in *Rutaganda;* see ICTR-96-3-A, 26 May 2003, AT. 1. In *Kamuhanda,* ICTR-99-54A-A, 19 September 2005, the judgement was delivered in The Hague; the appellant was brought there from Arusha.

crime.[31] Such a construction is justified on the view that the whole regime was concerned to demonstrate to an accused that he would not be punished without his having a right to be present in court at all times. Where the liberty of an accused is concerned, it is cheese-paring to cut down that approach.[32]

28. Though, as I have recognised, a right to self-representation does not follow from a right to be present, the non-existence of a right to be present seems to be the unspoken premise of the argument in favour of a denial of the right to self-representation. Indeed, in *Martinez* the United States Supreme Court noted that its holding that the absence of a right to self-representation on appeal would not have any significant impact on the law "because a lay appellant's rights to participate in appellate proceedings have long been limited by the well-established conclusions that he has no right to be present during appellate proceedings."[33] As has been seen, the premise that an appellant has no right to be physically present at appeal does not hold good at the Tribunal. The fact that the appellant has a right to be present during the hearing of his appeal favours a right to self-representation. It at any rate provokes this question: why does an appellant have a right to be present during the hearing of his appeal if he must sit there condemned to silence while he watches an assigned lawyer speak on his behalf – a lawyer whom he may not want and with whose statements he may disagree? There is difficulty in locating a convincing answer which would justify the Appeals Chamber in taking the radical step of what, despite the sanitised reference to "restricting" the right to self-representation, has the effect of altogether removing the right.

(ii) Additional evidence

29. The Appeals Chamber may admit additional evidence at the instance of the appellant. This may involve witnesses testifying and documents being tendered. In one case, the evidentiary portion of the appeal lasted four days.[34] Extensive documentation was admitted from a national archive which had been closed during the trial stage.[35] The Appeals Chamber rightly remarked that this "long appeal has, in part, been characterized by the filing of an enormous amount of additional **[page 11]** evidence".[36] An informed and fair-minded observer might take the view that, especially from the standpoint of the appellant, the trial, in part, was in substance reopened on appeal. If, as is not disputed, the appellant had a right to self-representation at trial,[37] and if, as it appears to me, he also had a right to be physically present during the hearing of his appeal, there would be difficulty in understanding why he should not have the right to self-representation during the hearing of the appeal. As has been seen, in *Belziuk v. Poland,*[38] the European Court of Human Rights gave the circumstance that the appellant had the right to adduce additional evidence on appeal as one of the factors supportive of what amounted to a right to self-representation during the hearing of his appeal.

(iii) The prosecution may appeal

30. There is the possibility of appeals by the prosecution. In this matter, for example, the prosecution has appealed. If the prosecution's appeal succeeds, the appellant may be punished.[39] On the opposing view, that

---

31 See the reasoning in *Delcourt v. Belgium,* ECtHR, App. No. 2689/65, 17 January 1970, paras. 23–26. Paragraph 25 stated: "In criminal matters, especially, accused persons do not disappear from the scene when the decision of the judges at first instance or appeal gives rise to an appeal in cassation."

32 *See Delcourt, supra,* para. 25, last sentence.

33 528 U.S. 152, 163 (2000).

34 *Blaškić,* IT-95-14-A, Judgement, 29 July 2004, para. 6.

35 *Ibid.,* paras. 4 and 6. The former stated that the appellant "sought to admit over 8,000 pages of material as additional evidence on appeal"; the latter stated that a "total of 108 items were admitted, and as a consequence, several witnesses were heard in the evidentiary portion of the hearing on appeal...".

36 *Ibid.,* para. 4.

37 *See Milosević,* Decision on Interlocutory Appeal of the Trial Chamber's Decision on Assignment of Counsel, IT-02-54-AR73.7, 1 November 2004, para. 11; and *Faretta,* 422 U.S. 806 (1975).

38 *Belziuk v. Poland,* ECtHR, App. No. 45/1997/829/1035, 25 March 1998, para. 38.

39 In some states, the sentence may even be increased on appeal without further appeal. In *Kremzow v. Austria,* ECtHR, App. No. 12350/86, 21 September 1993, para. 67, the European Court of Human Rights referred to that possibility, stating: "The Court observes that the Supreme Court [of Austria] was called upon in the appeal proceedings to examine whether the applicant's sentence should be increased from twenty years to life imprisonment". In paragraph 4(b) of her statement of ratification of the International Covenant on Civil and Political Rights, Austria stated that she did not consider that article 14(5) of the covenant was "in conflict with legal regulations which stipulate that after an acquittal or lighter sentence passed by a court of the first instance,

could happen with the appellant himself being forbidden to present new material or to argue. These things would have to be done by a lawyer whom the appellant possibly does not want. The appellant himself would have had nothing to do with the processes by which he is punished. He is not likely to regard the result as fair; neither would the international community. The reason is that fairness inextricably and inevitably includes fairness as seen by the appellant, though it may be qualified by other factors. I am not satisfied that the possibility of the appellant being punished as a result of an appeal by the prosecution was fully taken into account in arguments favouring the opposite view.

(iv) The international status of the Tribunal

31. There is the international status of the Tribunal to be considered. The Tribunal, as a judicial body established on behalf of practically the whole of the international community, has to satisfy the highest possible standards. True, the opposite argument is that these standards will include the fairness of the appeal hearing and that this can be jeopardised by the exercise of a right to self- **[page 12]** representation. But there could be a preliminary question as to what in the first instance is unfair. In determining what is unfair, any apparent shortcoming in the exercise of the right to self-representation to achieve fairness has to be balanced by the status of the Tribunal as an international judicial body. In my view, that international judicial body is designed to satisfy the sense of fairness felt by the individual appellant by, among other things, permitting him a right to self-representation. Moreover, in making that balance, also to be considered are the powers of the Appeals Chamber to take remedial or corrective measures during the hearing in respect of any abuse of the right to self-representation. When the balance is struck on this basis, the result is a trial which is fair.

(v) The effect of special features

32. If differences between trial procedures and appeal procedures suggest that representation at an appeal has to be by counsel (even if not wanted by the appellant), the special features of ICTY appeals, when considered in the light of the international status of the Tribunal, return those appeals to self-representation. That is to say, the international status of the Tribunal, when applied to the special features, produces a rule that in all appeals to the Appeals Chamber from a conviction or acquittal[40] there is a right to self-representation in accordance with the practice of those national courts which allow such a right. It is not in dispute that there are such courts; specific examples need not be given.[41]

Self-representation may be unwise but is a right

33. It may be unwise of an appellant to insist on self-representation; the right has probably never been used in this Appeals Chamber. The task before the appellant in the instant case is daunting. Further, the implementation of a right to self-representation might prove burdensome to the Appeals Chamber. But the Appeals Chamber should shoulder its responsibilities.[42] If the right is abused, the Appeals Chamber has available remedies: in the last analysis, it can impose counsel. But, subject to remedial and corrective measures, the right exists and is important. Paragraph 9 of today's decision aptly describes it as a "cornerstone" right. *Faretta* concerned self-representation at trial, not at appeal, but it is still appropriate to recall the principle enunciated by the Supreme Court of the **[page 13]** United States in that case that to "force a lawyer on a defendant can only lead him to believe that the law contrives against him. ... The right to defend is personal. The defendant, and not

---

a higher tribunal may pronounce conviction or a higher sentence for the same offence, while they exclude the convicted person's right to have such conviction or heavier sentence reviewed by a still higher tribunal".

40 That is to say, not interlocutory appeals.

41 However, reference may be made to *Blackstone's Criminal Practice 2007* (Oxford, 2006), p. 1949, para. D25.9. And see *R. v. Commissioner of Police of the Metropolis, Ex parte Blackburn,* [1968] 2 Q.B. 118, CA, and *R. v. Commissioner of Police of the Metropolis, Ex parte Blackburn (No. 2),* [1968] 2 Q.B. 150, CA, in which the defendant personally argued in a criminal appeal before the Court of Appeal of England and Wales. See likewise the position in Scotland, as recalled in *Granger v. United Kingdom,* ECtHR, App. No. 11932/86, 28 March 1990, paras. 18–21.

42 The Tribunal (including of course its Appeals Chamber) is under an obligation, without acting as defence counsel, to give to a self-representing appellant such information and advice as is necessary to ensure that the hearing is fair. See *R. v. Zorad* (1990) 19 NSWLR 91, 99. The observations of the Court of Criminal Appeal of New South Wales related to the duties of a trial judge, but those duties appear to be transposable to the Appeals Chamber of the ICTY.

his lawyer or the State, will bear the personal consequences of a conviction. It is the defendant, therefore, who must be free personally to decide whether in his particular case counsel is to his advantage"[43] The pertinence of these observations does not evaporate with the conclusion of a trial at first instance; their rationale extends to the entire judicial process ending in a final declaration of guilt or innocence.

Self-representation and assignment of counsel are not consistent

34. I agree to the appointment of *amicus curiae.* He can raise issues within the field of competence delineated for him by the Appeals Chamber. The Appeals Chamber can in turn select from among those issues, using its power to administer justice, provided of course that all parties have had an opportunity to respond to the point. The point is really being raised by the Appeals Chamber itself acting in the interests of justice. This differentiates the case from the workings of the general rule that an appellant is not entitled to argue a ground not specified in his notice of appeal. Also, it is not relevant to consider restrictions applicable to the raising by a party of a point which, however important, does not affect the outcome of the case. The power of the Appeals Chamber to decide an issue raised by *amicus curiae* does not convert *amicus* into a *de facto* defence counsel. He does not represent the accused; he is a friend of the court.

35. By contrast, an assigned counsel is defence counsel;[44] he represents the accused. It is true that, normally, authority for representation flows from the person represented. But there are circumstances in which an accused cannot or will not give authority. The court judges that. If it holds that the accused cannot or will not give authority in a proper case, it may in his place give the authority. In this way, an assigned counsel represents the accused; he is defence counsel.

36. However, the court cannot grant authority to counsel to represent the appellant where the court itself recognises that the appellant has a right to self-representation. In asserting his right to self-representation, the appellant is saying (as in this case) that he does not wish to be represented by counsel – that he will act as his own counsel. It is not therefore correct to take the position that the Appeals Chamber is granting the appellant's request for self-representation while it is at the same time placing him alongside an assigned counsel and by implication requiring him to act in cooperation with the latter. That would not be accepting a right to self-representation, but denying it. **[page 14]**

Conclusion

37. The appellant has a right to self-representation at his appeal. For the reasons given in the second section above, it was competent for the Appeals Chamber to select that method of achieving fairness even if representation by counsel was in some states considered to be the superior method. In any event, having regard to the special features of an appeal to the Appeals Chamber, the reasoning underlying representation by counsel in appeals to other courts of appeal would itself admit self-representation in appeals to the Appeals Chamber.

Done in English and French, the English text being authoritative.

Dated 11 May 2007,
The Hague,
The Netherlands

Mohamed Shahabuddeen

[Seal of the International Tribunal] [page 1]

43 *Faretta v. California,* 422 U.S. 806, 834 (1975).

44 It is submitted that so are other forms of legal aid counsel to the accused – "duty" counsel, "court-appointed" counsel, "independent" counsel, i.e., as long as they are acting for the accused.

FUNDAMENTALLY DISSENTING OPINION OF JUDGE SCHOMBURG ON THE RIGHT TO SELF-REPRESENTATION[1]

A. Introduction

1. If I were tasked to show that international criminal jurisdiction cannot work I would draft the decision in the same way as was done by the majority of the Appeals Chamber. Therefore, with all due respect, I have to fundamentally disagree with the decision.

2. I am deeply convinced that international criminal tribunals dealing with mega crimes can only carry out their important task of balancing the interests of victims with the interests of an accused by requiring the latter to be assisted by counsel for his own benefit. Indeed, the overarching right to a fair, expeditious and public trial (Articles 20(1) and 21(2) of the Statute of the International Tribunal ("Statute")) demand that counsel acting in open court be assigned even against an accused's wishes if the interests of fair proceedings so demand. In interpreting Article 21(4)(d) of the Statute,[2] which guarantees an accused the right "to defend himself in person or through legal assistance of his own choosing," rights emanating from the aforementioned fundamental right enshrined in Article 20(1) of the Statute, the Appeals Chamber's jurisprudence is based on a false dichotomy which assumes that the right to defend oneself negates the right to be assisted by counsel. This fundamental misunderstanding that both rights are mutually exclusive adversely affects the fairness of the proceedings. There is no fair procedure before international tribunals without public legal assistance.

3. For historical reasons human rights instruments ratified by countries from different legal systems have stipulated that at least one of the two rights set out in Article 21(4)(d) of the Statute has to be granted. This, however, does not mean that the competent authority cannot grant both rights cumulatively. On the contrary, in serious cases like those before international criminal tribunals it is impossible for an accused to defend himself. It is the accused, not the court by appointing *amicus curiae*,[3] who needs the legal assistance of a professional counsel, well-trained in criminal matters. At the same time, an accused's right to present his defence can never be denied. The international community has come to accept that an accused must never become the mere **[page 2]** object of criminal proceedings. In this context, it has to be noted that in the practice of the International Tribunal an accused is to a large degree excluded from his own defence the very moment that counsel is engaged,[4] and usually sits in the last row of the courtroom, well apart from his counsel. He is only allowed to give a "statement"[5] or to testify as a witness in his own case,[6] thereby altering his own role as an accused. This unsatisfactory situation – once counsel is engaged, any accused has only limited influence over his defence – is the main obstacle to an accused being willing to be represented by counsel.

4. The decision in this case is a glaring example in a long line of unfortunate decisions by the Appeals Chamber, such as the decision in *Prosecutor v. Milošević* of 1 November 2004[7] and most recently the decision in *Prosecutor v. Šešelj* of 8 December 2006.[8] These decisions completely disregard the fact that, in the interests

---

1 I would like to thank Matthias Schuster, Associate Legal Officer, and Christine Schön, Interna, for their extraordinary support and careful research in preparation of this opinion.

2 It has to be noted that this Article almost verbatim repeats Article 14(3)(d) of the ICCPR. Both must be read in their entirety: Article 14(3)(d) of the ICCPR reads: In the determination of any criminal charge against him, everyone shall be entitled to the following minimum guarantees, in full equality: [...] (d) To be tried in his presence, and to defend himself in person or through legal assistance of his own choosing; to be informed, if he does not have legal assistance, of this right; and to have legal assistance assigned to him, in any case where the interests of justice so require, and without payment by him in any such case if he does not have sufficient means to pay for it; [...].

3 Latin "friend of the court", see Black's Law Dictionary 93 (8th ed. 2004).

4 *See* Code of Professional Conduct for Counsel Appearing Before the International Tribunal, as amended on 29 June 2006, IT/125/Rev.2, Article 8(B) reads as follows: When representing a client, counsel shall: (i) abide by the client's decisions concerning the objectives of representation; (ii) consult with the client about the means by which those objectives are to pursued, but *is not bound by the client's decision* [...]. Italics added for emphasis.

5 Rule 84*bis* of the Rules.

6 Rule 85(C) of the Rules.

7 *Prosecutor v. Slobodan Milošević,* Case No. IT-02-54-AR73.7, Decision on Interlocutory Appeal of the Trial Chamber's Decision on the Assignment of Defense Counsel, 1 November 2004 *("Milošević* Decision").

8 *Prosecutor v. Vojislav Šešelj,* Case No. IT-03-67-AR73.4, Decision on Appeal Against the Trial Chamber's Decision (No.2) on Assignment of Counsel, 8 December 2006, which apparently was drafted under the impression of an accused blatantly exerting pressure on the judiciary.

of fair proceedings, a huge number of countries assign counsel both at trial and on appeal from the very moment that a case reaches a certain degree of gravity or a specifically serious sentence is to be expected, *i.e.* in scenarios in which it cannot be reasonably expected that an individual will be able to represent himself adequately. The same applies to all other international tribunals. Domestic law rarely regards obstructive behaviour as a reason to impose counsel, although this is certainly possible. Rather, such conduct is usually addressed by sanctioning an accused without touching upon issues of representation.

5. Due to time constraints and considering the particular question before this bench of the Appeals Chamber, I have to restrict my analysis to whether there is a right to self-representation in proceedings at the appellate level.[9] This does not mean, however, that I hold the Appeals **[page 3]** Chamber's past jurisprudence on self-representation during trial to be correct, having never been assigned to a bench of the Appeals Chamber ruling on this issue. My necessary self-restraint is based on the fact that this is the first Appeals Chamber decision dealing with self-representation on appeal. Thus, *stare decisis* does not apply.

6. Moreover, the attempt to ameliorate the effects of the Appellant's self-representation by assigning *amicus curiae*, which as a permanent institution is not at all covered by the International Tribunal's Rules of Procedure and Evidence ("Rules"), will only obfuscate the proceedings while doing little to safeguard the Appellant's right to a fair and expeditious trial, as past experiences have shown. Also here, *stare decisis* is not applicable as the Appeals Chamber has never ruled on this issue before.

B. The Applicable Law on Self-Representation with Special Reference to the Appellate Level

7. Article 21(4) of the Statute reads as follows:

> In the determination of any charge against the accused, pursuant to the present Statute, the accused shall be entitled to the following minimum guarantees, in full equality:
>
> (d) to be tried in his presence, and to defend himself in person or through legal assistance of his own choosing; to be informed, if he does not have legal assistance, of this right; and to have legal assistance assigned to him, in any case where the interests of justice so require, and without payment by him in any such case if he does not have sufficient means to pay for it.

1. The Right to Self-Representation on Appeal – Comparative Analysis

8. As mentioned above, the Appeals Chamber has not been previously seized of a convicted person's request to represent himself on appeal. I note that earlier decisions of the International Tribunal were limited to addressing the question of an accused's wish for self-representation either during trial (in *Milošević, Krajišnik and Šešelj)* or during pre-trial (in *Šešelj).* In those decisions, the International Tribunal has created certain guidelines and principles. I have to stress that I do not agree with these principles, which disregard the established practice under transnational/supranational and domestic law in most States.

9. In the case before us, the Appellant argues that his right to self-representation at the appellate level is the same as that at trial. However, even if assumed, *arguendo*, that there is a right to self-representation during trial, the role of an accused changes dramatically on appeal. This is primarily due to the fact that there is a fundamental difference between the role of an accused at trial, where he bears no burden of persuasion,

---

9 For an analysis of the issue *see, inter alia,* (in chronological order) Nina H. B. Jørgensen, *The Right of the Accused to Self-Representation Before International Criminal Tribunals,* 98 Am. J. Int'l L. 711–726 (2004); Göran Sluiter, *'Fairness and the Interests of Justice,' Illusive Concepts in the Milošević Case,* 3 J. Int'l Crim. Just. 9–19 (2005); Nina H. B. Jørgensen, *The Right of Self-Representation Before International Criminal Tribunals: Further Developments,* 99 Am. J. Int'l L., 663–668 (2005); Gideon Boas, *The Right to Self-Representation in International and Domestic Criminal Law – Limitations and Qualifications on that Right, in* The Dynamics of International Criminal Justice 39–93, (Hirad Abthai & Gideon Boas eds., 2005); Stefan Trechsel, Human Rights in International Criminal Proceedings 251–266 (2005); Michael P. Scharf, *Self-Representation versus Assignment of Defence Counsel before International Criminal Tribunals,* 4 J. Int'l Crim. Just. 31–46 (2006); Nina H. B. Jørgensen, *The Problem of Self-Representation at International Criminal Tribunals, Striking a Balance between Fairness and Effectiveness,* 4 J. Int'l Crim. Just. 64–77 (2006); Göran Sluiter, *Compromising the Authority of International Criminal Justice, How Vojislav Šešelj Runs His Trial,* 5 J. Int'l Crim. Just. 1–8 (2007).

and at the appellate level where an accused is confronted with the task of convincing the Appeals Chamber to quash the judgement of the first instance in whole or in part: **[page 4]**

> "[T]here are significant differences between the trial and appellate stages of a criminal proceeding." [...] "By contrast, it is ordinarily the defendant, rather than the State, who initiates the appellate process, seeking not to fend off the efforts of the State's prosecutor but rather to overturn a finding of guilt made by a judge or a jury below."[10]

10. In claiming that he has the right to self-representation on appeal, the Appellant relies upon the authority of various other jurisdictions. I have already felt compelled to emphasize in the context of another decision that the International Tribunal is not bound by any national and/or regional jurisprudence, but that at the same time it is the Tribunal's obligation "not to turn a blind eye to these and to show open-mindedness, respect and tolerance [...] by accepting internationally recognized legal interpretations[,] [...] theories"[11] and principles. However, in the case at hand, the decision of the Appeals Chamber even lacks a serious discussion of the matter. It is therefore again necessary – with the limited resources available to a Judge of this Tribunal – to conduct a comparative analysis of (a) transnational/ supranational law and jurisprudence, (b) national law and jurisprudence and (c) the law and jurisprudence of other international criminal tribunals and courts.

11. I am aware that many jurisdictions do not draw a clear distinction between trial proceedings on the one hand and appellate proceedings on the other when determining the scope of the right to self-representation. However, turning now to the comparative analysis of the applicable transnational/ supranational and national law and jurisprudence, and also the approach taken by other international criminal tribunals and courts, the aim is to come to a solution which draws on the shared values of these different legal systems.

(a) <u>Transnational/Supranational Law and Jurisprudence.</u>

12. From the outset it must be considered that Article 21(4) of the Statute is a reflection of the relevant provisions contained in various global and regional human rights conventions and therefore cannot be viewed in isolation. In fact, the question of a right to self-representation (during trial or on appeal) is not new and has often arisen in the context of the application of these global or regional instruments. The International Tribunal is not a party to any of these conventions. However, the International Covenant on Civil and Political Rights of 19 December 1966 (ICCPR/Covenant)[12] was adopted by resolution of the General Assembly of the United Nations. It can easily be assumed that the Security Council felt obliged to respect the rights as guaranteed under the Covenant when establishing the ICTY as a measure under Chapter VII of the U.N. **[page 5]** Charter.[13] Moreover, as an accused would enjoy the guarantees of some of these agreements, such as the Convention for the Protection of Human Rights and Fundamental Freedoms of 4 November 1950 (ECHR),[14] had he been charged with crimes on the territory of the former Yugoslavia, it is an obligation of the Tribunal to fully respect the rights as granted under this convention as well. To quote the report of the Secretary-General:

> It is axiomatic that the International Tribunal must fully respect internationally recognized standards regarding the rights of the accused at all stages of its proceedings. In the view of the Secretary-General, such internationally recognized standards are, *in particular,* contained in article 14 of the International Covenant on Civil and Political Rights.[15]

---

10 *Martinez v. Court of Appeal of California*, 528 U.S. 152, 162–163 (2000), referring to *Ross v. Moffitt,* 417 U.S. 600, 610(1974).

11 *Prosecutor v. Blagoje Simić,* Case No. IT-95-9-A, Judgement, Dissenting Opinion of Judge Schomburg, 28 November 2006, para. 17.

12 999 U.N.T.S. 171.

13 *See Georges Anderson Nderubumwe Rutaganda v. The Prosecutor,* Case No. ICTR-96-3-A, Judgement, Dissenting Opinion of Judge Pocar, 26 May 2003.

14 213 U.N.T.S. 221, CETS 005.

15 The Secretary General, *Report of the Secretary-General pursuant to Paragraph 2 of the Security Council Resolution 808 (1993),* U.N. Doc S/25704 (3 May 1993), para. 106 (italics added for emphasis).

13. Both the ICCPR and the ECHR contain provisions almost identical to Article 21(4)(d) of the Statute:

Article 14(3)(d) of the ICCPR

In the determination of any criminal charge against him, everyone shall be entitled to the following minimum guarantees, in full equality: [...]

(d) To be tried in his presence, and to defend himself in person or through legal assistance of his own choosing [...].

Article 6(3)(c) of the ECHR

Everyone charged with a criminal offence shall have the following minimum rights: [...]

(c) to defend himself in person or through legal assistance of his own choosing or, if he has not sufficient means to pay for legal assistance, to be given it free when the interests of justice so require [...].

14. The jurisprudence of the European Court of Human Rights (ECtHR) is particularly instructive because of its abundance of case-law related to alleged violations of Article 6(3)(c) of the ECHR. Furthermore, a number of judgements have specifically addressed the right of an accused to self-representation on appeal. It is clear from ECtHR's jurisprudence that this right must be considered in particular with a view to the overarching right of an accused to fair proceedings: In *Granger v. United Kingdom* the ECtHR emphasized that the rights as guaranteed in Article 6(3) are nothing but specific aspects of the right to a fair trial in criminal proceedings as regulated in Article 6(1) of the Convention,[16] which provides that "*everyone is entitled to a fair and public hearing.*"[17] **[page 6]** The ECtHR therefore drew the conclusion that it was "appropriate to examine the applicant's complaints from the angle of paragraphs 3(c) and (1) [of Article 6] taken together."[18]

15. The ECtHR also held that as a basic principle those rights as guaranteed in Article 6 of the Convention apply to any part of the proceedings, *i.e.* including appellate proceedings.[19] However, in the case of *Monnell and Morris v. The United Kingdom*, the ECtHR ruled that when applying Article 6 in relation to appellate proceedings the special features of the proceedings had to be taken into consideration. The ECtHR emphasized that "account must be taken of the entirety of the proceedings conducted in the domestic legal order and of the role of the appellate or cassation court therein."[20] In order to determine whether the procedure met the requirements of the right to a fair trial, the ECtHR considered matters such as the scope of powers of the court of appeal and the manner in which the applicant's interests were actually presented and protected before the court of appeal.[21] Similarly, in *Tripodi v. Italy* the ECtHR emphasized that the manner in which Articles 6(1) and (3)(c) of the Convention were applied depended on the "special features of the proceedings in question."[22] The ECtHR took into consideration that the Italian court of cassation decided on points of law, that its proceedings were essentially written and that at the hearing the appellant's lawyer was only allowed to present arguments in relation to submissions already made in the appeal brief and the memorials.[23]

16. In the case of *Croissant v. Germany* the Court was seized of a case where the defendant was initially represented by two lawyers of his own choice. The president of the regional court then designated a third

---

16 *Granger v. The United Kingdom,* ECtHR, App. No. 11932/86, 28 March 1990, para. 43 (with further references).

17 Italics added for emphasis. Article 6(1) of the ECHR reads as follows: "In the determination of his civil rights and obligations or of any criminal charge against him, everyone is entitled to a fair and public hearing within a reasonable time by an independent and impartial tribunal established by law. Judgement shall be pronounced publicly but the press and public may be excluded from all or part of the trial in the interest of morals, public order or national security in a democratic society, where the interests of juveniles or the protection of the private life of the parties so require, or the extent strictly necessary in the opinion of the court in special circumstances where publicity would prejudice the interests of justice."

18 *Granger v. The United Kingdom,* ECtHR, App. No. 11932/86, 28 March 1990, para. 43.

19 *Meftah v. France,* ECtHR, App. No. 32911/96, 26 April 2001, para. 42: "La Cour rappelle en effet que selon la jurisprudence, un Etat qui se dote d'une Cour de cassation a l'obligation de veiller à ce que les justiciables jouissent auprès d'elle des garanties fondamentales de l'article 6." *See also Kremzow v. Austria,* ECtHR, App. No. 12350/86, 21 September 1993, para. 58: "The Court recalls that Article 6 extends to nullity and appeal proceedings [...]."

20 *Monell and Morris v. United Kingdom* , ECtHR, App. No. 9562/81; 9819/82, 2 March 1987, para. 56.

21 *Id.*

22 *Tripodi v. Italy,* ECtHR, App. No. 13743/88, 22 February 1994, para. 27.

23 *Id.* at para. 28.

defence counsel who, unlike the first two lawyers, practiced in the jurisdiction of this court. The applicant objected to the appointment of defence counsel itself and not only to the choice of the person. In this context the ECtHR significantly held:

> The requirement that a defendant be assisted by counsel at all stages of the Regional Court's proceedings [...] – which finds parallels in the legislation of other Contracting States – cannot, in the Court's opinion, be deemed incompatible with the Convention.[24] **[page 7]**

The ECtHR further emphasized that despite the importance of a relationship of trust between lawyer and client, the right to self-representation could not be considered absolute. "It is necessarily subject to certain limitations [...] where [...] it is for the courts to decide whether the interests of justice require that the accused be defended by counsel appointed by them."[25]

17. In *Lagerblom v. Sweden*, the ECtHR confirmed again that "[a] legal requirement that an accused be assisted by counsel in criminal proceedings cannot be deemed incompatible with the Convention."[26] The ECtHR moreover held:

> When appointing defence counsel the courts must certainly have regard to the accused's wishes but these can be overridden when there are relevant and sufficient grounds for holding that this is necessary in the interests of justice.[27]

18. Quite recently, in *Mayzit v. Russia*, the ECtHR came to the following conclusion:

> In examining questions under Article 6(3)(c) the Court takes account of the treatment of the defence as a whole rather than the position of the accused taken in isolation, with particular regard to the principle of equality of arms as included in the concept of a fair hearing.[28]
>
> Article 6(3)(c) guarantees that proceedings against the accused will not take place without an adequate representation for the defence, but does not give the accused the right to decide himself in what manner his defence should be assured. The decision as to which of the two alternatives mentioned in the provision should be chosen, namely the applicant's right to defend himself in person or to be represented by a lawyer of his own choosing, or in certain circumstances one appointed by the court, depends upon the applicable legislation or rules of court.[29]

19. Even before the recent ruling of the ECtHR in *Mayzit v. Russia*, there has been unambiguous jurisprudence, some of it directly related to the question of the right to self-representation during criminal appeal proceedings, of the European Commission of Human Rights (EComHR).[30] In one of the first decisions on the matter, the EComHR ruled in relation to civil proceedings that

> it should be noted that the right to a fair hearing guaranteed by Article 6(1) of the Convention does not imply an obligation on the Contracting Party to allow litigants free access to the *Court of last resort* [...]. Article 6(1) does not debar Contracting Parties from making regulations governing the access of litigants to the said Court, provided that such regulations do not deviate from their exclusive purpose of assuring justice according to law.[31]

---

24 *Croissant v. Germany*, ECtHR, App. No. 13611/88, 25 September 1992, para. 27.

25 *Id.* at para. 29.

26 *Lagerblom v. Sweden*, ECtHR, App. No. 26891/95, 14 January 2003, para. 50.

27 *Id.* at para. 54.

28 *Mayzit v. Russia*, ECtHR, App. No. 63378/00, 20 January 2005, para. 64.

29 *Id.* at para. 65.

30 Until its abolishment in 1998 (by Protocol No. 11 to the ECHR – CETS No. 155 – which entered into force on 1 November 1998), the Commission played the role of an intermediary body by filtering the numerous complaints the Court received and declaring them either admissible or inadmissible with a view to the ECtHR's jurisprudence.

31 *X. v. Germany*, EComHR, App. No. 727/60, 5 August 1960 (italics added for emphasis). In relation to civil proceedings, the ECtHR explicitly accepted in the *Gillow v. United Kingdom*, ECtHR, App. No. 9063/80, 24 November 1986, para. 69, the requirement of representation by lawyer to lodge an appeal as a "common feature of the legal systems in several Member States of the Council of Europe."

20. As regards criminal proceedings, the EComHR considered that Article 6(3)(c) **[page 8]**

> does not confer upon the person charged with a criminal offence the right to decide in what way provision should be made for his defence. [...] The competent authorities are entitled to decide whether the person charged shall defend himself in person or shall be represented by a lawyer of his own choice or appointed ex officio as the case may be.[32]

21. In a later decision the EComHR held the following:

> It is true that in the wording of Art. 6(3)(c) of the convention everyone charged with a criminal offence shall have the right to defend himself in person or through legal assistance of his own choosing [...].
>
> In its case law the Commission has considered complaints by applicants that they were not allowed to defend themselves in person. These applications concerned appeal proceedings. However, the Commission expressed certain general principles. It took account of the treatment of the defence as a whole rather than the position of the accused taken in isolation, and it had particular regard to the principle of equality of arms as included in the concept of a fair hearing.
>
> Consequently, the Commission held that Art. 6(3)(c) guarantees that proceedings against the accused will not take place without an adequate representation for the defence, but does not give the accused the right to decide himself in what manners his defence should be assured. The decision as to which of the two alternatives mentioned in the provision should be chosen, namely the applicant's right to defend himself in person or to be represented by a lawyer of his own choosing, or in certain circumstances one appointed by the court, depends upon the applicable legislation or rules of the court.[33]

The ECtHR adopted this language not only in *Mayzit v. Russia.*[34]

22. With regard to the legal complexities of an appeals case, the EComHR decided that

> [...] it is apparent to the Commission from the Court of Appeal's judgment that it was in the interest of the applicant in this particular case that he should be represented by a barrister on the appeal. This follows from the fact that no merit was found in the applicant's own grounds of appeal and that leave to appeal was granted by the Court of Appeal on a legal issue specified by the court itself, on which clearly the applicant needed the services of a lawyer.[35]

23. Therefore, the jurisprudence of the ECtHR clarifies that a restriction of the right to self-representation on appeal does not violate the rights granted under Article 6(3)(c) of the Convention. Indeed, none of the cases in which the ECtHR found Article 6(3)(c) of the Convention to be violated can be compared to the case at hand. For example, in the case of *Belzuik v. Poland* the ECtHR ruled that an appellant's right to be present at his appeal and to defend himself in person **[page 9]** had been violated. However, in that case the appellant was denied even the right to be present at the appeal hearing. At the same time, he was not represented by a counsel, *i.e.* the accused was not represented at that hearing.[36] Consequently, the underlying facts of the case decided by the ECtHR differ fundamentally from the present case.

---

32 *Scheichelbauer v. Austria*, EComHR, App. No. 2645/65, 1969, para. 28.

33 *X. v. Norway,* EComHR, App. No. 5923/72, 30 May 1975.

34 *See also Philis v. Greece,* EComHR, App. No. 16598/90, 11 December 1990 and *Philis v. Greece*, EComHR, App. No. 19773/92, 31 August 1994, recalling the "constant case-law under Article 6 para 3. (c)." In this context, *see* Jørgensen, *The Right of the Accused to Self-Representation Before International Criminal Tribunals*, *supra* note 9, 715–716: "The case of *Philis v. Greece* similarly suggests that a provision in the Greek Code of Criminal Procedure stating that at a hearing before the Court of Cassation the parties must be presented by a lawyer must not be incompatible with Article 6(3)(c) of the European Convention. Invoking Article 6(3)(c), the applicant had presented his case before the Greek Court of Cassation submitting that this provision gave him the right to defend himself in person, notwithstanding the provision in the Greek code requiring that he be represented by a lawyer. The applicant's appeal was declared inadmissible because he was not duly represented and the European Commission did not accept any complaint in that regard."

35 EComHR, App. No. 5730/72, 11 December 1973 (unpublished), printed in 2 Council of Europe, Digest of Strasbourg Case-law relating to the European Convention on Human Rights (Article 6) 826 (1984).

36 *Belzuik v. Poland*, ECtHR, App. No. 45/1997/829/1035, 25 March 1998, para. 38.

24. Another case where the ECtHR found a violation of Article 6(3)(c) is the case of *Kremzow v. Austria.*[37] As happened in *Belzuik v. Poland*, the accused was not allowed to be present at all during his appeal hearing at which he was represented by a lawyer. The ECtHR held "that given the gravity of what was at stake for the applicant, he ought to have been able 'to defend himself in person' as required by Article 6(3)(c) and that the State was under a positive duty, notwithstanding his failure to make a request, to ensure his presence in such circumstances."[38] As in *Belzuik v. Poland*, the ECtHR did see a violation of Article 6(3)(c) of the ECHR, not because the applicant was represented by defence counsel against his own will, but because he was not allowed to be present at one specific hearing where important matters were at stake. If anything, the case shows that the ECtHR understands the right to "defend oneself in person" as relating to the fact of being present at a hearing. Therefore, it cannot be concluded from this case that the right to self-representation would be violated by the requirement of defence counsel on appeal.

25. In sum, under the ECHR, an accused does not have an absolute right to represent himself either at trial or, as in this case, on appeal. Both the ECtHR and the EComHR held that Article 6(3)(c) of the ECHR, being almost identical to Article 21(4)(d) of the Statute, must be interpreted in a holistic way, considering the right to self-representation in the context of the overarching fair trial guarantees, thus sometimes restricting the right to self-representation in the interests of a fair trial.[39] Moreover, the jurisprudence shows that it is not only the behaviour of an appellant during the proceedings that may justify the imposition of counsel, but primarily the nature of those proceedings as well.

26. The Human Rights Committee, established under the ICCPR, was seized of a case relating to the issue of self-representation and addressed this question only at the trial level. The Committee found Article 14 to be violated in the case of *Michael and Brian Hill v. Spain* because Hill's right to defend himself had not been respected.[40] However, the *Hill* case is not comparable to the case at hand as it relates solely to proceedings at trial and not on appeal. Moreover, the holding of the Human Rights Committee merely relates to a specific case where the defendant was not allowed to **[page 10]** cross-examine or call witnesses, or in fact to participate in the proceedings at all. It is already clear therefore, that little weight can be afforded to this decision when assessing the case before the Appeals Chamber. On the other hand, this case shows the importance of recognizing the accused as a subject of the proceedings, *i.e.* a human being actively participating in the proceedings.

27. Another important international legal instrument is the American Convention on Human Rights of 22 November 1969 (AMCHR),[41] Article 8(2) of which reads as follows (again similar to Article 21(4)(d) of the Statute):

> [...] During the proceedings, every person is entitled, with full equality, to the following minimum guarantees: [...]
>
> (d) the right of the accused to defend himself personally or to be assisted by legal counsel of his own choosing, and to communicate freely and privately with his counsel; (e) the inalienable right to be assisted by counsel provided by the state, paid or not as the domestic law provides, if the accused does not defend himself personally or engage his own counsel within the time period established by law; [...].

In an Advisory Opinion, the Inter-American Court of Human Rights (IACHR) stated that under sub-paragraphs (d) and (e) of Article 8(2) an accused had a right to defend himself personally or to be assisted by legal counsel of his own choosing. In this context, however, the IACHR held:

> Thus, a defendant may defend himself personally, but it is important to bear in mind that this would only be possible where permitted under domestic law. If a person refuses or is unable to defend himself personally, he has the right to be assisted by counsel of his own choosing. [...] To that extent the Convention guarantees the right to counsel in criminal proceedings. [...] Article 8 must, then, be read to require legal counsel only when that is necessary for a fair hearing.[42]

---

37 *Kremzow v. Austria,* ECtHR. App. No. 12350/86, 21 September 1993, para. 69.

38 *Id.* at para. 68.

39 *See also* TRECHSEL, *supra* note 9, 263–266.

40 *Michael and Brian Hill v. Spain*, Communication No. 526/1993, U.N. Doc. CCPR/C/59/D/526/1993, 2 April 1997, Para. 14.2.

41 1144 U.N.T.S. 123.

42 Exceptions to the Exhaustion of Domestic Remedies (Arts. 46(1), 46(2)(a) and 46 (2)(b) of the American Convention on Human Rights), Advisory Opinion OC-11/90, 10 August 1990, Inter-Am. Ct. H.R. (Ser. A) No. 11 (1990), paras 25–26.

Therefore, the IACHR assumed that the right to self-representation could be limited by domestic legislation without violating the rights guaranteed under Article 8 of the AMCHR as long as the general requirements of a fair trial were observed.

28. The African (Banjul) Charter on Human and Peoples' Rights of 26 June 1981[43] reads:

> Article 7(1): Every individual shall have the right to have his cause heard. This comprises: [...] (c) the right to defence, including the right to be defended by counsel of his choice.

From the wording it is clear that the right to self-representation is not explicitly included in the Charter.[44] Moreover, the African Commission on Human and Peoples' Rights held that, if **[page 11]** defendants at a criminal trial are not represented by counsel for all or part of the trial, this will violate the right to defence as stipulated in Article 7(1)(c).[45]

(b) National Law and Jurisprudence

29. I am conscious of the fact that one distinctive feature of Romano-Germanic law influenced proceedings is that an accused is still presumed innocent until the final judgment is rendered whereas the Anglo-Saxon law influenced systems retain the presumption of innocence only until the conclusion of the trial phase.[46] This *de jure* difference however does not change the *de facto* role of a convicted person. As already explained above, the role of an accused changes dramatically[47]once he has been convicted on trial. In both legal systems he must convince the judges in a higher instance to overturn the judgement of the lower court in whole or in part.

(i) Jurisdictions Influenced by Anglo-Saxon Legal Traditions

30. The **United States of America** has ratified the ICCPR and is bound by it. In recognition of the right to self-representation as granted under Article 14(3)(d) of the Covenant the Supreme Court of the United States held in *Faretta v. California*:

> The right to defend is personal. The defendant, and not his lawyer or the State, will bear the personal consequences of a conviction. It is the defendant therefore, who must be free personally to decide whether in his particular case counsel is to his advantage. And although he may conduct his own defense ultimately to his own detriment, his choice must be honoured out of "that respect for the individual which is the lifeblood of the law."[48]

However, the Supreme Court also indicated certain restrictions to the right to self-representation. It referred to a trial judge's option to terminate self-representation in cases where the defendant deliberately engaged in serious and obstructionist misconduct.[49]

31. In *Farhad v. United States* a United States Court of Appeal followed the ruling in *Faretta v. California* and affirmed the right to self-representation in the trial phase.[50] However, Judge *Reinhardt* emphasized the following points in his concurring opinion:

> The Constitution guarantees every defendant the fundamental, absolute right to fair trial. By contrast, the right to counsel (or even the implied right to self-representation) is not absolute. It, like all other procedural

43 1520 U.N.T.S. 217. The African Charter of Human and Peoples' Rights was adopted on 27 June 1981.

44 *See also* M. Cherif Bassiouni, *Human Rights in the Context of Criminal Justice: Identifying International Procedural Protections and Equivalent Protections in National Constitutions,* 3 Duke J. Comp. & Int'l L. 235, 283 (1993): "The right to self-representation is guaranteed by the ICCPR, the Fundamental Freedoms, the AMCHR, and *possibly* the Banjul Charter." (Italics added for emphasis).

45 *See* Rachel Murray, *Decisions by the African Commission on Individual Communications under the African Charter on Human and Peoples' Rights,* 46 Int'l & Comp. L.Q. 412, 429 (1997).

46 *See Martinez v. Court of Appeal of California,* 528 U.S. 152, 162 (2000).

47 *Id.*

48 *Faretta v. California,* 422 U.S. 806, 834 (1975), referring to *Illinois v. Allen*, 397 U.S. 337, 350–351 (Brennan, J., concurring).

49 *Id.* at 806, note 46, referring to *Illinois v. Allen*, 397 U.S. 337.

50 *U.S. v. Farhad*, 190 F.3d 1097, 1098 (1999).

> guarantees found in the Sixth Amendment, is intended primarily to **[page 12]** achieve the substantive objective of a fair trial. Where the right to self-representation conflicts with the paramount Fifth Amendment right to a fair and reliable trial, I believe that the former and not the latter, must yield. [...] I strongly question whether such a waiver [of the right to a fair trial], express or implied, is permissible.[51]

Judge *Reinhardt* further pointed out that permitting self-representation regardless of the consequences threatened to divert criminal trials from their clearly defined purpose of providing a fair and reliable determination of guilt or innocence.[52] He also observed that a defendant should not be able to waive his right to a fair trial[53] and that this right touched upon not only the interests of an accused, but also the institutional interests of the judicial system.[54]

32. In the same vein, the Supreme Court of the United States restricted the right to self-representation in *Martinez v. Court of Appeal of California* and made clear that the decision of *Faretta v. California* applied only to the right to defend oneself at the trial stage.[55] The Supreme Court held that the issue was fundamentally different once the defendant became an appellant:

> Our conclusion in Faretta extended only to a defendant's "constitutional right to conduct his own defense." Accordingly, our specific holding was confined to the right to defend oneself at trial. We now address the different question whether the reasoning in support of that holding also applies when the defendant becomes an appellant and assumes the burden of persuading a reviewing court that the conviction should be reserved. We have concluded that it does not.[56] [...]
>
> In the appellate context, the balance between the two competing interests surely tips in favour of the State. The status of the accused defendant, who retains a presumption of innocence throughout the trial process, changes dramatically when a jury returns a guilty verdict.[57] [...] The requirement of representation by trained counsel implies no disrespect for the individual inasmuch as it tends to benefit the appellant as well as the court.[58]

Recognizing this shifting focus the Supreme Court referred to an earlier decision:

> "[T]here are significant differences between the trial and appellate stages of a criminal proceeding." [...] "By contrast, it is ordinarily the defendant, rather than the State, who initiates the appellate process, seeking not to fend off the efforts of the State's prosecutor but rather to overturn a finding of guilt made by a judge or a jury below."[59]

Furthermore, the Supreme Court stressed that there was neither a "historical consensus establishing a right of self-representation on appeal" nor a "long-respected right of self-representation on appeal."[60] **[page 13]**

33. There are several other decisions by United States high courts that follow the Martinez precedent.[61] To quote only a few:

> Initially, we note that Mr. Reyes did not have a constitutional right to appear *pro se* on direct appeal.[62]

---

51 *Id.* at 1102.
52 *Id.* at 1106.
53 *Id.* at 1102, 1107.
54 *Id.* at 1107.
55 *Martinez v. Court of Appeal of California,* 528 U.S. 152, 154 (2000).
56 *Id.*
57 *Id.* at 162.
58 *Id.* at 163.
59 *Id.* at 162–163, referring to *Ross v. Moffitt*, 417 U.S. 600, 610 (1974).
60 *Martinez v. Court of Appeal of California*, 528 U.S. 152, 159 (2000).
61 *U.S. v. Frazier-El*, 204 F.3d 553 (2000); *see also Fudge v. State* 341 Ark. 652, 653 (2000), "While the Court in *Martinez* left to the State appellate courts the discretion to allow a lay person to proceed *pro se* on appeal, it also recognized that representation by trained appellate counsel is of distinct benefit to the appellant as well as the court. We conclude that appellant, who is represented by counsel qualified to represent defendants in capital cases, has not demonstrated that there is any good cause to permit him to serve as co-counsel or to file a supplemental *pro se* brief."
62 *Reyes v. Sedillo*, 2007 WL 867175 (10th Cir.(Kan.)), 1 (March 23, 2007).

> Rufus does not have a constitutional right to proceed on appeal pro se.[63]
>
> But, there is no federal constitutional right to self representation on direct appeal from a criminal conviction.[64]
>
> And where the defendant chooses neither attorney representation nor self-representation, the default position for the court should be to mandate attorney representation. After all, while there are competing fundamental rights to counsel and to self-representation, "it is representation by counsel that is the standard, not the exception."[65]

34. In **Australia** an accused has the right to self-representation at any stage of the criminal proceedings.[66] However, in cases where sexual offences are at stake, the accused cannot cross-examine the alleged victim.[67] Thus, the right to self-representation can be restricted under certain conditions.

35. There is a general right to self-representation in **Canada**.[68] However, the Criminal Code includes a provision under which defence counsel can be assigned at appellate level.

> **Section 684(1)**
>
> A court of appeal or a judge of that court may, at any time, assign counsel to act on behalf of an accused who is a party to an appeal or to proceedings preliminary or incidental to an appeal where, in the opinion of the court or judge, it appears desirable in the interests of justice that the accused should have legal assistance and where it appears that the accused has not sufficient means to obtain that assistance.

A similar provision can be found in Section 694(1) in relation to an appeal to the Supreme Court of Canada.[69] Those regulations have to be read in the context of the legal aid system provided for in **[page 14]** the Canadian Criminal Code. Assigning counsel on appeal is accordingly only possible in cases where justice so requires but the appellant lacks sufficient means to obtain such aid. Nevertheless, they are relevant to the case at hand. As a corresponding regulation does not exist for proceedings at trial level,[70] those provisions clarify that the role of an accused is decisively different on appeal and that the interests of justice might require the assignment of defence counsel on appeal even where that was not necessary at trial level.

36. In *R. v. Bernardo*[71] the Ontario Court of Appeal specified the criteria in which this rule was applicable:

> In deciding whether counsel should be appointed, it is appropriate to begin with an inquiry into the merits of the appeal. [...] Having decided that the appeal raises arguable issues, the question becomes whether the appellant can effectively advance his grounds of appeal without the assistance of counsel. This inquiry looks to the complexities of the arguments to be advanced and the accused's ability to make an oral argument in support of the grounds of appeal. The complexity of the argument is a product of the grounds of appeal, the length and content of the record on appeal, the legal principles engaged, and the application of those principles to the facts of the case. An accused's ability to make arguments in support of his or her grounds of appeal turns on a number of factors, including the accused's ability to understand the written word, comprehend the applicable legal principles, relate those principles to the facts of the case, and articulate the end product of that process before the court.[72]

---

63 *United States v. Rufus*, 114 Fed.Appx. 56, 56 (2004).

64 *Kenney v. Massachusetts*, 111 Fed.Appx. 20, 21 (2004).

65 *Fischetti v. Johnson*, 384 F.3d 140, 147 (2004).

66 *See* Mark Findlay, Stephen Odgers & Stanley Yeo, Australian Criminal Justice 142, 160 (2nd ed. 1999).

67 Section 294A of the Criminal Procedure Act reads: Arrangement for complainant in sexual offence proceedings giving evidence when accused person is unrepresented. (1) This section applies to sexual offence proceedings during which the accused person is not represented by counsel. (2) The complainant cannot be examined in chief, cross-examined or re-examined by the accused person, but may be so examined instead by a person appointed by the court. (3) The person appointed by the court is to ask the complainant only the questions that the accused person requests that person to put to the complainant. [...]

68 *R. v. Romanowicz*, 14 C.R. (5th) 100, [1998] O.J. No. 12, 6 January 1998, para. 30.

69 This provision reads: "The Supreme Court of Canada or a judge thereof may, at any time, assign counsel to act on behalf of an accused who is a party to an appeal to the Court or to proceedings preliminary or incidental to an appeal to the Court where, in the opinion of the Court or judge, it appears desirable in the interests of justice that the accused should have legal assistance and where it appears that the accused has not sufficient means to obtain that assistance."

70 *See* David Watt & Michelle Fuerst, The 2007 Annotated Tremeear's Criminal Code 1337 (2006).

71 *R v. Bernardo*, 12 C.R. (5th) 310, 121 C.C.C. (3d) 123 (Ont. C.A.) (1997).

72 *Id.* at paras 22, 24.

37. The legal system of **England** and **Wales** clearly recognizes the right to self-representation at any stage of proceedings.[73] However, the Youth Justice and Criminal Evidence Act 1999 includes provisions for the protection of witnesses from cross-examination by the accused in person. In proceedings for sexual offences, in cases where children are concerned, and in any other cases where it appears to the court that the quality of evidence given by the witness in cross-examination is likely to be diminished if the cross-examination is conducted by the accused in person, the court may give, where it is not contrary to the interest of justice, a direction prohibiting the accused from cross-examining the witness in person.[74] In such cases the court can assign defence counsel. The relevant provision reads:

> **Section 38**
>
> (2) Where it appears to the court that this section applies, it must-
>
> (a) invite the accused to arrange for a legal representative to act for him for the purpose of cross-examining the witness; and **[page 15]**
>
> (b) require the accused to notify the court, by the end of such a period as it may specify, whether a legal representative is to act for him for that purpose.
>
> (3) If by the end of the period mentioned in subsection 2(b) either-
>
> (a) the accused has notified the court that no legal representative is to act for him for the purpose of cross-examining the witness, or
>
> (b) no notification has been received by the court and it appears to the court that no legal representative is to so act,
>
> the court must consider whether it is necessary in the interests of justice for the witness to be cross-examined by a legal representative appointed to represent the interests of the accused.
>
> (4) If the court decides that it is necessary in the interests of justice for the witness to be so cross-examined, the court must appoint a qualified legal representative (chosen by the court) to cross-examine the witness in the interests of justice.

Thus, these provisions clearly show that the right to self-representation is not absolute and has to be seen in the overall context of fair proceedings. It can be restricted under certain conditions and defence counsel can be assigned *proprio motu.*

38. The rules of the Supreme Court of **India**[75] provide in relation to criminal appeals that "where an accused is not represented by an Advocate on Record of his choice the Court may in a proper case direct the engagement of an Advocate at the cost of the Government."

39. In **New Zealand** the right to self-representation is recognized at any stage of proceedings.[76] The same applies in **Scotland**.[77]

(ii) <u>Jurisdictions Influenced by Romano-Germanic Legal Traditions</u>

40. Many countries influenced by Romano-Germanic legal traditions restrict the right to self-representation and impose mandatory defence counsel in serious cases. For obvious reasons I will first turn to the law of the **States on the territory of the former Yugoslavia:**

- The Criminal Procedure Code of **Bosnia and Herzegovina** recognizes mandatory defence counsel in cases of serious crimes until the verdict becomes final, *i.e.* also on appeal. The relevant provision reads:

---

73 Peter Murphy, Blackstone's Criminal Practice 1137 (2005).

74 *See* Section 34–36 of the Youth Justice and Criminal Evidence Act 1999.

75 Supreme Court Rules, 1966, as amended, Order XXI, para 25.

76 *R. v. Cumming,* 2 N.Z.L.R. 597, 2 November 2005, para. 40.

77 Criminal Procedure Act (Scotland) 1995, Sections 92 and 110.

Article 59

(1) A suspect shall have a defence attorney at the first questioning [...] if he is suspected of a criminal offence for which a penalty of long-term imprisonment may be pronounced. [...] **[page 16]**

(4) If the suspect, or the accused in the case of a mandatory defence, does not retain a defence attorney himself, or if the persons referred to in Article 53, Paragraph 3, of this Code do not retain a defence attorney, the preliminary proceeding judge, preliminary hearing judge, the judge or the Presiding judge shall appoint him a defence attorney in the proceedings. In this case, the suspect or the accused shall have the right to a defence attorney *until the verdict becomes final* and, if a long-term imprisonment is pronounced, for proceedings under legal remedies [...].

(5) If the Court finds it necessary for *the sake of justice, due to the complexity of the case* or the mental condition of the suspect or the accused, it shall appoint an attorney for his defence.[78]

- Similarly, the Criminal Procedure Code of **Serbia** reads:

Article 71

(1) If the defendant is [...] unable successfully to defend himself or if the proceedings are carried out for a criminal offence punishable by imprisonment for a term of more than ten years or by a more severe punishment, the defendant must have a defence counsel even at his first interrogation. [...]

(4) When in the case of mandatory defence referred to in the preceding paragraphs of this Article the defendant fails to retain a defence counsel by himself, the president of the court shall, by virtue of the office, appoint a defence counsel to represent him in further criminal proceedings up *until the judgement becomes final*, and if the punishment by imprisonment for a term of twenty years or a more severe punishment is imposed – then in proceedings upon extraordinary judicial remedies as well [...].[79]

- The law of the **former Socialist Federal Republic of Yugoslavia**[80] and the laws of the other successor States[81] on the territory of the former Yugoslavia contain similar provisions. **[page 17]**

---

78 Italics added for emphasis.

79 Italics added for emphasis.

80 Criminal Procedure Code of the **Federal Socialist Republic of Yugoslavia,** Article 70 (1): If the accused is [...] incapable of effectively defending himself, or if proceedings are being conducted for a crime for which the death penalty may be pronounced, the accused must have defence counsel from the first examination. [...] (4) If in the cases of mandatory defence referred to in the previous cases the accused does not himself engage defence counsel, the president of the court shall automatically appoint counsel for his defence. [...]

81 Code of Criminal Procedure of **Croatia:** *Article 65* (1) If the defendant [...] unable successfully to defend himself or if the proceedings are carried out for an offence punishable by long-term imprisonment, the defendant must have a defence counsel even at his first interrogation. [...] (5) When in the case of mandatory defence referred to in paragraph 1, 2, 3, and 4 of this Article the defendant fails to retain a defence counsel, the president of the court shall, by virtue of the office, appoint a defence counsel to represent him in further criminal proceedings; up until the judgement becomes final, and if the punishment by imprisonment for a term of twenty years is imposed then in proceedings upon extraordinary judicial remedies as well. [...]

Code of Criminal Procedure of the **Former Yugoslav Republic of Macedonia**: *Article 66*: (1) If the Accused is [...] incapable to defend himself successfully or if a criminal procedure is conducted against him for a crime for which, according to the Code a sentence to life imprisonment is proscribed, then he must have a counsel during his first hearing. (5) If the accused in cases of obligatory defence according to the previous paragraphs of this Article does not provide a counsel for himself, the President of the court will assign a counsel ex officio for the further duration of the criminal procedure until the final legally valid verdict. [...]

Code of Criminal Procedure of **Montenegro:** *Article 69*: (1) If the defendant is [...] unable to defend himself successfully or if the proceedings are conducted for a criminal offence punishable by the maximum term of imprisonment, the defendant must have a defence attorney as early as his first interrogation. (2) When the indictment is brought for the criminal offence punishable by imprisonment of ten years, the defendant must have a defence attorney when the indictment is served on him. [...] (5) When in the case of mandatory defence referred to in the preceding paragraphs of this Article the defendant fails to retain a defence attorney by himself, the President of the Court shall, by virtue of an office, appoint a defence attorney to represent the defendant in the further criminal proceedings up until the judgement becomes final [...] If in the case of mandatory defence, the defendant is left without a defence attorney, the President of the Court before which the proceedings are being conducted shall appoint by virtue of an office a defence attorney to the defendant. [...]

Code of Criminal Procedure of **Slovenia**: *Article 70*: (1) If the accused is [...] incapable of defending himself successfully, or if criminal proceedings are conducted against the accused for a criminal offence punishable by twenty years of imprisonment, the accused shall have defence counsel from the very first interrogation. [...] (4) If in the cases of mandatory defence referred to in the

41. Likewise, the codes of criminal procedure and the respective jurisprudence of other civil law countries restrict the right to self-representation, especially on appeal. To give only a few examples:

42. The Criminal Procedure Code of **Argentina**[82] reads:

Article 104

An accused has the right to be represented by a registered lawyer of his choice or by a public defence counsel; an accused may also represent himself when to do so does not prejudice the effectiveness of the defence and does not interfere with the ordinary course of the proceedings. In this case the Court will order him to elect counsel **within three days**, failing which he will be assigned the public defence counsel *ex officio.*[83]

43. The Code of Criminal Procedure of **Austria** reads:

Section 41

(1) Defence counsel is mandatory in the following cases (mandatory defence counsel): [...] 4. to carry out the plea of nullity and for the public hearing of it or of an appeal against a judgement of the court of assize [...].[84]

44. The *Code d'Instruction Criminelle* of **Belgium** reads:

Section 293

Au moins quinze jours avant l'ouverture de la session et au plus tard le jour de la première audience, le président vérifiera si l'accusé a fait choix d'un conseil pour l'aider dans sa défense. Sinon le président lui en désignera un sur-le-champ, à peine de nullité de tout ce qui suivra.

Cette désignation sera considérée comme non avenue, et la nullité ne sera pas prononcée si l'accusé choisit un conseil.

Le président pourra interroger l'accusé. Dans ce cas, l'interrogatoire est constaté par un procès-verbal que signent le président, le greffier, l'accusé et s'il y a lieu, l'interprète.

45. The Penal Procedure Code of **Bulgaria** reads:

Article 70

(1) Participation of the defence counsel or the defender in the penal proceedings shall be mandatory in cases where: [...] (3.) the case refers to crime for which the punishment provided is life imprisonment or deprivation of liberty not less than ten years; [...] **[page 18]**

(3) Where the participation of defence counsel is mandatory, the respective authority shall be obliged to appoint as defence counsel a person practising the legal profession. [...]

46. The Bill to Institute the Criminal Procedure Code of **Cameroon** reads:

Section 490

Where an appellant sentenced to life imprisonment or to death has not briefed counsel, the President of the Supreme Court shall of his own motion, assign one to him as soon as the application for appeal is received in the registry of the said court.[85]

---

preceding paragraphs the accused fails to retain defence counsel by himself, the president of the court shall appoint defence counsel ex officio for the further course of criminal proceedings until the finality of the judgement: if the accused has been sentenced to twenty years in prison he shall have defence counsel appointed for him for the extraordinary judicial review as well. [...].

82 A similar provision can be found in Articles 80 and 83 of the Criminal Procedural Code of Costa Rica.

83 Unofficial courtesy translation. Italics added for emphasis.

84 Unofficial courtesy translation.

85 As cited in Book of Authorities for the Prosecution Submission in Relation to the Right to Self-Representation and the Role of Amicus Curiae in Appellate Proceedings, 3 April 2007, IV 34.

47. In **Denmark**, Section 731 of the Law on Criminal Procedure describes a number of situations where a suspect/an accused must have counsel.[86]

48. The *Code de Procédure Pénale* of **France** reads:

Article 274

L'accusé est ensuite invité à choisir un avocat pour l'assister dans sa défense.

Si l'accusé ne choisit pas son avocat, le président ou son délégué lui en désigne un d'office.

Cette désignation est non avenue si, par la suite, l'accusé choisit un avocat.

Article 317

A l'audience, la présence d'un défenseur auprès de l'accusé est obligatoire.

Si le défenseur choisi ou désigné conformément à l'article 274 ne se présente pas, le président en commet un d'office.

Article 380-1

Les arrêts de condamnation rendus par la cour d'assises en premier ressort peuvent faire l'objet d'un appel dans les conditions prévues par le présent chapitre.

Cet appel est porté devant une autre cour d'assises désignée par la chambre criminelle de la Cour de cassation et qui procède au réexamen de l'affaire selon les modalités et dans les conditions prévues par les chapitres II à VII du présent titre.

Article 576

La déclaration de pourvoi doit être faite au greffier de la juridiction qui a rendu la décision attaquée.

Elle doit être signée par le greffier et par le demandeur en cassation lui-même ou par un avoué près la juridiction qui a statué, ou par un fondé de pouvoir spécial; dans ce dernier cas, le pouvoir est annexé à l'acte dressé par le greffier. Si le déclarant ne peut signer, le greffier en fera mention.

Elle est inscrite sur un registre public, à ce destiné et toute personne a le droit de s'en faire délivrer une copie. **[page 19]**

Article 584

Le demandeur en cassation, soit en faisant sa déclaration, soit dans les dix jours suivants, peut déposer, au greffe de la juridiction qui a rendu la décision attaquée, un mémoire, signé par lui, contenant ses moyens de cassation. Le greffier lui en délivre reçu.

49. **Germany**'s Code of Criminal Procedure reads:

Section 140

(1) The assistance of defence counsel shall be mandatory if [...]: 2. the accused is charged with a serious criminal offence;

(2) In other cases the presiding judge shall appoint defence counsel upon application or *ex officio* if the assistance of defence counsel appears necessary because of the seriousness of the offence, or because of the difficult factual or legal situation, or if it is evident that the accused cannot defend himself, particularly where an attorney-at-law has been assigned to the aggrieved person pursuant to Sections 397a and 406g subsections [...].

---

86 *See* Lars Bo Langsted et al., Criminal Law in Denmark 128 (1998).

Section 345

(1) Notices of appeal together with the grounds therefore shall be submitted to the court whose judgment is being contested no later than one month after expiry of the time limit for seeking the appellate remedy. If the judgment has not been served by then, the time limit shall commence upon service thereof.

(2) The defendant may *only* act in the form of a notice signed by defence counsel or by an attorney-at-law, or to be recorded by the court registry.[87]

50. In general, the question of whether a defence counsel has to be assigned on appeal is determined pursuant to section 140(2) of the Code of Criminal Procedure. Additionally, according to settled jurisprudence this is always necessary in cases where there is a possibility that the court of appeal could increase the sentence of the court of first instance. Otherwise, not assigning a defence counsel would ultimately lead to a breach of the right to a fair trial.[88]

51. Under German law, even in cases where the rules of mandatory defence counsel do not apply, it is still required to file the leading documents for appellate proceedings with the help of legal assistance. Thus, these regulations show that the legislator has recognized the difficulty of filing a legally valid Notice of Appeal or Appeal Brief by requiring legal assistance, regardless of whether or not the conditions for mandatory defence counsel are met.

52. The Code of Criminal Procedure of **Italy** reads:

Section 97 [page 20]

An accused who has not designated Counsel of his own choosing or has no access to such a Counsel shall be assisted by *ex officio* defence counsel.[89]

53. The Code of Criminal Procedure of **The Netherlands** reads:

Article 437(2)

The accused, who or on whose behalf an appeal has been lodged, is obliged at the sanction of inadmissibility, to file with the *Hoge Raad*[90] within two months after the notification pursuant to Article 435(1) a written submission through his counsel stating the reasons for the appeal.[91]

54. The *Code de Procédure Pénale* of **Senegal** reads:

Article 257

L'accusé est ensuite invité à choisir un conseil pour l'assister dans sa défense.

Si l'accusé ne choisit pas son conseil, le président ou son délégué lui en désigné un d'office.

Cette désignation est non avenue, si par la suite, l'accusé choisit un conseil.

55. Summarizing these national approaches one can state that, in any event on appeal the principle of fair proceedings calls for, warrants, or sometimes even demands assignment of counsel either when a serious sanction is at stake and/or when the case at hand is factually and/or legally extraordinarily difficult. On appeal

---

87 Unofficial courtesy translation.

88 Bundesverfassungsgericht [BVerfG] [Federal Constitutional Court] 19 October 1977, 46 Entscheidungen des Bundesverfassungsgerichts [BVerfGE] 202, paras. 32–33; Oberlandesgericht Düsseldorf [OLG Düsseldorf] [Court of Appeals Düsseldorf] 9 September 1983, 4 Neue Zeitschrift für Strafrecht [NStZ] 44–46 (1984); Heinrich Laufhütte, *§ 140, in* KARLSRUHER KOMMENTAR ZUR STRAFPROZESSORDNUNG, § 140, marginal number 6 (Gerhard Pfeifer, ed., 5th ed. 2003).

89 Unofficial courtesy translation.

90 The *Hoge Raad* is the highest court in criminal matters in The Netherlands.

91 Unofficial courtesy translation.

there is an almost unanimous approach[92] that, because of the inherent difficulties of appellate proceedings before a higher court, an appellant cannot refuse the assistance of counsel as this would amount to a waiver of a fair trial. Furthermore, some regulations clearly show that the assignment of mandatory defence counsel does not exclude an active role of an accused.

(iii) Law and Jurisprudence of International Tribunals and Courts

56. The legal provisions of international courts and the decisions rendered by them addressing the issue of self-representation must also be considered:

57. Article 20(4)(d) of the Statute of the **International Criminal Tribunal for Rwanda** (ICTR) has the same wording as Article 21(4)(d) of the Statute of the ICTY. When faced with a **[page 21]** request by assigned counsel to withdraw in light of the accused's non-cooperation, Trial Chamber I of the ICTR held that

> [...] Counsel is assigned, not appointed. In the view of the Chamber, this does not only entail obligations towards the client, but also implies that he represents the interest of the Tribunal to ensure that the Accused receives a fair trial. The aim is to obtain efficient representation and adversarial proceedings.[93]

In *Prosecutor v. Nyiramasuhuko and Ntahobali*, the Trial Chamber recognized in relation to trial proceedings an accused's "right, pursuant to Rule 45(F) and Article 20 of the Statute, to conduct his own defence."[94] The Chamber explained, however, that:

> Nonetheless, the Chamber has duly considered the seriousness of the charges pending against the Accused who is currently being tried and has taken note of the Prosecution's arguments as to the Accused directly cross-examining witnesses. In light of these factors, and by virtue of its inherent powers to control its own proceedings, the Chamber decides *proprio motu* that it is in the interest of justice that a Duty Counsel be immediately appointed so as to ensure that the Accused is assisted in the conduct of his defence [...].[95]

58. Significantly, in 2002, the ICTR Rules of Procedure and Evidence were amended by consensus with Rule 45*quater* ("Assignment of Counsel in the Interests of Justice"), which reads as follows:

> The Trial Chamber may, if it decides that it is in the interests of justice, instruct the Registrar to assign a counsel to represent the interests of the accused.

Rule 45*quater* is also applicable to the ICTR's appeal proceedings.[96] Moreover, the Rules of Procedure and Evidence of the ICTR were adopted pursuant to Article 14 of the ICTR Statute. It is clear that the Judges of the ICTR, who are authorized pursuant to Article 14 of its Statute and Rule 6 of its Rules of Procedure and Evidence to adopt and to amend the Rules, did not view Rule 45*quater* as being in conflict with Article 20(4)(d) of its Statute. In sum, the jurisprudence of the ICTR and the existence of Rule 45*quater* illustrate that the right given to an accused in Article 20(4)(d) of the ICTR's Statute is not unrestricted, and that, indeed, at any stage of the proceedings, including appeals, counsel may be assigned to an accused if it is in the interests of justice to do so.

---

92 Out of more than twenty countries randomly analyzed, a large number have come to accept mandatory defence counsel, both on trial but at least on appeal. In particular, a number of countries, *inter alia,* Austria, Germany, The Netherlands, and the United States, draw a clear or further distinction between the trial and the appeals stage when determining whether counsel must be assigned.

93 *Prosecutor v. Jean-Bosco Barayagwiza,* Case No. ICTR-97-19-T, Decision on Defence Counsel Motion to Withdraw, 2 November 2000, para. 21.

94 *Prosecutor v. Pauline Nyiramasuhuko and Arsène Ntahobali,* Case No. ICTR-97-21-T, Decision on Ntahobali's Motion for Withdrawal of Counsel, 22 June 2001, para. 19.

95 *Id.* at para. 20.

96 Rule 107 of the ICTR Rules of Procedure and Evidence specifies that the Rules that "govern proceedings in the Trial Chambers shall apply *mutatis mutandis* to proceedings in the Appeals Chamber."

59. The Statute of the **Special Court for Sierra Leone**[97] in Article 17(4)(d) also contains the same wording as Article 21(4)(d) of the Statute of the ICTY. In *Prosecutor v. Sam Hinga Norman* **[page 22]** *et al.*,[98] a Trial Chamber of the Court held that in the context of trial proceedings the right to self-representation is "qualified and not absolute."[99] It stressed that

> [t]he philosophy of the Chamber on this crucial issue compels us to factor into the equation, certain critical issues namely: (i) that the right of counsel which is statutorily guaranteed by Article 17(4)(d) of our Statute is predicated upon the notion that representation by Counsel is an essential and necessary component of a fair trial. (ii) The right to counsel relieves trial Judges of the burden to explain and enforce basic rules of courtroom protocol and to assist the accused in overcoming routine and regular legal obstacles which the accused may encounter if he represents himself, for, the Court, to our mind, is supposed, in the adversarial context, to remain the arbiter and not a pro-active participant in the proceedings. (iii) Given the complexity of the trial in the present case, it cannot be denied that a joint trial of such magnitude, having regard to the gravity of the offences charged, and considering the number of witnesses to be called by the Prosecution and the Defence, make for a trial fraught with a high potential of complexities and intricacies typical of evolving international criminal law. (iv) There is also the public interest, national and international, in the expeditious completion of the trial. (v) Furthermore, there is the high potential for further disruption to the Court's timetable and calendar which we are already witnessing in this case. [...] (vi) The tension between giving effect to the 1st Accused's right to self representation and that of his co-accused, to a fair and expeditious trial as required by law.[100]

The Chamber further stated that all these factors were to be "taken into consideration and weighed individually and cumulatively."[101] The decision was not appealed and the Chamber later assigned standby-counsel to "provide legal assistance to the Accused and [to] ensure the safeguard to his right to a fair and expeditious trial."[102]

60. In conclusion, the Special Court for Sierra Leone has also allowed for a limitation of the right to self-representation; in particular by assessing the complexity of the proceedings, their expeditiousness and the right to a fair trial.

61. Article 67(l)(d) of the Rome Statute for an **International Criminal Court** (ICC)[103] provides an accused with the right

> [...] to conduct the defense in person or through legal assistance of the accused's choosing, to be informed, if the accused does not have legal assistance or the accused's choosing, of this right *and to have legal assistance assigned by the Court in any case where the interests of justice so require*, and without payment if the accused lacks sufficient means to pay for it.[104]

The ICC's Regulations, adopted by the judges of the court pursuant to Article 52 of its Statute, provide in Regulation 76(1) a norm that allows for the appointment of defence counsel by a Chamber of the court: **[page 23]**

> A Chamber, following consultation with the Registrar, may appoint counsel in the circumstances specified in the Statute and the Rules or where the interests of justice so require.

62. Again, this overview shows that the general test is whether or not in an individual case the interests of fair proceedings require the legal assistance by court assigned counsel.

---

97 2178 U.N.T.S. 138.

98 *Prosecutor v. Sam Hinga Norman et al.,* SCSL-04-14-T, Decision on the Application of Samuel Hinga Norman for Self Representation under Art. 17(4)(d) of the Statute of the Special Court, 8 June 2004.

99 *Id.* at para 27.

100 *Id.* at para 26.

101 *Id.* at para. 27.

102 *Prosecutor v. Sam Hinga Norman et al.,* SCSL-04-14-T, Consequential Order on Assignment and Role of Standby Counsel, 14 June 2004, p. 3, cited by Boas, *supra* note 9, at 60.

103 2187 U.N.T.S. 90.

104 Italics added for emphasis.

(c) Comparative Analysis – Conclusion

63. The analysis of transnational/supranational law and jurisprudence, national law and jurisprudence and the law and jurisprudence of other international criminal tribunals and courts shows that in appellate proceedings it is not only the behaviour of an accused as such that justifies a restriction of the right to self-representation but the nature of those proceedings. The different role of an accused at the appellate level allows for a greater restriction of the right to self-representation than may be justified at trial.

2. Application of these Parameters to the Case at Hand

64. Having found guidance from sources of transnational/supranational and national law and, in particular, jurisprudence, I will now turn to apply the principles found therein to the specific case before this Appeals Chamber.

65. Let me note in passing that even though I do not agree with the Appeals Chamber's stance that disallows self-representation at the trial stage only when there is obstructive behaviour by an accused, it is clear that the Appellant in this case has indeed been obstructive. Although he first indicated that the wanted counsel[105] he did not make a *bona fide* effort to actually obtain it.[106] It has to be recalled that for several months after the rendering of the Trial Judgement,[107] the Appellant stalled in finding a defence counsel even though he was provided with the International Tribunal's list of counsel prepared and willing to appear before the Tribunal. Specifically, the Appellant only proposed counsel who were unwilling and/or unable to represent him for the purposes of his appeal. I note that in the system before the International Tribunal it is for the Registrar to assign counsel. Despite of all the efforts of the Registry, the Appellant did not select a counsel from the list presented to him. It has to be noted that an appellant can be reasonably expected to select counsel within three days or one week. In this case, the Appellant had ample time – from September 2006 up to the present – to select counsel. Furthermore, it was only after a considerable delay of more than two and half months from the rendering of the Trial Judgement that the Appellant for the first **[page 24]** time indicated that he wanted to represent himself on appeal, however with the assistance of a "legal team."[108]

66. Returning to the legal question at stake, the point of departure for any assessment of the right to self-representation on appeal must be the fundamental requirement, enshrined in Article 21(2) of the Statute, that an accused shall be entitled to a "fair and public hearing."

67. It follows that Article 21(4)(d), stating that an accused has a right to defend himself in person, must be interpreted in the overall context of the fair trial requirement of the Statute and cannot be viewed in isolation from other rights and guarantees ensuring the fairness of proceedings.[109] Indeed, the fairness and expeditiousness of appeal proceedings cannot be seen in a legal vacuum and directly benefits an appellant.

68. The right to self-representation at the appellate level must be seen against the backdrop of the nature of the appellate proceedings. Conversely, the general principle of fairness depends on how the specific minimum guarantees afforded to an accused – among them the right to self-representation and the right to be assisted by counsel – are observed. This interdependency can be viewed as a form of reciprocal interaction whose components must be delicately balanced. In that regard, I would refer to the Appeals Chamber's decision in *Prosecutor v. Milošević*, which considered that restrictions of that right at trial "must be limited to the minimum extent necessary to protect the Tribunal's interest in assuring a reasonably expeditious trial."[110] The same line of reasoning applies to the fairness of the proceedings at

---

105 *See* Request to Extend the Deadline for Filing an Appeal Against the Judgement, 17 October 2006.

106 *See* Registrar's Submission on Counsel's Request for Review of the Registrar's Decisions on Assignment of Counsel, 16 January 2007, paras. 2–27.

107 *Prosecutor v. Momčilo Krajišnik,* Case No. IT-00-39-T, Judgement, 27 September 2006 ("Trial Judgement").

108 *See* Krajišnik Response to the Prosecution's Appeal Brief Against the Judgement of 27 September 2006, 12 February 2007 (filed 20 February 2007), p. 1.

109 *See Evrenos Önen v. Turkey,* ECtHR, App. No. 29782/02, 15 February 2007, para. 29: "The Court considers that, in the instant case, it is more appropriate to deal with the applicant's complaints under Article 6(1) globally due to the overlapping nature of the issues and since the sub-paragraphs of Article 6(3) may be regarded as specific aspects of the general fairness guarantee of the first paragraph."

110 *Milošević* Decision, *supra* note 7, para. 17.

the appellate level. The expeditiousness and fairness of the proceedings are intertwined. Therefore, when deciding whether the right to self-representation can be limited or qualified in appellate proceedings, it must be assessed whether such a step would benefit an appellant by ensuring his fundamental right to be the subject, not the object, of a fair and expeditious appeals process. An accused cannot waive his right to fair proceedings, under whatever circumstances.[111]

69. That said, I am aware of the importance of a correct assessment of the relationship between the general right to fair appeal proceedings and the right to self-representation. Again I refer to the **[page 25]** *Milošević* Decision's recognition of the general principle of proportionality[112] as being useful when determining whether and to what extent the restriction of one right is required to safeguard the important objective of another, potentially conflicting, right. Indeed, the application of this principle is also called for in the context of this decision. This means that if there is a balancing of potentially conflicting rights of an accused, the restriction of one right to the advantage of another right is contingent on three factors: it must be suitable, it must be necessary, and the degree and scope of the restriction must remain in a reasonable relationship to the preference given to the other right.

70. Consequently, in this case it must be assessed whether and to what extent the Appellant's wish to represent himself at this stage of the case against him affects the general fairness of the proceedings and vice versa. In light of the nature of appellate proceedings I am convinced that there are circumstances other than obstructive behaviour by an appellant that allow for the assignment of counsel, if need be even against the will of an appellant in his well-understood own interests. It is clear that there is a difference between pre-trial and trial proceedings on the one hand and the appeals stage on the other. Indeed, the difference is nothing less than dramatic:[113] The Appellant has already been convicted by the Trial Chamber for five counts of crimes against humanity and sentenced to 27 years of imprisonment. According to the Trial Judgement, the "trial record contains a vast amount of evidence", with presentation of evidence lasting for more than two years and more than 27,000 pages of transcript. The burden is now on the Appellant to consider this entire material, make a meaningful and legally sound assessment of its contents in relation to the reasoning of the Trial Judgement, point with specificity to purported errors of fact and errors of law by the Trial Chamber, formulate such allegations of error in a comprehensive and precise manner, and, at the same time, respond to the appeal by the Prosecution. It is difficult to envisage how the Appellant could muster the significant legal resources necessary to successfully exercise his right to have the Trial Judgement reviewed and – in the case of errors – revised or reversed. Indeed, the Appellant has on several occasions pointed out that he is not able to present his appeal without the assistance of professional counsel. The following exchange in the recent Status Conference is just one example:

> The Appellant: "At the moment there are certain items for which we would have to engage two Defence lawyers who would analyse, in professional terms, the appeal. *I cannot do this myself* [...]."
>
> Judge Schomburg: "So it is your submission that you can't exercise your defence yourself? Am I correct in reading this on the transcript?" **[page 26]**
>
> The Appellant: "[...] I am convinced that I can defend myself in a more professional way than the team that I currently have could do, but *I believe that the appeal procedure is specific and I would need counsel's assistance to deal with this appeals procedure.* So when I'm defending myself, *I would like to have a very experienced lawyer as a member of the Defence team.*"[114]

71. In this context it should also be recalled that it is for an appellant to *inter alia* provide precise references to relevant pages of transcript or paragraphs in the judgement to which challenge is made.[115] The

111 *See also Prosecutor v. Issa Hassan Sesay et al.*, Case No. SCSL-04-15-AR73, Gbao – Decision on Appeal Against Decision on Withdrawal of Counsel, 23 November 2004, para. 46, quoting the Trial Chamber Decision.

112 *Milošević* Decision, *supra* note 7, paras 17–18.

113 *See Martinez v. Court of Appeal of California*, 528 U.S. 152, 162 (2000); *see further* Judge Reinhardt's Concurring Opinion, *supra* at para. 31.

114 Transcript, p. 32 (26 March 2007), italics added for emphasis.

115 *See Prosecutor v. Stanislav Galić*, Case No. IT-98-29-A, Judgement, 30 November 2006, para. 11.

Appeals Chamber's jurisprudence is moreover abundantly clear that when an appellant's submissions are obscure, contradictory, vague, or suffer from other formal and obvious insufficiencies, the Appeals Chamber will not consider those submissions.[116] The Practice Directions on Formal Requirements for Appeals from Judgement,[117] the Practice Direction on Procedure for the Filing of Written Submissions in Appeal Proceedings before the International Tribunal,[118] and the Practice Directions on the Length of Briefs and Motions[119] illustrate the complicated nature of appellate proceedings before the International Tribunal and highlight that formal requirements are not easily met. Sometimes even trained lawyers cannot effortlessly navigate the proceedings on appeal. Much less so could the Appellant, to his own detriment.

72. Aside from the complex formalities of appellate proceedings, it must be further taken into consideration that the substantive case-law of the International Tribunal is extensive and legally sophisticated. The Appellant's convictions for persecution, extermination, murder, deportation and inhumane acts, as crimes against humanity pursuant to Article 5 of the Statute, relate to a time period of 18 months,[120] and he was found to have committed these crimes as a member of a joint criminal enterprise,[121] a legal concept unknown in his home country. The heavy burden to have these findings overturned now rests solely on the Appellant's shoulders. Consequently, the complexity of the proceedings, for instance the proper filing of a motion for additional evidence pursuant to Rule 115 of the Rules, renders the appeal proceedings unfair if he is left to his own devices – even when he so wishes. Already a comparison of the two Notices of Appeal submitted by the Appellant and by properly assigned counsel clearly shows the advantage of having the assistance of a professional lawyer acting in public appellate proceedings. For the Appeals Chamber to rely solely on the Appellant's own Notice of Appeal would render the proceedings unfair.

73. In conclusion, even though I am not in agreement with the prior jurisprudence of the Appeals Chamber, which gives precedence to an accused's right to self-representation during trial **[page 27]** over his right to a fair trial, on top of that there is a fundamental difference between trial and appeals proceedings. While during trial an accused has ample occasion to rebut the evidence against him, his role is by its nature far more challenging during the appeals proceedings as he has already been convicted by the Trial Chamber and it is now up to him to contest the findings and holdings of the impugned judgement.

74. A related consideration pertains to the expeditious disposal of the Appellant's appeal. As noted previously, expeditiousness has to be seen as a twin to the concept of fairness in criminal proceedings. Even if all other concerns were disregarded, it can hardly be ignored that the Appellant's self-representation would lead to significant delays in appeal proceedings. It is evident that the swiftness of the judicial process before the International Tribunal is in direct correlation with the rights of the Appellant. Of particular concern in this context, disregarded and mitigated by nothing in the decision of the Appeals Chamber, are the foreseeable translation delays. The Appellant apparently does not speak either of the official working languages of the International Tribunal well enough to enable him to participate, which is highly problematic in light of the primarily document-driven procedure before the Appeals Chamber. All filings by the Appellant will have to be translated into at least one of the official working languages of the International Tribunal. Likewise, all filings by the Prosecution and decisions of the Chamber will have to be translated into B/C/S. Even assuming that the translation requirements of this case are given priority, it is clear that appeal proceedings will fall victim to constant hold-ups. A conservative estimate of the translation delays shows that with this decision briefing will be completed at the earliest in December 2007. However, it would be more realistic to assume that all briefs will be before the Appeals Chamber only in 2008, making the preparation of an appeal hearing possible at the earliest in the spring if not summer of 2008. Given the length of the time spent in detention by the Appellant, the need for a prompt hearing and decision on the pending appeals carries extraordinary weight, the timely hearing of a case being part of the sound administration of justice.[122]

---

116 *Id.*

117 IT/201, 7 March 2002.

118 IT/155/Rev. 3, 16 September 2005.

119 IT/184/Rev. 2, 16 September 2005.

120 Trial Judgement, para. 5.

121 *Id.*, para. 1078.

122 *See Foti et al. v. Italy*, EComHR, Opinion, 15 October 1980, para. 97 (unpublished), printed in 2 COUNCIL OF EUROPE, *supra* note 35, at 505.

C. Remarks in Relation to the Decision's Disposition

75. In sum, it is predictable that there will be a significant disruption of the appeal proceedings in this case if the Appellant is allowed to represent himself without the assistance of defence counsel, endangering the integrity of the proceedings, rendering them fundamentally unfair from the outset and in all likelihood provoking a miscarriage of justice. It is obvious that under such **[page 28]** circumstances the Appellant will be deprived of his right to fair proceedings if he were allowed to represent himself.

76. Indeed, the disposition of the decision supported by the majority shows several major flaws:

1. No Guidelines for Modalities of Self-Representation

77. The decision grants the Appellant's request to be allowed to represent himself and orders the Registrar "to take the necessary steps." However, it fails to stipulate what these "necessary steps" mean. While I recognize that the modalities of counsel-related issues lie within the purview of the Registrar, the Appeals Chamber should have given clear guidelines to the Registrar on how to proceed. This is particularly true in light of the Appellant's statements that he intends to hire outside lawyers, who are not on the International Tribunal's Rule 45 list of counsel and will not be acting in public, to help him in the preparation of his appeal.[123]

78. Indeed, Mr. Brašić, one of the lawyers that the Appellant tried to hire[124] was recently fined and reprimanded for violating the Code of Professional Conduct for Counsel Appearing before the International Tribunal.[125] The decision neglects to establish how, for instance, the Appellant will be permitted to communicate with outside lawyers or non-lawyers. This raises the concern that the Appellant will be allowed to have unsupervised communications with individuals about whom the International Tribunal has no knowledge, thereby circumventing the strict requirements of Rules 44 and 45 of the Rules, which exist to ensure that only legal professionals of integrity are allowed to practice before the Tribunal. It is particularly worrisome in relation to potential access to confidential material, including the identities of protected witnesses, when the Appeals Chamber fails to address the Appellant's openly expressed wish to employ a defence team working behind the scenes, unknown to the Appeals Chamber and without any ethical obligations. The question arises whether this concept of undercover counsel is reconcilable with the fundamental principle of a public hearing. **[page 29]**

2. The Appointment of an *Amicus Curiae*

79. Before considering the fact that appointing an *amicus curiae* does not adequately address the fundamental problems arising from a situation where an accused wishes to be self-represented on appeal, I draw attention to the fact that the decision is not founded on any legal basis in this regard. I note that in the *Milošević* case, the *amici curiae* were initially appointed during the trial,[126] but that this, as can be clearly stated in hindsight, had adverse consequences for the trial. Indeed, in that case, the decision to appoint the *amici curiae* was never appealed, thus, the Appeals Chamber is not bound by any prior jurisprudence.

80. The wording of Rule 74 of the Rules is clear in that it is applicable in situations where the court might find it useful to hear from a State, organization or individual about "any issue specified by the Chamber." In general, this means that an *amicus curiae* shall assist the court only in relation to specific issues, usually

---

123 *See, e.g.*, Transcript, p. 73 *et seq.* (5 April 2007).

124 *See* Letter of the Appellant to the Pre-Appeal Judge, 2 April 2007 (filed 5 April 2007) and Transcript, p. 75–76 (5 April 2007). In his Letter to the Appeals Chamber, 7 May 2007 (filed 10 May 2007), the Appellant again emphasized "that Mr Brašić had agreed to work on the appeal *pro bono*. The only obligation [the Appellant] would have was to cover the costs of his stay in The Hague. [...] I would ask [the Appeals Chamber] [...] to enable me to finance my defence myself and involve Mr Brašić, Karganović and others in work on the appeal [...]" (emphasis in the original).

125 *See* Decision in the Appeal by the Disciplinary Board in the Matter of Mr. Deyan Ranko Brashich, Attorney at Law From the United States, Case No. IT-00-39-A, 22 March 2007. I also note the fact that Mr. Brašić's assignment as defence counsel in the *Krajišnik* case was withdrawn by the Registry on 2 May 2003. This decision was based on the fact that Mr. Brašić had been suspended from the practice of law in the United States for one year. As a result of the withdrawal, the start of the *Krajišnik* trial was delayed for more than nine months, not to mention the substantial costs. *See* Trial Judgement, paras 1226 and 1235.

126 *Prosecutor v. Milošević*, Case No. IT-01-51-PT, Order Inviting Designation of *Amicus Curiae*, 23 November 2001.

on points of law. It is thus obvious that the rule was not meant to introduce a third party to the courtroom. However, this is exactly what the decision does: the *amicus curiae* is supposed to "make submissions to the Appeals Chamber similar to those which a party would make (including a notice of appeal, appeal brief, response brief, and reply brief) [...]."[127] The artificial construct of an *amicus curiae* acting as *de facto* counsel must inevitably lead to a conflict of interest in the mind of any lawyer appointed as an *amicus curiae* who takes his role seriously.[128]

81. Furthermore, even disregarding the fact that the International Tribunal's Statute and Rules do not have a provision explicitly allowing for such an appointment instead of the assignment of Counsel, it begs the question of how the *amicus curiae* could do anything to mitigate the negative effects of the Appellant's self-representation. Moreover, as was acknowledged even by then assigned counsel during a recent Status Conference, the *amicus curiae* could indeed make submissions that run contrary to the Appellant's best interests or defence tactics.[129] Therefore, considering again what is at stake for the Appellant following his conviction by the Trial Chamber, it must be concluded, as explained in detail above, that in appeal proceedings before the **[page 30]** International Tribunal only defence counsel, working solely in the interests of the Appellant, can guarantee that the Appellant's right to fair and expeditious proceedings is fully respected.

3. Competing Briefs

82. The decision orders both the Appellant and the *amicus curiae*, once appointed, to file each their own appeal brief. It also allows for the dual filings of the notices of appeal and response briefs to the Prosecution appeal.[130] Once again, it is not clear how the *amicus curiae* could assist the court by filing his own appeal brief. Moreover, the decision does not clarify what happens in the event there is a conflict between the appeal brief filed by the Appellant and the one filed by *amicus curiae* or why the Chamber should accept grounds of appeal that were explicitly not raised or even rejected by the Appellant. Indeed, the majority wants to have it both ways – on the one hand it allows the Appellant to represent himself, on the other, it seeks the involvement of a professional lawyer, acting, however, not as a friend of the Appellant, but as a friend of the court. With all due respect, these two conflicting desiderata cannot be reconciled: the ensuing melee is a recipe for disaster.

127 Decision, para. 21.

128 *See* the statement by Mr. Nicholls, at that time assigned counsel, during a recent Status Conference, Transcript, p. 53 (26 March 2007): MR. NICHOLLS: Well, the function of an amicus curiae is normally to assist the Court, not to take instructions from the client but to read, listen to the arguments advanced by others and to put forward such arguments as the amicus considers are appropriate. Those arguments may be on the – in the interests of the client or may be against the interests of the client. That is the normal position of an amicus curiae. JUDGE SCHOMBURG: So you would submit that it might even happen that you, acting as an amicus curiae, would have to act when exercising your work conscientiously, also to act against the interests of Mr. Krajišnik? MR. NICHOLLS: As amicus curiae, yes. As Defence counsel, of course, totally different situation. [...]

129 *Id.*

130 In passing I note that the effect of an *amicus curiae* making submissions – even though only up to two thirds the length of those by the Appellant and the Prosecution – will be that further delays in the appeal proceedings can safely be expected.

D. Conclusion

83. When it conflicts with the overarching right to a fair, public and expeditious trial, the right to self-representation must yield. I firmly believe that a waiver of the right to a fair trial is not possible under any circumstances. I must therefore respectfully come to the conclusion that the decision supported by majority has no basis in law and from the outset renders these appellate proceedings before us unfair. Furthermore, I doubt that the disposition as it stands now can serve as a sound basis for the appeal proceedings in this case.

For these reasons, with all due respect, I fundamentally dissent from the decision of the Appeals Chamber.

Done in English and French, the English text being authoritative.

Dated this 11th day of May 2007,
At The Hague, The Netherlands.

Judge Wolfgang Schomburge

[Seal of the International Tribunal]

UNITED NATIONS

International Tribunal for the Prosecution of Persons Responsible for Serious Violations of International Humanitarian Law Committed in the Territory of the Former Yugoslavia since 1991	Case No.	IT-06-90-AR73.2
	Date:	29 June 2007
	Original:	English

IN THE APPEALS CHAMBER

Before: **Judge Andrésia Vaz, Presiding**
Judge Mohamed Shahabuddeen
Judge Liu Daqun
Judge Theodor Meron
Judge Wolfgang Schomburg

Registrar: **Mr. Hans Hothuis**

Decision : **29 June 2007**

PROSECUTOR

v.

ANTE GOTOVINA
IVAN ČERMAK
MLADEN MARKAČ

PUBLIC

DECISION ON IVAN ČERMAK'S INTERLOCUTORY APPEAL AGAINST TRIAL CHAMBER'S DECISION ON CONFLICT OF INTEREST OF ATTORNEYS ČEDO PRODANOVIĆ AND JADRANKA SLOKOVIĆ

Office of the Prosecutor
Mr. Alan Tieger
Ms. Laurie Sartorio

Counsel for Ante Gotovina
Mr. Luka Mišetić
Mr. Gregory Kehoe
Mr. Payam Akhavan

Counsel for Ivan Čermak
Mr. Cedo Prodanović
Ms. Jadranka Sloković

Counsel for Mladen Markač
Mr. Goran Mikuličić

[page 1] 1. The Appeals Chamber of the International Criminal Tribunal for the Prosecution of Persons Responsible for Serious Violations of International Humanitarian Law Committed in the Territory of the former Yugoslavia Since 1991 ("Appeals Chamber" and "International Tribunal", respectively) is seized of "Ivan Čermak's Interlocutory Appeal against Trial Chamber's Decision on Conflict of Interest of Attorneys Čedo Prodanović and Jadranka Sloković" filed on 4 May 2007 ("Appeal"), by Counsel for Ivan Čermak ("Appellant").

2. Ante Gotovina responded on 11 May 2007[1] and the Prosecution filed its response on 14 May 2007.[2] In conformity with the Appeals Chamber's Decision of 16 May 2007,[3] the Appellant filed his consolidated reply on 18 May 2007.[4]

I. PROCEDURAL BACKGROUND

3. On 20 February 2006 the Prosecution filed a consolidated motion to amend the Indictments against Mladen Markač, Ivan Čermak and Ante Gotovina ("Gotovina") and to jointly charge and try these three accused.[5] Gotovina objected to the said motion arguing, *inter alia*, that the joinder would create a conflict of interests between himself and the Appellant, as the Appellant's Counsel, Čedo Prodanović and Jadranka Sloković ("Prodanović" and "Sloković", respectively or "Counsel" when used jointly), also represented Rahim Ademi ("Ademi"), who is currently awaiting trial in Croatia following his transfer from the International Tribunal pursuant to Rule 11*bis* of the Rules of Procedure and Evidence of the International Tribunal ("Rules").[6] More specifically, Gotovina claimed that he intended to call Ademi as a witness "critical to his defence", since during and after "Operation Storm" Ademi was Gotovina's "second-in-command as chief of staff to the Commander of the Split Military District, and became Acting Commander of the Split Military District from on or about 9 August 1995 to on or about 15 August 1995 while General Gotovina was away on his **[page 2]** honeymoon".[7] According to Gotovina, the Appellant's Counsel indicated that their defence line may contend that Gotovina was the Appellant's "commanding officer and therefore certain incidents alleged in the Indictments were outside the scope of Čermak's duties, and thus the responsibility of Gotovina".[8] Gotovina anticipated that Ademi's testimony would rebut this potential defense of the Appellant.[9] The joinder would impair on Gotovina's ability to call this witness, since, *inter alia*, the Appellant's Counsel "would be privy to attorney-client privileged information that could be used to undermine the credibility of Ademi".[10]

4. On 14 July 2006, the Trial Chamber granted the Prosecution request to join the case against Mladen Markač and Ivan Čermak[11] with that of Ante Gotovina[12] pursuant to Rule 48 of the Rules. With respect to a possible conflict of interest between Gotovina and the Appellant as a result of the joinder, the Trial Chamber noted that no charges arising out of the events alleged in the proposed Joinder Indictment had been brought against Ademi either in the International Tribunal or in the Republic of Croatia and concluded that "there is no factual basis on which it is demonstrated that a conflict of interests will arise between the two Accused".[13]

---

1 Defendant Ante Gotovina's Response in Opposition to Ivan Cermak's [*sic*] Interlocutory Appeal against the Trial Chamber's Decision on Conflict of Interest of Attorneys Cedo Prodanovic [*sic*] and Jadranka Slokovic [*sic*], 11 May 2007 ("Gotovina's Response").

2 Prosecution's Response Brief to Ivan Čermak's Interlocutory Appeal against Trial Chamber's Decision on Conflict of Interest of Attorneys Čedo Prodanović and Jadranka Sloković, 14 May 2007 ("Prosecution's Response").

3 Decision on Ivan Čermak's Urgent Motion for Leave to File a Consolidated Reply to Responses Filed by the Prosecutor and Ante Gotovina, 16 May 2007.

4 Ivan Čermak's Consolidated Reply to the Prosecutor and Ante Gotovina's Responses to Ivan Čermak's Interlocutory Appeal against the Trial Chamber's Decision on Conflict of Interests of Attorneys Čedo Prodanović and Jadranka Sloković, 18 May 2007 ("Reply").

5 *Prosecutor v. Ivan Čermak and Mladen Markač*, Case No. IT-03-73-PT, Prosecution's Consolidated Motion to Amend the Indictment and for Joinder, 20 February 2006; *see* subsequently, *Prosecutor v. Ante Gotovina et al.*, Case No. IT-06-90-PT, Joinder Indictment *Modified by Order Pursuant to Rule 73Bis (D) to Reduce the Indictment, 21 February 2007*, filed on 6 March 2007 ("Joinder Indictment"), para. 98.

6 *Prosecutor v. Ante Gotovina,* Case No. IT-01-45-PT, Defedant Ante Gotovina's Response in Opposition to the Prosecution's Consolidated Motion to Amend the Indictment and for Joinder, 4 April 2006 ("Gotovina's Opposition to Joinder"), paras 5–7 and 54–62.

7 Gotovina's Opposition to Joinder, paras 6 and 56.

8 *Ibid.*, paras 6 and 54–55, 57.

9 *Ibid.*, paras 6 and 54–55, 57.

10 *Ibid.*, paras 7, 60.

11 IT-03-73-PT.

12 IT-01-45-PT.

13 *Prosecutor v. Ivan Čermak and Mladen Markač*, Case No. IT-03-73-PT and *Prosecutor v. Ante Gotovina*, Case No. IT-01-45-PT, Decision on Prosecution's Consolidated Motion to Amend the Indictment and for Joinder, 14 July 2006 ("Decision on Joinder"),

5. All three accused appealed the Trial Chamber's Decision on Joinder.[14] On 25 October 2006, the Appeals Chamber dismissed these appeals.[15] With regard to the potential Gotovina-Čermak conflict of interest the Appeals Chamber found that (i) it was uncertain at that stage in the proceedings "that Prodanović and Sloković's duty of loyalty to Čermak will be compromised because they will be unable to effectively cross-examine their other client, Ademi, due to a desire to avoid causing Ademi to incriminate himself" or that they "will be unable to effectively cross-examine Ademi in defense of Čermak without revealing privileged attorney-client communication arising out of representing Ademi in Croatia";[16] (ii) even if such conflict of interest arose, it would be with regard to the simultaneous representation of the Appellant and Ademi "regardless of joinder **[page 3]** of Čermak's case with Gotovina's";[17] (iii) even if the Appellant's Counsel were to choose between their two clients, it was not sure that they would choose Ademi over the Appellant;[18] and (iv) even if they were to make such choice, it would not cause serious prejudice to the Appellant as he would still have the possibility to choose another counsel to represent him before the commencement of the trial.[19]

6. On 17 January 2007, the Disciplinary Council of the Association of Defence Counsel of the International Tribunal ("Disciplinary Council") issued its confidential Advisory Opinion on the issues related to possible conflicts of interests in the present case ("Advisory Opinion"). With respect to Prodanović and Sloković, the Disciplinary Council concluded that (i) there is "no current conflict of interest" in relation to their representation of the Appellant and Ademi;[20] (ii) there is "an appreciable risk of conflict of interest arising in future" and it is "reasonably to be expected that such a conflict would adversely affect their representation" of either accused;[21] (iii) if such conflict were to arise, it is likely to be "one that would require compulsory withdrawal under Article 14(D), as opposed to the possibility of management under 14(E)ii2 by obtaining the consent of both clients to that course";[22] and (iv) while no criticism can be made of Prodanović and Sloković at this point, "if they were to *continue* to risk a conflict of interest arising with knowledge of this advisory opinion, [they would] be guilty of misconduct under Article 14(B) or (D)".[23] The Trial Chamber ordered the disclosure of the Advisory Opinion to "all Defence counsel, their clients and the Prosecution" on 26 January 2007.[24]

7. On 8 February 2007 Prodanović and Sloković filed Appellant's and Ademi's Undertakings "for the purpose of dealing with the matter of the potential conflict of interest in the current proceeding", by which both the Appellant and Ademi undertook not to raise their Counsel's dual representation as a legal impediment affecting their respective right to a fair trial.[25] **[page 4]**

---

para. 64. The Joinder Indictment was filed on 24 July 2006, and was further amended on 6 March 2007 in accordance with Order Pursuant to Rule 73bis(D) to Reduce the Indictment, 21 February 2007.

14 Appellant Mladen Markač's Interlocutory Appeal From the Trial Chamber's Decision on Prosecution's Consolidated Motion to Amend the Indictment and For Joinder, 21 August 2006; Appellant Ivan Čermak's Interlocutory Appeal Against the Trial Chamber's Decision on Prosecution's Consolidated Motion to Amend the Indictment and For Joinder, 23 August 2006; Brief of Interlocutory Appellant Ante Gotovina, 25 August 2006 ("Gotovina's Joinder Appeal").

15 Prosecutor v. *Ante Gotovina and Prosecutor v. Ivan Čermak and Mladen Markač*, Case Nos. IT-01-45-AR73.1, IT-03-73-AR73.1, IT-03-73-AR73.2, Decision on Interlocutory Appeals against the Trial Chamber's Decision to Amend the Indictment and for Joinder, 25 October 2006 ("Appeals Chamber Decision on Joinder").

16 *Ibid.*, para. 27.

17 *Ibid.*, paras 28–29.

18 *Ibid.*, para. 30.

19 *Ibid.*, para. 30.

20 Advisory Opinion, para. 45.

21 *Ibid.*, para. 46.

22 *Ibid.*, para. 47.

23 *Ibid.*, paras 50 and 53 (emphasis in the original).

24 *Prosecutor v. Ante Gotovina et al.*, Case No. IT-06-90-PT, *Confidential and Ex Parte* Order to Disclose Letter Containing the Advisory Opinion of the Association of Defence Counsel Dated 18 January 2007, 26 January 2007. The Appeals Chamber notes that, while the Advisory Opinion remains a confidential document, it can be referred to and quoted in the present public Decision inasmuch as it has been cited, in relevant parts, by the Trial Chamber in its public Impugned Decision (para. 3) and by the parties in their submissions at trial and on appeal (*cf.* in particular, Appeal, para. 11; Prosecution's Response, para. 8).

25 *Prosecutor v. Ante Gotovina et al.*, Case No. IT-06-90-PT, Notice to the Trial Chamber Concerning Undertakings Provided by Ivan Čermak and Rahim Ademi, 8 February 2007 ("Notice of Undertakings", "Appellant's Undertaking" and "Ademi's Undertaking", respectively).

8. The Trial Chamber rendered the Impugned Decision on 5 April 2007.[26] In its findings on the existence of a conflict of interests, the Trial Chamber relied, *inter alia*, on the Advisory Opinion as well as the Appellant's and Ademi's Undertakings.[27] It held that, in view of a commander-subordinate relationship between Gotovina and Ademi, on the one hand, and the Appellant on the other, the representation of both Ademi and the Appellant by Prodanović and Sloković raised a conflict of interest under Article 14(D)(i) of the Code of Professional Conduct for Counsel Appearing before the International Tribunal[28] ("Code of Conduct").[29]

9. On 25 April 2007, the Appellant submitted a request for certification to appeal the Impugned Decision.[30] On 27 April 2007, the Trial Chamber granted the said request.[31]

10. On 22 May 2007, the Prosecution notified the Appeals Chamber that on 17 May 2007 it identified, in compliance with the Trial Chamber's decision of 19 March 2007, Ademi as one of the "key military figures" of the joint criminal enterprise ("JCE") alleged in the Joinder Indictment.[32] The Appellant responded on 31 May 2007 opposing the Notice "on the basis that it has no bearing or relevance to the [...] Appeal and is nothing more than a supplementary attempt to influence the Appeals Chamber".[33] The Appeals Chamber notes that on 17 May 2007, the Prosecution filed the public "Motion to Amend the Indictment" seeking, *inter alia*, revisions of the pleading of the JCE in light of the new case-law of the Appeals Chamber, notably in relation with its judgement in the *Prosecutor v. Brđanin* case.[34]. The Trial Chamber has not yet rendered a decision on the Proposed Amended Joinder Indictment. **[page 5]**

II. STANDARD OF REVIEW

11. The Appeals Chamber recalls that an interlocutory appeal is not a *de novo* review of the Trial Chamber's decision.[35] Since decisions on matters relating to the calling of witnesses and assignment of counsel at trial fall squarely within the discretion of the Trial Chamber,[36] the question before the Appeals Chamber is not

---

26 *Prosecutor v. Ante Gotovina et al.*, Case No. IT-06-90-PT, Decision on Conflict of Interest of Attorneys Čedo Prodanović and Jadranka Sloković, 5 April 2007 ("Impugned Decision"). *See also, Prosecutor v. Ante Gotovina et al.*, Case No. IT-06-90-PT, Judge Orie's Dissenting Opinion on decision on Conflict of Interest of Attorneys Čedo Prodanović and Jadranka Sloković of 5 April 2007, 18 April 2007 ("Judge Orie's Dissenting Opinion").

27 Impugned Decision, paras 3 and 6.

28 IT/125 Rev.2, 29 June 2006 promulgated by the Registrar on 11 July 2006.

29 Impugned Decision, para. 10.

30 *Prosecutor v. Ante Gotovina et al.*, Case No. IT-06-90-PT, Ivan Čermak's Request for Certification to File Interlocutory Appeal against Trial Chamber's Decision on Conflict of Interest of Attorneys Čedo Prodanović and Jadranka Sloković, 25 April 2007.

31 *Prosecutor v. Ante Gotovina et al.*, Case No. IT-06-90-PT, Decision on Request for Certification to File Interlocutory Appeal against Trial Chamber's Decision on Conflict of Interest of Attorners Čedo Prodanović and Jadranka Sloković, 27 April 2007.

32 *Confidential* Prosecution's Notice Regarding Ivan Čermak's Interlocutory Appeal against Trial Chamber's Decision on Conflict of Interest of Attorneys Čedo Prodanović and Jadranka Sloković, 22 May 2007 ("Notice"), paras 1-2.

33 *Confidential* Ivan Čermak's Response to Prosecution's Notice Regarding Ivan Čermak's Interlocutory Appeal against Trial Chamber's Decision on Conflict of Interest of Attorneys Čedo Prodanović and Jadranka Sloković, 31 May 2007 ("Response to Notice"), para. 1.

34 *Prosecutor v. Ante Gotovina et al.*, Case No. IT-06-90-PT, Public Filing Motion to Amend the Indictment, 17 May 2007 and Annex A ("Proposed Amended Joinder Indictment"). Paragraph 15 of the Proposed Amended Joinder Indictment lists four persons who allegedly participated in the same JCE as the co-accused in the present case: Franjo Tuđman, Gojko Šušak, Janko Bobetko and Zvonimir Červenko. On the same date, the Prosecution filed a "Clarification of Indictment" listing another seven names, including Rahim Ademi, as "key military or political figures among the many persons who were members of the JCE" (*Prosecutor v. Ante Gotovina et al.*, Case No. IT-06-90-PT, Confidential Clarification of Indictment, 17 May 2007 ("Clarification to the Proposed Amended Joinder Indictment")). Following the motions from Gotovina and Mladen Markač seeking to lift the confidentiality of the Clarification to the Proposed Amended Joinder Indictment (*Prosecutor v. Ante Gotovina et al.*, Case No. IT-06-90-PT, *Confidential* Defendant Ante Gotovina's Emergency Motion to Lift the Confidentiality of Prosecution's Clarification of Indictment Filed 17 May 2007, 22 May 2007; Confidential Defendant Mladen Markač's Joinder to Defendant Ante Gotovina's Emergency Motion to Lift the Confidentiality of Prosecution's Clarification of Indictment Filed 17 May 2007, 24 May 2007), the Trial Chamber lifted the confidential status of the Clarification to the Proposed Amended Joinder Indictment. See also, *Prosecutor v. Ante Gotovina et al.*, Case No. IT-06-90-PT, Public Order to the Prosecutor under Rule 77, 1 June 2007.

35 *Prosecutor v. Ante Gotovina et al.*, Case No. IT-06-90-AR73.1, Decision on Miroslav Šeparović's Interlocutory Appeal against Trial Chamber's Decisions on Conflict of Interest and Finding of Misconduct, 4 May 2007 ("4 May 2007 Decision"), para. 11; *Prosecutor v. Milan Lukić and Sredoje Lukić*, Case No. IT-98-32/1-AR65.1, Decision on Defence Appeal Against Trial Chamber's Decision on Sredoje Lukić's Motion for Provisional Release, 16 April 2007 ("Lukić Provisional Release Decision"), para. 4; *Prosecutor v. Mico Stanišić*, Case No. IT-04-79-AR65.1, Decision on Prosecution's Interlocutory Appeal of Mićo Stanišić's Provisional Release, 17 October 2005 ("*Stanišić* Provisional Release Decision"), para. 6.

36 4 May 2007 Decision, para. 11; *Prosecutor v. Ante Gotovina,* and *Prosecutor v. Ivan Čermak and Mladen Markač*, Case Nos IT-01-45-AR73.1, IT-03-73-AR73.1 and IT-03-73-AR73.2, Decision on Appellant Malden Markač's Motion for Clarification,

whether it "agrees with that decision" but "whether the Trial Chamber has correctly exercised its discretion in reaching that decision."[37] The party challenging a discretionary decision by the Trial Chamber must demonstrate that the Trial Chamber has committed a "discernible error".[38] The Appeals Chamber will overturn a Trial Chamber's exercise of its discretion where it is found to be "(1) based on an incorrect interpretation of governing law; (2) based on a patently incorrect conclusion of fact; or (3) so unfair or unreasonable as to constitute an abuse of the Trial Chamber's discretion".[39]

III. PRELIMINARY MATTERS

12. In his Reply, the Appellant contests Gotovina's standing for filing a response to the Appeal as such right is reserved for the "opposite party", which in this instance, according to the Appellant, is the Prosecution.[40] The Appellant further submits that in order to be granted such standing, Gotovina should have shown specific interest in the matter which he failed to do.[41] The Appeals **[page 6]** Chamber finds that, while the Practice Direction does not specifically provide for the possibility for a co-accused to file submissions in appeals proceedings initiated by another co-accused, it is clear from the procedural background of the case that Gotovina does have a specific interest in the matter and it is therefore in the interests of justice to consider Gotovina's Response as validly filed. Moreover, the Appeals Chamber notes that the Appellant suffers no prejudice from such finding since he was granted the opportunity to reply to Gotovina's Response.[42]

IV. DISCUSSION

13. The Appellant essentially raises five grounds of appeal. In particular, he argues that (i) the Trial Chamber failed to give sufficient weight to and draw appropriate inference from the fact that Ademi did not provide to Prodanović and Sloković any privileged information which would be useful for the Appellant in his defence;[43] (ii) the Trial Chamber misdirected itself regarding the degree of counsel's duty of loyalty;[44] (iii) the Trial Chamber erred in law by concluding the Appellant's and Ademi's Undertakings were not fully informed;[45] (iv) the Trial Chamber committed a discernible error by ordering Prodanović and Sloković to withdraw from the case whereas less severe measures were available,[46] including Prodanović's and Sloković's withdrawal from Ademi's defence and retaining the services of a third counsel;[47] and (v) the Trial Chamber erred in law by failing to give sufficient consideration to the hardship for the Appellant as a result of Prodanović's and Sloković's withdrawal from his defence.[48]

---

12 January 2007, p. 4. *See* also, *Slobodan Milošević v. Prosecutor*, Case No. IT-02-54-AR73.7, Decision on Interlocutory Appeal of the Trial Chamber's Decision on the Assignment of Defense Counsel, 1 November 2004 ("*Milošević* Decision on Defence Counsel"), para. 9.

37 4 May 2007 Decision, para. 11.

38 *Ibid.*, para. 11.

39 *Ibid.*, para. 11; *Milošević* Decision on Defence Counsel, para. 10, *Prosecutor v. Vojislav Šešelj*, Case No. IT-03-67-AR73.4, Decision on Appeal Against the Trial Chamber's Decision (No.2) on Assignment of Counsel, 8 December 2006, para. 16.

40 Reply, para. 3 citing Practice Direction on Procedure for the Filing of Written Submissions in Appeal Proceedings before the International Tribunal, IT/155/Rev.3, 16 September 2005 ("Practice Direction"), para. 10.

41 Reply, para. 3. The Appellant also notes that at the Status Conference of 9 February 2007, Gotovina's Counsel stated, with respect to the alleged conflict of interest at stake, that he would "render no opinion about that whatsoever [...] since Gerenal Gotovina really isn't part of this" – *ibid.*, footnote 5 citing Status Conference, 9 February 2007 (Private Session), T. 93. The Appeals Chamber finds this argument to be misleading since Gotovina's Counsel did offer his position on the issue of conflicts of interest in this case (T.91-T.93) and his above-cited remark in fact concerned the issue of whether those matters should be discussed in private or public session (T.93, lines 6–17).

42 Decision on Ivan Čermak's Urgent Motion for Leave to File a Consolidated Reply to Responses Filed by the Prosecutor and Ante Gotovina, 16 May 2007, pp. 3–4.

43 Appeal, paras 30(i) and 31; Reply, paras 7(2), 13–14, and 18–20.

44 Reply, paras 7(1) and 8–14. The Appeals Chamber notes that this ground does not appear as a separate ground of appeal set out in the Appeal. However, the Appeals Chamber accepts it as validly pleaded in light of the fact that it is closely interlinked with the grounds listed in the Appeal and was further developed in the Reply following the arguments exposed in Gotovina's and Prosecution's Responses. Moreover, the Appeals Chamber notes that this issue in closely related to and intertwined with the Appellant's submissions on privileged information. Therefore, the Appeals Chamber will address these grounds in combination.

45 Appeal, paras 30(iii) and 35; Reply, para. 7(5).

46 *Ibid.*, paras 30(ii), 32–34 and 36; Reply, para. 7(3).

47 *Ibid.*, paras 30(iv) and 32.

48 *Ibid.*, paras 30(v) and 37–38; Reply, paras 7(6) and 30–32.

14. Both Gotovina and the Prosecution object to the Appeal in its entirety.[49] **[page 7]**

A. Applicable Law

15. Article 14 of the Code of Conduct reads in relevant parts:

(A) Counsel owes a duty of loyalty to a client. [...]

(B) Counsel shall exercise all care to ensure that no conflict of interest arises. [...]

(D) Counsel or his firm shall not represent a client with respect to a matter if:

(i) such representation will be, or may reasonably be expected to be, adversely affected by representation of another client;

(ii) representation of another client will be, or may reasonably be expected to be, adversely affected by such representation;

(iii) the matter is the same or substantially related to another matter in which counsel or his firm had formerly represented another client ("former client"), and the interests of the client are materially adverse to the interests of the former client; [...].

(E) Where a conflict of interest does arise, counsel shall:

(i) promptly and fully inform each potentially affected present and former client of the nature and extent of the conflict; and

(ii) either:

(1) take all steps necessary to remove the conflict; or

(2) obtain the full and informed consent of all potentially affected present and former clients to continue the representation unless such consent is likely to irreversibly prejudice the administration of justice.

16. The Appeals Chamber also recalls that a conflict of interest between an attorney and a client arises in any situation where, by reason of certain circumstances, representation by such an attorney prejudices, or could prejudice, the interests of the client and the wider interests of justice.[50] Safeguarding the interests of justice requires the prevention of potential conflicts of interest before they arise.[51] If a Chamber determines that the risks and damage that could be caused are such as to jeopardise the right of the accused to a fair and expeditious trial or proper administration of justice, it takes the appropriate measure to restore and protect the fairness of trial and the integrity of the proceedings.[52] It has been held that such measures can include ordering the withdrawal of counsel.[53] **[page 8]**

B. Duty of loyalty and Privileged Information

1. Submissions of the Parties

17. The Appellant submits that, in light of Ademi's explicit confirmation that he did not provide Prodanović and Sloković with "any confidential information which would be useful for Čermak in his defense there were

49 Gotovina's Response, para. 27; Prosecution's Response, para. 30.

50 4 May 2007 Decision, para. 23 citing Prosecutor v. *Jadranko Prlić et al.*, Case No. IT-04-74-AR73.1, Decision on Appeal by Bruno Stojić against Trial Chamber's Decision on Request for Appointment of Counsel, 24 November 2004 ("*Prlić* Appeal Decision"), para. 22.

51 Ibid., para. 25.

52 *See Prosecutor v. Jadranko Prlić et al.,* Case No. IT-04-74-PT, Decision on Requests for Appointment of Counsel, 30 July 2004 ("*Prlić* Trial Decision"), para. 16.

53 *Prosecutor v. Željko Mejakić et al.*, Case No. IT-02-65-AR73.1, Decision on Appeal by the Prosecution to Resolve Conflict of Interest Regarding Attorney Jovan Simić, 6 October 2004 ("*Mejakić* Decision"), para. 7; *Prlić* Trial Decision, para. 16.

other measures open to the Trial Chamber to take".[54] In the Appellant's view, the fact that no such confidential information was shared by Ademi with counsel "demonstrates that there is no substantial relationship between the two cases".[55] The Appellant also argues that the issue of whether such information was shared or not is a decisive factor in a decision as to whether there is a breach of loyalty to a current or former client.[56] The Prosecution responds that "the Trial Chamber's concern went beyond the possible use of confidential information to Counsel's duty of loyalty to Mr. Ademi".[57] Both Gotovina and the Prosecution argue that the conflict of interest exists regardless of whether such privileged information was indeed transmitted by Ademi to his Counsel.[58]

18. Referring to Judge Orie's Dissenting Opinion, the Appellant submits that in the absence of any confidential information in Counsel's possession, "the duty of loyalty to both clients would be in jeopardy 'only in the abstract' and that the conflict of loyalty had not resulted in a concrete conflict of interest".[59] He argues that the conflict of loyalty at stake "was an unforeseen consequence of the Prosecutor's indictment policy as opposed to counsel's failure to predict that such a conflict would arise".[60] In this sense, the Appellant insists that Ademi and he were indicted for unrelated crimes, since before the joinder Čermak was not prosecuted for Operation Storm charges, which had only been filed with respect to Gotovina, and Ademi was indicted for crimes committed in Medak Pocket which are "geographically and temporally unconnected to the Storm investigation".[61]

19. Gotovina and the Prosecution argue that because of the duty of loyalty with respect to Ademi, it would be impossible for Prodanović and Sloković to pursue a line of defence in favour of the Appellant as it would implicate Ademi and "potentially subject him to another war crimes indictment in Croatia".[62] Gotovina further argues that such conflict of interest has already been **[page 9]** demonstrated as it has forced the Appellant's Counsel "to abandon a potential defence of Čermak which they had already advanced to the Trial Chamber".[63]

20. In his Reply, the Appellant argues that the Trial Chamber erroneously speculated on the defences open to the Appellant which are issues that lie within the professional judgement of the Counsel[64] and elaborates on his understanding of the duty of loyalty with respect to a former client.[65] The Appeals Chamber will address the latter issue under the third ground of appeal below.

2. Analysis

21. The Appeals Chamber has already held that if a conflict of interest were to arise for Prodanović and Sloković with respect to the dual representation of the Appellant and Ademi, it would exist regardless of whether or not Gotovina or the Appellant decided to call on Ademi as a witness, since their duty of loyalty to Ademi would prevent them from making any arguments incriminating Ademi in order to defend Čermak.[66] It is therefore unnecessary to address the issues concerning Ademi's potential appearance as a witness in this case for the purposes of the present Decision.

22. In the Impugned Decision, the Trial Chamber held that this duty of loyalty would indeed be breached due to "a commander-subordinate relationship between Gotovina and Ademi, his second-in-command, on the one hand, and Čermak on the other".[67] The Trial Chamber also noted that Prodanović and Sloković "have neither explicitly excluded nor adopted" a line of defence for the Appellant that would incriminate

54 Appeal, para. 31.
55 Reply, para. 14.
56 *Ibid.*, paras 13–14.
57 Prosecution's Response, para. 20.
58 Gotovina's Response, paras 13–14; Prosecution's Response, para. 20.
59 Appeal, para. 31 citing Judge Orie's Dissenting Opinion, para. 11; Reply, para. 19.
60 Appeal, para. 26.
61 *Ibid.*, para. 26; *see also* Reply, paras 8–14.
62 Gotovina's Response, para. 14; Prosecution's Response, para. 20.
63 Gotovina's Response, para. 14.
64 Reply, para. 14.
65 *Ibid.*, paras 8–14.
66 Appeals Chamber Decision on Joinder, paras 28–29.
67 Impugned Decision, para. 10.

Ademi.[68] It went on to observe "with some concern" that "Prodanović and Sloković have not addressed the allegation that Ademi, as Gotovina's Chief of Staff and his second-in-command, may have been in charge temporarily in Gotovina's absence, when certain alleged crimes with which Čermak is charged during the Relevant Timeframe were committed".[69] Finally, the Trial Chamber held that what mattered most, at that point, was not whether Prodanović and Sloković would indeed raise this line of defence, but whether "all potential defences remain[ed] available to Čermak".[70] In these circumstances, the Trial Chamber was not satisfied that the Appellant's Counsel have demonstrated a "complete analysis of the matter"[71] and concluded that their duty of loyalty *vis-à-vis* Ademi was at serious risk regardless the fact that no **[page 10]** confidential information potentially useful to the Appellant had been provided by Ademi to Prodanović and Sloković.[72]

23. The Appeals Chamber is not satisfied that the Appellant has identified any discernible error in the Trial Chamber's conclusion in this regard. At the outset, the Appeals Chamber notes that the Trial Chamber was satisfied that no confidential information that would be potentially useful to the Appellant came into Prodanović's and Sloković's possession through Ademi.[73] However, in light of the findings below, the Appeals Chamber agrees with the Trial Chamber that, in the circumstances of the present case, the fact that Ademi did not provide his Counsel with any such confidential information is without bearing, since this factor is not the only basis on which a conflict of interest can be reasonably anticipated.[74] Indeed, where a Chamber can reasonably expect that, due to a conflict of interest, a counsel "may be reluctant to pursue a line of defence, to adduce certain items in evidence, or to plead certain mitigating factors at the sentencing stage, in order to avoid prejudicing another client", it can no longer presume that counsel has fulfilled his or her professional obligations under the Code of Conduct and has the power and the duty to intervene in order to guarantee or restore the integrity of the proceedings without delay.[75]

24. Also, while it is true that such conflicts of interest are more obvious in cases where counsel represents two accused who are, at least partly, charged with the same criminal acts, committed during the same period of time and in the same area,[76] this is clearly not the only situation where a conflict of interest may arise. In this regard, the Appeals Chamber emphasizes that the provisions of Article 14(D)(i) and (ii) of the Code of Conduct do not require that there be substantial relationship between matters in which the current clients are represented – what is prohibited is a simultaneous representation that will, or may reasonably be expected to, adversely affect the representation of either client.

25. In the present case, the Appellant, as Commander of the Knin Garrison, which encompassed a number of municipalities of the Krajina region, is charged for crimes committed under articles 3, 3(b), 3(e), 5(a), 5(d), 5(h), 5(i), 7(1) and 7(3) of the Statute of the International Tribunal ("Statute") **[page 11]** in the framework of the JCE related to the Operation Storm from at least July 1995 to about 30 September 1995.[77] Under the same Joinder Indictment, Gotovina is charged for the same crimes as Commander of the Split Military District of the *Hrvatska Vojska* ("HV") "and the overall operational commander of Operation Storm in the southern

68 *Ibid.*, para. 11.

69 *Ibid.*, para. 12.

70 *Ibid.*, para. 19.

71 *Ibid.*, para. 12.

72 *Ibid.*, paras 17–18.

73 *Ibid.*, para. 17.

74 *Cf.* First *Miletić* Decision, para. 33.

75 *See Prlić* Trial Decision, paras 15–16. *See also Perillo v. Johnson,* 205 F.3d 775, 781 (5th Cir. 2000): "'adverse effect' may be established with evidence that 'some plausible alternative defense strategy or tactic' could have been pursued, but was not because of the actual conflict impairing counsel's performance"; *Holloway v. Arkansas* 435 U.S. 475, 489–490, 98 S.Ct. 1173, 1181, 55 L.Ed.2d 426 (1978): "[j]oint representation of conflicting interests is suspect because of what it tends to prevent the attorney from doing [...] [A] conflict may [...] prevent an attorney from challenging the admission of evidence prejudicial to one client but perhaps favourable to another, or from arguing at the sentencing hearing the relative involvement and culpability of his clients in order to minimize the culpability of one by emphasizing that of another".

76 *See Prlić* Trial Decision, para. 16; *see also Prlić* Appeal Decision, para. 24.

77 Joinder Indictment, paras 6, 12–18, 20, 25–26 (with reference to the Medak Pocket Operation), 37 and 49–54 (*cf.* Proposed Amended Joinder Indictment, paras 6, 12–15, 17, 19, 24, 36 and 48–53). The Appeals Chamber also notes that the original version of the indictment against the Appellant also charged him for participation in the JCE (under modes of responsibility provided for by Articles 7(1) and 7(3) of the Statute) in the southern portion of the Krajina region during Operation Storm (*Prosecutor v. Ivan Čermak and Mladen Markač*, Case No. IT-03-73-I, Indictment, 19 February 2004, paras 4, 10–11, 15, 17–18; *see also* paras 55–56 with respect to Gotovina).

portion of the Krajina region".[78] According to the Joinder Indictment, the Split Military District included the Knin Garrison.[79] Therefore, the Appellant is alleged to be Gotovina's subordinate. It is true that the latest version of the indictment against Ademi before the International Tribunal only deals with the Medak Pocket military operation, which allegedly occurred from 9 September 1993 to on or about 17 September 1993 and of which he allegedly was Acting Commander.[80] The Appeals Chamber notes that the Current Ademi Indictment of 22 November 2006 filed by the State Prosecutor before the Zagreb County Court also only deals with the Medak Pocket military operation but refers to a chain of command "made of Supreme commander Tuđman, Minister of Defence Šušak, General Bobetko, Naval Captain Domazet, General Markač, Rojs Ćesić, Gotovina, second accused Mirko Norac and others".[81] On 7 February 2007, the Zagreb County Court found that the Current Ademi Indictment became "legally effective" at the moment of its confirmation by the International Tribunal (*i.e.* on 30 July 2004) and no objections against it were permissible as of that date.[82] It is unclear, at this stage, whether the fact that the Prosecution presently seeks to include Ademi in the list of key participants of the JCE pleaded under the Proposed Amended Joinder Indictment in the present case will have any bearing on the Current Ademi Indictment in Croatia. However, the Appeals Chamber finds that the current dual representation of the Appellant and Ademi by the same Counsel has a clear potential for a conflict of interest in this case, since it may, in any event, reasonably be expected to adversely affect the representation of either or both clients.[83] **[page 12]**

26. Indeed, while the Appellant and Ademi are currently charged with crimes committed in the course of two distinct military operations lead by the HV, given the nature of the factual basis of the charges for which the Appellant is now indicted, it cannot be said that the Current Ademi Indictment has exhausted charges against him and that there is no risk of Ademi being prosecuted in respect of the Operation Storm before any of the competent jurisdictions.[84] In fact, being an indictable member of the same JCE as the Appellant, Ademi may be viewed as much a potential witness as a potential co-defendant.

27. In this regard, what is particularly pertinent in the instant case is the fact that, in the relevant period in 1995, Ademi claims to have been Gotovina's second-in-command[85] and therefore exercised commander-subordinate functions with respect to the Appellant. In this situation, the Appellant's Counsel simultaneously representing Ademi are bound by their duty of loyalty to exclude any defence strategy that would result in implicating Ademi with respect to the crimes charged on the Appellant, and this is regardless of whether Ademi is currently being prosecuted for such crimes.[86]

28. Finally, the Appeals Chamber considers that, in a case of this kind, "safeguarding the interests of justice requires not only the existence of a mechanism for removing conflicts of interests *after* they have arisen but also the *prevention* of such conflicts *before* they arise".[87] It was hence not unreasonable for the Trial Chamber to find that the dual representation by Prodanović and Sloković risks to considerably prejudice the Appellant as it would limit the choice of defence strategies due to his Counsel's duty of loyalty to Ademi and that they therefore would not be able to serve best the Appellant's interests.

---

78 Joinder Indictment, paras 4, 12–19, 37 and 49–54 (*cf.* Proposed Amended Joinder Indictment, paras 4, 12–15, 18, 36 and 48–53).

79 Annex A to Joinder Indictment and to Proposed Amended Joinder Indictment.

80 *Prosecutor v. Rahim Ademi* and *Prosecutor v. Mirko Norac*, Case No. IT-01-46-PT & IT-04-76-I, Consolidated Indictment, 27 May 2004, paras 4–5, 13, 28–35. *See also, Prosecutor v. Rahim Ademi and Mirko Norac*, Case No. IT-04-78-PT, Decision for Referral to the Authorities of the Republic of Croatia Pursuant to Rule 11*bis*, 14 September 2005 ("*Ademi* Referral Decision"), paras 15–17.

81 Indictment of County Prosecutor to the Zagreb County Court, K-DO-349/05, 22 November 2006, CLSS translation OTP110317 ("Current Ademi Indictment"), p. 70.

82 Zagreb County Court, Case No. Kv-rz-2/07, Ruling K-rz-1/06, 7 February 2007 (unofficial translation by the Organization for Security and Co-operation in Europe). The Appeals Chamber also notes that the trial in relation to Ademi commenced, as scheduled, on 18 June 2007 (Zagreb County Court, Case No. K-rz-1/06, Order [unofficial translation by the International Tribunal's Outreach Office]).

83 *Cf. Prosecutor v. Zdravko Tolimir et al.,* Case No. IT-05-88-PT, Decision on Appointment of Co-Counsel for Radivoje Miletić, 28 September 2005 ("First *Miletić* Decision") (confidentiality lifted by Order of 30 September 2005), para. 29.

84 *Cf.* First *Miletić* Decision, para. 31.

85 Ademi's Undertaking, p.1, para. 5; *see also* Response to Notice, para. 10: "Ademi has already been implicated by reason of his position as Gotovina's deputy commander during Operation Storm. The Prosecutor's Notice on the new status of Rahim Ademi in this case does not have any additional impact on counsel's duty to his as a (former) client represented in a *distinct matter*" (emphasis in the original).

86 *Cf. Prlić Appeal* Decision, para. 24.

87 *Ibid.*, para. 25 (emphasis added).

29. Consequently, the Appeals Chamber dismisses the first and the second grounds of Appeal subject to its considerations below in relation to the duty of loyalty to a former client.

C. Appellant's and Ademi's Undertakings

1. Submissions of the Parties

30. The Appellant submits that the Trial Chamber erred in concluding that the Appellant's and Ademi's Undertakings were inadequate and suggests that, in any case, it should have instructed the **[page 13]** Counsel to address such inadequacies, in particular by having the Appellant's consent confirmed during the Status Conference held on 9 February 2007.[88] According to Prodanović and Sloković, both the Appellant and Ademi provided their free consent which clearly demonstrates that "they understood the potential nature of a conflict of interest arising".[89]

31. Gotovina responds that the Undertakings only concern "the issue of Ademi's appearance as a witness at trial" and no do not address the matter of pursuing "a defense of Čermak which would potentially incriminate Ademi".[90] He further notes that Ademi never provided "a waiver which would allow Prodanović and Sloković to withdraw from their representation of him on the eve of his trial in Croatia".[91] The Prosecution also submits that both Undertakings are deficient in that the Appellant did not refer to the possible defences that could be raised in light of the commander-subordinate relationship and Ademi's Undertaking did not contemplate the Counsel's potential withdrawal from his case.[92] It adds that, in any case, it would be hardly possible to get the Appellant's fully informed undertaking at this stage of proceedings and that it was within the Trial Chamber's discretion to consider whether his Undertaking could outweigh the interests of the administration of justice.[93]

2. Analysis

32. The Trial Chamber was not satisfied that the Appellant's and Čermak's Undertakings would constitute an appropriate measure in the presence of a conflict of interest in this case, notably because (i) "Ademi's Undertaking makes no reference to the details of Čermak's case and how he might be implicated as Gotovina's second-in-command" during the events pleaded in the Joinder Indictment;[94] (ii) the Appellant's Undertaking does not refer to "the potential defence which could be raised on his behalf in the light of information that Ademi was Gotovina's Chief of Staff and second-in-command and was allegedly Acting Commander of the Split Military District in Gotovina's stead".[95] The Trial Chamber found that Prodanović and Sloković were "duty-bound" to discuss these matters with both of their clients and held that these lacunae showed that the Undertakings were not fully informed for the purposes of Article 14(E) of the Code of Conduct.[96] **[page 14]**

33. The Appeals Chamber recalls that "consent provided by a potentially affected client or former client to remove a conflict of interests upon consultation with the counsel should generally be regarded as fully informed in the absence of an indication to the contrary".[97] However, such presumption could only be made in this case if the Appellant and Ademi had been fully conscious of *all possible implications, and possible limitations* that their simultaneous representation could impose upon either of their defence strategies.[98] Having

---

88 Appeal, para. 35.
89 *Ibid.*, para. 12.
90 Gotovina's Response, paras 20, 22.
91 *Ibid.*, para. 20.
92 Prosecution's Response, paras 21 and 23.
93 *Ibid.*, paras 22 (citing the Advisory Opinion, para. 44) and 24.
94 Impugned Decision, para. 20.
95 *Ibid.*, para. 21.
96 *Ibid.*, paras 20–22.
97 *Prlić* Appeal Decision, para. 27 citing *Prosecutor v. Milan Martić*, Case No.: IT-95-11-PT, 2 August 2002, Decision on Appeal Against Decision of Registry, p. 7.
98 *Cf. Prlić* Appeal Decision, para. 27 (emphasis added).

Also compare with Wheat v. United States, 486 U.S. 153, 162–163: "The likelihood and dimensions of nascent conflicts of interest are notoriously hard to predict, even for those thoroughly familiar with criminal trials [...] A few bits of unforeseen testimony or a single previously unknown or unnoticed document may significantly shift the relationship between multiple

examined both Undertakings, the Appeals Chamber is of the view that the Appellant has not demonstrated any discernible error in the Trial Chamber's findings, as they did not refer to any discussion on possible implications of such dual representation on any of the defence strategies with the exception of Ademi being potentially called as a witness in the present case.

34. The Appeals Chamber also disagrees with the Appellant's argument that the Trial Chamber should have ordered the Counsel to present new, more satisfactory, undertakings before rendering the Impugned Decision. The Trial Chamber was under no obligation to do so since the duty to inform promptly and fully each potentially affected client (current or former) and to take all steps to remove it or to obtain the full and informed consent of the said persons lies squarely upon the counsel.[99] The Trial Chamber decided on the matter taking into account the Undertaking that had been submitted to it by Prodanović and Sloković "for the purpose of dealing with the matter of the potential conflict of interest in the current proceeding".[100]

35. In any case, the Appeals Chamber recalls that such consent, even if found to be fully informed, is not conclusive of there being no conflict of interest.[101] The fact that the Appellant agreed to common representation does not relieve the Trial Chamber of its responsibility to ensure that the integrity of the proceedings would be preserved if such representation is maintained.[102] In **[page 15]** the present case, the Trial Chamber concluded otherwise and the Appeals Chamber has found no error in such conclusion.[103] Moreover, the Appeals Chamber finds that the Appellant's consent is in fact of no relevance to the present issue, as the point of concern is whether, by participating in the Appellant's defence, Prodanović and Sloković will be led into conflict with *their* professional responsibilities to Ademi.[104]

36. The third ground of appeal is therefore dismissed.

D. Measures to Remedy the Conflict of Interest

1. Submissions of the Parties

37. The Appellant submits that the Trial Chamber erred in concluding that Prodanović and Sloković must withdraw from the Appellant's representation, since it should have (i) offered them the opportunity to decide from which case to withdraw;[105] and (ii) take into account the general principle of proportionality in imposing such measures.[106] The Appellant adds that even if the Trial Chamber's conclusion on the potential conflict of interest were to be confirmed, other, less drastic, measures were available to the Trial Chamber as means to avoid or resolve it, such as giving the Counsel the possibility to withdraw from Ademi's representation

---

defendants. These imponderables are difficult enough for a lawyer to assess, and even more difficult to convey by way of explanation to a criminal defendant untutored on the niceties of legal ethics. Nor is it amiss to observe that the willingness of an attorney to obtain such waivers from his clients may bear an inverse relation to the care with which he conveys all the necessary information to them".

99 Article 14(E) of the Code of Conduct.

100 Notice of Undertakings, para. 2.

101 *Prlić* Appeal Decision, para. 27; First *Miletić* Decision, para. 32.

102 *See supra, para. 16.*

Also compare: United States v. Vasquez, 995 F.2d 40, 45 (5th cir. 1993); *Wheat v. United States*, 486 U.S 153, 162–163, 108 S.Ct. 1692, 1698–1699; *United States v. Medina*, 161 F.3d 867, 870 (5th Cir.1998), *United States v. Rico*, 51 F.3d 495, 511 (5th Cir. 1995): "In determining the validity of a waiver, the district court is afforded 'substantial latitude in refusing waivers of conflicts of interest not only if an actual conflict is demonstrated, but in cases where a potential for conflict exists which may result in an actual conflict as the trial progresses'. The court must also evaluate the potential effect on the integrity of the judicial system".

In the UK, such consent may also be found insufficient to save the professional from breaching fiduciary obligations to act for one client without being inhibited by the existence of the other client, and to avoid any actual conflict (whereby it is impossible to fulfil obligations to one client without breaching obligations to the other) (see *Hollander C. and Salzedo S.*, Conflicts of Interest & Chinese Walls (London: Sweet & Maxwell, 2000), 98, 117–18).

The French case-law also defines situations where a client's consent is without bearing on the counsel's duty of loyalty: "[...] *puisque les intérêts pécuniaires des deux époux étaient en opposition, l'accord allégué de M. Y... étant sans portée, en l'espèce, sur le devoir de prudence qui s'imposait à l'avocat [...] » (Cour de Cassation, 1ère ch. civile, 20 Janvier 1993, Bull. 1993 I No 22, p. 14).*

103 *See supra,* para. 28.

104 *Cf.* First *Miletić* Decision, para. 33.

105 Appeal, para. 32.

106 Ibid., para. 33.

and appointing a third counsel engaged by the Appellant for the purposes of cross examination of Ademi should he be called as a witness in this case.[107] Finally, he argues that in deciding which case the Counsel should withdraw, the Trial Chamber had no jurisdiction to consider the possible implications of the dual representation for Ademi's case.[108]

38. Gotovina responds that the Trial Chamber correctly imposed the Counsel's withdrawal from the Appellant's case since "the continued representation of Ademi will not have any impact on Prodanovic and Slokovic's duty of loyalty to Cermak, provided that Slokovic and Prodanovic do not advise Ademi concerning his testimony in this case [*sic*]".[109] He explains that, should **[page 16]** Prodanović and Sloković choose to withdraw from Ademi's defence they would nevertheless face a breach of duty of loyalty to their former client by continuing to represent the Appellant.[110] Gotovina further submits that withdrawing from Ademi's case while his trial is scheduled to commence imminently would have a material adverse effect on Ademi's interests contrary to Article 9(B) of the Code of Conduct.[111] With references to American case-law, Gotovina argues that abandoning Ademi at this stage of proceedings would be contrary to the "hot potato" rule according to which "[a] firm may not drop a client like a hot potato, especially if it is in order to keep happy a far more lucrative client".[112] He suggests that allowing Prodanović and Sloković to withdraw from Ademi's defence in these circumstances "would diminish public confidence in the [International] Tribunal, particularly with Ademi's upcoming trial and in light of the possibility that Ademi's lawyers eventually may attempt to implicate him".[113] Finally, Gotovina submits that the engagement of a third attorney to cross-examine Ademi would not be a satisfactory solution, as such third attorney would be precluded from implicating Ademi just as Prodanović and Sloković due to their duty of loyalty to the latter.[114] Moreover, Prodanović and Sloković would similarly be precluded from raising a defence implicating Ademi throughout the trial, including in closing argument.[115]

39. The Prosecution also submits that it was not unreasonable for the Trial Chamber to find that the Counsel's withdrawal from the Appellant's defence was the only option.[116]

40. In his Reply, the Appellant argues that the Counsel's duty of loyalty to Ademi would not be violated if they withdrew from the representation of the latter and continued to represent the Appellant.[117] He explains that the duty to decline representation of a client where counsel must take a position adverse to a former client only applies to "substantially related matters and is therefore a matter of degree".[118] Since, according to the Appellant, the present case is not substantially related to Ademi's case, the implications for the former client in the current proceedings are no more than speculative".[119]

41. The Appellant further reiterates that the provisions of the Code of Conduct do not apply to Ademi's case and that the Trial Chamber had no jurisdiction to consider the issues related to his **[page 17]** representation.[120] He adds that the Appeals Chamber should not take into account Gotovina's arguments in connection to the potential withdrawal from Ademi's case, as these matters are outside its jurisdiction and knowledge.[121] The Appellant insists that, in accordance with the Appeals Chamber Decision on Joinder, the Trial Chamber should have allowed the Counsel to decide for themselves from which case to withdraw in conformity of their duty of loyalty.[122]

---

107 *Ibid.*, paras 33 and 36.
108 *Ibid.*, para. 32.
109 Gotovina's Response, para. 15.
110 *Ibid.*, para. 15.
111 *Ibid.*, para. 16.
112 *Ibid.*, para. 17.
113 *Ibid.*, para. 18.
114 *Ibid.*, para. 23.
115 *Ibid.*, para. 23.
116 Proesecution's Response, para. 27.
117 Reply, para. 8.
118 *Ibid.*, paras 9 (emphasis omitted), 10-13 citing Article 14(D)(iii) of the Code of Conduct, Rule 1.9(a) of the American Bar Association Model Rules of Professional Conduct and related American case-law.
119 Reply, para. 9.
120 *Ibid.*, para. 28.
121 *Ibid.*, para. 29.
122 *Ibid.*, para. 28.

2. Analysis

42. Having reached the conclusion that the dual representation must be terminated, the Trial Chamber held that because "it has not been suggested that Čermak may be implicated in Ademi's case or be called as a witness in it" since their cases "are temporally and spatially separated", there was no need for Prodanović and Sloković to withdraw from Ademi's defence.[123] Therefore, it ordered that Prodanović and Sloković withdraw from representing the Appellant.[124] The Trial Chamber also considered that engaging a third attorney to represent the Appellant when dealing with Ademi's potential testimony in this case would not be sufficient to avoid the conflict of interest, as such attorney would be on the same defence team as Prodanović and Sloković which is equivalent to the position of a co-member of "firm" in the sense of Article 14(D) of the Code of Conduct.[125]

43. The Appeals Chamber considers that there is, at this stage, no need for it to address the question as to whether it has jurisdiction to consider matters related to Ademi's representation in the proceedings in Croatia. What is important in this instance is to examine whether the alternative solutions suggested by the Appellant, namely his Counsel's withdrawing from Ademi's defence and engaging a third counsel to cross-examine Ademi were he to testify in the present case, would be sufficient to ensure that the Appellant's representation is not impaired by the identified conflict of interest. Moreover, the Appeals Chamber notes that Article 14(D) of the Code of Conduct prohibits a representation with an adverse effect on either of the clients, regardless of whether they are represented in matters before the International Tribunal or other jurisdictions. At the same time, the Appeals Chamber emphasizes that Prodanović and Sloković have, at this stage, neither withdrawn from Ademi's defence, nor obtained a fully informed consent from Ademi with respect to the successive representation of the Appellant if Ademi's representation is terminated.[126] Therefore, the present discussion is rather hypothetical and is solely based on the Appellant's implicit suggestion **[page 18]** that had the Trial Chamber left the Counsel the choice to decide from which representation to withdraw, they would have withdrawn from Ademi's.[127]

(a) Withdrawal from Ademi's defence

44. The Appeals Chamber turns to consider whether withdrawal from Ademi's defence would allow Prodanović and Sloković to represent the Appellant to the best of his interests without breaching their duty of loyalty to Ademi under Article 14(D). While the said provision does not seem to distinguish between the duty of loyalty to a current and a former client,[128] the Appeals Chamber observes that a conflict of interest may be more difficult to discern when it arises from the context of successive or serial representation rather than concurrent representation. Parties made extensive references to national case-law and the Appeals Chamber finds it instructive to have a brief overview of underlying principles with respect to a counsel's duty of loyalty to a former client in national jurisdictions.

45. According to the relevant US and UK case-law on the matter, a conflict of interest *vis-à-vis* a former client exists when the subject matter of the two representations are substantially related so as to put at risk the confidences received from that client.[129] It is however important to note that such conflict of interest is

---

123 Impugned Decision, para. 24.

124 *Ibid.*, para. 25.

125 *Ibid.*, para. 23.

126 Article 14(E)(ii)(2) of the Code of Conduct.

127 *See* supra, para. 37.

128 The Appeals Chamber notes that the provisions of Article 14(D)(i) and (ii) of the Code of Conduct applicable to simultaneous representations do not require that the matters be substantially related, while Article 14(D)(iii) applicable to successive representations refers to both factors – substantial relationship and the materially adverse effect to the interests of the former client. However, Article 14(D) does not seem to differentiate the scope of the duty of loyalty that a counsel owes to a current or former client. *Also cf.* First *Miletić* Decision, paras 28–37.

129 *Perillo v. Johnson*, 205 F.3d 775, 798 (5th Cir. 2000); *Westinghouse v. Gulf*, 588 F.2d 221, 223-226; *Silver Chrysler v. Chrysler Motors* 518 F.2d 751, 754-756, *Santacroce v. Neff*, 134 F. Supp.2d 366, 372; *American Airlines v. Sheppard, Mullin, Richter & Hampton*, 96 Cal.App.4th 1017, 1019; *Duncan v. Merill Lynch, Pierce, Fenner & Smith*, 646 F.2d 1020, 1028-1029 (1981); *Steel* v. General Motors Corp., 912 F.Supp. 724, 735 (D.N.J. 1995); *see also* ABA Model Rules of Professional Conduct, 1983, Rule 1.9. For the UK, *see e.g. Bolkiah v. KPMG* [1999] 2 AC 222 (Lord Millett).

considered to exist in *all* situations "when defense counsel is compelled to compromise his or her duty of loyalty or zealous advocacy to the accused by choosing between or blending the divergent or competing interests of a former or current client".[130] Generally, it would be a case-by-case assessment by the judiciary of the character and extensiveness of the prior **[page 19]** representation to ensure that the interests of both former and current clients are preserved.[131] In any case, doubts as to the existence of an asserted conflict of interest with respect to a former client should be resolved in favour of disqualification.[132]

46. As a general principle in French law, apart from confidentiality issues, a counsel can only accept a new representation in which he or she may be led to plead against a former client where such new case is *entirely* different from the previous one, so as to fully conform to his or her duty of loyalty.[133] Similar principles are provided for by the Code of Conduct for European Lawyers, according to which a lawyer "must [...] refrain from acting for a new client if there is a risk of breach of a confidence entrusted to the lawyer by a former client or if the knowledge which the lawyer possesses of the affairs of the former client would give an undue advantage to the new client".[134]

47. While the Croatian Attorney's Code of Ethics is only explicit with respect to prohibiting legal assistance to an adverse party in a subsequent representation, it provides for duties of faithfulness and loyalty to a client which do not necessarily cease with the end of representation.[135] In Bosnia and Herzegovina, it is impermissible to represent clients with conflicting interests, and should such a conflict (or risk of infringing the confidentiality of information or the attorney's **[page 20]** independence) arise during litigation, the attorney has an obligation to return the power of attorney to *all* the parties involved.[136]

48. Having concluded that the simultaneous representation of the Appellant and Ademi by Prodanović and Sloković raises a high risk of a conflict of interest due to the fact that the Counsel would be limited in their choice of defence strategies in order to conform to their duty of loyalty,[137] the Appeals Chamber is of the view

---

It is also important to note that, in US case-law, the court generally presumes that confidential information was provided to the counsel by the former client and only needs to ensure that such information will not be used or disclosed in the current representation (Westinghouse v. Gulf, 588 F.2d 221, 224; *American Airlines v. Sheppard Mullin, Richter & Hampton*, 96 Cal.App.4th 1017, 1038-1039); *Gray v.* Commercial Union Insur. Co., 191 N.J.Super. 590, 598, 468 A.2d 721, 726 (App.Div.1983).

130 *See, e.g. Perillo v. Johnson*, 205 F.3d 775, 781 and 798 (5th Cir. 2000) citing *United States v. Alvarez*, 580 F.2d 1251, 1255, 1258 (5th Cir. 1978); *see generally Enoch v. Gramley*, 70 F.3d 1490, 1496 (7th Cir.1995); *Maiden v. Bunnell, Vvan De Kamp*, 35 F.3d 477, 480 (9th cir. 1994); *Westinghouse v. Gulf*, 588 F.2d 221, 224. *See also* on the "duty of undivided loyalty", "fiduciary relation" and "appearance of professional impropriety": *Harte Biltmore Ltd. v. First Pennsylvania Bank*, 655 F. Supp. 419, 421-422; *State of N.J. in the interest of S.G.*, 175 N.J. 138 (2003); Santacroce v. Neff, 134 F. Supp.2d 366, 370; *American Airlines v. Sheppard Mullin, Richter & Hampton*, 96 Cal.App.4th 1017, 1044; *Steel v. General Motors Corp.*, 912 F.Supp. 724, 740-741 (D.N.J. 1995).

131 *Perillo v. Johnson*, 205 F.3d 775, 799 (5th Cir. 2000) citing *Vega v. Johnson*, 149 F.3d 354, 360 (5th Cir. 1998); *Satellite Fin. Planning v. 1st Nat. BK. Wilmington*, 652 F.Supp. 1281, 1285 (D.Del.1987).

132 *Westinghouse v. Gulf*, 588 F.2d 221, 225; *International Business Machines Corp. v. Levin*, 579 F.2d 271, 283 (3d Cir. 1978); *Hull v. Celanese Corp.*, 513 F.2d 568, 571 (2d Cir. 1975); *Sitz v. Bethlehem Steel Corp.*, 650 F.Supp. 914, 916 (D.Md. 1987).

133 *Hamelin J., Nouvel abrégé des règles de la profession d'avocat* (Dalloz 1968) : *« ... dès lors qu'un avocat accepte de plaider une cause qui n'est pas entièrement distincte de celle à propos de laquelle il avait été précédemment consulté, il peut porter atteinte à la délicatesse qu'il doit observer et commettre un manquement professionnel pouvant être sanctionné par la Cour. »* A counsel can neither accept a new representation when the counsel's knowledge of his or her former client's case can be of unjustifiable benefit to the new client (*Décret No 91-1197 du 27 novembre 1991 organisant la profession d'avocat, article 155; Règlement Intérieur Unifié (R.I.U.) des Barreaux de France, (Décision à caractère normatif n° 2004-001 du Conseil National des Barreaux instituant le Règlement intérieur unifié (R.I.U) des Barreaux de France, article 4.3 : «* [...] *Il* [*l'avocat*] *ne peut accepter l'affaire d'un nouveau client si le secret des informations données par un ancien client risque d'être violé ou lorsque la connaissance par l'avocat des affaires de l'ancien client favoriserait le nouveau client de façon injustifiée.* [...] ».

See also, *Cour de cassation, 1ère Ch. civile, 30 juin 1981, Bull. des arrêts C. Cass. Ch. civile 1 No 237 Dalloz, 1982, p. 165: «* [...] *la prohibition édictée par l'article 84 du Décret du 9 juin 1972 [d'assister ou représenter des parties ayant des intérêts opposés] n'exige pas pour son application l'identité des affaires, mais la seule existence d'intérêts opposés* [...] *» ; Cour de Cassation, 1ère Ch. civile, 20 Janvier 1993, Bull. 1993 I No 22, p. 14 : «* [...] *en retenant que M. X..., dès lors qu'il avait été le conseil commun des époux Y..., dans <u>une procédure</u> de divorce par requête conjointe devait refuser d'être ensuite le conseil de Mme Z... dans <u>une autre procédure</u> de divorce pour faute puisque <u>les intérêts</u> pécuniaires des deux époux étaient <u>en opposition</u>* [...] *la cour d'appel a pu estimer que M. X... avait manqué à la délicatesse qui s'imposait à lui* [...] *» (emphasis added).*

134 28 October 1988 as amended on 19 May 2006, Article 3.2.2; see also Article 3.2.3: "must cease to act for both or all of the clients concerned when a conflict of interests arises between those clients and also whenever there is a risk of a breach of confidence or where the lawyer's independence may be impaired" (emphasis added).

135 The Attorney's Code of Ethics, (adopted at the Assembly of the Croatian Bar Association on 18 February 1995 with amendments of 12 June 1999), Articles 40–61.

136 *Kodeks advokatske etike advokata FBiH*, 5 November 2004 as amended on 4 May 2005, Article 21 (emphasis added).

137 *See supra*, paras 27–28.

that, even if Prodanović and Sloković withdrew from Ademi's defence, they would still be unable to represent the Appellant to the best of his interests as they would remain bound by their duty of loyalty to Ademi as a former client.[138] This potential conflict of interest is even more contoured considering the high probability that Ademi will be called as witness in the present case.[139]

(b) Third lawyer

49. As the Appeals Chamber has already held that the conflict of interest is very likely to arise even if Ademi is not called to testify in the present case[140] and if the Counsel withdrew from Ademi's defence,[141] there is no need to address the possibility of engaging a third lawyer for the purposes of cross-examination of Ademi. In any case, in light of the Appeals Chamber's findings above, this solution would not be sufficient to satisfy the duty of loyalty to a current or former client as it would constitute too limited an understanding thereof.[142] The Appeals Chamber also agrees with the observation made in a different case that "the defence cannot be compartmentalised, as is suggested, to get around a conflict situation".[143]

(c) Conclusion

50. In light of the foregoing, the Appeals Chamber dismisses the fourth ground of Appeal in its entirety. **[page 21]**

E. Hardship Caused to the Appellant

1. Submissions of the Parties

51. The Appellant finally argues that the Trial Chamber erred in failing to pay sufficient regard to the hardship that the removal of Counsel would cause to the Appellant. He explains that the relationship of trust between the Appellant his Counsel who have been acting for him for the past eight years, predates his charges before the International Tribunal and was the crucial factor in his choice of counsel in the present case.[144] He also argues that the withdrawal of Prodanović and Sloković at this stage would result in considerable financial burden for the Appellant who, in addition to the funds already spent on his defence in this case, will have to bear the costs of instructing the new counsel who will have no familiarity with the case.[145] He adds that the removal of his current Counsel and appointment of the new ones would necessarily delay the commencement of the trial for at least six months and thus prejudice his right to an expeditious trial.[146] The Appellant finally emphasizes that all this hardship would be borne by him in "a situation in which he is blameless".[147]

52. Referring to the Impugned Decision and the Appeals Chamber Decision on Joinder, Gotovina responds that the Appellant's "long-term interests are better served by counsel who are not limited in the defences that they are able to advance on his behalf, despite the short-term hardships that will result from having to obtain new counsel".[148] The Prosecution takes a similar position and adds that Article 14 of the Code of Conduct does not contain a "substantial hardship" exception.[149]

53. In his Reply, the Appellant accepts the absence of the notion of "substantial hardship" in the relevant provision of the Code of Conduct, but insists that in a case where the conflict of interest at stake is only a

[138] In this sense, the Appeals Chamber agrees with the Impugned Decision that counsel's duty of loyalty to a client under Article 14(A) of the Code of Conduct affects both present and former clients (Impugned Decision, para. 15).

[139] *Cf. Prosecutor v. Vujadin Popović et al.*, Case No. IT-05-88-T, *Confidential* Decision on Request for Review of the Registry Decision on the assignment of Co-Counsel for Radivoje Miletić, 16 November 2006 ("Second *Miletić* Decision"), paras 29–30.

[140] *See supra*, para. 22.

[141] *See supra*, para. 48.

[142] *Cf. First Miletić* Decision, para. 35.

[143] *Ibid.*, para. 34.

[144] Appeal, para. 37.

[145] *Ibid.*, para. 37.

[146] *Ibid.*, para. 38.

[147] *Ibid.*, para. 37.

[148] Gotovina's Response, paras 24–25.

[149] Prosecution's Response, paras 28–29.

potential one, the Trial Chamber should have taken the Appellant's hardship into account as a relevant factor in deciding on measures necessary to prevent or remove such conflict.[150] **[page 22]**

2. Analysis

54. In the Impugned Decision, the Trial Chamber concluded that the conflict of interest posed by continued dual representation by Prodanović and Sloković of both the Appellant and Ademi "is likely to irreversibly prejudice the administration of justice".[151] The Trial Chamber did not consider the hardship element when ordering the Counsel to withdraw from the Appellant's representation and the Appeals Chamber is not convinced that it was obliged to do so to the point where such an omission would constitute an abuse of discretion. The Appeals Chamber recalls that the question of prejudice was indeed discussed by the Trial and Appeal Chambers in their previous decisions related to the impact of the joinder on the Appellant's right to have a counsel of his choice.[152] In the present instance, there is nothing that would oblige the Trial Chamber to consider this factor in relation to the conflict of interest.

55. The Appeals Chamber reiterates that "[o]ne of the limits to the accused's choice [of counsel] is a conflict of interest affecting his counsel".[153] It further finds that, even though the replacement of counsel is generally likely to cause obvious inconveniences, including a delay in the proceedings, if the conflict of interests regarding the representation of the Appellant and Ademi is not resolved at the present stage of the proceedings, the administration of justice may be seriously prejudiced and have much more disastrous consequences in future.[154] The Appeals Chamber also notes that no imminent date has been established for the commencement of the trial in this case and, considering the current trial schedule of the International Tribunal,[155] it is not likely to commence within the next six months which the Appellant affirms to be necessary for the new counsel to get familiarized with the case.

56. The fifths ground of Appeal is therefore dismissed. **[page 23]**

---

150 Reply, para. 30.

151 Impugned Decision, para. 22.

152 *Decision* on Joinder, para. 64 and Appeals Chamber Decision on Joinder, para. 30. The Appeals Chamber then noted that any potential prejudice arising from having new counsel (situation that could arise regardless the joinder) could be mitigated by allowing additional time.

153 Appeals Chamber Joinder Decision, para. 30 citing *Prosecutor v. Željko Mejakić et al.*, Case No IT-02-65-AR73.1, Decision on Appeal by the Prosecution to Resolve Conflict of Interest Regarding Attorney Jovan Simić, 6 October 2004 ("*Mejakić* Decision"), para. 8.

154 *See supra*, para. 16; *cf. Prlić* Appeal Decision, para. 32; *Mejakić* Decision, para. 14.
Also compare with Steel v. General Motors Corp., 912 F.Supp. 724, 746 (D.N.J. 1995): "The court emphasised that 'only in extraordinary cases should a client's right to counsel of his or her choice outweigh the need to maintain the highest of the profession.'".

155 *See* Assessment and Report of Judge Fausto Pocar, President of the International Criminal Tribunal for the Former Yugoslavia, Provided to the Security Council Pursuant to Paragraph 6 of Council Resolution 1534 (2004), S/2007/283, 16 May 2007, paras 5 and 14 and Enclosures II, IV, XII.

V. DISPOSITION

57. On the basis of the foregoing, the Appeals Chamber (Judge Shahabuddeen dissenting),

DISMISSES the Appeal in its entirety.

Done in both English and French, the English text being authoritative.

Done this 29th day of June 2007
At The Hague, The Netherlands

Judge Andrésia Vaz
Presiding Judge

Judge Shahabuddeen appends a dissenting opinion.

[Seal of the International Tribunal] [page 1]

DISSENTING OPINION OF JUDGE SHAHABUDDEEN

1. The question raised in this interlocutory appeal by Čermak is whether defence counsel are entitled to represent a client if their representation of another client in a different case may prevent them from putting forward all the defences possible in the case of the first client. To that, the answer is in the negative: defence counsel are not so entitled. It is a fundamental rule that counsel are to be zealous in the representation of a client; they are not to be unreasonably inhibited from advancing his case. My opinion, however, is that in the instant case there will be no such inhibition.

A. The cases of Čermak and Ademi are different

2. The case against Čermak and that against Ademi call for separate conclusions by different courts as to guilt on temporally and spatially distinct facts. There is no common basis between the two cases. Defence counsel, Mr Prodanović and Mr Sloković (Prodanović and Sloković), are representing Čermak in Čermak's case and Ademi in Ademi's case. In principle, nothing prevents defence counsel from so acting. Further, but subject to the following, there is no reason why they cannot submit that Ademi does not have criminal responsibility in his own case, but that he has criminal responsibility in the case of Čermak. I may add that Ademi is not an accused in Čermak's case and that Prodanović and Sloković are not representing him in that case.

B. Defence counsel are not inhibited by any information from Ademi, because they do not have any such information

3. Prodanović and Sloković will only be inhibited from submitting that Ademi has criminal responsibility in the case of Čermak if there was an inhibiting element in any confidential information given by Ademi to Prodanović and Sloković in Ademi's case. But, in paragraph 17 of its decision of 5 April 2007, the Trial Chamber states explicitly that it "is satisfied that no such confidential information is in Prodanović's and Sloković's possession". Prodanović and Sloković, not being in possession of the confidential information, cannot be inhibited by anything in it.

C. Defence counsel are not inhibited by their position on Ademi's criminal responsibility

4. If there is no confidential information involved, will Prodanović and Sloković be inhibited in Čermak's case by virtue of the mere fact that they are also representing Ademi in Ademi's case? Though the two cases are different, they are pending at the same time; so it may be awkward for their counsel to submit that Ademi does not have criminal responsibility in one case but that he has **[page 2]** criminal responsibility in the other. It is not certain that Ademi will be called as a witness in Čermak's case, but, assuming that he is called, the Trial Chamber observes, in paragraph 13 of its decision, that the "question is whether Prodanović's and Sloković's attitude to Ademi as a witness would be materially different if he were not their client". This reflects the view that a conflict of interest includes not only an actual conflict of interest but potential ones also. I will not go into the question whether the awkwardness involved in this case rises to the level of a conflict of interest; for purposes of the present argument, I assume that it does.

5. If so, that is a usual situation in which defence counsel seeks the consent of his client to continuation of representation. Such consent was duly obtained in this case. In fact, consents were obtained from both Ademi and Čermak; they were both obtained in writing; and both texts made it clear that Ademi and Čermak took the view that Prodanović and Sloković would not be placed in a "conflict of interest situation" if Ademi was called as a witness in Čermak's case and had to be cross-examined by Prodanović and Sloković.[1] In my

---

[1] Paragraphs (b) and (c) of Ademi's consent of 6 February 2007 stated as follows:

b. Even if I was ordered to testify for one of the parties in those proceedings involving my Counsel – representing one of the Co-Accused, i.e. Ivan Čermak – I take the view that my Counsel would not be placed in a conflict of interest situation by having to cross-examine me; and, in any event,

c. I HEREBY UNDERTAKE not to raise my Counsel's dual representation of Ivan Čermak and myself as a legal impediment affecting my right to a fair trial in the Republic of Croatia and accordingly waive my right to do so.

Čermak's consent of 7 February 2007 was to similar effect.

view, the consents so given to dual representation would hold good even if the question of incrimination of Ademi was raised through evidence other than Ademi's; it is the substance which matters. But the majority in the Trial Chamber rejected the consents for not having been informed. Was that correct?

D. Whether the written consents to dual representation were informed

6. In reading the consents, I find value in an observation which Judge Orie made in paragraph 17 of his dissenting opinion. This observation, which in my opinion reflects the practice, runs as follows (footnote omitted):

> I have no reason to doubt that the consent given by both Čermak and Ademi are sufficiently informed. The expression of consent does not have to set out in full detail the potential situations that might arise and that are covered by such consent. I further consider both Čermak and Ademi sufficiently competent so as not to be easily misled.

With respect, I am not persuaded by an overcritical analysis which seeks to make good the proposition that the consents were not informed. Both consents authorised continuation of "dual representation" in circumstances in which it was clear that there could be divergent interests; that is **[page 3]** the material point. Without entering into further details, I join Judge Orie in holding that the consents were informed.

E. Conclusion

7. Prodanović and Sloković not having acquired any confidential information from Ademi, there is no reason to trouble on that account. The concern is only with the integrity of any evidence given by Ademi in Čermak's case, as that evidence may be affected by the fact that Prodanović and Sloković are representing Ademi in Ademi's case. But the consent of Ademi shows that he is willing to be cross-examined by Prodanović and Sloković despite his relationship to them. As to other evidence (Ademi may not be called as a witness in Čermak's case), this is a matter for defence counsel in the ordinary way.

8. In my view, Prodanović and Sloković are entitled unconditionally to represent Čermak. I would allow Čermak's interlocutory appeal.

Done in English and French, the English text being authoritative.

29 June 2007
The Hague
The Netherlands

Mohamed Shahabuddeen

[Seal of the International Tribunal]

UNITED NATIONS

International Tribunal for the Prosecution of Persons Responsible for Serious Violations of International Humanitarian Law Committed in the Territory of the Former Yugoslavia since1991	Case No.	IT-04-83-T
	Date:	24 July 2007
	Original:	English

IN TRIAL CHAMBER I

Before: **Judge Bakone Justice Moloto, Presiding**
Judge Frederik Harhoff
Judge Flavia Lattanzi

Registrar: **Mr. Hans Holthuis**

Decision of: **24 July 2007**

PROSECUTOR

v.

RASIM DELIĆ

PUBLIC

DECISION ADOPTING GUIDELINES ON THE ADMISSION AND PRESENTATION OF EVIDENCE AND CONDUCT OF COUNSEL IN COURT

The Office of the Prosecutor
Mr. Daryl A. Mundis
Ms. Laurie Sartorio
Mr. Kyle Wood
Mr. Aditya Menon

Counsel for the Accused
Ms. Vasvija Vidović
Mr. Nicholas David Robson

* Editor's note: the editors have incorporated in this decision the addendum of 22 October 2007 (Addendum to decision adopting guidelines on the admission and presentation of evidence and conduct of counsel in court, *Prosecutor v. Delić,* Case No. IT-04-83-T, T. Ch. I, 22 October 2007).

[page 2] TRIAL CHAMBER I ("Trial Chamber") of the International Tribunal for the Prosecution of Persons Responsible for Serious Violations of International Humanitarian Law Committed in the Territory of the former Yugoslavia since 1991 ("Tribunal");

NOTING that at the pre-Trial Conference on 2 July 2007, the Trial Chamber informed the Parties of its intention to adopt guidelines covering the presentation and admission of evidence and the conduct of counsel in court;[1]

NOTING that on 9 July 2007, the Trial Chamber requested the Parties to provide it with any comments by way of email by close of business on Monday, 16 July 2007;

NOTING that such comments were received from both Parties on Monday, 16 July 2007;

NOTING in particular, that the Defence proposed the addition of a paragraph stipulating that the Prosecution not be permitted to adduce new evidence which would attempt to prove the alleged guilt of the Accused during the Defence case;

NOTING that on 17 July 2007, the Trial Chamber gave the Parties an opportunity to provide it with responses on the comments of the other side, by way of email by 19 July 2007;

NOTING that a response was received from the Prosecution on 19 July 2007 in which the Prosecution objected to the Defence's proposed addition on the basis that, *inter alia,* the proposed addition was inconsistent with Rule 90(H) of the Rules of Procedure and Evidence ("Rules"), which it stated, gives parties considerable latitude in conducting their cross-examinations;

CONSIDERING that the Guidelines attached in the Annex to the present Decision will promote fair and expeditious trial proceedings;

CONSIDERING that the attached Guidelines are in conformity with the Statute and the Rules, notably Rules 89 and 90 of the Rules of Procedure and Evidence ("Rules"), and that the Guidelines are reflective of the jurisprudence of the Tribunal;

NOTING that Rule 90 (H) provides:

> (i) Cross-examination shall be limited to the subject-matter of the evidence-in-chief and matters affecting the credibility of the witness and, where the witness is able to give evidence relevant to the case for the cross-examining party, to the subject-matter of that case. **[page 3]**
>
> (ii) In the cross-examination of a witness who is able to give evidence relevant to the case for the cross-examining party, counsel shall put to that witness the nature of the case of the party for whom that counsel appears which is in contradiction of the evidence given by the witness.
>
> (iii) The Trial Chamber may, in the exercise of its discretion, permit enquiry into additional matters.

CONSIDERING that Trial Chamber finds that the terms of Rule 90 (H) apply to cross-examinations carried out during both the Prosecution and Defence cases and that the Defence's proposed additional paragraph is therefore not in keeping with the provisions of Rule 90 (H);

PURSUANT TO Article 20(1) of the Statute of the Tribunal and Rules 54, 89 and 90 of the Rules,

---

1 Pre-Trial Conference, 2 July 2007, T. 190.

HEREBY adopts the Guidelines, attached as an Annex to this Decision, which shall govern the admission and presentation of evidence and the conduct of counsel in court in this case.

Done in English and French, the English version being authoritative.

Dated this twenty-fourth day of July 2007
At The Hague
The Netherlands

Judge Bakone Justice Moloto
Presiding

[Seal of the Tribunal] [page 4]

ANNEX

A. Standards governing presentation of evidence and conduct of counsel in court

(a) Order of calling witnesses

1. Each Party shall provide the other Party and the Trial Chamber with a list indicating the order of witnesses due to testify and the scheduled date of their appearance at trial. The Trial Chamber requires the Parties to inform it of the calling order of witnesses at the end of every week for the coming two weeks. Furthermore, the Parties shall inform the Trial Chamber five working days in advance of any changes to the calling order. Moreover, the Parties shall provide a list of documents which they intend to use for the examination-in-chief of each witness at least two working days before the start of the testimony.

(b) Long, complicated or compound questions

2. The Parties are requested to bear in mind that long, complicated or compound questions risk confusing witnesses and making the trial record unclear and unnecessarily lengthy. Therefore, in the interest of effective presentation of evidence, the Parties are advised to put one question at a time to the witnesses.

(c) Admission into evidence of a prior statement of a testifying witness

3. In accordance with the principle of orality, which is expressed in Rule 89 (F),[2] prior statements of a witness should not be tendered into evidence where relevant portions thereof have been read out and entered on the record or where the witness has otherwise commented on the statement in his or her live testimony.[3]

(d) Referring to prior testimony or statements of a witness

4. The Parties are requested to avoid interpreting or paraphrasing what a witness has previously either stated or testified.[4] The Trial Chamber considers that such interpreting or **[page 5]** paraphrasing increases the risk of mischaracterising the prior statement or testimony and unnecessarily lengthens the trial record.

5. Instead, the Parties are encouraged to quote from the statement or transcript. However, the Parties are requested to restrict such quoting to situations when it is *strictly necessary* for the understanding of the question asked. In such cases, the quote shall be restricted to the part of the transcript that is directly relevant to the question. Furthermore, when referring to a prior statement or testimony, the Parties are asked to provide exact page and line references to the statement or transcript in question.

(e) Refreshing the memory of a witness using a prior statement

6. Prior statements of the testifying witness, whether in evidence or not, may be used to refresh a witness's memory both during examination-in-chief and during cross-examination.[5] The Trial Chamber

---

2 *Prosecutor v. Sefer Halilović,* Case No. IT-01-48-AR73.2, Decision on Interlocutory Appeal Concerning Admission of Record of Interview of the Accused from the Bar Table, 19 Aug 2005, paras 16-17. *See also Prosecutor v. Miroslav Kvočka et al.*, Case No. IT-98-30/1-A, Judgement, 28 Feb 2005, paras 122-126; *Prosecutor v. Zlatko Aleksovski*, Case No. IT-95-14/1-AR73, Decision on Prosecutor's Appeal on Admissibility of Evidence, Dissenting Opinion of Judge Patrick Robinson, 16 Feb 1999, para. 10; *Prosecutor v. Zoran Kupreškić et al.*, Case No. IT-95-16, Decision on Appeal by Dragan Papić Against Ruling to Proceed by Deposition, 15 Jul 1999, para. 18.

3 *Prosecutor v. Miroslav Kvočka et al.*, 04 Jul 2000, T. 3490. *See also Prosecutor v. Milan Martić*, Case No. IT-91-11, Revised Version of the Decision Adopting Guidelines on the Standards Governing the Presentation of Evidence and the Conduct of Counsel in Court, 19 May 2006.

4 This concerns both what the testifying witness has stated, or testified at prior hearings, and what other witnesses, whose testimony has concluded, have stated or testified.

5 *Prosecutor v. Enver Hadžihasanović and Amir Kubura*, Case No. IT-01-47-AR73.2, Decision on Interlocutory Appeal Relating to the Refreshment of the Memory of a Witness, 02 Apr 2004, p. 2, referring to *Prosecutor v. Blagoje Simić et al.*, Case Nos IT-95-9-AR73.6 & IT-95-9-AR73.7, Decision on Prosecution Interlocutory Appeals on the Use of Statements not Admitted into

recalls the Appeals Chamber's finding that also unadmitted portions of a statement made pursuant to Rule 92 *bis* may be used to refresh the memory of a witness during examination-in-chief[6] and during cross-examination.[7]

7. The Trial Chamber may consider the means and circumstances by which this process was conducted when assessing the reliability and credibility of the witness's testimony.[8]

(f) Scope of the cross-examination

8. The Trial Chamber recalls Rule 90 (H)(i) of the Rules of Procedure and Evidence, which requires the parties to restrict cross-examination to:

> the subject-matter of the evidence-in-chief and matters affecting the credibility of the witness and, where the witness is able to give evidence relevant to the case for the cross-examining party, to the subject-matter of that case.

9. In this respect, the Parties are reminded that, when dealing in cross-examination with questions relating to the historical, political and military context of the case, they are requested to state the purpose and relevance of questions to the allegations raised in the Indictment against the **[page 6]** Accused.[9] Furthermore, it is recalled that this Tribunal does not recognise *tu quoque* as a valid defence and has accepted, but only to a very limited extent, evidence relating to crimes allegedly committed by other parties to the conflict.[10] As a consequence, the Trial Chamber may disallow questions which are irrelevant either because they are beyond the Indictment's temporal scope or are unrelated to the specific facts of the violations alleged in the Indictment.[11]

10. The Trial Chamber acknowledges that Rule 90 (H)(i) does not limit the matters that may be raised during a cross-examination which is directed solely at the credibility of the witness. However, cross-examination must still be conducted within some reasonable limits.[12] The Trial Chamber may therefore disallow improper, repetitive, irrelevant or unfair questions, including those which constitute an unwarranted attack on the witness or which fall outside the above parameters.[13]

11. In this respect, the Trial Chamber notes that the cross-examining party may confront a witness with the testimony[14] of another witness **who has previously appeared in the present case** in order to impeach

---

Evidence Pursuant to Rule 92bis as a Basis to Challenge Credibility and to Refresh Memory, 23 May 2003, paras 18–20. See also Prosecutor v. Milan Martić, Case No. IT-91-11, Revised Version of the Decision Adopting Guidelines on the Standards Governing the Presentation of Evidence and the Conduct of Counsel in Court, 19 May 2006.

6 Ibid.

7 Prosecutor v. Blagoje Simić et al., Case No. IT-95-9 & IT-95-9-AR73.7, Decision on Prosecution Interlocutory Appeals on the Use of Statements not Admitted into Evidence Pursuant to Rule 92bis as a Basis to Challenge Credibility and to Refresh Memory, 23 May 2003, paras 18, 20.

8 Ibid.

9 Prosecution v. Zoran Kupreškić et al., Case No. IT-95-16, Decision on Evidence of the Good Character of the Accused and the Defence of Tu Quoque, 17 Feb 1999; Prosecutor v. Enver Hadžihasanović et al., Case No. IT-01-47, Decision on Defence Motion for Clarification on the Oral Decision of 17 December 2003 Regarding the Scope of Cross-examination Pursuant to Rule 90 (H) of the Rules, 28 Jan 2004, p. 3.

10 *Prosecution v. Zoran Kupreškić et al.*, Case No. IT-95-16, Decision on Evidence of the Good Character of the Accused and the Defence of *Tu Quoque*, 17 Feb 1999, pp 3–5; *Prosecutor v. Enver Hadžihasanović et al.*, Case No. IT-01-47, Decision on Defence Motion for Clarification on the Oral Decision of 17 December 2003 Regarding the Scope of Cross-examination Pursuant to Rule 90 (H) of the Rules, 28 Jan 2004, p. 4; and *Prosecutor v. Kupreškić et al.*, Trial Judgement, paras 515–520; *Prosecutor v. Kordić and Čerkez* Trial Judgement, para. 520.

11 The Trial Chamber recalls in this regard that, for example, certain adjudicated or agreed facts may fall outside of the temporal scope of the Indictment.

12 *Prosecution v. Momčilo Krajišnik*, Case No. IT-00-39-T, Decision on Cross-Examination of Milorad Davidović, 15 Dec 2005.

13 *Ibid.* In that case the Trial Chamber, by recalling its duty to protect witnesses set out in Article 22 of the Statute, retained the discretion to disallow a question or sustain an objection against a question in cross-examination where, in the Trial Chamber's view, it constituted an unwarranted attack on a witness. An example of such an attack was the allegation by the cross-examining party that a witness had engaged in serious criminal conduct, without showing reasonable grounds to do so at the time the allegation was made. A similar solution is found in the practice of the ICTR, *see Prosecutor v. Bagosora*, Case No. ICTR-96-7, Oral Decision on Cross Examination, 9 May 2005, T. 27–28.

14 **The Trial Chamber considers this to include statements pursuant to Rule 92 *bis*, Rule 92 *ter* or Rule 92 *quater* which have been admitted in evidence.**

or challenge the credibility of that witness or the testifying witness. The cross-examining party shall put to the testifying witness the evidence of the previous witness *without* from whom the information has come.[15] **Where the testimony has been made by a person who has previously appeared as a protected witness or where the prior testimony has been led in private or closed session, the presentation of that testimony to the testifying witness must be done in private or closed session.** Moreover, the Trial Chamber reminds the Parties that while they may ask the witness whether or **[page 7]** not he agrees or disagrees with the evidence of the previous testimony, the Parties should not ask witnesses to comment on the credibility of other witnesses.[16]

11*bis* The Parties may confront a witness in court with the statement of another witness of transcript of prior testimony from another case before this Tribunal (hereinafter "transcript") only where that person will come to testify in the present case. The presenting party must identify to the Trial Chamber and the other party the name of the statement maker or prior witness, the date of the statement or transcript and the page references of the portion(s) of the statement or transcript which will be read out in or referred to. However this information shall not be disclosed to witness in court. Where the witness statement or transcript has been made by a person who has previously appeared as a protected witness or where the prior testimony has been led in private or closed session, the presentation of that statement or transcript to the testifying witness must be done in private or closed session. Finally, the statement shall not ordinarily be admitted into evidence.

11*ter* Where a witness is confronted in court with the statement or transcript of another witness who is scheduled to come to testify in the present case, and where that witness ultimately does not testify, the Trial Chamber shall disregard the part of the testimony where the witness was confronted with the statement or transcript of the witness who ultimately did not testify.

12. The Trial Chamber recalls that Rule 90 (H)(ii) requires the cross-examining party to put to a witness, who is able to give evidence relevant to the case for that party, the nature of its case that is in contradiction to the witness' evidence. The Trial Chamber, in accordance with the practice of the Tribunal, notes that Rule 90 (H)(ii) allows for certain flexibility depending on the various circumstances at trial and interprets the rule to mean that the cross-examining party is required to put the *substance* of the contradictory evidence and not every detail that the party does not accept.[17]

(g) <u>Length of examination</u>

13. A system for monitoring the use of time shall be established by the Registry, who will be responsible for recording time used.

14. The examination-in-chief of a witness will be limited to the time indicated by each Party, under the control of the Trial Chamber.

15. In the interest of ensuring fair and expeditious conduct of the trial proceedings, the Parties are requested to adhere to the principle that the time for cross-examination of a witness should not exceed the time allotted for the examination-in-chief of that witness, unless there are particular circumstances requiring

---

[15] *Prosecutor v. Blagoje Simić et al.*, Case No. IT-95-9 & IT-95-9-AR73.7, 13 Mar 2003, T. 16636; *ibid.*, 29 Apr 2003, T. 18809-10; *Prosecutor v. Radoslav Brđanin and Momir Talić*, Case No. IT-99-36-T, 14 Oct 2002, T. 10654:

JUDGE AGIUS: [...] it's not right that you present the witness with information leading him to understand that another witness also coming from the political arena gives a completely different story to his with regard to some details at least.

Miroslav Kvočka et al., Case No. IT-98-30/1, 28 Aug 2000, T. 4220–21. *Prosecution v. Momčilo Krajišnik*, Case No. IT-00-39-T, 05 Dec 2005, T. 19215.

[16] *Prosecutor v. Blagoje Simić et al.*, Case No. IT-95-9, 04 Jun 2002, T. 8820–8821; *Prosecutor v. Miroslav Kvočka et al., ibid; Prosecutor v. Kordić and Čerkez*, Case No. IT-95-14/2, 24 Nov 1999, T. 10336-7; *Prosecutor v. Radoslav Brđanin and Momir Talić*, Case No. IT-99-36-T, 14 Oct 2002, T. 10651.

[17] *Prosecutor v. Blagoje Simić et al.*, Case No. IT-95-9 & IT-95-9-AR73.7, 13 Mar 2003, T. 16636; ibid., 29 Apr 2003, T. 18809-10; *Prosecutor v. Radoslav Brđanin and Momir Talić*, Case No. IT-99-36-T, 14 Oct 2002, T. 10654: JUDGE AGIUS: [...] it's not right that you present the witness with information leading him to understand that another witness also coming from the political arena gives a completely different story to his with regard to some details at least.

Miroslav Kvočka et al., Case No. IT-98-30/1, 28 Aug 2000, T. 4220–21. *Prosecution v. Momčilo Krajišnik*, Case No. IT-00-39-T, 05 Dec 2005, T. 19215.

that the cross-examination be extended.[18] Such circumstances include situations where there has been a particularly brief examination-in-chief, where the witness is an expert witness, or where fairness to the accused so requires.

16. Re-examination of a witness shall be limited to matters raised in cross-examination. **[page 8]**

(h) 92 *bis* witnesses appearing for cross-examination

17. Where a witness whose previous testimony or statement has been admitted into evidence pursuant to Rule 92 *bis*, has been called solely for the purposes of cross-examination, the *calling party* should not introduce new evidence through examination-in-chief. Furthermore, the cross-examination of such witnesses shall be carried out in accordance with Rule 90 (H)(i) and (ii) with the limitation that questions relating to the "subject matter of the evidence-in-chief":

1. shall be restricted to the matters for which the Trial Chamber has decided to allow the witness to be called for cross-examination;[19] and
2. shall not include questions relating to the summary of the witness's 92 *bis* statement or transcript, which the calling party reads out at the start of the testimony, unless related to item 1, above.

(i) 92 *ter* witnesses

18. The party calling a witness under Rule 92 *ter* may be permitted by the Trial Chamber to conduct a limited direct examination of the witness where such examination is focused on clarifying or highlighting particular aspects of the statements which have been admitted pursuant to that Rule. In addition, the calling party will be permitted to show documents to the witness during the direct examination of a 92 *ter* witness and such documents may be tendered into evidence.

(j) Use of large documents in court

19. The Trial Chamber considers that it is not an efficient use of in-court time to read out large passages of a document which is subsequently tendered for admission into evidence. This is particularly so where the party does not ask concise and specific questions on the information contained in the document but merely requests the witness to verify what is written on the page in front of the witness. In this respect, counsel are reminded of the possibility of tendering such evidence from the bar table.[20] Where the Parties wish to present passages of a long document to a witness, they are urged to provide the relevant parts of the document to the witness and give the witness time to study it either in court or, preferably, during a break, and then ask concise questions **[page 9]** on the substance of the relevant parts of the document. Smaller portions of a document may be read out by counsel in court.

20. Barring exceptional circumstances with the leave of the Trial Chamber, the Parties may not tender into evidence lengthy documents, such as books, where only portions thereof are relevant to the evidence of the witness through whom the document is tendered. Rather, when seeking the admission into evidence of such documents, be it during examination-in-chief, cross-examination or re-examination, each Party is requested to specify which portions of the document it seeks to have admitted. Each tendering Party is also requested to submit electronic versions of the portions of the document sought to be admitted.

18 *Prosecutor v. Blagoje Simić et al.*, Case No. IT-95-9, 04 Jun 2002, T. 8820–8821; *Prosecutor v. Miroslav Kvočka et al., ibid; Prosecutor v. Kordić and Čerkez*, Case No. IT-95-14/2, 24 Nov 1999, T. 10336-7; *Prosecutor v. Radoslav Brđanin and Momir Talić*, Case No. IT-99-36-T, 14 Oct 2002, T. 10651.

19 *See e.g.*, Prosecutor v. Milan Martić, Case No. IT-95-11-T, Decision on Prosecution's Motion For the Admission of Written Evidence Purusant to Rule 92 *bis* of the Rules, 16 Jan 2006.

20 Rule 89 (C) provides "a Chamber may admit any relevant evidence which it deems to have probative value"; Prosecutor v. Sefer Halilović, Case No. IT-01-48-AR73.2, Decision on Interlocutory Appeal Concerning Admission of Record of Interview of the Accused from The Bar Table, 19 Aug 2005, para. 14. *See also* Prosecutor v. Milan Martić, Case No. IT-91-11, Revised Version of the Decision Adopting Guidelines on the Standards Governing the Presentation of Evidence and the Conduct of Counsel in Court, 19 May 2006.

(k) Use of hardcopies of documents

21. Parties are reminded that as this trial uses E-Court, the principle is that all documents shall be handled through the E-Court system. Hardcopies of a document may be used by a party only where the party has been unable, due to unforeseen circumstances, to put a document into the E-Court system. Parties are also reminded that when the use of hardcopies of a document is permitted, sufficient copies should be provided to the witness, the opposite party, the Bench, the Registrar and the interpreters. Finally, the Parties are reminded to make use of the drawing functionality of E-Court when asking a witness to make a drawing or annotate a document.

(l) Tendering of exhibits through witnesses

22. Where one of the Parties seeks the admission of a document through a witness it must demonstrate to the Trial Chamber the relation between the witness and the document. The Trial Chamber may not allow the admission, through that particular witness, of documents which lack such relation.

(m) General terms of behaviour

23. The Parties are encouraged to contact the Trial Chamber Legal Officer to resolve issues that can be addressed informally.

24. The Parties should endeavour to take all steps to preserve the public character of the proceedings. In particular, the Parties should seek only those specific protective measures, such as face or voice distortion, which they deem strictly necessary for the protection of the witnesses. It should be noted that closed session will only be ordered on an exceptional basis, after a party has presented the Trial Chamber with sufficient information warranting the taking of such a measure. **[page 10]**

B. The admission of evidence

25. The Trial Chamber will begin any analysis on the admissibility of evidence by recalling Rule 89(C) of the Rules, which provides that "[a] Chamber may admit any relevant evidence which it deems to have probative value", and Rule 89(D) of the Rules, which provides that "[a] Chamber may exclude evidence if its probative value is substantially outweighed by the need to ensure a fair trial."

26. Parties should always bear in mind the basic distinction that exists between the admissibility of documentary evidence and the weight that documentary evidence is given under the principle of free evaluation of evidence. The practice will be, therefore, in favour of admissibility.

27. The admission of a document into evidence does not, in itself, signify that the information contained therein will necessarily be deemed to be an accurate portrayal of the facts.[21] Factors such as authenticity and proof of authorship will naturally assume the greatest importance in the Trial Chamber's assessment of the weight to be attached to individual pieces of evidence. As has previously been stated, "[t]he threshold standard for the admission of evidence [...] should not be set excessively high, as often documents are sought to be admitted into evidence, not as ultimate proof of guilt or innocence, but to provide a context and complete the picture presented by the evidence in general".[22]

28. The fact that this Trial Chamber may rule on the admissibility of a particular document or other piece of evidence will not prevent that ruling from being reversed. Therefore, a decision not to admit a piece of evidence may be quashed at a later stage if good cause is shown for doing so, for example, where further evidence emerges which is relevant, has probative value and thus justifies the admission of the evidence in question.[23]

29. There is no general prohibition on the admission of documents simply on the grounds that their

21 *Prosecutor v. Zejnil Delalić et. al*, Case No. IT-96-21-T, Decision on the Motion of the Prosecution for the Admissibility of Evidence, 19 January 1998, para. 20.

22 *Ibid.*

23 *Prosecutor v. Milan Martić*, Case No. IT-95-11-T, Decision Adopting Guidelines on the Standards Governing the Admission of Evidence, 19 January 2006, Annex A, para. 4.

purported author has not been called to testify. Similarly, the fact that a document is unsigned or unstamped does not, *a priori,* render it void of authenticity.[24]

30. When objections are raised on grounds of authenticity or reliability, this Trial Chamber will follow the practice of this Tribunal, namely, to admit documents and/or video recordings and then **[page 11]** decide on the weight to be given to them within the context of the trial record as a whole.[25] As provided for in Rule 89(E) of the Rules, the tendering party may be requested to provide the Trial Chamber with verification of the authenticity of evidence obtained out of court. Additionally, when an objection is made on the ground of reliability, the tendering party may be required to produce sufficient indicia of reliability to make a *prima facie* case for the admission of the document, audio tape or video in question.[26] On the request of a party or *proprio motu*, the Trial Chamber may order the party tendering copies of evidence to present the original or the best legible, audible or visible copy available.

31. The "best evidence rule" will be applied in the determination of matters before this Trial Chamber. This means that the Trial Chamber will rely on the best evidence available in the circumstances of the case, and parties are directed to keep this rule in mind when submitting evidence to the Trial Chamber. What is considered the best evidence will depend on the particular circumstances attached to each document the complexity of the case and the preceding investigations.

32. Hearsay evidence is admissible. Out of court statements, which a Trial Chamber considers relevant and probative, are admissible under Rule 89(C).[27] As stated by the Appeals Chamber in *Aleksovski*:

> Trial Chambers have a broad discretion under Rule 89(C) to admit relevant hearsay evidence. Since such evidence is admitted to prove the truth of its contents, a Trial Chamber must be satisfied that it is reliable for that purpose, in the sense of being voluntary, truthful and trustworthy, as appropriate; and for this purpose may consider both the content of the hearsay statement and the circumstances under which the evidence arose; or, as Judge Stephen described it, the probative value of a hearsay statement will depend upon the context and character of the evidence in question. The absence of the opportunity to cross-examine the person who made the statements, and whether the hearsay is "first-hand" or more removed, are also relevant to the probative value of the evidence. The fact that the evidence is hearsay does not necessarily deprive it of probative value, but it is acknowledged that the weight or probative value to be afforded to that evidence will usually be less than that given to the testimony of a witness who has given it **[page 12]** under a form of oath and who has been cross-examined, although even this will depend upon the infinitely variable circumstances which surround hearsay evidence.[28]

33. Rule 95 of the Rules provides for the exclusion of improperly obtained evidence. It declares that no evidence shall be admissible if obtained by methods which cast substantial doubt on its reliability or if its admission is antithetical to, and would seriously damage the integrity of, the proceedings. Accordingly, the Trial Chamber makes it clear at the very outset that statements which are not voluntary, but rather are obtained by means including oppressive conduct, cannot be admitted. If there are *prima facie* indicia that there was such oppressive conduct, the burden is on the party seeking to have the evidence admitted to prove that the statement was voluntary and not obtained by oppressive conduct.

---

24 Ibid., para. 5.

25 *See Prosecutor v. Zejnil Delalić et. al*, Case No. IT-96-21-T, Decision on the Motion of the Prosecution for the Admissibility of Evidence, 19 January 1998; *Prosecutor v. Dario Kordić and Mario Čerkez*, Decision on Appeal Regarding Statement of a Deceased Witness, Case No. IT-95-14/2-AR73.5, 21 July 2000; *Prosecutor v. Tihomir Blaškić*, Case No. IT-95-14-T, Decision on the Defence Motion for Reconsideration of the Ruling to Exclude from Evidence Authentic and Exculpatory Documentary Evidence, 30 January 1998.

26 See Prosecutor v. Zejnil Delalić et. al, Case No. IT-96-21-AR 73.2, Decision on the Application of Defendant Zejnil Delalić for Leave to Appeal against the Decision of the Trial Chamber of 19 January 1998 for the Admissibility of Evidence, 4 March 1998, para. 20: "The implicit requirement that a piece of evidence be prima facie credible – that it have sufficient indicia of reliability – is a factor in the assessment of its relevance and probative value. To require absolute proof of a document's authenticity before it could be admitted would be to require a far more stringent test than the standard envisioned by Sub-rule 89(C)."

27 Since "evidence is admissible only if it is relevant and it is relevant only if has probative value", the reliability of hearsay evidence is a necessary prerequisite of its probative value under Rule 89(C), Prosecutor v. *Galić*, Case No. IT-98-29-AR73.2, Decision on Interlocutory Appeal Concerning Rule 92*bis*(C), 7 June 2002, para. 35. See also Prosecutor v. Milutinović at. al., Case No. IT-05-87-T, Order on Procedure and Evidence, 11 July 2006, para. 4.

28 Prosecutor v. Zlatko Aleksovski, Case No. IT-95-14/1-T, Decision on Prosecutor's Appeal on Admissibility of Evidence, 16 February 1999, para. 15.

34. The Trial Chamber considers circumstantial evidence as being evidence of circumstances surrounding an event or an offence from which a fact at issue may be reasonably inferred.[29] The Trial Chamber recognises that circumstantial evidence may be necessary in order to establish an alleged fact, particularly in criminal trials such as those before this Tribunal, where there is often no eye-witness or conclusive documents relating to a particular alleged fact. The Trial Chamber does not consider circumstantial evidence to be of less value than direct evidence.[30] The Trial Chamber further considers that while individual items of evidence by themselves may be insufficient to establish a fact, when taken together, they may be revealing and decisive. In evaluating circumstantial evidence, this Trial Chamber takes particular notice of the Trial Chamber in *Krnojelac*, which stated that "[a] circumstantial case consists of evidence of a number of different circumstances which, taken in combination, point to the existence of a particular fact upon which the guilt of the accused person depends because they would usually exist in combination only because a particular fact did exist."[31] The Appeals Chamber further added that "[t]he standard is only satisfied if the inference drawn was the only reasonable one that could be drawn from the evidence presented."[32]

35. The Trial Chamber emphasises what it considers to be an over-riding principle in matters of admissibility of evidence. The Trial Chamber is, pursuant to the Statute of the Tribunal, the guardian and guarantor of the procedural and substantive rights of the accused. In addition, it has the obligation to strike a balance in seeking to protect the rights of victims and witnesses. As a trial **[page 13]** is often a complex journey in search for the truth in relation to the alleged individual criminal responsibility of the Accused, bearing in mind that "the truth" can never be fully satisfied, the Trial Chamber considers that questions of admissibility of evidence do not arise only when one of the parties raises an objection to a piece of evidence sought to be brought forward by the other party. This Trial Chamber has an inherent right and duty to ensure that only evidence which qualifies for admission under the Rules will be admitted. For this purpose, as may turn out to be necessary from time to time, the Trial Chamber will intervene *ex officio* to exclude from these proceedings those pieces of evidence which, in its opinion, for one or more of the reasons laid down in the Rules, ought not to be admitted in evidence.[33]

36. Finally, pursuant to Rule 98 of the Rules, the Trial Chamber may be obliged *proprio motu* to summon witnesses and order their attendance in order to address any outstanding questions regarding the individual criminal responsibility of the Accused emanating from the presentation of evidence by the parties.

---

29 Richard May and Stephen Powell, Criminal Evidence, 5th Edition, Sweet & Maxwell Ltd., London, 2004.

30 The Appeals Chamber noted that "[t]here is nothing to prevent a conviction being based upon such evidence. Circumstantial evidence can often be sufficient to satisfy a fact finder beyond reasonable doubt." Kupreskić Appeal Judgement, para. 303.

31 Krnojelac Trial Judgement, para. 67.

32 *Stakić* Appeal Judgement, para. 219. See also Krnojelac Trial Judgement, para. 67.

33 Prosecutor v. Milan Martić, Case No. IT-95-11-T, Decision Adopting Guidelines on the Standards Governing the Admission of Evidence, 19 January 2006, Annex A, para. 11.

UNITED
NATIONS

International Tribunal for the Prosecution of Persons Responsible for Serious Violations of International Humanitarian Law Committed in the Territory of the Former Yugoslavia since 1991	Case No.	IT-00-39-A
	Date:	20 July 2007
	Original:	English

IN THE APPEALS CHAMBER

Before: **Judge Fausto Pocar, Presiding**
Judge Mohamed Shahabuddeen
Judge Mehmet Güney
Judge Andrésia Vaz
Judge Theodor Meron

Registrar: **Mr. Hans Holthuis**

Decision of: **20 July 2007**

PROSECUTOR

v.

MOMČILO KRAJIŠNIK

PUBLIC

DECISION ON MOTION OF *AMICUS CURIAE* REGARDING APPELLATE GROUND OF INEFFECTIVE ASSISTANCE OF COUNSEL

The Office of the Prosecutor:
Mr. Peter Kremer QC

The Accused
Mr. Momčilo Krajišnik

Amicus Curiae
Mr. Colin Nicholls QC

[page 1] 1. The Appeals Chamber of the International Tribunal for the Prosecution of Persons Responsible for Serious Violations of International Humanitarian Law Committed in the Territory of the Former Yugoslavia since 1991 ("Appeals Chamber" and "Tribunal", respectively) is seized of a "Motion Regarding Appellate Ground of Ineffective Assistance of Counsel", filed confidentially on 28 June 2007 by *amicus curiae* ("Motion").[1]

I. BACKGROUND

2. In the "Decision on Momčilo Krajišnik's Request to Self-Represent, on Counsel's Motions in Relation to Appointment of *Amicus Curiae*, and on the Prosecution Motion of 16 February 2007", filed on 11 May 2007 ("11 May Decision"), the Appeals Chamber ordered the appointment of *amicus curiae* to "assist the Appeals Chamber by arguing in favour of Mr. Krajišnik's interests".[2] The Appeals Chamber specified that *amicus curiae* "is not requested to conduct any new factual investigations" but rather "in light of the evidence at issue in the trial record, *amicus curiae* is to put forth grounds of appeal seeking reversal of convictions or reduction in sentence and to argue against grounds of appeal advanced by the Prosecution."[3]

3. In the Motion, *amicus curiae* makes two requests. First, *amicus curiae* observes that in his previous role as assigned counsel for Mr. Krajišnik, he "conducted certain investigations into the alleged ineffective assistance of former counsel" for Mr. Krajišnik, including "accessing and utilising documents which were generated by the Appellant's pre-trial, trial and appeal defence teams which do not form part of the trial record."[4] *Amicus curiae* notes that his notice of appeal includes a ground of ineffective assistance of counsel in relation to the conduct of two prior counsel for Mr. Krajišnik,[5] and that Mr. Krajišnik's notice of appeal includes a ground of ineffective assistance of counsel in relation to one of these individuals.[6] *Amicus curiae* suggests that the mandate given to *amicus curiae* in the 11 May Decision does not adequately address "the unique difficulties associated with an ineffective assistance of counsel ground of appeal"[7] and requests that he be allowed to use the documents mentioned above (namely, those generated by earlier defence teams that are not part of the trial record) in preparing his appeal brief. *Amicus curiae* notes that these documents are now in the hands of Mr. Krajišnik, but expresses concerns that Mr. Krajišnik **[page 2]** "may have difficulty accessing and utilising this information in his Appeal Brief because the documents are in English and [Mr. Krajišnik] is currently without translation facilities."[8]

4. As to the second request in the Motion, *amicus curiae* states that "[i]f, after considering amicus curiae's appellate brief, the Appeals Chamber considers that it is in the interests of justice to address the ineffective assistance ground of appeal raised by *amicus curiae*, the Appeals Chamber is invited to appoint an independent person to conduct a limited factual investigation into the issue."[9] *Amicus curiae* suggests that such an investigation could involve the taking of witness statements and the preparation of a report regarding information that could not be determined from the trial record.[10]

5. In the "Prosecution Response to Motion by Amicus Curiae Regarding Appellate Ground of Ineffective Assistance of Counsel," filed confidentially on 9 July 2007 ("Response"), the Prosecution opposes both requests made in the Motion. As to the request that *amicus curiae* be able to access and use the documents of prior defence teams for Mr. Krajišnik that did not become part of the trial record, the Prosecution objects to this request for several reasons. First, the Prosecution claims that these materials are privileged and should not be disclosed to *amicus curiae* without the consent of Mr. Krajišnik.[11] Second, the Prosecution considers that "[n]othing to date indicates that [Mr.] Krajišnik is unable to safeguard his own interests in respect of the

---

1 Although this Motion was filed confidentially, the Appeals Chamber lifts confidentiality with regard to it. *See infra* para. 7.
2 11 May Decision, para. 19.
3 11 May Decision, para. 19.
4 *Amicus* Motion, para. 7.
5 *Amicus* Motion, para. 2.
6 *Amicus* Motion, para. 1.
7 *Amicus* Motion, para. 5.
8 *Amicus* Motion, para. 8.
9 *Amicus* Motion, para. 11.
10 *Amicus* Motion, para. 11.
11 Response, paras 6–8.

ground of appeal of ineffective representation by his former counsel", that concerns about Mr. Krajišnik's access to translation facilities are premature, and that in any event the Motion does not clarify why materials outside the trial record are needed to support *amicus curiae*'s ground of appeal dealing with ineffective assistance of counsel.[12] Third, the Prosecution argues that *amicus curiae*'s request is in any event too broad and amounts to a fishing expedition.[13] As to the request that the Appeals Chamber appoint an independent person to conduct further investigations upon receiving *amicus curiae*'s appeal brief, the Prosecution considers that this request should be dismissed as "premature" and notes that such an appointment "would be a novel course of action" and might in any event be "entirely unnecessary".[14] Finally, the Prosecution notes that while it filed its Response confidentially because the Motion was filed confidentially, the "Prosecution is not aware of any **[page 3]** reasons for these filings to be confidential and is content for them to be made public, provided the *Amicus* consents."[15]

6. On 13 July 2007, *amicus curiae* confidentially filed a "Reply to Prosecution Response to Motion by Amicus Curiae Regarding Appellate Ground of Ineffective Assistance of Counsel" ("Reply"). *Amicus curiae* states that with regard to documents protected by legal privilege, a waiver of privilege could be sought from Mr. Krajišnik upon the Appeals Chamber ruling in favour of *amicus curiae*'s request for an expanded mandate.[16] *Amicus curiae* adds that "[u]se of this material is absolutely vital to the Appeals Chamber being adequately briefed on [Mr. Krajišnik's] own ineffective assistance of counsel ground of appeal against [one prior counsel], as well as the amicus curiae's grounds" with regard to ineffective assistance, since "[r]eferences from the trial record in isolation are simply not representative of the quality of the legal assistance rendered to the Appellant by these persons."[17] *Amicus curiae* also suggests that Mr. Krajišnik "does not have the facilities to review and incorporate these materials in the time presently allowed for his Appellate Brief" and that without expanding the mandate of *amicus curiae*, "it is almost certain that they will not be considered in these appellate proceedings at all" which would "in effect amount to a denial of the Appellant's right to a full and fair appeal."[18] *Amicus curiae* further rejects the Prosecution's characterization of the request as a fishing expedition.[19] On the question of appointing an independent investigator after reviewing *amicus curiae's* brief, *amicus curiae* disputes the submission that the request is premature and explains that the request was made now "in order to avoid any additional hold-ups in the briefing schedule."[20] With regard to confidentiality, *amicus curiae* suggests confidentiality is appropriate "in order to fully uphold established principles of due process in respect of the as yet unparticularised allegations against" the two prior counsel; that confidentiality should currently be lifted as to only these two individuals; that they should be given a chance to respond to the allegations made against them; and that only after they have had a chance to respond should all filings on this issue be made public.[21] *Amicus curiae* also attaches as Annex A a guidance approved by the Lord Chief Justice and the Bar Council in England & Wales on "Criticism of Former Counsel in Criminal Cases" and invites the Appeals Chamber to consider adopting a similar protocol. **[page 4]**

II. DISCUSSION

7. As a preliminary matter, the Appeals Chamber will consider the issue of whether the filings in relation to the ground of ineffective assistance of counsel – namely, the Motion, the Response, the Reply, and a portion of "Amicus Curiae's Notice of Appeal"[22] – should be kept confidential. Pursuant to Rules 78 and 107 of the Rules of Procedure and Evidence of the Tribunal ("Rules"), "all proceedings before an Appeals Chamber

12 Response, paras 9–13.
13 Response, paras 2, 14–16.
14 Response, paras 17–18.
15 Response, para. 21.
16 Reply, paras 6–7. *Amicus curiae* further suggests that he be provided with access to these documents in the interim, while consent is being sought, "so that it may be included in amicus curiae's Appellate Brief".
17 Reply, para. 12.
18 Reply, para. 13.
19 Reply, para. 17.
20 Reply, para. 19.
21 Reply, paras 20–24.
22 Amicus Curiae's Notice of Appeal, 8 June 2007, paras 10–14 (confidential filing). Only this portion of Amicus Curiae's Notice of Appeal was redacted from the public version of Amicus Curiae's Notice of Appeal that was filed the same day. *See generally* Amicus Curiae's Notice of Appeal, 8 June 2007 (public and redacted version).

shall be public unless there are exceptional reasons for keeping them confidential."[23] As noted earlier, the only justification offered by *amicus curiae* in favour of confidentiality is that somehow this confidentiality is necessary "to fully uphold established principles of due process" with respect to the two attorneys whose alleged conduct forms the basis for these grounds of appeal.[24] *Amicus curiae* fails to explain, however, how confidentiality in this regard advances principles of due process, and the Appeals Chamber sees no such exceptional reasons. Indeed, the Appeals Chamber notes that in the past, ineffective-assistance-of-counsel claims have been made and considered publicly in this Tribunal.[25] Accordingly, the Appeals Chamber requests the Registry to lift confidentiality on the above-mentioned filings.[26]

8. Turning to the merits of *amicus curiae*'s request for an expanded mandate, the Appeals Chamber declines to grant such request. In the 11 May Decision, the Appeals Chamber set out a carefully calibrated mandate for *amicus curiae*. Recognizing that Mr. Krajišnik had chosen to self-represent and "must accept responsibility for the disadvantages this choice may bring,"[27] the Appeals Chamber did not vest *amicus curiae* with the full responsibilities that the counsel for defendants normally possess. Instead, recognizing that the role of *amicus curiae* was largely to help the Appeals Chamber to assess "whether the interest of justice requires the Appeals Chamber to consider, *proprio motu*, issues not raised in Mr. Krajišnik's appeal or in his responses to the **[page 5]** Prosecution's appeal," the Appeals Chamber limited *amicus curiae* to consulting "the evidence at issue in the trial record" rather than "conduct[ing] any new factual investigations."[28] Although *amicus curiae* frames his current request for an extension of the mandate as involving "unique difficulties associated with an ineffective assistance of counsel ground of appeal", the Appeals Chamber considers that the reasoning of *amicus curiae* would apply to any ground of appeal where *amicus curiae* had reason to think that evidence outside the trial record would assist him in promoting this ground of appeal. Under this reasoning, *amicus curiae's* role would become essentially equivalent to that of a defence counsel rather than limited to helping the Appeals Chamber assess whether the Trial Judgement and other relevant rulings of the Trial Chamber are fair to Mr. Krajišnik in light of the evidence at trial and the applicable law. While arguments with regard to evidence outside the trial record may thus go unmade (should Mr. Krajišnik fail to make these arguments himself), the Appeals Chamber considers that fairness does not require it to mitigate this further potential consequence of Mr. Krajišnik's own choice to self-represent.

9. The Appeals Chamber thus denies *amicus curiae*'s request for an expanded mandate. Accordingly, the Appeals Chamber declines to address the further arguments of the parties in relation to issues of privilege and to the breadth of *amicus curiae*'s request.

10. With regard to *amicus curiae*'s request that the Appeals Chamber appoint an independent person to conduct further investigations into the ineffective-assistance-of-counsel ground of appeal upon receiving *amicus curiae*'s appeal brief, the Appeals Chamber agrees with the Prosecution that this request is at least premature. The Appeals Chamber could of course address this concern by taking the issue under advisement and delaying a ruling until after the appeal brief of *amicus curiae* is filed. With the interests of judicial economy in mind, however, the Appeals Chamber instead denies the request as premature while retaining the power to revisit this issue *proprio motu* if it deems this necessary after reviewing the briefs of the parties and *amicus curiae*. **[page 6]**

---

23 *Prosecutor v. Milan Lukić and Sredoje Lukić*, Case No. IT-98-32/1-AR65.1, Decision on Defence Appeal Against Trial Chamber's Decision on Sredoje Lukić's Motion for Provisional Release, 16 April 2007, fn. 2.

24 Reply, para. 20.

25 *See, e.g., Prosecution v. Vidoje Blagojević and Dragan Jokić*, Case No. IT-02-60-A, Defence of Mr. Vidoje Blagojević Brief on Appeal, 20 October 2005, paras 2.14-2.20; *Prosecution v. Vidoje Blagojević and Dragan Jokić*, Case No. IT-02-60-A, Appeals Judgement, 9 May 2007, paras 22–25.

26 The Appeals Chamber declines at this time to consider *amicus curiae*'s suggestions with regard to giving former counsel a right of response where an ineffective-assistance claim with regard to their conduct is included as a ground of appeal and with regard to adopting a protocol similar to the one set out in Annex A of the Reply. The Appeals Chamber notes that these suggestions occur in *amicus curiae*'s Reply rather than in the original Motion. The Appeals Chamber also notes that while ineffective-assistance-of-counsel claims have been raised on appeal in past cases of this Tribunal and of the International Criminal Tribunal for Rwanda, *amicus curiae* neither suggests that a right of response for prior counsel has been granted in these past cases nor shows in the alternative why, if this is not the case, a departure from past practice is required.

27 11 May Decision, para. 18 (internal quotation marks and brackets omitted).

28 11 May Decision, paras 19–20.

III. DISPOSITION

11. For the foregoing reasons, the Appeals Chamber **DENIES** the Motion in its entirety. The Appeals Chamber also **REQUESTS** the Registry to lift the confidentiality of the Motion, Response, and Reply, and the currently confidential portion of Amicus Curiae's Notice of Appeal.

Done in English and French, the English text being authoritative.

Dated this 20th day of July 2007,
At The Hague, The Netherlands.

Fausto Pocar
Presiding Judge

[Seal of the Tribunal]

UNITED
NATIONS

International Tribunal for the Prosecution of Persons Responsible for Serious Violations of International Humanitarian Law Committed in the Territory of the Former Yugoslavia since 1991	Case No.:	IT-03-67-PT	
	Date:	30 July 2007	
		ENGLISH	
	Original:	French	

BEFORE THE PRE-TRIAL JUDGE

Before: **Judge Jean-Claude Antonetti**

Registrar: **Mr Hans Holthuis**

Decision of: **30 July 2007**

THE PROSECUTOR

v.

VOJISLAV ŠEŠELJ

PUBLIC DOCUMENT

DECISION ON THE FINANCING THE DEFENCE OF THE ACCUSED

The Office of the Prosecutor:
Ms Christine Dahl

The Accused:
Mr Vojislav Šešelj

[page 2] I. INTRODUCTION

1. I, Jean-Claude Antonetti, Judge of the International Tribunal for the Prosecution of Persons Responsible for Serious Violations of International Humanitarian Law Committed in the Territory of the Former Yugoslavia since 1991 ("Tribunal"), am seized of the motion on the financing of the defence, filed by Vojislav Šešelj ("the Accused") on 4 June 2007 (" the Motion").[1]

2. In the Motion, the Accused seeks the application of Rule 21 (4) (d) of the Statute of the Tribunal ("the Statute") and requests that the costs incurred for the preparation and presentation of his defence be covered by the Tribunal, on the ground of his demonstrated indigence.[2] Consequently, the Accused requests Trial Chamber III ("Chamber III") to review two decisions rendered by the Registry[3] in this respect and to order the Registry "to determine a Defence budget to correspond with the total cost of the Prosecution in the case,"[4] for each phase of the trial.[5]

II. PROCEDURAL BACKGROUND

3. The pre-trial Judge will briefly recall the numerous written submissions on the financing of the defence of the Accused which have been filed by the Registry and the Accused up to this decision.[6]

4. Two days after he was transferred to the seat of the Tribunal on 24 February 2003, the Accused stated his intention to represent himself.[7] On 31 October 2003, the **[page 3]** Accused formally requested the financing of his defence before the Tribunal.[8] An investigation procedure by the Registry ensued as to the financial situation of the Accused, as did many consultations between them, during which the Registry informed the Accused of the modalities of the legal aid generally granted to Accused before the Tribunal who claim to be indigent or partially indigent. On 7 December 2004, the Accused, however, categorically refused to provide the Registry with the information and documentation necessary for the examination of the financial situation of his close relations.[9]

5. After submitting an initial invoice on 23 July 2004 for the work his expert team is said to have carried out in 2003, the Accused submitted two other invoices, for 2004 and 2005 respectively, on 21 December 2004 and 3 January 2006. On 3 January 2006, the Accused also filed a motion for payment of the cost of his defence ("the First Motion").[10] On 31 January 2006, the Registry filed its submissions pursuant to Rule 33 (B) of the Rules of Procedure and Evidence of the Tribunal ("the Rules") concerning the First Motion.

6. As the issue of the assignment of standby Counsel remained undecided and no decision on the First Motion had been made, the question of financing the defence resurfaced when the Accused began his hunger strike and thus made a certain number of demands, concerning in particular the facilities which should be given to him in order to prepare and present his defence case.[11]

---

1 Original in BCS with English translation titled "Professor Vojislav Šešelj's Motion for a Decision by Trial Chamber III on Financing His Defence In Accordance with the Statute," submitted on 4 June 2007 and English version filed on 14 June 2007.

2 The Motion, p. 16.

3 For the sake of clarity, the generic term "Registry" is used to refer to all of the subordinate organs of the Registrar of the Tribunal, without distinction.

4 The Motion, p. 16.

5 In particular, the Accused requests the Chamber to order that "the Registrar, when approving the payment of the United Nations funds to finance the defence, set a monthly remuneration for the three legal advisers during the Prosecution case and Defence case, as well as during the appeal, which should be at least equal to that of defence teams in other cases before the ICTY, and one case manager up to the amount paid to the Prosecution's case manager in addition to an appropriate reimbursement of the cost of accommodation rental in the Hague", *Id.* p. 17.

6 For a more detailed procedural background, *see* the Registry Submission pursuant to Rule 33 (B) of the Rules regarding Vojislav Šešelj's Motion for a Decision by the Trial Chamber on Financing His Defence, 29 June 2007 ("the Submissions"), paras. 3–38.

7 The Submissions, para. 4; Decision on Appeal Against the Trial Chamber's Decision on Assignment of Counsel, 20 October 2006 ("The Decision of 20 October"), para. 2.

8 The Submissions, para. 7; The Motion, p. 2.

9 The Motion, pp. 7–11; The Submissions, paras. 8–11.

10 The Submissions, paras. 13, 17–18; Decision on Appeals Against Decisions of the Registrar of 4 January 2007 and 9 February 2007, 25 April 2007 ("The Interlocutory Decision of 25 April"), para. 7.

11 The Submissions, para. 25; The Interlocutory Decision of 25 April, para. 5.

7. By letters of 7 and 8 December 2006, the Registry attempted to meet the demands of the Accused by informing him that Mr Vučić, Mr Krasić and Mr Jerković had been accepted as "legal advisers" and would, in that capacity, be granted privileged access to the Accused. Moreover, the Registry notified the Accused that **[page 4]** some reasonable costs associated with his defence would be covered by the Registry, in particular the remuneration of a case manager.[12]

8. By letter of 19 December 2006, the Registry specified the nature and scope of the costs that it could cover, despite the absence of specific information concerning the financial situation of the Accused:

(i) the cost of the first trip to The Hague for the legal assistants and case manager, including travel costs, accommodation as well a daily subsistence allowance for each of them;

(ii) monthly remuneration of 1,500 euros (€) for the case manager;

(iii) a maximum allowance of € 1,200 for the rental of an apartment, to serve as a residence and office for the legal assistants and case manager; and

(iv) provided they go through the registration procedures, the case manager and the legal assistants would have access to the Tribunal under the same conditions as any other defence team.[13]

9. On 22 December 2006 the Accused simultaneously filed three motions requesting the reimbursement of costs incurred since 2003 for the preparation of his defence, which amounted to 6,395,000 dollars.[14] The motions were denied by the Registry on 4 January 2007 on the ground that the legal aid system in place at the Tribunal only allowed for cases of demonstrated indigence of the Accused and cases in which a counsel was assigned or appointed.[15] **[page 5]**

10. On 22 January 2007, the Accused lodged an appeal of the Registry decision of 19 December 2006 with the President of the Tribunal ("the President" and "the First Appeal to the President").[16] On 9 February 2007 the Registry filed its submissions on the appeal in accordance with Rule 33 (B) of the Rules.

11. On 19 February 2007 the Accused lodged an appeal of the Decision of 4 January with the President ("the Second Appeal to the President").[17]

12. The President ruled on the First Appeal to the President on 12 March 2007 in his "Decision on Appeal Against Registry Decision of 19 December 2006" ("the Interlocutory Decision of 12 March"), and held that "Šešelj's arguments are to be raised before the Trial Chamber presently seized with Šešelj's case."[18]

13. On 25 April 2007 the President denied the Second Appeal to the President ("the Interlocutory Decision of 25 April").

14. On 28 June 2007 the Office of the Prosecutor ("the Prosecution") filed its response to the Motion. The pre-trial Judge is of the view that the issues raised in the Motion are to be dealt with in light of the submissions made by the Accused and the Registry, the latter being responsible for granting legal aid. Therefore, the pre-trial Judge considers that the Prosecution has no *locus standi* to file its response and, consequently, will not address its content.

15. On 29 June 2007 the Registry filed its submissions on the Motion pursuant to Rule 33 (B) of the Rules ("the Submissions").[19]

---

12 The Submissions, paras. 28–29; Letters dated 7 and 8 December 2006, attached to the Decision on Appeal Against Registry Decision of 19 December 2006, 12 March 2007 ("The Interlocutory Decision of 12 March").

13 Letter dated 19 December attached to the Interlocutory Decision of 12 March.

14 The Motion, p. 3; The Submissions, para. 31.

15 The Motion, para. 32.

16 Filed on 5 January 2007.

17 The Motion, para. 35.

18 The Interlocutory Decision of 12 March, p. 5.

19 Registry Submission pursuant to Rule 33 (B) of the Rules regarding Vojislav Šešelj's Motion for a Decision by the Trial Chamber on Financing His Defence, 29 June 2007

16. On 19 July the Accused received the Submissions in a language he understands.[20] As the Accused did not request leave to file a reply within seven days **[page 6]** of receiving the Submissions in a language he understands,[21] the pre-trial Judge rules on the Motion as follows.

III. ARGUMENTS OF THE PARTIES

A. <u>The Motion of the Accused</u>

17. As a preliminary matter, the Accused seeks leave to exceed the number of words allowed to him under the Practice Direction on the Length of Briefs and Motions ("the Practice Direction")[22] and by Decision of the pre-trial Judge of 19 June 2006 on the Filing of Motions.[23]

18. The Accused also requests the Trial Chamber to recognize his entitlement to legal aid on the ground that he has demonstrated his indigence. Moreover, concerning the amount to be allocated for the legal aid, the Accused demands complete equality in respect of the financial means available the Prosecution for each phase of the trial, while wishing to be informed of the expenses of other defence teams and of the three Standby Counsel in the instant case.[24]

19. As to whether the Chamber has jurisdiction to rule on the Motion, the Accused submits that the procedures he has undertaken since his transfer to the Tribunal in February 2003 in order to obtain financing for his defence have yet to be finalized, even though the issue of this financing goes to the very heart of the fairness of the trial. In his Motion, the Accused submits that the President of the Tribunal, by Interlocutory Decision of 25 April, invited the Accused to raise this matter, which goes to the issues of a fair trial and the right of the Accused to have adequate time and resources to exercise and prepare his defence, with the Trial Chamber seized of the case. The Accused therefore requested Chamber III to review the Registry decisions of 19 December 2006 and 4 January 2007, in the light of the Motion thus exercising its judicial control over the administrative decisions made by the Registry.[25] **[page 7]**

20. On the merits, the Accused first submits that pursuant to Article 21 (4) (d) of the Statute, a fair trial requires the financing of the defence of the Accused, whether a counsel has been assigned or not.[26] He submits that this financing "is the equivalent of all the resources and the equivalent of the cost of engaging legal advisers, technical duties, translation, photocopying, and everything else."[27] Such financing is claimed to be necessary to remedy the fact that the Accused has been detained for several years and therefore is not in a position to alone deal with the elementary aspects of the preparation of a defence before the Tribunal.[28]

21. In addition, the Accused argues that the equality of arms requires that he enjoy "approximately the same" resources as those of the Prosecution,[29] which has absolutely not been the case to date, he submits.[30] For there to be equality of arms, the Accused requests disclosure to him of the costs incurred by the Prosecution in this case and by the defence teams in the other cases before the Tribunal as well as the cost of the fees paid to Standby counsel assigned in the present case.[31] He contends that this is all the more justified since this is the most complex case considering its geographic scope and the inclusion of a new criminal offence, i.e. hate speech.[32]

---

20 *Procès-verbal* D21130, 23 July 2007, showing that the Accused received the Submissions on 19 July 2007 at 17.00 hours.

21 *See* Rule 126 *bis* of the Rules.

22 Practice Direction on the Length of Briefs and Motions (IT/184 Rev. 2), 16 September 2005 ("the Practice Direction").

23 The Motion, p. 2.

24 *Id.*, p. 16.

25 *Id.*, pp. 2–4.

26 *Id.*, pp. 5–6.

27 *Id.*, p. 11.

28 "Professor Vojislav Šešelj cites the fact that he is wholly unable to maintain even elementary communication with potential defence witnesses or persons who could elucidate certain events for the purpose of, for example, elementary checking of a statement by a Prosecution witness," *Id.*, p. 14.

29 *Id.*, p. 6.

30 "In other words, the Office of the Prosecutor has everything and in quantities it requires, whereas Professor Vojislav Šešelj has nothing," *Id.*, p. 7.

31 *Id.*, pp. 11–13.

32 *Id.*, p. 13.

22. The Accused is of the view that

> with regard to legal aid the ICTY Statute does not differentiate between types of defence, but only in terms of the financial situation of the accused. If the accused is indigent, then he receives United Nations legal aid, and the form of his defence is entirely irrelevant for the purposes of legal aid.[33] **[page 8]**

Consequently, the Accused considers that he has demonstrated his indigence, with the exception of a sum of $70,000 currently frozen in an account in the United States, which the Accused has accepted to contribute whenever it becomes available.[34]

B. <u>The Submissions of the Registry</u>

> The Registrar will establish that there is no basis in law upon which the Tribunal can grant the Accused's request as formulated. A decision to disburse public funds to the persons retained by the Accused to assist him in his capacity as a self-represented accused outside the Tribunal's legal aid system would be illegal. In order to qualify for "payment of his defence costs", the Accused needs to comply with the requirements of the Tribunal's legal aid system.[35]

23. The Registry considers that its decision to deny reimbursement of the costs of preparing his defence must be confirmed because it satisfies the criteria for an administrative decision by a judicial organ.[36]

24. First, the Registry considers that any interpretation, be it literal,[37] systemic[38] or teleological,[39] leads to the conclusion that Article 21 (4) (d) of the Statute does not guarantee legal aid to an Accused who defends himself.[40] According to the Registry, this conclusion is confirmed by its study of national law and jurisprudence, which shows that legal aid "is equated with the assignment of defence counsel to an indigent accused and the coverage of contingent court fees and the like."[41]

25. Beyond Article 21 (4) (d) of the Statute cited by the Accused, the Registry argues that despite its duty to guarantee the effective exercise of the Accused's right **[page 9]** to defend himself, that exercise does not go beyond the "time and facilities necessary for the preparation of his defence" and can in no way cover the payment of fees or the allocation of funds to the Accused.[42] The Registry thus notes that

> While it is conceivable that a self-represented accused who is in detention may need to be assigned an investigator and/or (an) expert(s), paid for by the Tribunal if the accused is indigent, to gather or verify facts or to provide an expert report respectively, it is unimaginable that persons who draft legal submissions, analyse evidence and perform other functions normally performed by defence counsel be remunerated under the notion of facilities provided by the Tribunal to a self- represented accused. While the Tribunal will be required to facilitate the self- represented accused's communication with such persons, it cannot be expected to pay them.[43]

---

33 *Id.*, p. 7.
34 *Id.*, pp. 7–11.
35 The Submissions, para. 43.
36 *Id.*, para. 97.
37 *Id.*, para. 49. The Registry submits that the expression "legal assistance" used in Article 21 (4) (d) of the Statute can only be understood as assistance provided by a "counsel". *Ibid.*
38 *Id.*, paras. 50–52. The Registry further submits that that its literal interpretation of Article 21 (4) (d) of the Statute is in conformity with the Rules and the Directive on the Assignment of Defence Counsel ("the Directive"). According to the Registry, "the so-called 'defence costs' are a consequence of the assignment of counsel and do not exist independently of the assignment of counsel." *Ibid.*
39 *Id.*, paras. 54–57. Moreover, the Registry contends that the Tribunal's system of legal aid perfectly matches the national systems where there is provision for the assignment of counsel to indigent accused in order to ensure the proper administration of justice, the fairness of a trial as well as the public trust. *Ibid.*
40 *Id.*, paras. 44–48, 57.
41 *Id.*, para. 53.
42 *Id.*, paras. 58–65. *See* the Submissions, note 25 for a detailed examination of national and international jurisprudence in respect of the allocation of facilities necessary for the preparation of the defence.
43 *Id.*, para. 63.

26. The Registry further states that the equality of arms, a basic principle of the right to a fair trial, guarantees procedural equality but not complete equality of resources.[44] According to the Registry, "self-representation is an informed choice which an accused makes, accepting the limitations on his ability to prepare and present a professional defence."[45]

27. The Registry considers therefore that the assignment or appointment of a counsel paid by the legal aid system is not incompatible with the right of the Accused to present his own defence and that "the Accused's objective to compel the Tribunal to bear his defence costs can be achieved through the Tribunal's legal aid system in a manner which is not inconsistent with the Accused's right to represent himself."[46]

28. It is therefore suggested by the Registry that legal aid to the Accused must be contingent on the same conditions as those applicable to other accused before the Tribunal in accordance with the Rules and the Directive:

a. the Accused needs to prove that he is unable to pay for his defence; **[page 10]**

b. he needs to identify one or more persons who meet the qualification requirements of Rule 45 of the Rules and are available for assignment;

c. as in all other cases, the Registrar shall determine the amount of reasonable and necessary resources for the preparation and presentation of the Accused' s case based on a determination of the level of complexity and duration (where applicable), in accordance with the standard Registry payment policies; and

d. as in all other cases, the Registrar shall disburse such legal aid payments in accordance with the applicable UN rules and regulations, and must be in a position to fulfil his duty of controlling the expenditure of Tribunal legal aid funds.[47]

29. Regarding the burden of the Accused to prove his indigence, the Registry recalls Article 10 of the Directive which requires that account be taken of the financial resources of the Accused, his spouse, as well as those persons with whom he habitually resides, by means of the applicant's declaration of means form or by way of an investigation. By failing to duly fill out his declaration of means form and by refusing to cooperate with the Registry investigation, the Accused is said to have prevented the Registry from taking a position in respect of the indigence of the Accused.[48]

30. Furthermore, the Registry argues that at least one of the associates of the Accused must meet the requirements of Rule 45 of the Rules and thus qualify to be assigned to the defence of the Accused. Such associates will not only be required to respect the protective measures granted to witnesses and documents, but will also be authorized to be present in court. Associates who do not meet the requirements of Rule 45 will be able to perform other tasks within the team and be paid as such.[49]

31. Finally, with regard to the financing modalities, the Registry applies the same payment policies to all of the accused by examining the complexity of the case as well as the estimated length of the trial.[50] Moreover, the Registry must also "be entitled to **[page 11]** closely monitor the expenses incurred by the Accused and his defence team."[51] The Registry therefore requests that the same procedure be followed for the Accused in the present case.

IV. APPLICABLE LAW

A. Jurisdiction of the pre-trial Judge to Rule on the Motion

32. Before ruling on the merits of the Motion, it is appropriate to address the pre-trial Judge's jurisdiction in the matter. It is necessary to recall the order issued by the President of Trial Chamber III on 27 February 2007

44 *Id.*, para. 67.
45 *Id.*, para. 68.
46 *Id.*, para. 77.
47 *Id.*, para. 79.
48 *Id.*, paras. 80–87.
49 *Id.*, paras. 88–89.
50 *Id.*, para. 90.
51 *Id.*, para. 91.

in which the pre-trial Judge was entrusted with *all* of the functions relating to the pre-trial phase of the trial set out in Rules 66, 67, 73, 73 *bis* and 73 *ter* of the Rules.[52] As the Motion falls within the scope of Rule 73 (A), the pre-trial Judge has jurisdiction to rule on it.

33. Article 20 (1) of the Statute provides that "the Trial Chamber[...] shall ensure that a trial is fair and expeditious and that proceedings are conducted in accordance with the rules of procedure and evidence, with full respect for the rights of the accused." Moreover, the Appeals Chamber explicitly recalled that the Trial Chamber seized of the case must ensure the fairness of the trial.[53]

34. The rights of the Accused before the Tribunal are set out in Article 21 of the Statute. The article provides in particular that:

> 4. In the determination of any charge against the accused pursuant to the present Statute, the accused shall be entitled to the following minimum guarantees, in full equality:
>
> [...]
>
> (b) to have adequate time and facilities for the preparation of his defence [...];
>
> [...] **[page 12]**
>
> (d) to be tried in his presence, and to defend himself in person or through legal assistance of his own choosing; to be informed, if he does not have legal assistance, of this right; and to have legal assistance assigned to him, in any case where the interests of justice so require, and without payment by him in any such case if he does not have sufficient means to pay for it;
>
> (e) to examine, or have examined, the witnesses against him and to obtain the attendance and examination of witnesses on his behalf under the same conditions as witnesses against him;
>
> [...].

35. Pursuant to Rules 20 and 21 of the Statute, the Trial Chamber, sitting as the pre-trial Judge, not only has the power but also the inherent duty to ensure a fair trial and a proper administration of justice.[54] In the *Blagojević* case, the Appeals Chamber reaffirmed this position, specifying nonetheless that "the only inherent power that a Trial Chamber has is to ensure that the trial of an accused is fair; it cannot appropriate for itself a power which is conferred elsewhere."[55]

36. The President of the Tribunal applied this same reasoning when he held that he lacked jurisdiction to rule on the motions of the Accused for legal aid to pay his team of experts. Accordingly, the President of the Tribunal mentioned that

> it is appropriate for that Chamber to review decisions of the Registrar alleged to directly impact upon an accused's right to a fair trial, unless the power of review is specifically conferred on me elsewhere. Such is not the case here. In addition, as I have previously noted, "issues relating to an accused's exercise of the right to self-representation under the Statute of the International Tribunal are expressly for a Chamber to decide in light of its inherent power and duty to ensure the fair and expeditious management of its proceedings. Furthermore, review of a decision by the Registrar on allocation of funds in terms of its impact upon the right of an accused to 'equality of arms' with the Prosecution lies with the relevant Chamber." Therefore, only the Trial Chamber presently seized with the case may consider the issues **[page 13]** raised in his Appeals with respect to the Registrar's Decision of 24 January 2007 and Decision of 9 February 2007.[56]

37. The pre-trial Judge therefore has jurisdiction to rule on the Motion.

---

52 Order Entrusting Functions to Pre-Trial Judge, 27 February 2007.

53 *The Prosecutor v. Vidoje Blagojević,* Public and Redacted Reasons for Decision on Appeal by Vidoje Blagojević to Replace His Defence Team, Case No. IT-02-60-AR73.4, 7 November 2003 ("the *Blagojević* Interlocutory Decision"), para. 12.

54 *The Prosecutor v. Vidoje Blagojević,* Decision on Independent Counsel for Vidoje Blagojević's Motion to Instruct the Registrar to Appoint New Lead and Co-Counsel, 3 July 2003 ("the *Blagojević* Decision"), para. 112. The Chamber went further considering that "any steps which the Trial Chamber takes are discretionary and in its overarching interest and commitment to ensuring that in the case of the Accused, justice is not only done but justice is seen to be done, including by the Accused himself." *Ibid.*

55 The *Blagojević* Interlocutory Decision, para. 7.

56 The Interlocutory Decision of 25 April, para. 12.

B. Applicable Law in Respect of the Payment of Defence Costs of a Self-Represented Accused

1. The Right to Self-Representation

38. Pursuant to Article 20 (1) of the Statute it is incumbent upon the pre-trial Judge to ensure that the rights of the accused are duly respected. These rights are set out in Article 21 of the Statute. Beyond the principles of equality, equity and publicity, as well as that of the presumption of innocence, paragraph 4 of Article 21 of the Statute provides a number of *minimal* guarantees to which all accused are entitled, including the right to "have adequate time and facilities for the preparation of his defence", to defend himself, "to examine, or have examined, the witnesses against him and to obtain the attendance and examination of witnesses on his behalf under the same conditions as witnesses against him." Accordingly, Article 21 (4) echoes the wording of Article 14 of the International Covenant on Civil and Political Rights.[57]

39. The Statute therefore establishes the right to represent oneself as one of the rights the Trial Chamber must guarantee to any Accused before the Tribunal. **[page 14]** Moreover, this was emphasized by the Appeals Chamber of the Tribunal on several occasions when it held that the right to defend oneself was a fundamental right[58] and that

> the Appeals Chamber sees no reasonable way to interpret Article 21 except as a guarantee of the right to self-representation. Nor should this right be taken lightly. The drafters of the Statute clearly viewed the right to self-representation as an indispensable cornerstone of justice, placing it on a structural par with defendants' right to remain silent, to confront the witnesses against them, to a speedy trial, and even to demand a court-appointed attorney if they cannot afford one themselves.[59]

In the present case, the Appeals Chamber has on two occasions restored the right of the Accused to represent himself.[60]

40. In the *Krajišnik* Interlocutory Decision, the Appeals Chamber held that while self-representation may never be to the Accused's advantage, the fact remains that by virtue of Article 21 (4) (d), which is a "cornerstone", he always has the right to do so.[61]

2. The Status of Costs for the Defence of a Self-Represented Accused

41. In the Statute, as well as in the Rules and the Directive, payment of the defence costs of an Accused lacking the financial means to cover them is organized through the assignment of a counsel and the payment

---

57 Article 14 (3) of the International Covenant on Civil and Political Rights, adopted and opened for signature, ratification and accession by the General Assembly in resolution 2200 A (XXI) of 16 December 1966, entry into force on 23 March 1979, provides: "In the determination of any criminal charge against him, everyone shall be entitled to the following minimum guarantees, in full equality: [...](b) To have adequate time and facilities for the preparation of his defence and to communicate with counsel of his own choosing; [...] (d) To be tried in his presence, and to defend himself in person or through legal assistance of his own choosing; to be informed, if he does not have legal assistance, of this right; and to have legal assistance assigned to him, in any case where the interests of justice so require, and without payment by him in any such case if he does not have sufficient means to pay for it; (e) To examine, or have examined, the witnesses against him and to obtain the attendance and examination of witnesses on his behalf under the same conditions as witnesses against him; (f) To have the free assistance of an interpreter if he cannot understand or speak the language used in court; [...]" *See The Prosecutor v. Vojislav Šešelj,* Case No. IT-03-67-AR73.3, Decision on Appeal Against the Trial Chamber's Decision on Assignment of Counsel, 20 October 2006 ("the Decision of 20 October"), footnote 23.

58 *Slobodan Milošević v. The Prosecutor*, Case No. IT-02-54-AR73.7, Decision on Interlocutory Appeal of the Trial Chamber's Decision on the Assignment of Defence Counsel, 1 November 2004, ("the *Milošević* Interlocutory Decision"), para. 17.

59 The *Milošević* Interlocutory Decision, para. 11 (footnotes omitted). *See* also *The Prosecutor v. Momčilo Krajišnik,* Case No. IT-00-39-A, Decision on Momčilo Krajišnik's Request to Self-Represent, on Counsel's Motions in Relation to Appointment of *Amicus Curiae*, and on the Prosecution Motion of 16 February 2007," 11 May 2007 ("the *Krajišnik* Interlocutory Decision"), para. 9.

60 The Decision of 20 October, paras, 8, 22, 52; *The Prosecutor v. Vojislav Šešelj,* Case No. IT-03-67-AR73.4, "Decision on Appeal Against the Trial Chamber's Decision (No. 2) on Assignment of Counsel," 8 December 2006 ("the Decision of 8 December"), paras. 19, 30.

61 The *Krajišnik* Interlocutory Decision

of his fees.[62] Accordingly, even though they are on an equal footing as the right of the accused "to have legal assistance assigned to him, in any case where the interests of justice so require, and without payment by him in any such case if he does not have sufficient means to pay **[page 15]** for it," the implementing provisions of his right to represent himself are not set out in the Statute.

42. The Statute, the Rules and the Directive are silent on the issue of payment of the defence costs of a self-represented Accused who claims indigence, which leaves a gap in the law. In order to ensure the effective exercise of the right of any accused to represent himself and for this right not to remain a dead letter, in the absence of an *ad hoc* judicial decision, it is incumbent upon the pre-trial Judge to bridge this gap in the law and to address the issue of the implementing provisions of this right, should the said accused declare to be indigent.

43. Another international tribunal, the International Criminal Court ("the ICC"), had endeavoured to bridge this gap in the law. During the drafting of the regulations applicable before the ICC, the issue of granting "legal aid" to a self-represented accused arose. Accordingly, in the initial draft Regulations of the Registry of the ICC, it was proposed that the Registry of the ICC provide for the appointment of professional investigators and legal assistants to a self-represented accused.[63] Although this provision was not adopted in the end, the fact remains that the regulations currently in force may be interpreted as providing for such a possibility.

44. Accordingly, Regulation 83 (1) of the ICC Regulations of the Court provides that

> Legal assistance paid by the Court shall cover all costs reasonably necessary as determined by the Registrar for an effective and efficient defence, including the remuneration of counsel, his or her assistants as referred to in regulation 68 and staff, expenditure in relation to the gathering of evidence, administrative costs, translation and interpretation costs, travel costs and daily subsistence allowances.[64]

On the basis of Regulation 83 (1) mentioned above and Regulation 119 (2) of the Regulations of the Registry of the ICC,[65] it appears therefore that "legal assistance" is **[page 16]** not strictly contingent upon the assignment of counsel and would be allowed to a self-represented accused.

45. Based on this example, the pre-trial Judge considers that an accused representing himself without the assistance of counsel before an international court has the right to have associates paid by the international court subject to certain conditions.

V. DISCUSSION

A. <u>Preliminary Issue</u>

46. In response to the preliminary request of the Accused to exceed the word-limit, the pre-trial Judge would first remind the Accused that he is no longer bound by the 800-word limit imposed by Chamber I on 19 June 2006. In a decision dated 17 May 2007, the pre-trial Judge found that the circumstances which had led Chamber I to set a limit of 800 words had ceased to exist and ordered that "any submission from the Accused shall be submitted in accordance with the provisions set forth in the Practice Direction."[66]

47. Nevertheless, as the Motion totals 5,430 words in the original BCS version, it significantly exceeds the 3,000 words prescribed by the Practice Direction. However, given the fundamental importance of the issues raised in the Motion, the pre-trial Judge considers that "exceptional circumstances"[67] justify exceeding the 3,000-word limit, and will therefore address the Motion in its entirety.

---

62 Rule 45 (A); Articles 6 and 22 of the Directive.

63 "Registrar's Submission Pursuant to the Trial Chamber's Request for Further Information on the Request by Vojislav Šešelj for Payment of Expenses for the Preparation of His Defence," 21 September 2006, footnote 6.

64 Regulations of the Court, ICC-BD/01-01-04/Rev. 01/05.

65 Regulations of the Registry, ICC-BD/03-01-06-Rev. 1.

66 Decision Amending the Criteria for the Filing of Submissions from the Accused, 17 May 2007, pp. 2–3.

67 Practice Direction, para. 7.

B. Payment of Costs Incurred by the Accused in the Preparation and Presentation of His Defence

48. The pre-trial Judge stated above that it was necessary to bridge the existing gap in the law in respect of the payment of costs incurred for the preparation and **[page 17]** presentation of the defence of an accused claiming indigence.[68] This reasoning will be further explained in this section.

1. Ensuring a Fair Trial

49. The pre-trial Judge primarily must ensure that the rules for a fair trial are respected. Additionally, the fact that an accused represents himself or is represented by counsel, either assigned or appointed by him, must not affect the other rights arising from the fair trial requirements guaranteed by Article 21 (4) of the Statute, including the right to have the necessary time and facilities to prepare his defence, and to examine, or have examined, the witnesses against him and to obtain the attendance and examination of witnesses on his behalf under the same conditions as witnesses against him. Nevertheless, it is impracticable for an accused, who is detained at the Tribunal's detention unit and represents himself, to go into the field in search of evidence crucial for the cross-examination of witnesses and to conduct investigations to find defence witnesses. These tasks are quite simply impossible for him to perform. Additionally, a fair trial requires that a team be constituted for this purpose.

50. Otherwise, an accused who claims to lack the means to pay such a team and still wishes, for reasons of his own, to represent himself, will therefore find himself forced to go to the trial with no other facilities to prepare his defence than the documents disclosed by the Prosecution under Rules 65 *ter,* 66 and 68 of the Rules. In a memorandum drafted at the request of the Registry, the United Nations Office of Legal Affairs considered that "the Registry's reasoning entails that all accused who do not have financial means to ensure their own defence – for instance, to cover the expenses incurred for their own investigators or advisors – will be compelled to be represented by a defence counsel. It would mean that the exercise of the right of the accused to defend himself or herself in person – as enshrined in Article 21 (4) (d) of the ICTY Statute – would be entirely dependent on the financial means available to him or her."[69] Similarly, the pre-trial Judge considers that the effective exercise of a right guaranteed by the Statute cannot be curtailed by the financial resources of an accused. **[page 18]**

51. Under Article 21 (4) of the Statute, all accused are entitled to the "minimum" guarantees set forth in this provision. As the rights enshrined in Article 21 (4) are minimum rights, they are not an exhaustive list. In its Submissions, the Registry refers to national law and jurisprudence which tend to indicate that "the issues discussed in the scope of the provision of adequate facilities are purely of a technical nature."[70] The pre-trial Judge notes that these references are of little relevance in light of the complexity of the cases over which the Tribunal has jurisdiction.[71] Additionally, it is entirely reasonable to think that guaranteeing a fair trial for an accused who claims indigence and who is self-represented before the Tribunal requires *facilités*[72] /facilities/ which go beyond those necessary in a national setting.

2. Ensuring Equality of Arms

52. Second, with respect to the principle of equality of arms, the pre-trial Judge can only concur with the jurisprudence referred to by the Registry in its Submissions, in that the equality of arms does not require equality of resources but procedural equality, meaning that the parties must enjoy the same procedural

---

68 *See* para. 42 *supra.*

69 Internal Memorandum titled "ICTY – Application of the ICTY's Legal Aid System to a Self-Represented Accused" ("the Memorandum of 22 May"), para. 3.

70 The Submissions, para. 25.

71 Memorandum of 22 May, para. 3: "It may be true that, in most national systems where cases are not necessarily complex, an accused, when he chooses to represent himself or herself, must self-finance the costs of his or her own assistants or investigators. However, circumstances are fundamentally different in the context of the ICTY, where cases are all extremely complex and cannot be adequately handled by an accused without the assistance of legal advisors and investigators."

72 As defined in the *Nouveau Petit Robert de la Langue Française,* 2007, p. 998: "A means enabling something to be done effortlessly, without difficulty".

guarantees and conditions during the trial.[73] It is inconceivable that the financial situation of an accused should result in an inequality of arms. Therefore, in order to restore balance to the situation of a self-represented accused and to guarantee him "procedural equality", it may be necessary to grant him more facilities and financial resources than to those afforded to an accused who is represented by counsel. The pre-trial Judge must ensure that the Accused, who claims indigence, has sufficient means to examine or have examined the witnesses against him and to obtain the attendance and examination of witnesses on his behalf *under the same conditions* as witnesses against **[page 19]** him. Consequently, these rights become ineffective if an accused is in a situation of demonstrated indigence, who is provisionally detained in the detention unit and without a team to assist him.

3. Ensuring the Proper Administration of Justice

53. Third, the pre-trial Judge has the duty to "[ensure] the proper administration of justice, a power that falls clearly within the primary, if not exclusive, responsibility of the Chamber."[74] The pre-trial Judge considers that this duty can be fulfilled only if a team of associates assists the Accused in preparing and presenting his defence at every stage of the proceedings.

54. It is crucial for a team of associates to assist the accused before, during and after hearings. Prior to the hearings, such a team is necessary to communicate with the Registry or the Chamber in order to address administrative and organizational matters and to disclose to the Prosecution the documents which the Accused intends to present during cross-examination. During hearings, it is necessary that the team be able to follow the proceedings and the English transcription in real time, and to organize visual aids if necessary. After hearings, all teams have a duty to check the court transcripts for accuracy and to prepare the presentation of defence evidence. All of these tasks cannot reasonably be accomplished by the Accused alone. The Registry acknowledged this in its Submissions noting that

> it is conceivable that a self-represented accused who is in detention may need to be assigned an investigator and/or (an) expert(s), paid for by the Tribunal if the accused is indigent, to gather or verify facts or to provide an expert report respectively...[75]

55. However, the pre-trial Judge agrees in part with the position of the Registry which considers it unimaginable that associates who draft the written submissions of the Accused be paid for carrying out the work of a counsel whereas the Accused has chosen to represent himself. By choosing to represent himself, the Accused accepts at a minimum the burden of drafting his submissions, as he has stated that he is qualified **[page 20]** to carry out these tasks, considering his qualifications and title of professor of law. While the pre-trial Judge does not doubt the abilities of the Accused, he finds nevertheless that the recent written submissions drafted by the assistants of the Accused are more concise, better argued and reasoned than those previously filed. It is therefore in the interests of the proper administration of justice to succeed in ensuring that the associates of the Accused, who undeniably play a positive role in his defence, may be decently paid for the services they perform.

C. Implementing Provisions

56. Having established the principle of the absolute need to constitute a team in order to assist the Accused, who has chosen to represent himself, in the preparation and presentation of his defence, it is incumbent upon the Registry to take the specific steps to apply the principle after the pre-trial Judge has recalled certain guidelines. The pre-trial Judge concurs with the principal conditions set out by the Registry in its Submissions.[76]

---

[73] The Submissions, para. 67, referring to *The Prosecutor v. Clément Kayishema and Obed Ruzindana,* Case No. ICTR-95-1-A, Judgement (Reasons), 1 June 2001, para. 69; *The Prosecutor v. Naser Orić,* Case No. IT-03-68-AR73.2, Interlocutory Decision on Length of Defence Case, 20 July 2005, para. 7.

[74] *The Prosecutor v. Enver Hadžihasonvić, Mehmed Alagić and Amir Kubura,* Case No. IT-01-47-PT, Decision on Prosecution's Motion for Review of the Decision of the Registrar to Assign Mr. Rodney Dixon as Co-Counsel to the Accused Kubura, 26 May 2002, para. 24.

[75] The Submissions, para. 63.

[76] *Ibid,* para. 79.

1. Burden of Proof of Indigence

57. Pursuant to Article 8 (A) of the Directive, the Accused, like any accused applying for legal aid, must prove that he does not have the financial means to pay for his defence.

58. In this case, the Accused submits that he duly submitted to the formalities necessary to assess his indigence. On the contrary, the Registry claims that the lack of cooperation from the Accused and his close relations has prevented it from making any determination as to the state of the financial resources of the Accused.

59. While the Registry must implement the generally applicable procedure, the pre-trial Judge reminds the Accused that it is absolutely necessary for him to cooperate with the Registry by filling out *the entire* declaration of means form and by enabling the Registry to use appropriate means to assess the financial situation of the **[page 21]** Accused in a satisfactory manner. The pre-trial Judge would point out that the Accused gave an overview of his financial situation during the status conferences.[77] He now has to provide the Registry with the necessary documents in support of his prior statements.

2. Qualifications of One or More Associates

60. Furthermore, the Accused must designate one or more persons who possess the qualifications required under Rule 45 of the Rules and are willing and able to work as his associates.

61. These are public and uncontroversial criteria. The Accused must simply designate among his associates *one* associate who satisfies the conditions of Rule 45. Besides indigence, the obligation under Rule 45 is the *sina qua non* for the granting of legal aid.

62. The pre-trial Judge also invites the Accused to designate a person in his team who will work as case manager and who will liaise with the organs of the Tribunal. It is of paramount importance that this person speak one of the two official languages of the Tribunal.

3. Funds Allocated for the Preparation and Presentation of the Defence of the Accused

63. Under the Defence Counsel Payment Scheme for the Trial Stage ("the Payment Scheme"), the Registry must set, depending on the resources of the Tribunal, the reasonable and necessary amounts to be allocated to the Accused for the preparation and presentation of his defence, taking into account the complexity of the case and the estimated length of the trial (where appropriate).

64. The pre-trial Judge reminds the Accused that the allotment of funds is done in a public and equitable manner for all cases, in accordance with the Payment Scheme. **[page 22]**

4. Monitoring of Expenses

65. In accordance with the Directive and the Payment Scheme, the Registry must disburse the allocated amounts for legal aid granted to accused persons before the Tribunal, and monitor their use.

VI. DISPOSITION

66. For the foregoing reasons, pursuant to Article 21 (4) of the Statute and Rules 44 and 45 of the Rules, **PARTIALLY GRANT** the Motion and **ORDER** the Registry:

(i) to implement immediately, in respect of the Accused, the procedures applicable to the provision of legal aid in accordance with the Rules and the Directive as detailed above; and

[77] Status conference of 4 April 2007, T(F) pp. 1005–1008; Status conference of 2 May 2007, T(F) pp. 1052, 1087–1089; Status conference of 5 June 2007, T(F) pp. 1206–1207.

(ii) to inform, without delay, the pre-Trial Judge of the effective implementation of the facilities granted to the Accused.

URGE the Accused to provide the Registry with all the useful information to assess his state of indigence and the requisite qualifications of his associates.

Done in English and in French, the French version being authoritative.

Done this thirtieth day of July 2007
At The Hague
The Netherlands

Jean-Claude Antonetti
Pre-Trial Judge

[Seal of the Tribunal]

UNITED NATIONS

International Tribunal for the Prosecution of Persons Responsible for Serious Violations of International Humanitarian Law Committed in the Territory of the Former Yugoslavia since 1991	Case No.	IT-00-39-A
	Date:	11 September 2007
	Original:	English

IN THE APPEALS CHAMBER

Before: **Judge Fausto Pocar, Presiding**
Judge Mohamed Shahabuddeen
Judge Mehmet Güney
Judge Andrésia Vaz
Judge Theodor Meron

Registrar: **Mr. Hans Holthuis**

Decision of: **11 September 2007**

PROSECUTOR

v.

MOMČILO KRAJIŠNIK

PUBLIC

DECISION ON KRAJIŠNIK REQUEST AND ON PROSECUTION MOTION

The Office of the Prosecutor
Mr. Peter Kremer QC

The Accused
Mr. Momčilo Krajišnik

Amicus Curiae
Mr. Colin Nicholls QC

[page 1] 1. The Appeals Chamber of the International Tribunal for the Prosecution of Persons Responsible for Serious Violations of International Humanitarian Law Committed in the Territory of the Former Yugoslavia since 1991 ("Appeals Chamber" and "Tribunal", respectively) is seized of a "Request to Provide Conditions to Work and to Reverse the Decision of the Registry of 7 June 2007", filed by Momčilo Krajišnik on 18 June 2007 ("Krajišnik Request") and of a "Motion for Clarification of the Order of Filings and the Calculation of Time Limits for Filings", filed by the Prosecution on 5 July 2007 ("Prosecution Motion").

I. KRAJIŠNIK REQUEST

A. Background and Submissions

1. The Request Itself

2. In the "Decision on Momčilo Krajišnik's Request to Self-Represent, on Counsel's Motions in Relation to Appointment of *Amicus Curiae*, and on the Prosecution Motion of 16 February 2007", filed on 11 May 2007 ("11 May 2007 Decision"), the Appeals Chamber held that Momčilo Krajišnik ("Mr. Krajišnik") could represent himself on his appeal and requested "the Registry to take any necessary steps to implement" this holding.[1]

3. Since the 11 May 2007 Decision, the Registry and Mr. Krajišnik have been in communication as to the modalities of his self-representation. The Registry and Mr. Krajišnik have not always seen eye-to-eye on these modalities, however, and the Krajišnik Request asks the Appeals Chamber to reverse certain of the Registry's determinations and to provide him with specified work conditions.[2] Citing to a number of provisions in Article 21 of the Statute of the Tribunal ("Statute"),[3] Mr. Krajišnik asks for access to particular individuals, for financial support, and for various resources.

4. In relation to access, Mr. Krajišnik raises two concerns. First, he states that the Registry has not approved Deyan Brashich to serve as his legal associate and Stefan Karganović to serve as his translator/case-manager.[4] He challenges the Registry's rulings with regard to these specific individuals. Second, Mr. Krajišnik states that he has not been permitted direct contact with **[page 2]** investigators from his team at trial.[5] He claims that in order to be on equal footing with represented accused, he should "be allowed to contact all members of [his] Defence team directly".[6]

5. In relation to financial support, Mr. Krajišnik makes several requests. First, he asks that he "be provided the free assistance of an interpreter".[7] Second, making reference to the principle of "equality (limited)", he asks for "means to finance members of the Defence team as for a case at level III difficulty".[8] He also presents various arguments why, in his view, this case is complex enough to require level III status.[9]

6. As to resources, the Krajišnik Request makes several general statements.[10] More specifically, Mr. Krajišnik seeks use of "a telephone, scanner, fax and photocopier without time constraints during the whole day".[11] In addition, Mr. Krajišnik asks "that the documents [he] receive [s] from the Prosecution and from the Appeals Chamber be sent to [him] with a Serbian translation or that these documents be translated by the interpreter [whom he] requested visit [him] in the prison".[12]

7. The Krajišnik Request also asks the Appeals Chamber to extend the deadline for the filing of Mr. Krajišnik's Appeal Brief. Mr. Krajišnik suggests that an extension is warranted for four apparently

---

1 11 May 2007 Decision, paras 24–25.
2 Krajišnik Request, paras 16, 18, 20–21.
3 *Id.*, para. 14.
4 *Id.*, para. 12.
5 *Id.*, para. 12.
6 *Id.*, para. 16.
7 *Id.*, para. 14.
8 *Id.*, para. 18.
9 *Id.*, para. 20.
10 *Id.*, para. 21.
11 *Id.*, para. 21 and fn. 10.
12 *Id.*, para. 11–13.

independent reasons: first, because he has lost time because "technical conditions" have not been met for his "unhindered work on the appeal"; second, in light of "the length of time the submission announcing the appeal was considered (30 days, as prescribed by the [R]ules)"; third, "due to the complexity and scope of the appeal"; and fourth, because his former counsel on appeal (now the current *amicus curiae*) has not yet provided him with "the archive and documentation".[13]

8. Finally, Mr. Krajišnik asks for an "extraordinary status conference" so that he can present his requests orally to the Appeals Chamber.[14]

2. The Prosecution Response and the Replies

9. The Prosecution submitted the "Prosecution Response to Momčilo Krajišnik's Request" on 28 June 2007 ("Prosecution Response"). The Prosecution raises several technical objections to the Krajišnik Request, including its failure to attach the correspondence between Mr. Krajišnik and the **[page 3]** Registry as exhibits[15] and its failure to abide by the Practice Directions in various ways, including the absence of precise citations to portions of the referenced documents and the absence of a word count.[16] On the merits, the Prosecution opposes the Krajišnik Request for the most part. The Prosecution considers that as to issues of access, the Registry has the discretion to grant or withhold access to particular persons, and Mr. Krajišnik has not shown the Registry's decisions to jeopardize his right to a fair proceeding.[17] Similarly, the Prosecution considers that Mr. Krajišnik has not shown how a lack of direct contact with investigators impinges on his fair trial rights.[18] With regard to financial support, the Prosecution suggests that the language of Article 21(4)(d) of the Statute makes clear that "Tribunal funds are available only to those who request assigned legal assistance and not for those persons choosing to defend themselves in person or through legal assistance of their own choosing".[19] Since Mr. Krajišnik is not entitled to legal aid, the Registry has no need to designate the case's level of complexity.[20] The Prosecution considers, however, that Mr. Krajišnik is entitled to "the provision of adequate language facilities to enable him to participate effectively in an appeal which is being conducted in English".[21] In this regard, the Prosecution observes that Mr. Krajišnik should "receive[] filings from the other parties and from the Appeals Chamber in a language he understands".[22] As to Mr. Krajišnik's other requests for resources, the Prosecution considers that they are too vague to enable the Appeals Chamber to identify the challenged actions of the Registry.[23]

10. The Prosecution also opposes Mr. Krajišnik's requests for an extension of time with regard to his Appeal Brief and for an extraordinary status conference. As to the request for the extension of time, the Prosecution considers that the request is premature and in any event lacks good cause. In particular, the Prosecution notes that as of the date of its filing, the B/C/S translation of the Trial Judgement had not yet issued and hence the 75- day clock for Mr. Krajišnik's appeal had not yet begun to run.[24] In the Prosecution's view, no extensions should be given for delays that occurred before this clock began ticking,[25] and Mr. Krajišnik's submissions with regard to complexity should be dismissed as cursory.[26] Finally, with regard to the request for an extraordinary status conference, the Prosecution states that no provision in the Rules of Procedure and Evidence ("Rules") provides **[page 4]** for such status conferences and that in any event the Krajišnik Request does not warrant such measures.[27]

---

13 *Id.*, para. 17.
14 *Id.*, para. 21.
15 Prosecution Response, para. 3.
16 *Id.*, paras 30, 33–34.
17 *Id.*, para. 19; *see also id.*, paras 24–28.
18 *Id.*, para. 16.
19 *Id.*, para. 12.
20 *Id.*, para. 32.
21 *Id.*, para. 17.
22 *Id.*, para. 22.
23 *Id.*, para. 36.
24 *Id.*, para. 38.
25 *See id.*, para. 40.
26 *Id.*, para. 43.
27 *Id.*, para. 44.

11. On 2 July 2007 *amicus curiae* filed a document styled as "*Amicus Curiae*'s Reply to Prosecution Response to Momčilo Krajišnik's Request" ("*Amicus* Reply"). The *Amicus* Reply submits that while "the plain language of Article 21(4)(d) is not conclusive as to whether legal aid funds are available for both assigned counsel and self-represented litigants", "in order for [Mr. Krajišnik] to effectively represent himself in this Appeal, it is realistic and necessary that he be provided with some sort of language, case management, investigation, and legal support", particularly in light of Article 21(4)(b)'s provision of a right to "adequate time and facilities for the preparation of his defence".[28] *Amicus curiae* suggests the appointment of a *pro se* officer as a possible step in this regard.[29] *Amicus curiae* further informs the Appeals Chamber that with regard to the case files mentioned in the context of Mr. Krajišnik's request for an extension of time, these case files are due to be delivered to Mr. Krajišnik on 5 July 2007.[30] *Amicus curiae* notes that these case files are substantial (including more than 150 boxes of papers, predominantly in English), and suggests that Mr. Krajišnik might need an extension of time in order to adequately review them.[31] *Amicus curiae* also disputes the Prosecution's suggestion that the Rules do not allow for extraordinary status conferences and suggests that, pursuant to Rules 65*ter*(B) and 107, the Pre-Appeal Judge has the authority to convene such a status conference.[32] Finally, *amicus curiae* notes that the Krajišnik Request is Mr. Krajišnik's first filing since the 11 May 2007 Decision and implies that this factor may be taken into account in considering any technical failure to comply with Practice Directions.[33]

12. On 28 July 2007, four days after receiving a B/C/S translation of the Prosecution Response, Mr. Krajišnik submitted a "Reply by the Accused to the Prosecution Response to Momčilo Krajišnik Request" ("Krajišnik Reply to Prosecution").[34] Mr. Krajišnik acknowledges that the Krajišnik Request failed to comply with the Practice Directions in certain respects, but urges the Appeals Chamber to focus on the merits of his arguments.[35] As to the merits, he suggests that the Prosecution mistakenly focused only on Article 21(4)(b) of the Statute, while overlooking the **[page 5]** guarantees in Article 21(1) and (2).[36] In Mr. Krajišnik's view, his waiver of the right to counsel means that he should be treated as an unreimbursed lead counsel but entitled to legal aid funding for advisors, a translator, and a case manager.[37] In his view, this will bring him closer to equal footing with Prosecution, *amicus curiae* in this case, and accuseds in other cases.[38] He further suggests that the preparation of his own appeal is more complicated than what the Prosecution must do, and therefore that he should receive greater funding than the Prosecution or at the very least receive funding at level III complexity.[39] Mr. Krajišnik reiterates some points made in the Krajišnik Request,[40] and also indicates that his initial request for translated documents refers not only to filings but also to certain witness statements.[41] He suggests, however, that there are "positive" developments on this front.[42] With regard to the issue of a time extension, Mr. Krajišnik references the quantity and unsorted state of the documents sent by prior counsel as a reason he needs a significant extension.[43] Regarding the extraordinary status conference, Mr. Krajišnik states that Rule 65*bis* (B) of the Rules does in fact permit such conferences, but notes that he "does not insist on holding an extraordinary status conference if the Appeals Chamber does not consider it necessary".[44] In closing, Mr. Krajišnik expresses his appreciation for the 11 May 2007 Decision; urges the Appeals Chamber to grant him the resources that he considers necessary to implement this decision; and states that he "feels bound to respect all the orders of the … Chamber, and he will do so".[45]

---

28 *Amicus* Reply, paras 9–10.
29 *Id.*, para. 15.
30 *Id.*, para. 17.
31 *Id.*, paras 17–19.
32 *Id.*, para. 20.
33 *Id.*, paras 21–22.
34 The English translation was filed on 21 August 2007. On 28 July 2007, Mr. Krajišnik submitted a Corrigendum to the Krajišnik Reply to Prosecution. The English translation of this Corrigendum was also filed on 21 August 2007.
35 *See* Krajišnik Reply to Prosecution, p. 9.
36 *Id.*, para. 11.
37 *Id.*
38 *Id.*, para. 11 and fns 8–9, 11.
39 *Id.*, para. 15.
40 *See id.*, paras 19–20, 23, 25.
41 *Id.*, para. 21.
42 *Id.*
43 *Id.*, para. 28.
44 *Id.*, para. 29.
45 *Id.*, p. 9.

3. The Registry Submission and the Reply

13. On 19 July 2007 and pursuant to Rule 33(B) of the Rules, the Registry filed the "Registry Submission on Momčilo Krajišnik's Request to Reverse the Decision of the Registry of 7 June 2007" ("Registry Submission"), with several confidential and *ex parte* Annexes. In this submission, the Registry urges that the Appeals Chamber dismiss the Krajišnik Request.

14. With regard to access, the Registry clarifies that it has not denied Mr. Krajišnik access to the particular individuals mentioned by Mr. Krajišnik. Mr. Krajišnik may communicate with his investigators and others in "accordance with standard procedures" at the United Nations Detention **[page 6]** Centre (UNDU).[46] Rather, the Registry has denied him *privileged* access to these individuals.[47] The Registry considers that privileged access to these individuals would damage "the security and good order of the UNDU" as well as pose risks to "the integrity of the appellate proceedings".[48] The Registry states that it has offered Mr. Krajišnik the right to have privileged access to up to three legal associates, provided that these individuals meet certain "minimum qualification requirements" that the Registry deems "fundamental and necessary to safeguard the integrity of the proceedings and the security, and good order of the UNDU".[49] As of the date of the Registry's filing, no such legal associates have been designated.[50] The Registry notes that it has rejected Mr. Krajišnik's attempt to designate Mr. Braschich as a legal associate in light of the fact that Mr. Braschich was found guilty of professional misconduct by the Tribunal's Disciplinary Board.[51]

15. With regard to funding, the Registry makes detailed submissions. The Registry informs the Appeals Chamber that these submissions track ones made by the Registry in *Prosecutor v. Vojislav Šešelj*, where a similar question has arisen with regard to funding a self-represented accused's defence.[52] To begin with, the Registry considers that it "has no authority to allocate money to a self-represented accused".[53] The Registry considers that Article 24(d) of the Statute, Rule 45 of the Rules, and the Directive on the Assignment of Defence Counsel (IT/073/Rev.11) do not afford it with the authority to "disburse public funds to the Appellant, or to persons ultimately retained by the Appellant to assist him in his capacity as a self-represented accused outside the Tribunal's legal aid system".[54] In this regard, the Registry notes that "[t]here is no legal aid system known to the Registrar that offers the option to disburse funds directly or indirectly to a self-represented accused".[55] The Registry considers that Article 21(4)(d)'s provision of the right to have "legal assistance assigned" to an accused relates solely to counsel and cannot apply to persons acting in a different capacity.[56] The Registry further considers that while Article 21(4)(b)'s requirement that an accused "have adequate time and facilities for the preparation of his defence" does necessitate certain technical and logistical support to self-represented accused (such as "access to certain office **[page 7]** facilities, library, documentation, technical assistance" and "conceivabl[y]" to the assignment of a Tribunal-paid "investigator and/or (an) expert(s), depending on the stage of the proceedings"), this clause does not cover reimbursement for "persons who draft legal submissions, analyse evidence and perform other functions normally performed by defence counsel".[57] The Registry disputes Mr. Krajišnik's claim that principles of equality require him to have resources equal to those of the Prosecution.[58] The Registry considers that Mr. Krajišnik is entitled only to procedural equality,

---

46 Registry Submission, para. 26.

47 *Id.*, paras 26–27. The Registry implies that Mr. Krajišnik may have privileged communications with his investigators when a designated legal associate is also present. *See id.*, para. 21(d).

48 *Id.*, para. 29.

49 *Id.*, para. 22. Although the Registry Submission does not spell out what these qualification requirements are, the Appeals Chamber considers it appropriate to observe that the Registry has elsewhere defined these qualifications as "the basic qualification requirements of Rule 44 of the Rules". *Id.*, Confidential and *Ex Parte* Annex 1, p. 1.

50 *Id.*, para. 23.

51 *Id.* Accordingly, Mr. Brashich did not *prima facie* fulfill the requirement of Rule 44(A)(iv), and the Registry declined to waive this requirement in light of the gravity of the professional misconduct at issue. *Id.*

52 *Id.*, para. 34.

53 *Id.*, para. 33.

54 *Id.*, para. 35.

55 *Id.*, para. 43.

56 *Id.*, para. 39. Once counsel is assigned, the Registry may then fund support staff for assigned counsel pursuant to the Directive on the Assignment of Defense Counsel. *Id.*, para. 42.

57 *Id.*, paras 52–54.

58 *Id.*, para. 57.

not substantive equality, and that in any event Mr. Krajišnik's decision to self-represent constitutes voluntary waiver of his right to legal assistance.[59] In light of its position, the Registry considers that it has no need to classify Mr. Krajišnik's appeal based on a level of complexity, since the Registry only classifies cases where the legal aid system is in use.[60]

16. With regard to funding, the Registry further suggests that "the right to represent oneself and the right to have counsel assigned are not necessarily mutually incompatible".[61] To the extent that these rights are not incompatible and the Tribunal can fund assistance for a self-represented accused, "then this, it is submitted, can only be done through the Tribunal's legal aid system. That is, if the Appellant wants his assistants to be remunerated by the Tribunal, he must comply with the legal aid requirements", such as by demonstrating partial or complete indigency and by having his proposed legal advisors meet the requirements of Rule 45 of the Rules.[62] The Registry emphasizes that any legal aid disbursed in this way must be done pursuant to the same conditions that apply to fully represented accused.[63]

17. As to a translator/case manager, the Registry states that "there is no negative decision of the Registry that could be reviewed by the Appeals Chamber at this stage".[64] Regarding Mr. Karganović, the Registry states that it is in the process of assessing his acceptability and that in "the meantime, [Mr. Krajišnik] has not been denied the assistance of another translator".[65] The Registry acknowledges that "a paid translator/interpreter may be provided by the Tribunal to assist" Mr. Krajišnik, but suggests that "it must be a person whose qualifications and conduct are acceptable to the Registry".[66] **[page 8]**

18. Finally, with regard to resources, the Registry explains that it has offered Mr. Krajišnik access to a privileged telephone and fax line for communication with designated legal associates and the ability to exchange electronic documents with such associates, but that these offers have not been implemented due to the absence of legal associates.[67] The Registry does not specifically address either Mr. Krajišnik's request for 24-hour access to a telephone, scanner, fax, and copier or his request for the provision of certain documents in Serbian.

19. On 13 August 2007, within four days of receiving a B/C/S translation of the Registry Submission, Mr. Krajišnik submitted a "Reply of the Accused to Registry Submission on Momčilo Krajišnik's Request" ("Krajišnik Reply to Registry").[68] With regard to access, Mr. Krajišnik reiterates his concerns that the Registry has not approved Mr. Braschich as a legal associate and Mr. Karganović as a translator.[69] He also reiterates his need for "unrestricted communication" with his investigators, although he accepts that meetings with these investigators can only take place in the company of individuals whom the Registry has granted privileged access.[70] In his view, standard methods of communication with investigators is not adequate because the mail takes a long time and because "other prisoners use the standard [telephone] line" which in any event is costly.[71] As to funding, Mr. Krajišnik considers that he is entitled to funds, although he is willing not to control the disbursal of these funds.[72] Mr. Krajišnik wants these funds to be paid to Mr. Dershowitz, an American lawyer whom he seeks to have involved in his case.[73] Mr. Krajišnik explains that "it matters to him whether these funds are at level III in order to secure funding for engaging Mr. Dershowitz".[74] Mr. Krajišnik

59 *Id.*, paras 57–58.
60 *Id.*, para. 33.
61 *Id.*, para. 64.
62 *Id.*, paras 63, 66.
63 *Id.*, para. 66.
64 *Id.*, para. 24.
65 *Id.*
66 *Id.*, para. 55.
67 *Id.*, paras 21, 31.
68 The English translation was filed on 21 August 2007.
69 Krajišnik Reply to Registry, paras 12–15. Mr. Krajišnik also makes reference to a third individual, Zdenko Tomanović. Since Mr. Tomanović was not mentioned in the Krajišnik Request, the Appeals Chamber disregards this reference as going beyond the scope of a reply.
70 Krajišnik Reply to Registry, para. 11.
71 *Id.*, paras 18–19.
72 *Id.*, para. 33.
73 *Id.*
74 *Id.*, para. 27.

emphasizes that he does not think that the right to self-representation is compatible with having the Registry assign him counsel.[75] He does suggest, however, that to the extent that the Registry requires him to act through legal associates, then the Registry should take part in remunerating such associates.[76] With regard to a translator, Mr. Krajišnik states that no translator has been offered to him.[77] Mr. Krajišnik indicates his willingness to work with a **[page 9]** translator other than the one he initially requested, at least until concerns about his preferred translator have been resolved.[78]

B. Discussion

1. Preliminary Issues

20. Five preliminary issues merit addressing.

21. First, as the Prosecution Response observes, the Krajišnik Request fails to comply with certain provisions of the Practice Directions, including the requirements that where "filings of the parties refer to passages in a judgement, decision, transcript, exhibits or other authorities, they shall indicate precisely the date, exhibit number, page number and paragraph number of the text or exhibit referred to"[79] and that "[p]arties shall conduct a word count of any document they file which is subject to the length limitations set forth ... and shall include this information in the form 'Word count: __' at the end of the document, before the signature line".[80] The Appeals Chamber reminds Mr. Krajišnik of his obligation to comply with the Practice Directions and warns him that in the future the Appeals Chamber may sanction any noncompliance.[81] At the same time, the Appeals Chamber notes with approval that Mr. Krajišnik now appears aware of the obligations imposed by the Practice Directions,[82] and that both the Krajišnik Reply to Prosecution and the Krajišnik Reply to Registry demonstrate significant compliance with the provisions of the Practice Directions referenced above.

22. Second, the Appeals Chamber observes that there is some confusion over whether and in what way *amicus curiae* can file a "Reply" where Mr. Krajišnik has filed a motion and the Prosecution has filed a response. The Appeals Chamber provides guidance on this issue for the future in Part II of this decision, but in the present instance the Appeals Chamber accepts the *Amicus* Reply as validly filed.

23. Third, the Appeals Chamber notes that the Registry Submission was filed on 19 July 2007, just over one month after the filing of the Krajišnik Request. The Appeals Chamber acknowledges that the Rules and the Practice Directions do not specify time limits for the filing of Registry submissions pursuant to Rule 33(B). In the interests of ensuring that this case progresses as efficiently as possible, however, the Appeals Chamber requests that in the future the Registry make **[page 10]** any Rule 33(B) submissions in response to motions brought by Mr. Krajišnik within ten days of the filing of the English translation of such motions.

24. Fourth, the Appeals Chamber notes that the Rules do not specify whether and under what circumstances a party is entitled to reply to Registry Submissions made pursuant to Rule 33(B).[83] The Appeals Chamber nonetheless considers that where a party seeks judicial review of a Registry determination, it is appropriate to allow that party a right of reply to a Rule 33(B) submission (with the timeline for the reply to be the same as the timeline for replies made to responses).[84] Accordingly, the Appeals Chamber accepts the Krajišnik Reply to Registry as validly filed.

---

75 *Id.*, para. 48.
76 *Id.*, para. 47.
77 *Id.*, para. 25.
78 *Id.*
79 Practice Direction on Procedure for the Filing of Written Submissions in Appeal Proceedings before the International Tribunal (IT/155/Rev. 3), 16 September 2005 ("Practice Direction on Procedure"), para. 17.
80 Practice Direction on the Length of Briefs and Motions (IT/184/Rev.2), 16 September 2005, para. 8.
81 *See, e.g.,* Practice Direction on Procedure, para. 20.
82 *See* Krajišnik Reply to Prosecution, p. 9.
83 *See* Order Regarding Time Limits, 31 July 2007, p. 1 (before the Pre-Appeal Judge).
84 *See, e.g., Prosecutor v. Miroslav Kvočka et al.,* Case No. IT-98-30/1-A, Decision on Review of Registrar's Decision to Withdraw Legal Aid from Zoran Žigić, 7 February 2003 ("*Žigić* Decision"), para. 6 (referencing an acccused's reply to a filing by the Registry).

25. Fifth, the Appeals Chamber notes that although the Registry Submission does not contain a word count, it appears to exceed the 3000 words allotted for motions, responses, and replies pursuant to paragraph 5 of the Practice Direction on the Length of Briefs and Motions. Of course, the Registry Submission does not need to comply with this word limit requirement, as it is neither a motion, a response, nor a reply, but rather a filing pursuant to Rule 33(B) of the Rules. Nonetheless, as Mr. Krajišnik has implied,[85] this may lead to a problematic disparity: while the Registry has no word limit, Mr. Krajišnik is bound by a word limit in replying to the Registry. The Appeals Chamber accordingly requests the Registry to include a word count in future Rule 33(B) submissions. The Appeals Chamber further informs Mr. Krajišnik that, in the future, where he is entitled to reply to such a submission (as discussed in the previous paragraph) and where this submission exceeds 3000 words, his reply may have a word count up to but not exceeding the word count of the submission.

2. Merits

26. The Appeals Chamber now turns to the merits of the Krajišnik Request.

(a) Extraordinary Status Conference and Time Extension

27. To begin with, the Appeals Chamber dismisses the request for an extraordinary status conference. Such a conference is not required by the Rules, and the Appeals Chamber considers that it can adequately dispose of the Krajišnik Request on the basis of the written filings.[86] **[page 11]**

28. The Appeals Chamber further dismisses Mr. Krajišnik's request for an extension of time to file his appeal brief.[87] In this respect, the Appeals Chamber notes that the seventy-five-day clock for Mr. Krajišnik to file his appeal brief did not start running until 24 July 2007, when Mr. Krajišnik received a B/C/S translation of the Trial Judgement.[88] Any possible complications that occurred prior to that date, such as the fact that the transfer of files from prior counsel to Mr. Krajišnik did not take place until 5 July 2007, are thus irrelevant to the question of whether a time extension is merited.[89] To the extent that Mr. Krajišnik claims that the complexity of his case merited additional time, the Appeals Chamber rejects this contention. Mr. Krajišnik has not shown how his appeal is so complex as to warrant a time extension. Moreover, the fact that Mr. Krajišnik has had the opportunity to conduct some preparations for his appeal brief during the nearly ten-month lag between the issuance of the Trial Judgement and the issuance of its B/C/S translation cuts against the claim that a further time extension is currently warranted.

(b) Registry Determinations and Conditions of Work

29. The Appeals Chamber now turns to Mr. Krajišnik's challenges involving the determinations of the Registry and his conditions of work. The Appeals Chamber notes several difficulties inherent in addressing these challenges. For one thing, Mr. Krajišnik raises a large number of challenges, and the procedural background to these challenges is not always clear. As an example, it is often difficult to tell when a specific decision of the Registry is being challenged and what that decision is. For another thing, the briefing has taken a long time, due in large part to the time needed for translation. Because the Registry and Mr. Krajišnik have continued to communicate during this period, the state of affairs now may be different from what it was when the Krajišnik Request was filed. Given the need for efficient resolution of the issues presented, the Appeals Chamber passes over some of these difficulties and prioritizes the provision of guidance to the parties and the Registry.

30. To the extent that Mr. Krajišnik seeks judicial review of an administrative determination, the standard of review is clear. The Appeals Chamber will quash this determination if "the Registrar has failed

85 *See* Krajišnik Reply to Registry, fn. 27.

86 *See, e.g., Prosecutor v. Pavle Strugar*, Case No. IT-01-42-Misc.1, Decision on Strugar's Request to Reopen Appeal Proceedings, 7 June 2007, para. 19.

87 While issues regarding extensions of time limits could be left to the Pre-Appeal Judge, the Appeals Chamber considers it appropriate to deal with this particular request, since the request occurs in the context of a broader filing.

88 *See* 11 May 2007 Decision, para. 15; Procès Verbal of 24 July 2007, filed 26 July 2007.

89 The Appeals Chamber also rejects Mr. Krajišnik's and *amicus curiae*'s suggestions that the quantity of case files justifies an extension. Among other things, it is not clear why review of all these files is needed to mount an effective appeal.

to comply with [relevant] legal requirements" or "if the Registrar has failed to observe any basic rules of natural justice or to act with procedural fairness towards the person affected by the decision, or if he has taken into account irrelevant material or failed to take into account relevant material, or if he has reached a conclusion which no sensible person who has properly **[page 12]** applied his mind to the issue could have reached".[90] At least "in the absence of established unreasonableness", there "can be no interference with the margin of appreciation of the facts or merits of that case to which the maker of such an administrative decision is entitled".[91]

31. Most of the matters at issue relate to Article 21 of the Statute. This provides in relevant part that:

> 1. All persons shall be equal before the International Tribunal.
>
> 2. In the determination of charges against him, the accused shall be entitled to a fair and public hearing, subject to article 22 of the Statute.
>
> ...
>
> 4. In the determination of any charge against the accused pursuant to the present Statute, the accused shall be entitled to the following minimum guarantees, in full equality:
>
> ...
>
> (b) to have adequate time and facilities for the preparation of his defense and to communicate with counsel of his own choosing;
>
> ...
>
> (d) to be tried in his presence, and to defend himself in person or through legal assistance of his own choosing; to be informed, if he does not have legal assistance, of this right; and to have legal assistance assigned to him, in any case where the interests of justice so require, and without payment by him in any such case if he does not have sufficient means to pay for it;
>
> ...
>
> (f) to have the free assistance of an interpreter if he cannot understand or speak the language used in the International Tribunal;
>
> ...

Pursuant to Article 21(4)(d), Mr. Krajišnik has opted to represent himself. Today, the Appeals Chamber considers how this choice affects the application and/or implementation of other guarantees under Article 21 of the Statute.

(i) <u>Access</u>

32. The Appeals Chamber considers that there are four questions at issue in terms of access. First, there is the question of whom a self-represented accused may have privileged communications with. Second, there is the question of whom a self-represented accused may share confidential information with. Third, there is a question of quantity – namely, where a self-represented accused is confined to the UNDU and seeks the assistance of others in preparing his **[page 13]** appeal, to what extent, if any, is he entitled to more opportunities to communicate with others that are accorded to other accused? Lastly, there is the question of the reasonableness of the Registry's decision as to a specific individual proposed by Mr. Krajišnik to be a designated legal associate. The Appeals Chamber considers these issues in turn.

---

90 *Žigić* Decision, para. 13.

91 *Id. See also Prosecutor v. Vidoje Blagojević & Dragan Jokić*, Case No. IT-02-60-T, Decision on Independent Counsel for Vidoje Blagojević's Motion to Instruct the Registrar to Appoint New Lead and Co-Counsel, 3 July 2003, paras 23–25; *Nahimana et al. v. Prosecutor*, Case No. ICTR-99-52-A, Decision on Appellant Jean-Bosco Barayagwiza's Motion Contesting the Decision of the President Refusing to Review and Reverse the Decision of the Registrar Relating to the Withdrawal of Co-Counsel, 23 November 2006, para. 9.

33. With regard to privileged communication, the Appeals Chamber sees no error in the Registry's determination that Mr. Krajišnik may have privileged access to up to three designated legal associates (and presumably to team members who visit the accused in the company of these associates), but to no one else.[92] Privilege stems from the attorney-client relationship, as indicated in Article 21(4)(b) of the Statute and as set forth in Rule 97 of the Rules, which provides that all "communications between lawyer and client shall be regarded as privileged". Where an accused has opted to self-represent instead of to have counsel represent him, the basis for the privilege is removed. Mr. Krajišnik accordingly has no entitlement to privileged communications. Since the Registry has no obligation to provide him with privileged access to anyone, Mr. Krajišnik has no basis for objecting to the Registry's willingness to provide him with privileged access to up to three designated legal associates.[93]

34. With regard to confidential information, the Appeals Chamber generally sees no error in the Registry's determination that Mr. Krajišnik may only discuss confidential material with designated legal associates. This is a difficult issue. On the one hand, given Mr. Krajišnik's distance from the region and confinement in the UNDU, it is virtually impossible for him to personally undertake investigations relating to confidential material – investigations which may prove helpful in the preparation of his defence. If he cannot discuss confidential material with those outside the UNDU, then he has no mechanism for enabling such investigations.[94] On the other hand, if Mr. Krajišnik is permitted to share confidential information with anyone he considers to be part of his team, then the risks of leakage of confidential information or of inappropriate conduct of investigations are significantly higher than where investigations are conducted under the supervision of a legal professional. Such an approach could endanger the protection of witnesses and victims (protections so important that they are specifically referenced in Article 22 of the Statute). The Registry has sought to strike a balance between these competing interests by enabling Mr. Krajišnik to share confidential information only with designated legal associates, who in turn **[page 14]** can provide the professional supervision needed to ensure appropriate use of the confidential information. The Appeals Chamber considers that this approach does indeed strike a reasonable balance and upholds it, subject to one caveat that will be discussed in paragraph 44.

35. The third issue is quantity of access. The Registry has authorized Mr. Krajišnik to have unlimited communications with any designated legal associates, and Mr. Krajišnik can contact all other persons (*e.g.*, investigators) in accordance with standard procedures at the UNDU. When designated legal associates exist, this approach is a reasonable one. The unlimited access to the designated legal associates would provide Mr. Krajišnik with a conduit for exchanging appropriate information with other members of his team where time limitations (or other limitations) imposed by UNDU standard procedures impede direct exchange. This in turn would satisfy the requirement pursuant to Article 21(4)(b) of the Statute that an accused have "adequate time and facilities for the preparation of his defence".

36. If no legal associates have been designated, however, then the Appeals Chamber has some concerns about the Registry's approach. In this situation, pursuant to the Registry's approach a self-represented accused is limited only to the standard UNDU procedures for communication with the outside. If these procedures do not provide a self-represented accused with sufficient opportunity to exchange appropriate information with team members outside the UNDU during the preparation of his case, then this may amount to a lack of "adequate time and facilities for the preparation of his defence" in violation of Article 21(4)(b) of the Statute. The Appeals Chamber considers, however, that it lacks the necessary information to assess whether the standard procedures do indeed provide sufficient opportunity for communication with the outside during the preparation of his case. The Registry does not provide specifics about these procedures, and Mr. Krajišnik's allegations of limited time (and substantial expense) for telephone exchanges are vague. The Appeals Chamber thus does not know whether standard procedures permit Mr. Krajišnik's communication with his team for only a minute a day (which would seem insufficient), for several hours a day

92 *See* Registry Submission, paras 21, 27–29.

93 Although Mr. Krajišnik has no formal entitlement to privileged communications, the Appeals Chamber considers that the Registry's willingness to provide him with privileged access to up to three designated legal associates is a salutary practice.

94 Since Mr. Krajišnik's case is at the appeal stage, there is presumably little (if any) need for outside investigations. Nonetheless, the Appeals Chamber cannot rule out *a priori* the possibility that some need exists, and so the Appeals Chamber addresses this issue. *Cf. Nahimana et al. v. Prosecutor*, Case No. ICTR-99-52-A, Decision on Appellant Hassan Ngeze's Motions for Approval of Further Investigations on Specific Information Relating to the Additional Evidence of Potential Witnesses, 20 June 2006, para. 27.

(which would seem more than sufficient), or for some other period of time. The Appeals Chamber accordingly dismisses this issue for want of specificity. Nonetheless, the Appeals Chamber informs the Registry that in the event that no legal associates are designated, the Registry should ensure that Mr. Krajišnik has adequate means of communicating with his defence team while he is preparing his appeal brief and his reply brief. If accommodations beyond those provided under standard UNDU procedures are thus necessary, the Appeals Chamber expresses its conviction that the Registry will **[page 15]** provide such accommodations in the manner it deems most consistent with preserving order and security in the UNDU.

37. Finally, the Appeals Chamber sees no error in the Registry's decision that Mr. Deyan Brashich does not qualify as a designated legal associate. The Registry reasonably requires that designated legal associates meet the requirements of Rule 44 of the Rules. Rule 44(A)(iv) excludes any individual who has "been found guilty or otherwise disciplined in relevant disciplinary proceedings against him in a national or international forum, including proceedings pursuant to the Code of Professional Conduct for Defence Counsel Appearing Before the International Tribunal, unless the Registrar deems that, in the circumstances, it would be disproportionate to exclude such counsel". Mr. Brashich has been found guilty of professional misconduct by the Disciplinary Board.[95] The Registry reasonably explains that it did not deem the exclusion of Mr. Brashich disproportional given the gravity of Mr. Brashich's misconduct.[96]

(ii) Funding

38. Two broad issues arise in relation to funding. First and most notably, there is the question of whether and to what extent Article 21 of the Statute requires that funding for legal aid be made available to an indigent accused who self-represents.[97] If so, subsidiary questions arise as to what conditions shall attach to this legal aid funding and who shall control the disbursal. Second, there is the question of what else the Registry must fund for an indigent self-represented accused and in what manner it must do so. The Appeals Chamber addresses these questions in turn.

39. The parties and the Registry take a range of positions on whether an indigent self-represented accused is entitled to funding for legal assistance. Mr. Krajišnik believes that he is entitled to such funding; the Prosecution argues that an accused who self-represents has no entitlement to legal aid; and the Registry considers it may be able to use its legal aid system to assign counsel to a self-represented accused. The Appeals Chamber also notes the recent decision of the Pre-Trial Judge in *Prosecutor v. Vojislav Šešelj*, which appears to contemplate that, under certain circumstances, the Registry might have to provide some legal aid funding for an indigent self-represented accused.[98] **[page 16]**

40. In the Appeals Chamber's view, Article 21(4)(d) of the Statute does not support the proposition than an accused who elects to self-represent is nonetheless entitled to legal aid. Article 21(4)(d) gives the accused the right "to defend himself in person or through legal assistance of his own choosing". We have held that these two options stand in "binary opposition".[99] An accused who chooses to self-represent is not entitled to legal assistance. Hence, he is not entitled to the subsidiary right mentioned later in Article 21(4)(d) to have legal assistance paid for by the Tribunal if he is indigent.[100]

---

95 *In the Matter of Mr. Deyan Ranko Brashich, Attorney at Law from the United States*, Decision in the Appeal by the Registrar to the Disciplinary Board, 22 March 2007, para. 52.

96 Registry Submission, para. 23.

97 For brevity's sake, the Appeals Chamber uses the term "indigent" as a shorthand for "indigent or partially indigent".

98 *Prosecutor v. Vojislav Šešelj*, Case No. IT-03-67-PT, Decision on the Financing [of] the Defence of the Accused, 30 July 2007 ("*Šešelj* Decision"), paras 63-64; *see also id*., para. 55 (suggesting that legal associates should receive funding for their work drafting written submissions).

99 *Slobodan Milošević v. Prosecutor*, Case No. IT-02-54-AR73.7, Decision on Interlocutory Appeal of the Trial Chamber's Decision on the Assignment of Counsel, 1 November 2004 ("*Milošević* Decision"), para 11. *See also Nahimana et al. v. Prosecutor*, Case No. ICTR-99-52-A, Scheduling Order for Appeals Hearing and Decision on Hassan Ngeze's Motion of 24 January 2006, 16 November 2006, p. 3.

100 The Appeals Chamber notes that where stand-by or other counsel have been assigned to a self-represented accused, this has not been seen as complementary to the accused's right to self-represent but rather as an imposed limitation on the accused's right to self-represent. *See Milošević* Decision, para. 17 (describing the appointment of counsel for a self-represented accused as a restriction on the accused's right to self-represent). Similarly, an accused "is not entitled to *amicus curiae*", even where the relevant Chamber chooses to appoint *amicus curiae*. 11 May 2007 Decision, para. 18.

41. The question nonetheless remains whether some other provision of the Statute or source of law requires the Registry to provide an indigent self-representing accused with funded legal aid. Mr. Krajišnik suggests that the principle of equality referenced in Article 21(1) of the Statute and the fair trial rights referenced in Article 21(2) of the Statute have this effect.[101] The Appeals Chamber does not find these arguments convincing. While Article 21(1) may require that accused in similar circumstances receive roughly comparable treatment, it does not require that an accused who opts for self-representation receive all the benefits held by an accused who opts for counsel. To the contrary, as "part of the choice to self-represent, Mr. Krajišnik must accept responsibility for the disadvantages this choice may bring".[102] Moreover, the Appeals Chamber considers that where an accused elects to self-represent, he is asserting his ability to conduct his case without legal assistance and thus Tribunal funding for legal aid for him can be presumed to be unnecessary to the conduct of a fair trial. To the extent that the accused lacks the ability to conduct his own case and his self-representation is thus "substantially and persistently obstructing the proper and expeditious conduct of his trial", then the remedy is restriction of his right to self-representation.[103] To allow an **[page 17]** accused to self-represent and yet also to receive full legal aid funding from the Tribunal would, as the saying goes, let him have his cake and eat it too.

42. Finally, the Appeals Chamber considers whether Article 21(4)(b) of the Statute requires the Tribunal to provide some funding for the legal associates of self-represented accused. The Appeals Chamber agrees with the Registry that the term "facilities" in Article 21(4)(b) does not normally encompass legal assistance.[104] Nonetheless, the Appeals Chamber considers that in seeking otherwise to give effect to Article 21(4)(b) for a self-represented accused, the Registry has relied heavily on the concept of designated legal associates. To the extent that the Registry requires or encourages indigent self-representing accused to coordinate their defences through designated legal associates, it is appropriate for the Tribunal to provide some funding for such associates. Such funding should not be comparable to that paid to counsel for represented accused (particularly since work such as the drafting of written filings should be considered the responsibility of the self-representing accused), but nonetheless should adequately reimburse the legal associates for their coordinating work and for related legal consultation.[105] The Registry may impose additional criteria on designated legal associates who seek funding from the Tribunal (comparable to the Registry's ability to require that Tribunal-funded counsel meet the requirements of Rule 45 of the Rules as well as of Rule 44 of the Rules). As always, the Registry should disburse any such payments in accordance with applicable UN Rules and Regulations.

43. The Appeals Chamber now turns to the question of what else the Registry must fund for an indigent self-represented accused pursuant to Article 21(4)(b) of the Statute. Mr. Krajišnik's submissions on this front are vague, and the Appeals Chamber sees no reason for disturbing the Registry's finding that Article 21(4)(b) requires it to provide "certain technical and logistical support" and "conceivabl[y]" the assignment of a Tribunal-paid "investigator and/or (an) expert(s), depending on the stage of the proceedings".[106] **[page 18]**

---

101 The Appeals Chamber notes that while the *Šešelj* Decision does not clearly ground its holding that an indigent self-represented accused is entitled to funded legal aid in any particular provision of the Statute, it appears to draw on these same principles. *See Šešelj* Decision, paras 42, 49–50. The Appeals Chamber also notes that the Registry does not clearly explain the legal basis for its conclusion that counsel may be assigned to a self-represented accused pursuant to the legal aid program. *See generally* Registry Submission, paras 62–65.

102 11 May 2007 Decision, para. 17 (internal quotation marks and alteration omitted). *See also Prosecutor v. Slobodan Milošević*, Case No. IT-02-54-AR73.6, Decision on the Interlocutory Appeal by the Amici Curiae against the Trial Chamber Order Concerning the Presentation and Preparation of the Defence Case, 20 January 2004, para. 19 ("There is no doubt that, by choosing to conduct his own defence, the Accused deprived himself of resources a well-equipped legal defence team could have provided. A defendant who decides to represent himself relinquishes many of the benefits associated with representation by counsel").

103 *Prosecutor v. Vojislav Šešelj*, Case No. IT-03-67-AR-73.3, Decision on Appeal against the Trial Chamber's Decision on Assignment of Counsel, 20 October 2006, para. 20. The Appeals Chamber also notes the possibility of alternative measures, such as the appointment of *amicus curiae*, in certain circumstances. See 11 May 2007 Decision, para. 18.

104 *See* Registry Submission, paras 52–53. Accordingly, the Appeals Chamber agrees with the Registry's view that it does not need to assign a level of complexity to a case where an accused is self-representing. The Registry's designated levels of complexity may be reserved for cases where indigent accused assert the right to counsel.

105 The Appeals Chamber considers that this conclusion, combined with the observations made in the next paragraph, are not necessarily incompatible with the point made in a United Nations Office of Legal Affairs memorandum and quoted in the *Šešelj* Decision at para 50 and fn. 71. The Appeals Chamber further observes that the quoted portions of this memorandum nowhere suggest that this funding should be comparable to that provided for a represented accused.

106 Registry Submission, paras 52–54. In light of minimal briefing on the subject, the Appeals Chamber does not address under what circumstances, if any, the Registry should fund a case manager and/or *pro se* officer for an indigent accused who self-represents.

44. The Appeals Chamber further notes that all sides appear to agree that as an indigent self-represented accused, Mr. Krajišnik is entitled to Tribunal-funded translation assistance.[107] This does not mean, however, that Mr. Krajišnik is entitled to assistance from a translator/interpreter of his choosing, and the Appeals Chamber sees no error in the Registry's efforts to assess whether Mr. Karganović can acceptably fill the role. The Appeals Chamber notes, however, that should the Registry deem Mr. Karganović to be unacceptable, it must take steps to identify an acceptable translator/interpreter and to offer Mr. Krajišnik this person's services. Finally, the Appeals Chamber considers that in certain circumstances it might prove necessary for Mr. Krajišnik to be able to share confidential material with this translator/interpreter. For example, where no legal associate is designated and Mr. Krajišnik is working with the translator/interpreter, he may need to ask the translator/interpreter to translate a confidential document for him. Should such an eventuality arise, the Appeals Chamber considers that the Registry should take steps to accommodate it.

(iii) Resources

45. The Appeals Chamber declines to rule on Mr. Krajišnik's request for translated documents. Mr. Krajišnik currently receives translations of filings on an ongoing basis. To the extent that the Krajišnik Request seeks translations of additional documents, the Appeals Chamber concludes that this issue is now moot in light of the "positive" developments referenced in the Krajišnik Reply to Prosecution.[108]

46. As to Mr. Krajišnik's request for 24-hour access to a telephone, scanner, fax, and photocopier, the Appeals Chamber considers that the Registry's denial of such resources is reasonable. While in the absence of designated legal associates, some variation from standard UNDU procedures may be warranted to enable an accused adequate means of exchanging appropriate information with his defence team,[109] 24-hour access to such means of communication goes far beyond what is necessary to ensure the provision of adequate facilities.

II. PROSECUTION MOTION

47. The Prosecution Motion requests that the Appeals Chamber clarify two issues. One issue involves the question of how time spent translating filings from B/C/S to an official language of the **[page 19]** Tribunal and *vice versa* affects the calculation of time limits set forth in the 11 May 2007 Decision.[110] This issue has subsequently been clarified by the Pre-Appeal Judge in a status conference[111] and thus will not be discussed further by the Appeals Chamber. The second issue involves the question of whether, upon Mr. Krajišnik filing a motion and the Prosecution filing a response, *amicus curiae* is entitled to file a reply and, if so, whether and within what time frame the Prosecution is allowed to respond to such a reply.[112] The Prosecution suggests that "there may be circumstances where the need for the Amicus Curiae to make a submission only arises out of the Prosecution's response" and that the Prosecution should have a right of response where *amicus curiae* makes such a submission.[113]

48. On 16 July 2007, *amicus curiae* filed a "Response to Prosecution's Motion for Clarification of the Order of Filings and the Calculation of the Time Limits for Filings" ("*Amicus* Response"). Like the Prosecution, *amicus curiae* considers that "there may be certain circumstances where the need for the amicus curiae to make a submission only arises out of the Prosecution's response" and that the Prosecution should have a right of

---

107 In light of this general agreement, the Appeals Chamber need not specifically determine whether this right is rooted in Article 21(4)(b) of the Statute, Article 21(4)(f) of the Statute, or in some other principle. While most of Mr. Krajišnik's translation needs may be met by existing translations of documents (such as the existing translation of the Trial Judgement into B/C/S), the Appeals Chamber considers that provision of an interpreter/translator is necessary to enable Mr. Krajišnik to access certain residual material that has not been translated.

108 *See* Krajišnik Reply to Prosecution, para. 21.

109 *See* para. 36 *supra* (identifying possible yardsticks).

110 Prosecution Motion, paras 12–15.

111 Transcript of Status Conference of 5 July 2007, pp. 102–104 (explaining that the "Prosecution's clock for its response will not start running until it receives the English translation of Mr. Krajišnik's appeal brief" and similarly that where Mr. Krajišnik must meet a deadline, that deadline applies to his B/C/S submission rather than to its English translation).

112 Prosecution Motion, paras 4–11.

113 *Id.*, paras 10–11.

response to *amicus curiae* in such circumstances.[114] *Amicus curiae* further requests that *amicus curiae* have a right of reply to such a response.[115] *Amicus curiae* also suggests that if he "is going to step in at a late stage of a Motion" in the future, he could do so by way of a "Submission" rather than a "Reply".[116] Finally, *amicus curiae* proposes an expedited time frame for such circumstances whereby *amicus curiae* would file any submission within four days of a Prosecution response to a motion by Mr. Krajišnik, the Prosecution would then have four days to respond to *amicus curiae*, and *amicus curiae* would then have four days to file a reply.[117]

49. On 20 July 2007, the Prosecution filed the "Prosecution Reply to Amicus Response to Motion for Clarification of the Order of Filings and the Calculation of the Time Limits for Filings" ("Prosecution Reply"). The Prosecution considers that where Mr. Krajišnik has filed a motion, the Prosecution has responded, and *amicus curiae* has filed a "reply", then the Prosecution should have a right of response to this "reply" but no further filings should be authorized.[118] In the **[page 20]** Prosecution's view, a further right of reply for *amicus curiae* would elongate the briefing cycle of motions unduly.[119] The Prosecution further objects to the suggestion that *amicus curiae* instead be allowed to make a "Submission" in relation to a Prosecution response to a motion by Mr. Krajišnik, as such a submission (and the subsequent response and reply) would "effectively double the filings on any given issue".[120] While the Prosecution recognizes that such doubling "may be a natural consequence" of the 11 May 2007 Decision, the Prosecution points out that this will result in nearly twice as much work for the Prosecution, as it may wish to respond to both Mr. Krajišnik and *amicus curiae*.[121] The Prosecution observes that in the event that the Appeals Chamber permits *amicus curiae* to make such submissions – and then permits the Prosecution to respond and *amicus curiae* to reply – the Prosecution would prefer a normal briefing schedule.[122] The Prosecution also notes that the expedited briefing schedule proposed by *amicus curiae* primarily encumbers the Prosecution rather than *amicus curiae*.[123]

50. Like the Prosecution and *amicus curiae*, the Appeals Chamber considers that there may be rare occasions where, in line with the mandate given to *amicus curiae* in the 11 May 2007 Decision, it is appropriate for *amicus curiae* to make a filing in relation to a Prosecution response to a motion brought by Mr. Krajišnik. The Appeals Chamber requests that, for clarity's sake, *amicus curiae* title such a submission as a "Submission" rather than as a "Reply" in the future. The Appeals Chamber also agrees with the Prosecution and *amicus curiae* that the Prosecution should have a right of response to such a submission. Finally, the Appeals Chamber agrees with *amicus curiae* that *amicus curiae* has a right to reply to any such response. The Appeals Chamber acknowledges that this approach may result in double the number of usual filings in relation to a particular motion, but considers that this is a consequence of the 11 May 2007 Decision.[124] Should *amicus curiae* wish to make a "Submission" upon viewing the Prosecution response to a motion by Mr. Krajišnik, then, in the absence of specific instructions from the Appeals Chamber or the Pre-Appeal Judge otherwise, *amicus curiae* should do so within 4 days of the Prosecution response. With regard to time frame for a Prosecution response to the Submission and for a reply from *amicus curiae*, the normal briefing schedule should be followed in the absence of specific instructions otherwise from the Appeals Chamber or the Pre-Appeal Judge.[125] **[page 21]**

---

114 *Amicus* Response, paras 6, 8.
115 *Id.*, para. 11.
116 *Id.*
117 *Id.*, para. 12.
118 *See* Prosecution Reply, para. 3.
119 *Id.*
120 *Id.*, para. 4.
121 *Id.*.
122 *Id.*, para. 5.
123 *Id.*, para. 6.
124 Contrary to the Prosecution's suggestion, this approach is unlikely to elongate the briefing time in practice due to the concurrent time needed to translate the original Prosecution response into B/C/S and to then to translate into English the reply (if any) to this response submitted by Mr. Krajišnik.
125 *See* 11 May 2007 Decision, paras 21–22.

III. DISPOSITION

51. For the foregoing reasons, the Appeals Chamber **DISMISSES** the Krajišnik Request, but **REQUESTS** the Registry to ensure that it facilitates Mr. Krajišnik's self-representation in line with the reasoning given in this decision. The Appeals Chamber also **REQUESTS** the Registry in the future to make any Rule 33(B) submissions in response to motions brought by Mr. Krajišnik within ten days of the filing of the English translation of such motions. The Appeals Chamber further **REQUESTS** the Registry to include a word count with any such submission. Finally, as set out in paragraph 50, the Appeals Chamber also **GRANTS** the Prosecution Motion to the extent that clarification is sought with regard to the applicable procedure when *amicus curiae* makes a submission upon consideration of Prosecution response to a motion brought by Mr. Krajišnik.

Done in English and French, the English text being authoritative.

Dated this 11th day of September 2007,
At The Hague, The Netherlands.

Fausto Pocar
Presiding Judge

[Seal of the Tribunal]

Commentary

The Trial Chamber's decision of 5 April 2007 in the case of Gotovina *et al.* is procedurally interesting.[1] One of the accused in that case is Čermak. Čermak's two counsel were simultaneously representing an accused person from an earlier ICTY case, that of Ademi. Gotovina, Ademi, and Čermak were part of the same command structure, with Gotovina at the top and Čermak at the bottom. There was a possibility that Ademi would be called in the Gotovina *et al.* case as a witness. This would mean that Čermak's counsel could find themselves having to cross-examine their own client, Ademi. Worse still, it was conceivably in Čermak's interest to pass any blame for his actions up the chain of command to Ademi. But Čermak's counsel, who as noted were also Ademi's counsel, could never contemplate such a line of defence because it would be in breach of their duty of loyalty towards Ademi.

The situation described closed off a particular line of defence for Čermak that was at least theoretically open to him. This was true irrespective of whether or not Ademi was called as a witness in the Gotovina *et al.* trial. The crucial point is that Čermak's counsel had tied their own hands in relation to Ademi, and could not shift any blame onto him, whether in order to advantage Čermak or for any other reason related to the Gotovina *et al.* case. They were thus stymied by the fact of dual representation of these two persons with their particular histories. It was a consequence intolerable for the majority of the Trial Chamber, which ordered Čermak's two counsel to withdraw from his case (although it allowed them to stay on in Ademi's). We might feel that they should not have been appointed to Čermak in the first place. The Appeals Chamber, in its decision of 29 June 2007,[2] agreed, by majority, with the Trial Chamber's own majority, emphasizing in addition that any consent given by Čermak and Ademi to the dual representation, even if fully informed, was not determinative, because it could have no impact on the two counsel's independent professional duty to their clients. The dissenting judges (Orie[3] in the Trial Chamber and Shahabuddeen[4] in the Appeals Chamber) analysed the situation differently. They decided that the consent given by Čermak and Ademi neutralized any conflict of interest they might have experienced in the Gotovina *et al.* case. This is what consent *means,* in the dissenters' view.

The decision in the Krajišnik case of 11 May 2007[5] is notorious mainly on account of Judge Schomburg's "fundamentally" dissenting opinion.[6] To say that one dissents "fundamentally" from something probably has a precise technical meaning in German, but in English it adds no more than the verbal equivalent of thumping one's fist on the table. As it happens, by 2007 Judge Schomburg had become so irritated with the tribunal and the incompetence of some of its judges that he was regularly in the mood of table-thumping his fist. Those undercurrents aside, the decision in question is quite peculiar. The majority takes about a page to set out its argument to the effect that, if the tribunal allows self-representation at trial, then it must also allow it on appeal. There follows Judge Shahabuddeen's lengthy separate opinion, demonstrating that the case for that result is perhaps not so simple.[7] And the decision wraps up with Schomburg's rambunctious dissent, which itself runs to a fair number of pages.

---

1 ICTY, Decision on Conflict of Interest of Attorneys Čedo Prodanović and Jadranka Sloković, *Prosecutor v. Gotovina et al.*, Case No. IT-06-90-PT, T. Ch. I, 5 April 2007, in this volume, p. 53.

2 ICTY, Decision on Ivan Čermak's Interlocutory Appeal Against Trial Chamber's Decision on Conflict of Interest of Attorneys Čedo Prodanović and Jadranka Sloković, *Prosecutor v. Gotovina et al.*, Case No. IT-06-90-AR73.2, A. Ch., 29 June 2007, in this volume, p. 125.

3 ICTY, Judge Orie's Dissenting Opinion on Decision on Conflict of Interest of Attorneys Čedo Prodanović and Jadranka Sloković of 5 April 2007, *Prosecutor v. Gotovina et al.*, Case No. IT-06-90-PT, T. Ch. I, 18 April 2007, in this volume, p. 60.

4 ICTY, Dissenting Opinion of Judge Shahbuddeen, *Prosecutor v. Gotovina et al.*, Case No. IT-06-90-AR73.2, A. Ch., 29 June 2007, in this volume, p. 142.

5 Decision on Momčilo Krajišnik's Request to Selfrepresent, on Counsel's Motions in Relation to Appointment of *Amicus Curiae,* and on the Prosecution Motion of 16 February 2007, *Prosecutor v. Krajišnik,* Case No. IT-00-39-A, A. Ch., 11 May 2007, in this volume, p. 85.

6 Fundamentally Dissenting Opinion of Judge Schomburg, *Prosecutor v. Krajišnik,* Case No. IT-00-39-A, A. Ch., 11 May 2007, in this volume, p. 102.

7 ICTY, Separate Opinion of Judge Shahabuddeen, *Prosecutor v. Krajišnik*, Case No. IT-00-39-A, A. Ch., 11 May 2007, in this volume, p. 93.

By now, many scholars, in addition to judges, have given their opinion about self-representation at the tribunal.[8] I cannot see any clear winner in these exchanges. In some cases (Krajišnik, Karadžić) self-representation works well enough; in the case of Šešelj it has been one endless sickening train smash. The right of the accused to put his own case to the court is no weaker, and no stronger, it seems to me, than the right of the "state" in an adversarial proceeding to ensure that the prosecution's case is competently answered. The former right might seem more real when looked at from the political right, whereas "socialists" might emphasize the value in the latter. Most of us, I suspect, cannot tell the difference, and would rather focus on the arrangements to be put in place in each case to ensure that everything that needs to get done is done at some level of acceptability..

The special arrangements that went into the Krajišnik case (at the appellate stage) and the Karadžić case (at trial) – purely *ad hoc*, purely pragmatic – were all for this purpose of securing the middle ground, because from a non-ideological point of view, self-representation is just about enabling the accused to be as involved in his defence as the circumstances permit. The pragmatic approach to workable self-representation designs is evident also in the follow-up decisions in the Krajišnik case, of 20 July 2007[9] and 11 September 2007.[10] Thus, in its more recent decisions, the Appeals Chamber does not let us down by being non-pragmatic; it lets us down by its disingenuousness in pretending that it is acting on legal principle, when there is none. The only thing there is, is a choice to support self-representation at the tribunal up to a certain point.

The fact that self-representation has been supported to the extent it has in the Šešelj case – that is, absolutely and unconditionally – has more to do with the mind of Judge Antonetti than with the facilitative role and incomprehensible decisions made by the Appeals Chamber in the early stages of the case. Judge Antonetti's desire to twist logic so as to always deliver a favourable result for Šešelj can be seen again in the decision of 30 July 2007—but how is such perversity to be explained? I have argued elsewhere that Judge Antonetti's driving desire has been to see through a trial with Šešelj self-represented at whatever cost.[11] In Judge Antonetti's lengthy decision of 30 July 2007,[12] the answer should have been determined with reference to the principle that legal aid is reserved for the indigent and Šešelj has refused to cooperate in proving his alleged indigence. It follows that he cannot be entitled to legal aid. This supremely simple and entirely universal and self-evident point is lost in Judge Antonetti's narrative, and he somehow reaches the conclusion that the Registry must proceed with the grant of legal aid to Šešelj.

Alexander Zahar

---

8 See, for example, G. Boas, Self-Representation Before the ICTY: A Case for Reform, 9 Journal of International Criminal Justice 2011, p. 53, and J. Temminck Tuinstra, The ICTY's Continuing Struggle With the Right to Self-representation, in B. Swart *et al.* (eds), The Legacy of the International Criminal Tribunal for the Former Yugoslavia, Oxford University Press, Oxford 2011, p. 345-376, as well as the court decisions and scholarly literature cited therein.

9 ICTY, Decision on Motion of *Amicus Curiae* Regarding Appellate Ground of Ineffective Assistance of Counsel, *Prosecutor v. Krajišnik*, Case No. IT-00-39-A, A. Ch., 20 July 2007, in this volume, p. 155.

10 ICTY, Decision on Krajišnik Request and on Prosecution Motion, *Prosecutor v. Krajišnik*, Case No. IT-00-39-A, A. Ch., 11 September 2007 in this volume, p. 175.

11 A. Zahar, Legal Aid, Self-Representation, and the Crisis at the Hague Tribunal, 19 Criminal Law Forum 2008, p. 241.

12 ICTY, Decision on Financing the Defence of the Accused, *Prosecutor v. Šešelj*, Case No. IT-03-67-PT, T. Ch. III., 30 July 2007, in this volume, p. 161.

UNITED
NATIONS

International Tribunal for the Prosecution of Persons Responsible for Serious Violations of International Humanitarian Law Committed in the Territory of Former Yugoslavia since 1991	Case No.	IT-04-81-PT
	Date:	18 June 2007
	Original:	English

IN THE TRIAL CHAMBER

Before: **Judge Patrick Robinson, presiding**
Judge Krister Thelin
Judge Frank Höpfel

Registrar: **Mr. Hans Holthuis**

Decision: **18 June 2007**

PROSECUTOR

v.

MOMČILO PERISIĆ

PUBLIC FILING

DECISION ON MOTION TO APPOINT *AMICUS CURIAE* TO INVESTIGATE EQUALITY OF ARMS

The Office of the Prosecutor:
Mr. Mark B. Harmon
Ms. Susan L. Somers

Counsel for the Accused:
Mr. James Castle
Mr. Novak Lukić

[page 2] 1. Trial Chamber III of the International Tribunal for the Prosecution of Persons Responsible for Serious Violations of International Humanitarian Law Committed in the Territory of the former Yugoslavia since 1991 ("Tribunal") is seised of a motion filed by counsel for Momčilo Perišić ("Counsel") seeking the imposition of an *amicus curiae* to investigate, evaluate and report to the Chamber on whether there exists an inequality of arms between the Office of the Prosecutor ("Prosecution") and the Defence and hereby renders a decision ("Decision") thereon.

Motion and Response

2. On 1 February 2007, Counsel filed a "Motion for appointment of amicus counsel to report to Chamber on equality or arms afforded the Defence" (*sic*) ("Motion"). The Motion essentially contains two requests. First, Counsel requests the Trial Chamber, pursuant to Rule 74 of the Rules of Procedure and Evidence ("Rules"), to appoint an *amicus* counsel to investigate, evaluate and report to the Chamber on the issue of whether an inequality of arms exists in this case.[1] Secondly, Counsel requests the Chamber to "increase the defence resources to a level which allows the defence team to continue working on the case during the remainder of the Pre-Trial period".[2]

3. On 14 February 2007, the Prosecution filed a response to the Motion ("Response").[3] The Prosecution takes no position on the Motion, but filed its Response in order to correct what the Prosecution argues are two 'factual inaccuracies' contained in the Motion.[4]

4. Counsel's principal argument is that there is a fundamental inequality of resources between the Prosecution and the Defence. Counsel submits he was afforded a budget which amounted to 9.5 months of work for lead counsel and five support staff,[5] while the Prosecution has allegedly had more[6] and better paid[7] staff, whose work does not appear to be limited in time or subject to restricted resources. For example, Counsel submits that when the pre-trial phase has ended and where no trial date has been set, the Prosecution can continue to work on the case,[8] while the Defence "will need to be terminated and the defence of Momcilo Perisic will come to a grinding **[page 3]** halt."[9] Furthermore, Counsel alleges that the limitation of resources and staff has a serious impact on Counsel and his staff's ability to examine, review and summarise the great volume of materials in this case submitted to him by the Prosecution.[10] Counsel's alleged lack of resources has also affected his ability to generate the same amount and quality of expert reports that were proffered by the Prosecution.[11] In short, the Counsel claims he "has no realistic opportunity to meet the efforts of [his] adversary."[12]

Discussion

5. The right of an accused to a fair trial implies the principle of equality of arms between the Prosecution and the Defence.[13] The Appeals Chamber has held on several occasions that the principle of equality of arms, taken from the jurisprudence of the Human Rights Committee (HRC) under Article 14 of the International Covenant on Civil and Political Rights (ICCPR) and the European Court of Human Rights under the Article 6

---

1 Counsel requests that such amicus counsel should be selected from counsel who has defended criminally accused and is familiar with the costs associated with such. Furthermore, such amicus counsel should be an attorney independent of other obligations to the Tribunal so his or her findings, in addition to being fair and unbiased, are regarded as such. The defence requests both parties be ordered to cooperate in the investigation of the amicus counsel and open their books for inspection, Motion, para. 6.

2 Motion, para. 7.

3 Prosecution's Response to Defence Motion for Appointment of Amicus Counsel to Report to Chamber on Equality of Arms Afforded to Defence, 14 February 2007.

4 Response, para. 3–7.

5 Motion, para. 4.a.

6 Motion, para. 4.e.

7 Motion, para. 4.d.

8 Motion, para. 4.b.

9 Motion, para. 4.b.

10 Motion, paras 4.f. and 4.g.

11 Motion, para. 4.g.

12 Motion, para. 4.g.

13 *Prosecutor v. Tadić*, Case No. 94-I-A, Appeal Judgement, 15 July 1999 ("*Tadić* Appeal Judgement"), para. 48.

of the European Convention on Human Rights, is laid down in the fair trial guarantee provided in Article 21 of the Statute of the Tribunal ("Statute").[14]

6. In deciding on the scope of the principle of equality of arms, the Appeals Chamber in *Tadić* held that "equality of arms obligates a judicial body to ensure that neither party is put at a disadvantage when presenting its case."[15] The principle also must be viewed with respect to the **[page 4]** different functions which the parties have in various systems. The Trial chamber recalls what was said by the European Commission of Human Rights in the case of *Jespers v. Belgium:*

> "[i]n any criminal proceedings brought by a state authority, the prosecution has at its disposal, to back the accusation, facilities deriving from its powers of investigation supported by judicial and police machinery with considerable technical resources and means of coercion. It is in order to establish equality, as far as possible, between the prosecution and the defence that national legislation in most countries entrusts the preliminary investigation to a member of the judiciary or, if it entrusts the investigation to the Public Prosecutor's Department, instructs the latter to gather evidence in favour of the accused as well as evidence against him. It is also, and above all, to establish that same equality that the 'rights of the Defence'... have been instituted."[16]

7. The Appeals Chamber, in the context of discussing the concept of "equality of arms", specifically described the Prosecution's role as acting "on behalf of and in the interests of the [international] community, including the interests of the victims of the offence charged."[17] In order to fulfil that role, the Security Council vested the Prosecution with certain important powers and resources. A balance was created in both the Statute and the Rules to grant the parties to the proceedings procedural equality before the Court. In accordance with internationally recognised human rights instruments, substantial rights were accorded to accused persons that protect accused persons before the Tribunal against a powerful Prosecutor. In this context, the *Prlić* Trial Chamber correctly pointed out that "'equality' of arms must not be taken literally, evidenced by the fact that a person accused before the Tribunal is presumed innocent whereas the Prosecution must prove that person's guilt beyond reasonably doubt."[18] Another such example can be found in Rule 68 of the Rules, which places an extensive burden on the Prosecution for discovery and disclosure of *exculpatory* material to the Defence. Finally, as mentioned above, both the Statute and the Rules were designed to ensure that the proceedings adhere to internationally recognised principles of fair trial, such as, *inter alia*, the legal aid programme which provides counsel for indigent defendants at the expense of the Tribunal, the right to be tried without undue delay and the right to examine adverse witnesses.

---

14 *See* e.g. *Tadić* Appeal Judgement, para. 48–52; *Prosecutor v. Kayishema and Ruzindana*, Case No. ICTR-95-1-A, Appeal Judgement, para. 67; *Prosecutor v. Milutinović et al.*, Case No. IT-99-37-AR73.2, Decision on interlocutory appeal on motion for additional funds, paras 23 and 24; *Prosecutor v Aleksovski*, Case IT-95-14/1-AR73, Decision on Prosecutor's Appeal on Admissibility of Evidence, 16 February 1999, par 23.; *Prosecutor v. Dusko Tadić*, Case No. IT-94-1-AR72, Decision on the Defence Motion for Interlocutory Appeal on Jurisdiction (AC), 2 October 1995, para. 46; *Prosecutor v. Kordić and Čerkez*, Case: IT-95-14/2-A Appeal Judgement, para. 175; *Prosecutor v. Kordić and Čerkez*, Case: IT-95-14/2-A, Decision on Application by Mario Čerkez for Extension of Time to File his Respondent's Brief, 11 September 2001, para. 5; *Prosecutor v. Kayishema and Ruzindana*, Case No. ICTR-95-1-A, Appeal Judgement, para. 67, referring to *Prosecutor v. Kayishema and Ruzindana*, Case No. ICTR-95-1-T, Judgement, para. 55; In his report (S/25704), the UN Secretary-General noted that it was axiomatic that the Tribunal must fully respect internationally recognised standards regarding the rights of the suspect or accused at all stages of its proceedings. In the view of the Secretary-General, such internationally recognized standards are, in particular, contained in article 14 of the ICCPR, S/25704, 1993, paras 23 and 106; In his first annual report of 1994 to the General Assembly and the Security Council, the President of the Tribunal stated that "there is absolute respect for the principle of 'equality of arms' (...) [as derived from] Article 14 of the International Covenant on Civil and Political Rights, art. 14, paras. 1 and 3", annual report of the international tribunal for the prosecution of persons responsible for serious violations of international humanitarian law committed in the territory of the former yugoslavia since 1991, report of 1994, para. 23; *see also* CCPR Commentary by Manfred Nowak, 1993, at article 14 (1) of the ICCPR: "[t]he most important criterion of a fair trial is the principle of "equality of arms" between (...) the prosecutor and defendant", p.246.

15 *Tadić* Appeal Judgement, para. 48, referring to several cases brought before the European Commission on Human Rights.

16 *Jespers v. Belgium*, No. 8493, Report of the European Commission of Human Rights, 27 D.R [1981] 61 at 87, quoted in *The Prosecutor v. Tadić*, Case No. IT-94-1-T, Separate Opinion of Judge Vohrah on Prosecution Motion for Production of Defence Witness Statements, 27 November 1996, pp. 4 to 5.

17 *Prosecutor v Aleksovski*, Case IT-95-14/1-AR73, Decision on Prosecutor's Appeal on Admissibility of Evidence, 16 February 1999, para. 25.

18 *Prosecutor v. Prlić et al*, Case No. IT-04-74-T, Decision on the Oral Request of the Accused Jadranko Prlić for Authorisation to Use a Laptop Computer at Hearings or to Be Seated Next to his Counsel, 29 June 2006, pp. 3 and 4.

8. The rights of the accused and equality between the parties should however not be confused with the equality of means and resources.[19] The Trial Chamber endorses the view expressed by the **[page 5]** Appeals Chamber that equality of arms between the Defence and the Prosecution does not necessarily amount to the material equality of possessing the same financial and/or personal resources.[20] The Appeals Chamber in *Kordić* expressly stated that the right of an accused to have 'adequate time and facilities for the preparation of his Defence', as laid down in Article 21 (4) of the Statute, "does not imply that the Chambers are charged to ensure parity of resources between the Prosecutor and the Defence, such as the material equality of financial or personal resources".[21] Rather, as was held by the Human Rights committee, the principle of equality of arms was designed to provide the parties rights and guarantees that are *procedural* in nature.[22]

9. The Trial Chamber concludes that, although the right to a fair trial encompasses an equality of arms between the parties, there is no support in either customary international law, the case law of the HRC or that of the ECHR which supports the proposition that the principle of equality of arms affords a party a right to receive resources that are similar to his opponent.

10. In the instant case the Chamber is of the view that the Motion of the Accused does not amount to anything more than a complaint that he does not have the same material resources than the Prosecution. In this regard, the Chamber endorses the dictum of Judge Hunt that the purpose of the principle of equality of arms is "[t]o give to each party equal access to the processes of the Tribunal, or an equal opportunity to seek procedural relief where relief is needed."[23] The Accused has not demonstrated any equal lack of access to the processes of the Tribunal or opportunity to seek procedural relief. In fact, if the Accused is aggrieved by the level of his payment made by the Registrar in respect of this case, he can take this matter up with the Registrar. If he is not satisfied with the decision of the Registrar, he can appeal that decision with the President.[24] **[page 6]**

11. The Chamber now turns to Counsel's second request, namely, for the Chamber to "increase the defence resources to a level which allows the defence team to continue working on the case during the remainder of the Pre-Trial period". By this, the Trial Chamber understands Counsel to mean that, when his pre-trial funding has been depleted by or after 30 April 2007 and no date is yet set for trial, he will require additional funding in order to maintain a minimum of defence staff to work on this case until the start of trial. Such a request for additional funding should however be put before the Registrar, who has the primary responsibility to determine matters relating to remuneration of counsel under the legal aid system of the International Tribunal.[25] If an issue of fair trial arises from the Registrar's decision, Counsel may request the Trial Chamber to review it.[26]

---

19 *Prosecutor v. Kayishema and Ruzindana*, Case No. ICTR-95-1-T, Judgement, para. 20, referring to *Prosecutor v. Kayishema and Ruzindana*, Order on the Motion by the Defence Counsel for Application of Article 20 (2) and (4) (b) of the Statute of the International Tribunal for Rwanda, 5 May 1997, p. 3; *Prosecutor v. Milutinović et al.*, Case No. IT-99-37-AR73.2, Decision on interlocutory appeal on motion for additional funds, paras 23 and 24, where the Appeals Chamber found that "[t]he principle of equality of arms would be violated only if either party is put at a disadvantage when presenting its case. In the circumstances of this case, the Appeals Chamber finds that the Appellant cannot rely on the alleged inadequacy of funds during the pre-trial stage to establish such a disadvantage".

20 *Prosecutor v. Kayishema and Ruzindana*, Case No. ICTR-95-1-A, para. 69, referring to *Hentrich v. France*, Eur. Court H. R., Judgement of 22 September 1994, para. 56; *see also Prosecutor v. Prlić et al*, Case No. IT-04-74-T, Decision on the Oral Request of the Accused Jadranko Prlić for Authorisation to Use a Laptop Computer at Hearings or to Be Seated Next to his Counsel, 29 June 2006, pp. 3 and 4: "(…) the term "equality of arms" does not require that the parties to the trial have the same financial or technical resources."

21 *Prosecutor v. Kordić and Čerkez*, Case: IT-95-14/2-A Appeal Judgement, para. 176.

22 *Tadić* Appeal Judgement, para.50, referring to, *inter alia, B. d. B et al. v. The Netherlands*, Communication No. 273/1989, 30 March 1989, U.N. Doc. A/44/40, 442 and Nqalula Mpandanjila et al. v. Zaire, Communication No 138/1983, 26 March 1986, U.N. Doc. A/41/40, 121.

23 *Prosecutor v. Kordić and Čerkez*, Case: IT-95-14/2-A, Decision on Application by Mario Čerkez for Extension of Time to File his Respondent's Brief, 11 September 2001, para. 5 (*emphasis added*).

24 Directive on the Assignment of Defence Counsel, Article 31 (c).

25 *Prosecutor v. Hadžihasanović et al.*, Case No. IT-01-47-PT, Decision on Urgent Motion for *Ex Parte* Oral Hearing on Allocation of Resources to the Defence and Consequences Thereof for the Rights of the Accused to a Fair Trial, 17 June 2003, p. 2.

26 *Prosecutor v. Blagojević*, Case No. IT-02-60-AR73.4, Public and Redacted Reasons for Decision on Appeal by Vidoje Blagojević to Replace his Defence Team, 7 November 2003, para. 7 and footnote 23; For review of administrative decisions, *see Prosecutor v. Kvočka et al.*, Case No. IT-98-30/1-A, Decision on Review of Registrar's Decision to Withdraw Legal Aid from Zoran Žigić, 7 February 2003, para. 13.

Disposition

For the reasons stated above,

The Trial Chamber **DENIES** the Motion.

Done in English and French, the English text being authoritative.

Dated this eighteenth day of June 2007
At The Hague
The Netherlands

Patrick Robinson
Presiding

[Seal of the Tribunal]

UNITED NATIONS

International Tribunal for the Prosecution of Persons Responsible for Serious Violations of International Humanitarian Law Committed in the Territory of the former Yugoslavia since 1991	Case No.	IT-05-87-T
	Date:	27 August 2007
	Original:	English

IN THE TRIAL CHAMBER

Before: **Judge Iain Bonomy, Presiding**
Judge Ali Nawaz Chowhan
Judge Tsvetana Kamenova
Judge Janet Nosworthy, Reserve Judge

Registrar: **Mr. Hans Holthuis**

Decision of: **27 August 2007**

PROSECUTOR

v.

MILAN MILUTINOVIĆ
NIKOLA ŠAINOVIĆ
DRAGOLJUB OJDANIĆ
NEBOJŠA PAVKOVIĆ
VLADIMIR LAZAREVIĆ
SRETEN LUKIĆ

PUBLIC

DECISION ON OJDANIĆ THIRD MOTION FOR STAY OF PROCEEDINGS

The Office of the Prosecutor
Mr. Thomas Hannis
Mr. Chester Stamp

Counsel for the Accused
Mr. Eugene O'Sullivan and Mr. Slobodan Zečević for Mr. Milan Milutinović
Mr. Toma Fila and Mr. Vladimir Petrović for Mr. Nikola Šainović
Mr. Tomislav Višnjić and Mr. Norman Sepenuk for Mr. Dragoljub Ojdanić
Mr. John Ackerman and Mr. Aleksandar Aleksić for Mr. Nebojša Pavković
Mr. Mihajlo Bakrač and Mr. Đuro Čepić for Mr. Vladimir Lazarević
Mr. Branko Lukić and Mr. Dragan Ivetić for Mr. Sreten Lukić

[page 2] THIS TRIAL CHAMBER of the International Tribunal for the Prosecution of Persons Responsible for Serious Violations of International Humanitarian Law Committed in the Territory of the former Yugoslavia since 1991 ("Tribunal") is seised of "General Ojdanić's Third Motion for Stay of Proceedings," filed by the Ojdanić Defence ("Defence") on 23 July 2007 ("Third Motion"), and hereby renders its decision thereon.[1]

BACKGROUND

1. This is General Ojdanić's ("Accused") third motion to stay the proceedings on the ground that the purported inability of his Defence to conduct investigations of alleged crime sites or to interview witnesses in Kosovo interferes with his right to a fair trial under Articles 20 and 21 of the Statute of the Tribunal ("Statute"). The history of events leading up to this motion is complex, as has been acknowledged by the Defence.[2] The Trial Chamber therefore finds it appropriate to set out at length the procedural background leading up to the filing of the Motion.

2. On 6 December 2004, the Defence sent a request to the Registry of the Tribunal for the authorisation and arrangement of security for Lead Counsel Tomislav Višnjić and (then) Co-Counsel Peter Robinson to travel to Kosovo in order to view the alleged crime scenes and to interview witnesses.[3] The Defence was referred by the Registry to the United Nations Mission in Kosovo ("UNMIK").[4] On 10 March 2005, the Defence contacted the Special Representative of the United Nations Secretary-General in Kosovo, Mr. Soren Jessen-Petersen, requesting UNMIK to arrange security for a mission to Kosovo in April 2005 by Defence team members, namely Messrs Višnjić, Robinson, and Isak.[5] On 8 April 2005, UNMIK advised the Registrar of the Tribunal that, due to the dangerous security situation in Kosovo, a visit could not be accommodated at that time.[6] This letter was conveyed to the Defence; and, on 19 April 2005, Ojdanić's defence team requested that UNMIK notify it when it was safe to travel in Kosovo.[7]

3. After a trial date had been set for 10 July 2006, the Defence contacted UNMIK and requested that a visit to Kosovo be arranged.[8] UNMIK agreed to facilitate this mission and **[page 3]** arranged for Messrs Višnjić and Isak to travel to Kosovo in May 2006. That trip was undertaken. However, during the mission, the Defence team and UNMIK personnel were attacked when their convoy was surrounded by villagers in Mala Kruša/Krushe e Vogël in the Prizren Municipality on 25 May 2006.[9] Consequently, the mission was aborted.

4. On 31 May 2006, the Defence was advised by Mr. Steven Schook, Principal Deputy Special Representative of the Secretary-General in Kosovo, of the following:

> I am certain that you will understand that due to security concerns and the emotional impact of last week events UNMIK will need to be provided with all the necessary information in order to be able to make sound decisions and to ensure the smooth conduct of any similar visits in the future.
>
> Thus, I would ask you to furnish us with the following details:
>
> 1. The purpose of the visit;
>
> 2. A detailed itinerary for your planned visit;
>
> 3. Details of all the delegation members (full names, citizenship, passport numbers);
>
> 4. Exact time and location of your entry into and exit out of Kosovo.

---

1 General Ojdanić's Third Motion for Stay of Proceedings, 23 July 2007.
2 Motion for Leave to File Pleading in Excess of Word Limitations: General Ojdanić's Third Motion for Stay of Proceedings, 23 July 2007, paras. 3–4.
3 General Ojdanić's Motion for Stay of Proceedings, 2 June 2006 ("First Motion"), Annex A.
4 First Motion, Annex B.
5 First Motion, Annex C.
6 First Motion, Annex D.
7 First Motion, Annex E.
8 Third Motion, para. 8.
9 First Motion, paras. 1–11; Third Motion, paras. 9–11.

> Please note that in order to safeguard proper planning and preparation of future visits, the request for political clearance must be received no later than three full working days before the scheduled entry into Kosovo.[10]

5. On 2 June 2006, the Ojdanić Defence filed a motion, asking for a stay of proceedings until the Defence team was able to safely investigate in Kosovo.[11] The Accused Milutinović, Pavković, Šainović, and Lazarević joined this motion.[12]

6. On 9 June 2006, the Chamber issued its decision denying the Defence's first motion.[13] In doing so, the Chamber took into consideration the fact that, "while, during the Defence team's last visit to Kosovo, UNMIK was unable to provide the security necessary for the team to conduct and complete its investigations, this does not mean that UNMIK will continue indefinitely to be unable to do so."[14] The Chamber emphasised that "it is not faced at present with the situation wherein UNMIK has refused the Defence team access to Kosovo or represented to it that it is unable or **[page 4]** unwilling to provide security for future visits."[15] It was upon this basis that the Chamber denied the first motion to stay the proceedings and requested UNMIK to take "all reasonable and necessary measures, as soon as possible, in order to assist the Defence teams of the Accused in their investigations in Kosovo for the preparation of their defence."[16]

7. Following the Chamber's first decision on this matter, the Defence resumed its efforts to communicate with UNMIK, in order to conduct investigations of crime sites in Kosovo.[17] In particular, on 14 July 2006, the Defence sent a letter to Mr. Schook stating that the "sole purpose of our visit is to carry out our Investigation of the crime sites."[18] The letter listed 13 sites and details of the proposed members of the mission, including Mr. Isak. The letter was re-sent by email on 14 July 2006 and again on 17 July 2006, with an urgent notation. On 19 July 2006, a further email was sent repeating the request.[19] On 22 July 2006, the Defence sent a further letter to Mr. Schook, asking UNMIK to facilitate a visit and additionally requesting UNMIK to arrange a meeting with Prime Minister Çeku.[20]

8. On 26 July 2006, Mr. Schook replied, repeating the request made in the letter of 31 May 2006 for information on the purpose of the visit, the sites to be visited, and information on members of the team who would be visiting.[21] That same day, Mr. Višnjić responded by email, repeating the request and attaching the previous correspondence sent to UNMIK.[22]

9. On 28 July 2006, UNMIK indicated that, before arrangements could be made for the trip, it would require (a) "detailed information on what the intentions of the team are in each of the locations, i.e. are the members of the team intending to walk around the site, take photographs, do they intend to enter any premises, how much time will be spent in each location etc." and (b) "confirmation that you do not intend to interview any witnesses during this visit."[23] The letter continued that UNMIK had "begun making the necessary arrangements" and that, once the details of the visit were provided, representatives of UNMIK would be available to meet the Defence in "Pristina or Belgrade" to discuss the details of the visit.[24] **[page 5]**

10. On 29 July 2006, the Defence responded, indicating its disappointment that the visit was not arranged and stating that "we are now not in a position to provide you with an alternate date for our visit, since, as

---

10 First Motion, Annex G.
11 First Motion, para. 1.
12 Mr. Milutinović's Motion to Join General Ojdanić's Motion for Stay of Proceedings, 6 June 2006 (requesting hearing on Motion); Joinder by Nebojša Pavković in General Ojdanić's Motion for Stay of Proceedings, 6 June 2006 (suggesting hearing on Motion); Joint Defence Motion: Joining General Ojdanić's Motion for Stay of Proceedings, 6 June 2006 (Šainović and Lazarević).
13 Decision on Ojdanić Motion for Stay of Proceedings, 9 June 2006 ("Decision on First Motion").
14 Decision on First Motion, para. 4.
15 Decision on First Motion, para. 4.
16 Decision on First Motion, para. 6.
17 General Ojdanić's Second Motion for Stay of Proceedings, 31 July 2006 ("Second Motion"), pp. 2–4; Annexes H, J, L, N, O, P, Q.
18 Second Motion, Annex H.
19 Second Motion, Annexes I–J.
20 Second Motion, Annex L.
21 Second Motion, Annex N.
22 Second Motion, Annex O.
23 Second Motion, Annex P.
24 Second Motion, Annex P.

we repeatedly informed UNMIK, the trial will recommence on 7 August and there is no recess planned until Christmas. Winter conditions in Kosovo will not permit us to adequately view the crime scenes at that time."[25] The letter informed UNMIK of the Defence's intent to file for a stay of the proceedings until UNMIK would be able to facilitate the visit. In order to place UNMIK "in a position to act quickly" if the Trial Chamber were to order relief, the Defence provided further detail of its intentions for the mission, namely to "walk around the sites visited, to take photographs of the sites, and to seek permission to enter premises on the sites if criminal activity is alleged to have taken place inside those premises."[26] In the letter, the Defence confirmed that it did not intend to interview witnesses, but stated that the plan was to "arrive at the site, enlist the help of local citizens in pointing out the exact places where the events occurred, walk around those areas, photograph them, and leave."[27]

11. On 31 July 2006, the Defence filed a second motion on the matter.[28] The motion stated that "General Ojdanić's defence team did everything it could to arrange [the] visit [to Kosovo] before the trial recommences" and that "[i]t would be fundamentally unfair to proceed with the testimony of prosecution crime-base witnesses under these circumstances. General Ojdanić is simply unable to effectively cross-examine these witnesses."[29]

12. On 31 July 2006, UNMIK re-contacted the Defence, stating that it remained willing to facilitate the visit and proposing to meet in Priština/Prishtinë to review the list of proposed sites and any additional details of the Defence team's potential visit to Kosovo.[30] This meeting occurred on 3 August 2006 in Priština/Prishtinë. The next day, on 4 August 2006, UNMIK notified the Defence of its continued readiness to facilitate site visits. UNMIK noted changes to the proposed itinerary, including the fact that "four sites have been cancelled and several others added" and the requests for "interaction with the local population and unrestricted movement at some of the sites."[31] On that basis, UNMIK requested a formal amended request, "as agreed during the meeting", in order to carry out the further necessary preparations. UNMIK indicated that it had engaged in preliminary **[page 6]** preparations, including "consultations with the Kosovo authorities at the local and central level." A revised request outlining the intended activities at the sites on the new list was transmitted by the Defence to UNMIK on 6 August 2006.[32]

13. On 9 August 2006, UNMIK transmitted a more detailed plan of action in relation to the security aspects of the Defence team's anticipated visit, emphasising that "the reason for the detailed correspondence and recent face-to-face meeting on the issue of the site visits is mainly to ensure that security considerations, not only your personal security, but also UNMIK's responsibilities for general security and the maintenance of public order, are properly and effectively addressed."[33] UNMIK further stated:

> Accordingly, UNMIK would like to reiterate its general parameters for the requested visit, as pointed out during the 3 August meeting:
>
> 1. At this stage, we believe that the requested visit to eleven localities should be divided into two or three separate visits, each involving a limited number of sites, with an appropriate intervening time between each visit. This is advisable for operational and security reasons.
>
> 2. UNMIK has serious reservations regarding the participation of the Team's investigator, Mr. Isak Ilija, in the site visits to the crime scenes. As an ex-VJ member of high rank, who was active in Kosovo during the Milosevic period, the possibility of recognition and negative response in areas where individuals have been traumatized by security personnel cannot be excluded.

25 Second Motion, Annex Q.
26 Second Motion, Annex Q.
27 Second Motion, Annex Q.
28 General Ojdanić's Second Motion for Stay of Proceedings, 31 July 2006.
29 Second Motion, pp. 4–5.
30 Supplemental Materials in Support of General Ojdanić's Second Motion for Stay of Proceedings, 7 August 2006, Annex R.
31 Supplemental Materials in Support of General Ojdanić's Second Motion for Stay of Proceedings, 7 August 2006, Annex S.
32 Supplemental Materials in Support of General Ojdanić's Second Motion for Stay of Proceedings, 7 August 2006, Annex T.
33 Letter from the UNMIK Acting Special Representative of the Secretary-General, Mr. Steven P. Schook, to Lead Counsel for General Ojdanić, Mr. Tomislav Višnjić, 9 August 2006; Final Submissions in Support of General Ojdanić's Second Motion for Stay of Proceedings, 14 September 2006, Annex U.

3. UNMIK will not be able to facilitate spontaneous or unplanned interaction with the local population, in the manner described in the amended request as "speak to residents and find out their version of what happened there". Anyone familiar with Kosovo and the atrocities committed at the sites in question will understand that it is insensitive and provocative to randomly speak to residents about events related to the violent conflict. However, UNMIK stands ready to facilitate and arrange for meetings between you and specific individuals, provided that the person concerned is in agreement. Such meetings will have to be formally requested prior to any visit.

4. UNMIK will follow a very careful media policy. UNMIK will take a reactive approach, meaning that there will be no media announcement, in advance, of an impending visit, although we will have a press-line ready to use if asked. We expect you to take the same approach, in the interest of ensuring a smooth visit.

14. The letter ended with the statement that "UNMIK will expedite its evaluation of [the] amended request of 6 August" and would "revert with a detailed answer within three weeks." **[page 7]**

15. On 11 August 2006, a meeting took place between the Chamber and the Defence, during which the Defence's efforts to arrange with UNMIK an investigative trip to Kosovo were discussed.[34] Following this meeting, on 16 August 2006, the Senior Legal Officer of the Chamber wrote to UNMIK, emphasising the Chamber's readiness to assist in "finalising arrangements that are satisfactory to all to enable the investigations to be carried out."[35] The communication conveyed the representations of the Defence in the previous meeting with the Chamber, to the effect that Mr. Isak was an important member of the team, required to identify particular localities within Kosovo, and that the Defence team had no intentions of engaging in interactions which could provoke reactions.

16. On 30 August 2006, UNMIK indicated to the Defence and the Chamber that it would be able to facilitate visits to six out of the eleven requested locations. UNMIK set out specific conditions in relation to the six visits, including the requirement that Mr. Isak not be present during three of the site visits, along with time limits upon particular locations. UNMIK reiterated that it was willing to facilitate visits during the week of 2 October 2006 to the six sites.[36] With regard to four of the sites listed by the Defence, UNMIK indicated that it was unable, at that time, to facilitate visits and invited the Defence to propose alternative means of obtaining the information it sought in respect of each site.

17. On 6 September 2006, the Defence replied that the conditions surrounding the proposed visit were "such that the visit would not be meaningful" and that the Defence "would simply not be able to accomplish [its] duties to investigate the allegations against General Ojdanić."[37]

18. On 11 September 2006, a meeting was held between the Senior Legal Officer of the Chamber and the Defence concerning UNMIK's letter of 30 August 2006. At this meeting, the Defence stated that the conditions outlined by UNMIK for the visit were unacceptable and that it would be akin to a tourist visit and not yield the results they were after.[38] The Chamber asked several times whether it would not be helpful for further appropriate intervention from the Chamber with UNMIK, so as to yield a more favourable outcome with UNMIK on the issue. However, the **[page 8]** Chamber was told by the Defence that, although it appreciated the offer, it now wished to proceed on the record.

19. On 14 September 2006, the Defence filed further submissions in support of the second motion to stay proceedings, arguing, *inter alia*, that it had come to the conclusion that the restrictions imposed by UNMIK upon the investigation of the alleged crime sites made such a visit "of little value, and [did] not justify the substantial risk to the safety of defence team members."[39]

---

34 Internal Memorandum, 11 August 2006.

35 Letter from the Chamber's Acting Senior Legal Officer, Mr. Gideon Boas, to the UNMIK Acting Special Representative of the Secretary-General, Mr. Steven P. Schook, 16 August 2006.

36 Final Submissions in Support of General Ojdanić's Second Motion for Stay of Proceedings, 14 September 2006, Annex V.

37 Final Submissions in Support of General Ojdanić's Second Motion for Stay of Proceedings, 14 September 2006, Annex W.

38 E-mail from the Chamber's Acting Senior Legal Officer, Mr. Gideon Boas, to Judge Iain Bonomy (Presiding), 11 September 2006.

39 Final Submissions in Support of General Ojdanić's Second Motion for Stay of Proceedings, 14 September 2006, paras. 4–5, 7; Annex X.

20. On 4 October 2006, UNMIK sent a letter to the Chamber, informing it that the Defence had cancelled its trip to Kosovo. In the letter, UNMIK stated:

> In accordance with our letter of 30 August and within the time-frame indicated by your acting senior legal officer, UNMIK was ready to facilitate an initial visit by the defence team to at least six sites in Kosovo, which was planned to take place from 3 to 6 October....
>
> As you are aware, UNMIK has asked the Ojdanic defence team to suggest alternatives to the participation of their consultant Mr. Isak Ilija in visits to crimes scenes in Kosovo. We have also invited the defence team to propose alternative ways of obtaining the relevant material regarding those sites to which UNMIK cannot facilitate visits at this time....
>
> In accordance with its mandate under UN Security Counsel [sic] resolution 1244 (1999), and its obligations towards the ICTY, in particular the Trial Chamber's Request as set out in the Decision of 9 June 2006, UNMIK went through great effort to facilitate the requested visit. The preparations involved systematic coordination at central and local levels, including, but not limited to: both UNMIK and Kosovo Police; KFOR; UNMIK Civil Administration; the Office of the Prime Minister of Kosovo; local municipalities and village leaders. Detailed assessments of sites were made from numerous perspectives, including the security perspective, by experts in relevant fields. Moreover, the Prime Minister of Kosovo assigned a senior political advisor to work with the local leadership at the sites to be visited, in order to advance their cooperation with the visit of the Ojdanic defence team.
>
> Please be assured that UNMIK will continue to take all reasonable and necessary measures to assist the defence team. We stand ready to facilitate a visit in the event that defence counsel renews his request.[40]

21. On 19 October 2006, the Trial Chamber issued its "Decision on General Ojdanić's Second Motion for Stay of Proceedings", denying the motion.[41] The Trial Chamber noted:

> 9. ... the efforts that have been made by UNMIK to take all reasonable and necessary measures, as soon as possible, in order to assist the Defence in its investigations in Kosovo; however, the Chamber also acknowledges that UNMIK must **[page 9]** balance the needs of the Defence with its overall mission in connection with the administration of Kosovo. ...
>
> 10. In this regard, the Chamber considers that UNMIK, in its last communication with the Chamber on 4 October 2006, explained the extensive measures it took, and was continuing to take, in order to facilitate the investigations of the Defence in Kosovo .... As is plain from the letter of 9 August 2006, UNMIK was continuing to make arrangements to satisfy some of the outstanding requests and sought from the Defence proposals of alternative methods of accomplishing those visits that UNMIK stated it could not facilitate at that time. The Defence was not satisfied with the arrangements that were made; and, instead of accepting UNMIK's offer to continue to discuss how its outstanding requests might be satisfied and the Chamber's offer to intercede with a view to finding ways of satisfying these requests, the Defence has unilaterally broken off cooperative efforts with UNMIK in this matter, and has opted for the course of attempting to bring these criminal proceedings to a halt. The fact that the Ojdanić Defence is not satisfied with the arrangements for its visit to Kosovo does not necessarily lead to the conclusion that the Accused's rights under Article 21 are being violated. The cooperation between UNMIK, the Tribunal, and the Defence is a developing, dynamic process whence the Defence has withdrawn, despite UNMIK's continued participation in trying to make the investigations come to fruition.[42]

22. On this basis, the Chamber found that UNMIK's efforts had been sufficient to provide the Defence with adequate time and facilities for the preparation of its case and had not caused undue prejudice to the Accused's right to a fair trial.[43] The Chamber urged the Defence to reopen communications with UNMIK on the matter.

---

40 Letter from the UNMIK Principal Deputy Special Representative of the Secretary-General, Mr. Steven P. Schook, to Judge Iain Bonomy (Presiding), 4 October 2006.

41 Decision on Second Ojdanić Motion for Stay of Proceedings, 19 October 2006.

42 Decision on Second Ojdanić Motion for Stay of Proceedings, 19 October 2006, paras. 9–10.

43 Decision on Second Ojdanić Motion for Stay of Proceedings, 19 October 2006, para. 11.

23. On 15 March 2007, the Ojdanić Defence contacted UNMIK asking it to make preparations for a visit of the Defence team in April 2007, with the stated purpose of "contact[ing] various people who have been mentioned in the testimony to date and ask them about the incidents in which they had been named, and to speak with other people whose names we would get as 'leads' and who also participated in or witnessed the same events."[44] The letter contained a list of sites, including a number of sites that had not been mentioned in either of the previous lists of sites provided to UNMIK.

24. On 23 March 2007, UNMIK responded by letter indicating that it remained ready to organise a visit to Kosovo, but requested the following information in order to make the necessary preparations:

> 1. The identity of each person whom you would like to contact so that we can assist in locating the individuals and ask if they are willing to speak with members of the Ojdanic defence team. **[page 10]**
>
> 2. The identity of each site that you would like to visit, and the purpose of visiting each site, so that we can begin making security and logistical arrangements.
>
> 3. Details of the members of the Ojdanic defence team that would visit Kosovo, including full names, citizenship, passport numbers, and any relevant background.[45]

25. On 26 March 2007, the Defence wrote to UNMIK, changing the dates of the proposed visit to the week of 14 May and stating in relation to the preparations for the mission that the team did not want UNMIK representatives contacting the people the team intended to interview as "[t]hat would be counterproductive to obtaining their consent to speak with us and to the spontaneity and truthfulness of the information we receive… Instead, we want to knock on doors and interview people spontaneously." The Defence team clarified that the sites proposed had altered as the opportunity for cross-examination had passed and that the new ones were intended to allow for the location of potential witnesses. The letter listed the people travelling as Messrs Višnjić, Robinson, and Isak.[46]

26. On 30 March 2007, UNMIK responded by letter to the Defence request, repeating its security concerns and the parameters for the proposed trip, which it had detailed in its letter to the Defence of 9 August 2006.[47] UNMIK expressed its continued reservations regarding the inclusion of Mr. Isak in visits to sites in Kosovo, and asked the Defence to propose an alternate investigator. UNMIK further stated that it was unable to facilitate spontaneous interactions by members of the Defence team with the local population. As an alternative, UNMIK offered to organise secure locations in each of the municipalities and/or villages listed by the Defence and to provide police transport for the team members to and from the secure locations, so as to facilitate the Defence team speaking with relevant persons within Kosovo.

27. On 10 April 2007, the Defence wrote to UNMIK, stating in relation to the mission to Kosovo that:

> [W]e appreciate your suggestions but continue to find the conditions too restrictive to enable us to accomplish our work. We need Mr. Isak with us because he has the best knowledge of what happened on the ground and is in the best position to conduct the interviews. We also need to meet the witnesses under conditions that will allow them to speak to us freely, and your proposal, while interesting, doesn't allow us to do that.
>
> Therefore, while we appreciate very much your willingness to assist us, it seems that the conditions in Kosovo remain too dangerous for our defence team to travel there at this **[page 11]** time. We are not willing to risk our lives for very little prospect of success in actually obtaining any potential witnesses.[48]

---

44 Third Motion, Annex X. The previous lists are those included in the letter to UNMIK of 6 August 2006. Supplemental Materials in Support of General Ojdanić's Second Motion for Stay of Proceedings, 7 August 2006, Annex T (letter to UNMIK of 14 July 2006); Second Motion, Annex H. The letter of 15 March also contained a request concerning documents in the KLA archives, which is not relevant to the Motion.

45 Third Motion, Annex Y.

46 Third Motion, Annex Z.

47 General Ojdanić's Supplemental Filing of Annex AA to General Ojdanić's Third Motion for Stay of Proceedings, (10 August 2007).

48 Third Motion, Annex BB.

28. On 9 May 2007, UNMIK wrote to the Defence stating, "we regret your assessment that what we proposed is not to your satisfaction. We therefore invite you to propose an alternate solution, albeit within the security parameters as carefully developed by UNMIK.... We are open to your suggestions and look forward to your response."[49] This opportunity was not taken up by the Defence, for the stated reason that "given the continuing violence against Serbs in Kosovo, and tensions over the unresolved status of Kosovo, General Ojdanić's team considered that the security risk was too great to return to Kosovo at this time."[50]

29. Subsequently, on 23 July 2007, the Defence filed this Third Motion.

SUBMISSIONS

30. The Ojdanić Defence considers it a necessary and standard practice in providing effective assistance of counsel to contact people identified in the written statements and oral testimony of the witnesses of the Office of the Prosecutor of the Tribunal ("Prosecution"), in order to either confirm or contradict the accounts given by the witnesses called by the Prosecution, or to better identify the affiliation of the perpetrators.[51] On this basis, the Defence has prepared a list of 730 persons that it desires to contact.[52] The Defence submits that virtually all of these people reside in Kosovo and that a number of these people were only partially identified, thus necessitating further investigations in the field.[53]

31. However, the Defence considers that the security situation has not improved since its last abortive mission to Kosovo. It thus fears for the safety of its members if a further mission to Kosovo is carried out under the current conditions. Conseqntly, the Defence submits that it has been prevented from investigating its case in Kosovo and from obtaining defence witnesses, and that this violates the Accused's right to a fair trial, right to equality of arms, right to adequate **[page 12]** facilities for the preparation of his defence, and right to effective assistance of counsel, under Articles 20 and 21 of the Statute.[54]

32. With regard to the right of equality of arms, the Defence submits that, in contrast with the Prosecution's "unhindered" opportunity to investigate within Kosovo, the Defence has been subjected to "life-threatening physical attack" when it has sought to "view the scenes of the crimes and to locate and interview eyewitnesses" and "prevented from returning to Kosovo to locate and interview potential witnesses identified in the prosecution's case as having relevant information to the events which form the 'crime base' in his case" and consequently "will not even be in a position to call such witnesses, let alone in proportion to the number of witnesses called by the prosecution."[55]

33. The Defence submits that the restrictions on its abilities to conduct its defence are due to the inability of UNMIK to provide secure conditions within Kosovo. It argues that, as UNMIK is administered by the same body as the Tribunal, namely the United Nations, the Chamber is obliged to stay the trial until such time as UNMIK is able to provide secure conditions within Kosovo.[56] The Defence further submits that its inability to observe the scenes of the alleged crimes and its lack of access to potential witnesses, prevents it from providing effective assistance to Ojdanić, in particular by limiting its ability to effectively cross-examine witnesses called by the Prosecution and by limiting its ability to identify witnesses able to contradict these witnesses.[57] On this basis, the Defence submits that the Chamber should invoke its inherent power to order a stay of the proceedings "until such time as the security situation in Kosovo allows for adequate defence investigation."[58]

---

49 Third Motion, Annex CC.

50 Third Motion, para. 44.

51 Third Motion, paras. 45–46.

52 Prosecution Response to General Ojdanić's Third Motion for Stay of Proceedings, 1 August 2007, ("Prosecution Response"), para. 5.

53 Third Motion, para. 47. The list of people that the Defence wishes to contact is contained is attached as Annex DD to the Third Motion.

54 Third Motion, paras 50–54.

55 Third Motion, paras. 57–59, 71.

56 Third Motion, para. 64.

57 Third Motion, paras. 66–67.

58 Third Motion, para. 71.

34. The Prosecution urges the Chamber to deny the Third Motion due to the lack of an adequate and sufficiently detailed showing in support of a stay of the proceedings.[59]

35. The Prosecution submits that the Defence has failed to avail itself of the alternative means available for the conduct of Ojdanić's defence. The Prosecution argues that the Defence:

> [Has] access to numerous former VJ and MUP witnesses who served in Kosovo during the events in question. In addition they have access to the archives of those agencies as well as to public sources of maps, photographs and video footage of the relevant areas. **[page 13]** Finally, it seems that the Ojdanić Defence at this stage no longer desires or needs to visit the crime sites.[60]

36. In relation to the list of persons that the Defence has prepared, the Prosecution submits that the Defence has failed to assess the relevance, importance, or necessity of contacting these individuals. The Prosecution points out that the list includes "witnesses who already testified in this case; children who were under the age of five at the time of the events; individuals now living in Western Europe or Canada; and even some deceased persons listed in the Schedules to the Indictment."[61] The Prosecution submits that the Defence has failed to enquire into alternate means of contacting those people, such as by mail or by telephone.

37. In relation to the Defence team's intended activities during its prior proposed mission to Kosovo, including by spontaneous door-to-door investigations, the Prosecution submits that this would not be an effective or professional way to proceed, and in fact would be "counterproductive".[62] On this basis, the Prosecution urges the Chamber to deny the motion.

DISCUSSION

38. As noted in its previous decisions on Ojdanić's first and second motions to stay the proceedings, the Trial Chamber considers that United Nations Security Council Resolution 1244 ("UNSC Resolution 1244") obliges UNMIK to cooperate with the Tribunal, including through efforts to provide assistance to Defence teams of accused before the Tribunal in respect of investigations inside of Kosovo for the preparation of their defences.[63] However, the Chamber acknowledges that UNMIK must balance the needs of the Defence with its overall mission in connection with the administration of Kosovo, which includes "[m]aintaining civil law and order".[64]

39. In its Decision on the Second Motion, the Chamber noted the extensive measures undertaken by UNMIK to arrange a further mission by the Defence team to Kosovo, and UNMIK's continued willingness to enter into dialogue with the Defence team to explore alternative means of accommodating the visit within the required security parameters.[65] The Chamber detailed the efforts made by UNMIK to take all reasonable and necessary measures, in order to assist the **[page 14]** Defence in its investigations in Kosovo.[66] The Chamber's decision on the Second Motion on 19 October 2006 urged the Defence to reopen communications with UNMIK.

40. Upon the Defence's renewed request to visit Kosovo, on 15 March 2007, the Chamber considers that UNMIK continued to endeavour to make all necessary and reasonable efforts to facilitate the visit.[67] Noting its concerns over the Defence's stated intent to engage in spontaneous interactions with the local population,

---

59 Prosecution Response, para. 5.
60 Prosecution Response, para. 4.
61 Prosecution Response, para. 4.
62 Prosecution Response, para. 11.
63 Decision on Ojdanić Motion for Stay of Proceedings, 9 June 2006, para. 3 (citing S.C. Res. 1244, U.N. Doc. S/RES/1244 (1999), para. 14; *Prosecutor v. Haradinaj et al.*, Case No. IT-04-84-AR65.1, Decision on Ramush Haradinaj's Modified Provisional Release, 10 March 2006, para. 14).
64 United Nations Security Council Resolution 1244, Clause 11(i).
65 Decision on Second Ojdanić Motion for Stay of Proceedings, 19 October 2006, para. 10.
66 *See* Final Submissions in Support of General Ojdanić's Second Motion for Stay of Proceedings, 14 September 2006, Annex V (letter from the UNMIK Acting Special Representative of the Secretary General, Mr. Steven P. Schook, to Lead Counsel for General Ojdanić, Mr. Tomislav Višnjić, 30 August 2006 ("We have striven to achieve a careful balance between UNMIK's obligations toward the ICTY and the proper administration of international justice, and UNMIK's mandate under UN Security Council resolution 1244 (1999) to maintain a stable and safe security environment in Kosovo in light of the current political climate in Kosovo, as well as the local sensitivities in the specific locations that you request to visit.")).
67 Third Motion, Annex X.

UNMIK prepared and presented an alternative plan to the Defence team, whereby it would provide secure facilities and police escorts in the sites which the Defence sought to visit.[68] When this proposal was turned down, UNMIK again offered to explore alternative means to accommodate visits by the Defence team to the various sites within Kosovo.[69] In contrast, the Defence, rather than suggest alternative means of conducting the visits, discontinued the communications. The Defence determined of its own accord that the "security risk was too great to return to Kosovo at this time."[70]

41. In the view of the Chamber, UNMIK has made sufficient efforts to provide the Defence with adequate time and facilities for the preparation of its defence. In response to the Chamber's efforts to intercede directly on the behalf of the Defence, UNMIK has been willing to enter into constructive dialogue.[71] Its efforts to accommodate the mission by the Defence team have been extensively listed within this decision. The obligation of UNMIK to cooperate with the Tribunal, including by endeavouring to provide assistance to Defence teams, is not absolute or unqualified, but rather stands alongside its other obligations under UNSC Resolution 1244. Reasonable efforts have been made to accommodate the requests of the Defence, taking into account the security parameters repeatedly outlined by UNMIK; and, alternative proposals have not been forthcoming from the Defence. Thus, the Chamber considers that sufficient efforts have been made by UNMIK to provide assistance, should the Defence decide to avail itself of those efforts. **[page 15]**

42. The Chamber does not consider that the list of names prepared by the Defence, indicating persons that it intends to contact within Kosovo, adds any significant weight to the claimed violations of the Accused's fair trial rights. The list appears to contain a number of individuals that may be contacted by means other than entering Kosovo, such as persons apparently residing outside of Kosovo at this point in time, as well as a number of individuals whom it would not be appropriate to contact, such as children who were under the age of five at the time of the events and deceased persons listed in the Schedules to the Indictment. The Chamber considers that the Defence has failed to indicate with sufficient specificity the relevance of these individuals to the ongoing proceedings and the necessity of undertaking a mission to Kosovo in order to contact them. Indeed, the very list itself demonstrates that means other than entering Kosovo are available to the Defence in order to carry out its investigations.

43. In light of the detailed background of interactions between UNMIK and the Defence, the Chamber considers that the Accused has failed to demonstrate how his rights to equality of arms, to adequate facilities for the preparation of his defence, and to effective assistance of counsel have been specifically prejudiced by the actions of UNMIK. On this basis, the Chamber considers that the Accused's allegations that his fair trial rights have been violated are without foundation. **[page 16]**

---

[68] General Ojdanić's Supplemental Filing of Annex AA to General Ojdanić's Third Motion for Stay of Proceedings, 10 August 2007, Annex AA.

[69] Third Motion, Annex CC.

[70] Third Motion, para. 44.

[71] Letter of 30 August 2006 from UNMIK, Final Submissions in Support of General Ojdanić's Second Motion for Stay of Proceedings, 14 September 2006, Annex V; Letter from the UNMIK Principal Deputy Special Representative of the Secretary-General, Mr. Steven P. Schook, to Judge Iain Bonomy (Presiding), 4 October 2006; Letter of 9 May 2007 from UNMIK to the Defence, Third Motion, Annex CC.

DISPOSITION

44. The Chamber again recalls its duty pursuant to Article 20 to ensure that these proceedings are conducted in both a fair *and* expeditious manner.[72] The Chamber considers that, in light of all the circumstances, particularly the history of the current and previous motions to stay the trial and the refusal of the Defence to engage in further dialogue with UNMIK about alternate arrangements for carrying out investigations, the Defence has not demonstrated a sufficient basis for the requested relief to be granted. Accordingly, the Trial Chamber, pursuant to Articles 20 and 21 of the Statute and Rule 54 of the Rules of Procedure and Evidence of the Tribunal, hereby DENIES the Motion.

Done in English and French, the English text being authoritative.

Judge Iain Bonomy
Presiding

Dated this twenty-seventh day of August 2007
At The Hague
The Netherlands

[Seal of the Tribunal]

[72] *See* Decision on Second Ojdanić Motion for Stay of Proceedings, 19 October 2006 (citing *Prosecutor v. Prlić et al.*, Case No. IT-04-74-AR73.2, Decision on Joint Defence Interlocutory Appeal Against the Trial Chamber's Oral Decision of 8 May 2006 Relating to Cross-Examination by Defence and On association of Defence Counsel's Request for Leave to File an *Amicus Curiae* Brief, 4 July 2006, p. 4 (stating that "time and resource constraints exist in all judicial institutions and ... a legitimate concern in this trial, which involves six accused, is to ensure that the proceedings do not suffer undue delays and that the trial is completed within a reasonable time, which is recognized as a fundamental right of due process under international human rights law") (footnotes omitted)).

UNITED NATIONS

International Tribunal for the Prosecution of Persons Responsible for Serious Violations of International Humanitarian Law Committed in the Territory of the former Yugoslavia since 1991	Case No.: IT-04-81-PT Date: 23 November 2007 Original: English

IN THE TRIAL CHAMBER

Before: **Judge Patrick Robinson, Presiding**
Judge Krister Thelin
Judge Frank Höpfel

Registrar: **Mr. Hans Holthuis**

Decision of: **23 November 2007**

THE PROSECUTOR

v.

MOMČILO PERIŠIĆ

PUBLIC FILING

DECISION ON MOTION FOR SANCTIONS FOR FAILURE TO BRING THE ACCUSED TO TRIAL WITHOUT UNDUE DELAY

Office of the Prosecutor
Mr. Mark Harmon

Counsel for the Accused
Mr. James Castle
Mr. Novak Lukić

[page 2] I. PROCEDURAL BACKGROUND

1. **TRIAL CHAMBER III** ("Chamber") of the International Tribunal for the Prosecution of Persons Responsible for Serious Violations of International Humanitarian Law Committed in the Territory of the former Yugoslavia since 1991 ("Tribunal") is seised of the "Motion for Sanctions for Failure to Bring the Accused to Trial Without Undue Delay" filed by Counsel for Momčilo Perišić ("Defence" and "Accused", respectively) on 10 August 2007 ("Motion"), wherein the Defence submits that the Accused has suffered prejudice from delays in the proceedings both before and after the indictment against him was filed, and therefore requests "the imposition of specific remedial sanctions designed to address the prejudice suffered by the [A]ccused".[1]

2. The Office of the Prosecutor ("Prosecution") filed its "Prosecution's Response to Defence Motion for Sanctions for Failure to Bring the Accused to Trial Without Undue Delay" on 23 August 2007 ("Response"), in which its contends that the Defence failed to establish any prejudice to the Accused and further submits that any delay in the proceedings, both prior to and after issuance of the indictment against the Accused, was necessary to safeguard his rights.[2]

II. SUBMISSIONS OF THE PARTIES

3. In particular the Defence argues that a cumulative analysis of the following factors demonstrates that the trial against the Accused has been unduly delayed: i) length of the delay; ii) complexity of the proceedings; iii) conduct of the Parties; iv) conduct of the relevant authorities; and v) prejudice to the Accused.[3]

4. Although the Defence does not specify the date from which it alleges the delay begins, it submits, variously, that "[t]he factual basis of the indictment occurred 13 – 15 years ago"[4], that "the prosecution has known about the basis for the indictment since 1996, eleven years ago,"[5] and notes that the indictment "was issued on 22 February 2005, two months after the Completion Strategy's limitation on the termination of investigations".[6] The Defence submits that the Accused cannot **[page 3]** receive a fair trial "at this point in time" due to: i) the delay in filing the indictment and ii) the delay in the post-indictment progress of this case towards trial.[7]

5. The Defence requests the following relief from the Trial Chamber: i) that a hearing on the cause of such 'undue delay' be conducted;[8] ii) that the Prosecution be precluded from using prior testimony or statements of deceased witnesses whom the Defence lost the ability to cross-examine;[9] iii) that the Prosecution be precluded from tendering transcripts or minutes of the Federal Republic of Yugoslavia Supreme Defence Council;[10] iv) that the Prosecution be precluded from using adjudicated facts as well as statements obtained pursuant to Rule 92*bis* of the Rules of Procedure and Evidence of the Tribunal ("Rules");[11] v) that the Trial Chamber consider the delay and prejudice suffered by the Accused in assessing the facts presented at trial;[12] and ultimately vi) that the Trial Chamber apply the 'abuse of process' doctrine to assess whether the delay in bringing the Accused to trial makes it impossible to give him a fair trial and, if that is the case, to dismiss the case against him with prejudice.[13]

6. While the Prosecution agrees that the five factors set forth by the Defence should indeed be examined when conducting an 'undue delay' assessment,[14] it first contends that on the length of the delay, it was within

---

1 Motion for Sanctions for Failure to Bring the Accused to Trial Without Undue Delay, 10 August 2007 (submitted on 9 August 2007) ("Motion"), para. 30; *see also Id.*, paras 23–27.

2 Prosecution's Response to Defence Motion for Sanctions for Failure to Bring the Accused to Trial Without Undue Delay, 23 August 2007 ("Response"), paras 1, 11.

3 Motion, paras 13–27.

4 Motion, para. 13.

5 *Id.*

6 *Id.*, para 1.

7 *Id.*, para 28.

8 *Id.*, para. 20.

9 *Id.*, para. 30(a).

10 *Id.*, para. 30(b).

11 *Id.*, para. 30(c).

12 *Id.*, para. 31.

13 *Id.*, para. 32.

14 Response, para. 7.

its prosecutorial duty to gather a *prima facie* case against the Accused before issuing an indictment against him and adds that the lack of State co-operation in this case contributed to such delay.[15]

7. Second, as regards the complexity of the proceedings, the Prosecution argues that given the broad geographical and temporal scope of the indictment against the Accused as well as the number of proposed witnesses and volume of documents, any delay in the proceedings both prior to and after issuance of the indictment was necessary to protect the right of the Accused to a fair trial.[16] **[page 4]**

8. Third, as to the conduct of the Parties, the Prosecution submits that "[n]o evidence in the record shows that the prosecution acted inappropriately or deliberately delayed the submission of the indictment".[17]

9. Fourth, on the conduct of relevant authorities, the Prosecution opines that this case is progressing at the same speed as other cases before the Tribunal of similar complexity.[18]

10. Finally, as to the prejudice to the Accused, the Prosecution submits that the Defence failed to establish the following:

i) that the deceased witnesses referred to by the Defence possessed exculpatory information other witnesses would not have had;

ii) that potentially exculpatory documents were lost or destroyed; and

iii) how the filing of Prosecution motions to admit evidence pursuant to Rules 92*bis*, 92*quater* and 94(B) were not in conformity with the work plan established by the Pre-Trial Judge on 22 October 2006 pursuant to Rule 65*ter*(D) (ii) ("Work Plan") but rather were used to benefit from the alleged delay in the proceedings.

Furthermore, the Prosecution submits that the issue of the alleged unequal access of the Defence to the processes of the Tribunal has already been decided by a decision of the Chamber of 18 June 2007.[19]

III. APPLICABLE LAW

11. The obligation to ensure that proceedings are conducted expeditiously and without undue delay is incumbent upon the Chamber pursuant the Statute of the Tribunal ("Statute") and the Rules.[20]

12. While the issue of 'undue delay' has not yet been examined in the case law of the Tribunal, the Appeals Chamber of the International Criminal Tribunal for Rwanda ("ICTR") has held that **[page 5]**

> it is necessary to consider, inter alia, the following factors when determining whether there has been a violation of the right to be tried without undue delay:
>
> (1) The length of the delay;
>
> (2) The complexity of the proceedings, such as the number of charges, the number of accused, the number of witnesses, the volume of evidence, the complexity of facts and law;
>
> (3) The conduct of the parties;
>
> (4) The conduct of the relevant authorities; and
>
> (5) The prejudice to the accused; if any
>
> [...]

15 *Id.*, paras 11–14.

16 *Id.*, paras 15–16.

17 *Id.*, para. 18; *see also Id.*, paras 17–19.

18 *Id.*, para. 21.

19 *Id.*, paras 22–33.

20 Article 20(1) of the Statute provides: "The Trial Chambers shall ensure that a trial is fair and expeditious [...]"; Article 21(4) of the Statute provides: "In the determination of any charge against the accused pursuant to the present Statute, the accused shall be entitled to the following minimum guarantees, in full equality: (c) to be tried without undue delay". *See also* Rule 65*ter*(B) of the Rules, according to which "[t]he pre-trial Judge shall ensure that the proceedings are not unduly delayed and shall take any measure necessary to prepare the case for a fair and expeditious trial."

> [and] that the Trial Chamber, by stating, "(t)hat there is no need to inquire into any role that the Prosecutor might have played about the alleged undue delay", has failed to conduct a full enquiry and thus failed to take into account a necessary factor to determine whether there has been undue delay.[21]

13. Examining the *Mugiraneza* case, it is clear that the circumstances are closely related to the present case, and thus the Chamber considers that the standard set forth by the ICTR Appeals Chamber is helpful in analysing the instant case. Specifically, as recounted in the decision of the Trial Chamber, the Accused, Mugiraneza, was arrested in Cameroon on 6 April 1999 pursuant to a request by the Prosecutor for the ICTR.[22] The indictment was confirmed on 13 May 1999, and the Accused was transferred to the United Nations Detention Facilities on 31 July 1999.[23] The Indictment alleges offenses which occurred between 1 January and 31 December 1994.[24] The Defence filed its motion to dismiss on 2 August 2003, nearly four years after the indictment was confirmed,[25] and nearly nine years after the offenses allegedly occurred. Prior to filing its motion, the Defence in the *Mugiraneza* case also submitted that it had "called for a speedy trial on several occasions".[26] The Appeals Chamber, in reviewing the Trial Chamber's decision denying the motion, established the five factors above, indicating the analysis of the motion turns on these five **[page 6]** criteria.[27] As the cases contain very similar arguments and the facts are closely related, the Chamber finds it useful to use the analysis set out by the Appeals Chamber in this case, and will proceed to such an analysis below.

14. The Defence suggests that a period of 11 years must be taken into account in the instant case, arguing that the time for which the Prosecution must be held accountable begins at the point at which it became aware of the Accused's alleged offences.[28] The indictment against the Accused was issued on 22 February 2005, and the Accused surrendered to the Tribunal on 7 March 2005.[29] In the instant case, the Accused was granted provisional release on 9 June 2005.[30]

15. According to the Work Plan, adopted on 22 October 2006, the case against the Accused was to be trial ready on 30 April 2007. The period between the issuance of the indictment and the adoption of a Work Plan to complete pre-trial is less than two years, and the period between the adoption of the Work Plan and the case achieving a status of trial readiness was, therefore, only six months. In addition, the Defence concedes in its motion that this is a complex case.[31]

16. In *Case of W. v. Switzerland* heard before the European Court of Human Rights ("ECHR"),[32] the Accused, a Swiss businessman, was prosecuted along with eleven accomplices for a series of economic offences, including frauds in the management of some sixty companies.[33] The first complaints were made to the criminal police concerning the conduct of the Accused in 1982, and investigation revealed that the conduct which eventually led to charges against the Accused began as far back as 1977.[34] The Accused remained under investigation until 1986.[35] In 1985 and 1987, money and valuables belonging to the Accused and his co-accused were seized following orders or searches.[36] The Accused was arrested on 27 March 1985 and placed in pre-trial detention, where he remained until he was eventually convicted and sentenced to

---

21 *Prosecutor v. Prosper Mugiraneza*, Case No. ICTR 99-50-AR73, Decision on Prosper Mugiraneza's Interlocutory Appeal from Trial Chamber II Decision of 2 October 2003 Denying the Motion to Dismiss the Indictment, Demand Speedy Trial and for Appropriate Relief, 27 February 2004, p. 2.

22 *Prosecutor v. Prosper Mugiraneza*, Case No. ICTR 99-50-I, Decision on Propser Mugiraneza's Motion to Dismiss the Indictment for Violation of Article 20(4)(C) of the Statute, Demand for Speedy Trial and for Appropriate Relief, 2 October 2003, para. 1.

23 *Id.*

24 *Prosecutor v. Prosper Mugiraneza*, Case No. ICTR 99-50-I, Indictment, para. 2.1.

25 *Id.* at preamble paragraph.

26 *Id.*, at para. 4.

27 *Prosecutor v. Prosper Mugiraneza*, Case No. ICTR 99-50-AR73, Decision on Prosper Mugiraneza's Interlocutory Appeal from Trial Chamber II Decision of 2 October 2003 Denying the Motion to Dismiss the Indictment, Demand Speedy Trial and for Appropriate Relief, 27 February 2004, p. 2.

28 Motion, para. 13.

29 Motion, para. 2

30 *Prosecutor v. Momčilo Perišić*, Case No. IT-04-81-PT, Decision on Momčilo Perišić's Motion for Provisional Release, 9 June 2005.

31 Motion, para. 14, "The case against the Accused is extremely complex."

32 Application No. 14379/88, European Court HR, 26 January 1993.

33 *Id.*, para. 7.

34 *Id.*, para. 9.

35 *Id.*, paras. 7, 9.

36 *Id.*, para. 9.

eleven years' imprisonment on 30 **[page 7]** March 1989.[37] During his pre-trial detention, the Accused and his co-accused submitted some 25 applications for release, eight of which were made by the Accused, W.[38]

17. Claiming a violation of Article 5, paragraph 3 of the European Convention on Human Rights ("Article 5-3"), the Accused W argued that the period between his arrest and his conviction, which spanned four years and three days, constituted an unreasonable delay.[39] The Accused W also complained that he was held unreasonably in pre-trial detention for an excessive period.[40]

18. Article 5-3 states:

> Everyone arrested or detained in accordance with the provisions of paragraph 1.c of this article shall be brought promptly before a judge or other officer authorised by law to exercise judicial power and shall be entitled to trial within a reasonable time or to release pending trial. Release may be conditioned by guarantees to appear for trial.

19. In its determination that there had been no violation of Article 5-3, the ECHR held that the Prosecution's responsibility for delay began on the date of the Accused, W's, arrest.[41] The Court reasoned that, among other factors, the difficulty of a case is an appropriate consideration when determining whether pre-trial detention is unreasonable. In the case of W., pre-trial detention exceeded five years. The Court also noted that the presence of "intensive continuous review" of the case ensured that the rights of the Accused were respected. The Court went on to state, "the right of an accused in detention to have his case examined with particular expedition must not hinder the efforts of the courts to carry out their tasks with proper care."[42]

IV. DISCUSSION

20. Against the backdrop of this ECHR decision, an examination of the five factors outlined in *Mugiraneza* is appropriate here.

21. First, the Chamber rejects the contention of the Defence that the Prosecution should be held to account for time prior to the Accused's surrender to the Tribunal on 7 March 2005. While *Case of W.* serves as only persuasive, and not controlling authority, the Chamber agrees with the reasoning, that it is from the date of arrest or surrender forward that the obligation to proceed with a fair and expeditious trial begins. To adopt any other date on which the Prosecution is accountable would, in **[page 8]** the Chamber's view, be unreasonable. Using this reasoning, therefore, the length of the delay has extended now to two years and seven months from the date of the surrender.

22. With respect to the complexity of the proceedings, as noted above, the case is accepted by all parties and the Chamber, to be of great complexity. The Chamber notes that, in addition to the concession of the Defence in its Motion, acknowledging the complexity of the case[43], the Registry of the Tribunal informed the Defence, by letter of 25 August 2005, that the case against the Accused would be ranked at the highest level of complexity for the purposes of payment during the pre-trial stage. Therefore, the Chamber accepts for purposes of determining this motion that this case is amongst the most complex cases before the Tribunal.[44]

23. With respect to the conduct of the parties, the Chamber first notes that the period of time from the adoption of the Work Plan on 22 October 2006, until the case was placed in a trial ready state on 30 April 2007, was only six months. Clearly, under the terms of *Mugiraneza*, as well as under the standards applied in *Case of W.*, this is not an unreasonable delay, particularly in light of the agreed level of complexity of the case.

---

37 *Id.*, paras. 7, 24.
38 *Id.*, para. 14.
39 *Id.*, para. 29.
40 *Id.*, para. 28.
41 *Id.*, para. 29.
42 *Id.*, paras. 41, 42.
43 Motion, para. 14.
44 Pursuant to Article 1 of the Statute, the mandate of the Tribunal is to try already complex cases of "persons responsible for serious violations of international humanitarian law".

24. Further with respect to the conduct of the parties, the Chamber is of the view that the parties, both Prosecution and Defence have, to date, exercised due diligence in their respective obligations to prepare this case in the pre-trial phase.

25. The Chamber also notes one factor considered in *Case of W.* was the "intensive and continuous review" of the Accused W's pre-trial detention when the Court concluded there had not been a violation of Article 5-3.[45] In each case of an accused appearing before the Tribunal, there is a Status Conference at least every 120 days, where a Pre-Trial Judge ensures a case is moved expeditiously toward trial.[46] As in the *Case of W.*, the Chamber concludes that the active involvement in the present case has served to ensure that the proceedings move forward in as expeditiously as is possible.

26. The Chamber is mindful that one of the allegations of harm submitted by the Defence in its motion is that it suffers a lack of funding. The Chamber notes that while the Prosecution has no role to play in determining the funding level of the Defence, the relief sought by the motion is a request **[page 9]** for sanction against the Prosecution.[47] Where the harm which is alleged is not capable of remedy by the Prosecution, such as in the case of a complaint of inadequate funding, the sanction requested against the Prosecution is not well-founded. This matter has been previously raised by this Defence, and the Chamber has previously dealt with it.[48]

27. Further, as to the Defence claim of prejudice to the Accused, the Chamber merely recalls its previous finding that

> [t]he Accused has not demonstrated any equal lack of access to the processes of the Tribunal or opportunity to seek procedural relief. In fact, if the Accused is aggrieved by the level of his payment made by the Registrar in respect of this case, he can take this matter up with the Registrar [...][49]

28. The Chamber also takes note of the various sources of alleged prejudice to the Accused and acknowledges the difficulties encountered by the Defence. However, the Chamber does not consider that the Defence Motion successfully demonstrated that exculpatory material was irreparably lost due to a delay in the proceedings.

29. Therefore, the Chamber, which does not see the need for a hearing on the matter, holds that the Defence has not established the existence of a failure to bring the Accused to trial without undue delay.

V. DISPOSITION

30. For the foregoing reasons and pursuant to Articles 20(1) and 21(4)(c) of the Statute and Rule 65*ter*(B) of the Rules, the Chamber **DENIES** the Motion. **[page 10]**

Done in English and French, the English text being authoritative.

Dated this twenty-third day of November 2007
At The Hague
The Netherlands

Patrick Robinson
Presiding

[Seal of the Tribunal]

45 *Case of W. v. Switzerland,* para. 42.
46 Rule 65 *bis*(A), Rules of Procedure and Evidence.
47 Motion, paras. 28–31.
48 Decision on Motion to Appoint *Amicus Curiae* to Investigate Equality of Arms, 18 June 2007.
49 Decision on Motion to Appoint *Amicus Curiae* to Investigate Equality of Arms, 18 June 2007, para. 10.

Commentary

1. Introduction

The three decisions discussed in this commentary illustrate the tribunal's approach to probably the most criticized issues regarding the defence in international criminal proceedings. These concern the resource discrepancy between the defence and the prosecutor, the difficulties surrounding defence (on-site) investigations for trial preparation and the long duration of the international criminal process. The argument of the defence in all three decisions relates to the principle of equality of arms, which is "one of the most assiduously argued arenas" in international criminal proceedings.[1] This commentary highlights and discusses the central arguments and deliberations of the three decisions in the chronological order of their issuance.

2. Perišić equality of arms decision[2]

2.1 Position of the defence

The resource inequality, or the appearance thereof, between the prosecution and the defence represents one of the main "equality of arms" arguments in international criminal proceedings. The defence has found creative ways to bring this issue to the attention of the judges. In this case, the defence requested the appointment of an *amicus* counsel to investigate and report to the chamber on the possible imbalance created by the allocated resources to both parties.[3] According to the defence "the inequality of resources in this case is now at a crisis point".[4] It then offered several examples of the resource inequality between parties.

The defence argued that, although it was very cautious in stretching its overall budget to the limit, as the available pre-trial funds would soon be exhausted, the "[d]efence staff will need to be terminated and the defence of Momčilo Perišić will come to a grinding halt".[5] This inequality is extended by the length of the pre-trial process, which means "more trips need to be conducted on a *pro bono* basis, overhead costs accumulate without reimbursement, and staff defections cause lost knowledge and increased start up costs for replacement personnel".[6]

Moreover, the amount of disclosed material that is relevant to the case and/or exculpatory is such that using all the pre-trial funds the defence "would not be able to look at 75% of the printed relevant materials", let alone at the video/audio disclosure.[7] The defence also alleged a severe discrepancy in the quality of investigative staff and expert resources of the defence and prosecution. According to the defence, the "OPT's investigative staff in this case includes doctorates in history and philosophy, professional accountants and high ranking military personnel",[8] while "[t]he hard truth is defence teams at this tribunal are staffed by a single overwhelmed attorney and a single case manager until shortly before trial".[9]

The defence thus invited the chamber to appoint an *amicus curiae* to investigate the issue neutrally and thus provide the chamber with the opportunity to objectively determine whether any inequality of arms exists in this case.[10] Although the defence did not seek a specific remedy, because the extent of the inequality had not yet

---

1 H. Morrison, Foreword, Symposium The Role of Defence in International Criminal Trials, 8 Journal of International Criminal Justice 2010, p. 449.

2 ICTY, Decision on Motion to Appoint *Amicus Curiae* to Investigate Equality of Arms, *Prosecutor v. Perišić*, Case No. IT-04-81-PT, T. Ch. III, 18 June 2007, in this volume, p. 193.

3 ICTY, Motion for Appointment of Amicus Counsel to report to Chamber on Inequality of arms afforded the defence, *Prosecutor v. Perišić*, Case No. IT-04-81-PT, T. Ch. III, 1 February 2007, par. 1.

4 *Ibid.*, par. 3.

5 *Ibid.*, par. 4 , sub a.

6 *Ibid.*, par. 4, sub b.

7 *Ibid.*, par. 4, sub c.

8 *Ibid.*, par. 4, sub d.

9 *Ibid.*, par. 4, sub e.

10 *Ibid.*, par. 5.

been established, it did request the chamber, "at a minimum [...] to increase defence resources to a level which allows the defence team to continue working on the case during the remainder of the Pre-Trial period".[11]

2.2 Comparing the resources

According to the chamber, the argument of the general appearance of inequality between parties before the tribunal "does not amount to anything more than a complaint that he [the accused] does not have the same material resources than the Prosecution".[12] In that regard, the *ad hoc* tribunals have time and again repeated the dictum of the Appeals Chamber in the Kayishema and Ruzindana case, that "equality of arms between the Defence and the Prosecution does not necessarily amount to the material equality of possessing the same financial and/ or personal resources".[13] Next to the rather obscure foundation of this observation, the meaning of this statement is not elaborated any further.[14]

If equality of arms *does not necessarily* reflect equality of resources between prosecution and defence, could there be instances where it does? Common sense advises that a mathematical parity between the staff and resources of the prosecution and the defence, particularly in the pre-trial phase, is principally and practically unattainable. Equality of arms cannot be assessed on the basis of comparing the available pre-trial resources between the prosecution and defence; that is comparing apples and oranges. There is no reciprocity on the issue of resources due to the differing roles of the prosecution and the defence in the proceedings.

Yet the principle of equality of arms can only be violated if the defence or the prosecution is put at a disadvantageous position when presenting its case *as compared to each other*. This reasoning would imply that resources as such fall outside the operating scope of the principle of equality of arms; simply stated, this is because resources cannot be compared and the principle of equality of arms implies a comparison.

However, this reasoning seems defective to the extent that equality of arms is one of the fundamental principles of the legal aid system that secures "equality of arms" by providing quality defence to indigent accused.[15] The "playing field" would undeniably be manifestly tilted in a case where an indigent accused would not be afforded legal assistance; our understanding of a fair trial does not envisage a criminal trial where a poor individual alone is facing a powerful prosecutor. Thus, the legal aid system is established to provide for "equality of arms", but following the Kayishema and Ruzindana reasoning, defence counsel cannot appeal to that principle when requesting additional funds. This confusing conclusion might be explained by reference to differing notions of equality of arms.

2.3 Two notions of equality of arms

As noted by Cassesse, the principle of equality of arms has two distinct notions: as a concept developed in the case law of the European Court of Human Rights (ECtHR) and as an essential element of the adversarial

[11] *Ibid.*, par. 7.

[12] Decision on Motion to Appoint *Amicus Curiae* to Investigate Equality of *Arms, Prosecutor v. Perišić*, T. Ch. III, *supra* note 2, par. 10.

[13] ICTR, Judgment (Reasons), *Prosecutor v. Kayishema and Ruzindana*, Case No. ICTR-95-1-A, A. Ch., 1 June 2001, par. 69, Klip/ Sluiter, ALC-X-495.

[14] The Appeals Chamber refers in footnote 84 to ECtHR, Judgment, *Hentrich v. France*, 22 September 1994, par. 56 as an example; however, this case concerns a civil case and the particular passage from the judgment does not seem to provide any support for Appeals Chamber's assumption.

[15] ICTY, Decision on Interlocutory Appeal on Motion for Additional Funds, *Prosecutor v. Milutinović, Ojdanić and Šainović*, Case No. IT-99-37-AR73.2, A. Ch., 13 November 2003, Klip/ Sluiter, ALC-XV-4, par. 3: "The international Tribunal's Legal Aid System [...] bears the costs of a defence for indigent accused; it is not in dispute that the system is designed to give the defence quality representation to secure equality of arms with the Prosecution". See also ICTY Decision on accused motion for adequate facilities and equality of arms: legal associates, *Prosecutor v. Karadžić and Mladić*, Case No. IT-95-5/18, T. Ch. III, 28 January 2009, to be published in volume XXXVII, par. 29: "The Tribunal has a fully funded, flexible scheme for the provision of legal aid through counsel and associated staff for indigent accused. Thus is equality of arms with the Prosecution generally secured." See also ICC, Report to the Assembly of States Parties on options for ensuring adequate defence counsel for accused persons, ICC-ASP/3/16, Third Session, 17 August 2004, par. 16: "Equality of arms: The payment system must contribute to maintaining equilibrium between the resources and means of the accused and those of the prosecution. In this respect, the fees of the members of the defence team are based on the salaries paid in the Office of the Prosecutor (OPT) of the ICC and at the ad hoc Tribunals, increased by 40% to compensate for the increment in professional charges resulting from an appointment".

structure of proceedings.[16] Arguably, the first notion relates equality of arms to the (minimum) human rights of the defence, as presented in the international human rights conventions (the human rights notion of equality of arms). The ECtHR explicitly acknowledged "equality of arms" as an indivisible aspect of the right to a fair trial. It based the principle on Article 6, paragraph 1 ECHR, thus applying more generally to all proceedings, while Article 6, paragraph 2 and 3 only apply to criminal cases.[17] Clearly, the rights laid down in the human rights conventions are intended for the benefit of individuals and, as such, the human rights bodies make no judgment on the position of the prosecutor, a state body, in their deliberations.

However, that is not to say that the principle of equality of arms as a corollary of adversarial process is not included in the definition as given by the human rights bodies. This second notion of equality of arms is "hidden" in the principle of adversarial proceedings. Indeed, equality of arms as the corollary of adversarial process implies reciprocity of entitlements between parties and thus "works both way".[18] The reciprocal procedural devices, such as the ability to cross-examine witnesses or to advance evidence, "can and must exist in symmetrical balance".[19] The function of this notion of equality of arms is to maintain the formal equality in regard to procedural opportunities.

In the case at hand, the human rights notion of equality of arms seems to come to the fore. Rather then arguing general inequality of arms based on the difference of resources between the prosecution and the defence, the latter in this case should have focused its submissions on the (minimum) rights of the accused. The important question remains as to whether the defence was able to adequately prepare for trial, and not whether unequal distribution of resources between prosecution and defence had created an - appearance of - inequality of arms. The issue at hand concerns a non-reciprocal advantage of the prosecution, and an argument of inequality based on a comparison between prosecution and defence in this regard is bound to be dismissed as an inappropriate[20] request for additional funding.[21]

The adequacy of resources for the defence can only be made in the framework of a particular procedural system having due consideration to the difference in functions that the prosecution and defence are to assume at different stages of a criminal trial. Regarding this, the Trial Chamber reiterated the Tadić formula, that "equality of arms obliges a judicial body to ensure that neither party is put at a disadvantage when presenting its case".[22] It furthermore added that "[t]he principle also must be viewed with respect to the different functions which the parties have in various systems".[23]

---

16 A. Cassese, International Criminal Law, Oxford University Press, Oxford 2008, p. 384. First, there is a concept developed in the case law of the European Court of Human Rights over the years. It implies that the accused may not be put at a serious procedural disadvantage with respect to the prosecutor. This applies to the accused only: human rights treaties do not grant the prosecutor the right to be put on a par with the defence. On the other hand, human rights treaties do not forbid, and sometimes even require, the accused to be put in a "better" or more advantageous position than the prosecution in order to preserve an overall balance in the proceedings (the prosecutor normally being better equipped that the defence for the collection of evidence).

Secondly, equality of parties is an essential ingredient of the adversarial structure of proceedings, based on the notion of the trial as a contest between two parties. Under this approach, it is indispensable for both parties to the proceedings to have the same rights; otherwise, there is no fair fight between the two "contestants", and the spectators will not be convinced by the outcome. Here fairness works both ways and therefore also the prosecutor is entitled not to be put in a disadvantageous position. Similar worries do not exist in inquisitorial systems of justice, where proceedings are conceived of as an "official inquiry."

17 The independent meaning of "equality of arms" was ascertained in European Court of Human Rights, Judgment, Vidal v. Belgium, Application. No. 12351/86, 22 April 1992, par. 33: "The concept of "equality of arms" does not, however, exhaust the content of paragraph 3 (d) of Article 6 (art. 6-3-d), nor that of paragraph 1 (art. 6-1), of which this phrase represents one application among many others".

18 *Cf.* J. S. Silver, Equality of Arms and the Adversarial Process: A New Constitutional Right, 1007 Wisconsin Law Review 1990, p. 1039.

19 *Ibid.*

20 In the sense that requests for additional funding would have to be directed to the appropriate body, the registrar. This decision could be reviewed by the chamber.

21 Decision on Motion to Appoint *Amicus Curiae* to Investigate Equality of Arms, *Prosecutor v. Perišić*, T. Ch. III, *supra* note 2, par. 10 and 11. To be allowed additional funds, the defence has to demonstrate exceptional circumstances, or circumstances beyond its control, which would warrant additional resources during a particular stage of proceedings: see Decision on Interlocutory Appeal on Motion for Additional Funds, *Prosecutor v. Milutinović, Ojdanić and Šainović*, A. Ch., *supra* note 15 par. 21.

22 Decision on Motion to Appoint *Amicus Curiae* to Investigate Equality of Arms, *Prosecutor v. Perišić*, T. Ch. III, *supra* note 2, par. 6.

23 *Ibid.*

Obviously, the only system relevant here is the ICTY system, and in that regard the Trial Chamber repeats the Aleksovski Appeals Chamber conclusion that the role of the prosecution is to represent not only the victims of the charged offences, but also the whole international community.[24] To equalize to the powerful position of the prosecutor, the tribunal's legal system, "in accordance with internationally recognized human rights instruments", affords the accused substantial rights.[25] This is evidenced by the presumption of innocence an accused enjoys, contrasted to the burden of proof resting upon the prosecution; the "extensive burden on the Prosecution for discovery and disclosure of *exculpatory* material to the Defence"; and the fact that proceedings before the tribunal were designed to "adhere to internationally recognized principles of fair trial".[26]

This is as far as theory is concerned; the practice seems rather "worlds apart", sometimes. What is the practical value of this "presumption of innocence" for someone so widely "judged" beforehand, such as Milošević, Karadžić, Taylor? If even the prosecutor complains about his ability to conduct meaningful investigations in the framework of international criminal trials due to institutional dependency on state cooperation, what is the defence to do? What is the value of the burden to disclose exculpatory evidence to the defence, if there is no accompanying responsibility of the prosecutor to actively search for that evidence, considering the problematic defence investigations? Or that the obligation to disclose such evidence can be limited by counter balancing considerations like state interests?

These questions only touch the surface of the underlying, very complex, issues that cannot adequately be addressed in this commentary. However, one critical issue will be considered in the next section, namely the defence's ability to conduct its own investigations by visiting the crime scene/area.

3. Ojdanić stay of proceedings decision[27]

In this decision, the Trial Chamber addressed Ojdanić's third motion to stay the proceedings "on the grounds that he cannot presently receive a fair trial as guaranteed in Article 20 of the Tribunal's Statute", due to defence's inability to safely conduct on-site investigations in Kosovo.[28] After an aborted field mission in May 2006, during which the Ojdanić defence team was attacked, and numerous attempts to visit the crime sites in Kosovo since then, the defence team argued in its third motion to stay the proceedings, since "the reality was that it was not possible for a Serbian accused to conduct investigation in Kosovo at that time".[29]

3.1 Position of the defence

The defence asserted a violation of equality of arms and the right to effective assistance of a counsel in this case. Relying on the Orić Appeals Chamber decision,[30] the defence proposed a two step approach in the assessment of equality of arms, namely "(1) was the defence put at a disadvantage vis-à-vis the Prosecution, taking into account the "principle of basic proportionality" and (2) was the accused permitted a fair opportunity to present his case".[31]

As the prosecution was indeed able to investigate "freely in Kosovo and was able to bring witnesses from Kosovo"[32] and the defence was not, the latter was unable to fairly present its case. Although the case law of the tribunal indicates that the failure of a government to cooperate with the defence is insufficient to establish

---

24 *Ibid,* par. 7, referring to ICTY, Decision on Prosecutor's Appeal on Admissibility of Evidence, *Prosecutor v. Aleksovski,* Case No. IT-95-14/1-AR73, A. Ch., 16 February 1999, Klip/ Sluiter, ALC-III-241, par. 25.

25 *Ibid.*

26 *Ibid.,* (emphasis in original).

27 ICTY, Decision on Ojdanić Third Motion for Stay of Proceedings, *Prosecutor v. Milutinović et al.*, Case No. IT-05-87-T, T. Ch. III, 27 August 2007, in this volume, p. 199.

28 ICTY, General Ojdanić's Third Motion for Stay of Proceedings, *Prosecutor v. Milutinović et al.,* Case No. IT-05-87-T, T. Ch. III, 23 July 2007, par. 1.

29 *Ibid.,* par. 37.

30 ICTY, Interlocutory decision on length of defence case, *Prosecutor v. Orić*, Case No. IT-03-68-AR73.2, A. Ch., 20 July 2005, Klip/ Sluiter, ALC-XXVII-311.

31 General Ojdanić's Third Motion for Stay of Proceedings, Prosecutor v. Milutinović et al., T. Ch. III, *supra* note 28, par. 56.

32 Decision on Ojdanić Third Motion for Stay of Proceedings, *Prosecutor v. Milutinović et al.,* T. Ch. III, *supra* note 27, par. 1.

inequality of arms, the defence distinguished this case from Tadić and Kayishema and Ruzindana in that "[h]ere, the same United Nations which proposes to put General Ojdanić on trial is responsible for security in the areas to which his defence tams needs access".[33] Thus, the tribunal "cannot shift the responsibility for a fair trial away from its own institution - the United Nations", but must stay the proceedings until it will be possible for the Ojdanić defence team to conduct "basic defence investigations".[34]

3.2 Position of the prosecution

The prosecution urged the chamber to deny Ojdanić's third motion "due to the lack of an adequate and sufficiently detailed showing in support of a stay of proceedings", as the defence "has not fully availed itself of alternatives" that are available to overcome the difficulties the defence "has encountered in its efforts to carry our on-site investigations in Kosovo".[35] The defence thus failed to assess the relevance, importance, or necessity of contacting the persons on its potential witness list, or to contact some of these individuals by alternate means, such as by phone or email.[36]

3.3 Trial Chamber's evaluation

The Trial Chamber's discussion interestingly completely bypasses the "equality of arms" discussion, but rather focuses on the "efforts" undertaken by different parties to facilitate defence investigations. From the outset, the chamber "acknowledges that UNMIK must balance the needs of the Defence with the overall mission in connection with the administration of Kosovo".[37] In the decision on the first motion to stay the proceedings, the chamber requested UNMIK "to take all reasonable and necessary measures, as soon as possible, in order to assist the Defence teams of the Accused in their investigations in Kosovo for the preparation of their defence".[38] It denied Ojdanić's motion to stay the proceedings, considering that the fact that UNMIK was not able to provide the security conditions to the defence team at its first visit to Kosovo does not imply that UNMIK will "indefinitely" be unable to do so.[39]

Moreover, UNMIK has not shown its inability or unwillingness to secure future defence team visits to Kosovo. According to the Trial Chamber, "in these circumstances, it cannot be said that the Accused will not have a fair trial or that their rights will not be respected".[40]

It is the Trial Chamber's responsibility to ensure a fair trial, "having regard to all the circumstances of the trial".[41] In addition to the email sent by the senior officer of the chamber to UNMIK in August 2006, emphasizing the "Chamber's readiness to assist in finalizing arrangements that are satisfactory to all to enable the investigations to be carried out",[42] the chamber had several times indicated its willingness to assist the defence further "so as to yield a more favorable outcome with UNMIK".[43] The defence, however, while appreciating the offer, replied that "it now wished to proceed on the record".[44] The security parameters as indicated by UNMIK, under which the defence would possibly be able to conduct (part of) its intended investigations in Kosovo, were not deemed satisfactory to the defence.[45] It thus indicated that the security

33 *Ibid.*, par. 64.

34 *Ibid.*

35 ICTY, Prosecution Response to General Ojdanić's Third Motion for Stay of Proceedings, *Prosecutor v. Milutinovic et al.*, Case No. IT-05-87-T, 31 July 2007, T. Ch. III, par. 4.

36 *Ibid., par. 5.*

37 Decision on Ojdanić Third Motion for Stay of Proceedings, *Prosecutor v. Milutinović et al.*, T. Ch. III, *supra* note 27, par. 38.

38 *ICTY, Decision on Ojdanić Motion for Stay of Proceedings, Prosecutor v. Milutinović et al.*, Case No. IT-05-87-PT, T. Ch. III, 9 June 2006, par. 6.

39 *Ibid.*, par. 4.

40 *Ibid.*, par. 5.

41 *Ibid.*

42 Decision on Ojdanić Third Motion for Stay of Proceedings, *Prosecutor v. Milutinović et al.*, T. Ch. III, *supra* note 27, par. 15.

43 *Ibid.*, par. 18.

44 *Ibid.*

45 UNMIK was only able to facilitate site visits to six out of eleven requested sites, under stringent conditions, "including the requirement that Mr. Isak Ilija [defence investigator] not be present during three of the site visits and various other constraints such as time limits upon particular locations and prohibitions upon contact with citizens". According to the defence, such a visit would be useless, as it would constitute a mere tourist visit; ICTY, Decision on Second Ojdanić Motion For Stay of Proceedings,

risk was obviously still too great for the defence team to conduct, in their view, meaningful on-site investigation.

According to the Trial Chamber, "UNMIK has made sufficient efforts to provide the Defence with adequate time and facilities for the preparation of its defence [...] should the Defence decide to avail itself of those efforts".[46] In the chamber's view, the defence has been less than cooperative due to its unilateral discontinuance of the "constructive dialogue" offered by UNMIK, and its unwillingness to provide alternative proposals.[47] The cooperation between UNMIK, the ICTY and the defence is "a developing, dynamic process whence the Defence has withdrawn, despite UNMIK's continued participation to trying to make the investigations come to fruition".[48]

Additionally, the chamber found merit in the prosecution's assertion that the defence had failed to indicate the specific relevance or necessity of the individuals it intended to contact in Kosovo. In fact, according to the chamber, "the very list itself demonstrates that means other than entering Kosovo are available to the Defence in order to carry out its investigations".[49] The defence had compiled this list on the basis of witness testimony during the prosecution's case.[50] Of course, compiling this list can be seen as an investigatory act of the defence, indeed a necessary first investigatory step in the absence of other means. Seemingly, the defence has neglected to demarcate the list more specifically, thus including individuals who had already testified, had died, were too young, or were living abroad at the moment.[51] This is unfortunate, as it undermines, to some extent, the importance of this list.

The chamber cannot, however, be implying that this necessary first step is a sufficient means to conduct meaningful defence investigations outside the direct crime scene. It seems that the best chance for the defence to prepare meaningfully is to scrutinize the prosecution's case to its maximum, and to try to "poke holes in it" from the inside.[52] This clear civil law approach to a defence preparation is not explicit in the chamber's reasoning, and the chamber unfortunately did not elaborate on the other possible means that are available to the defence, in order to carry out its investigations without entering Kosovo.

In conclusion, the chamber considered that accused's rights to equality of arms, to adequate time and facilities for the preparation of his defence, and to effective assistance of counsel, had not been "specifically prejudiced by the actions of UNMIK".[53] These stringent conditions - UNMIK's actions should specifically prejudice the defence to comprise a violation of the rights of the accused - accord to the tribunal's approach towards the difficulties encountered by defence teams in their investigations. As may be remembered, already in Tadić, the Appeals Chamber indicated that the chamber cannot be expected to regulate conditions beyond the control of the international tribunal preventing a party from securing the attendance of certain witnesses.[54] In Kayishema and Ruzindana, the Appeals Chamber agreed with Trial Chamber's reasoning that the mere fact that the defence counsel was unable to visit Rwanda does not imply an inequality of arms between the prosecution and the defence.[55] Here again, the argument seems to be advanced that the institution of legal aid systems as such is sufficient to secure equality of arms. Investigators, paid by the tribunal were available to the defence, and thus the Trial Chamber was satisfied that "all the necessary provisions for the preparation of a comprehensive defence were available, and were afforded to all Defence Counsel in this

Prosecutor v. Milutinović et al., Case No. IT-05-87-T, T. Ch. III, 19 October 2006, par. 6 and 7.

46 Decision on Ojdanić Third Motion for Stay of Proceedings, *Prosecutor v. Milutinović et al.*, T. Ch. III, *supra* note 27, par. 41.

47 *Ibid.*, par. 40–41.

48 Decision on Second Ojdanić Motion For Stay of Proceedings, *Prosecutor v. Milutinović et al.*, T. Ch. III, *supra* note 45, par. 10.

49 Decision on Ojdanić Third Motion for Stay of Proceedings, *Prosecutor v. Milutinović et al.*, T. Ch. III, *supra* note 27, par. 42.

50 General Ojdanić's Third Motion for Stay of Proceedings, *Prosecutor v. Milutinović et al.*, T. Ch. III, *supra* note 28, par. 46.

51 Prosecution Response to General Ojdanić's Third Motion for Stay of Proceedings, *Prosecutor v. Milutinović et al., supra* note 35, par. 5.

52 Interlocutory Decision on Length of Defence Case, *Prosecutor v. Orić, A. Ch.*, *supra* note 30, par. 7: "The Prosecution has the burden of telling an entire story, of putting together a coherent narrative and proving every necessary element of the crimes charged beyond a reasonable doubt. Defense strategy, by contrast, often focuses on poking specifically targeted holes in the Prosecution's case".

53 Decision on Ojdanić Third Motion for Stay of Proceedings, *Prosecutor v. Milutinović et al.*, T. Ch. III, *supra* note 27, par. 43.

54 ICTY, Judgment, *Prosecutor v. Tadić, Case* No. IT-91-1-A, 15 July 1999, A. Ch., Klip/ Sluiter, ALC-III-761, par. 49.

55 Judgment (Reasons), *Prosecutor v. Kayishema and Ruzindana,* Case No. ICTR-95-1-A, A. Ch., *supra* note 13, par. 72.

case."[56] Indeed, "the utilization of those resources is not a matter for the Trial Chamber".[57] However, with all the available means and resources, if the defence investigator cannot enter the state of the crime scene, what is left of the "meaningful", "adequate" or "effective" defence an accused is entitled to? In fact, it was the defence investigator against whose participation in on-site investigations UNMIK had expressed its serious reservations, this restricting his access to certain crime sites.[58]

According to Article 21, paragraph 4, sub e, of the ICTY Statute, an accused has the minimum right to "obtain the attendance and examination of witnesses on his behalf under the same conditions as witnesses against him". Part of a more general right to present evidence, this gives the defence an opportunity to actively participate in shaping the proceedings.[59] Clearly, the tribunal has to draw the line somewhere, and it is understandable that it is drawn here: the chamber assists the defence as much as possible, but cannot administer factors outside its control. In fact, the obligation of the Trial Chamber to assist the parties in presenting their case is "especially pressing when outside forces seek to undermine the ability to present its evidence at trial".[60]

In Tadić, the Appeals Chamber explained that it could imagine a situation where a fair trial is not possible due to the obstructionist efforts of a state to hinder the appearance of defence witnesses.[61] In such a case, the option to submit a motion to stay the proceedings is available to the defence.[62] The Ojdanić defence made avail of this option, but failed to satisfy the high threshold that such relief required.[63]

3.4 Defence appeal

The last opportunity to raise the issue is taken up by Ojdanić defence on appeal, where he advanced virtually the same grounds as in his Third Motion to Stay the Proceedings.[64] Additionally, he referred to the prosecutor's appeal brief in the Haradinaj case, following the Trial Chamber's acquittal, where the prosecution asserted that there had been a violation of its right to a fair trial, due to the failure of the Trial Chamber to take all reasonable steps to secure the testimony of crucial witnesses.[65] The Ojdanić defence reasoned that "[i]f the Prosecution contends that it, with the weight of international community and its substantial resources behind it, could not get witnesses in Kosovo to testify on behalf of Serbs, how could General Ojdanić's Serbian Defence team possibly be expected to do the same?"[66]

Interestingly, the Appeals Chamber in Haradinaj allowed the prosecutor's appeal, and considered that the Trial Chamber's failure to take sufficient steps to obtain the testimony of the important witnesses undermined the fairness of proceedings and resulted in a miscarriage of justice.[67] The fact that the two witnesses never meaningfully testified during the trial deprived the prosecutor of vital support for its case, resulting in a subsequent acquittal on "almost all of the counts that the two witnesses' testimony might have helped to

---

56 Judgment and Sentence, *Prosecutor v. Kayishema and Ruzindana,* Case No. ICTR-95-1-T, T. Ch. II, 21 May 1999, Klip/ Sluiter, ALC-II-555, par. 61. Endorsed by Appeals Chamber in Judgment (Reasons), *Prosecutor v. Kayishema and Ruzindana, supra* note 35, par. 72.

57 *Ibid.,* par. 61.

58 ICTY, Decision on Second Ojdanić Motion For Stay of Proceedings, *Prosecutor v. Milutinović et al.,* Case No. IT-05-87-T, T. Ch. III, 19 October 2006, Klip/ Sluiter, ALC-XXXIII-209, par. 4 and 6.

59 S. Trechsel, Human Rights in Criminal Proceedings, Oxford University Press, Oxford 2005, p. 323.

60 ICTY, Judgment, *Prosecutor v. Haradinaj et al.,* Case No. IT-04-84-A, A. Ch., 19 July 2010, par. 35.

61 Judgment, *Prosecutor v. Tadić,* A. Ch., *supra* note 54, par. 55. See also ICTY, Decision on Second Motion by Brđanin to Dismiss the Indictment, *Prosecutor v. Brđanin and Talić,* Case No. IT-99-36-PT, T. Ch. II, 16 May 2001, Klip/ Sluiter, ALC-VII-37, par. 5.

62 Judgment, *Prosecutor v. Tadić,* A. Ch., *supra* note 61, par. 55.

63 For a recent decision highlighting the "drastic" nature of the remedy of stay of proceedings, see ICC, Judgment on the Appeal of the Prosecutor Against the Decision of Trial Chamber I of 8 July 2010 entitled "Decision on the Prosecution's Urgent Request for Variation of the Time-Limit to Disclose the Identity of Intermediary 143 or Alternatively to Stay Proceedings Pending Further Consultations with the VWU", *Prosecutor v. Dyilo,* Case No. ICC-01/04-01/06 CA 18, A. Ch., 8 October 2010.

64 ICTY, General Ojdanić's Motion Submitting Amended Appeal Brief, *Prosecutor v. Milutinović et al.,* Case No. IT-05-87-A, A. *Ch.,* 11 December 2009, p. 124–132.

65 ICTY, Notice of Filling of Public Redacted Version of Prosecution Appeal Brief, *Prosecutor v. Haradinaj et al.,* Case No. IT-04-84-A, A. Ch., 17 July 2008, par. 1

66 General Ojdanić's Motion Submitting Amended Appeal Brief, *Prosecutor v. Milutinović et al., supra* note 64, p. 132.

67 Judgment, *Prosecutor v. Haradinaj et al.,* A. Ch., *supra* note 60, par. 49.

establish".[68] Considering the Trial Chamber's discretion in this matter, the Appeals Chamber emphasized that each of the decisions of the Trial Chamber concerning the witnesses in question, "taken individually and outside the context of the trial [...] could be considered as falling within its scope of discretion".[69] However, considered together, and in the context of serious witness intimidation during trial, the error on the part of the Trial Chamber is apparent.[70]

It is questionable however, whether the Appeals Chamber would consider that the Trial Chamber in the Ojdanić case "failed to appreciate the gravity of the threat" that the defence's inability to conduct investigations in Kosovo, "posed to the trial's integrity".[71] The fact that the defence unilaterally decided not to pursue any investigations in Kosovo, however limited they would be, places a burden on the defence to demonstrate its complete inability to conduct meaningful investigations.

4. Perisić Undue Delay Decision[72]

One of the major frustrations about the *ad hoc* and hybrid tribunals has been the pace of their trials.[73] The adage "justice delayed is justice denied" has been fully employed in the criticisms expressed by different observers, particularly victims, donors, but also accused persons. Seemingly, both the effectiveness and efficiency of these institutions is measured by their ability to conduct trials "as soon as possible, as quick as possible and as cheap as possible".[74] The ICTY and ICTR are seen as "too costly, too inefficient and too ineffective", and more so the "delays in bringing detainees to trial - and the trials themselves - have generally been so lengthy that questions have been raised as to the violation by the tribunals of the basic human rights guarantees set out in the International Covenant on Civil and Political Rights (ICCPR)".[75] Momčilo Perišić's "Motion for Sanctions for Failure to Bring the Accused to Trial Without Undue Delay" indeed advances the violation of his right to be tried without undue delay, a right that finds protection in Article 14, paragraph 3, ICCPR, Article 6, paragraph 1, ECHR and Article 8, paragraph 1, ACHR.

4.1 Position of the defence

The defence submitted that the pre- and post-indictment delay in this case makes a fair trial at this stage impossible. According to the defence, the pre-indictment period, which would amount to approximately 15 years, is relevant for the evaluation of "undue delay", because "[d]uring the pre-indictment period the accused is actually at a more vulnerable position as he has no procedural mechanisms to preserve evidence, nor resources to conduct an investigation and no ability to seek a speedy resolution".[76]

Admittedly, outside the framework of a formal accusation, the suspect is subject to (police) investigation and enjoys considerably less procedural rights, as compared to an accused person.

Further, "the right to be free from undue delay is multifaceted",[77] as the principle of fairness demands that it is in the interest of the society, the victim and the suspected person to deliver speedy justice through a criminal prosecution. In fact, this forms the underlying rationale of the statutes of limitations enforced in national criminal systems. These statutes, however, are deemed inapplicable in the context of international crimes, due

68 *Ibid.*, par. 38.

69 *Ibid.*, par. 40.

70 *Ibid.*

71 Judgment, *Prosecutor v. Haradinaj et al.*, A. Ch., *supra* note 60, par. 40: "This misplaced priority [to the time schedule] demonstrates that the Trial Chamber failed to appreciate the gravity of the threat that witness intimidation posed to the trial's integrity".

72 ICTY, Decision on Motion for Sanctions for Failure to Bring the Accused to Trial Without Undue Delay, *Prosecutor v. Perišić*, Case No. IT-04-81-PT, T. Ch. III, 23 November 2007, in this volume, p. 211.

73 For an evaluation of the pace of such trials, see generally J. Galbraith, The Pace of International Criminal Justice, 31 Michigan Journal of International Law 2009, p. 79.

74 J. Rabkin, Global Criminal Justice: An Idea Whose Time Has Passed, 38 Cornell International Law Journal 2005, p. 768.

75 See, for a harsh critique, R. Zacklin, The Failings of Ad Hoc International Tribunals, 2 Journal of International Criminal Justice 2004, p. 543 and 545.

76 ICTY, Motion for Sanctions for Failure to Bring the Accused to Trial Without Undue Delay, *Prosecutor v. Perišić*, Case No. IT-04-81-PT, T. Ch. III, 9 August 2007, par. 10.

77 *Ibid.*, par. 12.

to their grave nature. Thus, the interest of prevention and prosecution of these crimes outweighs the interest of an individual not to be kept too long in uncertainty and anxiety of a possible criminal prosecution.[78]

The defence, moreover, argued that the prosecution had been aware of the factual underpinnings of the indictment for at least for a decade and the delay in the start of the trial was due to delays in disclosure and the tribunal's "docket – overload".[79] According to the defence, "the combined effect" of the delays caused by the prosecution (pre-indictment delay), the chamber (post-indictment delay) and the registrar (funding delay) on the right of the accused to a fair trial must be assessed.[80]

Regarding the prejudice caused by the delay to the accused, the defence argued that numerous witnesses had died without providing exculpatory evidence in this case.[81] In addition, the defence was disadvantaged as compared to prosecution, in obtaining evidence 13–15 years after the events underlying the indictment. Memory and documents had been lost or destroyed.[82] Referring to the defence motion on the appointment of *amicus curiae* to investigate equality of arms (discussed above), the defence felt that the lack of funds to adequately defend the accused caused the delay. Additionally, the prejudice arising from "an inequity with respect to the presentation of the case" is apparent.[83] According to the defence, the prosecution "seeks to benefit by the various delays through the use of procedural mechanisms allowing them to reduce required proof and the opportunity for the defence to confront such evidence".[84] As an example, the defence advanced the prosecution's admission at a status conference, that a delay of the trial in this case until after the appeals decision in the Galić case would be beneficial for the prosecutorial presentation of evidence.[85]

All these factors lead the defence to conclude that the chambers should exercise its supervisory power to issue sanctions in this case to ensure a fair trial. The defence advanced several specific remedial sanctions: exclusion of prior statements of witnesses who the defence is not in a position to question (due to their death), of transcripts and minutes the defence has no access to, and of Rule 92 statements. Moreover, the chamber should be mindful of the delay and the prejudice the defence has suffered through the loss of exculpatory material in its assessment of the evidence. Last but not least, the defence advanced that, where the loss of evidence cannot be adequately addressed through traditional remedial sanctions, the chamber must determine whether a fair trial is still possible under the doctrine of abuse of process.

4.2 Relevant factors for evaluation

In its analysis, the Trial Chamber draws a parallel to the ICTR case in Mugiraneza, where the Appeals Chamber had the chance to provide five factors relevant to the determination of a violation of the right to be tried without undue delay.[86] The five factors include: (1) the length of the delay; (2) the complexity of the case; (3) the conduct of the parties; (4) the conduct of relevant authorities; and (5) the prejudice to the accused. Both the defence and the prosecution structured their arguments according to these five factors.

In addition, the Trial Chamber takes guidance from the ECtHR case of *W. v. Switzerland*.[87] These factors correspond for the most part to the relevant factors found in the case law of the ECtHR. There, the court

78 Convention on the Non-Applicability of Statutory Limitations to War Crimes and Crimes Against Humanity, U.N. Doc. A/7218 (1968), entered into force 11 November 1970. Also, Article 29 ICC Statute: "The crimes within the jurisdiction of the Court shall not be subject to any statute of limitations".

79 Motion for Sanctions for Failure to Bring the Accused to Trial Without Undue Delay, *Prosecutor v. Perišić,* T. Ch. III, *supra* note 76, par. 19.

80 *Ibid.*, par. 22.

81 *Ibid.,* par. 24.

82 *Ibid.*, par. 25.

83 *Ibid.,* par. 27.

84 *Ibid.*

85 *Ibid.*

86 ICTR, *Prosecutor v. Mugiraneze,* Decision on Prosper Mugiraneza's Interlocutory Appeal from Trial Chamber II Decision of 2 October 2003 Denying the Motion to Dismiss the Indictment, Demand Speedy Trial and for Appropriate Relief, Case No. ICTR-99-50-AR73, A. Ch., 27 February 2004.

87 Decision on Motion for Sanctions for Failure to Bring the Accused to Trial Without Undue Delay, *Prosecutor v. Perišić,* T. Ch. III, *supra* note 72, par. 16.

looks at the conduct of the applicant, the complexity of the case, the importance of what is at stake for the applicant, and the conduct of the authorities.[88] The ECtHR's examination appears to proceed according to a *prima facie* indication as to whether the proceedings appear to be excessively long;[89] the length of the delay factor considered by the tribunals. Substantive differences lie, however, in the fact that the tribunals look at the prejudice to the accused, while this factor is missing from the list of the ECtHR. On the other hand, the ECtHR addresses the issue of the importance of what is at stake for the applicant. In considering this factor, the court takes into account, for example, the fact of detention on remand, or the ill health of the applicant, both aggravating factors upon the obligation of the state to avoid any delay.[90]

International criminal tribunals do not address the "reasonable time" standard in the case of deprivation of liberty,[91] or more generally as part of the "fair trial" principle, and do not emphasize the fact that the accused is detained.[92] Considering prejudice to the accused in the context of international criminal proceedings, as a factor, seems rather unwarranted, as any substantial delay would seem prejudicial to the accused.

In the context of international human rights case law, a state can avoid liability in a case where the delay is compensated, for example through an express and adequate reduction of sentence.[93] Considering this, the "prejudice to the accused factor" could play a role in this context: although the accused has suffered unjustifiable delay in his case, he is duly compensated for that and thus no prejudice to his rights arises.

However, the tribunals' use of this factor is independent and mostly perfunctory.[94] As stated below, it would seem rather difficult for the defence to substantiate any prejudice suffered from loss of evidence, for example, that is caused by the delay in pre-trial process. Perhaps the reasoning should be that, in a case where the delay is not *prima facie* excessive or "undue" considering the other factors, the delay would still be "undue" if it has caused some prejudice to the defence.

4.3 The clock starts running...

Crucial to the determination of undue delay is the start of the relevant period. The Trial Chamber rejected the submission of the defence as to the relevance of the pre-indictment period, and determined that the date of the arrest or surrender indicates the "start" of the obligation to proceed expeditiously and without undue delay. It would be unreasonable to hold the prosecution accountable from any other date, according to the chamber.[95] This brings the length of the relevant period to 2 years and 7 months.

In coming to this conclusion, the chamber referred to the above mentioned case of *W. v. Switzerland.* However, the chamber neglected to pay attention to the fact that that ECtHR case deals with an unreasonably long pre-trial detention and revolves around Article 5, paragraph 3, ECHR. This article lays down a clear beginning of the reasonable time period: the date of the arrest. For the purposes of Article 6, paragraph 1 - fair trial - the ECtHR applies an autonomous interpretation of "criminal charge", and the reasonable time period starts running when the situation of the suspect is substantially affected.[96] In this regard, the ECtHR has held that

---

88 S. Trechsel, Human Rights in Criminal Proceedings, *supra* note 59, p. 142.

89 *Ibid.* When the period is excessively long, it "falls to the respondent State to come forward with explanations": see, for example, ECtHR, Judgment, *Eckle v. Germany,* Application No. 8130/78, 15 July 1982, par. 80.

90 S. Trechsel, Human Rights in Criminal Proceedings, p. 144. Perišić was provisionally released: see ICTY, Decision on Momčilo Perišić's Motion for Provisional Release, *Prosecutor v. Perišić,* Case No. IT-04-81-PT, T. Ch. III, 9 June 2005.

91 Article 5 ECHR, Article 9 ICCPR.

92 Article 6 ECHR, Article 14 ICCPR.

93 *Ibid.,* p. 148.

94 See, for example, ICTR, Decision on Prosper Mugiraneza's Application for a Hearing or Other Relief on his Motion for Dismissal for Violation of his Right to a Trial Without Undue Delay, *Prosecutor v. Bizimungu, Mugenzi, Bicamumpaka and* Mugiraneza, Case No. ICTR-99-50-T, T. Ch. II, 3 November 2004, Klip/ Sluiter, ALC-XVIII-71; ICTR, Decision on Prosper Mugiraneza's Second Motion to Dismiss for Deprivation of his Right to Trial Without Undue Delay, *Prosecutor v. Bizimungu, Mugenzi, Bicamumpaka and Mugiraneza,* Case No. ICTR-99-50-T, T. Ch. II, 29 May 2007, Klip/ Sluiter, ALC-XXV-419.

95 Decision on Motion for Sanctions for Failure to Bring the Accused to Trial Without Undue Delay, *Prosecutor v. Perišić,* T. Ch. III, *supra* note 72, par. 21.

96 For a recent case of European Court of Human Rights, see ECtHR, *McFarlane v. Ireland,* Application No. 31333/06, 10 September 2010, par. 143: "The Court reiterates that in criminal matters, the "reasonable time" referred to in Article 6 § 1 begins to run as soon as a person is "charged". "Charge, for the purposes of Article 6 § 1, may be defined as "the official notification

the preliminary investigation stage as such cannot be included in the period of criminal proceedings where there have been no measures taken against the suspect, as there existed a possibility that the investigation would come to an end without any steps taken that would affect the position of the suspect.[97]

In Perišić, the date of the confirmation of the indictment and the surrender of the accused coincide. In the context of international criminal tribunals, the indictment as the "official notification" usually precedes the arrest or surrender of the accused. Arguably, the dependence of international criminal tribunals on state cooperation for apprehension of the accused persons as a factor cannot be neglected, when considering the starting point for the assessment of undue delay period. This, however, does not negate the period prior to the transfer of the accused to the tribunal, or make the tribunals' responsibility during that period non-existent. A case-by-case approach is warranted, and the Trial Chamber's agreement with the reasoning in *W. v. Switzerland* as to the start of the relevant period cannot serve as a given in all cases.

5. The loss of exculpatory evidence

Notably, the prosecution advances arguments as explanations for the delay in the pre-indictment proceedings, namely the lack of state cooperation and the protection of the rights of the accused. The prosecution sought corroborating evidence to support the allegations before presenting an indictment; however, the national authorities of the Republic of Serbia had been less than cooperative in production of this evidence. In fact, in the evaluation of the conduct of relevant authorities, the ECtHR has noted that there rests a particular obligation of expedition on the state in a case when criminal proceedings began a considerable time after the alleged criminal events occurred, because the lapse of time can do considerable damage to the evidence in case.[98]

In Perišić, the defence made an attempt to substantiate the submission that (potentially) exculpatory evidence had been lost due to the lapse of time (witnesses dying), something that seems rather difficult to do in the first place, let alone to support the allegation that this loss has prejudiced the accused. Right at the end, in a rather concise deliberation, the chamber agreed with the prosecution and considered that the defence was not persuasive in demonstrating that any exculpatory evidence was "irreparably" lost due to the delay, notwithstanding the fact that the chamber "acknowledges the difficulties encountered by the Defence".[99] It seems that this factor was not deemed relevant enough, considering that all other factors did not contribute to a violation of the right to be brought to trial without undue delay.

6. Evaluation of relevant factors

Not contested is the fact that the case can be characterized as involving the highest level of complexity before the international tribunal.[100] Moreover, nothing in the conduct of the parties amounts to less than due diligence. In fact, in the case law of ECtHR, the most decisive factor for the evaluation of undue delay is the conduct of the relevant authorities.[101] Of course, it would be difficult to attribute delay directly to the prosecution; however, it cannot be denied that the prosecutorial conduct can advance delay in the proceedings, by submitting complex indictments, rushed through due to the completion strategy of the tribunal,[102] in a system that cannot proceed more expeditiously.

---

given to an individual by the competent authority of an allegation that he has committed a criminal offence", a definition that also corresponds to the test whether "the situation of the [suspect] has been substantially affected".

97 ECtHR, *Massey v. the United Kingdom,* Application No. 14399/02, 16 November 2004, par. 25. However, in the recent case of ECtHR, *McFarlane v. Ireland, supra* note 96, par. 144, the ECtHR has indicated that "police and prosecution activity prior to that date [arrest] could, in principle, have some relevance to the fairness aspect of Article 6 § 1." However, what the 'relevance' was isnot elaborated, as the charges were dismissed in this case and, as such, no violation of Article 6 could have occurred.

98 For example, *ibid.,* par. 27.

99 Decision on Motion for Sanctions for Failure to Bring the Accused to Trial Without Undue Delay, *Prosecutor v. Perišić,* T. Ch. III, *supra* note 72, par. 28.

100 *Ibid.,* par. 22.

101 *Ibid.,* p. 142 and 141.

102 The defence references to the completion strategy in the first paragraph of its motion as part of "procedural history", emphasizing the fact that the indictment in this case was issued two months after the completion strategy's limitation on the termination of investigations. Neither the prosecution nor the chamber touch upon this remark.

The Trial Chamber itself, through regular status conferences, has ensured that the case moved towards trial in an expeditious manner.[103] Here again, the chamber referred to the ECtHR case of *W v. Switzerland,* where the court considered that there has been regular reviewing of the accused' detention. The Trial Chamber drew a parallel, and reasoned that active involvement of the Pre-Trial Judge through status conferences ensures expeditiousness of the proceedings.

In regard to the inadequacy of funding alleged by the defence as harm suffered through the delay, the Chamber noted that "[w]here the harm which is alleged is not capable of remedy by the prosecution, such as in the case of a complaint of inadequate funding, the sanction requested against the prosecution is not well-founded".[104] The defence argued that the prosecution continues to prepare for trial at a constant level of funding, while the defence has exhausted its resources for the trial preparation. A longer pre-trial period enlarges the gap between the resources, which is prejudicial to the defence.[105] Without any further substantiation of its argument, the defence referred to its equality of arms motion, discussed above. Of course, the fact the pre-trial process was longer than approximated in relation to pre-trial defence funding, does not automatically lead to a prejudice to the accused in relation to the violation of his right to be tried without undue delay. The chamber did not give too much attention to this argument either, and reasoned that it had already dealt with the issue of inequality of arms in the Perišić equality of arms decision, and any other grievances of the defence in regard to the funding should be taken up with the registrar.

Masha Fedorova

---

103 Decision on Motion for Sanctions for Failure to Bring the Accused to Trial Without Undue Delay, *Prosecutor v. Perišić, T. Ch.* III, supra note 72, par. 23–25.

104 *Ibid.*, par. 26.

105 Motion for Sanctions for Failure to Bring the Accused to Trial Without Undue Delay, *Prosecutor v. Perišić*, T. Ch. III, *supra* note 76, par. 26.

UNITED NATIONS

International Tribunal for the Prosecution of Persons Responsible for Serious Violations of International Humanitarian Law Committed in the Territory of Former Yugoslavia since 1991	**Case No.**	**IT-04-84-T**
	Date:	**23 May 2007**
	Original:	**English**

IN TRIAL CHAMBER I

Before: **Judge Alphons Orie, Presiding**
Judge Frank Höpfel
Judge Ole Bjørn Støle

Registrar: **Mr Hans Holthuis**

Decision of: **23 May 2007**

PROSECUTOR

v.

RAMUSH HARADINAJ
IDRIZ BALAJ
LAHI BRAHIMAJ

PUBLIC

DECISION ON DEFENCE REQUEST FOR AUDIO-RECORDING OF PROSECUTION WITNESS PROOFING SESSIONS

Office of the Prosecutor
Mr David Re
Mr Gramsci di Fazio
Mr Gilles Dutertre
Mr Philip Kearney

Counsel for Ramush Haradinaj
Mr Ben Emmerson, QC
Mr Rodney Dixon

Counsel for Idriz Balaj
Mr Gregor Guy-Smith
Ms Colleen Rohan

Counsel for Lahi Brahimaj
Mr Richard Harvey
Mr Paul Troop

[page 2] 1. The Chamber is seised of a request by the Defence seeking an order to the Prosecution to audio-record the proofing sessions with its witnesses.[1]

2. On 8 March 2007, Witness 38 testified before this Chamber that she was mistreated at a certain location, before a vehicle, allegedly carrying one of the Accused, arrived at that location.[2] However, the proofing notes produced by the Prosecution record the witness as saying that there had been no mistreatment prior to the arrival of the vehicle.[3] Witness 38 responded to the Chamber's question as to what she had said to Prosecution counsel during the proofing session as follows:

> I really don't know. I honestly can't remember. I told him [Prosecution counsel] how we were mistreated. But when I told my story, it wasn't in chronology. I skipped from one thing to another.[4]

The following exchange between Defence Counsel for Mr Haradinaj and Witness 38 ensued:

> Q. Witness 38, did you or did you not tell Mr Di Fazio on Tuesday that the jeep – by the time the jeep arrived, you had already been stripped naked and assaulted? Did you tell him that or not.
>
> A. I think I did, yes.[5]

According to the Defence, another such instance of discrepancy between in-court testimony and proofing notes occurred on 13 March 2007, when Witness Radošević testified in court that a certain person was "only a distant relative",[6] whereas the proofing notes record this witness as stating that the person in question was his "cousin".[7] In a third instance, which concerned Witness 60, there was a discrepancy between the witness's in-court testimony, on the one hand, and the contents of a Prosecution letter addressed to the Defence and containing notes of a communication between Witness 60 and the Prosecution, on the other.[8]

3. As a way of preventing similar problems in the future, the Defence proposed that the Prosecution should audio-record the proofing sessions with its witnesses. On 15 March 2007, **[page 3]** the Chamber ordered the Prosecution, as a provisional measure, to audio-record proofing sessions until a final decision on the matter.[9] The Chamber then invited the parties to make written submissions on the issue in order to assist the Chamber to make its ruling.[10]

I. Submissions received

4. On 22 March 2007, the Prosecution filed the "Prosecution's Written Submissions Opposing Verbatim Recording of 'Proofing' Sessions with Witnesses" ("Prosecution Submission").[11] Also on 22 March, counsel for all three Accused filed the "Defence Submissions on the Procedure for the Proofing of Prosecution Witnesses". On 23 March 2007, the Prosecution filed a "Corrigendum to Prosecution's Written Submissions Opposing Verbatim Recording of 'Proofing' Sessions with Witnesses" and a "Book of Authorities for the Prosecution's Written Submissions Opposing Verbatim Recording of 'Proofing' Sessions with Witnesses".[12]

---

1 Defence Submissions on the Procedure for the Proofing of Prosecution Witnesses, 22 March 2007 ("Defence Submission"), para. 31. Already on 19 January 2007, Counsel for Mr Balaj had sent a letter to the Prosecution suggesting that it audio-record its proofing sessions. Further letters regarding this issue were sent to the Prosecution by Mr Balaj's Counsel on 6 February 2007 and 12 March 2007. The Chamber did not consider these letters when deciding the current issue.

2 T. 730–732.

3 Exh. D2 (Proofing notes of Witness 38), p. 5.

4 T. 789.

5 T. 792.

6 T. 1035.

7 Defence Submission, para. 6.

8 T. 2292–2293, 2259–2265 and 3872–3873.

9 T. 1260 and 1398.

10 T. 1302.

11 This was supplemented on 30 March 2007 with the "Prosecution Submission of Further Authority in Relation to 'Prosecution's Written Submissions Opposing Verbatim Recording of 'Proofing' Sessions with Witnesses'".

12 In supplementation of the last-mentioned filing, on 26 March 2007, the Prosecution filed the "Prosecution's Notice of Unofficial English Translations of the Authorities Cited in the Prosecution's Written Submissions Opposing Verbatim Recording of 'Proofing' Sessions with Witnesses".

5. On 23 March 2007, the Chamber requested the parties to file further written submissions[13] and to address therein whether an order to audio-record proofing sessions should bind both parties.[14] Furthermore, the Chamber requested the Prosecution to file the Prosecution's staff guidelines for proofing sessions.[15] On 28 March 2007, the Prosecution filed the "Prosecution's Written Submissions in Response Opposing Verbatim Recording of 'Proofing' Sessions with Witnesses" ("Prosecution Response"). Also on 28 March, the Defence for Mr Haradinaj filed the "Response of the Defence for Ramush Haradinaj to Prosecution Submissions on the Procedure for the Proofing of Prosecution Witnesses" ("Haradinaj Response"),[16] and the Defence for Mr Balaj filed the "Response by the Defence for Idriz Balaj to Prosecution's Written Submission Opposing Verbatim Recording of 'Proofing' Sessions with Witnesses" ("Balaj Response"). The Defence for Mr Brahimaj filed **[page 4]** its "Defence Response to Prosecution Submissions on the Procedure for the Proofing of Prosecution Witnesses", belatedly, on 16 April 2007.

6. On 30 March 2007, the Prosecution filed the "Prosecution Reply to 'Response for Ramush Haradinaj to Prosecution Submissions on the Procedure for the Proofing of Prosecution Witnesses'".

7. On 14 May 2007, the Prosecution filed the "Prosecution's Reference to Supplementary Authority in Relation to 'Prosecution's Written Submissions Opposing Verbatim Recording of 'Proofing' Sessions with Witnesses'". On 15 May 2007, the Defence for Mr Haradinaj filed a partly confidential "Submission of Additional Information in Regards to 'Prosecution's Written Submissions Opposing Verbatim Recording of 'Proofing' Sessions with Witnesses' with Confidential Annex". Counsel for Mr Balaj and Mr Brahimaj joined this filing.[17] On 16 May 2007, Counsel for Mr Balaj filed "Idriz Balaj's Response to the Prosecution's Supplementary Authority Regarding Verbatim Recording of 'Proofing' Sessions with Prosecution Witnesses". On 18 May 2007, the Prosecution filed the "Prosecution Submission Concerning *Karemera* Appeals Chamber Decision re Witness Proofing Interviews". On 21 May 2007, the Defence for Mr Brahimaj filed "Lahi Brahimaj's Response to the Prosecution's Supplementary Authority Regarding Verbatim Recording of Proofing Sessions with Prosecution Witnesses". On 23 May 2007, Counsel for Mr Haradinaj filed an "Additional Submission on behalf of Ramush Haradinaj in Respect of a Further Authority on 'Witness Proofing' filed by the Prosecution".

II. Proofing defined

8. Despite the fact that the practice of proofing witnesses, by both the Prosecution and the Defence, has been in place since the inception of the Tribunal,[18] there is no set definition of proofing at the Tribunal. The ICTR Appeals Chamber has found that the definition of acceptable witness proofing adopted by the Trial Chamber in the *Karemera et al.* case "is consistent with the approach sanctioned by the Appeals Chamber in the *Gacumbitsi* Appeal **[page 5]** Judgment".[19] The Prosecution in a case before this Tribunal offered another definition of proofing.[20] In the view of this Chamber, the term "proofing" refers to a meeting held between a

13 T. 1823–1824.

14 T. 1841.

15 T. 1825.

16 On 29 March 2007, the Defence for Mr Haradinaj supplemented this filing with a "Book of Authorities for Defence Submissions on the Procedure for the Proofing of Prosecution Witnesses".

17 See Notice by the Defence for Idriz Balaj of Joinder, filed on 16 May 2007, and Notice by the Defence for Lahi Brahimaj of Joinder, filed on 17 May 2007.

18 See also *Prosecutor v. Limaj et al.*, Decision on Defence Motion on Prosecution Practice of 'Proofing' Witnesses, 10 December 2004 ("*Limaj* Decision"), p. 2.

19 *Prosecutor v. Karemera et al*, Decision on Interlocutory Appeal Regarding Witness Proofing, 11 May 2007, paras 4 and 9. The definition adopted by the Trial Chamber in that case is as follows: "Provided that it does not amount to the manipulation of a witness'[s] evidence, this practice may encompass preparing and familiarizing a witness with the proceedings before the Tribunal, comparing prior statements made by a witness, detecting differences and inconsistencies in recollection of the witness, allowing a witness to refresh his or her memory in respect of the evidence he or she will give, and inquiring and disclosing to the Defence additional information and/or evidence of incriminatory or exculpatory nature in sufficient time prior to the witness'[s] testimony", *Prosecutor v. Karemera et al.*, Decision on Defence Motions to Prohibit Witness Proofing, 15 December 2006, para. 15.

20 See the Prosecution's filing in the *Milutinović et al.* case, referred to in fn. 25 of the Prosecution Submission: "The Prosecution understand witness proofing to be meetings or other contacts with witnesses prior to their testimony. Witness proofing includes informing the witness about the purpose of the trial and its procedure. This would include the role of the judges, prosecution, defence and the accused, the purpose and method of examination in chief, cross-examination and re-examination amongst other similar matters; informing the witness on the areas likely to be asked in examination, cross-examination and re-examination as well as the form in which questions are likely [to] be asked and expected to be answered; informing the witness of appropriate

party to the proceedings and a witness, usually shortly before the witness is to testify in court, the purpose of which is to prepare and familiarize the witness with courtroom procedures and to review the witness's evidence.[21] The Trial Chamber in the *Limaj et al.* case found that witness proofing assists in (i) providing a detailed review of relevant and irrelevant facts in light of the precise charges to be tried; (ii) aiding the process of human recollection; (iii) enabling the more accurate, complete, orderly and efficient presentation of the evidence of a witness in the trial; and (iv) identifying and putting the Defence on notice of differences in recollection, thereby preventing undue surprise.[22] This finding was endorsed by the *Milutinović et al.* Trial Chamber.[23]

9. In the *Limaj et al.*, *Milutinović et al.*, and *Karemera et al.* cases, the Trial Chambers were faced with a challenge to the practice of proofing itself, as the Defence in those cases sought an order disallowing proofing entirely.[24] This Chamber is not seised of such a challenge, as counsel for the Accused in this case do not object to the practice of proofing.[25] **[page 6]** The issue before this Chamber is whether proofing sessions between counsel and witnesses should be audio-recorded.

III. Arguments for and against audio-recording of proofing sessions

10. Several arguments for and against the audio-recording of proofing sessions were advanced by the parties:

(1) The Prosecution submits that the issuance of an order to audio-record proofing sessions "would amount to an improper exercise of the Trial Chamber's discretion".[26] The Prosecution submits further that such an order would "encroach upon powers that the Statute expressly delegates to the Prosecutor", namely the responsibility to investigate and to prosecute.[27] The Prosecution argues that its "broad inherent power to determine the manner in which it should conduct its case … must extend to witness preparation".[28] Balaj's Defence responds that "*none* of the cases cited by the Prosecution stand for the proposition that a trial court in a common law jurisdiction has no power … to order that witness interviews be tape recorded".[29]

(2) The Prosecution submits that the order sought by the Defence "would also be contrary to the Tribunal's Rules and practice".[30] It adds that "by way of contrast the Rules require that questioning of suspects or accused persons be audio or video taped".[31] Balaj's Defence responds that the Tribunal's Rules of Procedure and Evidence ("Rules") are silent on proofing in general, and yet proofing is accepted practice at the Tribunal.[32] In its Response, the Prosecution states that an earlier version of Rule 66 of the Rules required the Prosecution to disclose to the Defence an audio-recorded statement of an "accused or witness", and that the fact that this provision was deleted after eleven months, supports the Prosecution's position in this case.[33] The Prosecution refers to

---

and effective witness behaviour. Witness proofing can also include showing the witness their prior statements for the purpose of refreshing their memory; showing the witness exhibits likely to be used during the witness's testimony or any other relevant material; questioning the witness on areas relevant to their testimony which should include questions on inconsistencies between prior statements and information provided in witness proofing. Witness proofing is not used for 'coaching' the witness. In particular, witness proofing cannot include informing the witness about the specific substance of an answer they are expected to give during testimony", *Prosecutor v. Milutinović et al.*, Prosecution Response to General Ojdanić's Motion to Prohibit Witness Proofing, 29 November 2006, fn. 2.

21 *Prosecutor v. Milutinović et al.*, Decision on Ojdanić Motion to Prohibit Witness Proofing, 12 December 2006 ("*Milutinović* Decision"), paras 10, 16 and 20.

22 *Limaj* Decision, p. 2.

23 *Milutinović* Decision, para. 20.

24 This was also an issue recently at the International Criminal Court (see *Prosecutor v. Dyilo*, Decision on the Practices of Witness Familiarisation and Witness Proofing, 8 November 2006 ("*Dyilo* Decision")).

25 See Defence Submission, para. 2; see also Balaj Response, para. 4. See further T. 1303–1304.

26 Prosecution Submission, paras 5, 14–19.

27 *Ibid.*, para. 20.

28 *Ibid.*, para. 21.

29 Balaj Response, paras 26 and 31.

30 Prosecution Submission, paras 5, 20–21.

31 *Ibid.*, para. 15.

32 The Balaj Defence adds that "the fact that a practice is not specifically 'authorized' under the rules does not mean that it is therefore specifically prohibited under the rules", Balaj Response, para. 9.

33 Prosecution Response, paras 29–31.

Rules 89(D) and 95 of the **[page 7]** Rules as the appropriate mechanisms to "deal with any issues surrounding the circumstances of obtaining evidence such as to warrant exclusion of evidence".[34]

(3) The Prosecution argues that an order to audio-record proofing sessions would "go against the trend of domestic practice and be counter to evidence regarding the current state of customary international law".[35] The Prosecution submits that its "survey of the practices of 25 countries" reveals that the requested order "would be inconsistent with the practice of the most relevant domestic jurisdictions".[36] The Prosecution proceeds to make an extensive submission, based on the negotiating history establishing the Rules of Procedure and Evidence of the International Criminal Court ("ICC Rules"), that an order to audio-record proofing sessions would be in contradiction with customary international law.[37] The Prosecution relies on Rules 111 and 112 of the ICC Rules, which require the audio- or video-recording of interviews with suspects or accused before the ICC, but not of other persons interviewed in the course of an investigation.[38] Haradinaj's Defence responds that the *Dyilo* Decision shows that the ICC state parties did not contemplate witness proofing at all.[39] It further responds that it is not sufficient to assert that there is no customary international rule which requires proofing, but that "the Prosecution would need to be able to show that there is a rule of Customary International Law which *forbids*" audio-recording of proofing sessions.[40] Haradinaj's Defence also notes that only eight out of the twenty-five countries surveyed by the Prosecution allow for witness proofing, and that therefore "there is no consensus on whether witnesses can be proofed at all, let alone whether proofing sessions should be taped".[41] Balaj's Defence adds that the cases cited by the Prosecution which arise from civil-law jurisdictions "provide little to no guidance on the subject at issue in this case".[42]

(4) The Prosecution submits that an order to audio-record proofing sessions would "not serve the aims and objectives of proofing and could potentially cause delays in the conduct of this trial".[43] The Defence argues that following the Trial Chamber's provisional order to audio-record the proofing sessions, "the Prosecution has not identified any concrete **[page 8]** problems with the implementation" of that order.[44] The Defence also argues that audio-recording of proofing sessions will "enhance the effective fulfilment" of the objectives of proofing as set out by the *Limaj* Trial Chamber.[45] Haradinaj's Defence states that there are "three critical distinctions between statements taken in the investigation stage, and proofing sessions", namely that (i) proofing is immediately related to trial proceedings; (ii) the principle of equality of arms requires both parties to know what the witness has said during proofing; and (iii) in relation to statements taken during the investigation phase, investigators can be called to give evidence whereas trial counsel cannot in relation to what was said during proofing "without being placed in a situation of potential professional embarrassment".[46] The Defence submits that audio-recording of proofing sessions will protect the Prosecution from allegations of "coaching or rehearsing witnesses", and that it "will provide the parties and the Trial Chamber with an accurate record of the discussions that have taken place with witnesses".[47] The recordings would in turn "permit evaluation and resolution of any differences that arise between a witness'[s] evidence in court and the record of what the witness stated during a proofing session with the Prosecution" and will avoid "unnecessary litigation about witness proofing".[48]

---

34 Prosecution Submission, paras 5, 75–76.
35 *Ibid.*, para. 5.
36 *Ibid.*, para. 44.
37 *Ibid.*, paras 53–74.
38 *Ibid.*, paras 54–59.
39 Haradinaj Response, para. 8.
40 *Ibid.*, para. 9 (emphasis in the original).
41 *Ibid.*, para. 16.
42 Balaj Response, para. 27.
43 Prosecution Submission, para. 5.
44 Defence Submission, para. 29.
45 Defence Submission, para. 16; see *supra* para. 8.
46 Haradinaj Response, para. 11.
47 Defence Submission, para. 21.
48 *Ibid.*, paras 22–23.

(5) The Prosecution submits that "audio, video or digital recording would discourage witnesses from openly sharing and discussing their anxieties and fears about testifying",[49] and that such recording "could discourage witnesses from freely speaking about any inconsistencies in their prior statements" or a refusal by the witness to have the proofing session audio-recorded or even to "a refusal to appear at the Tribunal".[50] Relying on unspecified provisions of the European Convention on Human Rights ("ECHR") and the International Covenant on Civil and Political Rights, the Prosecution adds that the privacy rights of a witness should also be considered.[51] The Haradinaj Defence responds that Article 8 of the ECHR does not apply to the issue at hand and that audio-recording would promote the right to a fair hearing protected by Article 6 of the ECHR.[52] The Balaj Defence also submits that "there is no reason to conclude ... that witnesses willing to **[page 9]** testify at trial, under oath, where their statements will be audio taped, video taped, stenographically transcribed and broadcast to the world on the internet, will be unduly uncomfortable if asked to speak, with a tape recorder running in the background".[53] The Prosecution also asserts that the procedure of audio-recording would be "inefficient and costly".[54] The Balaj Defence responds that "simply listening to the tape or the relevant portion of it" will be sufficient to resolve any future dispute between testimony and proofing notes and that in most cases there would be no need for the Chamber to listen to the recordings or to transcribe the recordings.[55]

(6) The Prosecution has offered to "provide the defence with supplementary statements signed by witnesses. These would set out any new, additional or different evidence gleaned from such witnesses during proofing. They would be translated into the language of the witness wherever practicable".[56] With such a mechanism in place the Defence would, according to the Prosecution, have the possibility to cross-examine witnesses on any new, additional or different evidence, request additional information from the Prosecution about witness preparation and seek time for additional investigations.[57] The Defence does not object to the proposal of supplementary statements, but nevertheless insists that audio-recordings be made.[58] The Defence proposes a detailed procedure for the proofing of Prosecution witnesses which would not require the automatic disclosure of audio-recordings by the Prosecution to the Defence.[59] Balaj's Defence submits that cross-examination of the witness or a request for additional information from the Prosecution is not a sufficient remedy, as demonstrated in the case of Witnesses 38 and Radošević.[60] In relation to Witness Radošević, the Prosecution submits that there was a simple mistake in the translation of a particular Serbian word, which can mean both "cousin" and "relative" in English.[61]

IV. Discussion [page 10]

(a) Does the Chamber have the discretion to order the Prosecution to audio-record proofing sessions?

11. The Prosecution did not refer to any provision in the Tribunal's Rules or Statute that would prevent a Trial Chamber order to the Prosecution to audio-record proofing sessions. The Chamber does not agree

49 Prosecution Submission, para. 28.
50 *Ibid.*, paras 29–30.
51 *Ibid.*, para. 31.
52 Haradinaj Response, paras 20–22.
53 Balaj Response, para. 23.
54 Prosecution Submission, para. 32.
55 Balaj Response, para. 16.
56 Prosecution Submission, para. 2; see also para. 37. See further Prosecution Response, paras 24–26.
57 Prosecution Submission, para. 38.
58 Defence Submission, para. 3(v).
59 *Ibid.*, paras 2–3. In para. 3(ii), the Defence suggests that it "should have the right to request the recordings or portions thereof should any matter arise which necessitates a review of the recordings" and that "any disagreement over the disclosure of the recordings ... should be referred to the Trial Chamber to resolve it". See also Balaj Response, paras 6 and 34.
60 Balaj Response, para. 22.
61 Prosecution Response, paras 19–22.

with the Prosecution's interpretation of the amendment to Rule 66 of the Rules, as the amendment does not specifically address witness proofing, but is rather related to the investigation phase of the Prosecution's case.

12. The Prosecution contends that an order to audio-record proofing sessions would "encroach" upon its investigative powers vested in the Statute. However, by the time a trial has commenced, the Prosecution's investigations should be largely complete, save for the investigative work prompted by new information which was unavailable at an earlier stage. Moreover, the purpose of proofing is not investigation, but the preparation and familiarization of the witness with courtroom procedures and the review of the witness's evidence, these being matters closely related to the trial proceedings and their streamlining.[62] It should be noted that the Defence is not seeking an order to extend audio-recording to the interviewing of witnesses during the investigation phase.[63] The Chamber considers that the requested order is limited to witness proofing and would not have any effect on the taking of witness statements during an investigation. The Prosecution has failed to show how such an order would infringe upon its statutory role to investigate and prosecute crimes under the Tribunal's jurisdiction.

13. The Trial Chambers in the *Milutinović et al.* and *Limaj et al.* cases, on which the parties rely in their submissions, have considered whether proofing itself should be allowed before the Tribunal. The Chamber considers that if a Trial Chamber possesses the discretion to consider that question, it surely must also have the authority to determine how the proofing of witnesses may be conducted in the interests of justice and with respect to the fairness of the trial.

14. Article 20 of the Statute provides that it is the duty of Trial Chambers to ensure that a trial is fair and expeditious. The Chamber recalls Rule 54 of the Rules, which provides: **[page 11]**

> At the request of either party or *proprio motu*, a Judge or a Trial Chamber may issue such orders, summonses, subpoenas, warrants and transfer orders as may be necessary for the purposes of an investigation or for the preparation or conduct of the trial.

Considering that witness proofing assists in the preparation and conduct of the trial, the Chamber finds that Rule 54, together with the Chamber's duty to ensure a fair and expeditious trial, give it the discretion to issue an order to the Prosecution on the conduct of proofing sessions with witnesses.

(b) Would it be contrary to customary international law to order the Prosecution to audio-record proofing sessions?

15. In order to prove the existence of a rule of customary international law, Article 38(1)(b) of the Statute of the International Court of Justice ("ICJ") requires a general practice accepted as law. In the *Asylum* case, the ICJ found that:

> The party which relies on a custom ... must prove that this custom is established in such a manner that it has become binding on the other party ... that the rule invoked ... is in accordance with a constant and uniform usage, practised by the States in question, and that this usage is the expression of a right appertaining to the State granting asylum and a duty incumbent on the territorial State ...[64]

In the *Continental Shelf* case, the ICJ further stated that in order for state practice to constitute the necessary *opinio juris*, two conditions must be fulfilled:

> Not only must the acts concerned amount to a settled practice, but they must also be such, or be carried out in such a way, as to be evidence of a belief that this practice is rendered obligatory by the existence of a rule of law requiring it. The need for such a belief, i.e., the existence of a subjective element, is implicit in the very notion of the *opinio juris sive necessitatis*. The States concerned must therefore feel that they are conforming to what amounts to a legal obligation. The frequency, or even habitual character of the acts is not in itself enough. There are many international acts, e.g., in the field of ceremonial and protocol, which are performed

---

62 *Milutinović* Decision paras 10, 16, 20, relying on the *Limaj* Decision.
63 Haradinaj Response, para. 28; Balaj Response, para. 13.
64 ICJ Reports (1950), pp. 276–277.

> almost invariably, but which are motivated only by considerations of courtesy, convenience or tradition, and not by sense of legal duty.[65]

16. The Prosecution maintains that a general order to audio-record proofing sessions is "not support[ed]"[66] by a rule of customary international law, or "would go far beyond"[67] the provisions of customary international law, as evidenced by the negotiations behind the ICC **[page 12]** Rules. The Prosecution would need to show that there is a rule against such a procedure to be found in customary international law; and in order to show that, the Prosecution would have to prove that there is settled practice which prohibits the ordering of the audio-recording of witness proofing and that this prohibition amounts to a legal obligation.

17. The Chamber takes into account the fact, acknowledged by the Prosecution,[68] that witness proofing is a common practice only in jurisdictions following an adversarial system of criminal justice, and is not to be found in civil-law jurisdictions.[69] Considering that in a large number of states (including, but not limited to, states within the civil-law tradition) proofing of witnesses does not occur, it is difficult to see how the ICC negotiating process could be interpreted as reflecting a general practice. Furthermore, the Prosecution's own review of the ICC negotiating process does not identify any explicit reference to the audio-recording of witness proofing. In the Chamber's view, the Prosecution has failed to prove the existence of a general practice, and therefore has failed to prove the existence of a rule of customary international law prohibiting the ordering of audio-recording of witness proofing. Therefore, the closely related question, to what extent, if any, a permissive or prohibitive rule of customary international law may, in this respect, affect the development of procedural law at the Tribunal need not be addressed.

(c) Do the circumstances of the present case merit an order to the Prosecution to audio-record proofing sessions?

18. The proofing notes of Witness 38 were not read back to the witness before the commencement of her testimony.[70] It is not contested that there was a discrepancy between what Witness 38 stated in court and what the proofing notes reflect. Had there been an audio-recording of Witness 38's statement during proofing, the Defence would have had the ability to challenge the credibility of the witness on that basis. Thus the Defence may have suffered some disadvantage in relation to the testing of a part of Witness 38's evidence, but the Chamber finds that any possible disadvantage was, in the context of this case, very slight. In **[page 13]** any case, the Chamber will take into account the potential disadvantage when assessing the weight of Witness 38's evidence.

19. In relation to the alleged contradiction between the testimony and the proofing notes of Witness Radošević, the Chamber is satisfied that this instance involved nothing more than a difference in translation during in-court testimony and proofing. The Chamber is satisfied that the word the witness used in his own language is "very general" and does not specify whether the family relationship is close or distant.[71]

20. Concerning the incident in relation to Witness 60, the Prosecution conceded making an "error in transcribing" the notes it had made during the interview with that witness, and therefore the letter sent to the Defence also contained an error.[72] The error was of relatively minor significance as it gave an impression that certain allegations were conveyed to Witness 60 on two occasions in recent years, when in fact that was done

---

65 ICJ Reports (1969), p. 44.

66 Prosecution Submission, para. 70.

67 *Ibid.*, para. 71.

68 *Ibid.*, para. 22.

69 Annex B to the Prosecution Submission, entitled "Countries that permit witness preparation" refers to States with a common-law tradition (Australia, Canada, India, Pakistan, South Africa, Tanzania, England and Wales and United States of America). By contrast, Annex C to the Prosecution Submission, entitled "Countries that do not use proofing" refers to States with a civil-law tradition (Argentina, Austria, Belgium, Cameroon, Chile, Croatia, Denmark, France, Germany, Italy, Netherlands, Norway, Peru, Serbia, Spain, Sweden and Switzerland).

70 T. 788.

71 T. 1058–1059.

72 See Submission of Additional Information in Regards to 'Prosecution's Written Submissions Opposing Verbatim Recording of 'Proofing' Sessions with Witnesses' with Confidential Annex, 15 May 2007, Confidential Annex A, p. 1.

on only one occasion.[73] In this case the Prosecution was able to remedy the error by reviewing its written notes and did not strictly need to review the audio-recording of the witness's proofing.

21. The Chamber will now consider what measures should be taken in order to prevent the reoccurrence of the problem which arose with Witness 38. The Prosecution proposes as a remedy the exclusion of evidence pursuant to Rules 89(D) and 95 of the Rules. While this is a possibility, it is not the most efficient solution, as it assumes litigation of the issue, and does not necessarily serve the interests of justice and the discovery of the truth.

22. Although the Chamber is concerned about the possibility of a similar problem arising in the future, it is not convinced that the audio-recording of Prosecution proofing sessions is the most appropriate way at this stage to avoid such a problem. While the audio-recording of proofing sessions is consistent with, and may indeed facilitate some or all of the above-mentioned purposes of witness proofing, the incident on which the Defence bases its request is not sufficient to justify a general measure which will have considerable implications for the Prosecution and which may be remedied just as well by a more diligent and cautious approach by Prosecution counsel when taking notes during witness proofing. In particular, the Chamber endorses the Prosecution's offer to provide the Defence with a supplementary statement signed by the witness that would set out any new, additional or different evidence gleaned **[page 14]** from the witness during proofing, and which is to be translated into the language of the witness wherever practicable.[74] The Chamber finds that such a practice would ensure that proofing notes are attested to by the witness – something that did not happen in the case of Witness 38 – and, in turn, this would lessen any concern that proofing notes are not a correct record of what the witness said during proofing. Such attestation can be achieved, as a minimum, by having the witness sign the proofing notes in his or her language or by having the witness sign the English version of proofing notes after they are read back to the witness in a language he or she understands.

23. If future circumstances demonstrate that the above remedy is insufficient, the Chamber may reconsider its decision not to order audio-recording of proofing sessions.

24. Finally, the parties made submissions, upon the Chamber's request, on how any order to audio-record Prosecution proofing sessions might apply to Defence witness proofing. The parties also briefly touched upon the issue of whether proofing should be recorded when dealing with witnesses who give evidence pursuant to Rule 70 of the Rules. In light of the foregoing discussion, it is premature to consider these matters at this stage, as the Prosecution is not being ordered to audio-record proofing sessions. **[page 15]**

73 *Ibid.*, p. 2.

74 Prosecution Submission, para. 2; see also para. 37. and Prosecution Response, paras 24–26.

DISPOSITION

For the foregoing reasons:

1. The Defence request is denied;
2. The Chamber's interim order is revoked and the Prosecution is no longer required to audio-record witness proofing sessions;
3. The Prosecution shall preserve the audio-recordings made prior to the filing of this decision;
4. The Prosecution is instructed to produce its proofing notes in accordance with the practice described in paragraph 22.

Done in English and French, the English version being authoritative.

Dated this 23rd day of May 2007
At The Hague
The Netherlands

Judge Alphons Orie
Presiding Judge

[Seal of the Tribunal]

UNITED NATIONS

International Tribunal for the Prosecution of Persons Responsible for Serious Violations of International Humanitarian Law Committed in the Territory of Former Yugoslavia since 1991	**Case No.**	**IT-04-84-T**
	Date:	**31 May 2007**
	Original:	**English**

IN TRIAL CHAMBER I

Before: **Judge Alphons Orie, Presiding**
Judge Frank Höpfel
Judge Ole Bjørn Støle

Registrar: **Mr. Hans Holthuis**

Decision of: **31 May 2007**

PROSECUTOR

v.

RAMUSH HARADINAJ
IDRIZ BALAJ
LAHI BRAHIMAJ

PUBLIC

DECISION ON NOTIFICATION OF CROSS-EXAMINATION MATERIAL

Office of the Prosecutor
Mr David Re
Mr Gramsci di Fazio
Mr Gilles Dutertre
Mr Philip Kearney

Counsel for Ramush Haradinaj
Mr Ben Emmerson, QC
Mr Rodney Dixon
Ms Susan L. Park

Counsel for Idriz Balaj
Mr Gregor Guy-Smith
Ms Colleen Rohan

Counsel for Lahi Brahimaj
Mr Richard Harvey
Mr Paul Troop

[page 2] 1. On 23 March 2007, the Prosecution moved the Chamber to order the Defence to disclose to the Prosecution in advance of the cross-examination of witnesses the documents which the Defence intends to use with each witness in cross-examination.[1] The Prosecution contends that there is an established practice at the Tribunal of providing such documents to the Prosecution in advance.[2] While this is factually correct and is not resisted as such by the Defence, the question remains how far in advance. Here the Prosecution concedes that the practice is not so well established.[3]

2. Different Trial Chambers have set different deadlines: after the witness is sworn in but before examination-in-chief begins;[4] immediately after examination-in-chief ends;[5] at least twenty-four hours before a document is due to be used in cross-examination;[6] before cross-examination begins;[7] and piecemeal disclosure in the course of cross-examination.[8] The **[page 3]** Prosecution asks for the earliest of these deadlines, namely provision of the relevant information just prior to the commencement of examination-in-chief.[9] It sees such a deadline as necessary to ensure procedural fairness and efficiency in complex, document-heavy

1 Prosecution's Motion for a Cross-Examining Party to Provide Advance Copies of Documents Used to Cross-Examine Witnesses, 23 March 2007.

2 Ibid., paras 3–4.

3 Ibid., paras 6–9.

4 *Prosecutor v. Milutinović et al.*, Decision on Joint Defence Motion for Modification of Order on Procedure and Evidence, 16 August 2006 ("A list of documents or other material to be used by a party when cross-examining a witness must be disclosed to the opposing party or parties at the commencement of the direct examination of that witness and after he or she has made the solemn declaration … At the same time, the cross-examining party must release to the opposing party or parties, via the eCourt system, any documents or other material not already in the possession of the opposing party or parties that form part of the list"). Orders by two other Trial Chambers closely follow the *Milutinović* wording: *Prosecutor v. Popović et al.*, Order on Production of Defence Documents Used in Cross-Examination of Prosecution Witnesses, 24 August 2006 ("a list of documents or other material to be used by the Defence when cross-examining a Prosecution witness must be disclosed to the Prosecution at the commencement of the examination in chief of that witness, after the witness has made the solemn declaration … concurrently, the Defence must release to the Prosecution, via the eCourt system, any documents or other material not already in the possession of the Prosecution that form part of the list"); and *Prosecutor v. Dragomir Milošević*, Decision on Time-Limits for Disclosure of Documents to be Used During a Witness's Testimony, 18 January 2007 ("the Defence [is] to provide the Prosecution, the Registry, and the Trial Chamber with a list of exhibits it intends to use in court during cross-examination at the commencement of the examination-in-chief of that witness and after he or she has made the solemn declaration … [and] to release to the Prosecution, the Registry and the Trial Chamber, via the eCourt system, any documents or material that form part of the list … insofar as they are not already in the possession of the Prosecution, the Registry, and the Trial Chamber").

5 *Prosecutor v. Prlić et al.*, Oral Decision, 8 May 2006, T. 1475 ("these documents [which the Defence intends to use in the course of cross-examination] will be disclosed before the beginning of the cross-examination, but also just after the end of the examination-in-chief. That means that if the examination-in-chief is concluded at 1500 hours, at 1500 hours and one second Defence counsel shall disclose the documents. But if the examination-in-chief is concluded at 1900 hours, in that case the Defence shall disclose the documents at 1900 hours and one second. The cross-examination shall then commence on the following day").

6 *Prosecutor v. Mrkšić et al.*, Oral Decision, 6 December 2005, T. 2953 ("from the 23rd of January on, applying equally to both sides, documents ought to be subject to 24 hours' notice").

7 *Prosecutor v. Martić*, Oral Decision, 20 February 2006, T. 1578–1579 ("the Prosecution requested that the Trial Chamber rule … that the cross-examining party should provide to the opposing party no later than the commencement of the cross-examination, a list of those documents or exhibits which it intends to use during the cross-examination of a witness. … The Trial Chamber notes that the Defence … has agreed … Considering the above positions of the parties, the Trial Chamber grants the motion").

8 *Prosecutor v. Naletilić and Martinović*, Decision on the Accused Naletilić's Request for Enforcement of Trial Chamber's Previous Order Regarding Documents During Cross-Examination, 3 May 2002 ("the party conducting the cross-examination may give to the other party and to the Chamber the exhibits it intends to use during the cross-examination at the time that the document is submitted to the witness; that an earlier distribution is encouraged as it facilitates the conduct of the proceedings; and that a list of the exhibits intended to be used should be distributed in advance to allow the Chamber as well as the other party to bring the relevant documents into court"); *Prosecutor v. Blagojević and Jokić*, Oral Decision, 28 April 2004, T. 8406-8407 ("before the cross-examination, the party conducting the cross-examination should furnish at least a list of the documents they are going to use during the cross-examination, which will greatly facilitate the proceedings of the present case"); and *Prosecutor v. Halilović*, Decision on Motion for Prosecution Access to Defence Documents Used in Cross-Examination of Prosecution Witnesses, 9 May 2005, para. 9 ("during the Prosecution case the Defence is not obliged to provide in advance (not even at the beginning of cross-examination) the Prosecution with the documents or a list of documents which it intends to use during cross-examination of a witness … The Defence is therefore entitled to provide the Prosecution only with those documents actually used in court during cross-examination, at the time the documents are shown to the witness").

9 Prosecution's motion, paras 4, 17.

trials.[10] It maintains that without timely notification it might not be in a position to make informed objections on authenticity or content, or to adequately re-examine witnesses.[11]

3. Mr Haradinaj's response to the Prosecution's motion was joined by the other Accused.[12] The Defence does not object to disclosure of the relevant information to the Prosecution at the conclusion of the examination-in-chief of a witness.[13] However, it submits that the obligation at that point is to reveal to the Prosecution only those documents which the Defence has "definitively" resolved to use in cross-examination.[14] The Defence does not explain why it should not also reveal documents that it is likely, or very likely, to use.

4. In opposing disclosure at any earlier point in time, the Defence relies on the argument that "If a witness is given advance notice of a line of cross-examination which the opposing party intends to pursue, he/she will have the opportunity to prepare a response in advance and to tailor his/her evidence accordingly".[15] This argument could have been expressed more accurately; for once a witness is sworn in, the Prosecution's communication with that witness is so heavily regulated that "advance notice" of an intended line of cross-examination – even if the line were evident to the Prosecution from a reading of the document – could not so **[page 4]** easily be communicated to the witness. Moreover, the suggestion that the benefit to the court of cross-examination is attenuated in cases where the Prosecution examiner modifies a line of questioning (or abandons it) in light of documents disclosed by the Defence following the swearing in of a witness is too speculative.

5. While the Chamber generally agrees with the Defence that a witness must not be "forewarned and afforded an opportunity to prepare a response" to cross-examination,[16] it does not follow from this principle alone that Defence material should not be turned over to the Prosecution prior to the conclusion of examination-in-chief. The usual objectives of the Prosecution's examination of witnesses, pursued in the context of significant communication constraints between examiner and witness, ensure that if early disclosure by the Defence makes the lines of witness cross-examination less surprising overall for Prosecution counsel, the possibilities of exposure of the witness to unexpected challenges by the Defence remain largely unaffected. Additionally, while it is true, as the Defence observes, that the Prosecution "seek[s] to elicit answers which are aimed at weakening or undermining the line of cross-examination to be pursued",[17] this is true *generally*, and experienced Prosecution counsel anticipate lines of cross-examination even without full knowledge of the documents to be used by the Defence. This does not lessen the effectiveness or value of cross-examination.

6. The Defence cites an English authority, *R. v. Brown*,[18] to the effect that, in the common law, not even the *prosecutor* is under a legal duty to disclose material which adversely affects only the credibility of defence witnesses (and is thus detrimental only to the defence case). The burden of such a duty is seen in the common law to be excessive and unnecessary. A fortiori, goes the Defence argument, the Accused are under no legal duty to disclose material relevant to the credibility of Prosecution witnesses.

7. *Brown* concerned a question of disclosure prior to testimony – had the relevant information in the prosecutor's possession about two defence witnesses been disclosed to the defence, the defence would not have called those two witnesses.[19] Thus *Brown* answers a question about how far the prosecutor must go to assist the defence case in deciding which witnesses to call. But that aspect of the law does not generate an argument relevant to the present case, because the question here is not how far the Defence must go to assist the Prosecution case but the extent to which the Defence is entitled to ambush the Prosecution **[page 5]** when

10 Ibid., paras 10–12, 14.

11 The Prosecution would also dismiss as misguided and internally inconsistent a decision in the *Halilović* case which declined to order notification of cross-examination material prior to the actual use of such material (ibid., para. 13). Considering that the Defence in the present case is not pressing for an order in line with *Halilović*, this argument need not be evaluated here.

12 Confidential Response on Behalf of Ramush Haradinaj to Prosecution Motion for a Cross-Examining Party to Provide Copies of Documents Used to Cross-Examine Witnesses, 30 March 2007; the notifications by Mr Balaj and Mr Brahimaj, joining the main response, were filed on the same date.

13 Response, para. 2.

14 Ibid., para. 3.

15 Ibid., para. 4, grounded in *R. v. Brown*, [1998] AC 367, at 380A (per Lord Hope).

16 Response, para. 7; the argument is developed ibid., paras 10–17.

17 Ibid., para. 14.

18 [1998] A.C. 367.

19 Ibid., at 378E.

the Prosecution's witness is already in the box. The Defence[20] cites the Canadian case of *R. v. Stinchcombe*[21] for the proposition that "the defence has no obligation to assist the prosecution and is entitled to assume a purely adversarial role toward the prosecution".[22] Yet in the same case the Supreme Court of Canada made the following observation:

> Production and discovery were foreign to the adversary process of adjudication in its earlier history when the element of surprise was one of the accepted weapons in the arsenal of the adversaries. This applied to both criminal and civil proceedings. Significantly, in civil proceedings this aspect of the adversary process has long since disappeared, and full discovery of documents and oral examination of parties and even witnesses are familiar features of the practice. This change resulted from acceptance of the principle that justice was better served when the element of surprise was eliminated from the trial and the parties were prepared to address issues on the basis of complete information of the case to be met. Surprisingly, in criminal cases in which the liberty of the subject is usually at stake, this aspect of the adversary system has lingered on.[23]

8. As is evident from the ICTY decisions cited above in footnotes 4 through 8, the practice at this Tribunal has changed over time, with the three most recent decisions (footnote 4) shifting the deadline for disclosure of cross-examination material to the moment following the swearing in of a witness. The Defence, in expounding the asymmetrical disclosure obligations found in the Tribunal's Rules of Procedure and Evidence, implies that this trend rests not on legal principle but on grounds of pragmatism and efficient trial management.[24] Yet the Rules do require the Defence to notify the Prosecution about a range of matters concerning the Defence case.[25] These requirements are not reducible to pragmatism but underscore the legal principle that for the purposes of fair play the Defence must show part of its hand to the Prosecution. Disclosure obligations may be asymmetrical at this Tribunal but they are not entirely one-sided. The Defence does acknowledge that its preferred later deadline may at times prove unfair to the Prosecution,[26] thus recognizing the possibility, at least, that legal principle is involved in the observed trend towards early disclosure.

9. The Defence notes that it is only when a witness has completed his or her evidence-in-chief that a final decision can be made about documents to be put to the witness in cross-examination.[27] The consequence, however, is not a later deadline, but that the Defence **[page 6]** notifies the Prosecution of the material which it is *likely* to use with each witness, and not only of the material which it has definitively resolved to use. Use of unannounced material is not foreclosed, as seen from the *Milutinović* order:

> A list of documents or other material to be used by a party when cross-examining a witness must be disclosed to the opposing party or parties at the commencement of the direct examination of that witness and after he or she has made the solemn declaration pursuant to Rule 90(A). At the same time, the cross-examining party must release to the opposing party or parties, via the eCourt system, any documents or other material not already in the possession of the opposing party or parties that form part of the list of documents or material for use during cross-examination. Should a party seek to use a document or material during cross-examination that has not been so listed and disclosed, that party may be permitted to do so on showing good cause for not so listing and disclosing it. The opposing party or parties may then request a short adjournment in order to examine the material.[28]

---

20 Response, para. 21.
21 [1991] 3 S.C.R. 326.
22 Ibid., at 333.
23 Ibid., at 332.
24 Response, paras 20–24.
25 Chiefly Rules 65 ter (F)-(G) and 67.
26 Response, paras 27–29; hence the need for the compensation discussed in these paragraphs of the Defence response.
27 Ibid., para. 18.
28 *Prosecutor v. Milutinović et al.*, Decision on Joint Defence Motion for Modification of Order on Procedure and Evidence, 16 August 2006, para. 4.

FOR THE FOREGOING REASONS,

The motion is **ALLOWED**. The procedure to be followed in the present case is that set out in the *Milutinović* order, quoted above.

Done in English and French, the English version being authoritative.

Dated this 31st day of May 2007
At The Hague
The Netherlands

Judge Alphons Orie
Presiding Judge

[Seal of the Tribunal]

FOR THE FOREGOING REASONS,

UNITED NATIONS

International Tribunal for the Prosecution of Persons Responsible for Serious Violations of International Humanitarian Law Committed in the Territory of the Former Yugoslavia Since 1991	Case No.	IT-04-74-AR73.5
	Date:	24 August 2007
	Original:	English

IN THE APPEALS CHAMBER

Before: **Judge Fausto Pocar, Presiding**
Judge Mohamed Shahabuddeen
Judge Mehmet Güney
Judge Andrésia Vaz
Judge Wolfgang Schomburg

Registrar: **Mr. Hans Holthuis**

Order of: **24 August 2007**

PROSECUTOR

v.

Jadranko PRLIĆ
Bruno STOJIĆ
Slobodan PRALJAK
Milivoj PETKOVIĆ
Valentin ĆORIĆ
Berislav PUŠIĆ

Public

DECISION ON PRALJAK'S APPEAL OF THE TRIAL CHAMBER'S 10 MAY 2007 DECISION ON THE MODE OF INTERROGATING WITNESSES

Office of the Prosecutor
Mr. Kenneth Scott
Mr. Daryl Mundis

Counsel for the Accused
Mr. Michael Karnavas and Ms. Suzana Tomanović for Jadranko Prlić
Ms. Senka Nožica and Mr. Peter Murphy for Bruno Stojić
Mr. Božidar Kovačić and Ms. Nika Pinter for Slobodan Praljak
Ms. Vesna Alaburić and Mr. Nicolas Stewart for Milivoj Petković
Ms. Dijana Tomašegović-Tomić and Mr. Dražen Plavec for Valentin Ćorić
Mr. Fahrudin Ibrišimović and Mr. Roger Sahota for Berislav Pušić

[page 2] 1. The Appeals Chamber of the International Tribunal for the Prosecution of Persons Responsible for Serious Violations of International Humanitarian Law Committed in the Territory of the Former Yugoslavia Since 1991 ("Appeals Chamber" and "International Tribunal", respectively) is seized of an appeal of Slobodan Praljak ("Appellant")[1] against the Trial Chamber's "Decision on the Mode of Interrogating Witnesses" ("Impugned Decision"). The Prosecution has not filed a response to the Appeal.

Background

2. The Impugned Decision[2] of the Trial Chamber was rendered on 10 May 2007, and certified by the Trial Chamber on 28 June 2007 for appeal.[3] The part of the Impugned Decision appealed by the Appellant concerns the Appellant's participation in the questioning of witnesses. In the Impugned Decision, the Trial Chamber recalled Guideline C of the "Decision Adopting Guidelines on Conduct of Trial Proceedings" in its revised version of 28 April 2006, which states as follows:

> Article 21(e) of the Statute reiterates the right of the accused to examine, or have examined, the witnesses against him. In the present case, the Accused are represented by counsel. Witnesses shall primarily be questioned by counsel for the Accused. In exceptional circumstances and after authorisation of the Chamber, an Accused may directly address a witness and put questions to him or her.[4]

3. Having recalled Guideline C, the Trial Chamber considered that it had been very flexible in its application and in particular, had allowed the Appellant "to speak and question witnesses about all issues and even, at least in part, to conduct the cross examination himself".[5] The Trial Chamber considered that while it was not in principle opposed to allowing an accused to speak, "[t]he experience of previous months...has shown that the complexity of this trial compels the Chamber to strictly control the modes of witness interrogation".[6] Accordingly, it determined that Guideline C would be applied more strictly and that the Appellant would no longer be permitted to ask questions without the prior approval of the Chamber. "Consequently, witnesses shall first be cross-examined by Counsel for the Accused. In exceptional circumstances and with the authorisation of the Chamber, an Accused may directly address a witness and put questions to him or her".[7] **[page 3]**

4. In his Appeal, the Appellant complains that the Impugned Decision of the Trial Chamber places unreasonable restrictions on his right to participate in the proceedings.[8] The Appellant claims that under the Guidelines laid down by the Trial Chamber in the Decision of 28 April 2006, he was granted a right to "directly address a witness and put questions to him or her" with a proviso (a) that a "witness shall primarily be questioned by counsel", (b) that there exist "exceptional circumstances", and (c) "after authorisation of the Chamber".[9] He argues that prior to the issuing of the Impugned Decision, the Trial Chamber was "implementing the guidelines wisely and with flexibility", allowing him to "cross-examine all the witnesses he wished to".[10] He alleges that the Impugned Decision "imposes additional and unjustified constraints" on his right to "personally interrogate the witnesses" and "unnecessarily and unreasonably restricts his right to personally cross-examine the witnesses to such an extent that it effectively amounts to a violation of his right of confrontation".[11] Further, he claims that to change his right to participate in his defence at this "late stage of the proceedings results in manifest prejudice and injustice" to him.[12] He requests the Appeals Chamber to

---

1 Slobodan Praljak's Appeal of the Trial Chamber's 10 May 2007 "Decision on the Mode of Interrogating Witnesses", 4 July 2007 ("Appeal").

2 Decision on the Mode of Interrogating Witnesses, 10 May 2007.

3 Decision on Certification to Appeal the Decision on the Mode of Interrogating Witnesses, 28 June 2007.

4 Impugned Decision, para. 8, citing Revised Version of the Decision Adopting Guidelines on Conduct of Trial Proceedings. 28 April 2006 ("Decision of 28 April 2006").

5 *Ibid.*, para. 9.

6 *Ibid.*, para. 10.

7 *Ibid.*

8 Appeal, para. 5.

9 *Ibid.*

10 *Ibid.*

11 *Ibid.*, para. 6.

12 *Ibid.*

overturn the Impugned Decision with respect to his right to directly cross-examine those witnesses that he wishes to cross-examine.[13]

Standard of Review

5. It is well-established in the jurisprudence of the International Tribunal that Trial Chambers exercise discretion in relation to the conduct of proceedings before them.[14] In the present case, the Impugned Decision's holding to more strictly apply Guideline C is a discretionary decision of the Trial Chamber, to which the Appeals Chamber accords deference. This deference is based on the Appeals Chamber's recognition of the Trial Chamber's familiarity with the day-to-day conduct of the parties and practical demands of the case.[15] The Appeals Chamber's examination is therefore **[page 4]** limited to establishing whether the Trial Chamber abused its discretion by committing a discernible error.[16] The Appeals Chamber will only overturn a Trial Chamber's exercise of its discretion where it is found to be (1) based on an incorrect interpretation of governing law; (2) based on a patently incorrect conclusion of fact; or (3) so unfair or unreasonable as to constitute an abuse of discretion.[17]

Alleged Violation of the Appellant's Right to Participate in the Proceedings

6. In his Appeal, the Appellant argues that the Impugned Decision unacceptably restricts his ability to cross-examine witnesses.[18] The Appellant claims that while the Impugned Decision does not "unequivocally" prevent him from cross examining witnesses, it places "additional severe restrictions on his right to participate in the proceedings" and that these restrictions have the effect of vitiating that right. He claims that the restrictions imposed go beyond the proper exercise of discretion and "may substantially and unacceptably exclude" him from participation in his own defence.[19]

7. The restrictions complained of by the Appellant are that Defence Counsel must cross-examine witnesses first; the Appellant is only entitled to directly address the witness with the prior authorisation of the Trial Chamber; the Appellant is only permitted to cross examine with respect to events that he directly participated in or has special knowledge of; and prior to being permitted to directly examine a witness, the Appellant must explain to the Trial Chamber the special circumstances that warrant his permission to do so.[20]

---

13 *Ibid.*, para. 23.

14 *Prosecutor v. Jadranko Prlić et al.*, Case No. IT-04-74-AR73.2, Decision on Prosecution Appeal Concerning the Trial Chamber's Ruling Reducing Time for the Prosecution Case, 6 February 2007 ("*Prlić* Decision on Reduction of Time") para. 8, referring to Decision on Joint Defence Interlocutory Appeal against the Trial Chamber's Oral Decision of of 8 May 2006 Relating to Cross-Examination By Defence and on Association of Defence Counsel's Request for Leave to File an *Amicus Curiae* Brief, 4 July 2006 ("*Prlić* Decision on Cross-Examination"), p. 3; *Prosecutor v. Zdravko Tolimir et al.*, Case No. IT-04-80-AR73.1, Decision on *Radivoje Miletić's* Interlocutory Appeal Against the Trial Chamber's Decision on Joinder of Accused, 27 January 2006 ("Decision on *Radivoje Miletić's* Interlocutory Appeal") para. 4; *Prosecutor v. Slobodan Milošević*, Case No. IT-02-54-AR73.7, Decision on Interlocutory Appeal of the Trial Chamber's Decision on the Assignment of Defence Counsel, 1 November 2004 (*Milošević* Decision on the Assignment of Defence Counsel"), para. 9; *Prosecutor v. Slobodan Milošević*, Case No. IT-02-54-AR73, Reasons for Refusal of Leave to Appeal from Decision to Impose Time Limit, 16 May 2002 ("*Milošević* Decision to Impose Time Limit"), para. 14.

15 *Prlić* Decision on Reduction of Time, para. 8, which refers to Decision on *Radivoje Miletić's* Interlocutory Appeal, para. 4; *Milošević* Decision on Defence Counsel, para. 9.

16 *Prlić* Decision on Cross-Examination, p. 3 citing *Prosecutor v. Milošević*, Case Nos. IT-99-37-AR73, IT-01-50-AR73, and IT-01-51-AR73, Reasons for Decision on Prosecution Interlocutory Appeal from Refusal to Order Joinder, 18 April 2002, para. 4: "Where an appeal is brought from a discretionary decision of a Trial Chamber, the issue in that appeal is not whether the decision was correct, in the sense that the Appeals Chamber agrees with that decision, but rather whether the Trial Chamber has correctly exercised its discretion in reaching that decision", see also paras. 5-6; see also *Milošević* Decision on the Assignment of Defence Counsel, para. 10; Decision on *Radivoje Miletić's* Interlocutory Appeal, para. 6 citing *Prosecutor v. Mićo Stanišić*, Case No. IT-04-79-AR65.1, Decision on Prosecution's Interlocutory Appeal of *Mićo Stanišić's* Provisional Release, 17 October 2005 ("*Stanišić* Provisional Release Decision"), para. 6.

17 Decision on *Radivoje Miletić's* Interlocutory Appeal, para. 6 citing *Stanišić* Provisional Release Decision, para. 6 and n. 10. The Appeals Chamber will also consider whether the Trial Chamber "has given weight to extraneous or irrelevant considerations or that it has failed to give weight or sufficient weight to relevant considerations" *Ibid*".

18 *Prosecutor v. Jadranko Prlić et al.*, Case No. IT-04-74-AR73.5, Slobodan Praljak's Appeal of the Trial Chamber's 10 May 2007 "Decision on the Mode of Interrogating Witnesses", 4 July 2007 ("*Praljak* Appeal").

19 Appeal, para. 7.

20 *Ibid.*, para. 7

8. In the Impugned Decision, the Trial Chamber made abundantly clear why the adoption of a stricter approach to the application of Guideline C of the Decision of 28 April 2006 was warranted. Namely, it considered that the lee-way it had given to the Appellant was impacting upon the rights **[page 5]** of his co-accused to an expeditious and fair trial.[21] Additionally, it did not consider that the flexibility it had accorded the Appellant was of benefit to his defence. As it stated:

> The Accused Praljak, although full of good intentions, had repeatedly proved to lack both the legal expertise and the experience required to interrogate witnesses in conformity with the Rules and the jurisprudence of the Tribunal. It is true that some of his questions were interesting and pertinent. Nevertheless, most of the questions were irrelevant and frequently concentrated on *tu quoque*. Many times the questions were not put to the appropriate Witness. Moreover, the Chamber has observed that the Accused Praljak sometimes makes a habit of substituting his own thoughts or elements of defence for witnesses' answers. Rather than ask true questions, he regularly invited the witnesses to share his opinions. The Chamber cannot but find that interventions of this type entail a useless waste of time.[22]

9. In light of the above reasoning, the Appeals Chamber is satisfied that there was good reason for the Trial Chamber to determine that a stricter application of Guideline C was justified in order to protect the rights of the Appellant's co-accused to a fair and expeditious trial, as well as the rights of the Appellant. The Trial Chamber's experience of the Appellant's direct participation in the proceedings satisfied it that such interventions were a waste of time. Accordingly, the Appeals Chambers is not satisfied that the Appellant has identified an error in the exercise of the Trial Chamber's discretion or justified his claim that the Trial Chamber abused its discretion by restricting his examination of witnesses in the Impugned Decision.

Alleged Right of the Appellant to Participate in the Proceedings

10. The Appellant next claims that, while he recognises that he is represented by Counsel, he has always maintained that he wants to participate directly in the proceedings through cross-examination of the witnesses. He argues that prior to the rendering of the Impugned Decision his wish was respected by the Trial Chamber and he was permitted to cross-examine witnesses whenever he requested to do so. However, "it remains to be seen" whether he will be so permitted following the Impugned Decision.[23] He claims that it is well established that he "has a right to self-representation or a right to legal counsel, as well as a right to examine or have examined witnesses against him" and refers in this respect to Article 21(4) of the Statute.[24] The Appellant relies upon various decisions of this International Tribunal to argue that the right to counsel and the right to self-representation are not mutually exclusive and that the assignment of counsel does not negate the right of the accused to also participate directly in the proceedings.[25] He notes that while these authorities dealt with situations where accused refused to recognise counsel assigned, to limit the **[page 6]** right to participate directly in proceedings to those accused who refused counsel and obstruct proceedings would penalise accused who have cooperated with the International Tribunal and accepted assigned counsel.[26]

11. The Appeals Chambers finds that the Appellant's arguments in this regard are misguided. In the Impugned Decision, the Trial Chamber did not hold that the Appellant did not have a right to participate in the proceedings.[27] Rather, the Impugned Decision held that in the interests of a fair and expeditious trial for the Appellant and his co-accused, the right of the Appellant to participate directly would be subject to the restrictions it identified to avoid the Appellant wasting court time. Accordingly, the Trial Chamber has not removed the right of the Appellant to participate directly in the proceedings alongside his counsel. It has merely placed reasonable restrictions on that right to prevent the Appellant's needless waste of court time and to protect the rights of all accused to a fair and expeditious trial.

---

21 *Ibid.*, para. 10

22 *Ibid.*

23 *Ibid.*, para. 9.

24 *Ibid.*, para. 10.

25 *Ibid.*, paras. 11-17.

26 *Ibid.*, para. 18.

27 Impugned Decision, para. 8.

Alleged Prejudice Shown to Appellant as a Result of the Impugned Decision

12. The Appellant argues that his trial has been proceeding for over one year and that during that time a practice has evolved whereby he has been permitted to directly participate in the proceedings by the cross examination of witnesses. He argues that this practice "has formed a fundamental component" in his defence and "has shaped the preparation and strategy for trial".[28] He claims that to fundamentally change this practice at this late stage of the proceedings "would be highly prejudicial and severely disruptive" to him and his defence team in the conduct of his case and "would result in manifest unfairness [...] thereby violating his right to a fair trial as outlined in Article 21 of the Statute".[29]

13. The Appeals Chamber is not satisfied that the Appellant's argument has any merit. The Impugned Decision in fact highlights the right to a fair trial as a prime consideration of the Trial Chamber in deciding to place limits upon the Appellant's ability to cross-examine witnesses.[30] The Trial Chamber made quite clear that the Appellant's lack of legal experience meant that his interventions were of little or no value to his defence.[31] Therefore, far from jeopardizing fair trial rights, the Impugned Decision was made in direct response to a perceived threat to these very same rights resulting from the actions of the Appellant. **[page 7]**

Disposition

On the basis of the foregoing, the Appeals Chamber **DISMISSES** the Appeal.

Done in English and French, the English text being authoritative.

Done this 24th day of August 2007
At The Hague,
The Netherlands.

Judge Fausto Pocar
Presiding Judge

[Seal of the International Tribunal]

[28] Appeal., para. 19.
[29] Ibid., paras. 19-20.
[30] Impugned Decision., para. 10.
[31] Ibid.

UNITED NATIONS

International Tribunal for the Prosecution of Persons Responsible for Serious Violations of International Humanitarian Law Committed in the Territory of Former Yugoslavia since 1991	Case No. IT-04-84-T Date: 5 September 2007 Original: English

---

IN TRIAL CHAMBER I

Before: **Judge Alphons Orie, Presiding**
Judge Frank Höpfel
Judge Ole Bjørn Støle

Registrar: **Mr Hans Holthuis**

Decision of: **5 September 2007**

PROSECUTOR

v.

RAMUSH HARADINAJ
IDRIZ BALAJ
LAHI BRAHIMAJ

PUBLIC

DECISION ON MOTION BY WITNESS 28 TO SET ASIDE SUBPOENA OR FOR ALTERNATIVE RELIEF

Office of the Prosecutor
Mr David Re
Mr Gramsci di Fazio
Mr Gilles Dutertre
Mr Philip Kearney

Counsel for Witness 28
Ms Virginia Lindsay

Counsel for Ramush Haradinaj
Mr Ben Emmerson, QC
Mr Rodney Dixon
Ms Susan L. Park

Counsel for Idriz Balaj
Mr Gregor Guy-Smith
Ms Colleen Rohan

Counsel for Lahi Brahimaj
Mr Richard Harvey
Mr Paul Troop

[page 2] 1. Witness 28 is subject to a subpoena to testify, served on her on 13 August 2007.[1] It contains a standard clause ordering the witness "to appear as a witness before the Trial Chamber ... or to show cause why this subpoena cannot be complied with". On 15 August, Witness 28 filed a motion to have the subpoena set aside, or, in the alternative, to have her testimony received in closed session (and related relief).[2]

2. The Chamber understands Witness 28's motion to be a response to the aforementioned "show cause" clause in the subpoena. A subpoena is an invasive measure that should not be issued lightly. When a Chamber issues a subpoena, it relies on the facts presented to it by the applicant, in this case the Prosecution. These facts may be wrong or incomplete, and where this is thought to be the case, the subpoenaed witness is entitled to address the Chamber, showing cause why he or she believes that the subpoena should be set aside.

3. The Chamber considers Witness 28's motion to be a valid action before it, except as it relates to protective measures, as explained in paragraph 9, below.

4. The Prosecution and the Accused made submissions in response to the motion.[3] The Prosecution asks for the motion to be dismissed, for reasons similar to those set out in the present decision. There is no reason to reiterate the Prosecution's points here. The submissions of the Accused, which concern the significance and reliability of the witness's potential evidence, would have been relevant to this decision only if the Chamber had found that the witness was a "war correspondent" at the relevant time. For the reasons given below, that is not the Chamber's finding. Thus the Accused's concerns fall to be considered at a later stage, in the course of Witness 28's testimony, and not now. **[page 3]**

5. Witness 28 claims a "qualified testimonial privilege" on the strength of her work as a war correspondent and investigative journalist. (In order to protect the identity of the witness and preserve the public status of this decision, the Chamber will not discuss her career in detail.) By her own account, Witness 28 worked as a war correspondent some years *prior* to the period covered by the indictment in this case.[4] During the indictment period, when Witness 28 was interviewing victims and witnesses about their experiences in Kosovo, she was neither a war correspondent nor a journalist. She worked for a human rights organization whose function it was to research human rights violations by means of such interviews. The organization had been cooperating with the Tribunal since before the indictment period.[5] Witness 28 did not return to professional journalism until some time after the indictment period.[6] She gave two statements to the Office of the Prosecutor, one in 1999 and another in 2002, concerning her work and observations during the indictment period, and her eventual testimony is expected to focus on those earlier statements.

6. Witness 28 is not covered by the testimonial privilege which she invokes. Not only was she not a war correspondent at the relevant time, she worked for an organization whose very purpose it was to gather information about, and assist the prosecution of, human rights violations.[7] Witness 28 relies on a decision in the *Brđanin* case, wherein the Appeals Chamber postulated a testimonial privilege for "war correspondents". It defined war correspondents as "individuals who, for any period of time, report (or investigate for the

---

1 Subpoena ad testificandum, 12 July 2007.

2 Motion to Set Aside Subpoena ad Testificandum and in the Alternative, Motion to Protect Confidential Sources and for Closed Session Testimony, 15 August 2007. The motion was first filed as a confidential and ex parte document (excluding the Defence). On 17 August, following a telephone conversation between the Trial Chamber's legal officer and Ms Lindsay, the motion was refiled as a confidential document, but with the two annexes remaining ex parte. In the meantime, also on 17 August, the Prosecution filed a request to have Witness 28's motion refiled inter partes. At this point, the dispute had been narrowed down to the filing status of the two annexes. On 21 August 2007, Witness 28 responded to the Prosecution's request, giving reasons why the two annexes should retain their ex parte status. The Prosecution replied on the same day, and on 22 August 2007 Witness 28 refiled Annex B as an interpartes confidential document. The Chamber's decision on the outstanding issue of the final status of Annex A will be given at the time of Witness 28's testimony.

3 Prosecution's Response to Witness [28's] Motion to Set Aside the Subpoena ad Testificandum, 28 August 2007; Response on Behalf of Ramush Haradinaj to Application of [Witness 28] to Set Aside Subpoena, 28 August 2007; Idriz Balaj's Submissions on Witness [28]'s Motion to Set Aside Subpoena ad Testificandum, 28 August 2007; and Response on Behalf of Lahi Brahimaj to Application of [Witness 28] to Set Aside Subpoena, 28 August 2007. An email application from Witness 28 for leave to file a reply to the Prosecution's response was denied by the Chamber on 30 August 2007.

4 Motion, para. 7. The indictment covers the period 1 March 1998 to 30 September 1998.

5 Motion, para. 8; see also the Prosecution's response, para. 9.

6 Motion, para. 11.

7 Ibid., para. 8.

purposes of reporting) from a conflict zone on issues relating to the conflict."[8] Witness 28 suggests that this covers her circumstances, since she was, for a time, a war correspondent.[9]

7. This is an insupportable interpretation. The *Brđanin* case concerned a war correspondent who was subpoenaed to testify about an interview he had conducted while working as a war correspondent.[10] The *Brđanin* decision sought to obviate the creation of a public perception "that war correspondents can be forced to become witnesses against their interviewees" and thus be made to breach source confidentiality, with the potential result that war correspondents can no longer perform their jobs effectively.[11] The *Brđanin* decision does **[page 4]** not bestow testimonial privilege on a war correspondent for activities carried out in a capacity other than that of war correspondent.

8. Witness 28 argues, apparently in the alternative, that "Those who defend human rights are often in a position that warrants the recognition of a testimonial privilege."[12] The phrase "are often" is a concession that this proposition, even if true, is not conclusive. Witness 28's attempted analogy between the work performed and privileges enjoyed by employees of the International Committee of the Red Cross, on the one hand, and members of the human rights organization which Witness 28 belonged to during the indictment period, on the other, fails for the reason that ICRC privileges are specific to the ICRC and cannot be extended to other groups by analogy. As a Trial Chamber of this Tribunal has said:

> the right to non-disclosure of information relating to the ICRC's activities in the possession of its employees in judicial proceedings is necessary for the effective discharge of the ICRC of its mandate. The Trial Chamber therefore finds that the parties to the Geneva Conventions and their Protocols have assumed a conventional obligation to ensure non-disclosure in judicial proceedings of information relating to the work of the ICRC in the possession of an ICRC employee, and that, conversely, the ICRC has a right to insist on such non-disclosure by parties to the Geneva Conventions and the Protocols.[13]

Apart from anything else, the human rights organization which Witness 28 worked for at the relevant time had as one of its aims to disclose information gathered from its activities to this Tribunal for use in judicial proceedings.[14] Thus there is no analogy.

9. The other issues raised by Witness 28 in her motion concern trial-related protective measures to which the witness may be entitled. It is for the calling party, in this case the Prosecution, to move the Chamber for protective measures for its witnesses. The Chamber does not receive motions on such matters directly from witnesses. This part of the motion is therefore not validly filed before the Chamber and is hereby dismissed without consideration of the merits of the arguments therein. **[page 5]**

---

8 Decision on Interlocutory Appeal, Prosecutor v. Radoslav Brđanin and Momir Talić, 11 December 2002 (Brđanin decision), para. 29.

9 Motion, para. 16.

10 Brđanin decision, paras 3–4.

11 Ibid., paras 42–43.

12 Motion, para. 26.

13 Decision on the Prosecution Motion Under Rule 73 for a Ruling Concerning the Testimony of a Witness, Prosecutor v. Blagoje Simić et al., 27 July 1999, para. 73.

14 Motion, para. 8.

FOR THE FOREGOING REASONS,

The motion is **DISMISSED** in its entirety;

Witness 28 is **ORDERED** to comply with the subpoena and to appear to give testimony in this case on a date to be communicated to her by the Tribunal's Registry.

Done in English and French, the English version being authoritative.

Dated this 5th day of September 2007
At The Hague
The Netherlands.

Judge Alphons Orie
Presiding Judge

[Seal of the Tribunal]

UNITED NATIONS

International Tribunal for the Prosecution of Persons Responsible for Serious Violations of International Humanitarian Law Committed in the Territory of the Former Yugoslavia since 1991	Case No.	IT-05-88-AR73.1
	Date:	14 December 2007
	Original:	English

IN THE APPEALS CHAMBER

Before: **Judge Fausto Pocar, Presiding**
Judge Mehmet Güney
Judge Andrésia Vaz
Judge Theodor Meron
Judge Wolfgang Schomburg

Registrar: **Mr Hans Holthuis**

Decision of: **14 December 2007**

PROSECUTOR

v.

VUJADIN POPOVIĆ
LJUBIŠA BEARA
DRAGO NIKOLIĆ
LJUBOMIR BOROVČANIN
RADIVOJE MILETIĆ
MILAN GVERO
VINKO PANDUREVIĆ

Public

DECISION ON APPEALS AGAINST DECISION ADMITTING MATERIAL RELATED TO BOROVČANIN'S QUESTIONING

The Office of the Prosecutor:
Mr Peter McCloskey

Counsel for the Appellants:
Mr Zoran Živanović and Ms Mira Tapušković for Vujadin Popović
Mr John Ostojić and Mr Christopher Meek for Ljubiša Beara
Ms Jelena Nikolić and Mr Stéphane Bourgon for Drago Nikolić
Mr Aleksandar Lazarević and Mr Miodrag Stojanović for Ljubomir Borovčanin
Ms Natacha Fauveau Ivanović and Mr Nenad Petrušić for Radivoje Miletić
Mr Dragan Krgović and Mr David Josse for Milan Gvero
Mr Peter Haynes and Mr Đorde Sarapa for Vinko Pandurević

[page 1] 1. The Appeals Chamber of the International Tribunal for the Prosecution of Persons Responsible for Serious Violations of International Humanitarian Law Committed in the Territory of the Former Yugoslavia Since 1991 ("Appeals Chamber" and "Tribunal", respectively) is seized of four appeals, respectively filed by Ljubomir Borovčanin, Milan Gvero, Ljubiša Beara, and by the Office of the Prosecutor ("Prosecution") against the "Decision on the Admissibility of the Borovčanin Interview and the Amendment of the Rule 65*ter* Exhibit List" ("Impugned Decision") issued on 25 October 2007 by Trial Chamber II ("Trial Chamber").

I. PROCEDURAL HISTORY

2. The Prosecution questioned Ljubomir Borovčanin ("Borovčanin") on 20 February, 11 March, and 12 March 2002. The questioning was audio recorded and transcribed (collectively referred to as "Borovčanin Recordings and Transcript").[1] On 6 September 2002, a judge of the Tribunal confirmed an indictment against Borovčanin. On 31 October 2005, the Trial Chamber granted a motion by the Prosecution and ordered the consolidation of the indictments previously issued against: Vujadin Popović ("Popović");[2] Ljubiša Beara ("Beara");[3] Drago Nikolić;[4] Ljubomir Borovčanin;[5] Zdravko Tolimir, Radivoje Miletić, and Milan Gvero ("Gvero");[6] Vinko Pandurević;[7] Milorad Trbić.[8] The present proceedings, against seven accused (when referred to collectively, "Co-Accused"),[9] started on 14 July 2006.

3. On 6 July 2007, the Trial Chamber was seized of the confidential "Prosecution's Motion for Leave to Amend 65*ter* Exhibit List with 18 Exhibits Pertaining to Alistair Graham" ("Rule 65 *ter* List Amendment Motion"). In this motion, the Prosecution requested the addition of the Borovčanin Recordings and Transcript and related materials to its list of exhibits prepared pursuant to Rule 65 *ter* ("Exhibit List"). The related material consists of a number of documents and audio-visual material brought by Borovčanin to the meeting with the Prosecution, some documents produced by Borovčanin himself during the questioning, as well as papers detailing the efforts by the **[page 2]** Prosecution to question Borovčanin (collectively, "Borovčanin Documents").[10] In the period between 6 and 16 July 2007, the Co-Accused filed their responses to the Rule 65 *ter* Amendment Motion[11] and the Prosecution

---

1 Prosecution's Motion for Leave to Amend 65 *ter* Exhibit List with 18 Exhibits Pertaining to Alistair Graham, 6 July 2007, para. 4 (quoted in Impugned Decision, para. 2). The parties and the Trial Chamber used the expression "Borovčanin Interview" or "Borovčanin's Statements" to describe the transcript and audio recording of Borovčanin's questioning.

2 Case No. IT-02-57-I, Amended Indictment, 28 April 2002.

3 Case No. IT-02-58-I, Indictment, 28 March 2002.

4 Case No. IT-02-63-I, Indictment, 2 September 2002.

5 Case No. IT-02-64-I, Indictment, 6 September 2002.

6 Case No. IT-04-80-I, Indictment, 8 February 2005.

7 Case No. IT-05-86-I, Indictment, 24 March 2005.

8 Case No. IT-05-86-I, Indictment, 24 March 2005.

9 Zdravko Tolimir's case was severed on 26 June 2006 and 15 August 2006 (see *Prosecutor v. Vujadin Popović et al.*, Case No. IT-05-88-T, Order on Operative Indictment and Severance of Case against Zdravko Tolimir, 15 August 2006). Milorad Trbić's case was also severed and later transferred to Bosnia and Herzegovina pursuant to Rule 11*bis* of the Rules of Procedure and Evidence ("Rules" or, individually, "Rule") (see *Prosecutor v. Milorad Trbić*, Case No. IT-05-88/1-PT, Decision on Referral of Case under Rule 11 *bis* with Confidential Annex, 27 April 2007).

10 Rule 65 *ter* List Amendment Motion, paras 1–6.

11 *Prosecutor v. Vujadin Popović et al.*, Case No. IT-05-88-T: Response of General Miletić to Prosecution Motion for Leave to Amend the List of Exhibits by Adding 18 Exhibits Related to Alistair Graham, 12 July 2007 (French original), 26 July 2007 (English translation); Defence Response on Behalf of Ljubiša Beara to the Prosecution's Motion for Leave to Amend 65*ter* Exhibit List with 18 Exhibits Pertaining to Alistair Graham, 12 July 2007; Borovčanin Defence Response and Motion in Opposition to 'Prosecution's Motion for Leave to Amend 65*ter* Exhibit List with 18 Exhibits Pertaining to Alistair Graham', 12 July 2007; Motion on Behalf of Drago Nikolić Joining the Borovčanin and Miletić Defence Responses to "Prosecution's Motion for Leave to Amend 65*ter* Exhibit List with 18 Exhibits Pertaining to Alistair Graham", 12 July 2007; Motion on Behalf of Vinko Pandurević Joining the Defence Responses to Prosecution's Motion for Leave to Amend 65*ter* Exhibit List with 18 Exhibits Pertaining to Alistair Graham, 13 July 2007; Defence Response on Behalf of Ljubiša Beara to Prosecution Motion for Leave to Supplement Prosecution's 6 July 2007 65*ter* Motion, 13 July 2007; Borovčanin Defence Notification on Joining "Defence Response on Behalf of Ljubiša Beara to the Prosecution's Motion for Leave to Amend 65*ter* Exhibit List with 18 Exhibits Pertaining to Alistair Graham", 13 July 2007; Borovčanin Defence Response to Prosecution 12 July 2007 65*ter* Motion, Notification on Joining Beara Defence Response to Prosecution 12 July 2007 65*ter* Motion, and Motion for Leave to Supplement "Borovčanin Defence Response and Motion in Opposition to 'Prosecution's Motion for Leave to Amend 65*ter* Exhibit List with 18 Exhibits Pertaining to Alistair Graham'", 16 July 2007; Corrigendum to Response of General Miletić to Prosecution Motion for Leave to Amend the Exhibits List by Adding 18 Exhibits Related to Alistair Graham, 16 July 2007 (French original), 25 July 2007 (English translation).

filed a consolidated Reply.[12] On 17 and 18 July 2007, the Trial Chamber heard Mr Alistair Graham's testimony about the procedures followed during the questioning of Borovčanin.[13] Between 17 and 20 July 2007, the parties filed additional written submissions on whether, if admitted, the Borovčanin Recordings and Transcript could be used with respect to the co-accused other than Borovčanin.[14] The parties further made submissions in court on 19 July 2007.[15]

4. On 25 October 2007, the Trial Chamber granted the Prosecution's request to amend the Exhibit List, adding the Borovčanin Recordings and Transcript as well as the Borovčanin Documents.[16] In particular, it admitted the Borovčanin Recordings and Transcript to be used "as evidence concerning" Borovčanin[17] and the other co-accused but, in the case of the latter, not to be used to prove their acts and conduct.[18] The Trial Chamber further admitted the Borovčanin **[page 3]** Documents without qualification. Lastly, the Trial Chamber granted the parties certification to appeal the Impugned Decision.[19]

5. On 1 November 2007, the Prosecution filed an appeal against the Impugned Decision.[20] Popović and Beara responded on 8 and 9 November.[21] On 13 November 2007, the Prosecution filed its Reply.[22]

6. On 1 November, Borovčanin,[23] Beara,[24] and Gvero,[25] also filed their appeals. The Prosecution reacted with two separate responses on 12 November[26] and on 16 November 2007 Borovčanin filed his reply to the Prosecution Response to Borovčanin.[27]

---

12 *Prosecutor v. Vujadin Popović et al.*, Case No. IT-05-88-T, Prosecution's Request for Leave to Reply and Prosecution's Consolidated Reply to Defence Responses to "Prosecution's Motion for Leave to Amend 65*ter* Exhibit List with 18 Exhibits Pertaining to Alistair Graham", 16 July 2007.

13 T. 13834–13891, 13894–13946.

14 Addendum to the Defence Submission Regarding the Admissibility of the Interview of Accused Ljubomir Borovčanin as Evidence Against the Co-Accused Ljubisa Beara, 17 July 2007; Arguments of the Defence for General Miletić Regarding the Admissibility of the Interview with Ljubomir Borovčanin Against General Miletić, 19 July 2007 (French original), 27 July 2007 (English translation); Submission on Behalf of Milan Gvero on the Admissibility of an Accused's Interview in the Case of a Co-Accused, 20 July 2007; Prosecution's Further Submission Regarding Admissibility of the Interviews of Ljubomir Borovčanin as Evidence Against the Co-Accused, 20 July 2007; Book of Authorities for the Prosecution Submission Regarding Admissibility of the Interview of Ljubomir Borovčanin as Evidence Against the Co-Accused, 24 July 2007.

15 T. 13956–13978.

16 Impugned Decision, para. 83(a).

17 Impugned Decision, para. 83(d).

18 Impugned Decision, paras 77, 83(e). On the reasoning informing this holding of the Trial Chamber, see also paras 70–72, 77–80.

19 Impugned Decision, paras 82, 83(g).

20 Prosecution's Appeal on Refusal to Admit Borovčanin's Interview with Regard to Acts and Conduct of Co-accused, 1 November 2007 ("Prosecution Appeal").

21 Popović Response to Prosecution's Appeal on Refusal to Admit Borovčanin's Interview with Regard to Acts and Conduct of Co-accused, 8 November 2007 ("Popović Response") and *Prosecutor v. Vujadin Popović et al.*, Case No. IT-05-88-AR73.1, Response to the Prosecution's Appeal on Refusal to Admit Borovčanin's Interview with Regard to Acts and Conduct of Co-accused, 9 November 2007 ("Beara Response").

22 Prosecution Consolidated Reply to Popović's and Beara's Responses Regarding Admission of Borovčanin's Interview, 13 November 2007 ("Prosecution Reply").

23 Borovčanin Defence Interlocutory Appeal of the Trial Chamber's Decision on the Admissibility of the Borovčanin Interview and the Amendment to the Rule 65 *ter* Exhibit List, 1 November 2007 ("Borovčanin Appeal").

24 Interlocutory Appeal on Behalf of Ljubiša Beara to the Decision on the Admissibility of the Borovčanin Interview and the Amendment of the Rule 65*ter* Exhibit List and Joinder of the Appeal of Milan Gvero against the Decision (in part) on the Admissibility of the Borovčanin Interview, 1 November 2007 ("Beara Appeal").

25 Appeal of Milan Gvero against the Decision (in part) on the Admissibility of the Borovčanin Interview, 1 November 2007 ("Gvero Appeal").

26 Prosecution Response to Beara and Gvero Interlocutory Appeals Concerning Borovčanin Interviews, 12 November 2007 ("Prosecution Response to Beara and Gvero"); *Prosecutor v. Vujadin Popović et al.*, Case No. IT-05-88-AR73.1, Prosecution Response to Accused Borovčanin Interlocutory Appeal Concerning His Interview, 12 November 2007 ("Prosecution Response to Borovčanin").

27 Borovčanin Defence Reply to Prosecution Response to Accused Borovčanin's Interlocutory Appeal Concerning His Interview, 16 November 2007.

II. STANDARD OF APPELLATE REVIEW

7. Trial Chambers exercise broad discretion as regards admission of evidence.[28] In this context, the Appeals Chamber notes that it is seized only of the issue of the admission of evidence: the substantial assessment of the evidence is for the Trial Chamber, subject to an appeal – if any – against the Trial Chamber's judgement and will be properly undertaken when the trial record is complete. Considering that this type of decision must therefore be given a margin of deference, the Appeals Chamber will reverse such decisions only when an abuse of such discretion is established. The Appeals Chamber will overturn a Trial Chamber's exercise of its discretion where it is found to **[page 4]** be (i) based on an incorrect interpretation of governing law; (ii) based on a patently incorrect conclusion of fact; or (iii) so unfair or unreasonable as to constitute an abuse of the Trial Chamber's discretion. The Appeals Chamber will also consider whether the Trial Chamber has given weight to extraneous or irrelevant considerations or has failed to give weight or sufficient weight to relevant considerations in reaching its decision.[29]

8. The question before the Appeals Chamber is thus not whether it agrees with a decision but whether the Trial Chamber has correctly exercised its discretion in reaching this decision.[30] For the Appeals Chamber to intervene in a discretionary decision of a Trial Chamber, it must be demonstrated that the Trial Chamber has committed a "discernible error" resulting in prejudice.[31]

III. SUBMISSIONS OF THE PARTIES

A. The Appeal by the Prosecution

1. Reliability of the Borovčanin Recordings and Transcript

9. The Prosecution contends that the Trial Chamber committed an error by assuming *in abstracto* that a suspect has an incentive to shift the blame to persons who only subsequently become his co-accused in a joint trial, arguing that a more specific and concrete analysis is necessary.[32] According to the Prosecution, *prima facie* reliable evidence has to be admitted and the weight given to it must be determined at the end of the case.[33] Beara responds that the Trial Chamber adequately considered the problems fundamental to the issue, namely the incentive for Borovčanin to place the blame on the other co-accused.[34] He argues that the Prosecution bears the burden of proving beyond reasonable doubt that, in a particular case, the inherent lack of reliability of suspect interviews does not exist.[35] **[page 5]**

2. Interpretation of Rules 89, 92 *bis*, 92 *ter*, and 92 *quarter*

10. The Prosecution argues that, pursuant to Rule 89(C) and (D), the Borovčanin Recordings and Transcript are admissible as against the Co-Accused without qualifications, that is, including those portions which go to prove their acts and conduct.[36] It submits that Rule 89(D) provides for the exclusion of evidence only in cases

---

28 *Prosecutor v. Zejnil Delalić et al.*, Case No. IT-96-21-A, Judgement, 20 February 2001 ("*Delalić et al.* Appeal Judgement"), para. 533. See also: *Prosecutor v. Sefer Halilović*, Case No. IT-01-48-A, Judgement, 16 October 2007, para. 38; *Prosecutor v. Dario Kordić and Mario Čerkez,* Case No. IT-95-14/2-AR73.5, Decision on Appeal Regarding Statement of a Deceased Witness, 21 July 2000, para. 20; *Prosecutor v. Dario Kordić and Mario Čerkez,* Case No. IT-95-14/2-AR73.6, Decision on Appeal Regarding the Admission into Evidence of Seven Affidavits and One Formal Statement, 18 September 2000, para. 24.

29 *Prosecutor v. Jadranko Prlić et al.*, Case No. IT-04-74-AR73.6, Decision on Appeals against Decision Admitting Transcript of Jadranko Prlić's Questioning into Evidence, 23 November 2007 ("*Prlić* Decision on Admission of Transcript"), para. 8; *Prosecutor v. Milan Milutinović et al.,* Case No. IT-05-87-AR108bis.2, Decision on the Request of the United States of America for Review, 12 May 2006 ("*Milutinović* Decision on Review"), para. 6.

30 *Prosecutor v. Slobodan Milošević*, Case Nos. IT-99-37-AR73, IT-01-50-AR73, and IT-01-51-AR73, Reasons for Decision on Prosecution Interlocutory Appeal from Refusal to Order Joinder, 18 April 2002, para. 4; *Milutinović* Decision on Review, para. 6.

31 *Prlić* Decision on Admission of Transcript, para. 9.

32 Prosecution Appeal, paras 9, 11.

33 Prosecution Appeal, para. 11; Prosecution Reply, paras 5–8 and 17, referring to *Prosecutor v. Zejnil Delalić et al.*, Case No. IT-96-21-AR73.2, Decision on Application of Defendant Zejnil Delalić for Leave to Appeal against the Decision of the Trial Chamber of 19 January 1998 for the Admissibility of Evidence, 4 March 1998, para. 17.

34 Beara Response, para. 14.

35 Beara Response, para. 13.

36 Prosecution Appeal, paras 2–4.

where "its probative value is substantially outweighed by the need to ensure a fair trial".[37] The Prosecution alleges that the Trial Chamber's reliance on the finding by the Appeals Chamber in *Galić* that questions concerning reliability have arisen in connection with witness statements before the Tribunal is mistaken[38] because, in the present case, the evidence in question stems from a *verbatim* record of the questioning of Borovčanin by Prosecution representatives in accordance with Rule 43.[39]

11. Beara avers that the Prosecution's interpretation of Rules 89(C) and 92 *bis* is inconsistent with the *Galić* Decision, wherein the Appeals Chamber held that Rule 89(C) cannot be used so as to "avoid the stringency" of Rule 92 *bis*.[40] The concerns raised in the *Galić* Decision with regard to hearsay evidence apply *a fortiori* in the present case, according to Beara, because Borovčanin was questioned as a suspect and, therefore, had an even stronger reason not to tell the truth.[41] In any event, according to Beara, the Prosecution has disregarded the interpretation of Rule 92 *bis* by the Appeals Chamber in the *Galić* Decision, which is the relevant issue in the present case, rather than the question of how statements are compiled.[42]

12. The Prosecution replies that the conclusion in the *Galić* Decision, that Rule 92 *bis*(C) bars admission of evidence going to the acts and conduct of an accused has been superseded by the new Rule 92 *quater*(B), which explicitly contemplates the admission of such evidence.[43] The Prosecution further replies that the letter of Rules 92 *bis* and 92 *quater* also shows that they are inapplicable to the present case.[44] Rule 92 *quater* is not applicable as it concerns evidence which is unavailable for "factual reasons", such as the death of a witness as opposed to "legal reasons", such as the inability to compel the testimony of an accused.[45] Moreover, Rule 92 *bis* and Rule 92 *ter* are inapplicable because they use the term "witness" which does not encompass "a suspect interview **[page 6]** originating from an accused".[46] The Prosecution argues that the word "witness" shows that these Rules deal with instances where the evidence is in principle available *viva voce*, but can be admitted in writing, under certain conditions, so as to accelerate the proceedings. In the present case, however, if the Borovčanin Recordings and Transcript are not introduced in writing, they would be lost.[47]

3. The Requirement of Cross-examination

13. The Prosecution alleges that the exclusion of the Borovčanin Recordings and Transcript with respect to the acts and conduct of the other co-accused, is inconsistent with the prior holding of the Appeals Chamber in the *Martić* case, that evidence not tested by cross-examination does not necessarily need to be excluded.[48] The Prosecution argues that the present case is actually similar to the one dealt with in the *Martić* Decision, where a witness died before the defence was able to complete his cross-examination. Indeed, the Appeals Chamber in *Martić* relied on the European Court on Human Rights ("ECtHR") case-law to support the proposition that evidence not tested through cross-examination should not be excluded as a matter of principle from the trial record.[49] The same jurisprudence has repeatedly upheld the admission of "uncrossed hearsay evidence" originating from one accused against co-accused.[50]

---

37 Prosecution Appeal, para. 10 (referring to Rule 89(D)).

38 Prosecution Appeal, paras 20–21, referring to *Prosecutor v. Galić*, Case No. IT-98-29-AR73.2, Decision on Interlocutory Appeal Concerning Rule 92 *bis*(C), 7 June 2002 (*Galić* Decision).

39 Prosecution Appeal, para. 22; Prosecution Reply, para. 11.

40 Beara Response, para. 10, referring to *Galić* Decision, para. 31.

41 Beara Response, paras 11–12.

42 Beara Response, para. 15.

43 Prosecution Reply, para. 10.

44 Prosecution Reply, paras 12–16.

45 Prosecution Reply, para. 15.

46 Prosecution Reply, para. 13 (emphasis omitted).

47 Prosecution Reply, paras 14, 15.

48 Prosecution Appeal, para. 3, referring to *Prosecutor v. Milan Martić*, Case No. IT-95-11- AR73.2, Decision on Appeal against the Trial Chamber's Decision on the Evidence of Witness Milan Babić, 14 September 2006 ("Martić Decision"), para. 20; Prosecution Reply para. 3.

49 Prosecution Reply, para. 4, referring to the *Martić* Decision para. 19.

50 Prosecution Reply, para. 4, referring to *Carta v. Italy*, Application No. 4548/02, Judgement, 20 April 2006, paras 46–55; *Ferrantelli & Santangello v. Italy*, Application No. 19874/92, Judgement, 26 June 1996, paras 51–52; *Gossa v. Poland*, Application No. 47986/99, 9 January 2007, paras 57–65.

14. Beara and Popović distinguish the Borovčanin Recordings and Transcript from the evidence given by Milan Babić ("Babić"), which was allowed in *Martić* on two grounds. First, Babić was a witness in the *Martić* case, whereas Borovčanin's statements are those of an accused and would be used against his co-accused in a joint trial.[51] Popović submits in this respect that the "inherent conflict of interest between co-accused" was not considered in the *Martić* Decision.[52] Second, Beara and Popović argue that the present situation is also distinguishable because Borovčanin has the right to remain silent under Article 21(4)(g) of the Tribunal's Statute ("Statute").[53] Popović adds that, if Borovčanin makes use of his right to remain silent, the other co-accused will be prevented from exercising their right to cross-examine him pursuant to Article 21(4)(e) of the Statute.[54] Beara **[page 7]** points out that Borovčanin has not been subjected to any cross-examination.[55] Thus, the present situation is further distinguishable from the one analyzed in *Martić*, where the witness in question (Milan Babić) was cross-examined for a certain amount of time.[56]

15. Moreover, the Prosecution claims that the Trial Chamber erred on three grounds when it held that ECtHR jurisprudence is irrelevant in the present case. First, the Appeals Chamber has explicitly considered ECtHR jurisprudence as a "useful source of guidance".[57] Second, in this specific case, the right of the accused to cross-examine witnesses is spelled out identically under the European Convention for the Protection of Human Rights and Fundamental Freedoms of 4 November 1950, as amended by Protocol No. 11 ("ECHR")[58] and under the Statute.[59] Third, the Trial Chamber erroneously regarded the test on the propriety of admission as distinct from the question of the right to a fair trial, which is the test to be met under the ECHR. The Prosecution maintains that, in ascertaining the propriety of a decision under Rule 89(C), the Trial Chamber needs – on the basis of Rule 89(B) and (D) – to consider whether fair trial guarantees are met.[60]

4. Joinder of Proceedings

16. The Prosecution further argues that the Trial Chamber erroneously applied Rule 82(A), when it held that accused in a joint trial must have the same "technical rights" that they would enjoy if they were tried individually.[61] The Prosecution claims that the system provides other safeguards, such as the requirement that untested evidence be corroborated if relied upon to ground a conviction. Otherwise, an accused would always be able to argue that "were he tried alone he would have the right to examine or cross-examine his co-accused whereas in a joinder case he does not."[62] Popović responds that cross-examination is the only way to adequately assess whether or not Borovčanin told the truth when questioned by the Prosecution.[63] **[page 8]**

B. The Appeals by the Co-Accused

1. Borovčanin Appeal

17. Borovčanin submits that the Trial Chamber erred in allowing the Prosecution to add the Borovčanin Recordings and Transcript, as well as the Borovčanin Documents, to its Exhibit List.[64] Borovčanin claims that the Trial Chamber failed to give adequate weight to arguments opposing this late addition and to the lack of a valid reason for the Prosecution's late request to amend. Moreover, he claims that the Trial Chamber

---

51 Beara Response, para. 4; Popović Response, paras 7–8.
52 Popović Response, para. 5.
53 Beara Response, para. 19; Popović Response, para. 6.
54 Popović Response, para. 6.
55 Beara Response, para. 19.
56 Beara Response, paras 18–19; see also Popović Response, para. 4.
57 Prosecution Appeal, para. 13, referring to *Martić* Decision, para. 19.
58 213 UNTS 221, CETS 005. See http://conventions.coe.int/Treaty/en/Treaties/Html/005.htm.
59 Prosecution Appeal, para. 14, referring to the ECHR and the Statute.
60 Prosecution Appeal, para. 15.
61 Prosecution Appeal, paras 23–24; Prosecution Reply, para. 19.
62 Prosecution Appeal, para. 24, quoting Impugned Decision, Partial Dissenting Opinion of Judge Kimberly Prost, para. 36.
63 Popović Response, para. 8.
64 Borovčanin Appeal, para. 12.

abused its discretion by concluding that the Prosecution inadvertently omitted the Borovčanin Recordings and Transcript, as well as the Borovčanin Documents, from the original Exhibit List.[65]

18. The Prosecution responds that the Trial Chamber applied the Tribunal's jurisprudence and gave adequate weight to the relevant facts before allowing the Prosecution to amend its Exhibit List.[66] Noting Borovčanin's failure to identify any prejudice suffered,[67] the Prosecution recalls the factors listed in the Impugned Decision: (i) the Prosecution's evidence that the exhibits were of *prima facie* relevance to the Indictment; (ii) the lack of prejudice to the Accused; and (iii) the fact that the Prosecution's disclosure had provided enough time for the Co-Accused to prepare for Mr Graham's cross-examination.[68]

19. Borovčanin further challenges the admissibility, in relation to himself, of the Borovčanin Recordings and Transcript and of the Borovčanin Documents, claiming that the Trial Chamber's finding that Borovčanin was adequately represented during the questioning, considering the totality of the circumstances, was erroneous.[69] The circumstances that the Trial Chamber should have taken into account included (i) Counsel's relative silence during most of the questioning; (ii) Counsel's absence during the first three hours of the First Interview; (iii) Counsel's failure to inquire about the portion of the questioning that he missed; (iv) Counsel's failure to ask how Borovčanin was related to the investigation; (v) Counsel's failure to clarify Borovčanin's status as a potential suspect and his corresponding procedural rights; and (vi) the representative of the Prosecution's failure to ensure that Counsel understood the relevant Rules.[70]

20. Borovčanin insists that his waiver of the right to have counsel present during the whole of the questioning was invalid as he was informed that he was a "possible" rather than an "actual" **[page 9]** suspect. He refers to ECtHR and United States of America's jurisprudence to support the contention that his waiver was therefore not done voluntarily, knowingly or intelligently, thus concluding that nothing said thereafter should be admitted, pursuant to Rules 42 and 95.[71] Borovčanin submits that pursuant to the fair trial guarantees enshrined in Article 21 of the Statute, the summons, which did identify him as a suspect, was nullified when Mr Graham subsequently stated that he "may be a suspect". He therefore assigns error to the Trial Chamber's conclusion that Mr Graham confirmed Borovčanin's status as described in the summons.[72]

21. While conceding that Rule 42(a)(iii) does not require the Prosecution to explicitly warn that material gathered during a suspect's questioning could be used "against him", Borovčanin however argues that, since Mr Graham did tell Borovčanin that the questioning could be used "against him" but these words were not translated into Borovčanin's own language, Borovčanin was misled as to his status and therefore deprived of due process.[73]

22. In relation to Counsel's representation and to Borovčanin's waiver of the right to remain silent, the Prosecution avers that Borovčanin's description of Counsel's conduct is "incomplete",[74] as Borovčanin did not mention Counsel's meeting with Borovčanin or his suggestion that the session be terminated to discuss matters with his client.[75] Rejecting Borovčanin's interpretation of ECtHR and U.S. case law as inapplicable before the Tribunal, the Prosecution claims that the waiver of the right to remain silent was valid pursuant to Rule 42[76] and that the Trial Chamber's decision on this matter reflects its assessment of the circumstances enumerated in Borovčanin's appeal.[77] The Prosecution also faults Borovčanin for failing to identify the specific breach of his rights or to link any such breach to the admissibility issue.[78]

---

65 Borovčanin Appeal, paras 11–12.
66 Prosecution Response to Borovčanin, paras 4–5.
67 Prosecution Response to Borovčanin, para. 8.
68 Prosecution Response to Borovčanin, paras 4–7.
69 Borovčanin Appeal, paras 14, 22.
70 Borovčanin Appeal, paras 14, 17–19.
71 Borovčanin Appeal, paras 24–30.
72 Borovčanin Appeal, paras 32–38.
73 Borovčanin Appeal, paras 39–42.
74 Prosecution Response to Borovčanin, para. 11.
75 Prosecution Response to Borovčanin, paras 11–12.
76 Prosecution Response to Borovčanin, para. 15.
77 Prosecution Response to Borovčanin, para. 15.
78 Prosecution Response to Borovčanin, para. 16.

23. In his reply, Borovčanin suggests that the finding in the Impugned Decision that the admission of the Borovčanin Recordings and Transcript and of the Borovčanin Documents "in no way alters the Prosecution's case" is unsubstantiated.[79] Borovčanin submits that the Prosecution has not provided a reasonable excuse for its late amendment to the Exhibit List,[80] and that the Trial Chamber unduly allowed the Prosecution to make such unsubstantiated and untimely amendments **[page 10]** without regard to these amendments' prejudicial effect on the Co-Accused.[81] Pointing to the cross-examination of Alistair Graham[82] and to the Trial Chamber's statement regarding his Counsel's conduct,[83] Borovčanin argues that Counsel's failure to "effectively and diligently" represent him is reflected in his failure to terminate the questioning instead of merely raising the issue after several hours of interviewing.[84] Borovčanin avers that Counsel's ineffectiveness was based not only on his experience, but on his relative unwillingness to educate himself on the applicable procedural rules.[85] Addressing the Prosecution's treatment of foreign case-law, Borovčanin submits that Rule 89(A) provides for the application of other sources of law when "lacunae in its rules of evidence" exist.[86]

2. Gvero Appeal

24. Gvero appeals the Impugned Decision in part. He argues generally that Trial Chamber did not properly distinguish between the status of a witness and that of an accused in deciding to admit the Borovčanin Recordings and Transcript.[87] Gvero submits that Borovčanin, has the choice of testifying during his defence case, and so cannot also be a Prosecution witness in his own trial against the Co-accused.[88] By "joining Borovčanin to the case", the Prosecution thus effectively lost the opportunity to use him as a witness in the case.[89]

25. Gvero argues that the Trial Chamber erred by referring to Rules 92 *bis* and 92 *ter*, which apply specifically to witnesses and not to accused persons: any analogy between the situation of Borovčanin and those of witnesses under these Rules is therefore fundamentally unfair.[90] Gvero agrees with the Trial Chamber's position that Rule 92 *quater* refers to circumstances that are inapplicable to the present case,[91] but argues that the Trial Chamber's interpretation of Rule 82(A) – dealing with the rights of an accused in joint and separate trials – should extend the prohibition of using the Borovčanin Recordings and Transcript as proof of the co-accused's acts and conduct to prevent their use as to *all* evidentiary issues.[92] Gvero further claims that since the Rules do not speak of the evidentiary value of a previous statement of an accused in relation to his co-accused, it would be improper to settle the issue through a Trial Chamber's judicial interpretation.[93] **[page 11]**

26. In its response, the Prosecution addresses a number of Gvero's arguments. It rejects Gvero's propositions that the joinder of cases renders Borovčanin unavailable as a witness, since the Borovčanin Recordings and Transcript are documentary evidence rather than witness testimony.[94] In any event, according to the Prosecution, the joinder decision was issued by the Trial Chamber.[95] The Prosecution also objects to Gvero's interpretation of Rule 82(A) as requiring identical rights for accused tried separately and jointly, insisting that such rights must only be "equivalent". The Prosecution specifically notes that the right to cross-examine in joint proceedings is protected by requiring corroboration for evidence not tested by cross-examination.[96]

---

79 Borovčanin Reply, para. 8.
80 Borovčanin Reply, para. 10.
81 Borovčanin Reply, para. 11.
82 Borovčanin Reply, para. 12.
83 Borovčanin Reply, para. 14.
84 Borovčanin Reply, para. 15.
85 Borovčanin Reply, paras 16–17.
86 Borovčanin Reply, paras 20–21.
87 Gvero Appeal, para. 7
88 Gvero Appeal, para. 13.
89 Gvero Appeal, para. 9.
90 Gvero Appeal, paras 10–11.
91 Gvero Appeal, para. 12.
92 Gvero Appeal, para. 14.
93 Gvero Appeal, para. 15.
94 Prosecution Response to Beara and Gvero, paras 22–23.
95 Prosecution Response to Beara and Gvero, para. 27.
96 Prosecution Response to Beara and Gvero paras 28–29.

3. Beara Appeal

27. Beara joins Gvero's submissions on appeal in their entirety, further elaborating that the Trial Chamber erred by granting the Prosecution's request to add the Borovčanin Recordings and Transcript and the Borovčanin Documents to its Exhibit List.[97]

28. First, Beara points to the Prosecution's failure to address the need to ensure a fair trial under Rule 89(D)[98] by failing to show "good cause" in requesting permission to amend the Exhibit List,[99] and by disclosing the Borovčanin Recordings and Transcript and the Borovčanin Documents at a late stage of the proceedings, despite having had them in its possession for more than five years.[100] Beara then argues that his fair trial rights pursuant to Articles 20 and 21 of the Statute were prejudiced by numerous late amendments to the Exhibit List,[101] averring that the Trial Chamber erred in finding that the Defence only provided "general assertions of prejudice" since even the late submission of relatively short documents has affected its preparation in relation to other material.[102]

29. Second, Beara submits that the Trial Chamber's admission of the Borovčanin Recordings and Transcript against the other co-accused violates his right to examine the witnesses against him. He questions the reasoning supporting the application by analogy of Rule 92 *quater* to the situation under consideration.[103] Noting that the jurisprudence of the Tribunal is inconclusive on the admission of a statement by an accused against another co-accused, Beara further cites both Trial **[page 12]** Chamber decisions and external authorities to support his argument that such evidence should be excluded.[104]

30. As noted above, the Prosecution filed a joint response to the Gvero Appeal and to the Beara Appeal. In this Response, the Prosecution notes that the rights of all co-accused featured prominently in the Trial Chamber's decision.[105] The Prosecution submits that the Trial Chamber correctly allowed the amendment of the Exhibit List because the Prosecution had shown good cause: the exhibits were *prima facie* relevant to the Indictment and the disclosure did not prejudice the rights of the accused in the particular circumstances of the case.[106] As evidence of the absence of prejudice, the Prosecution notes that most of the new material was disclosed in 2005[107] and that the July 2007 disclosure of the remaining materials, which were "neither lengthy nor complicated", were either referenced in the interview transcripts disclosed in 2005 or only became relevant after the Prosecution became able to anticipate Defence challenges.[108]

31. The Prosecution submits that, contrary to Beara's arguments, Rules 89(C) and (D) do address the admission of the Borovčanin Recordings and Transcript against the other co-accused by treating them as hearsay evidence.[109] The Prosecution rejects Beara's reference to the Tribunal's jurisprudence as well as to external authorities as incorrect, inapplicable, or unhelpful.[110] The Prosecution assigns further error to Beara and Gvero's application of Rules 92 *bis*, 92 *ter*, and 92 *quater* to the admissibility issue,[111] arguing that, contrary to Beara's argument, the Trial Chamber did not rely on, but rather noted the limited applicability of the Rule 92 *quater*(A) cases.[112] The Prosecution submits that, while Rule 92 *quater*(A) involves mentally or physically unavailable witnesses, the reasons for unavailability do not matter: this provision is relevant, by analogy, to the admission of interview transcripts of a legally unavailable person.[113] The Prosecution therefore

---

97 Beara Appeal, para. 9.
98 Beara Appeal, para. 13.
99 Beara Appeal, para. 17.
100 Beara Appeal, paras 14–15.
101 Beara Appeal, para. 19.
102 Beara Appeal, paras 20–23.
103 Beara Appeal, para. 24.
104 Beara Appeal, paras 31–39.
105 Prosecution Response to Beara and Gvero, paras 8–9.
106 Prosecution Response to Beara and Gvero, paras 10–12.
107 Prosecution Response to Beara and Gvero, para. 13.
108 Prosecution Response to Beara and Gvero, para. 14.
109 Prosecution Response to Beara and Gvero, paras 16–17.
110 Prosecution Response to Beara and Gvero, paras 18–21.
111 Prosecution Response to Beara and Gvero, para. 24.
112 Prosecution Response to Beara and Gvero, para. 24.
113 Prosecution Response to Beara and Gvero, para. 26.

reiterates its position that the Trial Chamber erred in automatically excluding the Borovčanin Recordings and Transcript as proof of the acts and conduct of the co-accused other than Borovčanin.[114] **[page 13]**

IV. DISCUSSION

A. Borovčanin's Right to Effective Assistance of Counsel

32. A preliminary matter to the issue of admission of the Borovčanin Recordings and Transcript and the Borovčanin Documents is the question of whether, as Borovčanin submits, he was not adequately represented by Counsel during his questioning by the Prosecution.[115] Indeed, the questioning of a suspect pursuant to Rules 42 and 43 demands stringent safeguards in order to protect the questioned individual's right not to incriminate himself.[116]

33. In this respect, the Trial Chamber considered two relevant principles: (i) whether the procedural safeguards set forth in Rules 42 and 43 were satisfied; and (ii) whether the admissibility test laid down in Rules 89(C) and 89(D) (relevant evidence with probative value and not substantially outweighed by the need to ensure a fair trial) was met.[117] It further carefully analyzed the Tribunal's case law applying these principles[118] and took into account the investigator's examination and cross-examination in court in order to reach its conclusion on whether the rights of Borovčanin had been breached.[119]

34. The Appeals Chamber recalls that the Prosecution or another competent authority who is obliged to inform a suspect or an accused about his right to counsel must do so in an unambiguous way and in a language that the suspect or accused understands.[120] This procedure is essential to ensure the rights of each suspect. On the basis of the parties' arguments, the Appeals Chamber is not convinced that the Trial Chamber abused its discretion or otherwise erred in concluding that the Prosecution unambiguously advised Borovčanin about his right to counsel. Moreover, when Borovčanin appeared for his questioning, he was advised that he could wait for his attorney to arrive; notwithstanding this assurance, he agreed that the questioning could begin.[121]

35. Furthermore, the Appeals Chamber notes that Borovčanin has not brought specific evidence showing his former Counsel's misconduct, lack of necessary qualification and competence, or otherwise inappropriate behaviour.[122] In particular, Borovčanin does not contest the Prosecution's **[page 14]** suggestion that he had originally misrepresented the conduct of Counsel, omitting to mention the fact that Counsel did have a meeting with him and did request termination of the questioning in order to discuss matters with Borovčanin.[123] From the moment when Counsel arrived, and considering that Borovčanin has not shown any misbehaviour by his former Counsel, it was not unreasonable for the Trial Chamber to conclude that Borovčanin's right to effective representation had been ensured.

36. In light of these circumstances, and taking into consideration all of the relevant arguments of the parties in this respect, the Appeals Chamber finds that in this case the Trial Chamber did not abuse its discretion in concluding that Borovčanin's procedural rights – both his right to be informed about the right to counsel and his right to effective representation – had been effectively safeguarded during the questioning by the Prosecution, both before and after Counsel's arrival at the location of the questioning.

---

114 Prosecution Response to Beara and Gvero, para. 26.

115 Borovčanin Appeal, paras 14–22.

116 *Prlić* Decision on Admission of Transcript, para. 45.

117 Impugned Decision, para. 28.

118 Impugned Decision, paras 29–39.

119 See, for example, Impugned Decision, paras 6, 33 and 37.

120 *Delalić et al.* Appeal Judgement, paras 551–552.

121 Impugned Decision, para. 33.

122 *Prosecutor v. Duško Tadić*, Case No. IT-94-1-A, Decision on Appellant's Motion for the Extension of the Time-Limit and Admission of Additional Evidence, 15 October 1998, para. 65 ("lurking doubt that injustice may have been caused to the accused by gross professional incompetence"); *Prosecutor v. Vidoje Blagojević and Dragan Jokić*, Case No. IT-02-60-A, 9 May 2007, para. 23. *Cf.*, for example, *Prosecutor v. Sefer Halilović*, Case No. IT-01-48-AR73.2, Decision on Interlocutory Appeal Concerning Admission of Record of Interview of the Accused from the Bar Table, paras 61–62. See also *Prosecutor v. Jean-Paul Akayesu*, Case No. ICTR-96-4-A, Judgement, 1 June 2001, paras 67–84 (in particular para. 80 on requirement to show some "tangible example of gross professional misconduct by his Counsel such as resulted in a miscarriage of justice") and *Ferdinand Nahimana et Consorts c. Procureur, affaire n° ICTR-99-52-A, Arrêt*, 28 November 2007 ("*Nahimana et al.* Appeal Judgement"), paras 130–131.

123 Prosecution Response to Borovčanin, paras 11–16; Borovčanin Reply, paras 12–19.

B. Amendment to the Exhibit List

37. Rule 65 *ter* (E)(iii) provides, *inter alia*, that the Prosecution shall file, within a time-limit set by the pre-trial Judge and not less than six weeks before the Pre-Trial Conference, "the list of exhibits the Prosecution intends to offer", serving on the Defence copies of the listed exhibits. In the exercise of its inherent discretion in managing the trial proceedings and if satisfied that this is in the interests of justice, a Trial Chamber may, however, grant a Prosecution's request to amend the above-mentioned list. In doing so, a Trial Chamber must be satisfied that, taking into account the specific circumstances of a case, good cause is shown for amending the original list and that the newly offered material is relevant and of sufficient importance to justify the late addition. Moreover, a Trial Chamber must carefully balance any amendment to the lists in Rule 65 *ter* with an adequate protection of the rights of the accused.[124]

38. In the present case, the Trial Chamber carefully assessed the arguments of the parties on the amendment of the Exhibit List[125] and came to the conclusion that allowing the proposed amendments to the Exhibit List was in the interest of justice. This conclusion was based on the **[page 15]** *prima facie* relevance of the newly proposed material and on the fact that enough time had been provided to the Co-Accused to familiarize themselves with the new material. Moreover, the Co-Accused had not demonstrated what prejudice would arise in the particular circumstances by allowing the amendment of the Exhibit List.[126] The Trial Chamber found that the Prosecution had only inadvertently omitted the Borovčanin Recordings and Transcript and the Borovčanin Documents from its original Exhibit List.[127] It further considered that, "in the context of a complex multi-accused trial in which a considerable amount of evidence is presented by the Prosecution, a certain level of flexibility must be maintained".[128]

39. The Appeals Chamber finds that, in the circumstances of this case, the Trial Chamber has not abused its discretion in allowing a late amendment to the Exhibit List. Contrary to what Borovčanin[129] and Beara[130] argue, the Trial Chamber did not err in setting out the applicable law and in applying it to the circumstances of the case. In particular, it fell within the Trial Chamber's discretion to conclude that the failure to add the material in question to the original Exhibit List was an inadvertent omission and that the rights of the accused could be safeguarded through means other than excluding potentially relevant material.

C. Joinder of Proceedings

40. The parties are not in disagreement that the present trial proceedings originate from a request of joinder filed by the Prosecution, which the Trial Chamber granted on 31 October 2005, despite subsequent severance of the trial of two accused.[131]

41. Rule 82 provides that:

> (A) In joint trials, each accused shall be accorded the same rights as if such accused were being tried separately.
>
> (B) The Trial Chamber may order that persons accused jointly under Rule 48 be tried separately if it considers it necessary in order to avoid a conflict of interests that might cause serious prejudice to an accused, or to protect the interests of justice.

---

124 *Cf.* Rule 73 *bis* (E) of the Rules of Procedure and Evidence of the International Criminal Tribunal for the Prosecution of Persons Responsible for Genocide and Other Serious Violations of International Humanitarian Law Committed in the Territory of Rwanda and Rwandan Citizens Responsible for Genocide and Other Such Violations Committed in the Territory of Neighbouring States, between 1 January 1994 and 31 December 1994. See, in this respect, *Nahimana et al.* Appeal Judgement, paras 228–233.

125 Impugned Decision, paras 10–17.

126 Impugned Decision, paras 19–20.

127 Impugned Decision, para. 21.

128 Impugned Decision, para. 18.

129 Borovčanin Appeal, paras 11–12.

130 Beara Appeal, paras 9–23.

131 See *supra*, para. 2.

Severance or joinder of cases is a matter falling within the discretion of Trial Chambers.[132] **[page 16]**

42. The Trial Chamber recalled the import of this Rule and took it into account when reaching its conclusions, holding that, since the Prosecution elected to try Borovčanin jointly with the other accused in this trial, Borovčanin's absolute right not to testify in his own trial operates as a bar preventing the six other co-accused from calling him for cross-examination.[133]

43. Undoubtedly, the situation posed by the request for admission of the Borovčanin Recordings and Transcript into evidence does indeed modify the situation for Borovčanin's co-accused – had the trials been separate, each of them could conceivably request to have Borovčanin examined as a witness in their own trials, for he would not have benefited from the right to remain silent in those proceedings. The issue is whether such different treatment would result in prejudice.[134] The Appeals Chamber notes that one of the elements to be taken into account when joining different proceedings is indeed "the protection of the rights of the accused pursuant to Article 21 of the Statute"[135] and not whether the protection of the accused's rights would be identical in a separate and in a joint trial.

44. Even if the Co-Accused were tried separately, they would not necessarily have the opportunity to conduct an effective cross-examination of Borovčanin. If the Prosecution were to tender the Borovčanin Recordings and Transcript, the various Co-Accused could call Borovčanin as a witness and subject him to cross-examination; however, Borovčanin might refuse to answer questions pursuant to Rule 90(E), which stipulates that a witness may object to giving self-incriminating statements.[136] Nonetheless, the Trial Chamber, in principle, could still admit all of the documents in question as such into evidence. Thus, it cannot be said *a priori* that a joinder in such circumstances would entail prejudice to Borovčanin's co-accused.

45. Moreover, the Appeals Chamber does not accept that Rule 82(A) bars *in abstracto* any difference of treatment between accused in a joint trial and those in separate trials. The consequence of such reasoning would be that an accused could *always* successfully oppose joinder on the basis of the fact that, were he tried alone, he would have the right to examine or cross-examine his co-accused – whereas in the joint case he does not. The Appeals Chamber has already stated that, as long as a Trial Chamber considers potential prejudice to an accused stemming from joinder, his right to examine Prosecution witnesses is not unduly impaired by the fact that Counsel for another **[page 17]** accused will examine those witnesses before, or even instead of, him in a joint trial.[137] Similarly, a Trial Chamber will have to be vigilant in ensuring the exercise of all the accused's rights related to a fair trial in such a situation – but this may not translate into barring any difference of treatment across the board.

46. The Appeals Chamber concludes that, though different safeguards apply in the two instances, there is no prejudice *per se* against Borovčanin's co-accused by allowing the Borovčanin Recordings and Transcript and the Borovčanin Documents into evidence in a joint trial. This does not, however, exclude the possibility that in certain circumstances, it might be appropriate for a Trial Chamber to take additional measures in order to ensure the right to a fair trial of an accused, including – but not limited to – severing proceedings, excluding certain evidence, and calling or recalling certain witnesses to be examined in court.

---

132 *Prosecutor v. Ante Gotovina* and *Prosecutor v. Ivan Čermak and Mladen Markač*, Case Nos. IT-01-45-AR73.1, IT-03-73-AR73.1 and IT-03-73-AR73.2, Decision on Interlocutory Appeals against the Trial Chamber's Decision to Amend the Indictment and for Joinder, 25 October 2006 ("*Gotovina* Decision of 25 October 2006"), para. 6; *Prosecutor v. Zdravko Tolimir et al.*, Case No. IT-04-80-AR73.1, Decision on Radivoje Miletić's on Interlocutory Appeal Against the Trial Chamber's Decision on Joinder of Accused, 27 January 2006 ("*Miletić* Decision on Joinder"), para. 5; *Prosecutor v. Radoslav Brđanin and Momir Talic*, Case No. IT-99-36-AR72.2, Decision on Request to Appeal, 16 May 2000, p. 4. See, *e.g.*, *Prosecutor v. Milan Milutinović et al.*, Case No. IT-05-87-T, Decision on Pavković Motion for Partial Severance, 27 September 2007, para. 7; *Prosecutor v. Jadranko Prlić et al.*, Case No. IT-04-74-T, Decision on Jadranko Prlić's Motion for Severance, 17 August 2007, para. 22.

133 Impugned Decision, paras 73 and 75.

134 *Gotovina* Decision of 25 October 2006, para. 17.

135 *Prosecutor v. Vinko Pandurević and Milorad Trbić*, Case No. IT-05-86-AR73.1, Decision on Vinko Pandurević's Interlocutory Appeal Against the Trial Chamber's Decision on Joinder of Accused, 24 January 2006, para. 8.

136 The basis of this rule is the fundamental right to remain silent enshrined in Art. 14(3)(g) of the International Covenant on Civil and Political Rights of 16 December 1966 (999 UNTS 171). For the ECHR, see *Funke v. France*, ECtHR, App. No. 10828/84, 25 February 1993, para. 44.

137 *Miletić* Decision on Joinder, para. 29.

D. Admissibility of Borovčanin Recordings and Transcript

47. As mentioned above, the Trial Chamber admitted the Borovčanin Recording and Transcripts in relation to all Co-Accused in the instant proceedings.[138] However, it limited their admission as evidence concerning Borovčanin's co-accused, ordering that they not be used as evidence which goes to proof of the acts and conduct of co-accused other than Borovčanin.[139] The Appeals Chamber notes that several arguments raised by the parties in relation to the admissibility of the Borovčanin Recordings and Transcript in general[140] as well as in relation to the acts and conduct of Borovčanin's co-accused are interrelated.[141]

48. In the *Prlić* Decision on Admission of Transcript, the Appeals Chamber has recently reasoned that "[a] request to admit a transcript of a suspect's questioning into the trial record cannot be equated with a request to add the person in question to the Prosecution's witness list".[142] Moreover, "as a matter of principle nothing bars the admission of evidence that is not tested or might not be tested through cross-examination" as long as findings that a trier of fact has to reach beyond reasonable doubt (*i.e.*, on facts indispensable for a conviction or to find aggravating circumstances) require sufficient corroboration.[143] The Appeals Chamber has further remarked that this "does not mean that a trier of fact would always abuse its discretion in limiting, or even **[page 18]** denying, the admission of certain statements of a co-accused in light of Rules 89 and 95 and depending on the circumstances of the case".[144]

49. Trial Chambers faced with exceptional circumstances might indeed need to take steps additional to the requirement of corroboration described above in order to ensure the rights of all accused in a trial. In particular, the Appeals Chamber notes that there are indeed differences between the *Prlić et al.* case and the instant proceedings such as, for example, the fact that the investigator who questioned the suspect – Mr Alistair Graham – testified as a witness and that, therefore, the Trial Chamber had the opportunity to assess in greater detail the modalities of the questioning.

50. However, it would be wrong to exclude certain evidence solely because of the supposedly intrinsic lack of reliability of the content of a suspect's questioning in relation to persons who later became that suspect's co-accused. In this context, the Appeals Chamber notes that there is a fundamental distinction between admitting evidence and according weight to it.[145]

51. The Appeals Chamber further notes that, in order to properly ensure the rights of all Co-Accused in the present proceedings, a trier of fact is required to carry out a careful balancing of the probative value of the suspect's questioning to be admitted into evidence, taking into account all of the circumstances of the case.[146]

52. In light of the foregoing, the Appeals Chamber finds that the Trial Chamber committed a discernible error. Taking into account that a proper assessment of the material in question should be done on the basis of the trial record,[147] and considering that the Impugned Decision is partly premised on an incorrect interpretation of the governing law and consequent lack of reasoning in relation to the content and modalities of the Borovčanin Recordings and Transcript, the Appeals Chamber finds it necessary to remand the issue to the Trial Chamber. **[page 19]**

---

138 Impugned Decision, para. 83(d) and (e).
139 Impugned Decision, para. 83(e).
140 See, *inter alia*, Gvero Appeal, paras 10–15, Beara Appeal, paras 24, 31–39.
141 See, *inter alia*, Prosecution Appeal, paras 2–4, 9–15, 20–22.
142 *Prlić* Decision on Admission of Transcript, para. 38.
143 *Prlić* Decision on Admission of Transcript, paras 55–61.
144 *Prlić* Decision on Admission of Transcript, para. 62, in particular fn. 104.
145 See already, *mutatis mutandis*, *Prlić* Decision on Admission of Transcript, para. 62.
146 *Prlić* Decision on Admission of Transcript, paras 61–62.
147 *Prlić* Decision on Admission of Transcript, para. 62.

V. DISPOSITION

In light of the foregoing, the Appeals Chamber

DISMISSES the Borovčanin Appeal;

DISMISSES the Beara Appeal;

DISMISSES the Gvero Appeal;

ALLOWS the Prosecution Appeal in part;

REMANDS the issue to the Trial Chamber for further action consistent with the present decision;

DISMISSES the remainder of the Prosecution Appeal.

Done in English and French, the English version being authoritative.

Done this 14th day of December 2007
At The Hague,
The Netherlands.

Judge Fausto Pocar
President

[Seal of the Tribunal]

UNITED NATIONS

International Tribunal for the Prosecution of Persons Responsible for Serious Violations of International Humanitarian Law Committed in the Territory of the former Yugoslavia since 1991	Case No.:	IT-05-88-T
	Date:	25 October 2007
	Original:	English

IN TRIAL CHAMBER II

Before: **Judge Carmel Agius, Presiding**
Judge O-Gon Kwon
Judge Kimberly Prost
Judge Ole Bjørn Støle – Reserve Judge

Registrar: **Mr. Hans Holthuis**

Decision of: **25 October 2007**

PROSECUTOR

v.

VUJADIN POPOVIĆ
LJUBIŠA BEARA
DRAGO NIKOLIĆ
LJUBOMIR BOROVČANIN
RADIVOJE MILETIĆ
MILAN GVERO
VINKO PANDUREVIĆ

PUBLIC

DECISION ON THE ADMISSIBILITY OF THE BOROVČANIN INTERVIEW AND THE AMENDMENT OF THE RULE *65 TER* EXHIBIT LIST

Office of the Prosecutor
Mr. Peter McCloskey

Counsel for the Accused
Mr. Zoran Živanović and Ms. Julie Condon for Vujadin Popović
Mr. John Ostojić and Mr. Christopher Meek for Ljubiša Beara
Ms. Jelena Nikolić and Mr. Stéphane Bourgon for Drago Nikolić
Mr. Aleksandar Lazarević and Mr. Miodrag Stojanović for Ljubomir Borovčanin
Ms. Natacha Fauveau Ivanović and Mr. Nenad Petrušić for Radivoje Miletić
Mr. Dragan Krgović and Mr. David Josse for Milan Gvero
Mr. Peter Haynes and Mr. Đorđe Sarapa for Vinko Pandurević

[page 1] THIS TRIAL CHAMBER of the International Tribunal for the Prosecution of Persons Responsible for Serious Violations of International Humanitarian Law Committed in the Territory of the former Yugoslavia since 1991 ("Tribunal"), is seised of the "Prosecution's Motion for Leave to Amend 65 *ter* Exhibit List with 18 Exhibits Pertaining to Alistair Graham", filed confidentially on 6 July 2007 ("Rule 65 *ter* List Amendment Motion"); the "Motion for Leave to Supplement Prosecution's 6 July 2007 65 *ter* Motion", filed on 12 July 2007 ("Supplemental Rule 65 *ter* Motion"); the "Corrigendum to Prosecution's 6 July 2007 and 12 July 2007 Motions Seeking Leave to Amend 65 *ter* Exhibit List", filed on 13 July 2007 ("Prosecution Corrigendum")—colleetively, "Amendment Motions." In the course of considering the motions and Defence objections, this Trial Chamber has become seised of the issue of whether statements taken by the Prosecution from one of the accused, Ljubomir Borovčanin ("Borovčanin"), should be admitted as evidence against the other accused in this case ("co-Accused").

I. INTRODUCTION

1. On 28 April 2006, the Prosecution indicated intent to call its investigator Alistair Graham ("Graham") to testify about statements taken by the Prosecution from Borovčanin, one of seven accused in this case.[1]

2. Borovčanin was interviewed by the Prosecution on 20 February 2002 and 11 to 12 March 2002. The interview resulted in audio recordings and transcripts ("Borovčanin Recordings" and "Borovčanin Transcripts", collectively referred to as "Borovčanin Interview" or "Borovčanin's statements")[2] Multiple documents were also referenced during the interviews ("Borovčanin Documents").[3]

3. On 6 July 2007, the Prosecution sought to amend its Rule 65 *ter* Exhibit List to add the materials related to its 2002 interview with Borovčanin.[4] Defence teams filed responses to the Prosecution's motion to amend its 65 *ter* list,[5] and the Prosecution filed a reply,[6] between 6 and 16 July 2007. **[page 2]**

4. On 28 June 2007, defence counsel for Borovčanin and Gvero orally asked whether Borovčanin's statements to the Prosecution would be treated as admissible evidence against the co-Accused.[7] The prosecutor

---

1 *See* Prosecution's Filing of Pre-Trial Brief Pursuant to Rule 65 *ter* and List of Exhibits Pursuant to Rule 65 *ter* (E)(v), 28 April 2006, Annex B, p. 2 (listing Graham as witness in 65*ter* pre-trial brief).

2 Rule 65 *ter* List Amendment Motion, para. 4.

3 *Ibid.*, para. 5.

4 *Ibid.*, para. 1.

5 Response of General Miletić to Prosecution Motion for Leave to Amend the List of Exhibits by Adding 18 Exhibits Related to Alistair Graham, 12 July 2007 (French original), 26 July 2007 (English translation), ("Miletić Response"); Defence Response on Behalf of Ljubisa Beara to the Prosecution's Motion for Leave to Amend 65 *ter* Exhibit List with 18 Exhibits Pertaining to Alistair Graham, 12 July 2007 ("Beara Response"); Borovčanin Defence Response and Motion in Opposition to "Prosecution's Motion for Leave to Amend 65 *ter* Exhibit List with 18 Exhibits Pertaining to Alistair Graham", 12 July 2007 ("Borovčanin Response"); Motion on Behalf of Drago Nikolić Joining the Borovčanin and Miletić Defence Responses to "Prosecution's Motion for Leave to Amend 65 *ter* Exhibit List with 18 Exhibits Pertaining to Alistair Graham", 12 July 2007 ("Nikolić Response"); Motion on Behalf of Vinko Pandurević Joining the Defence Responses to Prosecution's Motion for Leave to Amend the 65 *ter Exhibit* List with 18 Exhibits Pertaining to Alistair Graham, 13 July 2007 ("Pandurević Response"); Defence Response on Behalf of Ljubisa Beara to Prosecution Motion for Leave to Supplement Prosecution's 6 July 2007 65 *ter* Motion, 13 July 2007 ("Second Beara Response"); Borovčanin Defence Notification on Joining "Defence Response on Behalf of Ljubisa Beara to the Prosecution's Motion for Leave to Amend 65 *ter* Exhibit List with 18 Exhibits Pertaining to Alistair Graham", 13 July 2007 ("Second Borovčanin Response"); Borovčanin Defence Response to Prosecution 12 July 2007 65 *ter* Motion, Notification on Joining Beara Defence Response to Prosecution 12 July 2007 65 *ter* Motion, and Motion for Leave to Supplement "Borovčanin Defence Response and Motion in Opposition to "Prosecution's Motion for Leave to Amend 65 *ter* Exhibit List with 18 Exhibits Pertaining to Alistair Graham"", 16 July 2007 ("Third Borovčanin Response"); Corrigendum to Response of General Miletić to Prosecution Motion for Leave to Amend the Exhibits List by Adding 18 Exhibits Related to Alistair Graham, 25 July 2007 (English translation), 16 July 2007 (French original) ("Miletić Corrigendum").

6 Prosecution's Request for Leave to Reply and Prosecution's Consolidated Reply to Defence Responses to "Prosecution's Motion for Leave to Amend 65 *ter* Exhibit List with 18 Exhibits Pertaining to Alistair Graham", 16 July 2007 ("Prosecution Reply").

7 *See, e.g.*, T. 13516-13517, 28 June 2007 (statement of Aleksandar Lazarević, counsel for Borovčanin) ("The other issue is, well, it is of course relevant for Mr. Borovčanin's Defence but it's also relevant for all other defences and that's the impact that the admissibility of – the admission of Mr. Borovčanin's interview into evidence will have towards other Defences."); T. 13522–13523 (28 June 2007) (statement of David Josse, counsel for Milan Gvero) ("[I]n due course, those of us representing the co-accused will need to know in terms, whether this interview, if admitted into evidence, in part or in whole, has any evidential effect as against our clients. . . . I know as well that it was a live issue in the *Blagojević-Jokić* case and indeed I hope Mr. McCloskey will forgive me for saying this but in that case he conceded that Jokić's interview had no evidential effect as against Blagojević.")

stated that "that the policy of the Office of the Prosecutor is now that a statement can be used against fellow accused and it's up to the Court to decide what weight they give it."[8]

5. The Trial Chamber heard extensive oral argument on 11 and 12 July 2007 about whether Borovčanin's statements should be admitted against the co-Accused.[9] Beara also filed a written submission on the issue on 12 July 2007.[10]

6. Without prejudice to these submissions or pending Amendment Motions, the Trial Chamber heard Graham's testimony, limiting examination-in-chief and cross-examination to the **[page 3]** circumstances surrounding the Prosecution's taking of statements from Borovčanin.[11] Graham testified on 17 and 18 July 2007 about the procedures followed during the Borovčanin interview.[12]

7. Following Graham's testimony, the Prosecution sought to further examine him to lay the foundation for the introduction of documents and materials used, generated, and/or viewed during the interviews with Borovčanin.[13] These documents are the subject of the Amendment Motions. The Defence argued that the attempt at further examination was premature pending the decision on whether, and for what purposes, Borovčanin's statements would be admitted as evidence.[14] The Trial Chamber concurred.[15]

8. Between 17 and 20 July 2007, the parties filed further written submissions on the issue of the admissibility of the Borovčanin interview with respect to the other Accused.[16] The parties presented additional oral submissions on the admissibility of the Borovčanin interview on 19 July 2007.[17]

9. Collectively, the various written and oral submissions of the parties present three issues to be decided by the Trial Chamber: (1) the addition of documents to the Prosecution's Rule 65 *ter* Exhibit List; (2) whether Borovčanin's statements should be admitted as evidence against him; and (3) whether Borovčanin's statements should be admitted as evidence against the co-Accused in this case. **[page 4]**

---

[8] T. 13524 (28 June 2007) (statement of Peter McCloskey, Office of the Prosecutor).

[9] On 11–12 July 2007, the Trial Chamber heard oral submissions on the following three questions: (1) If the statement is admissible against Borovčanin, what probative value, if any, does it have with respect to the other Accused? T. 13709–13751 (11 July 2007); (2) If the Chamber determines the statement has probative value with respect to the other accused, what is the permissible scope of cross-examination of witness Alistair Graham by the other accused as to admissibility? T. 13756 (11 July 2007)–13764 (12 July 2007); (3) If instead the Chamber determines the statement has no probative value with respect to the other accused, what if any redactions should be made to the statement? T. 13767–13800 (12 July 2007). The Trial Chamber then invited the parties to supplement their oral submissions on the broader issue of the use of the Borovčanin Interview vis-à-vis the co-accused with further written submissions and/or authorities by 20 July 2007. T. 13802–13804 (12 July 2007).

[10] Defence Submission Regarding the Admissibility of the Interview of Accused Ljubomir Borovčanin as Evidence Against the Co-Accused Ljubisa Beara, 12 July 2007 ("Beara Submissions").

[11] T. 13827–13832 (17 July 2007).

[12] T. 13834–13891, 13894–13946 (17–18 July 2007).

[13] T. 13946–13947 (18 July 2007).

[14] T. 13947–13948 (18 July 2007).

[15] T. 13948–13949 (18 July 2007).

[16] Addendum to the Defence Submission Regarding the Admissibility of the Interview of Accused Ljubomir Borovčanin as Evidence Against the Co-Accused Ljubisa Beara, 17 July 2007 ("Further Beara Submissions"); Arguments of the Defence for General Miletić Regarding the Admissibility of the Interview with Ljubomir Borovčanin Against General Miletić, 19 July 2007 (French original), 27 July 2007 (English translation), ("Miletić Submissions"); Submission on Behalf of Milan Gvero on the Admissibility of an Accused's Interview in the Case of a Co-Accused, 20 July 2007 ("Gvero Submissions"); Prosecution's Further Submission Regarding Admissibility of the Interviews of Ljubomir Borovčanin as Evidence Against the Co-Accused, 20 July 2007 ("Prosecution's Further Submission") including Appendix 1: Book of Authorities for the Prosecution Submission Regarding Admissibility of the Interview of Ljubomir Borovčanin as Evidence Against the Co-Accused, filed separately on 24 July 2007.

[17] T. 13956–13978 (19 July 2007).

II. ADDITION OF DOCUMENTS TO THE PROSECUTION'S RULE 65 *TER* EXHIBIT LIST AND THE ADMISSIBILITY OF THE BOROVČANIN DOCUMENTS

A. Submissions of the Parties

1. Prosecution Motions

10. Pursuant to Rule 73,[18] the Prosecution seeks to add the Borovčanin Interview to its existing Rule 65 *ter* Exhibit List together with the Borovčanin Documents.[19]

11. Relying on the Trial Chamber's previous decisions on similar motions,[20] the Prosecution submits that the Borovčanin Documents are "procedurally and substantively probative and relevant to the testimony of Graham and the issues raised by the Indictment".[21] The Borovčanin Documents were either "created, obtained, and/or utilised" during the Borovčanin Interview[22] or "pertain directly to the anticipated legal challenges to the admissibility and reliability of the interviews".[23] Accordingly, the Prosecution argues the introduction of the Borovčanin Documents "will enable the Trial Chamber to better understand the testimony of Graham and the interviews made by Borovčanin".[24] Furthermore, the Defence will suffer no undue prejudice by the Borovčanin Interview,[25] as they have been (1) on notice of the Prosecution's intention to introduce the Borovčanin Interview since the beginning of the case; (2) in possession of the draft Borovčanin Transcripts since September 2005; and (3) provided with copies of the Borovčanin Documents.[26] **[page 5]**

2. Defence Responses

12. Miletić objects to the addition of the Borovčanin Interview on the grounds that (1) the Prosecution has failed to show a valid reason for the addition at such a late stage in the proceedings;[27] and (2) the Borovčanin Interview is devoid of probative value based on its inherent lack of credibility given the circumstances under which it was made. [28] Miletić takes no position with respect to the Borovčanin Documents.[29]

13. Beara opposes the Amendment Motions in their entirety, arguing that (1) the Prosecution has previously failed to show "just cause" for its failure to disclose the Borovčanin Interview and Borovčanin Documents;[30] and (2) the Accused have been unjustly prejudiced by the Prosecution's "constant" practice of amending its Rule 65 *ter* Exhibit List.[31]

---

18 Prosecution Corrigendum, paras. 2–3 (where the Prosecution indicates that its previous reference to Rule 72 *bis*(F) was in error and that it meant to refer only to Rule 73).

19 The Borovčanin Documents are the following: (1) five documents brought to the 20 February 2002 interview by Borovčanin regarding his employment from 1982 through 1998 (Rule 65 *ter* List Amendment Motion, para. 5(i)); (2) four documents created during the 20 February 2002 interview by Borovčanin, including a sheet of paper indicating his name, date of birth, and occupation; an organisational chart of the Republika Srpska Ministry of the Interior in 1995; an organisational chart of the Republika Srpska Supreme Command and Armed Forces in 1995; and a list of the units comprising the First Company Zvornik PJP in 1995 and the number of individuals assigned to each unit (Rule 65 *ter* List Amendment Motion, para. 5(ii)); (3) a DVD shown to Borovčanin during the 12 March 2002 interview consisting of footage from the Srebrenica area in July 1995 (Rule 65 *ter* List Amendment Motion, para. 5(iii)); and (4) documents chronicling the Prosecution's efforts to interview Borovčanin, including three summonses; and one receipt of summons with attached cover letter (Rule 65 *ter* List Amendment Motion, paras. 6, 10); as well as an additional summons and two letters to the Republika Srpska Ministry of Justice requesting assistance in delivering summonses (Supplemental Rule 65 *ter* Motion, para. 2, see also T. 13533–13534, 9 July 2007).

20 Rule 65 *ter* List Amendment Motion, para. 8.

21 *Ibid.*, para. 2.

22 *Ibid.*

23 *Ibid*; *See also ibid.*, para. 7; Supplemental Rule 65 *ter* Motion, para. 1.

24 Rule 65 *ter* List Amendment Motion, para. 7; *See also* Supplemental Rule 65 *ter* Motion, para. 1.

25 Rule 65 *ter* List Amendment Motion, para. 11.

26 *Ibid.*, paras. 3–6, 9, 10.

27 Miletić Response, paras. 5–9.

28 *Ibid.,* paras. 5, 10–11. Miletić also argues that the admission of the Borovčanin Interview without cross-examination would unduly prejudice the rights of the co-accused (Miletić Response, paras. 5,12–13)

29 *Ibid.*, para. 2.

30 Beara Response, paras. 7–11.

31 *Ibid.*, para. 16.

14. Borovčanin states that (1) the Rule 65 *ter* List Amendment Motion is untimely;[32] (2) the Prosecution's mere intention to seek the additions of the Borovčanin Interview and the Borovčanin Documents does not amount to good cause for not having done so to date;[33] and (3) granting the Rule 65 *ter* List Amendment Motion would unfairly prejudice Borovčanin's rights.[34] Additionally, Borovčanin joins the Beara Response.[35] With respect to the Supplemental Rule 65 *ter* Motion, Borovčanin (1) argues that no good cause has been shown with respect to the summons,[36] but does not object to the other two documents–the letters of the Republika Srpska Ministry of Justice dated 12 February and 7 March 2002 respectively–being added to the list;[37] (2) joins the Second Beara Response;[38] (3) notes that two of the Borovčanin Documents are already on the 65 *ter* Exhibit List ("Two Documents");[39] and (4) seeks leave to supplement its Borovčanin Response and Second **[page 6]** Borovčanin Response by submitting that the Prosecution's arguments and the relief sought in the 65 *ter* Motion should be deemed moot with regard to these two Borovčanin Documents.[40]

15. Nikolić (1) joins the Borovčanin Response and Miletić Response;[41] and (2) contends that the Prosecution has not shown good cause for failing to include them previously on the Rule 65 *ter* Exhibit List.[42] Nikolić further objects to the Supplemental Rule 65 *ter* Motion for the same reasons.[43]

16. Pandurević joins the "various Defence responses filed to date",[44] while Popović and Gvero do not make any submission in response to either of the Amendment Motions.

3. Prosecution Reply

17. Asking for leave to reply and addressing the arguments raised by the various responses, the Prosecution argues that (1) it has made clear its intention to use the Borovčanin Interview and some of the Borovčanin Documents since 2005 and that the timing of the disclosure of the Borovčanin Documents causes no prejudice to the Defence;[45] (2) as a general matter, Prosecution requests to amend its Rule 65 *ter* Exhibit List are made in good faith;[46] (3) the Borovčanin Interview and the Borovčanin Documents would in no way alter the case against the Accused;[47] and (4) the question of the admissibility of the Borovčanin Interview and Borovčanin Documents is not germane to the Amendment Motions and should be dealt with separately.[48]

B. Discussion on the Addition of Documents to the 65 *ter* List

18. Pursuant to Rule 65 *ter*(E)(iii), the Prosecution is required to file "the list of exhibits [it] intends to offer" and to "serve on the defence copies of the exhibits so listed". However, the Prosecution is not strictly bound by this initial filing. When exercising its discretion in this regard, "the Trial Chamber should balance the Prosecution's duty to present the available evidence to prove its case with the right of the accused to have adequate time and facilities to prepare a defence and to be tried without undue delay".[49] In striking

32 Borovčanin Response, para. 13.
33 *Ibid.*, para. 16.
34 *Ibid.*, para. 22.
35 Second Borovčanin Response, para. 2.
36 Third Borovčanin Response, para. 9.
37 *Ibid.*, para. 10.
38 *Ibid.*, para. 11.
39 *Ibid.*, paras. 12–13. The Trial Chamber notes that the Two Documents, (1) RS MUP Ministerial Order 64/95, dated 10 July 1995 and (2) the article entitled "The Whitewashing of the Town Has Begun" from the newspaper "Intervju", dated 21 July 1995 are already on the 65 *ter* Exhibit List under numbers P00057 and P00469 respectively.
40 *Ibid.*, para. 14.
41 Nikolić Response, para. 2.
42 *Ibid.*, paras. 5, 10, 14.
43 *Ibid.*, para. 17.
44 Pandurević Response, para. 1.
45 Prosecution Reply, paras. 4–5.
46 *Ibid.*, para. 6.
47 *Ibid.*, para. 7.
48 *Ibid.*, para. 9.
49 Decision on Prosecution's Motions for Leave to Amend Rule 65 *ter* Witness List and Rule 65 *ter* Exhibit List, 6 December 2006 ("6 December Decision"), p. 6 (internal citations omitted).

that balance "in the context of a complex multi-accused **[page 7]** trial in which a considerable amount of evidence is presented by the Prosecution, a certain level of flexibility must be maintained."[50] However, the primary concern should be "whether the rights of the Accused will be adequately protected if exhibits [...] will be added to the Prosecution Exhibit List".[51] Additional factors to consider include "whether the proposed evidence is *prima facie* relevant and of probative value to issues raised in the indictment, and whether good cause for amending the [...] exhibit list was shown, taking into consideration the complexity of the case, on-going investigations, and translation of documents and other materials".[52]

19. The Trial Chamber is satisfied that it is in the interest of justice to allow the proposed amendments to the Prosecution's Rule 65 *ter* Exhibit List. The information contained in the Borovčanin Interview is clearly *prima facie* relevant to issues raised in the indictment vis-à-vis Borovčanin, as well as potentially probative with regard to the co-Accused. The Borovčanin Documents are also relevant in so far as they relate directly to the circumstances surrounding the taking of the Borovčanin Interview and may therefore assist the Trial Chamber in its evaluation of Graham's testimony relative to the admissibility of the Borovčanin Interview.

20. The Prosecution's intention to introduce the Borovčanin Interview has been clear at the least since April 2006 and the defence have long been in possession of the Borovčanin Transcripts. The Accused have made general assertions of prejudice arising from the addition of the Borovčanin Interview and the Borovčanin Documents to the 65 *ter* Exhibit List.[53] However they have not demonstrated to the satisfaction of the Trial Chamber how that prejudice arises in the particular circumstances. Although several of the Borovčanin Documents were not disclosed to the Defence by the Prosecution until early July 2007, these Borovčanin Documents—all related to the Borovčanin Interview—are neither lengthy nor complicated. Moreover, the Defence was provided with copies of the Borovčanin Documents two weeks prior to Graham's testimony, giving counsel for the Accused sufficient time to prepare for Graham's preliminary cross-examination.[54] Accordingly, the Trial Chamber finds that the Accused will suffer no prejudice as a result of the proposed modifications to the 65 *ter* Exhibit List. **[page 8]**

21. The Trial Chamber acknowledges the Prosecution's desire to resolve any issues regarding the Borovčanin Interview and the Borovčanin Documents by stipulation with the Defence.[55] It further serves to evidence the intent to introduce the Borovčanin Interview as evidence in the case. Considering this and the other surrounding circumstances, the Trial Chamber concludes that the non-inclusion of the Borovčanin Interview and the Borovčanin Documents in the 65 *ter* Exhibit List was however an inadvertent omission by the Prosecution. As noted, the Accused have suffered no prejudice from this omission and inclusion of the Borovčanin Interview and the Borovčanin Documents at this stage of the proceedings in no way alters the Prosecution's case. Taking all these factors into account, the Trial Chamber holds that the Prosecution has shown good cause as to why the 65 *ter* Exhibit List should be amended and will accordingly allow the additions requested to the 65 *ter* Exhibit List.

---

[50] Decision on Nikolić's Motion for Disclosure Pursuant to Rules 65 *ter* and 66, 30 January 2007, p. 4.

[51] 6 December Decision, p. 6 (internal citations omitted); *See also* Decision on Prosecution's Third Motion for Leave to Amend Rule 65 *ter* Exhibit List, 10 January 2007 ("10 January Decision"), p. 2.

[52] 6 December Decision, p. 7 (internal citations omitted); *See also* Decision Permitting the Addition of One Exhibit to the Prosecution's Rule 65 *ter* List and Denying an Oral Request for Certification Pursuant to Rule 73(B), 16 January 2007, p. 4; 10 January Decision, p. 2.

[53] *See supra* paras. 8–12.

[54] *See supra* para. 7.

[55] *See* Rule 65 *ter* List Amendment Motion, para. 3.

III. ADMISSIBILITY OF THE BOROVČANIN INTERVIEW VIS-À-VIS BOROVČANIN

A. Submissions of the Parties

1. Defence Submissions

22. According to Borovčanin, in order for the Borovčanin Interview to be admitted into evidence it must have been given voluntarily.[56] He submits that the burden of proof rests with the Prosecution,[57] and the analysis is two-pronged.[58] First, it must be shown that no "compulsion, coercive force, or serious threat was applied" in order to extract the Borovčanin Interview.[59] Second, the Trial Chamber must evaluate "whether, when giving his interview, Mr. Borovčanin was aware of his position" and "his rights which emanate from his position".[60] While Borovčanin concedes that he was not compelled, coerced, or threatened in any way, he argues that the second prong of the test was not met and therefore the statement should not be admitted into evidence.[61]

23. Specifically, Borovčanin considers the following putative errors to be significant: (1) although his summons indicated that he was regarded as suspect, it did not list his rights as **[page 9]** such;[62] (2) because Graham informed Borovčanin at the interview that he "may be a suspect", Borovčanin believed he was only a potential or possible suspect and such concepts do not exist in the Rules or in the "relevant legislation of other jurisdictions";[63] (3) although Graham cautioned Borovčanin in English that his statement could be used "against him", that portion was not translated into Bosnian-Croat-Serbian ("BCS") as would have been required under his domestic legal system;[64] (4) "at no time was it clearly stated to him that he did not have to speak to the Office of the Prosecutor at all" or that "he was free to stop and leave the interview";[65] (5) Borovčanin was never informed of the particular crimes of which he was suspected;[66] (6) because Borovčanin is not a lawyer, "his ability to understand such cautions or lack of them" was somehow hampered by "the fact that his legal counsel was not present at the time";[67] (7) although Borovčanin's counsel was present for much of the time, Borovčanin "was deprived [...] of effective legal representation" because counsel did not "effectively protect his rights";[68] and (8) although Borovčanin was given an opportunity to clarify his statement, he could not have made any meaningful clarifications or corrections because he was not provided with copies of the Borovčanin Recordings.[69]

24. Beara submits that (1) the provisions of Rule 42 are mandatory;[70] (2) the Prosecution has the burden of showing that the suspect "knowingly, intelligently and voluntarily waived his rights" and "thereafter [...] voluntarily gave his statement";[71] and (3) Graham's use of the aide-memoire was "nothing less than subterfuge [...], a ruse, a trick, a device, to obtain an advantage over [Borovčanin] to get him to give the statement".[72] For the reasons canvassed by Borovčanin, Beara submits that the Prosecution has failed to demonstrate that there was a "knowing, intelligent, and voluntary waiver".[73] **[page 10]**

---

56 T. 13956 (19 July 2007).
57 *Ibid.*
58 *Ibid.*
59 *Ibid.*
60 *Ibid.*
61 T. 13956–13957 (19 July 2007).
62 T. 13957–13958 (19 July 2007).
63 T. 13958–13959 (19 July 2007); *See also* T. 13963–13965 (19 July 2007) where Borovčanin argues that certain provisions of the Bosnia and Herzegovina criminal procedure code related to the questioning of suspects should apply to the instant proceedings.
64 T. 13959–13960 (19 July 2007).
65 T. 13961 (19 July 2007).
66 *Ibid.*
67 T. 13962–13963 (19 July 2007); *See also* T. 13965 (19 July 2007).
68 T. 13966–13967 (19 July 2007).
69 T. 13968 (19 July 2007).
70 T. 13969 (19 July 2007).
71 T. 13970 (19 July 2007).
72 T. 13971 (19 July 2007); *See also* T. 13972 (19 July 2007).
73 T. 13971 (19 July 2007); *See also* T. 13972 (19 July 2007).

2. Prosecution Submissions

25. The Borovčanin Interview is admissible because it is "probative" and "reliable",[74] and the "crux [...] of the issue" is whether Rule 42 was followed.[75] The Prosecution submits that "all the procedural safeguards required under the Statute were fully complied with" and the Borovčanin Interview "was given voluntarily and knowingly and intelligently by Mr. Borovčanin".[76]

26. Regarding the right to counsel, the Prosecution submits that Borovčanin was advised "in a very simple fashion" that he was under no obligation to begin without his lawyer, and he indicated that he wanted to proceed.[77] Borovčanin, a highly educated man with an extensive background in law enforcement, made an intelligent, unambiguous, and express waiver of his right.[78] Once his lawyer arrived, the fact that the lawyer did not ask questions or interrupt the interview does not constitute ineffective assistance of counsel.[79]

27. With respect to the caution given, the Prosecution notes that an investigator is not obliged to go further than clearly informing the suspect in a language he understands of his rights under Rule 42.[80] By attempting to inform Borovčanin that the Borovčanin Interview could be used "against him", Graham "went beyond the rule".[81] Further, Rule 42 does not require that a suspect be advised of his status as such,[82] and the jurisprudence of the Tribunal rejects arguments regarding cultural differences.[83]

B. Discussion

28. Tribunal jurisprudence has addressed the issue of the admissibility of a suspect's interview in proceedings brought subsequently against him or her. The legal test to be met is two-pronged: (1) whether the procedural safeguards set forth in Rules 42 and 43 are satisfied, and (2) whether the admissibility test laid down in Rules 89(C) and 89(D) is met.[84] **[page 11]**

1. Procedural safeguards set forth in Rules 42 and 43

29. The interview of a suspect who subsequently becomes an accused may be admitted into evidence if the Trial Chamber is satisfied "that the interview was obtained voluntarily and that it was conducted in compliance with the requirements set out in the Rules".[85] In such a case, the "principal question at issue is what *safeguards* should have been applied by the Prosecution in order for a former statement of a now accused person to be admissible into evidence".[86]

---

74 T. 13972 (19 July 2007).

75 *Ibid.*

76 *Ibid.*

77 T. 13974–13975 (19 July 2007).

78 T. 13975–13977 (19 July 2007).

79 T. 13975 (19 July 2007).

80 T. 13974 (19 July 2007).

81 *Ibid.*

82 T. 13976 (19 July 2007).

83 T. 13973 (19 July 2007).

84 *Prosecutor v. Kvočka, Radić, Žigić, and Prcać*, Case No. IT-98-30/1-A, Judgement, 28 February 2005, para. 128; *Prosecutor v. Halilović*, Case No. IT-01-48-AR73.2, Decision on Interlocutory Appeal Concerning Admission of Record of Interview of the Accused from the Bar Table, 19 August 2005 ("*Halilović* Appeal Decision"), para. 14; *Prosecutor v. Blagojević and Jokić*, Case No. IT-02-60-T, Decision on Prosecution's Motion for Clarification of Oral Decision Regarding Admissibility of Accused's Statement, 18 September 2003 ("*Blagojević* September 2003 Decision"), paras. 6–8, 13.

85 *Prosecutor v. Halilović*, Case No. IT-01-48-T, Decision on Motion for Exclusion of Statement of Accused, 8 July 2005 ("*Halilović* Trial Decision"), para. 18. Certification to appeal this decision was denied by the Trial Chamber. *See Prosecutor v. Halilović*, Case No. IT-01-48-T, Decision on Prosecution Request for Certification for Interlocutory Appeal of "Decision on Motion for Exclusion of Statement of Accused", 25 July 2005.

86 *Halilović* Trial Decision, para. 19 (emphasis added); *See also ibid.*, para. 21. ("The Trial Chamber finds that in order to protect the right of the Accused to a fair trial, in accordance with Article 21 of the Statute, it should be taken into account whether the safeguards of Rules 42, 43, and 63 of the Rules have been fully respected when deciding on the admission of *any* former statement of an accused irrespective of the status of the accused at the time of taking the statement.").

30. The specific *safeguards* are set forth in the Statute which bestows certain fundamental guarantees on behalf of suspects, namely the "right to have legal assistance [...] as well as to necessary translation into and from a language [the suspect] speaks and understands".[87] Rule 42 contains these guarantees and sets forth a third—the right to remain silent, and to be cautioned that any statement made would be recorded and could be used in evidence:

> (A) A suspect who is to be questioned by the Prosecutor shall have the following rights, of which the Prosecutor shall inform the suspect prior to questioning, in a language that the suspect understands: (i) the right to be assisted by counsel of the suspect's choice or to be assigned legal assistance without payment if the suspect does not have sufficient means to pay for it; (ii) the right to have the free assistance of an interpreter if the suspect cannot understand or speak the language to be used for questioning; and (iii) the right to remain silent, and to be cautioned that any statement the suspect makes shall be recorded and may be used in evidence.
>
> (B) Questioning of a suspect shall not proceed without the presence of counsel unless the suspect has voluntarily waived the right to counsel. In case of waiver, if the suspect subsequently expresses a desire to have counsel, questioning shall thereupon cease, and shall only resume when the suspect has obtained or been assigned counsel.[88]

31. The right to be assisted by counsel of the suspect's choice during questioning, as provided by Rule 42, "is neither ambiguous nor difficult to understand. As long as the suspect is clearly informed of it in a language he or she understands, the Prosecution fulfils its obligations. Contrary **[page 12]** to [Defence] submissions, an investigator is not obliged to go further."[89] The duty of an investigator is "only to interpret to the suspect the rules in a language he or she understands".[90] With regard to the right to be assisted by counsel, a Trial Chamber is obliged to assess a lawyer's "actual competence to adequately represent the interests"[91] of the suspect, but only where substantive evidence is adduced to the contrary.[92]

32. The Appeals Chamber has held that Rule 42 "should be construed objectively" and explicitly rejected the notion of a "subjective standard of informed consent".[93] Any different or additional procedures provided under the suspect's national legal system are simply inapplicable to proceedings before the Tribunal, and the suspect's familiarity with such rules is irrelevant.[94]

33. Borovčanin was clearly advised on multiple occasions of his right to counsel.[95] With regard to the initial portion of the 20 February 2002 interview, the Trial Chamber is satisfied that Borovčanin provided a knowing and voluntary waiver of this right after being advised in conformity with the requirements of

---

87 Article 18(3). *Prosecutor v. Delalić, Mucić a/k/a "Pavo", Delic, and Landzo a/k/a "Zenga"*, Case No. IT-96-21-T, Decision on Zdravko Mucić's Motion for the Exclusion of Evidence, 2 September 1997 ("*Mucić* Decision"), para. 47 ("[T]he litmus test of the right of the suspect is clearly laid down in Article 18 of the Statute as elaborated in Rule 42.").

88 *See also Halilović* Trial Decision, para. 21 (quoting *Mucić* Decision, para. 43), ("Rule 42 embodies the essential provisions of the right to a fair hearing as enshrined in Article 14(3) of the International Covenant on Civil and Political Rights and Article 6(3) (c) of the European Convention of Human Rights. These are the internationally accepted basic and fundamental rights accorded to the individual to enable the enjoyment of a right to a fair hearing during trial.").

89 *Prosecutor v. Delalić, Mucić a/k/a "Pavo", Delić, and Landžo a/k/a "Zenga"*, Case No. IT-96-21-A, Judgement, 20 February 2001 ("Delalić Appeal Judgement"), para. 551, *affirming Mucić* Decision.

90 *Delalić* Appeal Judgement, para. 552, (*quoting Mucić* Decision, para. 58).

91 *Halilović* Appeal Decision, para. 61.

92 *Ibid.*, para. 62.

93 *Delalić* Appeal Judgement, para. 553; *See also Mucić* Decision, para. 59 (Rule 42 "should be objectively construed"), para. 60 ("Rule 42 is an adaptation *mutatis mutandis* of Article 6(3) of the European Convention on Human Rights and Article 14(3) of the International Covenant on Civil and Political Rights ('ICCPR'). These are supranational conventions based on the most elementary and fundamental provisions for the protection of individual human rights. The former Yugoslavia was a party to the ICCPR. It will, therefore, be anomalous to rely on cultural differences for their interpretation.").

94 *Mucić* Decision, para. 59 ("If we were to accept the cultural argument, it would be tantamount to every person interpreting the rights read to him subject to his personal or contemporary cultural environment."); *See also Delalić* Appeal Judgement, para. 552 ("[P]rovided that the suspect's rights are explained in a language that the suspect understands, it shouldn't matter in what country the suspect is at the time, particularly in the case of an international tribunal which may interview suspects in many different countries and which has a legal system that's different to that in any particular national jurisdiction.") (internal citation omitted).

95 Ex. P02852 (Interview of 20 February 2002), pp. 2, 23, 44, 63; Ex. P02853 (Interview of 11 March 2002), pp. 2, 50, 73, 91; Ex. P02853 (Interview of 12 March 2002), p. 115.

Rule 42(B).[96] As for the remaining portions of the 20 February 2002 interview and the entirety of the 11–12 March 2002 interviews, Borovčanin was repeatedly advised of his right to **[page 13]** counsel, and his attorney was present throughout.[97] The Trial Chamber finds Borovčanin's argument that his counsel failed to adequately represent his interests during the interviews[98] to be unsubstantiated by objective evidence. That counsel stood mute during the majority of the interviews[99] does not, in the circumstances of the Borovčanin Interview, suggest that the representation was in any way deficient.[100]

34. The Trial Chamber notes that at the beginning of each session Borovčanin was advised of his right to an interpreter,[101] and one was present throughout the interviews, which were audio-recorded and conducted in English with simultaneous translation.[102] Borovčanin was advised that he "may be a suspect who is responsible for committing acts which may be chargeable under the Tribunal statute".[103] Borovčanin's submission that this particular language was equivocal and therefore led him to believe he was only a potential or possible subject[104] is both immaterial and objectively unsound. Borovčanin was previously informed—by way of summonses accompanied by undertakings of safe passage—that the Prosecution wished to speak to him as a suspect.[105] Any reasonable person would have understood Graham's comments as simply confirming this fact.

35. On multiple occasions throughout the Borovčanin Interview, he was informed of the right to remain silent and was further cautioned that any statement he made could be used in evidence before the Tribunal.[106] This is sufficient to satisfy Rule 42, and Graham was under no obligation to go further in his caution to Borovčanin, although he did—by including the language "against you".[107] The fact that these words were not translated into BCS is immaterial to the application of the objective test set out in Rule 42. Further, the fact that such additional language may be required **[page 14]** under the criminal procedure of Republika Srpska is not of relevance.[108] Accordingly, Borovčanin's submission that he did not understand that his statement could be used *against him* is untenable.[109] Moreover, Graham was not required by the Rules to inform Borovčanin that he was at liberty to leave the interview or not required to speak "at all",[110] nor was he obliged to advise Borovčanin of the particular crimes for which he was a suspect at the time.[111]

---

96 When Borovčanin appeared for his interview on the morning of 20 February 2002 without his attorney, he was advised by Graham as well as Mr. McCloskey that there was no need for the interview to commence until his attorney arrived; notwithstanding this assurance, Borovčanin agreed to begin. T. 13837, 13852 (17 July 2007). Ex. P02852 (Interview of 20 February 2002), pp. 2–3, 23. Borovčanin was further advised—and he acknowledged—that he could suspend the interview at any time, Ex. P02852 (Interview of 20 February 2002), pp. 3, 23. After the first break in the interview, Graham further advised Borovčanin that he had the right to stop and wait for his lawyer to arrive. T. 13852–13853 (17 July 2007). Borovčanin indicated that he was "happy to continue without legal presentation at [that] time". T. 13853 (17 July 2007). Sometime before the lunch break, Graham was informed that Borovčanin's lawyer had arrived, and he "stopped the tape immediately". T. 13853 (17 July 2007). Ex. P02852 (Interview of 20 February 2002), p. 42.

97 Upon resuming the interview, Graham again advised Borovčanin of his rights, including his right to counsel, in the presence of his counsel. T. 13854 (17 July 2007). Borovčanin's counsel remained until the interview was completed. T. 13857 (17 July 2007). During the interviews of 11–12 March 2002, Borovčanin was again advised of his right to counsel, who was present throughout. T. 13858–13860, 13862 (17 July 2007).

98 *See supra* note 69, para. 20.

99 T. 13966–13977 (19 May 2007).

100 In fact, Borovčanin met with his lawyer Goran Bubić for two hours after the latter's arrival on 20 February 2002—presumably to receive advice about the interview—and after meeting privately with Peter McCloskey later in the day, Bubić suggested terminating the session in order to discuss matters further with Borovčanin. Ex. P02852 (Interview of 20 February 2002), pp. 43, 89–90.

101 Ex. P02852 (Interview of 20 February 2002), pp. 1–2; Ex. P02853 (Interview of 11 March 2002), pp. 1–2; Ex. P02853 (Interview of 12 March 2002), p. 115.

102 T. 13838, 13843 (17 July 2007).

103 T. 13845 (17 July 2007). Ex. P02852 (Interview of 20 February 2002), pp. 2, 43–44; Ex. P02853 (Interview of 11 March 2002), pp. 2, 50; Ex. P02853 (Interview of 12 March 2002), p. 115.

104 *See supra* note 64, para. 20.

105 T. 13834–13836, 13857 (17 July 2007).

106 T. 13844–13845, 13854, 13858–13860, 13862 (17 July 2007). Ex. P02852 (Interview of 20 February 2002), pp. 2, 23, 44, 63; Ex. P02853 (Interview of 11 March 2002), pp. 2, 50, 73, 91; Ex. P02853 (Interview of 12 March 2002), p. 115.

107 T. 13858, 13879 (17 July 2007).

108 T. 13963 (19 July 2007).

109 *See supra* note 65, para. 20.

110 *See supra* note 66, para. 20. In fact, Borovčanin was advised—and he acknowledged—that he was not required to say anything or to answer any questions unless he wanted to do so. Ex. P02852 (Interview of 20 February 2002), pp. 2, 23, 44, 63; Ex. P02853 (Interview of 11 March 2002), pp. 2, 50, 73, 91; Ex. P02853 (Interview of 12 March 2002), p. 115.

111 *See supra* note 67, para. 20.

36. Additionally, Rule 43 sets out the necessary procedures to be followed for the recording of the questioning of suspects:[112]

> Whenever the Prosecutor questions a suspect, the questioning shall be audio-recorded or video-recorded, in accordance with the following procedure:
>
> (i) the suspect shall be informed in a language the suspect understands that the questioning is being audio-recorded or video-recorded;
>
> (ii) in the event of a break in the course of the questioning, the fact and the time of the break shall be recorded before audio-recording or video-recording ends and the time of resumption of the questioning shall also be recorded;
>
> (iii) at the conclusion of the questioning the suspect shall be offered the opportunity to clarify anything the suspect has said, and to add anything the suspect may wish, and the time of conclusion shall be recorded;
>
> (iv) a copy of the recorded tape will be supplied to the suspect or, if multiple recording apparatus was used, one of the original recorded tapes;
>
> (v) after a copy has been made, if necessary, of the recorded tape, the original recorded tape or one of the original tapes shall be sealed in the presence of the suspect under the signature of the Prosecutor and the suspect; and
>
> (vi) the tape shall be transcribed if the suspect becomes an accused.

37. No one has argued that the requirements laid down in Rule 43(i), (ii), (v), and (vi) were not met. With regard to the requirement set forth in Rule 43(iii), Borovčanin was given an opportunity to add to and/or clarify his statement at the conclusion of each session but he declined to do so.[113] Borovčanin, however, now argues that, given the length of the interviews, because he was not provided with copies of the audiotapes of his interviews, he was effectively prevented from making **[page 15]** additions or clarifications.[114] The Trial Chamber does not accept this argument. Although Rule 43(iv) requires the Prosecution to provide copies of the "recorded tape" to the suspect, the Trial Chamber is not convinced that the delay in providing the recordings to Borovčanin had any impact on his decision not to make further comment when offered the opportunity by Graham.[115] As to the failure to provide the Borovčanin Recordings immediately after the interviews, the Trial Chamber does not consider that this affected the content or reliability of the Borovčanin Interview or created such prejudice so as to implicate fair trial standards. Therefore this delay does not warrant exclusion of the Borovčanin Interview. Finally, at the end of each session, Borovčanin confirmed that he had answered the questions of his own free will, that he was not threatened, promised, or induced in any way, and that he had no complaints about the way he had been treated before and during the Borovčanin Interview.[116]

38. For the foregoing reasons, the Trial Chamber holds that the procedural safeguards contained in Rules 42 and 43 were afforded to Borovčanin during the Borovčanin Interview.

---

[112] *See Halilović* Trial Decision, para. 24 ("The Trial Chamber finds that Rule 43 is a fundamental provision to protect the rights of a suspect and an accused. Moreover, it is a safeguard for a full and accurate reflection of the questions and answers during the interview and thus enables the parties and the Trial Chamber to verify the exact wording of what was said during the interview.").

[113] T. 13856, 13861–13863 (17 July 2007). Ex. P02852 (Interview of 20 February 2002), p. 90; Ex. P02853 (Interview of 11 March 2002), p. 113.

[114] *See supra* note 70, para. 20.

[115] Copies of the Borovčanin Recordings were not immediately available following the 20 February 2002 interview due to, according to the Prosecution, certain limitations of the recording equipment. T. 13857 (17 July 2007). It is not clear from the record exactly when the Prosecution subsequently provided the Borovčanin Recordings to Borovčanin. T. 13858 (17 July 2007), T.13902 (18 July 2007). However, Borovčanin was informed that he would be provided with copies of the Borovčanin Recordings and Borovčanin Transcripts as soon as possible. Ex. P02852 (Interview of 20 February 2002), p. 4; Ex. P02853 (Interview of 11 March 2002), p. 3; Ex. P02853 (Interview of 12 March 2002), pp. 116, 162.

[116] Ex. P02852 (Interview of 20 February 2002), p. 91; Ex. P02853 (Interview of 11 March 2002), pp. 113–114; Ex. P02853 (Interview of 12 March 2002), p. 163.

2. The Admissibility test under Rules 89 (C) and (D)

39. The Trial Chamber notes that no one argues that the Borovčanin Interview is not relevant or probative and given that this is the statement of an accused relating to the events in the Indictment, such an argument would be difficult to sustain. The Trial Chamber is fully satisfied that the Borovčanin Interview is both relevant and probative. Accordingly, considering that the Borovčanin Interview meets the procedural safeguards set forth in Rules 42 and 43, is both relevant and has probative value to the Prosecution's case against Borovčanin, the Trial Chamber will admit it against Borovčanin. **[page 16]**

IV. ADMISSIBILITY OF BOROVČANIN'S STATEMENTS AGAINST HIS CO-ACCUSED

A. Submissions of the Parties

1. Prosecution Submissions

40. The Prosecution assumes for purposes of argument that "Borovčanin will not testify and that his co-accused will not have the right to cross-examine him on the contents of his interview".[117] So assuming, the Prosecution argues for the admission of Borovčanin's statements to the Prosecution against his co-Accused for any purpose, including proof of the acts and conduct of the co-Accused.[118]

41. The Prosecution argues in the alternative that Borovčanin's statements should be admitted against the co-Accused only with respect to matters other than "acts and conduct" as that phrase has been "interpreted and applied under Rule 92 *bis*".[119]

42. The Prosecution first contends that admission of Borovčanin's statements against the co-Accused for any purpose would not violate the co-Accused's right to a fair trial.[120] The Prosecution points to the Trial Chamber's broad discretion to admit evidence, including hearsay, under Rules 89(C) and (D), and submits that the "primary considerations" should be "probative value and fairness".[121] While the right to cross-examine witnesses is an important aspect of a fair trial, "'it is settled law before the International Tribunal that the right of an accused to cross-examine a witness is not absolute'".[122] In certain circumstances, Chambers have admitted statements or prior testimony of witnesses who were not available for cross-examination or where cross-examination was curtailed.[123] The Prosecution argues that the strong motive of an Accused to exculpate himself **[page 17]** by shifting blame to others does not render such statement inadmissible,[124] but rather goes to the weight to be attached to it "in relation

---

117 Prosecution's Further Submission, para. 7; *See also* T. 13718 (11 July 2007) (statement of Peter McCloskey, Office of the Prosecutor) ("I am assuming this—Mr. Borovčanin would not testify, because I have no way of knowing at this point whether he would or would not. And aside from asking Defence counsel, but Defence counsel, that's a decision they have to make and it can change. So I have assumed for this argument that he is not testifying, though he may, and of course if he does testify he will be open for cross-examination by everyone and the door is all open and no one would have any objection, I take it.").

118 Prosecution's Further Submission, paras. 3–4.

119 *Ibid.*, para. 5.

120 *Ibid.*, paras. 8–18.

121 *Ibid.*, para. 9; T. 13714 (11 July 2007).

122 *Ibid.*, para. 10; *See also ibid.*, paras. 12–15 (quoting *Prosecutor v. Martić*, Case No. IT-95-11-AR73.2, Decision on Appeal Against the Trial Chamber's Decision on the Evidence of Witness Milan Babić, 14 September 2006, para. 12 ("*Martić* Appeals Chamber Decision").

123 *Ibid.*, paras. 11, 16–18. *Compare Prosecutor v. Aleksovski*, Case No. IT-95-14/1-AR73, Decision on Prosecutor's Appeal on Admissibility of Evidence, 16 February 1999, para. 27 ("*Aleksovski* Appeals Chamber Decision")(permitting transcript of evidence from witness "extensively cross-examined" in prior proceeding by defence with "common interest" with the accused); *Martić* Appeals Chamber Decision, paras. 14–15, 20, 26 (affirming Trial Chamber's admission of evidence from a witness who committed suicide before the accused's cross-examination was complete based on the finding that the accused had an adequate opportunity to cross-examine the witness for about 10.5 hours); *Prosecutor v. Brdanin and Talić*, Case No. IT-99-36-AR73.9, Decision on Interlocutory Appeal, 11 December 2002, paras. 52–53 (admitting *Washington Post* news article as hearsay evidence without requiring former war correspondent to appear to testify about the veracity and accuracy of the contents). *But see Prosecutor v. Kordić and Čerkez*, Case No. IT-95-14/2-AR73.5, Decision on Appeal Regarding Statement of a Deceased Witness, 21 July 2000, paras. 5, 18, 21–27 ("*Kordić and Čerkez* Appeals Chamber Decision") (ruling it was an abuse of discretion to admit the unsworn, uncross-examined, out of-court statement of a witness taken by a Prosecution investigator).

124 *See* Prosecution's Further Submission, para. 3.

to each co-accused in light of the totality of the evidence at the end of the trial."[125] Cases before this Tribunal are decided by professional judges,[126] and an accused may not be convicted solely on the basis of uncorroborated hearsay evidence.[127] The Prosecution represents that it "has called, or will be calling, evidence corroborating those portions of his [Borovčanin's] interview which relate to the acts and conduct of the co-accused".[128]

43. Second, the Prosecution contends that Rule 92 *quater* should be applied by analogy to this case where Borovčanin is essentially an "unavailable witness" if he chooses not to testify.[129] Rule 92 *quater* concerns "[t]he evidence of a person in the form of a written statement or transcript who has subsequently died, or who can no longer with reasonable diligence be traced, or who is by reason of bodily or mental condition unable to testify orally". The Prosecution points out that under Rule 92 *quater*, "if the evidence in the statement goes to proof of 'acts and conduct' of an accused, this 'may be a factor against the admission of such evidence, or that part of it.' However, such evidence is not automatically disqualified for that reason."[130]

44. The Prosecution's third point is that the "common-law rule against admission [...] should not be applied wholesale in this Tribunal",[131] as the "procedural system at the ICTY is distinct from most common-law ones".[132] Cases at the Tribunal are heard before professional judges who, unlike members of a common law jury, are better able to "consider factors such as a co-accused's possible motives to try and exculpate himself or to implicate others".[133] Further, the general approach of the Trial Chamber should be to consider individual pieces of evidence "in light of the totality of the evidence in this case, and in particular with reference to witness and documentary evidence that **[page 18]** plainly supports and corroborates it".[134] In the final analysis, the Trial Chamber will assign little or no weight to evidence it determines is not credible or has not been sufficiently corroborated.[135]

45. Fourth, the Prosecution argues that its position is supported by the jurisprudence of the European Court of Human Rights,[136] which has ruled that the use at trial of a co-accused's statement does not amount to a violation of Articles 6(1) and 6(3)(d) of the European Convention on Human Rights provided the rights of the defence have been "respected".[137] The European Court of Human Rights has held that where a conviction is not based "solely or to a decisive extent" on a co-accused's interview, the inability of an accused to cross-examine the co-accused does not so undermine the right to a fair trial as to violate the Convention.[138] The Prosecution contends that the position of the European Court of Human Rights "accords with the Tribunal's jurisprudence providing that convictions cannot be based on uncorroborated hearsay."[139]

46. If the Trial Chamber chooses not to admit Borovčanin's statements against the co-Accused, the Prosecution submits that—pursuant to Rule 92 *bis* and the normal rule on hearsay—redactions are inappropriate with respect to background material and facts associated with underlying crimes.[140]

---

125 *Ibid.*, para. 4; *See also* T. 13716 (11 July 2007) where the Prosecution submitted that an untested statement of one accused which implicates his co-accused is a piece of evidence a Chamber will look at with "a great critical eye and would be able to give [...] the appropriate weight, if any, it needed."
126 Prosecution's Further Submission,para. 10.
127 *Ibid.*, para. 10.
128 *Ibid.*, paras. 3 n.1, 29.
129 *Ibid.*, para. 21.
130 *Ibid.*
131 *Ibid.*, para. 23.
132 Ibid., para. 26.
133 *Ibid.*
134 *Ibid.*, para. 28.
135 *Ibid.*, para. 29.
136 *Ibid.*, paras. 30–42; *See also* T. 13715–13716 (11 July 2007).
137 Prosecution's Further Submission, para. 32.
138 *Ibid.*, paras. 33–40.
139 *Ibid.*, para. 42.
140 T. 13767 (12 July 2007); Nor are redactions necessarily appropriate with respect to material related to the acts or conduct of the co-accused, as the mention of such acts or conduct by the maker of the statement could be probative of matters relevant to the maker, for example his participation in a JCE or his state of mind. *See* T. 13767–13768 (12 July 2007); redactions are essentially a safeguard for juries. *See* T. 13768–13769 (12 July 2007); in a common law bench trial, the judge would review the material and if he felt it was not admissible, he would simply set it aside." *See* T.13770 (12 July 2007); the distinction between 92 *bis* redactions and the instant case is that, in the former scenario all references to all accused are redacted, whereas in the latter, the evidence remains with respect to the maker of the statement. *See* T. 13772–13773 (12 July 2007).

2. Defence Submissions

47. The various Defence submissions raise three major objections. The first is that admission of Borovčanin's statements to the Prosecution against the co-Accused would violate their rights under Article 21(4)(e) of the Statute, which guarantees an accused the right "to examine, or have examined, the witnesses against him".[141] Beara cites the Rules,[142] the established practice of certain **[page 19]** national jurisdictions,[143] the jurisprudence of the Tribunal[144] and the ECHR[145] in support of the Defence position. He suggests a fair balance would be struck between the right of the co-Accused to confront their accuser and Borovčanin's right not to testify by admitting the evidence against Borovčanin pursuant to Rule 89(C) but excluding it against the others with respect to their acts, conduct, and mental state pursuant to Rules 89(D) and 95.[146] Additionally, Pandurević submits that the Tribunal's jurisprudence is in accordance with the common law and ECHR positions on the issue,[147] while Borovčanin argues that because all of the Accused are charged with participation in a joint criminal enterprise, it would be unfair to allow the Borovčanin interview to negatively impact the others.[148]

48. Beara argues that statements of an accused against co-accused are a particularly problematic category of hearsay due to the strong motive of an accused to shift blame away onto others.[149] The probative value of such evidence is so intrinsically dubious as to render it insufficient to establish any fact in issue as proven beyond a reasonable doubt.[150] To admit such a problematic species of hearsay into evidence untested by cross-examination would be manifestly unfair.[151] Hearsay evidence, though generally admissible at the Tribunal, must be subject to some measure of regulation, and it would be imprudent to depart from the widely-accepted municipal rules and procedures that govern the exceptional type of hearsay at issue in the instant case.[152]

49. Finally, Miletić argues that any limitation on the general right of cross-examination should be "regulated by specific rules"[153] and therefore the question of the admissibility of an accused's statement should be assessed "within the framework of the Rules concerning the admission of written statements",[154] namely Rules 89(F), 92 *bis*, 92 *ter*,[155] and 92 *quater*.[156] In Miletić's view, "[t]he fact that the Rules contain specific rules governing the admission of written statements into **[page 20]** evidence but do not provide the possibility of admitting the statement of one accused against his co-accused resolutely speaks against" admission.[157] Miletić argues that Rule 82(A), guaranteeing accused in a joint trial the same rights as if each were tried separately, is implicated because the Borovčanin interview would not be admitted if Miletić were tried separately without Borovčanin being called to testify.[158]

---

141 Beara Submissions, paras. 5–6; *See also* T. 13728–13731 (11 July 2007); Miletić Submissions, paras. 5, 20–24 (Miletić also refers to Article 82(A). *See infra* para. 52); *See also* T. 13723, 13726–13727 (11 July 2007); Gvero Submissions, para. 6; *See also* T. 13735–13736, 13738 (11 July 2007); *See* T. 13743–13744 (11 July 2007) for Popović; *See* T. 13745–13747 (11 July 2007) for Pandurević, Borovčanin and Nikolić).

142 Beara Submissions, para. 17.

143 *Ibid.*, paras. 11–14, 28–30; *See also* Further Beara Submissions, para. 2.

144 Beara Submissions, paras. 7–8.

145 *Ibid.*, paras. 9–10.

146 *Ibid.*, paras. 19–21, 24. However, Beara concedes that it is legally possible that the value of the statement in relation to the co-Accused could remain in limbo until the moment it is known whether there will be the possibility of cross-examination. T. 13731–13732 (11 July 2007); Miletić and Gvero expressly endorse the Beara Submissions (Miletić Submissions, para. 2; Gvero Submissions, para. 5).

147 T. 13745 (11 July 2007).

148 T. 13743–13744 (11 July 2007).

149 T. 13730 (11 July 2007); *See also* Beara Submissions, paras. 16, 25–26.

150 Miletić Submissions, para. 19; *See also* T. 13721–13722 (11 July 2007); *See* T. 13728–13729 (11 July 2007) for Beara ; *See* T. 13744 (11 July 2007) for Nikolić.

151 *See supra note* 153, para. 51.

152 T. 13745–13746 (11 July 2007).

153 Miletić Submissions, para. 6.

154 *Ibid.*, para. 7.

155 *Ibid.*, paras. 9–11.

156 *Ibid.*, para. 13.

157 *Ibid.*, para. 14.

158 Ibid., paras. 20.

50. Defence teams take varying positions on whether redaction is warranted if the Trial Chamber decides not to admit Borovčanin's statements against his co-Accused. Beara submits that if the material has no probative value, then redactions are generally appropriate regardless of whether the Judges can "put it out of [their] minds or not."[159] Further, as a practical matter, any redactions he would seek would have no effect on the Prosecution's case against Borovčanin.[160] Pandurević suggests that redactions are preferable in order to give the appearance to the co-Accused and the public that justice is being done.[161] Popović and Borovčanin also favour redactions.[162] Miletić is not opposed to redactions.[163] Nikolić argues that although redactions would prevent any confusion as to the exact use made of Borovčanin's statements, where the Trial Chamber is very clear in this regard, redaction is not required.[164] Finally, Gvero accepts that on occasion professional judges will view material which they might be required to disregard as a matter of law and therefore considers redaction unnecessary.[165]

B. Discussion

1. Introduction

51. As more joint trials are proceeding and the Prosecution has begun advocating for use of statements by an accused against co-accused, Trial Chambers are being confronted with the question of whether to admit statements taken by the Prosecution from an accused against co-accused.[166] Except for a recent Trial Chamber decision in *Prosecutor v. Prlić*,[167] there has been no **[page 21]** written decision by any Chamber of this Tribunal on the important issue.[168] Now this Trial Chamber, which is presiding over the largest joint trial in the Tribunal's history, is faced with the question.

52. The Prosecution references European Court of Human Rights (ECHR) cases holding that the admission of statements by an accused against his co-accused without opportunity for cross-examination does not amount to a violation of the fair trial provisions of the European Convention on Human Rights if the evidence is not the sole or decisive basis for conviction.[169] But the ECHR has repeatedly emphasized that as a supranational court of review, it does *not* examine the propriety of admission.[170] Rather the ECHR simply reviews whether the admission of statements amounted to a defect that invalidated the fairness of the trial altogether.[171]

---

159 T. 13775 (12 July 2007); T. 13777–13778 (12 July 2007).

160 T. 13779 (12 July 2007).

161 T. 13790 (12 July 2007).

162 T. 13774 (12 July 2007); T. 13787 (12 July 2007).

163 T. 13787–13786 (12 July 2007).

164 T. 13783–13784 (12 July 2007).

165 T. 13788–13789 (12 July 2007).

166 *See, e.g.*, *Prosecutor v. Milutinović, Šainović, Ojdanić, Pavković, Lazarević and Lukić*, Case No. IT-05-87-T, T. 12596–12599 (3 May 2007) (considering but not deciding question); Prosecution's Further Submission, p. 2 n. 2 (noting question will not be decided until end of the *Milutinović* trial). *Compare Prosecutor v. Blagojević and Jokić*, Case No. IT-02-60-T, Prosecution's Motion for Clarification of Oral Decision Regarding Admissibility of Accuseds' Statements, 30 June 2003, paras. 13, 15-20 (stating that the Accused Jokić's statements will not be used against co-Accused Blagojević and arguing that admission of Jokić's statements will not "improperly taint[]" his co-Accused's defence because professional judges will properly limit the use of the statement); T. 13524 (28 June 2007) (statement of Peter McCloskey, Office of the Prosecutor) (acknowledging that during the *Blagojević and Jokić* trial he indicated that statements by an Accused should not be used against a co-Accused, but stating, "I can tell everyone that the policy of the Office of the Prosecutor is now that a statement can be used against fellow accused and it's up to the Court to decide what weight they give it.").

167 *Prosecutor v. Prlić, Stojić, Praljak, Petković, Ćorić and Pušić*, Case No. IT-04-74-T, Decision on Request for Admission of the Statement of Jadranko Prlić, 22 August 2007 ("*Prlić* Trial Chamber Decision"), For the reasons stated below, the Trial Chamber reaches a different outcome than that in *Prlić*.

168 *See ibid.*, para. 13 (stating that "no Chamber of the Tribunal has expressed itself" on the use of an accused's statement against co-accused in a joint trial).

169 Prosecution's Further Submission, paras. 30–32, 34, 36–40.

170 *See, e.g.*, *Carta v. Italy*, Application No. 4548/02, Définitif, European Court of Human Rights, 13 September 2006, para. 47 ["*Carta v. Italy*, ECHR Decision"] ("La Cour rappelle qu'elle n'est pas compétente pour se prononcer sur le point de savoir si des dépositions de témoins ont été à bon droit admises comme preuves ou encore sur la culpabilité du requérant.") (available only in French); *Lucà v. Italy*, Application No. 33354/96, Judgement, European Court of Human Rights, 27 February 2001, para. 38 ("The Court's task under the Convention is not to give a ruling as to whether statements of witnesses were properly admitted as evidence, but rather to ascertain whether the proceedings as a whole, including the way in which evidence was taken, were fair.").

171 *See, e.g.*, *Carta v. Italy*, ECHR Decision, para. 47 ("La mission confiée à la Cour par la Convention consiste uniquement à rechercer si la procédure considérée dans son ensemble, y compris le mode de présentation des moyens de preuve, a revêtu un

53. As a Trial Chamber, the duty to decide whether to exercise our discretion under Rules 89(C) and (D) to admit or exclude the statements of an accused against co-accused falls squarely on us.[172] Exercising discretion informed by the principles of fair trial undergirding the Tribunal's Rules, including the concern demonstrated by Rules 92 *bis* and *ter* for safeguards concerning evidence used as proof of the acts and conduct of an accused and the guarantee at Rule 82(A) that if accused are jointly tried, each accused shall have the same rights as if separately tried, the Trial Chamber by **[page 22]** majority declines to use Borovčanin's statements to the Prosecution as proof of the acts and conduct of the co-Accused.[173]

2. Analysis

54. The Trial Chamber must assume at this juncture for purposes of analysis that Borovčanin will exercise his absolute right not to be called to testify during his trial. The co-Accused will therefore have no meaningful opportunity to cross-examine Borovčanin about the accuracy and veracity of his statements taken by the Prosecution in anticipation of legal proceedings.

55. If Borovčanin ultimately chooses to testify, the Trial Chamber will re-evaluate the issue of the admissibility of his statements against the co-Accused.[174]

a) The Right of Cross-Examination

56. We begin with fundamental principles. The Appeals Chamber has explained that "the right to cross-examine witnesses is a fundamental right recognized under international human rights law and restated in Article 21(4) of the Statute of this Tribunal".[175] Article 21(4) of the Tribunal's Statute guarantees to an accused, "in fully equality" the right "to examine, or have examined, the witnesses against him".

57. Invoking the right of cross-examination, the co-Accused argue that the admission of Borovčanin's statements against them would be a violation because they would be unable to cross-examine Borovčanin.[176] This argument does not end the analysis, however, because the Appeals Chamber has explained that the right to cross-examination "is not absolute" and this Tribunal does not generally bar hearsay evidence.[177] **[page 23]**

58. Counsel for Beara has argued that at issue here "is a special kind of hearsay" that is particularly problematic because the statements come from someone with powerful self-interest in shifting blame away from himself and onto others.[178] In a written submission, Beara invokes the United States' rule on the

caractère equitable et si les droits de la défense ont été respectés revêtu un caractère équitable et si les droits de la défense ont été respectés.") (available only in French); *Gossa v. Poland*, Application No. 47986/99, Judgement, European Court of Human Rights, 9 January 2007, paras. 52, 64 (observing that "[t]he Court's task under the Convention is not to give a ruling as to whether statements of witnesses were properly admitted as evidence" and ruling, after reviewing the proceedings as a whole, that the Court could not find "that the applicant's trial as a whole was unfair").

172 *See Prosecutor v. Bagosora, Kabiligi, Ntabakuze and Nsengiyumva*, Case Nos. ICTR-98-41-AR93 & ICTR-98-41-AR93.2, Decision on Prosecutor's Interlocutory Appeals Regarding Exclusion of Evidence, 19 December 2003, para. 11 ("The decision to admit or exclude evidence pursuant to Rule 89(C) is one within the discretion of the Trial Chamber and, therefore, appellate intervention is warranted only in limited circumstances."). Rule 89(C) of the Rules of the International Criminal Tribunal for Rwanda referenced by the Appeals Chamber is worded identically to Rule 89(C) of this Tribunal's Rules.

173 Judge Prost dissents in part. Her dissent in part is appended.

174 *See Prosecutor v. Orić,* Case No. IT-03-68-T, Order Concerning Guidelines on Evidence and the Conduct of Parties during Trial Proceedings, 21 October 2004, p. 5 ("The fact that the Trial Chamber may, at some point in the course of the proceedings, issue a ruling upon the admissibility of a particular document or other piece of evidence, will not prevent that ruling being reversed at a later stage as further evidence emerges that is relevant to the admissibility of the evidence in question.").

175 *Prosecutor v. Prlić, Stojić, Praljak, Petković, Ćorić and Pušić* Case No. IT-04-74-AR73.2, Decision on Joint Defence Interlocutory Appeal Against the Trial Chamber's Oral Decision of 8 May 2006 Relating to Cross-Examination by Defence and on Association of Defence Counsel's Request for Leave to File an Amicus Brief, 4 July 2006, p. 2 ("*Prlić* Appeals Chamber Decision on Management of Cross-Examination").

176 Beara Submissions, paras. 5–6; *See also* T. 13728–13731 (11 July 2007); Miletić Submissions, paras. 5, 20–24; Gvero Submissions, para. 6; T. 13743–13744 (11 July 2007) (Popović defence arguments); T. 13745–13747 (11 July 2007) (Pandurević, Borovčanin and Nikolić defence arguments).

177 *See, e.g., Martić* Appeals Chamber Decision, paras. 12, 25 (noting the right of cross-examination is not absolute and permitting admission of testimony by a witness who committed suicide after the defence had conducted about 10.5 hours of cross-examination, but had not completed cross-examination); *Kordić and Čerkez* Appeals Chamber Decision, paras. 18, 23 (noting that admission of an "unsworn, uncross-examined, out-of-court statement of a deceased witness" is "in marked tension with the guarantee in Article 21(4) that the accused has the right to examine the witnesses against him" but that it is "well-settled that this provision does not create a general prohibition on hearsay evidence").

178 T. 13730 (11 July 2007) (statement of Christopher Meek, counsel for Beara).

exclusion of uncross-examined statements of a defendant concerning a co-defendant.[179] The United States Supreme Court has held "that when one person accuses another of a crime under circumstances in which the declarant stands to gain by inculpating another, the accusation is presumptively suspect and must be subjected to the scrutiny of cross-examination."[180]

59. The Trial Chamber's decision does not turn on the presumption or *per se* bar of a particular domestic jurisdiction. Arguments trying to turn reliability concerns into a *per se* bar do not end the analysis because the Trial Chamber does not adopt such a position. Rather, in analyzing how to exercise discretion to admit or exclude evidence, the Trial Chamber finds guidance in the balances struck by the international and hybrid set of Rules forged at the Tribunal[181] and the principles of fair trial that undergird the Rules and jurisprudence.

b) Rules 89(C) and (D)

60. Rule 89(C) provides that the Trial Chamber "may admit any relevant evidence which it deems to have probative value" while Rule 89(D) provides: "A Chamber may exclude evidence if its probative value is substantially outweighed by the need to ensure a fair trial."

61. The Prosecution's transcript and recording of Borovčanin's statement is hearsay that implicates fairness as well as reliability concerns if used against the co-accused. Both concerns are relevant to the analysis. In *Kordić and Čerkez*, the Appeals Chamber ruled that "the reliability of a statement is relevant to its admissibility, and not just to its weight" and ruled that the evidence "may be so lacking in terms of the indicia of reliability" that admission would be an abuse of discretion.[182] While the Appeals Chamber has since noted that "[t]o some extent, the *Kordić & Čerkez* Decision **[page 24]** was dependent upon the preference in the Rules at the time for 'live, in court' testimony" and this preference has since been qualified by Rules 89(F) and 92 *bis*, the Appeals Chamber has restated and left unperturbed the principle in *Kordić and Čerkez* that reliability of hearsay is relevant to its admissibility, and not just to its weight.[183] Rule 89(D) explicitly prescribes "the need to ensure a fair trial" as a consideration.

c) The Special Concerns Posed

62. The hearsay at issue is problematic and "special" for two reasons. First, it involves statements by an accused—a suspect at the time the Prosecution questioned him–with powerful incentive to shift blame away to others. Second, the statements were taken by the Prosecution in anticipation of legal proceedings. The only materials or person the co-Accused have to examine or cross-examine were produced by, or affiliated with, the party seeking their conviction in this case.

63. Considering the admissibility of statements made by prospective witnesses to investigators of the Office of the Prosecutor ("OTP"), the Appeals Chamber in *Galić* underscored that statements prepared for purposes of legal proceedings constitute "hearsay material of a very special type, with very serious issues raised as to its reliability."[184] The *Galić* Appeals Chamber described "the recognised potential [...] of such documents

---

179 Beara's Submissions, paras. 11–12, n. 7, 28–29 (citing *Bruton v. United States*, 391 U.S. 123 (1968)). Beara also underscores U.S. jurisprudence on the Sixth Amendment right to confront witnesses which mandates that that the reliability of "testimonial statements" be tested "in the crucible of cross-examination". Beara's Submissions, paras. 12–13 (quoting *Crawford v. Washington*, 541 U.S. 36, 61 (2004)). As explained *supra*, at paragraph 57, however, this Tribunal generally admits hearsay statements, in marked contrast to the common law position.

180 *Lee v. Illinois*, 476 U.S. 530, 541 (1986).

181 *See* O-Gon Kwon, *the Challenge of An International Criminal Trial as Seen from the Bench*, 5 J. Int'l Crim. Justice 360, 361–64, 367, 376 (2007) (analyzing how provisions of the Rules represent "the internationalization of criminal procedure" and "combine different features of the common-law and civil-law systems in a unique hybrid fashion unknown to any domestic jurisdiction in the world" and describing the duty of the Tribunal's judges, drawn from a diverse array of domestic jurisdictions "to continue to think 'internationally'").

182 *Kordić and Čerkez* Appeals Chamber Decision, paras. 24, 27.

183 *Prosecutor v. Milošević*, Case No. IT-02-54-AR73.2, Decision on Admissibility of Prosecution Investigator's Evidence, 30 September 2002, para. 18(2), (3), 19 ("*Milošević* Appeals Decision on Admissibility of Prosecution Investigator's Evidence"). *See also Prosecutor v. Galić*, Case No. IT-98-29-AR73.2, Decision on Interlocutory Appeal Concerning Rule 92 *bis*(C), 7 June 2002, para. 27 ("*Galić* Appeals Chamber Decision") ("To some extent, the *Kordić & Čerkez* Decision by the Appeals Chamber was dependent upon the preference in the Rules a the time for 'live, in court' testimony, but its insistence upon the reliability of hearsay evidence was maintained in relation to hearsay written statements, despite the qualification of that preference [.....] when Rule 92*bis* was introduced as a result of that decision.").

184 *Galić* Appeals Chamber Decision, paras. 1, 28.

being carefully devised by lawyers or others to ensure that they contained only the most favourable version of the facts stated."[185]

64. The need to ensure reliability was particularly salient, the *Galić* Appeals Chamber wrote, "in relation to written statements given by prospective witnesses to OTP investigators, as questions concerning the reliability of such statements have unfortunately arisen, from knowledge gained in many trials before the Tribunal as to the manner in which those written statements are compiled."[186]

65. The *Prlić* Chamber has endeavoured to distinguish suspect statements taken by the Prosecution pursuant to Rules 42 and 43, emphasizing that transcripts are more complete following such interviews and the suspect interviewed may have counsel present.[187] These factors do not lessen the **[page 25]** fundamental problems with using the statements of an accused against co-accused–the high incentive to shift the blame away to others by a suspect undergoing prosecution questioning, and the fundamental fact that the only person or materials the co-Accused have to cross-examine or examine are affiliated with, or produced in anticipation of legal proceedings by, the entity seeking their conviction in this case.

66. Cross-examining the Prosecution investigator does little to mitigate reliability concerns because the Prosecution investigator's testimony can shed scant light on the nature and force of Borovčanin's incentive to shift blame, which will be left largely unexplored and untested by cross-examination.

67. Cross-examining the prosecution investigator is also no substitute for exploring with Borovčanin the circumstances under which he claims to have seen or heard relevant events and the accuracy and veracity of his account.[188] Where the Appeals Chamber has permitted evidence despite abrogation of cross-examination, the Appeals Chamber has carefully considered other protections, such as subjection to extensive cross-examination by a defence team with a common interest in a prior proceeding,[189] or the ability of the defence to cross-examine a witness for ten and a half hours before he committed suicide.[190] Here there are no such indicia.

d) Rule 89(B)

68. The parties do not dispute, and the Trial Chamber readily recognizes, that no provision of the Rules is directly on point as to whether, and under what conditions, the statements of an accused relevant to co-accused are admissible. Rule 89(B) provides that "[i]n cases not otherwise provided for" by the Rules of Evidence, "a Chamber shall apply rules of evidence which will best favour a fair determination of the matter before it and are consonant with the spirit of the Statute and the general principles of law." In carrying out this task, the Trial Chamber finds guidance by analogy to the Rules, which have evolved over the years to balance the interests in having information available, expediency, and the need for fairness and reliability. **[page 26]**

e) Applying the Safeguard in Rules 92 *bis* and *ter* by Analogy

69. As the *Galić* Appeals Chamber detailed, Rule 92 *bis* was fashioned to address the special circumstances of written statements taken for purposes of legal proceedings.[191] The introduction of the initial version of Rule 92 *bis* in December 2001 was accompanied by the qualification of the Tribunal's preference for "live, in court" testimony by Rule 89(F), which permits evidence in written form "where the interests of justice allow".[192] In 2003, the Appeals Chamber clarified that written evidence that did not meet the strictures of Rule 92 *bis* may be admitted under Rule 89(F) where the witness is available for cross-examination and attests to the accuracy of the written statement.[193] This holding was codified in Rule 92 *ter*, introduced in 2006

185 *Ibid.*, para. 29.

186 *Ibid.*, para. 30.

187 *Prlić* Trial Chamber Decision, paras. 26–27.

188 *Compare Milošević* Appeals Decision on Admissibility of Prosecution Investigator's Evidence, para. 22 ("Contrary to the submission of the prosecution, the opportunity to cross-examine the person who summarized those statements does not overcome the absence of the opportunity to cross-examine the persons who made them.").

189 *E.g.*, *Aleksovski* Appeals Chamber Decision, para. 27.

190 *Martić* Appeals Chamber Decision, paras. 25–26.

191 *Galić* Appeals Chamber Decision, paras. 28–29.

192 *Milošević* Appeals Decision on Admissibility of Prosecution Investigator's Evidence, para. 18(3).

193 *Prosecutor v. Milošević*, Case No. IT-02-54-AR73.4, Decision on Interlocutory Appeal on the Admissibility of Evidence-in-Chief in the Form of Written Statements, 30 September 2003, paras. 1, 21.

together with an amended version of Rule 92 *bis* and the insertion of Rule 92 *quater*.[194] This trio of Rules—92 *bis*, 92 *ter*, and 92 *quater*—reflect a balancing of the special concerns posed by witness statements taken for purposes of legal proceedings that can inform our analysis.

70. Rule 92 *bis* "strikes a balance between the procedural rights of the Accused and the interest of expediency".[195] The Rule gives a Trial Chamber discretion to "dispense with the attendance of a witness in person" and to admit "the evidence of a witness in the form of a written statement or a transcript of evidence, which was given by a witness in proceedings before the Tribunal, in lieu of oral testimony which goes to proof of a matter other than the acts and conduct of the accused as charged in the indictment." Evidence may thus potentially be admitted under Rule 92 *bis* absent cross-examination—but is limited to proof of a matter other than the acts and conduct of an accused.

71. The acts and conduct limitation is an important safeguard for fairness and reliability and has been applied by the Appeals Chamber analogously in the context of judicial notice. Reasoning by analogy to Rule 92 *bis*, the Appeals Chamber ruled that "judicial notice should not be taken of **[page 27]** adjudicated facts relating to the acts, conduct, and mental state of the accused."[196] The Appeals Chamber found instructive the balance between expediency and procedural protections struck by Rule 92 *bis* and reasoned there is cause "to be particularly sceptical of facts adjudicated in other cases when they bear specifically on the actions, omissions, or mental states of an individual not on trial in those cases" because "the defendants in those other cases would have had significantly less incentive to contest those facts than they would facts related to their own actions; indeed, in some cases such defendants might affirmatively choose to allow blame to fall on another."[197] The Appeals Chamber's analogical reasoning and fashioning of a fair limitation in light of the principles balanced in Rule 92 *bis* is instructive.

72. Also instructive is Rule 92 *ter*, which provides that written witness statements or transcripts going to proof of acts and conduct may be admitted under three conditions—including, importantly, that the witness is present in court and available for cross-examination. Read in conjunction with Rule 92 *bis*, Rule 92 *ter* underscores the special sensitivity for procedural protections and ensuring a meaningful right of cross-examination where evidence goes to the acts and conduct of an accused.

73. The Prosecution argues that the Trial Chamber should reason by analogy to Rule 92 *quater* rather than Rules 92 *bis* and *ter*.[198] The argument elides the point of Rule 92 *quater* and raises concerns of conflict with Rule 82(A)'s guarantee that persons jointly tried shall have the same rights as if tried separately.

74. By its terms, Rule 92 *quater* governs evidence by a person "who has subsequently died, or who can no longer with reasonable diligence be traced, or who is by reason of bodily or mental condition unable to testify orally"[199]—in short, a person who cannot appear for reasons beyond control. As a further safeguard, Rule 92 *quater* requires a finding "from the circumstances in which the statement was made and recorded that it is reliable."[200] Only such compelling circumstances trigger Rule 92 *quater*'s permission to potentially admit the written statement of the person unable to appear because of uncontrollable circumstances—and even then, the fact that evidence goes to proof of acts and conduct is a factor against the admission of the evidence or that part of the evidence.[201]

---

194 *See Prosecutor v. Milutinović, Šainović, Ojdanić, Pavković, Lazarević, and Lukić*, Case No. IT-05-87-T, Decision on Use of Time, 9 October 2006, pp. 3–4 n. 9 (noting that Rule 92 *ter* "codifies the existing jurisprudence on admission of evidence under Rule 89(F)").

195 *Prosecutor v. Karemera, Ngirumpatse & Nzirorera*, Case No. ICTR-98-44-AR73(C), Decision on Prosecutor's Interlocutory Appeal of Decision on Judicial Notice, 16 June 2006, para. 51 ("*Karemera* Appeals Chamber Decision on Judicial Notice"). The *Karemera* Appeals Chamber wrote regarding Rule 92 *bis* of the Rules of the International Criminal Tribunal for Rwanda, which, is in substance if not in full text, largely identical to this Tribunal's Rule 92 *bis* and concerns the admission of "the evidence of a witness in the form of a written statement in lieu of oral testimony which goes to proof of a matter other than the acts and conduct of the accused as charged in the indictment." *Compare, e.g.*, Rule 92 *bis* (this Tribunal's Rule) (concerning "the evidence of a witness in the form of a written statement or a transcript of evidence, which was given by a witness in proceedings before the Tribunal, in lieu of oral testimony which goes to proof of a matter other than the acts and conduct of the accused as charged in the indictment").

196 *Karemera* Appeals Chamber Decision on Judicial Notice, para. 50.

197 *Ibid.*, para. 51.

198 Prosecution's Further Submissions, para. 21.

199 Rule 92 *quater*(A).

200 Rule 92 *quater*(A)(ii).

201 Rule 92 *quater*(B).

75. A potential witness made unavailable by the Prosecution's seeking of joinder plainly cannot be likened to witnesses made unavailable by the uncontrollable circumstances defined in Rule 92 **[page 28]** *quater*. The position would be perverse and perverse incentive indeed. The position also poses potential conflict with Rule 82(A)'s guarantee that each accused in a joint trial "shall be accorded the same rights as if such accused were being tried separately." The Prosecution elected to try Borovčanin jointly with the other accused in this trial. As a result, Borovčanin's absolute right not to testify in his own trial operates as a bar preventing the six other co-Accused from calling him for cross-examination.

76. The interaction between, and principles behind, Rules 92 *bis* and 92 *ter* are the most fair and analogous guide to the circumstances at issue here.[202] There is no need to slip beneath the balance of protections borne of concern for ensuring a fair trial struck in Rules 92 *bis* and 92 *ter*. To do so would be anomalous indeed given the particularly special nature of the hearsay at issue, involving not only statements taken by a party in anticipation of legal proceedings but the statements of an accused with strong self-interest in shifting blame away onto others.[203]

3. Conclusion

77. Exercising discretion informed by analogy, the Trial Chamber decides that, absent cross-examination, Borovčanin's statements to the Prosecution cannot be used as proof of the acts and conduct of his co-accused.

78. The phrase "acts and conduct of the accused" is "a plain expression and should be given its ordinary meaning: deeds and behaviour of the accused."[204] The meaning of the terms "should not be extended by fanciful interpretation."[205] The Trial Chamber directs the parties' attention to the *Galić* Appeals Chamber's detailed list of what constitutes statements going to acts and conducts of an accused excluded under Rule 92 *bis*.[206] The *Galić* Appeals Chamber listed statements that the Prosecution relies on to establish: **[page 29]**

(a) that the accused committed (that is, that he personally physically perpetrated) any of the crimes charged himself, or

(b) that he planned, instigated or ordered the crimes charged, or

(c) that he otherwise aided and abetted those who actually did commit the crimes in their planning, preparation or execution of those crimes, or

(d) that he was a superior to those who actually did commit the crimes, or

(e) that the knew or had reason to know that those crimes were about to be or had been committed by his subordinates, or

(f) that he failed to take reasonable steps to prevent such acts or to punish those who carried out those acts.[207]

---

202 Even if Rule 92 *quater* were applied analogously, moreover, it does not counsel for admitting Borovčanin's statements as proof of the acts and conducts of his co-Accused. As noted, Rule 92 *quater* requires a finding from the circumstances in which the statement was made and recorded that it is reliable—and even then, the fact that evidence goes to proof of the acts and conduct of an accused may be a factor against admission of the evidence, or that part of it.

203 The dissent aptly notes this powerful self-interest but posits that suspects videotaped and interrogated by the Prosecution might be more careful with the truth. This creative speculation does not undercut the strong and obvious self-interest of a suspect warned and questioned by the Prosecution in trying to shift blame away onto others.

204 *Prosecutor v. Slobodan Milošević*, Case No. IT-02-54-T, Decision on Prosecution Motion for the Admission of Transcripts in Lieu of Viva Voce Testimony Pursuant to 92*bis*(D) – Foča Transcripts, 30 June 2003, para. 11; *Prosecutor v. Slobodan Milošević*, Case No. IT-02-54-T, Decision on Prosecution's Request to Have Written Statements Admitted Under Rule 92*Bis,* 21 March 2002, para. 22 ["*Milošević* Trial Chamber 2002 Decision on Written Statements"]

205 *Milošević* Trial Chamber 2002 Decision on Written Statements, para. 22.

206 *Galić* Appeals Chamber Decision, para. 10.

207 *Ibid.*

Where the prosecution alleges participation in a joint criminal enterprise, statements going to acts or conduct of an accused also include those used to establish:

(g) that he had participated in that joint criminal enterprise, or

(h) that he shared with the person who actually did commit the crimes charged the requisite intent for those crimes.[208]

79. Additionally, the *Galić* Appeals Chamber ruled that the limitation concerning evidence of "conduct" includes a statement that goes to proof of any act or conduct, or relevant omission to act, used to establish the state of mind of an accused.[209]

80 Borovčanin's statements may be used as evidence in the case pertaining to the co-Accused for purposes other than proving the acts and conduct of the co-Accused.[210] Redactions are unnecessary because professional judges are entrusted with, and well-able to, properly use evidence for the prescribed purposes.

V. THE ADMISSIBILITY OF DOCUMENTS RELATED TO THE BOROVČANIN INTERVIEW

81. The Trial Chamber recalls the parties' submissions on the admissibility of the Borovčanin Documents related to the Borovčanin Interview.[211] The Borovčanin Documents consist of (1) **[page 30]** documents regarding Borovčanin's employment from 1982 through 1998; (2) documents that Borovčanin generated during the 20 February 2002 interview, including a sheet of paper stating his personal details, organisational charts of the Republika Srpska Ministry of the Interior and Supreme Command, and a list of the units and number of people per unit in the First Company Zvornik PJP in 1995; (3) a DVD of footage from the Srebrenica area in July 1995 that Borovčanin viewed during his interview on 12 March 2002; (4) documents related to the Prosecution's efforts to interview Borovčanin, including multiple summonses, one receipt of summons with attached cover letter, and two letters to the Republika Srpska Ministry of Justice requesting assistance in delivering summonses.[212] As such, the Borovčanin Documents do not go to proof of the acts and conduct of the co-Accused. In view of the foregoing decisions on the admissibility of the Borovčanin Interview, the Borovčanin Documents are admitted.

VI. CERTIFICATION TO FILE INTERLOCUTORY APPEAL

82. The Trial Chamber envisages that a party may wish to file a request for certification pursuant to Rule 73. Rule 73(B) provides that "[d]ecisions on all motions are without interlocutory appeal save with certification by the Trial Chamber, which may grant such certification if the decision involves an issue that would significantly affect the fair and expeditious conduct of the proceedings or the outcome of the trial, and for which, in the opinion of the Trial Chamber, an immediate resolution by the Appeals Chamber may materially advance the proceedings." Satisfied that both these requirements are met and because of the importance of the issues involved in this decision, the Trial Chamber will grant certification.

---

208 *Ibid.*,

209 *Ibid.*, para. 11.

210 Because Borovčanin's statements are admitted with the limitation that they may not go to proof of the acts and conduct of the accused, the statements will not have sole or decisive weight in proving the case against the co-accused in keeping with ECHR jurisprudence *See Kaste & Mathisen v. Norway*, Application Nos. 18885/04 & 21166/04, Judgement, 9 November 2006, paras. 9–13, 54, 56 (finding denial of a fair trial where statements of an accused not subject to cross-examination may have had decisive influence on the outcome of the cases of the co-accused). *Compare Galić* Appeals Chamber Decision, para. 12, n. 34 (analysing consistency between Tribunal's practice under Rule 92 *bis* and ECHR jurisprudence).

211 *See supra* paras. 6–12.

212 Rule 65 *ter* List Amendment Motion, paras. 5–6, 10; Supplemental Rule 65 *ter* Motion, para. 2.

VII. DISPOSITION

83. For these reasons, pursuant to Rules 54, 73(A), 73(C), 89(B), 89(C) and 89(D) of the Rules, the Trial Chamber hereby decides as follows:

a) **GRANTS** the Amendment Motions and **ORDERS** that the Prosecution's 65 *ter* Exhibit List be amended to include the Borovčanin Interview and Borovčanin Documents;

b) **GRANTS** Borovčanin leave to supplement the Borovčanin Response and the Second Borovčanin Response and **DECLARES** the 65 *ter* Motion with regard the Two Documents which are already on the 65 *ter* Exhibit List as moot; **[page 31]**

c) **GRANTS** the Prosecution leave to file its Prosecution Reply and to exceed the word limit of 3,000 words in the Prosecution Submissions;

d) **ADMITS** the Borovčanin Interview as evidence concerning Borovčanin;

e) **ADMITS** the Borovčanin Interview as evidence concerning the co-Accused except that, as decided on by majority, Judge Prost dissenting, it will not be used as evidence which goes to proof of the acts and conduct of the co-Accused;

f) **ADMITS** the Borovčanin Documents; and

g) **GRANTS** certification to file an interlocutory appeal of this decision within seven days of the filing of this decision.

Done in English and French, the English text being authoritative.

Dated this twenty-fifth day of October 2007
At The Hague
The Netherlands

Carmel Agius
Presiding

[Seal of the Tribunal] [page 1]

PARTIAL DISSENTING OPINION OF JUDGE KIMBERLY PROST

1. I depart from the position of the majority on the issue of whether the Borovčanin Interview is admissible against the co-Accused in so far as it goes to the proof of their acts and conduct as charged in the Indictment.

A. The Right of Cross-Examination

2. As is noted in the majority decision, the submissions from the Defence cited several authorities from national jurisdictions in support of exclusion of the Borovčanin Interview with reference to the Accused.[1] Almost without exception, these precedents come from common law jurisdictions where the answer to this question is an easy one; an out-of-court statement given by an accused is, with reference to the other accused, inadmissible hearsay.[2] However, when the question is raised before a Tribunal where there is no general exclusionary rule with reference to hearsay, it is a much more complex matter.

3. The co-Accused argue that the central obstacle to admissibility is that the introduction of this evidence would offend the right prescribed by Article 21(4)(e) of the Statute "to examine, or have examined, the witnesses against him."[3] Because Borovčanin cannot be compelled by the co-Accused to appear to be examined or cross-examined, the Borovčanin Interview should be excluded as evidence with reference to them.[4]

4. However, as acknowledged by the majority, the jurisprudence and rules of this Tribunal establish clearly that this right in the Statute, which has been interpreted as a right to cross-examine a witness, is not absolute.[5] The majority has discussed this at some length with reference to the authorities of this Tribunal regarding the admissibility of witness evidence which has not been fully tested by cross-examination.[6] While this is of some relevance, my starting point is a much simpler one, flowing from the early decisions of this Tribunal which held that generally hearsay evidence is admissible.[7] As a result, if Borovčanin had made comments relating to the acts and conduct of his co-Accused, before, during or after the events, other than in the circumstances of an interview with **[page 2]** the OTP, those comments would be admissible for all purposes. If for example he had told a fellow officer that Mr. X had ordered executions or he told a journalist that Mr. Y was in charge of it all, those statements could be considered by the Trial Chamber in relation to Borovčanin and with respect to X and Y. Because hearsay evidence is generally admissible in this Tribunal,[8] Trial Chambers often consider such out-of-court statements of persons without the maker of the statement being produced for cross-examination. It therefore cannot be the case that the mere absence of an opportunity to cross-examine the maker of a statement is *per se* sufficient to make the statement inadmissible before this Tribunal. Instead, the crux of the issue is whether the very particular circumstances of this hearsay statement - made by a co-accused, as a suspect, in an interview with the OTP – render the statement inadmissible in these proceedings with reference to the acts and conduct of the other accused.

5. Like the majority, I agree that statements made in this context do not constitute ordinary hearsay. These are a) made by a person who is involved in the same events, ultimately as a co-accused and b) given to OTP authorities in the course of an investigation. Because of these special characteristics, the resulting interviews are quite distinct from other hearsay which is admissible and they deserve separate consideration. I move, therefore, to examine if there are features to this particular evidence which make it inadmissible in part before this Tribunal, given its special context. In so doing, I agree with the majority that the only directly applicable

---

1 *See supra* paras. 47–48, 58.

2 In the case of jurisprudence of the United States it is restricted even more to its national context by virtue of a constitutionally enshrined right to "confrontation" neither found in other jurisdictions nor in the Statute of this Tribunal.

3 *See supra* para. 47.

4 See *supra* paras. 47–50.

5 *See supra* para. 56–57.

6 *See supra* paras. 60–76.

7 *Prosecutor v.Duško Tadić a/k/a/ "Dule"*, Case No. IT-94-1-T, Decision on Defence Motion on Hearsay, 5 August 1996, paras. 5,7,15.

8 *See supra* note 177, para. 57; *See also*, *supra*. note 183, para. 61.

rules are 89(C) and (D) which provide for the admissibility of evidence which has probative value, when it is not outweighed by the need to ensure a fair trial.

B. Statements in anticipation of legal proceedings

6. To begin, I do not concur with the majority position that these interviews can be categorised as "statements taken in anticipation of legal proceedings" subject to the dangers outlined by the *Galić* Appeals Chamber in dealing with witness statements with reference to Rule 92 *bis*.

7. At issue in *Galić* were statements that were taken from witnesses in anticipation of legal proceedings **against other persons**. The Appeals Chamber was concerned that in this situation the party putting forward the evidence, in conjunction with the witness, could "construct" the statement in the most favourable light for the particular legal proceedings and it would be admitted in that form, without subsequent testing through cross-examination. In contrast, a suspect is questioned in anticipation of legal proceedings against himself or herself. The adversarial dynamic that will exist between the Prosecution and a suspect clearly will not support a collaborative effort to craft a favourable statement for use at trial. **[page 3]**

8. The purposes of the two statements are also very different. The statement of a witness has as its main, if not sole, purpose the compiling of evidence from a witness to be adduced in a legal proceeding against others, generally with a very specific proceeding in mind. It is this single-minded focus which enhances the danger that evidence will be carefully crafted to fit its intended purpose.

9. Suspect statements do not have as their sole or main purpose the gathering of evidence against others. In fact, it would be highly unusual for the Prosecutor to use the very restrictive process delineated in Rules 42 and 43 for that purpose. If that is the intent, the Prosecution would be far better off interviewing the person as a witness, without any of the procedural constraints or the psychological impact attached to a suspect statement.

10. Admittedly, the Prosecution may use the opportunity, especially in a case such as this with many suspects, to explore evidence against others. Even more likely, the interview may result in the suspect giving information relevant to other individuals. But that is not when the dangers of "constructed" statements arise. Such dangers surface when the party interviewing the person is focused on crafting a statement in a favourable way with the purpose of introducing it in specific legal proceedings, against individuals other than the maker of the statement.

11. Taking these differences into account, at best what can be said is that the suspect may use the opportunity to put forward the most favourable account of his acts and conduct and shift blame to others. But that, in my view, is no more than a different way of characterising the fundamental issue—which the majority seems to treat as a separate inquiry- what effect does the motivation of the suspect have on admissibility?

12. Finally, we must focus on the concern of the Appeals Chamber which is aptly summarised in the quotation cited by the majority—"in relation to written statements given by prospective witnesses to OTP investigators, as questions concerning the reliability of such statements have unfortunately arisen, from knowledge gained in many trials before the Tribunal as to the manner in which those written statements are compiled."[9] Albeit the OTP may have in place protocols and procedures for the conduct of witness interviews, nothing in the Tribunal Rules provides that they must do so or sets any conditions as to the conduct of such questioning. Because of this difference, there is scope for the slanted "compilation" of statements as the Appeals Chamber rightly identifies. **[page 4]**

13. In contrast, the interview of a suspect is circumscribed by the rigorous requirements of Rules 42 and 43. These provisions ensure a process, where the accused is fully informed as to his or her rights and has the opportunity to have counsel present. A verbatim record exists of the proceedings which makes the circumstances surrounding the taking of the statement transparent and subsequently open to close scrutiny. This is well illustrated in this case where the Accused each had an opportunity to review the transcript and question the investigator who took the statement. In so far as these conditions are followed, the possibility of "compiling" evidence against others simply does not exist in the context of a suspect interview.

---

9 *Galić* Appeals Chamber Decision, para. 30; *See also, supra* para. 64.

14. The majority says that these procedures bring little comfort to the co-Accused because they do not go to the motivation of the suspect. I agree–motivation remains the live and central issue. But what these procedures do safeguard against are the dangers associated with witness statements "taken in anticipation of legal proceedings" as described by the *Galić* Appeals Chamber.

15. For all these reasons I do not consider that the jurisprudence surrounding the taking of statements in anticipation of legal proceedings has any relevance to a suspect interview, either directly or by analogy.

C. Reliability of the Borovčanin Interview

16. I move then to what I consider to be the crucial question. While I agree that the context of the Borovčanin Interview mandates that it be considered on a distinct basis in terms of admissibility under Rules 89(C) and (D), I do not agree with the manner in which the majority treats the interviews or with their conclusion as how context affects its reliability.

17. The majority draws no distinction between the written statement of a witness and the questioning of a suspect and thus relies heavily, if not exclusively, upon the jurisprudence and rules relating to the introduction of witness statements and testimony. As discussed above, the statement of a suspect is very distinct from a witness statement most notably in terms of the protections enshrined in the Rules for the process by which suspect interviews are conducted.

18. In this regard, I agree with the finding of the *Prlić* Trial Chamber that:

> the transcript of the suspect interview that was carried out pursuant to Rules 42 and 43 of the Rules, offers further indications of reliability with regard to the written statements taken pursuant to Rule 92 *bis*(B) of the Rules. The latter reflect only the words of the witness; they do not include the questions asked of the witness; nor do they recount the circumstances under which the interview was held. On the other hand, the transcript of a suspect interview reflects not only the questions asked of the witness but also the answered [*sic*] given. It even includes pauses in the interview. As such, the Chamber has not only indications of external reliability but also indications of intrinsic reliability of the "statement". It can place the answers given by a suspect in their proper context; it knows the questions asked; it sees what subject-matter has been omitted; it is aware of **[page 5]** any possible pressure exerted on the suspect.[...] a suspect interview must take place in the presence of Counsel, unless the suspect voluntarily renounced his right to assistance from Counsel.[10].

19. My second point of departure from the majority is the view of the effect of the context of the Borovčanin Interview on its content. Clearly the situation is a unique and special one. Questions are constructed and posed by an investigating authority. The individual is informed that he or she is a suspect. A formal caution is administered outlining the right to silence and to counsel and the whole of the interview is taped.

20. There is no doubt that in these grave circumstances, a suspect faced with a real possibility of arrest and prosecution may indeed be motivated to mislead or lie to the investigators and to cast blame for the events on to others. On this I agree with the majority. However, in this situation, a suspect might be equally motivated to be careful and precise as to his words when he knows the interview is being given to investigative authorities with access to other witnesses and information, especially when he is under caution and every word is being recorded.[11] In addition, a suspect of course is presumed innocent and as such he or she may use the interview as an opportunity to describe his or her version of the events as truthfully and precisely as possible. Therefore, I do not presume, as does the majority, that the sole effect of the circumstances is a negative one that leads invariably to unreliable statements in terms of the acts and conduct of other persons who might possibly one day become a co-accused. On balance, the circumstances of an interview can affect its reliability positively or negatively. But there is certainly nothing in my view about this special hearsay which would make it so intrinsically unreliable that it should be *per se* excluded in all cases.

---

10 *Prlić* Trial Chamber Decision, para. 27.

11 *Ibid.*

21. Further, I cannot subscribe to the view that because the statement is taken by the authorities advancing the prosecution, there is a presumed bias in the questioning or presentation which makes this evidence suspect. As is the case with any hearsay statement, the Trial Chamber must look carefully at the context of the statement and its content and determine what if any weight to give to it. In fact, I see no reason why such evidence is less reliable than off-hand comments made to a friend several months after an incident; comments admissible in this Tribunal. To the contrary, I believe that the grave circumstances in which this evidence was taken make it more reliable than other forms of evidence which are routinely admissible before us. In any event, I certainly see no basis to exclude any particular portion of the statement as unreliable *per se*.

22. I come then to my most significant point of departure from the majority in terms of the reliability of this evidence. The majority decision rests on the presumption that in giving this **[page 6]** statement to investigative authorities, the accused has a powerful motive to construct the facts in his favour and to shift blame from to others. As I have said, I agree. However, that is unquestionably a concern that must be carefully weighed by the Trial Chamber in examining the entirety of a suspect interview. The motivation to construct evidence in his or her favour would extend to all parts of the statement. What he says about general events, chronology, command structure, the acts of others and, most importantly, how he describes his own acts, conduct and intent; all of these comments must be viewed with the knowledge that the suspect may have a powerful motive to lie. In admitting the evidence against Borovčanin in totality and against the other accused, save with reference to their acts and conduct, the majority draws a distinction that, for me, is unsupportable. I fail to understand why the Trial Chamber considers itself capable of weighing part of the evidence in light of the circumstances of the interview but not the totality.[12] In my view, it is not possible to conclude that the circumstances under which the Borovčanin Interview occurred – the very circumstances which give it reliability for some of its content – suddenly have no value when it comes to comments that the Accused may have made about others. It is important to note in this regard that the phrase "acts and conducts as charged in the indictment" is a very broad one. It is not like the situation the majority cites from the United States jurisprudence where "one person accuses another of a crime under circumstances in which the declarant stands to gain by inculpating others."[13]

23. It is far more complex. This is particularly so in a case of this nature with many accused and the alleged existence of two joint criminal enterprises. In my opinion, the mere possibility that a suspect may be motivated to place the blame on someone else should not have the effect of excluding from the Trial Chamber's consideration such a broad category of evidence as every statement made that goes to the acts and conduct of other individuals who later became his co-accused. Such an exclusionary rule is vastly disproportionate in terms of striking an appropriate balance between available information, probative value and possible prejudice to the accused in terms of the fairness of the trial.

D. The analogy to Rules 92 *bis*, *ter* and *quater*

24. To inform its reasoning, the majority looks to other rules which address statements of a similar nature – namely Rules 92 *bis,* 92 *ter* and 92 *quater*. I agree that while these rules are not of direct application in the instant case, it is important to consider them in analysing the issue before us. **[page 7]**

25. However, I attach a significant caveat particularly when dealing with Rules 92 *bis* and 92 *ter*. As highlighted by the Appeals Chamber in *Galić*, the intention in the introduction of Rules 92 *bis* and subsequently Rule 92 *ter* was the facilitation of the trial process by allowing for the introduction of written statements or transcripts in lieu of oral evidence. The rules were introduced simultaneously with amendments that qualified the previous preference for live, in-court testimony. As a result, as discussed by the majority, both rules are designed to strike a balance between efficiency and fairness in the trial process.

26. However, considerations of the efficacy of the trial do not arise in the context of the statement of an accused. There is no suggestion that the Prosecution is adducing the_interviews as written evidence in lieu of oral testimony. There is no question of advancing the efficiency of the trial. If the recording equipment had failed and no written evidence existed, the same issue would be before us for consideration – whether

12 *See supra* paras. 77–80.

13 *Lee v. Illinois*, 476 U.S. 530, 541 (1986); *see supra* para. 58.

the out-of-court comments of Borovčanin to OTP authorities on the acts and conduct of the co-Accused are admissible. The only distinction would be that the comments would be adduced not by the tendering of a statement but by the recounting of the investigator through oral testimony. While certainly there would be more questions as to accuracy, the crux of the issue would not change. For that reason, while I agree these rules are relevant to the analysis, there are limits as to what analogies can be drawn.

27. It is correct, as pointed out by the majority, that Rule 92 *bis* does not permit the introduction of written evidence which involves the acts and conduct of the accused.[14] The majority argues that this reflects a balancing of the interests of efficiency and fairness, a balance which should be replicated in the case before us. Thus, references to acts and conduct in Borovčanin's statements should be similarly inadmissible.[15] As stated above, I do not agree that the same factors are to be balanced in considering an interview of a suspect. Further, what this overlooks is that Rule 92 *bis* does not address instances where the author of the written evidence in question is not available for cross-examination. In the situations governed by that Rule, the evidence relating to acts and conduct can be presented to the Trial Chamber simply by calling the witness either for full *vive voce* testimony or for cross-examination in accordance with Rule 92 *ter*. It is understandable that evidence of acts and conduct are excluded under Rule 92 *bis* where there is no compelling reason to allow such evidence to be adduced in the absence of cross-examination. In every instance actually covered under Rule 92 *bis*, there is no possibility that evidence may be denied to the Trial Chamber due to the unavailability of the witness. It is no surprise therefore that the balance between fairness and efficiency is so struck under that rule as the evidence can be made available to the Chamber, albeit **[page 8]** in a more protracted manner. In my view, an analogy cannot be drawn between Rule 92 *bis* and the Borovčanin Interview.

28. The same must be said of the Appeals Chamber jurisprudence relating to adjudicated facts. It is not a question as to whether or not a fact can be demonstrated to the Trial Chamber, it is a question of how it must be established. Even though a fact may be outside the realm of adjudicated facts it is always open to the party to call evidence on it.

29. Even more so, Rule 92 *ter* is not helpful in the analysis of the issue before us. It is a procedural provision designed to facilitate the introduction of direct examination in written form. It is predicated entirely on the requirement that the witness appear for cross-examination and thus is not analogous at all to a situation where that is not possible.

30. In my view, what is most helpful is Rule 92 *quater*. Under this Rule, statements or transcripts of persons who have subsequently died or are by reason of bodily or mental condition unable to testify orally, can be admitted. And in this instance, even if the evidence goes to proof of acts and conduct, the Trial Chamber has the discretion to admit the statement or transcript. The underlying difference between Rule 92 *bis* and Rule 92 *quater* in terms of the treatment of evidence of acts and conduct of the accused is that the evidence in the case of Rule 92 *quater* will not be available at all to the Trial Chamber if it cannot be adduced under this Rule. In contrast, the narrow category of evidence excluded under Rule 92 *bis* can always be introduced if necessary by calling the relevant witness – either for full *viva voce* testimony or for cross-examination pursuant to Rule 92 *ter*.

E. Prejudice resulting from the Joinder

31. By contrast, the situation facing the Trial Chamber is very similar to that under Rule 92 *quater*. The difference in the two situations is the reason for the unavailability of the maker of the statement. For legal reasons, as opposed to physical or mental ones, the person who made the statement is not available for cross-examination. I fail to see how the reasons for unavailability can affect the evidence – in terms of its reliability or otherwise - so as to exclude one category of statement completely but allow for possible admissibility in the other instance. In my view, given the similarity of circumstance and underlying rationale, Rule 92 *quater* supports, at the least, discretion to admit the Borovčanin statements with reference to the acts and conduct of the co-Accused.

---

14 *See supra* note 195, para. 70.

15 *See supra* para. 77.

32. The majority is of the view that it would be perverse to apply Rule 92 *quater* by analogy to situations where the unavailability of the witness was brought about by the Prosecution's **[page 9]** application for joinder.[16] The majority fears it would constitute a perverse incentive, though I am unclear as to what the incentive would be towards. As I read the majority opinion, because the Prosecution's joinder application has acted as a bar to the right of the co-Accused to cross-examine Borovčanin on his statements, fairness dictates that the evidence with reference to the acts and conduct of the co-Accused must be excluded.

33. I find that argument to be somewhat artificial. Such a position ignores a fundamental fact that it was not the application of the Prosecution which triggered the limitations on cross- examination but rather the decision of the Trial Chamber to grant joinder. It is at that juncture – when the decision on joinder was at issue - that an argument as to possible prejudice to cross- examination rights should have been advanced. However, after the fact, in a Tribunal where the question of the admissibility of the statement of one co-accused against another has not been decided, it does not seem appropriate to me that the Prosecution's application for joinder constitutes any basis upon which to exclude evidence.

34. More significantly, in a Tribunal of this nature, not strictly adversarial, the issue of admissibility of evidence in my view should not be couched in terms of choices by the parties. Rather the question is: did the joinder application and decision so alter the circumstances surrounding this evidence such that its admission by the Trial Chamber would affect the fairness of the trial? In considering this question I refer also to the related argument advanced by Miletić. He has argued that the Rules and jurisprudence mandate that an accused should not be prejudiced in his or her position as a result of joinder. Here, because of joinder, Miletić is denied the right to cross-examine Borovčanin, which would have been an option if they had been tried separately. In his view, the admission of Borovčanin's statements against him would thus prejudice his position as a result of joinder.

35. In response to both points, I agree fully that the situation with reference to this evidence would have been different if the Accused had been tried separately. But where I differ from the majority is as to whether Miletić or any of the co-Accused is prejudiced as a result of this difference.[17] In the case of separate trials the Prosecution would have been required to call Borovčanin to adduce this evidence and the co-Accused would have had the opportunity to cross-examine him. That is true. At the same time, in that case the evidence of Borovčanin would be admissible without question or qualification and would carry any weight the Trial Chamber chose to accord to it. It could in fact form the sole basis for conviction. In the instance case, if the evidence is admitted, untested by cross-examination, it can never be accorded full weight nor can it possibly serve as the sole or **[page 10]** decisive evidence upon which to found a conviction. This for me strikes the appropriate balance between consideration of relevant evidence and possible prejudice to the co-accused. Complete exclusion is an unnecessary step which would deprive the Trial Chamber access to potentially relevant evidence whatever weight to be ascribed to it.

36. As to the related argument that Rule 82(A) has been breached in that there is no right to cross-examine Borovčanin as would have been the case in a separate trial, I note that the Rule must be read in light of the Statute and the relevant jurisprudence. As discussed previously and by the majority, there is no absolute right to cross-examination under the Tribunal regime. Thus, Rule 82(A) cannot be interpreted so as to mandate the exact same opportunity for cross-examination in joinder cases as exists in a separate trial. Taken to its logical conclusion, that would lead to an impossible situation in terms of joinder. An accused could always successfully oppose the motion on the basis of the principle that were he tried alone he would have the right to examine or cross-examine his co-accused whereas in the joint case he does not. While that may be a relevant consideration on the facts of a particular case, it cannot be argued in the abstract as is advanced here. The provisions of Rule 82(A) do not assist in terms of the admissibility of this evidence.

37. For these reasons, to the extent that existing Rules provide guidance on the question of the admissibility of this evidence, I am of the view that 92 *quater* is of most significance and it clearly supports, at the least, a discretion to admit the evidence.

---

[16] *See supra* para. 75.

[17] *See supra* paras. 49, 53.

F. Admissibility

38. But there is an important distinction between the question at hand and the circumstances governed by Rule 92 *quater*. This is not an instance where the evidence in question will be admitted or not. The Trial Chamber has decided to admit the full text of Borovčanin's statements with reference to Borovčanin. I clearly recognise that the factors leading to the admission with reference to Borovčanin are different. They are his own statements, arguably against his interests. However, I cannot accept that evidence, which we consider sufficiently reliable to meet the threshold of admissibility with respect to one accused, is at the same time so unreliable with reference to others as to require its exclusion from consideration as evidence. If, for example, Borovčanin places himself and Mr. X, a co-accused, at the command of the Zvornik Brigade on a certain date, I fail to see why that statement should be considered as reliable with reference to one accused but totally unreliable and inadmissible with reference to the other. Where that leaves us in practical terms is within the uncomfortable realm that often exists in the common law where evidence is admissible and reliable for some purposes but not for others. While such an analysis can be conducted by **[page 11]** professional judges and even by juries, I see no necessity for it in the instant case. In my view, the civil law concept of free evaluation of this evidence should prevail. In essence, it should all be a question of weight.

39. In conclusion, in my view the proper analysis here is not whether the evidence in question has *per se* sufficient indicia of reliability to allow for its admissibility. I do not reach that point. Under the prevailing jurisprudence of this Tribunal, I can find no principled basis upon which to treat this evidence differently than any other evidence governed directly by Rule 89(C) and (D). Similarly, I do not consider that its nature is such that in every instance its probative value is substantially outweighed by possible prejudice that affects fair trial rights under Rule 89(D).

G. Conclusion

40. For these reasons, I would have held Borovčanin's statements to be admissible in their entirety with reference to all of the Accused. I find it necessary however to go further and make it clear that there is, of course, a fundamental distinction between admitting evidence and according weight to it. While I would be prepared to admit the evidence for consideration, a totally separate question would be the weight that I would attribute to it. I am in complete agreement with the authorities cited from the ECHR whereby a conviction cannot be founded solely or to a decisive extent on evidence such as this, which is untested.[18] Further, in my view such evidence can never be given the full weight accorded to other types of evidence which have been the subject of cross-examination.

Done in English and French, the English text being authoritative.

Dated this twenty-fifth day of October 2007
At The Hague
The Netherlands

Kimberly Prost
Judge

[Seal of the Tribunal]

18 *Martić* Appeals Decision, paras. 20, 22; *Prlić* Trial Chamber Decision, para. 28.

Commentary

1. Introduction

This commentary concerns six decisions on ICTY evidence and procedure.[1] Two decisions (a trial and an appeals decision) concern the same issue in the same case, i.e. the admissibility of suspect interviews against co-accused in multi-accused trials. The other four each concern different aspects of witness examination and, as such, are dealt with separately.

2. Admissibility of suspect interviews against co-accused in multi-accused trials

2.1 Procedural background

On 20 February, 11 and 12 March 2002, the Office of the Prosecutor (OTP) questioned Ljubomir Borovčanin as a suspect (within the meaning of Rules 42 and 43 of the ICTY Rules of Procedure and Evidence (RPE)). The interview was audio-recorded and transcribed (Borovčanin Recordings and Transcript). On 6 July 2007, the prosecution in the case of Popović *et al.*, in which Borovčanin was an accused, filed a confidential motion seeking the addition of, *inter alia*, the Borovčanin Recordings and Transcript to its Rule 65 *ter* list of exhibits.[2] On 17 and 18 July 2007, OTP investigator Alistair Graham testified about the procedures followed during Borovčanin's interview. On 25 October 2007, the Trial Chamber rendered its decision on the prosecution motion (Popović *et al.* Trial Decision)[3] and admitted the Borovčanin Recordings and Transcript into evidence in the case against all of the accused, on the proviso that they could not be used as proof of the acts and conduct of Borovčanin's co-accused (Vujadin Popović, Ljubiša Beara, Drago Nikolić, Radivoje Miletić, Milan Gvero and Vinko Pandurević). On 14 December 2007 the Appeals Chamber rendered its decision on the prosecution and defence appeals against the Popović *et al.* Trial Decision, remanding the issue back to the Trial Chamber on the basis of a discernible error.[4]

2.2 Applicable law and practice

Neither the ICTY Statute nor RPE make special provision for the admission of an out-of-court statement of a suspect (be it in the form of a written statement or a record of interview) in his or her (multi-accused) trial. Nevertheless, several ICTY Trial Chambers have admitted such statements pursuant to Rule 89 (C) of the ICTY RPE, which provides for wide discretion in admitting evidence. According to ICTY case-law, an accused's statement may be admitted in his own trial if it is relevant, has probative value and all the procedural guarantees and protections were respected at the time the statement was made.[5] The admission of a statement given in accordance with such guarantees and protections is dependent neither on the agreement of the

---

1 ICTY, Decision on Defence Request for Audio-Recording of Prosecution Witness Proofing Sessions, *Prosecutor v. Haradinaj et al.*, Case No. IT-04-84-T, T. Ch. I, 23 May 2007, in this volume, p. 229; ICTY, Decision on Notification of Cross-Examination Material, *Prosecutor v. Haradinaj et al.*, Case No. IT-04-84-T, T. Ch. I, 31 May 2007, in this volume, p. 239; ICTY, Decision on Praljak's Appeal of the Trial Chamber's 10 May 2007 Decision on the Mode of Interrogating Witnesses, *Prosecutor v. Prlić et al.*, Case No. IT-04-74-AR73.5, A. Ch., 24 August 2007 in this volume, p. 245; ICTY, Decision on Motion by Witness 28 to Set Aside Subpoena or for Alternative Relief, *Prosecutor v. Haradinaj et al.*, Case No. IT-04-84-T, T. Ch. I, 5 September 2007, in this volume, p. 251; ICTY, Decision on Appeal Against Decision Admitting Material Related to Borovčanin's Questioning, *Prosecutor v. Popović et al.*, Case No. IT-05-88-Ar73.1, A. Ch., 14 December 2007, in this volume, p. 255; ICTY, Decision on the Admissibility of the Borovčanin Interview and the Amendment of the Rule 65*ter* Exhibit List, *Prosecutor v. Popović et al.*, Case No. IT-05-88-T, T. Ch. II, 25 October 2007 in this volume, p. 269.

2 ICTY, Prosecution's Motion for Leave to Amend 65*ter* Exhibit List with 18 Exhibits Pertaining to Alistair Graham (Confidential), *Prosecutor v. Popović et al.*, Case No. IT-05-88, T. Ch. II, 6 July 2007.

3 Decision on the Admissibility of the Borovčanin Interview and the Amendment of the Rule 65*ter* Exhibit List, *Prosecutor v. Popović et al.*, T. Ch. II, *supra* note 1.

4 Decision on Appeals against Decision Admitting Material Related to Borovčanin's Questioning, *Prosecutor v. Popović et al.*, A. Ch., *supra* note 1.

5 See *e.g.* ICTY, Decision on interlocutory appeal concerning admission of record of interview of the accused from the Bar Table, *Prosecutor v. Halilović*, Case No. IT-01-48-AR73.2, A. Ch., 19 August 2005, Klip/ Sluiter, ALC-XXVII-383, par. 14 and 15.

accused, nor on any testimony he might give in court.[6] Prior to the Prlić case, however, no ICTY chamber had ruled on the use of out-of-court statements of accused against co-accused in multi-accused trials.[7] It is this last issue with which this commentary is concerned. Before discussing the Prlić case, however, a brief overview of the relevant fair trial considerations is in order.

The fair trial considerations particular to the admissibility of suspect interviews in multi-accused trials have been summarised by Khan and Dixon as follows:

> In cases where the Prosecution seeks to introduce a statement it has taken from a suspect or accused as evidence, not only against the accused who gave the statement, but also against other accused, the rights of the accused who made the statement and the other accused against whom such evidence may be used, are at stake. Unless the accused whose statement was taken is called as witness [for the prosecution], the co-accused is deprived of an opportunity to cross-examine him on the contents of the statement. Moreover, given that the suspect or accused may have had reason to put the blame on others in an attempt to limit their own responsibility, the reliability of such a statement may be dubious. Such statements constitute hearsay of a potentially unreliable source.[8]

Although hearsay is not *per se* inadmissible at the *ad hoc* Tribunals, "hearsay statements prepared by the Prosecution for the purposes of litigation constitute hearsay of a very special kind, which involves the need for additional judicial scrutiny."[9] After all, such statements raise serious questions as to their reliability, due to the fact that they tend to be drafted "to ensure that they [contain] only the most favourable version of the facts stated".[10] According to the Trial Chamber in the ICTY case of Prlić,

> [t]hough Tribunal case law has identified a certain number of indicators to establish the reliability of hearsay evidence, it is clear from Rules 92*bis* and *ter* [of the ICTY RPE] that the reliability of a written statement on the acts and conduct of the Accused may only be established through cross-examination.[11]

Therefore, the written statement of a suspect who later becomes an accused, prepared for the purpose of criminal proceedings and going to the acts or conduct of the accused, cannot otherwise be admitted under Rule 89 (C) of the ICTY RPE, in order to sidestep the requirements of Rules 92 *bis* and 92 *ter*. By contrast, a suspect interview conducted in accordance with Rules 42 and 43 of the ICTY RPE is admissible pursuant to Rule 89 (C). In other words, according to the Trial Chamber in Prlić, a distinction may be made between suspect interviews on the one hand and Rule 92 *bis* and 92 *ter* statements on the other:

> The latter reflect only the words of the witness; they do not [include] the questions asked of the witness; nor do they recount the circumstances under which the interview was held. On the other hand, the transcript of a suspect interview reflects not only the questions asked of the witness but also the answers given. It even includes pauses in the interview. As such, the Chamber has not only indications of external reliability but also indications of intrinsic reliability of the "statement". It can place the answers given by a suspect in their proper context; it knows the questions asked; it sees what subject matter has been omitted; it is aware of any possible pressure exerted on the suspect. The reliability of the circumstances surrounding a suspect interview is further enhanced by the provisions of Rule 42 (B) of the [ICTY RPE], according to which a suspect interview must take place in the presence of Counsel. The suspect also enjoys further protection from any possible pressure exerted upon him by the Prosecution.[12]

---

6 *Ibid*, par. 15; ICTY, Decision on Request for Admission of the Statement of Jadranko Prlić (Public), *Prosecutor v. Prlić et al.*, Case No. IT-04-74-T, T. Ch. III, 22 August 2007, par. 12.

7 Although in Blagojević and Jokić the Trial Chamber acknowledged the dangers of relying on such statements, it did not get around to ruling on the matter. ICTY, Decision on Prosecution's Motion for Clarification of Oral Decision Regarding Admissibility of Accused's Statement, *Prosecutor v. Blagojević and Jokić*, Case No. IT-02-60-T, T. Ch. I, 18 September 2003, Klip/ Sluiter, ALC-XIV-427, par. 24, 25, 26 and 27.

8 K. Khan, R. Dixon, Archbold International Criminal Courts Practice, Procedure and Evidence, Sweet & Maxwell, London 2009, par. 9–115.

9 *Ibid*, referring to ICTY, Decision on Interlocutory Appeal Concerning Rule 92*bis*(C), *Prosecutor v. Galić*, Case No. IT-98-29-AR73.2, A. Ch., 7 June 2002, Klip/ Sluiter, ALC-VIII-281.

10 *Ibid.*, par. 27.

11 ICTY, Decision on Request for Admission of the Statement of Jadranko Prlić (Public), *Prosecutor v. Prlić et al.*, T. Ch. III, *supra* note 6, par. 25.

12 *Ibid.*, par. 27.

Accordingly, "the transcript of a suspect interview [...] may be admitted and used without cross-examination even if it goes to the acts and conduct of the co-[a]ccused." Nevertheless, on the basis of jurisprudence from the European Court of Human Rights (which the ICTY Appeals Chamber adopted in an interlocutory appeal in the case of Martić), the Trial Chamber stressed that a conviction may not be based solely or substantially upon evidence not subjected to cross-examination, that any lack of cross-examination would be taken into account in determining the probative value of the suspect interview and that before giving such evidence any weight, it must be corroborated by other evidence.[13] In other words, the lack of opportunity to cross-examine the accused (*i.e.* the person to have been interviewed) and the incentive of the accused to shift blame on others (*i.e.* the co-accused) are, according to the Prlić Trial Chamber, matters of weight and not of admissibility. The Prlić Trial Chamber's decision was upheld on appeal.[14]

2.3 The Popović *et al.* Trial Decision

For the purposes of its decision, the Trial Chamber in Popović *et al.* assumed that the accused, Borovčanin, would exercise his right to silence and would therefore be unavailable for cross-examination by his co-accused.[15] According to the Trial Chamber, the factors enumerated by the Trial Chamber in Prlić, which 'enhance' the reliability of suspect interviews conducted in compliance with Rules 42 and 43 of the ICTY RPE, "do not lessen the fundamental problems with using the statements of an accused against co-accused", *i.e.* the incentive of the accused to shift blame on others and the fact that such statements are produced in anticipation of legal proceedings by the entity seeking to convict the accused. The Trial Chamber further noted that making the prosecution investigator who took the statement available for cross-examination is no substitute for cross-examining the maker of the statement, because (i) the prosecution investigator is affiliated with the entity seeking conviction of the accused, (ii) the prosecution investigator's evidence "can shed scant light on the nature and force of [an accused's] incentive to shift blame, and (iii) the prosecution investigator is "no substitute for exploring with [the maker of the statement] the circumstances under which he claims to have seen or heard relevant events and the accuracy and veracity of his account".[16] Accordingly, the Trial Chamber decided that the Borovčanin Recordings and Transcript were inadmissible as evidence of the acts and conduct of the co-accused.[17]

2.4 The Popović *et al.* Appeals Decision

Regarding the admissibility of out-of-court statements of an accused against his or her co-accused, the Appeals Chamber noted that "there is a fundamental distinction between admitting evidence and according weight to it".[18] Therefore, "it would be wrong to exclude certain evidence solely because of the supposedly intrinsic lack of reliability of the content of a suspect's questioning in relation to persons who later became that suspect's co-accused."[19] On these grounds, the Appeals Chamber found that the Trial Chamber had committed a discernible error and remanded the issue back to the Trial Chamber. On 18 June 2008, the Trial Chamber in an oral decision admitted the Borovčanin Recordings and Transcript for all purposes.[20]

2.5 Discussion

The Popović *et al.* appeals decision is in line with the approach in Prlić, according to which a suspect interview is, in principle, admissible as evidence (even if it goes to the acts and conduct of the suspect's co-accused) and, further, that any lack of opportunity to cross-examine the accused (i.e. the suspect interviewed)

---

13 *Ibid.*, par. 28 and 33.

14 ICTY, Decision on Appeals Against Decision Admitting Transcript of Jadranko Prlić's Questioning into Evidence, *Prosecutor v. Prlić et al.*, Case No. IT-04-74-AR73.6, A. Ch., 23 November 2007.

15 Decision on the Admissibility of the Borovčanin Interview and the Amendment of the Rule 65*ter* Exhibit List, *Prosecutor v. Popović et al.*, T. Ch. II, *supra* note 1, par. 54. This assumption turned out to be correct; Borovčanin did not testify.

16 *Ibid.*, par. 65, 66 and 67.

17 *Ibid.*, par. 77 and 80.

18 Decision on Appeals against Decision Admitting Material Related to Borovčanin's Questioning, *Prosecutor v. Popović et al.*, A. Ch., *supra* note 1, par. 50.

19 *Ibid.*

20 ICTY, Oral Decision, *Prosecution v. Popović et al.*, Case No. IT-05-88, T. Ch. II, 18 January 2003, transcript 19993.

or incentive of the accused to shift blame on others (i.e. the co-accused) are matters of weight and not of admissibility. This approach represents a shift away from the principle in Kordić and Čerkez (as endorsed in the Popović *et al.* Trial Decision, among others),[21] that "the reliability of a statement is relevant to its admissibility, and not just to its weight" because "evidence may be so lacking in terms of [...] reliability that [it] is not "probative" and is therefore inadmissible".[22] According to the Appeals Chamber in Milošević, "[t]o some extent, the [the approach in Kordić and Čerkez] was dependent upon the preference in the [ICTY RPE] at the time for "live, in court" testimony".[23] As noted by the Trial Chamber in Popović *et al.*, "this preference has since been qualified by Rules 89(F) and 92 *bis*",[24] which provide for the admission of written evidence. Arguably, the shift referred to above may (in part) be explained by the increased acceptance of written evidence at the ICTY. According to the Trial Chamber in Prlić, it may (also) be explained by the "recognition that professional judges are better able to weigh evidence and consider it in its proper context than members of a jury" and by the fact that, "as opposed to a jury's verdict, professional judges have to write a reasoned decision, which is subject to appeal".[25] Either way, it is clear that where a suspect interview is admitted into evidence for all purposes, without having been tested, corroboration is essential, in order to ensure that a conviction is not based solely or substantially upon untested evidence.

3. Witness examination

3.1 Recording witness proofing sessions

3.1.1 Procedural background

On 22 March 2007, counsel for all three accused in the case of Haradinaj *et al.* filed a joint request for an order that the prosecution audio-record proofing sessions with its witnesses.[26] The request was made following a number of instances of discrepancy between the in-court testimony of a witness and the proofing notes provided by the prosecution to the defence shortly before the witness concerned was due to testify. According to counsel for the accused, such discrepancies were potentially important in assessing the credibility and reliability of the evidence of the witnesses concerned. Moreover, the audio-recording of proofing sessions would "provide the parties and the Trial Chamber with an accurate record of the discussions that have taken place with witnesses" and "permit evaluation and resolution of any differences that arise between a witness' evidence in court and the record of what the witness stated during a proofing session with the Prosecution".[27] The defence was not seeking the automatic disclosure of such recordings, but rather to be entitled to request such recordings when necessary.[28] The prosecution opposed the request, arguing that it would not serve the aims and objectives of proofing and could potentially cause delays in the trial. Instead, the prosecution offered to provide the defence with supplementary statements signed by the witness, which would set out any new, additional or different evidence gleaned from such witnesses during proofing.[29] On 23 May 2007, the Trial Chamber issued its decision,[30] some aspects of which are addressed below.

---

21 Decision on the Admissibility of the Borovčanin Interview and the Amendment of the Rule 65ter Exhibit List, *Prosecutor v. Popović et al.,* T. Ch. II, *supra* note 1, par. 61.

22 ICTY, Decision on Appeal Regarding Statement of a Deceased Witness, *Prosecutor v. Kordić and Čerkez*, Case No. IT-95-14/2-AR73.5, A. Ch., 21 July 2000, Klip/ Sluiter, ALC-V-157, par. 24.

23 ICTY, Decision on Admissibility of Prosecution Investigator's Evidence, *Prosecutor v. Milošević*, Case No. IT-02-54-AR73.2, A. Ch., 30 September 2002, Klip/ Sluiter, ALC-XI-359, par. 18, sub 2.

24 Decision on the Admissibility of the Borovčanin Interview and the Amendment of the Rule 65ter Exhibit List, *Prosecutor v. Popović et al.,* T. Ch. II, *supra* note 1, par. 61.

25 Decision on Appeals Against Decision Admitting Transcript of Jadranko Prlić's Questioning into Evidence, *Prosecutor v. Prlić et al.,* A. Ch., *supra* note 14, par. 57.

26 ICTY, Defence Submissions on the Procedure for the Proofing of Prosecution Witnesses, *Prosecutor v. Haradinaj et al.*, Case No. IT-04-84-T, T. Ch. I, 22 March 2007.

27 *Ibid.*, par. 22.

28 *Ibid.*, par. 3, sub ii.

29 ICTY, Prosecution's Written Submissions Opposing Verbatim Recording of "Proofing" Sessions with Witnesses, *Prosecutor v. Haradinaj et al.,* Case No. IT-04-84-T, T. Ch. I, 22 March 2007, par. 2.

30 ICTY, Decision on Defence Request for Audio-Recording of Prosecution Witness Proofing Sessions, *Prosecutor v. Haradinaj et al.*, Case No. IT-04-84-T, T. Ch. I, 23 May 2007.

3.1.2 Applicable law and practice

Witness proofing is a practice by which parties to trial proceedings meet with witnesses they intend to call shortly before they are due to testify in order to proof or prepare them. At the *ad hoc* Tribunals, the purpose of such meetings is not limited to procedural preparation of the witness for the examination in court, whereby the witness is acquainted with the process and applicable procedures in the courtroom. Proofing sessions may also be used to substantively prepare witnesses for examination, to review witnesses' evidence by providing them with their statement(s) (taken in the investigative stage of the proceedings) and by allowing them to refresh their memory in respect of their prospective testimony, provided that such preparation does not amount to rehearsing, practicing or coaching.[31] During such sessions, it is not unusual for new, additional or different facts or circumstances to come to light. Proofing notes provide a non-verbatim record of such sessions, usually in the form of an unsigned 'supplementary information sheet', sometimes in the form of a signed statement. In the event of discrepancy between in-court testimony and the record of the proofing session, signed statements allow the cross-examining party to challenge the credibility and reliability of the witness on that basis. Proofing notes are subject to disclosure to the opposing (cross-examining) party and, due to the fact that proofing often only occurs upon arrival of witnesses in The Hague (shortly before they are due to testify in court), are often disclosed a day or so before the witness concerned is sworn in. The 'practice' of substantively preparing witness during proofing sessions raises serious concerns for the cross-examining party in terms of preparation for cross-examination. Two situations may arise in this regard. In the first situation, the proofing notes, which will have been provided to the cross-examining party shortly before the examination-in-chief of the witness concerned is due to commence, contain something new, additional or different than in the previous witness statement(s). In the second, the proofing notes reflect the content of the previous statement(s), but the witness testifies to something new, additional or different during examination-in-chief. Either way, the cross-examining party may not have had sufficient time to prepare for cross-examination and, by extension, to effectively challenge the credibility of the witness concerned.

As counsel for the accused in the case under discussion were not challenging the practice of witness proofing *per se* and as much has been written on the (legitimacy of the) practice of witness proofing already,[32] this commentary will not include a general discussion of (the legitimacy of) such practice, but will be limited to the issue of recording proofing sessions.

3.1.3 The Haradinaj *et al.* Witness Proofing Decision

Before ruling on the merits, the Trial Chamber confirmed that it had the discretion, pursuant to Rule 54 and pursuant to its duty to ensure a fair and expeditious trial, to order the prosecution to audio-record proofing sessions.[33] Moreover, the Trial Chamber found that it would not be contrary to customary international law to make such an order.[34]

As to the merits, the Trial Chamber first observed that audio-recordings of proofing sessions allow the cross-examining party, in this case the defence, to challenge the credibility of the witness on the basis of any discrepancy between the in-court testimony of that witness and what the witness said during the proofing session. Not being able to challenge the witness' credibility on this basis may disadvantage the cross-examining party.[35] In the particular circumstances of the case, however, the Trial Chamber considered the disadvantage caused by the audio-recording not having been made (available) to have been 'very slight', but nevertheless resolved to "take into account the potential disadvantage when assessing the weight of [the evidence of the witness concerned]".[36] As to what measures should be taken in order to prevent the

---

[31] S. Vasiliev, Commentary, Klip/ Sluiter, ALC-XXIII-313.

[32] See e.g. C.E.F. Coracini, Commentary, Klip/ Sluiter ALC-XX-139, S. Vasiliev, Commentary, Klip/ Sluiter, ALC-XXIII-313 and S. Bock, Commentary, Klip/ Sluiter, ALC-XXV-130.

[33] Decision on Defence Request for Audio-Recording of Prosecution Witness Proofing Sessions, *Prosecutor v. Haradinaj et al.*, T. Ch. I, *supra* note 30, par. 11–14.

[34] *Ibid.*, par. 17.

[35] *Ibid.*, par. 18.

[36] *Ibid.*

aforementioned disadvantage, the Trial Chamber considered that, while the exclusion of evidence pursuant to Rules 89 (D) and 95 of the ICTY Rules of Procedure and Evidence "is a possibility, it is not the most efficient solution, as it assumes litigation of the issue, and does not necessarily serve the interests of justice and the discovery of the truth".[37] Moreover, the incident(s) on which the request was based were "not sufficient to justify a general measure [the audio-recording of proofing sessions] which will have considerable implications for the Prosecution and which may be remedied just as well by a more diligent and cautious approach by Prosecution counsel when taking notes during witness proofing".[38] Instead, the Trial Chamber adopted the approach put forth by the prosecution, i.e. that the defence be provided with a supplementary statement signed by the witness, setting out any new, additional or different evidence gleaned from the witness during proofing. According to the Trial Chamber, "such a practice would ensure that proofing notes are attested to by the witness...and, in turn, this would lessen any concern that proofing notes are not a correct record of what the witness said during proofing".[39] In the event of such an approach proving to be insufficient, the Trial Chamber indicated its willingness to reconsider its decision not to order the audio-recording of proofing sessions.[40]

3.1.4 Discussion

The Decision on Defence Request for Audio-Recording of Prosecution Witness Proofing Sessions,[41] is not the first ICTY decision to address the issue of (audio) recording proofing sessions. In the case of Limaj *et al.*, the Trial Chamber denied the request for an order "that a representative of the Defence be allowed to attend the prosecution's proofing sessions, or that the Defence be provided with a video or tape-recording of proofing sessions". The defence in that case was "seeking to avoid rehearsals of testimony that may undermine a witness's ability to give a full and accurate recollection of events". However, the Trial Chamber was not persuaded that the "clear standards of professional conduct which apply to Prosecuting counsel when proofing witnesses" were not being observed in that case, "as to warrant some intervention by the Chamber". The Trial Chamber also declined to order the prosecution to provide the defence with signed supplementary statements (as opposed to unsigned supplementary information sheets) of witnesses to have been proofed. According to the Trial Chamber, "[e]xcept perhaps where the subject of a notice of a new item of evidence, or a change of evidence is extensive, there is not any sufficient reason to require a signed statement". Although these findings were made in the particular circumstances of the case, generally speaking such an approach may be too restrictive, since evidence that is new, additional or different, but not significantly so, may also give rise to legitimate concerns as to its credibility. Moreover, such an approach, in order to be efficient, would require the party calling the witness to make an (initial) assessment as to whether the proposed evidence is new or significantly different, such as to warrant a signed statement. Given the (largely) adversarial character of the proceedings at the ICTY, it is questionable whether such an assessment should be left to a party to the proceedings, both in view of that party's inherent procedural bias and of the potential for unnecessary litigation. In this regard, the *Haradinaj et al.* Witness Proofing Decision, which prescribes the provision of signed supplementary statements to the defence (the cross-examining party), is to be applauded. It is questionable, however, whether this approach goes far enough. There is a clear difference between a signed statement and an audio-recording or transcript of an interview, as acknowledged by different ICTY Trial Chambers and the Appeals Chamber, albeit in a different context.[42] As such, the reasons for stopping short of ordering the audio-recording of all proofing sessions are best sought in more practical considerations, such as potentially far-reaching consequences for other Trial Chambers seized of the same matter.

[37] *Ibid.*, par. 21. Rule 89 (D) prescribes that "[a] Chamber may exclude evidence if its probative value is substantially outweighed by the need to ensure a fair trial." Rule 95 prescribes that "[n]o evidence shall be admissible if obtained by methods which cast substantial doubt on its reliability or if its admission is antithetical to, and would seriously damage, the integrity of the proceedings."

[38] *Ibid.*, par. 22.

[39] *Ibid.*

[40] *Ibid.*, par. 23.

[41] Decision on Defence Request for Audio-Recording of Prosecution Witness Proofing Sessions, *Prosecutor v. Haradinaj et al.*, T. Ch. I, *supra* note 30.

[42] See the case-law on admissibility of suspect interviews against co-accused in multi-accused trials, as set out above.

3.2 (Timely) disclosure of material to be used during cross-examination

3.2.1 Procedural background

On 23 March 2007, the prosecution in the case of Haradinaj *et al.* filed a motion requesting the Trial Chamber to order the defence to disclose to the prosecution, in advance of the cross-examination of prosecution witnesses, (a list of) the documents that the defence intended to use during such cross-examination. Specifically, the prosecution sought disclosure of such documents "at least by the commencement of the examination in chief".[43] The defence indicated its willingness to disclose the relevant information to the prosecution at the conclusion of the examination-in-chief of the witness, but only those documents which the defence had "definitively" resolved to use in cross-examination.[44] On 31 May 2007, the Trial Chamber rendered its decision.

3.2.2 Applicable law and practice

Although not provided for in the RPE, the practice of parties disclosing to the opposing party the (list of) documents they intend to use during cross-examination is well-established at the ICTY. Different ICTY Trial Chambers have set different deadlines in this regard: after the witness is sworn in (after the witness has made the solemn declaration pursuant to Rule 90 (A) of the RPE) but before examination-in-chief commences;[45] immediately after examination-in-chief ends;[46] at least twenty-four hours before a document is due to be used in cross-examination;[47] before cross-examination begins;[48] and piecemeal disclosure in the course of cross-examination.[49] Arguments in favour of the timely disclosure of cross-examination materials to the opposing party include procedural fairness and efficiency. Procedural fairness should be understood to ensure (within reason) not only that the opposing party be in a position to make informed objections on authenticity and to adequately re-examine the witness, but also that the cross-examining party be in a position to effectively challenge the credibility of the witness. Such a reading of procedural fairness flows from the largely adversarial mode of presentation of evidence prescribed at the ICTY. In this way, procedural fairness may also count as an argument against too early a deadline for disclosure of cross-examination materials.

In more recent ICTY decisions, the deadline for disclosing cross-examination material to the opposing party appears to have shifted to the moment following the solemn declaration (the first of the deadlines set out above). The first Trial Chamber to order such a deadline was the Milutinović Trial Chamber, which was closely followed in a number of other ICTY cases.[50] Regarding the use of undisclosed material during cross-examination, the Milutinović Trial Chamber held that, "[s]hould a party seek to use a document or material during cross-examination that has not been so listed and disclosed, that party may be permitted to do so on

---

43 ICTY, Prosecution's Motion for a Cross-Examining Party to Provide Advance Copies of Documents Used to Cross-Examine Witnesses, *Prosecutor v. Haradinaj et al.,* Case No. IT-04-84-T, 23 March 2007, par. 4.

44 ICTY, Decision on Notification of Cross-Examination Material, *Prosecutor v. Haradinaj et al.,* Case No. IT-04-84-T, T. Ch. I, 31 May 2007.

45 ICTY, Decision on Joint Defence Motion For Modification of Order on Procedure and Evidence, *Prosecutor v. Milutinović et al.*, Case No. IT-05-87, T. Ch. III, 16 August 2006; ICTY, Order on Production of Defence Documents Used in Cross-Examination of Prosecution Witnesses, *Prosecutor v. Popović et al.*, Case No. IT-05-88-T, T. Ch. II, 24 August 2006; and ICTY, Decision on Time-Limits for Disclosure of Documents to be Used During a Witness' Testimony, *Prosecutor v. Milošević*, Case No. IT-98-29/1-T, T. Ch. III, 18 January 2007.

46 ICTY, Oral Decision, *Prosecutor v. Prlić et al.*, Case No. IT-04-74, T. Ch. III, 8 May 2006, t. 1475.

47 ICTY, Oral Decision, *Prosecutor v. Mrkšić, Radić and Šljivančanin*, Case No. IT-95-13/1-T, T. Ch. II, 6 December 2005, transcript 2953.

48 ICTY, Oral Decision, *Prosecutor v. Martić*, Case No. IT-95-11-T, T. Ch. I, 20 February 2006, transcript 1578–1579.

49 ICTY, Decision on the Accused Naletilić's Request for Enforcement of Trial Chamber's Previous Order Regarding Documents During Cross-Examination, *Prosecutor v. Naletilić and Martinović*, Case No. IT-98-34-T, T. Ch. I, 3 May 2002; and ICTY, Decision on Motion for Prosecution Access to Defence Documents Used in Cross-Examination of Prosecution Witnesses, *Prosecutor v. Halilović*, Case No. IT-01-48-T, T. Ch. I, 9 May 2005, par. 9.

50 Decision on Joint Defence Motion For Modification of Order on Procedure and Evidence, *Prosecutor v. Milutinović et al.*, T. Ch. III, *supra* note 45; Order on Production of Defence Documents Used in Cross-Examination of Prosecution Witnesses, *Prosecutor v. Popović et al.*, T. Ch. II, *supra* note 45; and Decision on Time-Limits for Disclosure of Documents to be Used During a Witness' Testimony, *Prosecutor v. Milošević*, T. Ch. III, *supra* note 45.

showing good cause for not listing and disclosing it". In such situations, "the opposing party or parties may then request a short adjournment in order to examine the material".[51]

3.2.3 The Haradinaj *et al.* Disclosure Decision

In relation to the defence concern that advance disclosure of cross-examination material and, by extension, a line of cross-examination, may provide the witness with "the opportunity to prepare a response in advance and to tailor his/her evidence accordingly", the Trial Chamber observed that "once a witness is sworn in, the Prosecution's communication with that witness is so heavily regulated that "advance notice" of an intended line of cross-examination – even if the line were evident to the Prosecution from reading the document – could not so easily be communicated to the witness".[52] Moreover, whilst advance disclosure may render the lines of cross-examination "less surprising overall to prosecution counsel", this "does not lessen the effectiveness or value of cross-examination".[53] According to the Trial Chamber, the shifting of the deadline for disclosure of cross-examination material to the moment following the swearing in of the witness is not due to pragmatism (alone), but (also) by "the legal principle that for the purposes of fair play the Defence must show part of its hand to the Prosecution".[54] In this regard, the Trial Chamber observed that although disclosure obligations may be asymmetrical at the ICTY, they are not entirely one-sided. In relation to the defence argument that it is only when a prosecution witness has completed his or her evidence-in-chief that a final decision can be made about documents to be put to the witness cross-examination, the Trial Chamber held that the consequence was "not a later deadline, but that the Defence notifies the Prosecution of the material which it is likely to use with each witness, and not only of the material which it has definitively resolved to use". Accordingly, the Trial Chamber ordered that the procedure to be followed was that set out in the case of Milutinović, noting that the "[u]se of unannounced material is not foreclosed".[55]

3.2.4 Discussion

The reasons for the cross-examining party to seek a later deadline for disclosure of cross-examination material are evident: to prevent witnesses from being given advance notice of a line of cross-examination so that he or she is able prepare a response in advance and to prevent the (directly) examining party from eliciting answers from the witness aimed at weakening or undermining the cross-examination. Whilst shifting the deadline for disclosure to the moment following the solemn declaration, in principle sidesteps this problem (due to the communication constraints placed on the examiner and witness from the moment the witness is sworn in), it may still put the (directly) examining party in a stronger position to undermine or weaken the line of cross-examination to be pursued and, as such, may lessen the cross-examination's effectiveness. As the Haradinaj *et al.* Trial Chamber noted, however, "experienced Prosecution counsel anticipate lines of cross-examination even without full knowledge of the documents to be used by the Defence".[56] In other words, the possibility that the opposing party might read into the disclosed cross-examination materials a potential line of cross-examination does not by definition render the deadline set by, *inter alia*, the Haradinaj *et al.* Trial Chamber procedurally unfair nor any subsequent cross-examination ineffective. Nevertheless, there are situations imaginable in which the aforementioned deadline for disclosure may seriously impede the cross-examining party's ability to challenge the witness' credibility. Such situations call for a more flexible approach to the disclosure of cross-examination materials, an approach that the Milutinović and Haradinaj *et al.* decisions appear to provide for. After all, according to those decisions, the use of unannounced, undisclosed material is permissible, provided that "good cause" is shown. The question, then, is what constitutes "good cause". That "good cause" is intended to cover exceptional circumstances only is evident from an 'efficiency' point of view. It should be recalled that where good cause is shown, the opposing party or parties may request a "short adjournment" in order to examine the material. An obvious example of "good cause" is where the non-disclosure of a document is attributable to

---

51 Decision on Joint Defence Motion For Modification of Order on Procedure and Evidence, *Prosecutor v. Milutinović et al.*, T. Ch. III, *supra* note 45, par. 4.

52 Decision on Notification of Cross-Examination Material, *Prosecutor v. Haradinaj et al.*, T. Ch. I, *supra* note 44, par. 4.

53 *Ibid.*, par. 5.

54 *Ibid.*, par. 8.

55 *Ibid.*, par. 9.

56 *Ibid.*, par. 5.

practical or logistical constraints (which is not implausible, given the ongoing nature and piecemeal approach of defence investigations in international criminal proceedings). Whether it also applies to situations in which the cross-examining party has withheld material on the grounds that its effect would be significantly compromised by an earlier disclosure is, however, unclear. This will depend on a number of factors, including the subject matter of the witness' testimony, the type of witness testifying (for example, expert or not) and the frequency with which the party concerned invokes the "good cause" exception.

3.3 Participation of the accused in witness examination

3.3.1 Procedural background

On 28 April 2006, the Trial Chamber in Prlić *et al.* issued (revised) guidelines on the conduct of proceedings in that case. On the matter of witness examination, the Trial Chamber noted that the accused in that case were represented by counsel and (therefore) that witnesses were to be "primarily [...] questioned by counsel for the Accused". However, in "exceptional circumstances" and with the permission of the Trial Chamber, the accused would also be allowed to put questions to the witness.[57] On 10 May 2007, the Trial Chamber indicated in a further written decision that while it was not, in principle, opposed to an accused putting questions to witnesses, "[t]he experience of previous months [...] has shown that the complexity of this trial compels the Chamber to strictly control the modes of witness interrogation", since "in every multiple-accused trial, a Chamber must make sure that the intervention of an accused does not affect the rights of the other accused to an expeditious trial". The experience on which the Trial Chamber based this determination consisted, *inter alia*, of "irrelevant" questions and interventions by the accused Slobodan Praljak, which, according to the Trial Chamber, were "a useless waste of time".[58] Accordingly, the Trial Chamber determined that the guideline on witness examination referred to above would be applied more strictly. In particular, the Trial Chamber stated that witnesses would first be cross-examined by counsel for the accused, that the accused would only be able to put questions to witnesses with the Trial Chamber's prior approval and, finally, that the "exceptional circumstances" referred to in the original guidelines "shall be linked either to the examination of events in which the Accused personally took part or to the examination of issues about which he is specifically competent."[59] On 24 August 2007, the Appeals Chamber rendered its decision on the accused Praljak's appeal against the Trial Chamber's decision of 10 May 2007.[60]

3.3.2 Applicable law and practice

Article 21, paragraph 4, sub e of the ICTY Statute guarantees the accused's right "to examine, or have examined, the witnesses against him or her". Both the ICTY Statute and RPE are otherwise silent on the participation of the accused in the examination of witness, where the accused is represented by counsel. Nevertheless, such practice is not unheard of at the ICTY.[61] Also relevant in this regard is Rule 90 (F) of the ICTY RPE, pursuant to which "The Trial Chamber shall exercise control over the mode and order of interrogating witnesses and presenting evidence so as to (i) make the interrogation and presentation effective for the ascertainment of the truth; and (ii) avoid needless consumption of time".

3.3.3 The Prlić *et al.* Appeals Decision

In relation to the defence contention that the restrictions imposed by the Trial Chamber in its decision of 10 May 2007 go beyond the proper exercise of discretion and "may substantially and unacceptably exclude"

57 ICTY, Revised version of the decision adopting guidelines on conduct of trial proceedings, *Prosecutor v. Prlić et al.*, Case No. IT-04-74, T. Ch. II, 28 April 2006, Klip/ Sluiter, ALC-XXIX-109, par. 9, sub c.
58 ICTY, Decision on the Mode of Interrogating Witnesses, *Prosecutor v. Prlić et al.,* Case No. IT-04-74-T, T. Ch. III, 10 May 2007, par. 10.
59 *Ibid*, par. 11 and 12.
60 Decision on Praljak's Appeal of the Trial Chamber's 10 May 2007 Decision on the Mode of Interrogating Witnesses, *Prosecutor v. Prlić et al.*, A. Ch., 24 August 2007, *supra* note 1.
61 See, for example, ICTY, Transcript, *Prosecutor v. Krajišnik*, Case No. IT-00-39-T, T. Ch. I, 3 June 2005.

him from participation in his own defence, the Appeals Chamber found that "there was good reason for the Trial Chamber to determine that a stricter application of [the guideline] was justified in order to protect the rights of [Praljak's] co-accused to a fair and expeditious trial, as well the rights of [Praljak]" and, as such, that the Trial Chamber had committed no discernible error.[62] In relation to the defence argument that the right to counsel and the right to self-representation are not mutually exclusive and that the assignment of counsel does not negate the right of the accused to also participate directly in the proceedings, the Appeals Chamber observed that the Trial Chamber never held that the accused did not have a right to participate in the proceedings alongside his counsel.[63] The Trial Chamber "merely placed reasonable restrictions on that right to prevent [Praljak's] needless waste of court time and to protect the rights of all accused to a fair and expeditious trial".[64]

3.3.4 Discussion

The Prlić *et al.* Appeals Decision confirms that an accused's participation in the examination of witnesses may be restricted pursuant to an accused's (and, in multi-accused trials, the co-accused's) right to a fair and expeditious trial.[65] It is, however, unclear on the issue of whether such participation can be limited solely on the grounds that, when an accused is represented by counsel, it is primarily counsel's task to examine witnesses. Since the Prlić *et al.* Appeals Decision, the shared Appeals Chamber of the *ad hoc* Tribunals has held that where an accused is represented by counsel, it for counsel, in principle, to conduct the examination of witnesses.[66] According to the Appeals Chamber in the ICTR case of Nahimana *et al.*, Article 20, paragraph 4, sub d of the ICTR Statute and Article 21, paragraph 4, sub d of the ICTY Statute provide for "a choice as between the right of an accused to conduct his own defence and his right to have legal assistance".[67] It further referred to the (ICTR) Directive on the Assignment of Defence Counsel, according to which assigned counsel "shall deal with all stages of the procedure and all matters arising out of the representation of the accused or of the conduct of his Defence".[68] In finding that it is for counsel to examine witnesses, the Appeals Chamber does not appear to have been ruling out the possibility that, in exceptional circumstances, the accused may be permitted to participate in the examination of witnesses.

As to the "exceptional circumstances" under which an accused is permitted to participate in the examination of witnesses, the Appeals Chamber in Prlić *et al.* (in another decision) held that the additional restrictions imposed by the Trial Chamber in this regard constituted an abuse of discretion.[69] According to the Trial Chamber, the "issues about which he is specifically competent" referred to "the expertise held by an Accused at the time of the alleged facts and owing to which he was charged in the Amended Indictment of 11 June 2008".[70] The Trial Chamber "should have allowed more flexibility for its assessment of the notion of specific expertise and perform such assessment on a case-by-case basis when faced with a specific request".[71] Finally, according to the Appeals Chamber the Trial Chamber's approach "could potentially lead to a violation of the Appellant's rights under Article 21 of the [ICTY] Statute".[72] If that is correct, barring an accused represented by counsel from participating in the examination of witnesses altogether would surely constitute a violation of such rights.

62 Decision on Praljak's Appeal of the Trial Chamber's 10 May 2007 Decision on the Mode of Interrogating Witnesses, *Prosecutor v. Prlić et al.*, A. Ch., 24 August 2007, *supra* note 1, par. 9.

63 *Ibid.*, par. 11.

64 *Ibid.*

65 *Ibid.*, par. 9.

66 ICTR, Judgement, *Nahimana, Barayagwiza and Ngeze v. Prosecutor*, Case No. ICTR-99-52-A, A. Ch., 28 November 2007, Klip/ Sluiter, ALC-XXXI-257, par. 267 and footnote 651.

67 *Ibid.*, footnote 651.

68 *Ibid.*

69 ICTY, Decision on Slobodan Praljak's Appeal of the Trial Chamber's Decision on the Direct Examination of Witnesses dated 26 June 2008, *Prosecutor v. Prlić et al.*, Case No. IT-04-74-AR73.11, A. Ch., 11 September 2008, par. 21, to be published in volume XXXVII.

70 ICTY, Decision on Motion for Reconsideration Presented by the Praljak Defence, *Prosecutor v. Prlić et al.*, Case No. IT-04-74-T, T. Ch. III, 26 June 2008, par. 5.

71 Decision on Slobodan Praljak's Appeal of the Trial Chamber's Decision on the Direct Examination of Witnesses dated 26 June 2008, *Prosecutor v. Prlić et al.*, A. Ch., *supra* note 69.

72 *Ibid.*

3.4 Testimonial privilege of witnesses

3.4.1 Procedural background

On 13 August 2007, Witness 28 was subpoenaed to appear as a witness before the Trial Chamber in the case of Haradinaj *et al.* On 15 August 2007, Witness 28 filed a motion to have the subpoena set aside or, in the alternative, to have her testimony received in closed session, claiming a "qualified testimonial privilege" on the basis of her work as a war correspondent and investigative journalist.[73] On 5 September 2007, the Trial Chamber rendered its decision.[74]

3.4.2 Applicable law and practice

There are different ways of protecting confidential information from being 'exposed' in international criminal proceedings, depending on, *inter alia*, the source, nature and (proposed) mode of the information concerned. In this regard, a distinction may be drawn between immunities on the one hand and privileges on the other.[75] In the context of testimonial immunity and testimonial privilege, Friman has noted that,

> [w]hile testimonial immunity means that a person cannot be compelled to appear before the court and to give evidence, testimonial privilege is typically more limited in scope – confidential information or communications – and does not automatically prevent the testimony as such. The concept of a privilege is an exception to a duty to speak, which in turn implies that the witness can be compelled.[76]

In the case-law of the ICTY, privileges can be both testimonial and documentary and have been afforded to a variety of individuals and entities, including ICRC workers,[77] war correspondents[78] and state officials acting in their official capacity.[79] Privileges at the ICTY are therefore not limited to the lawyer-client privilege provided for in Rule 97 of the ICTY RPE. It is the second of the aforementioned privileges, *i.e.* war correspondents, with which this commentary is concerned.

According to the Appeals Chamber in Brđanin and Talić, war correspondents are "individuals who, for any period of time, report (or investigate for the purposes of reporting) from a conflict zone on issues relating to the conflict".[80] In view of the fact that "society's interest in protecting the integrity of the newsgathering process is particularly clear and weighty in the case of war correspondents,"[81] the Appeals Chamber set forth a two-pronged test for Trial Chambers issuing subpoenas to a war correspondents: "First, the petitioning party must demonstrate that the evidence sought is of direct and important value in determining a core issue in the case. Second, it must demonstrate that the evidence sought cannot reasonably be obtained elsewhere."[82]

---

73 Decision on motion by Witness 28 to Set Aside Subpoena or for Alternative Relief (Public), *Prosecutor v. Haradinaj et al.*, T. Ch. I, *supra* note 1, par. 1.

74 *Ibid.*

75 For a comprehensive overview of immunities and privileges in international proceedings, see K.A.A. Khan and G. Azarnia, Evidentiary Privileges, in K.A.A. Khan, C. Buisman and C. Gosnell (eds.), Principles of Evidence in International Criminal Justice, Oxford University Press, New York 2010, p. 551–598. See also H. Friman, Commentary, Klip/ Sluiter, ALC-XXI-311.

76 H. Friman, Commentary, Klip/ Sluiter, ALC-XXI-313.

77 ICTY, Decision on the Prosecution Motion under Rule 73 for a Ruling Concerning the Testimony of a Witness (*Ex Parte* Confidential), *Prosecutor v. Simić, Simić, Tadić, Todorović and Zarić*, Case No. IT-95-9-PT, T. Ch. III, 27 July 1999, Klip/ Sluiter, ALC-IV-231, par. 73.

78 ICTY, Decision on Interlocutory Appeal, *Prosecutor v. Brđanin and Talić*, Case No. IT-99-36-AR73.9, A. Ch., 11 December 2002, Klip/ Sluiter, ALC-XI-325.

79 ICTY, Judgement on the Request of the Republic of Croatia for Review of the Decision of Trial Chamber II of 18 July 1997, *Prosecutor v. Blaškić*, Case No. IT-95-14-AR108*bis*, A. Ch., 29 October 1997, Klip/ Sluiter, ALC-I-245.

80 Decision on Interlocutory Appeal, *Prosecutor v. Brđanin and Talić*, A. Ch., *supra* note 78, par. 29.

81 *Ibid.*, par. 36.

82 *Ibid.*, par. 50.

3.4.3 The Haradinaj *et al.* Subpoena Decision

In relation to witness 28's claim that she was covered by the testimonial privilege afforded to war correspondents, the Trial Chamber noted first that, during the Haradinaj *et al.* indictment period, "when Witness 28 was interviewing victims and witnesses about their experiences in Kosovo, she was neither a war correspondent nor a journalist".[83] Moreover, during that period, "she worked for an organization whose very purpose it was to gather information about, and assist the prosecution of, human rights violations".[84] Accordingly, witness 28 was not covered by the testimonial privilege which she invoked. As to her claim that she was otherwise covered by testimonial privilege on the basis of her human rights work, the Trial Chamber held that "Witness 28's attempted analogy between the work performed and privileges enjoyed by employees of the International Committee of the Red Cross, on the one hand, and members of the human rights organization which Witness 28 belonged to during the indictment period, on the other, fails for the reason that ICRC privileges are specific to the ICRC and cannot be extended to other groups by analogy."[85]

3.4.4 Discussion

As Khan and Dixon have noted, the definition of "war correspondent" provided by the Appeals Chamber in Brđanin and Talić is somewhat ambiguous.[86] The Haradinaj *et al.* subpoena decision confirms that, in determining whether a person may claim testimonial privilege as a war correspondent, the question is whether or not the person concerned was a war correspondent during the period in relation to which he or she is expected to give evidence.[87] In this way, the Haradinaj *et al.* subpoena decision restricts the privilege afforded to war correspondents, which goes some way to mitigate the criticism that the privilege established in Brđanin and Talić is overly broad and therefore potentially undermines the right of an accused to examine (or have examined) the witnesses against him or her (where documents authored by a "war correspondent" are admitted into evidence).[88]

Kelly Pitcher

83 Decision on motion by Witness 28 to Set Aside Subpoena or for Alternative Relief (Public), *Prosecutor v. Haradinaj et al.*, T. Ch. I, *supra* note 1, par. 5.

84 *Ibid.*, par. 6.

85 *Ibid.*, par. 8.

86 K. Khan, R. Dixon, Archbold International Criminal Courts Practice, Procedure and Evidence, *supra* note 8, par. 9–197.

87 See also the following (earlier) decision: ICTY, Decision on Prosecution's Motion for Issuance of a Subpoena, *Prosecutor v. Popović et al.*, Case No. IT-05-88, T. Ch. II, 21 August 2007, par. 3.

88 See, for example, M. A. Fairlie, Prosecutor v. Brdjanin & Talić. Case No. IT-99-36-AR73.9, 98 American Journal of International Law 2004, p. 805–809.

UNITED
NATIONS

International Tribunal for the Prosecution of Persons Responsible for Serious Violations of International Humanitarian Law Committed in the Territory of Former Yugoslavia since 1991	Case No.	IT–98–29/1–T
	Date:	10 April 2007
	Original:	English

IN TRIAL CHAMBER III

Before: **Judge Patrick Robinson, Presiding**
Judge Antoine Kesia–Mbe Mindua
Judge Frederik Harhoff

Registrar: **Mr. Hans Holthuis**

Decision of: **10 April 2007**

PROSECUTOR

v.

DRAGOMIR MILOŠEVIĆ

DECISION ON PROSECUTION'S MOTION FOR JUDICIAL NOTICE OF ADJUDICATED FACTS AND PROSECUTION'S CATALOGUE OF AGREED FACTS WITH DISSENTING OPINION OF JUDGE HARHOFF

The Office of the Prosecutor:
Mr. Alex Whiting
Mr. Stefan Waespi
Ms. Carolyn Edgerton
Mr. John Docherty

Counsel for the Accused:
Mr. Branislav Tapušković
Ms. Branislava Isailović

[page 2] I. INTRODUCTION

1. **TRIAL CHAMBER III** ("Trial Chamber") of the International Tribunal for the Prosecution of Persons Responsible for Serious Violations of International Humanitarian Law Committed in the Territory of the Former Yugoslavia since 1991 ("Tribunal") is seised of the "Prosecution's Motion for Judicial Notice of Adjudicated Facts", filed by the Office of the Prosecutor ("Prosecution") on 18 December 2006 ("Motion"). The Trial Chamber is also seised of the "Response to Prosecution's Motion for Judicial Notice of Adjudicated Facts", filed by the Defence ("Defence") on 19 January 2007 ("Response") and the "Prosecution's Request for Leave to Reply and Reply to Response to Prosecution's Motion for Judicial Notice of Adjudicated Facts", filed by the Prosecution on 25 January 2007 ("Reply").

2. In the Motion, the Prosecution requests, pursuant to Rule 94(B) of the Rules of Procedure and Evidence ("Rules"), that the Trial Chamber take judicial notice of 181 facts ("Proposed Facts") which it claims were adjudicated in the case of *Prosecutor v. Galić*, Case No. IT–98–29 ("*Galić* Case") in the Trial Chamber Judgement rendered on 5 December 2003 ("*Galić* Trial Judgement") and in the Appeals Chamber Judgement rendered on 30 November 2006 ("*Galić* Appeal Judgement").

3. The Trial Chamber is further seised of oral submissions by the Parties in response to questions posed by the Trial Chamber, given during a hearing of 12 February 2007.[1]

4. The Trial Chamber is also seised of the "Prosecution's Catalogue of Facts Agreed Between the Prosecution and Defence", filed by the Prosecution on 28 February 2007 ("Agreed Facts") and endorsed by the Defence[2], informing the Trial Chamber of twenty–nine facts to which the parties have agreed, pursuant to Rule 65 *ter* (E) and listed in the Annex to the Catalogue.

II. SUBMISSIONS

A. Written submissions

5. With regard to judicial notice pursuant to Rule 94(B) of the Rules, the Prosecution submits that the Proposed Facts meet the criteria which must be satisfied in order for a fact to be judicially noticed. In particular, the Prosecution argues that the Proposed Facts: (a) are relevant to the case the Prosecution must prove, (b) are distinct, concrete and identifiable, (c) represent the Galić **[page 3]** Chambers' factual findings, (d) are in the same or substantially similar form as expressed in the *Galić* Trial Judgement and *Galić* Appeal Judgement, (e) are not subject to pending appeal or review and (f) do not attest to the criminal responsibility of the Accused.[3]

6. The Prosecution further submits that taking judicial notice of the Proposed Facts will serve the interests of justice by allowing the Prosecution to forego the introduction of unnecessary evidence, thus making the trial more efficient and expeditious.[4] The Prosecution argues that the right of the Accused to a fair trial will not be prejudiced, since the Proposed Facts must fulfil strict criteria before they can be noticed and the Defence has the opportunity to challenge a noticed fact at trial.[5]

7. In its Response, the Defence submits that Proposed Facts 1 to 53 concern the general context of the conflict with respect to the acts allegedly committed by the Accused[6] and defers to the Trial Chamber's decision with regard to these Proposed Facts.[7]

---

1 Trial Hearing, 12 February 2007, T. 1891–1935.
2 Trial Hearing, 14 Mars 2007, T. 3707.
3 Motion, paras 8–13.
4 Motion, paras 2, 14–16.
5 Motion, paras 17–18.
6 Response, para. 8.
7 Response, p. 3. While the Defence here states that it takes no position with regard to Proposed Facts 1 to 54, the Trial Chamber notes the Defence's submission that it does object to Proposed Fact 54 (para. 11). The Trial Chamber will interpret the Defence submission as being that it takes no position only with respect to Proposed Facts 1 to 53.

8. The Defence, however, objects to the judicial notice of Proposed Facts 54 and 55, alleging that these are not facts but rather definitions of concepts contained in the Indictment.[8] The Defence also opposes the judicial notice of Proposed Facts 56 to 181, arguing that facts 57 to 181 occurred outside the time covered by the Indictment, are not relevant to matters at issue in the current proceedings and are solely relevant to the criminal responsibility of Mr. Galić and not that of the Accused.[9] The Defence provides no basis for opposing Proposed Fact 56.

9. In its Reply, the Prosecution argues that Proposed Facts 54 and 55 only contain relevant factual findings rendered in the *Galić* Trial Judgement.[10] During oral submissions, however, the Prosecution abandoned its request for judicial notice of these two facts.[11]

10. The Prosecution further contends in its Reply that Proposed Facts 57 to 181 relate to matters at issue in the current proceedings, in that they go to establishing that the Accused was on notice, had knowledge of, and, in fact, inherited and continued a campaign of shelling and sniping by the Sarajevo Romanija Corps ("SRK") against civilians in Sarajevo between September 1992 and August 1994.[12] Specifically, the Prosecution argues that these Proposed Facts—albeit outside the **[page 4]** Indictment period—go to proving Paragraph 19 of the Amended Indictment,[13] which alleges that the Accused implemented and/or furthered a campaign of sniping and shelling of civilians and knew of such a campaign as early as May 1992.[14]

11. The Prosecution argues, however, that, while relevant for establishing notice and knowledge, Proposed Facts 57 to 181 do not "attest, directly or indirectly, to the criminal responsibility of the Accused, nor to the Accused's acts, conduct or mental state."[15] The Prosecution refers to the *Karemera* Appeal Decision,[16] which it claims prohibits judicial notice only of those facts which go to the acts and conduct of the accused.[17] The Prosecution argues that none of the Proposed Facts 57 to 181 relates to the acts, conduct or mental state of the Accused and that they are thus suitable for judicial notice.[18]

B. Oral submissions

12. During a hearing of 12 February 2007, the Parties made oral submissions in response to questions posed by the Trial Chamber regarding judicial notice of adjudicated facts. These questions focused on two main issues: (1) how the Parties distinguish between a *factual* finding and a finding of an *essentially legal* nature and (2) in cases where the Proposed Facts do not go to the acts, conduct or mental state of the Accused, whether the facts should nonetheless be excluded, following the *Karemera* Appeal Decision, if they do not advance Rule 94(B)'s objective of achieving expediency without compromising the rights of the accused, particularly the right to cross–examine.[19]

13. The Prosecution responded to the first question by arguing that the *Karemera* Appeal Decision clearly differentiates between a factual finding and an essentially legal conclusion.[20] According to the Prosecution, a factual finding is one that may contain legal terms but nonetheless describes a factual situation, allowing the legal term to be re–characterised using other words. The Prosecution submitted that a legal conclusion, in contrast, is "purely a legal finding" which can not be described factually in any other way.[21] The Prosecution

---

8 Response, para. 11.
9 Response, paras 8–10.
10 Reply, para. 6.
11 Trial Hearing, 12 February 2007, T. 1927.
12 Reply, paras 8–9.
13 Amended Indictment, 18 December 2006, para. 19.
14 Reply, para. 8.
15 Reply, para. 10.
16 *Prosecutor v. Édouard Karemera et al.*, Case No. ICTR–98–44–AR73, Decision on Prosecutor's Interlocutory Appeal of Decision on Judicial Notice, 16 June 2006 ("*Karemera* Appeal Decision").
17 Reply, para. 10.
18 Reply, para. 10.
19 Trial Hearing, 12 February 2007, T. 1891.
20 Trial Hearing, 12 February 2007, T. 1897.
21 Trial Hearing, 12 February 2007, T. 1900.

argued that the Karemera Appeals Decision establishes that the category of essentially legal characterisations is rather narrow.[22] **[page 5]**

14. In supporting this submission, the Prosecution gave examples of facts which the Appeals Chamber in *Karemera* deemed suitable for judicial notice. Specifically, the Prosecution cited facts containing the characterisations "widespread or systematic attacks",[23] "serious bodily or mental harm",[24] "armed conflict not of an international character"[25] and "genocide".[26] The Prosecution claimed that, by taking judicial notice of these facts, the *Karemera* Appeal Decision had the effect of ruling that they were "factual characterisations and not essentially legal characterisations."[27]

15. The Prosecution submitted that the Proposed Facts are similar to those deemed suitable for judicial notice in the *Karemera* Appeal Decision.[28] Further, the Prosecution argued that, while some of the Proposed Facts contain legal terms, they all describe factual situations.[29]

16. The Defence submitted that terms such as "civilians", "indiscriminate attacks" and "legitimacy of targets" constitute legal matters rather than factual ones and that judicial notice of Proposed Facts containing these terms would prejudice the rights of the Accused.[30] The Defence, however, offered no criteria for distinguishing between a factual finding and an essentially legal one.

17. To the second question, the Prosecution first responded that facts which do not go to the acts, conduct or mental state of the accused should be judicially noticed, following the *Karemera* Appeal Decision. The Prosecution argued that the balance between the rights of the accused—in particular the right to cross–examine—and the purpose of Rule 94(B) was struck by the *Karemera* Appeal decision's holding that facts proposed for judicial notice should not go to the acts, conduct or mental state of the accused.[31]

18. Secondly, the Prosecution alleged that the fact that the Defence took the position that the Proposed Facts are irrelevant indicates that there is no danger to the rights of the Accused, including the right to cross—examine.[32]

19. Thirdly, the Prosecution submitted that the rights of the Accused are not prejudiced because the Proposed Facts, although relevant to the Prosecution's case, are not crime—based facts. Rather than going to the crime—base of the crimes charged in the Indictment, they are one step further away, going to the crimes committed by Galić. **[page 6]**

20. Lastly, the Prosecution further contended that the Proposed Facts go directly to the guilt of Galić. In this regard, the Prosecution submitted that the Proposed Facts were tested and found by the Trial and Appeals Chamber in the course of the Galić proceedings, where it was in Galić's interest to rebut these facts and where he was given the opportunity to do so. The Prosecution argued that not admitting these facts would render Rule 94(B) a dead letter. [33]

21. The Defence argued that, although the formal conditions for the application of Rule 94(B) have been met, the Proposed Facts are not relevant and are not helpful to the proceedings. The Defence was of the view that judicially noticing the Proposed Facts could infringe upon the rights of the Accused, stating that the objective of expeditiousness of Rule 94(B) only applies under the condition that the right of the accused to a fair trial is not prejudiced. The Defence also argued that the Prosecution's submissions were inconsistent and that the Prosecution "here proposed a twisted application [...] of the relevant jurisprudence."[34]

---

22 Trial Hearing, 12 February 2007, T. 1907, T. 1908.
23 Trial Hearing, 12 February 2007, T. 1897, referring to *Karemera* Appeal Decision, para. 26.
24 Trial Hearing, 12 February 2007, T. 1897, referring to *Karemera* Appeal Decision, para. 26.
25 Trial Hearing, 12 February 2007, T. 1898, referring to *Karemera* Appeal Decision, para. 26.
26 Trial Hearing, 12 February 2007, T. 1898, referring to *Karemera* Appeal Decision, para. 33.
27 Trial Hearing, 12 February 2007, T. 1898.
28 Trial Hearing, 12 February 2007, T. 1904, T. 1909, T. 1910.
29 Trial Hearing, 12 February 2007, T. 1905, T. 1906, T. 1910.
30 Trial Hearing, 12 February 2007, T. 1928.
31 Trial Hearing, 12 February 2007, T. 1910, T. 1912, T. 1914.
32 Trial Hearing, 12 February 2007, T. 1914.
33 Trial Hearing, 12 February 2007, T. 1915–1917.
34 Trial Hearing, 12 February 2007, T. 1928–1929.

III. APPLICABLE LAW

22. Judicial notice of facts is governed by Rule 94 of the Rules, which provides as follows:

> (A) A Trial Chamber shall not require proof of facts of common knowledge but shall take judicial notice thereof;
>
> (B) At the request of the party or *proprio motu*, a Trial Chamber, after hearing the parties, may decide to take judicial notice of the adjudicated facts or documentary evidence from other proceedings of the Tribunal relating to matters at issue in the current proceedings;

23. Rule 94(A) of the Rules concerns facts of common knowledge, while Rule 94(B) of the Rules allows a Trial Chamber to take judicial notice of relevant facts adjudicated in a previous trial or appeal judgement ("original judgement"), after having heard the parties, even if a party objects to the taking of judicial notice of a particular fact.[35] The basis upon which judicial notice is taken, pursuant to Rule 94(A) of the Rules, is that the fact is notorious.[36] In deeming a fact to be notorious, **[page 7]** a Trial Chamber likewise determines that the matter is not the subject of reasonable dispute[37] and, as a result, the fact cannot normally be challenged during trial.[38] Conversely, pursuant to Rule 94(B) of the Rules, the basis upon which judicial notice is taken is that the fact is the subject of adjudication by another Chamber.[39] Consequently, while Rule 94(B) of the Rules confers a discretionary power on the Trial Chamber to determine whether or not to take judicial notice of a fact[40] and allows for the challenging of this fact during trial, it is mandatory for the Trial Chamber to take notice of a fact of common knowledge under Rule 94 (A), and the consequence is that it cannot be challenged.[41]

24. With regard to the Agreed Facts, Rule 65 *ter* (H) provides that "[t]he pre–trial Judge shall record the points of agreement and disagreement on matters of law and fact", Rule 65 *ter* (M) provides that "[t]he Trial Chamber may *proprio motu* exercise any of the functions of the pre–trial Judge" and Rule 89 (C) provides that "[a] Chamber may admit any relevant evidence which it deems to have probative value".

IV. DISCUSSION AND FINDINGS

25. In the instant case, the Prosecution has made no submission that the Proposed Facts are notorious or that they should be judicially noticed pursuant to Rule 94(A).[42] The Trial Chamber must, however, determine whether the facts are admissible under rule 94(A), because it is mandatory for a Trial Chamber to take notice of a notorious fact, irrespective of any application by any party. Further, the Trial Chamber notes that

---

35 *Prosecutor v. Zoran Kupreškić et al.*, Case No. IT–95–16–A, Decision on the Motions of Drago Josipović, Zoran Kupreškić and Vlatko Kupreškić to Admit Additional Evidence pursuant to Rule 115 and for Judicial Notice to be Taken pursuant to Rule 94(B), 8 May 2001 ("*Kupreškić et al.* Appeal Decision"), para. 6; *Prosecutor v. Vujadin Popović et al.*, Case No. IT–05–88–T, Decision on Prosecution's Motion for Judicial Notice of Adjudicated Facts with Annex, 26 September 2006 ("*Popović et al.* Decision"), para. 3; *Prosecutor v. Vidoje Blagojević and Dragan Jokić*, Case No. IT–02–60–T, Decision on Prosecution's Motion for Judicial Notice of Adjudicated Facts and Documentary Evidence, 19 December 2003 ("*Blagojević and Jokić* Decision"), para. 16.

36 *Prosecutor v. Momir Nikolić,* Case No. IT–02–60/1–A, Decision on Appellant's Motion for Judicial Notice, 1 April 2005 (*Momir Nikolić* Appeal Decision"), para. 10; *Prosecutor v. Slobodan Milošević*, Case No. IT–02–54–AR73.5, Decision on the Prosecution's Interlocutory Appeal Against the Trial Chamber's 10 April 2003 Decision on Prosecution Motion for Judicial Notice of Adjudicated Facts, 28 October 2003 ("*Slobodan Milošević* Appeal Decision"), pp. 3–4.

37 *Momir Nikolić* Appeal Decision, para. 10; *Prosecutor v. Blagoje Simić et al.*, IT–95–9–PT, Decision on the Pre–Trial Motion by the Prosecution Requesting the Trial Chamber to take Judicial Notice of the International Character of the Conflict in Bosnia–Herzegovina, 25 March 1999, pp. 4–5.

38 *Momir Nikolić* Appeal Decision, para. 10; *Prosecutor v. Mom~ilo Krajišnik*, Case No. IT–00–39–PT, Decision on Prosecution's Motions for Judicial Notice of Adjudicated Facts and for Admission of Written Statements of Witnesses Pursuant to Rule 92*bis*, 28 February 2003 ("*Krajišnik* February 2003 Decision"), para. 16.

39 *Slobodan Milošević* Appeal Decision, p. 4; *Kupreškić et al.* Appeal Decision, para. 6.

40 *Karemera* Appeal Decision, para. 41; *Slobodan Milosević* Appeal Decision, pp. 3–4; *Popović et al.* Decision, para. 3; *Prosecutor v. Jadranko Prlić et al.*, Case No. IT–04–74–PT, Decision on Motion for Judicial Notice of Adjudicated Facts Pursuant to Rule 94(B), 14 March 2006 ("*Prlić et al* Pre–Trial Decision"), para. 9.

41 *Karemera* Appeal Decision, para. 41; *Momir Nikolić* Appeal Decision, para. 11; *Slobodan Milošević* Appeal Decision, p. 4; *Krajišnik* February 2003 Decision, para. 16.

42 *See* Hearing, T. 1903–1904 where the Prosecution stated that the basis upon which it sought judicial notice was that the Proposed Facts had been adjudicated in past proceedings, not that they were facts of common knowledge.

the standard of notoriety is particularly rigorous; in the *Karemera* case, the Appeals Chamber relied on a variety of sources confirmed by numerous unanimous decisions of the Tribunal.[43] The Trial Chamber notes that the Prosecution has made no **[page 8]** submission that these conditions exist with respect to the Proposed Facts, and holds that they do not exist.

26. Therefore, the Trial Chamber now turns to consider whether the facts are judicially noticeable under Rule 94(B).

27. Several criteria may be derived from the Tribunal's case—law to determine whether to exercise discretion to take judicial notice of a proposed adjudicated fact.[44] The Appeals Chamber has held that:

(i) The fact must have some relevance to an issue in the current proceedings;[45]

(ii) The fact must be finalised, meaning that it is not subject to pending appeal or review;[46]

(iii) The fact must not be "related to the acts, conduct, or mental state" of an accused;[47]

(iv) The fact must not be unclear or misleading in the context in which it is placed in the moving party's motion;[48]

(v) The fact must be identified with adequate precision by the moving party.[49]

Trial Chambers have considered the following criteria in the exercise of the Chamber's discretion to judicially notice adjudicated facts:

(i) The fact must be distinct, concrete, and identifiable in the findings of the original judgement.50 In making such a determination, the Trial Chamber must consider the proposed fact in the context of the original judgement, with specific reference to the place referred to in the judgement and to the indictment period of that case;[51] **[page 9]**

(ii) The fact, as formulated by the moving party, must not differ in any significant way from the formulation in the original judgement.[52] The Trial Chamber does not, however, endorse the notion that the formulation must be reproduced exactly;

---

43 *See for example Karemera* Appeal Decision, para. 35 where the Appeals Chamber relies on the fact that: "Trial and Appeal Judgements [...] have unanimously and decisively confirmed the occurrence of genocide in Rwanda, which has also been documented by countless books, scholarly articles, media reports, U.N. reports and resolutions, national court decisions, and government and NGO reports."

44 *Popović et al.* Decision, para. 4; *Prosecutor v. Momćilo Krajišnik*, Case No. IT–00–39–PT, Decision on Third and Fourth Prosecution Motions for Judicial Notice of Adjudicated Facts, 24 March 2005 ("*Krajišnik* Decision on Third and Fourth Motions"), para. 14; *Blagojević and Jokić* Trial Decision, para. 16; *Prosecutor v. Slobodan Milošević*, Case No. IT–02–54–T, Decision on Prosecution's Motion for Judicial Notice of Adjudicated Facts, 10 April 2003 ("*Slobodan Milošević* April 2003 Trial Decision"), p. 4; *Krajišnik* February 2003 Decision, para. 15.

45 *Momir Nikolić* Appeal Decision, para. 11; *Laurent Semanza v. Prosecutor*, Case No. ICTR–97–20–A, Judgement, 20 May 2005, para. 189; *Prosecutor v. Eliézer Niyitegeka*, Case No. ICTR–96–14–A, Reasons for Oral Decision Rendered 21 April 2004 on Appellant's Motion for Admission of Additional Evidence and for Judicial Notice, 17 May 2004, para. 16; *Popović et al.* Decision, para. 5; *Krajišnik* Decision on Third and Fourth Motions, para. 17.

46 *Kupreškić et al.* Appeal Decision, para. 6; *Popović et al.* Decision, para. 14; *Prlić et al.* Pre–Trial Decision, paras 12, 15; *Krajišnik* Decision on Third and Fourth Motions, para. 14.

47 Karemera Appeal Decision, paras 50–53 (quotation at para. 53); *Popović et al.* Decision, para. 12.

48 *Karemera* Appeal Decision, para. 55; *Popović et al.* Decision, para. 8.

49 *Momir Nikolić* Appeal Decision, paras 47, 56; *Kupreškić et al.* Appeal Decision, para. 12; *Popović et al.* Decision, para. 9; *Prosecutor v. Casimir Bizimungu et al.*, Case No. ICTR–99–50–T, Decision on Prosper Mugiraneza's First Motion for Judicial Notice Pursuant to Rule 94(B), 10 December 2004, para. 13.

50 *Prlić et al* Pre–Trial Decision, para. 12; *Popović et al.* Decision, para. 6; *Prosecutor v. Enver HadŽihasanović and Amir Kubura*, Case No. IT–01–47–T, Decision on Judicial Notice of Adjudicated Facts Following the Motion Submitted by Counsel for the Accused HadŽihasanović and Kubura on 20 January 2005, 14 April 2005, p. 5; *Blagojević and Jokić* Decision, para. 16; *Krajišnik* Decision on Third and Fourth Motions, para. 14; *Krajišnik* February 2003 Trial Decision, para. 15.

51 *Krajišnik* Decision on Third and Fourth Motions, para. 14, fn. 44.

52 *Popović* Decision, para. 7; *Blagojević and Jokić* Decision, para. 16; *Krajišnik* Decision on Third and Fourth Motions, para. 14.

(iii) The fact must be adjudicated, meaning that it is not based on a plea agreement or on facts voluntarily admitted in a previous case. The fact must have been the subject of adjudication rather than an agreement between parties in previous proceedings;[53]

(iv) The fact must represent the *factual findings* of a Trial Chamber or Appeals Chamber. It must not, therefore, contain any findings or characterisations that are of an essentially legal nature;[54]

28. In determining whether to exercise its discretion to take judicial notice of a proposed adjudicated fact, the Trial Chamber must also consider whether doing so would serve the interests of justice.[55] In this respect, a Trial Chamber is guided primarily by the need to ensure that the proceedings are both fair and expeditious and that the rights of the accused are preserved, as enshrined in Articles 20 and 21 of the Statute of the Tribunal ("Statute").[56] As the Krajišnik Trial Chamber emphasised, the "first concern is always to ensure that the Accused is offered a fair trial. As long as this principle is accomplished, the Chamber is under a duty to avoid that unnecessary time and resources are wasted on unnecessary disputes."[57]

29. In this respect, a key consideration is whether taking judicial notice of a fact pursuant to Rule 94(B) of the Rules will advance judicial economy while still safeguarding the rights of an accused. Judicially noticing a fact can enhance judicial economy by avoiding the rehearing of allegations already proven in past proceedings, thereby shortening the duration of the trial. However, judicially noticing a fact has the legal effect of establishing a "presumption for the accuracy of this fact, which therefore does not have to be proven again at trial, but which, subject to that presumption, may be challenged at that trial";[58] judicial notice, therefore, shifts the burden of **[page 10]** production of evidence to the accused such that, if the Defence does not rebut the adjudicated fact, the Chamber is entitled to presume the adjudicated fact to be accurate.[59] However, adjudicated facts which are judicially noticed pursuant to Rule 94(B) of the Rules remain to be assessed in light of all the evidence brought at trial to determine what conclusions, if any, can be drawn from them and what weight should be attributed to them.[60] Further, it is important to recall that, while the initial burden of producing evidence is shifted to the accused, the burden of proof beyond a reasonable doubt remains on the Prosecution.[61]

30. The Appeals Chamber's decision in *Karemera* explicitly permits the taking of judicial notice of facts relating directly or indirectly to the defendant's guilt, provided they do not go specifically to the acts, conduct or mental state of the accused.[62] However, if the Proposed Facts do not go to the acts, conduct or mental state of the accused, the Trial Chamber must still assess whether under the circumstances of the case admitting them will advance Rule 94 (B)'s objective of expediency without compromising the rights of the accused.[63]

---

53 *Popović et al.* Decision, para. 11; *Krajišnik* Decision on Third and Fourth Motions, para. 14; *Prosecutor v. Željko Mejakić et al.*, Case No. IT–02–65–PT, Decision on Prosecution Motion for Judicial Notice pursuant to Rule 94(B), 1 April 2004, p. 4; *Prosecutor v. Slobodan Milošević*, Case No. IT–02–54–T, Decision on Prosecution Motion for Judicial Notice of Adjudicated Facts, 10 April 2003 ("*Slobodan Milošević* April 2003 Trial Decision"), p. 3; *Krajišnik* February 2003 Trial Decision, para. 15.

54 The phrase "essentially legal" stems from the *Krajišnik* Decision on Third and Fourth Motions, para. 15. *See also Popović et al.* Decision, para. 11; *Prlić et al.* Pre–Trial Decision, para. 12; *Blagojević and Jokić* Trial Decision, para. 16; *Slobodan Milošević* April 2003 Trial Decision, p. 3; *Krajišnik* February 2003 Trial Decision, para. 15; *Prosecutor v. Blagoje Simić*, Case No. IT–95–9–PT, Decision of 25 March 1999, p. 3.

55 *See, e.g., Popović et al.* Decision, para. 4; *Prlić et al.* Pre–Trial Decision, para. *Krajišnik* Decision on Third and Fourth Motions, para. 12.

56 *Karemera* Appeal Decision, para. 41; *Momir Nikolić* Appeal Decision, para. 12; *Popović et al.* Decision, para. 16; *Krajišnik* February 2003 Decision, para. 15.

57 *Krajišnik* February 2003 Decision, para. 11.

58 *Momir Nikolić* Appeal Decision, para. 11, *quoting Slobodan Milošević* Appeal Decision, p. 4.

59 *Karemera* Appeal Decision, para. 42; *Popović et al.* Decision, para. 21; *Krajišnik* February 2003 Decision, para. 16.

60 *Popović et al.* Decision, para. 21, citing *Krajišnik* March 2005 Trial Decision, para. 17, *Accord Prlić et al.* Pre–Trial Decision, para. 11; *See also Prosecutor v. Vujadin Popović et al.*, Case No. IT–05–88–T, Decision on Defence Motion for Certification to Appeal Decision on Prosecution Motion for Judicial Notice of Adjudicated Facts, p. 3–4.

61 *Karemera* Appeal Decision, para. 49; *Popović et al.* Decision, para. 21; *Krajišnik* February 2003 Decision, para. 16.

62 *Karemera* Appeal Decision, para. 50.

63 *Karemera* Appeal Decision, para. 53.

31. The Trial Chamber is of the view that the Prosecution's submission with regard to the balance struck by the *Karemera* Appeal Decision[64] between the purpose of Rule 94(B) and the rights of the Accused does not fully reflect the substance of that Decision. The *Karemera* Decision did hold, as argued by the Prosecution, that facts going to the acts, conduct or mental state of the accused cannot be noticed. However, it also held—and this was omitted in the Prosecution submissions—that, regarding facts which do not, "it is for the Trial Chambers, in the careful exercise of their discretion, to assess each particular fact in order to determine whether taking judicial notice of it—and thus shifting the burden of producing evidence rebutting it to the accused—is consistent with the accused's rights under the circumstances of the case. This includes [...] facts related to the conduct of physical perpetrators of a crime for which the accused is being held criminally responsible through some other mode of liability."[65]

32. The Trial Chamber is satisfied that none of the Proposed Facts go to the acts, conduct or mental state of the Accused. However, following the *Karemera* Appeals Decision, it must still assess whether taking judicial notice of them would be consistent with the rights of the accused, particularly the right to examine witnesses against him, as enshrined in Article 21(4)(e) of the Statute. The Trial Chamber is of the view that this right is particularly important with regard to **[page 11]** Proposed Facts which go to crimes committed under the command of Galić, the Accused's predecessor, and which, as acknowledged by the Prosecution, have a strong link with the crimes charged in the indictment, particularly those facts which may in effect put the Accused on notice.[66] The Trial Chamber considers that shifting the burden to produce evidence to the Accused, and thereby obliging him to rebut them, would not be consistent with his rights. Regardless of whether or not the Defence considers these Proposed Facts relevant to this case, it remains the duty of the Trial Chamber to safeguard the rights of the Accused.

33. Further, the Trial Chamber recalls that the purpose of Rule 94(B) is to enable a Trial Chamber to take judicial notice of *factual* findings. Judicial notice pursuant to Rule 94(B) is not designed for the importing of legal conclusions from past proceedings. In determining whether a proposed fact is truly a factual finding, the *Krajišnik* Trial Chamber observed that "many findings have a legal aspect, if one is to construe this expression broadly. It is therefore necessary to determine on a case–by–case basis whether the proposed fact contains findings or characterizations which are of an essentially legal nature and which must, therefore, be excluded."[67]

34. The Trial Chamber notes the Prosecution's submission that an essentially legal finding or characterisation is one that can not be described factually in any other way, whereas a factual finding is one that may contain legal terms but nonetheless describes a factual situation, allowing the legal term to be re–characterised using other words.[68] As outlined above, the Prosecution relied extensively on examples of facts deemed suitable for judicial notice in the *Karemera* Appeal Decision in supporting this submission.[69]

35. The Trial Chamber considers the Prosecution's submission in this respect to be flawed. The facts from the *Karemera* Appeals Decision to which the Prosecution refers were judicially noticed pursuant to Rule 94(A) rather than Rule 94(B) of the Rules. Under Rule 94(A), a Chamber must satisfy itself *only* that the fact is notorious and beyond reasonable dispute.[70] Upon making this finding, the Chamber is *bound* to take judicial notice of the fact and can not consider any other criteria.[71] Indeed, in discussing the submission that the term "genocide" is a legal characterisation, **[page 12]** the Appeals Chamber in *Karemera* ruled that it could not even consider the submission, as "Rule 94(A) does not provide the Trial Chamber with discretion to refuse judicial notice on this basis."[72]

36. Thus, the Trial Chamber observes that in no part of its Decision in *Karemera* did the Appeals Chamber hold that the facts it deemed suitable for judicial notice did not contain essentially legal conclusions or characterisations; it simply ruled that these facts were notorious. The Prosecution submission relies extensively

64 See surpa para. 15.

65 *Karemera* Appeal Decision, para. 52.

66 See supra para. 8 the Prosecution's submission on the relevance of the crimes committed under *Galić* to the present case.

67 *Krajisnik* Decision on Third and Fourth Motions, para. 19.

68 Hearing, T. 1900; *see supra* para. 16.

69 Hearing, T. 1897–1898, 1907–1908.

70 *Karemera* Appeal Decision, para. 22; *Momir Nikolić* Appeal Decision, para. 10; *Slobodan Milošević* Appeal Decision, pp. 3–4.

71 *Karemera* Appeal Decision, paras 22, 23; *Momir Nikolić* Appeal Decision, para. 10; *Prosecutor v. Semanza*, Case No. ICTR–97–20–A, Judgement, 20 May 2005, para. 14; *Slobodan Milošević* Appeal Decision, pp. 3–4.

72 *Karemera* Appeal Decision, para. 37.

on an erroneous comparison with these facts. It is not necessary for the Trial Chamber to determine the scope of the category of essentially legal conclusions, that is, whether it is narrow or broad. It is sufficient to point out that, in arriving at its conclusion as to the narrowness of that category, the Prosecution relied on a flawed interpretation of the *Karemera* Appeals Decision.

37. With regard to the Catalogue of Agreed Facts, the Trial Chamber finds that the recording of points of agreement between the parties at the trial stage results in the acceptance of those agreed points as evidence pursuant to Rule 89 (C).[73]

V. DISPOSITION

The Trial Chamber understands rule 94(B) as giving a Trial Chamber a discretionary power to admit adjudicated facts when it advances the expeditiousness of the proceedings and is in the interests of justice. Accordingly, the Trial Chamber will identify, in light of the foregoing analysis, those facts which it admits, leaving aside those which it rejects.

PURSUANT TO Rules 126 *bis*, 94 (B), 65 *ter* (H), 65 *ter* (M) and 89 (C) of the Rules

HEREBY GRANTS IN PART the Motion and decides as follows:

(a) The Trial Chamber grants leave to the Prosecution to file the Reply;

(b) The Trial Chamber takes judicial notice of the following Proposed Facts:

1–53, 56, 60, 64–71, 73–76, 81–85, 88, 90–93, 99–104, 108–110, 112–116, 122, 123, 125–130, 143, 147, 156, 158, 159 and 161–164, admitted unanimously; facts 62 and 176 are admitted by majority, Judge Robinson dissenting;

(c) The Trial Chamber admits into evidence the list of Agreed Facts. **[page 13]**

Done in English and French, the English version being authoritative.

Dated this tenth day of April 2007
At The Hague
The Netherlands

Judge Patrick Robinson
Presiding

[Seal of the Tribunal] [page 14]

73 *See Prosecutor v. Sefer Halilović*, Case No. IT–01–48–T, Decision on Motion Concerning Further Agreed Facts, 25 July 2005, p. 2.

I. DISSENTING OPINION OF JUDGE HARHOFF

1. Taking "judicial notice" of facts adjudicated in other trials before this Tribunal appears to be a fundamentally flawed idea because of the very nature of judicial litigation. If a certain fact has been the subject of a reasonable dispute at trial, and if it was ultimately adjudicated by a Chamber, this very circumstance would seem to suggest that the fact in question was not and could not have been an indisputable fact of so–called "common knowledge"—like the facts contemplated in Rule 94 (A) of the Tribunal's Rules of Procedure and Evidence. Had the fact in question been of common knowledge, there would have been no reason to dispute it at trial. Taking "judicial notice" of facts which have been litigated in earlier proceedings may, depending on the context, affect the presumption of innocence of the Accused.

2. In this trial, the Prosecution has requested the Chamber to take "judicial notice" of 181 facts adjudicated in the Galić case, *viz.* the Trial Chamber's judgement of 5th December 2003 and the Appeals Chamber's judgement of 30th November 2006. The first 53 of these facts relate to the history and background of the armed conflict and do not pose any problem with regard to the presumption of innocence. Two facts have been dropped by the Prosecution and the Chamber has decided, in the present Decision, to take "judicial notice" of another 57 facts.

3. In its Decision, thus, the Trial Chamber has taken judicial notice of altogether 110 of the proposed adjudicated facts under Rule 94 (B) and has partly rejected the Prosecution's interpretation of the Appeals Chamber's Decision of 16th June 2006 in *Karemera et al.* I fully support these findings of the Trial Chamber and the reasons behind them.

4. However, I respectfully disagree with the majority's decision to decline from accepting judicial notice of the remaining 69 proposed adjudicated facts. All of these remaining facts relate to the factual situation or to particular incidents occurring in Sarajevo during General Galić's time in power, and they all imply somehow that the SRK—under Galić—deliberately and indiscriminately targeted civilians or civilian objects in Sarajevo. In this opinion, I shall try to set out my reasons for departing from the majority's views.

5. As reflected in the Tribunal's judicial practice, there are indeed valid and acceptable reasons for relying, under certain conditions, on facts which have been adjudicated in other proceedings before this Tribunal. All the trials here, notably, deal with inter–related conflicts unfolding within a limited geographical space during a limited time–span, and it is therefore only natural, as the proceedings have developed, that certain factual findings made by the Tribunal's Chambers in previous trials are assumed by Chambers in subsequent trials without having to establish, once again, the veracity of these findings. The justification for this assumption lies not only in the quest for judicial economy, as frequently adduced in the Tribunal's Decisions on judicial notice, but also **[page 15]** in the need to spare our crime–base witnesses from having to relive their traumas once more by returning to the Tribunal to offer their testimony over and over again. Rule 94, in this respect, shares the same purpose as Rules 92 *bis* and *ter*, but Rule 94 goes further in that it allows for accepting the adjudicated fact without requiring submission of any further evidence in proof thereof. In this respect, judicial notice of adjudicated also relieves the Trial Chamber from having to review evidence relating to facts which have already been considered and established by previous Chambers.

6. From the point of view of criminal law, however, the Tribunal's practice of taking "judicial notice" of adjudicated facts appears to run contrary to the presumption of innocence of the Accused, mainly because it places an onus of proof on the latter and prevents him or her from cross–examining the witnesses who previously bore testimony to the facts which are now being judicially noticed in his or her trial. This, obviously, represents a disadvantage to any defendant.

7. In many or most of the Tribunal's recent decisions, however, Trial Chambers as well as the Appeals Chamber have sought to remedy this deficiency, at least partially, by asserting that previously adjudicated facts are only admitted into evidence in the new trial as "rebuttable presumptions", so as to allow the defendant to challenge the adjudicated facts at trial. The impact of this notion, in other words, is that the new Trial Chamber or the Appeals Chamber is not compelled to rely unconditionally on such facts—as it would have been if the fact in question were truly a fact of common knowledge. This, to be sure, does place an onus of proof upon the Accused in the sense that he or she then has to prove that the adjudicated fact is unsafe.

8. In the end, thus, the onus to adduce evidence will have shifted from the Prosecution to the Accused, and this is what constitutes the controversial and highly sensitive aspect of taking "judicial notice" of adjudicated facts. In the present Decision, the Trial Chamber does not claim that judicial notice directly establishes a "burden of proof" on the Accused, but rather that judicial notice of adjudicated facts partly *shifts* the burden of proof to the Accused, who now has to actively submit evidence to rebut the adjudicated fact.

9. There is another inherent problem arising out of the Tribunal's practice in respect of adjudicated facts, namely that of showing a viable distinction between truly factual findings on the one hand, and facts which are of an essentially legal nature on the other. This problem becomes apparent when one looks at the facts proposed by the Prosecution; when the Galić judgement establishes, for instance, that *"civilians* were targeted in Novo Sarajevo between September 1992 and August 1994 from the SRK—controlled area of Grbavica" (see proposed fact nr. 77; italics added), then it is open to interpretation whether the term "civilians" refers to persons specifically protected by International Humanitarian Law—thus being a legal finding within the meaning of International Humanitarian Law–or merely establishes that the status of the victims was that they **[page 16]** were *de facto* civilian in the sense that they were not members of the armed forces or in any way affiliated to these, in which case the adjudicated fact appears to be a purely factual finding. In the Tribunal's practice, it has been established that adjudicated facts cannot be judicially noticed if they are of "an essentially legal nature", but this qualification is still unclear as it offers no guidance as to whether the concept of "a civilian" is of a purely factual or an essentially legal nature. It all depends on the context and is therefore subject to the Trial Chamber's discretion.

10. The Accused–in his capacity as commander of the Sarajevo Romanija Corps (the SRK)—is charged in the Indictment with having carried on and continuously conducted a campaign of terror against the civilian population in the City of Sarajevo when he took power over the SRK after General Galić in August 1994. While the latter was in power from 1992 to August 1994, however, the Accused served as Chief of Staff directly under general Galić from July 1993—more than a year before he himself became commander of the SRK after Galić. This fact is agreed upon by the Parties.

11. If this Trial Chamber were to admit adjudications in Galić regarding the deliberate and indiscriminate sniping and shelling, by forces under Galić's command, on civilian persons and civilian objects in Sarajevo, one might easily infer from such facts that the Accused in the present trial *was put on notice* that these crimes were being committed under the authority of his predecessor. He must have known that this was going on and should have taken steps to prevent these crimes and punish the perpetrators—at least from the time when he himself took power.

12. This inference may not in itself have any direct bearing on the responsibility of the Accused for the particular crimes charged in the Indictment against him, but it might suggest that the Accused would then have to prove that he was *not* put on notice and had no knowledge of the deliberate targeting of civilians in Sarajevo. In this respect, the issue of the Accused being put on notice indirectly points to the mode of his liability as alleged by the Prosecution, either directly under Article 7.1 of the Statute or as command responsibility under Article 7.3. Admitting such facts, in other words, would seem to be prejudicial to the rights of the Accused.

13. This concern, however, is misperceived because it is still for the Prosecutor to prove that the Accused was in fact put on notice about the crimes. Although it may seem very likely that the Accused knew about the campaign of terror under Galić, the Prosecution still has to prove beyond a reasonable doubt that the Accused knew of the campaign and also, according to the Indictment, that he himself intended to support and continue this campaign and failed to take the necessary measures to prevent the sniping of civilians and the shelling of civilian objects and/or to punish the perpetrators.

14. There is, undoubtedly, a procedural advantage for the Prosecution in this, but it does on the other hand appear somewhat artificial if the Chamber were to completely disregard the facts **[page 17]** established in *Galić* and require the Prosecution to prove it all again. The Chamber, in my view, must be afforded the freedom of being able to take into consideration the *context* in which the Accused held command of the SRK during his time in power and the *circumstances* under which he assumed and exercised control of the Serbian forces around Sarajevo. It should be recalled, in this regard, that the Chamber already enjoys a large degree of discretion under Rule 89 (C) and (D) to attach whatever probative value to the evidence before it which it deems to be appropriate. Taking "judicial notice" of facts adjudicated in Galić does not, in other words,

compel the Chamber to rely unconditionally on these facts, even if the defence does not raise any challenge against them. The Chamber will still require proof beyond a reasonable doubt that the Accused had knowledge of the campaign and committed himself to its extension and failed to prevent the crimes and punish the perpetrators.

15. For this same reason, in my view, the taking of "judicial notice" of the remaining facts in this case does not impair *the interests of justice.* Even if the Chamber were to require the Prosecution to prove that the SRK deliberately and indiscriminately targeted civilians in Sarajevo under Galić's command, the Accused would still have to seek evidence to rebut the Prosecution's allegation that he was indeed put on notice. The Chamber is tasked to strike a reasonable balance between judicial economy, expeditiousness and concerns for the witnesses on the one hand, and the rights of the Accused on the other, but this balance is not overthrown by taking "judicial notice" of facts relating to crimes committed outside the scope of the Indictment by perpetrators outside his command. This aspect, in my view, is a strong argument in favour of taking judicial notice of all the proposed facts.

16. As far as the qualification of the facts is concerned, none of the proposed facts contain, as far as I can see, elements which are of an "essentially legal nature". Even if terms such as "civilians", indiscriminate attacks" and others do have legal importance in terms of International Humanitarian Law, the use of these terms in the present context and the proposed facts is exclusively to establish that the victims did not have any affiliation to the armed forces of the ABiH.

17. I am therefore of the opinion that the remaining 69 proposed adjudicated facts from Galić could have been admitted in this trial as "judicially noticed" facts. **[page 18]**

Done in English and French, the English version being authoritative.

Dated this tenth day of April 2007
At The Hague
The Netherlands

Judge Frederik Harhoff

[Seal of the Tribunal]

UNITED
NATIONS

International Tribunal for the Prosecution of Persons Responsible for Serious Violations of International Humanitarian Law Committed in the Territory of the Former Yugoslavia since 1991	Case No.	IT-98-29/1-AR73.1
	Date:	26 June 2007
	Original:	English

IN THE APPEALS CHAMBER

Before: **Judge Mehmet Güney, Presiding**
Judge Mohamed Shahabuddeen
Judge Liu Daqun
Judge Andrésia Vaz
Judge Theodor Meron

Registrar: **Mr. Hans Holthuis**
Decision of: **26 June 2007**

PROSECUTOR

v.

Dragomir MILOŠEVIĆ

PUBLIC FILING

DECISION ON INTERLOCUTORY APPEALS AGAINST TRIAL CHAMBER'S DECISION ON PROSECUTION'S MOTION FOR JUDICIAL NOTICE OF ADJUDICATED FACTS AND PROSECUTION'S CATALOGUE OF AGREED FACTS

The Office of the Prosecutor:
Mr. Alex Whiting
Mr. Stefan Waespi
Ms. Carolyn Edgerton
Mr. John Docherty

Counsel for the Accused:
Mr. Branislav Tapušković
Ms. Branislava Isailović

[page 2] 1. The Appeals Chamber of the International Tribunal for the Prosecution of Persons Responsible for Serious Violations of International Humanitarian Law Committed in the Territory of the Former Yugoslavia Since 1991 ("Appeals Chamber" and "Tribunal", respectively) is seized of the "Prosecution's Interlocutory Appeal Brief against Trial Chamber's Decision on Prosecution's Motion for Judicial Notice of Adjudicated Facts and Prosecution's Catalogue of Agreed Facts with Dissenting Opinion of Judge Harhoff" filed on 10 May 2007 ("Prosecution's Interlocutory Appeal") and of the "*Appel contre la Décision prise par la Chambre d'appel de première instance sur la demande du Procureur aux fins de dresser le constat judiciaire de faits*" filed by Dragomir Milošević ("Milošević") on 10 May 2007 ("Defence's Interlocutory Appeal").

I. BACKGROUND

2. On 18 December 2006, the Prosecution filed before Trial Chamber III of the Tribunal ("Trial Chamber") its "Prosecution's Motion for Judicial Notice of Adjudicated Facts". In the Motion, the Prosecution requested, pursuant to Rule 94(B) of the Rules of Procedure and Evidence of the Tribunal ("Rules"), that the Trial Chamber takes judicial notice of 181 facts which were adjudicated in the case of *Prosecutor v. Galić,* Case No. IT-98-29 ("*Galić* Case"), in the Trial Judgement rendered on 5 December 2003 ("*Galić* Trial Judgement") and in the Appeals Chamber Judgement of 30 November 2006 ("*Galić* Appeals Judgement"), and pertaining to the "deliberate targeting of civilians by forces of the Sarajevo Romanija Corps ("SRK") under the command of General Galić in the period of time preceding the indictment period in this case"[1] ("Proposed Facts"). On 19 January 2007, Milošević filed his response in which he deferred to the Trial Chamber's decision with regard to Proposed Facts 1 through 53. He opposed, however, judicial notice of Proposed Facts 54 through 181.[2] The Prosecution replied on 25 January 2007.[3] During a hearing held on 12 February 2007, both parties presented oral submissions on questions posed by the Trial Chamber.[4] At this occasion, the Prosecution abandoned its request for judicial notice of Proposed Facts 54 and 55.[5] On 28 February 2007, the Prosecution filed its Catalogue of Agreed Facts.[6] It was endorsed by the Defence on 14 March 2007.[7] **[page 3]**

3. On 10 April 2007, the Trial Chamber issued its "Decision on Prosecution's Motion for Judicial Notice of Adjudicated Facts and Prosecution's Catalogue of Agreed Facts with Dissenting Opinion of Judge Harhoff" ("Impugned Decision"). The Trial Chamber gave leave to the Prosecution to file its Prosecution's Reply, and unanimously took judicial notice of the following Proposed Facts: 1–53, 56, 60, 64–71, 73–76, 81–85, 88, 90–93, 99–104, 108–110, 112–116, 122, 123, 125–130, 143, 147, 156, 158, 159, and 161–164, and by majority, Judge Robinson dissenting, Proposed Facts 62 and 176.[8] It rejected, by majority, Judge Harhoff dissenting,[9] the other Proposed Facts, but admitted into evidence the Catalogue of Agreed Facts.[10]

4. Both Interlocutory Appeals, filed following certification to appeal the Impugned Decision granted by the Trial Chamber on 3 May 2007,[11] rely on the *Karemera* Appeals Decision.[12] The Prosecution's Interlocutory Appeal challenges the Impugned Decision regarding the 69 Proposed Facts 56 through 181 rejected by the

---

1 Prosecution's Interlocutory Appeal, para. 2 (emphasis and footnote omitted).

2 *Prosecutor v. Dragomir Milošević*, Case No. IT-98-29/1-T, *Conclusion en Réponse de la Requête du Procureur aux fins de constat judiciaire de faits (Article 94B du Règlement de procédure et de preuve),* 19 January 2007.

3 *Prosecutor v. Dragomir Milošević,* Case No. IT-98-29/1-T, Prosecution's Request for Leave to Reply and Reply to Response to Prosecution's Motion for Judicial Notice of Adjudicated Facts, 25 January 2007.

4 Trial Hearing, 12 February 2007, T. 1891-1935; *See* also, Trial Chamber III's Memorandum on Issues Relating to Judicial Notice for Clarification by the Parties, 9 February 2007 (Annex A to the Prosecution's Interlocutory Appeal).

5 Trial Hearing, 12 February 2007, T. 1927.

6 *Prosecutor v. Dragomir Milošević*, Case No. IT-98-29/1-T, Prosecution's Catalogue of Facts Agreed between the Prosecution and the Defence, 28 February 2007 ("Catalogue of Agreed Facts").

7 Trial Hearing, 14 March 2007, T. 3707. The parties agreed, pursuant to Rule 65*ter* (E) of the Rules, to 29 facts.

8 Impugned Decision, p. 12.

9 Dissenting Opinion of Judge Harhoff, paras 4, 17.

10 Impugned Decision, p. 12.

11 Prosecutor *v. Dragomir Milošević*, Case No. IT-98-29/1-T, Decision on Defence and Prosecution Motions for Certification to Appeal Decision on Prosecution's Motion for Judicial Notice of Adjudicated Facts, 3 May 2007; *See* also, *Demande de certification d'appel contre la décision prise par la Chambre de première instance le 10 avril 2007 sur la demande du Procureur aux fins de dresser le constat judicaire des faits*, 16 April 2007, and Prosecution's Rule 73(B) Request for Interlocutory Appeal Certification of Trial Chamber's 10 April 2007 Decision on Adjudicated Facts, 17 April 2007.

12 *Prosecutor v. Édouard Karemera et al.*, Case No. ICTR-98-44-AR73(C), Decision on Prosecutor's Interlocutory Appeal of Decision on Judicial Notice, 16 June 2006 ("*Karemera* Appeals Decision").

majority of the Trial Chamber.[13] The Prosecution submits that "the [m]ajority discernibly erred in the exercise of its discretion pursuant to Rule 94(B) by incorrectly interpreting the law set out by the Appeals Chamber in the *Karemera* Appeal[s] Decision and by abusing its discretion",[14] and "requests that the Appeals Chamber [...] remand the matter to the Trial Chamber directing it to apply the reasoning and holdings of the *Karemera* Appeal[s] Decision to its consideration of the Prosecution's Proposed Facts."[15] The Defence's Interlocutory Appeal requests the partial reversal of the Impugned Decision insofar as it judicially noticed 57 Proposed Facts from 56 to 181.[16] In its response filed on 21 May 2007,[17] the **[page 4]** Prosecution seeks dismissal of the Defence's Interlocutory Appeal.[18] Milošević did not respond to the Prosecution's Interlocutory Appeal nor did he reply to the Prosecution's Response.

II. STANDARD OF REVIEW

5. Ruling on requests for judicial notice under Rule 94(B) of the Rules forms part of the discretionary power that lies with Trial Chambers, so as to allow them "to determine which adjudicated facts to recognize on the basis of a careful consideration of the accused's right to fair and expeditious trial".[19] A Trial Chamber's exercise of its discretion will only be overturned by the Appeals Chamber if it is found to be "(1) based on an incorrect interpretation of governing law; (2) based on a patently incorrect conclusion of fact; or (3) so unfair or unreasonable as to constitute an abuse of the Trial Chamber's discretion".[20]

III. SUBMISSIONS OF THE PARTIES AND DISCUSSION

1. Submissions of the Parties

6. In the present case, the Prosecution sought judicial notice, under Rule 94(B) of the Rules, of 179 adjudicated facts. The Trial Chamber took judicial notice of 110 of them and rejected the other 69. The Prosecution appeals the rejection of these 69 Proposed Facts, while Milošević challenges the admission of 57 Proposed Facts.[21] Both appeals relate to the judicial notice of Proposed Facts comprised between 56 and 181.

7. In the Prosecution's Interlocutory Appeal, the Prosecution requests that the Impugned Decision be remanded regarding the 69 Proposed Facts excluded by the Trial Chamber. The Prosecution submits that these facts, adjudicated by the Trial Judgement and the Appeals Judgement in the *Galić* Case, "were those showing that civilians were deliberately targeted by SRK forces under the command of General Galić".[22] The Prosecution alleges that the majority of the Trial Chamber, by refusing admission of these Proposed Facts, erred in exercising "its **[page 5]** discretion in a manner that is inconsistent with the principles set forth in the *Karemera* Appeal[s] Decision".[23]

8. The Prosecution firstly submits that the majority of the Trial Chamber erroneously "concluded that taking judicial notice of facts that have 'a strong link with the crimes charged' would be inconsistent with the rights of the Accused, in particular his right to examine witnesses against him".[24] It explains that "the

---

13 Prosecution's Interlocutory Appeal, paras. 2, 3, 8.
14 Prosecution's Interlocutory Appeal, para. 3.
15 *Ibid.*, para. 35.
16 Defence's Interlocutory Appeal, p. 5.
17 Article IV.10. of the Practice Direction on Procedure for the Filing of Written Submissions in Appeal Proceedings before the International Tribunal (IT/155/Rev. 3), 16 September 2005, requires a party to file a response within ten days of the filing of an interlocutory appeal. Because 20 May 2007 fell on a Sunday – a non-working day of the International Tribunal – the deadline to file a response to both interlocutory appeals was Monday 21 May 2007.
18 Prosecution's Response to Defence Appeal against the Trial Chamber's Decision on Prosecution Motion for Judicial Notice of Adjudicated Facts, 21 May 2007 ("Prosecution's Response").
19 *Karemera* Appeals Decision, para. 41.
20 *Karemera* Appeals Decision, para. 43; *See* also, *Prosecutor v. Vojislav Šešelj,* Case No. IT-03-67-AR73.5, Decision on Vojislav Šešelj's Interlocutory Appeal against the Trial Chamber's Decision on Form of Disclosure, 17 April 2007, para. 14.
21 The Prosecution's Interlocutory Appeal erroneously refers to 56 admitted facts at paragraph 8 and footnote 14.
22 Prosecution's Interlocutory Appeal, para. 8.
23 *Ibid.*, para. 9.
24 *Ibid.*, para. 12 (footnote omitted).

[m]ajority rebalanced the interests" at stake, *e.g.*, the procedural rights of the accused vis-à-vis expediency, "drew the line elsewhere" than in the *Karemera* Appeals Decision and "applied this new line to the present case".[25] The Prosecution further alleges that the Trial Chamber's approach was "explicitly rejected by" the *Karemera* Appeals Decision and resulted in rendering Rule 94(B) of the Rules a "dead letter".[26] In this respect, it contends that "[i]f facts pertaining to crimes committed before the time period of the indictment cannot be judicially noticed because they 'have a strong link' with the crimes charged in the indictment, then facts pertaining to the crime base actually charged in the indictment could never be judicially noticed, since in that case the 'strong link' will be even more prevalent".[27] Concerning this issue, the Prosecution submits that "if the Proposed Facts were judicially noticed the Trial Chamber could rely on them, *together with other evidence,* to draw inferences about notice to the Accused of crimes being committed by SRK forces".[28]

9. The Prosecution secondly submits that the Trial Chamber erred in law and abused its discretion when "it apparently rejected Proposed Facts on the basis that they contained findings of an essentially legal nature".[29] In support of this submission, the Prosecution contends that the "determination of what constitutes a 'fact' under Rule 94(A) [as established in the *Karemera* Appeals Decision] provides apposite guidance on the question of what may constitute a 'fact' under Rule 94(B)".[30] It further argues that in reaching a contrary conclusion, the Trial Chamber read a sentence extracted from paragraph 37 of the Impugned Decision "out of context",[31] and erred in finding from that sentence that the Appeals Chamber in the *Karemera* Appeals Decision intended to "hold that legal conclusions could be judicially noticed under Rule 94(A)".[32] It also **[page 6]** emphasizes that the Trial Chamber had itself "demonstrated the propriety of using 'legal language' to describe facts"[33] pending trial proceedings. It concludes that this conduct considered together with the "plain language" of Rules 94(A) and 94(B) of the Rules, the *Karemera* Appeals Decision and the *Prlić*[34] and *Popović*[35] Trial Chamber Decisions "demonstrate the validity of describing as 'factual' the Proposed Facts in this case".[36] Alleging that a review of the challenged Proposed Facts "shows that none of them are legal conclusions", the Prosecution claims that "judicial notice should have been taken of all of them".[37]

10. Milošević requests that the judicial notice of 57 Proposed Facts 56 through 181 be reversed and that the remaining part of the Impugned Decision be affirmed, thus amounting, in fact, to seeking rejection of all Proposed Facts from 56 to 181. In support of his appeal, Milošević submits that all these facts "deal with the period which falls outside that of the Indictment"[38] and relate "to the acts, conducts and *mens rea* of Stanislav Galić",[39] and thus "are in no way relevant" to the present case.[40] He further points out that despite that and the finding that "none of the[se] Proposed Facts go to the acts, conducts [sic] or mental state" of Milošević,[41] the Trial Chamber took judicial notice of them.[42] He concludes that in light of the *Karemera* Appeals Decision which ruled, *inter alia,* that "judicial notice under Rule 94(B) is in fact available only for adjudicated facts that bear, at least in some respect, on the criminal responsibility of the accused",[43] Proposed Facts 56 through 181 "cannot be the subject of judicial notice".[44]

---

25 *Ibid.*, paras 13, 14.
26 *Ibid.*, para. 15.
27 *Ibid.* (footnote and emphasis omitted).
28 *Ibid.*
29 Ibid., para. 19.
30 *Ibid.*, para. 26.
31 *Ibid.*, para. 27.
32 *Ibid.*, para. 29.
33 *Ibid.*, para. 32.
34 *Prosecution v. Jadranko Prlić et al.*, Case No. IT-04-74-T, *Décision relative aux requêtes des 14 et 23 juin 2006 de l'Accusation aux fins de dresser le constat judiciaire de faits admis*, 7 September 2006 ("*Prlić* Decision").
35 *Prosecutor v. Vujadin Popović at al.*, Case No. IT-05-88-T, Decision on Prosecution Motion for Judicial Notice of Adjudicated Facts with Annex, 26 September 2006 ("*Popović* Decision").
36 Prosecution's Interlocutory Appeal, para. 34.
37 *Ibid.*
38 Defence's Interlocutory Appeal, para. 11.
39 *Ibid.*, para. 16.
40 *Ibid.*
41 *Ibid.*, para. 15, citing the Impugned Decision, para. 32.
42 *Ibid.*, para. 16.
43 *Ibid.*, para. 17, citing the *Karemera* Appeals Decision, para. 48.
44 *Ibid.*, para. 18.

11. The Prosecution responds that the Defence's Interlocutory Appeal should be dismissed on the ground that the "Proposed Facts that were judicially noticed by the Trial Chamber aré plainly relevant to the current proceedings."[45] In this respect, it submits that because of the allegations against Milošević contained in the Amended Indictment,[46] the positions he held within the SRK **[page 7]** before he became Commander[47] and "the evidence adduced at trial concerning the unchanging nature of the campaign of shelling and sniping from 1992 to 1995",[48] the Trial Chamber did not err when it found that the 57 Proposed Facts it judicially noticed were relevant.[49] The Prosecution also points out that Defence Counsel for Milošević have themselves "frequently elicited evidence concerning" the time period preceding the time period of the Amended Indictment, and that Milošević concedes that Proposed Facts 1 through 53, despite pertaining to the time period comprised before the Amended Indictment, are relevant.[50] It finally submits that while Milošević's arguments "may ultimately go to the weight that should be afforded [to] the judicially noticed Proposed Facts, [they should not go] to their admissibility."[51]

2. <u>Discussion</u>

12. Relying on the *Karemera* Appeals Decision, the Trial Chamber found that "none of the Proposed Facts go to the acts, conduct or mental state of the Accused".[52] It then went on to "assess whether taking judicial notice of them would be consistent with the rights of the accused, particularly the right to examine witnesses against him".[53] It held in this respect that "this right is particularly important with regard to Proposed Facts which go to crimes committed under the command of Galić, the Accused's predecessor, and which [...] have a strong link with the crimes charged in the indictment, particularly those facts which may in effect put the Accused on notice."[54] The Trial Chamber thus considered that if the Proposed Facts that relate to the crimes committed under the command of Milošević's predecessor were to be judicially noticed, it would shift the burden of producing evidence onto Milošević and oblige him to rebut those facts, which would be inconsistent with his rights.[55]

a. <u>Relevance of the Proposed Facts</u>

13. Milošević challenges taking judicial notice of all Proposed Facts from 56 to 181 on the sole ground that they relate to the time period before the Amended Indictment and to the acts, conduct and *mens rea* of Stanislav Galić ("Galić"), and are thus irrelevant to the present case.[56] In this **[page 8]** respect, the Trial Chamber correctly held that the adjudicated facts sought to be judicially noticed must be relevant to the matters at issue in the current proceedings.[57]

14. Proposed Facts 56 through 181 are grouped under the heading "Campaign against Civilians between September 1992 and August 1994".[58] The Amended Indictment against Milošević alleges that the SRK implemented a campaign of shelling and sniping the civilian population in Sarajevo during a forty-four

45 Prosecution's Response, para. 4.
46 *Prosecutor v. Dragomir Milošević*, Case No. IT-98-29/1-T, Amended Indictment, 26 December 2006, ("Amended Indictment").
47 Prosecution's Response, paras 4, 6.
48 Prosecution's Response, para. 6, *see* also para. 5.
49 *Ibid.*, para. 6.
50 *Ibid.*, para. 5.
51 *Ibid.*, para. 6.
52 Impugned Decision, para. 32.
53 *Ibid.*
54 *Ibid.*
55 *Ibid.*
56 Defence's Interlocutory Appeal, para. 16.
57 Impugned Decision, para. 27; *See, inter alia,* regarding this issue, *Prosecutor v. Momir Nikolić,* Case No. IT-02-60/1-A, Decision on Appellant's Motion for Judicial Notice, 1 April 2005, para. 11; *Prosecutor v. Elizaphan Ntakirutimana and Gerard Ntakirutimana,* Case Nos. ICTR-96-10 and ICTR-96-17-T, Decision on the Prosecutor's Motion for Judicial Notice of Adjudicated Facts – Rule 94(B) of the Rules of Procedure and Evidence, 22 November 2001, para. 27; *Prosecutor v. Laurent Semanza,* Case No. ICTR-97-20-T, Decision on the Prosecutor's Motion for Judicial Notice and Presumptions of Facts Pursuant to Rules 94(B) and 54, 6 February 2002, para. 14.
58 *See* Annex C to the Prosecution's Interlocutory Appeal.

month period from 1992 through 1995, and that Milošević inherited this campaign when he succeeded Galić as Commander of the SRK on or about 10 August 1994 and proceeded to maintain and further it through his own conduct.[59] The charges also allege that from May 1992, Milošević was Commander of the SRK's 1st Romanija Infantry Brigade, and from July 1993 the SRK's Chief of Staff, and that therefore he knew of the campaign against the civilian population when he himself became Commander of the SRK.[60] Even though these Proposed Facts fall outside the time period charged in the Amended Indictment and are related to the acts, conduct and *mens rea* of his predecessor, Galić, the Appeals Chamber finds that they are clearly relevant to the present case inasmuch as they concern the campaign against civilians between September 1992 and August 1994. While the Trial Chamber did not specifically state whether Proposed Facts 56 through 181 present any relevance for this case - except for those which go to crimes committed under Galić's command[61] - such a finding can be inferred from the Impugned Decision.[62] Therefore, Milošević has failed to demonstrate that the Trial Chamber committed an error in considering that the Proposed Facts it judicially noticed were relevant, and his appeal is dismissed.

b. Judicial Notice of Adjudicated Facts of Crimes Having a Strong Link with the Crimes against Milošević

15. At the outset, the Appeals Chamber notes that the Trial Chamber did not clearly articulate on which ground it relied to exclude the 69 Proposed Facts that are the subject of the Prosecution's Interlocutory Appeal. In light of the introductory statement of the Impugned Decision's **[page 9]** Disposition[63] as well as of the Dissenting Opinion of Judge Harhoff,[64] it seems, however, that in declining to take judicial notice of these 69 Proposed Facts the Trial Chamber mostly – if not exclusively - relied upon its finding that if the Proposed Facts which go to the crimes committed under the command of Galić and which have a strong link with the crimes charged in the Amended Indictment against Milošević, "particularly those facts which may in effect put the Accused on notice", were to be judicially noticed, the burden to produce evidence would be shifted to Milošević in such a manner that it would jeopardize his rights.[65]

16. The *Karemera* Appeals Decision established that it is prohibited to take judicial notice of "adjudicated facts relating to the acts, conduct, and mental state of the accused."[66] This means that, when an accused is charged with crimes committed by others, while it is possible to take judicial notice of adjudicated facts regarding the existence of such crimes, the *actus reus* and the *mens rea* supporting the responsibility of the accused for the crimes in question must be proven by other means than judicial notice.[67] Thus, the Appeals Chamber sees no reason why judicial notice could not be taken of adjudicated facts providing evidence as to the existence of crimes committed by others and which the accused is not even charged with, as in the instant case, as long as the burden remains on the Prosecution to establish, by means other than judicial notice, that the accused had knowledge of their existence. The Appeals Chamber recalls, in this respect, that judicial notice of adjudicated facts "does not shift the ultimate burden of persuasion, which remains with the Prosecution" and that the facts "established under Rule 94(B) are merely presumptions that may be rebutted by the defence with evidence at trial".[68]

---

59 Amended Indictment, paras 11, 12, 13, 17, 19.

60 *Ibid.*, para. 19.

61 Impugned Decision, para. 32.

62 At paragraph 27 of the Impugned Decision, the Trial Chamber stated that one of the criteria to be considered when deciding to judicially notice a proposed adjudicated fact is that "[t]he fact must have some relevance to an issue in the current proceedings". Although this matter was not specifically addressed by the Trial Chamber, it can be inferred from that stipulation and from the Trial Chamber's finding that the Proposed Facts which go to crimes committed under Galić's command have a strong link with the current case, that the Trial Chamber did indeed deem all Proposed Facts relevant.

63 "The Trial Chamber understands [R]ule 94(B) as giving a Trial Chamber a discretionary power to admit adjudicated facts when it advances the expeditiousness of the proceedings and is in the interests of justice. Accordingly, the Trial Chamber will identify, in light of the foregoing analysis, those facts which it admits, leaving aside those which it rejects." Impugned Decision, p. 12.

64 "However, I respectfully disagree with the majority's decision to decline from accepting judicial notice of the remaining 69 proposed adjudicated facts. All of these remaining facts relate to the factual situation or to particular incidents occurring in Sarajevo during General Galić's time in power, and they all imply somehow that the SRK – under Galić – deliberately and indiscriminately targeted civilians or civilian objects in Sarajevo." Dissenting Opinion of Judge Harhoff, para. 4.

65 Impugned Decision, para. 32.

66 *Karemera* Appeals Decision, para. 50.

67 *Ibid.*, para. 52.

68 *Ibid.*, para. 42.

17. Taking judicial notice of adjudicated facts related to crimes committed under the command of Galić, *e.g.* facts regarding the deliberate and indiscriminate sniping and shelling by forces under Galić's command on civilian persons and objects in Sarajevo, would provide evidence of the commission of such crimes. Milošević has full latitude to rebut the presumption that these crimes were committed by introducing reliable and credible evidence to the contrary. Furthermore, establishing the very existence of these crimes does not imply that Milošević had knowledge of **[page 10]** their commission. Whether proof that the SRK deliberately and indiscriminately targeted civilians in Sarajevo under Galić's command is adduced through judicial notice or through other means, the Prosecution will be required to demonstrate beyond reasonable doubt that Milošević knew of the campaign under Galić's command, supported its continuation when he took over command, and failed to prevent the crimes committed under his command and punish the perpetrators. In this respect, the Appeals Chamber finds ambiguous the Prosecution's statement that "if the Proposed Facts were judicially noticed the Trial Chamber could rely on them, *together with other evidence*, to draw inferences about notice to the Accused of crimes committed by SRK forces",[69] and recalls that evidence of the accused's notice of the crimes has to be produced separately from judicial notice of their existence.

18. Considering the above, the Trial Chamber therefore committed a discernable error when it found that shifting the burden to produce evidence would be inconsistent with Milošević's rights and refused to take judicial notice of Proposed Facts relating to the very existence of crimes committed by others and for which Milošević is not charged.

c. Adjudicated Facts Containing Findings of an Essential Legal Nature

19. Concerning the second Prosecution's ground of appeal that the Trial Chamber erred in law and abused its discretion by rejecting any of the 69 Proposed Facts at stake "on the basis that they contained findings of an essentially legal nature",[70] as a preliminary remark, and as already noted above,[71] the Appeals Chamber remains uncertain as to whether the Trial Chamber relied on this ground to deny judicial notice to any of these Proposed facts, but will consider this issue.

20. The Trial Chamber found that facts sought to be judicially noticed "must represent the *factual findings* of a Trial Chamber or Appeals Chamber. It must not, therefoere, contain any findings or characterisations that are of an essentially legal nature".[72] It rejected the Prosecution's submission drawing a distinction between an essentially legal finding and a factual finding based on the *Karemera* Appeals Decision, because it found that "in no part [in this decision] did the Appeals Chamber hold that the facts it deemed suitable for judicial notice did not contain essentially legal conclusions or characterizations; it simply ruled that these facts were notorious."[73] Considering further that the "Prosecution submission relied extensively on an erroneous comparison of these facts",[74] the Trial Chamber declined to "determine the scope of the category of **[page 11]** essentially legal conclusions" and deemed it "sufficient to point out that, in arriving at its conclusion as to the narrowness of that category, the Prosecution relied on a flawed interpretation of the *Karemera* Appeals Decision".[75]

21. Contrary to the Prosecution's allegations, the Trial Chamber did not err in its analysis of the *Karemera* Appeals Decision. In that decision, the Appeals Chamber held that the key question regarding admission of facts of common knowledge, pursuant to Rule 94(A) of the Rules, is "whether the proposition can reasonably be disputed" and "not whether a proposition is put in legal or layman's terms."[76] When a Trial Chamber determines that a fact is notorious and not subject to reasonable dispute, it is obliged to take judicial notice of it under Rule 94(A) of the Rules. It has no discretion to act otherwise.[77] It is irrelevant whether the fact

---

69 Prosecution's Interlocutory Appeal, para. 15.
70 Prosecution's Interlocutory Appeal, para. 19.
71 Para. 15.
72 Impugned Decision, para. 27 (footnote omitted).
73 Impugned Decision, para. 36.
74 *Ibid.*
75 Impugned Decision, para. 36.
76 *Karemera* Appeals Decision, para. 29.
77 *Ibid.*, paras 29, 37.

in question is defined by terms with a legal meaning as long as these terms describe factual situations.[78] In this respect, the Appeals Chamber does not agree with the Prosecution that the Trial Chamber held "that legal conclusions could be judicially noticed under Rule 94(A)" of the Rules.[79] The Trial Chamber limited itself to noting that the Appeals Chamber in *Karemera* ruled that "the submission that the term 'genocide' is a legal characterisation" could not even be considered given that "Rule 94(A) does not provide the Trial Chamber with discretion to refuse judicial notice on this basis."[80] This constitutes an accurate reflection of the *Karemera* Appeals Decision.[81] Furthermore, "whereas judicial notice under Rule 94(A) is mandatory, judicial notice under Rule 94(B) is discretionary."[82] Thus, the Trial Chamber correctly interpreted the *Karemera* Appeals Decision when it ruled that its conclusions with regard to Rule 94(A) could not be apposite to Rule 94(B) of the Rules.

22. The Appeals Chamber additionally notes that the Trial Chamber correctly held that "[j]udicial notice pursuant to Rule 94(B) is not designed for the importing of legal conclusions from past proceedings".[83] To determine "whether a proposed fact is truly a factual finding", the Trial Chamber referred to the *Krajišnik* Decision which adjudicated that "many findings have a legal aspect, if one is to construe this expression broadly. It is therefore necessary to determine on a case-by-case basis whether the proposed fact contains findings or characterizations which are of an essentially legal nature and which must, therefore, be excluded."[84] Thus, the Prosecution does **[page 12]** not accurately represent the findings in the Impugned Decision when it claims that the Trial Chamber held "that facts could not be judicially noticed if they were described with legal language".[85] The Appeals Chamber also observes that the Trial Chamber's conclusion is fully in line with the jurisprudence of the Trial Chambers on this issue[86] – including after the issuance of the *Karemera* Appeals Decision.[87] The Prosecution's Interlocutory Appeal on this ground is therefore dismissed.

---

78 *Ibid.*

79 Prosecution's Interlocutory Appeal, para. 29.

80 Impugned Decision, para. 35, citing the *Karemera* Appeals Decision, para. 37.

81 *Karemera* Appeals Decision, para. 37.

82 *Ibid.*, para. 41.

83 Impugned Decision, para. 33.

84 Impugned Decision, para. 33, quoting *Prosecutor v. Momčilo Krajišnik,* Case No. IT-00-39-T, Decision on Third and Fourth Prosecution Motions for Judicial Notice of Adjudicated Facts, 24 March 2005 ("*Krajišnik* Decision"), para. 15 (In this decision, the Trial Chamber further observed that findings of an essentially legal nature "must, therefore, be excluded. In general, findings related to the *actus reus* or the *mens rea* of a crime are deemed to be factual findings. As long as they also comply with the other criteria [...] they may be admitted." (para. 15)).

85 Prosecution's Interlocutory Appeal, para. 33.

86 *Krajišnik* Decision, para. 15; *See* also, *inter alia, Prosecution v. Enver Hadžihasanović et al.*, Case No. IT-01-47-T, Decision on Judicial Notice of Adjudicated Facts Following the Motion Submitted by Counsel for the Accused Hadžihasanović and Kubura on 20 January 2005, 14 April 2005, p. 5, and Final Decision on Judicial Notice of Adjudicated Facts, 20 April 2004, pp. 7, 8; *Prosecutor v. Željko Mejakić,* Case No. IT-02-65-PT, Decision on Prosecution Motion for Judicial Notice pursuant to Rule 94(B), 1 April 2004, p. 4; *Prosecution v. Vidoje Blagojević et al.,* Case No. IT-02-60-T, Decision on Prosecution's Motion for Judicial Notice of Adjudicated Facts and Documentary Evidence, 19 December 2003, para. 16; *Prosecution v. Jadranko Prlić et al.*, Case No. IT-04-74-PT, Decision on Motion for Judicial Notice of Adjudicated Facts pursuant to Rule 94(B), 14 March 2006, para. 12.

87 *Prlić* Decision, para. 23, ("*Quant à la condition n° 3 relative à l'absence de qualification juridique, la Chambre considère qu'elle doit être appréciée au cas par cas et interprétée de façon restrictive. En effet, certains paragraphes de jugements et arrêts proposés pour constat judiciaire, tout en décrivant essentiellement des réalités factuelles, renferment également, souvent, des termes juridiques. Ces paragraphes sont susceptibles d'être admis en application de l'article 94 B) du Règlement. Ce n'est que lorsque des paragraphes tirent principalement des conclusions juridiques qu'ils ne feront pas l'objet de constat judicaire.* " (footnotes omitted)); *Popović* Decision, para. 10 (The Trial Chamber endorsed the above-quoted position in the *Krajišnik* Decision).

IV. DISPOSITION

Based on the foregoing reasons, the Appeals Chamber

DISMISSES the Defence's Interlocutory Appeal;

ALLOWS the Prosecution's Interlocutory Appeal **IN PART**;

AFFIRMS the Impugned Decision regarding judicial notice of the 57 Proposed Facts 56 through 181 appealed by Milošević;

REMANDS the remaining 69 Proposed Facts 56 through 181, which are the subject of the Prosecution's Interlocutory Appeal, to the Trial Chamber for further consideration in a manner consistent with the present Decision. **[page 13]**

Done in English and French, the English version being authoritative.

Done this 26th day of June 2007,
At The Hague,
The Netherlands.

Mehmet Güney
Presiding Judge,

[Seal of the Tribunal]

UNITED
NATIONS

International Tribunal for the Prosecution of Persons Responsible for Serious Violations of International Humanitarian Law Committed in the Territory of Former Yugoslavia since 1991	Case No.	IT-04-83-PT
	Date:	9 July 2007
	Original:	English

IN TRIAL CHAMBER I

Before: **Judge Bakone Justice Moloto, Presiding**
Judge Frederik Harhoff
Judge Flavia Lattanzi

Registrar: **Mr. Hans Holthuis**

Decision of: **9 July 2007**

PROSECUTOR

v.

RASIM DELIĆ

PUBLIC

DECISION ON PROSECUTION'S MOTION FOR JUDICIAL NOTICE OF ADJUDICATED FACTS AND JOINT MOTION CONCERNING AGREED FACTS

The Office of the Prosecutor:
Mr. Daryl A. Mundis
Ms. Laurie Sartorio
Mr. Kyle Wood
Mr. Aditya Menon

Counsel for the Accused:
Ms. Vasvija Vidović
Mr. Nicholas David Robson

I. INTRODUCTION

[page 2] 1. **TRIAL CHAMBER I** ("Trial Chamber") of the International Tribunal for the Prosecution of Persons Responsible for Serious Violations of International Humanitarian Law Committed in the Territory of the former Yugoslavia since 1991 ("Tribunal") is seised of the "Prosecution's Motion for Judicial Notice of Adjudicated Facts" ("Motion"), filed by the Prosecution on 29 September 2006, and of the Joint Motion Concerning Agreed Facts ("Joint Motion"), filed on 29 May 2007, and hereby renders its decision.

II. PROCEDURAL HISTORY

2. The Prosecution filed the Motion on 29 September 2006, requesting the Trial Chamber to take judicial notice, pursuant to Rule 94(B) of the Rules of Procedure and Evidence of the Tribunal ("Rules"), of 325 facts ("Proposed Facts") listed in an Annex to the Motion, which it submits were adjudicated by the judgement in the case of *Prosecutor v. Hadžihasanović and Kubura.*[1] On 6 October 2006, the Defence filed a response to the Motion requesting a stay as the Annex to the Motion was in French and an order to the Prosecution to re-file the Annex in English when an official translation of the *Hadžihasanović et al.* Judgement was available.[2] On 11 October 2006, the Prosecution replied that it had no objection to the Defence's request.[3] On 18 October 2006, the Trial Chamber ordered a stay and the re-filing of the Annex listing the proposed adjudicated facts in English once the English translation of the Judgement was available.[4] The English Annex of the proposed adjudicated facts was filed by the Prosecution on 27 November 2006.[5] The Defence filed its response to the Motion on 11 December 2006 objecting to the admissibility of the proposed facts on the basis of several grounds which will be illustrated in detail below ("Response of 11 December 2006").[6] Finally, on 29 May 2007, a Joint Motion Concerning Agreed Facts ("Joint Motion") was filed, by which motion the Defence indicated that a number of the Proposed Facts were acceptable and that they may now be considered as Agreed Facts. As a result of this agreement, the Prosecution withdrew 75 listed Proposed Facts from the Motion. The Trial Chamber therefore has **[page 3]** to decide whether to take judicial notice of the remaining 250 Proposed Facts. The Trial Chamber also has to decide whether to admit into evidence a list of 163 Agreed Facts which has been attached by the parties to the Joint Motion.

III. SUBMISSIONS

3. The Prosecution submits that the Proposed Facts meet the criteria which must be satisfied in order for the Trial Chamber to take judicial notice thereof pursuant to Rule 94(B) of the Rules. In particular, the Prosecution argues that the Proposed Facts: (a) are relevant to the case the Prosecution must prove;[7] (b) they

---

1 *Prosecutor vs. Hadžihasanović and Kubura*, Case No. IT-01-47-T, Judgement, 15 Mar 2006 (*Hadžihasanović et al.* Trial Judgement"). On 5 October 2006, the Prosecution filed a Corrigendum to the Motion and an Annex thereto in which the proposed adjudicated facts were reorganised and reformatted so as to make them easier to understand ("Corrigendum to the Prosecution Motion for Judicial Notice of Adjudicated Facts").

2 Defence Response to the Prosecution Motion for Judicial Notice of Adjudicated Facts, 6 Oct 2006 ("6 October Response").

3 Prosecution Reply to Defence Response to the Prosecution Motion for Judicial Notice of Adjudicated Facts, 6 Oct 2006

4 Decision Regarding the Prosecution Motion for Judicial Notice of Adjudicated Facts" ("Decision"), 18 Oct 2006.

5 Submission pursuant to the Decision regarding the Prosecution Motion for Judicial Notice of Adjudicated Facts, 27 Nov 2006.

6 Defence Response to the Prosecution Motion for Judicial Notice of Adjudicated Facts, 11 Dec 2006. On 12 December 2006. The Defence filed a corrigendum to correct some mistakes in the text, Defence Corrigendum to Defence Response to the Prosecution Motion for Judicial Notice of Adjudicated Facts, 12 Dec 2006.

7 Motion, para. 7. The Prosecution submits that the Proposed Facts are of relevance to the proceedings because a significant number of the factual findings in *Hadžihasanović et al.* are directly relevant to a number of legal and factual issues in the *Delić* case by establishing the necessary background to place the crimes charged in context. They are also relevant to establishing the criminal responsibility of the Accused without being related to his specific acts, conduct or mental state. The Prosecution also submits that the case of *Hadžihasanović et al.* was related to the armed conflict between the Army of Bosnia and Herzegovina ("ABiH") and Croatian Defence Council ("HVO") in the territory of Central Bosnia in 1993. Like Rasim Delić, Enver Hadžihasanović and Amir Kubura were charged with murder and cruel treatment pursuant to Article 3 of the Statute for the crimes committed in Maline/Bikoši on 8 June 1993. Enver Hadžihasanović was Commander of the 3rd Corps of the ABiH and Amir Kubura was Commander of 7th Muslim Mountain Brigade of the ABiH. The Prosecution further notes that those facts which attest to the *modus operandi* of these units in 1992 and 1993 and their way of functioning in battle, are therefore relevant to the *Delić* case. Moreover, the Prosecution argues that the military and civilian system of justice is the same system applicable in the case against Rasim Delić, Motion, paras 7–9.

have been "truly" adjudicated in the proceedings before the Tribunal and they are not the subjects of the appeal of either party in the original case;[8] (c) they do not include any legal characterisations[9] and (d) they are distinct, concrete and identifiable.[10] The Prosecution further submits that the Proposed Facts will serve to promote efficient conduct of the proceedings.

4. The Defence's primary submission in its Response of 11 December 2006 is that the *Hadžihasanović et al.* Judgement in its entirety is unsuitable for judicial notice of facts adjudicated in light of the fact that, *inter alia*, the methodology of the conduct of the trial is subject to appeal, and no final decision has been rendered thereon. In particular, among the grounds for appeal referred to by the Defence are: (a) the submission of the Appellant *Hadžihasanović* that the Trial Chamber erred in law because "through its practice of systematically questioning witnesses [...] gave the impression that the court was not impartial";[11] (b) the submission of the Appellant *Hadžihasanović* that the Trial Chamber erred in admitting the "War Diaries" as a full Chambers **[page 4]** Exhibit,[12] and (c) that the Trial Chamber wrongly failed to grant relief when the Defence applied for access to the EUMM Archives, thereby "seriously affect[ing] the ability of the Defence to prepare for trial and to effectively challenge the evidence led by the Prosecution during the presentation of its case".[13]

5. Without prejudice to its primary contention, the Defence further submits that many of the individual proposed facts fail to meet the requirements of the legal test to be applied when determining whether a given proposed fact may be judicially noticed by a Trial Chamber.[14] In particular, the Defence submits that some of them (i) are not facts but speculations or equivocal assertions;[15] (ii) consist merely of the "Trial Chamber's recitation of evidence that they heard before them"; [16] (iii) merely amount to partial descriptions of documents and are not appropriate to be submitted as "adjudicated facts" because this is improperly advancing the content of a document as proof that the matters contained therein occurred;[17] (iv) are only partially complete or taken out of context;[18] (v) concerns "acts or conduct of the Accused";[19] (vi) "are not shown to not be based substantially on agreement between the parties".[20]

6. Finally, the Defence submits that numerous facts are "subject to reasonable dispute between the Parties". Therefore, they cannot be judicially noticed because it would be wholly unfair if the **[page 5]** Accused was bound by facts that go to material matters relevant to the case against him and that were adjudicated by another Trial Chamber.[21]

---

8 Motion, paras 11–12.

9 Motion, paras 14.

10 Motion, paras 15–16. In this regard, the Prosecution contends that the Proposed Facts meet all of the requirements established by the jurisprudence of the Tribunal.

11 Response of 11 December 2006, para. 6.

12 Response of 11 December 2006, para. 8.

13 Response of 11 December 2006, para. 8.

14 The parties disagree regarding the legal test to be applied when determining whether a given proposed fact may be judicially noticed by a Trial Chamber. The Defence indicated seven requirements to be met in light of the jurisprudence, while the Prosecution listed only four.

15 Response of 11 December 2006, para. 11. The Defence cited the following Proposed Facts: 17, 20, 38, 65, 67, 68, 73, 74, 77, 79, 83, 86, 88, 113, 116, 134, 141, 151, 161, 170, 177, 192, 193, 194, 209, 215, 290. It also refers to the following Proposed Facts which it considers "imprecise" or unclear: 16, 24, 25, 41, 87, 107, 139, 235, 237, 238, 242,248, 310. The Defence notes that many proposed facts contain expressions of equivocation such as "seems" or "it would appear" or involve estimates. The Defence argues that such facts are not "distinct, concrete and identifiable". It further argued that when facts are formulated with insufficient precision they should be rejected on the ground that they will not promote judicial economy, *ibid.*

16 The Defence cited the following Proposed Facts: 73, 74, 81, 82, 116, 156, 157, 159–165, 175, 176, 177, 180, 182, 218, 219, 222, 223, 227, 228, 229, 235, 239, 240, 241, 243, 244, 254, 281, 282, 298, 299, 300, 312. The Defence also refers to the following Proposed Facts which it says "do not accurately reflect the document etc cited in the footnote as authority": 59, 64, 105, 204. Response of 11 December 2006, para. 13.

17 The Defence cited the following Proposed Facts: 4, 12–16, 21–23, 25, 26, 44, 45–47, 89, 110, 190, 206, 210, 249, 261–264, 267–270, 297. The Defence notes that none of the "facts" cited therein will advance judicial economy as they consist of (partial) excerpts from documents which will, as a matter of fairness to the Accused, have to be produced at his trial and "to alter the status of documentary exhibits by admitting them by way of Rule 94(B) is an impermissible reversal of the burden of proof which would otherwise fall on the Prosecution and is inconsistent with the Trial Chamber's obligations to ensure that the fairness of the Accused's trial is protected". Response of 11 December 2006, para. 16.

18 The Defence cited the following Proposed Facts: 142, 284, 301, 307, 308, 309. Response of 11 December 2006, para. 17.

19 The Defence cited the following Proposed Facts: 26, 27, 149. Response of 11 December 2006, para. 18.

20 Response of 11 December 2006, para. 19.

21 The Defence submits also that no judicial economy will be achieved because the Accused will need to call evidence to establish the inaccuracy of these facts, Response of 11 December 2006, paras 20–22.

IV. APPLICABLE LAW

7. Rule 94(B) of the Rules provides that:

> At the request of a party or *proprio motu*, a Trial Chamber, after hearing the parties, may decide to take judicial notice of adjudicated facts or documentary evidence from other proceedings of the Tribunal relating to matters at issue in the current proceedings.

8. Rule 94(B) aims at achieving judicial economy and harmonising judgements of the Tribunal by conferring the Trial Chamber with discretionary power to take judicial notice of facts or documents from other proceedings. This power has to be exercised "on the basis of a careful consideration of the accused's right to a fair and expeditious trial", that is in keeping with the principle of a fair trial enshrined in Articles 20 and 21 of the Statute.[22]

9. The Appeals Chamber has clarified that a request for the admission of adjudicated facts "must specifically point out the paragraph(s) or parts of the judgement of which it wishes judicial notice to be taken, and refer to *facts*, as found by the trial chamber".[23] In relation to the effects of taking judicial notice, the Appeals Chamber has further held that "by taking judicial notice of an adjudicated fact, a Chamber establishes a well-founded presumption for the accuracy of this fact, which therefore does not have to be proven again at trial, but which, subject to that presumption, may be challenged at that trial."[24] Thus, "in the case of judicial notice under Rule 94 (B), the effect is only to relieve the Prosecution of its initial burden to produce evidence on the point; the defence may then put the point into question by introducing reliable and credible evidence to the contrary." It is however important to note that the burden of proof beyond reasonable doubt remains on the Prosecution.[25] **[page 6]**

10. According to the settled jurisprudence of the Tribunal, the Trial Chamber, in the exercise of its discretion to judicially notice adjudicated facts, has to consider whether the purported adjudicated facts meet at least the following requirements:

(i) The fact must be distinct, concrete and identifiable;[26]

(ii) It must be pertinent and relevant to the case;[27]

(iii) It must not include findings or characterisations that are of an essentially legal nature;[28]

(iv) It must not be based on a plea agreement or on facts voluntarily admitted in a previous case;[29]

(v) It must be "truly adjudicated" i.e. it must not have been contested on appeal, or, if it has, the fact has been settled on appeal;[30]

---

22 *Prosecutor v. Karemera et al.*, Case No. ICTR-98-44-AR73, Decision on Prosecutor's Interlocutory Appeal of Decision on Judicial Notice, 16 Jun 2006 ("*Karemera et al.* Appeal Decision"), para. 41.

23 See *Prosecutor v. Zoran Kupreškić et al.*, Case No. IT-95-16, Decision on the Motions of Drago Jospović, Zoran Kupreškić and Vlatko Kupreškić to admit additional evidence pursuant to Rule 115 and for judicial notice taken pursuant to rule 94(B), 8 May 2001, ("*Kupreškić et al.* Decision*")*, para. 12.

24 See *Prosecutor v. Slobodan Milošević*, Case No. IT-02-54-AR73.5, Decision on the Prosecution's Interlocutory Appeal against the Trial Chamber's 10 April 2003 Decision on Prosecution Motion for Judicial Notice of Adjudicated Facts, 28 Oct 2003, ("*Slobodan Milošević* Appeal Decision"), p. 4 (footnote omitted). The Appeals Chamber in *Karemera* reaffirmed this holding, and clarified that judicial notice of adjudicated facts only "relieve the Prosecution of its initial burden to produce evidence on the point; the defence may then put the point into question by introducing reliable and credible evidence to the contrary", *Karemera et al.* Appeal Decision, para. 42. *See also Prosecutor v. Popović et al.*, Case No. IT-05-88-T, Decision on Prosecution's Motion for Judicial Notice of Adjudicated Facts with Annex, 26 Sep 2006 ("*Popović et al.* Decision"), para. 20.

25 *Karemera et al.* Appeal Decision, para. 41.

26 *See*, for example, *Prosecutor v. Krajišnik*, Case No. IT-00-39-PT, Decision on Third and Fourth Prosecution Motions for Judicial Notice of Adjudicated Facts, 24 March 2005, ("*Krajišnik* Decision"), para. 14.

27 *Prosecutor v. Momir Nikolić*, Case No. IT-02-60/1-A, Decision on Appellant's Motion for Judicial Notice, 1 April 2005 (*"Nikolić* Appeal Decision"), para. 52

28 *Prosecutor v. Dragomir Milošević*, Case No. IT-98-29/1-AR73.1, Decision on Interlocutory Appeals Against Trial Chamber's Decision on Prosecution's Motion for Judicial Notice of Adjudicated Facts and Prosecution's Catalogue of Agreed Facts, 26 June 2007, paras 19–22.

29 *Popović et al.* Decision, para. 11 The Trial Chamber noted that such would be the case where the structure of the relevant footnote in the original judgement cites the agreed facts between the parties as a primary source of authority.

30 *Kupreškić et al.* Decision, para. 6; *Krajišnik* Decision, para. 14; *Prosecutor v. Prlić et al.*, Case No. IT-04-74-PT, Decision on Motion for Judicial Notice of Adjudicated Facts Pursuant to Rule 94(B), 14 March 2006, ("*Prlić et al.* Pre-Trial Decision"), paras 12, 15.

(vi) It must not go to the act, conduct or mental state of the accused;[31]

(vii) The formulation proposed in the moving party's motion for admission must not differ in any significant way from the way the fact was expressed when adjudicated in the previous proceeding.[32]

11. It is not required that the proposed facts not be subject to reasonable dispute between the parties.[33] However, as taking of judicial notice under Rule 94(B) is discretionary, the Trial Chamber always retains the right to withhold judicial notice of a fact even if it fulfils all the requirements above, when it believes that such notice would not serve the interests of justice.[34] Indeed, as held by **[page 7]** the Appeals Chamber, a key factor in the Trial Chamber's determination as to the admission of adjudicated facts lies in the consideration that taking judicial notice of such facts will achieve judicial economy while preserving the right of the accused to a fair, public and expeditious trial.[35]

12. With regard to the law applicable to the Agreed Facts, Rule 65 *ter* (H) provides that "[t]he pre-trial Judge shall record the points of agreement and disagreement on matters of law and fact". Moreover, Rule 65 *ter* (M) provides that "[t]he Trial Chamber may *proprio motu* exercise any of the functions of the pre-trial Judge" and Rule 89(C) provides that "[a] Chamber may admit any relevant evidence which it deems to have probative value". The Trial Chamber will assess the proposed Agreed Facts in light of these Rules.

V. DISCUSSION

13. The Trial Chamber will address the primary submission of the Defence, according to which the judgement in its entirety is not yet suitable for judicial notice in light of the fact that, *inter alia*, the methodology of the conduct of the trial is subject to appeal.[36] The Trial Chamber recalls that the test to be applied is whether those facts, of which judicial notice is sought, are subject to appeal.[37] As held by the Appeal Chamber, "[o]nly facts in a judgement, from which there has been no appeal, or as to which any appellate proceedings have concluded, can truly be deemed "adjudicated facts" within the meaning of Rule 94(B)".[38]

14. The Trial Chamber notes the submission of the Appellant *Hadžihasanović* contained in its first ground of Appeal on the fairness of the trial that the Trial Chamber erred in law because "through its practice of systematically questioning witnesses [...] gave the impression that the court was not impartial."[39] The Trial Chamber cannot fail to note that this submission alleges an irregularity in the conduct of the trial, which, if upheld by the Appeal Chamber, would undermine the integrity of the entire *Hadžihasanović et al.* Judgement. The Trial Chamber is therefore of the view that this ground of appeal amounts to a direct challenge to the factual findings of that Judgement. It follows that the Proposed Facts of which judicial notice is sought cannot be **[page 8]** considered truly adjudicated and, consequently, the Trial Chamber cannot take judicial notice of them. The Trial Chamber further notes, having reviewed the 65 *ter* witness list, that it appears that evidence concerning most of the Proposed Facts will be introduced through the witnesses coming to testify and the documents which the Prosecution has indicated it will submit.

---

31 *Karemera et al.* Appeal Decision, para. 51.

32 *Krajišnik* Decision, para. 14; *Prlić et al.* Pre-Trial Decision , para. 21.

33 *Karemera et al.* Appeal Decision, para. 40. *See also Prosecutor v. Dragomir Milošević,* Case No. IT-98-29/1-T, Decision on Prosecution's Motion for Judicial Notice of Adjudicated Facts and Prosecution's Catalogue of Agreed Facts with Dissenting Opinion of Judge Harhoff, 10 April 2007 ("*Milošević* Decision"), para. 27; *Popović et al.* Decision, fn. 19.

34 *Karemera et al.* Appeal Decision, para. 41; *Popović et al.* Decision, para. 16.

35 *Nikolić* Appeal Decision, para. 11, with further references.

36 *See supra*, para. 4.

37 *Popović et al.* Decision para. 14.

38 *Kupreškić et al.* Decision, para. 6; *Krajišnik* Decision, para. 14; *Prlić et al.* Pre-Trial Decision, paras 12, 15. The Trial Chamber notes that subsequent jurisprudence interpreted this holding to mean that "judicial notice of adjudicated facts should generally not be taken of facts which are *themselves* being appealed", *Prosecutor v. Paško Ljubicić*, Case No. IT-00-41-PT, Decision on Prosecution's Motion for Judicial Notice of Adjudicated Facts, 23 January 2003,(" *Ljubicić* Decision"), p. 5. In *Popović et al.*, the Trial Chamber stated that if an appeal is pending in respect of a judgement, a fact may only be judicially noticed if "the fact itself is clearly not among, or inextricably commingled with, those findings that have been challenged by a party." *Popović et al.* Decision, para. 14.

39 *Hadžihasanović and Kubura*, Case No.IT-01-47-T, Notice of Appeal from Judgement on Behalf of Enver Hadžihasanović and Request for Leave to Exceed the Page Limit, 18 April 2006, p. 6.

15. The primary submission of the Defence being upheld, the Trial Chamber does not need to discuss the Proposed Facts further.

16. As regards the list of Agreed Facts, the Trial Chamber has carefully assessed those facts and has found them of relevance and probative value to the current case.

VI. DISPOSITION

17. On the basis of the reasoning set forth above, and recalling the discretionary power of the Trial Chamber in relation to adjudicated facts, the Trial Chamber decides as follows.

PURSUANT TO 65 *ter* (H), 65 *ter* (M) 89(C), and 94(B) of the Rules;

DENIED the Motion;

GRANTS the Joint Motion; and

ADMITS the 163 Agreed Facts.

Done in English and French, the English version being authoritative.

Dated this ninth day of July 2007
At The Hague
The Netherlands

Judge Bakone Justice Moloto
Presiding

[Seal of the Tribunal]

UNITED NATIONS

International Tribunal for the Prosecution of Persons Responsible for Serious Violations of International Humanitarian Law Committed in the Territory of Former Yugoslavia since 1991	Case No.	IT-98-29/1-T
	Date:	18 July 2007
	Original:	English

IN TRIAL CHAMBER III

Before: **Judge Patrick Robinson, Presiding**
Judge Antoine Kesia-Mbe Mindua
Judge Frederik Harhoff

Registrar: **Mr. Hans Holthuis**

Date: **18 July 2007**

PROSECUTOR

v.

DRAGOMIR MILOŠEVIĆ

DECISION ON APPEALS CHAMBER REMAND OF JUDICIAL NOTICE OF ADJUDICATED FACTS WITH SEPARATE OPINION OF JUDGE ROBINSON

The Office of the Prosecutor:
Mr. Stefan Waespi
Ms. Carolyn Edgerton
Mr. John Docherty

Counsel for the Accused:
Mr. Branislav Tapušković
Ms. Branislava Isailović

[page 2] 1. **TRIAL CHAMBER III** ("Trial Chamber") of the International Tribunal for the Prosecution of Persons Responsible for Serious Violations of International Humanitarian Law Committed in the Territory of the former Yugoslavia since 1991 ("Tribunal") is seised of the Appeals Chamber "Decision on Interlocutory Appeals Against Trial Chamber's Decision on Prosecution's Motion for Judicial Notice of Adjudicated Facts and Prosecution's Catalogue of Agreed Facts" ("Appeals Chamber Decision") of 26 June 2007, in which the Appeals Chamber remands 69 Proposed Facts 56 through 181 to the Trial Chamber for further consideration in a manner consistent with the Appeals Chamber Decision.

I. INTRODUCTION

2. On 18 December 2006, the Prosecution filed a "Motion for Judicial Notice of Adjudicated Facts" ("Prosecution Motion"), to which the Defence responded on 19 January 2007 ("Defence Response"), and the Prosecution replied on 25 January 2007 ("Reply"). After hearing additional oral submissions from the parties on 12 February 2007, the Trial Chamber ruled upon the Motion on 10 April 2007 in its "Decision on Prosecution's Motion for Judicial Notice of Adjudicated Facts and Prosecution's Catalogue of Agreed Facts with Dissenting Opinion of Judge Harhoff" ("Trial Chamber Decision"). The Trial Chamber granted certification to appeal the decision on 3 May 2007. In its Decision, the Appeals Chamber ruled on both parties' appeals of the Trial Chamber Decision.

3. The Appeals Chamber dismissed the Defence appeal in its entirety. The Prosecution's appeal focused on the decision of the Trial Chamber not to take judicial notice of 69 Proposed Facts.[1] The Appeals Chamber granted, in part, the Prosecution's appeal, directing the Trial Chamber to further consider the 69 Proposed Facts in a manner consistent with its Decision.[2]

II. APPLICABLE LAW

4. The Appeals Chamber saw "no reason why judicial notice could not be taken of adjudicated facts providing evidence as to the existence of crimes committed by others and which the accused is not even charged with, as in the instant case, as long as the burden remains on the Prosecution to establish, by means other than judicial notice, that the accused had knowledge of their existence."[3] In addressing the Prosecution's appeal, the Appeals Chamber held that, according to the *Karemera* **[page 3]** Appeals Decision,[4] "when an accused is charged with crimes committed by others, while it is possible to take judicial notice of adjudicated facts regarding the existence of such crimes, the *actus reus* and the *mens rea* supporting the responsibility of the accused for the crimes in question must be proven by other means than judicial notice."[5] As such, the Appeals Chamber held that establishing the existence of these crimes committed during the period in which Stanislav Galić was the commander of the SRK does not imply that Dragomir Milošević ("the Accused") had knowledge of their commission.[6]

5. The distinction drawn by the Appeals Chamber between the existence of crimes prior to the indictment period and the notice of the Accused during the indictment period appears to rest on its finding that the Prosecution, regardless of any judicial notice of facts going to the existence of crimes under Stanislav Galić, will be required to demonstrate beyond reasonable doubt that the Accused knew of the crimes committed under the command of Stanislav Galić, supported its continuation when he took over command, and failed to prevent the crimes committed under his command and punish the perpetrators.[7] The Appeals Chamber dismissed the Prosecution's proposition that the Trial Chamber could rely on such adjudicated facts, *together with other evidence*, to draw inferences about notice to the Accused of crimes committed by SRK forces and

1 Facts numbered 57–59, 61, 63, 72, 77–80, 86, 87, 89, 94–98, 105–107, 111, 117–121, 124, 131–142, 144–146, 148–155, 157, 160, 165–175, 177–181 in the Prosecution's Motion for Judicial Notice of Adjudicated Facts and Prosecution's Catalogue of Agreed Facts filed by the Prosecution on 18 December 2006.

2 Appeals Chamber Decision, p. 12.

3 *Ibid.*, para. 16.

4 *Prosecutor v. Edouard Karemera et al.,* Case No. ICTR-98-44-AR73(C), Decision on Prosecutor's Interlocutory Appeal of Decision on Judicial Notice, 16 June 2006 ("*Karemera* Appeals Decision").

5 Appeals Chamber's Decision, para. 16.

6 *Ibid.*, para. 17.

7 *Ibid.*

it affirmed that evidence of the Accused's notice of the crimes has to be produced separately from judicial notice of their existence.[8]

6. The Appeals Chamber also recalled that judicial notice of adjudicated facts "does not shift the ultimate burden of persuasion, which remains with the Prosecution" and that the facts "established under Rule 94(B) are merely presumptions that may be rebutted by the defence with evidence at trial".[9] In this regard, the Appeals Chamber emphasised the ability of the Accused to rebut the presumption, which would arise as a consequence of the admission of the 69 Proposed Facts, that certain crimes were committed under the command of Stanislav Galić.[10]

7. The Appeals Chamber held that the Trial Chamber had therefore committed a "discernable error when it found that shifting the burden to produce evidence would be inconsistent with [the **[page 4]** Accused's] rights and refused to take judicial notice of Proposed Facts relating to the very existence of crimes committed by others and for which [the Accused]is not charged".[11]

8. The Appeals Chamber upheld the decision of the Trial Chamber in all other aspects of its ruling.

III. DISCUSSION

9. The Appeals Chamber upheld the decision of the Trial Chamber except for its interpretation of the *Karemera* Appeals Decision concerning crimes committed by physical perpetrators other than the Accused before the time period mentioned in the Indictment. In light of the Appeals Chamber decision, the Trial Chamber finds that it must reconsider the 69 remaining Proposed Facts it initially refused to judicially notice, taking into account the Appeals Chamber Decision and the criteria identified in the Trial Chamber Decision.[12]

10. Of the 69 remaining facts, only facts which represent factual findings of the *Galić* Trial Chamber or the *Galić* Appeals Chamber and which do not contain any findings or characterisations that are of an essentially legal nature can be admitted.[13] The Trial Chamber also retains its discretion to take judicial notice of adjudicated facts under Rule 94(B) for the purpose of expediting the proceedings, if it finds it to be in the interest of justice and provided the rights of the Accused are not thereby compromised.[14] Furthermore, adjudicated facts, even in conjunction with other evidence, cannot be used to establish notice of the Accused of the crimes he is charged with.

11. The Trial Chamber understands a finding to be legal when it involves the interpretation or application of legal principles while a finding is factual when it requires a description of circumstances surrounding the case at hand.[15] **[page 5]**

12. The adjudicated facts at issue are relevant to the background of the case,[16] or could provide circumstantial evidence from which the notice of the Accused of crimes committed under his command could be inferred.[17]

---

8 *Ibid.*

9 *Ibid.*

10 *Ibid.*, para. 17.

11 *Ibid.*, para. 18.

12 Trial Chamber Decision, 10 April 2007, paras 25–30.

13 Trial Chamber Decision, para. 27.

14 *See Prosecutor v. Edouard Karemera et al.*, Case No. ICTR-98-44-T, Decision on Appeals Chamber Remand on Judicial Notice, 11 December 2006.

15 *See also Prosecutor v. Pauline Nyiramasuhuko et al.*, Case No. ICTR-98-42-T, Décision Relative à la Requête du Procureur aux Fins de Constat Judiciaire et d'Admission de Présomptions Factuelles , 15 May 2002, para. 39 in which the Trial Chamber held that "facts involving interpretation or legal characterisation of facts are not capable of admission under Rule 94."

16 In this regard, the Trial Chamber notes that the Prosecutor submitted that the adjudicated facts are "relevant to establish the historical and factual background of the Prosecution's case" in the Prosecution's Motion for Judicial Notice of Adjudicated Facts, 18 December 2006, para. 8. Further, the Prosecution orally submitted that the adjudicated facts go to prove that "the Accused was instrumental and a part of putting together [... the] criminal scheme into place [...] and [...] in August of 1994, when he became the commander of the SRK, he continued that scheme and did nothing to stop it", Trial Hearing, 12 February 2007, T. 1896.

17 *See Čelebići* Appeal Judgement, 20 February 2001, para. 238 in which the Appeals Chamber held that "A showing that a superior had some general information in his possession, which would put him on notice of possible unlawful acts by his subordinates would be sufficient to prove that he "had reason to know" [...] As to the form of the information available to him, it may be written or oral, and does not need to have the form of specific reports submitted pursuant to a monitoring system.

In light of the Appeals Chamber directions as to the type of evidence on which a finding on the notice of the Accused must be based, these facts cannot be used to establish notice. However, in light of the significance of the adjudicated facts for the historical and factual background of the Prosecution's case, the Trial Chamber concludes that facts related to crimes committed under the command of *Galić*, but which do not contain findings of an essentially legal nature, should be judicially noticed.

13. **FOR THOSE REASONS, THE TRIAL CHAMBER**

GRANTS IN PART the Prosecution's Motion with regard to the remaining adjudicated facts number 57, 58, 63, 72, 78, 79, 89, 105, 111, 117, 119, 132, 134, 142, 145, 146, 148, 150–152, 171, 172.

Done in English and French, the English version being authoritative.

Judge Patrick Robinson
Presiding

Dated this eighteenth day of July 2007
At The Hague
The Netherlands.

[Seal of the Tribunal] [page 6]

This information does not need to provide specific information about unlawful acts committed or about to be committed. For instance, a military commander who has received information that some of the soldiers under his command have a violent or unstable character, or have been drinking prior to being sent on a mission, may be considered as having the required knowledge".

I. SEPARATE OPINON OF JUDGE ROBINSON

1. I fully support the Decision of the Trial Chamber. However, I have a difficulty with the statement in paragraph 11 that "a finding is factual when it requires a description of circumstances surrounding the case at hand."

2. In the first place, if there is a need for a definition of any term in relation to the issue at hand, it is the term "legal" that should be defined, and I am quite content with the statement in the same paragraph that "a finding is legal when it involves the interpretation or application of legal principles." It is a mistake to define terms that do not need definition. There is no need to define "factual". Moreover, I find the definition offered vague and unhelpful.

Done in English and French, the English version being authoritative.

Dated this eighteenth day of July 2007
At The Hague
The Netherlands

Judge Patrick Robinson

[Seal of the Tribunal]

Commentary

1. Introduction

These four decisions,[1] three from *Prosecutor v. Dragomir Milošević* and one from *Prosecutor v. Delić*, concern the application of judicial notice under Rule 94 of the Rules of Procedure and Evidence. Despite extensive case law on this topic, certain aspects of judicial notice remain unclear and are applied in various ways by the Trial and Appeals Chamber. This commentary will consider some of these.

First, the considerations of the Trial and Appeals Chamber in *Dragomir Milošević* will be discussed, involving the reasoning on taking judicial notice of legal terms and characterizations under Rule 94 (A). Then, I will argue that Rule 94 (B) is best understood and, in fact, can only be applied properly, when chambers make a strict distinction between admissibility requirements and discretionary considerations.

The second part of this commentary will discuss the decision in *Prosecutor v. Delić*, concerning the clarification of the admissibility requirement that proposed facts should be truly adjudicated.

2. Rule 94 (A) - Facts of Common Knowledge and Legal Terms

A recurring topic in the application of judicial notice is whether legal terms or legal characterizations can be judicially noticed as facts of common knowledge. Under Rule 94 (B), chambers are not allowed to take judicial notice of adjudicated facts that contain essentially legal terms. Whether the Trial Chamber may judicially notice legal terms as facts of common knowledge under Rule 94 (A) is controversial. In the present case, the Trial Chamber applied the standard formulated by the Appeals Chamber in Karemera to determine whether a proposed fact is a fact of common knowledge: is it notorious and beyond reasonable dispute?[2] If so, the chamber is obliged to take judicial notice: Rule 94 (A) leaves the chamber no room for discretion. This means that it is irrelevant whether the proposed fact contains a legal term: when the fact is notorious and beyond reasonable dispute, judicial notice has to be taken, without discussing the nature of the proposed fact, or the legal term contained in it.

In the present case, the Appeals Chamber observed that the question as to whether a term is a legal one could not even be considered under Rule 94 (A): the only test the chamber must apply is whether the proposed fact is notorious and beyond reasonable dispute.[3] The prosecution's ground of appeal on this point, arguing that the Trial Chamber erred in its reading of the Karemera Appeals Chamber decision, was dismissed.

3. Rule 94 (B) - Admissibility and discretionary considerations

The prosecution in Dragomir Milošević requested the Trial Chamber, pursuant to Rule 94 (B), to judicially notice 181 facts that were finally settled on appeal in *Prosecutor v. Galić*.[4] The proposed facts concerned crimes

---

1 ICTY, Decision on Prosecution's Motion for Judicial Notice of Adjudicated Facts and Prosecution's Catalogue of Agreed Facts with Dissenting Opinion of Judge Harhoff, *Prosecutor v. Dragomir Milošević*, Case No. IT-98-29/1-T, T. Ch. III, 10 April 2007, in this volume, p. 311; ICTY, Decision on Interlocutory Appeals Against Trial Chamber's Decision on Prosecution's Motion for Judicial Notice of Adjudicated Facts and Prosecution's Catalogue of Agreed Facts, *Prosecutor v. Dragomir Milošević*, Case No. IT-98-29/1-AR73.1, A. Ch., 26 June 2006, in this volume, p. 323; ICTY, Decision on Prosecution's Motion for Judicial Notice of Adjudicated Facts and Joint Motion Concerning Agreed Fact, *Prosecutor v. Delić*, Case No. IT-04-83-PT, T. Ch. I, 9 July 2007, in this volume, p. 333; ICTY, Decision on Appeals Chamber Remand of Judicial Notice of Adjudicated Facts with Seperate Opinion of Judge Robinson, *Prosecutor v. Dragomir Milošević*, Case No. IT-98-29/1-T, T. Ch. III, 18 July 2007, in this volume, p. 339.

2 Reference is made to ICTR, Decision on Prosecutor's Interlocutory Appeal of Decision on Judicial Notice, *Prosecutor v. Karemera, Ngirumpatse and Nzirorera*, Case No. ICTR-98-44-AR73(C), A. Ch., 16 June 2006, Klip/ Sluiter, ALC-XXIV-283, par. 22; ICTY, Decision on appellant's motion for judicial notice, *Prosecutor v. Momir Nikolić*, Case No. IT-02-60/1-A, A. Ch., 1 April 2005, Klip/ Sluiter, ALC-XXVII-345, par. 10; ICTY, Decision on the Prosecution's Interlocutory Appeal Against the Trial Chamber's 10 April 2003 Decision on Prosecution Motion for Judicial Notice of Adjudicated Facts, *Prosecutor v. Milošević*, IT-02-54-AR73.5, A. Ch, 28 October 2003, Klip/ Sluiter, ALC-XV-73, p. 3–4.

3 Decision on Interlocutory Appeals Against Trial Chamber's Decision on Prosecution's Motion for Judicial Notice of Adjudicated Facts and Prosecution's Catalogue of Agreed Facts, *Prosecutor v. Dragomir Milošević*, A. Ch., *supra* note 1, par. 21.

4 Decision on Prosecution's Motion for Judicial Notice of Adjudicated Facts and Prosecution's Catalogue of Agreed Facts with Dissenting Opinion of Judge Harhoff, *Prosecutor v. Dragomir Milošević*, T. Ch. III, *supra* note 1, par. 2.

committed under the command of Stanislav Galić, the predecessor of the accused as commander of the Sarajevo Romanija Corps of the VRS. Although those proposed facts do not directly concern the charges the accused is facing, they have, according to the prosecution, "a strong link with the crimes charged in the Indictment."[5]

It is further argued that the proposed facts prove that the accused "inherited and continued" the sniping and shelling campaign against the city and civilians of Sarajevo. Consequently, the accused had knowledge, or at least was put on notice, of these crimes.[6]

According to well established case law, chambers may judicially notice facts that relate to the defendant's guilt, but may not notice facts that go to the acts, conduct or mental state of the accused.[7] This distinction remains a contested one, and is discussed in most motions on judicial notice.[8] The Appeals Chamber in Karemera convincingly commented on the rationale and application of judicial notice of adjudicated facts under Rule 94 (B):

> "The purpose of a criminal trial is to adjudicate the criminal responsibility of the accused. Facts that are not related, directly or indirectly, to that criminal responsibility are not relevant to the question to be adjudicated at trial, and, [...] thus may neither be established by evidence nor through judicial notice. So judicial notice under Rule 94 (B) is in fact available *only* for adjudicated facts that bear, at least in some respect, on the criminal responsibility of the accused."[9]

The Appeals Chamber emphasizes that chambers may only admit evidence that is relevant to the current proceedings, which means that it must have some probative value for the establishment of the accused's guilt.[10] The determination of whether a proposed fact touches upon the criminal responsibility of the accused, but at the same time does not go to the acts, conduct and mental state of the accused, remains difficult and the outcome is not predicted easily.

In the present case, the Trial Chamber concluded that the proposed facts are relevant to the proceedings and do not go to the acts, conduct or mental state of the accused and, therefore, comply with the admissibility requirements for judicial notice. However, the Trial Chamber enjoys discretion to withhold judicial notice in the interests of justice, even when all admissibility requirements have been fulfilled. The Trial Chamber denied judicial notice, because to judicially notice the proposed facts would be inconsistent with the rights of the accused, protected under Article 21 of the statute.

The proposed facts, relating to crimes committed by the accused's predecessor, have "a strong link" with the charges in the indictment, and to take judicial notice of them would violate the right to examine witnesses. The strong link refers to the fact that, if judicial notice was taken, it would be established, or it could be inferred, that the accused was put on notice of the existence of crimes committed under the command of his predecessor. Consequently, the burden to prove that crimes continued to be committed under the command of the accused with his knowledge would be lowered.[11]

---

5 *Ibid.*, par. 32.

6 *Ibid.*, par. 10.

7 Among many other authorities; Decision on Prosecutor's Interlocutory Appeal of Decision on Judicial Notice, *Prosecutor v. Karemera, Ngirumpatse and Nzirorera*, A. Ch., *supra* note 2, par. 50. It is for each chamber to carefully distinguish between facts that bear upon the criminal responsibility of the accused without going to the acts, conduct or mental state of the accused, and those facts that tend to prove *mens rea* elements. A chamber may take judicial notice of the former category, but not the latter.

8 For example, ICTY, Prosecution's Sixth Motion for Judicial Notice of Adjudicated Facts, *Prosecutor v. Stanišić and Župljanin*, Case No. IT-08-91-T, T. Ch. II, 2 February 2010; ICTY, Second Set of Objections to Prosecution's Motion for Judicial Notice of Adjudicated Facts Concerning Sarajevo, *Prosecutor Perišić*, Case No. IT-04-81-PT, T. Ch. III, 8 March 2007; ICTR, Decision on the Prosecution Motion for Judicial Notice, *Prosecutor v. Kanyarukiga*, Case No. ICTR-2002-78-I, T. Ch. II, 14 May 2009, par. 22; ICTR, Decision on Prosecution's Motion for Judicial Notice Pursuant to Rule 73, 89 and 94, *Prosecutor v. Bizimungu et al.*, Case No. ICTR-99-50-I, T. Ch. II, 2 December 2003, par. 12; SCSL, Decision on the Prosecution Motion for Judicial Notice, *Prosecutor v. Taylor*, Case No. SCSL-03-1-T, T. Ch. II, 7 December 2007, par. 5 and 6; SCSL, Decision on Appeal Against "Decision on Prosecution's Motion for Judicial Notice and Admission of Evidence, *Prosecutor v. Norman et al.*, Case No. SCSL-2004-14-AR73, A. Ch., 16 May 2005, par. 7.

9 Decision on Prosecutor's Interlocutory Appeal of Decision on Judicial Notice, *Prosecutor v. Karemera, Ngirumpatse and Nzirorera*, A. Ch., *supra* note 2, par. 48, (emphasis in original). The Appeals Chamber acknowledges that it departs from the view held by several Trial Chambers that denied judicial notice of facts that went, directly or indirectly, to the criminal responsibility of the accused.

10 *Cf.* Rule 89 (C): "A Chamber may admit any relevant evidence which it deems to have probative value."

11 Decision on Prosecution's Motion for Judicial Notice of Adjudicated Facts and Prosecution's Catalogue of Agreed Facts with Dissenting Opinion of Judge Harhoff, *Prosecutor v. Dragomir Milošević*, T. Ch. III, *supra* note 1, par. 32.

In reaching this conclusion, the Trial Chamber does not discern between what I would call admissibility requirements ("is the proposed fact truly adjudicated?"), and discretionary considerations ("is it in the interest of justice to judicially notice the adjudicated fact?"). The Trial Chamber stated that, in exercising its discretion to withhold judicial notice, it must consider whether the proposed fact is distinct, concrete and identifiable. Moreover, the fact may not differ substantively from the original judgement, it must not be subject to appeal or review, or be the result of agreements between the parties, such as a plea agreement. The proposed fact must be a factual one, and it must be in the interests of justice to take judicial notice. To determine whether it is in the interests of justice to take judicial notice, regard must be had to judicial economy and the fair trial rights of the accused.[12]

This is reminiscent of the 2003 Krajišnik requirements, where the Trial Chamber for the first time enumerated the criteria for judicial notice in a comprehensive manner. The present decision, though, differs from Krajišnik in the categorisation of the requirements. In my opinion, Rule 94 (B) provides for a two pronged test: first, the proposed fact must meet the nine Krajišnik admissibility requirements.[13] The first requirement, ("The fact must have some relevance to an issue in the current proceedings"), repeats the general requirement of relevance of Rule 89 (C) and is, in fact, redundant.

Secondly, when the proposed fact complies with the admissibility requirements, it remains within the Trial Chamber's discretion to deny judicial notice. Reasons to deny judicial notice on discretionary grounds include fair trial and judicial economy considerations.[14] The Trial Chamber in the present case does not distinguish clearly between admissibility considerations and discretionary ones. In fact, the Trial Chamber considers both categories to fall under the discretionary power of the chamber under Rule 94 (B), whereas other chambers do make a strict separation between the two categories.[15]

The distinction is not insignificant. In appellate proceedings, findings of the Trial Chamber based on a discretionary power are overturned only when the Trial Chamber incorrectly applied governing law, when the finding is based on a patently incorrect conclusion of fact, or when the finding is so unreasonable as to constitute abuse of the discretionary power.[16] Appellate proceedings are, therefore, not trials *de novo*. To maintain that the considerations of the Trial Chamber to grant or deny judicial notice fall under the overall discretionary power of the Trial Chamber under Rule 94 (B) would result in denying the accused the right to have the decision reviewed on appeal in a substantive way.

---

12 Decision on Prosecution's Motion for Judicial Notice of Adjudicated Facts and Prosecution's Catalogue of Agreed Facts with Dissenting Opinion of Judge Harhoff, *Prosecutor v. Dragomir Milošević*, T. Ch. III, *supra* note 1, par. 27.

13 These nine requirements are: 1) The fact must have some relevance to an issue in the current proceedings; 2) The fact must be distinct, concrete and identifiable; 3) The fact as formulated by the moving party must not differ in any substantial way from the formulation of the original judgement; 4) The fact must not be unclear or misleading in the context in which it is placed in the moving party's motion; 5) The fact must be identified with adequate precision by the moving party; 6) The fact must not contain characterizations of an essentially legal nature; 7) The fact must not be based on an agreement between the parties to the original proceedings; 8) The fact must not relate to the acts, conduct, or mental state of the accused; and 9) The fact must clearly not be subject to pending appeal or review. ICTY, Decision on Prosecution Motions for Judicial Notice of Adjudicated Facts and for Admission of Written Statements of Witnesses Pursuant to Rule 92bis, *Prosecutor v. Krajišnik*, Case No. IT-00-39-PT, T. Ch. I, 28 February 2003, par. 15. This two-pronged test is also applied in: ICTY, Decision on Prosecution Motion for Judicial Notice of Adjudicated Facts Pursuant to Rule 94 (B), *Prosecutor v. Tolimir*, Case No. IT-05-88/2-PT, T. Ch. II, 17 December 2009; ICTY, Decision on Popović Motion for Judicial Notice of Adjudicated Facts with Annex, *Prosecutor v. Popović et al.*, Case No. IT-05-88-T, T. Ch. II, 2 June 2008.

14 ICTY, Decision on Motion for Judicial Notice of Adjudicated Facts Pursuant to Rule 94 (B), *Prosecutor v. Prlić et al.*, Case No. IT-04-74-PT, T. Ch. II, 14 March 2006, par. 21; ICTY, Decision on prosecution motion for judicial notice of adjudicated facts with annex, *Prosecutor v. Popović et al.*, Case No. IT-05-88, T. Ch. II, 26 September 2006, Klip/ Sluiter, ALC-XXX-139, par. 16.

15 For example, Decision on Prosecution Motion for Judicial Notice of Adjudicated Facts with Annex, *Prosecutor v. Popović et al.*, T. Ch. II, *supra* note 14, par. 4; Decision on Motion for Judicial Notice of Adjudicated Facts Pursuant to Rule 94 (B), *Prosecutor v. Prlić et al.*, T. Ch. II, *supra* note 14, par. 12; ICTY, Decision on Judicial Notice of Adjudicated Facts Following the Motion Submitted by Counsel for the Accused Hadžihasanović and Kubura on 20 January 2005, *Prosecutor v. Hadžihasanović and Kubura*, Case No. IT-01-47-T, T. Ch. II, 14 April 2005, p. 4. An example of such a separation can be found in ICTY, Decision on Third Prosecution's Motion for Judicial Notice of Adjudicated Facts, *Prosecutor v. Stanišić and Simatović*, Case No. IT-03-69-T, T. Ch. I, 23 July 2010; Decision on Prosecution's Motion for Judicial Notice of Adjudicated Facts and Prosecution's Catalogue of Agreed Facts with Dissenting Opinion of Judge Harhoff, *Prosecutor v. Dragomir Milošević*, T. Ch. III, *supra* note 1, par. 27.

16 Decision on Interlocutory Appeals Against Trial Chamber's Decision on Prosecution's Motion for Judicial Notice of Adjudicated Facts and Prosecution's Catalogue of Agreed Facts, *Prosecutor v. Dragomir Milošević*, A. Ch., *supra* note 1, par. 5.; Decision on Prosecutor's Interlocutory Appeal of Decision on Judicial Notice, *Prosecutor v. Karemera, Ngirumpatse and Nzirorera*, A. Ch., *supra* note 2, par. 43.

The Appeals Chamber in the present case, however, does not agree with the Trial Chamber, and reviews the admissibility considerations of the Trial Chamber thoroughly.[17] The Appeals Chamber first considered that the proposed facts, although concerning crimes committed before the time period in the indictment, are relevant to the present case.[18] The Appeals Chamber reiterated the reasoning in Karemera: it is prohibited to take judicial notice of adjudicated facts that relate to the acts, conduct and mental state of the accused, but it does not follow from Karemera that it is prohibited to take judicial notice of facts relating to the commission of crimes the accused is not even charged with.[19]

The Appeals Chamber emphasized that judicial notice is taken only of the *existence* of the crimes, and not whether the accused had knowledge of these crimes or was put on notice. Knowledge of the crimes must be proven by means other than judicial notice, such as witness testimony. This follows logically from the requirement that the *actus reus* and *mens rea* can only be proven by means other than judicial notice. The Appeals Chamber underlined this by opposing the prosecution's submission that knowledge of the crimes could be inferred from the adjudicated facts, together with other evidence. The Appeals Chamber held that the Trial Chamber may not infer conclusions from the adjudicated facts when it comes to notice of the accused: evidence of notice must be presented separately and by means other than judicial notice.[20]

This is in line with Karemera: to act otherwise would be equal to judicially noticing facts that relate to the mental state of the accused. In conclusion, the Trial Chamber, in its discretion, committed a discernable error in denying judicial notice of all proposed facts. The case was remanded to the Trial Chamber that made the contested decision for further consideration.

4. Remanded procedure

The reasoning of the Trial Chamber, reconsidering its earlier decision, is somewhat ambiguous:

> "The adjudicated facts at issue are relevant to the background of the case, or could provide circumstantial evidence from which the notice of the Accused of crimes committed under his command could be inferred. In light of the Appeals Chamber directions as to the type of evidence on which a finding on the notice of the Accused must be based, these facts cannot be used to establish notice. However, in light of the significance of the adjudicated facts for the historical and factual background of the Prosecution's case, the Trial Chamber concludes that facts related to crimes committed under the command of Galić, but which do not contain findings of an essentially legal nature, should be judicially noticed."[21]

The facts are relevant and significant for the prosecution's case, but no notice of the accused can be derived from them, so the Trial Chamber concludes. It remains unclear, then, how these facts could provide circumstantial evidence. If the notice or knowledge of the accused of certain crimes is derived in any way from the judicially noticed facts, then the right of the accused to examine the witnesses is still violated. The conclusion must be that judicially noticed facts cannot be used to prove any mental element of the accused: not as a rebuttable presumption, nor as circumstantial evidence.

What is meant by "historical and factual background" remains vague and it is questionable whether the adjudicated facts are background facts at all. As referred to by the Trial Chamber itself, the prosecution submitted to the chamber that the adjudicated facts go to prove that:

---

17 Decision on Interlocutory Appeals Against Trial Chamber's Decision on Prosecution's Motion for Judicial Notice of Adjudicated Facts and Prosecution's Catalogue of Agreed Facts, *Prosecutor v. Dragomir Milošević*, A. Ch., *supra* note 1, par. 13–14, 19–22. The Appeals Chamber thoroughly reviews the findings of the Trial Chamber on "relevance" and "facts of an essential nature".

18 Decision on Interlocutory Appeals Against Trial Chamber's Decision on Prosecution's Motion for Judicial Notice of Adjudicated Facts and Prosecution's Catalogue of Agreed Facts, *Prosecutor v. Dragomir Milošević*, A. Ch., *supra* note 1, par. 13–14.

19 Decision on Interlocutory Appeals Against Trial Chamber's Decision on Prosecution's Motion for Judicial Notice of Adjudicated Facts and Prosecution's Catalogue of Agreed Facts, *Prosecutor v. Dragomir Milošević*, A. Ch., *supra* note 1, par. 16.

20 Decision on Appeals Chamber Remand of Judicial Notice of Adjudicated Facts with Seperate Opinion of Judge Robinson, *Prosecutor v. Dragomir Milošević*, T. Ch. III, *supra* note 1, par. 5.

21 Decision on Appeals Chamber Remand of Judicial Notice of Adjudicated Facts with Seperate Opinion of Judge Robinson, *Prosecutor v. Dragomir Milošević*, T. Ch. III, *supra* note 1, par. 12.

> "the Accused was instrumental and a part of putting together [...the] criminal scheme into place [...] and [...] in August of 1994, when he became the commander of the SRK, he continued that scheme and did nothing to stop it."[22]

This remark seems to indicate that the adjudicated facts do not represent historical or factual background to the case, but rather relate to the *mens rea* of the accused: did he know that the crimes had taken place under the command of his predecessor and did he fail to prevent their continued occurrence under his command? This way, more than the mere existence of the crimes is judicially noticed. The inferences the prosecution wishes to draw from these proposed facts do not seem to be in line with settled case law on judicial notice.

The Trial Chamber commented on the distinction between legal and factual findings. As stated above, this distinction results in a lot of discussion, and a sound definition of the two categories is to be welcomed. In older case law, the following definition is often used:

> "many findings have a legal aspect, if one is to construe this expression broadly. It is therefore necessary to determine on a case-by-case basis whether the proposed fact contains findings or characterizations which are of an *essentially* legal nature, and which must, therefore be excluded."[23]

This is actually more a specification than a definition: only essentially legal characterizations are not to be judicially noticed. What a legal characterization actually is, remains unclear. The Milošević Trial Chamber defined a finding as legal "when it involves the interpretation or application of legal principles". A finding is factual "when it requires a description of circumstances surrounding the case at hand."[24] Some examples could have clarified the distinction even more, but the Trial Chamber did not provide any. In his Separate Opinion, Judge Robinson agrees with the definition of a legal term, but considers the definition of a factual finding "vague and unhelpful."[25]

5. Rule 94 (B) – Appeal Proceedings and Judicial Notice

The decision in *Prosecutor v. Delić* concerns the question as to when a proposed fact is truly adjudicated. Under the Krajišnik admissibility requirements, a fact may be judicially noticed when the fact is clearly not subject to appeal or review.[26] This is obviously the case when a Trial Chamber judgement is not appealed and has become final, or when the appeal is concentrated on a specific part of the judgement, such as sentencing.

The prosecution in Delić argued that the 250 proposed facts it sought judicial notice of, complied with this requirement. The proposed facts were derived from the Trial Chamber's judgement in *Prosecutor v. Hadžihasanović et al.*[27] Although this judgement is under appeal, the prosecution argued that this did not result in the inadmissibility of all facts contained in the Trial Chamber's judgement: only those facts that were specifically addressed in the parties' notices of appeal are inadmissible, because they cannot be considered truly adjudicated.[28]

---

22 Decision on Appeals Chamber Remand of Judicial Notice of Adjudicated Facts with Seperate Opinion of Judge Robinson, *Prosecutor v. Dragomir Milošević*, T. Ch. III, *supra* note 1, par. 12, footnote 16.

23 ICTY, Decision on Third and Fourth Prosecution Motions for Judicial Notice of Adjudicated Facts, *Prosecutor v. Krajišnik*, Case No. IT-00-39-T, T. Ch. I, 24 March 2005, par. 15, (emphasis in original).

24 Decision on Appeals Chamber Remand of Judicial Notice of Adjudicated Facts with Seperate Opinion of Judge Robinson, *Prosecutor v. Dragomir Milošević*, T. Ch. III, *supra* note 1, par. 11.

25 ICTY, Separate Opinion Judge Robinson, *Prosecutor v. Dragomir Milošević*, Case No. IT-98-29/1-T, T. Ch. III, 18 July 2007, in this volume, p. 343, par. 2.

26 Decision on Prosecution Motions for Judicial Notice of Adjudicated Facts and for Admission of Written Statements of Witnesses Pursuant to Rule 92bis, *Prosecutor v. Krajišnik*, T. Ch. I, *supra* note 13, par. 15.

27 ICTY, Prosecution Motion for Judicial Notice of Adjudicated Facts, *Prosecutor v. Delić*, Case No. IT-04-83-PT, T. Ch. III, 29 September 2006, par. 1.

28 *Ibid.*, par. 11–12. References are made to: Decision on Third and Fourth Prosecution Motions for Judicial Notice of Adjudicated Facts, *Prosecutor v. Momcilo Krajišnik*, T. Ch. I, *supra* note 23, par. 14.; Decision on Motion for Judicial Notice of Adjudicated Facts Pursuant to Rule 94 (B), *Prosecutor v. Prlić et al.*, T. Ch. II, *supra* note 14, par. 12.

The defence argued, predictably, that all the proposed facts are not truly adjudicated, not because they were under appellate scrutiny, but because the "methodology of the conduct of the trial" is subject to appeal.[29] The argument was raised in Hadžihasanović that the bench erred in law, because it systematically questioned witnesses. This, according to the Hadžihasanović defence, resulted in partiality of the court.[30]

The Delić Trial Chamber considered that the case law of the Tribunals forbids taking judicial notice of *facts* that are subject to appeal: a judgement under appeal does not, as such, render the proposed facts inadmissible.[31] The Trial Chamber further stated that the ground of appeal raised by the Hadžihasanović defence, if upheld by the Appeals Chamber, would "undermine the integrity of the entire *Hadžihasanović et al.* judgement."[32] Therefore, the ground of appeal directly challenges the factual findings of the judgement rendering the proposed facts not truly adjudicated. Judicial notice was accordingly denied.

To me, this reasoning is not entirely convincing. The defence in Hadžihasanović indeed filed an important ground of appeal, but the Delić Trial Chamber, in dismissing the motion for judicial notice, could have distinguished between the sources supporting the facts that were proven in the Hadžihasanović trial judgement. It is unclear whether all the proposed facts were derived from witness testimony. If that were the case, the reasoning of the Trial Chamber, despite its limited reasoning, is correct: witness testimony is challenged in Hadžihasanović, rendering facts that are based on that testimony not truly adjudicated. One could even distinguish between each witness testimony: did the bench question the particular witness? If not, the proposed fact is truly adjudicated.

If the proposed facts are derived from sources other than witness testimony, judicial notice could have been granted. After all, the ground of appeal is concerned with witness testimony, and not with other means of proof. What is more, the fact that a judgement in its entirety is labelled unfair on appeal, does not necessarily mean that all facts contained in it are unsound.

In this respect, the Delić Trial Chamber could have distinguished between different categories of facts. In not doing so, the chamber creates a precedent that might slow down the pace of ongoing trials: if there is mere allegation that a trial has been unfair because of "activist" judges, judicial notice of facts based on witness testimony can only be based on final judgements, being either appeal judgements or trial judgement where no appeal was lodged. The defence's ground of appeal might be substantiated by proof, but the limited reasoning of the chamber in denying judicial notice is rather disappointing.

6. Conclusion

The guidance provided by the Appeals Chamber on the separation between admissibility and discretionary considerations in deciding on judicial notice motions is to be welcomed. Not only does the Appeals Chamber provide us with a clear test, it also ensures that the discretion the Trial Chamber enjoys under Rule 94 (B) is not extended to the formal, technical admissibility requirements. The Appeals Chamber also stated unequivocally that judicial notice may not be taken of facts that relate to the mental state of the accused. To prove *mens rea* elements, the prosecution must present means of proof other than judicial notice.

Despite the clear reasoning of the Appeals Chamber, the Milošević Trial Chamber in the remanded procedure creates some ambiguity on the probative value of the judicially noticed facts: the facts cannot be used to establish notice, but are, nevertheless, relevant to the historical and factual background of the case.

---

29 Prosecution Motion for Judicial Notice of Adjudicated Facts, *Prosecutor v. Delić*, T. Ch. III, *supra* note 27, par. 4.

30 *Ibid.*, par. 4.

31 As referred to by the Trial Chamber, the Ljubičić Trial Chamber stated that "judicial notice of adjudicated facts should generally not be taken of facts which are *themselves* being appealed"; Prosecution Motion for Judicial Notice of Adjudicated Facts, *Prosecutor v. Delić*, T. Ch. III, *supra* note 27, par. 13, footnote 38. Unlike the Trial Chamber in Dragomir Milošević, the Delić Trial Chamber made a strict separation between admissibility considerations and discretionary ones. *Cf.* Decision on Prosecution Motions for Judicial Notice of Adjudicated Facts and for Admission of Written Statements of Witnesses Pursuant to Rule 92bis, *Prosecutor v. Krajišnik*, T. Ch. I, *supra* note 13, par. 14.

32 Prosecution Motion for Judicial Notice of Adjudicated Facts, *Prosecutor v. Delić*, T. Ch. III, *supra* note 27, par. 14.

The Appeals Chamber reiterated that the only test that Trial Chambers are to conduct in determining whether a fact is a fact of common knowledge is whether the proposed fact is notorious and beyond reasonable dispute. The nature of the fact, legal or factual, cannot, by definition, be considered.

The decision in *Prosecutor v. Delić,* concerning the requirement that a proposed fact must be truly adjudicated, can be detrimental to the pace of proceedings at the *ad hoc* tribunals. In my opinion, the Trial Chamber should have distinguished between different categories of facts, instead of denying the motion for judicial notice in its entirety.

Koen Vriend

UNITED
NATIONS

International Tribunal for the Prosecution of Persons Responsible for Serious Violations of International Humanitarian Law Committed in the Territory of the former Yugoslavia since 1991	Case No.: IT-05-88/1-PT Date: 1 June 2007 Original: English

---

TRIAL CHAMBER II

Before: **Judge Carmel Agius, Presiding**
Judge O-Gon Kwon
Judge Kimberly Prost

Registrar: **Mr. Hans Holthuis**

Decision of: **1 June 2007**

PROSECUTOR

v.

MILORAD TRBIĆ

PUBLIC

DECISION ON TRIAL CHAMBER'S COMPETENCE TO ENTERTAIN MOTION FILED AFTER ENTRY INTO FORCE OF DECISION UNDER RULE 11 BIS

Office of the Prosecutor
Mr. Peter McCloskey
Mr. Kweku Vanderpuye

Counsel for the Accused
Mr. Stéphane Piletta-Zanin

[page 1] THIS TRIAL CHAMBER of the International Tribunal for the Prosecution of Persons Responsible for Serious Violations of International Humanitarian Law Committed in the Territory of the former Yugoslavia since 1991 ("Tribunal");

NOTING the "Motion to Suspend Following Registry Decision of 7 May 2007", filed confidentially in the original French on 17 May 2007;[1]

NOTING the "Decision on Referral of Case Under Rule 11 *bis*" of 27 April 2007 ("Referral Decision"), in which the Referral Bench decided to refer the Accused's case to the authorities of Bosnia and Herzegovina;[2]

NOTING that Rule 11 *bis*(I) of the Rules of Procedure and Evidence of the Tribunal provides, in pertinent part, that "[a]n appeal by the accused or the Prosecutor shall lie as of right from a decision of the Referral Bench whether or not to refer a case", and that "[n]otice of appeal shall be filed within fifteen days of the decision";[3]

CONSIDERING that neither the Accused nor the Prosecution filed notice of appeal against the Referral Decision within the 15-day limit prescribed by Rule 11 *bis*(I),[4] and that the Referral Decision therefore became final on 14 May 2007;[5]

CONSIDERING that, while the Referral Bench retains the power to issue certain orders in a referred case after its decision on referral has become final,[6] the Trial Chamber seised of pre-trial **[page 2]** proceedings in a referred case lacks competence to consider any motions filed subsequent to the date on which the Bench's decision becomes final, including through the issuance of a decision by the Appeals Chamber upholding the Bench's decision,[7] and where neither party has filed notice of appeal against the decision within the 15-day time limit in Rule 11 *bis*(I);

---

1 This motion was signed on 16 May 2007 and the English translation was filed on 29 May 2007.

2 Referral Decision, para. 49(a).

3 Rule 11 *bis*(I).

4 In a letter dated 2 May 2007 and filed publicly on 3 May 2007, the Accused informed the Registrar that he did not intend to file an appeal against the Referral Decision. *See* Letter from Milorad Trbić to Hans Holthuis, 3 May 2007, p. 1. Since this filing was not made by Counsel for the Accused, it cannot be regarded as a formal waiver of the right of appeal having the effect of making the Referral Decision final. *See* Registry Submission Pursuant to Rule 33(B) of the Rules of Procedure and Evidence Regarding the Status of Defence Counsel, 4 May 2007, p. 2 (stating that, as of 4 May 2007, Counsel for the Accused "is still officially assigned to the Accused").

5 Counting from the day after the day on which the Referral Decision was issued, the deadline to file notice of appeal would have fallen on 12 May 2007. *Cf. Prosecutor v. Popović, Beara, Nikolić, Borovčanin, Miletić, Gvero, and Pandurević*, Case No. IT-05-88-T, Decision Regarding Evidence of General Rupert Smith and the Calculation of Time Limits Under Rule 126 *bis*, 30 March 2007, p. 2 (interpreting the language "within fourteen days" in Rule 126 *bis* as "excluding the day the original motion is filed"). As 12 May 2007 was a Saturday, and thus "a day when the Registry of the Tribunal does not accept documents for filing", such notice would have been considered timely had it been filed "on the first day thereafter when the Registry does accept documents for filing"—that is, Monday, 14 May 2007. *See* Rule 126(B).

6 *See* Rules 11 *bis*(D)–(F). *See also, e.g., Prosecutor v. Mejakić, Gruban, Fuštar, and Knežević*, Case No. IT-02-65-PT, Order on Prosecution Request for an Extension of Time to File Progress Report, 25 September 2006 (issued five months after Appeals Chamber decision upholding referral); *Prosecutor v. Ljubičić*, Case No. IT-00-41-PT, Decision on Defence Request for Handover of Confidential Material, confidential, 22 September 2006 (issued two months after Appeals Chamber decision upholding referral); *Prosecutor v. Janković*, Case No. IT-96-23/2-PT, Decision on Former Counsel's Motion for Leave to Hand Over Confidential Documents to New Counsel, partly confidential, 23 June 2006 (issued seven months after Appeals Chamber decision upholding referral); *Prosecutor v. Trbić*, Case No. IT-05-88/1-PT, Decision on Referral of Case Under Rule 11 *bis*, 27 April 2007, para. 41 (Referral Bench "recall[ing] its power under Rules 11 *bis*(F) and (G) to revoke the referral of this case and compel the Accused's return to the seat of the Tribunal if [...] it will not be possible for him to receive a fair trial").

7 *See Prosecutor v. Janković*, Case No. IT-96-23/2-PT, Decision on Prosecution's Motion for Reconsideration, confidential, 6 October 2005, p. 3 (considering that "the Prosecutor prejudges [...] the Appeals Chamber's decision on the [Referral Bench's decision to refer the case] when assuming that the pre-trial status of the case ceases with the [Bench's decision]", and that "the pre-trial status of the case will effectively cease when and if the Appeals Chamber renders a decision that confirms the Decision on Referral"). Several decisions have been taken by Trial Chambers after an order by the Referral Bench for referral under Rule 11 *bis*, but before the issuance of a decision by the Appeals Chamber upholding such referral. *See, e.g., ibid.*; *Prosecutor v. Janković*, Case No. IT-96-23/2-PT, Decision on Prosecution's Motion for Reconsideration, confidential, 6 October 2005; *Prosecutor v. Janković*, Case No. IT-96-23/2-PT, Decision on Janković's Motion for Provisional Release, 21 September 2005; *Prosecutor v. Rašević and Todović*, Case No. IT-97-25/1-PT, Decision on Savo Todović's Application for Provisional Release, 22 July 2005. Moreover, one Trial Chamber has held status conferences during this period. *See Prosecutor v. Rašević and Todović*, Case No. IT-97-25/1-PT, T. 175–187 (20 October 2005); *Prosecutor v. Rašević and Todović*, Case No. IT-97-25/1-PT, T. 188–195 (21 February 2006).

CONCLUDES that the Trial Chamber is not competent to deal with the Motion.

Done in English and French, the English text being authoritative.

Dated this first day of June 2007
At The Hague
The Netherlands

Carmel Agius
Presiding

[Seal of the Tribunal]

UNITED NATIONS

International Tribunal for the Prosecution of Persons Responsible for Serious Violations of International Humanitarian Law Committed in the Territory of the Former Yugoslavia since 1991	Case No.	IT-98-32/1-AR11*bis*.1
	Date:	11 July 2007
	Original:	English

IN THE APPEALS CHAMBER

Before: **Judge Theodor Meron, Presiding**
Judge Mohamed Shahabuddeen
Judge Mehmet Güney
Judge Liu Daqun
Judge Andrésia Vaz

Registrar: **Mr. Hans Holthuis**

Decision of: **11 July 2007**

PROSECUTOR

v.

MILAN LUKIĆ &
SREDOJE LUKIĆ

PUBLIC

DECISION ON MILAN LUKIĆ'S APPEAL REGARDING REFERRAL

The Office of the Prosecutor:
Mr. David Tolbert
Ms. Marie-Ursula Kind
Mr. Aleksandar Kontić

Counsel for Milan Lukić
Mr. Alan L. Yatvin
Ms. Jelena Đ. Lopičić Jančić

Counsel for Sredoje Lukić
Mr. Đuro Čepić
Mr. Jens Dieckmann

[page 1] 1. The Appeals Chamber of the International Tribunal for the Prosecution of Persons Responsible for Serious Violations of International Humanitarian Law Committed in the Territory of the Former Yugoslavia since 1991 ("Appeals Chamber" and "Tribunal", respectively) is seized of an appeal by Milan Lukić ("Appellant") against the Referral Bench's "Decision on Referral of Case Pursuant to Rule 11*bis* with Confidential Annex A and Annex B", filed on 5 April 2007 ("Referral Decision").[1]

I. BACKGROUND

2. On 21 October 1998, the Prosecutor issued an indictment ("Indictment") against the Appellant and Sredoje Lukić, both Bosnian Serbs from the Višegrad municipality.[2] The Indictment alleged that the two men had belonged to a paramilitary unit known as the White Eagles[3] and that they had committed atrocities "from in or about April 1992 through in or about October 1994 in the Višegrad municipality and the surrounding area in the Republic of Bosnia and Herzegovina".[4] The Indictment charged both men with extermination, persecution, murder, and inhumane acts as crimes against humanity, and with murder, cruel treatment, and violence to life and person as violations of the laws or customs of war.[5] The charge of persecution was framed in general terms.[6] The other charges related to two specific occasions on which the two men were alleged to have forced Bosnian Muslim civilians into houses and set the houses on fire (resulting in a total of around 135 deaths) and to the accuseds' alleged periodic abuse of Bosnian Muslim men in a detention camp.[7] The Indictment also charged the Appellant with murder and inhumane acts as crimes against humanity, and with murder and violence to life and person as violations of the laws or customs of war, in relation to three other incidents involving attacks on 13 Bosnian Muslims (11 of whom were alleged to have been murdered in the course of the attacks).[8] The Indictment was confirmed on 26 October 1998.[9]

3. In July 2001, arrest warrants for both accused were issued.[10] By February 2005, however, they were still at large. That month, the Prosecutor filed a motion requesting that the case be **[page 2]** referred to Bosnia and Herzegovina ("BiH") pursuant to Rule 11*bis* of the Rules of Procedure and Evidence ("Rules") and seeking the appointment of a Referral Bench to consider this issue.[11] Rule 11*bis* provides a way for the Tribunal to send certain cases to domestic jurisdictions for trial. Specifically, Rule 11*bis*(A) provides that a Referral Bench appointed by the President may "determine whether [a] case should be referred to the authorities of a State: (i) in whose territory the crime was committed; or (ii) in which the accused was arrested; or (iii) having jurisdiction and being willing and adequately prepared to accept such a case." Rule 11*bis*(C) further specifies that in "determining whether to refer the case … the Referral Bench shall, in accordance with Security Council resolution 1534 (2004),[12] consider the gravity of the crimes charged and the level of responsibility of the accused". Finally, pursuant to Rule 11*bis*(B), the Referral Bench may only order referral upon "being satisfied that the accused will receive a fair trial [in the State to which the case is referred] and that the death penalty will not be imposed or carried out."

4. The President of the Tribunal accordingly convened a Referral Bench for the purpose of considering the appropriateness of referral to BiH.[13] Then, in September 2005, the ICTY gained custody over Sredoje

---

1 Notice of Appeal of Milan Lukić from 5 April 2007 Decision on Referral of Case Pursuant to Rule 11*bis*, 18 April 2007 ("Notice of Appeal"); Brief of Appellant Milan Lukić, 3 May 2007 ("Appeal Brief").

2 The Indictment also covered a third accused, Mitar Vasiljević, whose case was subsequently severed and who will not be discussed further in this decision. *See generally* Indictment; *see also Prosecutor v. Mitar Vasiljević*, Case No. IT-98-32-A, Judgement, 25 February 2004.

3 Indictment, paras 9–11. The Indictment suggested that the Appellant was the leader of this paramilitary unit. *See ibid.*, para. 11 (describing Sredoje Lukić as "join[ing the Appellant's] paramilitary unit").

4 Indictment, para. 13.

5 Indictment, paras 18–30, 38–40.

6 Indictment, paras 19–20.

7 Indictment, paras 18, 21–30, 38–40.

8 Indictment, paras 31–37.

9 Confidential Review of the Indictment, 26 October 1998.

10 *See* Motion by the Prosecutor Under Rule 11*bis*, 1 February 2005, paras 2, 4 ("Motion of 1 February 2005").

11 Motion of 1 February 2005; *see also* Request by the Prosecutor under Rule 11*bis*, 1 February 2005 ("Request of 1 February 2005").

12 U.N. Doc. S/RES/1534 (2004).

13 Order Appointing a Trial Chamber for the Purpose of Determining Whether an Indictment Should be Referred to Another Court under Rule 11*Bis*, 2 February 2005.

Lukić after his voluntary surrender. Also in the fall of 2005, the Argentine police apprehended the Appellant. He was transferred to the ICTY in February 2006, following a decision of the Argentine Federal National Criminal and Correctional Court No. 8 ("Argentine Court Order"). This decision authorized the Appellant's transfer to the Tribunal for trial and also authorized his subsequent extradition to Serbia (which has criminal charges pending against the Appellant and had requested his extradition).[14]

5. Shortly after the Appellant's transfer to the ICTY, the Prosecution sought to amend the indictment in relation to him.[15] Among other things, the revised indictment ("Second Amended Indictment") (1) specifically alleged that the Appellant had organised the White Eagles (also known as the Avengers);[16] (2) identified the factual bases for the crime of persecution;[17] (3) clarified the dates (or the range of dates) on which the alleged crimes occurred;[18] and (4) specified that all the **[page 3]** alleged crimes occurred within the Višegrad municipality.[19] The Trial Chamber granted leave to amend on 22 March 2006.[20]

6. In the meantime, the request for referral remained pending before the Referral Bench. The Referral Bench received submissions not only from the parties, but also, at its invitation, from Argentina and BiH.[21] In addition, the Referral Bench received submissions from Serbia, which requested that the case be referred to it rather than to BiH.[22] Along with the parties, representatives of all three countries participated in the oral hearing held by the Referral Bench on 15 September 2006.[23]

7. On 5 April 2007, the Referral Bench issued a decision referring the case to BiH. Looking to the allegations set forth in the Second Amended Indictment, the Referral Bench determined that while the crimes alleged were very serious, neither Sredoje Lukić nor the Appellant could be considered to hold the level of responsibility of "most senior leaders".[24] In light of these factors, the Referral Bench found that the case was "not *ipso facto* incompatible" with referral.[25] The Referral Bench further found that the most appropriate State for the referral was BiH – a conclusion it reached in part by taking note of the fact that "the victims were allegedly Bosnian Muslims and other non-Serb nationals or residents of Bosnia and Herzegovina."[26] Having considered the applicable substantive law in BiH, the Referral Bench went on to find that Sredoje Lukić and the Appellant would receive a fair trial if the case were referred to BiH and that the death penalty would not be imposed or carried out.[27] With regard to concerns raised by the Appellant about his personal safety in the event of a referral to BiH, the Referral Bench concluded that these concerns were unsubstantiated.[28] Finally, the Referral Bench concluded that the circumstances of the Appellant's capture in Argentina and his transfer to the ICTY did not preclude referral to BiH, although these circumstances did place restrictions on BiH's ability to try the Appellant for crimes other than those within the Tribunal's jurisdiction.[29] Further particulars in relation to the Referral **[page 4]** Bench's decision will be discussed in the course of considering the Appellant's specific grounds of appeal.

---

14 Argentine Court Order, p. 9, *in* Registry Submission Pursuant to Rule 33(B) of the Rules of Procedure and Evidence Regarding the Referral Bench's Order to File the Decision of the Federal Court of Argentina, 7 July 2006.

15 *See* Prosecution's Motion to Amend Indictment, 27 February 2006 ("Motion of 27 February 2006") and the attached Second Amended Indictment. The Prosecution had sought and received permission to amend the Indictment on two prior occasions, but these prior amendments were not significant with regard to the Appellant. *See generally* Prosecution Motion to Amend Indictment, 12 July 2001; and Prosecution's Motion to Amend Indictment, 17 November 2005.

16 Second Amended Indictment, paras 1, 31.

17 Second Amended Indictment, paras 3–4.

18 *See* Motion of 27 February 2006, para. 27.

19 *See* Motion of 27 February 2006, para. 28; Second Amended Indictment, para. 17. As compared to the Indictment, the Second Amended Indictment also increased the number of deaths resulting from the alleged fire-burning incidents somewhat, raising the tally from approximately 135 deaths to approximately 140 deaths. *See* Second Amended Indictment, paras 7, 11.

20 *See* Decision Granting Prosecution's Motion to Amend Indictment with regard to Milan Lukić, 22 March 2006, p. 2; *see also* Decision on the Form of the Indictment, 11 May 2006, para. 1.

21 Referral Decision, para. 8 and accompanying footnotes (identifying the submissions).

22 Referral Decision, para. 9 and accompanying footnotes (identifying the submission and related filings).

23 Referral Decision, para. 10.

24 Referral Decision, paras 29–30.

25 Referral Decision, para. 31.

26 Referral Decision, paras 37–41.

27 Referral Decision, paras 42–93

28 Referral Decision, paras 63–68.

29 Referral Decision, para. 122.

8. Sredoje Lukić did not appeal the Referral Decision, but the Appellant has appealed it.[30] In his Notice of Appeal and his Appeal Brief, he raises 14 grounds of appeal. The Prosecution has responded to this appeal,[31] and the Appellant has filed a reply to this response.[32]

II. STANDARD OF REVIEW

9. "The Appeals Chamber recalls that a decision on whether or not a case should be referred to the authorities of a State which meets the requirements set out in Rule 11*bis* of the Rules is a discretionary one."[33] Therefore, "the party challenging a decision pursuant to Rule 11*bis* of the Rules must show that the Referral Bench misdirected itself either as to the principle to be applied, or as to the law which is relevant to the exercise of its discretion, or that the Referral Bench gave weight to extraneous or irrelevant considerations, failed to give weight or sufficient weight to relevant considerations, or made an error as to the facts upon which it has exercised its discretion, or that its decision was so unreasonable and plainly unjust that the Appeals Chamber is able to infer that the Referral Bench must have failed to exercise its discretion properly."[34]

III. GROUNDS OF APPEAL RELATED TO THE REFERRAL BENCH'S FINDINGS ON GRAVITY AND LEVEL OF RESPONSIBILITY

A. First Ground of Appeal

10. In his first ground of appeal, the Appellant challenges the Referral Bench's use of the Second Amended Indictment in assessing the gravity of his crimes and level of responsibility. In the Appellant's view, the Referral Bench instead should have used the version of the indictment that was operative in February 2005 (the time when the Prosecution originally sought referral) instead of the Second Amended Indictment, which had neither been filed nor confirmed at the time the Prosecution sought referral.[35] The Appellant suggests that the Prosecution manipulated the Second Amended Indictment "to eradicate the facts averred in the [earlier indictment] which undermined **[page 5]** the Rule 11*bis* Request."[36] In this regard, the Appellant points specifically to the "constrict[ion of] the geographic and temporal scope of the alleged conduct" in the Second Amended Indictment.[37]

11. The Prosecution responds that the Referral Bench appropriately used the indictment that, pursuant to the ruling of the Trial Chamber, was operative at the time of the Referral Decision.[38] The Prosecution points out that the Referral Bench considered and rejected the same arguments by the Appellant with regard to any tailoring of the indictment by the Prosecution for the purpose of furthering referral.[39]

12. The Appeals Chamber sees no error in the Referral Bench's use of the currently operative indictment at the time of its decision (in this case, the Second Amended Indictment) in evaluating gravity and level of responsibility. Indeed, the Appeals Chamber's decisions in *Prosecutor v. Mitar Rašević and Savo Todović* plainly support this approach.[40] In that case, the Appeals Chamber indicated that the Referral Bench should

---

30 After it became clear that only one of the two accused had appealed the Referral Decision, the Referral Bench issued an order staying the execution of Sredoje Lukić's transfer to BiH until after the resolution of the Appellant's appeal. *See generally* Order Concerning Submissions of the Registrar Pursuant to Rule 33(B), 17 May 2007.

31 Prosecution Response to Brief of Milan Lukić, 14 May 2007 ("Response Brief").

32 Reply Brief of Appellant Milan Lukić, 17 May 2007 ("Reply Brief").

33 *Prosecutor v. Mitar Rašević and Savo Todović*, Case Nos. IT-97-25/1-AR11*bis*.1 & IT-97-25/1-AR11*bis*.2, Decision on Savo Todović's Appeals Against Decisions on Referral under Rule 11*bis*, 4 September 2006 ("*Todović* Decision of 4 September 2006"), para. 8.

34 *Todović* Decision of 4 September 2006, para. 8.

35 *See* Appeal Brief, paras 8–9.

36 Appeal Brief, para. 10.

37 Appeal Brief, para. 11.

38 *See* Response, para. 2.4.

39 Response, para. 2.5.

40 *Prosecutor v. Savo Todović*, Case No. IT-97-25/1-AR11*bis*.1, Decision on Rule 11*bis* Referral, 23 February 2006 ("*Todović* Decision of 23 February 2006"), paras 12–14, 18–19; *Todović* Decision of 4 September 2006, paras 3–4, 6, 13.

rely on the most recently confirmed version of the indictment, even where the Prosecution sought and received leave to use this version after the appointment of the Referral Bench.[41]

13. The Appeals Chamber further rejects the Appellant's claim that manipulation of the Indictment by the Prosecution justifies a different approach in this case. The Appeals Chamber need not address whether or not such manipulation, if proved, would justify a different approach, because here the Appellant fails to offer any credible evidence of manipulation.[42] In the absence of support for an assertion of manipulation, "the Appeals Chamber takes it for granted that the **[page 6]** Prosecution would not seek to influence the proceedings in such a way that by [changing] the charges alleged, this Tribunal would have decided the referral request differently."[43]

B. Second Ground of Appeal

14. In his second ground of appeal, the Appellant objects to the Referral Bench's exclusive reliance on the Second Amended Indictment in assessing his alleged level of responsibility pursuant to Rule 11*bis* (C) of the Rules. Although acknowledging that precedent supports this approach,[44] the Appellant considers that "neither the pronouncements of the Security Council, nor the Tribunal's Rules of Procedure anywhere declare that the operative indictment is the *sole* source of the facts" that the Referral Bench should use for such determinations.[45] He considers that in this case the Referral Bench should have made use of extrinsic evidence. In particular, he points to statements made at various times by the Prosecution (either in the course of his case or in other cases before the Tribunal) suggesting (1) that the Appellant's "paramilitary unit was one of the most feared and notorious during the conflict" and the Appellant himself "is considered to be perhaps the person who killed more people with his own hands than any other during the course of the Bosnian conflict";[46] (2) that the ethnic cleansing in Višegrad constituted "one of the most brutal campaigns of ethnic cleansing in the Bosnian conflict";[47] and (3) that the Appellant was also involved in the events of Srebrenica.[48]

15. The Prosecution responds that the "Referral Bench did not only look at the indictment but took into account all the factors relevant for a determination under Rule 11*bis*."[49]

---

41 *Todović* Decision of 23 February 2006, paras 18–19 (ordering the Referral Bench to suspend its proceedings until the Trial Chamber had resolved whether to accept proposed amendments to the indictment); Decision of 4 September 2006, paras 4, 6, 13 (seeming to view the most recently confirmed indictment as the relevant one for the Rule 11*bis* proceedings, but accepting that the differences between this indictment and the prior one were not material enough to justify a revised analysis based on this indictment).

42 The crimes charged in the two versions of the Indictment remain the same, although the Second Amended Indictment provides more details with regard to the factual allegations supporting these charges. While the Second Amended Indictment does provide more specific dates with regard to the factual allegations and does limit the geographic location of the crimes to within the municipality of Višegrad, these changes do not give rise to an inference of manipulation. In this regard, the Appeals Chamber notes that (1) the changes with respect to dates and geographic location primarily clarify rather than limit the specific factual allegations, as the only reference in the specific charges of the Indictment to events outside the Višegrad municipality occurred in the very general allegation of persecution, *see* Indictment, paras 19–20; and (2) the Second Amended Indictment provides more information with regard to the Appellant's leadership role in the White Eagles, *see* Second Amended Indictment paras 1, 31, a point which cuts against the Appellant's claim that the Second Amended Indictment sought to minimize his level of responsibility. The Appeals Chamber also notes that the Trial Chamber rejected a claim by Sredoje Lukić that similar amendments to the Indictment implied manipulation. *See* Decision Granting Prosecution's Motion to Amend Indictment and Scheduling Further Appearance, 11 February 2006, para. 13.

43 *Prosecutor v. Gojko Janković*, Case No. IT-96-23/3-AR11*bis*.2, Decision on Rule 11*bis* Referral, 15 November 2005 ("*Janković* Appeal Decision on Referral"), para. 25.

44 Appeal Brief, para. 12 & fn. 17.

45 Appeal Brief, para. 6.

46 Appeal Brief, para. 13 (quoting Request of 1 February 2005, para. 17) (emphasis omitted); *see also Prosecutor v. Mitar Vasiljević*, Case No. IT-98-32-T, Judgement, 29 November 2002, para. 72.

47 Appeal Brief, para. 15 (quoting *Prosecutor v. Mitar Vasiljević*, Case No. IT-98-32-T, Transcript of 10 September 2001, p. 105); *see also ibid.*, para. 16.

48 Appeal Brief, paras 17–19 (citing various filings by the Prosecution and alleged testimony from a BiH proceeding). Neither the Indictment nor the Second Amended Indictment charges the Appellant with crimes in relation to the events of Srebrenica. *Cf.* Motion of 1 February 2005, para. 23 (stating that "Milan LUKIĆ's crimes extended to his alleged involvement in some of the massacres arising out of the fall of Srebrenica in July of 1995").

49 Response, para. 2.7.

16. In reply, the Appellant asserts that the "Prosecution is simply incorrect in its response that, as to level of responsibility, the Referral Bench did not limit its inquiry to the Second Amended Indictment."[50] In the Appellant's view, the Referral Bench committed a legal error in looking only **[page 7]** to the Second Amended Indictment in assessing the level of responsibility, and this legal error led it to make a factual error in its findings on the level of responsibility.[51]

17. The Appeals Chamber agrees with the Appellant that, in assessing the Appellant's level of responsibility, the Referral Bench relied solely on the factual allegations made in the Second Amended Indictment.[52] But the Appeals Chamber disagrees with the Appellant's suggestion that this approach was wrong. Existing case law clearly endorses the approach taken by the Referral Bench.[53] Indeed, in *Prosecutor v. Gojko Janković*, the Appeals Chamber explicitly rejected the accused's argument that the Trial Chamber should have considered allegations that were not in the indictment in assessing the gravity of his alleged crimes.[54] The Appeals Chamber declines to revisit its existing approach, which is supported both by the text of the Rules and by sound policy reasons. Rule 11*bis* (C) of the Rules speaks of the "charge[s]", not of possible future charges. The ultimate case brought against an accused (whether in the Tribunal or in BiH State Court following a referral) may include additional charges, not present in the operative indictment at the time of referral,[55] that affect ultimate findings with regard to gravity and level of responsibility. But this is not sufficient justification to abandon the existing approach. Were the Referral Bench required to look beyond the four corners of an indictment, it would find itself in the untenable position of making speculation upon speculation with regard to whether there are other possible charges that could be brought against the accused, whether these charges may in fact be brought, and how these possible charges might relate to the issues of gravity and level of responsibility. Thus, at least in the absence of a showing that the Prosecution has withheld charges against an accused in order to promote the possibility of referral, the Referral Bench appropriately assesses gravity and level of responsibility solely in light of the allegations in the operative indictment. Accordingly, the Referral Bench had no obligation in this case to consider extrinsic evidence with regard to the Appellant's notoriety or to his possible involvement in criminal acts other than those charged in the Second Amended Indictment. In the present case, the Appeals Chamber is of the view that the fact that the Prosecution may now possess some evidence suggesting that the Appellant was also involved in the events of Srebrenica is not enough, standing alone, to raise concerns that the Prosecution has withheld charges against the Appellant in order to promote referral. **[page 8]**

C. <u>Third Ground of Appeal</u>

18. In his third ground of Appeal, the Appellant claims that the Referral Bench erred in concluding that the Appellant could not be characterized as one of the "most senior leaders" with regard to level of responsibility. In this regard, the Appellant cites a statement made by the President of the Security Council that the "Security Council recognizes … that the ICTY should concentrate its work on the prosecution and trial of the civilian, military, and paramilitary leaders … rather than on minor actors."[56] In the Appellant's view, this statement implies that paramilitary leaders are not suitable for referral.[57] Since he is alleged to be a paramilitary leader, he considers that his case accordingly should not be referred.[58] He also points out that in its decision in *Prosecutor v. Dragomir Milošević*, the Referral Bench stated that the phrase "most senior leaders" did not merely apply to leaders at the highest policy-making levels.[59]

---

50 Reply, para. 2.

51 Reply, para. 2.

52 *See* Referral Decision, paras 16, 26–31.

53 *Prosecutor v. Mejakić et al.*, Case No. IT-02-65-AR11*bis*.1, Decision on Joint Defence Appeal Against Decision on Referral under Rule 11*bis*, 7 April 2006 ("*Mejakić et al.* Appeal Decision on Referral"), para. 22 ("When assessing the gravity of the crimes charged against the Appellants and their level of responsibility, the Referral Bench properly considered only those facts alleged in the Indictment before reaching a determination concerning the appropriateness of referring the case to a national jurisdiction").

54 *Janković* Appeal Decision on Referral, para. 21.

55 *See Todović* Decision of 23 February 2006, paras 15–16.

56 United Nations Security Council, Statement by the President of the Security Council, 23 July 2002, S/PRST/2002/21, cited in Appeal Brief, para. 14.

57 Appeal Brief, para. 23.

58 Appeal Brief, para. 23.

59 Appeal Brief, para. 22 (citing *Prosecutor v. Dragomir Milošević*, Case No. IT-98-29/1-PT, Decision on Referral of Case Pursuant to Rule 11*bis*, 8 July 2005, para. 22).

19. The Prosecution responds that the Referral Bench considered and rejected these arguments in the Referral Decision; that the "findings of the Referral Bench taken in their entirety do not place [the Appellant] in the category of 'most senior leaders'"; and that the Appellant has not shown how these findings are unreasonable.[60]

20. To begin with, the Appeals Chamber rejects the Appellant's suggestion that the statement by the President of the Security Council precludes the referral of paramilitary leaders as a matter of law. The Appeals Chamber does not read this statement to bar referral of *all* cases involving civilian, military, and paramilitary leaders. Were that to be the case, then the Security Council would not have referenced "most senior leaders" in Resolutions 1503 (2003) and 1534 (2004), but would instead have spoken of *all* leaders. Instead, the Appeals Chamber understands the statement of the President of the Security Council simply to indicate that "most senior leaders" may come from positions of civilian, military, or paramilitary leadership (rather than simply from military leadership positions, for example). The reasoning of the Referral Bench was in keeping with this approach, as it plainly recognized that paramilitary leaders could fall within the category of "most senior leaders". **[page 9]**

21. The Appeals Chamber finds more merit in the Appellant's contention that the Referral Bench erred in its factual assessment of whether he amounted to a "most senior leader". The Referral Bench set out the following standard for considering his level of responsibility:

> The level of responsibility of an accused relates both to the role of the accused in the commission of the alleged offences and to the position and rank of the accused in the civil, political, or military hierarchy .... [A] high level of responsibility may arise from the alleged level of participation in the commission of the crimes charged in the indictment. A person holding a high rank or position may have the authority to orchestrate the actions of other people: because he may inflict more damage than he would be able to inflict absent such a rank or position, he therefore bears a higher level of responsibility. The accused must have exercised such a significant degree of authority that it is appropriate to refer to him as being among the 'most senior', rather than 'intermediate' [leaders]. The notion of 'most senior leaders' is, however, not limited to the architects of an overall policy forming the basis of the alleged crimes.[61]

Yet the Referral Bench's application of this standard was sparse. The Referral Bench simply stated that "[i] rrespective of the alleged local notoriety of Milan Lukić and his paramilitary group, neither of the Accused can sensibly be characterised as one of the 'most senior leaders', as envisioned by the Security Council in Resolution 1534."[62] This conclusory statement appears to presume that a "local" paramilitary leader can never constitute a "most senior leader". In doing so, it fails to take into account the "alleged level of participation in the commission of the crimes charged in the indictment."[63] The Second Amended Indictment not only alleges that the Appellant directly "committed" the crimes charged, but also suggests that he was a leader and orchestrator of these crimes[64] – which were part of "one of the most notorious campaigns of ethnic cleansing in the conflict".[65] There is no suggestion in the Second Amended Indictment that the Appellant was acting under the orders of others, although he may have coordinated with others in carrying out a "reign of terror upon the local Muslim population."[66] Rather, it seems that within his own sphere, he was a dominant presence.

22. The Appeals Chamber also considers that the Referral Bench placed too much stress on the local character of the Appellant's crimes. Of course, this is a relevant factor and in some situations can be a significant one.[67] But while, as discussed above, the President of the Security Council's statement did not show an intent for the Tribunal to retain all paramilitary leaders, it certainly gives rise to the inference that

---

60 Response, paras 2.9–2.11.

61 Referral Decision, para. 28.

62 Referral Decision, para. 30.

63 Referral Decision, para. 28.

64 *See* Second Amended Indictment, para. 31 (describing the Appellant as "form[ing] a group of paramilitaries which worked with local police and military units in exacting a reign of terror upon the local Muslim population").

65 Second Amended Indictment, paras 1, 27; *see also* para. 14 (suggesting that the beatings were done by the Appellant and "other members of [the Appellant's] group of paramilitaries").

66 Second Amended Indictment, para. 31.

67 *See Todović* Decision of 4 September 2006, para. 16.

the cases of at least some paramilitary leaders should be retained rather **[page 10]** than referred.[68] Since the criminal acts of paramilitary leaders are likely to be limited to a municipal (or at most regional) scope, an undue emphasis on geographic scope might thwart the intent of the Security Council that the Tribunal retain jurisdiction over at least the most significant paramilitary leaders. There is no necessary nexus between, on the one hand, leadership responsibility for the most serious crimes and, on the other hand, a broad geographic area. In light of the number and nature of his alleged criminal acts, and given the absence of any suggestion in the Indictment that the Appellant answered to a higher authority, the Appeals Chamber considers the Appellant's case falls into this category of most significant paramilitary leaders. The Appeals Chamber also takes note of the fact that the Appellant's paramilitary group appears to have operated for at least two years.[69] In light of these facts, the Appeals Chamber considers that the Referral Bench underestimated the level of responsibility allegedly held by the Appellant. The Appeals Chamber will consider the effect of this error in the next section.

D. Fourth Ground of Appeal

23. In his fourth ground of appeal, the Appellant claims that the Referral Bench erred "in finding that the gravity of the crimes charged, in combination with the level of responsibility, does not demand trial before the Tribunal."[70] This assertion appears to rest on the claim[71] that had the Referral Bench properly evaluated the Appellant's level of responsibility (discussed in regard to the third ground of appeal), it would have come to a different conclusion overall with regard to the criteria set forth in Rule 11*bis* of the Rules, namely "the gravity of the crimes charged and the level of responsibility of the accused".[72]

24. The Prosecution does not address whether, if the Appellant is correct in identifying an error with regard to the level of responsibility, this will materially affect the overall assessment for purposes of Rule 11*bis*(C) of the Rules.

25. The Appeals Chamber grants this ground of appeal. As the Referral Bench found, the crimes allegedly committed by the Appellant were grave indeed. They included a number of horrific incidents that resulted in the deaths of a total of more than 150 people – namely, two incidents where Bosnian Muslim men, women, and children were forcibly barricaded into houses that were then set on fire,[73] two incidents in which Bosnian Muslim men were seized and then **[page 11]** gunned down along the banks of a river,[74] one incident in which a Bosnian Muslim woman was questioned and then shot repeatedly,[75] and repeated incidents of inhumane acts and cruel treatment aimed at Bosnian Muslim men held at a detention camp.[76] Of course, gravity alone is not dispositive. The alleged crimes in this case are comparable to those alleged with regard to Paško Ljubičić, an intermediate-level military leader whose case was referred by the Tribunal pursuant to Rule 11*bis*.[77] But when the Appellant's alleged crimes are taken in conjunction with the earlier-discussed role allegedly played by him as a paramilitary leader, this case becomes too significant to be appropriate for referral. As noted earlier, the Security Council intended for the Tribunal to try top paramilitary leaders[78] and the allegations against the Appellant put him into this category. In this regard, his case differs substantially from that of Gojko Janković ("Janković"), another paramilitary leader whose case was referred pursuant to Rule 11*bis* of the Rules. Although a paramilitary leader, Janković was also acting at an intermediate level

---

68 *See* United Nations Security Council, Statement by the President of the Security Council, 23 July 2002, S/PRST/2002/21 (also cited in Security Council Resolutions 1503 (2003) and 1534 (2004)).

69 *See* Second Amended Indictment, paras 3, 5–7, 11–13, and 17.

70 Appeal Brief, p. 2.

71 *See* Appeal Brief, para. 23.

72 *See* Rule 11*bis* (C) of the Rules.

73 Second Amended Indictment, paras 7–11.

74 Second Amended Indictment, paras 5–6.

75 Second Amended Indictment, para. 12.

76 Second Amended Indictment, paras 13–15.

77 *See Prosecutor v. Paško Ljubičić*, Case No. IT-00-41-AR11*bis*.1, Decision on Appeal Against Decision on Referral under Rule 11*bis*, para. 3 (noting that the Indictment alleged that he had a role in crimes committed over a three-month period in a town and neighboring villages resulting in to the deaths of over 100 civilians, the detention and abuse of many more, and the destruction of Muslim property).

78 *See supra* footnote 68 and accompanying text.

within the military hierarchy as a sub-commander of the military police.[79] Moreover, Janković was charged with crimes in relation to a series of rapes and sexual assaults which, while serious indeed, involved far fewer victims and fewer varied incidents than the charges set out against the Appellant in the Second Amended Indictment.[80]

26. Indeed, the Prosecution has not identified any paramilitary leader indicted by the Tribunal in whose case the gravity of crimes charged and the level of responsibility of the accused are, when taken in conjunction, as significant as those in the present case. Nor is the Appeals Chamber aware of any such case, with the possible exception of the indictment issued against the now-deceased Željko Ražnjatović (also known as "Arkan").[81] In light of the notorious role played by paramilitary organizations and their leaders during the conflict in the former Yugoslavia, and in light of the Security Council's recognition that the Tribunal should try at least some of these leaders, the Appeals Chamber considers that the Appellant's case should be retained by the Tribunal. Based on **[page 12]** the allegations set forth in the Second Amended Indictment, the Appellant will be perhaps the most significant paramilitary leader tried by the Tribunal to date.

26. Accordingly, the Appeals Chamber reverses the Referral Decision and instructs that the Trial Chamber proceed with the trial in this case. Since the remaining grounds of appeal are rendered moot in light of this reversal, the Appeals Chamber declines to address them.

27. In light of this decision of the Appeals Chamber, it would be open to the Referral Bench to reconsider its decision relating to Sredoje Lukić, after giving him and the Prosecution an opportunity to be heard, on the ground that it would be judicially more appropriate for both cases to be heard by the same judicial body.

IV. DISPOSITION

28. For the foregoing reasons, the Appeals Chamber **GRANTS** the Appellant's appeal.

Done in English and French, the English text being authoritative.

Dated this 11th day of July 2007,
At The Hague, The Netherlands.

Theodor Meron
Presiding Judge

[Seal of the Tribunal]

[79] *See Janković* Appeal Decision on Referral, paras 4, 20.

[80] *See Janković* Appeal Decision on Referral, para. 4 (describing the changes); *see also Prosecutor v. Gojko Janković*, Case No. IT-96-23/2-PT, Decision on Rule 11*bis* Referral, 15 November 2005, para. 19 (considering the alleged "incidents of torture and rape involving sixteen females and within a time frame of four months" to be limited in terms of the number of victims).

[81] *Prosecutor v. Željko Ražnjatović*, Case No. IT-97-27, Indictment, 26 September 1997 (charging that Željko Ražnjatović, a notable paramilitary leader, bore responsibility for a series of crimes committed in September 1995, including the detention and cruel treatment of roughly 70 individuals, the murder of roughly 80 individuals, the rape of another individual, and several related crimes).

Commentary

1. Introduction

Both of these decisions[1] pertain to appeals of Rule 11*bis* decisions, referring the defendants to the domestic legal system of Bosnia and Herzegovina. Under Rule 11*bis* (I),[2] the prosecutor or an accused individual whose case has been referred to a national jurisdiction by the Referral Bench shall be given the right to appeal that decision within 15 days of the issuance of the referral judgment.[3]

2. Post-referral motions: *Prosecutor v. Trbić*

Milorad Trbić was deputy chief of security with the Zvornik Brigade of the Republika Srpska Army, serving under Dragan Nikolić.[4] The first indictment issued against him charged him solely with murder as a crime against humanity.[5] His case was joined with that of Popović *et. al.* in 2005, but severed from that case a number of months subsequent, as it was feared that issues relating to the mental health of the accused might cause delay in the trials of his co-accused.[6] The individual indictment then issued against Trbić, as amended, alleged that he had committed, in a joint criminal enterprise with his former co-accused: genocide, conspiracy to commit genocide, extermination, murder (both as a war crime and a crime against humanity), persecution, and forcible transfer of a civilian population at Srebrenica.[7]

A Referral Bench of the International Criminal Tribunal for the former Yugoslavia, comprised of Judges Orie, Parker and Kwon, decided to refer the case of Trbić to the authorities of Bosnia and Herzegovina on 27 April 2007,[8] a move agreed upon by both prosecution and defence teams.[9] Following the decision, the accused made the somewhat uncommon move of affirming his support of the decision by way of a personal letter to the registrar.[10] The registrar could not accept this letter as a waiver of the right to appeal, as Trbić was still assigned counsel and thus such a waiver must be made by that counsel for the accused, not by the accused himself.[11] As a result, it was determined that the referral decision had entered into force on 14 May 2007,[12] taking into account the decision in Popović *et al.* that interpreted the phrase "within fourteen days" as excluding the day the original notice - or in this instance, appealable decision - was filed.[13]

On 17 May 2007, the accused filed a confidential motion entitled "Motion to Suspend Following Registry Decision of 7 May 2007". The purported decision of the Registry of 7 May 2007 is nowhere to be found on

1 ICTY, Decision on Trial Chamber's Competence to Entertain Motion Filed After Entry into Force of Decision under Rule 11bis, *Prosecutor v. Trbić*, Case No. IT-05-88/1-PT, T. Ch. II, 1 June 2007, in this volume, p. 351; ICTY, Decision on Milan Lukić's Appeal Regarding Referral, *Prosecutor v. Lukić and Lukić*, Case No. IT-98-32/1- AR11bis.1, A. Ch., 11 July 2007, in this volume, p. 355.

2 Rules of Procedure and Evidence of the International Criminal Tribunal for the former Yugoslavia, IT/32/Rev. 44, 10 December 2009, as amended by IT/32/Rev.34, 11 February 2005.

3 Unless the accused was not present at the judgment, in which case the time limit shall run from the date he or she is informed of the decision.

4 ICTY, Case Information Sheet, *Prosecutor v. Trbić*, Case No. IT-05-88/1-PT, Referral Bench.

5 ICTY, Indictment, *Prosecutor v. Pandurević and Trbić*, Case No. IT-05-88/1, 3 March 2005.

6 ICTY, Decision on Severance of Case against Milorad Trbić with Confidential and *Ex Parte* Annex, *Prosecutor v. Popović, Beara, Nikolić, Borovčanin, Tolimir, Miletić, Gvero, Pandurević and Trbić*, Case No. IT-05-88-PT, Referral Bench, 26 June 2006, p. 2.

7 ICTY, Indictment, *Prosecutor v. Trbić*, Case No. IT-05-88/1-PT, Referral Bench, 18 August 2006.

8 ICTY, Decision on Referral of Case under Rule 11*bis* with Confidential Annex, *Prosecutor v. Trbić*, Case No. IT-05-88/1-PT, Referral Bench, 27 April 2007.

9 *Ibid.*, par. 9.

10 Decision on Trial Chamber's Competence to Entertain Motion Filed After Entry into Force of Decision under Rule 11bis, *Prosecutor v. Trbić*, T. Ch. II, *supra* note 1, footnote 4.

11 ICTY, Registry Submission Pursuant to Rule 33(B) of the Rules of Procedure and Evidence Regarding the Status of Defence Counsel, *Prosecutor v. Trbić*, Case No. IT-05-88/1-PT, Referral Bench, 4 May 2007.

12 Decision on Trial Chamber's Competence to Entertain Motion Filed After Entry into Force of Decision under Rule 11bis, *Prosecutor v. Trbić*, T. Ch. II, *supra* note 1, par. 5.

13 ICTY, Decision Regarding Evidence of General Rupert Smith and the Calculation of Time Limits Under Rule 126 *bis*, *Prosecutor v. Popović, Beara, Nikolić, Borovčanin, Tolimir, Miletić, Gvero, Pandurević and Trbić*, Case No. IT-05-88-T, T. Ch. II, 30 March 2007, par. 2.

the tribunal's court records,[14] and the motion remains confidential so it is impossible to determine what the substance of the suspension request was. Nevertheless, Trial Chamber II held that it had no competence to handle such motions once the referral decision has entered into force.[15]

This is not to say that the accused is left without remedy once the referral motion is affirmed. The Referral Bench retains, for example, the power to revoke an order made pursuant to Rule 11 *bis* and demand that the accused be transferred back to the seat of the tribunal.[16] In this case, after the accused had been transferred to Bosnia and Herzegovina on 11 June 2007, an urgent motion for payment of Trbić's defence counsel was filed before the Trial Chamber in July.[17] The Trial Chamber once again held that it had no competence to deal with motions relating to an accused whose transfer had been approved, but in the later decision, it took the added (and in this author's view, more pragmatic) action of remitting the matter to the tribunal's president "for whatever further action he deems appropriate".[18] The president, in turn, ordered the Referral Bench to consider the motions, noting that "in accordance with Rule 11*bis* [...] the Referral Bench remains seized of post-referral matters after its decision on referral has become final".[19]

The Trial Chamber's decision of 1 June 2007 reflects a fair and correct assessment of its competence as regards motions once a referral decision has come into force. However, it is submitted that the Trial Chamber should have taken the added step of remitting the motion to the president of the tribunal who could then have sent it to the Referral Bench for consideration. The fact that the suggested step was taken as regards the motion for payment of defence counsel a month later reflects an implicit value judgment on the importance of that motion over the confidential motion to suspend filed on 17 May 2007. It ought to have been left to the Referral Bench, still responsible for the consideration of post-referral matters, to deny any motion which was scurrilous or unfounded in law, but Trial Chamber II's 1 June decision has the effect of informally dismissing the motion incorrectly filed before it.

2. Appeal of 11 bis referral decision: *Prosecutor v. Lukić*

Milan Lukić was alleged, along with his cousin Sredoje Lukić, to have been part of a paramilitary group known as the White Eagles, who allegedly committed atrocities in and around the Višegrad municipality of Bosnia and Herzegovina between April 1992 and October 1994.[20] Both men were charged with persecution, a charge framed in general terms, and also with the crimes against humanity of extermination, murder and other inhumane acts, and with the war crimes of murder, cruel treatment and violence to life and person as war crimes. The latter charges related to two incidents whereby the two men allegedly forced Bosnian Muslims into houses and set those houses on fire, and further alleged incidents of mistreatment against Bosnian Muslim men in detention camps.[21] The charges against Milan Lukić further referred to three separate attacks on 13 Bosnian Muslim men, 11 of whom were killed.[22]

In February 2005, when the two accused were still at large, the prosecutor filed a motion requesting that their cases be transferred to Bosnia and Herzegovina pursuant to Rule 11 *bis*.[23] A Referrals Bench was convened for this purpose.[24] However, in September 2005, Sredoje Lukić surrendered himself to the ICTY, and Milan Lukić was apprehended by the Argentinean police in the autumn of 2005, and transferred to the seat of the tribunal in February 2006.[25]

---

14 ICTY Court Records http://icr.icty.org

15 Decision Regarding Evidence of General Rupert Smith and the Calculation of Time Limits Under Rule 126 *bis*, *Prosecutor v. Popović, Beara, Nikolić, Borovčanin, Tolimir, Miletić, Gvero, Pandurević and Trbić*, T. Ch. II, *supra* note 13, par. 6–7.

16 Rule 11*bis* (G) RPE.

17 ICTY, Decision on Motion to Order the Registry to Pay Invoices due from January 2007 to June 2007, *Prosecutor v. Trbić*, Case No. IT-05-88/1, T. Ch. II, 13 July 2007.

18 *Ibid.*

19 ICTY, Order to the Referral Bench to consider Motions filed before Trial Chamber II and before me, *Prosecutor v. Trbić*, Case No. IT-05-88/1, President, 20 July 2007.

20 Decision on Milan Lukić's Appeal Regarding Referral, *Prosecutor v. Lukić and Lukić*, A. Ch., *supra* note 1, par. 2.

21 *Ibid.*

22 *Ibid.*

23 *Ibid.*, par. 3.

24 *Ibid.*, par. 4.

25 *Ibid.*

On 5 April 2007, the Referral Bench referred the cases of the two accused to Bosnia and Herzegovina. While it was acknowledged that the crimes alleged were very serious, the Referral Bench was of the view that neither Sredoje Lukić nor Milan Lukić could be considered to hold the level of responsibility of 'most senior leaders' and that the case was 'not ipso facto incompatible' with referral.[26] Milan Lukić appealed the referral decision, while Sredoje Lukić did not.

Milan Lukić's first ground of appeal referred to the fact that the Referral Bench had relied on the second amended indictment - that is, the indictment which was in force at the time of the decision, as opposed to the indictment in force when the bench was established to examine the possibility of referral - in deciding his case. The Appeals Chamber held that it had not erred in this regard.[27] Further, there had been no error in the Referral Bench's sole reliance on the indictment as a measure of the seriousness of the crimes; to look outside the four corners of the indictment would mean that the bench would have to make 'speculation upon speculation' with regard to whether there were additional charges that could be brought against the accused and how these possible charges might relate to the issues of gravity and level of responsibility.[28]

However, the Appeals Chamber held that the Referral Bench had erred in its assessment of the seriousness of the allegations contained in the indictment. The allegations against the accused include a number of incidents that resulted in the death of over 150 people in horrific circumstances. That being said, gravity alone is not dispositive; the seriousness of the alleged crimes must be assessed in light of the accused's position of command.[29]

The Referral Bench had stated that in spite of the accused men's "local notoriety", their status as "most senior leaders" was not established.[30] According to the Appeals Chamber, this insinuated that a "local" paramilitary leader could never constitute a "most senior leader" as envisioned by Security Council Resolution 1534. The Referral Bench's reasoning placed "undue emphasis" on geographic scope, which could thwart the intention of the Security Council.[31] There was no evidence put forward in the amended indictment that Milan Lukić was answerable to the orders of another, thus the indictment squarely alleged that he was the leader and orchestrator of the crimes charged.[32]

4. Conclusion

The Appeals Chamber's decision, which limits the importance of geographic scope in assessing who is to be considered a "most senior leader" is well-reasoned and a welcome development. It has been cited with approval by the Extraordinary Chambers in the Courts of Cambodia.[33] However, there is one element of the decision which this author finds somewhat perturbing.

Having upheld the Milan Lukić's appeal against referral, the Appeals Chamber went on to suggest that it would be open to the Referral Bench to "reconsider" its decision relating to Sredoje Lukić. The reasoning given is that it would be "judicially more appropriate for both cases to be heard by the same judicial body."[34]

Be that as it may, there is no legal basis in Rule 11*bis* or anywhere else in the Statute or Rules to justify a "reconsideration" of this sort. As neither Sredoje Lukić nor the prosecutor lodged their appeals pursuant to Rule 11*bis* (I), and following the Trial Chamber's reasoning in Trbić, discussed above, the referral decision became final fifteen days after the issuance of the judgment, on 20 April 2007. As discussed above, Trial Chamber II in Trbić declined to assess a motion three days after the decision entered into force, which was

26 ICTY, Decision on referral of case pursuant to Rule 11*bis*, *Prosecutor v. Lukić and Lukić*, Case No. IT-98-32/1-PT, T. Ch. III, 5 April 2007.

27 Decision on Milan Lukic's Appeal Regarding Referral, *Prosecutor v. Lukić and Lukić*, A. Ch., *supra* note 19, par. 12.

28 *Ibid.*, par. 17, following the decision in Decision on rule 11*bis* referral, *Prosecutor v. Janković*, Case No. IT-96-23/2-AR11bis.2, A. Ch., 15 November 2005, Klip/ Sluiter, ALC-XXVII-435.

29 *Ibid.*, par. 25.

30 *Ibid.*, par. 21.

31 *Ibid.*, par. 21 and 22.

32 *Ibid.*

33 ECCC, Judgment, *Prosecutor v. Kaing Guek Eav (alias 'Duch')*, Case No. 001/18-07-2007/ECCC/TC, T. Ch., 26 July 2010, par. 29.

34 *Ibid.*, par. 27.

a logical consequence of the elapsed time limit, but in this case, the Appeals Chamber opted to effectively nudge the prosecutor into filing a Rule 11*bis* (F) motion. Under Rule 11*bis* (F), a referral order can be revoked and a motion for deferral can be entered upon the prosecutor's request, and once the state authorities have been given a chance to be heard, provided that no final judgment has been reached in the national court.

In this author's view, the consequence of neither the accused Sredoje Lukić nor the prosecutor appealing the original decision within the permissible timeframe ought to have been that the Lukić cases were separated and that Sredoje Lukić was sent to Bosnia and Herzegovina, while Milan Lukić was tried in the tribunal. Instead, the Appeals Chamber issued a value judgment on both facets of the original decision *ex post facto* the passage of the deadline for appeals, despite the fact that only one of the accused had exercised his right of appeal.

The Lukić referral decision shows an application of double standards within the tribunal - the defence is supposed to respect strict deadlines in lodging an appeal, but the prosecutor can essentially ask for a revocation order at any time after the decision is issued and before the national court has come to a verdict of guilty or not guilty.

Yvonne McDermott

UNITED NATIONS

International Tribunal for the Prosecution of Persons Responsible for Serious Violations of International Humanitarian Law Committed in the Territory of the Former Yugoslavia since 1991	Case No.	IT-03-67-AR77.1
	Date:	14 December 2007
	Original:	English

IN THE APPEALS CHAMBER

Before:	**Judge Fausto Pocar, Presiding** **Judge Mohamed Shahabuddeen** **Judge Mehmet Güney** **Judge Andrésia Vaz** **Judge Theodor Meron**
Registrar:	**Mr. Hans Holthuis**
Decision of:	**14 December 2007**

PROSECUTOR

v.

VOJISLAV ŠEŠELJ

PUBLIC

DECISION ON VOJISLAV ŠEŠELJ'S APPEAL AGAINST THE TRIAL CHAMBER'S DECISION OF 19 JULY 2007

The Office of the Prosecutor:
Ms. Christine Dahl

The Accused:
Mr. Vojislav Šešelj

[page 1] THE APPEALS CHAMBER of the International Tribunal for the Prosecution of Persons Responsible for Serious Violations of International Humanitarian Law Committed in the Territory of the Former Yugoslavia Since 1991 ("Appeals Chamber" and "International Tribunal", respectively),

NOTING that it is seized of "Professor Vojislav Šešelj's Notice of Appeal against the Trial Chamber III Decision of 19 July 2007" ("Notice of Appeal") submitted by Vojislav Šešelj ("Mr. Šešelj") on 2 November 2007 pursuant to Rule 77(J) of the Rules of Procedure and Evidence ("Rules");[1]

NOTING the "Prosecution's Response to Šešelj's Notice of Appeal" filed on 26 November 2007 ("Response"), in which the Prosecution informs the Appeals Chamber of its intention not to file a Response;[2]

NOTING "Professor Vojislav Šešelj's Appeal against the Decision of Trial Chamber III of 19 July 2007" ("Appeal") submitted by Mr. Šešelj on 22 November 2007;[3]

NOTING that, by the Order of 15 May 2007,[4] Trial Chamber III ("Trial Chamber") postponed the determination of a request for initiation and execution of contempt proceedings against members of the Office of the Prosecutor ("Alleged Contemnors"), filed by Mr. Šešelj on 23 March 2007;[5]

NOTING that, in its Decision of 19 July 2007 ("Impugned Decision"),[6] the Trial Chamber denied a motion filed by Mr. Šešelj[7] seeking review of the Order of 15 May 2007;

NOTING that on 15 August 2007, Mr. Šešelj filed an application for leave to appeal the Impugned Decision;[8] **[page 2]**

NOTING that on 14 September 2007, the Trial Chamber denied the Request for Certification on the grounds that (i) the Impugned Decision was a decision "relating in its essential parts to contempt", (ii) consequently, it had "no jurisdiction to determine [Mr. Šešelj's] request for certification" and (iii) Mr. Šešelj had a right to appeal directly to the Appeals Chamber pursuant to Rule 77(J) of the Rules;[9]

CONSIDERING that, pursuant to Rule 77(D) of the Rules, contempt proceedings are initiated upon determination by a Chamber that there are sufficient grounds to proceed against a person for contempt;

CONSIDERING further that the parties to a contempt proceedings are, on the one hand, the alleged contemnor and, on the other hand, the prosecuting authority, which can be, depending on the Chamber's choice, (i) the Prosecutor of the International Tribunal, (ii) an *amicus curiae* appointed by the Registrar pursuant to Rule 77(C)(ii) of the Rules or (iii) the Chamber itself;

CONSIDERING that no decision to initiate contempt proceedings against the Alleged Contemnors has been rendered yet;

CONSIDERING that the Trial Chamber, rather, decided to postpone its determination on whether or not to initiate contempt proceedings[10] and that, until such determination, this decision remains within its exclusive discretion pursuant to Rule 77 of the Rules;

---

1 English translation filed on 12 November 2007.

2 *Prosecutor v. Vojislav Šešelj*, IT-03-67-AR77.1, Prosecution's Response to Šešelj's Notice of Appeal, 26 November 2007.

3 *Prosecutor v. Vojislav Šešelj*, IT-03-67-AR77.1, Professor Vojislav Šešelj's Appeal against the Decision of Trial Chamber III of 19 July 2007, 22 November 2007. English translation filed on 6 December 2007.

4 *Prosecutor v. Vojislav Šešelj*, IT-03-67-PT, Order Regarding Mr. Šešelj's Motion for Contempt Proceedings, 15 May 2007 ("Order of 15 May 2007").

5 *Prosecutor v. Vojislav Šešelj*, IT-03-67-PT, Motion by Professor Šešelj for Trial Chamber III to Instigate Proceedings for Contempt of the Tribunal Against Carla Del Ponte, Hildegard Uertz-Retzlaff and Daniel Saxon, 8 March 2007. English translation filed on 23 March 2007.

6 *Prosecutor v. Vojislav Šešelj*, IT-03-67-PT, Decision on the Accused's Motion for Review of the Order of 15 May 2007, 19 July 2007 ("Impugned Decision").

7 *Prosecutor v. Vojislav Šešelj*, IT-03-67-PT, Professor Vojislav Šešelj's Motion for Trial Chamber III to Review its Order of 15 May 2007 Postponing a Decision on the Motion to Instigate Contempt Proceedings Until After the Completion of the Trial, 5 June 2007.

8 *Prosecutor v. Vojislav Šešelj*, IT-03-67-PT, Professor Vojislav Šešelj's Motion for Leave to File an Interlocutory Appeal Against the Decision of Trial Chamber III of 19 July 2007, 15 August 2007 ("Request for Certification"). English translation received on 28 August 2007.

9 *Prosecutor v. Vojislav Šešelj*, IT-03-67-PT, Decision on the Accused's Request for Certification to Appeal the Trial Chamber's Decision of 19 July 2007, 14 September 2007 ("Decision on Certification"). B/C/S translation received on 22 October 2007.

10 Order of 15 May 2007, p. 3.

CONSIDERING, therefore, that there are currently no contempt proceedings pending against the Alleged Contemnors;

CONSIDERING, further, that both the Order of 15 May 2007[11] and the Impugned Decision[12] were issued pursuant to Rule 54 of the Rules;

CONSIDERING, further, that Rule 77(J) of the Rules shall be interpreted as allowing for appeals against decisions disposing of the contempt case only;[13] **[page 3]**

CONSIDERING, therefore, that Rule 77(J) of the Rules is not applicable in the present case and that the Trial Chamber erred in law in directing Mr. Šešelj to file an appeal pursuant to this rule;[14]

NOTING further that Mr. Šešelj's request to initiate contempt proceedings addressed only issues relating to contempt proceedings, in which he cannot be a party[15] and has no standing,[16] rather than questions that directly affect his rights to a fair trial, such as evidentiary rulings, which he does have standing to contest;

On the basis of the foregoing,

FINDS that the Trial Chamber erred in holding that Rule 77 of the Rules was applicable to the issue before it;

FINDS further that Mr. Šešelj lacks standing to appeal any decision by the Trial Chamber regarding the initiation of contempt proceedings; and

CONSEQUENTLY DISMISSES the Appeal.

Judge Mohamed Shahabuddeen appends a Declaration to the present Decision.

Done in English and French, the English version being authoritative.

Done this 14th of December 2007,
At The Hague,
The Netherlands.

Judge Fausto Pocar
President

[Seal of the International Tribunal] [page 4]

[11] Order of 15 May 2007, p. 3.

[12] Impugned Decision, p. 4.

[13] *See Prosecutor v. Josip Jović*, IT-95-14&14/2-R77-AR.72.1, Decision on Interlocutory Appeal Challenging the Jurisdiction of the Tribunal, 2 March 2006, para. 5 where the Appeals Chamber addresses an appeal under Rule 72(B)(i) of the Rules in contempt proceedings. The Appeals Chamber notes that the Appeals Chamber of the Special Court for Sierra Leone has followed the same reasoning with regard to applicability of Rule 77(J) of its Rules of Procedure and Evidence, the contents of which was then similar to the one of Rule 77(J) of the Rules of the Tribunal - *See* Special Court for Sierra Leone ("SCSL"), *Prosecutor v. Brima, Kamara and Kanu ("AFRC")*, SCSL-04-16-AR77, Decision on Defence Appeal Motion Pursuant to Rule 77(J) on Both Imposition of Interim Measures and an Order Pursuant to Rule 77(C)(iii), 23 June 2005, para. 29 ("*AFRC* Decision").

[14] Decision on Certification, p. 1.

[15] *See Prosecutor v. Zlatko Aleksovski*, IT-95-14/1-AR77, Decision on Application of Mr. Nobilo for Leave to Appeal the Trial Chamber Finding of Contempt, 22 December 1998, p.1, where the Bench of the Appeals Chamber did "not consider the Office of the Prosecutor ("Prosecution") to be a party to the contempt proceedings". *See also, Prosecutor v. Zlatko Aleksovski*, IT-95-14/1-AR77, Judgement on Appeal by Anto Nobilo against Finding of Contempt, 30 May 2001, para. 24; *Prosecutor v. Duško Tadić*, IT-94-1-A-AR77, Order on the Prosecution Motion for Leave to Participate in the Present Appeal, 26 February 2001.

[16] *See* SCSL, *AFRC* Decision, para. 33. *See also* SCSL, *The Prosecutor v. Brima, Kamara and Kanu ("AFRC")*, SCSL-04-16-AR77, Decision on Joint Defence Appeal Against the Decision on the Report of the Independent Counsel pursuant to Rules 77(C)(iii) and 77(D), 17 August 2005, para. 16.

DECLARATION OF JUDGE SHAHABUDDEEN

1. I agree with the outcome of the decision of the Appeals Chamber but not with the reasoning. I give my views below.

Introduction

2. Trial Chamber III had before it a motion by Mr. Šešelj for leave to file an interlocutory appeal (certification). The Trial Chamber denied the motion, holding that it had no jurisdiction to determine it for the reason that, in the view of the Trial Chamber, Mr. Šešelj had a right under Rule 77(J) to appeal directly to the Appeals Chamber, that, in other words, he did not need certification. So Mr. Šešelj's subsequent 'Notice of Appeal' relates to an appeal, and not to an interlocutory appeal as he would have preferred.

3 The Appeals Chamber considers that the Trial Chamber's interpretation of Rule 77(J) was incorrect – a view which I respectfully share and which corresponds to a view held by Mr. Šešelj.[1] The remedy should be to remand the matter to the Trial Chamber for it to resume consideration of Mr. Šešelj's motion for certification in the light of the correct interpretation of the Rule. But it is not necessary to do so, because all the elements of a final decision by the Appeals Chamber are at hand. And so I agree with the dismissal of Mr. Šešelj's[1] appeal.

Mr. Šešelj's right to request the Trial Chamber to exercise its power to 'initiate' contempt proceedings did not depend on whether he had 'standing' in the proposed contempt case

4. However, I am not able to support the view that the decision of the Appeals Chamber should be based on 'standing'. Mr. Šešelj was really interested in getting the Trial Chamber to 'initiate' contempt proceedings against members of the prosecution team engaged in a prosecution against him. It is argued that he could not be party to the contempt case and would have no 'standing' in it, that he therefore had no right to request the Trial Chamber to 'initiate' contempt proceedings, and that consequentially he also had no right to bring other proceedings in relation thereto.

5. I accept that Mr. Šešelj would have no 'standing' in the contempt case, but am not persuaded that such 'standing' was a prerequisite of his right to request the Trial Chamber to **[page 5]** 'initiate' contempt proceedings or to seek leave to appeal a related decision of the Trial Chamber. 'Standing' in the contempt case is different from capacity to request the Trial Chamber to 'initiate' contempt proceedings. 'Standing' is usually employed in connection with capacity to participate in legal proceedings. Here what is in issue is the capacity of a person to ask the Trial Chamber to 'initiate' proceedings. Has he got the capacity, or has he not? I do not see that 'standing' provides an answer one way or another: a legal tag is not helpful. The answer has to be given by the application of normal principles of law to the question whether a person has legal capacity to do a given act.

6. Rule 77(C) of the Rules provides that when 'a Chamber has reason to believe that a person may be in contempt of the Tribunal, it may [among other things] (iii) initiate proceedings itself'. Mr. Šešelj's motion of 23 March 2007 'requests that Trial Chamber III, in accordance with Rule 77 of the Rules, instigate and execute proceedings for contempt …'.[2]. In its order postponing a determination of this request, the Trial Chamber correctly referred to the request as a 'request for the initiation and execution of contempt proceedings …'.[3].

7. Thus, it was clear that Mr. Šešelj recognized that the power to 'initiate' contempt proceedings lay with the Trial Chamber. He did not suggest that he himself had a right to 'initiate' such proceedings. But it seems to me that he had a right to request the Trial Chamber to exercise its power to 'initiate' such proceedings. Why? Because, although he would have no 'standing' in the contempt case proper, he had a right to a fair trial in

---

1 *Prosecutor v. Vojislav Šešelj*, IT-03-67-PT, Professor Vojislav Šešelj's Notice of Appeal against Trial Chamber III Decision of 19 July 2007, submitted on 2 November 2007, pp. 4–5, 12–13.

2 *Prosecutor v. Vojislav Šešelj*, IT-03-67-PT, Motion by Professor Vojislav Šešelj for Trial Chamber III to Instigate Proceeding for Contempt of the Tribunal against Carla Del Ponte, Hildegard Uertz-Retzlaff and Daniel Saxon, 8 March 2007. English translation filed 23 March 2007, p. 23.

3 *Prosecutor v. Vojislav Šešelj*, IT-03-67-PT, Order Regarding Mr. Šešelj's Motion for Contempt Proceedings, 15 May 2007, p. 3.

his own case. That right to a fair trial is meaningless unless it gives a right to complain to the Trial Chamber about the prosecution against him being conducted in a manner which may do harm to his right to a fair trial and to move it to exercise its power to initiate contempt proceedings.

8. The contempt case, if it were brought, would, according to Mr. Šešelj, involve serious allegations against members of the Office of the Prosecutor of suborning, threatening and otherwise illegally pressuring potential witnesses for the prosecution in the case now pending against Mr. Šešelj. It is lamentable if an accused in those circumstances has no competence to request the Trial Chamber to exercise its power to 'initiate' contempt proceedings; nor does the law command so curious a result. **[page 6]**

9. In sum, I am unable to agree with the proposition that, since, in respect of contempt proceedings, Mr. Šešelj 'cannot be a party and has no standing', he has no capacity to move the Trial Chamber to initiate those proceedings. The question is not whether he would have 'standing' in the contempt case; the question is whether he had the legal capacity for the limited purpose of requesting the Trial Chamber to exercise its power to 'initiate' contempt proceedings. The former question does not govern the latter. His right to a fair trial indicates an affirmative answer to the latter question.

Mr. Šešelj did raise questions that directly affect his rights to a fair trial

10. The decision of the Appeals Chamber states that Mr. Šešelj did not raise 'questions that directly affect his rights to a fair trial, such as evidentiary rulings, which he does have standing to contest'.[4] I am puzzled: the whole thesis of Mr. Šešelj's case was that the fairness of his own trial would be directly affected, in the sense that there were serious allegations of misconduct of members of the prosecution team committed in relation to the trial.[5]

11. The pleadings have to be read as a whole. Statements are not to be construed as if they were each made in hermetically sealed compartments. As was noted by Mr. Šešelj at page 15 of his 'Notice of Appeal':

> Although formally this motion can be considered only with respect to the Trial Chamber Decision of 19 July 2007, Professor Vojislav Šešelj points out that it is important to bear in mind that his Motions (of 8 March 2007 and 14 June 2007) make up a unified whole, as do the Order and the Decision of the Trial Chamber (of 15 May 2007 and 19 July 2007 respectively), because they deal with contempt of the International Tribunal, of which the most senior representatives of the prosecution are 'suspected'.

Thus, Mr. Šešelj was not relying merely on his formal Notice of Appeal; he was relying on all of his connected pleadings. **[page 7]**

12. Mr. Šešelj's 'Notice of Appeal', at page 4, refers to his 'Motion for Review' of 14 June 2007. At page 6, the latter noted that he requested that the representatives of the prosecution 'be found criminally responsible for contempt of court, because they knowingly and wilfully interfered with the administration of justice'. At page 9, he alleged that 'potential witnesses ... were threatened, intimidated, bribed or otherwise improperly coerced by Prosecution representatives ...'; the context makes it clear that what was being spoken of was evidence to be given in the prosecution case against Mr. Šešelj. At page 6, there are references to his right to a 'fair trial'. It is clear from the last paragraph of his 'Notice of Appeal' that what he was saying was that coercion of potential prosecution witnesses interfered with his 'right to a fair trial'.

13. Thus, it is the case that Mr. Šešelj was alleging that his right to a fair trial in the prosecution now pending against him would be prejudiced by a failure to initiate contempt proceedings. In other words, he

---

4 *Prosecutor v. Vojislav Šešelj*, IT-03-67-PT, Appeals Chamber Decision on Vojislav Šešelj's Appeal Against the Trial Chamber's Decision of 19 July 2007, p. 3.

5 See *Prosecutor v. Vojislav Šešelj*, IT-03-67-PT, Order Regarding Mr. Šešelj's Motion for Contempt Proceedings, 15 May 2007, pp. 13, 14 and 15, for Mr. Šešelj's use of the words 'fair trial' or their cognates. See also on this point, as well as on the issue of consequences of threats to witnesses, *Prosecutor v. Vojislav Šešelj*, IT-03-67-PT, Professor Vojislav Šešelj's Motion for Leave to File an Interlocutory Appeal Against the Decision of Trial Chamber III of 19 July 2007, 15 August 2007. English translation received on 28 August 2007, pp. 4–5. On the latter point, see further *Prosecutor v. Vojislav Šešelj*, IT-03-67-PT, Professor Vojislav Šešelj's Motion for Trial Chamber III to Review its Order of 15 May 2007 Postponing a Decision on the Motion to Instigate Contempt Proceedings Until After the Completion of the Trial, 5 June 2007, p. 9.

was raising 'questions that directly affect his rights to a fair trial', to use the words of the Appeals Chamber's present decision. It is enough to observe that the Appeals Chamber accepts that Mr. Šešelj 'does have standing to contest' such questions.

But, in the specific case, Mr. Šešelj's right to a fair trial could be satisfied by his right to examine and cross-examine witnesses

14. However, in the specific case, Mr. Šešelj's right to a fair trial could be satisfied by his right to examine and cross-examine witnesses; the prosecution against him is not a case in which the relevant material could not be made available to the court through the exercise of the latter right. In this respect, the Trial Chamber correctly observed that –

> a challenge to the admissibility of any evidence should be dealt with during the trial and, particularly, through the examination and cross-examination of the witnesses identified in the Motion. [6]

Since Mr. Šešelj's right to a fair trial could be satisfied in that way – a way that has been accepted by the Trial Chamber – it would be incorrect to take the view that a motion inviting the Trial Chamber to 'initiate' separate proceedings was in order. It is this consideration, and not considerations of 'standing', which justifies today's decision to dismiss his appeal. **[page 8]**

15. I would add that there appears to be no good reason why Mr. Šešelj's trial in the case against him must await the conclusion of a new case. Whatever may have led to that approach, it is enough to observe that the approach could stretch into the future to exceed tolerable limits of Mr. Šešelj's right to an expeditious trial, as was in substance pointed out by the Trial Chamber.[7]

Done in English and in French, the English text being authoritative.

Dated 14 December 2007
At The Hague
The Netherlands

Mohamed Shahabuddeen

[Seal of the Tribunal]

---

6 *Prosecutor v. Vojislav Šešelj*, IT-03-67-PT, Order Regarding Šešelj's Motion for Contempt Proceedings, 15 May 2007, p. 2, penultimate paragraph.

7 *Ibid.*, p. 3.

Commentary

1. Introduction

Rule 77 of the International Criminal Tribunal of the Former Yugoslavia's (ICTY) Rules of Procedure and Evidence (RPE) is a powerful tool to penalise parties who demonstrate an obstructionist attitude towards the proceedings of the tribunal. However, the Rule can only be activated through the chamber itself rather than by any or all of the parties to the proceedings.[1] One of the decisions in the *Prosecutor v. Šešelj* case dealt with the possibility that the defendant could request the relevant chamber to initiate proceedings against the prosecution.[2] Although the Appeals Chamber, in the 2007 decision,[3] reached the conclusion that Šešelj did not have any standing with regard to the Trial Chamber initiating contempt proceedings, Judge Shahabuddeen declared that their reasoning was flawed. Judge Shahabuddeen's declaration will be the basis of this commentary.[4]

2. Standing in contempt proceedings

The first ground of reasoning that Judge Shahabuddeen challenged was that the Appeals Chamber had declared that Šešelj's right to request the Trial Chamber to exercise its power to "initiate" contempt proceedings depended upon whether or not he had "standing" in the proposed contempt case.[5] A traditional interpretation of who has standing in contempt proceedings before the ICTY would include those who are direct parties to the issue, for example the person alleged to have committed the act or acts of contempt, and the relevant chamber that brought contempt proceedings under Rule 77 (C) (iii). It is therefore logical to claim that Šešelj did not in fact have standing in the potential contempt proceedings in question.

Judge Shahabuddeens' objections to the Appeals Chamber's initial reasoning is based on Šešelj's original request, which merely asked the Trial Chamber to initiate contempt proceedings under Rule 77 C iii, rather than attempt to establish that he himself had a right to initiate those proceedings.[6] In Judge Shahabuddeen's opinion, Šešelj "had the right to request the Trial Chamber to exercise its power to 'initiate' such proceedings."[7] This does appear to be the most appropriate interpretation since if one rejects Judge Shahabudeen's arguments, it will leave every potential defendant with no remedy in the face of acts they perceive as amounting to contempt of the tribunal. The Appeals Chamber decision demonstrates a certain rigidity in the way they are willing to perceive allegations of contempt of the tribunal arising from the side of defendants. A relevant concern might be that some defendants would make endless and groundless requests of the Trial Chambers to initiate contempt proceedings, which would delay their trials. However, this should not weigh more heavily than the consideration that, in some instances, the allegations will be valid, and to ignore them would be a violation of the defendant's right to a fair trial.

---

1 Rules of Procedure and Evidence, U.N. Doc. IT/32 Rev. 46, 20 October 2011, Rule 77 (C):

"(C) When a Chamber has reason to believe that a person may be in contempt of the Tribunal, it may:

(i) direct the Prosecutor to investigate the matter with a view to the preparation and submission of an indictment for contempt;

(ii) where the Prosecutor, in the view of the Chamber, has a conflict of interest with respect to the relevant conduct, direct the Registrar to appoint an *amicus curiae* to investigate the matter and report back to the Chamber as to whether there are sufficient grounds for instigating contempt proceedings; or

(iii) initiate proceedings itself."

2 ICTY, Decision on Vojislav Šešelj's appeal against the Trial Chamber's decision, *Prosecutor v. Šešelj*, Case No. IT-03-67-AR77.1, A. Ch., 19 July 2007.

3 ICTY, Decision on Vojislav Šešelj's Appeal Against the Trial Chamber's Decision of 19 July 2007, *Prosecutor v. Šešelj*, Case No. IT-03-67-AR77.1, A. Ch., 14 December 2007, in this volume, p. 369.

4 ICTY, Declaration of Judge Shahabuddeen, *Prosecutor v. Šešelj*, Case No. IT-03-67-AR77.1, A. Ch., 14 December 2007, in this volume, p. 372.

5 Decision on Vojislav Šešelj's appeal against the Trial Chamber's decision, *Prosecutor v. Šešelj*, A. Ch., *supra* note 2, par. 4.

6 ICTY, Motion by Professor Vojislav Šešelj for Trial Chamber III to Instigate Proceeding for Contempt of the Tribunal against Carla Del Ponte, Hildegard Uertz-Retzlaff and Daniel Saxon, *Prosecutor v. Šešelj*, Case No. IT-03-67-PT, T. Ch. III, 8 March 2007, p. 23.

7 Decision on Vojislav Šešelj's appeal against the Trial Chamber's decision, *Prosecutor v. Šešelj*, A. Ch., *supra* note 2, par. 7.

3. Contempt and the right to a fair trial

Judge Shahabuddeen's second objection was to the argument that, because Šešelj had raised no questions that affected his rights to a fair trial, he could have no standing on that basis.[8] Issues that affect his rights to a fair trial are, of course, immediately accepted as something he would have "standing" on, since the right to a fair trial is enshrined within numerous international conventions, as well as within the ICTY Statute itself.[9] However, the Appeals Chamber held that the issue of contempt proceedings would not affect his rights to a fair trial, or at the very least, it would not automatically raise any such issues. Judge Shahabuddeen raised the issue of Šešelj's notice of appeal, where he reiterated his allegations that the prosecution had in fact intimidated, threatened and coerced witnesses on whom they wanted to rely, to the detriment of Šešelj.[10] It seems impossible to claim that allegations such as these, in the event that they were true, would not affect a defendant's right to a fair trial. In no way is this commentary suggesting that the tribunal's differing chambers would overlook actual acts of contempt against the tribunal, however circumstances may arise when a defendant becomes aware of such matters before the tribunal itself. In such circumstances, how else should a defendant notify the tribunal that some of the parties to their proceedings are in violation of a specific part of Rule 77 of the RPE?

4. Conclusion

Judge Shahabuddeen concludes his declaration by agreeing with the result of the Appeals Chamber decision, if not the reasoning, on the basis that Šešelj's "right to a fair trial could be satisfied by his right to examine and cross-examine witnesses."[11] As Šešelj's concern was focused on the witnesses and the evidence they would present, any inadmissibility issues with respect to them should have been dealt with in the natural course of the trial proceedings.

Although having the authority to request instigation of contempt proceedings is not necessarily a specific right under the tribunal's fair trial principle,[12] leaving a defendant with no possible recourse to challenge potentially contemptuous acts by the prosecution, or any other party, must be considered as violating the general fair trial principle. Sluiter establishes that the fact that no specific established right of fair trial has been violated "does not automatically warrant the conclusion that the trial as a whole is fair."[13] Considering the stringent penalties that Rule 77 (G) sets out - up to a 100 000 Euros fine or up to seven years imprisonment - there is no question that the ICTY considers acts of contempt against the tribunal as a very serious matter. Therefore, preventing defendants from merely requesting that the tribunal look into an allegation of contempt on the simple basis that he does not have "standing," does not rely on entirely sound reasoning. At the very least, the Appeals Chamber failed to provide them in this instance.

This commentary would support Judge Shahabuddeen's suggestion that the question that should be asked in such circumstances is whether or not the defendant "had the legal capacity for the limited purpose of requesting the Trial Chamber to exercise its power to 'initiate' contempt proceedings."[14]

Birgitte Hagem

---

8 *Ibid.*, p. 3.

9 Article 21, ICTY statute, Article 14, International Covenant on Civil and Political Rights, Article 6, European Convention on the Protection of Human Rights, as well as, Article 67 of the International Criminal Court Statute.

10 ICTY, Professor Vojislav Šešelj's Notice of Appeal against Trial Chamber III Decision of 19 July 2007, *Prosecutor v. Šešelj*, Case No. IT-03-67-PT, T. Ch. III, 2 November 2007, p. 9.

11 Decision on Vojislav Šešelj's appeal against the Trial Chamber's decision, *Prosecutor v. Šešelj*, A. Ch., *supra* note 2, par. 14.

12 Article 21 ICTY statute lists specific rights that the defendant must have afforded to him to ensure he has a fair trial. Article 21, paragraph 2, mentions the right to a fair trial in general.

13 G. Sluiter and A. Zahar, International Criminal Law, Oxford University Press, Oxford 2008, p. 293.

14 Decision on Vojislav Šešelj's appeal against the Trial Chamber's decision, *Prosecutor v. Šešelj*, A. Ch., *supra* note 2, par. 9.

UNITED
NATIONS

International Tribunal for the Prosecution of Persons Responsible for Serious Violations of International Humanitarian Law Committed in the Territory of Former Yugoslavia since 1991	Case No.:	IT-02-60-A
	Date:	9 May 2007
	Original:	English

IN THE APPEALS CHAMBER

Before: **Judge Fausto Pocar, Presiding**
Judge Mohamed Shahabuddeen
Judge Mehmet Güney
Judge Andrésia Vaz
Judge Theodor Meron

Registrar: **Mr. Hans Holthuis**

Judgement of: **9 May 2007**

PROSECUTOR

v.

VIDOJE BLAGOJEVIĆ
AND
DRAGAN JOKIĆ

JUDGEMENT

The Office of the Prosecutor:
Mr. Norman Farrell
Ms. Antoinette Issa
Ms. Marie-Ursula Kind
Mr. Matteo Costi

Counsel for Vidoje Blagojević:
Mr. Vladimir Domazet

Counsel for Dragan Jokić:
Mr. Peter Murphy
Ms. Chrissa Loukas

[page 1] I. INTRODUCTION

1. The Appeals Chamber of the International Tribunal for the Prosecution of Persons Responsible for Serious Violations of International Humanitarian Law Committed in the Territory of the Former Yugoslavia since 1991 ("Appeals Chamber" and "International Tribunal", respectively) is seized of three appeals from the written Judgement rendered by Trial Chamber I, Section A, on 17 January 2005 in the case of *Prosecutor v. Vidoje Blagojević and Dragan Jokić*, Case No. IT-02-60-T ("Trial Judgement").[1]

2. The events giving rise to these appeals took place in the immediate aftermath of the take-over of the Srebrenica "safe area" by the Army of the Republika Srpska ("VRS").[2] Srebrenica, a predominantely Muslim municipality before the war, is in eastern Bosnia and Herzegovina near the border with Serbia.[3] On 16 April 1993, the United Nations Security Council declared it a "safe area which should be free from any armed attack or any other hostile act."[4] Between 6 and 11 July 1995, the VRS attacked and gained control of Srebrenica.[5] In the following days, various elements of the VRS detained and killed thousands of Bosnian Muslim men, while transporting the women, children, and elderly out of Srebrenica on buses.[6] This case has focused primarily on the role played in these events by the Bratunac and Zvornik Brigades of the Drina Corps of the VRS and, in particular, by two of their respective officers at the time, Colonel Vidoje Blagojević and Major Dragan Jokić.[7]

3. Vidoje Blagojević ("Blagojević") was born on 22 June 1950 in the Bratunac municipality, located in what is now the Republika Srpska region of Bosnia and Herzegovina.[8] After serving in the Army of the Socialist Federal Republic of Yugoslavia, Blagojević rose to the rank of colonel in the VRS, commanding the Bratunac Brigade in July 1995.[9] Based on his actions as well as those of the Bratunac Brigade in the events following the fall of Srebrenica, the Trial Chamber convicted Blagojević under Article 7(1) of the Statute for complicity in genocide, aiding and abetting murder as a violation of the laws or customs of war, and aiding and abetting murder, persecutions, and **[page 2]** other inhumane acts (forcible transfer) as crimes against humanity and sentenced him to eighteen years' imprisonment.[10]

4. Dragan Jokić ("Jokić") was born on 20 August 1957 in the Zvornik municipality, located in what is now the Republika Srpska region of Bosnia and Herzegovina.[11] Jokić joined the VRS on 16 May 1992 and, in July 1995, held the position of Chief of Engineering of the Zvornik Brigade, with the rank of major.[12] Based on his actions as well as those of the Zvornik Brigade in the events following the fall of Srebrenica, the Trial Chamber convicted Jokić under Article 7(1) of the Statute for aiding and abetting murder as a violation of the laws or customs of war and aiding and abetting extermination and persecutions as crimes against humanity and sentenced him to nine years' imprisonment.[13]

5. The Appeals Chamber heard oral submissions regarding these appeals on 5 and 6 December 2006. Having considered the written and oral submissions of Blagojević, Jokić, and the Prosecution, the Appeals Chamber hereby renders its Judgement. **[page 3]**

---

1 *See* Annex A – Procedural Background, section A.

2 Trial Judgement, para. 136 ("The Trial Chamber recognises that the attack on the enclave is not charged in the Indictment. Furthermore, the crimes charged in the Indictment are alleged to have commenced on 11 July 1995 – after the fall of the Srebrenica enclave.") (internal citations omitted).

3 Trial Judgement, para. 94.

4 Trial Judgement, para. 100, quoting UN Security Council resolution 819 (1993).

5 Trial Judgement, paras. 125–133.

6 *See generally* Trial Judgement, paras. 141–379.

7 The Appeals Chamber recalls that the International Tribunal previously considered the criminal responsibility of Radislav Krstić, the commander of the Drina Corps. *See Krstić* Appeal Judgement; *Krstić* Trial Judgement.

8 Trial Judgement, para. 4.

9 Trial Judgement, paras. 4, 41.

10 Trial Judgement, Chapter X (Disposition).

11 Trial Judgement, para. 11.

12 Trial Judgement, para. 11.

13 Trial Judgement, Chapter X (Disposition).

II. STANDARD OF APPELLATE REVIEW

6. On appeal, the parties must limit their arguments to errors of law that invalidate the decision of the Trial Chamber and to errors of fact that result in a miscarriage of justice. These criteria are set forth in Article 25 of the Statute and are well established.[14] The Appeals Chamber also exceptionally hears arguments where a party has raised a legal issue that would not lead to the invalidation of the judgement but that is of general significance to the International Tribunal's jurisprudence.[15]

7. Any party alleging an error of law must identify the alleged error, present arguments in support of its claim, and explain how the error invalidates the decision.[16] An allegation of an error of law which has no chance of changing the outcome of a decision may be rejected on that ground.[17] However, even if the party's arguments are insufficient to support the contention of an error, the Appeals Chamber may find, for other reasons, that there is an error of law.[18]

8. The Appeals Chamber reviews the Trial Chamber's impugned findings of law to determine whether or not they are correct.[19] Where the Appeals Chamber finds an error of law in the trial judgement arising from the application of an incorrect legal standard, the Appeals Chamber may articulate the correct legal standard and review the relevant factual findings of the Trial Chamber accordingly.[20] In so doing, the Appeals Chamber not only corrects the legal error, but applies the correct legal standard to the evidence contained in the trial record, where necessary, and determines whether it is itself convinced beyond reasonable doubt as to the factual findings challenged by the appellant before affirming them.[21]

9. When considering an alleged error of fact with respect to a particular ground where no additional evidence has been admitted on appeal, the Appeals Chamber will apply a standard of **[page 4]** reasonableness in reviewing the finding.[22] Where the convicted person is appealing, the Appeals Chamber will reverse only if it finds that no reasonable trier of fact could have made the particular finding of fact beyond reasonable doubt and the conviction relied on this finding. Where the Prosecution is appealing, the Appeals Chamber will reverse only if it finds that no reasonable trier of fact could have failed to make the particular finding of fact beyond reasonable doubt and the acquittal relied on the absence of this finding.[23] In determining whether or not a Trial Chamber's finding was reasonable, the Appeals Chamber does not lightly disturb findings of fact made by a Trial Chamber.[24] The Appeals Chamber recalls, as a general principle, the approach adopted by the Appeals Chamber in the *Kupreškić et al.* case, wherein it was stated that:

> Pursuant to the jurisprudence of the Tribunal, the task of hearing, assessing and weighing the evidence presented at trial is left primarily to the Trial Chamber. Thus, the Appeals Chamber must give a margin of deference to a finding of fact reached by a Trial Chamber. Only where the evidence relied on by the Trial Chamber could not have been accepted by any reasonable tribunal of fact or where the evaluation of the evidence is "wholly erroneous" may the Appeals Chamber substitute its own finding for that of the Trial Chamber.[25]

---

14 *See, e.g., Simić* Appeal Judgement, para. 7; *Stakić* Appeal Judgement, para. 8; *Kvočka et al.* Appeal Judgement, para. 14; *Tadić* Appeal Judgement, para. 64; *Furundžija* Appeal Judgement, paras. 34–40; *Čelebići* Appeal Judgement, paras. 434, 435; *Kupreškić et al.* Appeal Judgement, para. 29; *Kunarac et al.* Appeal Judgement, paras. 35–48; *Vasiljević* Appeal Judgement, paras. 4–12. For jurisprudence under Article 24 of the ICTR Statute *see, e.g., Kajelijeli* Appeal Judgement, para. 5; *Semanza* Appeal Judgement, para. 7; *Akayesu* Appeal Judgement, para. 178; *Kayishema and Ruzindana* Appeal Judgement, paras. 177, 320; *Musema* Appeal Judgement, para. 15.

15 *See, e.g., Simić* Appeal Judgement, para. 7; *Stakić* Appeal Judgement, para. 7.

16 *See, e.g., Simić* Appeal Judgement, para. 8; *Kvočka et al.* Appeal Judgement, para. 16; *Vasiljević* Appeal Judgement, para. 6.

17 *See, e.g., Simić* Appeal Judgement, para. 8; *Kvočka et al.* Appeal Judgement, para. 16; *Vasiljević* Appeal Judgement, para. 6.

18 *See, e.g., Simić* Appeal Judgement, para. 8; *Stakić* Appeal Judgement, para. 8; *Ntagerura et al.* Appeal Judgement, para. 11.

19 *Simić* Appeal Judgement, para. 9; *Krnojelac* Appeal Judgement, para. 10.

20 *See, e.g., Simić* Appeal Judgement, para. 9; *Stakić* Appeal Judgement, para. 9; *Naletilić and Martinović* Appeal Judgement, para. 10.

21 *See, e.g., Simić* Appeal Judgement, para. 9; *Stakić* Appeal Judgement, para. 9; *Naletilić and Martinović* Appeal Judgement, para. 10.

22 *Simić* Appeal Judgement, para. 10; *Naletilić and Martinović* Appeal Judgement, para. 11; *Blaškić* Appeal Judgement, paras. 16, 19; *Kordić and Čerkez* Appeal Judgement, paras. 18, 20.

23 *See Brđanin* Appeal Judgement, paras. 12–14.

24 *Naletilić and Martinović* Appeal Judgement, para. 11; *Kvočka et al.* Appeal Judgement, para. 18; *Furundžija* Appeal Judgement, para. 37, referring to *Tadić* Appeal Judgement, para. 64. *See also Aleksovski* Appeal Judgement, para. 63; *Krnojelac* Appeal Judgement, para. 11; *Musema* Appeal Judgement, para. 18.

25 *Kupreškić et al.* Appeal Judgement, para. 30. *See also Stakić* Appeal Judgement, para. 10; *Kvočka et al.* Appeal Judgement, paras. 18, 19; *Kordić and Čerkez* Appeal Judgement, para. 19 fn. 11; *Blaškić* Appeal Judgement, paras. 17, 18.

10. The Appeals Chamber reiterates that a party may not merely repeat on appeal arguments that did not succeed at trial, unless that party can demonstrate that rejecting them constituted such error as to warrant the intervention of the Appeals Chamber. Arguments of a party that do not have the potential to cause the impugned decision to be reversed or revised may be immediately dismissed by the Appeals Chamber and need not be considered on the merits.[26]

11. With regard to form, the parties are expected to provide precise references to relevant transcript pages or paragraphs in the judgement to which the challenge is being made, as well as exact references to the parts of the record on appeal invoked in its support.[27] If a party makes submissions that are obscure, contradictory, or vague, or if they suffer from other formal and obvious insufficiencies, the Appeals Chamber will dismiss the submissions as unfounded without providing detailed reasoning.[28] Additionally, arguments will be dismissed without detailed reasoning where the argument advanced by the appealing party is clearly irrelevant or the appealing **[page 5]** party's argument unacceptably seeks to substitute its own evaluation of the evidence for that of the Trial Chamber.[29] **[page 6]**

III. THE APPEAL OF VIDOJE BLAGOJEVIĆ

A. Fair Trial (Ground 1)

12. Blagojević submits that his trial was not fair because he was denied the right to counsel of his choice, the right to competent counsel, and the right to appear as a witness in his own trial.[30] The origin of these complaints involves a dispute between Blagojević and his assigned counsel which led to a complete breakdown in trust and communication, ultimately pervading the entire trial. This dispute was the subject of extensive litigation before the start of trial, culminating in an interlocutory appeal, as Blagojević repeatedly and unsuccessfully sought to replace his entire assigned defence team.[31]

13. The history of the assignment of Blagojević's trial counsel and of their dispute is set forth in a number of decisions in this case.[32] It suffices to note here that Blagojević is a long-time beneficiary of the International Tribunal's legal aid system. Shortly after his arrest, Blagojević requested the Registrar to appoint Mr. Michael Karnavas as his lead counsel, which was done as of 31 August 2001.[33] More than a year later, Mr. Karnavas requested the Registrar to appoint Ms. Suzana Tomanović as his co-counsel, which was done on 25 September 2002.[34] The selection of Ms. Tomanović as co-counsel, as opposed to another lawyer preferred by Blagojević, apparently began the deterioration in the relationship between Blagojević and his assigned counsel.[35] Blagojević initially sought to replace only Ms. Tomanović.[36] He later requested to replace his entire defence team, claiming the denial of the right to counsel of his choice and complaining about the lack of competence and professionalism of his lawyers.[37] In particular, Blagojević complained before the Appeals Chamber that

---

26 *Simić* Appeal Judgement, para. 12; *Naletilić and Martinović* Appeal Judgement, para. 13; *Blaškić* Appeal Judgement, para. 13; *Kordić and Čerkez* Appeal Judgement, para. 21; *Ntagerura et al.* Appeal Judgement, para. 13.

27 Practice Direction on Formal Requirements for Appeals from Judgement, para. 4(b). *See also Simić* Appeal Judgement, para. 13.

28 *Simić* Appeal Judgement, paras. 13, 14; *Naletilić and Martinović* Appeal Judgement, para. 14; *Blaškić* Appeal Judgement, para. 13; *Kordić and Čerkez* Appeal Judgement, paras. 22, 23.

29 *Simić* Appeal Judgement, para. 14.

30 Blagojević Notice of Appeal, paras. 1, 2; Blagojević Appeal Brief, paras. 1.1–1.4, 2.1–2.40. *See also* AT. 88–108.

31 Trial Judgement, paras. 888–892.

32 *See generally Blagojević, Ex Parte* and Confidential Reasons for Decision on Appeal by Vidoje Blagojević to Replace His Defence Team, paras. 2–5; *Blagojević and Jokić*, Decision on Independent Counsel for Vidoje Blagojević's Motion to Instruct the Registrar to Appoint New Lead and Co-Counsel, paras. 1–22; *Blagojević et al.*, Decision by the Registrar, 8 April 2003, pp. 1–2; *Blagojević et al.*, Decision on Oral Motion to Replace Co-Counsel, pp. 2–6.

33 *See* Trial Judgement, para. 865; *Blagojević and Jokić*, Decision on Vidoje Blagojević's Oral Request, p. 2 fn. 3; *Blagojević*, Decision by the Registrar, 5 September 2001, p.1.

34 Trial Judgement, para. 865.

35 AT. 91–93, 107–108, 121.

36 *Blagojević, Ex Parte* and Confidential Reasons for Decision on Appeal by Vidoje Blagojević to Replace His Defence Team, para. 2. *See also Blagojević et al.*, Decision on Oral Motion to Replace Co-Counsel, pp. 2–6.

37 *Blagojević, Ex Parte* and Confidential Reasons for Decision on Appeal by Vidoje Blagojević to Replace His Defence Team, para. 3. *See also Blagojević and Jokić*, Decision on Independent Counsel for Vidoje Blagojević's Motion to Instruct the Registrar to Appoint New Lead and Co-Counsel, paras. 28–42.

his counsel had irreparably destroyed the trust between them by accusing him of seeking to replace his lawyers in an attempt to engage in fee-splitting.[38] **[page 7]**

14. The Appeals Chamber ultimately confirmed that as a participant in the International Tribunal's legal aid program, Blagojević did not have the absolute right to choose his counsel;[39] that the Registrar had properly assigned competent counsel committed to representing Blagojević's interests;[40] that good cause did not exist for removing his duly assigned defence team;[41] and that he was not justified in unilaterally refusing to cooperate with his lawyers.[42] In dismissing Blagojević's interlocutory appeal, the Appeals Chamber further added that, in such circumstances, the assigned counsel had the professional obligation to continue representing Blagojević.[43] In addition, the Appeals Chamber found no error in the Trial Chamber's conclusion that the retention of Blagojević's assigned counsel would not only protect his right to be tried fairly but also his right to be tried expeditiously.[44]

15. As the trial proceeded, Blagojević persisted in not communicating with his counsel and resisted attempts by the Trial Chamber to restore the communication.[45] Blagojević claims that his counsel devised a defence strategy and conducted the case without his input and, as a result, in a manner that was ineffective and prejudicial to his interests.[46] In addition, he notes that the Trial Chamber's requirement that his counsel examine him if he appeared as a witness prevented him from testifying in his own defence.[47]

16. Blagojević now requests the Appeals Chamber to grant him a new trial to rectify the alleged violations of his right to counsel of his choice, right to competent counsel, and right to appear as a witness in his own trial.[48] The Appeals Chamber considered many of the issues raised by Blagojević on the composition and competence of his defence team when it dismissed his interlocutory appeal at the outset of trial. The purpose of an interlocutory appeal is to decide the presented issues with finality.[49] Therefore, in assessing the alleged violations under this ground of appeal, the Appeals Chamber focuses primarily on events following its interlocutory appeal **[page 8]** decision that either would call into question the basis of the decision or that might constitute previously unconsidered violations.

1. Alleged Violation of Right to Choice of Counsel

17. Blagojević submits that the Trial Chamber violated his right to counsel of his choice when it refused to replace his entire defence team after the breakdown in trust and communication between him and his assigned counsel.[50] This submission consists of two principal arguments. First, Blagojević maintains that, even as a participant in the International Tribunal's legal aid system, he has a right to counsel of his choice.[51] This argument has no merit. An accused who lacks the means to remunerate counsel shall have the right to have counsel assigned to him by the Registrar from the list drawn up in accordance with Rule 45(B), provided

38 *Blagojević*, *Ex Parte* and Confidential Reasons for Decision on Appeal by Vidoje Blagojević to Replace His Defence Team, paras. 34–41.
39 *Blagojević*, *Ex Parte* and Confidential Reasons for Decision on Appeal by Vidoje Blagojević to Replace His Defence Team, paras. 22, 33, 54.
40 *Blagojević*, *Ex Parte* and Confidential Reasons for Decision on Appeal by Vidoje Blagojević to Replace His Defence Team, para. 54.
41 *Blagojević*, *Ex Parte* and Confidential Reasons for Decision on Appeal by Vidoje Blagojević to Replace His Defence Team, paras. 16–22, 24–33, 42–54.
42 *Blagojević*, *Ex Parte* and Confidential Reasons for Decision on Appeal by Vidoje Blagojević to Replace His Defence Team, paras. 31, 51, 54.
43 *Blagojević*, *Ex Parte* and Confidential Reasons for Decision on Appeal by Vidoje Blagojević to Replace His Defence Team, paras. 52, 54.
44 *Blagojević*, *Ex Parte* and Confidential Reasons for Decision on Appeal by Vidoje Blagojević to Replace His Defence Team, para. 50. *See also Blagojević and Jokić*, Decision on Independent Counsel for Vidoje Blagojević's Motion to Instruct the Registrar to Appoint New Lead and Co-Counsel, paras. 112, 113.
45 *See Blagojević and Jokić*, Decision on Vidoje Blagojević's Oral Request, pp. 3, 4. *See also* Blagojević Appeal Brief, para. 2.32; AT. 95, 96, 122, 125, 126.
46 Blagojević Appeal Brief, paras. 2.14–2.20, 2.23, 2.35, 2.37, 2.38; T. 90, 96–97, 122–123.
47 Blagojević Appeal Brief, paras. 2.4, 2.30; AT. 96, 124–125.
48 Blagojević Appeal Brief, paras. 2.40–2.42; AT. 98–100.
49 *Čelebići* Appeal Judgment, para. 122.
50 Blagojević Appeal Brief, paras. 2.4–2.14.
51 Blagojević Appeal Brief, paras. 2.4–2.6; Blagojević Reply Brief, para. 2.12.

that there is no impediment to the assignment of that counsel.[52] While there is the additional limitation placed on the right of an indigent accused to choose counsel in so far as the choice is limited to the list of counsel maintained in accordance with Rule 45, as previously explained in this case, the Registrar normally takes account of an accused's preferences in assigning counsel, as was done in the present case, but it is also within the Registrar's discretion to override that preference in the interests of justice.[53] Once counsel has been properly assigned, as was the case here, counsel has a professional obligation to continue representing the accused and may only be withdrawn or replaced, if sufficient cause exists.[54]

18. Second, Blagojević disputes the conclusion of the Appeals Chamber and Trial Chamber that he was not justified in resisting his assigned legal representation and that he did not show good cause for removing his assigned counsel.[55] Blagojević contends that the breakdown was not, in fact, unilateral because his counsel falsely accused him of trying to engage in fee-splitting.[56] Blagojević argues that this "false and tendentious accusation" destroyed all possibility of re-establishing any form of cooperation between them because in his view his counsel had accused him of being a "common criminal".[57] Though the Appeals Chamber found this argument to be without merit at the **[page 9]** pre-trial stage,[58] Blagojević points to an exchange at a status conference during the trial where Mr. Karnavas, in his view, acknowledged and apologized for making false accusations against him, thereby vindicating his refusal to deal with his counsel.[59]

19. The Appeals Chamber previously explained that the matter of alleged fee-splitting had no bearing on the Trial Chamber's decision to maintain Blagojević's assigned counsel.[60] The Appeals Chamber nonetheless considered the nature and possible impact of such an allegation on the lawyer-client relationship "for completeness and to ensure finality".[61] The Appeals Chamber noted that the assigned counsel did not breach any client confidence by raising the issue of fee-splitting, as he was ethically bound to bring such issues to the attention of the Registrar.[62] The Appeals Chamber also determined that this issue should not unduly impact the relationship, in particular, noting that Mr. Karnavas did not place blame on Blagojević for attempting to enter into a fee-splitting arrangement and instead explained that it resulted from "family pressures".[63] The Appeals Chamber observed that this was consistent with Blagojević's own explanation.[64] A review of the transcripts of the status conference pointed to by Blagojević does not, contrary to his submissions, indicate that Mr. Karnavas admitted to falsely accusing him of trying to engage in fee-splitting. Rather, Mr. Karnavas simply made clear, consistent with the submissions previously considered by the Appeals Chamber, that he never accused Blagojević himself of trying to engage in fee-splitting.[65]

20. In addition, Blagojević seeks to reopen the issues considered and decided in the interlocutory appeal by arguing that the Appeals Chamber and Trial Chamber failed to appreciate that the breakdown of his relationship with his counsel would last throughout the trial and prevent him from playing any meaningful

---

52 Rules, Rule 45; Directive on Assignment of Defence Counsel, Articles 6 and 11(D)(i).

53 *Blagojević*, *Ex Parte* and Confidential Reasons for Decision on Appeal by Vidoje Blagojević to Replace His Defence Team, para. 22 fn. 54. *See also Mejakić et al.*, Decision on Appeal by the Prosecution to Resolve Conflict of Interest Regarding Attorney Jovan Simić, para. 8; *Nahimana et al.*, Decision on Appellant Jean-Bosco Barayagwiza's Motion Contesting the Decision of the President Refusing to Review and Reverse the Decision of the Registrar relating to the Withdrawal of Co-Counsel, para. 10; *Akayesu* Appeal Judgement, para. 61; *Kambanda* Appeal Judgement, para. 33.

54 *Blagojević*, *Ex Parte* and Confidential Reasons for Decision on Appeal by Vidoje Blagojević to Replace His Defence Team, paras. 52, 54.

55 Blagojević Appeal Brief, paras. 2.8–2.14.

56 AT. 94–96, 108.

57 AT. 94, 95, 103, 108, 122.

58 *Blagojević*, *Ex Parte* and Confidential Reasons for Decision on Appeal by Vidoje Blagojević to Replace His Defence Team, paras. 42–48.

59 AT. 95–96.

60 *Blagojević*, *Ex Parte* and Confidential Reasons for Decision on Appeal by Vidoje Blagojević to Replace His Defence Team, para. 45.

61 *Blagojević*, *Ex Parte* and Confidential Reasons for Decision on Appeal by Vidoje Blagojević to Replace His Defence Team, paras. 9–11, 42.

62 *Blagojević*, *Ex Parte* and Confidential Reasons for Decision on Appeal by Vidoje Blagojević to Replace His Defence Team, para. 46.

63 *Blagojević*, *Ex Parte* and Confidential Reasons for Decision on Appeal by Vidoje Blagojević to Replace His Defence Team, para. 47.

64 *Blagojević*, *Ex Parte* and Confidential Reasons for Decision on Appeal by Vidoje Blagojević to Replace His Defence Team, para. 47.

65 T. 11858 ("I just want to reiterate, one, I have done nothing for which I need to explain or apologise. I have never divulged any attorney/client privileges, nor have I ever accused Mr. Blagojević of making any attempts to fee split as he seems to indicate. I've never accused him of that, nor has he ever made any efforts himself. So I want to make sure that's very clear on the record. I have nothing more, Your Honour.").

role in his defence.[66] However, Blagojević's submissions before **[page 10]** trial clearly indicated that he considered the breakdown irreparable.[67] Nonetheless, Blagojević correctly notes that both the Appeals Chamber and Trial Chamber expressed measured optimism that the situation between him and his counsel would improve.[68] This view resulted from the determination that there was no objective basis for Blagojević to be dissatisfied with his counsel's performance.[69] Blagojević has not called this conclusion into question. More importantly, however, Blagojević's argument on this point fails to address the key aspect of the Appeals Chamber's earlier holding. In dismissing Blagojević's interlocutory appeal, the Appeals Chamber stated:

> In circumstances such as this, where an Appellant unjustifiably resists legal representation from assigned Counsel, Counsel's professional obligations to continue to represent the accused remain. The Appeals Chamber is satisfied that Counsel in this case is committed to representing the Appellant, and that the Appellant will receive a fair trial with the assistance of his assigned Counsel. In dismissing the Appellant's appeal, the Appeals Chamber wishes to make it clear to the Appellant that he has now exhausted all avenues available to him to voice his objections that he has not been accorded that to which he has no justifiable reason to demand. The Tribunal will not entertain a demand by an Appellant for that to be granted to him to which he has established no legal entitlement.[70]

21. Blagojević's own submissions under the present ground of appeal reflect that the continued breakdown during the trial and the resulting complaints about the conduct of his defence also resulted from his unilateral refusal to communicate with his counsel, rather than from any action on the part of his counsel and Defence team.[71] The Trial Chamber's decision on Blagojević's request to testify is exemplary of Mr. Karnavas's continued willingness to meet with and assist him and of Blagojević's unilateral resistance to any cooperation.[72] The Appeals Chamber considers that an **[page 11]** appellant cannot premise a request for a new trial on a claim of a total breakdown in communication in circumstances where the appellant unjustifiably refused to cooperate with his or her assigned counsel throughout the trial proceedings.

2. <u>Alleged Violation of Right to Competent Counsel</u>

22. Blagojević submits that his assigned counsel conducted his defence without his input and thus provided ineffective representation that was prejudicial.[73]

---

66 Blagojević Appeal Brief, paras. 2.22, 2.31; AT. 91, 94.

67 *See, e.g., Blagojević, Ex Parte* and Confidential Reasons for Decision on Appeal by Vidoje Blagojević to Replace His Defence Team, para. 41 ("[Blagojević] says that he 'categorically refuses to accept assignment of a legal representative as decided by the Trial Chamber,' and that the conflict between him and his assigned Counsel is of such seriousness that he cannot envisage that he could ever work with them again.").

68 Blagojević Appeal Brief, para. 2.33. *Blagojević, Ex Parte* and Confidential Reasons for Decision on Appeal by Vidoje Blagojević to Replace His Defence Team, para. 51.

69 *Blagojević, Ex Parte* and Confidential Reasons for Decision on Appeal by Vidoje Blagojević to Replace His Defence Team, para. 49.

70 *Blagojević, Ex Parte* and Confidential Reasons for Decision on Appeal by Vidoje Blagojević to Replace His Defence Team, para. 54.

71 Blagojević Appeal Brief, para. 2.33 ("[...] the Decisions of both Trial Chamber and the Appeals Chamber were passed when the trial was at the beginning [...] and [...] it was expected that the rebuilding of confidence between the Accused and Mr. Karnavas would take place during the course of the trial or at least up to the beginning of the Defence case. It did not happen since the Accused stayed at his opinion against imposing Mr. Karnavas as his Defence counsel as from the very beginning[...]. Expectations that the change will take place in any of the procedure stage was really without any grounds."); AT. 96 ("[Blagojević] abided by his position that he could have no contact with the counsel who had been appointed by the Registry against his will."); AT 126 ("this was a complete breakdown of communication, making it impossible to cooperate because of the accusations that were made. After the serious accusation was made, no further contact was possible until the end of the trial.").

72 *See, e.g., Blagojević and Jokić*, Decision on Vidoje Blagojević's Oral Request, pp. 8–10 ("Considering Therefore that the Trial Chamber ordered the Accused to meet with Mr. Karnavas to discuss the three options available to him[...]. Considering that the Accused refused to meet with Mr. Karnavas, as instructed by the Trial Chamber[...]. Considering that Mr. Karnavas indicated he would be prepared to proceed with the direct examination on the next day of the proceedings, indicating that it would be Mr. Blagojević's choice of whether to prepare for the direct examination with him[...]. Considering that after the Accused indicated that he needs preparation before his testimony but would not conduct any preparations with Mr. Karnavas [...] the Accused responded that he would not answer any questions put to him on direct examination by Mr. Karnavas.").

73 Blagojević Appeal Brief, paras. 2.14–2.20, 2.23, 2.35, 2.37, 2.38; AT. 90, 96–97, 122–123.

23. A participant in the International Tribunal's legal aid system has the right to competent assigned counsel.[74] An assigned counsel is presumed to be competent and such a presumption can only be rebutted by evidence to the contrary.[75] Among other things, an appellant must demonstrate "gross incompetence" on the part of the assigned counsel.[76]

24. Blagojević points to four principal examples of alleged deficient representation in his case. First, he claims that his counsel did not properly characterize his relationship with and authority over Momir Nikolić and the Bratunac Brigade Military Police.[77] Second, he complains about the selection of the expert witness for the defence and the fact that this witness was not called to testify.[78] Third, Blagojević faults his counsel's examination of witnesses as well as his selection of Witnesses Ljubomir Beatović, DP-106, and Dragomir Keserović, who, he claims, incriminated him.[79] Fourth, he refers to two decisions where the Trial Chamber criticized Mr. Karnavas's performance.[80]

25. As a general matter, in his submissions Blagojević simply disagrees or complains about decisions made by his counsel.[81] Moreover, Blagojević's complaints about his counsel's performance during trial stem from his refusal to communicate with his counsel and instruct his **[page 12]** Defence team. The Appeals Chamber considers that this is not an acceptable basis for challenging counsel's conduct. His cursory submissions therefore fail to demonstrate that his counsel's performance constituted "gross incompetence".

3. Alleged Violation of Right to Appear as a Witness

26. Blagojević submits that the Trial Chamber denied him the right to appear as a witness by requiring that he be examined by his assigned counsel if he wished to testify in his defence.[82] The Trial Chamber summarized, as follows, the three possibilities it presented to Blagojević in connection with exercising his right to be heard as well the manner in which this issue was resolved during trial:

> On various occasions during the trial, Vidoje Blagojević expressed the intention to address the Trial Chamber, including as a witness. On 17 June 2004, the Trial Chamber held a motion hearing during which it explained to Vidoje Blagojević the options available to him in relation with his right to remain silent and his right to address the Trial Chamber. These options were "to exercise his right to remain silent", "to make a statement under the control of the Trial Chamber" or "to testify under oath like any other witnesses," meaning that he would answer the questions put to him by his counsel. Vidoje Blagojević indicated that he wished to testify before the Trial Chamber in open session, but that it would be impossible for him to answer his counsel's questions. On 30 July 2004, the Trial Chamber decided that under these circumstances, only two options remained available to Vidoje Blagojević: either to remain silent, or to make a sworn or unsworn statement under the control of the Trial Chamber pursuant to Rule 84*bis*. The Blagojević Defence requested certification to appeal this decision; the Trial Chamber denied the request. On 9 September 2004, a hearing was held in order to permit Vidoje Blagojević an opportunity to be heard, should he choose to waive his right to remain silent. Refusing again to follow the procedure Vidoje Blagojević declined to choose another possibility than testifying under oath and therefore remained silent.[83]

---

[74] *Akayesu* Appeal Judgement, para. 76. *See also Halilović*, Decision on Interlocutory Appeal Concerning Admission of Record of Interview of the Accused from the Bar Table, paras. 61, 62. *See also* Rules, Rule 45(A)-(B); Directive on Assignment of Defence Counsel, Article 14.

[75] *Akayesu* Appeal Judgement, paras. 77, 78. *See also Tadić*, Decision on Appellant's Motion for the Extension of the Time-Limit and Admission of Additional Evidence, para. 48.

[76] *Akayesu* Appeal Judgement, paras. 77, 78, 80. *See also Tadić*, Decision on Appellant's Motion for the Extension of the Time-Limit and Admission of Additional Evidence, para. 49.

[77] Blagojević Appeal Brief, paras. 2.14, 2.19, 2.20; AT. 123–124.

[78] Blagojević Appeal Brief, paras. 2.17, 2.18, 2.37, 2.38; Blagojević Reply Brief, paras. 2.32–2.37; AT. 97, 123.

[79] Blagojević Appeal Brief, paras. 2.17, 2.18; Blagojević Reply Brief, paras. 2.24–2.31; AT. 96, 123–124.

[80] Blagojević Appeal Brief, para. 2.17.

[81] *See, e.g.*, Blagojević Appeal Brief, paras. 2.16–2.20; AT. 96 ("Mr. Blagojević had no influence on the course of the trial during the Prosecution case; and, which is far worse, he had no influence in the course of the Defence case, which was handled by a team of counsel imposed on him without his knowledge and influence. That is why some witnesses of the so-called Defence were hostile and detrimental to his case. These, however, are details.").

[82] Blagojević Appeal Brief, paras. 2.4, 2.30; Blagojević Reply Brief, paras. 2.41–2.45; AT. 96, 124–125.

[83] Trial Judgement, para. 907 (internal citations omitted). *See also Blagojević and Jokić*, Decision on Vidoje Blagojević's Oral Request, pp. 5–10.

27. In the *Galić* Appeal Judgement, the Appeals Chamber confirmed that an accused has the right to appear as a witness in his defence.[84] The Appeals Chamber equally determined that this right does not prevent a Trial Chamber from exercising its authority to control the conduct of a trial by imposing conditions on the right to appear as a witness, provided these conditions do not unreasonably interfere with the right to testify.[85]

28. In the present case, the only condition imposed on Blagojević's right to testify was that his assigned counsel would be responsible for examining him. The Appeals Chamber notes that Blagojević stated that he would answer questions put to him by the parties that "incorporate[ed] the examination-in-chief and cross-examination"[86] and that he needed assistance in preparing for his **[page 13]** testimony.[87] In these circumstances, it was not unreasonable for the Trial Chamber to require Blagojević to be examined by his assigned counsel if he chose to testify, notwithstanding his persistent refusal to communicate with Mr. Karnavas. The Appeals Chamber is of the view that the Trial Chamber made extensive efforts to ensure that Blagojević was advised of the consequences of testifying and was given the opportunity to testify or otherwise be heard before the end of the case.[88] It was Blagojević's unjustified and unilateral refusal to communicate with his assigned counsel that resulted in his failure to testify, rather than any action or unjustified restriction imposed on his right by the Trial Chamber.

29. Therefore, the Appeals Chamber is not satisfied that the conditions placed by the Trial Chamber on Blagojević's right to testify on his own behalf, namely that his counsel conduct the examination, so unreasonably interfered with his right to testify that his right to a fair trial was infringed.

4. Conclusion

30. Accordingly, the Appeals Chamber dismisses this ground of appeal. Judge Shahabuddeen dissents on the ground that Blagojević was denied the right to a fair trial and considers that his case should be remanded for a new trial. **[page 14]**

B. Alleged Errors relating to Factual Findings (Ground 2)

31. Blagojević submits that the Trial Chamber committed a number of errors of fact resulting in his convictions for complicity in genocide, aiding and abetting murder as a violation of the laws or customs of war, and aiding and abetting murder, persecutions, and other inhumane acts (forcible transfer) as crimes against humanity. The Appeals Chamber will address the individual alleged errors in turn.

1. Blocking of Humanitarian Convoys to Srebrenica

32. The Trial Chamber found that, beginning in February 1995, elements of the Bratunac Brigade restricted the movement of international convoys of humanitarian aid and supplies into the Srebrenica "safe area" at the Žuti Most checkpoint, impacting the rotation and readiness of troops of the Dutch Battalion of UNPROFOR ("DutchBat") and causing a further deterioration of the humanitarian situation in the Srebrenica enclave.[89]

---

[84] *Galić* Appeal Judgement, paras. 19, 22.

[85] *Galić* Appeal Judgement, paras. 19, 20, 22. In the *Galić* Appeal Judgement, the restriction at issue related to the timing of the accused's testimony.

[86] T. 12267.

[87] *Blagojević and Jokić*, Decision on Vidoje Blagojević's Oral Request, pp. 7–8, 10.

[88] The Trial Chamber also offered Blagojević the opportunity to make a sworn or unsworn statement under the control of the Trial Chamber. Blagojević explained to the Trial Chamber that he did not want to pursue this option because the Trial Chamber indicated that it might not carry the same weight as testimony given under oath and subject to cross-examination and further inquiry from the Trial Chamber. *See Blagojević and Jokić*, Decision on Vidoje Blagojević's Oral Request, pp. 7, 10. However, the Appeals Chamber observes that, in explaining that the statement might carry less weight, the Trial Chamber referred specifically to the situation where a statement would be unsworn. In addition, in making its observation, the Trial Chamber did not state that it would definitively accord such a statement less weight, in particular if it were sworn. Blagojević has made no submissions suggesting that this would have been an unreasonable alternative to being examined by his counsel or that it would fail to satisfy his right to appear as a witness in his defence.

[89] Trial Judgement, paras. 111, 138, 474.

33. Blagojević submits that the Trial Chamber erred in fact in making its factual findings on the role of the Bratunac Brigade in blocking humanitarian convoys bound for Srebrenica as well as its findings on the sufficiency of supplies in the Srebrenica enclave.[90] He argues that the VRS Main Staff, and not the command of the Bratunac Brigade, controlled the flow of humanitarian supplies into the Srebrenica enclave at žuti Most.[91] In addition, he points to Defence Exhibit 55, a top-secret report from the defences of the municipality of Srebrenica to the secretariat of defence in Tuzla, dated 5 June 1995, reflecting that several tons of food and other supplies reached the enclave in addition to humanitarian supplies received from the United Nations High Commissioner for Refugees and DutchBat.[92] Blagojević argues that this credible defence evidence from the archives of the Army of Bosnia-Herzegovina ("ABiH") as well as his own characterization of the situation demonstrate that the enclave had sufficient supplies.[93]

34. Blagojević has not demonstrated under this sub-ground of appeal that any alleged error on the part of the Trial Chamber resulted in a miscarriage of justice. The Trial Chamber considered the blocking of humanitarian convoys as an unpleaded "background issue" that "pre-date[s] the start of the Accused's criminal liability."[94] While the Trial Chamber acknowledged that events other than **[page 15]** those charged in the Indictment could be used to prove an issue relevant to the charges,[95] Blagojević has not articulated how any specific finding by the Trial Chamber on his criminal responsibility or sentence is implicated by this challenge. Blagojević's assertions concerning the control of the check-point were not at issue in the trial. The Trial Chamber did not place any direct responsibility on Blagojević in connection with the blocking of humanitarian convoys.[96] In addition, the Trial Chamber also expressly declined to consider these events as an *actus reus* of genocide.[97] The only conclusions the Trial Chamber drew from the evidence on this point were Blagojević's awareness of the basic need for supplies in the enclave and the DutchBat's inability to deal with the humanitarian situation following the military assault against Srebrenica.[98] The Trial Chamber used its findings on the blocking of humanitarian aid only generally as background, along with a substantial body of other evidence, to reflect that Blagojević had knowledge that his own acts occurred as part of the larger attack.[99]

35. Accordingly, the Appeals Chamber dismisses this sub-ground of appeal. Judge Shahabuddeen dissents on the ground that Blagojević was denied the right to a fair trial and considers that his case should be remanded for a new trial.

2. Role of Blagojević and the Bratunac Brigade in the Attack on Srebrenica

36. The Trial Chamber determined that, on 2 July 1995, the commander of the Drina Corps issued "Krivaja 95", an order for active combat operations, with the stated objective of reducing the Srebrenica enclave to its urban area.[100] However, as the operation progressed, the Trial Chamber noted, the military objective changed to the taking-over of Srebrenica town and the enclave as a whole.[101] The Trial Chamber found that on 6 July 1995, the VRS commenced an assault against Srebrenica, leading to its fall on 11 July 1995 and resulting in a humanitarian crisis impacting the approximately 40,000 people who lived in the enclave.[102] The Trial Chamber found that the attack was directed against the Bosnian Muslim civilian population in the Srebrenica enclave.[103] In making this finding, the Trial Chamber considered that, at the time, between 1,000 and 4,000 **[page 16]** soldiers of the 28th Division of the Army of Bosnia-Herzegovina ("28th Division") also operated within the enclave.[104]

---

90 Blagojević Notice of Appeal, para. 4; Blagojević Appeal Brief, paras. 3.3–3.9.
91 Blagojević Appeal Brief, paras. 3.4, 3.6–3.8.
92 Blagojević Appeal Brief, para. 3.9. The exhibit referred to by Blagojević as Defence Exhibit 55 was filed as D232/1.
93 Blagojević Appeal Brief, paras. 3.5, 3.9.
94 Trial Judgement, paras. 136–137, 140.
95 Trial Judgement, paras. 137, 473.
96 Trial Judgement, paras. 474, 475.
97 Trial Judgement, para. 641 fn. 2056.
98 Trial Judgement, paras. 474, 475, 484.
99 Trial Judgement, paras. 551, 553.
100 Trial Judgement, para. 120.
101 Trial Judgement, para. 130.
102 Trial Judgement, paras. 125–133, 551.
103 Trial Judgement, para. 552.
104 Trial Judgement, para. 552.

37. Blagojević submits that the Trial Chamber erred in fact in its characterization of the attack against Srebrenica as an illegitimate attack directed at the civilian population as well as in its findings on the role he and the Bratunac Brigade played in the attack.[105] Blagojević describes the attack against Srebrenica, pursuant to "Krivaja 95", as a legitimate military operation directed against the 28th Division of the ABiH in response to attacks on Serbian civilians and the VRS and in response to anticipated offensive military operations.[106] Moreover, according to Blagojević, the role of the Bratunac Brigade under "Krivaja 95" was to maintain its defensive position between the enclave and Bratunac town in the event of an attack by the ABiH.[107] Blagojević asserts that although he issued an order of active combat on 5 July 1995, the Bratunac Brigade never engaged in combat with the 28th Division because, contrary to expectations, the 28th Division formed a column leaving the enclave in a direction away from the Bratunac Brigade.[108] He submits that the Bratunac Brigade did not leave its positions until 17 July 1995 when the high command ordered it to go to žepa.[109]

38. In challenging the Trial Chamber's characterization of the attack, Blagojević first addresses the legitimacy of the attack. He supports his position that the attack had a legitimate military purpose by pointing to two exhibits which he alleges emanate from the Main Staff of the ABiH referring to an anticipated offensive by the 28th Division, which was operating in the enclave.[110] The record does not reflect that the Trial Chamber admitted the exhibits referred to by Blagojević into evidence. In any event, the Trial Chamber expressly considered evidence of the activities and the presence of the 28th Division of the ABiH in the enclave in making its findings on the nature of the attack.[111] In addition, a review of the Trial Judgement reveals that in assessing the issues concerning the nature of the attack, the Trial Chamber relied on first-hand and expert testimony as **[page 17]** well as official reports in connection with its findings on the general factual context of the events.[112] Significantly, Blagojević does not identify any specific deficiencies in the evidence referred to by the Trial Chamber.

39. In particular, the Trial Chamber explained that "[t]he attack continued after the fall of Srebrenica and affected the approximately 40,000 people who lived within the Srebrenica enclave at the time of that attack."[113] The Trial Chamber also expressly focused its findings on "the effect of the attack on the civilians."[114] Blagojević does not address the broader attack as defined by the Trial Chamber.

40. Furthermore, Blagojević's submissions on the actions of the Bratunac Brigade appear to be his own view of what transpired, unsupported by any reference to the trial record. Such submissions do not call into question the reasonableness of the Trial Chamber's findings.

41. In any event, the Appeals Chamber notes that Blagojević has not demonstrated that any alleged error on the part of the Trial Chamber on this point resulted in a miscarriage of justice. The Trial Chamber considered the military assault against Srebrenica from 6 July 1995 as an unpleaded "background issue" that "pre-date[s] the start of the Accused's criminal liability",[115] and Blagojević has not articulated how this challenge implicates any specific finding by the Trial Chamber on his criminal responsibility. The Appeals Chamber notes that the Trial Chamber considered this evidence only as background in connection with its assessment of the general requirements of Articles 3 and 5 of the Statute as well as the *mens rea* of the crime of genocide.[116]

---

105 Blagojević Notice of Appeal, para. 5; Blagojević Appeal Brief, paras. 3.10–3.19. Blagojević addresses the Trial Chamber's findings on the specific actions of the Bratunac Brigade in his other factual grounds of appeal. *See* Ground 2.3 (Firing on Civilians in Srebrenica and *en route* to Potočari), Ground 2.4 (Removal of Civilians from Potočari), Ground 2.5 (Searching the Terrain and Attack on the Column), Ground 2.6 (Detention, Mistreatment, and Murders in Bratunac Town), Ground 3 (Murder), Ground 4 (Forcible Transfer), and Ground 7 (Aiding and Abetting) of the Appeal Judgement.

106 Blagojević Appeal Brief, paras. 3.10–3.14.

107 Blagojević Appeal Brief, para. 3.15.

108 Blagojević Appeal Brief, paras. 3.16, 3.17.

109 Blagojević Appeal Brief, paras. 3.17–3.19.

110 Blagojević Appeal Brief, paras. 3.13, 3.14, citing Defence Exhibits 59, 60. Blagojević describes Defence Exhibit 59 as an order dated 17 June 1995 from the ABiH Main Staff to the command of the 28th Division ordering it to implement all preparations for an "offensive" directed at liberating territory. He describes Defence Exhibit 60 as a report referring to preparations for an offensive to liberate territory.

111 *See* Trial Judgement, paras. 115, 522. *See also Musema* Appeal Judgement, para. 20; *Kajelijeli* Appeal Judgement, para. 75.

112 Trial Judgement, para. 553 fn. 1869 (referring to sections II, III, and IV of the Trial Judgement).

113 Trial Judgement, para. 551.

114 Trial Judgement, para. 140.

115 Trial Judgement, paras. 136, 137, 140.

116 Trial Judgement, paras. 551, 552, 674, 786.

42. Accordingly, the Appeals Chamber dismisses this sub-ground of appeal. Judge Shahabuddeen dissents on the ground that Blagojević was denied the right to a fair trial and considers that his case should be remanded for a new trial.

3. Firing on Civilians in Srebrenica and *en route* to Potočari

43. The Trial Chamber found that, in the months before the attack on Srebrenica, elements of the Bratunac Brigade shelled and opened sniper fire on the enclave.[117] In addition, with respect to the events occurring on 11 July 1995, the Trial Chamber found that the VRS, including elements of **[page 18]** the Bratunac Brigade, shelled and shot at a column of civilian refugees headed from Srebrenica town to Potočari.[118] Blagojević submits that the Trial Chamber erred in fact in finding that the Bratunac Brigade fired on Srebrenica during the period before and after the fall of the enclave on 11 July 1995.[119]

(a) Alleged Error related to Firing on Srebrenica before 11 July 1995

44. Blagojević submits that there is no evidence to support the finding that the Bratunac Brigade fired on Srebrenica in the months before the attack and notes that this, in any event, would have predated the assumption of his command.[120]

45. A review of the Trial Judgement reveals that the Trial Chamber relied primarily on the evidence of Momir Nikolić and Mićo Gavrić to support its conclusion that the Bratunac Brigade fired on the enclave in the months before the July 1995 military assault on Srebrenica.[121] In particular, the Trial Chamber referred to the testimony of Momir Nikolić, a former member of the Bratunac Brigade, who stated generally that elements of the brigade opened sniper fire on members of the army and civilians in the enclave both before and after Blagojević assumed command.[122] In addition, the Trial Chamber relied on the evidence of Mićo Gavrić, the head of the brigade's Mixed Artillery Group, who acknowledged firing into the enclave on one occasion on 25 May 1995.[123] However, referring to the evidence of Robert Franken, the deputy commander of DutchBat, stationed in Potočari at the time, the Trial Chamber found that the VRS generally shelled the western part of the enclave.[124] The Appeals Chamber observes that Franken stated that "mostly it was done in the area of the Milici Brigade."[125] Blagojević has not pointed to any deficiencies in the evidence related to the firing by the Bratunac Brigade. Consequently, Blagojević has not demonstrated that the Trial Chamber erred in its findings on the pre-attack fire on the enclave.

46. In any event, the Appeals Chamber notes that Blagojević has not articulated how any of the alleged errors concerning the limited evidence of the shelling and sniping by the Bratunac Brigade before the attack invalidated any part of the Trial Judgement. The Trial Chamber did not ascribe **[page 19]** any criminal responsibility to Blagojević based on these events and only considered them as background in connection with its assessment of the general requirements of Articles 3 and 5 of the Statute.[126]

---

117 Trial Judgement, paras. 117, 139.
118 Trial Judgement, paras. 131, 144.
119 Blagojević Notice of Appeal, para. 6; Blagojević Appeal Brief, paras. 3.20–3.27. The Appeals Chamber notes that in his brief, under this sub-ground of appeal, Blagojević also challenges the Trial Chamber's findings in paragraph 484 of the Trial Judgement concerning his criminal responsibility for the inhumane conditions facing the refugees in Potočari on 12 April 1995. These events do not directly relate to shelling of the civilians as described in the Notice of Appeal and are therefore not considered here. The Appeals Chamber will consider these arguments in connection with Blagojević's fourth ground of appeal concerning his conviction for inhumane acts. *See infra* section III.D.
120 Blagojević Appeal Brief, para. 3.26.
121 Trial Judgement, para. 117, fns. 371–373.
122 Trial Judgement, para. 117, citing Momir Nikolić, T. 1626–1627,1629–1634.
123 Trial Judgement, para. 117, citing Mićo Gavrić, T. 8605–8606.
124 Trial Judgement, para. 117 fn. 370.
125 T. 1478.
126 Trial Judgement, paras. 551–553, referring generally to all findings in Chapters I-III of the Trial Judgement. *See also* Trial Judgement, paras. 136, 137, 140.

(b) Alleged Errors related to Firing on a Column of Civilian Refugees on 11 July 1995

47. Blagojević submits that the Trial Chamber misinterpreted the evidence of Defence Witness Mićo Gavrić, the head of the Bratunac Brigade's Mixed Artillery Group, in finding that the brigade also fired on a column of civilians walking from Srebrenica town to Potočari after the fall of Srebrenica on 11 July 1995.[127] Blagojević notes that Gavrić's testimony, cited by the Trial Chamber for this proposition, expressly denies the targeting of civilians.[128] Furthermore, Blagojević alleges that the Trial Chamber erred in interpreting the general combat order, which he issued on 5 July 1995, as specifically authorizing the brigade to fire artillery on "the enclave".[129]

48. With respect to the role of the Bratunac Brigade in firing on the refugee column on 11 July 1995, which is within the period covered by the Indictment, the Appeals Chamber observes that the Trial Chamber took note of the testimony of various civilians forming part of the column, who attested to being fired on by the VRS.[130] In placing responsibility for at least a portion of this firing on the Bratunac Brigade, the Trial Chamber relied on the testimony of Momir Nikolić who stated that the Second Battalion of the Bratunac Brigade fired on civilians moving toward Potočari.[131] In addition, the Trial Chamber relied on the testimony of Mićo Gavrić who acknowledged adjusting his barrage to approximately three kilometres away from the refugees.[132]

49. Blagojević does not address the specific evidence given by Momir Nikolić in support of the Trial Chamber's findings. Rather, he primarily contends that the Trial Chamber misinterpreted Gavrić's testimony, emphasizing that Gavrić denied targeting civilians and fired from several kilometres away.[133] A review of the Trial Judgement and the underlying record reveals that, in relying on Gavrić's testimony, the Trial Chamber expressly acknowledged Gavrić's account of targeting an uninhabited village and correcting his line of fire to go beyond the civilians.[134] In the view of the Appeals Chamber, the Trial Chamber did not act unreasonably in relying on this testimony in support of its findings that the Bratunac Brigade fired on the refugees. Indeed, Gavrić **[page 20]** admitted firing in the general direction of the column.[135] Moreover, the Trial Chamber focused its findings generally on the fear and panic generated by the shelling, rather than any resultant death or bodily injury.[136]

50. Blagojević, moreover, stresses that Gavrić never stated that the general combat order authorized firing on the enclave, as the Trial Chamber indicated in describing his testimony.[137] In the view of the Appeals Chamber, however, Blagojević has failed to demonstrate the unreasonableness of the Trial Chamber's use of the expression "on the enclave" to describe the direction in which Gavrić actually fired. Indeed, the Appeals Chamber notes that Blagojević's order authorized Gavrić's Mixed Artillery Group to open fire on targets in the Potočari sector, which was in the enclave.[138]

51. The Appeals Chamber finds unpersuasive Blagojević's challenge to the sufficiency of the evidence underlying the Trial Chamber's general finding, made in paragraph 144 of the Trial Judgement, that the Second Battalion of the Bratunac Brigade fired on the column.[139] The Appeals Chamber notes that, in footnote 475 of the Trial Judgement, the Trial Chamber stated: "Mićo Gavrić testified that the 2nd Battalion of the Bratunac Brigade was firing on civilians who 'were on the move' toward Potočari." A review of the relevant transcripts reveals that this statement is misattributed to Mićo Gavrić. However, the statement is supported by the relevant references to Momir Nikolić's evidence, which are equally cited by the Trial Chamber in support

127 Blagojević Appeal Brief, paras. 3.23–3.25.
128 Blagojević Appeal Brief, para. 3.23.
129 Blagojević Appeal Brief, para. 3.24.
130 Trial Judgement, para. 144 fn. 474.
131 Trial Judgement, para. 144.
132 Trial Judgement, paras. 131, 144, citing Mićo Gavrić, T. 8485–8488, 8490, 8492.
133 Blagojević Appeal Brief, para. 3.23
134 Trial Judgement, paras. 131 fns. 430, 431; 144 fn. 475.
135 *See* Trial Judgement, para. 131.
136 Trial Judgement, paras. 207, 611.
137 Blagojević Appeal Brief, para. 3.24, referring to Trial Judgement, para. 131 ("[Gavrić] testified that [the written combat order from Colonel Blagojević on 5 July] was sufficient authorisation to use artillery fire on the enclave, which he did on 11 July.").
138 Trial Judgement, para. 124, citing Prosecution Exhibit 406.
139 Blagojević Appeal Brief, para. 3.27.

of the same finding.[140] Blagojević, however, makes no submissions concerning the reliability of this specific underlying evidence. Consequently, Blagojević has failed to demonstrate that the Trial Chamber erred in concluding that elements of the Bratunac Brigade participated in firing on the column.

(c) Conclusion

52. Accordingly, the Appeals Chamber dismisses this sub-ground of appeal. Judge Shahabuddeen dissents on the ground that Blagojević was denied the right to a fair trial and considers that his case should be remanded for a new trial. **[page 21]**

4. Removal of Civilians from Potočari

53. The Trial Chamber found that, after the fall of Srebrenica on 11 July 1995, several thousand Bosnian Muslims sought refuge in Potočari in part due to firing on the enclave by the VRS, including the Bratunac Brigade.[141] The Trial Chamber found that, on 12 and 13 July 1995, elements of the VRS transported Bosnian Muslim women, children, and the elderly from Potočari to Bosnian Muslim-held territory after separating them from the men, who in turn were transferred to Bratunac town.[142] The Trial Chamber noted that the MUP, acting on General Mladić's orders, played the principal role in the transport of refugees out of Potočari.[143] The Trial Chamber found that the Bratunac Brigade participated in this operation by contributing two buses and fuel, and by regulating traffic.[144] In addition, the Trial Chamber found that Momir Nikolić and other members of the Bratunac Brigade's Military Police, acting under orders of the security organ of the VRS Main Staff, took part in the separation process of Bosnian Muslim men from the women, children, and elderly by actively separating men from their families, providing security for other units engaged in the separations, counting people as they boarded buses, and participating in the transfer.[145] In addition, the Trial Chamber found that the mere presence of the Bratunac Brigade Military Police and members of the first, second, and third battalions in Potočari generally contributed to the atmosphere of fear there.[146]

54. Blagojević submits that the Trial Chamber erred in fact in connecting him and the Bratunac Brigade to the removal of civilians from Potočari.[147] Blagojević contends that the Bratunac Brigade was not under orders to take part in the transport and that, as such, neither he nor the brigade was involved in it.[148] He contends that Momir Nikolić and other members of the brigade's military police, who participated in the separation and transfer, acted exclusively under the authority of the VRS Main Staff.[149] In addition, Blagojević argues that any driver or vehicle with connections to the Bratunac Brigade that participated in the transfer did so on the basis of mobilization orders of the **[page 22]** Bratunac town's civil protection program as authorized by the Minister of Defence.[150] Moreover, according to Blagojević, other members of the Bratunac Brigade, who happened to be in Potočari at the time, either passed through the town on the way to other assignments or had returned there against orders to check on family members.[151]

140 Trial Judgement, para. 144 fn. 475. The correct reference is to Momir Nikolić's testimony at T. 1639–1640, cited at the beginning of the footnote.

141 Trial Judgement, paras. 141–146, 207.

142 Trial Judgement, paras. 180–192.

143 Trial Judgement, para. 191. MUP refers to the Ministry of the Interior of Republika Srpska. *See* Trial Judgement, Annex (1)(D)(6).

144 Trial Judgement, paras. 180, 186, 216.

145 Trial Judgement, paras. 181, 212, 216.

146 Trial Judgement, paras. 208, 214.

147 Blagojević Notice of Appeal, para. 7; Blagojević Appeal Brief, paras. 3.40–3.47. In his appeal brief under this sub-ground of appeal, Blagojević also challenges the Trial Chamber's findings concerning the involvement of two Bratunac Brigade soldiers in burials at Glogova. Blagojević Appeal Brief, paras. 3.48-3.54. However, these arguments exceed the scope of the notice of appeal. Moreover, Blagojević has not articulated how any specific finding by the Trial Chamber on his criminal responsibility is implicated by this challenge. Consequently, the Appeals Chamber declines to address these arguments.

148 Blagojević Appeal Brief, paras. 3.41–3.47.

149 Blagojević Appeal Brief, paras. 3.44, 3.45.

150 Blagojević Appeal Brief, para. 3.47.

151 Blagojević Appeal Brief, para. 3.46.

55. A review of the relevant portion of the Trial Judgement reveals that the Trial Chamber considered the testimony of numerous Prosecution and Defence witnesses, including former members of the Bratunac Brigade, before finding that elements of the brigade were involved in the separation and transfer.[152] Blagojević does not point to any deficiencies in this evidence nor does he dispute that certain members of the brigade participated in these events or were present in Potočari. Consequently, the Appeals Chamber finds that Blagojević has not demonstrated that no reasonable trier of fact could have found that elements of the brigade participated in the transfer. The Appeals Chamber notes that Blagojević primarily contests whether, under the circumstances, he can be held criminally responsible for the actions of these individuals. The Appeals Chamber will address these arguments below in connection with the grounds of Blagojević's appeal concerning his legal responsibility for the crimes committed by members of the Bratunac Brigade.[153]

56. Accordingly, the Appeals Chamber dismisses this sub-ground of appeal. Judge Shahabuddeen dissents on the ground that Blagojević was denied the right to a fair trial and considers that his case should be remanded for a new trial.

5. Searching the Terrain and Attack on the Column

57. The Trial Chamber observed that, on 12 July 1995, as the crisis deepened in Srebrenica, 10,000 to 15,000 mostly Bosnian Muslim men and boys, both civilians and members of the 28th Division of the ABiH, formed a column and proceeded toward Muslim-held territory in Tuzla.[154] The Trial Chamber concluded that, between 12 and 17 July 1995, the Drina Corps carried out searches of the area with the purpose of capturing the men from the column.[155] The Trial Chamber concluded that, in the end, elements of the VRS captured, mistreated, and killed thousands of men from this column in what it called a mass execution or murder operation.[156] The Trial Chamber found that members of the Bratunac Brigade's four battalions as well as its military police **[page 23]** participated in searching the terrain for members of the column with instructions to capture and disarm them.[157] The Trial Chamber concluded that these acts, among others, were a form of practical assistance in the murder operation that followed, but did not place any criminal responsibility on Blagojević for this because it found that he lacked knowledge of the perpetrators' intent to kill those captured.[158]

58. Blagojević submits that the Trial Chamber erred in fact in finding that the Bratunac Brigade played a role in the attack on the column.[159] He contends that the searches carried out by the Bratunac Brigade's four battalions near their locations had no connection to the actual interception of the column, which was conducted far from the brigade's positions by other VRS and special police units.[160] Blagojević further asserts that the Bratunac Brigade never came into contact with the 28th Division of the ABiH, highlighting the Trial Chamber's findings related to the interception of the column near Konjević Polje as well as a report from the commander of the Special Police, neither of which mentions the involvement of the brigade.[161]

59. In challenging the Trial Chamber's findings on this point, Blagojević does not dispute that members of the Bratunac Brigade searched the terrain, but rather focuses on the fact that they did not actually intercept members of the column.[162] A review of the Trial Judgement reveals, however, that the Trial Chamber agreed that, other than in a few cases, the brigade's participation in the search operation did not extend to actually capturing members of the column.[163] Relying, *inter alia*, on daily combat reports and first-hand accounts of participants of the search operation, the Trial Chamber concluded that armed and uniformed members

---

152 Trial Judgement, paras. 172, 173, 174, 176, 180, 181, 186, 189, 190, 191, 212–214, 216, 217.

153 *See generally* Blagojević Appeal Brief, Ground 4 (Forcible Transfer), Ground 6 (Complicity in Genocide), and Ground 7 (Aiding and Abetting), challenging the Trial Chamber's legal conclusion that Blagojević's acts constituted substantial assistance to the crimes.

154 Trial Judgement, paras. 218–221.

155 Trial Judgement, para. 222.

156 Trial Judgement, paras. 569, 732, 733, 736, 738.

157 Trial Judgement, paras. 258–263, 489.

158 Trial Judgement, paras. 736, 742, 745.

159 Blagojević Notice of Appeal, para. 8; Blagojević Appeal Brief, paras. 3.57–3.68.

160 Blagojević Appeal Brief, paras. 3.60–3.66

161 Blagojević Appeal Brief, paras. 3.65–3.68.

162 Blagojević Appeal Brief, paras. 3.58, 3.61.

163 Trial Judgement, paras. 224, 229, 258, 263.

of the Bratunac Brigade searched "in the area where the column was located on 12, 13, and 14 July".[164] Blagojević has not pointed to any deficiencies in the assessment of the specific evidence relied upon by the Trial Chamber in reaching its findings. Furthermore, Blagojević makes no specific submissions challenging the Trial Chamber's findings or the underlying evidence related to the few cases where the brigade captured individuals from the column. Therefore, he has not demonstrated that the Trial Chamber erred on this point.

60. In any event, the Appeals Chamber notes that Blagojević has not shown under this sub-ground of appeal that the alleged error resulted in a miscarriage of justice. Although determining **[page 24]** that the participation of the Bratunac Brigade in the search operation, taken together with other actions of the brigade, had a substantial effect on the commission of murder,[165] the Trial Chamber did not place any criminal responsibility on Blagojević for this, given his lack of knowledge that the capture and detention of the Bosnian Muslim men from the column would result in their killing.[166]

61. Accordingly, the Appeals Chamber dismisses this sub-ground of appeal. Judge Shahabuddeen dissents on the ground that Blagojević was denied the right to a fair trial and considers that his case should be remanded for a new trial.

6. Detention, Mistreatment, and Murders in Bratunac Town

62. The Trial Chamber held Blagojević criminally responsible for the killing of more than fifty Bosnian Muslim men and the inhumane treatment of thousands of others detained in and around the Vuk Karadžić School in Bratunac town between 12 and 14 July 1995.[167] The Trial Chamber found that, on the nights of 12 and 13 July 1995, members of the Bratunac Brigade Military Police played a role in guarding and controlling access to the detainees.[168] For the Trial Chamber, members of the Bratunac Brigade Military Police contributed to the mistreatment and murders which occurred there by providing "security".[169] The Trial Chamber concluded that Blagojević permitted brigade resources and personnel to be used in this detention operation which substantially contributed to the crimes committed against the detainees.[170] The Trial Chamber inferred that Blagojević knew about these crimes and the role played by the Bratunac Brigade in them, on the basis that he was in Bratunac town during this period, he ordered at least two brigade members to check on the detainees, and the crimes were widespread and visible.[171]

63. Blagojević does not dispute the detention of Bosnian Muslim men in and around the Vuk Karadžić School in Bratunac town nor the fact that a number of them were killed.[172] Rather, he submits that the Trial Chamber erred in fact in making findings on both his knowledge of and contribution to these crimes.[173] The Appeals Chamber will address these submissions in turn. **[page 25]**

(a) Blagojević's Knowledge of the Detention, Mistreatment, and Murders

64. The Trial Chamber found that Blagojević had knowledge of the detention, mistreatment, and murders in and around the Vuk Karadžić School in Bratunac town based primarily on his presence in the area coupled with the widespread and apparent nature of the crimes. In particular, the Trial Chamber determined that Blagojević was at the brigade headquarters where he would have reviewed reports and issued orders concerning the detainees.[174] The Trial Chamber also found that Blagojević spent the nights of 12 and 13 July 1995 at his

164 Trial Judgement, paras. 221–231, 259.
165 Trial Judgement, paras. 259, 733, 736, 738.
166 Trial Judgement, paras. 742, 745.
167 Trial Judgement, paras. 264, 271, 289, 564, 747-749, 755, 756, 759, 784.
168 Trial Judgement, paras. 286, 287, 289, 492, 493.
169 Trial Judgement, paras. 289, 747, 755.
170 Trial Judgement, paras. 729, 747–749, 759.
171 Trial Judgement, paras. 288, 449, 492–494, 748, 756.
172 Blagojević Appeal Brief, paras. 3.75, 4.21, 4.22. However, under Ground 3 challenging his convictions for murder, Blagojević asserts the number of victims was too high. Blagojević Appeal Brief, paras. 4.21, 4.22.
173 Blagojević Notice of Appeal, para. 9; Blagojević Appeal Brief, para. 3.69.
174 Trial Judgement, para. 493.

apartment near the school and as such could not have missed the toll of human suffering: screams followed by gunshots and streets lined with buses packed with detainees guarded by VRS units and civilian authorities.[175] In addition, the Trial Chamber accepted the evidence of Prosecution Witness P-210 and Defence Witness Ljubomir Beatović that Blagojević ordered them to check on the detainees at the Vuk Karadžić School.[176]

(i) Blagojević's Presence in Bratunac Town between 12 and 14 July 1995

65. Blagojević submits that the Trial Chamber erred in fact in its findings concerning his presence in and around Bratunac town during this period, in particular at the apartment in question on the nights of 12 and 13 July 1995.[177] He submits that, during this period, he was either at the brigade's forward command post in Pribićevac, some two and a half hours away, or at the brigade's headquarters in Bratunac town where he slept.[178] Blagojević further contends that it would have been impossible for him to stay at the apartment near the school because it had been sealed off by the authorities.[179] Blagojević emphasizes that Prosecution Witness P-210, who placed him at the apartment, only saw him depart and arrive at brigade headquarters, and thus the witness's testimony alone is insufficient to support the conclusion that he stayed at the apartment in question.[180] Blagojević further disputes the witness's credibility based on his status as a suspect implicated in the crimes and his cooperation with the Prosecution.[181]

66. Blagojević does not dispute that he was in Bratunac town during this period, and he concedes that he spent time at the Bratunac Brigade's headquarters.[182] He primarily contests that he spent the nights of 12 and 13 July 1995 at an apartment near the Vuk Karadžić School. The Appeals **[page 26]** Chamber observes that Blagojević's proximity to the detention site was one of the main factors relied on by the Trial Chamber in inferring his knowledge of the detention, mistreatment, and murder which occurred there.[183]

67. A review of the Trial Judgement indicates that the Trial Chamber relied exclusively on the evidence of Prosecution Witness P-210 for the finding that Blagojević stayed at the apartment.[184] As the transcripts of this witness's testimony reflect, Witness P-210 did not provide an eye-witness account of Blagojević staying at the apartment.[185] Rather, the witness testified that he saw Blagojević depart in the evening of 11 July 1995 for the apartment.[186] In addition, on 13 July 1995, the witness saw Blagojević arrive at the brigade headquarters from the apartment around 7 a.m. and leave for the apartment later that evening.[187] The witness also noted that Blagojević "mostly" spent the nights at the apartment in question,[188] which he identified in a photograph of Bratunac town.[189] In this respect, the Appeals Chamber notes that Witness P-210 was a brigade member familiar with Blagojević's comings and goings in this small town because he spent a lot of time at the reception of the brigade's headquarters.[190]

68. In disputing the Trial Chamber's inference based on Witness P-210's evidence that he stayed at the apartment, Blagojević does not offer a reasonable explanation for his whereabouts on 12 and 13 July 1995, and his version of the events is not supported by any reference to the trial record. In any event, Witness P-210's account of Blagojević regularly leaving the brigade headquarters at night, at the very least,

175 Trial Judgement, paras. 494, 748.
176 Trial Judgement, paras. 275, 287, 449.
177 Blagojević Appeal Brief, paras. 3.78–3.85.
178 Blagojević Appeal Brief, paras. 3.79, 3.81.
179 Blagojević Appeal Brief, para. 3.78. He also submits that he was unable to put this proposition to Witness P-210 during cross-examination due to the breakdown of communication with his counsel described in Ground 1 of his appeal. Blagojević Appeal Brief, paras. 3.80, 3.83, 3.102.
180 Blagojević Appeal Brief, paras. 3.80, 3.83.
181 Blagojević Appeal Brief, para. 3.104.
182 Blagojević Appeal Brief, para. 3.79.
183 Trial Judgement, paras. 493, 494, 748.
184 Trial Judgement, paras. 265, 438, 748.
185 T. 7374, 7375.
186 T. 7374, 7375, 7404.
187 T. 7384, 7385.
188 T. 7395. *See also* T. 7384, 7385, 7404, 7424.
189 T. 7382, 7383. *See also* Ex. P681.
190 T. 7395 ("A. Well, mostly he would go to his apartment to spend the night there. He was at the brigade during working hours, and then he would go home. Q. Okay. And how do you know that? A. I was there. I spent quite a lot of time at the reception desk."). *See also* Trial Judgement, paras. 265, 275, 493.

undermines Blagojević's assertion of sleeping at the brigade headquarters. The Appeals Chamber also finds that Blagojević's challenge to the credibility of Prosecution Witness P-210, based on his cooperation with the Prosecution and status as a suspect, is unpersuasive and does not in itself call into question the reasonableness of the Trial Chamber's reliance on his testimony. The Trial Chamber expressly stated that it gave "due regard to the individual circumstances" of witnesses, including those testifying with the status of "suspect".[191]

69. In any event, the Appeals Chamber notes that Blagojević has not demonstrated that the alleged error concerning his stay at the apartment resulted in a miscarriage of justice. For the Trial Chamber, the significance of Blagojević's presence at the apartment was that he would have **[page 27]** observed the buses and heard screams and gunshots "as he traveled the short distance from the Bratunac Brigade headquarters to his apartment, which was located nearby the Vuk Karadžić School."[192] However, as the Trial Chamber observed from the evidence on the record and from its visit to the site, distances in Bratunac town are short, and, in any event, the Vuk Karadžić School was only around 200 meters from the brigade headquarters.[193] Therefore, regardless of whether Blagojević spent the nights of 12 and 13 July 1995 at the apartment in question or at the brigade's headquarters, it remains undisputed that he was present in Bratunac town during this period.[194]

(ii) Blagojević's Orders to Members of the Bratunac Brigade to Visit the School

70. Blagojević further submits that the Trial Chamber erred in fact in finding that he ordered Prosecution Witness P-210 and Defence Witness Ljubomir Beatović to check on the detainees at the school.[195] He primarily asserts that these witnesses lack credibility due to their status as suspects and their cooperation, respectively, with the Prosecution and his assigned Defence counsel.[196] The Appeals Chamber finds Blagojević's arguments on this point unpersuasive. The Trial Chamber gave due regard to the individual circumstances of the witnesses,[197] and these arguments do not call into question the Trial Chamber's reliance on their testimony to support the finding that Blagojević was aware of the presence of Bosnian Muslim detainees and Bratunac Brigade Military Police in and around the Vuk Karadžić School.

(iii) The Scope and Visibility of the Crimes

71. Blagojević further submits that the Trial Chamber erred in fact in its findings on the scope and visibility of the crimes. First, he disputes the number of detainees and buses as well as the duration of their stay in Bratunac town.[198] He submits that the buses only arrived in the night of 13 July 1995 and departed before the morning.[199] He further alludes to the evidence of Prosecution Witness P-210 and Defence Witness Ljubomir Beatović who both visited the school and did not **[page 28]** observe any mistreatment.[200] Finally, Blagojević relies on the Trial Chamber's observation that Momir Nikolić only learned of the murders at the school on 15 July 1995, after the detainees had departed.[201] Blagojević asserts that it was not reasonable to find that he would have been aware of the murders during the course of the detention at the school while Momir Nikolić, who was involved in this operation on the ground, only learned of them later.[202]

---

191 Trial Judgement, para. 23.

192 Trial Judgement, paras. 493, 494 (" [...] Colonel Blagojević was present in the small town of Bratunac on both nights and would have seen the buses parked throughout the town as he traveled the short distance from the Bratunac Brigade headquarters to his apartment, which was located nearby the Vuk Karadžić School. [...] [I]t would have been common knowledge to anyone walking the streets of Bratunac on the nights of 12 and 13 July that the Bosnian Muslim men were being detained in overcrowded conditions in an environment of constant threat of abuse and serious mistreatment, including the threat of death.").

193 Trial Judgement, paras. 265, 493, 494, 748.

194 *See also* Trial Judgement, paras. 441–447.

195 Blagojević Appeal Brief, paras. 3.105–3.107.

196 Blagojević Appeal Brief, paras. 3.104, 3.106. Blagojević's objections to his assigned counsel at trial are discussed under his first ground of appeal. *See supra* section III.A (Fair Trial).

197 Trial Judgement, para. 23.

198 Blagojević Appeal Brief, para. 3.75.

199 Blagojević Appeal Brief, paras. 3.76, 3.88.

200 Blagojević Appeal Brief, para. 3.107.

201 Blagojević Appeal Brief, paras. 3.159, 3.160, 4.23–4.25.

202 Blagojević Appeal Brief, paras. 3.91, 3.160. *See also* AT. 105–106.

72. Relying on accounts of Bosnian Muslim men, members of the Bratunac Brigade, and civilian authorities, the Trial Judgement describes "a picture of shear [*sic*] horror",[203] lasting from 12 to 14 July 1995, for the several thousand Bosnian Muslim men detained without adequate provision of food and water in and around the Vuk Karadžić School and on board the between 80 to 120 buses lining the streets of Bratunac town.[204] The Trial Chamber found that screams and gunshots were heard throughout the night in the relatively small area of Bratunac town.[205] Blagojević does not point to any deficiencies in the evidence relied on by the Trial Chamber in making its findings concerning the detention in Bratunac town. Rather, he simply advances a different view of how these events unfolded, pointing primarily to the evidence of Witnesses Beatović and P-210. This is insufficient to call into question the reasonableness of the impugned findings.

73. The Appeals Chamber is not satisfied that Blagojević's reliance on the apparent lack of knowledge of Witnesses P-210 and Ljubomir Beatović of the mistreatment of the detainees calls into question the reasonableness of the Trial Chamber's findings on this point. Given the weight of evidence detailing the manifest nature of the horrific conditions, the Appeals Chamber finds that it was entirely reasonable for the Trial Chamber to prefer this evidence over that of the above-named former members of the Bratunac Brigade.

74. In addition, a close examination of the Trial Judgement and the record undermines Blagojević's arguments with respect to the timing of Momir Nikolić's knowledge of the killings. Blagojević correctly notes that the Trial Judgement states, without a supporting reference, that Nikolić learned of the killings on 15 July 1995.[206] The transcripts, however, do not specify the exact date when Momir Nikolić learned of the killings and, in fact, his testimony suggests that he knew of **[page 29]** them earlier.[207] Furthermore, Blagojević simply points to the more direct role of Momir Nikolić in the detention and transfer operation and has thus not demonstrated that the Trial Chamber acted unreasonably in finding that he had knowledge of the killings before Momir Nikolić.

75. In this regard, the Appeals Chamber recalls that the Trial Chamber based its finding that Blagojević had knowledge of the killings on the fact that he "was present in Bratunac town between 12 and 14 July" and that "[o]n these days, where shooting is reported to have been heard throughout the night, Colonel Blagojević was at the brigade headquarters and slept at his apartment located close to the Vuk Karadžić School".[208] The Appeals Chamber also notes that the Trial Chamber concluded that Blagojević "was aware of the situation in Bratunac", both with respect to the killings and with respect to the conditions of detention, referring to its factual findings as regards the events in the Vuk Karadžić School.[209] In those findings the Trial Chamber particularly referred to "an environment of constant threat of abuse and serious mistreatment, including the threat of death"[210] and the fact that, through the night, witnesses who were in the same town attested to hearing the sounds of "horrific screams followed by gunshots, after which silence ensued."[211]

76. Accordingly, the Appeals Chamber is not satisfied that Blagojević has demonstrated the unreasonableness of the Trial Chamber's findings on his knowledge of the detention, mistreatment, and murders which occurred in and around the Vuk Karadžić School.

---

203 Trial Judgement, para. 494.

204 Trial Judgement, paras. 264–282, 288, 493, 494, 748.

205 Trial Judgement, paras. 266, 288, 493, 494, 748.

206 Trial Judgement, para. 288 ("Finally, Momir Nikolić testified that on 15 July he was informed that men had been killed in the school").

207 *See* T. 1763 ("[Dragan Mirkovic] told me what he knew about [...] the Muslims that had been killed between the 13th and the 14th [...] Again, I must say on the 14th, no official meeting with Colonel Blagojevic took place. However, we talked mainly about what I had found out in relation to those killed at the Vuk Karadzic elementary school [...]"). The Trial Chamber recounts this exchange in another part of the judgement at paragraph 458. *See also* Trial Judgement, para. 282 with reference to T. 1701 where Momir Nikolić testified that he met Blagojević on the evening of 12 July and told him about, *inter alia*, the plan to kill the men detained at the Vuk Karadžić School.

208 Trial Judgement, para. 748.

209 Trial Judgement, para. 748 with reference to paras. 271–282, 492–496.

210 Trial Judgement, para. 494.

211 Trial Judgement, para. 494. *See also* Trial Judgement, paras. 269, 274.

(b) Blagojević's Contribution to the Detention, Mistreatment, and Murders

77. The Trial Chamber found that Bratunac Brigade Military Police played a role in guarding and controlling access to the detainees at the Vuk Karadžić School and thus contributed to their detention, mistreatment, and murder.[212] The Trial Chamber based Blagojević's criminal responsibility for these crimes on making brigade resources available.[213]

78. Blagojević does not dispute the participation of the Bratunac Brigade Military Police in this operation.[214] Rather, he contests his responsibility for their actions, pointing to a parallel chain of **[page 30]** command in such situations in which the military police answered directly to the VRS Main Staff and not to him.[215] He further argues that, in any event, the role of the brigade's military police in guarding the Bosnian Muslim detainees in and around the Vuk Karadžić School was insufficient to constitute substantial assistance to the crimes committed against them.[216] The Appeals Chamber will address these arguments below in connection with Blagojević's challenges to his convictions for aiding and abetting the crimes.[217]

79. Blagojević, however, raises additional arguments concerning his contribution to the crimes. First, he disputes any responsibility for the general welfare of the detainees. He explains that the Bratunac Brigade did not capture these men and that the civilian authorities and other elements of the VRS were responsible for them.[218] He adds that he received no order or request for assistance in connection with the detainees.[219] Second, he disputes that any other member of the Bratunac Brigade besides its military police was present in and around the Vuk Karadžić School, explaining that all four battalions were stationed in their positions surrounding Srebrenica.[220] With respect to these arguments, however, Blagojević has failed to demonstrate how any alleged error resulted in a miscarriage of justice. A review of the Trial Judgement reveals that the Trial Chamber based the finding of his criminal responsibility on the role played by the Bratunac Brigade Military Police in guarding the detainees at the Vuk Karadžić School, not on any overarching duty he had toward them or on actions by brigade members present at the school other than the military police.[221] Accordingly, the Appeals Chamber dismisses these arguments. Judge Shahabuddeen dissents in respect of this sub-ground of appeal on the ground that Blagojević was denied the right to a fair trial and considers that his case should be remanded for a new trial. **[page 31]**

7. Evaluation of the Testimonies of Momir Nikolić and Dragan Obrenović

80. The Prosecution charged Momir Nikolić and Dragan Obrenović as co-accused with Blagojević in relation with the events that occurred after the fall of Srebrenica.[222]Both Momir Nikolić and Dragan Obrenović pleaded guilty at the outset of the trial and testified for the Prosecution in this case before their sentencing.[223]

---

212 Trial Judgement, paras. 286, 287, 492, 747, 755.

213 Trial Judgement, paras. 729, 749, 759, 784.

214 Blagojević Appeal Brief, para. 3.112.

215 Blagojević Appeal Brief, paras. 3.113, 3.115–3.117, 3.136–3.147. This is also discussed below in section III.B.8 (Alleged Errors relating to Factual Findings: Blagojević's Authority over Momir Nikolić and the Bratunac Brigade Military Police).

216 Blagojević Appeal Brief, paras. 3.118–3.120, 3.130–3.133.

217 *See infra* section III.G (Alleged Errors relating to Aiding and Abetting).

218 Blagojević Appeal Brief, paras. 3.71–3.73, 3.86, 3.87, 3.89, 3.97–3.99, 3.108–3.110.

219 Blagojević Appeal Brief, para. 3.109.

220 Blagojević Appeal Brief, paras. 3.108, 3.109, 3.111.

221 *See, e.g.,* Trial Judgement, paras. 289 ("*Through the guarding of detention sites*, members of the Bratunac Brigade Military Police contributed to the continuation of the detention of the Bosnian Muslim men in overcrowded buses and buildings, without food, water or medical treatment, as was needed in some cases.") (emphasis added), 747 ("*By ensuring the further detention of the men and indeed by helping to control who entered and left the Vuk Karadžić school*, members of the Bratunac Brigade permitted these murders to take place.") (emphasis added), 755 ("The Trial Chamber found that cruel and inhumane treatment and terrorising the civilian population were established through [...] detention in Bratunac [...]. The Trial Chamber finds that members of the Bratunac Brigade Military Police [...] rendered practical assistance which had a substantial effect on these acts by [...] guarding detainees in Bratunac.").

222 Trial Judgement, paras. 869, 873, 874.

223 Trial Judgement, paras. 876, 877.

81. Blagojević submits that the Trial Chamber erred in law in its treatment of the evidence of Momir Nikolić and Dragan Obrenović, contending that their testimonies are inherently unreliable given their plea agreements with the Prosecution.[224] Blagojević's arguments, however, focus entirely on Momir Nikolić. In particular, Blagojević points to the Trial Chamber's willingness to accept Momir Nikolić's incriminating testimony in situations where the witness inculpated himself, even while rejecting it in other instances absent corroboration.[225]

82. Accomplice testimony is not *per se* unreliable, and its use by a Trial Chamber, in and of itself, does not constitute error.[226] Such evidence, however, must be carefully considered in light of the circumstances under which it was given.[227] A review of the Trial Judgement reveals that the Trial Chamber expressly considered the totality of the circumstances in which the evidence of Momir Nikolić and Dragan Obrenović was tendered;[228] this was particularly so with respect to Nikolić's testimony that tended to incriminate Blagojević.[229] In the view of the Appeals Chamber, the Trial Chamber treated this evidence with appropriate caution. Moreover, the Appeals Chamber observes that it is not unreasonable for a Trial Chamber to accept certain parts of a witness's testimony and reject others.[230]

83. Accordingly, the Appeals Chamber dismisses this sub-ground of appeal. Judge Shahabuddeen dissents on the ground that Blagojević was denied the right to a fair trial and considers that his case should be remanded for a new trial. **[page 32]**

8. Blagojević's Authority over Momir Nikolić and the Bratunac Brigade Military Police

84. The Trial Chamber concluded that Blagojević remained in command and control of all units of the Bratunac Brigade, including Momir Nikolić and the brigade's military police, and thus incurred criminal responsibility for their actions throughout the Indictment period.[231] Blagojević submits that the Trial Chamber erred in fact in making these findings. In particular, Blagojević contests his authority over Momir Nikolić and the Bratunac Brigade Military Police.[232] He argues that, at the time, a parallel chain of command existed between the brigade's security organ and the Main Staff of the VRS.[233] He points to four documents which, in his view, demonstrate this: the Rules of Service; the 2 July 1995 Order from General Milenko Zivanovic for operation Krivaja 95; the 24 October 1994 Instructions of General Ratko Mladić; and the Plan of Counter Intelligence Duties.[234] Blagojević argues that he was only a superior to Momir Nikolić in precisely defined areas, limited to twenty percent of Nikolić's work in administrative, military police, and criminal and legal matters.[235] Blagojević further explains that Momir Nikolić acted solely as a direct subordinate of the security organ of the VRS Main Staff in matters of counter-intelligence, including the securing of prisoners of war, constituting eighty percent of his duties.[236]

85. In considering Blagojević's authority over Momir Nikolić and the Bratunac Brigade Military Police, the Trial Chamber heard considerable evidence and in the Trial Judgement expressly referred to three of the documents highlighted by Blagojević under this sub-ground of appeal.[237] The Trial Chamber accepted,

224 Blagojević Notice of Appeal, para. 10; Blagojević Appeal Brief, paras. 3.155–3.157. The Appeals Chamber observes that Blagojević devotes the remainder of his argument under this sub-ground of appeal to issues specifically related to his knowledge of the killings in Bratunac town, which are treated in section III.B.6 (Alleged Errors relating to Factual Findings: Detention, Mistreatment, and Murders in Bratunac Town). Blagojević Appeal Brief, paras. 3.158-3.161.

225 Blagojević Appeal Brief, paras. 3.156, 3.157.

226 *Niyitegeka* Appeal Judgement, para. 98. *See also Ntagerura et al.* Appeal Judgement, paras. 203, 204.

227 *Niyitegeka* Appeal Judgement, para. 98. *See also Ntagerura et al.* Appeal Judgement, para. 204.

228 Trial Judgement, para. 24.

229 Trial Judgement, paras. 262, 472, 495.

230 *Kupreškić et al.* Appeal Judgement, para. 333. *See also Ntagerura et al.* Appeal Judgement, para. 214; *Kamuhanda* Appeal Judgement, para. 248.

231 Trial Judgement, para. 419.

232 Blagojević Appeal Brief, paras. 3.162–3.169.

233 Blagojević Appeal Brief, para. 3.163.

234 Blagojević Appeal Brief, para. 3.165.

235 Blagojević Appeal Brief, para. 3.166.

236 Blagojević Appeal Brief, para. 3.167.

237 Trial Judgement, paras. 391–418. Blagojević provides no reference for the document he refers to as the "Plan of Counter-Intelligence". However, the relevant paragraphs of the Trial Judgement discuss counter intelligence matters.

as Blagojević contends, that the security and intelligence organs were controlled centrally by the security and intelligence organ of the superior command.[238] In addition, the Trial Chamber also heard evidence that Lieutenant Colonel Popović, the Drina Corps assistant commander for security, Colonel Ljubiša Beara, the Main Staff chief of security, and General Mladić, the commander of the VRS Main Staff, issued orders directly to Momir Nikolić and to members of the Bratunac Brigade Military Police.[239] The Trial Chamber, ultimately, concluded that a functional chain of command in relation to security existed between the security and intelligence organs of the VRS Main Staff and the Bratunac Brigade that could be considered parallel to the brigade command.[240] The Trial Chamber emphasized, however, that the parallel **[page 33]** command of the Main Staff security organ was not disconnected from the brigade command.[241] In other words, the security organs of the brigade could receive orders from two commanders, the superior command for security and the unit commander.[242] The Trial Chamber noted that the security section remained duty-bound to consult with the brigade commander in certain circumstances and, ultimately, that "the functional chain of command was not operating in isolation from military chain of command of the unit."[243] For the Trial Chamber, the situation surrounding the crimes committed at the time necessitated such consultation.[244] In addition, the Trial Chamber also relied on General Mladić's instruction that "the security and intelligence organs are directly commanded by the unit or institution of which they form part."[245]

86. In the Appeals Chamber's view, Blagojević's argument is premised on a misinterpretation of the Trial Chamber's finding on his authority over Momir Nikolić and the Bratunac Brigade Military Police. In holding that Blagojević remained in command and control of all elements of the Bratunac Brigade, the Trial Chamber was accepting that the Prosecution had established his *de jure* authority over what, according to General Mladić's instruction quoted above, were clearly formally subordinate units. It appears that the Trial Chamber examined the facts as they existed on the ground at the time of a given crime to determine whether Blagojević had responsibility for the actions of these units.

87. The Trial Chamber concluded that Blagojević lacked effective control over Momir Nikolić in view of the existence of the functional chain of command as well as the presence of other senior members of the VRS in the Srebrenica area issuing orders and instructions at the time.[246] Further, the Trial Chamber's legal findings on Blagojević's criminal responsibility do not reflect that he was held liable as a superior for Momir Nikolić's actions.[247] Accordingly, Blagojević has failed to identify any error in the findings concerning his authority over Momir Nikolić which would result in a miscarriage of justice.

88. A review of the Trial Judgement reveals that, while there are instances where the VRS Main Staff issued orders directly to the military police,[248] the record also reflects that Blagojević issued orders to members of the Bratunac Brigade Military Police. For example, the Trial Chamber found that Blagojević asked two members of the brigade to check on the detainees and to tell the military **[page 34]** police to ensure proper treatment of detainees.[249] These men were granted access by the Bratunac Brigade Military Police after explaining to the guards that Blagojević had instructed them to go to the school.[250] Prosecution Witness P-210 noted that Blagojević instructed him to inform the Bratunac Brigade Military Police to ensure that there were no problems.[251] Blagojević has not pointed to anything in the trial record that would call into question his legal authority in this instance. Consequently, in the Appeals Chamber's view, Blagojević has failed to demonstrate that no reasonable trier of fact could have made the Trial Chamber's findings on his authority over the Bratunac Brigade Military Police.

---

238 Trial Judgement, para. 417.
239 Trial Judgement, para. 409.
240 Trial Judgement, para. 417.
241 Trial Judgement, para. 417.
242 Trial Judgement, para. 417.
243 Trial Judgement, para. 418.
244 Trial Judgement, para. 418.
245 Trial Judgement, para. 417.
246 Trial Judgement, para. 795.
247 Trial Judgement, paras. 748, 755.
248 Trial Judgement, paras. 413–416.
249 Trial Judgement, paras. 275, 278.
250 Trial Judgement, paras. 275, 278.
251 Trial Judgement, para. 275.

89. Accordingly, the Appeals Chamber dismisses this sub-ground of appeal. Judge Shahabuddeen dissents on the ground that Blagojević was denied the right to a fair trial and considers that his case should be remanded for a new trial.

9. Zone of Responsibility of the Bratunac Brigade

90. Blagojević submits that the Trial Chamber erred in fact in finding that the Bratunac Brigade had a specific geographic "zone of responsibility".[252] He argues that the Trial Chamber erroneously employed this concept to implicate the Bratunac Brigade in criminal conduct simply by virtue of its occurrence within such a zone.[253] For instance, Blagojević points to the events in the Sandići Meadow, Kravica, the opportunistic killings in Bratunac town, and the reburial operation in Glogova.[254]

91. Recalling the analysis of the Defence military expert Schifanelli, Blagojević asserts that VRS military units, such as the Bratunac Brigade, did not have "zones of responsibility", but rather operated in a "zone of action" defined by specific orders and subject to change given the exigency of the situation.[255] To illustrate this, Blagojević highlights the Trial Chamber's finding that many other authorities and units also operated in areas near Bratunac Brigade command posts.[256] Moreover, Blagojević indicates that Bratunac Brigade operated at times several hundred kilometres from the seat of its command, in places such as žepa and Sarajevo.[257] **[page 35]**

92. The Appeals Chamber observes that the Trial Judgement makes reference in several instances to the Bratunac Brigade's zone or area of responsibility.[258] Blagojević, however, has not demonstrated that the use of this descriptive phrase was unreasonable.[259] In any event, a review of the Trial Judgement does not reveal that the Trial Chamber defined a fixed geographic area as the Bratunac Brigade's zone of responsibility, as Blagojević suggests, and then, as a consequence, imposed liability on him for what transpired there. Instead, the Trial Chamber imposed criminal responsibility on Blagojević based on his own conduct of permitting the use of specific Bratunac Brigade resources and personnel in the commission of certain crimes.[260]

93. Accordingly, the Appeals Chamber dismisses this sub-ground of appeal. Judge Shahabuddeen dissents on the ground that Blagojević was denied the right to a fair trial and considers that his case should be remanded for a new trial.

10. Conclusion

94. For the foregoing reasons, the Appeals Chamber finds that the second ground of Blagojević's appeal related the Trial Chamber's factual findings is unfounded and, therefore, dismisses it in its entirety. Judge Shahabuddeen dissents on the ground that Blagojević was denied the right to a fair trial and considers that his case should be remanded for a new trial. **[page 36]**

C. Alleged Errors relating to Murder (Ground 3)

95. The Trial Chamber convicted Blagojević for aiding and abetting murder as a crime against humanity and as a violation of the laws and customs of war.[261] These convictions are based on Blagojević's knowledge

[252] Blagojević Notice of Appeal, para. 12; Blagojević Appeal Brief, paras. 3.170–3.185.
[253] Blagojević Appeal Brief, paras. 3.171, 3.172, 3.175–3.178, 3.180.
[254] Blagojević Appeal Brief, paras. 3.172–3.174.
[255] Blagojević Appeal Brief, paras. 3.179, 3.182, 3.183, 3.185.
[256] Blagojević Appeal Brief, para. 3.181.
[257] Blagojević Appeal Brief, para. 3.181.
[258] *See* Trial Judgment, paras. 6, 7, 384–386, 392, 418, 742.
[259] The Appeals Chamber itself has used this phrase in other judgements dealing with similar factual issues. *See Krstić* Appeal Judgement, para. 135.
[260] Trial Judgement, paras. 729, 784.
[261] Trial Judgement, para. 797, Chapter X (Disposition). The Trial Chamber also convicted Blagojević for the killings in Bratunac town under the counts of persecutions and complicity in genocide. Trial Judgement, paras. 754, 759, 784, 797. Under this ground, Blagojević only addresses his convictions for murder as a crime against humanity and as a violation of the laws and customs of war.

of and contribution to the killing of more than fifty Bosnian Muslim men in and around the Vuk Karadžić School in Bratunac town between 12 and 14 July 1995.[262] The Appeals Chamber has already addressed a number of the alleged factual errors[263] related to these convictions in its assessment of the detention and killings in Bratunac town under Ground 2.

96. The Appeals Chamber considers here Blagojević's remaining claims that the Trial Chamber erred in fact in its estimation of the number of murder victims and in finding that these crimes formed part of a widespread or systematic attack against a civilian population and his knowledge thereof.[264] In Ground 7 (Aiding and Abetting), the Appeals Chamber will address Blagojević's submissions that the Trial Chamber erred in fact in characterizing the role played by the members of the Bratunac Brigade Military Police in connection with the detention of the men in and around the Vuk Karadžić School as providing substantial assistance to the murders.[265]

1. Number of Murders

97. Blagojević submits that the Trial Chamber erred in fact in finding that more than fifty detainees were executed between 12 and 14 July 1995 in and around the Vuk Karadžić School in Bratunac town, arguing that this number does not comport with the evidence given at trial.[266] In support of this position, Blagojević points to two transcript pages from the evidence of Srbislav Davidović, in which the witness recounts that he heard that "some corpses" were left behind around the school, without specifying a number.[267]

98. In the view of the Appeals Chamber, Blagojević has not demonstrated that no reasonable trier of fact could have made the Trial Chamber's finding on the number of victims murdered. A review of the Trial Judgement reveals that the testimony of Srbislav Davidović is only a part of the evidence expressly relied on by the Trial Chamber in estimating the number of detainees killed in **[page 37]** and around the school.[268] Blagojević does not address, for example, the evidence that detainees from the Vuk Karadžić School loaded a number of corpses of people killed on the night of 12 July 1995 onto trucks.[269] In addition, he also fails to deal with the evidence of Momir Nikolić, who heard that between eighty and one hundred Bosnian Muslim men had been killed in and around the Vuk Karadžić School during the night of 13 to 14 July 1995, or that of Witness DP-101, who saw between forty and fifty dead bodies in the classrooms of the Vuk Karadžić School on 15 July 1995.[270]

2. Widespread or Systematic Attack

99. The Trial Chamber concluded that Blagojević's acts formed part of a widespread or systematic attack against the civilian population of Srebrenica and that, given his role as a high-ranking officer of a brigade participating in the attack on the Srebrenica enclave, Blagojević had knowledge of the wider context of his actions.[271]

100. Blagojević submits that the Trial Chamber erred in fact in finding that there was a widespread or systematic attack against the civilian population of Srebrenica.[272] He describes the attack against Srebrenica pursuant to the "Krivaja 95" operation, and the Bratunac Brigade's participation in it, as legitimate and directed at the "well-armed" members of the 28th Division of the ABiH, not at the civilian population.[273]

101. The Appeals Chamber recalls that it has addressed and rejected under Ground 2 above portions of Blagojević's argument related to the legitimacy of the attack against Srebrenica and the role of the Bratunac

262 Trial Judgement, paras. 264, 271, 289, 564, 747–749, 755, 756, 759, 784.

263 Blagojević raises again the arguments related to his general knowledge of and contribution to the killings. *See supra* section III.B.6 (Alleged Errors relating to Factual Findings: Detention, Mistreatment, and Murders in Bratunac Town).

264 Blagojević Notice of Appeal, paras. 13–16; Blagojević Appeal Brief, paras. 4.1–4.36.

265 Blagojević Appeal Brief, para. 4.32.

266 Blagojević Appeal Brief, para. 4.22.

267 Blagojević Appeal Brief, para. 4.22 fn. 99, referring to T. 7753, 7756.

268 Trial Judgement, paras. 277, 281.

269 Trial Judgement, para. 277.

270 Trial Judgement, para. 281.

271 Trial Judgement, paras. 551–554.

272 Blagojević Appeal Brief, paras. 4.2–4.11.

273 Blagojević Appeal Brief, paras. 4.3–4.11.

Brigade in it.[274] Furthermore, in the Appeals Chamber's view, Blagojević has misinterpreted the Trial Chamber's factual findings on the widespread or systematic nature of the attack underlying the convictions for crimes against humanity in this case. Blagojević focuses his submissions on justifying the initial military assault on the enclave from 6 to 11 July 1995, which was a background consideration[275] and fails to address the main aspect of the Trial Chamber's findings on the nature of the attack, which concerns the resulting impact on the civilian population after the fall of the enclave on 11 July 1995. His argument, therefore, is insufficient to call into question the reasonableness of the Trial Chamber's findings that the attack carried out pursuant to **[page 38]** the "Krivaja 95" order continued after the fall of Srebrenica, was directed at the Bosnian Muslim civilian population, affected the approximately 40,000 people living in the enclave at the time, and constituted a widespread or systematic attack against the civilian population.[276] The totality of evidence relating to the forcible transfer and the detention and mistreatment in Bratunac town, in particular when coupled with the humanitarian crisis that followed the fall of the Srebrenica enclave, leaves no room for any other reasonable conclusion about the nature of the attack.

102. Blagojević also submits that the Trial Chamber erred in fact in finding that he was aware of this broader context.[277] His simple denial that he lacked knowledge of the context in which the attack occurred is insufficient to call into question the reasonableness of the Trial Chamber's findings on this point. As discussed elsewhere in this Judgement, the Trial Chamber reasonably concluded that he was aware, among other things, of the dire humanitarian situation, the forcible transfer, and the detention and mistreatment of thousands of Bosnian Muslim men in Bratunac town, as well as the role played by brigade personnel in these events.[278] Moreover, it was also reasonable for the Trial Chamber to conclude that given his role as a commanding officer of a brigade operating in the area at the time, Blagojević would have had knowledge of the wider context in which his own acts occurred, namely the widespread or systematic attack against the civilian population of Srebrenica. Though the Trial Chamber concluded that he lacked knowledge of the mass murder operation,[279] the events of which he had knowledge, mentioned above, were sufficient to put him on notice of the nature of the attack.

103. Accordingly, the Appeals Chamber dismisses this ground of appeal. Judge Shahabuddeen dissents on the ground that Blagojević was denied the right to a fair trial and considers that his case should be remanded for a new trial. **[page 39]**

D. <u>Alleged Errors relating to Forcible Transfer (Ground 4)</u>

104. The Trial Chamber held Blagojević criminally responsible for the forcible transfer of thousands of Bosnian Muslims from Srebrenica and, as a result, entered convictions against him for aiding and abetting inhumane acts and persecutions as crimes against humanity.[280] In challenging these convictions, Blagojević submits that the Trial Chamber first erred in fact in finding that a forcible transfer of Bosnian Muslims occurred in Srebrenica[281] and, second, in finding that he contributed to and had knowledge of the transfer.[282]

---

274 *See supra* section III.B.2 (Alleged Errors relating to Factual Findings: Role of Blagojević and the Bratunac Brigade in the Attack on Srebrenica).

275 Trial Judgement, paras. 136, 137, 140.

276 Trial Judgement, paras. 551, 552, 554.

277 Blagojević Appeal Brief, paras. 4.12–4.20.

278 Trial Judgement, paras. 473–496. *See supra* sections III.B.1 (Alleged Errors relating to Factual Findings: Blocking of Humanitarian Convoys to Srebrenica), III.B.2 (Alleged Errors relating to Factual Findings: Role of Blagojević and the Bratunac Brigade in the Attack on Srebrenica), III.B.3 (Alleged Errors relating to Factual Findings: Firing on Civilians in Srebrenica and *en route* to Potočari), III.B.4 (Alleged Errors relating to Factual Findings: Removal of Civilians from Potočari), III.B.5 (Alleged Errors relating to Factual Findings: Searching the Terrain and Attack on the Column), III.B.6 (Alleged Errors relating to Factual Findings: Detention, Mistreatment, and Murders in Bratunac Town), III.C (Alleged Errors relating to Murder), III.D (Alleged Errors relating to Forcible Transfer).

279 Trial Judgement, paras. 497–500. *See also infra* section V.A (Alleged Errors relating to Blagojević's Knowledge of Mass Killing).

280 Trial Judgement, paras. 616-618, 631, 757, 759, 760. The Trial Chamber also convicted Blagojević for forcible transfer under the count of complicity in genocide as an act of serious bodily or mental harm. Trial Judgement, paras. 654, 671, 675, 784, 787. Under this ground, Blagojević only challenges his convictions for inhumane acts and persecutions as a crime against humanity.

281 Blagojević Notice of Appeal, para. 17; Blagojević Appeal Brief, paras. 5.1, 5.12–5.14, 5.16–5.18.

282 Blagojević Notice of Appeal, paras. 17–19; Blagojević Appeal Brief, paras. 5.3–5.9, 5.15, 5.20–5.23.

1. Existence of Forcible Transfer

105. The Trial Chamber found that the VRS forcibly transferred thousands of Bosnian Muslim civilians from the Srebrenica enclave.[283] The Trial Chamber explained that women, children, and the elderly were transported from Potočari in the enclave to Kladanj while the men were initially taken to Bratunac town.[284] The Trial Chamber concluded that the refugees in Potočari did not have a genuine choice of whether to remain in the Srebrenica enclave.[285] Further, the Trial Chamber found that the evidence demonstrated that the perpetrators did not intend for the displaced people to return once the situation normalized.[286]

106. Blagojević submits that the Trial Chamber erred in fact in finding that women and children were forcibly transferred from the Srebrenica enclave.[287] He raises four principal points to support this contention. First, he argues that the refugees and the international community in fact demanded that General Mladić effectuate the transfer.[288] Second, he points to the deteriorating humanitarian situation which necessitated a quick transfer.[289] Third, he claims that many of the refugees were not voluntarily in Srebrenica and thus were happy to have the opportunity to leave.[290] Fourth, Blagojević submits that the refugees took few possessions, reflecting that they only intended to depart temporarily.[291] **[page 40]**

107. In determining that the transfer was forcible in nature, the Trial Chamber relied on evidence of the prevalent knowledge among displaced persons of the serious crimes being committed by members of the Bosnian Serb forces in Potočari, the inhumane and aggressive separation process, the dire humanitarian situation in Potočari during the nights of 11 and 12 July 1995, the threats of slaughter by VRS soldiers against the Bosnian Muslim refugees, and the VRS attack on Potočari on the morning of 12 July 1995.[292]

108. Blagojević does not point to any errors made by the Trial Chamber in the assessment of the evidence underlying these findings. Rather, he simply advances alternative theories, unsupported by any reference to the trial record, that are clearly implausible when weighed against the evidence relied upon by the Trial Chamber.

109. In light of the circumstances taken into account by the Trial Chamber, it was reasonable for it to find that the request on the part of the Bosnian Muslims to leave Srebrenica was not the result of a genuine choice, but rather stemmed from the coercive circumstances in which they found themselves and the humanitarian disaster caused by what the Trial Chamber described as the VRS's unlawful activity.[293] Blagojević's arguments on this point do not demonstrate that no reasonable trier of fact could have found that the transfer of Bosnian Muslims from Srebrenica was forcible.

2 Blagojević's Participation in and Knowledge of the Forcible Transfer

110. The Trial Chamber found that Blagojević contributed to the transfer by making Bratunac Brigade resources available to assist in the operation, which included vehicles, fuel, and personnel.[294] In particular, the Trial Chamber concluded that elements of the Bratunac Brigade assisted in patrolling the area, in counting and separating people, in loading the buses, in regulating traffic, and in escorting the buses out of Potočari for Bratunac town.[295] The Trial Chamber noted that these elements included some members of the Bratunac Brigade's Military Police as well as its battalions.[296]

283 Trial Judgement, paras. 175, 191, 216, 217, 616.
284 Trial Judgement, paras. 190, 192, 616.
285 Trial Judgement, para. 617.
286 Trial Judgement, para. 618.
287 Blagojević Appeal Brief, para. 5.1.
288 Blagojević Appeal Brief, para. 5.13.
289 Blagojević Appeal Brief, para. 5.14.
290 Blagojević Appeal Brief, paras. 5.16, 5.17.
291 Blagojević Appeal Brief, para. 5.17.
292 Trial Judgement, paras. 141–192, 617, 618.
293 Trial Judgement, paras. 617, 618. *See also Stakić* Appeal Judgement, paras. 279–287.
294 Trial Judgement, paras. 216, 217, 482–484, 486, 487, 713, 729, 757–759.
295 Trial Judgement, paras. 216, 217, 482–484, 486, 487, 757.
296 Trial Judgement, paras. 181, 191, 208, 483, 487, 757.

111. Blagojević disputes that he contributed to or had any knowledge of the forcible transfer.[297] In this respect, he argues primarily that the responsibility for the transfer rested with the civilian authorities and the VRS Main Staff and submits that any involvement by the Bratunac Brigade was **[page 41]** limited to Momir Nikolić and the Bratunac Brigade Military Police.[298] Blagojević contends that he lacked authority over these elements of the brigade and points to the existence of a parallel chain of command to the VRS Main Staff in such matters.[299] The Appeals Chamber has addressed and rejected the argument with respect to his authority over Momir Nikolić and the military police under Ground 2 above.[300] In addition, Blagojević also asserts that he had no connection to or responsibility for the overall welfare of the displaced people in Potočari, who were under the care of the local civilian authorities.[301] The Appeals Chamber observes, however, that the Trial Chamber did not impose criminal liability on Blagojević based on an overarching duty to the civilians there, but rather based on making his brigade's resources available to render practical assistance to the operation.[302] Consequently, Blagojević has failed to demonstrate that no reasonable trier of fact could have reached the Trial Chamber's findings concerning the involvement of brigade members in the forcible transfer.

112. In disputing his knowledge of the forcible transfer, Blagojević points primarily to his absence from various meetings where the transfer was planned or discussed.[303] He further adds that he was not present in Potočari.[304] In this respect, Blagojević clearly misunderstands the basis of the Trial Chamber's findings as to his knowledge of the forcible transfer. The Trial Chamber determined that he had knowledge of these events based on: (1) his presence at Bratunac Brigade headquarters, where he would have received updates about the activities of his troops and units and reviewed daily combat reports and logbook entries; and (2) his presence in Bratunac town, in general, where he would have witnessed the results of the transfer as buses filled with women, children, and the elderly passed through town, and buses filled with men lined the streets.[305] Under this ground, Blagojević points to no error in the assessment of the relevant evidence, and the Appeals Chamber has addressed and rejected his challenges to the findings on his presence in Bratunac town elsewhere in this Judgement.[306] Consequently, in the Appeals Chamber's view, Blagojević has failed to demonstrate that no reasonable trier of fact could have found that he had knowledge of the forcible transfer. **[page 42]**

113. Accordingly, the Appeals Chamber dismisses this ground of appeal. Judge Shahabuddeen dissents on the ground that Blagojević was denied the right to a fair trial and considers that his case should be remanded for a new trial. **[page 43]**

E. Alleged Errors relating to Persecutions (Ground 5)

114. The Trial Chamber concluded that the widespread or systematic attack against the civilian population of Srebrenica was committed on racial, religious, or political grounds.[307] Consequently, the Trial Chamber convicted Blagojević for aiding and abetting persecutions as a crime against humanity through murder, cruel and inhumane treatment, terrorising of Bosnian Muslim civilians in Srebrenica and Potočari and through the forcible transfer of Bosnian Muslims from the Srebrenica enclave.[308] Blagojević submits that the Trial Chamber erred in fact in finding that he was aware of the discriminatory intent of the perpetrators as well as the discriminatory context in which the underlying crimes were committed.[309]

---

297 Blagojević Appeal Brief, paras. 5.3–5.9, 5.15, 5.20–5.23.
298 Blagojević Appeal Brief, paras. 5.20–5.23.
299 Blagojević Appeal Brief, para. 5.20.
300 *See supra* section III.B.8 (Alleged Errors relating to Factual Findings: Blagojević's Authority over Momir Nikolić and the Bratunac Brigade Military Police).
301 Blagojević Appeal Brief, paras. 3.30–3.36.
302 Trial Judgement, paras. 729, 755, 757, 759, 784.
303 Blagojević Appeal Brief, paras. 5.5–5.8.
304 Blagojević Appeal Brief, paras. 3.29, 5.15.
305 Trial Judgement, paras. 483, 493, 758.
306 *See supra* section III.B.6 (Alleged Errors relating to Factual Findings: Detention, Murder, and Mistreatment in Bratunac Town).
307 Trial Judgement, para. 619.
308 Trial Judgement, paras. 759, 797.
309 Blagojević Notice of Appeal, paras. 20–22; Blagojević Appeal Brief, paras. 6.1–6.28. In addition, Blagojević disputes that members of the Bratunac Brigade participated in the crimes and that he had knowledge of such participation. Blagojević Appeal Brief, para. 6.1. However, he does not develop this argument under this ground of appeal, and the Appeals Chamber does not address it here further.

115. Blagojević attempts to justify the attack as a legitimate military operation against the 28th Division of the ABiH and to characterize the resulting civilian transfer as voluntary.[310] He does not, however, address the majority of the evidence relied on by the Trial Chamber in determining that the attack against the civilian population of Srebrenica was discriminatory in nature, beyond disagreeing with the conclusions reached from it, nor does he support his arguments with any relevant reference to the trial record. In particular, in reaching its conclusions on the discriminatory nature of the attack, the Trial Chamber pointed to General Mladić's statement that it was time to take revenge on the "Turks".[311] It further noted the insulting comments made by VRS soldiers to the refugees, referring to their departure from "Serb country" and "greater-Serbia" as well as forcing them to read pro-Serb texts.[312] Moreover, the Trial Chamber concluded that Blagojević would have had knowledge of the discriminatory purpose of the attack and the perpetrators' discriminatory intent given his general knowledge of the attack and his familiarity with the purpose of the "Krivaja 95" operation, which changed from reducing the enclave to the urban area to taking it over as a whole, as well as his knowledge of the impact on the civilian population, including the humanitarian crisis in Potočari, the bussing of civilians, and the mistreatment of Bosnian Muslim detainees in Bratunac town.[313]

116. The Appeals Chamber has already addressed and rejected Blagojević's arguments disputing the Trial Chamber's characterization of the nature and purpose of the attack against the civilian **[page 44]** population of Srebrenica under other grounds of his appeal.[314] These arguments, therefore, do not demonstrate any error in the Trial Chamber's findings concerning the discriminatory purpose of the attack or the discriminatory intent of the perpetrators.

117. In disputing his overall knowledge about the nature of the attack, Blagojević takes specific issue with the Trial Chamber's findings that Miroslav Deronjić, the Serbian civilian commissioner of Srebrenica, informed him on 11 July 1995 that the military plan had changed to taking over the entire enclave.[315] As noted above, this finding formed part of the Trial Chamber's basis for concluding that Blagojević was informed of the overall progress of the attack and its ultimate purpose.[316] Blagojević challenges Miroslav Deronjić's credibility given his plea agreement and resulting cooperation with the Prosecution.[317] However, the Appeals Chamber considers that, Miroslav Deronjić's cooperation with the Prosecution alone is insufficient to call into question the reasonableness of the Trial Chamber's reliance on his testimony. In any event, the Appeals Chamber notes that the Trial Chamber was expressly mindful of this factor in assessing Deronjić's testimony.[318]

118. Accordingly, the Appeals Chamber dismisses this ground of appeal. Judge Shahabuddeen dissents on the ground that Blagojević was denied the right to a fair trial and considers that his case should be remanded for a new trial. **[page 45]**

F. Alleged Errors relating to Complicity in Genocide (Ground 6)

119. The Trial Chamber convicted Blagojević for complicity in genocide as an aider and abettor.[319] It concluded that the Bosnian Serb forces committed genocide in Srebrenica through the killing of more than 7,000 Bosnian Muslim men and by inflicting serious bodily and mental harm on Bosnian Muslim civilians resulting from the inhumane treatment surrounding their forcible transfer from Potočari.[320] The Trial Chamber

310 Blagojević Appeal Brief, paras. 6.8–6.14, 6.18–6.26.
311 Trial Judgement, para. 619.
312 Trial Judgement, para. 619.
313 Trial Judgement, paras. 754, 758.
314 *See supra* sections III.B.2 (Alleged Errors relating to Factual Findings: Role of Blagojević and the Bratunac Brigade in the Attack on Srebrenica), III.C (Alleged Errors relating to Murder), III.D (Alleged Errors relating to Forcible Transfer).
315 Blagojević Appeal Brief, paras. 6.15–6.17.
316 Trial Judgement, para. 478.
317 Blagojević Appeal Brief, paras. 6.16. In addition, based on the breakdown between him and his assigned trial counsel, Blagojević argues that he was unable to raise this objection or to cross-examine Deronjić. Blagojević Appeal Brief, para. 6.17. The Appeals Chamber has addressed and rejected Blagojević's challenges to errors flowing from his relationship with his trial counsel under Ground 1 (Fair Trial).
318 Trial Judgement, para. 24 fn. 59.
319 Trial Judgement, paras. 787, 797.
320 Trial Judgement, paras. 671–677.

concluded that these acts formed a single scheme to commit genocide as reflected in the "Krivaja 95" operation, the ultimate objective of which was to eliminate the enclave.[321] The Trial Chamber determined that Blagojević was complicit in this genocide by allowing Bratunac Brigade resources and personnel to be used in connection with the forcible transfer from Potočari and the mistreatment and murder of the Bosnian Muslim detainees in Bratunac town.[322] For the Trial Chamber, the forcible transfer of the women and others was a "manifestation of the specific intent to rid the Srebrenica enclave of its Bosnian Muslim population" and the killings and mistreatment at Bratunac town were a similar "manifestation of this intent to destroy the group."[323]

120. Blagojević submits that the Trial Chamber erred in fact in finding that he had knowledge of the commission of the crime of genocide or the genocidal intent of the principal perpetrators.[324] In disputing his awareness of the commission of genocide and of the genocidal intent of the principal perpetrators, Blagojević points to the Trial Chamber's finding that he lacked knowledge about the mass killings, which the Trial Chamber determined formed part of the genocide.[325] The Prosecution responds that the fact that Blagojević was unaware of the mass killings is irrelevant to his liability as an aider and abettor of the crime of genocide.[326]

121. A review of the Trial Judgement reflects that the Trial Chamber based its finding that Blagojević knew of the genocidal intent of the principal perpetrators on the following facts: (1) his knowledge that the purpose of the "Krivaja 95" operation was to create conditions for the **[page 46]** elimination of the Srebrenica enclave; (2) his knowledge that the Bosnian Muslim population was driven out of Srebrenica town in its entirety to Potočari; (3) his knowledge that Bosnian Muslim men were separated from the rest of the population; (4) his knowledge that Bosnian Muslim women, children, and the elderly were forcibly transferred to non-Serb held territory; (5) his knowledge that Bosnian Muslim men were detained in inhumane conditions in temporary detention centres pending further transport; (6) his knowledge that the Bratunac Brigade contributed to the murder of Bosnian Muslim men detained in Bratunac town; and (7) his knowledge of and participation in an operation to search the terrain with the purpose of capturing and detaining Bosnian Muslim men from the column so as to prevent them from reaching territory under Bosnian Muslim control.[327]

122. The main question for the Appeals Chamber is whether, in the absence of knowledge about the mass killings, the above findings form a sufficient basis to conclude that Blagojević knew of the principal perpetrators' genocidal intent. It follows from the *Krstić* Appeal Judgement that the existence of the mass killings which followed the take-over of Srebrenica was key to the finding that genocide had been committed.[328] In this respect, the Appeals Chamber stated: "[t]he main evidence underlying the Trial Chamber's conclusion that the VRS forces intended to eliminate all the Bosnian Muslims of Srebrenica was the massacre by the VRS of all men of military age from that community."[329] Moreover, the Appeals Chamber also placed significant weight on Radislav Krstić's awareness of the mass killings in determining that he had knowledge of the genocidal intent of the principal perpetrators.[330] In this respect, the Appeals Chamber refers to its assessment of the impact of Radislav Krstić's awareness of the forcible transfer operation, the separations in Potočari, and the detention and mistreatment of Bosnian Muslim men in Bratunac town on his knowledge of the genocidal intent of the principal perpetrators.[331] **[page 47]**

---

321 Trial Judgement, paras. 674, 677.

322 Trial Judgement, paras. 784, 787. More specifically, the Trial Chamber concluded that the following acts of practical assistance had had a substantial effect on the commission of genocide: (1) aiding and abetting the murders committed in Brutanac town; (2) aiding and abetting persecutions committed through the underlying acts of murder, cruel and inhumane treatment, terrorizing the civilian population and forcible transfer; (3) aiding and abetting the commission of other inhumane acts through forcible transfer; and, thus, rendering practical assistance in the killings and in causing serious bodily or mental harm to the Bosnian Muslims from Srebrenica.

323 Trial Judgement, paras. 675–676.

324 Blagojević Notice of Appeal, paras. 23–25; Blagojević Appeal Brief, paras. 7.9, 8.7, 8.9. Blagojević also asserts three other specific arguments against his conviction for complicity in genocide related to the genocidal intent of the principal perpetrators, the identity of the principal perpetrators, and the nature of his assistance to them. *See* Blagojević Appeal Brief, paras. 7.3, 7.4, 7.8, 7.10, 8.9.

325 Blagojević Appeal Brief, para. 8.6.

326 *See* Prosecution Response Brief, para. 8.11.

327 Trial Judgement, para. 786.

328 *See, e.g., Krstić* Appeal Judgement, paras. 26, 28, 29, 37, 83, 98, 100, 137.

329 *Krstić* Appeal Judgement, para. 26.

330 *Krstić* Appeal Judgement, paras. 104, 106, 112, 137.

331 *Krstić* Appeal Judgement, paras. 99, 100 (internal citations omitted):

> 99. The Trial Chamber based its finding as to Krstić's intent on a number of other facts as well. The men separated at Potočari were transported to Bratunac, along with other Bosnian Muslim prisoners captured in the wooded terrain. The Trial Chamber found

123. The Appeals Chamber notes that genocidal intent may be inferred, among other facts, from evidence of other culpable acts systematically directed against the same group.[332] Thus, the Appeals Chamber accepts that the forcible transfer operation, the separations, and the mistreatment and murders in Bratunac town are relevant considerations in assessing whether the principal perpetrators had genocidal intent.[333] However, the Appeals Chamber is not convinced by the Trial Chamber's reasoning that the forcible transfer operation alone or coupled with the murders and mistreatment in Bratunac town would suffice to demonstrate the principal perpetrators' intent to "destroy" the protected group.[334] The *Krstić* Appeal Judgement clearly held that "forcible transfer does not constitute in and of itself a genocidal act", and it is simply a relevant consideration as part of the overall factual assessment.[335] Similarly, the Appeals Chamber notes that "opportunistic killings" by their very nature provide a very limited basis for inferring genocidal intent. Rather, as the Appeals Chamber determined in the *Krstić* Appeal Judgement, these culpable acts simply assist in placing the mass killings in their proper context.[336] Consequently, no reasonable trier of fact could find beyond a reasonable doubt that, without knowledge of the mass killings, Blagojević's awareness of the other facts related to the forcible transfer operation shows that he had knowledge of the principal perpetrators' genocidal intent.[337] **[page 48]**

124. On the basis of the foregoing, the Appeals Chamber grants Blagojević's sixth ground of appeal and reverses his conviction for complicity in genocide. The Appeals Chamber will address the consequences of this finding on Blagojević's sentence below under Ground 8 of his appeal. Judge Shahabuddeen dissents on the ground that Blagojević was denied the right to a fair trial and considers that his case should be remanded for a new trial. **[page 49]**

G. Alleged Errors relating to Aiding and Abetting (Ground 7)

125. The Trial Chamber determined that Blagojević permitted the use of the Bratunac Brigade's resources, including personnel, to facilitate the commission of the crimes for which he was convicted.[338] The Trial Chamber considered that aiding and abetting constituted the most appropriate form of participation under Article 7(1) of

that the Bratunac Brigade would have informed the Drina Corps Command about the arrival of the prisoners, and that the Drina Corps Command must have known that the prisoners were not being transferred to regular prisoner of war facilities, but were being detained in Bratunac without any provision for food and water etc. From Radislav Krstić's presence in Potocari and his role in organising the transportation, the Trial Chamber concluded that he must known that the men were being separated from women and children and either detained, or were being transported elsewhere.

100. This evidence does not by itself establish that Krstic knew about the joint criminal enterprise to destroy the Bosnian Muslim population. As the Trial Chamber itself acknowledged, the separation of the men and their detention elsewhere may have been equally consistent with General Mladić's publicly stated intention that they be screened for possible war criminals. The separation and detention of the men was also consistent with an intention to exchange the prisoners for the Serbian soldiers captured by the Bosnian Muslims. The Trial Chamber heard evidence that such exchanges were frequent during the military conflict in the former Yugoslavia and that "a new infusion of Bosnian Muslim prisoners would have been a potentially useful bargaining tool for the Bosnian Serbs in future exchange negotiations." Indeed, the decision to execute the Bosnian Muslim civilians was, according to the Prosecution expert, "unfathomable in military terms". If this decision was so unexpected and irrational, it is surely unreasonable to expect Radislav Krstić to anticipate such a course of events on the basis of observations that are equally (if not more so) consistent with an innocent outcome. Krstić's knowledge of the detention of prisoners in Bratunac is therefore not sufficient to support an inference of actual knowledge about the execution plan, and by extension, an inference of genocidal intent on the part of Krstić.

332 *Krstić* Appeal Judgement, para. 33. *See also Jelisić* Appeal Judgement, para. 47; *Semanza* Appeal Judgement, paras. 261, 262; *Kayishema and Ruzindana* Appeal Judgement, para. 159.

333 *See, e.g., Krstić* Appeal Judgement, para. 33 ("the Trial Chamber [...] was entitled to conclude that the evidence of the transfer supported its finding that some members of the VRS Main Staff intended to destroy the Bosnian Muslims in Srebrenica.").

334 Trial Judgement, paras. 665, 675, 676.

335 *Krstić* Appeal Judgement, para. 33.

336 *Krstić* Appeal Judgement, para. 35 ("As already explained, the scale of the killing, combined with the VRS Main Staff's awareness of the detrimental consequences it would have for the Bosnian Muslim community of Srebrenica and with the other actions the Main Staff took to ensure that community's physical demise, is a sufficient factual basis for the finding of specific intent.").

337 The Trial Chamber's conclusion to the contrary may have been based on a view that in removing a group from a particular location, the removers are "destroying" the group. *See* Trial Judgement, paras. 657–666. The Appeals Chamber emphasizes, however, that displacement is not equivalent to destruction. *See Case Concerning the Application of the Convention on the Prevention and Punishment of the Crime of Genocide*, Judgement, para. 334.

338 Trial Judgement, paras. 747, 749, 755, 757, 759–760, 784, 794–796.

the Statute to describe his criminal responsibility.[339] Under this ground of appeal, Blagojević raises four errors of law and fact in connection with his conviction for aiding and abetting, including an alleged legal error in the definition of aiding and abetting and alleged factual errors related to his knowledge of the underlying crimes, whether he made Bratunac Brigade resources available, and whether this constituted substantial assistance.[340]

1. Alleged Error in Defining Aiding and Abetting

126. Initially, Blagojević submits that the Trial Chamber erred in law in setting forth the elements of aiding and abetting.[341]

127. The Appeals Chamber has explained that an aider and abettor carries out acts specifically directed to assist, encourage, or lend moral support to the perpetration of a certain specific crime, which have a substantial effect on the perpetration of the crime.[342] The *actus reus* need not serve as condition precedent for the crime and may occur before, during, or after the principal crime has been perpetrated.[343] The Appeals Chamber has also determined that the *actus reus* of aiding and abetting may be satisfied by a commander permitting the use of resources under his or her control, including personnel, to facilitate the perpetration of a crime.[344] The requisite mental element of aiding and abetting is knowledge that the acts performed assist the commission of the specific crime of the principal perpetrator.[345] In cases of specific intent crimes such as persecutions or genocide, the aider and abettor must know of the principal perpetrator's specific intent.[346] **[page 50]**

128. A review of the Trial Judgement reveals that in describing the applicable law for aiding and abetting, the Trial Chamber restated the above-mentioned formulations and principles, citing the *Vasiljević, Blaškić, Aleksovski, Čelebići*, and *Tadić* Appeal Judgements.[347] Blagojević has not pointed to any specific deficiencies in the Trial Chamber's statement of the applicable law beyond disagreeing with it. Accordingly, Blagojević has failed to identify any legal error on the part of the Trial Chamber in setting forth the applicable law on aiding and abetting.

2. Alleged Error in Finding that Blagojević Was Aware of the Crimes

129. Blagojević submits that the Trial Chamber erred in fact in finding that he was aware of the commission of the underlying crimes.[348] In this respect, Blagojević first challenges his conviction for complicity in genocide based on the Trial Chamber's finding that he had no knowledge of the mass killing operation.[349] The Appeals Chamber considered and accepted this argument under Ground 6 above.[350] In addition, with respect to his other convictions for aiding and abetting murder, persecutions, and inhumane acts, which relate to the forcible transfer of Bosnian Muslim civilians out of Srebrenica and the detention, mistreatment, and murders occurring in and around the Vuk Karadžić School in Bratunac town, Blagojević simply incorporates by reference arguments advanced elsewhere in his appeal challenging those factual findings.[351] The Appeals Chamber, however, has addressed and rejected those arguments in other grounds of this appeal.[352]

---

339 Trial Judgement, para. 796.

340 Blagojević Notice of Appeal, paras. 26, 27; Blagojević Appeal Brief, paras. 8.1–8.18. In addition, Blagojević makes additional arguments concerning his conviction for complicity in genocide. These arguments overlap to some extent with those raised under Ground 6 and are dealt with there.

341 Blagojević Appeal Brief, paras. 8.1, 8.2.

342 *Simić* Appeal Judgement, para. 85; *Blaškić* Appeal Judgement, paras. 45, 46; *Vasiljević* Appeal Judgement, para. 102; *Ntagerura et al.* Appeal Judgement, para. 370.

343 *Blaškić* Appeal Judgement, para. 48. *See also Simić* Appeal Judgement, para. 85; *Ntagerura et al.* Appeal Judgement, para. 372.

344 *Krstić* Appeal Judgment, paras. 137, 138, 144.

345 *Simić* Appeal Judgement, para. 86; *Vasiljević* Appeal Judgement, para. 102; *Blaškić* Appeal Judgement, para. 46; *Ntagerura et al.* Appeal Judgement, para. 370.

346 *Simić* Appeal Judgement, para. 86; *Krstić* Appeal Judgment, paras. 140, 141.

347 Trial Judgement, paras. 726–728.

348 Blagojević Appeal Brief, paras. 8.3–8.9, 8.18.

349 Blagojević Appeal Brief, paras. 8.3–8.7.

350 *See supra* section III.F (Alleged Errors relating to Complicity in Genocide).

351 Blagojević Appeal Brief, paras. 8.8, 8.9.

352 *See supra* sections III.B.3 (Alleged Errors relating to Factual Findings: Firing on Civilians in Srebrenica and *en route* to Potočari), III.B.4 (Alleged Errors relating to Factual Findings: Removal of Civilians from Potočari), III.B.6 (Alleged Errors relating

3. Alleged Error in Finding that Blagojević Permitted Bratunac Brigade Resources to Facilitate the Crimes

130. Blagojević submits that the Trial Chamber erred in fact in finding that he permitted the use of Bratunac Brigade resources to facilitate the commission of the crimes.[353] Blagojević does not dispute the role played by Momir Nikolić and the Bratunac Brigade Military Police in the transfer of Bosnian Muslim civilians from Potočari on 12 and 13 July 1995 or in the detention of Bosnian Muslim men in and around the Vuk Karadžić School in Bratunac town from 12 to 14 July 1995. Rather, he contests his legal authority over Momir Nikolić and the Bratunac Brigade Military Police, pointing to the parallel chain of command between these elements of the brigade and the **[page 51]** VRS Main Staff.[354] He notes that his criminal liability is almost exclusively predicated on their conduct over which he claims to have had no control.[355] Blagojević further challenges the Trial Chamber's findings concerning the role played by elements of the Bratunac Brigade other than the military police by describing it as inconsequential, noting that only a few brigade members were spotted in Potočari and Bratunac town and that they were likely there of their own volition or functioning under a separate, civilian chain of command.[356]

131. A review of the Trial Judgement reveals that the Trial Chamber concluded that Blagojević permitted members of the Bratunac Brigade Military Police to participate in the separations of Bosnian Muslim men from the women, children, and elderly in Potočari on 12 and 13 July 1995 and in the subsequent transfer from the Srebrenica enclave of the women, children, and the elderly as well as in guarding the Bosnian Muslim men detained in Bratunac town from 12 to 14 July 1995.[357] The Appeals Chamber has already addressed and rejected Blagojević's arguments on the Trial Chamber's findings that he had authority over the Bratunac Brigade Military Police and has further noted that his liability is not predicated on the actions of Momir Nikolić.[358] Moreover, the Trial Chamber also concluded that members of the Bratunac Brigade's Second Battalion and Third Artillery Group played a role in shelling and shooting around civilians *en route* to Potočari on 11 July 1995, in patrolling the area in and around Potočari on 12 and 13 July 1995, and in assisting in the transfer operation.[359] The Trial Chamber further concluded that Blagojević had command and control over these elements.[360] Blagojević does not dispute in any detail the role played by these additional elements of the Bratunac Brigade other than offering an alternative basis for their participation which is unsupported by any reference to the trial record. This is insufficient to call into question the reasonableness of the Trial Chamber's findings that Blagojević permitted these brigade resources to facilitate the commission of the crimes.

4. Alleged Error in Finding that Blagojević and the Bratunac Brigade Substantially Contributed to the Crimes

132. Blagojević submits that the Trial Chamber erred in fact in finding that any act of the Bratunac Brigade substantially contributed to the crimes.[361] A review of the Trial Judgement reveals that the Trial Chamber based Blagojević's criminal responsibility on permitting Bratunac **[page 52]** Brigade resources to be used to facilitate the crimes.[362] In connection with Blagojević's conviction for the mistreatment and murder, which occurred in and around the Vuk Karadžić School in Bratunac town from 12 to 14 July 1995, the Trial Chamber concluded that members of the Bratunac Brigade Military Police gave "practical assistance"

to Factual Findings: Detention, Mistreatment, and Murders in Bratunac Town), III.C (Alleged Errors relating to Murder), III.D (Alleged Errors relating to Forcible Transfer), III.E (Alleged Errors relating to Persecutions).

353 Blagojević Appeal Brief, paras. 8.11–8.18.

354 Blagojević Appeal Brief, paras. 8.11–8.16.

355 Blagojević Appeal Brief, para. 8.14.

356 Blagojević Appeal Brief, paras. 8.15–8.17.

357 Trial Judgement, paras. 729, 747, 755, 757, 784.

358 *See supra* section III.B.8 (Alleged Errors relating to Factual Findings: Blagojević's Authority over Momir Nikolić and the Bratunac Brigade Military Police).

359 Trial Judgement, paras. 755, 757, 784.

360 Trial Judgement, para. 419.

361 Blagojević Appeal Brief, paras. 3.118–3.120, 3.130-3.133, 5.21–5.23, 7.8, 8.14–8.17.

362 Trial Judgement, paras. 729, 749, 759, 784.

by guarding the detainees and helping to control access to them which ensured their further detention and allowed the murders to take place.[363] In addition, in connection with Blagojević's conviction for persecutions, the Trial Chamber concluded that members of the Bratunac Brigade gave practical assistance to terrorising the civilian population and to creating the inhumane conditions in Potočari and Bratunac town from 11 to 14 July 1995 by shelling and shooting around the civilians moving toward Potočari on 11 July; by participating in the separation process; by patrolling in Potočari on 12 and 13 July; and by guarding the detainees in Bratunac town from 12 to 14 July.[364] In addition, in connection with Blagojević's conviction for forcible transfer, the Trial Chamber concluded that members of the Bratunac Brigade gave practical assistance by separating the men from the women, children, and the elderly; loading buses; counting people as they entered buses; escorting the buses; and patrolling the area where the population was being held pending the completion of the transfer.[365]

133. In his submissions, Blagojević points to the relatively few members of the Bratunac Brigade who participated in the crimes when compared with the overall operation as well as the fact that the brigade members were not direct participants in the mistreatment or murder.[366]

134. The Appeals Chamber observes that the question of whether a given act constitutes substantial assistance to a crime requires a fact-based inquiry. Blagojević's primary argument on the point of substantial assistance is that the role played by the Bratunac Brigade was inconsequential in the overall context of the event. The Appeals Chamber, however, has already held that it is not required that the act of assistance serve as a condition precedent for the commission of the crime.[367] In making its findings, the Trial Chamber was aware of the more limited scope of assistance provided by the Bratunac Brigade in relation to other elements of the VRS and civilian authorities.[368] Nonetheless, the Trial Chamber described the contribution of the resources made available by Blagojević as "practical assistance" to the crimes which had a **[page 53]** substantial effect on the commission of the crimes.[369] The Appeals Chamber recalls that, in a similar context, it reached the same conclusion in the *Krstić* Appeal Judgement.[370] Blagojević has therefore failed to demonstrate that the Trial Chamber erred on this point.

5. Conclusion

135. For the foregoing reasons, the Appeals Chamber grants Blagojević's seventh ground of appeal with respect to the crime of genocide, as discussed in detail in his sixth ground of appeal. In all other respects, the Appeals Chamber finds that Blagojević's appeal against the Trial Chamber's findings related to aiding and abetting is not founded and, therefore, dismisses it. Judge Shahabuddeen dissents in all respects on the ground that Blagojević was denied the right to a fair trial and considers that his case should be remanded for a new trial. **[page 54]**

H. Alleged Errors relating to Sentencing (Ground 8)

136. The Trial Chamber sentenced Blagojević to a single sentence of eighteen years' imprisonment.[371] Blagojević submits that the Trial Chamber erred in law in assessing the aggravating and mitigating factors in assessing his sentence.[372] His submissions however do not address the factors discussed by the Trial Chamber in relation to aggravation and mitigation, but rather focus exclusively on its discussion of the gravity of the

---

363 Trial Judgement, para. 747.
364 Trial Judgement, para. 755.
365 Trial Judgement, para. 757.
366 Blagojević Appeal Brief, paras. 3.118–3.120, 3.130–3.133, 5.21–5.23, 7.8, 8.14.
367 *Simić* Appeal Judgement, para. 85; *Blaškić* Appeal Judgement, para. 48.
368 *See, e.g.,* Trial Judgement, para. 191 (noting the primary role played by the MUP in the transport of Bosnian Muslim refugees out of Potočari on 13 July 1995); para. 835 ("In relation to Vidoje Blagojević, the Trial Chamber finds that he was not one of the major participants in the commission of the crimes").
369 Trial Judgement, paras. 747, 755, 757.
370 *Krstić* Appeal Judgement, paras. 135–138.
371 Trial Judgement, Chapter X (disposition).
372 Blagojević Notice of Appeal, para. 28; Blagojević Appeal Brief, paras. 9.1–9.7. Blagojević in his notice of appeal and his appeal brief argued that his counsel at trial failed to make sentencing submissions. However, during the appeal hearing, Blagojević's counsel explained that this was not part of his appeal. *See* AT. 106.

crimes.[373] The Appeals Chamber considers these alleged errors first and then determines the impact on the sentence of its decisions to reverse Blagojević's conviction for genocide.

1. Alleged Errors in Assessing the Gravity of the Crimes

137. Trial Chambers are vested with a broad discretion in determining an appropriate sentence, due to their obligation to individualize penalties to fit the circumstances of the accused and the gravity of the crime.[374] As a rule, the Appeals Chamber will not revise a sentence unless the Trial Chamber has committed a discernible error in exercising its discretion or has failed to follow the applicable law.[375] It is for the appealing party to demonstrate how the Trial Chamber erred in imposing the sentence.[376]

138. Blagojević takes issue with the Trial Chamber's conclusion that persecutions warrant special attention and are particularly grave given the discriminatory nature of the crimes.[377] He argues that this cannot be the case for him as the Trial Chamber did not conclude that he possessed discriminatory intent.[378] The Appeals Chamber observes that the Trial Chamber expressly noted **[page 55]** that Blagojević did not have this intent, but aided and abetted others with knowledge that they acted on a discriminatory basis.[379]

139. Blagojević contends that the Trial Chamber's emphasis on the gravity of the discriminatory nature of the crime of persecutions reflects that it impermissibly aggravated his sentence based on a factor that is also an element of the crime.[380] The Appeals Chamber notes that in considering sentencing the Trial Chamber found that persecutions as a crime against humanity warrant "special attention" because they involve the "targeting of groups" on "discriminatory grounds".[381] The Trial Chamber also considered the crime of persecutions as "particularly grave because it incorporates manifold acts committed with discriminatory intent."[382] The Appeals Chamber sees no error in the Trial Chamber's approach because, in making these observations, the Trial Chamber has simply noted the inherent gravity of the crimes and did not refer to this as a specific aggravating factor.

140. Finally, Blagojević submits that the Trial Chamber did not properly take into account that he was not among the major participants in the crimes; that his role in the crime was that of an aider and abettor; and that he lacked knowledge of the mass killings.[383] However, a review of the Trial Judgement reveals that the Trial Chamber considered Blagojević's knowledge and the form of assistance that he provided to the principal perpetrators in determining his sentence, after it expressly stated that he was not one of the major participants in the commission of the crimes.[384]

141. The Appeals Chamber finds that Blagojević has not pointed to any discernible error on the part of the Trial Chamber in determining his sentence. Accordingly, the Appeals Chamber dismisses this ground of appeal in its entirety. Judge Shahabuddeen dissents on the ground that Blagojević was denied the right to a fair trial and considers that his case should be remanded for a new trial.

---

373 In his notice of appeal and appeal brief, Blagojević asserts error in paragraphs 841, 844, 845, and 850 in the portions of the Trial Judgement devoted to assessing aggravating and mitigating circumstances. *See* Blagojević Notice of Appeal, para. 28; Blagojević Appeal Brief, para. 9.1. Blagojević however does not develop this argument and thus his submissions fail to satisfy the threshold for consideration on appeal.

374 *Čelebići* Appeal Judgement, para. 717; *Dragan Nikolić* Sentencing Appeal Judgement, para. 9; *Babić* Sentencing Appeal Judgement, para. 7; *Deronjić* Sentencing Appeal Judgement, para. 8; *Miodrag Jokić* Sentencing Appeal Judgement, para. 8.

375 T*adić* Sentencing Appeal Judgement, para. 22; *Aleksovski* Appeal Judgement, para. 187; *Furundžija* Appeal Judgement, para. 239; *Čelebići* Appeal Judgement, para. 725; *Jelisić* Appeal Judgement, para. 99; *Kupreškić et al.* Appeal Judgement, para. 408; *Krstić* Appeal Judgement, para. 242; *Blaškić* Appeal Judgement, para. 680; *Deronjić* Sentencing Appeal Judgement, para. 8; *Miodrag Jokić* Sentencing Appeal Judgement, para. 8.

376 *Čelebići* Appeal Judgement, para. 725.

377 Blagojević Appeal Brief, paras. 9.4, 9.5, citing Trial Judgement, para. 834. Blagojević makes the same argument with respect to the crime of genocide. However, as that conviction has been reversed, the Appeals Chamber addresses his arguments only with respect to the crime of persecutions.

378 Blagojević Appeal Brief, para. 9.4.

379 Trial Judgement, para. 834.

380 Blagojević Appeal Brief, para. 9.5.

381 Trial Judgement, para. 834.

382 Trial Judgement, para. 834.

383 Blagojević Appeal Brief, paras. 9.6, 9.7.

384 Trial Judgement, paras. 835, 836.

2. Impact of the Appeals Chamber's Findings on Sentencing

142. The Appeals Chamber has reversed Blagojević's conviction for complicity in genocide on the basis that his knowledge of the forcible transfer operation, the separations, and the mistreatment and murders in Bratunac town were insufficient, without knowledge of the mass killings, to allow a reasonable trier of fact to find genocidal intent beyond reasonable doubt. However, the Appeals Chamber has upheld Blagojević's convictions for aiding and abetting murder as a violation of the **[page 56]** laws or customs of war, and aiding and abetting murder, persecutions, and other inhumane acts (forcible transfer) as crimes against humanity. The Appeals Chamber proceeds with the adjustment of Blagojević's sentence in light of its findings, and in accordance with the requirements of the Statute and the Rules. In light of the circumstances of this case, as well as the gravity of the crimes for which Blagojević is responsible, the Appeals Chamber, taking into account the principle of proportionality, considers that the sentence imposed by the Trial Chamber should be reduced to fifteen years. Judge Shahabuddeen dissents on the ground that Blagojević was denied the right to a fair trial and considers that his case should be remanded for a new trial. **[page 57]**

IV. THE APPEAL OF DRAGAN JOKIĆ

A. Alleged Errors relating to *Mens Rea* of Aiding and Abetting (Grounds 1 and 2)

143. The Trial Chamber convicted Jokić of aiding and abetting murder as a violation of the laws and customs of war and murder, extermination, and persecutions as crimes against humanity based on his acts of practical assistance, including co-ordinating, sending, and monitoring the deployment of Zvornik Brigade resources, which had a substantial effect on the mass executions at Orahovac, Pilica School/Branjevo Military Farm, and Kozluk between 14 and 17 July 1995.[385] The Trial Chamber concluded that Jokić rendered this assistance with the knowledge that his acts assisted in the commission of these crimes.[386]

144. Under the first ground of his appeal, Jokić submits that the Trial Chamber erred in law because it reached factual findings in relation to aiding and abetting by applying an incorrect legal standard.[387] However, Jokić expressly does not dispute the definition of the requisite *mens rea* for aiding and abetting which was adopted by the Trial Chamber.[388] Rather, he argues that the Trial Chamber erred in the application of the standard because its factual conclusions were not supported by the evidence and were not sufficient to prove his *mens rea* beyond reasonable doubt.[389] Under his second ground of appeal, Jokić argues that the Trial Chamber erred in fact regarding his *mens rea* in relation to aiding and abetting. In particular, he challenges the Trial Chamber's conclusion that he knew about the impending mass executions of prisoners at the sites of Orahovac, Pilica School/Branjevo Military Farm, and Kozluk.[390]

145. The Appeals Chamber has previously noted that, although a Trial Chamber's factual findings are governed by the legal rule that facts essential to establishing the guilt of an accused have to be proven beyond reasonable doubt, this does not affect their nature as factual conclusions.[391] A party arguing that a Trial Chamber based its factual conclusions on insufficient evidence therefore submits that the Trial Chamber committed an error in fact, not an error in law.

146. Accordingly, the Appeals Chamber considers that Jokić submits both under his first and second grounds of appeal that the Trial Chamber erred in fact when it found that he acted with the requisite *mens rea* in relation to the events at Orahovac, Pilica School/Branjevo Military Farm, and **[page 58]** Kozluk. The Appeals Chamber therefore addresses the arguments advanced under these grounds of appeal together.

---

385 Trial Judgement, paras. 770, 772, 775, Chapter X (disposition).

386 Trial Judgement, paras. 770, 772, 775.

387 Jokić Appeal Brief, para. 39. For the procedural aspects of this ground of appeal, *see Blagojević and Jokić*, Decision on Motion to Strike, paras. 2–4.

388 Jokić Appeal Brief, para. 38.

389 Jokić Appeal Brief, paras. 39, 55; Jokić Reply Brief, para. 2.

390 Jokić Appeal Brief, paras. 58, 62, 66.

391 *Blagojević and Jokić*, Decision on Motion to Strike, para. 8.

1. Orahovac

147. The Trial Chamber concluded that between 1,000 and 2,500 Bosnian Muslim men detained at Grbavci School in Orahovac were executed in a nearby field beginning on the afternoon of 14 July 1995 and continuing until around 5 a.m. on 15 July 1995.[392] The Trial Chamber found that, around 12 p.m. on 14 July 1995, Jokić told Cvijetin Ristanović, a machine operator with the Zvornik Brigade Engineering Company, in the presence of Slavko Bogičević, the deputy commander of the Zvornik Brigade Engineering Company, to go to Orahovac with an excavator where Bogičević instructed Ristanović as to how to dig mass graves.[393] The Trial Chamber concluded as follows:

> The Trial Chamber is convinced that Dragan Jokić knew that Bosnian Muslim prisoners were detained at the Grbavci School awaiting their execution when he told Ristanović to go there. The Trial Chamber therefore finds that Dragan Jokić knew that Ristanović was sent to Orahovac specifically in order to dig mass graves for the victims of the executions. By telling Cvijetin Ristanović to take the excavator to Orahovac, Dragan Jokić provided practical assistance that had a substantial effect on the commission of the crime.[394]

148. Jokić submits that the Trial Chamber erred in fact in finding that he was aware of the impending executions at Orahovac when he told Cvijetin Ristanović to go there with an excavator.[395] He asserts that the Trial Chamber's findings on his knowledge of the mass killings are inconsistent with the undisputed facts in relation to the massacre.[396] In this respect, he points primarily to the chronology of the events, noting that Cvijetin Ristanović was sent to Orahovac around noon, well before the executions commenced in the early evening.[397] Further, he disputes that his role as duty officer provided the Trial Chamber with a reasonable basis for inferring his knowledge of the impending killings. Although the duty officer had to be informed about the activities of the brigade's units, Jokić argues that the executions were carried out in a clandestine way and information about them was not communicated to him.[398] He submits that, as late as 10.36 p.m. on 14 July 1995, the information about the mass executions was disclosed only on a "need to-know-basis", whereas he told Cvijetin Ristanović to go to Orahovac around noon on 14 July 1995 **[page 59]** and the executions started in the early evening.[399] Moreover, Jokić points to the evidence of Tanacko Tanić who stated that nobody knew in advance that there were going to be executions, but that it became common knowledge only after they occurred.[400] Jokić argues that it was unreasonable to conclude from his knowledge of the detention that he must have known about the killings to follow, as "detaining prisoners is a legitimate military operation, whereas executing them constitutes a heinous crime."[401] He argues that it was equally reasonable to conclude from the evidence that he was not aware of the criminal outcome of the detention at the time he told Cvijetin Ristanović to go to Orahovac.[402]

149. Finally, Jokić disputes that Cvijetin Ristanović's testimony on the presence of Slavko Bogičević provided the Trial Chamber with a reasonable basis for making the inference about his knowledge of the impending killings. In this respect, he first argues that the Trial Chamber erred in fact in relying on Ristanović's equivocal and contradictory account to establish the presence of Slavko Bogičević when Jokić gave Ristanović the instruction to go to Orahovac.[403] Second, Jokić argues that, even if Bogičević were present when Jokić instructed Ristanović to go to Orahovac, there was no reason to assume that Bogičević shared his knowledge about the impending executions with Jokić.[404]

---

392 Trial Judgement, para. 763.
393 Trial Judgement, paras. 763, 764.
394 Trial Judgement, paras. 763, 764.
395 Jokić Appeal Brief, paras. 40, 58, 61.
396 Jokić Appeal Brief, paras. 39(1), 41–43.
397 Jokić Appeal Brief, paras. 41–43.
398 Jokić Appeal Brief, paras. 42, 59(1).
399 Jokić Appeal Brief, paras. 41, 42. Jokić raises the same argument under his sixth ground of appeal. *See* Jokić Appeal Brief, para. 174.
400 Jokić Appeal Brief, para. 59(1), citing T. 12024–12027.
401 Jokić Appeal Brief, para. 59(1).
402 Jokić Appeal Brief, para. 59(1).
403 Jokić Appeal Brief, para. 59(2).
404 Jokić Appeal Brief, para. 59(2).

150. A review of the Trial Judgement reveals that the Trial Chamber based its findings on Jokić's *mens rea* on two principal facts: (1) Jokić's role as duty officer of the Zvornik Brigade at the relevant time, which provided him with knowledge about the movement of prisoners; and (2) the order he gave to Cvijetin Ristanović to go to Orahovac with his excavation machine in the presence of Slavko Bogičević, who, a short time later, instructed Ristanović to dig mass graves at the execution site.[405] The principal question before the Appeals Chamber is whether no reasonable Trial Chamber could find on the basis of these facts that Jokić knew about the impending executions of the Bosnian Muslim detainees in Orahovac.

151. With regard to Slavko Bogičević's presence when Jokić instructed Ristanović to take an excavator to Orahovac, Ristanović testified: "As far as I can remember, there was the lorry driver who transported a piece of equipment. There was another soldier, Risto Lazić, and I believe that **[page 60]** Slavko Bogičević was also present."[406] Later, after Cvijetin Ristanović's machine – a backhoe excavator – had been loaded on a truck and taken to Orahovac, Ristanović met Slavko Bogičević again:

> Q. Now, you said somebody came to tell you to unload the truck, do you remember who that was?
>
> A. I cannot remember with 100 percent certainty. When I went up there after having unloaded the things there, I saw Slavko Bogičević.
>
> Q. What did he tell you to do?
>
> A. He told me to take the machine up there – I mean after the underpass, to take it through the underpass and then to the other side.[407]

152. The Appeals Chamber finds that, based on the above-quoted testimony, a Trial Chamber could reasonably conclude that Slavko Bogičević was present when Jokić gave his orders to Cvijetin Ristanović. Contrary to Jokić's assertion,[408] the fact that Slavko Bogičević was at the railroad underpass in Orahovac not long after this conversation, which took place at the headquarters of the Engineering Company, is not inconsistent with his presence at the conversation. After he had received his orders from Jokić, Cvijetin Ristanović took some time to load the backhoe excavator on a truck.[409] It was therefore not unreasonable to conclude that Slavko Bogičević arrived at the same location earlier then Cvijetin Ristanović.

153. The expression used by Cvijetin Ristanović that he "believe[d]" Slavko Bogičević was present during the conversation with Jokić at the headquarters of the Engineering Company may indeed indicate that the witness was not certain. However, this is not necessarily so, and the Appeals Chamber defers to the assessment of the Trial Chamber, which was satisfied on the basis of Ristanović's testimony that Slavko Bogičević was present.[410] Regarding Slavko Bogičević's presence at the execution site in Orahovac, the Appeals Chamber notes that although Cvijetin Ristanović was not certain who told him to unload the backhoe excavator from the truck, he was positive that it was Slavko Bogičević who told him what to do with the machine afterwards. The Appeals Chamber finds that a Trial Chamber could reasonably conclude that Slavko Bogičević was present when Jokić gave his orders to Cvijetin Ristanović as well as at the execution site in Orahovac. **[page 61]**

154. With respect to the question of Jokić's knowledge, the Appeals Chamber is not convinced by Jokić's contention that it would be reasonable to infer from the chronology and clandestine nature of the events that he sent Cvijetin Ristanović to Orahovac without knowledge of the impending executions. Absent a reasonable alternative explanation for why earth-moving equipment might be needed at a temporary detention site – even accepting Jokić's submission that the true purpose of the operation was revealed on only a "need to-know-basis" – the nature of Jokić's instruction reasonably indicates that he was necessarily within this limited circle of knowledge. The presence of Slavko Bogičević, the deputy commander of the Engineering Company, both at the time of Jokić's instruction and again a short time later at a pre-marked site to give the specific instruction to dig mass graves provides, in the circumstances of this case, an even more compelling basis for concluding that Jokić had advance knowledge of the killings.

405 Trial Judgement, paras. 511, 526, 763, 764.
406 T. 5364–5365.
407 T. 5370.
408 Jokić Appeal Brief, para. 59(2).
409 T. 5367.
410 Trial Judgement, para. 526.

155. Jokić appears to accept that it was reasonable to infer that Slavko Bogičević was informed about the impending executions at the time Cvijetin Ristanović was instructed to go to Orahovac.[411] This was in any case, in the view of the Appeals Chamber, a reasonable conclusion open to the Trial Chamber.

156. At the relevant time, Slavko Bogičević was the deputy commander of the Engineering Company of the Zvornik Brigade. However, from 13 to 17 July 1995, he was in charge of the Engineering Company because its commander was absent.[412] At the same time, Jokić was the Chief of Engineering of the Zvornik Brigade.[413] The commander of the Engineering Company took his orders directly from the Brigade Commander; in theory, Jokić could not directly issue orders to the commander of the Engineering Company, but would assist him in carrying out the orders of the Brigade Commander, which in turn were based on the advice and proposals of the Chief of Engineering.[414] Because neither the commander of the Engineering Company nor Slavko Bogičević as his deputy had sufficient experience to carry out the complex tasks assigned to the Engineering Company,[415] Jokić had an advisory function and worked closely with the Engineering Company to ensure that the orders were properly carried out. In some instances, Jokić issued orders to the Engineering Company and went to the field to carry out engineering tasks himself.[416] Therefore, during the company commander's absence, "Slavko Bogičević would certainly have consulted Mr. Jokić on all matters", as Dragan Obrenović, the Deputy Brigade Commander and Chief of Staff of **[page 62]** the Zvornik Brigade, testified.[417] According to Cvijetin Ristanović, Jokić ordered him to go to Orahovac in his role as "Chief of Engineers",[418] as opposed to relaying an order from the Brigade Commander in his function as duty officer.

157. In sum, the Appeals Chamber notes that Jokić and Slavko Bogičević worked in close collaboration; that Jokić was, in the words of Dragan Obrenović, superior in practical terms to the commander of the Engineering Company and controlled the Engineering Company when it came to the professional part of its duties; and, that he was assigned this role because of his professional expertise and experience.[419] In these circumstances, the Appeals Chamber finds that a Trial Chamber could arrive at the conclusion that the only reasonable inference to be drawn from these facts was that Jokić knew about the intended mass executions when he sent Cvijetin Ristanović to Orahovac.

158. Jokić also takes issue with a number of other findings by the Trial Chamber which could be used to support the conclusion that he knew about the impending mass executions when he sent Cvijetin Ristanović to Orahovac.[420] Having found that the factual findings in paragraph 764 of the Trial Judgement were reasonable and having allowed the conclusion that Jokić had the requisite *mens rea* for aiding and abetting the mass executions committed at Orahovac, the Appeals Chamber need not address the remaining arguments on this point.

2. Pilica School and Branjevo Military Farm

159. The Trial Chamber concluded that, on 16 July 1995, Bosnian Muslim men, who had been detained for two days at the Pilica School, were taken by bus to the nearby Branjevo Military Farm and executed.[421] Additionally, the Trial Chamber found that, on 16 July 1995, the Zvornik Brigade First Battalion requested that a loader, an excavator, and a dump truck be brought to the Branjevo Military Farm.[422] The Trial Chamber further concluded that, on 17 July 1995, the Zvornik Brigade Engineering Company provided an excavator and that Cvijetin Ristanović used the excavator to dig a mass grave.[423] The Trial Chamber found that Jokić knew of the detention of the Bosnian Muslim men at the Pilica School as early as 14 July 1995, that he was

---

411 Jokić Appeal Brief, para. 59(2).
412 Trial Judgement, para. 523.
413 Trial Judgement, paras. 11, 516–519.
414 Trial Judgement, para. 519.
415 Trial Judgement, paras. 520, 523.
416 Trial Judgement, paras. 519–524.
417 Trial Judgement, para. 523, quoting Witness Dragan Obrenović, T. 3034. As to Dragan Obrenović's function, *see* Trial Judgement, para. 62.
418 T. 5364.
419 Trial Judgement, paras. 520, 521.
420 Jokić Appeal Brief, para. 60.
421 Trial Judgement, para. 766.
422 Trial Judgement, para. 766.
423 Trial Judgement, para. 766.

informed of the request for heavy machinery as Chief of Engineering for the Zvornik Brigade, and that he contacted the brigade's **[page 63]** Engineering Company to effectuate the request.[424] The Trial Chamber held that Jokić knew that the resources were sent to dig a mass grave.[425]

160. Jokić argues that the Trial Chamber relied on three factual findings to infer that he knew that the engineering equipment sent to the Branjevo Military Farm was used to dig mass graves: (1) Jokić knew of the detention of Bosnian Muslim men at the Pilica School from 14 July 1995; (2) Jokić, as Chief of Engineering, was informed about the request to send heavy machinery to the Branjevo Military Farm; and (3) Jokić was in contact with members of the Engineering Company to fulfil the request.[426] Jokić challenges the latter two findings and submits that, even if all three findings were admitted, the only reasonable inference would not be that he knew about the intended use of the equipment sent to the Branjevo Military Farm.[427] In addition, he argues that the request for heavy machinery was sent to the Zvornik Brigade only several hours after the mass murders had been committed.[428]

161. Regarding the finding that Jokić was informed about the request for engineering equipment to be sent to the Branjevo Military Farm, Jokić submits that the "evidence on which this assertion is based should have been disbelieved".[429] Jokić further submits that, according to Prosecution Witness P-130, two persons were contacted with a request for engineering equipment: Jokić and Sretin Milošević, the assistant commander of logistics.[430] Jokić argues that the request made to him for the equipment "must have been unsatisfactory, or a second person would not have been contacted".[431]

162. The Trial Judgement considered why Sretin Milošević was contacted in addition to Jokić: the First Battalion of the Zvornik Brigade had requested a loader, an excavator, and a dump truck for the Branjevo Farm, and "the logistics commander was notified in case the engineering company did not have a truck".[432] The Appeals Chamber concludes that Jokić has not shown why the finding that he was notified of the request for engineering equipment to be sent to the Branjevo Military Farm was unreasonable. **[page 64]**

163. Regarding the finding that Jokić was in contact with members of the Engineering Company to effectuate the request, Jokić argues that there was no evidence supporting such a finding.[433] The Appeals Chamber notes that the Trial Chamber did not refer in its Judgement to any direct evidence showing that Jokić was involved in sending engineering equipment to the Branjevo Military Farm. However, the Trial Chamber found that there was evidence showing that the request for equipment had been conveyed to Sretin Milošević and Jokić as Chief of Engineering and that the request had been fulfilled.[434] Considering the Trial Chamber's findings about the close relation between Jokić as Chief of Engineering and the Engineering Company,[435] the Appeals Chamber finds that a Trial Chamber could reasonably conclude that Jokić was also involved in the fulfilment of this particular request for engineering equipment.

164. The Appeals Chamber notes that the request for engineering equipment was dated 16 July 1995, and that the equipment was dispatched on 17 July 1995.[436] The Appeals Chamber recalls that it has already concluded that it was reasonable for the Trial Chamber to find that Jokić knew about the mass executions in Orahovac on 14 July 1995.[437] Jokić, referring to Tanacko Tanić's testimony, concedes that he, along with

424 Trial Judgement, paras. 766, 767.
425 Trial Judgement, para. 767.
426 Jokić Appeal Brief, para. 62.
427 Jokić Appeal Brief, para. 64.
428 Jokić Appeal Brief, para. 48.
429 Jokić Appeal Brief, para. 63(2) refers to para. 33 of the same document. However, in paragraph 33 no arguments as to the reliability of the evidence paraphrased in paragraph 362 of the Trial Judgement are to be found. In footnote 152 to paragraph 117 of his Appeal Brief, Jokić appears even to accept the finding that a request for heavy machinery was conveyed to him.
430 Jokić Reply Brief, para. 15.
431 Jokić Reply Brief, para. 15.
432 Trial Judgement, para. 352 fn. 1318.
433 Jokić Appeal Brief, para. 63(3).
434 Trial Judgement, para. 352.
435 *See* Trial Judgement, paras. 516–524.
436 Trial Judgement, para. 352.
437 *See supra* section IV.A.1 (Alleged Error relating to *Mens Rea* of Aiding and Abetting: Orahovac).

"everyone", knew about the mass executions of detainees at Orahovac on 15 July 1995.[438] Consequently, a Trial Chamber could reasonably conclude that Jokić also knew about the intended use of engineering equipment requested for other detention sites. The argument that Jokić acted only several hours after the mass murders had already been committed is discussed below.[439]

3. Kozluk

165. The Trial Chamber concluded that between 15 and 16 July 1995 around 500 men were executed and buried at the edge of the Drina River at Kozluk.[440] The Trial Chamber found that, around 8 a.m. on 16 July 1995, Jokić told Miloš Mitrović, a machine operator with the Zvornik Brigade Engineering Company, and Nikola Ricanović, another member of the Engineering Company, to go to Kozluk with an excavator where they would receive additional instructions from Damjan Lazarević, the commander of the Engineering Company's fortification platoon.[441] The Trial Chamber found that, on arrival, Damjan Lazarević ordered Miloš Mitrović to put earth on bodies already in mass graves, which he did until it was decided that the excavator, which was operating at **[page 65]** only 30 percent capacity, was not capable of completing the work.[442] Based on Jokić's instruction to Miloš Mitrović, the Trial Chamber concluded that Jokić not only knew about the intended use of the excavator at Kozluk but also about the killings which occurred there.[443]

166. Jokić submits that the Trial Chamber erred in fact in finding that he had knowledge of the mass killings at Kozluk at the time they were planned, prepared, or executed and in finding that he sent Miloš Mitrović and Nikola Ricanović there in order to dig mass graves.[444] At the outset Jokić argues that the Trial Chamber concluded that his knowledge about the massacre at Kozluk came only after the killings, which is insufficient for establishing his *mens rea*.[445] In this respect, Jokić points to the Trial Chamber's finding that he learned of the killings "by 17 July" whereas the relevant events occurred on 16 July.[446]

167. The Appeals Chamber is not persuaded by Jokić's contention that the Trial Chamber concluded that he only learned of the mass killings at Kozluk on 17 July 1995. In paragraph 769 of the Trial Judgement, the Trial Chamber stated: "With particular regard to Kozluk, therefore, by 17 July the evidence is clear as to Dragan Jokić's knowledge [...]". This language is misleading when quoted out of context. In the preceding paragraph in the Trial Judgement, the Trial Chamber stated:

> On 16 July at around 08:00, Miloš Mitrović, a machine operator of the fortification platoon of the Zvornik Brigade Engineering Company, was told by Dragan Jokić to take an excavator and go with another member of the Engineering Company, Nikola Ricanović, to Kozluk. This use of Engineering Company resources is corroborated by documentary evidence. While Dragan Jokić did not tell Mitrović what their tasks were going to be in Kozluk, he told Mitrović that Damjan Lazarević, commander of the fortification platoon of the Engineering Company, was going to inform them on-site. This establishes that Dragan Jokić, as Chief of Engineering, not only knew what the tasks were going to be but also that mass killings had been committed in Kozluk.[447]

168. It follows from this passage that the Trial Chamber concluded that Jokić had knowledge of the mass killings at Kozluk and the consequent need to dig mass graves at the time he dispatched Miloš Mitrović and Nikola Ricanović there with the excavator. In the view of the Appeals Chamber, this knowledge was sufficient to establish Jokić's *mens rea*.

---

438 Jokić Appeal Brief, para. 169 fn. 204.
439 *See infra* section IV.B (Alleged Errors relating to *Ex Post Facto* Assistance).
440 Trial Judgement, para. 357.
441 Trial Judgement, para. 768.
442 Trial Judgement, para. 768.
443 Trial Judgement, para. 768.
444 Jokić Appeal Brief, paras. 49–55, 66–75.
445 Jokić Appeal Brief, paras. 49–55.
446 Jokić Appeal Brief, para. 53, citing Trial Judgement, para. 769.
447 Trial Judgement, para. 768 (internal citations omitted).

168. Jokić next challenges the reasonableness of the Trial Chamber's conclusion that he had knowledge of the killings and of the purpose to which the Zvornik Brigade equipment and personnel he dispatched to Kozluk would be put. In this respect Jokić contends that, even if he sent Miloš Mitrović and Nikola Ricanović with excavator equipment to Kozluk in order to receive **[page 66]** instructions on-site from Damjan Lazarević, this evidence alone is insufficient to establish that he knew about the killings and that he deployed these brigade resources there to dig mass graves.[448] In particular, in disputing that he knew the equipment was sent to dig mass graves, he points to the fact that the excavator was not suited for the task and that it was substituted after only thirty minutes by a machine commandeered by the Zvornik Brigade from a private company.[449] Moreover, Jokić contends that no evidence connects him with the second machine, which the Trial Chamber erroneously described as "from the Zvornik Brigade Engineering Company".[450] He also highlights the Trial Chamber's error in describing this event as the "third time since 14 July that Dragan Jokić participated in deployment of Zvornik Brigade engineering resources", when the Trial Chamber's factual findings indicate that it was only the second time.[451] Jokić suggests that the evidence and the Trial Chamber's findings, therefore, support the equally reasonable conclusion that he did not know of the intended use of the equipment and simply acted in fulfilment of an order to mobilize it.[452]

169. The Trial Chamber expressly considered and rejected Jokić's argument that he lacked knowledge as evidenced by the unsuitability of the excavator for the task, reasoning as follows:

> First, while the evidence shows that the excavator did not work at full capacity and was designed for smaller road works, it was sent to the site by Dragan Jokić and was used there until another machine, also from the Zvornik Brigade Engineering Company, was sent to finish the task. Secondly, this was the third time since 14 July that Dragan Jokić participated in the deployment of Zvornik Brigade engineering resources to sites where Bosnian Muslims were detained awaiting execution or executed.[453]

The Appeals Chamber is not convinced that Jokić has called into question the reasonableness of this assessment. The Appeals Chamber considers that the alleged error in finding that this was the third – instead of the second – instance when Jokić sent engineering equipment to an execution site is immaterial to the reasonableness of the Trial Chamber's conclusion.

170. The Appeals Chamber is also not convinced by Jokić's argument on appeal that the deployment of the second machine shows that someone else was in charge of securing equipment for the Kozluk execution site. First, even assuming *arguendo* that Jokić was not involved in sending the second machine, this would not be inconsistent with the finding that he sent the first machine, and would not relieve him of his responsibility for its deployment. Second, the argument that the second machine did not "belong" to the Engineering Company, but was commandeered from a private company for the use of the Zvornik Brigade is immaterial. The Appeals Chamber notes that **[page 67]** Miloš Mitrović testified that the second machine was commandeered *for the use of* the Engineering Company.[454] In addition, the Appeals Chamber notes that also the excavator used by Miloš Mitrović did not "belong" to the Engineering Company, but was commandeered from a private company.[455]

171. Although it is not clear whether the Trial Chamber held Jokić responsible for sending the second machine to Kozluk, the Appeals Chamber finds that a Trial Chamber could reasonably arrive at the conclusion that he did so. This second machine arrived only half an hour after Miloš Mitrović had arrived at the site,[456] and its driver, like Miloš Mitrović, reported half an hour earlier to Damjan Lazarević for instructions.[457] On this

448 Jokić Appeal Brief, paras. 66–68.
449 Jokić Appeal Brief, paras. 69–72.
450 Jokić Appeal Brief, paras. 70, 71(1), citing Trial Judgement, para. 769.
451 Jokić Appeal Brief, paras. 54, 71(3), 73.
452 Jokić Appeal Brief, paras. 55, 68.
453 Trial Judgement, para. 769 (internal citations omitted).
454 T. 5608.
455 T. 5595.
456 T. 5606.
457 T. 5610.

date, the commander of the Engineering Company was still absent, and Damjan Lazarević reported to Jokić.[458] Considering Jokić's overall involvement in the activities of the Engineering Company, the short time-span between the arrival of the two machines and the almost identical manner in which their operators were instructed about the details of their task, it was not unreasonable to conclude that both of them were sent by Jokić.

173. For the foregoing reasons, the Appeals Chamber concludes that Jokić has not shown that the Trial Chamber erred when it dismissed his argument that he was not aware of the executions in Kozluk because he initially sent a machine which was not well suited for the task.

174. Further, the Appeals Chamber recalls that, at the time Jokić sent Miloš Mitrović with the excavator to Kozluk, he was aware that mass executions had taken place at Orahovac and that equipment of the Engineering Company had been used to dig mass graves for the victims.[459] Moreover, the Appeals Chamber confirmed the reasonableness of the Trial Chamber's conclusion that Jokić in fact dispatched Zvornik Brigade Engineering Company equipment and personnel to dig mass graves at the Orahovac site. There is a striking parallel between Jokić's action with regard to the Orahovac killing site and with regard to Kozluk: in both cases, he did not tell the operator of the equipment he sent to the site directly what he was to do, but instructed him to report to another officer on-site for further instructions. In the case of Orahovac, this was Slavko Bogičević, the deputy commander of the Engineering Company; in the case of Kozluk, it was Damjan Lazarević, the commander of the Fortification Platoon of the Engineering Company.[460] In light of the finding that "Slavko Bogičević would certainly have consulted Mr. Jokić on all matters",[461] a trier of fact **[page 68]** could reasonably infer that Damjan Lazarević would have done the same. Given Jokić's close involvement in the activities of the Engineering Company, the Trial Chamber reasonably concluded that Jokić was as well informed as the officers on-site about the intended use of the equipment he sent there.

175. Lastly, the Appeals Chamber rejects Jokić's argument that "Kozluk was not a previously known detention site."[462] Once it had been established that Jokić knew that he was sending equipment there to dig mass graves, it is immaterial whether he knew previously that prisoners were detained at this site, or whether the mass graves were intended for prisoners from other sites.

4. Conclusion

176. Accordingly, the Appeals Chamber dismisses Jokić's first and second grounds of appeal. **[page 69]**

B. Alleged Error relating to *Ex Post Facto* Assistance (Ground 4)

177. Jokić submits that the Trial Chamber erred in law by convicting him as an aider and abettor when the evidence against him clearly shows that his conduct was confined to *ex post facto* assistance.[463] According to Jokić, *ex post facto* assistance can only have a substantial effect on the commission of the crime, and thus lead to accomplice liability, when the accomplice and principal perpetrator have a prior agreement, a condition that was not met in this case.[464] Jokić points to the Trial Chamber's conclusion that "[i]t is required for *ex post facto* aiding and abetting that at the time of the planning, preparation or execution of the crime, a prior agreement exists between the principal and the person who subsequently aids and abets in the commission of the crime", and contends that it is a correct statement of the law.[465]

178. Jokić notes that in various legal systems a person who aids and abets before or during the commission of the crime is considered a party to the principal offence, whereas one who assists after the fact is considered

458 T. 5604.
459 *See supra* section IV.A.1 (Alleged Errors relating to *Mens Rea* of Aiding and Abetting: Orahovac).
460 Trial Judgement, para. 768.
461 Trial Judgement, para. 523, quoting witness Dragan Obrenović, T. 3034.
462 Jokić Reply Brief, para. 20.
463 Jokić Notice of Appeal, p. 6.
464 Jokić Notice of Appeal, p. 6; Jokić Appeal Brief, para. 143.
465 Jokić Appeal Brief, para. 140, citing Trial Judgement, para. 731.

guilty of a separate offence.[466] Jokić argues that criminal liability under Article 7(1) of the Statute encompasses only conduct that can be equated with that of a principal perpetrator, and intentionally precludes, by omission, liability as an accessory after the fact.[467] In the alternative, Jokić argues that if the Appeals Chamber considered that aiding and abetting after the fact is a form of liability encompassed by Article 7(1) of the Statute, the Appeals Chamber should nonetheless reverse his convictions because it was not proven beyond reasonable doubt that his acts were performed for the purpose of assisting the principal perpetrator to evade justice.[468]

179. In this ground of appeal, Jokić submits that the Trial Chamber committed an error of law, although he agrees with the Trial Chamber's statement of the law and appears instead to refute its factual findings.[469] Jokić concedes that he sent Zvornik Brigade Engineering Company assets to the Orahovac site before the killings there began and, therefore, accepts that this alleged act of assistance was not *ex post facto*.[470] He argues, however, that his alleged assistance to the killings at both the Pilica School/Branjevo Military Farm and Kozluk was *ex post facto* and, therefore, did not constitute the *actus reus* for aiding and abetting.[471] This ground thus turns on Jokić's assumption **[page 70]** that the Trial Chamber had before it no evidence on which it could reasonably conclude that he provided *ex ante* or contemporaneous assistance to the mass killings at Pilica School/Branjevo Military Farm and Kozluk. That, however, was not the case.

180. The Trial Chamber found that Jokić knew about the murder operation when he sent Cvijetin Ristanović to Orahovac in the afternoon of 14 July 1995 before the killings occurred there.[472] Consequently, all of his knowing assistance to the murders once he knew of the murder operation is culpable as aiding and abetting. As the Trial Chamber found, Jokić's "acts of assistance included co-ordinating, sending and monitoring the deployment of Zvornik Brigade resources and equipment to the mass execution sites between 14–17 July."[473] The Appeals Chamber therefore considers the Trial Chamber to have reasonably concluded that Jokić was integrally involved in the murder operation, spanning multiple mass killing sites.

181. Accordingly, the Appeals Chamber dismisses this ground of appeal. **[page 71]**

C. Alleged Errors relating to the *Actus Reus* of Aiding and Abetting (Ground 3)

182. Jokić submits that the Trial Chamber erred in law by holding that his acts, as found, constituted the *actus reus* of aiding and abetting.[474] While Jokić expressly does not challenge the Trial Chamber's definition of the *actus reus* of aiding and abetting, he argues that "[s]ome aspects of this definition need to be established in greater detail in order to enable them to be applied to the particular facts found by the Trial Chamber in this case."[475] Jokić posits as a legal element of the *actus reus* of aiding and abetting that the practical assistance given to the perpetrators, in addition to having a substantial effect on the commission of the crime, must be specifically or sufficiently directed to this end.[476] In this connection he argues that the mere performance by a person of his or her routine duties in an organized structure is not by its nature an act "specifically directed" to assist the perpetration of a crime.[477] Jokić contends that where such conduct fails to demonstrate the exercise of any independent power or initiative it could not, without more, constitute the *actus reus* of aiding and abetting.[478]

---

466 Jokić Appeal Brief, paras. 150–157 (referring to the Socialist Federal Republic of Yugoslavia, United Kingdom, Canada, France, and Italy).

467 Jokić Appeal Brief, paras. 158, 159.

468 Jokić Appeal Brief, para. 160.

469 The Prosecution suggests that since other grounds of Jokić's appeal do not raise the same argument, this ground must relate only to the killings that took place in Pilica School/Branjevo Military Farm. Prosecution Response Brief, para. 12.3. Jokić replied that this ground also relates to the mass killings at Kozluk. Jokić Reply Brief, para. 43.

470 Jokić Reply Brief, para. 43.

471 Jokić Reply Brief, para. 43.

472 Trial Judgement, paras. 763, 764.

473 Trial Judgement, para. 770.

474 Jokić Appeal Brief, para. 77.

475 Jokić Appeal Brief, para. 80.

476 Jokić Appeal Brief, paras. 88, 138.

477 Jokić Appeal Brief, paras. 95, 99.

478 Jokić Appeal Brief, paras. 112, 120, 123, 134, 135, 137.

183. In relation to the incidents which took place at the mass execution sites, Jokić argues that any assistance the principal perpetrators may have derived from his ordering a particular member of the Zvornik Brigade Engineering Company to go with equipment to a particular place at a particular time[479] was too remote or insubstantial to have had a substantial effect on the commission of the crime.[480] In particular, Jokić contends that he did not exercise any independent initiative or powers, but merely transmitted orders from his superiors in the course of his routine functions. Consequently, Jokić argues, his acts were not specifically directed to assist the perpetration of a crime.[481] Accordingly, he requests that his conviction be reversed and substituted with an acquittal.[482]

1. "Specifically Directed"

184. Jokić argues that in the *Tadić* Appeal Judgement the Appeals Chamber included specific direction as a required legal element in defining the *actus reus* of aiding and abetting and that it has not since departed from this definition.[483] To show that his acts were not "specifically directed" to **[page 72]** assist the perpetration of a crime, Jokić submits in relation to his conduct at Orahovac, Pilica School/Branjevo Military Farm, and Kozluk, that he merely performed his normal or routine duties in an organized structure, which, as such, could not be acts "specifically directed" to assist the perpetration of a crime.[484] Jokić further argues that the International Tribunal's jurisprudence indicates that "a person in an organized structure who merely continues to perform their routine duties does not become an aider and abettor of other members of the organized structure who commit crimes, even if the performance of their routine duties may in some way provide some practical assistance to the perpetrators of the crimes."[485]

185. In its consideration of the applicable law, the Trial Chamber found the *actus reus* for aiding and abetting to be that "the accused carried out an act which consisted of practical assistance, encouragement or moral support to the principal."[486] It further found that while the assistance need not have caused the act of the principal, it must have had a substantial effect on the commission of the crime.[487] Among other sources, the Trial Chamber cited the *Tadić* Appeal Judgement for this proposition. In the *Tadić* Appeal Judgement the Appeals Chamber stated that "[t]he aider and abettor carries out acts specifically directed to assist, encourage or lend moral support to the perpetration of a certain specific crime [...] and this support has a substantial effect upon the perpetration of the crime."[488] The Appeals Chamber notes that this statement followed a discussion of the *mens rea* and *actus reus* of joint criminal enterprise liability and was introduced for the purpose of distinguishing aiding and abetting from acting in pursuance of a common purpose or design to commit a crime, the latter requiring only that the participant perform acts that are "in some way directed" to the furtherance of the common plan or purpose.[489]

186. The contextual nature of the statement in the *Tadić* Appeal Judgement was acknowledged by the Appeals Chamber in the *Aleksovski* Appeal Judgement[490] which, as a consequence, concluded that the *Tadić* Appeal Judgement "does not purport to be a complete statement of the liability of the person charged with aiding and abetting".[491] It did, however, go on to quote the points made in the *Tadić* Appeal Judgement without departing from them, including the above-**[page 73]** referenced statement in relation to the aider and abettor carrying out acts which are specifically directed to assist.[492]

479 Jokić Appeal Brief, paras. 114, 129, 136.
480 Jokić Appeal Brief, paras. 110, 111, 121, 122, 135, 136.
481 Jokić Appeal Brief, paras. 106, 107,112, 120, 123, 134, 135, 137.
482 Jokić Appeal Brief, para. 77.
483 Jokić Appeal Brief, paras. 87, 88; Jokić Reply Brief, para. 39, citing *Tadić* Appeal Judgement, para. 229.
484 Jokić Appeal Brief, paras. 112, 123, 137.
485 Jokić Appeal Brief, para. 97.
486 Trial Judgement, para. 726.
487 Trial Judgement, para. 726.
488 *Tadić* Appeal Judgement, para. 229(iii).
489 *Tadić* Appeal Judgement, para. 229.
490 *Aleksovski* Appeal Judgement, para. 163.
491 *Aleksovski* Appeal Judgement, para. 163.
492 *Aleksovski* Appeal Judgement, para. 163(ii).

187. In the *Blaškić* Appeal Judgement, the Appeals Chamber considered whether the *actus reus* of aiding and abetting requires causation between the act of the accused and the act of the principal, or in other words, whether the contribution "must have a direct and important impact on the commission of the crime."[493] The Appeals Chamber found that "proof of a cause-effect relationship between the conduct of the aider and abettor and the commission of the crime, or proof that such conduct served as a condition precedent to the commission of the crime, is not required."[494] However, the Appeals Chamber reiterated that one of the requirements for the *actus reus* of aiding and abetting is that the support of the aider and abettor have a substantial effect upon the perpetration of the crime.[495]

188. In reaching this conclusion, in the *Blaškić* Appeal Judgement the Appeals Chamber referenced the definition of aiding and abetting in the *Vasiljević* Appeal Judgement, which is identical to that set out in the *Tadić* Appeal Judgement, and which, in specifying that the assistance given by an aider and abettor must be specifically directed, also contrasted aiding and abetting liability with that of joint criminal enterprise.[496] However, in the *Blaškić* Appeal Judgement the Appeals Chamber also found that the Trial Chamber correctly held that the standard for the *actus reus* was that set out in the *Furundžija* Trial Judgement: "consist[ing] of practical assistance, encouragement, or moral support which has a substantial effect on the perpetration of the crime."[497]

189. The Appeals Chamber observes that while the *Tadić* definition has not been explicitly departed from, specific direction has not always been included as an element of the *actus reus* of aiding and abetting.[498] This may be explained by the fact that such a finding will often be implicit in the finding that the accused has provided practical assistance to the principal perpetrator which had a substantial effect on the commission of the crime. The Appeals Chamber also considers that, to the extent specific direction forms an implicit part of the *actus reus* of aiding and abetting, where the accused knowingly participated in the commission of an offence and his or her participation **[page 74]** substantially affected the commission of that offence, the fact that his or her participation amounted to no more than his or her "routine duties" will not exculpate the accused.

190. Jokić seeks to rely on the statement of the Appeals Chamber in the *Čelebići* Appeal Judgement that it "would not accept that the circumstance alone of holding a position as a guard somewhere within a camp in which civilians are unlawfully detained suffices to render that guard responsible for the crime of unlawful confinement of civilians."[499] On this basis, Jokić argues that "while the work of camp guards directly contributed to the unlawful confinement of prisoners within the camp, the Appeals Chamber accepted, as a matter of law, that such contribution alone was too insignificant or insubstantial to constitute aiding and abetting that crime."[500] From this, Jokić extrapolates that "where a person holds a position within an organized structure to which certain lawful duties attach, the mere performance by that person of their routine duties will not of itself constitute aiding and abetting crimes that may be committed by others within that organized structure."[501]

191. The Appeals Chamber considers it unreasonable to compare Jokić's position within the Zvornik Brigade to that of a camp guard in the *Čelebići* case. At issue in the *Čelebići* case was the ability of the accused, Zejnil Delalić and Hazim Delić, to affect the continued detention of the civilians in the camp.[502] The Appeals Chamber considers that it was reasonable for the Trial Chamber in this case to find, with respect to the three execution sites, that Jokić's role, whether as duty officer or Chief of Engineering, went beyond that

493 *Blaškić* Appeal Judgement, para. 43.
494 *Blaškić* Appeal Judgement, para. 48. *See also Simić* Appeal Judgement, para. 85.
495 *Blaškić* Appeal Judgement, para. 48.
496 *Vasiljević* Appeal Judgement, para. 102.
497 *Blaškić* Appeal Judgement, para. 46, quoting *Blaškić* Trial Judgement, para. 283 (quoting *Furundzija* Trial Judgement, para. 249).
498 *Krnojelac* Appeal Judgement, para. 37, citing *Tadić* Appeal Judgment, para. 229; *Čelebići* Appeal Judgement, para. 345, citing *Tadić* Trial Judgement, para 688 (where the opposition is drawn between culpability where the accused "intentionally commits" a crime or where he "*knowingly* aids, abets or otherwise assists, *directly and substantially*, in the commission of such a crime" (emphasis added)). *But see Čelebići* Appeal Judgement, para. 352.
499 *Čelebići* Appeal Judgement, para. 364.
500 Jokić Appeal Brief, para. 94.
501 Jokić Appeal Brief, para. 95.
502 *Čelebići* Appeal Judgement, paras. 336–369.

of merely relaying orders up and down the chain of command.[503] The Trial Chamber's findings make it clear that Jokić's ability to affect the commission of the crime was substantial. In particular, the Trial Chamber found that, while Jokić did not directly issue orders in his capacity as Chief of Engineering, he assisted in carrying out the orders of the Brigade Commander which were based on his advice and proposals.[504]

192. Finally, Jokić's attempt to ground his argument in its apparent consistency with the principle that a person convicted of aiding and abetting "is convicted *of the crime itself*, in the same way as the principal perpetrator who actually commits the crime"[505] and thus must be specifically directed, is fundamentally misguided. The Appeals Chamber recalls that Article 7(1) of the Statute deals not only with individual responsibility by way of direct or personal participation in the criminal act but **[page 75]** also with individual participation by way of aiding and abetting in the criminal acts of others.[506] Aiding and abetting generally involves a lesser degree of directness of participation in the commission of the crime than that required to establish primary liability for an offence.[507]

193. The Appeals Chamber considers that Jokić's characterization of his conduct as the mere performance of routine duties in an organized structure is irrelevant to the principal question of whether his impugned conduct had a substantial effect on the perpetration of the crime.

2. Substantial Effect on the Commission of the Crime

194. Jokić next argues that his conduct was too insubstantial or remote from the commission of the underlying crimes. He reiterates that he did not himself participate or order anyone to participate in the digging of graves at the execution sites, nor did he exercise any independent initiative or powers with respect to the movement of equipment or personnel.[508] Jokić maintains that the sum total of his assistance, if any, consisted of ordering a particular member of the Zvornik Brigade Engineering Company to go with equipment to a particular place at a particular time. This, in his view, did not amount to substantial contribution to the killings at Orahovac, Pilica School/Branjevo Military Farm, and Kozluk.[509]

195. The Appeals Chamber rejects the proposition that independent initiative, power, or discretion must be shown in order for the *actus reus* of aiding and abetting to be established. It recalls its previous rejection of the contention that there exists a special requirement that a position of superior authority be established before liability for aiding and abetting under Article 7(1) of the Statute can be recognized.[510] The apparent implication of that argument was that a person lacking sufficient authority to be considered a superior or to be acting independently, rather than in the course of routine duties, would necessarily also lack the sufficient authority or capacity to make a significant contribution to the commission of the crime. The Appeals Chamber considers that such a determination is to be made on a case by case basis. In this sense, an accused's position of authority and ability to exercise independent initiative constitute contextual factors that may go to proving the significance of the accused's assistance in the commission of the crime.

196. The Trial Chamber found that Jokić rendered practical assistance which had a substantial effect on the commission of the mass executions in Orahovac, Pilica School/Branjevo Military **[page 76]** Farm, and Kozluk.[511] Jokić's acts of assistance were found to include co-ordinating, sending, and monitoring the deployment of Zvornik Brigade resources and equipment to the mass execution sites between 14 and 17 July 1995.[512] The Appeals

503 Trial Judgement, paras. 761–770.
504 Trial Judgement, para. 519.
505 Jokić Appeal Brief, para. 100.
506 *Aleksovski* Appeal Judgement, para. 170.
507 *Čelebići* Appeal Judgement, paras. 342, 343.
508 Jokić Appeal Brief, paras. 110, 121, 135.
509 Jokić Appeal Brief, paras. 114, 129, 136.
510 *Čelebići* Appeal Judgement, para. 338 (in the context of the offence of unlawful confinement); *Aleksovski* Appeal Judgement, para. 170 (in relation to the offence of outrages of personal dignity consisting of the use of detainees for forced labour and as human shields).
511 Trial Judgment, para. 770.
512 Trial Judgement, para. 770. *See also* Trial Judgement, para. 836 (finding that Jokić "substantially assisted the commission of the crimes by sending machinery of the Engineering Company to the execution sites and members of the Engineering Company to take part in the burial operation").

Chamber considers that by using the word "included" in paragraph 770 of the Trial Judgement, the Trial Chamber did not intend to encompass Jokić's conduct as duty officer from 14 to 15 July 1995. The Appeals Chamber notes that the Trial Chamber considered Jokić's role as duty officer solely in connection with his knowledge of the mass killings and not as part of the *actus reus* of aiding and abetting and that, in any event, it was reasonable for the Trial Chamber to conclude that the assistance Jokić provided in his capacity as Chief of Engineering in deploying engineering machinery and personnel for the burial operations at Orahovac, Pilica/Branjevo Military Farm, and Kozluk, had a substantial effect on the commission of the mass executions at these three sites.

197. The Appeals Chamber notes that Jokić advances the following arguments in support of his claim that the Trial Chamber erred in finding that his conduct had a substantial effect on the murder operation: (1) he did not himself participate in the digging of mass graves; (2) he did not order anyone to participate in the digging of graves; and (3) in ordering the deployment of resources and equipment of the Engineering Company to these sites, he was merely carrying out his routine duties.[513]

198. The Appeals Chamber finds that it was reasonable for the Trial Chamber to conclude that *de facto* Jokić not only had an advisory function, but worked closely with the Engineering Company, in some instances issued orders to the Engineering Company, and went to the field to carry out engineering tasks himself.[514] The Appeals Chamber further considers that Jokić, while perhaps not expressly, effectively ordered members of the Engineering Company to dig mass graves, having already affirmed the Trial Chamber's finding that Jokić knew the nature of the task to be given to the personnel he sent to the three execution sites.[515] The fact that Jokić did not himself participate in the digging of graves but ordered others to do so does not render his assistance any less substantial. Furthermore, the Appeals Chamber notes that there is nothing in the Trial Judgement to suggest that Jokić's role was limited to relaying orders up and down the chain of command. Rather, the Appeals **[page 77]** Chamber notes the Trial Chamber's finding that while Jokić did not directly issue orders in his capacity as Chief of Engineering, he assisted in carrying out the orders of the Brigade Commander which were based on his advice and proposals.[516]

199. The Appeals Chamber considers that Jokić has failed on appeal to demonstrate any error in the Trial Chamber's finding that he provided practical assistance which had a substantial effect on the murder operation. Assisting the organizers of the mass executions with the disposal of the victims was substantial to the achievement of murder operation.[517]

3. Conclusion

200. Accordingly, the Appeals Chamber dismisses this ground of appeal. **[page 78]**

D. Alleged Error relating to Equally Probable Explanation Consistent with Innocence (Ground 5)

201. Jokić submits that the Trial Chamber erred in law by convicting him when the evidence against him clearly showed that there was an equally probable explanation for his acts and omissions that was consistent with innocence: that it was in the interests of public health that the bodies of the victims be buried without delay. Jokić submits that the Prosecution neither proved that he had a prior agreement with the principal offenders to bury the victims, nor that he had been involved in the re-burial operation.[518] Jokić argues that it was only proved that, when confronted with a large number of unburied corpses, he took steps to bury them.[519] This could be construed as rendering assistance to the principal offenders, but equally probable was the interpretation that he acted in the interest of public health and safety.[520] To support this argument, Jokić

513 Jokić Appeal Brief, paras. 110–112; 121–123; 135–137. Jokić's arguments that any assistance provided at Kozluk or at the Pilica/ Branjevo Military Farm was provided *ex post facto* are addressed above under Ground Four.
514 Trial Judgement, paras. 519–524.
515 *See supra* section IV.A (Alleged Errors relating to *Mens Rea* of Aiding and Abetting).
516 Trial Judgement, para. 519.
517 *See infra* section IV.D (Alleged Error relating to Equally Probable Explanation Consistent with Innocence).
518 Jokić Appeal Brief, para. 164.
519 Jokić Appeal Brief, para. 164.
520 Jokić Appeal Brief, para. 164; Jokić Reply Brief, para. 59.

claims that he was confronted with the murders only after they had been committed.[521] In addition, Jokić maintains that he was legally obliged to act as he did under the Legal Act on the Organising and Functioning of Civilian Protection.[522] In sum, Jokić submits that his conduct was not criminal, and that, therefore, the Prosecution has not proved the *actus reus* of aiding and abetting.[523]

202. The Appeals Chamber notes that the issue raised under this ground of appeal is not one of law, but one of fact. The question whether the evidence allowed the conclusion that the *actus reus* of aiding and abetting had been proved is a factual one.[524] The Trial Chamber found, and the Appeals Chamber confirmed, that Jokić substantially contributed to the mass executions when he sent engineering equipment to the execution sites and that he did this knowing that the equipment would be used to dig mass graves for the victims.[525] Even if Jokić were concerned about public safety and health, this would not change the fact that his actions substantially contributed to the crimes or the conclusion that he did so with knowledge that his actions would assist the organizers of the "murder campaign". Rather his arguments go to the issue of motive. The Appeals Chamber recalls that personal motives are immaterial for the purposes of assessing an accused's intent and criminal responsibility.[526] Such considerations are only relevant to the Prosecutor's initial decision on whether to charge an accused with a crime and in determining the appropriate sentence.[527] **[page 79]**

203. In addition, the Appeals Chamber considers that Jokić's argument that his activities were somehow lawful and that there was no alternative open to him[528] must be viewed in the light of the fact that the victims were buried clandestinely in shallow unmarked mass graves. Given the circumstances, the Appeals Chamber does not find Jokić's arguments under this ground of appeal convincing.

204. Accordingly, the Appeals Chamber dismisses this ground of appeal. **[page 80]**

E. Alleged Error relating to Events of 15 July 1995 (Ground 6)

205. Jokić submits that the Trial Chamber erred in fact when it found that he was present at the duty officer's station in the early hours of 15 July 1995, when officers of the Zvornik Brigade returned from Orahovac and celebrated their "successful mission" in a neighbouring office.[529]

206. The Appeals Chamber notes that the Trial Chamber found that Jokić knew about the impending mass executions when he sent Cvijetin Ristanović with an excavator to Orahovac around noon on 14 July 1995.[530] The Appeals Chamber recalls its conclusion above that this was a reasonable finding.[531] The question whether Jokić was present when the officers returned from Orahovac around midnight on 14 July 1995 and celebrated the "success" of their mission is therefore immaterial to his knowledge about the mass executions. Jokić asserts that the alleged error occasioned a miscarriage of justice, without giving any reasons or showing the consequences of the alleged error on the outcome of the trial.[532]

207. Accordingly, the Appeals Chamber dismisses this ground of appeal. **[page 81]**

521 Jokić Appeal Brief, para. 164.
522 Jokić Appeal Brief, para. 165.
523 Jokić Appeal Brief, para. 166.
524 *Cf.* Decision on the Motion to Strike, para. 8.
525 Trial Judgement, paras. 764, 767, 769, 770.
526 *Kvočka et al.* Appeal Judgement, para. 106; *Jelisić* Appeal Judgement, para. 49, referring to *Tadić* Appeal Judgement, para. 269; *Krnojelac* Appeal Judgement, para. 102. The Appeals Chamber need not determine whether an accused could raise an affirmative defense of necessity where his or her actions responded to compelling concerns of safety and public health. The facts of this case do not amount to such a compelling situation.
527 *Tadić* Appeal Judgement, para. 269.
528 *Cf.* Jokić Reply Brief, para. 59.
529 Jokić Notice of Appeal, p. 7; Jokić Appeal Brief, para. 167.
530 Trial Judgement, para. 764.
531 *See supra* section IV.A.1 (Alleged Errors relating to *Mens Rea* of Aiding and Abetting: Orahovac).
532 Jokić Notice of Appeal, p. 7.

F. Alleged Error relating to Pilica School Burial Site (Ground 7)

208. The Trial Chamber found that Jokić knew that Bosnian Muslim prisoners were detained at the Pilica School between 14 and 16 July 1995.[533] The Trial Chamber further found that on 16 July 1995 the detainees were taken to the nearby Branjevo Military Farm where they were executed.[534] Paragraph 767 of the Trial Judgement reads in relevant part:

> [I]t has been established beyond reasonable doubt that Jokić, as Chief of Engineering, was informed of the 16 July request for heavy machinery and was in contact with Engineering Company members in order to effectuate the request. As a result of Dragan Jokić's actions Zvornik Brigade engineering resources and personnel were sent. The Trial Chamber is convinced that Dragan Jokić knew these resources were sent in order to dig mass graves.[535]

209. Jokić submits that the Trial Chamber erred in fact when it found that "engineering resources and personnel were sent to the Pilica School burial site 'as a result of Dragan Jokić's actions'".[536] He submits that the evidence of Prosecution Witness P-130 on which the Trial Chamber based its finding was not corroborated.[537] Jokić argues that the evidence in any case did not show that he, and not the commander for logistics, sent the equipment to the site and that there was no evidence to show that he knew "that the machinery was needed for something other than lawful purposes related to farming activities".[538] In fact, he adds, there was evidence showing that the same vehicles had been sent to the farm in July 1995 to move gravel and to dig up trees.[539]

210. The Appeals Chamber notes that the relevant entry in the workbook for 16 July 1995 reads: "At 2210 hrs. the 1st pb asked for one loader, one excavator and a dump-truck to be in Pilica at 0800 hrs. Conveyed to JOKIĆ and MILOŠEVIĆ."[540] Witness P-130 testified that the entry meant that Jokić and Milošević were notified that the equipment was needed.[541] Jokić, the witness explained, was the "chief of the engineer unit", and Milošević was the assistant to the commander for logistics.[542] Milošević, Witness P-130 added, was informed in case the engineering company did not have a truck available.[543]

211. The Trial Chamber found that part of Witness P-130's testimony was not truthful and "decided that weight can only be given to those parts of his testimony where sufficient **[page 82]** corroboration is found in the record".[544] The Appeals Chamber finds that it was open to the Trial Chamber to conclude that Witness P-130's testimony was corroborated by the entry in the workbook, showing that the request for engineering equipment was conveyed to Jokić and Milošević.

212. The argument that there was no evidence that Jokić, and not Milošević, sent the machinery to the farm, is unfounded. Witness P-130 explained that Milošević was only contacted in case the Engineering Company had no truck available.[545] The Appeals Chamber finds that a Trial Chamber could reasonably accept this explanation. In particular, there is no finding that Milošević, as the assistant to the logistics commander, had engineering equipment such as a loader or an excavator at his disposal, whereas the Engineering Company did.[546]

533 Trial Judgement, para. 766, referring to Trial Judgement, para. 347.
534 Trial Judgement, para. 766.
535 Trial Judgement, para. 767.
536 Jokić Notice of Appeal, p. 7, referring to Trial Judgement, para. 767.
537 Jokić Appeal Brief, para. 177.
538 Jokić Appeal Brief, para. 179. *See also* Jokić Reply Brief, paras. 15, 66.
539 Jokić Reply Brief, para. 66.
540 Ex. P133 "Zvornik Brigade – Duty Officer Workbook, English Translation of entries dated 13 to 20 July 1995", p. 34.
541 T. 6647.
542 T. 6647.
543 T. 6647.
544 Trial Judgement, para. 323.
545 T. 6647.
546 Trial Judgement, para. 70.

213. The Appeals Chamber finds Jokić's argument that the equipment may have been requested for "lawful purposes related to farming"[547] unpersuasive. First, the Appeals Chamber recalls that it was reasonable for the Trial Chamber to conclude that Jokić knew about the purpose for which engineering equipment was sent to Orahovac and Kozluk, namely to dig mass graves for executed detainees.[548] Jokić does not challenge the finding of the Trial Chamber that he knew about the detention of Bosnian Muslim men at the Pilica School, which was based on the testimony of Pero Petrović about a conversation he had with Jokić on 14 July 1995.[549] These findings alone would allow, in the view of the Appeals Chamber, a Trial Chamber to reasonably conclude that the equipment sent to Pilica was not intended for "lawful purposes related to farming".

214. Second, the Appeals Chamber notes that the evidence on which Jokić relies to support his argument is not persuasive. Exhibit P-873,[550] an article from a magazine, only notes that the Branjevo Military Farm was used for the production of food in June 1995. However, the article also notes that the "farm has its own tractor and borrows machinery from *Agroprom*".[551] This does not support the hypothesis that equipment of the Zvornik Brigade Engineering Company was used for farming purposes at the farm. Exhibit P-538, a vehicle log for a truck,[552] has only one entry related to the Branjevo Military Farm. This entry shows that the truck travelled to the farm on 17 July **[page 83]** 1995; the purpose of this trip is given as "[t]ransport of 700 loader", without any reference to farming activities.[553] Only Exhibit P-516 bears some relevance to the present issue. It is a vehicle log for a "Torpedo" excavator, used by Cvijetin Ristanović and Miloš Mitrović.[554] The log shows in fact an entry for 11 July 1995, stating that the machine was sent to a location identified as "Military Farm" with the purpose of "digging up cherry trees".[555] However, the Appeals Chamber notes that the next two entries in the log for 14 and 16 July 1995 respectively read "digging trenches in Orahovac" and "digging trenches in Kozluk",[556] when the machine was used to dig mass graves at these locations.[557] At a minimum this shows that the entries in the vehicle log are open to interpretation and have to be regarded with caution. In the view of the Appeals Chamber, none of this evidence shows that the Trial Chamber erred when it concluded that Jokić knew that the engineering resources and personnel were sent to the farm to dig mass graves.

215. Accordingly, the Appeals Chamber dismisses this ground of appeal. **[page 84]**

V. THE APPEAL OF THE PROSECUTION

A. Alleged Errors relating to Blagojević's Knowledge of Mass Killings (Ground 1)

216. The Trial Chamber found that, after the fall of Srebrenica on 11 July 1995, several thousand Bosnian Muslim men were executed by VRS and MUP forces and buried in different locations in the Srebrenica, Bratunac, and Zvornik municipalities.[558] Initially after the fall of Srebrenica, several thousand Bosnian Muslims sought refuge in Potočari.[559] On 12 and 13 July 1995, elements of the VRS separated the Bosnian Muslim men from the women, children, and the elderly and transferred them to Bratunac town.[560] In Bratunac town, they were detained in "unbearable conditions" at a school, a stadium, and on 80 to 120 buses for between one and three days.[561] On 12 July 1995, between 1,000 and 4,000 Bosnian Muslim men from a column of men that had fled Srebrenica toward

547 Jokić Appeal Brief, para. 179. *See also* Jokić Reply Brief, paras. 15, 66.
548 *See supra* sections IV.A.1 (Alleged Errors relating to *Mens Rea* of Aiding and Abetting: Orahovac), IV.A.3 (Alleged Errors relating to *Mens Rea* of Aiding and Abetting: Kozluk). *Cf.* Trial Judgement, paras. 764, 768, 769.
549 Jokić Appeal Brief, para. 63(1); Trial Judgement, paras. 347, 766.
550 Ex. P873, "Article from Drinski Magazine titled, 'They produce their own food'".
551 Ex. P873, "Article from Drinski Magazine titled, 'They produce their own food'", p. 1.
552 Ex. P538, "Zvornik Brigade Vehicle Log for Mercedes 2626 (M-5195) for July 1995".
553 Ex. P538, "Zvornik Brigade Vehicle Log for Mercedes 2626 (M-5195) for July 1995", p. 2; *cf.* Trial Judgement, para. 532.
554 Ex. P516, "Zvornik Brigade Vehicle Log for Rovakopac Torpedo from Birac Holding for July 1995".
555 Ex. P516, "Zvornik Brigade Vehicle Log for Rovakopac Torpedo from Birac Holding for July 1995", p. 2.
556 Ex. P516, "Zvornik Brigade Vehicle Log for Rovakopac Torpedo from Birac Holding for July 1995", p. 2.
557 Trial Judgement, paras. 530, 532.
558 Trial Judgement, para. 291.
559 Trial Judgement, para. 207.
560 Trial Judgement, paras. 180–192.
561 Trial Judgement, paras. 264, 270, 276.

Tuzla were captured at Sandići Meadow by MUP forces.[562] Approximately 1,000 of the men captured at Sandići Meadow were taken to an agricultural warehouse in Kravica ("Kravica Warehouse"), and others were taken to Bratunac town.[563] The men taken to the Kravica Warehouse were killed by Bosnian Serb forces in the evening of 13 July 1995.[564] Beginning on 13 July 1995 and lasting until 15 July 1995, the men held on buses in Bratunac town were transported to Orahovac, Petkovci, Pilica, and other localities in the Zvornik municipality.[565] Bosnian Serb forces killed and buried most of these men between 14 and 17 July 1995.[566]

217. At trial, the Prosecution submitted that Blagojević was criminally responsible for aiding and abetting the mass execution of these Bosnian Muslim men.[567] The Trial Chamber determined that Blagojević and members of the Bratunac Brigade assisted with the capture and detention of these men between 12 and 14 July 1995 and thus provided practical assistance to their ensuing mass execution.[568] The Trial Chamber, however, was not satisfied that there was sufficient evidence to establish that Blagojević knew, at the time he rendered this assistance, that the capture and detention of Bosnian Muslim men was a further step in a "murder operation".[569] Consequently, **[page 85]** because he lacked the requisite *mens rea*, the Trial Chamber did not convict Blagojević of aiding and abetting the mass executions.

218. The Prosecution submits that the Trial Chamber erred in finding that Blagojević did not know about the mass killings which occurred between 12 and 14 July 1995 and, consequently, erred in finding that he lacked the requisite *mens rea* for aiding and abetting these crimes.[570] The Prosecution requests the Appeals Chamber to enter convictions for aiding and abetting murder and extermination, and for complicity in genocide on the basis of the mass executions.[571] First, the Prosecution submits that the Trial Chamber erred in law by not applying the correct definition of the *mens rea* for aiding and abetting.[572] Second, according to the Prosecution, the Trial Chamber further erred in law in its application of the standard of proof beyond reasonable doubt.[573] Third, the Prosecution contests a number of factual findings and alleges that no reasonable Trial Chamber could have concluded that Blagojević did not have knowledge of the mass killings.[574]

1. Alleged Error of Law in the Definition of the *Mens Rea* for Aiding and Abetting

219. The Prosecution alleges that the Trial Chamber erred in law in its approach to the "knowledge" component of the *mens rea* for aiding and abetting.[575] The Prosecution contends that the Trial Chamber required proof that Blagojević knew, "in the sense of virtual certainty", that the mass killings would be committed.[576] According to the Prosecution, however, "the *mens rea* for aiding and abetting is awareness of a probability that the crime will be committed and that, if the crime will be committed, the acts of the accused assist the crime."[577] In the Prosecution's view, if the Trial Chamber would have applied this standard, it would have convicted Blagojević for aiding and abetting the mass killings.

---

562 Trial Judgement, paras. 219, 240.
563 Trial Judgement, para. 243.
564 Trial Judgement, paras. 296–299.
565 Trial Judgement, paras. 283–285, 316, 337, 347.
566 Trial Judgement, paras. 327–331, 337–346, 349–354, 357–362.
567 Trial Judgement, paras. 7–9.
568 Trial Judgement, paras. 733–738.
569 Trial Judgement, paras. 739–744. Thus, the only murders Blagojević was convicted of aiding and abetting were the "opportunistic killings" that occurred in Bratunac town between 12 and 14 July 1995. Trial Judgement, paras. 747–749.
570 Prosecution Appeal Brief, para. 2.3. The Prosecution submits that, for the purposes of this appeal, the relevant period for ascertaining Blagojević's knowledge is 12–14 July 1995, the period when he rendered practical assistance to the murder operation, but that, if he is found to have the requisite knowledge when he rendered assistance at that time, the Appeals Chamber should hold him responsible for all mass killings from 12 July through 17 July 1995. Prosecution Appeal, para. 2.4 fn. 1.
571 Prosecution Appeal Brief, para. 2.111.
572 Prosecution Appeal Brief, para. 2.16.
573 Prosecution Appeal Brief, para. 2.66.
574 Prosecution Appeal Brief, para. 2.71.
575 Prosecution Appeal Brief, paras. 2.6, 2.16, citing Trial Judgement, paras. 727, 782.
576 Prosecution Appeal Brief, para. 2.17.
577 Prosecution Appeal Brief, para. 2.18 (internal citations omitted). The Prosecution also submits that it is "awareness of a substantial likelihood that the crime will be committed and knowledge (or awareness) of a substantial likelihood that the acts of the accused will assist." Prosecution Appeal Brief, para. 2.62.

220. In support of its position concerning the *mens rea* of aiding and abetting, the Prosecution refers to the *Blaškić* Appeal Judgement, three trial judgements, and several national jurisdictions.[578] The Prosecution also argues that the standard for aiding and abetting should be consistent with other **[page 86]** forms of liability under Article 7(1) of the Statute, including ordering, instigating, and planning, which, in its view, require only an awareness of the substantial likelihood that the crime will be committed.[579]

221. In describing the applicable law for aiding and abetting, the Trial Chamber restated the formulation of the *mens rea* for aiding and abetting found in the *Vasiljević* Appeal Judgement:

> [I]t is not required that the aider and abettor shared the *mens rea* required for the crime; it is sufficient that the aider and abettor had knowledge that his or her own acts assisted in the commission of the specific crime by the principal offender. The aider and abettor must also be aware of the "essential elements" of the crime committed by the principal offender, including the state of mind of the principal offender.[580]

The Appeals Chamber has applied this formulation consistently in its judgements.[581] Consequently, the Appeals Chamber finds no legal error on the part of the Trial Chamber in this regard.

222. The Prosecution faults the Trial Chamber for not recalling the following additional language from the *Blaškić* Appeal Judgement and applying it in this case:

> The Trial Chamber agreed with the statement in the *Furundžija* Trial Judgement that "it is not necessary that the aider and abettor [...] know the precise crime that was intended and which in the event was committed. If he is aware that one of a number of crimes will probably be committed, and one of those crimes is in fact committed, he has intended to facilitate the commission of that crime, and is guilty as an aider and abettor." The Appeals Chamber concurs with this conclusion.[582]

The Appeals Chamber, however, recalls its position from the *Blaškić* Appeal Judgement that there are no reasons to depart from the definition of *mens rea* of aiding and abetting found in the *Vasiljević* Appeal Judgement.[583] The *Blaškić* Appeal Judgement did not extend the definition of *mens rea* of aiding and abetting.

223. The Prosecution also points to the Trial Chamber's statement that it had reasonable doubt that Blagojević "knew" that his acts furthered the mass killing operation,[584] suggesting that this indicates that the Trial Chamber examined the evidence to determine whether Blagojević knew that the mass killings were a virtual certainty. The Appeals Chamber, however, can identify no error on the part of the Trial Chamber based on the use of this formulation. The Appeals Chamber has employed the same formulation in its examination of the *mens rea* of aiding and abetting in other **[page 87]** cases.[585] Moreover, the Appeals Chamber observes that the Trial Chamber's reasonable doubt as to Blagojević's knowledge of the impending murder operation arose out of the equally plausible inference that "he saw [the detention and capture of Bosnian Muslim men] as further steps in transporting the Bosnian Muslim population out of Serb-held territory".[586] In this respect, the Trial Chamber also noted throughout the Trial Judgement that Bosnian Muslim men, who were captured, were told that they would be exchanged.[587] It is also telling that the Trial Chamber accepted as credible testimony from a former Bratunac Brigade officer who stated that he did not assist a particular detainee who was taken to the Vuk Karadžić School and later killed because he thought that the detainee was going to be exchanged.[588] Thus, the Trial Chamber did not decline to find that Blagojević knew about the mass killing operation because he lacked

---

578 *See* Prosecution Appeal Brief, paras. 2.28–2.58.
579 Prosecution Appeal Brief, paras. 2.35–2.38, 2.55–2.58.
580 Trial Judgement, para. 727.
581 *See, e.g., Blaškić* Appeal Judgement, para. 45; *Vasiljević* Appeal Judgement, para. 102; *Tadić* Appeal Judgement, para. 229.
582 *Blaškić* Appeal Judgement, para. 50 (internal citations omitted).
583 *Blaškić* Appeal Judgement, para. 45.
584 Prosecution Appeal Brief, para. 2.17, citing Trial Judgement, paras. 742, 743 (emphasis in Prosecution Appeal Brief).
585 *See, e.g., Kvočka et al.* Appeal Judgement, paras. 89, 90.
586 Trial Judgement, para. 742.
587 Trial Judgement, paras. 177, 227, 242, 251, 252, 254, 277, 316, 647, 736.
588 Trial Judgement, paras. 251–252, 736, fn. 2197. At the time, this officer was tasked with matters related to prisoners of war. Trial Judgement, paras. 50, 251.

certainty, but because it could not rule out the equally reasonable inference that he thought that his acts were directed towards another goal. Accordingly, the Trial Chamber did not err in its formulation of the *mens rea* requirement for aiding and abetting, and the Appeals Chamber dismisses this sub-ground of appeal.

2. Alleged Error of Law in the Application of the Standard of Proof Beyond Reasonable Doubt

224. The Prosecution submits that the Trial Chamber erred in law in its application of the standard of proof. Specifically, the Prosecution contends that the Trial Chamber applied the standard of proof in a two-stage process, first to the individual strands of evidence and then to the issue of *mens rea*, rather than reserving the application of the standard to the ultimate conclusion of guilt.[589] The Prosecution argues that this approach led the Trial Chamber to consider the evidence "piecemeal", failing to consider all of the established facts as a coherent whole in assessing Blagojević's *mens rea* for the mass killings.[590]

225. In particular, the Prosecution argues that the Trial Chamber failed to incorporate the following findings into its analysis of Blagojević's knowledge of the mass killings: (1) Blagojević's knowledge of the killings in Bratunac town on the nights of 12 and 13 July 1995 and the assistance provided by the Bratunac Brigade units in those killings;[591] (2) the vastness of the murder operation, involving many elements of VRS and MUP forces and occurring in many towns in a geographically **[page 88]** small area, including Potočari, Jadar River, Kravica Warehouse, and Tišca;[592] (3) Blagojević's knowledge of his units' participation in the separation and transport of Muslims from Potočari, in the detention of Muslim men in Bratunac town from 12 to 14 July 1995, and in the transfer of the men to Zvornik on 14 July 1995;[593] and (4) Blagojević's position in a functioning chain of command and his obligation to keep apprised of the activities of his subordinates.[594]

226. The standard of proof at trial requires that a Trial Chamber may only find an accused guilty of a crime if the Prosecution has proved each element of that crime and of the mode of liability, and any fact which is indispensable for the conviction, beyond reasonable doubt.[595] This standard applies whether the evidence evaluated is direct or circumstantial.[596] The Appeals Chamber has previously endorsed an approach where, similar in parts to the present case, a Trial Chamber individually examined evidence with respect to a number of incidents and subsequently assessed the accused's criminal responsibility for those incidents.[597]

227. In its analysis of Blagojević's *mens rea*, the Trial Chamber stated that it "carefully assessed all the evidence and in particular the evidence in relation to the detention of men in Sandići meadow" when making its finding that there was insufficient evidence to conclude that Blagojević knew that the detention and capture of the Bosnian Muslim men was a further step in the murder operation.[598] The Appeals Chamber notes that the vast majority of the Prosecution's appeal on this ground consists of reasserting findings of fact that were made in its favour throughout the Trial Judgement, but which were not individually referred to in the Trial Chamber's analysis of Blagojević's *mens rea*.[599] As the Appeals Chamber noted previously, where

589 Prosecution Appeal Brief, paras. 2.8, 2.66.

590 Prosecution Appeal Brief, para. 2.69.

591 Prosecution Appeal Brief, paras. 2.92–2.95.

592 Prosecution Appeal Brief, para. 2.88.

593 Prosecution Appeal Brief, para. 2.89.

594 Prosecution Appeal Brief, para. 2.90.

595 *See, e.g.*, *Stakić* Appeal Judgement, para. 219 ("A Trial Chamber may only find an accused guilty of a crime if the Prosecution has proved each element of that crime (as defined with respect to the relevant mode of liability) beyond a reasonable doubt."); *Ntagerura et al.* Appeal Judgement, para. 174.

596 *Stakić* Appeal Judgement, para. 219; *Kupreškić et al.* Appeal Judgement, para. 303; *Kordić and Čerkez* Appeal Judgement, para. 834.

597 *Kvočka et al.* Appeal Judgement, para. 70 (citing with approval the approach of the Trial Chamber in *Prosecutor v. Stanislav Galić* to determine whether certain incidents occurred beyond reasonable doubt before determining Galić's individual criminal responsibility for those incidents).

598 Trial Judgement, para. 742.

599 *See, e.g.*, Prosecution Appeal Brief, para. 2.75 (location of the Kravica Warehouse near the Bratunac Brigade 4th Battalion's IKM) (citing Trial Judgement, para. 742); Prosecution Appeal Brief, para. 2.75 (Muslim men captured at Sandići Meadow were taken to Kravica Warehouse) (citing Trial Judgement, para. 742); Prosecution Appeal Brief, para. 2.75 (many people in Bratunac knew of what happened at the Kravica Warehouse within 24 hours) (citing Trial Judgement, para. 742); Prosecution Appeal Brief, para. 2.75 (Blagojević was in Bratunac town on 12 to 14 July 1995) (citing Trial Judgement, para. 748); Prosecution Appeal Brief,

evidence is discussed in a Trial Judgement, it must be presumed to have been considered for each finding that it affects.[600] Therefore, the Appeals Chamber considers that the Prosecution has not demonstrated that the Trial **[page 89]** Chamber erred in its choice of method of assessment of evidence or in its application of the standard of proof. Accordingly, this sub-ground of appeal is dismissed.

3. Alleged Errors of Fact regarding Blagojević's Knowledge

228. The Prosecution challenges a number of factual findings made by the Trial Chamber regarding Blagojević's knowledge of specific mass killings and posits that the sum of these factual errors led to an erroneous conclusion regarding his knowledge of "a mass killing operation" in the Srebrenica enclave from 12 through 17 July 1995.[601] The Prosecution urges the Appeals Chamber to view the Trial Chamber's factual findings and the trial record together and in their totality to assess Blagojević's *mens rea* for aiding and abetting the mass killings.[602] In particular, it focuses on the reasonableness of the Trial Chamber's finding that the Prosecution failed to prove beyond reasonable doubt Blagojević's knowledge about the massacre at Kravica Warehouse on 13 July 1995, which was a key consideration in assessing his knowledge of the overall murder operation.[603]

(a) Alleged Common Knowledge of the Kravica Warehouse Massacre

229. The Trial Chamber found that there was insufficient evidence to establish that Blagojević knew about the mass executions at Kravica Warehouse until two to three days after they took place "and thereby did not know that his participation in the search operation was rendering practical assistance to a murder operation."[604]

230. The Prosecution argues that this finding was unreasonable in light of the following factual findings made by the Trial Chamber.[605] First, Kravica Warehouse was on the main road, near the forward command post of the Fourth Battalion of the Bratunac Brigade.[606] Second, Muslim men were detained within the Bratunac Brigade's area of responsibility and taken to Kravica Warehouse.[607] Third, the killings at Kravica Warehouse were open and notorious,[608] and news of the massacre spread to nearby towns, including Bratunac, within hours.[609] In this regard, the Prosecution argues that the Trial Chamber disregarded the testimony of six witnesses whose **[page 90]** testimony, in its view, indicated that Blagojević would have known about the killings.[610] Finally, Blagojević was at the Bratunac Brigade headquarters and slept in his apartment in Bratunac town between 12 and 14 July 1995.[611] The Prosecution also argues that the Trial Chamber erred in characterizing Blagojević as searching the woods in the days immediately following the killings at the Kravica Warehouse.[612]

---

para. 2.80 (a member of the Bratunac Brigade was injured in Kravica at the time of the massacre) (citing Trial Judgement, para. 364); Prosecution Appeal Brief, para. 2.82 (the Kravica Warehouse massacre was a matter of common knowledge) (citing Trial Judgement, paras. 296–303).

600 *Kvočka et al.* Appeal Judgement, para. 23.

601 Prosecution Appeal Brief, paras. 2.71, 2.74 fn. 1.

602 Prosecution Appeal Brief, para. 2.71.

603 Prosecution Appeal Brief, paras. 2.73, 2.85.

604 Trial Judgement, para. 742.

605 Prosecution Appeal Brief, paras. 2.71, 2.73.

606 Prosecution Appeal Brief, para. 2.75, citing Trial Judgement, para. 742.

607 Prosecution Appeal Brief, para. 2.75 (stating that Muslim men were detained in Sandići Meadow, near where members of the Bratunac Brigade were searching the terrain, and taken to Kravica Warehouse) (citing Trial Judgement, paras. 296–303).

608 The Prosecution submits that the Trial Chamber found that there were grenade explosions, gunfire, screaming, and hundreds of corpses lined up outside the warehouse the following morning and that it was widely known what happened there within 24 hours. Prosecution Appeal Brief, para. 2.75, citing Trial Judgement, paras. 296–303, 742.

609 Prosecution Appeal Brief, paras. 2.81–2.83. *See also* Trial Judgement, para. 742 fn. 2191.

610 Prosecution Appeal Brief, para. 2.81, citing testimony of Momir Nikolić, Witness DP-102, Tesić, Mirković, Gajić, and Davidović.

611 Prosecution Appeal Brief, para. 2.75, citing Trial Judgement, para. 748.

612 The Prosecution does not indicate where the Trial Chamber might have made this alleged error, but the Prosecution cites orders signed by Colonel Blagojević to battalions to sweep the terrain demonstrating that he was in Bratunac Headquarters. *See* Prosecution Appeal Brief, para. 2.78. The Prosecution is likely referring to the Trial Chamber's statement about Blagojević that "*he and his units* continued to participate in the search operation [emphasis added]" in the days following the Kravica Warehouse

231. A review of the Trial Judgement reflects that the Trial Chamber expressly noted much of the evidence that the Prosecution points to in support of its contention that the Trial Chamber gave scant or no regard to several findings indicating that Blagojević must have known about the killing at the Kravica Warehouse shortly after they occurred. Moreover, the Appeals Chamber finds no evidence that renders the Trial Chamber's finding on this point unreasonable.

232. The strongest evidence suggesting that Blagojević knew about the Kravica Warehouse killings came from Momir Nikolić's testimony that "already on the 14th" the Kravica Warehouse killings were "common knowledge" in Bratunac town, "[t]hat is, almost the entire town, all the soldiers, had heard about it."[613] The Trial Chamber did not reference this specific statement in the Trial Judgement; however, it clearly took account of this testimony because it cited the same transcript page when discussing when and how the Kravica Warehouse massacre became known.[614] The Trial Chamber, however, did not consider Nikolić to be a "wholly credible or reliable witness", and concluded that "on matters that bear directly on [Blagojević's] knowledge [...] such as what [Nikolić] reported to Colonel Blagojević [...] or was told to do [by Blagojević], it must require corroboration for such evidence, in order to enter a finding against [Blagojević]."[615] The Prosecution does not challenge the Trial Chamber's assessment of Nikolić's credibility, nor does the Prosecution make a specific argument as to why the testimony at issue here should be credited. In addition, the Trial Chamber found that, according to Momir Nikolić, he did not discuss the Kravica Warehouse killings with Blagojević until sometime around 24 July 1995.[616] **[page 91]**

233. The Trial Chamber also noted that, while many other persons learned of the Kravica Warehouse massacre in Bratunac town within twenty-four hours,[617] some learned of it later, citing the testimony of Dragomir Zekić,[618] who testified that he learned of the "genocide" at the Kravica Warehouse "probably sometime around the 14th or 15th of July."[619] Witnesses that the Trial Chamber noted learned of the killings on 14 July 1995 include Miroslav Deronjić, Witness DP-102, and Jovan Nikolić.[620] Contrary to the Prosecution's claim, there is no indication that the Trial Chamber disregarded the statements of Witness DP-102[621] and Jovan Nikolić as it cited their statements in key paragraphs concerning Blagojević's *mens rea*.[622]

234. The Prosecution also complains the Trial Chamber disregarded the testimony of Aleksander Tesić, Dragan Mirković, Nikola Gajić, and Srbislav Davidović, who were all aware of the massacre within twenty-four hours.[623] Aleksander Tesić, chief of the Department of Defence in Bratunac,[624] testified that he learned of the Kravica Warehouse massacre "when he saw it" – by which the Appeals Chamber understands him to say he saw the aftermath of the massacre – "on the 14th [of July 1995], just a bit before noon".[625] Witness Dragan Mirković, commander of the "Rad Utilities Company" unit,[626] testified that he witnessed some of the killings at the Kravica Warehouse from the road and that he returned to his home in Bratunac town by the evening of

massacre. This statement is made in the Trial Chamber's summary remarks regarding Blagojević's knowledge of that incident. *See* Trial Judgement, para. 742.

613 T. 1734.

614 Trial Judgement, para. 300 fn. 1080.

615 Trial Judgement, para. 472.

616 Trial Judgement, paras. 456 (Nikolić did not tell Blagojević of the Kravica Warehouse massacre until Blagojević returned from Žepa), 469 (Blagojević returned from Žepa on 24 July 1995). This evidence was referenced again by the Trial Chamber to support the possibility that Blagojević did not learn of the Kravica Warehouse killings until sometime after it occurred. *See* Trial Judgement, para. 498.

617 Trial Judgement, para. 742.

618 Trial Judgement, para. 742, citing Dragomir Zekić, T. 8899–8901.

619 T. 8901.

620 Trial Judgement, fn. 2191.

621 Witness DP-102 testified that from his position approximately 2 km down the road from Kravica he learned of the massacre "an hour or two later, perhaps more. People began to talk. Because people – you must understand, people were coming and going all the time, passing by that way." T. 8270. He later testified that he "heard about this incident two or three hours after it happened." T. 8272.

622 *See* Trial Judgement, para. 742, fn. 2191.

623 Prosecution Appeal Brief, para. 2.81.

624 Trial Judgement, para. 84.

625 T. 7808–7809.

626 Trial Judgement, fn. 289.

14 July 1995.[627] Although the Trial Chamber did not refer to the part of Mirković's testimony that related to witnessing some of the killings at Kravica Warehouse, in light of the number of references to his testimony in the Trial Judgement,[628] it can be inferred that that Trial Chamber fully considered his testimony. Indeed, as Dragan Mirković's and Aleksander Tesić's knowledge of the massacre at Kravica Warehouse derives from witnessing some of the killings or their aftermath, it does not help answer the question of whether Blagojević must have known about the events at the warehouse.

235. Nikola Gajić and Srbislav Davidović did not witness the Kravica Warehouse killings, but learned of them from others. Nonetheless, their statements also do not necessarily indicate whether **[page 92]** Blagojević had the requisite knowledge. Gajić, a member of the First Battalion of the Bratunac Brigade stationed in Magasiči,[629] testified that he learned of the Kravica Warehouse massacre in the evening of 13 July 1995 or the following day.[630] The Appeals Chamber observes that the Trial Chamber thoroughly reviewed Gajić's testimony and specifically referenced the transcript pages that the Prosecution alleges were disregarded.[631] Davidović, President of the Executive Board of Bratunac,[632] testified that he learned of the Kravica Warehouse killings at his office in the municipal building in Bratunac town in the morning of 14 July 1995.[633] The Trial Chamber cited Davidović's testimony several times.[634] The Appeals Chamber considers that the fact that some people learned of the massacre within twenty-four hours, either by witnessing the events or from others, does not compel the conclusion that Blagojević would have also learned of the massacre within the same time period. Notably, the record does not show that Blagojević witnessed the events at the Kravica Warehouse or that someone promptly informed him of them. Therefore it cannot be concluded that the measure of doubt that the Trial Chamber had about his knowledge of these killings was unreasonable.

236. Finally, on this point, the Prosecution also argues that the Trial Chamber ignored its own findings that Blagojević was at the Bratunac Brigade headquarters in Bratunac town from 12 to 14 July 1995, where, according to the Prosecution, the Kravica Warehouse killings were common knowledge and Blagojević thus would have learned of them.[635] The Trial Chamber's findings that Blagojević was present in Bratunac town between 12 and 14 July 1995 and slept at his apartment in Bratunac town on those nights contributed to its determination of Blagojević's responsibility for aiding and abetting the "opportunistic killings" that occurred there.[636] There is no indication that the Trial Chamber disregarded these findings when it found reasonable doubt that Blagojević had knowledge of the mass killings. Similarly, there is no indication that the Trial Chamber disregarded its finding that Bosnian Muslim men were detained within the Bratunac Brigade's zone of responsibility before being sent to the Kravica Warehouse, as the Prosecution argues.[637] This finding formed one of the bases for the Trial Chamber's finding that Blagojević "provided practical **[page 93]** assistance to the murder operation which had a substantial effect on the commission of murder."[638] In the view of the Appeals Chamber, there is no reason to consider that the Trial Chamber disregarded its finding that men were detained in the Bratunac Brigade zone of responsibility when, four paragraphs later in the Trial Judgement, it summarized its findings regarding Blagojević's *mens rea* as to the mass killings.

---

627 T. 7953.

628 *See* Trial Judgement, fns. 282, 289, 291, 292, 1024, 1026, 1090, 1092, 1093, 1097, 1100, 1102, 1112–1114.

629 Trial Judgement, para. 364.

630 T. 3373–3374. It is likely that Nikola Gajić learned of the massacre on or before 14 July, since he recalled talking about it at the 1st Battalion's Command Post in Magasiči and that command post was moved to Cizmiči after that date. *See* Trial Judgement, para. 52.

631 Trial Judgement, para. 364.

632 Trial Judgement, fn. 432.

633 T. 7721, 7723.

634 *See* Trial Judgement, fns. 266, 268, 269, 293, 432, 480, 544, 554, 889, 890, 945, 946, 948, 953-955, 959, 960, 969, 1022, 1592, 1593, 2197.

635 Prosecution Appeal Brief, para. 2.75.

636 Trial Judgement, para. 748.

637 Prosecution Appeal Brief, para. 2.75.

638 Trial Judgement, paras. 736, 738 ("The Trial Chamber further finds that the participation of the Bratunac Brigade battalions, and indeed, Colonel Blagojević himself, in the search operation was a form of practical assistance to the murder operation"). *See also* Trial Judgement, para. 261.

(b) Communication about the Kravica Warehouse Massacre within the Chain of Command

237. The Prosecution argues that the Trial Chamber's finding on Blagojević's knowledge of the Kravica Warehouse mass killings is unreasonable in light of the diligence with which Blagojević carried out his command functions and the well-functioning chain of communication that would have carried news of the massacre to Blagojević.[639] In this regard, the Prosecution points to the following omissions by the Trial Chamber: (1) the Trial Chamber's alleged failure to include any mention of its findings concerning Blagojević's position of command and the well-functioning chain of communication in its determination of when information about the Kravica Warehouse massacre reached Blagojević;[640] (2) the alleged failure to refer to its finding regarding the proximity of the Fourth Battalion's forward command post to the warehouse and the significance of that position to the likelihood that the mass killing would be reported to the Bratunac Brigade headquarters;[641] and (3) the alleged failure to adequately consider a medical report indicating that Miroslav Stanojević, one of Blagojević's Bratunac Brigade Red Berets, was wounded in Kravica at 5.30 p.m. on 13 July 1995, when no legitimate combat activity could account for that injury.[642]

238. A review of the Trial Judgement reveals that the Trial Chamber made extensive findings on the efficiency and control with which Blagojević commanded his subordinates[643] and the frequent communications within the chain of command,[644] although it did not expressly incorporate these findings into its analysis of the timing of Blagojević's knowledge of the Kravica Warehouse massacre. The Prosecution argues that such findings should have been the lens through which the Trial Chamber assessed the question of Blagojević's knowledge. The Prosecution, however, does not identify specific evidence of communications that would have carried the news of the Kravica Warehouse massacre to Blagojević. Nor does the Prosecution reference in this regard any **[page 94]** communication between the Fourth Battalion command post on the road leading to Kravica and the Bratunac Brigade headquarters in Bratunac town.

239. There are indications in the Trial Judgement that the Trial Chamber scrutinized the chain of command and communications to determine when Blagojević learned of the Kravica Warehouse killings. In paragraph 439 of the Trial Judgement, the Trial Chamber noted that Momir Nikolić regularly reported on the day's activities to Blagojević. The Trial Chamber observed that Momir Nikolić testified that he met Blagojević on the night of 13 to 14 July 1995.[645] However, the Trial Chamber noted that, according to Momir Nikolić, he did not discuss the Kravica Warehouse killings with Blagojević until sometime around 24 July 1995.[646]

240. The Prosecution places particular emphasis on a medical report showing that a member of the Bratunac Brigade Red Berets was wounded in Kravica at 5.30 p.m. on 13 July 1995.[647] The Trial Chamber noted that this report only indicated that the soldier was injured in Kravica, without specifying where, and determined that even if Blagojević had been aware of the report he may not necessarily have known that the soldier was injured at the warehouse.[648] On appeal, the Prosecution has not shown that Blagojević was indeed aware of the report at the relevant time, nor how that information would have informed Blagojević of the mass killings at the warehouse.

241. The Prosecution correctly notes that Blagojević remained in Bratunac town while his troops searched the terrain in the days after 14 July 1995; however, the Appeals Chamber does not find any error in the Trial Chamber's

---

639 Prosecution Appeal Brief, paras. 2.77, 2.90.

640 Prosecution Appeal Brief, para. 2.91.

641 Prosecution Appeal Brief, paras. 2.75, 2.77.

642 Prosecution Appeal Brief, para. 2.80.

643 Trial Judgement, paras. 41–61 (Bratunac Brigade structure and command overview), 393–419 (findings regarding the chain of command).

644 *See, e.g.*, Trial Judgement, paras. 438 (daily review of orders, report and instructions at the Bratunac Brigade command post), 439 (daily reporting from Momir Nikolić to Blagojević).

645 Trial Judgement, para. 456.

646 Trial Judgement, paras. 456 (Nikolić did not tell Blagojević of the Kravica Warehouse massacre until Blagojević returned from Žepa), 469 (Blagojević returned from Žepa on 24 July 1995). This evidence was referenced again by the Trial Chamber to support the possibility that Blagojević did not learn of the Kravica Warehouse killings until sometime after it occurred. *See* Trial Judgement, para. 498.

647 Prosecution Appeal Brief, para. 2.80.

648 Trial Judgement, para. 364.

description of this fact. The Trial Chamber merely stated that "[Blagojević] and his units continued to participate in the search operation" in the days following the Kravica Warehouse massacre.[649] Considering that the Trial Chamber found that Blagojević ordered his subordinates to carry out the search,[650] this could be considered as a form of participation in the search.[651] Thus, while describing Blagojević as a participant in the search operation is not precise, it is accurate and does not indicate an error on the part of the Trial Chamber. **[page 95]**

(c) Findings Relevant to the Conclusion on *Mens Rea* for Complicity in Genocide

242. The Prosecution argues that the Trial Chamber unreasonably failed to incorporate extensive factual findings supporting its conclusion that Blagojević had sufficient *mens rea* for complicity in genocide into its analysis of his *mens rea* for aiding and abetting mass killings.[652] The Appeals Chamber recalls its finding that the Trial Chamber erred in finding that Blagojević possessed the requisite *mens rea* for complicity in genocide.[653] Accordingly, the Prosecution's argument that such a finding should support the finding that Blagojević possessed the *mens rea* for aiding and abetting the mass killings is dismissed as moot.

(d) Communications regarding Blagojević

243. The Prosecution submits that the Trial Chamber failed to properly take into account a conversation regarding Blagojević that took place between General Radislav Krstić, the commander of the Drina Corps, and Colonel Ljubiša Beara, head of security administration in the VRS Main Staff that, in its view, suggests that Blagojević had knowledge of the mass killing operation.[654] In the intercepted conversation, Beara repeatedly told Krstić that he "need[ed] 15 to 30 men", apparently to assist in the murder operation.[655] Krstić first responded that Beara already had some men "down there at [...] Blagojević's."[656] Then, after Beara replied that he did not, Krstić stated: "Check with Blagojević, take his Red Berets."[657] In addition, the Prosecution further argues that the Trial Chamber failed to properly take into account the testimony of Momir Nikolić regarding his conversations with Blagojević.[658]

244. The Appeals Chamber observes that the intercept evidence in question is circumstantial in nature, and it is far from conclusive on the proposition that "Blagojević [...] was in the circle of knowledge of the murder operation."[659] It is impossible to conclude from the conversation whether Radislav Krstić, Ljubiša Beara, or *anyone* had already discussed the murder operation with Blagojević. Further, the Prosecution does not argue, and the Trial Judgement does not reveal, whether Ljubiša Beara subsequently discussed the murder operation with Blagojević. Because little can be concluded from this circumstantial evidence, the Appeals Chamber considers that the Trial **[page 96]** Chamber could reasonably have disregarded it when reaching a finding on Blagojević's knowledge of the mass killings.

245. The Appeals Chamber further notes that the Trial Chamber found Momir Nikolić not to be wholly credible, and specifically required his testimony to be corroborated before it could be used to support conviction.[660] The Prosecution does not challenge this finding,[661] and does not demonstrate under this sub-ground that aspects of Momir Nikolić's testimony were adequately corroborated but not properly weighed by the Trial Chamber.

---

649 Trial Judgement, para. 742.
650 *See* Trial Judgement, para. 230.
651 *See Čelebići* Appeal Judgement, paras. 350–352 (equating the modes of responsibility under Articles 7(1) and 7(3) of the Statute with "forms of participation").
652 Prosecution Appeal Brief, paras. 2.96, 2.97 (delineating seven specific facts that the Prosecution argues the Trial Chamber should have considered in the context of Blagojević's knowledge of the mass killings).
653 *See supra* section III.F (Alleged Errors relating to Complicity in Genocide).
654 Prosecution Appeal Brief, para. 2.103, 2.104.
655 Ex. P245/A.
656 Ex. P245/A.
657 Ex. P245/A.
658 Prosecution Appeal Brief, paras. 2.107–2.109.
659 Prosecution Appeal Brief, para. 2.104.
660 Trial Judgement, para. 472.
661 Prosecution Appeal Brief, para. 2.109.

(c) Bratunac Brigade Members' Alleged Knowledge of the Mass Killing Operation

246. The Prosecution submits that an incident in which two soldiers from the Bratunac Brigade saved a Muslim man by removing him from a bus of men in Potočari and enabling him to board a bus of women and children demonstrates that Bratunac Brigade soldiers knew that the Muslim men separated in Potočari would be murdered.[662] The Prosecution complains that the Trial Chamber did not take this evidence into account when assessing Blagojević's knowledge of the killing operation.[663]

247. The Trial Chamber considered that members of the Bratunac Brigade were involved in the separation of Bosnian Muslim men in Potočari and noted that two members of the brigade took measures to ensure that their friend was put on a bus with Bosnian Muslim women and children rather than with the men.[664] The Appeals Chamber considers that the Trial Chamber was not required on this basis to draw the inference that the two soldiers knew that the men were going to be killed, or much less that Blagojević knew of the mass killing operation.

248. Following this analysis, the Appeals Chamber finds that the Prosecution has not established as unreasonable the finding of the Trial Chamber that there was insufficient evidence on which to find that Blagojević had the requisite *mens rea* for aiding and abetting murder in relation to the mass executions. **[page 97]**

4. Conclusion

249. For the foregoing reasons, the Appeals Chamber finds that the Prosecution has failed to demonstrate that the Trial Chamber erred in assessing Blagojević's knowledge of the mass killings. Accordingly, the Appeals Chamber dismisses this ground of appeal. **[page 98]**

B. Alleged Error relating to Blagojević's Intent to Commit Forcible Transfer (Ground 2)

250. The Prosecution charged Blagojević as part of a joint criminal enterprise, which had two objectives:

> (1) to forcibly transfer the women and children from the Srebrenica enclave to Kladanj, on 12 July and 13 July 1995; and
>
> (2) to capture, detain, summarily execute by firing squad, bury, and rebury thousands of Bosnian Muslim men and boys aged 16 to 60 from Srebrenica enclave from 12 July 1995 until and about 19 July 1995. [...][665]

The Trial Chamber found that there was evidence of a joint criminal enterprise to commit forcible transfer.[666] The Trial Chamber also found that Blagojević voluntarily participated in the forcible transfer, but was not satisfied that he participated with the shared intent of committing forcible transfer.[667] Consequently, the Trial Chamber decided that his participation in the forcible transfer was more appropriately described as aiding and abetting rather than participation in a joint criminal enterprise.[668]

251. The Prosecution submits that the Trial Chamber erred in fact by finding that Blagojević did not have the requisite intent to commit forcible transfer as part of the joint criminal enterprise.[669] It argues that, in assessing Blagojević's *mens rea*, the Trial Chamber adopted an unduly restrictive focus on the physical aspects of the transfer, such as the separations, the loading of buses, and the transporting of people out of the enclave.[670] The Prosecution further claims that the Trial Chamber unduly focused on Blagojević's knowledge rather than addressing what the Prosecution characterizes as Blagojević's extensive involvement in the operation coupled with that knowledge.

---

662 Prosecution Appeal Brief, para. 2.106.
663 Prosecution Appeal Brief, para. 2.106.
664 Trial Judgement, para. 176.
665 Trial Judgement, para. 715, quoting Indictment, para. 30.
666 Trial Judgement, paras. 709, 710.
667 Trial Judgement, paras. 711, 712.
668 Trial Judgement, para. 713.
669 Prosecution Appeal Brief, paras. 3.1–3.56.
670 Prosecution Appeal Brief, para. 3.5.

252. The Prosecution contends that, if properly considered, the evidence and findings on Blagojević's role in making life in the Srebrenica enclave unbearable as well as his participation in the "Krivaja 95" operation, knowing its stated purpose, lead to the only reasonable conclusion that Blagojević shared the intent to commit forcible transfer.[671] The Prosecution further argues that the Trial Chamber erred in failing to convict Blagojević for several killings in Potočari, which the Prosecution claims, were a natural and foreseeable consequence of the joint criminal enterprise.[672] The Appeals Chamber will addresses in turn the Prosecution's principal arguments relating to, first, **[page 99]** the period prior to the attack on the Srebrenica enclave and, second, to the period of the attack pursuant to the "Krivaja 95" operation and its aftermath.

1. Findings and Evidence related to the Period Prior to the Attack on Srebrenica

253. The Prosecution first argues that the evidence and findings related to the role of Blagojević and the Bratunac Brigade in creating unbearable conditions in Srebrenica demonstrate his intent to commit forcible transfer. According to the Prosecution, Blagojević ensured that the Bratunac Brigade did what it could to further the VRS policy relating to Srebrenica during the pre-attack period.[673] The Trial Chamber found that the stated policy of Bratunac Brigade prior to Blagojević's command was "the expulsion of Muslims from the Srebrenica enclave [...]. [In order to do so] the enemy's life has to be made unbearable and their temporary stay in the enclave impossible so that they leave en masse as soon as possible, realising that they cannot survive there".[674] The Prosecution contends that this strategy was implemented[675] and that the policy did not change when Blagojević became the Bratunac Brigade's commander in May 1995.[676]

254. The Prosecution further argues that Blagojević knew that the Bratunac Brigade was blocking humanitarian assistance[677] in order to diminish the effectiveness of DutchBat to cope with a humanitarian crisis[678] and to create impossible and unbearable conditions for Bosnian Muslims in the Srebrenica enclave.[679] The Prosecution argues that the brigade's "checking" of convoys blocked the delivery of humanitarian aid to the enclave,[680] but that the Trial Chamber nevertheless concluded that the evidence "does not suggest that Blagojević either ordered or supported the blocking of humanitarian [aid]".[681]

255. The Prosecution argues that no reasonable trier of fact could have concluded that Blagojević neither ordered nor actively supported the blocking of humanitarian aid in light of the 4 July 1995 Analysis of Combat Readiness document he signed, which, the Prosecution says, shows that he ordered restrictions on humanitarian aid convoys.[682] The Prosecution posits that, since Blagojević issued instructions and orders to control access to Srebrenica knowing that the controls were **[page 100]** restricting humanitarian aid, the only reasonable conclusion is that Blagojević intended that result.[683] The Prosecution also points to the Trial Chamber's finding that Blagojević continued the practice of shelling and sniping the enclave in the months before the attack as a further indication that he continued his predecessor's policy to render life in the enclave unbearable.[684]

256. The Appeals Chamber is unconvinced by the Prosecution's argument that the Trial Chamber found that Blagojević actively furthered the VRS plan[685] and that this indicates that he intended the accomplishment

671 Prosecution Appeal Brief, paras. 3.5–3.9, 3.19–3.56.
672 Prosecution Appeal Brief, paras. 3.4, 3.57–3.73.
673 Prosecution Appeal Brief, para. 3.21.
674 Prosecution Appeal Brief, para. 3.22, quoting Trial Judgement, para. 103. *See* Ex. D132/1, Report for the Bratunac Brigade members, No. 04–1738–1/94, dated 4 July 1994, para. 2 ("4 July 1994 Report").
675 Prosecution Appeal Brief, para. 3.23, citing Trial Judgement, para. 104 fn. 326.
676 Prosecution Appeal Brief, para. 3.22, citing Trial Judgement, paras. 117, 475.
677 Prosecution Appeal Brief, paras. 3.25, 3.26, citing Trial Judgement, para. 475.
678 Prosecution Appeal Brief, paras. 3.25, 3.26, citing Trial Judgement, paras. 138, 474, 475.
679 Prosecution Appeal Brief, paras. 3.24; Trial Judgement, para. 475 (inferring that Blagojević knew that the Bratunac Brigade was blocking humanitarian aid, in part, to make life within the enclave impossible for the civilian population).
680 Prosecution Appeal Brief, para. 3.27.
681 Prosecution Appeal Brief, para. 3.28, quoting Trial Judgement, para. 474.
682 Prosecution Appeal Brief, para. 3.28, citing Ex. P391 ("4 July 1995 Analysis of Combat Readiness").
683 Prosecution Appeal Brief, para. 3.33.
684 Prosecution Appeal Brief, paras. 3.38, 3.39, citing Trial Judgement, paras. 117, 476.
685 Prosecution Appeal Brief, paras. 3.21, 3.22, citing Trial Judgement, paras. 117, 475.

of its objectives. The Prosecution cites paragraphs 117 and 475 of the Trial Judgement in support of this proposition. Paragraph 117 contains a discussion of skirmishes between ABiH and VRS soldiers occurring in the spring of 1995, sniper fire directed at combatants and civilians, and incursions made by the Bratunac Brigade into the Srebrenica enclave in the period before Blagojević became commander.[686] The Trial Chamber concluded, "[w]hen Colonel Blagojević became the commander of the Bratunac Brigade in May 1995, the policy towards the safe area adopted by his predecessor did not change."[687] The Prosecution argues that this finding indicates that Blagojević adopted and continued the "plans to defeat the Srebrenica enclave".

257. The Appeals Chamber disagrees that paragraph 117 indicates that the Trial Chamber found that Blagojević furthered the broad plan to make life in the enclave unbearable. Rather, the Trial Chamber found that Blagojević knew that elements of the Bratunac Brigade were involved in sniping and shelling the enclave in the months prior to the attack on Srebrenica on 6 July 1995;[688] this is, in fact, how the Trial Chamber later summarizes its findings,[689] and there is no reason to adopt the Prosecution's more expansive interpretation.

258. The Prosecution's reference to paragraph 475 of the Trial Judgement is similarly unpersuasive. Paragraph 475 states:

> Upon taking up his duties as commander of the Bratunac Brigade, Colonel Blagojević must have been informed that elements of his Brigade, namely his assistant commander for security and intelligence, Captain Momir Nikolić, and members of the Bratunac Brigade Military Police, were actively involved in checking the convoys that entered the Srebrenica enclave. Furthermore, Momir Nikolić testified that the purpose of blocking these supplies was to ensure that DutchBat would not be ready for combat and not be able to carry out its task in the enclave, and to make life within the enclave impossible for the civilian population. As Colonel Blagojević would have needed to know the state of preparedness of DutchBat before the attack began on 6 July, he would have been informed of *this information* by his superiors in meetings preparing for the operation as well as by Captain Nikolić, who also served as a liaison between the Bratunac Brigade and DutchBat. The Trial Chamber finds that *this information* would have put him on notice about **[page 101]** DutchBat's readiness – or rather, inability – to deal with the humanitarian situation created by the attack on the Srebrenica enclave.[690]

Although the finding in paragraph 475 is somewhat ambiguous, particularly the multiple, non-specific references to Blagojević's knowledge of "this information", the Appeals Chamber considers that the Trial Chamber concluded that Blagojević was aware that elements of the Bratunac Brigade were actively involved in checking the convoys with the aim of blocking supplies to DutchBat and making life within the enclave impossible for civilians. Thus, paragraph 475, like paragraph 117, supports the Trial Chamber's finding that Blagojević *knew* of the plan,[691] but does not necessarily demonstrate that he supported it.

259. According to the Prosecution, the Trial Chamber failed to appreciate the significance of the 4 July 1995 Analysis of Combat Readiness document, which the Prosecution claims provided, in "Blagojević's own words", his intent to cause forcible transfer.[692] The document, signed by Blagojević, states that the Bratunac Brigade checkpoint "functions in accordance with the [...] instructions and orders of the Brigade Commander."[693] The Prosecution argues that reading the 4 July 1995 Analysis of Combat Readiness document in light of Blagojević's awareness of the purpose of the restrictions on humanitarian aid indicates that he either actively supported or ordered the restrictions on humanitarian aid, and no reasonable trier of fact could have found otherwise.[694] The 4 July 1995 Analysis of Combat Readiness document was signed by Blagojević, written in the first-person, and sent from the Bratunac Brigade to the Drina Corps Command. It notes that in

686 Trial Judgement, para. 117.
687 Trial Judgement, para. 117.
688 *See* Trial Judgement, para. 125.
689 *See* Trial Judgement, para. 476.
690 Trial Judgement, para. 475 (emphasis added).
691 The Trial Chamber expressly inferred Blagojević's knowledge of the discriminatory intent of the perpetrators of the attack on the Srebrenica enclave and the consequences of the attack on the civilian population. Trial Judgement, para. 754.
692 Prosecution Appeal Brief, paras. 3.6, 3.30, citing Trial Judgement, para. 116 fn. 367.
693 Prosecution Appeal Brief, para. 3.29, quoting Ex. P391 ("4 July 1995 Analysis of Combat Readiness").
694 Prosecution Appeal Brief, para. 3.28.

"addition to verbal orders, all assignments were confirmed by written combat documents"[695] and describes that one such assignment in the brigade's area of responsibility was "a checkpoint [...] established for the control of all international organisations entering and leaving the enclave of Srebrenica."[696] According to the document, the "checkpoint function[ed] in accordance with the orders of the GŠ VRS and instructions and orders of the Brigade Commander."[697] The Trial Chamber relied on this document extensively, and, indeed, accepted the part noted by the **[page 102]** Prosecution as support for its conclusion that the restrictions on humanitarian aid affected the delivery of humanitarian supplies and the rotation of DutchBat troops.[698]

260. However, the Appeals Chamber notes other evidence on the record, not rebutted by the Prosecution, that suggests that Blagojević had no effective control over the restrictions on humanitarian aid. For example, Momir Nikolić testified that he "was personally responsible for everything concerning the entry of [...] humanitarian aid convoys [and] for everything to do with international organisations present in Srebrenica."[699] Contrary to the Prosecution's assertion that Blagojević ordered the restrictions on the convoys, Nikolić testified that the "Bratunac Brigade had no authority to keep convoys out or let them in. All orders that were issued in this respect went from the main staff through the Drina Corps command, through the Bratunac Brigade, trickling down to us eventually."[700] The Trial Chamber accepted and relied upon this testimony.[701]

261. Furthermore, contrary to the Prosecution's argument, the Trial Chamber expressly examined the "connection between [the 'Krivaja 95'] operation and the events which transpired following the fall of the Srebrenica enclave" in order to prove relevant issues such as "intent [...] or knowledge".[702] The Trial Chamber also examined the Bratunac Brigade's role in blocking humanitarian supplies and in the sniping and shelling of the Srebrenica enclave in the months before the "Krivaja 95" operation.[703] On the basis of this analysis, the Trial Chamber concluded that "elements of the Bratunac Brigade were involved [...] in blocking humanitarian supplies and convoys from entering the Srebrenica enclave";[704] however, as discussed above, the Trial Chamber may reasonably have relied on Nikolić's testimony that *he* controlled the humanitarian blockades. In the absence of conclusive evidence to the contrary, the Appeals Chamber considers that the Trial Chamber, having examined all of the evidence, reached a reasonable finding. Consequently, the Appeals Chamber finds that the Prosecution did not show error in the Trial Chamber's findings on this point.

262. For the foregoing reasons, to the Appeals Chamber dismisses this sub-ground of the appeal. **[page 103]**

2. Findings related to Blagojević's Participation in the "Krivaja 95" Operation

263. According to the Prosecution, Blagojević's knowing, wilful participation in the "Krivaja 95" operation indicated his intent to expel the Muslim population from Srebrenica.[705] The Prosecution argues: (1) "Srebrenica was the 'primary concern' of the Bratunac Brigade"[706] and Blagojević knew this;[707] (2) Blagojević knew that the initial objective of "Krivaja 95" was to reduce the Srebrenica enclave to its urban area and that this later changed to eliminating the enclave;[708] and (3) Blagojević willingly participated in the "Krivaja 95" operation.[709]

695 *See* Ex. P391/A, p. 2.
696 *See* Ex. P391/A, p. 8.
697 *See* Ex. P391/A, p. 8.
698 *See* Trial Judgement, para. 111 fns. 341, 343. The Trial Chamber also relied on it to determine facts regarding the logistics of the Bratunac Brigade, such as troop levels, the location of forward command posts, and the composition of the battalions within the Bratunac Brigade. *See* Trial Judgement, paras. 42 fn. 117, 43 fn. 119, 52 fn. 150, 56 fn. 169.
699 T. 1634.
700 T. 1634.
701 *See* Trial Judgement, paras. 111 fn. 340, 475 fn. 1677.
702 Trial Judgement, para. 137.
703 Trial Judgement, paras. 138, 139.
704 Trial Judgement, para. 138.
705 Prosecution Appeal Brief, paras. 3.40–3.43.
706 Prosecution Appeal Brief, para. 3.21, citing Trial Judgement, para. 476.
707 Prosecution Appeal Brief, para. 3.21, citing Trial Judgement, para. 476.
708 Prosecution Appeal Brief, paras. 3.41, 3.42, citing Trial Judgement, para. 478.
709 Prosecution Appeal Brief, para. 3.41, citing Trial Judgement, para. 478. *See also* Trial Judgement, paras. 120, 121.

264. Additionally, the Prosecution argues that the Trial Chamber failed to incorporate its findings related to Blagojević's knowledge and conduct during the attack.[710] Instead of focusing only on the Bratunac Brigade's role in separating the Muslim population, the Prosecution contends the Trial Chamber should have incorporated its findings on other Bratunac Brigade conduct during the attack.[711] According to the Prosecution, these acts and omissions include: (1) firing on civilians in the centre of Srebrenica, and between Srebrenica and Potočari, with Blagojević's knowledge and partly pursuant to his earlier order,[712] causing the civilians to flee toward Potočari;[713] and (2) Blagojević's failure to summon assistance to Potočari when he knew that 20,000 people had fled there from Srebrenica town and were crowded in inhumane conditions.[714]

265. The Prosecution also argues that the Trial Chamber failed to incorporate its findings that Blagojević knew about the scope of the Bratunac Brigade's participation in the forcible transfer[715] and that he knew about the key aspects of the transfer operation.[716] The Prosecution notes that the Trial Chamber found that Blagojević remained in command and control of all members of the Bratunac Brigade, including the Bratunac Brigade Military Police, and thus bore responsibility for their actions throughout the Indictment period.[717] The Prosecution argues that the Bratunac Brigade and Blagojević were involved in "all aspects" of the forcible transfer operation.[718] In its view, Blagojević knew of the changed objective to eliminate the enclave at least on 11 July 1995, having **[page 104]** met with Radislav Krstić and Miroslav Deronjić at the forward command post in Pribićevac,[719] and knowingly and willingly participated in key aspects of the forcible transfer operation thereafter.

266. A review of the Trial Judgement reflects that the Trial Chamber found that Blagojević knew the objectives of the "Krivaja 95" operation, issued an order to make the operation a success,[720] but nonetheless did not intend to commit forcible transfer.[721] The Trial Chamber appears to have considered that the element of forcible transfer became part of the "Krivaja 95" operation only later during the execution of the operation in the period from 2 to 11 July 1995. The Trial Chamber found that originally the "stated objective of the attack on the Srebrenica enclave was to reduce "the enclave to its urban area",[722] and that the "Krivaja 95" operation was designed from the beginning "to create conditions for the elimination of the [Srebrenica and Žepa] enclaves".[723] The Trial Chamber found that the objective then changed "to the taking-over of Srebrenica town and the enclave as a whole."[724] The Trial Chamber allowed that news of the operation's new objective might only have reached Blagojević on 11 July 1995.[725] Although the Trial Chamber found that the elimination of the enclave "necessarily entailed removing the Bosnian Muslim population from" the Srebrenica enclave,[726] it appeared to make no finding about whether the reduction of the enclave to its urban size, or the creation of conditions for the elimination of the enclave, also entailed forcible transfer.

267. The Trial Chamber may have found tacitly that Blagojević intended some of the operation's objectives, but that he did not intend to commit forcible transfer when he issued the 5 July 1995 Order and subsequently participated in the "Krivaja 95" operation. The Trial Chamber's finding that Blagojević intended the operation's objectives relies specifically on his 5 July 1995 Order.[727] That order, however, is

---

710 Prosecution Appeal Brief, para. 3.44.

711 Prosecution Appeal Brief, para. 3.44, citing *Krnojelac* Appeal Judgement, para. 229. The citation is inapposite because it stands for the holding that absence of genuine choice makes displacement unlawful, which is not at issue here because the *actus reus* for forcible transfer has been proved.

712 Prosecution Appeal Brief, para. 3.45, citing Trial Judgement, para. 477.

713 Prosecution Appeal Brief, para. 3.45 (without citation).

714 Prosecution Appeal Brief, para. 3.45, citing Trial Judgement, para. 484.

715 Prosecution Appeal Brief, para. 3.46, citing Trial Judgement, para. 486.

716 Prosecution Appeal Brief, paras. 3.46, 3.47, citing Trial Judgement, paras. 186, 486, 487.

717 Prosecution Appeal Brief, para. 3.48, citing Trial Judgement, para. 419.

718 Prosecution Appeal Brief, para. 3.55.

719 Prosecution Appeal Brief, para. 3.56, citing Trial Judgement, para. 478.

720 Trial Judgement, para. 478, citing Ex. P406, Bratunac Brigade Order for Active Combat, signed by Colonel Blagojević, 5 July 1995 ("5 July 1995 Order").

721 Trial Judgement, paras. 478, 712.

722 Trial Judgement, para. 120, quoting Ex. P543, Drina Corps Order No. 04/156–2, "Krivaja 95" Attack Plan, dated 2 July 1995, p. 3.

723 Trial Judgement, para. 137, quoting Ex. P543, Drina Corps Order No. 04/156–2, "Krivaja 95" Attack Plan, dated 2 July 1995, p. 3.

724 Trial Judgement, para. 130.

725 Trial Judgement, para. 130.

726 Trial Judgement, para. 758.

727 Trial Judgement, para. 478 fn. 1683.

an order to begin *combat activities*,[728] it does not mention the Bosnian Muslim civilian population in the enclave, and it could be construed reasonably as being aimed solely at obtaining the military defeat of the Bosnian Muslim forces in the Srebrenica enclave. Consequently, the Appeals Chamber considers that a reasonable trier of fact could have concluded, **[page 105]** as the Trial Chamber appears to have done, that Blagojević may not have intended to commit forcible transfer when he issued the order, but only intended to ensure the success of military objectives.

268. The Appeals Chamber now examines the Prosecution's remaining arguments in addition to the evidence discussed above to determine whether no reasonable trier of fact could have found that Blagojević did not intend to commit the forcible transfer. The Prosecution suggests that the Trial Chamber should have inferred Blagojević's intent to commit forcible transfer from its finding that, during the attack, the Bratunac Brigade shelled civilians pursuant to his orders.[729] The Trial Chamber, however, did not find that Blagojević issued orders with the intent to shell civilians. It found that Blagojević issued a written order for active combat operations on 5 July 1995 pursuant to the "Krivaja 95" order from the Drina Corps command.[730] Pursuant to the general authority granted under Blagojević's order, Mićo Gavrić "fired on 11 July in the area around which civilians were walking from Srebrenica to Potočari".[731] In testimony found credible and relied upon by the Trial Chamber,[732] Gavrić stated that he never fired at civilians and that he had no particular orders to carry out the attack on 11 July.[733] He testified that instead, the 5 July 1995 Order gave him "general competency to resort to artillery fire when and where necessary".[734] The Trial Chamber reasonably declined to make an inference about Blagojević's intent from the Bratunac Brigade's alleged shelling of civilians.

269. The Prosecution's second and third assertions posit that specific omissions by Blagojević demonstrate his state of mind: his failure to summon humanitarian assistance to Potočari, and his failure to take measures to stop the separations after learning of them. Regarding Blagojević's failure to summon assistance to Potočari, the Trial Chamber found that

> [A]s commander of the Bratunac Brigade for the six weeks before the attack, [Blagojević] was aware that DutchBat was facing severe food and water shortages, and was therefore not able to provide for the thousands upon thousands of refugees arriving at their base [in Potočari]. Colonel Blagojević was present in the town of Bratunac, including in Bratunac Brigade Headquarters with its communication centre, during this time. While the Bratunac Brigade itself may not have been able to provide the supplies necessary, Colonel Blagojević could have summoned assistance from other organizations or agencies. Instead, there is no evidence that he did anything in this respect.[735] **[page 106]**

Neither the Trial Chamber nor the Prosecution refer to evidence that supports the conclusion that Blagojević could have summoned assistance to Potočari. Nonetheless, the Trial Chamber inferred that Blagojević understood the situation facing the Bosnian Muslim refugees in Potočari: he knew that more than twenty-thousand people, the majority of whom were civilians, had been displaced and were being held in the small space around the UN base in Potočari.[736] The Trial Chamber also inferred from the circumstances that Blagojević knew that there was a severe shortage of food and water.[737]

270. The Prosecution does not show how Blagojević's failure to try to provide humanitarian aid invariably demonstrates his intent to commit forcible transfer, nor simply how the failure to provide humanitarian aid to

---

728 *See* Trial Judgement, para. 140. *See also* Ex. P406, 5 July 1995 Order.

729 *See* Prosecution Appeal Brief, para. 3.45 (stating, "the Bratunac Brigade fired on the civilians in the centre of Srebrenica and fired again on the civilians between Srebrenica and Potočari, driving the civilian population toward Potočari. Blagojević knew about these activities; in fact, he had ordered the shelling." [internal citations omitted]).

730 Trial Judgement, paras. 124, 435, 477.

731 Trial Judgement, para. 477.

732 *See* Trial Judgement, paras. 131, 478.

733 T. 8490.

734 T. 8490.

735 Trial Judgement, para. 484 (internal citations removed).

736 Trial Judgement, para. 484.

737 Trial Judgement, para. 484.

fleeing refugees furthered their forcible transfer.[738] Without such a showing, the Appeals Chamber will not set aside the Trial Chamber's reasoned analysis.

271. Finally, the Prosecution argues that Blagojević's failure to intervene, after he learned of the separations and that his subordinates were participating in them, demonstrates his intent. In part, the Prosecution complains that the Trial Chamber did not incorporate findings made elsewhere into its analysis of Blagojević's intent. However, the Trial Chamber need not have repeated each of its findings – summarized in other sections of the Trial Judgement – in considering each subsequent question that implicates those findings. The question is only whether those findings are incompatible with the Trial Chamber's conclusion.

272. The Trial Chamber found that Blagojević knew about key aspects of the forcible transfer operation,[739] and knew that members of the Bratunac Brigade Military Police were involved in the separations in Potočari on 13 July 1995 while they were still in progress.[740] However, the Trial Chamber did not describe any action taken by Blagojević to abate the separations. **[page 107]**

273. In the Appeals Chamber's view, Blagojević's failure to intervene, at least with respect to the participation of Bratunac Brigade resources, to prevent the forcible transfer operation might suggest that he had the intent to carry it out. However, it does not necessarily compel such a conclusion, particularly in light of the fact that the Trial Chamber also determined that senior members of the VRS including General Mladić, General Krstić, Colonel Janković, Colonel Popović, and Lieutenant Colonel Kosorić, as well as political leaders including Miroslav Deronjić, the newly-appointed Civilian Commissioner for Srebrenica, Ljubislav Simić, President of the Bratunac Municipal Assembly, and Srbislav Davidović, President of the Executive Board of the Bratunac Municipality, were in Potočari during the relevant time-period,[741] and that the MUP on the instructions of General Mladić played the primary role in the operation.[742] In such circumstances, the Appeals Chamber finds the Trial Chamber's characterization of the role played by Blagojević as aiding and abetting reasonable.

274. The Prosecution has not demonstrated that Blagojević's conduct and knowledge necessitated a finding that he intended to commit forcible transfer. Accordingly, the Appeals Chamber dismisses this sub-ground of appeal.

275. As the Prosecution has not shown that Blagojević committed forcible transfer as a member of a joint criminal enterprise, there is no need to address the Prosecution's other submissions related to his liability for the natural and foreseeable consequences of the common plan to commit forcible transfer.

3. Conclusion

276. Accordingly, the Appeals Chamber dismisses this ground of appeal. **[page 108]**

C. Alleged Errors relating to Liability under Article 7(3) of the Statute (Ground 3)

277. Examining Blagojević's responsibility under Article 7(3) of the Statute, the Trial Chamber found that "the participation of units of the Bratunac Brigade in the crimes [...] has been reflected in the responsibility

---

738 The Prosecution makes no additional argument except that Blagojević's knowing failure to summon assistance was an omission that demonstrated his state of mind. *See* Prosecution Appeal Brief, para. 3.45.

739 Trial Judgement, paras. 449 (Blagojević knew of the detention of the Bosnian Muslim men in Bratunac), 477 (Blagojević knew of the Bratunac Brigade's participation in the attack on the Srebrenica enclave included firing on civilians in the centre of Srebrenica town, which had the effect of causing those civilians and DutchBat to take the decision to leave Srebrenica town and go to Potočari, and again while the civilians were fleeing from Srebrenica to Potočari), 478 (Blagojević knew what the objective of the "Krivaja 95" operation, and that it changed from reducing the enclave to eliminating the enclave), and 758 (Blagojević knew: (i) members of the Bratunac Brigade rendered practical assistance to the forcible transfer of the Bosnian Muslim population out of the Srebrenica area; (ii) the objective and result of the Krivaja 95 operation was the elimination of the Srebrenica enclave; (iii) the role played by members of his brigade in the Krivaja 95 operation; and (iv) the forcible transfer was carried out on discriminatory grounds.).

740 *Compare* Trial Judgement, para. 483 (Blagojević knew on 13 July that the Bratunac Brigade Military Police was contributing to the separation process in Potočari), *with* Trial Judgement, para. 168 ("separations continued throughout 12 and 13 July").

741 Trial Judgement, para. 159.

742 Trial Judgement, para. 191.

of Colonel Blagojević for aiding and abetting",[743] with the exception of the participation in the "murder operation"[744] and the crimes committed by Momir Nikolić.[745] The Trial Chamber then analysed Blagojević's responsibility under Article 7(3) of the Statute for the crimes not covered by his responsibility under Article 7(1) of the Statute, and concluded that the requirements for command responsibility for the crimes charged in paragraph 46 of the Indictment were not met.[746]

278. The Prosecution submits that the Trial Chamber erred in law and fact in finding that Blagojević was not responsible for the participation of members of the Bratunac Brigade, including Momir Nikolić, in the "murder operation". The Prosecution divides its argument into four sub-grounds.[747] First, the Prosecution submits that the Trial Chamber erred in law in holding that liability under Article 7(3) of the Statute may attach only where the accused's subordinates have participated in a crime through "committing" under Article 7(1) of the Statute. Second, the Prosecution submits that the Trial Chamber erred in law in finding that a superior cannot be liable under Article 7(3) of the Statute for the acts of his subordinates when he does not know the exact identity of the perpetrators of the crimes. Third, the Prosecution submits that in light of the preceding errors, the Trial Chamber failed to consider the *mens rea* of members of the Bratunac Brigade. As a result of this alleged error, the Prosecution submits that the Trial Chamber failed to find that members of the Bratunac Brigade aided and abetted the murder operation, and failed to fully consider Blagojević's Article 7(3) liability. Fourth, the Prosecution submits that the Trial Chamber erred in law and in fact in finding that no superior-subordinate relationship existed between Blagojević and Momir Nikolić. The Prosecution requests the Appeals Chamber to enter convictions against Blagojević for Counts 2, 3, 4, and 5 of the Indictment pursuant to Article 7(3) of the Statute and revise his sentence accordingly.[748] **[page 109]**

1. Alleged Error in Finding that a Superior Cannot be Liable for the Acts of Subordinates When Such Acts Do Not Amount to "Committing"

279. The Prosecution submits that the Trial Chamber erred in law in paragraph 794 of the Trial Judgement in stating that liability under Article 7(3) of the Statute may attach only where the accused's subordinates have participated in a crime through "committing" under Article 7(1) of the Statute.[749]

280. As a threshold matter, the Appeals Chamber confirms that superior responsibility under Article 7(3) of the Statute encompasses all forms of criminal conduct by subordinates, not only the "committing" of crimes in the restricted sense of the term, but all other modes of participation under Article 7(1). The Appeals Chamber notes that the term "commit" is used throughout the Statute in a broad sense, encompassing all modes of responsibility covered by Article 7(1)[750] and that such a construction is clearly manifest in Article 29 (co-operation and judicial assistance) of the Statute, referring to States' obligation to co-operate with the International Tribunal "in the investigation and prosecution of persons accused of *committing* serious violations of international humanitarian law."[751]

281. The Appeals Chamber has previously determined that criminal responsibility under Article 7(3) is based primarily on Article 86(2) of Protocol I.[752] Accordingly, the meaning of "commit", as used in Article 7(3) of

---

[743] Trial Judgement, para. 794.

[744] The Appeals Chamber understands that the term "murder operation" which the Trial Chamber uses in paragraph 794 of the Trial Judgement refers to the "Organised Mass Executions", but not to the "Opportunistic Killings". This becomes clear from reading paragraph 577 of the Trial Judgement in conjunction with paragraphs 568 and 569. *See also* Trial Judgement, para. 797 (acquitting Blagojević of killings charged under paras 46.1–46.12 of the Indictment).

[745] Trial Judgement, paras. 794, 795.

[746] Trial Judgement, paras. 794–796.

[747] Prosecution Notice of Appeal, paras. 12, 13; Prosecution Appeal Brief, paras. 4.4, 4.5. The Prosecution Notice of Appeal was amended following a request by the Prosecution. *See* Decision on Prosecution's Request for Leave to Amend.

[748] Prosecution Appeal Brief, para. 4.78.

[749] Prosecution Appeal Brief, para. 4.9.

[750] *See, e.g.*, Statute, Articles 1, 2, 4, 5, 9, 16, 29.

[751] Emphasis added.

[752] *Hadžihasanović et al.*, Decision on Interlocutory Appeal Challenging Jurisdiction in Relation to Command Responsibility, para. 48. *See also Čelebići* Appeal Judgement, para. 237. Article 86(2) of Protocol I provides: "The fact that a breach of the Conventions or of this Protocol was committed by a subordinate does not absolve his superiors from penal or

the Statute, necessarily tracks the term's broader and more ordinary meaning, as employed in Protocol I.[753] The object and purpose of Protocol I, as reflected in its preamble, is to "reaffirm and develop the provisions protecting the victims of armed conflicts and to supplement measures intended to reinforce their application". The preamble of Protocol I adds further that "the provisions of the Geneva Conventions of 12 August 1949 and of this Protocol must be fully applied in all circumstances to all persons who are protected by those instruments." The purpose of superior responsibility, as evidenced in Articles 86(1) and 87 of Protocol I,[754] is to ensure compliance with **[page 110]** international humanitarian law. Furthermore, one of the purposes of establishing the International Tribunal, as reflected in Security Council Resolution 808, is to "put an end to [widespread violations of international humanitarian law] and to take effective measures to bring to justice the persons who are responsible for them".[755] And, more particularly, the purpose of superior responsibility in Article 7(3) is to hold superiors "responsible for failure to prevent a crime or to deter the unlawful behaviour of [their] subordinates."[756]

282. In this context, the Appeals Chamber cannot accept that the drafters of Protocol I and the Statute intended to limit a superior's obligation to prevent or punish violations of international humanitarian law to only those individuals physically committing the material elements of a crime and to somehow exclude subordinates who as accomplices substantially contributed to the completion of the crime. Accordingly, "commit" as used in Article 7(3) of the Statute must be understood as it is in Protocol I, in its ordinary and broad sense.

283. Turning to the present case, the Appeals Chamber notes that the relevant part of the impugned paragraph 794 of the Trial Judgement reads in relevant part:

> In relation to the participation of the units in the murder operation, the Trial Chamber is convinced that they rendered practical assistance that furthered the crimes of murder and extermination. However, the Trial Chamber is unable to determine that they "committed" any of the crimes charged under the counts of murder or extermination. Therefore, the Trial Chamber cannot, with any precision, identify the specific perpetrators for whom Colonel Blagojević had the duty to punish.

284. The Appeals Chamber understands paragraph 794 of the Trial Judgement as simply stating that it was not established that members of the Bratunac Brigade "committed", in the broad sense of the word, any of the crimes encompassed by the murder operation with which Blagojević was charged in paragraph 46 of the Indictment.[757] The Appeals Chamber notes, moreover, that this finding is not inconsistent with the Trial Chamber's conclusion that members of the Bratunac Brigade gave practical assistance to the murder operation. A finding that certain members of the Bratunac Brigade rendered practical assistance does not necessarily reflect that each given act constituted substantial assistance in order to satisfy the *actus reus* requirement of aiding and **[page 111]** abetting[758] or that, if it did, the given perpetrator in fact had the requisite *mens rea* at the time.[759] The Appeals Chamber, therefore, does not find any legal error on the part of the Trial Chamber in stating that it was not established that the members of the Bratunac Brigade "committed" any of the crimes charged.

---

disciplinary responsibility, as the case may be, if they knew, or had information which should have enabled them to conclude in the circumstances at the time, that he was committing or was going to commit such a breach and if they did not take all feasible measures within their power to prevent or repress the breach."

753 Article 31(1) of the Vienna Convention on the Law of Treaties provides: "A treaty shall be interpreted in good faith in accordance with the ordinary meaning to be given to the terms of the treaty in their context and in the light of its object and purpose".

754 Protocol I, Article 86(1) states: "The High Contracting Parties and the Parties to the conflict shall repress grave breaches, and take measures necessary to suppress all other breaches, of the Conventions or of this Protocol which result from a failure to act when under a duty to do so." Article 87(1) states: "The High Contracting Parties and the Parties to the conflict shall require military commanders, with respect to members of the armed forces under their command and other persons under their control, to prevent and, where necessary, to suppress and to report to competent authorities breaches of the Conventions and of this Protocol."

755 S/RES/808 (1993), p. 2.

756 Report of the Secretary-General, para. 56.

757 In other parts of the Trial Judgement, the Trial Chamber also used the term "committed" in a broad sense. *See, e.g.,* Trial Judgement, para. 814. Throughout the sentencing section, the Trial Chamber speaks of the crimes "committed" by Blagojević and Jokić (*e.g.*, Trial Judgement, para. 841) although both of them were convicted for aiding and abetting only.

758 The Trial Chamber determined that the various acts of the Bratunac Brigade members "taken together" had a substantial effect on the commission of murder. *See* Trial Judgement, para. 738.

759 *See Kayishema and Ruzindana* Appeal Judgement, para. 186. In any event, as the Appeals Chamber explains below, the Trial Chamber did not find that members of the Bratunac Brigade aided and abetted the murder operation. *See* Section V.C.3.

285. Accordingly, the Appeals Chamber dismisses this sub-ground of appeal.

2. Alleged Error in Finding that a Superior Cannot be Liable for the Acts of Subordinates Whose Identity He or She Does Not Know

286. The Prosecution submits that the Trial Chamber erred in law in stating that it could not "identify the specific perpetrators [...] whom Colonel Blagojević had the duty to punish", implying, in the view of the Prosecution, that liability under Article 7(3) of the Statute could not attach.[760] The Prosecution argues that it was not necessary for the Trial Chamber to establish the exact identity of Blagojević's subordinates engaged in criminal conduct to establish his responsibility under Article 7(3) of the Statute.[761]

287. The Appeals Chamber agrees that a superior need not necessarily know the exact identity of his or her subordinates who perpetrate crimes in order to incur liability under Article 7(3) of the Statute. As discussed above, the conclusion in paragraph 794 of the Trial Judgement demonstrates reasonable doubt on the part of the Trial Chamber that Blagojević's subordinates "committed" any crimes relevant to the murder operation that would provide a basis for his Article 7(3) liability.[762] Only after reaching this conclusion did the Trial Chamber determine as a consequence that it "cannot, with any precision, identify the specific perpetrators for whom [*sic*] Colonel Blagojević had the duty to punish."[763] This language does not appear to refer, as the Prosecution suggests, to a statement of law concerning the identity of Blagojević's subordinates. Rather, it appears to be the Trial Chamber's conclusion that it lacked sufficient evidence to find that one of Blagojević's subordinates "committed", in the broad sense of the word, one of the crimes encompassed in the murder operation. Indeed, the Trial Chamber specified on numerous occasions throughout the Trial Judgement the identity of the members of the Bratunac Brigade who rendered practical assistance to **[page 112]** the murder operation.[764] The Appeals Chamber, therefore, does not find any legal error on the part of the Trial Chamber in stating that it could not identify the specific perpetrators whom Blagojević had the duty to punish.

3. Alleged Error in Failing to Consider the *Mens Rea* of Bratunac Brigade Members with respect to the Murder Operation

288. The Prosecution contends that the Trial Chamber found that the *actus reus* for aiding and abetting the "murder operation" was established.[765] It argues that the factual findings also establish the *mens rea* element and submits that the Trial Chamber failed to consider whether members of the Bratunac Brigade could be held responsible for aiding and abetting the murder operation.[766] Specifically, the Prosecution points to the presence of members of the Bratunac Brigade Military Police in Potočari during the separation of the Bosnian Muslim men[767] and the presence of soldiers of the Bratunac Brigade during the mass executions at the Kravica Warehouse on 13 July 1995.[768] In the Prosecution's view, the only inference to be drawn from the findings is that members of the Bratunac Brigade knew that Bosnian Muslim men would be killed.[769]

289. The Trial Chamber identified the following facts as rendering "practical assistance" to the "murder operation": (1) members of the Bratunac Brigade Military Police participated in the separation of Bosnian Muslim men from the rest of the Bosnian Muslim population in Potočari;[770] (2) members of the Bratunac Brigade contributed through their presence in Potočari to the creation of an atmosphere of terror and assisted in the guarding of the detained Bosnian Muslim men;[771] (3) members of the Bratunac Brigade participated

---

760 Prosecution Appeal Brief, para. 4.15, referring to Trial Judgement, para. 794.

761 Prosecution Appeal Brief, para. 4.15.

762 Trial Judgement, para. 794 ("However, the Trial Chamber is unable to determine that [Bratunac Brigade units] "committed" any of the crimes charged under the counts of murder or extermination.").

763 Trial Judgement, para. 794.

764 *See, e.g.*, Trial Judgement, paras. 208, 258, 284, 287, 755, 757.

765 Prosecution Appeal Brief, para. 4.24.

766 Prosecution Appeal Brief, para. 4.25.

767 Prosecution Appeal Brief, paras. 4.28–4.30.

768 Prosecution Appeal Brief, para. 4.27.

769 Prosecution Appeal Brief, paras. 4.26–4.32.

770 Trial Judgement, paras. 212, 734.

771 Trial Judgement, paras. 213, 214, 734.

in the transport of Bosnian Muslim men from Potočari to Bratunac on 12 and 13 July 1995;[772] (4) members of the Bratunac Brigade guarded the Bosnian Muslim men from 12 to 14 July 1995 in Bratunac;[773] (5) the Bratunac Brigade battalions participated in the "search operation";[774] and (6) members of the Bratunac Brigade Military Police escorted a convoy of buses with Bosnian Muslim men from Bratunac to detention sites in Zvornik **[page 113]** on 14 July 1995.[775] The Trial Chamber concluded that "these acts *taken together* provided practical assistance to the murder operation which had a substantial effect on the commission of murder".[776]

290. The Prosecution submits that the Trial Chamber failed to consider the *mens rea* of Bratunac Brigade soldiers with respect to aiding and abetting the murder operation and, consequently, erred by failing to fully consider Blagojević's Article 7(3) liability.[777] The Appeals Chamber disagrees. While the Trial Judgement does not contain an explicit discussion of the *mens rea* possessed by Bratunac Brigade soldiers in connection with the individual role that they played in rendering practical assistance to the murder operation, the Appeals Chamber is not convinced, as the Prosecution argues, that this was not taken into account. Initially, the Appeals Chamber notes that the Trial Chamber concluded that it could not determine whether members of the Bratunac Brigade "committed" any of the crimes related to the murder operation.[778] Such a finding necessarily encompasses a determination as to *mens rea*.[779] While, the Trial Chamber could have been more explicit, the Appeals Chamber sees no error in the result. For clarity, however, the Appeals Chamber addresses the Prosecution's specific arguments regarding the *mens rea* of Bratunac Brigade soldiers in turn.

291. The Prosecution emphasizes that members of the Bratunac Brigade Military Police in Potočari were present during the separation of the Bosnian Muslim men[780] and points to the presence of soldiers of the Bratunac Brigade around the time of the mass executions at the Kravica Warehouse on 13 July 1995.[781] The Prosecution also highlights the Trial Chamber's assertion that "many people" knew what happened at the Kravica Warehouse within twenty-four hours.[782] It argues that, although Blagojević remained unaware of these killings for days, these findings demonstrate that brigade soldiers learned earlier and knew more about the events than he did.[783] These facts, coupled with the Trial Chamber's findings that the Bratunac Brigade's practical assistance had a substantial effect on the murder operation, in the Prosecution's view, prove that Bratunac Brigade members aided and abetted the murder operation, and that the underlying crimes supporting Blagojević's Article 7(3) liability have been established. **[page 114]**

292. With respect to Potočari, the Appeals Chamber recalls the Trial Chamber's finding that the practical assistance provided by Bratunac Brigade members in Potočari was one of several distinct acts that when "taken together" had a "substantial effect" on the murders.[784] However, assuming *arguendo* that the Bratunac Brigade's participation in separating Bosnian Muslim men and guarding detainees in Potočari had a substantial effect on the murder operation, satisfying the *actus reus* for aiding and abetting, the Trial Chamber's inability to find the underlying criminal acts required for Article 7(3) liability is reasonable. The Trial Chamber found that ten to fifteen members of the Bratunac Brigade Military Police were present in Potočari participating in separation, detention, and evacuation activities.[785] The Trial Chamber concluded that the assistance in loading

772 Trial Judgement, paras. 217, 734.

773 Trial Judgement, para. 735.

774 Trial Judgement, para. 736. The Trial Chamber refers to the search for Bosnian Muslim men who tried to leave the Srebrenica area in a column from 10 to 16 July 1995. *See* Trial Judgement, paras. 218–290.

775 Trial Judgement, paras. 290, 737.

776 Trial Judgement, para. 738 (emphasis added).

777 Prosecution Appeal Brief, para. 4.25.

778 *See* Trial Judgement, para. 794.

779 *See, e.g., Kayishema and Ruzindana* Appeal Judgement, para. 186 (noting that a finding of participation in a crime requires proof of both the *actus reus* and *mens rea*).

780 Prosecution Appeal Brief, paras. 4.28–4.30.

781 Prosecution Appeal Brief, para. 4.27.

782 Prosecution Appeal Brief, para. 4.27. Among them was Nikola Gajić, a member of the First Battalion of the Bratunac Brigade stationed in Magasiči, who learned about the massacre from "other soldiers" a day after it had occurred. *See* Trial Judgement, para. 364 fn. 1370.

783 Prosecution Appeal Brief, para. 427.

784 Trial Judgement, para. 738.

785 Trial Judgement, para. 173 fn. 616, para. 212. There is some indication that other Bratunac Brigade members, including a member of the Second Battalion of the Bratunac Brigade, were in and around Potočari as well. *See* Trial Judgement, paras. 144, 148, 164, 165, 168–170, 176, 213, 214, 734.

people onto buses could be seen as participation in the separation process.[786] The Prosecution argues that these soldiers "had to have seen" the burning of personal belongings and identity documents in front of the "White House", and their detailed knowledge of violence in Potočari left as the only reasonable inference that they knew that the Bosnian Muslim men would be murdered.[787] Additionally, the Prosecution emphasizes the fact that two members of the Bratunac Brigade rescued their friend from one of the buses loaded with men and allowed him to board a bus with women and children.[788]

293. The Appeals Chamber recalls the Trial Chamber's determination that the evidence failed to demonstrate that elements of the Bratunac Brigade participated in the destruction of personal property.[789] Furthermore, the Prosecution does not show that members of the Bratunac Brigade were actually deployed near the "White House" or that they saw the burning of belongings and documents. In any event, the Appeals Chamber is of the opinion that knowledge of such activities leaves several reasonable inferences about the Bratunac Brigade members' awareness of the detainees' fate. One such inference could be that burning personal items of Bosnian Muslim men was an attempt to further disorient, demoralize, and/or dehumanize the prisoners.[790] Furthermore, even if the act of the two Bratunac Brigade members assisting a friend to leave with women and children is an indication that these individuals were aware of dangers facing the separated Bosnian Muslim men, it does not establish that they knew about the planned mass executions. A reasonable trier of fact could conclude that these soldiers acted to save their friend from maltreatment or prolonged detention, unaware of the impending executions. Thus, the Appeals Chamber finds no error in the Trial Chamber's refusal to ground Article 7(3) liability upon these acts. **[page 115]**

294. With respect to the executions at the Kravica Warehouse, the Trial Chamber found that on the evening of 13 July 1995, approximately 1,000 Bosnian Muslim men were executed in a warehouse in Kravica.[791] The Prosecution emphasizes the Trial Chamber's finding in paragraph 497 that some members of the Bratunac Brigade were "around the Kravica Warehouse around the time that the mass executions took place".[792] The Prosecution argues that these facts lead to only one reasonable conclusion: Blagojević's subordinates knew from this event forward that Bosnian Muslim men would be channelled into a murder operation.[793]

295. The Appeals Chamber recalls that the Trial Chamber found the evidence insufficient to conclude that members of the Bratunac Brigade participated in the killing at Kravica Warehouse.[794] Moreover, the Trial Chamber noted that "evidence as to the presence of members of the Bratunac Brigade members [*sic*] at the Kravica Warehouse is limited"[795] and refused to conclusively determine that Bratunac Brigade members were present "*when* the mass executions were carried out".[796] Reading these findings together, the time-frame described in paragraph 497 of the Trial Judgement – "*around* the time the mass executions took place" – is properly interpreted to extend to periods beyond the precise moment the killings took place.[797] Such an interpretation, coupled with an absence of facts demonstrating that Bratunac Brigade members offered assistance to the executions as they occurred,[798] negates the finding that Bratunac Brigade members rendered practical assistance to these particular killings as they happened. Moreover, the Prosecution submissions fail to demonstrate that any assistance rendered by Bratunac Brigade members prior to or contemporaneously with the killings was done with knowledge that executions would occur at the Kravica Warehouse or elsewhere.[799] In light of the

786 Trial Judgement, paras. 173, 212.
787 Prosecution Appeal Brief, para. 4.28.
788 Prosecution Appeal Brief, para. 4.30.
789 Trial Judgement, para. 215.
790 *Cf.* Trial Judgement, para. 615.
791 Trial Judgement, paras. 296–303.
792 Prosecution Appeal Brief, para. 4.27, citing Trial Judgement, paras. 497, 742.
793 Prosecution Appeal Brief, para. 4.27.
794 Trial Judgement, paras. 366, 497.
795 Trial Judgement, para. 364.
796 Trial Judgement, para. 366 ("The Trial Chamber concludes that while members of the Bratunac Brigade *might* have been present around the Kravica Warehouse *when* the mass executions were carried out[...]." (emphasis added)).
797 *See, e.g.*, Trial Judgement, para. 364 fn. 1368 (finding that a member of the Bratunac Brigade went to the Kravica Warehouse on 13 July 1995 prior to the executions).
798 *See* Trial Judgement, paras. 298–303.
799 Momir Nikolić is an exception to this statement and his particular role will be discussed in the fourth sub-ground. *See* Trial Judgement, paras. 246, 247, 262. The Trial Chamber determined that those detained in the Kravica Warehouse were taken from Sandići Meadow and that members of the Bratunac Brigade were in the area at the time. Trial Judgement, paras. 261, 296 fns. 1062-1064.

Trial Chamber's findings, the Appeals Chamber finds no error in the Trial Chamber's refusal to ground superior liability pursuant to Article 7(3) of the Statute on the Kravica Warehouse killings.[800] **[page 116]**

296. The Prosecution also highlights the Trial Chamber's assertion that "many people" "knew" what happened at the Kravica Warehouse within twenty-four hours.[801] In addition, the warehouse was located "near" the forward command post for the Bratunac Brigade's Fourth Battalion.[802] The Prosecution argues that the only reasonable inference is that from 14 July 1995, Bratunac Brigade members searching the terrain knew that detainees would be channelled into a murder operation.[803]

297. Again, the Trial Chamber found that searching the terrain was among several separate and distinct acts that when "taken together" had a "substantial effect" on the commission of murder.[804] Moreover, the Trial Chamber's summary of the relevant evidence recounts that on 14 and 15 July 1995, Bratunac Brigade members searching the terrain did not come across or detain anyone, except in a few cases, mitigating the impact of such searches.[805] The Trial Chamber did, however, find that on 17 July 1995, 200 prisoners were taken by a search task force commanded by Mićo Gavrić, Bratunac Brigade's Chief of Artillery.[806] In addition, the Trial Chamber found that members of the Bratunac Brigade, upon the orders of Momir Nikolić, participated in the burial of the victims of the Kravica Warehouse massacre in Glogova on 14 July 1995.[807] Assuming *arguendo* that these activities provided practical assistance that had a substantial effect on the murder campaign, satisfying the *actus reus* for aiding and abetting, the Appeals Chamber concludes that the Trial Chamber did not err in not finding that members of the Bratunac Brigade committed crimes upon which Blagojević could incur Article 7(3) liability.

298. As discussed above, the Trial Chamber refrained from concluding that any Bratunac Brigade member participated in or was necessarily present when the killings at Kravica Warehouse occurred.[808] In asserting that "many people" knew of what happened there, the Trial Chamber pointed to the testimonies of Miroslav Deronjić,[809] Witness DP-102,[810] Jovan Nikolić,[811] and Dragomir Zekić[812] as examples of what was known and by whom.[813] These testimonies reflect that **[page 117]** knowledge Bratunac Brigade members possessed concerning the Kravica Warehouse killings was generally second-hand.[814] Dragomir Zekić's testimony provides arguably the most compelling basis to find that at least some Bratunac Brigade soldiers knew what happened at Kravica.[815] Zekić, commander of the Bratunac Brigade's Third Infantry Battalion at the time, testified that he heard that on 14 or 15 July 1995 an incident occurred at the Kravica Warehouse, and, at trial, stated "I know that genocide was committed in Kravica."[816] The statement remains ambiguous as to what precisely Zekić heard, and whether he concluded that the killings were a "genocide" from

800 Trial Judgement, para. 794.

801 Prosecution Appeal Brief, para. 4.27, citing Trial Judgement, para. 742.

802 Trial Judgement, paras. 43, 742.

803 Prosecution Appeal Brief, paras. 4.27, 4.32.

804 Trial Judgement, paras. 736, 738.

805 Trial Judgement, paras. 231, 232, 258.

806 Trial Judgement, paras. 235, 237, 259.

807 Trial Judgement, paras. 306, 307, 367.

808 *See also* Trial Judgement, para. 742 fn. 2191, citing Jovan Nikolić's Trial Testimony. Jovan Nikolić testified that although those involved in the killing were masked, he was "convinced that there were no men [...] from [...] the Bratunac Brigade" among them. T. 8013-8014.

809 Trial Judgement, para. 742 fn. 2191, citing KT. 124. A clerical error exists as the cited *Krstić* Transcript page is not from Deronjić's testimony. While T. 124 from *Blagojević* does reflect Deronjić's testimony, its content is not relevant to the finding the Trial Chamber seeks to support. *But see* Deronjić, T. 6461 (acknowledging that he learned from Borovčanin of the events at the Kravica Warehouse on the evening of 13 July 1995 and of more details in the early morning hours of 14 July 2006).

810 Trial Judgement, para. 742 fn. 2191, citing T. 8270–8271.

811 Trial Judgement, para. 742 fn. 2191, citing T. 8011–8016.

812 Trial Judgement, para. 742 fn. 2192, citing T. 8899–8901.

813 *See also* T. 7952–7953.

814 *But see* Trial Judgement, paras. 306, 307, 367 (finding that after the executions, a number of Bratunac Brigade members participated in removing bodies from the Kravica Warehouse and burying them on the orders of Momir Nikolić).

815 The Appeals Chamber notes that Jovan Nikolić provided a graphic first-hand account of observing prisoners being "liquidated" one by one and having notified civilian authorities in Bratunac. *See* T. 8012, 8015. However, he also affirmatively denied having relayed his observations to the Bratunac Brigade. *See* T. 8015.

816 T. 8901.

the moment he became aware of them, or if he reached this opinion later. The statement also remains ambiguous as to whether the incident was widely discussed among members of the Bratunac Brigade, and if so, what information was relayed.[817] The Prosecution's burden was to elicit clarifications, which it did not do.

299. For the above reasons, the Appeals Chamber dismisses this sub-ground of the appeal.

4. Alleged Error in Finding that No Superior-Subordinate Relationship Existed between Blagojević and Nikolić

300. The Prosecution submits that the Trial Chamber erred in law and in fact in finding that no superior-subordinate relationship existed between Blagojević and Momir Nikolić.[818] The Prosecution argues that the Trial Chamber appears to have applied an incorrect legal standard when determining whether Blagojević exercised effective control over Momir Nikolić.[819] The Prosecution argues that despite the presence of senior officers of the VRS directly issuing orders to Momir Nikolić, Blagojević had the power to punish or, at least, to initiate measures leading to proceedings against Nikolić.[820] The Prosecution posits that the Trial Chamber, in finding no effective control existed, determined that any measures Blagojević could have taken would have been unsuccessful.[821] The Prosecution asserts that "material ability to prevent or punish", a necessary component when determining effective control, is satisfied when the superior has the ability to *initiate* steps to prevent or punish crimes even where such actions would not lead to prevention or **[page 118]** punishment.[822] In the Prosecution's view, the Trial Chamber's conclusion that Blagojević had no effective control over Momir Nikolić, an officer of the Bratunac Brigade, is inconsistent with the finding that Blagojević bore responsibility for the actions of all members and units of the Bratunac Brigade.[823] Indeed, the Prosecution adds, the Trial Chamber even found Blagojević guilty for the conduct of members of the brigade under the direct orders of Momir Nikolić.[824]

301. The Appeals Chamber observes that, in determining the scope of Blagojević's *de jure* authority over Momir Nikolić, the Trial Chamber held:

> Colonel Blagojević remained in command and control of all units of the Bratunac Brigade, including those members of the security organ, as well as the Bratunac Brigade Military Police, and thus continued to bear responsibility for the actions of all members and units of the Bratunac Brigade throughout the Indictment period.[825]

Moreover, the Trial Chamber noted testimony indicating that during the relevant period, a functioning judicial system existed, which required reporting of incidents and investigations into criminal offences against humanity and international law.[826] Nonetheless, in assessing Blagojević's actual criminal responsibility as a superior for the actions of Momir Nikolić, the head of the Bratunac Brigade Security Organ, the Trial Chamber ultimately concluded that Blagojević exercised no effective control over Nikolić, reasoning as follows:

> [C]onsidering that during the period between July and November 1995 senior members of the VRS were in Srebrenica area issuing orders and instructions, and taking into consideration the Trial Chamber's findings in relation to the functional chain of command for the security organ, the Trial Chamber is unable to conclude

817 *See also* Nikola Gajic, T. 3373–3374 (testifying that he heard "from the soldiers" that "some people were killed [at Kravica Warehouse]").
818 Prosecution Appeal Brief, paras. 4.5, 4.34.
819 Prosecution Appeal Brief, paras. 4.39, 4.40.
820 Prosecution Appeal Brief, paras. 4.34, 4.43.
821 Prosecution Appeal Brief, paras. 4.39, 4.40.
822 Prosecution Appeal Brief, paras. 4.42–4.50.
823 Prosecution Appeal Brief, paras. 4.60, 4.61.
824 Prosecution Appeal Brief, para. 4.62.
825 Trial Judgement, para. 419.
826 Trial Judgement, paras. 420–427.

that Colonel Blagojević had 'effective control' over Momir Nikolić to the threshold required in order to establish a superior-subordinate relationship for the purpose of Article 7(3) of the Statute – namely, that he had the "material ability to prevent or punish the commission of the offences".[827]

302. The Appeals Chamber does not consider the conclusions regarding the scope of Blagojević's authority irreconcilable with the finding that he exercised no effective control over Momir Nikolić. In the *Čelebići* Appeal Judgement, the Appeals Chamber discussed the possibility that *de jure* authority alone may not lead to the imposition of command responsibility.[828] The relevant discussion indicated "possession of *de jure* power in itself may not suffice for the finding of command responsibility if it does not manifest in effective control."[829] In the view of the Appeals Chamber, the Trial Chamber's conclusion in paragraph 419 of the Trial Judgement that Blagojević remained in command and control of all units of the Bratunac Brigade reflects its assessment of his **[page 119]** *de jure* authority over all members of the brigade, including Nikolić, following a lengthy discussion of various legal provisions, orders, and expert testimony.[830] The Trial Chamber's subsequent finding in paragraph 795 of the Trial Judgement that Blagojević lacked effective control over Momir Nikolić reflected its assessment of the actual facts on the ground in light of the earlier legal discussion.

303. In such circumstances, the Trial Chamber's findings on this point cannot be considered to be legally incorrect or unreasonable. First, the Trial Chamber referenced its earlier *de jure* assessment of Blagojević's authority. This assessment included findings that a functional chain of command existed between the VRS Main Staff and the Bratunac Brigade security organ, which was headed by Momir Nikolić and that the VRS Main Staff controlled this organ centrally.[831] The Trial Chamber's finding that Blagojević had *de jure* authority is based on the fact that this functional chain of command did not operate in "isolation" and that the brigade's security and intelligence organs were equally under the authority of the unit's commander.[832] The Trial Chamber further alluded to its findings that these same authorities who centrally controlled the brigade's security organ were in the area at the time issuing orders and instructions.[833] In view of such evidence, it was open to a reasonable trier of fact to conclude that Blagojević lacked effective control over Momir Nikolić at the time of the commission of the crimes.

304. Accordingly, the Appeals Chamber dismisses this sub-ground of appeal.

5. Conclusion

305. For the foregoing reasons, the Appeals Chamber dismisses this ground of appeal in its entirety. **[page 120]**

D. Alleged Errors relating to Jokić's Acquittals for Mass Killings at Petkovci School and Petkovci Dam (Ground 4)

306. The Trial Chamber found that on 14 July 1995 approximately 1,000 of the Bosnian Muslim men detained in Bratunac town and in Kravica were transported to the Petkovci school in the Zvornik Municipality, where some of them were shot.[834] The Trial Chamber further determined that the majority of the detainees were transported that evening from the school to a nearby dam and killed.[835] The Trial Chamber found that around noon, Jokić, acting as the Zvornik Brigade's duty officer, contacted Marko Milošević, Deputy Commander of the Sixth Infantry Battalion of the Zvornik Brigade, and informed him that the Bosnian Muslim prisoners

[827] Trial Judgement, para. 795.
[828] *Čelebići* Appeal Judgement, para. 197.
[829] *Čelebići* Appeal Judgement, para. 197 (quoting the Trial Judgement approvingly).
[830] *See* Trial Judgement, paras. 396–419.
[831] Trial Judgement, para. 417.
[832] Trial Judgement, para. 418.
[833] *See, e.g.*, Trial Judgement, paras. 172, 186, 191, 795.
[834] Trial Judgement, paras. 337–339, 567(g).
[835] Trial Judgement, paras. 340, 341, 567(h).

would arrive and be detained at the Petkovci school.[836] The Trial Chamber was not satisfied that this phone call constituted substantial assistance to the mass execution committed at Petkovci.[837] Therefore, it did not place any criminal responsibility on Jokić for these killings.

307. On appeal, the Prosecution submits that the Trial Chamber erred in fact in concluding that Jokić did not substantially assist the mass execution at the Petkovci school and dam.[838] The Prosecution submits that the only reasonable conclusion from the Trial Chamber's own factual findings is that Jokić provided substantial assistance to the massacre at the Petkovci school and dam with knowledge that the Bosnian Muslim men detained there would be killed.[839]

308. The Prosecution submits that Jokić substantially assisted the commission of murder at Petkovci school and dam: (1) by remaining informed, as duty officer, of the activities of the Zvornik Brigade and facilitating the communication of that information amongst the principal players of the murder operation; and (2) as Chief of Engineering, by co-ordinating, sending and monitoring deployment of Zvornik Brigade resources and equipment.[840] The Prosecution also alleges that the evidence supporting this is the same or similar to evidence used by the Trial Chamber to convict Jokić for aiding and abetting the killings in Orahovac.[841] The Appeals Chamber will examine these submissions in turn. **[page 121]**

1. Jokić's Role as the Zvornik Brigade Duty Officer

309. The Prosecution argues that, through two communications Jokić had while functioning as the Zvornik Brigade duty officer, he facilitated the detention of prisoners at Petkovci.[842] First, the Prosecution argues that Jokić told Marko Milošević, Deputy Commander of the Sixth Infantry Battalion of the Zvornik Brigade, that prisoners were to be detained at the Petkovci school within two hours.[843] Second, the Prosecution argues that Jokić requested of Marko Milošević that Colonel Ljubiša Beara contact the brigade and that intercepts of a subsequent conversation between Jokić and Beara recorded Jokić stating that there were "big problems. Well with the people, I mean, with the parcel."[844] The Prosecution argues that this conversation "plainly shows that Jokić was coordinating the detention of *all* prisoners in the Zvornik area on that day, not only in Orahovac"[845] and that no reasonable trier of fact would consider this conversation to pertain only to the prisoners in Orahovac.[846]

310. The Prosecution's primary submission is that the Trial Chamber failed to consider Jokić's overall actions as duty officer in the context of assessing whether he substantially assisted the murders at Petkovci school and dam, as the Prosecution claims it did in the context of the Orahovac killings. The Appeals Chamber does not find this argument persuasive. A review of the Trial Judgement reveals that in making findings on the nature of Jokić's substantial assistance at Orahovac the Trial Chamber did not rely, as the Prosecution suggests, on Jokić's role and activities as duty officer. Rather, in holding Jokić responsible for aiding and abetting the killings in Orahovac, the Trial Chamber concluded that his act of substantial assistance involved making Zvornik Brigade Engineering Company resources available to assist in digging mass graves.[847] The Appeals Chamber notes that the Trial Chamber considered Jokić's role as duty officer in connection with the

836 Trial Judgement, paras. 343, 765.
837 Trial Judgement, para. 765.
838 Prosecution Appeal Brief, paras. 5.1–5.44.
839 Prosecution Appeal Brief, para. 5.8.
840 Prosecution Appeal Brief, para. 5.4.
841 Prosecution Appeal Brief, paras. 5.2, 5.11 (stating that the evidence used by the Trial Chamber to convict Jokić for aiding and abetting killings at Orahovac included evidence that he (1) ordered men and equipment to assist with burials; (2) facilitated communications between primary participants in the murder operation; (3) facilitated the detention of the prisoners at the Grbvaci school).
842 Prosecution Appeal Brief, para. 5.14.
843 Prosecution Appeal Brief, para. 5.14, citing Trial Judgement, paras. 343, 344.
844 Prosecution Reply Brief, para. 4.10, quoting Trial Judgement, para. 325. *See also* Prosecution Appeal Brief, para. 5.14.
845 Prosecution Appeal Brief, para. 5.15.
846 Prosecution Appeal Brief, paras. 5.15, 5.16.
847 Trial Judgement, para. 764 ("By telling Cvijetin Ristanović to take the excavator to Orahovac, Dragan Jokić provided practical assistance that had a substantial effect on the commission of the crime.").

massacres at both Orahovac and Petkovci in connection with his knowledge of those killings.[848] As such, the Appeals Chamber considers that the Trial Chamber implicitly determined that Jokić's role as duty officer did not have a substantial effect on the murder of men detained at Petkovci.[849] The Appeals Chamber considers this finding to be reasonable, particularly in light of **[page 122]** the lack of specific arguments by the Prosecution substantiating how such acts had a substantial effect on the killings at Petkovci.

2. Jokić's Role as the Chief of Engineering

311. According to the Prosecution, Jokić substantially assisted the killings at Petkovci by providing engineering machinery to dig mass graves.[850] The Prosecution submits that "after sending an excavator to Orahovac and learning of the mass killings there, Jokić sent equipment for the same purpose to [Petkovci] on the same day."[851] The Prosecution focuses on the Zvornik Brigade Engineering Company daily order book[852] indicating that an excavator and loader were present and working at Petkovci on 15 July 1995.[853] The Prosecution argues that the Trial Chamber erred to the extent that it concluded that it could not rely on that specific daily order book entry because it was "not specifically corroborated by witness testimony."[854] The Prosecution argues that the evidence in the daily order book, found reliable in other contexts, should have led the Trial Chamber to the only reasonable inference: that engineering equipment was sent to the sites, including Petkovci, to dig mass graves.[855] Moreover, the Prosecution argues, corroboration existed in the form of testimony given by Prosecution Witnesses P-111 and P-112 and accepted by the Trial Chamber, that an excavator and loader were present at the Petkovci site on 15 July 1995.[856]

312. The Appeals Chamber observes that the Trial Chamber, in the course of examining evidence "regarding [the] presence of Engineering Company resources", noted that it was "furnished" with evidence, "not specifically corroborated by witness testimony".[857] The Trial Chamber subsequently discussed entries in the daily order book potentially relevant to the crimes at Petkovci, including noting that "a loader and an excavator were present working at 'Petkovci'."[858] Rather than exclude the evidence, the Trial Chamber merely noted that this hearsay evidence was not corroborated and apparently accorded it minimal weight. In another context, the Trial Chamber noted that it saw "no reason to doubt the validity of [certain information contained in the daily order book] in light of the fact that other information contained in the daily order book has been corroborated by other **[page 123]** evidence."[859] Thus, the Trial Chamber appears to have applied the standards of ordinary evidence to the daily order book, which permit the Trial Chamber, depending on the circumstances, to exclude or give limited weight to material admitted pursuant to Rule 89(C) on account of the reliability or credibility concerns inherent to this category of evidence.[860]

313. With respect to the Prosecution's contention that the daily order book was in fact corroborated, the Appeals Chamber observes that its entries, if accurate, indicate that an ULT model loader was sent to

---

848 Trial Judgement, paras. 762–765. In paragraph 765, the Trial Chamber refers to the discussion between Jokić and Marko Milošević about the transfer of prisoners to the school, concluding that "[...] this evidence is in line with previous evidence regarding Dragan Jokić's knowledge as to the detention of prisoners in the Zvornik Brigade area [...]").

849 *Cf.* Trial Judgement, paras. 508, 836.

850 Prosecution Appeal Brief, paras. 5.21–5.25.

851 Prosecution Appeal Brief, paras. 5.11, 5.41.

852 The Prosecution alternatively refers to the evidence as the "daily order book" and "daily logbook". *See* Prosecution Appeal Brief, paras. 5.21, 5.28.

853 Prosecution Appeal Brief, para. 5.21, citing Trial Judgement, para. 534 fn. 1824.

854 Prosecution Appeal Brief, paras. 5.21, 5.22, quoting Trial Judgement, para. 533 (citing *Čelebići* Appeal Judgement, para. 506; *Blaškić* Appeal Judgement, para. 342 fn. 705).

855 Prosecution Appeal Brief, para. 5.25.

856 Prosecution Appeal Brief, para. 5.28, citing Trial Judgement, para. 342.

857 Trial Judgement, para. 533.

858 Trial Judgement, para. 534.

859 Trial Judgement, para. 529.

860 *Naletilic and Martinovic* Appeal Judgement, para. 228. The daily order book is a document made in the ordinary course of events by a person with no interest other than to record as accurately as possible the matters described therein. As such, its admissibility is governed by Rule 89 not Rule 92 *bis*.

Petkovci.[861] In the *Krstić* trial, Witness P-112 testified that he thought the loader was a model ULT-160.[862] The Engineering Company had two ULT model loaders available for use during July 1995.[863] It is possible that one of them was the one observed by Witnesses P-111 and P-112 at Petkovci, but the Prosecution has not attempted to demonstrate this. The Appeals Chamber observes, in any event, that the Trial Chamber found that other loaders were used in the area and that they were not attributable to Jokić's command.[864] Therefore, the observation that a loader was present at the Petkovci burial site does not specifically corroborate the daily order book entry. Moreover, the Prosecution has failed to demonstrate that the loader observed at the Petkovci dam was sent on Jokić's order. Thus, contrary to the Prosecution's argument, the evidence related to Petkovci dam is not the same or similar to that used by the Trial Chamber to connect Jokić to the murders at Orahovac as the Trial Chamber relied on Jokić's specific instruction to Cvijetin Ristanović to take an excavator to Orahovac in finding him guilty for aiding and abetting murders at that site.[865]

3. Conclusion

314. The Prosecution has not demonstrated that Jokić provided assistance that had a substantial effect on the mass killings at Petkovci through his communications about the detainees or by sending equipment there. The Appeals Chamber, therefore, need not assess the Prosecution's submissions that the Trial Chamber erred in fact in relation to its findings on Jokić's knowledge of the mass killings at Petkovci school and dam.[866] **[page 124]**

315. Accordingly, the Prosecution has not established that the Trial Chamber erred in its findings related to Jokić's participation in the Petkovci mass killings, and the Appeals Chamber dismisses this ground of appeal. **[page 125]**

E. Alleged Error relating to Corroboration of Testimony Admitted under Rule 92*bis*(D) (Ground 6)

316. The Prosecution's sixth ground of appeal concerns the use of transcript evidence admitted pursuant to Rule 92*bis*(D) of the Rules.[867] The Prosecution submitted several motions to the Trial Chamber for admission of transcripts of testimony from other trials of approximately thirty witnesses pursuant to Rule 92*bis*(D).[868] In its first decision on these motions,[869] the Trial Chamber determined, *inter alia*, that the testimony of three witnesses from the *Krstić* case admitted pursuant to Rule 92*bis*(D) might be the only evidence of certain facts alleged in the indictment.[870] The Trial Chamber ruled that, in such circumstances, the evidence that those witnesses' statements contain "may lead to a conviction only if there is other evidence which corroborates the statement[s]".[871] The Trial Chamber held, following the Appeals Chamber's guidance in the *Galić* case, that "other evidence would be necessary to corroborate evidence put forward by a single Rule 92*bis* witness who was not called for cross-examination in order to lead to a conviction on that charge of the Indictment".[872] When no corroborating evidence was submitted to support three witness transcripts admitted pursuant to Rule 92*bis*(D), the Trial Chamber disregarded the testimony contained therein as a matter of law.[873]

---

861 Ex. P521a.

862 Trial Judgement, fn. 1263.

863 Trial Judgement, para. 70.

864 Jokić Response Brief, para. 2.65, citing Trial Judgement, paras. 90, 306, 386.

865 *See* Trial Judgement, paras. 332–336, 526–529, 763, 764.

866 Prosecution Appeal Brief, paras. 5.34–5.43.

867 Prosecution Appeal Brief, paras. 7.1–7.24. The extraordinary plenary session of the International Tribunal held on 13 September 2006 amended Rule 92*bis*. In this case, however, the former version of Rule 92*bis* is applicable.

868 *See, e.g., Blagojević and Jokić*, First Rule 92*bis* Decision, para. 1 fn. 6.

869 *Blagojević and Jokić*, First Rule 92*bis* Decision.

870 The allegations are contained in Indictment paragraphs 43(c) ("On the morning of the 13 July, the bodies of six Bosnian Muslim women and five Bosnian Muslim men were found in a stream near the UN Compound in Potočari") and 46.2 ("At approximately 1100 hours on 13 July 1995, a small squad of soldiers consisting of at least one Bratunac police officer (Bratunac MUP), working with individuals and units of the VRS and/or MUP, captured approximately 16 Bosnian Muslim men from the column of men retreating from the Srebrenica enclave, transported them from Konjević Polje to an isolated area on the bank of the Jadar River and summarily executed 15 of them. One individual was wounded and managed to escape"), respectively.

871 *Blagojević and Jokić*, First Rule 92*bis* Decision, para. 25, quoting *Galić*, Rule 92*bis* Decision, fn. 34.

872 *Blagojević and Jokić* First Rule 92*bis* Decision, para. 25.

873 Trial Judgement, paras. 566, 567.

317. The Prosecution submits that the Trial Chamber erred in law by requiring that evidence admitted under Rule 92*bis*(D) of the Rules must be corroborated in order to be relied upon to lead to a conviction.[874] The Prosecution concedes that this error does not impact the verdict but argues that it raises an issue significant to the jurisprudence of the Tribunal, and that, as such, it should be considered on appeal.[875]

318. The Appeals Chamber observes that, in making the impugned finding, the Trial Chamber relied on an Appeals Chamber decision. In addition, the Trial Chamber gave clear notice to the Prosecution at the time it admitted the Rule 92*bis* material that it would require corroboration. The **[page 126]** Prosecution elected not to do so and, in any event, has not demonstrated that it was impractical to corroborate the evidence in question. Furthermore, the Prosecution has not made detailed submissions on the significance of this issue to the jurisprudence. In such circumstances, the Appeals Chamber declines to exercise its discretion in order to consider this ground of appeal. **[page 127]**

F. Alleged Errors relating to the Sentences (Ground 5)

319. The Trial Chamber sentenced Blagojević to a single sentence of eighteen years' imprisonment and Jokić to a single sentence of nine years' imprisonment.[876] The Prosecution submits that the Trial Chamber committed a number of errors in determining these sentences.[877] The Prosecution requests the Appeals Chamber to reverse these errors and increase the sentences accordingly.[878]

320. The sentencing provisions of the International Tribunal are contained in Articles 23 and 24 of the Statute and Rules 100 to 106 of the Rules. Both Article 24 of the Statute and Rule 101 of the Rules contain general sentencing guidelines for a Trial Chamber that amount to an obligation to take into account the following factors: the gravity of the offence, the individual circumstances of the convicted person, the general practice regarding prison sentences in the former Yugoslavia, and aggravating and mitigating circumstances.[879]

321. Trial Chambers are vested with a broad discretion in determining an appropriate sentence, due to their obligation to individualize penalties to fit the circumstances of the accused and the gravity of the crime.[880] As a rule, the Appeals Chamber will not revise a sentence unless the Trial Chamber has committed a discernible error in exercising its discretion or has failed to follow the applicable law.[881] It is for the appealing party to demonstrate how the Trial Chamber erred in imposing the sentence.[882]

1. Alleged Sentencing Errors relating to Blagojević

322. The Prosecution alleges errors with respect to the sentence imposed on Blagojević concerning the assessment of aggravating and mitigating factors as well as the adequacy of the sentence.[883] **[page 128]**

(a) Alleged Error regarding an Aggravating Circumstance

323. The Prosecution submits that the Trial Chamber erred in law by determining that Blagojević's position as a military leader was not an aggravating circumstance.[884] According to the Prosecution, the

874 Prosecution Appeal Brief, paras. 7.2, 7.5.
875 Prosecution Appeal Brief, para. 7.1.
876 Trial Judgement, Chapter X (disposition).
877 Prosecution Appeal Brief, paras. 6.29, 6.61.
878 Prosecution Appeal Brief, paras. 6.30, 6.62.
879 *Čelebići* Appeal Judgement, paras. 429, 716. In addition, Trial Chambers are obliged to take into account the extent to which any penalty imposed by a court of any State on the convicted person for the same act has already been served, as referred to in Article 10(3) of the Statute and in Rule 101(B)(iv) of the Rules.
880 *Čelebići* Appeal Judgement, para. 717; *Dragan Nikolić* Sentencing Appeal Judgement, para. 9; *Babić* Sentencing Appeal Judgement, para. 7; *Deronjić* Sentencing Appeal Judgement, para. 8; *Miodrag Jokić* Sentencing Appeal Judgement, para. 8.
881 *Tadić Sentencing Appeal Judgement, para. 22; Aleksovski Appeal Judgement, para. 187; Furundžija Appeal Judgement, para. 239; Čelebići Appeal Judgement, para. 725; Jelisić Appeal Judgement, para. 99; Kupreškić et al. Appeal Judgement, para. 408; Krstić Appeal Judgement, para. 242; Blaškić Appeal Judgement, para. 680; Deronjić Sentencing Appeal Judgement, para. 8; Miodrag Jokić Sentencing Appeal Judgement, para. 8.*
882 *Čelebići* Appeal Judgement, para. 725.
883 Prosecution Appeal Brief, para. 6.2.
884 Prosecution Appeal Brief, paras. 6.3, 6.9, referring to Trial Judgement, para. 848.

Trial Chamber did not take Blagojević's position of authority into account as an aggravating circumstance because it considered that he had a limited role in the commission of the crimes.[885] The Prosecution, however, argues that Blagojević's limited role is part of the consideration for the gravity of the offence, not position of authority as an aggravating circumstance.[886] Thus, the Prosecution considers the Trial Chamber to have mitigated Blagojević's punishment twice on account of his role: initially, by considering his "limited" role in the determination of the gravity of the offence, and again by declining to take his position of authority into account as an aggravating circumstance.[887]

324. The Appeals Chamber recalls that a Trial Chamber "shall take into account [...] any aggravating circumstances",[888] which may include the seniority, position of authority, or high position of leadership held by a person criminally responsible under Article 7(1) of the Statute.[889] What matters is not the position of authority taken alone, but that position coupled with the manner in which the authority was exercised: abuse of superior position may be considered an aggravating factor.[890]

325. When assessing Blagojević's position of authority as an aggravating circumstance, the Trial Chamber found:

> [T]he role of Vidoje Blagojević in relation to the crime for which he has been convicted was not that of a commanding officer issuing orders, but the role of a commander who facilitated the use of Bratunac Brigade personnel and assets under his command. Therefore, the Trial Chamber considers the role of Vidoje Blagojević in the commission of the crimes to have been a limited one. Accordingly, the Trial Chamber will not take the position of authority of, nor abuse of authority by, Vidoje Blagojević into account as an aggravating circumstance.[891]

326. From this passage, it is evident that the Trial Chamber considered Blagojević's position and his role as a commander in the context of assessing any relevant aggravating circumstances and determined that it did not warrant aggravation in the circumstances of the case. Beyond disagreeing **[page 129]** with this determination, the Prosecution does not identify any discernible error in the exercise of the Trial Chamber's sentencing discretion. Accordingly, the Appeals Chamber dismisses this sub-ground of appeal.

(b) Alleged Error regarding a Mitigating Circumstance

327. The Prosecution submits that the Trial Chamber erred in finding that Blagojević's participation in de-mining activities constituted a mitigating circumstance.[892] The Prosecution argues that the structure of the Trial Chamber's analysis indicates that it considered Blagojević's participation in de-mining activities as "remorse," but that Blagojević's conduct could not be considered as such because it did not demonstrate remorse for his own criminal conduct, a desire to alleviate the suffering of victims, or an intention to promote peace and reconciliation in the region.[893]

328. The Appeals Chamber holds that the Trial Chamber permissibly considered Blagojević's participation in de-mining activities under the broad category of post-conflict conduct that goes to the character of the accused. In the *Babić* Sentencing Appeal, the Appeals Chamber observed that "[n]either the Statute nor the Rules exhaustively define the factors which may be taken into account by a Trial Chamber in mitigation or aggravation of a sentence."[894] In that case, the Appeals Chamber provided a non-exhaustive list of twelve

885 Prosecution Appeal Brief, para. 6.10, citing Trial Judgement, para. 848.

886 Prosecution Appeal Brief, para. 6.10.

887 Prosecution Appeal Brief, para. 6.11.

888 Rules, Rule 101 (emphasis added).

889 *See Naletilić* and *Martinović* Appeal Judgement, para. 613; *Kupreškić et al.* Appeal Judgement, para. 451.

890 *Stakić* Appeal Judgement, para. 411. *See also Kayishema and Ruzindana* Appeal Judgement, paras. 358-359; *Babić* Sentencing Appeal Judgement, para. 80; *Kamuhanda* Appeal Judgement, para. 347; *Aleksovski* Appeal Judgement, para. 183; *Ntakirutimana* Appeal Judgement, para. 563, *Krstić* Trial Judgement, para. 709.

891 Trial Judgement, para. 848.

892 Prosecution Appeal Brief, para. 6.13.

893 Prosecution Appeal Brief, para. 6.17.

894 *Babić* Sentencing Appeal Judgement, para. 43.

factors that have been taken into account in connection with mitigation. Notably, the *Babić* Appeals Chamber placed remorse within the broader context of the "character of the accused after the conflict".[895] The Appeals Chamber did not specify how other post-conflict conduct – distinguishable from remorse – could evidence the character of the accused in mitigation of a sentence. Leaving such considerations to the Trial Chambers, the Appeals Chamber recognized that they are "endowed with a considerable degree of discretion in deciding on the factors which may be taken into account".[896] In the present case, the Trial Chamber considered that Blagojević's active engagement in planning, managing, and organizing a system of de-mining in the army of the Republika Srpska was a relevant mitigating circumstance, without placing it under the rubric of remorse.[897] **[page 130]**

329. The Prosecution argues that Blagojević's conduct needs to have been voluntary for the Trial Chamber to consider evidence thereof in mitigation, and argues that his conduct was not voluntary because it was required by his VRS position and the Dayton Peace Accords.[898] The Appeals Chamber notes that the Dayton Peace Accords imposed obligations on the parties to the treaty, not on specific members of their armed forces.[899] Further, the Prosecution did not demonstrate that Blagojević's post-conflict position in the VRS required him to participate in de-mining activities or that his participation in them was not in any way voluntary.

330. The Prosecution also asserts that Blagojević's de-mining activities are irrelevant because they are not sufficiently connected to the harm he caused. The Prosecution appears to locate support for this requirement in the *Plavsić* and *Miodrag Jokić* Sentencing Judgements.[900] The Appeals Chamber disagrees and considers that conduct of an accused that promotes reconciliation in the former Yugoslavia may be considered as a mitigating circumstance whether or not it is directly connected to the harm the accused caused. The Appeals Chamber observes that the *Plavsić* and *Miodrag Jokić* cases do not stand for a different proposition. In the *Plavsić* Sentencing Judgement, the Trial Chamber credited Biljana Plavsić for "ensuring that the Dayton Agreement was accepted and implemented in Republika Srpska."[901] In the case of Miodrag Jokić, the Trial Chamber credited him for post-war "participat[ion] in political activities programmatically aimed at promoting a peaceful solution to the conflicts in the region."[902] Similarly, the Trial Chamber here credited Blagojević for taking a leadership role in implementing one aspect of the Dayton Peace Accords, as previous Trial Chambers, cited by the Prosecution, have credited convicted persons for implementing that agreement.

331. In view of the foregoing, the Appeals Chamber finds that the Prosecution did not demonstrate that the Trial Chamber committed a discernible error in considering Blagojević's post-conflict conduct in mitigation of his sentence. **[page 131]**

(c) Alleged Inadequacy of the Sentence

332. The Prosecution argues that Blagojević's sentence is inadequate in light of the magnitude of his crimes, and in comparison to three persons either found guilty of or who pled guilty to participation in crimes that occurred in Srebrenica: Radislav Krstić, Momir Nikolić, and Dragan Obrenović.[903] According to the

---

895 *Babić* Sentencing Appeal Judgement, para. 43, citing *Miodrag Jokić* Sentencing Judgement, paras. 90, 92 (finding that Miodrag Jokić's "post-conflict conduct" "reflect[ed] his sincere remorse").

896 *Babić* Sentencing Appeal Judgement, para. 43, quoting *Čelebići* Appeal Judgement, para. 780.

897 The Appeals Chamber notes that remorse is not mentioned in the operative paragraphs considering Blagojević's de-mining activities. *See* Trial Judgement, paras. 858-860.

898 Prosecution Appeal Brief, para. 6.13.

899 *See* Dayton Peace Accords, Annex 1A: Agreement on the Military Aspects of the Peace Settlement, Article IV.2.d (stating "The Parties immediately after this Annex enters into force shall begin promptly and proceed steadily to complete the following activities within thirty (30) days after the Transfer of Authority or as determined by the IFOR Commander: (1) remove, dismantle or destroy all mines, unexploded ordnance, explosive devices, demolitions, and barbed or razor wire from the Agreed Cease-Fire Zone of Separation or other areas from which their Forces are withdrawn; (2) mark all known mine emplacements, unexploded ordnance, explosive devices and demolitions within Bosnia and Herzegovina; and (3) remove, dismantle or destroy all mines, unexploded ordnance, explosive devices and demolitions as required by the IFOR Commander.").

900 *See* Prosecution Appeal Brief, paras. 6.20, 6.21.

901 *Plavsić* Sentencing Judgement, para. 94.

902 *Miodrag Jokić* Sentencing Judgement, para. 91.

903 Prosecution Appeal Brief, para. 6.25.

Prosecution, sentences in those cases demonstrate an "unjustified disparity".[904] The Prosecution submits that, amongst the Srebrenica perpetrators, only Radislav Krstić and Blagojević have been convicted of genocide, and the Prosecution argues, given that Blagojević was also convicted of forcible transfer, murders, and persecutions, the sentence of eighteen years is manifestly inadequate.[905]

333. The Appeals Chamber has noted that the precedential effect of sentences rendered by the International Tribunal is very limited because: (1) comparisons between sentences can only be undertaken where the offences are the same and committed in substantially similar circumstances; and (2) each Trial Chamber has an overriding obligation to tailor a penalty to fit the individual circumstances of the accused and the gravity of the crime.[906]

334. The Prosecution suggests comparing Blagojević's sentence to the sentences of Momir Nikolić and Dragan Obrenović, who were originally jointly indicted in this case.[907] The Appeals Chamber previously found that the cases of Momir Nikolić and Dragan Obrenović were comparable in general.[908] Blagojević's conviction, however, is substantially distinguishable. Momir Nikolić and Dragan Obrenović plead guilty to Count 5 of the Indictment, the crime of persecutions on political, racial, and religious grounds, a crime against humanity under Article 5(h) of the Statute. Momir Nikolić admitted his conduct related to the opportunistic killings in Potočari and Bratunac town, organized mass executions, and the opportunistic killings that occurred in the Bratunac Brigade zone of responsibility.[909] Dragan Obrenović admitted his conduct related to the opportunistic killings in Bratunac town, the organized mass executions that occurred in the Zvornik municipality, and the opportunistic killings in the Zvornik Brigade Zone.[910] Both Momir Nikolić and Dragan Obrenović were held responsible for committing the crime of persecutions. Unlike Momir Nikolić and Dragan Obrenović, Blagojević was convicted of aiding and abetting, not commission, and "[a]iding and abetting the commission of a crime is generally considered a lesser degree of **[page 132]** individual criminal responsibility than committing a crime."[911] Blagojević's criminal liability is also distinguishable because, unlike Momir Nikolić and Dragan Obrenović, Blagojević was not convicted of participating in the mass killing operation.

335. Turning to the Prosecution's comparison with the sentence of Radislav Krstić, the differences are even more significant.[912] The Appeals Chamber recalls that Radislav Krstić was Blagojević's superior.[913] He was convicted of aiding and abetting genocide, aiding and abetting extermination and persecutions as crimes against humanity, and aiding and abetting murder as a violation of the laws or customs of war.[914] Moreover, unlike Blagojević, Radislav Krstić knew of the mass killing operation and the genocidal intent of the VRS officers in connection with it. Thus, Blagojević, Radislav Krstić, Momir Nikolić, and Dragan Obrenović were convicted of related, but distinct crimes, pursuant to distinct modes of liability. Therefore, comparing their sentences does not demonstrate the inadequacy of Blagojević's sentence. Accordingly, the Appeals Chamber finds that the Prosecution failed to show that the Trial Chamber in this case committed a discernible error by imposing an inadequate sentence on Blagojević. In addition, the Appeals Chamber notes that it has reversed Blagojević's conviction for genocide.

(d) Conclusion

336. For the foregoing reasons, the Appeals Chamber dismisses the Prosecution's appeal against Blagojević's sentence.

904 Prosecution Appeal Brief, para. 6.25, quoting *Čelebići* Appeal Judgement, para. 757.
905 Prosecution Appeal Brief, para. 6.27.
906 *See Babić* Sentencing Appeal Judgement, para. 32 (internal citations omitted); *Čelebići* Appeal Judgement, paras. 717, 720, 821.
907 *See* Trial Judgement, para. 874.
908 *Momir Nikolić* Sentencing Appeal Judgement, para. 42.
909 *Momir Nikolić* Sentencing Appeal Judgement, para. 42.
910 *Momir Nikolić* Sentencing Appeal Judgement, para. 42.
911 *Vasiljević* Appeal Judgement, para. 102.
912 The Appeals Chamber has held that the cases of Nikolić and Krstić were too dissimilar to make a comparison of their sentences meaningful. *Momir Nikolić* Sentencing Appeal Judgement, para. 50.
913 Trial Judgement, para. 38.
914 *Krstić* Appeal Judgement, p. 87.

2. Alleged Sentencing Errors relating to Jokić

337. The Prosecution alleges five errors in the Trial Chamber's determination of Jokić's sentence. The Prosecution submits that the Trial Chamber: (1) failed to adequately consider the gravity of the offence and form and degree of Jokić's participation; (2) erred in considering Jokić's de-mining activities as a mitigating factor; (3) erred in considering Jokić's helping Muslim boys through a minefield as a mitigating factor; (4) erred in considering Jokić's cooperation with the Prosecution as a mitigating factor; and (5) erred in handing down a sentence that is manifestly inadequate in light of the magnitude of the crimes. **[page 133]**

(a) Alleged Failure to Reflect the Overall Gravity of the Offence and the Form and Nature of Jokić's Participation

338. The Prosecution submits that the Trial Chamber failed to impose an appropriate sentence on Jokić based on its assessment of the gravity of the offence and the degree of his culpability.[915] The Prosecution argues that despite stating the legal test correctly, the Trial Chamber handed down a sentence that was "manifestly inadequate" in light of its own findings on the scale of the persecutions and extermination.[916] The Prosecution also argues that Jokić's sentence does not adequately reflect that he played a pivotal role in the Zvornik Brigade's operations and alleges that his sentence did not reflect the impact of his crimes upon the victims.[917]

339. The Appeals Chamber recalls that "the governing criterion in sentencing is that the sentence should reflect the totality of the offender's conduct (the 'totality' principle), and that it should reflect the gravity of the offences and the culpability of the offender so that it is both just and appropriate."[918] On appeal, the Prosecution simply points to facts that the Trial Chamber itself considered in finding that Jokić "did not play a major role in the commission of the crimes",[919] without demonstrating how the Trial Chamber erred in weighing those factors. Accordingly, this sub-ground of the Prosecution's appeal is dismissed.

(b) Alleged Error regarding Jokić's Participation in De-mining as a Mitigating Circumstance

340. The Prosecution repeats the same arguments in connection with the Trial Chamber's decision to consider Jokić's participation in de-mining activities as a mitigating circumstance as it made in relation to Blagojević's sentence, discussed above.[920] Accordingly, the Appeals Chamber dismisses this argument for the same reasons.[921]

(c) Alleged Error in Considering as a Mitigating Factor Jokić's Act of Ensuring Safe Passage through a Minefield

341. The Prosecution submits that the Trial Chamber erred in considering as a mitigating factor Jokić's "single act of ensuring the safe passage through a minefield of a group of Bosnian Muslim **[page 134]** boys" because Jokić was obligated to take all reasonable steps to protect civilians from the indiscriminate effects of land mines and to give special protection to children.[922]

---

915 Prosecution Appeal Brief, para. 6.32.
916 Prosecution Appeal Brief, paras. 6.34, 6.35.
917 Prosecution Appeal Brief, paras. 6.37-6.42.
918 *Mucić et al.* Sentencing Appeal Judgement, para. 21.
919 Trial Judgement, para. 836.
920 Prosecution Appeal Brief, para. 6.44.
921 *See supra* section V.F.1. (Alleged Errors relating to Sentences: Alleged Sentencing Errors relating to Blagojević).
922 Prosecution Appeal Brief, para. 6.46, citing Trial Judgement, para. 854; Prosecution Appeal Brief, para. 6.49; Prosecution Reply Brief, para. 5.25.

342. The Trial Chamber assessed the evidence that Jokić ensured the boys' safe passage through the minefield in light of the fact that Jokić was convicted for the crime of persecutions, and it considered that this merited mitigation in connection with his crimes involving discriminatory intent.[923] Mere compliance with the law is not ordinarily a factor in assessing an accused's good character, but the Appeals Chamber has noted that a Trial Chamber, in the exercise of its discretion, may credit an accused for fully complying with certain obligations, such as the terms and conditions of an accused's provisional release,[924] or may permissibly credit an accused for preventing the commission of crimes.[925] The Appeals Chamber therefore finds no discernible error in the treatment of Jokić's conduct as a mitigating factor by the Trial Chamber in the exercise of its discretion.

(d) Alleged Error in Crediting Jokić for Co-Operating with the Prosecution

343. The Trial Chamber considered that Jokić co-operated with the Prosecution by appearing for two interviews with the Prosecution and voluntarily surrendering to the International Tribunal and therefore mitigated his sentence.[926] The Prosecution submits in doing so the Trial Chamber abused its discretion because this cooperation was not sufficient to meet the threshold of "substantial cooperation", which the Prosecution claims Rule 101(B)(ii) requires for consideration as a mitigating circumstance.[927] The Prosecution submits that Jokić maintained his innocence and that his statement did not assist the International Tribunal either by limiting the resources required to determine his culpability or by assisting the Prosecution in other areas.[928] Moreover, the Prosecution argues that the evidence from the interviews was not properly before the Trial Chamber because on Blagojević's objection the Trial Chamber decided not to admit transcripts of the interviews into evidence.[929] The Prosecution argues that the Trial Chamber's exclusion of the evidence should have prevented it from considering it for the purposes of determining the sentence.[930] The Prosecution also argues that the Trial Chamber erroneously granted more than a **[page 135]** small amount of weight to Jokić's voluntary surrender because it incorporated the surrender into its finding on his cooperation.[931]

344. The Appeals Chamber recalls that the cooperation of the accused is not

> [A]ssessed solely by reference to the value of the information the accused provides, or that the Trial Chamber should accept the Prosecution assertions that the information provided was not as useful as it might have been. An accused before this Tribunal is not obliged to assist the Prosecution in proving its case, and any evidence of willingness on the part of an accused to be voluntarily interviewed by the Prosecution is evidence of a degree of cooperation that an accused is entitled to withhold, without adverse inference being drawn.[932]

The Trial Chamber, having found that Jokić voluntarily attended the interviews and waived his right to remain silent,[933] was within its discretion to consider his cooperation as a mitigating factor. With respect to the Prosecution's submission that an accused's cooperation must be "substantial" in order to be credited, the Appeals Chamber has previously affirmed that a Trial Chamber may consider less-than-substantial cooperation as a mitigating factor as long as it accords it less weight.[934] The Prosecution does not demonstrate

923 Trial Judgement, para. 854.
924 *See, e.g., Miodrag Jokić* Sentencing Appeal Judgement, para. 82.
925 *See, e.g., Kupreškić et al.* Appeal Judgement, para. 430 (permitting the Trial Chamber's consideration that Josipović stopped soldiers from killing a Muslim civilian woman).
926 Trial Judgement, para. 857.
927 Prosecution Appeal Brief, paras. 6.51, 6.52.
928 Prosecution Appeal Brief, para. 6.52.
929 Prosecution Appeal Brief, para. 6.53.
930 Prosecution Appeal Brief, para. 6.53.
931 Prosecution Appeal Brief, para. 6.54.
932 *Stanišić*, Decision on Prosecution's Appeal Against Decision Granting Provisional Release, para. 14.
933 *Blagojević and Jokić*, Decision on Prosecution's Motion for Clarification of Oral Decision regarding Admissibility of Accused's Statement, para. 9.
934 *See, e.g., Vasiljević* Appeal Judgement, para. 180.

error in the weight accorded by the Trial Chamber to Jokić's cooperation with the Prosecution. Nor does the Prosecution demonstrate error in the weight accorded by the Trial Chamber to Jokić's voluntary surrender. The Prosecution argues that an accused is under an obligation to surrender to the International Tribunal,[935] but this does not mean that doing so may not be considered in mitigation,[936] as the Trial Chamber did here. Although voluntary surrender is not cooperation with the Prosecution *per se*, it is cooperation with the International Tribunal, and the Trial Chamber could consider it a mitigating circumstance. Therefore, the Appeals Chamber dismisses this sub-ground of the appeal.

(e) Alleged Error in Imposing a Manifestly Inadequate Overall Sentence on Jokić

345. The Prosecution submits that the Trial Chamber erred in imposing a manifestly inadequate sentence on Jokić in light of the crimes for which he was convicted and in comparison to the other five persons convicted of participating in the attack on Srebrenica.[937] However, the Appeals Chamber considers that the Prosecution's submissions on this sub-ground fail to address the test for comparing sentences that is articulated clearly in the International Tribunal's jurisprudence. The **[page 136]** Prosecution argues that "in light of the fact that they deal with identical factual scenarios and crime bases" the disparity in sentences makes them "random and unjust",[938] but concedes that Jokić's case is not comparable to any of the cases with which the Prosecution attempts to compare it. Accordingly, the Prosecution has not demonstrated a discernible error in the Trial Chamber's exercise of discretion and, the Appeals Chamber dismisses this sub-ground of appeal.

(f) Conclusion

346. For the foregoing reasons, the Appeals Chamber dismisses the Prosecution's appeal against Jokić's sentence. **[page 137]**

VI. DISPOSITION

For the foregoing reasons, **THE APPEALS CHAMBER**

PURSUANT to Article 25 of the Statute and Rules 117 and 118 of the Rules;

NOTING the respective written submissions of the Parties and the arguments they presented at the hearings of 5 and 6 December 2006;

SITTING in open session;

ALLOWS Blagojević's appeal, in part, with respect to Grounds 6 and 7; **REVERSES** his conviction for Complicity in Genocide (Count 1B); **REDUCES** the sentence of eighteen years' imprisonment imposed on Blagojević by the Trial Chamber to a sentence of fifteen years' imprisonment, subject to credit being given under Rule 101(C) of the Rules for the period Blagojević has already spent in detention; and **DISMISSES** Blagojević's appeal in all other respects, Judge Shahabuddeen dissenting;

DISMISSES Jokić's appeal in its entirety;

DISMISSES the Prosecution's appeal in its entirety;

---

[935] Prosecution Appeal Brief, para. 6.54 (stating that an accused is required to submit themselves to the Tribunal pursuant to an Indictment).

[936] *See Blaškić* Appeal Judgement, para. 701 fn. 1512, citing *Kunarac et al.* Trial Judgement, para. 868 (stating "That an accused may be said to be under an obligation to surrender to the International Tribunal does not mean that doing so should not be considered in mitigation").

[937] Prosecution Appeal Brief, para. 6.56.

[938] Prosecution Appeal Brief, para. 6.57.

ORDERS in accordance with Rule 103(C) and Rule 107 of the Rules, that Blagojević and Jokić are to remain in the custody of the International Tribunal pending the finalization of arrangements for their transfer to the State(s) in which their sentences will be served.

Done in English and French, the English text being authoritative.

Judge Fausto Pocar Presiding	Judge Mohamed Shahabuddeen	Judge Mehmet Güney
Judge Andrésia Vaz		Judge Theodor Meron

Judge Mohamed Shahabuddeen appends a partly dissenting opinion. **[page 138]**

Dated this 9th day of May 2007

At The Hague,

The Netherlands

[Seal of the International Tribunal] [page 139]

VII. PARTLY DISSENTING OPINION OF JUDGE SHAHABUDDEEN

1. I support the judgement of the Appeals Chamber in respect of the appeals by Mr Jokić and the Prosecution. I regret that I am not in the same position in respect of Mr Blagojević's appeal. I consider that Mr Blagojević was unlawfully prevented from telling his story, that this meant that he did not have a fair trial and that, in all the circumstances, his case should be remanded for retrial.[1]

2. Mr Karnavas was appointed on 3 September 2001 as the legal aid counsel for Mr Blagojević. Almost from the beginning, the relationship proved a difficult one. Aspects of the relationship were before the Appeals Chamber on interlocutory appeal. The Appeals Chamber ruled on the matter and Mr Karnavas retained his assignment, but the relationship remained bad. Whatever the origin, in the words of the Appeals Chamber, there was "a complete breakdown in trust and communication, ultimately pervading the entire trial".[2] Mr Blagojević steadfastly refused to recognize Mr Karnavas as his counsel. Mr Karnavas examined and cross-examined witnesses, but it may be inferred that he did so on his own professional appreciation of the case and without instructions from Mr Blagojević.

3. As the trial progressed, Mr Blagojević stated that he wished to testify under oath on his own behalf.[3] According to the Trial Chamber, he said "initially that he would answer all questions put to him in examination-in-chief and cross-examination".[4] But a little later, again according to the Trial Chamber, he made it clear that he "would not conduct any preparations with Mr. Karnavas"[5] and "that he would not answer any questions put to him in direct examination by Mr. Karnavas".[6] "Direct examination" seemed to include any question asked by Mr Karnavas, for what Mr Blagojević had said on 17 June 2004 was that he did not "think that Mr. Karnavas should be allowed to ask me questions".[7]

4. This was in keeping with Mr Blagojević's declared stand, for on 7 April 2004, he had said that, while he wished to testify under oath, he did not "need advice of a lawyer who doesn't wish **[page 140]** me good".[8] The reference was of course to Mr Karnavas. So, while Mr Blagojević said that he needed assistance in preparing his testimony, he had made it clear that he was not thinking of any assistance from Mr Karnavas. Likewise, although he said that he would answer questions put to him by the parties, it was obvious that he did not consider Mr Karnavas a party: his position was that Mr Karnavas should not ask him any questions.[9] That was simple and unmistakable.

5. Of course, Mr Blagojević could have remained silent, or he could have made an unsworn statement, but those courses would not have had the advantage of a statement made by him under oath and subject to being tested in cross-examination. Mr Blagojević pointed this out to the Trial Chamber; he wished to have the benefit of his statement being so regarded. The Trial Chamber also indicated to Mr Blagojević that he could make a sworn statement under the control of the Trial Chamber; but then that statement would not have been tested in cross-examination. In the latter respect, the Trial Chamber stated that the appellant might "make a sworn or unsworn statement under the control of the Trial Chamber, the contents of which he shall not be examined about, pursuant to Rule 84 *bis*".[10]

6. The Trial Chamber was in a difficult position. It assumed that an accused who wished his statement to be tested in cross-examination was under a duty to be examined by his own counsel; therefore an accused

---

1 It is understood of course that the results of a retrial might have conflicted with paragraph 7 of the disposition, in which the Appeals Chamber dismisses all of the Prosecution's grounds of appeal, but this complication need not be considered in view of the Judgement of the Appeals Chamber.

2 Appeals Chamber Judgement, para. 12; *see also ibid.*, para. 15.

3 Decision on Vidoje Blagojević's Oral Request, IT-02-60-T, 30 July 2004, pp. 7-8.

4 *Ibid.*, p. 9.

5 Decision on Vidoje Blagojević's Oral Request, IT-02-60-T, 30 July 2004, p. 10. Mr Blagojević said that Mr "Karnavas is not somebody I can engage in preparations with". See the Trial Chamber's Transcript, 23 July 2004, T. 12273.

6 Decision on Vidoje Blagojević's Oral Request, IT-02-60-T, 30 July 2004, p. 10.

7 Trial Chamber's Transcript, 17 June 2004, T. 10928.

8 Pre-Defence Conference, 7 April 2004, T. 38-42, *quoted in* Decision on Vidoje Blagojević's Oral Request, IT-02-60-T, 30 July 2004, pp. 5-6.

9 The appellant said: "I have to be consistent. I will answer [questions put in direct examination] but not if those questions come from Mr Karnavas". *See* Trial Chamber's Transcript, 23 July 2004, T. 12277.

10 Decision on Vidoje Blagojević's Oral Request, IT-02-60-T, 30 July 2004, p. 10.

who did not comply with that duty lost his right to testify. That was not a duty; it was a right – a right to be assisted by counsel. The accused was free to waive that right, provided he did so knowingly, intelligently and voluntarily. In the circumstances, that right was properly waived; it could be waived without waiving the fundamental right to testify. If not, there is more than eloquence in Justice Frankfurter's remark that to require the acceptance of counsel "is to imprison a man in his privileges and call it the Constitution".[11]

7. It is important to remember that Mr Blagojević was the accused in this case. The Appeals Chamber has recognized that "there is a fundamental difference between being an accused, who might testify as a witness if he so chooses, and a witness", and that not all Rules relating to testimony are applicable to the accused.[12] While Trial Chambers have discretion to "exercise control over the mode and order of interrogating witnesses and presenting evidence,"[13] this **[page 141]** discretion is always "subject to [a] Trial Chamber's obligation to respect the rights of the accused".[14]

8. Mr Blagojević unsuccessfully requested certification to appeal the Trial Chamber's decision refusing to allow him to testify as he wished. I agree with the prosecution when it then said that "the right to appear as a witness in [one's] own defence [...] without question is central to the right to a fair trial" as "the testimony of the accused and the weight it is to be given are critical to the Trial Chamber's overall review and analysis of the evidence in the case".[15] It happens that Mr Blagojević's request for certification to appeal was denied.[16]

9. The Trial Chamber should have permitted Mr Blagojević to give his evidence on his own – under oath and subject to cross-examination. In the event, Mr Blagojević did not tell his story. The Trial Chamber convicted him. Mr Blagojević has appealed, complaining, *inter alia*, that his fundamental right to a fair trial was breached by the failure of the Trial Chamber to hear him. In my opinion, there was such a breach: he could not be convicted without having had an opportunity to tell his own story. His appeal on the point should be allowed.

10. Mr Blagojević asked for a new trial, alternatively to be acquitted on all grounds.[17] In the circumstances, I am of the view that his first request should be granted: his case should be remanded for retrial. **[page 142]**

Done in English and French, the English text being authoritative.

Dated this 9th day of May 2007,
The Hague,
The Netherlands

Mohamed Shahabuddeen

[Seal of the International Tribunal] [page 143]

11 *Adams v. United States* 317 U.S. 269, 280 (1942).

12 *Galić*, IT-98-29-A, Judgement, 30 November 2006 ("*Galić* Appeal Judgement"), para. 17.

13 *See* Rule 90(F) of the Rules of Procedure and Evidence of the International Tribunal.

14 *Galić* Appeal Judgement, para. 18.

15 Prosecution's Additional Submission on Vidoje Blagojević's Request for Certification to Appeal and Request for Modification of the Trial Chamber's Decision on Vidoje Blagojević's Oral Request, IT-02-60-T, 27 August 2004, pp. 3-4.

16 *See* Decision on Request for Certification to Appeal the Trial Chamber's Decision in Vidoje Blagojević's Oral Request & Request for the Appointment of an Independent Counsel for this Interlocutory Appeal Should Certification be Granted, IT-02-60-T, 2 September 2004.

17 *See* Defence of Accused Mr Vidoje Blagojević Brief on Appeal, IT-02-60-A, 20 October 2005, pp. 77-78.

VIII. ANNEX A – PROCEDURAL BACKGROUND

A. Pre-Trial and Trial Proceedings

1. Vidoje Blagojević was indicted on 30 October 1998; the indictment was subsequently amended on 27 October 1999.[1] He was arrested by SFOR on 10 August 2001 in Banja Luka and was transferred to the UNDU the same day.[2] At his initial appearance before Judge Liu Daqun on 16 August 2001, he pleaded not guilty to all counts and was ordered detained on remand.[3] His case was assigned to Trial Chamber III.[4]

2. Dragan Jokić was indicted on 28 May 2001.[5] He surrendered on 15 August 2001 and appeared before Judge Liu on 21 August 2001, pleading not guilty to all counts.[6] The case was assigned to Trial Chamber I.[7]

3. On 11 September 2001, the Prosecutor filed a motion to join the indictments of Blagojević and Jokić together with that of Dragan Obrenović, who was also charged in relation with the events following the fall of Srebrenica.[8] Notwithstanding the opposition of the three accused, Trial Chamber II ordered the joinder of the indictments.[9] To reflect the joinder, the Prosecutor submitted an amended indictment on 22 January 2002. Following a Prosecution motion,[10] Trial Chamber II issued a decision on 17 May 2002 to try Momir Nikolić jointly with Blagojević, Jokić, and Obrenović.[11]

4. Nikolić and Obrenović pleaded guilty and were sentenced to imprisonment for twenty-seven and seventeen years, respectively.[12] **[page 144]**

5. Jokić filed a motion for provisional release,[13] which Trial Chamber II denied.[14] Jokić appealed the decision;[15] the Appeals Chamber granted the appeal and ordered his provisional release subject to specific terms and conditions.[16] Blagojević also filed an application for provisional release,[17] which Trial Chamber II denied.[18] Blagojević appealed the decision, and the Appeals Chamber remanded the matter to the Trial Chamber for further consideration in light of Republika of Srpska guarantees in connection with the applications.[19] The Trial Chamber issued a second decision denying release, as it was not satisfied that the accused would return to stand trial.[20] The Appeals Chamber confirmed this decision.[21]

---

1 *Prosecutor v. Vidoje Blagojević*, Case No. IT-98-33/1-1, Amended Indictment, 27 October 1999.

2 *Prosecutor v. Vidoje Blagojević,* Case No. IT-98-33/1-1, Order of the President Assigning a Case to a Trial Chamber, 16 August 2001.

3 *Prosecutor v. Vidoje Blagojević,* Case No. IT-98-33-/1, Order for Detention on Remand, 16 August 2001.

4 *Id.*

5 *Prosecutor v. Dragan Jokić*, Case No. IT-01-44-I, Indictment. The indictment was filed on 31 May 2001.

6 *Prosecutor v. Dragan Jokić*, Case No. IT-01-44-I, Initial Appearance Transcript, 21 August 2001.

7 *Prosecutor v. Dragan Jokić*, Case No. IT-01-44-I, Order of the President, 16 August 2001.

8 *Prosecutor v. Dragan Obrenović*, Case No. IT-01-43. Obrenović was arrested on 15 April 2001 and after his initial appearance on 18 April 2001, his case was assigned to Trial Chamber II on 23 November 2001.

9 Written Reasons Following Oral Decision of 15 January 2002 on the Prosecution's Motion for Joinder, 16 January 2002.

10 *Prosecutor v. Vidoje Blagojević et al.*, Case No. IT-02-53-PT, Prosecution Motion for Joinder and to Stay the Deadline for the Accused Blagojević, Obrenović and Jokić to Challenge the Joinder Indictment in Case IT-02-53-PT, 3 April 2002.

11 *Prosecutor v. Momir Nikolić*, Case No. IT-02-56-PT, Decision on Prosecution's Motion for Joinder, 17 May 2002. The Indictment was confirmed on 28 March 2002, para. 3.

12 *Prosecutor v. Nikolić*, Sentencing Judgement, Case No. IT-02-60/1-S, 2 December 2003, para. 183; *Prosecutor v. Obrenović*, Sentencing Judgement, Case No. IT-02-60/2-S, 10 December 2003, para. 156.

13 *Prosecutor v. Dragan Jokić*, Case No. IT-01-44-PT, Proposal for a Provisional Release from Prison for the Defendant Dragan Jokić, 10 January 2002.

14 *Prosecutor v. Vidoje Blagojević et al.*, Case No. IT-02-53, Decision on Request for Provisional Release of Accused Jokić, 28 March 2002.

15 *Prosecutor v. Vidoje Blagojević et al.*, Case No. IT-02-53-AR65, Dragan Jokić's Appeal of Trial Chamber's Denial of Request for Provisional Release, 3 May 2002.

16 *Prosecutor v. Vidoje Blagojević et al.*, Case No. IT-02-53-AR65, Decision on Application from Dragan Jokić for Provisional Release, 28 May 2002.

17 *Prosecutor v. Blagojević et al.*, Case No. IT-02-60-PT, Pre-Trial Provisional Release Request of Accused Blagojević, 17 July 2002.

18 *Qrosecutor v. Blagojević et al.*, Case No. IT-02-60-PT, Decision on Vidoje Blagojević's Application for Provisional Release, 23 July 2002.

19 *Prosecutor v. Blagojević et al.*, Case Nos. IT-02-60-AR65 & IT-02-60-AR65.2, Decision on Provisional Release of Vidoje Blagojević and Dragan Obrenović, 3 October 2002.

20 *Prosecutor v. Blagojević et al.*, Case No. IT-02-60-PT, Decision on Vidoje Blagojević's Application for Provisional Release, 19 November 2002.

21 *Prosecutor v. Vidoje Blagojević et al.*, Case No. IT-02-53-AR65.4, Decision on Provisional Release Application by

6. On 1 April 2003, the President of the International Tribunal transferred the case from Trial Chamber II to Trial Chamber I.[22] The Bench consisted of Judge Liu Daqun, Presiding, Judge Volodymyr Vassylenko, and Judge Carmen Maria Argibay.[23]

7. On 23 June 2003, the Prosecution filed a motion requesting that the Trial Chamber take judicial notice of 419 facts and 165 pieces of documentary evidence from the Trial Chamber Judgement in *Prosecutor v. Radislav Krstić* (IT-98-33-T).[24] The Trial Chamber admitted only the facts and documentary evidence which had been agreed upon by the Parties, but declined to admit into evidence or take judicial notice of the remaining facts and documents proposed in the motion.[25]

8. The trial commenced on 14 May 2003.[26] The Trial Chamber heard the evidence of forty-eight Prosecution witnesses and admitted the evidence of thirty-seven witnesses pursuant to Rule **[page 145]** 92*bis* of the Rules.[27] Obrenović and Nikolić, the former co-accused, also testified.[28] In addition, the Prosecution case comprised eighteen experts and more than 800 exhibits.[29]

9. Following the conclusion of the Prosecution case on 2 March 2004, Blagojević and Jokić filed motions for full acquittals under Rule 98*bis* of the Rules.[30] The Trial Chamber entered a judgement of acquittal for Blagojević on Counts 2 to 4 of the Indictment, insofar as his individual criminal responsibility was alleged under Article 7(1) for planning, instigating, ordering, and committing the crimes.[31] The Trial Chamber further entered a judgement of acquittal on Counts 5 and 6 of the Indictment, insofar as Blagojević's individual criminal responsibility was alleged under Article 7(1) for planning, instigating, and ordering the crimes.[32] Jokić was acquitted on Counts 2 to 5 of the Indictment, insofar as his individual criminal responsibility was alleged under Article 7(1) for planning, instigating, and ordering the crimes.[33]

10. The Defence case started on 14 April 2004.[34] In total, fifty-six Defence witnesses were heard, and the statements of twenty witnesses were admitted pursuant to Rule 92*bis* of the Rules.[35]

11. Closing arguments for the Prosecution were heard on 29 September 2004.[36] Closing arguments for Blagojević and Jokić were heard respectively on 30 September 2004 and 1 October 2004.[37]

12. The Trial Chamber delivered its Judgement orally on 17 January 2005; the written Judgement was filed on 24 January 2005. The Trial Chamber found Blagojević not guilty of extermination (Count 2) and guilty, pursuant to Article 7(1) of the Statute, of complicity to commit genocide (Count 1B), murder as a crime against humanity (Count 3), murder as a violation of the laws or customs of war (Count 4), persecutions as a crime against humanity (Count 5), and inhumane acts (Count 6).[38] The Trial Chamber sentenced him to a single sentence of imprisonment for eighteen years.[39] **[page 146]**

Blagojević, 17 February 2003.

[22] *Prosecutor v. Vidoje Blagojević et al.*, Case No. IT-02-60-PT, Order Assigning Judges to a Case before a Trial Chamber, 1 April 2003.

[23] *Id.*

[24] Prosecution's Motion for Judicial Notice of Adjudicated Facts and Documentary Evidence, 23 June 2003.

[25] *Prosecutor v. Vidoje Blagojević et al.*, Case No. IT-02-60-T, Decision on Prosecution's Motion for Judicial Notice of Adjudicated Facts and Documentary Evidence, 19 December 2003, paras. 19-27, § IV.

[26] Trial Judgement, para. 898.

[27] *Id.*

[28] *See* T. 1, 2, 6-9 October 2003 (Obrenović). *See* T. 19, 22-23, 25-26, 29 September 2003 (Nikolić).

[29] Trial Judgement, para. 901.

[30] Vidoje Blagojević's Motion for Judgement of Acquittal Pursuant to Rule 98*bis*, Case No. IT-02-60-T, 2 March 2004; Redacted Defendant Dragan Jokić's Motion for Acquittal Pursuant to Rule 98*bis*, Case No. IT-02-60-T, 2 March 2004.

[31] *Prosecutor v. Vidoje Blagojević et al.*, Case No. IT-02-60-T, Judgement on Motions for Acquittal Pursuant to Rule 98*bis*, 5 April 2004, para. 47, § IV Disposition.

[32] *Id.*, paras. 54-59, § IV Disposition.

[33] *Id.*, para. 72, § IV Disposition.

[34] Trial Judgment, paras. 903-905.

[35] *Id.*

[36] *Id.*, para. 909

[37] *Id.*

[38] *Id.*, § X.

[39] *Id.*

13. The Trial Chamber declined to enter a conviction against Jokić for murder as a crime against humanity (Count 3).[40] Jokić was found guilty, pursuant to Article 7(1) of the Statute, of extermination as a crime against humanity (Count 2), murder as a violation of the laws and customs of war (Count 4), and persecutions as a crime against humanity (Count 5).[41] Jokić was sentenced to a single sentence of imprisonment for nine years.[42]

B. The Appeals

1. Extension of Time for Notices of Appeal

14. On 3 February 2005, the Prosecution filed a motion for extension of time in which to file its Notice of Appeal.[43] On 7 February 2005, Jokić requested an extension of time for the filing of his Notice of Appeal.[44] On 16 February 2005, Blagojević also requested an extension of time for the filing of his Notice of Appeal.[45] The Pre-Appeal Judge granted the Prosecution's and Jokić's motions in part, and ordered the parties to file their Notices of Appeal no later than 23 February 2005.[46] Blagojević was granted leave to file his Notice of Appeal no later than 26 April 2005.[47]

2. Assignment of Judges

15. On 14 February 2005, the President of the International Tribunal assigned Judge Theodor Meron, Judge Fausto Pocar, Judge Mohamed Shahabuddeen, Judge Mehmet Güney, and Judge Inés Mónica Weinberg de Roca to the case, designating Judge Shahabuddeen to serve as the Pre-Appeal Judge.[48] On 15 July 2005 Judge Andrésia Vaz was assigned to the Bench to replace Judge Weinberg de Roca effective 15 August 2005.[49] **[page 147]**

3. Notices of Appeal

16. The Prosecution filed its Notice of Appeal on 23 February 2005.[50] Jokić filed his Notice of Appeal on 23 February 2005[51] and an Amended Notice of Appeal on 25 February 2005.[52] Blagojević was granted two further extensions of time[53] and filed his Notice of Appeal on 31 May 2005.[54]

---

40 *Id.*

41 *Id.*

42 *Id.*

43 Prosecution Motion for Extension of Time in which to File Prosecution Notice of Appeal, 3 February 2005.

44 Defence Motion for Extension of Time in which to File Defence Notice of Appeal, 7 February 2005.

45 Vidoje Blagojević's Expedited Motion for Extension of Time in which to File his Notice of Appeal, 16 February 2005.

46 *Prosecutor v. Vidoje Blagojević et al.*, Case No. IT-02-60-A, Decision on Prosecution Motion for Extension of Time in which to File the Prosecution Notice of Appeal, 15 February 2005; *Prosecutor v. Vidoje Blagojević et al.*, Case No. IT-02-60-A, Decision on Defence Motion for Extension of Time in which to File the Defence Notice of Appeal, 15 February 2005.

47 *Prosecutor v. Vidoje Blagojević et al.*, Case No. IT-02-60-A, Decision on Vidoje Blagojević' Expedited Motion for Extension of Time in which to File his Notice of Appeal, 16 February 2005.

48 *Prosecutor v. Vidoje Blagojević et al.*, Case No. IT-02-60-A, Order Assigning Judges to a Case Before the Appeals Chamber, 14 February 2005.

49 *Prosecutor v. Vidoje Blagojević et al.*, Case No. IT-02-60-A, Order Replacing a Judge in a Case Before the Appeals Chamber, 15 July 2005.

50 *Prosecutor v. Vidoje Blagojević et al.*, Case No. IT-02-60-A, Prosecutor's Notice of Appeal, 23 February 2005.

51 *Prosecutor v. Vidoje Blagojević et al.*, Case No. IT-02-60-A, Defendant's Notice of Appeal, 23 February 2005.

52 *Prosecutor v. Vidoje Blagojević et al.*, Case No. IT-02-60-A, Defendant's Amended Notice of Appeal, 25 February 2005.

53 *Prosecutor v. Vidoje Blagojević et al.*, Case No. IT-02-60-A, Decision on Vidoje Blagojević's Expedited Motion for Extension of Time in which to File his Notice of Appeal, 16 February 2005; Decision on Vidoje Blagojević's Motion for Extension of Time in which to File his Notice of Appeal & on Dragan Jokić's Notion for and Extension of Time in which to File his Appeal Brief, 14 April 2005.

54 *Prosecutor v. Vidoje Blagojević et al.*, Case No. IT-02-60-A, Defence of Accused Mr. Vidoje Blagojević Notice of Appeal, 31 May 2005.

4. Appeal Briefs

(a) Prosecution

17. The Prosecution filed its Appeal Brief on 9 May 2005.[55]On 6 June 2005, the Prosecution sought leave amend its Notice of Appeal in relation to Blagojević,[56] which was granted on 20 July 2005.[57]

18. On 5 July 2005, the Prosecution filed a single Reply Brief to the Respondent's Briefs of Blagojević and Jokić.[58]

19. On 9 December 2005, the Prosecution responded to Blagojević's and Jokić's Appeal Briefs.[59]

20. On 20 July 2006, the Prosecution filed its Amended Consolidated Response Brief.[60]

(b) Blagojević

21. On 25 May 2005, Blagojević filed a request for an extension of time.[61] On 1 June 2005 the Pre-Appeal Judge denied this request.[62] **[page 148]**

22. On 20 June 2005, Blagojević filed his Respondent's Brief.[63]

23. On 5 October 2005, the Pre-Appeal Judge extended the time for Blagojević to file his Appeal Brief until 20 October 2005.[64] Blagojević filed his Appeal Brief on 20 October 2005.[65]

24. On 27 December 2005, Blagojević filed his Brief in Reply.[66]

(c) Jokić

25. On 26 May 2005, Jokić filed a request for an extension of time.[67] On 1 June 2005, the Pre-Appeal Judge denied this request.[68] On 20 June 2005, Jokić filed his Respondent's Brief.[69]

---

55 *Prosecutor v. Vidoje Blagojević et al.*, Case No. IT-02-60-A, Prosecution Appeal Brief, 9 May 2005.

56 Request for Leave to Amend Notice of Appeal in Relation to Vidoje Blagojević, 6 June 2005.

57 *Prosecutor v. Vidoje Blagojević et al.*, Case No. IT-02-60-A, Decision on Prosecution's Request for Leave to Amend Notice of Appeal in Relation to Vidoje Blagojević, 20 July 2005.

58 *Prosecutor v. Vidoje Blagojević et al.*, Case No. IT-02-60-A, Prosecution's Brief in Reply, 5 July 2005.

59 Prosecution Response to Appeal Brief of Vidoje Blagojević, 9 December 2005, as corrected by Corrigendum of 16 December 2005 to read Prosecution Consolidated Response to Appeal Briefs of Vidoje Blagojević and Dragan Jokić.

60 Prosecution Amended Consolidated Response Brief (Confidential and Partly *Ex Parte*), 20 July 2006. A public, redacted version of the Response Brief was filed on 4 August 2006.

61 Defence of Accused Mr. Vidoje Blagojević Motion for Extension of Time Limit in which to File a Respondent's Brief, 25 May 2005.

62 *Prosecutor v. Vidoje Blagojević et al.*, Case No. IT-02-60-A, Decision on Appellants' Motions for Extension of Time in which to File their Responses to the Prosecutor's Appeal Brief, 1 June 2005.

63 Response Brief of Dragan Jokić, 20 June 2005; Defence of Accused Mr. Vidoje Blagojević Response Brief on Prosecution's Brief on Appeal Filed on 9 May 2005, 20 June 2005.

64 *Prosecutor v. Vidoje Blagojević et al.*, Case No. IT-02-60-A, Decision on Blagojević's Motion for Extension of Time in which to File his Appeal's Brief, 5 October 2005.

65 Defence of Accused Mr. Vidoje Blagojević Brief on Appeal, 20 October 2005.

66 Defence of Vidoje Blagojević Response to Prosecution Response to Appeal Brief of Vidoje Blagojević (Confidential), 27 December 2005. A public, redacted version of the Response was filed on 28 December 2005.

67 Appellant, Dragan Jokic's Motion for Extension of Time to File Respondent's Brief Pursuant to Rule 112, 26 May 2005.

68 *Prosecutor v. Vidoje Blagojević et al.*, Case No. IT-02-60-A, Decision on Appellants' Motions for Extension of Time in which to File their Responses to the Prosecutor's Appeal Brief, 1 June 2005.

69 Response Brief of Dragan Jokić, 20 June 2005; Defence of Accused Mr. Vidoje Blagojević Response_Brief_on_Prosecution's Brief on Appeal Filed on 9 May 2005, 20 June 2005.

26. On 8 September 2005, the Pre-Appeal Judge granted Jokić's motion for an extension of time to file his Appeal Brief until 4 October 2005.[70] Jokić filed his Appeal Brief on 4 October 2005.[71]

27. On 2 December 2005, Jokić filed an Amended Notice of Appeal[72] along with an Amended Appeal Brief,[73] after the Appeals Chamber had granted him leave to amend on 24 November 2005.[74]

28. On 6 July 2006, Jokić filed his Third Amended Notice of Appeal and an Amended Appeal Brief[75] after being granted leave to do so by the Appeal Chamber on 26 June 2006.[76]

29. Jokić filed his Reply on 2 August 2006.[77] **[page 149]**

5. Status Conferences

30. Status Conferences in accordance with Rule 65*bis* of the Rules were held on 20 February 2005, 17 June 2005, 23 September 2005, 13 March 2006, 28 April 2006, 23 August 2006, and 30 January 2007.

6. Hearing of the Appeals

31. Pursuant to the Scheduling Order of 10 November 2006, the hearing of the appeals took place on 5 and 6 December 2006. **[page 150]**

IX. ANNEX B – CITED MATERIALS AND DEFINED TERMS

A. Jurisprudence

1. ICTY

Aleksovski

Prosecutor v. Zlatko Aleksovski, Case No. IT-95-14/1-A, Judgement, 30 May 2001 ("*Aleksovski* Appeal Judgement").

Babić

Prosecutor v. Milan Babić, Case No. IT-03-72-A, Judgement on Sentencing Appeal, 18 July 2005, ("*Babić* Sentencing Appeal Judgement").

Blagojević and Jokić

Prosecutor v. Vidoje Blagojević, Case No. IT-98-33/1-PT, Decision, 5 September 2001, dated 3 September 2001 ("*Blagojević*, Decision by the Registrar, 5 September 2001").

Prosecutor v. Vidoje Blagojević et al., Case No. IT-02-60-PT, Decision on Oral Motion to Replace Co-Counsel, 9 December 2002 ("*Blagojević et al.*, Decision on Oral Motion to Replace Co-Counsel").

Prosecutor v. Vidoje Blagojević et al., Case No. IT-02-60-PT, Decision, 8 April 2003 ("*Blagojević et al.*, Decision by the Registrar, 8 April 2003").

---

70 *Prosecutor v. Vidoje Blagojević et al.*, Case No. IT-02-60-A, Decision on Jokić's Motion for Extension of Time, 8 September 2005.

71 Appeal Brief of Dragan Jokić, 4 October 2005.

72 Second Amended Notice of Appeal, 2 December 2005.

73 Amended Appeal Brief of Dragan Jokić, 2 December 2005.

74 *Prosecutor v. Vidoje Blagojević et al.*, Case No. IT-02-60-A, Decision on Motions Related to the Pleadings in Dragan Jokić's Appeal, 24 November 2005, paras. 26–30.

75 Third Amended Appellate Brief of Dragan Jokić, 6 July 2006.

76 *Prosecutor v. Vidoje Blagojević et al.,* Case No. IT-02-60-A, Decision on Motion of Dragan Jokić for Leave to File Third Amended Notice of Appeal and Amended Appellate Brief, 26 June 2006, paras. 42–45.

77 Reply of Dragan Jokić to Prosecution Amended Consolidated Response Brief (20 July 2006) (Confidential), 2 August 2006.

Prosecutor v. Vidoje Blagojević and Dragan Jokić, Case No. IT-02-60-T, First Decision on Prosecution's Motion for Admission of Witness Statements and Prior Testimony Pursuant to Rule 92*bis*, 12 June 2003 ("*Blagojević and Jokić*, First Rule 92*bis* Decision").

Prosecutor v. Vidoje Blagojević and Dragan Jokić, Case No. IT-02-60-T, Decision on Independent Counsel for Vidoje Blagojević's Motion to Instruct the Registrar to Appoint New Lead and Co-Counsel, 3 July 2003 ("*Blagojević and Jokić*, Decision on Independent Counsel for Vidoje Blagojević's Motion to Instruct the Registrar to Appoint New Lead and Co-Counsel").

Prosecutor v. Vidoje Blagojević and Dragan Jokić, Case No. IT-02-60-T, Decision on Prosecution's Motion for Clarification of Oral Decision regarding Admissibility of Accused's Statement, 18 September 2003 ("*Blagojević and Jokić*, Decision on Prosecution's Motion for Clarification of Oral Decision regarding Admissibility of Accused's Statement"). **[page 151]**

Prosecutor v. Vidoje Blagojević, Case No. IT-02-60-AR73.4, *Ex Parte* and Confidential Reasons for Decisions on Appeal by Vidoje Blagojević to Replace his Defence Team, 7 November 2003 ("*Blagojević*, *Ex Parte* and Confidential Reasons for Decisions on Appeal by Vidoje Blagojević to Replace his Defence Team").

Prosecutor v. Vidoje Blagojević and Dragan Jokić, Case No. IT-02-60-T, Decision on Vidoje Blagojević's Oral Request, 30 July 2004 ("*Blagojević and Jokić*, Decision on Vidoje Blagojević's Oral Request").

Prosecutor v. Vidoje Blagojević and Dragan Jokić, Case No. IT-02-60-A, Decision on Motion to Strike Ground One of Jokić Appeal Brief, 31 August 2006 ("*Blagojević and Jokić*, Decision on Motion to Strike").

Blaškić

Prosecutor v. Tihomir Blaškić, Case No. IT-95-14-A, Judgement, 29 July 2004 ("*Blaškić* Appeal Judgement").

Brđanin

Prosecutor v. Radoslav Brđanin, Case No. IT-99-36-A, Judgement, 3 April 2007 (*Brđanin* Appeal Judgement).

Čelebići

Prosecutor v. Zejnil Delalić, Zdravko Mucić, a.k.a. "Pavo", Hazim Delić and Esad Landzo, a.k.a. "Zenga", Case No. IT-96-21-A, Judgment, 20 February 2001 ("*Čelebići* Appeal Judgement").

Deronjić

Prosecutor v. Miroslav Deronjić, Case No. IT-02-61-A, Judgement on Sentencing Appeal, 20 July 2005 ("*Deronjić* Sentencing Appeal Judgement").

Furundžija

Prosecutor v. Anto Furundžija, Case No. IT-95-17/1-T, Judgement, 10 December 1998 ("*Furundžija* Trial Judgement").

Prosecutor v. Anto Furundžija, Case No. IT-95-17/1-A, Judgement, 21 July 2000 ("*Furundžija* Appeal Judgement"). **[page 152]**

Galić

Prosecutor v. Stanislav Galić, Case No. IT-98-29-AR73.2, Decision on Interlocutory Appeal Concerning Rule 92*bis*(C), 7 June 2002 ("*Galić*, Rule 92*bis* Decision").

Prosecutor v. Stanislav Galić, Case No. IT-98-29-A, Judgement, 30 November 2006 ("*Galić* Appeal Judgement").

Hadžihasanović et al.

Prosecutor v. Enver Hadžihasanović et al., Case No. IT-01-47-AR72, Decision on Interlocutory Appeal Challenging Jurisdiction in Relation to Command Responsibility, 16 July 2003 ("*Hadžihasanović et al.*, Decision on Interlocutory Appeal Challenging Jurisdiction in Relation to Command Responsibility").

Halilović

Prosecutor v. Sefer Halilović, Case No. IT-01-48-AR73.2, Decision on Interlocutory Appeal Concerning Admission of Record of Interview of the Accused from the Bar Table, 19 August 2005 ("*Halilović*, Decision on Interlocutory Appeal Concerning Admission of Record of Interview of the Accused from the Bar Table").

Jelisić

Prosecutor v. Goran Jelisić, Case No. IT-95-10-A, Judgement, 5 July 2001 ("*Jelisić* Appeal Judgement").

Miodrag Jokić

Prosecutor v. Miodrag Jokić, Case No. IT-01-42/1-S, Sentencing Judgement, 18 March 2004 ("*Miodrag Jokić* Sentencing Judgement").

Prosecutor v. Miodrag Jokić, Case No. IT-01-42/1-A, Judgement on Sentencing Appeal, 30 August 2005 ("*Miodrag Jokić* Sentencing Appeal Judgement").

Kordić and Čerkez

Prosecutor v. Dario Kordić and Mario Čerkez, Case No. IT-95-14/2-A, Judgement, 17 December 2004 ("*Kordić and Čerkez* Appeal Judgement"). **[page 153]**

Krnojelac

Prosecutor v. Milorad Krnojelac, Case No. IT-97-25-A, Judgement, 17 September 2003 ("*Krnojelac* Appeal Judgement").

Krstić

Prosecutor v. Radislav Krstić, Case No. IT-98-33-T, Judgement, 2 August 2001 ("*Krstić* Trial Judgement").

Prosecutor v. Radislav Krstić, Case No. IT-98-33-A, Judgement, 19 April 2004 ("*Krstić* Appeal Judgement").

Kunarac et al.

Prosecutor v. Dragoljub Kunarac et al., Case No. IT-96-23 and IT-96-23/1-T, Judgement, 22 February 2001 ("*Kunarac et al.* Trial Judgement").

Prosecutor v. Dragoljub Kunarac et al., Case No. IT-96-23&IT-96-23/1-A, Judgement, 12 June 2002 ("*Kunarac et al.* Appeal Judgement").

Kupreškić et al.

Prosecutor v. Zoran Kupreškić et al., Case No. IT-95-16-A, Judgement, 23 October 2001 ("*Kupreškić et al.* Appeal Judgement").

Kvočka et al.

Prosecutor v. Miroslav Kvočka et al., Case No. IT-98-30/1-A, Judgement, 28 February 2005 ("*Kvočka et al.* Appeal Judgement").

Mejakić et al.

Prosecutor v. Zeljko Mejakić et al., Case No. IT-02-65-PT, Decision on Prosecutor's Motion for Referral of Case Pursuant to Rule 11*bis*, 20 July 2005 ("*Mejakić et al.*, Decision on Prosecutor's Motion for Referral of Case Pursuant to Rule 11*bis*").

Prosecutor v. Zeljko Mejakić et al., Case No. IT-02-65-AR73.1, Decision on Appeal by the Prosecution to Resolve Conflict of Interest Regarding Attorney Jovan Simić, 6 October 2004 ("*Mejakić et al.*, Decision on Appeal by the Prosecution to Resolve Conflict of Interest Regarding Attorney Jovan Simić"). **[page 154]**

Mucić et al.

Prosecutor v. Zdravko Mucić et al., Case No. IT-96-21-A*bis*, Judgement on Sentence Appeal, 8 April 2003 ("*Mucić et al.* Sentencing Appeal Judgement").

Dragan Nikolić

Prosecutor v. Dragan Nikolić, Case No. IT-94-2-A, Judgement on Sentencing Appeal, 4 February 2005 ("*Dragan Nikolić* Sentencing Appeal Judgement").

Momir Nikolić

Prosecutor v. Momir Nikolić, Case No. IT-02-60/1-A, Judgement on Sentencing Appeal, 8 March 2006 ("*Momir Nikolić* Sentencing Appeal Judgement").

Naletilić and Martinović

Prosecutor v. Mladen Naletilić and Vinko Martinović, Case No. IT-98-34-A, Judgement, 3 May 2006 ("*Naletilić and Martinović* Appeal Judgement").

Plavsić

Prosecutor v. Biljana Plavsić, Case No. IT-00-39&40/1, Sentencing Judgement, 27 February 2003 ("*Plavsić* Sentencing Judgement").

Simić

Prosecutor v. Blagoje Simić, Case No. IT-95-9-A, Judgement, 28 November 2006 ("*Simić* Appeal Judgement").

Stakić

Prosecutor v. Milomir Stakić, Case No. IT-97-24, Judgement, 21 July 2003 ("*Stakić* Trial Judgement").

Prosecutor v. Milomir Stakić, Case No. IT-97-24-A, Judgement, 22 March 2006 ("*Stakić* Appeal Judgement"). **[page 155]**

Stanišić

Prosecutor v. Jovica Stanišić, Case No. IT-03-69-AR65.1, Decision on Prosecution's Appeal Against Decision Granting Provisional Release, 17 October 2005 ("*Stanišić*, Decision on Prosecution's Appeal Against Decision Granting Provisional Release").

Tadić

Prosecutor v. Duško Tadić a/k/a "Dule", Case No. IT-94-1-T, Opinion and Judgement, 7 May 1997 ("*Tadić* Trial Judgement").

Prosecutor v. Duško Tadić a/k/a "Dule", Case No. IT-94-1-A, Decision on Appellant's Motion for the Extension of the Time-Limit and Admission of Additional Evidence, 16 October 1998 ("*Tadić*, Decision on Appellant's Motion for the Extension of the Time-Limit and Admission of Additional Evidence").

Prosecutor v. Duško Tadić a/k/a "Dule", Case No. IT-94-1-A, Judgement, 15 July 1999 ("*Tadić* Appeal Judgement").

Prosecutor v. Duško Tadić a/k/a "Dule", Case No. IT-94-1-A and IT-94-1-A*bis*, Judgement in Sentencing Appeals, 26 January 2000 ("*Tadić* Sentencing Appeal Judgement").

Todović

Prosecutor v. Savo Todović, Case No. IT-97-25/1-AR11*bis*.1, Decision on Rule 11 *bis* Referral, 23 February 2006 ("*Todović*, Decision on Rule 11 *bis* Referral").

Vasiljević

Prosecutor v. Mitar Vasiljević, Case No. IT-98-32-A, Judgement, 25 February 2004 ("*Vasiljević* Appeal Judgement").

2. ICTR

Akayesu

The Prosecutor v. Jean-Paul Akayesu, Case No. ICTR-96-4-A, Judgement, 1 June 2001 ("*Akayesu* Appeal Judgement"). **[page 156]**

Kajelijeli

Juvénal Kajelijeli v. The Prosecutor, Case No. ICTR-98-44A-A, Judgement, 23 May 2005 ("*Kajelijeli* Appeal Judgement").

Kambanda

Jean Kambanda v. The Prosecutor, Case No. ICTR-97-24-A, Judgement, 19 October 2000 ("*Kambanda* Appeal Judgement").

Kamuhanda

Jean de Dieu Kamuhanda v. The Prosecutor, Case No. ICTR-95-54A-A, Appeal Judgement, 19 September 2005 ("*Kamuhanda* Appeal Judgement").

Kayishema and Ruzindana

The Prosecutor v. Clément Kayishema and Obed Ruzindana, Case No. ICTR-95-1-A, Judgement (Reasons), 1 June 2001 ("*Kayishema and Ruzindana* Appeal Judgement").

Musema

Alfred Musema v. The Prosecutor, Case No. ICTR-96-13-A, Judgement, 16 November 2001 ("*Musema* Appeal Judgement").

Nahimana et al.

Ferdinand Nahimana et al. v. The Prosecutor, Case No. ICTR-99-52-A, Decision on Appellant Jean-Bosco Barayagwiza's Motion Contesting the Decision of the President Refusing to Review and Reverse the Decision of the Registrar Relating to the Withdrawal of Co-Counsel, 23 November 2006 ("*Nahimana et al.*, Decision on Appellant Jean-Bosco Barayagwiza's Motion Contesting the Decision of the President Refusing to Review and Reverse the Decision of the Registrar Relating to the Withdrawal of Co-Counsel").

Niyitegeka

Eliézer Niyitegeka v. The Prosecutor, Case No. ICTR-96-14-A, Judgement, 9 July 2004 ("*Niyitegeka* Appeal Judgement"). **[page 157]**

Ntagerura et al.

The Prosecutor v. André Ntagerura et al., Case No. ICTR-99-46-A, Arrêt, 7 July 2006 ("*Ntagerura et al.* Appeal Judgement").

Ntakirutimana

The Prosecutor v. Elizaphan Ntakirutimana and Gérard Ntakirutimana, Cases Nos. ICTR-96-10-A and ICTR-96-17-A, Appeal Judgement, 13 December 2004 ("*Ntakirutimana* Appeal Judgement").

Semanza

Laurent Semanza v. The Prosecutor, Case No. ICTR-97-20-A, Judgement, 20 May 2005 ("*Semanza* Appeal Judgement").

3. International Court of Justice

Case Concerning the Application of the Convention on the Prevention and Punishment of the Crime of Genocide (Bosnia and Herzegovina v. Serbia and Montenegro), Judgement of 26 February 2007 ("*Case Concerning the Application of the Convention on the Prevention and Punishment of the Crime of Genocide*, Judgement").

B. Defined Terms and Abbreviations

28th Division

28th Division of the Army of Bosnia-Herzegovina

ABiH

Army of Bosnia-Herzegovina

BiH

Bosnia and Herzegovina

Blagojević Appeal Brief

Defence of Accused Mr. Vidoje Blagojević Brief on Appeal (Partly Confidential – Annex A), filed 20 October 2005 **[page 158]**

Blagojević Defence

Vidoje Blagojević, and/or Blagojević's Counsel

Blagojević Notice of Appeal

Defence of Mr. Vidoje Blagojević Notice of Appeal, filed 31 May 2005

Blagojević Response Brief

Defence of Accused Mr. Vidoje Blagojević Response Brief on Prosecution's Brief on Appeal, filed 20 June 2005

Directive on Assignment of Defence Counsel

Directive on Assignment of Defence Counsel, Rev. 11, 11 July 2006.

DutchBat

Dutch Battalion of UNPROFOR

Ex. D

Defence Exhibit

Ex. P

Prosecution Exhibit

ICTR

International Criminal Tribunal for the Prosecution of Persons Responsible for Genocide and Other Serious Violations of International Humanitarian Law Committed in the Territory of Rwanda and Rwandan Citizens Responsible for Genocide and Other Such Violations Committed in the Territory of Neighbouring States, between 1 January 1994 and 31 December 1994

ICTY or International Tribunal

International Tribunal for the Prosecution of Persons Responsible for Serious Violations of International Humanitarian Law Committed in the Territory of the Former Yugoslavia since 1991 **[page 159]**

Indictment

Prosecutor v. Vidoje Blagojević and Dragan Jokić, Case No. IT-02-60-I, Amended Joinder Indictment, filed 26 May 2003

Jokić Appeal Brief

Third Amended Appellate Brief of Dragan Jokić, filed 6 July 2006

Jokić Defense

Dragan Jokić, and/or Dragan Jokić's Counsel

Jokić Notice of Appeal

Third Amended Notice of Appeal of Dragan Jokić, filed 6 July 2006

Jokić Reply Brief

Reply of Dragan Jokić to Prosecution Amended Consolidated Response Brief (20 July 2006), filed 2 August 2006

Jokić Response Brief

Response Brief of Dragan Jokić, filed 20 June 2005

KT.

Transcript page from hearings before the *Krstić* Trial Chamber, *Prosecutor v. Radislav Krstić*, Case No. IT-98-33-T

MUP

Ministry of the Interior in Republika Srpska, unless otherwise indicated

fn. (fns.)

footnote (footnotes)

Prosecution

Office of the Prosecutor **[page 160]**

p. (pp.)

page (pages)

para. (paras.)

paragraph (paragraphs)

Parties

The Prosecutor and the Defence in *Prosecutor v. Vidoje Blagojević and Dragan Jokić*

Practice Direction on Formal Requirements for Appeals from Judgement

Practice Direction on Formal Requirements for Appeals from Judgement, IT/201, 7 March 2002

Prosecution Appeal Brief

Prosecution's Brief on Appeal, filed 9 May 2005

Prosecution Notice of Appeal

Prosecution Notice of Appeal, filed 23 February 2005

Prosecution Reply Brief

Prosecution's Brief in Reply, filed 5 July 2005

Prosecution Response Brief

Prosecution Amended Consolidated Response Brief, filed 20 July 2006

Protocol I

Protocol Additional to the Geneva Conventions of 12 August 1949, and relating to the Protection of Victims of International Armed Conflicts (Protocol I), 8 June 1977

Report of the Secretary-General

Report of the Secretary-General pursuant to Paragraph 2 of Security Council Resolution 808 (1993), S/25704 **[page 161]**

Rules

Rules of Procedure and Evidence of the International Criminal Tribunal for the Former Yugoslavia

SFOR

Stabilisation Force (NATO - Bosnia)

Statute

The Statute of the International Tribunal for the Former Yugoslavia established by Security Council Resolution 827

T.

Transcript page from hearings at trial in the present case

Third Amended Notice of Appeal

The Prosecutor v. Vidoje Blagojević and Dragan Jokić, Case No. IT-02-60-A, Third Amended Notice of Appeal of Dragan Jokić, 6 July 2006

Trial Judgement

Prosecutor v. Vidoje Blagojević and Dragan Jokić, Case No. IT-02-60-T, 17 January 2005

UN

United Nations

UNPROFOR

United Nations Protection Force

VRS

Army of the Republika Srpska

Vienna Convention on the Law of Treaties

Vienna Convention on the Law of Treaties, May 1969, entered into force on 27 January 1980

Commentary

1. Introduction

In the Blagojević case, two officers of the Army of Republika Srpska (VRS) appealed against their January 2005 convictions for crimes committed in the immediate aftermath of the VRS takeover of the United Nations "safe haven" of Srebrenica in July 1995.[1] Vidoje Blagojević, formerly commanding the Bratunac Brigade of the VRS, was convicted of complicity in genocide; of aiding and abetting murder as a violation of the laws or customs of war; and of aiding and abetting murder, persecutions and other inhumane acts (forcible transfers) as crimes against humanity. Dragan Jokić, formerly chief of engineering in the Zvornik Brigade of the VRS, was convicted of aiding and abetting murder as a violation of the laws or customs of war; and of aiding and abetting extermination and persecutions through murder as crimes against humanity. The prosecution cross-appealed, alleging various errors as to both fact and law on the part of the Trial Chamber.

The Appeals Chamber allowed Blagojević's appeal in part, reversing his conviction for complicity in genocide and consequently reducing his sentence of imprisonment from 18 to 15 years; and dismissed the appeals by Jokić and the Prosecution in their entirety.[2]

The large majority of the Appeals Chamber's decision in the Blagojević case concerns matters of either procedure (Blagojević claimed that he had been denied the right to a fair trial because of a complete breakdown in trust and communication between him and his defence counsel, which he claimed meant that he had been denied counsel of his own choice, denied competent counsel and denied the right to appear as a witness in his own defence)[3] or of the interpretation of facts and evidence. In respect of most of the latter, Blagojević's appeal consisted largely of flatly denying or disagreeing with the relevant aspects of the Trial Chamber's Judgement, or advancing implausible alternative theories to explain the evidence, without however attempting to refute in any substantive detail the findings of the Trial Chamber as to the facts.[4]

Significant issues of law were discussed in relation to the crime of genocide: namely, complicity in genocide; and aiding and abetting genocide. Additionally, there was some discussion of the *actus reus* and *mens rea* of aiding and abetting more generally, and the distinction between these and the doctrine of joint criminal enterprise; and of certain components of the doctrine of command responsibility. However, it would be fair to say that the decision as a whole adds relatively little that is substantive to the sum of the tribunal's jurisprudence in international criminal law.

2. Complicity in genocide

Blagojević was not convicted for actually committing genocide, but rather for complicity in genocide as an aider and abettor,[5] in that he allowed resources and personnel of his Bratunac Brigade to be used in forcibly transferring Bosnian Muslim detainees from Potočari and their subsequent mistreatment and murder. The Trial Chamber had opined that the forcible transfer in and of itself was a "manifestation of the specific intent [required for genocide] to rid the Srebrenica enclave of its Muslim population",[6] as were the subsequent killings and mistreatment in Bratunac. However, in relation to the latter at least, the Trial Chamber had found that Blagojević had lacked knowledge of the mass killings,[7] although he had known of other aspects of the VRS operation, such as the segregation of Bosnian Muslim men from other detainees and their detention in inhumane conditions.

1 ICTY, Judgement, *Prosecutor v. Blagojević et al.*, Case No. IT-02-60, T. Ch. I, 17 January 2005, Klip/ Sluiter, ALC-XXVI-261.
2 ICTY, Judgement, *Prosecutor v. Blagojević and Jokić*, Case No. IT-02-60-A, A. Ch., 9 May 2007, in this volume, p. 377.
3 The Appeals Chamber dismissed this ground of appeal: *ibid.*, par. 12–30. Judge Shahabudeen dissented on this ground, holding that Blagojević's case should be remanded for a new trial.
4 For example, *ibid.*, par. 101–102.
5 Judgement, *Prosecutor v. Blagojević et al.*, T. Ch. I, *supra* note 1, par. 787 and 797.
6 *Ibid.*, par. 675.
7 *Ibid.*, par. 740 *et seq.*

The Appeals Chamber compared Blagojević's case with that of Radislav Krstić, the former commander of the VRS Drina Corps which carried out the massacres at Srebrenica, in which the Appeals Chamber had emphasised Krstić's awareness of the mass killings as a significant factor in determining that he had knowledge of the genocidal intent of the principal perpetrators.[8] However, the Appeals Chamber in that case had also clearly stated that, "forcible transfer does not constitute in and of itself a genocidal act", but is merely one factor as part of the assessment of the overall context of the crime.[9] Consequently, the Appeals Chamber found that it was unreasonable to infer Blagojević's knowledge of the principal perpetrators' genocidal intent on the basis of his awareness of other facts related to the forcible transfer operation, but without knowledge of the mass killings, and reversed his conviction for complicity in genocide.[10]

3. Aiding and abetting genocide

Although the Appeals Chamber curtly dismissed Blagojević's submission that the Trial Chamber had erred in law in defining the elements of aiding and abetting on the basis of its previous jurisprudence,[11] it upheld – without detailed discussion – his appeal against conviction for aiding and abetting genocide on the same grounds as those cited in reversing his conviction for complicity in genocide, namely, his lack of knowledge of the mass killings of Bosnian Muslim men at Bratunac.[12]

As a result of overturning his convictions for complicity in, and aiding and abetting, genocide, the Appeals Chamber reduced Blagojević's sentence from 18 to 15 years' imprisonment.[13]

4. Aiding and abetting generally: *actus reus* and *mens rea*

The appeal of Jokić raised some different points in relation to aiding and abetting more generally, not in specific connection with any charged offence of genocide. The first argument on point concerned the provision of *ex post facto* assistance to the commission of a crime, which Jokić contended was distinct from aiding and abetting *per se*; the latter, he submitted, required a prior agreement between the principal perpetrator and the person who subsequently aids and abets the commission of the offence. The Appeals Chamber dismissed this ground of appeal easily on the facts, finding that Jokić in fact knew of the murder operation before it commenced.[14] The Appeals Chamber then reaffirmed the tribunal's jurisprudence, primarily from the Tadić appeal,[15] on the *actus reus* of aiding and abetting, namely that "the accused carried out an act which consisted of practical assistance, encouragement or moral support to the principal", which must have had "a substantial effect on the commission of the crime".[16] It did not need to be "specifically directed" to the commission of the crime[17] but needed to have "a substantial effect" on its commission.

In this way liability by aiding and abetting was to be distinguished from joint criminal enterprise liability, which requires only that the participant perform acts that are "in some way directed" to the furtherance of the common plan or purpose".[18] The requirement of "substantial effect" as a result of aiding and abetting, the Appeals Chamber found, was satisfied in the instant case by Jokić having provided the organisers of mass executions with practical assistance in the disposal of the victims' bodies.[19]

---

8 ICTY, Judgement, *Prosecutor v.Krstić*, Case No. IT-98-33-A, A. Ch., 19 April 2004, Klip/ Sluiter, ALC-XIX-539, par. 104, 106, 112 and 137.

9 *Ibid.*, par. 33 and 35.

10 Judgement, *Prosecutor v.Blagojević and Jokić*, A. Ch., *supra* note 2, par. 123–124.

11 *Ibid.*, par. 127–128. The cases principally relied upon were ICTY, Judgement, *Prosecutor v. Simić et al.*, Case No. IT-95-9-A, A. Ch., 28 November 2006, Klip/ Sluiter, ALC-XXIX-313; ICTY, Judgement, *Prosecutor v. Blaškić*, Case No. IT-95-14-A, A. Ch., 29 July 2004, Klip/ Sluiter, ALC-XX-295; ICTY, Judgement, *Prosecutor v. Vasiljević*, Case No. IT-98-32-A, A. Ch., 25 February 2004, Klip/ Sluiter, ALC-XXIX-465; and ICTR, Judgement, *Prosecutor v. Ntagerura, Bagambiki and Imanishimwe*, Case No. ICTR-99-46-A, A. Ch., 7 July 2006, Klip/ Sluiter, ALC-XXIV-595.

12 *Ibid.*, par. 129 and 135.

13 *Ibid.*, par. 142.

14 *Ibid.*, par. 180.

15 ICTY, Judgement, *Prosecutor v. Tadić*, Case No. IT-94-1-A, A. Ch., 15 July 1999, Klip/ Sluiter, ALC-III-761.

16 Judgement, *Prosecutor v. Blagojević and Jokić*, A. Ch., *supra* note 2, par. 185.

17 *Ibid.*, par. 189.

18 *Ibid.*, par. 185, citing Judgement, *Prosecutor v. Tadić*, A. Ch., *supra* note 15, par. 229.

19 Judgement, *Prosecutor v. Blagojević and Jokić*, A. Ch., *supra* note 2, par. 199.

In respect of the *mens rea* for aiding and abetting, the Appeals Chamber, in dismissing the prosecution's appeal, reaffirmed previous judgements to the effect that the aider and abetter does not have to share the same *mens rea* for the crime with the principal perpetrator, but must simply know that his acts assisted in the commission of the crime and must be aware of the essential elements thereof, including the state of mind of the principal perpetrator. Thus, it was plausible that in the instant case Blagojević did not know about the impending murder operation against the Bosnian Muslim men because he could equally likely have inferred from the circumstances that they were to be exchanged for Serbian prisoners, or simply transferred out of the Serbian-occupied area.[20]

5. Joint Criminal Enterprise

Blagojević had originally been charged with participating in a joint criminal enterprise to forcibly transfer the women and children out of the Srebrenica enclave and to detain and murder the men, but the Trial Chamber had found that his participation in the forcible transfer operation was more akin to aiding and abetting because of his lack of shared intent with the principal perpetrators. The Appeals Chamber upheld this view, finding that Blagojević's activities in the operation in question had been directed to making it militarily successful in terms of combat activities. His lack of intention to commit forcible transfer meant, in the Appeals Chamber's view, that he could not be found guilty of participating in a joint criminal enterprise to that effect.[21]

6. Command Responsibility

The Trial Chamber had declined to find that Blagojević bore command responsibility for the participation of members of his Bratunac Brigade in the murder of the Bosnian Muslim men, a decision against which the Prosecution appealed. First, the Appeals Chamber held that command responsibility includes all forms of criminal conduct by subordinates and is not restricted to situations where subordinates have actually "committed" a crime: thus, a commander whose subordinates had acted as aiders and abetters to a crime could also be found guilty on the basis of command responsibility.[22] The Trial Chamber had found that it could not "identify the specific perpetrators [...] whom Colonel Blagojević had the duty to punish",[23] but the Appeals Chamber confirmed that such certainty was not necessary for a finding of command responsibility, and that the Trial Chamber's finding on this point had simply indicated that it had been unable to find that any of Blagojević's subordinates had actually committed the crime in question.[24]

Finally, the Appeals Chamber was not convinced that Blagojević, despite having de jure authority over the personnel of the Bratunac Brigade, actually possessed effective control over them at the material time, because the direct involvement of senior VRS officers from outside the Brigade's chain of command in issuing them with orders and instructions meant that Blagojević lacked effective control, in the sense that he "lacked the material ability to prevent or punish the commission of the offences".[25]

David Turns

---

20 *Ibid.*, par. 219–223.
21 *Ibid.*, par. 250–275.
22 *Ibid.*, par. 279–284.
23 Judgement, *Prosecutor v. Blagojević et al.*, T. Ch. I, *supra* note 1, par. 794.
24 Judgement, *Prosecutor v. Blagojević and Jokić*, A. Ch., *supra* note 2, par. 287.
25 *Ibid.*, par. 300, 301, 302 and 303.

UNITED NATIONS

International Tribunal for the Prosecution of Persons Responsible for Serious Violations of International Humanitarian Law Committed in the Territory of Former Yugoslavia since 1991	Case No.	IT-95-11-T
	Date:	12 June 2007
	Original:	English

IN TRIAL CHAMBER I

Before: **Judge Bakone Justice Moloto, Presiding**
Judge Janet Nosworthy
Judge Frank Höpfel

Registrar: **Mr. Hans Holthuis**

Judgement of: **12 June 2007**

PROSECUTOR

v.

MILAN MARTIĆ

JUDGEMENT

The Office of the Prosecutor:
Mr. Alex Whiting
Ms. Anna Richterova
Mr. Colin Black
Ms. Nisha Valabhji

Counsel for Milan Martić:
Mr. Predrag Milovančević
Mr. Nikola Perović

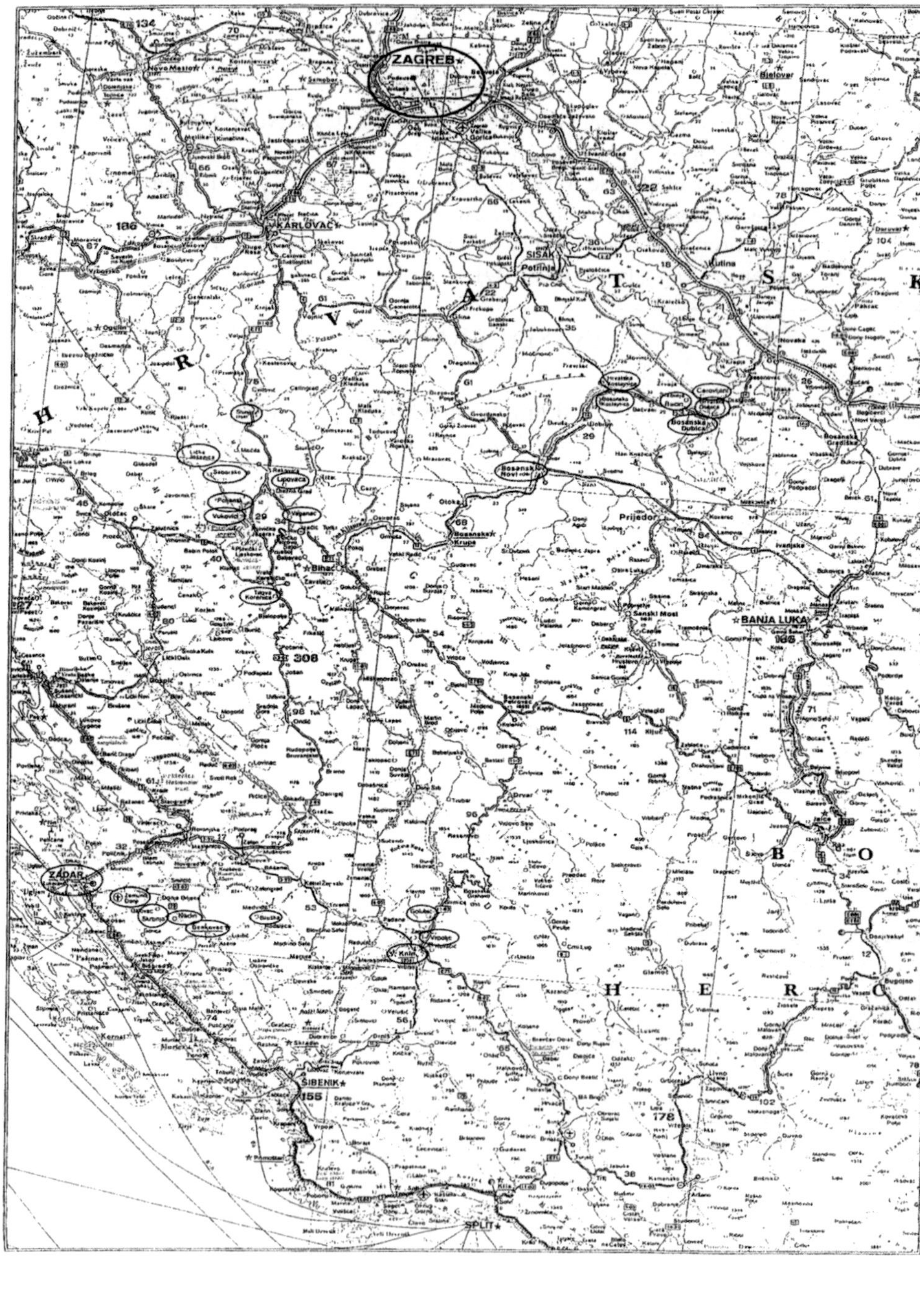
ZAGREB
KARLOVAC
SISAK
Petrinja
Prijedor
BANJA LUKA
Bihać
ZADAR
ŠIBENIK
SPLIT
Knin
H
R
V
A
T
S
K
B
O
H
E
R
C

[page 2] <u>Contents</u>

[page 5] List of abbreviations and acronyms

Additional Protocol I	Protocol Additional to the Geneva Conventions of 12 August 1949, and Relating to the Protection of Victims of International Armed Conflicts (Protocol I), Geneva, 12 December 1977
Additional Protocol II	Protocol Additional to the Geneva Conventions of 12 August 1949, and Relating to the Protection of Victims of Non-International Armed Conflicts (Protocol II), Geneva, 12 December 1977
APC	Armoured Personnel Carrier (vehicle)
BiH	Bosnia and Herzegovina
Common Article 3	Article 3 common to the four Geneva Conventions of 1949
Defence	Defence of Milan Martić
Defence Final Trial Brief	Final trial brief of Milan Martić, filed confidentially on 5 Jan 2007; public version filed on 17 Jan 2007
ECHR	European Convention for the Protection of Human Rights and Fundamental Freedoms, Rome, 4 November 1950
Ex.	Exhibit
fn	Footnote
FNU	First name unknown
Geneva Convention III	Geneva Convention Relative to the Treatment of Prisoners of War of 12 August 1949
Geneva Convention IV	Geneva Convention Relative to the Protection of Civilian Persons in Time of War of 12 August 1949
Geneva Conventions	Geneva Conventions I to IV of 12 August 1949
HDZ	Croatian Democratic Union
HVO	Croatian Armed Forces
ICCPR	International Covenant on Civil and Political Rights, G.A. res. 2200A (XXI), 21 U.N. GAOR Supp. (No. 16) at 52, U.N. Doc. A/6316 (1966), 999 U.N.T.S. 171
ICRC	International Committee of the Red Cross
Indictment	Second Amended Indictment in this case, filed on 9 Dec 2005
JCE	Joint criminal enterprise pursuant to Article 7(1) of the Statute
JNA	Yugoslav People's Army
MUP	Ministry of Interior
p.	Page
pp	Pages
para.	Paragraph
paras	Paragraphs

PJM	Special Police Brigade
Prosecution	The Office of the Prosecutor
Prosecution Final Trial Brief	Final Trial Brief of the Prosecution, filed confidentially on 5 Jan 2007; public version filed on 17 Jan 2007
Rules	Rules of Procedure and Evidence of the Tribunal
Rules of Detention	Rules Governing the Detention of Persons Awaiting Trial or Appeal Before the Tribunal or Otherwise Detained on the Authority of the ICTY
RS	Republika Srpska in Bosnia and Herzegovina
RSK	Republic of Serbian Krajina
SAO	Serbian Autonomous District
SDB	State Security Service
SDS	Serbian Democratic Party
SFRY	Socialist Federal Republic of Yugoslavia **[page 6]**
SJB	Public Security Station, *i.e.* police station
SNC	Serbian National Council
Statute	Statute of the International Tribunal for the Former Yugoslavia established by Security Council Resolution 827, as amended by Resolution 1481
SUP	Secretariat for Internal Affairs
SVK	Army of the Republic of Serbian Krajina
T.	Page in the transcript of this trial
TO	Territorial Defence
UN	United Nations
UNCIVPOL	United Nations Civilian Police
UNCRO	United Nations Confidence Restoration Operation
UNDU	United Nations Detention Unit
UNMO	United Nations Military Observers
UNPA	United Nations Protected Area
UNPROFOR	United Nations Protection Force
VRS	Army of the Republika Srpska
VJ	Army of the Federal Republic of Yugoslavia
Z-4 Plan	Zagreb 4 Plan
ZNG	Croatian National Guards Corps

[page 7] I. INTRODUCTION

A. The Accused Milan Martić

1. Milan Martić was born on 18 November 1954 in the village of Žagrović, Knin municipality in the Republic of Croatia, SFRY.[1] He graduated from the Post-Secondary Police School in Zagreb and between 1976 and 1981 worked as a policeman at the Public Security Station ("SJB") in Šibenik. After 1982, Milan Martić was a Junior Police Inspector in Knin and was eventually promoted to Chief of the SJB.[2]

2. From 4 January 1991 until August 1995, Milan Martić held various positions within the Serbian Autonomous Region of Krajina ("SAO Krajina") and the Republic of Serbian Krajina ("RSK") governments, including Chief of the Police in Knin, Secretary for Internal Affairs of the SAO Krajina, Minister of Defence of the SAO Krajina, Deputy Commander of the TO of the SAO Krajina, Minister of the Interior of the SAO Krajina and of the RSK, and President of the RSK.[3]

B. Overview of the case against Milan Martić

3. The Prosecutor ("Prosecution") charges Milan Martić with 19 counts brought under Article 3 and Article 5 of the Statute of the Tribunal ("Statute").[4]

4. The Prosecution alleges that Serb forces, comprised of, *inter alia*, units of the Yugoslav People's Army ("JNA"), later the Yugoslav Army ("VJ"), the Republika Srpska ("RS") army ("VRS"), the Territorial Defence ("TO"), and forces of the Ministry of the Interior ("MUP") of both the SAO Krajina, later the RSK, and the Republic of Serbia ("Serbia"), including the police forces of the SAO Krajina and the RSK, commonly referred to as "Martić's Police", and paramilitary units, committed persecutions in the SAO Krajina and the RSK between August 1991 and December 1995. It is further alleged that these acts of persecution included the extermination and murder of hundreds of Croats, Muslims and other non-Serb civilians, including in the villages of Hrvatska Dubica, Cerovljani, Baćin, Saborsko, Poljanak (including the hamlet of Vukovići), Lipovača (and neighbouring villages), Škabrnja, Nadin, and Bruška (including the hamlet of Marinovići), the prolonged and routine imprisonment of hundreds of Croats, Muslims and non-Serb **[page 8]** civilians in specified detention facilities, the torture and inhumane treatment of prisoners, and the deportation and forcible transfer of tens of thousands of non-Serb civilians from the territory of the SAO Krajina and the RSK. In addition, it is alleged that public and private property in the SAO Krajina and the RSK was intentionally destroyed or plundered, including buildings dedicated to religion or education, that restrictive and discriminatory measures were imposed against the Croat, Muslim and other non-Serb civilian population. Moreover, it is alleged that unlawful attacks were carried out on Zagreb and undefended Croat and Muslim villages.

5. For each count, individual criminal responsibility is charged under both Article 7(1) and (3) of the Statute. The Prosecution alleges that Milan Martić participated in a joint criminal enterprise ("JCE") together with, among others, Slobodan Milošević, Veljko Kadijević, Blagoje Adžić, Milan Babić, Jovica Stanišić, Franko "Frenki" Simatović, Radovan Karadžić, Ratko Mladić and other named and unnamed individuals of, *inter alia*, the JNA, later the VJ, the RSK army ("SVK"), the VRS, the TO, and forces of the MUP of both the SAO Krajina, later the RSK, and Serbia, including "Martić's Police", and the State Security Service ("SDB") of Serbia, and Serb paramilitary forces. It is alleged that the JCE came into existence before 1 August 1991 and continued until at least August 1995, and that the common purpose of the JCE was "the forcible removal of a majority of the Croat, Muslim and other non-Serb population from approximately one-third of the territory of the Republic of Croatia ["Croatia"] and large parts of the Republic of Bosnia and Herzegovina

---

[1] Ex. 76. *See also* Ex. 493, p. 1, which provides Milan Martić's birthplace as "Žagorić near Knin".

[2] Ex. 493, p. 1.

[3] *See infra* paras 135, 151, 156.

[4] Article 3: Counts 4 and 16: Murder, Count 8, Torture, Counts 9 and 18: Cruel treatment, Count 12: Wanton destruction of villages, or devastation not justified by military necessity, Count 13: Destruction or wilful damage done to institutions dedicated to education or religion, Count 14: Plunder of public or private property, Count 19: Attacks on civilians. Article 5: Count 1: Persecutions, Count 2: Extermination, Counts 3 and 15: Murder, Count 5: Imprisonment, Count 6: Torture, Count 7 and 17: Inhumane Acts, Count 10: Deportation, Count 11: Other inhumane Acts (Forcible transfer).

["BiH"] in order to make them part of a new Serb-dominated state."[5] The Prosecution alleges that all crimes charged in the Indictment were within the object of the JCE and that at all relevant times Milan Martić held the necessary state of mind for the commission of each of these crimes. In the alternative, the Prosecution alleges that the crimes enumerated in Counts 1 to 9 and 12 to 19 were a natural and foreseeable consequence of the execution of the common purpose of the JCE and that Milan Martić was aware that such crimes were the possible outcome of the execution of the JCE.

6. The Prosecution alleges that Milan Martić participated in the JCE by, *inter alia*, creating, financing, supplying, training and directing the "Martić's Police" and the TO of the SAO Krajina and the RSK, and by creating, training and directing special police forces of the SDB of Serbia. Moreover, the Prosecution alleges that Milan Martić participated in the planning, preparation and execution of the take-over of territories in the SAO Krajina and RSK territory, and that Milan Martić personally participated in military actions and subsequent crimes of these forces, including in the subsequent removal of the non-Serb population. **[page 9]**

7. The Prosecution also charges Milan Martić with responsibility for each count pursuant to Article 7(1) for having planned, instigated, ordered, committed or otherwise aided and abetted in the planning, preparation, execution and commission of these crimes.

8. The Prosecution alleges that Milan Martić, by virtue of the various positions he held from 1991 to 1995 in the SAO Krajina and the RSK, is individually criminally responsible pursuant to Article 7(3) of the Statute as a superior for failing to prevent or punish the crimes charged and allegedly committed by the above-mentioned forces.

C. Interpretation of the Indictment

9. Pursuant to Article 18(4) of the Statute, an indictment shall contain "a concise statement of the facts and the crime or crimes with which the accused is charged". According to the well established jurisprudence of the Tribunal, this means that the indictment must set out the material facts underpinning the charges "with enough detail to inform a defendant clearly of the charges against him so that he may prepare his defence."[6]

10. Some paragraphs of the Indictment identify specific victims and/or sites of alleged crimes,[7] while other paragraphs of the Indictment use a non-exhaustive enumeration of victims and crime sites.[8] The Trial Chamber also heard evidence regarding victims and sites of crimes, which are not specified in the Indictment. Having regard to the right of the accused to be informed promptly and in detail of the nature and cause of the charges against him,[9] and in view of the degree of specificity required in the Indictment, the Trial Chamber has considered the evidence as described below.[10] **[page 10]**

---

5 Indictment, paras 4, 6.

6 *Kupreškić et al.* Appeal Judgement, para. 88. *See also Naletilić and Martinović* Appeal Judgement, para. 23; *Stakić* Appeal *Judgement*, para. 116; *Kvočka et al.* Appeal Judgement, para. 28; *Blaškić* Appeal Judgement, para. 209.

7 *E.g.* paras 26, 28–29, 32–34 and 39 of the Indictment.

8 *E.g.* paras 23(a), 23(b)–(d), 30–31 of the Indictment.

9 Article 21(4) (a) of the Statute.

10 The Appeals Chamber in *Kupreškić et al.* held that: "A decisive factor in determining the degree of specificity with which the Prosecution is required to particularise the facts of its case in the indictment *is the nature of the alleged criminal conduct charged to the accused*," *Kupreškić et al.* Appeal Judgement, para. 89 (emphasis added). In a case based upon individual responsibility where it is *not* alleged that the accused personally committed the acts for which he is to be held responsible, what is most material is the conduct of the accused by which he may be found to have planned, instigated, ordered, committed or otherwise aided and abetted, *Prosecutor v. Milorad Krnojelac*, Case No. IT-97-25-PT, Decision on Preliminary Motion on Form of Amended Indictment, 11 Feb 2000, para. 18. Where it is alleged that the accused planned, instigated, ordered, or aided and abetted the alleged crimes, the Prosecution is required to identify the "particular acts" or "the particular course of conduct" on the part of the accused which forms the basis for the charges in question, *Naletilić and Martinović* Appeal Judgement, para. 24. If the Prosecution relies upon a theory of JCE, it must plead the purpose of the enterprise, the identity of the participants, and the nature of the accused's participation in the enterprise, *Kvočka et al.* Appeal Judgement, para. 28. The degree of precision required for the material facts relating to those acts of other persons is higher than that required for an allegation of superior responsibility, but lower than where the accused is alleged to have personally done the acts in question, *Prosecutor v. Milorad Krnojelac*, Case No. IT-97-25-PT, Decision on Preliminary Motion on Form of Amended Indictment, 11 Feb 2000, para. 18. *See also Prlić Decision*, para. 46. Furthermore, in certain cases "the sheer scale of the alleged crimes 'makes it impracticable to require a high degree of specificity in such matters as the identity of the victims and the dates for the commission of the crimes,'" *Kupreškić et al.* Appeal Judgement, para. 89.

11. In determining the innocence or guilt of Milan Martić in relation to the charges in paragraphs 26, 28, 29, and 32 to 34 of the Indictment, in light of the wording of these paragraphs,[11] the Trial Chamber has only considered evidence concerning victims listed in Annex 1 of the Indictment.

12. In determining the innocence or guilt of Milan Martić in relation to the charges in paragraphs 27, 30 and 31 of the Indictment, in light of the wording of these paragraphs, the Trial Chamber has considered evidence concerning victims who are not listed in Annex I to the Indictment but who are proven beyond reasonable doubt as having been killed during the events described in those paragraphs.[12]

13. In determining the innocence or guilt of Milan Martić under Count 1 (Persecutions), the Trial Chamber has considered evidence concerning unlisted victims of the events described in paragraph 23(a) of the Indictment only with respect to the events described in paragraphs 27, 30 and 31 of the Indictment.

14. Concerning the events described in paragraphs 23(b) to (d) of the Indictment relevant to crimes allegedly committed in detention facilities, the Trial Chamber is of the view that the range of crime sites shall correspond to the scope of paragraph 39 of the Indictment.

15. As to paragraph 39 of the Indictment, and in relation to Count 5 (Imprisonment), Counts 6 and 8 (Torture), Count 7 (Inhumane acts) and Count 9 (Cruel treatment), in light of the wording of paragraph 38 of the Indictment, the Trial Chamber finds that the relevant time period applicable to these counts is from August 1991 to December 1992. The Trial Chamber finds that this time period shall also govern paragraphs 23(b) to (d) of the Indictment relating to Count 1 (Persecutions), which concern the same events.

16. In determining the innocence or guilt of Milan Martić under Count 12 (Wanton destruction or devastation), Count 13 (Destruction or wilful damage done to institutions dedicated to education or religion) and Count 14 (Plunder), in light of the wording of paragraph 47 of the Indictment, the **[page 11]** Trial Chamber has considered only evidence concerning destruction and plunder allegedly committed in the villages listed in paragraph 47 during the period between August and December 1991. The Trial Chamber further finds that this time period shall also govern paragraph 23(j) of the Indictment relating to Count 1, which concerns the same events.

17. There are situations where the Trial Chamber is satisfied that the Defence has been put on notice of the Prosecution's case regarding a particular unspecified victim or crime site that is not specifically included in the Indictment, in a manner which has allowed the Defence to prepare its case adequately.[13] In such cases, the Trial Chamber has considered this evidence as a basis for a conviction under the relevant counts.

---

[11] These paragraphs provide an exhaustive enumeration of victims allegedly killed in each village and further identify each victim by referring to Annex I to the Indictment listing their names. Paragraph 26 refers to "fifty-six victims" allegedly killed in a location near the village of Baćin and "thirty civilians from Baćin and twenty-four from the villages Dubica and Cerovljani" allegedly killed into an unknown location. Paragraph 28 refers to "seven civilians" allegedly killed in Lipovača. Paragraph 29 refers to the alleged execution of "ten civilians" in Vukovići near Poljanak. Paragraph 32 refers to the killing of "seven non-Serb civilians" in the village of Nadin; paragraph 34 refers to "ten civilians, among them nine Croats" allegedly killed in the village of Bruška (emphasis in original).

[12] These paragraphs provide a non-exhaustive enumeration of victims allegedly killed in each village. Paragraph 27 alleges that members of Martić's Police and other Serb forces entered the villages of Saborsko, Poljanak and Lipovača and they allegedly killed "all remaining non-Serb inhabitants they found". Paragraph 30 alleges that "members of Martić's Police and the JNA and the TO entered the village of Saborsko where they allegedly killed at least twenty-nine Croat civilians". Paragraph 31 alleges that members of Martić's Police and other Serb forces entered Škabrnja and allegedly "killed at least thirty-eight non-Serb civilians in their homes or in the streets" (emphasis in original).

[13] The Prosecution Pre-Trial Brief, its opening statement and Rule 65 *ter* witness summaries provided to the Defence sufficiently in advance could satisfy this requirement, *Naletilić and Martinović* Appeal Judgement, paras 27, 45; *Kupreškić et al.* Appeal Judgement, paras 114–124; *Kvočka et al.* Appeal Judgement, paras 34, 43–54; *Gacumbitsi* Appeal Judgement, paras 55–58. The relevant factors to be considered should be: the timing of these filings, the relevance of the information to the ability of the accused to prepare his defence, and the impact of the newly-disclosed material facts on the Prosecution case, *Ntakirutimana* Appeal Judgement, para. 27; *Kupreškić et al.* Appeal Judgement, paras 119–121. The mere provision of witness statements or of potential exhibits by the Prosecution pursuant to the disclosure requirements does not suffice to inform an accused of material facts which the Prosecution intends to prove at trial, *Naletilić and Martinović* Appeal Judgement, para. 27; *Ntakirutimana* Appeal Judgement, para. 27, citing *Prosecution v. Radoslav Brđanin and Momir Talić*, Case No. IT-99-36-PT, Decision on Form of Further Amended Indictment and Prosecution Application to Amend, 26 Jun 2001, para. 62. The Defence's submissions at trial, for example in a motion for judgement of acquittal, Final Trial Brief or closing arguments, may in some instances assist in an assessment as to what extent the Defence was put on notice of the Prosecution's case and was able to respond to the Prosecution's allegations, *Naletilić and Martinović* Appeal Judgement, para. 27, citing *Kvočka et al.* Appeal Judgement, paras 52, 53; *Kordić and Čerkez* Appeal Judgement, para. 148. *Cf. Mrkšić et al. Decision*, para. 19.

18. The Trial Chamber notes that in cases where the evidence on unspecified victims and crime sites was not relied upon to determine the innocence or guilt of Milan Martić, such evidence has been utilised, where appropriate, as corroborative of a consistent pattern of conduct, from which inference may be drawn relevant to the elements of crimes with which Milan Martić is charged.[14]

19. The Trial Chamber notes that the Prosecution has decided "not to pursue those crimes alleged in the indictment that occurred in Bosnia and Herzegovina, with the exception of those crimes occurring in Bosanski Novi (including Bosanski [*sic*] Kostajnica [...])."[15] At the Rule 98 *bis* stage of the trial, the Prosecution stated that it had reviewed the evidence and concluded that the evidence did not, even under the standard applicable pursuant to Rule 98 *bis*, support a conviction on the factual allegations under Counts 5 to 9 concerning detention at the Bosanska Kostajnica SJB and the Bosanski Novi SJB.[16] The Trial Chamber will therefore only consider evidence relating to **[page 12]** Bosanski Novi and Bosanska Kostajnica under Counts 1 (except evidence under paragraph 23(b) of the Indictment, which concerns detention), 10 and 11.

D. General considerations regarding the evaluation of evidence

1. General

20. The Trial Chamber has considered the charges against Milan Martić in light of the entire trial record, and in this regard has carefully assessed and weighed the evidence in accordance with the Statute and its Rules of Procedure and Evidence ("Rules"). Where no guidance is given by these sources, it has assessed the evidence in such a way as will best favour a fair determination of the case and which is consistent with the spirit of the Statute and the general principles of law.[17]

21. Article 21(3) of the Statute provides that the accused shall be presumed innocent until proven guilty.[18] The Prosecution therefore bears the burden of proving the guilt of the accused, and in accordance with Rule 87(A) of the Rules, the Prosecution must do so beyond reasonable doubt.[19] In determining whether the Prosecution has done so with respect to each particular count, the Trial Chamber has carefully considered whether there is any reasonable conclusion available from the evidence other than the guilt of the accused.[20]

22. Article 21(4)(g) of the Statute provides that no accused shall be compelled to testify against himself. In the present case, Milan Martić exercised his right not to testify.[21] No adverse inferences were drawn from the fact that he did not testify.

23. Pursuant to Rule 84 *bis* of the Rules, Milan Martić made a statement on 13 December 2005.[22] In accordance with Rule 84 *bis* (B) of the Rules, the Trial Chamber has considered the probative value, if any, of the statement and has found that the statement does not have any probative value.[23] **[page 13]**

24. The Trial Chamber issued a decision adopting guidelines on the standards governing the admission of evidence.[24] In addition to direct evidence, the Trial Chamber has admitted hearsay and circumstantial

---

14 Rule 93 of the Rules; *Kvočka et al.* Trial Judgement, fn 7, paras 547, 556; *Krnojelac* Trial Judgement, para. 230.

15 Prosecution's Estimate of Time Required for Prosecution Case, 23 November 2005, para. 2; Pre-Trial Conference, 12 Dec 2005, T. 222.

16 Indictment, paras 39 (d) and (e), respectively; Rule 98 *bis* arguments, 26 Jun 2006, T. 5889–5890.

17 Rule 89(B) of the Rules.

18 This provision is in accordance with all major human rights instruments, *see e.g.* International Covenant on Civil and Political Rights, Article 14(2); European Convention on Human Rights, Article 6(2).

19 *E.g. Krnojelac* Trial Judgement, para. 66; *Limaj et al.* Trial Judgement, para. 10. *See also Ntakirutimana* Appeal Judgement, para. 140; *Niyitegeka* Appeal Judgement, para. 60. The fact that the Defence has not challenged certain factual allegations contained in the Indictment does not mean that the Trial Chamber has accepted these facts to be proven. Furthermore, the Trial Chamber interprets the standard "beyond reasonable doubt" to mean a high degree of probability; it does not mean certainty or proof beyond a shadow of a doubt.

20 *Čelibići* Appeal Judgement, para. 458.

21 Hearing, 24 Aug 2006, T. 7122.

22 Hearing, 13 Dec 2005, T. 296–318.

23 With respect to the opening statement of Milan Martić, *see* Rule 84 *bis* (B) of the Rules.

24 Decision Adopting Guidelines on the Standards Governing the Admission of Evidence, 19 Jan 2006 ("Guidelines").

evidence.[25] In evaluating the probative value of hearsay evidence, the Trial Chamber has carefully considered all indicia of its reliability, including whether the evidence was "voluntary, truthful and trustworthy", and has considered its content and the circumstances under which the evidence arose.[26] In some instances, the Trial Chamber has relied upon circumstantial evidence in order to determine whether or not a certain conclusion could be drawn. The Trial Chamber recalls that the conclusion must be the only reasonable conclusion available.[27]

25. In evaluating the evidence given *viva voce*, the demeanour and conduct of witnesses has been considered. The Trial Chamber has also given due regard to the individual circumstances of a witness, including the witness' possible involvement in the events and fear of self-incrimination, the witness' relationship with Milan Martić and any protective measures granted to the witness. The Trial Chamber has also assessed the internal consistency of each witness' testimony and other features of his or her evidence, as well as whether there is corroborating evidence. Mindful that the evidence presented in this case relates to events which occurred between 1991 and 1995, the Trial Chamber has in general not treated minor discrepancies between the evidence of witnesses, or between the evidence of a particular witness in court and his or her prior statement, as discrediting their evidence where that witness nevertheless recounted the essence of an incident charged in acceptable detail.[28]

26. In some instances only one witness has given evidence of an incident with which Milan Martić has been charged. In this regard the Trial Chamber recalls that the Appeals Chamber has held that the testimony of a single witness on a material fact does not, as a matter of law, require corroboration.[29]

27. Pursuant to Rule 92 *bis* and Rule 92 *ter*, which allow the admission of written statements and former testimony of witnesses with or without cross-examination, the Trial Chamber has admitted such statements and testimony in lieu of *viva voce* testimony. As regards evidence in **[page 14]** statements and testimony admitted without cross-examination, the Trial Chamber recalls that "evidence which the statement contains may lead to a conviction only if there is other evidence which corroborates the statement".[30] Such "other evidence" may include other witnesses' testimony, documentary evidence or video evidence.[31]

28. The Parties tendered into evidence a statement of agreed facts pursuant to Rule 65 *ter* (H). The Trial Chamber admitted the evidence based on the agreed facts subject "to the tests of relevance, probative value and reliability" in accordance with Rule 89 of the Rules.[32]

29. The Trial Chamber has also assessed and weighed the testimony of expert witnesses. When weighing an expert's oral and written evidence, the Trial Chamber considered factors such as "the professional competence of the expert, the methodologies used by the expert and the credibility of the findings made in light of these factors and other evidence accepted by the Trial Chamber."[33] In addition, the Trial Chamber has duly taken into consideration all factors relevant to the position or positions held by an expert witness, such as his or her status as an employee of the Prosecution or a party-related agency, as well as his or

---

25 Hearsay evidence is evidence of facts not within the testifying witness' own knowledge, *Halilović* Trial Judgement, para. 15; *Blagojević and Jokić Trial Judgement*, para. 21. *See also Prosecutor v. Zlatko Aleksovski*, Case No. IT-95-14/1-AR73, Decision on Prosecutor's Appeal on Admissibility of Evidence, 16 Feb 1999, para. 14. Circumstantial evidence is evidence of circumstances surrounding an event or offence from which a fact at issue may be reasonably inferred, *Blagojević and Jokić Trial Judgement*, para. 21; *Brđanin* Trial Judgement, para. 35; Guidelines, para. 10.

26 *Prosecutor v. Duško Tadić*, Case No. IT-94-1-T, Decision on Defence Motion on Hearsay, 5 Aug 1996, para. 16. *See also Prosecutor v. Zlatko Aleksovski*, Case No. IT-95-14/1-AR73, Decision on Prosecutor's Appeal on Admissibility of Evidence, 16 Feb 1999, para. 15, cited in the Guidelines, Annex, para. 8.

27 *Čelebići* Appeal Judgement, para. 458.

28 *Kupreškić et al.* Appeal Judgement, para. 31. *See also Čelebići* Appeal Judgement, paras 485, 496–498.

29 *Tadić* Appeal Judgement, para. 65; *Aleksovski* Appeal Judgement, para. 62; *Kupreškić et al.* Appeal Judgement, para. 33.

30 *Prosecutor v. Stanislav Galić*, Case No. IT-98-29-AR73.2, Decision on Interlocutory Appeal concerning Rule 92 *bis* (C), 7 Jun 2002, fn 34.

31 *Blagojević and Jokić Trial Judgement*, para. 26; *Halilović* Trial Judgement, para. 19.

32 *Halilović* Trial Judgement, para. 20; *Blagojević and Jokić Trial Judgement*, para. 28. *See also Prosecutor v. Vidoje Blagojević and Dragan Jović*, Case No. IT-02-60-T, Decision on Prosecution's Motion for Judicial Notice of Adjudicated Facts and Documentary Evidence, 19 Dec 2003, para. 13.

33 *Vasiljević* Trial Judgement, para. 20; *Blagojević and Jokić Trial Judgement*, para. 27.

her involvement in the respective party's case preparations.[34] The Trial Chamber also carefully examined the limitation of the expertise of each expert witness and the relevance and reliability of his or her evidence.[35] **[page 15]**

30. In order to assess the authenticity of documentary evidence, the Trial Chamber considered the source of the evidence and its chain of custody, to the extent known. The Trial Chamber did not consider unsigned, undated or unstamped documents *a priori* to be void of authenticity. Furthermore, when the Trial Chamber was satisfied of the authenticity of a particular document, it did not automatically accept the statements contained therein to be an accurate portrayal of the facts.[36] The Trial Chamber evaluated all evidence within the context of the trial record as a whole.[37]

31. Between 25 and 30 September 2006, the Trial Chamber and the Parties conducted a site visit to locations in the Republic of Croatia. The locations visited were Zagreb, Hrvatska Dubica, Cerovljani, Baćin, Slunj, Hrvatska Kostajnica, Dvor na Uni, Saborsko, Poljanak (including the hamlet of Vukovići), Lipovača, Vaganac, Hrvatska Korenica, Škabrnja, Nadin, Bruška (including the hamlet of Marinovići), Knin, Vrpolje and Golubić. The purpose of the site visit was to obtain first-hand observations of the geography and topography of the relevant areas, which are of direct consequence to the counts with which Milan Martić is charged.

2. Witnesses whose evidence has been assessed with particular caution

32. The Trial Chamber considers that the testimony of the following witnesses should be assessed with particular caution in light of the circumstances surrounding their testimony: Milan Babić, Ari Kerkkanen, Witness MM-003 and Witness MM-079.

33. On 15 to 17, 20 and 21 February and 2 and 3 March 2006, Milan Babić, who was previously convicted by this Tribunal, testified as a witness for the Prosecution. However, Milan Babić died prior to the completion of his cross-examination.[38] The Trial Chamber has assessed the evidence of Milan Babić in light of the entire trial record, taking into account the full range of circumstances surrounding his testimony.[39] The Trial Chamber has given due consideration to the fact that the Defence was unable to complete the cross-examination of Milan Babić. In this regard, the Trial Chamber recalls the practice of the Tribunal requiring corroboration of evidence which has not

34 The Trial Chamber notes in this regard Reynaud Theunens, who is an employee of the Office of the Prosecutor of the ICTY and who was accepted as a military expert for the Prosecution; Ivan Grujić, who is the President of the Croatian Government Commission for Detainees and Missing Persons and Assistant Minister of the government of the Republic of Croatia and who was accepted as an expert in the field of exhumation for the Prosecution; Davor Strinović, who is a member of the Croatian Government Commission for Detainees and Missing Persons and who was accepted as a forensic expert for the Prosecution; Jožef Poje who is an employee of the Ministry of Defence of the Republic of Slovenia and who was accepted as an artillery expert for the Prosecution; and Mladen Lončar who is a coordinator of the National Programme of Psychosocial Aid to the War Victims within the government of the Republic of Croatia and who was accepted as an expert in the field of psychiatry for the Prosecution. *See also* Decision on Defence's Motion to Exclude the Evidence of Reynaud Theunens and to Call an Independent Military Expert with Confidential Annexes A, B, C, D and E, 28 Nov 2006, p. 5; Decision on Prosecution's Motions for Admission of Transcripts Pursuant to Rule 92 *bis* (D) and of Expert Reports Pursuant to Rule 94 *bis*, 13 Jan 2006, paras 39–41. *See further Prosecutor v. Milan Milutinović et al.*, Oral Decision, 13 Jul 2006, T. 840–844. *See also Milutinović et al. Decision*, para. 10.

35 In this regard, the Trial Chamber is of the view that the factors to be examined in determining the admission of an expert report, indicated in its Decision on Defence's Submission of the Expert Report of Professor Smilja Avramov Pursuant to Rule 94 *bis*, 9 November 2006, paras 5–12, are *mutatis mutandis* applicable when assessing the weight to be attached to an expert's evidence in light of the entire trial record. The Trial Chamber further observes that an expert witness may not offer his opinion on the criminal liability of the accused, a matter which falls within the sole jurisdiction of the Chamber at the close of the trial, Decision on Defence's Submission on the Expert Report of Milisav Sekulić Pursuant Rule 94 *bis*, and on Prosecution's Motion to Exclude Certain Sections of the Military Expert Report of Milisav Sekulić, and on Prosecution Motion to Reconsider Order of 7 November 2006, 13 Nov 2006, p. 5 with further references.

36 Guidelines, para. 5. The Trial Chamber notes in this respect that it has admitted into evidence excerpts of books, *e.g.* Ex. 24, Ex. 860, Ex. 238, Ex. 793, Ex. 476, Ex. 870, Ex. 874, Ex. 937, Ex. 931, Ex. 1011. The Trial Chamber has considered only the parts of the books admitted in light of the trial record as a whole.

37 Guidelines, para. 6.

38 The Defence filed a motion to exclude the evidence of Milan Babić from the trial record as a result of the incomplete cross-examination. On 9 June 2006, the Trial Chamber denied the motion. This Decision was affirmed by the Appeals Chamber on 14 September 2006. *See infra* paras 537–540. As a result, the evidence of Milan Babić as a whole remains in the record.

39 In this regard, the Trial Chamber recalls its Decision on Defence Motion to Exclude the Testimony of Witness Milan Babić, Together with Associated Exhibits, From Evidence, 9 Jun 2006, paras 71–76.

been cross-examined when such evidence leads to a conviction of an accused.[40] In order to remedy or **[page 16]** ameliorate any potential unfairness which might arise out of the incomplete cross-examination, the Trial Chamber afforded the Defence an opportunity to file the following additional evidence: (i) a list of the portions of the evidence-in-chief of Milan Babić upon which it intended, but was unable, to cross-examine as a result of his death, and (ii) any documents it intended to use in order to challenge those specific portions of Milan Babić's evidence-in-chief.[41] The Defence availed itself of this opportunity and tendered excerpts of Milan Babić's interviews with the Prosecution.[42] In response, and in view of the fact that the Prosecution was unable to re-examine Milan Babić, the Prosecution tendered other portions of those same interviews.[43] The Trial Chamber gave close attention to these documents in its assessment of the parts of Milan Babić's testimony which were not subject to cross-examination or re-examination.

34. Furthermore, the Trial Chamber considered the alleged inconsistencies between Milan Babić's testimony and his prior testimony or statements as well as the fact that Milan Babić testified pursuant to a plea agreement.[44] In relation to the latter, the Trial Chamber took into consideration that some charges against Milan Babić were dropped without prejudice, that the Appeals Chamber had decided upon his appeal against his sentence at the time he appeared before this Trial Chamber, and that he testified under solemn declaration.[45] The Trial Chamber has also considered that Milan Babić pled guilty as co-perpetrator in a joint criminal enterprise which allegedly comprised, *inter alia*, Milan Martić. The Trial Chamber is therefore of the view that Milan Babić's evidence should be treated with caution and requires corroboration.

35. On 4, 5 and 9 May 2006, Ari Kerkkanen, who was previously employed as a Criminal Intelligence Analyst by the Prosecution, testified before the Trial Chamber as a witness for the Prosecution.[46] His written statement was admitted in redacted form on 19 April 2006.[47] The Trial Chamber recalls that Ari Kerkkanen was one of the organisers of, and participants in, several archive missions undertaken by the Prosecution, including to the Croatian State Archive, to collect documents on the MUP of the SAO Krajina and of the RSK.[48] The Trial Chamber observes that both during his testimony and in his written statement on the documents collected, Ari Kerkkanen presented views on and drew conclusions from the information contained in the documents, **[page 17]** although he neither possesses expertise in this area nor personal knowledge of the information.[49] Accordingly, the Trial Chamber has attached no weight whatsoever to such views, conclusions and analyses of Ari Kerkkanen.

36. Witness MM-003 testified from 8 to 10 March 2006. In its Final Trial Brief, the Prosecution accepted that the evidence of Witness MM-003 should be examined "with care" since "he sought and received assistance from the OTP in order to remain in the country where he is now living".[50] The Defence submitted that this would be a factor negating the credibility of his testimony.[51] On 9 April 2007, the Prosecution sent a letter to the Defence disclosing details of its assistance provided to Witness MM-003 in his asylum case.[52]

37. Witness MM-079 testified on 31 March, 3 and 4 April 2006. In its Final Trial Brief, the Prosecution acknowledged that the evidence of Witness MM-079 should be "scrutinized with care" since "he said that he

---

40 *Prosecutor v. Stanislav Galić*, Case No. IT-98-29-AR73.2, Decision on Interlocutory Appeal concerning Rule 92 *bis*, 7 Jun 2002, fn 34; *Brđanin* Trial Judgement, 1 Sep 2004, fn 944; Decision on Defence Motion to Exclude the Testimony of Witness Milan Babić, Together with Associated Exhibits, From Evidence, 9 Jun 2006, paras 73–75.

41 Decision on Defence Motion to Exclude the Testimony of Witness Milan Babić, Together with Associated Exhibits, From Evidence, 9 Jun 2006, para. 81.

42 Defence's Submission Pursuant to the Trial Chamber's Order of 9 Jun 2006, 4 Oct 2006.

43 Prosecution's Response to the Defence's Submission Pursuant to the Trial Chamber's Order of 9 June 2006, 16 Oct 2006.

44 Motion to Exclude the Testimony of Witness Milan Babić, Together with Associated Exhibits, From Evidence, 2 May 2006, paras 22–31 and Annex A.

45 Decision on Defence Motion to Exclude the Testimony of Witness Milan Babić, Together with Associated Exhibits, From Evidence, 9 Jun 2006, para. 76; *Blagojević and Jokić Trial Judgement*, para. 24.

46 Ex. 459, p. 2; Ari Kerkkanen, 4 May 2006, T. 3997.

47 Decision on the Prosecution Motion for the Admission of a Statement of a Witness Pursuant to Rule 89(F), with Confidential Annex A, filed confidentially on 28 Apr 2006.

48 Ex. 459, pp 2–4.

49 Prosecution's Reply to Defense Response to Prosecution's Motion for Admission of Statement of Witness MM-014 Pursuant to Rule 89 (F), filed confidentially on 19 Apr 2006, para. 6, where the Prosecution acknowledges that Ari Kerkkanen lacks expertise.

50 Prosecution Final Trial Brief, para. 44.

51 Witness MM-003, 10 Mar 2006, T. 2175–2188; Defence Closing Argument, 11 Jan 2007, T. 11330–11331.

52 Letter from Alex Whiting to Predrag Milovančević, dated 9 April 2007. The Trial Chamber was copied on this letter.

hoped to receive the assistance of the OTP to remain in the country where he is relocated."[53] Witness MM-079 testified that after his lawyer had suggested that he contact the Tribunal to seek assistance with his asylum, he was interviewed by the Prosecution, and that he was subsequently informed that the Prosecution had written a letter to the authorities of the state where he currently lives to ask that he be allowed to stay there until he finishes testifying at the Tribunal.[54] The Trial Chamber notes that the Defence did not raise objections as to the credibility of this witness.

38. The Trial Chamber notes that both Witness MM-003 and Witness MM-079 sought assistance from the Prosecution, which also provided such assistance to both witnesses. The Trial Chamber therefore considers that there is significant doubt as to the credibility of both witnesses and has consequently given weight only to the parts of their respective evidence which are corroborated by other evidence. **[page 18]**

II. APPLICABLE LAW

A. General requirements of Article 3 of the Statute

1. Generally

39. Milan Martić is charged with the following crimes as violations of the laws and customs of war punishable under Article 3 of the Statute: murder, torture and cruel treatment, based on Article 3 common to the four Geneva Conventions of 12 August 1949 ("Common Article 3"), and attacks on civilians based on Article 51(2) of Additional Protocol I and Article 13(2) of Additional Protocol II.[55] In addition, Milan Martić is charged with wanton destruction of villages, or devastation not justified by military necessity, destruction or wilful damage done to institutions dedicated to education or religion, and plunder of public or private property, punishable under Article 3 (b), (d) and (e), respectively.[56] Article 3 of the Statute provides in its relevant parts:

> The International Tribunal shall have the power to prosecute persons violating the laws or customs of war. Such violations shall include, but not be limited to: [...]
>
> (b) wanton destruction of cities, towns or villages, or devastation not justified by military necessity; [...]
>
> (d) seizure of, destruction or wilful damage done to institutions dedicated to religion, charity and education, the arts and sciences, historic monuments and works of art and science;
>
> (e) plunder of public or private property.

40. Article 3 of the Statute has been defined in the jurisprudence of the Tribunal as a general clause covering all violations of international humanitarian law not covered by Articles 2, 4 or 5 of the Statute.[57] The application of Article 3

---

53 Prosecution Final Trial Brief, para. 85; Witness MM-079, 31 Mar 2006, T. 3025–3028.

54 Witness MM-079, 31 Mar 2006, T. 3025–3026.

55 Counts 4 and 16 (murder), Count 8 (torture), Counts 9 and 18 (cruel treatment), Count 19 (attacks on civilians) of the Indictment. Common Article 3, in its relevant parts, reads:

> In case of armed conflict not of an international character occurring in the territory of one of the High Contracting Parties, each Party to the conflict shall be bound to apply, as a minimum, the following provisions;
>
> (1) Persons taking no active part in the hostilities, including members of armed forces who have laid down their arms and those placed *hors de combat* by sickness, wounds, detention, or any other cause, shall in all circumstances be treated humanely, without any adverse distinction founded on race, colour, religion or faith, sex, birth or wealth, or any other similar criteria.
>
> To this end the following acts are and shall remain prohibited at any time and in any place whatsoever with respect to the abovementioned persons:
>
> (a) violence to life and person, in particular murder of all kinds, mutilation, cruel treatment and torture; [...]

56 Counts 12–14 of the Indictment.

57 *Tadić* Jurisdiction Decision, para. 89, re-affirmed in *Čelebići* Appeal Judgement, paras 133–136.

of the Statute requires a determination that a state of armed conflict existed at the time the crime was committed and that the alleged crime was "closely **[page 19]** related" to the armed conflict.[58] Furthermore, four conditions, known as the *Tadić* conditions, must be fulfilled for a crime to fall within the jurisdiction of the Tribunal.[59]

2. Existence of an armed conflict and the nexus requirement

41. An armed conflict exists "whenever there is a resort to armed force between States or protracted armed violence between governmental authorities and organised groups or between such groups within a State."[60] Until a general conclusion of peace or a peaceful settlement is reached, international humanitarian law continues to apply "in the whole territory of the warring States or, in the case of internal conflicts, the whole territory under the control of a party, whether or not actual combat takes place there".[61]

42. Common Article 3 requires the warring parties to abide by certain fundamental humanitarian standards by ensuring "the application of the rules of humanity which are recognized as essential by civilized nations" and as such the provisions of Common Article 3 have general applicability.[62] When an accused is charged with violation of Article 3 of the Statute, it is immaterial whether the armed conflict was international or non-international in nature.[63]

43. When the alleged crime did not occur at a time and place in which fighting was actually taking place, "it would be sufficient [...] that the alleged crimes were closely related to hostilities occurring in other parts of the territories controlled by the parties to the conflict."[64] The crime "need not have been planned or supported by some form of policy".[65] The armed conflict "need not have been causal to the commission of the crime, but the existence of an armed conflict must, at a minimum, have played a substantial part in the perpetrator's ability to commit it, his decision to commit it, the manner in which it was committed or the purpose for which it was committed."[66] **[page 20]** However, "[i]t is essential, [...] that a Trial Chamber establish the existence of a geographical and temporal linkage between the crimes ascribed to the accused and the armed conflict."[67]

3. The *Tadić* conditions

44. The four *Tadić* conditions referred to above are: (i) the violation must constitute an infringement of a rule of international humanitarian law; (ii) the rule must be customary in nature, or, if it belongs to treaty law, the required conditions must be met;[68] (iii) the violation must be "serious", that is to say, it must constitute a breach of a rule protecting important values, and the breach must involve grave consequences for the victim; and (iv) the violation of the rule must entail, under customary or conventional law, the individual criminal responsibility of the person breaching the rule.[69]

---

58 *Tadić* Jurisdiction Decision, paras 67–70.

59 *Tadić* Jurisdiction Decision, para. 94. *See also Kunarac et al.* Appeal Judgement, para. 66.

60 *Tadić* Jurisdiction Decision, para. 70. The term "protracted" is significant in excluding mere cases of civil unrest or single acts of terrorism in cases of non-international conflicts, *see Kordić and Čerkez* Appeal Judgement, para. 341.

61 *Tadić* Jurisdiction Decision, para. 70. *See also Kunarac et al.* Appeal Judgement, paras 57, 64. In para. 64, the Appeals Chamber held that: "the Prosecutor did not have to prove that there was an armed conflict in each and every square inch of the general area. The state of armed conflict is not limited to the areas of actual military combat but exists across the entire territory under the control of the warring parties."

62 ICRC Commentary on Geneva Convention IV, p. 34.

63 *Tadić* Jurisdiction Decision, para. 137; *Čelebići* Appeal Judgement, paras 140, 147–150, 420, where the Appeals Chamber held that the provisions of Common Article 3 are applicable to both international and non-international conflicts. *See also Galić* Appeal Judgement, para. 120.

64 *Kunarac et al.* Appeal Judgement, para. 57. The Trial Chamber notes that the term "hostilities" is not synonymous with the term "armed conflict." An armed conflict may continue to exist after the hostilities in an area have ceased. The state of armed conflict ends when a peace agreement has been achieved or – in case of a non-international conflict – if a peaceful settlement has been reached, *see Tadić* Jurisdiction Decision, para. 70.

65 *Kunarac et al.* Appeal Judgement, para. 58.

66 *Kunarac et al.* Appeal Judgement, para. 58.

67 *Stakić* Appeal Judgement, para. 342.

68 These conditions are that the treaty (i) was unquestionably binding on the parties at the time of the alleged offence; and (ii) was not in conflict with or derogated from peremptory norms of international law, as are most customary rules of international humanitarian law, *Tadić* Jurisdiction Decision, para. 143.

69 *Tadić* Jurisdiction Decision, para. 94. *See also Kunarac et al.* Appeal Judgement, para. 66.

45. With regard to murder, torture and cruel treatment, the Appeals Chamber has held that Common Article 3 "is indeed regarded as being part of customary international law, and serious violations thereof would at once satisfy the four requirements".[70] In relation to attacks on civilians, the Appeals Chamber in *Strugar* held that "the principles" contained in Article 51(2) of Additional Protocol I and Article 13(2) of Additional Protocol II have attained the status of customary international law.[71] Moreover, it is clear that attacks against civilians undoubtedly breach rules protecting important values and involves grave consequences for the victim.[72] The Appeals Chamber in *Strugar* also found that "[c]ustomary international law establishes that a violation of these principles entails individual criminal responsibility."[73]

46. Concerning the crimes of wanton destruction of villages, or devastation, and destruction or wilful damage done to institutions dedicated to education or religion, it is established in the jurisprudence of the Tribunal that the crimes meet the four *Tadić* conditions.[74] Concerning the **[page 21]** crime of plunder, it is well-established that the first, second and fourth conditions are met.[75] As regards the third condition, the Trial Chamber finds that the jurisprudence establishes that the crime is a breach of a rule protecting important values,[76] and that whether the breach involves grave consequences for the victim has to be decided on a case-by-case basis.[77]

4. "Persons taking no active part in the hostilities"

47. In relation to charges based on Common Article 3, including in this case, the charges of murder, torture and cruel treatment, the Prosecution must prove that the victim was taking no active part in the hostilities when the crime was committed.[78] The perpetrator of the crime must have known or should have been aware that the victim was taking no active part in the hostilities.[79] It is the specific situation of the victim at the moment the crime was committed that must be taken into account in determining the victim's protection under Common Article 3.[80]

B. General requirements of Article 5 of the Statute

1. Elements

48. Milan Martić is charged with the following crimes against humanity punishable under Article 5 of the Statute: murder, extermination, deportation, imprisonment, torture, persecution, and other inhumane acts (including forcible transfer). Article 5 of the Statute provides:

---

70 *Kunarac et al.* Appeal Judgement, para. 68, referring to *Tadić* Jurisdiction Decision, paras 98–34 and *Čelebići* Appeal Judgement, para. 125.

71 *prosecutor v. Pavle Strugar et al.*, Case No. IT-01-42-AR72, Decision on Interlocutory Appeal, 22 Nov 2002, 22 Nov 2002, para. 9; *Blaškić* Appeal Judgement, paras 157–158.

72 *Galić* Trial Judgement, paras 27, 45; *Strugar* Trial Judgement, para. 221.

73 *Prosecutor v. Pavle Strugar et al.*, Case No. IT-01-42-AR72, Decision on Interlocutory Appeal, 22 Nov 2002, 22 Nov 2002, para. 10.

74 Regarding wanton destruction of villages, or devastation not justified by military necessity pursuant to Article 3(b) of the Statute, *see Hadžihasanović and Kubura* Rule 98 *bis* Appeal Decision, para. 30 (*see also* paras 28–29); *Brđanin* Trial Judgement, para. 157; *Strugar* Trial Judgement, para. 231. Regarding destruction or wilful damage done to institutions dedicated to education or religion pursuant to Article 3(d), *see Hadžihasanović and Kubura* Rule 98 *bis* Appeal Decision, paras 44–48, with further references; *Hadžihasanović and Kubura* Trial Judgement, para. 63; *Brđanin* Trial Judgement, para. 157; *Strugar* Trial Judgement, para. 232.

75 *Hadžihasanović and Kubura* Rule 98 *bis* Appeal Decision, paras 37–38, with further references.

76 *Kordić* and *Čerkez* Appeal Judgement, para. 81.

77 *Kordić* and *Čerkez* Appeal Judgement, paras 82–83.

78 *Čelebići* Appeal Judgement, para. 420; *Tadić* Trial Judgement, para. 615.

79 *Halilović* Trial Judgement, para. 36; *Krajišnik* Trial Judgement, para. 847.

80 *Tadić* Trial Judgement, paras 615–616; *Halilović* Trial Judgement, paras 33–34. *See also* ICRC Commentary on Geneva Convention III, p. 39: "a man who has surrendered individually is entitled to the same humane treatment as he would receive if the whole army to which he belongs had capitulated. The important thing is that the man in question will be taking no further part in the fighting."

> The International Tribunal shall have the power to prosecute persons responsible for the following crimes when committed in armed conflict, whether international or internal in character, and directed against any civilian population:
>
> (a) murder;
>
> (b) extermination;
>
> (c) enslavement;
>
> (d) deportation;
>
> (e) imprisonment;
>
> (f) torture;
>
> (g) rape;
>
> (h) persecutions on political, racial and religious grounds;
>
> (i) other inhumane acts.

In order to constitute a crime against humanity under Article 5 of the Statute, the acts of the accused must have been carried out during armed conflict, whether international or non-international in **[page 22]** character.[81] This is a jurisdictional requirement which is satisfied by proof that there was an armed conflict and that objectively the acts of the accused were linked geographically as well as temporally with the armed conflict.[82]

49. The acts of the accused must have formed part of a widespread or systematic attack directed against any civilian population.[83] Five elements have been set out in the jurisprudence for the establishment of this requirement:

(1) 'Attack' may be defined as a course of conduct involving the commission of acts of violence.[84] It is not limited to the use of armed force but may also encompass any mistreatment of the civilian population.[85] 'Attack' is a concept different from that of "armed conflict". The attack may precede, outlast or continue during the armed conflict and need not be part of it.[86]

(2) The attack must be directed against any civilian population, that is, it must be established that the civilian population was the primary object of the attack.[87] It is not required that the entire population be subjected to the attack, however the Chamber must be satisfied that the attack was in fact directed against a civilian "population", rather than against a limited and randomly selected number of individuals.[88]

(3) The attack must be widespread or systematic. 'Widespread' refers to the large-scale nature of the attack and the number of targeted persons, while the phrase 'systematic' refers to the organised

---

81 *Tadić* Jurisdiction Decision, paras 70, 142; *Kunarac et al.* Appeal Judgement, para. 86. *See infra* section II A.

82 *Kunarac et al.* Appeal Judgement, paras 83–84, referring to *Tadić* Appeal Judgement, paras 249, 251.

83 *Blaškić* Appeal Judgement, para. 98 (with further references).

84 *Kunarac et al.* Trial Judgement, para. 415, *affirmed by Kunarac et al.* Appeal Judgement, para. 89.

85 *Kunarac et al.* Appeal Judgement, para. 86.

86 *Tadić* Appeal Judgement, para. 251; *Kunarac et al.* Appeal Judgement, para. 86.

87 *Kunarac et al.* Appeal Judgement, para. 91. *See also Blaškić* Appeal Judgement, paras 110–115, where the Appeals Chamber discussed in detail the scope of the term "civilian population".

88 *Kunarac et al.* Appeal Judgement, para. 90. The Appeals Chamber also held (para. 91) that:

> [i]n order to determine whether the attack may be said to have been so directed, the Trial Chamber will consider, *inter alia*, the means and method used in the course of the attack, the status of the victims, their number, the discriminatory nature of the attack, the nature of the crimes committed in its course, the resistance to the assailants at the time and the extent to which the attacking force may be said to have complied or attempted to comply with the precautionary requirements of the laws of war. To the extent that the alleged crimes against humanity were committed in the course of an armed conflict, the laws of war provide a benchmark against which the Chamber may assess the nature of the attack and the legality of the acts committed in its midst.

[page 23] nature of the acts of violence and the improbability of their random occurrence.[89] It is settled jurisprudence that the existence of a plan need not be proven.[90]

(4) The acts of the perpetrator must objectively form part of the attack on the civilian population. However, it is not required that the acts be committed in the midst of the attack. A crime which is committed before or after the main attack or away from it must be sufficiently connected with the attack and not be an isolated act.[91]

(5) The perpetrator must have known of the attack on the civilian population and that his or her acts formed part of the attack, or at least have taken the risk that his or her acts were part of the attack.[92] However, the perpetrator need not know of the details of the attack.[93] It is the attack, not the acts of the accused, which must be directed against the target population.[94]

2. Applicability of Article 5 to non-civilians

50. As a preliminary point, the Trial Chamber notes that it is well established that the term "civilian population" in the general requirements of Article 5 should be given a broad definition and that the presence of combatants within a civilian population does not necessarily alter its characterisation as such.[95]

51. The Trial Chamber now turns to the question of the required status of the victims under Article 5. As held by the Appeals Chamber in *Blaškić*, "the status of the victim as a civilian" is one of the elements which characterises a crime against humanity.[96] In defining the term "civilian", the Appeals Chamber in *Blaškić* relied upon the provisions of Article 50 of Additional Protocol I, **[page 24]** which it found "may largely be viewed as reflecting customary law."[97] Article 50 of Additional Protocol I defines civilians as follows:

> 1. A civilian is any person who does not belong to one of the categories of persons referred to in Article 4 A (1), (2), (3) and (6) of the Third Convention and in Article 43 of this Protocol. In case of doubt whether a person is a civilian, that person shall be considered to be a civilian.[98]

---

89 *Kordić and Čerkez* Appeal Judgement, para. 94 (with further references). Relevant factors include "the consequences of the attack upon the targeted population, the number of victims, the nature of the acts, the possible participation of officials or authorities, and any identifiable patterns of crimes", *Kunarac et al.* Appeal Judgement, para. 95.

90 *Blaškić* Appeal Judgement, para. 120 (with further references), also holding that the existence of a plan "may be evidentially relevant in proving that an attack was directed against a civilian population and that it was widespread or systematic", *ibid.*

91 *Kunarac et al.* Appeal Judgement, paras 85, 99–101 (with further references). A crime would be regarded as an "isolated act" when it is so far removed from that attack that, having considered the context and circumstances in which it was committed, it cannot reasonably be said to have been part of the attack, *ibid.*

92 *Kunarac et al.* Appeal Judgement, paras 99, 102, also holding (para. 103) that "the motives of the accused for taking part in the attack are irrelevant and a crime against humanity may be committed for purely personal reasons."

93 *Kunarac et al.* Appeal Judgement, para. 102.

94 *Kordić and Čerkez* Appeal Judgement, para. 99; *Kunarac et al.* Appeal Judgement, para. 103.

95 Article 50 of Additional Protocol I provides that the "civilian population comprises all persons who are civilians" and that the "presence within the civilian population of individuals who do not come within the definition of civilians does not deprive the population of its civilian character." *See also Blaškić* Appeal Judgement, which held that "[t]hus, in order to determine whether the presence of soldiers within a civilian population deprives the population of its civilian character, the number of soldiers, as well as whether they are on leave, must be examined," para. 115.

96 *Blaškić* Appeal Judgement, para. 107.

97 *Blaškić* Appeal Judgement, para. 110.

98 Article 4 A (1), (2), (3) and (6), of Geneva Convention III provides:

> A. Prisoners of war, in the sense of the present Convention, are persons belonging to one of the following categories, who have fallen into the power of the enemy:
>
> 1. Members of the armed forces of a Party to the conflict as well as members of militias or volunteer corps forming part of such armed forces.
>
> 2. Members of other militias and members of other volunteer corps, including those of organized resistance movements, belonging to a Party to the conflict and operating in or outside their own territory, even if this territory is occupied, provided that such militias or volunteer corps, including such organized resistance movements, fulfil the following conditions:
>
> (a) That of being commanded by a person responsible for his subordinates;
>
> (b) That of having a fixed distinctive sign recognizable at a distance;

In light of this finding of the Appeals Chamber, the Trial Chamber finds no reason why Article 50 of Additional Protocol I should not also be applied when determining to the status of victims under Article 5 of the Statute.

52. The Appeals Chamber in *Blaškić* further held that, "[r]ead together, Article 50 of Additional Protocol I and Article 4A of Geneva Convention III establish that members of the armed forces, and members of militias or volunteer corps forming part of such armed forces, cannot claim civilian status".[99] The *Blaškić* Appeals Chamber continued that neither may "members of organized resistance groups" claim civilian status, provided that they are commanded by a person responsible **[page 25]** for his subordinates, that they have a fixed distinctive sign recognisable at a distance, that they carry arms openly, and that they conduct their operations in accordance with the laws and customs of war.[100] In determining the status of the victim at the time the crimes were committed, the Appeals Chamber held that:

> the specific situation of the victim at the time the crimes are committed may not be determinative of his civilian or non-civilian status. If he is indeed a member of an armed organization, the fact that he is not armed or in combat at the time of the commission of crimes, does not accord him civilian status.[101]

53. The Appeals Chamber in *Kordić and Čerkez* appears to have taken a different approach to that taken by the Appeals Chamber in *Blaškić*, by expanding the concept of "civilian". The Appeals Chamber in *Kordić and Čerkez* repeated the language of the Appeals Chamber in *Blaškić* in relying upon Article 50 of Additional Protocol I as part of customary international law.[102] It also followed the Appeals Chamber in *Blaškić*, finding that "during an armed conflict, until a soldier is demobilized, he is considered a combatant whether or not he is in combat, or for the time being armed."[103] However, the *Kordić and Čerkez* Appeals Chamber continued, concerning evidence underlying, *inter alia*, Count 7, murder under Article 5 of the Statute:

> read together, the above excerpts [...] constitute evidence that numerous persons were killed during their arrest, simply because they were Muslims, and ABiH soldiers were killed after their arrest, after being placed *hors de combat*. These persons, wilfully killed by Croat forces, were without doubt [...] "civilians" in the sense of Article 5 of the Statute.[104]

(c) That of carrying arms openly;

(d) That of conducting their operations in accordance with the laws and customs of war.

3. Members of regular armed forces who profess allegiance to a government or an authority not recognized by the Detaining Power. [...]

6. Inhabitants of a non-occupied territory, who on the approach of the enemy spontaneously take up arms to resist the invading forces, without having had time to form themselves into regular armed units, provided they carry arms openly and respect the laws and customs of war.

Article 43 of Additional Protocol I provides:

1. The armed forces of a Party to a conflict consist of all organized armed forces, groups and units which are under a command responsible to that Party for the conduct of its subordinates, even if that Party is represented by a government or an authority not recognized by an adverse Party. Such armed forces shall be subject to an internal disciplinary system which, inter alia, shall enforce compliance with the rules of international law applicable in armed conflict.

2. Members of the armed forces of a Party to a conflict (other than medical personnel and chaplains covered by Article 33 of the Third Convention) are combatants, that is to say, they have the right to participate directly in hostilities.

3. Whenever a Party to a conflict incorporates a paramilitary or armed law enforcement agency into its armed forces it shall so notify the other Parties to the conflict.

99 *Blaškić* Appeal Judgement, para. 113.

100 *Blaškić* Appeal Judgement, para. 113, referring to Article 4 A of Geneva Convention III.

101 *Blaškić* Appeal Judgement, para. 114.

102 *Kordić and Čerkez* Appeal Judgement, para. 97.

103 *Kordić and Čerkez* Appeal Judgement, para. 421. *See also* para. 50.

104 *Kordić and Čerkez* Appeal Judgement, paras 421–422. The Appeals Chamber thus upheld the Trial Chamber's finding of murder under Article 5 and wilful killing under Article 2.

Nevertheless, the Appeals Chamber appears to have followed the reasoning of the Appeals Chamber in *Blaškić* in overturning the finding of the Trial Chamber in relation to the killing of a man and a woman shot by the HVO in their apartment. It held that "as TO members, the two victims are to be considered as 'combatants' and cannot claim the status of civilians."[105]

54. The Appeals Chamber in *Galić* supported the view of the *Blaškić* Appeal Chamber that a person *hors de combat* is not a civilian in the context of international humanitarian law:

> Persons *hors de combat* are certainly protected in armed conflicts through Common Article 3 of the Geneva Conventions. This reflects a principle of customary international law. Even *hors de combat*, however, they would still be members of the armed forces of a party to the conflict and therefore fall under the category of persons referred to in Article 4(A)(1) of the Third Geneva **[page 26]** Convention; as such, they are not civilians in the context of Article 50, paragraph 1, of Additional Protocol I. Common Article 3 of the Geneva Conventions supports this conclusion in referring to "persons taking no active part in the hostilities, including *members of armed forces* who have laid down their arms *and those placed hors de combat* by sickness, wounds, detention, or any other cause" (emphasis added).[106]

55. The Trial Chamber agrees with the findings of the Appeals Chamber in *Blaškić* and *Galić* that the term civilian is one which is narrowly defined. The Trial Chamber does not, therefore, follow the logic of the Appeals Chamber in *Kordić and Čerkez*, which appeared to expand the term "civilian" to cover persons *hors de combat.* In the view of the Trial Chamber, such an interpretation is not in keeping with the definition of civilians as set out in Article 50 which the Appeals Chamber found "may be largely viewed as reflecting customary international law".[107] As held by the Appeals Chamber in *Blaškić* and *Galić*, the fact that a person, who is not a civilian according to Article 4A of Geneva Convention III and Article 43 Additional Protocol I, is not armed or in combat, or is *hors de combat* at the time of the commission of crime, does not render them civilian for the purposes of Article 5 of the Statute.

56. That Article 5 of the Statute is applicable to civilians is in keeping with the fundamental principle of the distinction between civilians and combatants, which permeates the laws of war and international humanitarian law. In this respect, the Trial Chamber recalls the ICRC Commentary to Article 50 of Additional Protocol I, which provides that:

> [t]he principle of the protection of the civilian population is inseparable from the principle of the distinction which should be made between military and civilian persons. In view of the latter principle, it is essential to have a clear definition of each of these categories.[108]

Article 5 of the Statute defines crimes against humanity more narrowly than required under customary international law by including a requirement of a nexus between the crime and the armed conflict.[109] This requirement in Article 5 necessarily links crimes against humanity to an armed conflict in which distinction must be made between combatants and non-combatants. Therefore, to allow for the term

---

105 *Kordić and Čerkez* Appeal Judgement, para. 458. The Appeals Chamber also found that "members of the armed forces resting in their homes in the area of the conflict, as well as members of the TO residing in their homes, remain combatants whether or not they are in combat, or for the time being armed," *Kordić and Čerkez* Appeal Judgement, para. 51. The Appeals Chamber also only applied the crime of imprisonment to those who were proved at trial to be civilians, *ibid.* paras 591–640.

106 *Galić* Appeal Judgement, fn 437.

107 *Blaškić* Appeal Judgement, para. 110. The Trial Chamber recalls that the Appeals Chamber in *Kordić and Čerkez* relied upon the Appeals Chamber in *Blaškić*: "The Appeals Chamber considers that Article 50 of Additional Protocol I contains a definition of civilians and civilian populations, and the provisions in this article may largely be viewed as reflecting customary law. As a result, they are relevant to the consideration at issue under Article 5 of the Statute, concerning crimes against humanity" (footnotes omitted), *Kordić and Čerkez* Appeal Judgement, para. 97.

108 ICRC Commentary on Additional Protocols, para. 1911.

109 *Tadić* Jurisdiction Decision, paras 140–141, wherein the Appeals Chamber stated (*ibid.* para. 141) that:

> It is by now a settled rule of customary international law that crimes against humanity do not require a connection to international armed conflict. Indeed, as the Prosecutor points out, customary international law may not require a connection between crimes against humanity and any conflict at all. Thus, by requiring that crimes against humanity be committed in either internal or international armed conflict, the Security Council may have defined the crime in Article 5 more narrowly than necessary under customary international law. There is no question, however, that the definition of crimes against humanity adopted by the Security Council in Article 5 comports with the principle of *nullum crimen sine lege.*

"civilians" to include all persons who were not actively participating in combat, **[page 27]** including those who were *hors de combat,* at the time of the crime would impermissibly blur this necessary distinction.

C. Murder

57. Milan Martić is charged with murder, both as a violation of the laws or customs of war pursuant to Article 3 of the Statute (Counts 4 and 16) and as a crime against humanity pursuant to Article 5(a) of the Statute (Counts 3 and 15).

58. The elements of the crime of murder under Article 3 and under Article 5 are identical, with the exception that the respective general requirements for the application of these provisions must be met.[110] The common elements are the following:

1. the death of a victim;
2. the death was the result of an act or omission of the accused or of one or more persons for whom the accused is criminally responsible;
3. the act or omission was committed with intent to kill, or in the knowledge that death was a probable consequence of the act or omission.[111]

59. For the proof of the death of the victim, there is no requirement that the body be recovered. Rather, the death may be established by circumstantial evidence, provided it is the only reasonable inference available from the evidence.[112]

60. The *mens rea* of murder is the intent to kill, including indirect intent, that is the knowledge that the death of the victim was a probable consequence of the act or omission.[113] This Trial Chamber does not consider it to be sufficient that the perpetrator knew that death would be a *possible* consequence of his act or omission.[114] In connection with the identity of victims, it is not required for the perpetrator to have intended to target a certain individual; indiscriminate intent to kill whoever is fatally injured as a result of his action is sufficient. **[page 28]**

D. Extermination

61. Milan Martić is charged with extermination, a crime against humanity under Article 5(b) of the Statute (Count 2).

62. Extermination is the act of killing on a large scale.[115] The crime of extermination subsumes the elements of murder.[116] The *actus reus* consists of any act or omission, which contributes directly or indirectly to the killing of a large number of individuals.[117] The *actus reus* also includes subjecting a large number of people "to conditions of living that would inevitably lead to death".[118]

---

110 *Kordić and Čerkez* Trial Judgement, paras 229, 233, 236; *Brđanin* Trial Judgement, para. 380; *Strugar* Trial Judgement, para. 236; *Orić* Trial Judgement, para. 345.

111 *Kvočka et al.* Appeal Judgement, para. 261.

112 *Kvočka et al.* Appeal Judgement, para. 260; *Brđanin* Trial Judgement, paras 383–385; *Krnojelac* Trial Judgement, paras 326–327; *Tadić* Trial Judgement, para. 240. Relevant factors to be considered include, but are not limited to, proof of incidents of mistreatment directed against the victim, patterns of mistreatment and disappearances of other victims, the coincident or near-coincident time of death of other victims, the fact that the victims were present in an area where an armed attack was carried out, when, where and the circumstances in which the victim was last seen, behaviour of soldiers in the vicinity, as well as towards other civilians, at the relevant time, and lack of contact by the victim with others whom he/she would have been expected to contact, such as his/her family, *Halilović* Trial Judgement, para. 37; *Krnojelac* Trial Judgement, para. 327.

113 *Strugar* Trial Judgement, paras 235–236; *Limaj et al.* Trial Judgement, para. 241. *See also Orić* Trial Judgement, para. 348. Neither negligence nor gross negligence on the part of the perpetrator is sufficient to satisfy the mental element, *Stakić* Trial Judgement, para. 587; *Brđanin* Trial Judgement, para. 386; *Orić* Trial Judgement, para. 348.

114 *Strugar* Trial Judgement, para. 236.

115 *Ntakirutimana* Appeal Judgement, para. 516 and fn 880; *Stakić* Appeal Judgement, para. 259.

116 *Krajišnik* Trial Judgement, para. 716. As regards the elements of murder, *see infra* section II C.

117 *Vasiljević* Trial Judgement, para. 229; *Brđanin* Trial Judgement, para. 389. *See also Rutaganda* Trial Judgement, para. 83; *Musema* Trial Judgement, para. 219.

118 *Stakić* Appeal Judgement, para. 259; *Ntakirutimana* Appeal Judgement, para. 522.

63. The requirement that killings occurred on a large scale does not suggest a numerical minimum.[119] An assessment of whether this requirement has been met must be made on the basis of a case-by-case analysis of all relevant factors.[120] Extermination may be established "on an accumulation of separate and unrelated incidents, meaning on an aggregated basis", where a large number of killings did not occur during a single incident in a concentrated place over a short period.[121]

64. It is not required that the perpetrator targeted the victims on national, ethnical, racial or religious grounds.[122] Neither is a "vast scheme of collective murder", nor knowledge of such a scheme, an element of extermination.[123] Moreover, it is not necessary that the victims of extermination be precisely identified by name; it is sufficient for it to be proven that killings occurred on a large scale.[124]

65. The *mens rea* element of extermination requires that the act or omission was committed with the intent to kill persons on a large scale or in the knowledge that the deaths of a large number of people were a probable consequence of the act or omission.[125] In other words, the *mens rea* encompasses direct intent and indirect intent.[126] **[page 29]**

E. Attacks on civilians

66. Milan Martić is charged with attacks on civilians, a violation of the laws or customs of war pursuant to Article 3 of the Statute (Count 19).

67. The crime of attacks on civilians is based upon Article 51(2) of Additional Protocol I and Article 13(2) of Additional Protocol II, both of which provide, in their relevant parts, that "[t]he civilian population as such, as well as individual civilians, shall not be made the object of attack."[127]

68. Article 49 of Additional Protocol I defines the term "attack" as "acts of violence against the adversary, whether in offence or in defence".[128] In relation to attacks on civilians, the Appeals Chamber in *Blaškić* held that there is an absolute prohibition in customary international law against the targeting of civilians.[129] In *Kordić and Čerkez*, the Appeals Chamber held that "the prohibition against attacking civilians and civilian objects may not be derogated from because of military necessity".[130] According to Article 52(2) of Additional Protocol I only military objectives may be lawfully attacked, that is "those objects which by their nature, location, purpose or use make an effective contribution to military action and whose total or partial destruction, capture or neutralization, in the circumstances ruling at the time, offers a definite military advantage".[131]

69. The prohibition against targeting the civilian population does not exclude the possibility of legitimate civilian casualties incidental to an attack aimed at military targets.[132] However, such casualties must not be disproportionate to the concrete and direct military advantage anticipated before the attack.[133] In particular,

[119] *Stakić* Appeal Judgement, para. 260; *Ntakirutimana* Appeal Judgement, para. 516.

[120] *Stakić* Trial Judgement, para. 640; *Brđanin* Trial Judgement, para. 391; *Blagojević and Jokić Trial Judgement*, para. 573. The relevant factors include "the time and place of the killings, the selection of the victims, and the manner in which they were targeted", *Krajišnik* Trial Judgement, para. 716. *See also Nahimana et al.* Trial Judgement, para. 1061.

[121] *Brđanin* Trial Judgement, para. 391. *See also Stakić* Trial Judgement, para. 640.

[122] *Krstić* Trial Judgement, paras 499–500; *Stakić* Trial Judgement, para. 639.

[123] *Stakić* Appeal Judgement, paras 258–259. *See also Krstić* Appeal Judgement, para. 225.

[124] *Ntakirutimana* Appeal Judgement, para. 521, endorsed by *Stakić* Appeal Judgement, fn 552.

[125] *Stakić* Appeal Judgement, para. 259; *Ntakirutimana* Appeal Judgement, para. 522.

[126] *Krstić* Trial Judgement, para. 495; *Stakić* Trial Judgement, paras 587, 641–642; *Brđanin* Trial Judgement, para. 395.

[127] The Indictment provides: "Count 19: Attacks on civilians, a Violation of the Laws or Customs of War, as recognised by Article 51(2) of Additional Protocol I and Article 13(2) of Additional Protocol II to the Geneva Conventions of 1949, punishable under Articles 3 and 7(1) and 7(3) of the Statute of the Tribunal".

[128] This definition of attack has been endorsed in *Kordić and Čerkez* Appeal Judgement, para. 47.

[129] *Blaškić* Appeal Judgement, para. 109; *Galić* Appeal Judgement, para. 190.

[130] *Kordić and Čerkez* Appeal Judgement, para. 54 (as revised by Corrigendum of 26 January 2005).

[131] Article 52(2) of Additional Protocol I. *See also Kordić and Čerkez* Appeal Judgement, para. 53. In this context, *see* the Trial Chamber's discussion on reprisals, *infra* section IV B 4 (c).

[132] *Galić* Appeal Judgement, para. 190.

[133] *Galić* Appeal Judgement, para. 190. The Appeals Chamber also endorsed the Trial Chamber's finding in *Galić* according to which the parties to a conflict have an obligation "to remove civilians, to the maximum extent feasible from the vicinity of military objectives and to avoid locating military objectives within or near densely populated areas". However, "the failure of a party to abide by this obligation does not relieve the attacking side of its duty to abide by the principles of distinction and proportionality when launching an attack", *Galić* Appeal Judgement, para. 194.

indiscriminate attacks, that is attacks which affect civilians or civilian objects and military objects without distinction, may also be qualified as direct attacks on **[page 30]** civilians.[134] In this regard, a direct attack against civilians can be inferred from the indiscriminate character of the weapon used.[135]

70. It is an element of the crime that the attacks resulted in death or serious bodily injury within the civilian population at the time of such attacks.[136]

71. The Trial Chamber recalls that the Appeals Chamber has considered that "Article 50 of Additional Protocol I contains a definition of civilians and civilian populations", which may largely be viewed as reflecting customary law.[137]

72. The *mens rea* required for attacks against civilians is direct and indirect intent.[138]

F. Torture

73. Milan Martić is charged with torture as a crime against humanity under Article 5(f) of the Statute (Count 6), and as a violation of the laws or customs of war under Article 3 of the Statute (Count 8), respectively.

74. The torture of persons not taking an active part in hostilities is expressly prohibited by the Geneva Conventions and the Additional Protocols, both in international and non-international **[page 31]** armed conflicts.[139] The definition of torture is identical under both Article 3 and Article 5 of the Statute.[140] It comprises the following elements:

1. The intentional infliction, by act or omission, of severe pain or suffering, whether physical or mental;
2. the act or omission must have occurred in order to obtain information or a confession, or to punish, intimidate or coerce the victim or a third person, or to discriminate, on any ground, against the victim or a third person ("prohibited purpose").[141]

---

134 *Galić* Appeal Judgement, para. 132, referring to *Galić* Trial Judgement, para. 57. *See also* ICJ Advisory Opinion: *Legality of the Threat or Use of Nuclear Weapons*, Advisory Opinion of 8 July 1996, I.C.J. Reports 1996, para. 78.

135 *Galić* Appeal Judgement, para. 132. The Appeals Chamber upheld the Trial Chamber's finding in *Galić* which relied, *inter alia*, on the *Martić* Rule 61 Decision, 8 Mar 1996, paras 23–31, according to which the Trial Chamber regarded the use of a cluster bomb warhead as evidence of Milan Martić's intent to deliberately attack the civilian population. The Appeals Chamber noted also that the Trial Chamber is, in principle, entitled to determine on a case-by-case basis that the indiscriminate character of an attack can assist it in determining whether the attack was directed against the civilian population. Among the elements that the Trial Chamber may take into account in its determination as to whether the attack was directed against civilians are "the means and method used in the course of the attack, the status of the victims, their number, [...] the nature of the crimes committed in its course, the resistance to the assailants at the time and the extent to which the attacking force may be said to have complied or attempted to comply with the precautionary requirements of the laws of war", *Galić* Appeal Judgement, para. 132 referring to *Kunarac et al.* Appeal Judgement, para. 91 and *Blaškić* Appeal Judgement, para. 106.

136 *Kordić and Čerkez* Appeal Judgement, paras 55–67.

137 *Kordić and Čerkez* Appeal Judgement, para. 97; *Blaškić* Appeal Judgement, para. 110. The Appeals Chamber based its holding on the ICRC Commentary on Additional Protocols, pp 611–612 (regarding Article 50(3) of Additional Protocol I), which explains the principle as follows:

> [I]n war time conditions it is inevitable that individuals belonging to the category of combatants become intermingled with the civilian population, for example, soldiers on leave visiting their families. However, provided that these are not regular units with fairly large numbers, this does not in any way change the civilian character of a population.

138 Article 85(3)(a) of Additional Protocol I qualifies as a grave breach the act of "wilfully [...] making the civilian population or individual civilians the object of attack". The ICRC Commentary on Additional Protocols, para. 3474, concerning this provision reads: "*wilfully*: the accused must have acted consciously and with intent, i.e., with his mind on the act and its consequences, and willing them ('criminal intent' or 'malice aforethought'); this encompasses the concepts of 'wrongful intent' or 'recklessness', viz., the attitude of an agent who, without being certain of a particular result, accepts the possibility of it happening; on the other hand, ordinary negligence or lack of foresight is not covered, i.e., when a man acts without having his mind on the act or its consequences." *See also Galić* Appeal Judgement, para. 140.

139 *Čelebići* Trial Judgement, para. 446, *referring* in fn 455 to Article 12 Geneva Conventions I and II; Article 50 Geneva Convention I; Article 51 Geneva Convention II; Articles 17, 87 and 130 Geneva Convention III; Articles 32 and 147 Geneva Convention IV; Common Article 3 Geneva Conventions I–IV; Article 75 Additional Protocol I; Article 4 Additional Protocol II.

140 The definition of torture is largely based on the 1984 Convention against Torture and Other Cruel, Inhuman or Degrading Treatment or Punishment, which entered into force on 26 June 1987.

141 *See e.g. Kunarac et al.* Appeal Judgement, paras 142–144; *Brđanin* Trial Judgement, para. 481; *Furunzđžija* Trial Judgement, para. 162.

75. The pain and suffering inflicted during acts of torture is more severe than the pain and suffering inflicted during other forms of mistreatment and cruel treatment.[142] The Trial Chamber will assess on a case-by-case basis whether the acts or omissions charged as torture, inflicted severe physical or mental pain or suffering on the part of the victim.[143] In its assessment of the severity of the pain or suffering inflicted, the Trial Chamber may take several factors into account, including the duration of the suffering inflicted, the nature of the crimes, the physical or mental condition of the victim, the effect of the acts on the victim, the victim's age, and the victim's position of inferiority to the perpetrator.[144]

76. In the jurisprudence of the Tribunal several acts have been listed as rising to the level of seriousness necessary to constitute torture. These acts include beatings, administering electric shocks, forcing victims to watch executions of others, rape, forcing victims to bury the bodies of their neighbours and friends, and causing burn injuries.[145]

77. As to the *mens rea*, the perpetrator's acts or omissions must be committed for a prohibited purpose. The definition of torture provides a non-exhaustive list of prohibited purposes.[146] There is no requirement that the act of the perpetrator be committed solely or predominantly to serve this prohibited purpose.[147] Once the conduct has been carried out for one of the prohibited purposes, it **[page 32]** is immaterial whether there is another purpose behind the conduct.[148] In addition, it needs to be established that the perpetrator acted or omitted to act with direct or indirect intent.

G. Cruel treatment

78. Milan Martić is charged with cruel treatment as a violation of the laws or customs of war, as recognised in Common Article 3, pursuant to Article 3(1)(a) of the Statute (Counts 9 and 18).

79. The crime of cruel treatment is defined in the jurisprudence as an intentional act or omission causing serious mental or physical suffering or injury, or constituting a serious attack on human dignity, committed against a person not taking an active part in hostilities.[149] The perpetrator must be shown to have acted with direct intent or with indirect intent, that is, in the knowledge that cruel treatment was a likely consequence of his act or omission.[150]

80. It is not required that the suffering caused by the cruel treatment be "lasting".[151] In its assessment of the seriousness of the act or omission, the Trial Chamber will take all circumstances into consideration, including factors such as the age and health of the victim, and the physical and mental effects of the crime upon the victim.[152] Moreover, it is not required that the seriousness of the suffering or injury amounts to the level of seriousness required for torture.[153]

---

142 *Brđanin* Trial Judgement, para. 483. *See also Čelebići* Trial Judgement, para. 468.

143 *Naletilić and Martinović* Appeal Judgement, para. 299; *Čelebići* Trial Judgement, para. 469.

144 *Naletilić and Martinović* Appeal Judgement, para. 300; *Brđanin* Trial Judgement, para. 484, citing *Kvočka et al.* Trial Judgement, para. 143 and *Krnojelac* Trial Judgement, para. 182.

145 *See e.g. Kunarac et al.* Appeal Judgement, para. 151; *Čelebići* Trial Judgement, para. 495–496, 971, 973, 976–77; *Naletilić and Martinović* Trial Judgement, paras 350–352; *Brđanin* Trial Judgement, paras 492, 503–511, 524.

146 *Čelebići* Trial Judgement, para. 470; *Brđanin* Trial Judgement, para. 487.

147 *Kunarac et al.* Appeal Judgement, para. 155; *Čelebići* Trial Judgement, para. 470.

148 *Kunarac et al.* Appeal Judgement, para. 155.

149 *Čelebići* Appeal Judgement, para. 424; *Limaj et al.* Trial Judgement, para. 231.

150 The Trial Chamber notes that in the jurisprudence "likely" is synonymous to "probable", *see e.g. Prosecutor v. Radoslav Brđanin and Momir Talić*, Decision on Form of Further Amended Indictment and Prosecution Application to Amend, 26 Jun 2001, para. 29; *Simić et al.* Trial Judgement, para. 76, citing *Vasiljević* Trial Judgement, para. 236; *Limaj et al.* Trial Judgement, para. 231.

151 *Kunarac et al.* Trial Judgement, para. 501.

152 *Simić et al.* Trial Judgement, para. 75; *Vasiljević* Trial Judgement, para. 235; *Krnojelac* Trial Judgement, para. 131.

153 *Čelebići* Trial Judgement, para. 510; *Kordić and Čerkez* Trial Judgement, para. 245. *See supra* section II F.

H. Other inhumane acts

81. Milan Martić is charged with three counts of other inhumane acts, as crimes against humanity pursuant to Article 5(i) of the Statute. Count 7 charges Milan Martić with "inhumane acts" in relation to events in detention centres, Count 11 charges Milan Martić with "inhumane acts (forcible transfers)" in relation to the removal of non-Serb inhabitants of the SAO Krajina and the RSK, and Count 17 charges Milan Martić with "inhumane acts" in relation to the shelling of Zagreb.[154] **[page 33]**

82. "Other inhumane acts" is a residual category of crimes against humanity recognised as forming part of customary international law.[155] It must be emphasised that the Trial Chamber must exercise great caution in finding that an alleged act, which is not regulated elsewhere in Article 5 of the Statute, amounts to "other inhumane acts" within the meaning of Article 5(i).[156]

83. In addition to meeting the general requirements for application of Article 5, an act or omission must satisfy the following elements to fall within the category of other inhumane acts:

1. the act or omission was of similar seriousness to the other crimes enumerated in Article 5;
2. the act or omission caused serious mental or physical suffering or injury, or constituted a serious attack on human dignity; and
3. the act or omission was carried out intentionally by the accused or by persons for whom the accused bears criminal responsibility.[157]

84. The element of "similar seriousness" is to be evaluated in light of all factual circumstances, including the nature of the act or omission, the context within which it occurred, the individual circumstances of the victim as well as the physical and mental effects on the victim.[158] There is no requirement that the effects on the victim be long-term, however any such effects will form part of the determination whether the act or omission meets the "similar seriousness" requirement.[159]

85. The *mens rea* required is that the perpetrator had direct or indirect intent to inflict, by act or omission, serious physical or mental suffering or to commit a serious attack on the victim's human dignity.[160]

I. Imprisonment

86. Milan Martić is charged with imprisonment as a crime against humanity pursuant to Article 5(e) of the Statute (Count 5). **[page 34]**

87. Imprisonment is defined as arbitrary imprisonment, that is the deprivation of liberty of an individual without due process of law.[161]

---

154 The elements of the crime of other inhumane acts (forcible transfer) are discussed in the context of deportation pursuant to Article 5(d) of the Statute, *see infra* section II M.

155 *Stakić* Appeal Judgement, para. 315, noting in fn 649 that the category of other inhumane acts was included in Art. 6(c) of the Nuremberg Charter, Art. 5(c) of the Tokyo Charter, and Art. II(1)(c) of Control Council Law No. 10, and that convictions have been entered on this ground. The Appeals Chamber also noted "that numerous human rights treaties also prohibit inhuman and degrading treatment", including the ICCPR and the ECHR, *ibid. Kordić and Čerkez* Appeal Judgement, para. 117, affirming *Kupreškić et al.* Trial Judgement, para. 563.

156 *Kordić and Čerkez* Appeal Judgement, para. 117. In that case, the Appeals Chamber noted that "'other inhumane acts' [were] charged exclusively as injuries", *ibid. See also Blagojević and Jokić* Trial Judgement, para. 625, which held in relation to Article 5(i) that "norms of criminal law must always provide individuals with sufficient notice of what is criminal behaviour and what is not."

157 *Kordić and Čerkez* Appeal Judgement, para. 117. *See also Krnojelac* Trial Judgement, paras 130–131; *Vasiljević* Trial Judgement, para. 234.

158 *Galić* Trial Judgement para. 153; *Vasiljević* Trial Judgement, para. 235; *Krnojelac* Trial Judgement, para. 131; *Čelebići* Trial Judgement, para. 536; *Kunarac et al.* Trial Judgement, para. 501.

159 *Vasiljević* Trial Judgement, para. 235.

160 *Krnojelac* Trial Judgement, para. 132; *Vasiljevic* Trial Judgement, para. 236; *Kayishema and Ruzindana* Trial Judgement, para. 153.

161 *Kordić and Čerkez* Appeal Judgement, para. 116. The Appeals Chamber noted that the Trial Chamber had used the term "individual" in the sense of the term "civilian", *Kordić and Čerkez* Appeal Judgement, fn 139. The Trial Chamber notes that the Appeals Chamber also included the requirement "as part of a widespread or systematic attack directed against a civilian population" in its definition of the crime of imprisonment. The Trial Chamber recalls that this is a general requirement for crimes against

88. Deprivation of liberty can be achieved by an act or omission on the part of the perpetrator.[162] The act or omission must be committed with the intent to deprive a civilian of his or her physical liberty without due process of law or in the reasonable knowledge that his act or omission was likely to cause the deprivation of physical liberty without due process of law.[163]

J. Wanton destruction of villages, or devastation not justified by military necessity

89. Milan Martić is charged with wanton destruction of villages, or devastation not justified by military necessity, violations of the laws or customs of war pursuant to Article 3(b) of the Statute.[164]

90. The following elements must be proven in relation to these violations:

1. the destruction of property has occurred on a large scale;
2. the destruction was not justified by military necessity; and
3. the perpetrator acted with the intent to destroy the property in question or in reckless disregard of the likelihood of its destruction.[165]

91. The Trial Chamber considers that there is no material difference between the elements of the crimes of wanton destruction and devastation in the context of this case.[166] **[page 35]**

92. The element of destruction of property "on a large scale" requires that a considerable number of objects were destroyed. However, it is not required that a city, town or village has been destroyed in its entirety.[167] The Trial Chamber will assess on a case-by-case basis whether the extent of any proven destruction of a particular village was of sufficient scale to meet this element.[168]

93. The destruction or devastation of property is prohibited, except where justified by military necessity.[169] The Trial Chamber considers that military necessity may justify the infliction of collateral damage to civilian objects and as such constitutes an exception to the principles of the protection of civilian objects.[170] The protection of civilian objects may cease entirely or be reduced or suspended when belligerents cannot avoid causing collateral

---

humanity. Accordingly, this requirement does not need to be included in the definition of elements of the crime of imprisonment.

162 *Krnojelac* Trial Judgement, para. 115, cited in *Simić et al.* Trial Judgement, paras 64–65.

163 *Simić et al.* Trial Judgement, paras 64–65, citing *Krnojelac* Trial Judgement, para. 115. The Trial Chamber notes that the Trial Chambers in *Krnojelac* and in *Simić et al.* included that the acts or omission be "performed by *the accused or a person or persons for whom the accused bears criminal responsibility*", *ibid.* (emphasis added). The Trial Chamber considers that these words comprise definitions included in elements of Article 7(1) and 7(3) and that there is no need to include them in the definition of a crime.

164 *Hadžihasanović and Kubura* Rule 98 *bis* Appeal Decision, para. 26; *Brđanin* Trial Judgement, para. 591. Article 3(b) of the Statute is derived from Article 23(g) of the Hague Convention (IV) of 1907 and the annexed Regulations ("Hague Regulations"). Article 23 of the Hague Regulations reads, in its relevant part:

> In addition to the prohibitions provided by special Conventions, it is especially forbidden: [...]
>
> (g) To destroy or seize the enemy's property, unless such destruction or seizure be imperatively demanded by the necessities of war; [...]

165 *Kordić and Čerkez* Appeal Judgement, para. 74, reiterating *Kordić and Čerkez* Trial Judgement, para. 346. *See also Naletilić and Martinović* Trial Judgement, para. 579; *Hadžihasanović and Kubura* Trial Judgement, para. 41; *Orić* Trial Judgement, para. 581.

166 For a similar opinion with which this Trial Chamber agrees, *see Strugar* Trial Judgement, paras 290–297, reaching this conclusion both from a linguistic point of view and with reference to international instruments (*e.g.* Article 6(B) of the Nuremberg Charter; Article II (1)(b) of Control Council Law No. 10) treating "destruction" and "devastation" together. *See also Brđanin* Trial Judgement, paras 591–593.

167 *Orić* Trial Judgement, para. 585; *Hadžihasanović and Kubura* Trial Judgement, para. 43.

168 *Orić* Trial Judgement, para. 585. The Trial Chamber in *Hadžihasanović and Kubura* held that "destruction is large scale either when a large quantity of property has been destroyed or when the value of a single destroyed object is sufficiently great", *Hadžihasanović and Kubura* Trial Judgement, para. 43.

169 *Kordić and Čerkez* Appeal Judgement, para. 495; *Kordić and Čerkez* Trial Judgement, para. 346; *Naletilić and Martinović* Trial Judgement, para. 579; *Brđanin* Trial Judgement, para. 592; *Strugar* Trial Judgement, para. 295; *Hadžihasanović and Kubura* Trial Judgement, para. 45. Article 14 of the 1863 Lieber Code provides that "[m]ilitary necessity, as understood in modern civilized nations, consists in the necessity of those measures which are indispensable for securing the ends of war, and which are lawful according to the modern law and usages of war".

170 *Hadžihasanović and Kubura* Trial Judgement, para. 45; *Galić* Appeal Judgement, para. 190.

damage to civilian property even though the object of a military attack is comprised of military objectives.[171] In order to establish that the destruction was not justified by military necessity, the Prosecution has to prove not only that the destruction occurred, but also when and how the destruction occurred.[172] An assertion of military necessity or the absence thereof will be assessed on a case-by-case basis. In principle, destruction carried out before fighting begins or after fighting has ceased cannot be justified by claiming military necessity.[173]

94. The *mens rea* of wanton destruction and devastation under Article 3(b) of the Statute is that the perpetrator acted with direct or indirect intent.[174] **[page 36]**

K. Destruction or wilful damage done to institutions dedicated to education or religion

95. Milan Martić is charged with destruction or wilful damage done to institutions dedicated to religion or education, a violation of the laws or customs of war pursuant to Article 3(d) of the Statute (Count 13).[175]

96. The crime of destruction or wilful damage done to institutions dedicated to religion or education has the following elements:[176]

1. an act has caused damage to, or destruction of, an institution dedicated to religion or education;
2. the damaged or destroyed institution was not used for military purposes at the time of the act; and
3. the act was carried out with intent to destroy or damage, or in reckless disregard of the likelihood of the destruction or damage to the institution in question.

97. Article 3(d) of the Statute is considered as comprising of two types of protection for cultural, historical, and religious monuments: general protection and special protection.[177] General protection applies to civilian objects, that is all objects which are not military objects.[178] Special protection is granted to "historic monuments, works of art, and places of worship, provided they constitute the cultural or spiritual heritage of peoples".[179] The "cultural or spiritual heritage of peoples" covers "objects whose value transcends geographical boundaries, and which are unique in character and are intimately associated with the history and culture of a people".[180] Thus, special protection does not encompass all the buildings or institutions dedicated to education or religion.[181] **[page 37]**

98. The protection of institutions dedicated to religion or education is lost if such institutions are used for a military purpose.[182] The Trial Chamber considers that this exception applies both to general protection

---

171 *Kupreškić et al.* Trial Judgement, para. 522, cited by *Hadžihasanović and Kubura* Trial Judgement, para. 45.

172 *Kordić and Čerkez* Appeal Judgement, para. 495.

173 *Orić* Trial Judgement, para. 588; *Naletilić and Martinović* Trial Judgement, para. 589. However, there may be rare occasions in which pre-emptive destruction could arguably fall within the scope of 'military necessity', when such destruction is reasonably connected with the overcoming of enemy forces, *Orić* Trial Judgement, para. 588.

174 *Kordić and Čerkez* Trial Judgement, para. 346; *Naletilić and Martinović* Trial Judgement, fn 1440; *Brđanin* Trial Judgement, para. 593; *Strugar* Trial Judgement, para. 296; *Hadžihasanović and Kubura* Trial Judgement, para. 40; *Orić* Trial Judgement, para. 589.

175 Article 3(d) of the Statute prohibits "seizure of, destruction or wilful damage done to institutions dedicated to religion, charity and education, the arts and sciences, historic monuments and works of art and science." Article 3(d) of the Statute is derived from Articles 27 and 56 of the Hague Regulations, and also has its basis in the Hague Convention for the Protection of Cultural Property in the Event of Armed Conflict of 14 May 1954 ("1954 Hague Convention"), Articles 52 and 53 of Additional Protocol I, and Article 16 of Additional Protocol II, *Kordić and Čerkez* Appeal Judgement, paras 89–91; *Hadžihasanović and Kubura* Rule 98 *bis* Appeal Decision, paras 45–46; *Brđanin* Trial Judgement, para. 595; *Strugar* Trial Judgement, paras 303–306.

176 *Strugar* Trial Judgement, para. 312.

177 *Kordić and Čerkez* Appeal Judgement, paras 89–91; *Hadžihasanović and Kubura* Rule 98 *bis* Appeal Decision, para. 45. General protection is codified, *inter alia*, in Article 52 of Additional Protocol I.

178 *Kordić and Čerkez* Appeal Judgement, para. 89; *Hadžihasanović and Kubura* Rule 98 *bis* Appeal Decision, para. 45.

179 *Kordić and Čerkez* Appeal Judgement, para. 90; *Hadžihasanović and Kubura* Rule 98 *bis* Appeal Decision, para. 46, both referring to Article 53 of Additional Protocol I. Article 16 of Additional Protocol II reiterates the protection for the same categories of property. *See also* Article 1(a) of the 1954 Hague Convention, which also codifies the special protection.

180 *Kordić and Čerkez* Appeal Judgement, para. 91; ICRC Commentary on Additional Protocols, paras 2063–2068 (regarding Article 53 of Additional Protocol I), paras 4840–4844 (regarding Article 16 of Additional Protocol II).

181 *Kordić and Čerkez* Appeal Judgement, paras 89–90, 92; *Brđanin* Trial Judgement, fn 1505.

182 *Kordić and Čerkez* Trial Judgement, paras 361–362; *Naletilić and Martinović* Trial Judgement, para. 605; *Brđanin* Trial Judgement, para. 598; *Strugar* Trial Judgement, para. 310; *Hadžihasanović and Kubura* Trial Judgement, paras 58, 60–61.

and special protection under Article 3(d) of the Statute.[183] However, the protection is not lost simply because military activities or military installations are situated in the immediate vicinity of the institution. It is the use of an institution and not its location which is the decisive factor.[184]

99. The *mens rea* of this crime is that the perpetrator acted with direct or indirect intent.[185]

L. Plunder of public or private property

100. Milan Martić is charged with plunder of public and private property, a violation of the laws or customs of war pursuant to Article 3(e) of the Statute (Count 14).[186]

101. Plunder of public or private property under Article 3(e) of the Statute is committed "when private or public property is appropriated intentionally and unlawfully".[187] The prohibition of plunder includes "all forms of unlawful appropriation of property in armed conflict for which individual criminal responsibility attaches under international law, including those acts traditionally described as 'pillage'".[188] There is no difference between public and private property under the Statute.[189]

102. For the crime of plunder to be established, the appropriation of private or public property must be done without lawful basis or legal justification. Belligerent occupants may, in certain instances, lawfully use private or public property in the occupied territory for their military needs.[190] A party to the conflict is also allowed to seise enemy military equipment captured or found on the battlefield as war booty, with the exception that the personal belongings of the **[page 38]** prisoners of war may not be taken away.[191] According to the Hague Regulations, forcible contribution of money, requisition for the needs of the occupying army, and seizure of material obviously related to the conduct of military operations, though restricted, are lawful in principle.[192]

103. It is required that the property unlawfully appropriated be of "sufficient monetary value" for its appropriation to involve grave consequences for the victim.[193] The assessment of whether a piece of property holds the required value "can only be made on a case-by-case basis and only in conjunction with the general circumstances of the crime".[194] This requirement could be met in cases where appropriations take place *vis-à-vis* a large number of

---

183 *Hadžihasanović and Kubura* Trial Judgement, paras 60–61. *See also* ICRC Commentary on Additional Protocols, paras 2069–2079 (regarding Article 53 of Additional Protocol I).

184 *Naletilić and Martinović* Trial Judgement, para. 605; *Strugar* Trial Judgement, para. 310.

185 *Brđanin* Trial Judgement, para. 599; *Hadžihasanović and Kubura* Trial Judgement, para. 59.

186 The offence of plunder has also been codified in the following instruments: Article 6(b) of the Nuremberg Charter and Article 2(1)(b) of Control Council Law No. 10, punishing the war crime of "plunder of public and private property"; Articles 28 and 47 of the Hague Regulations, Article 7 of Hague Convention IX, and Article 33 of Geneva Convention IV, Article 4(2)(g) of Additional Protocol II, prohibiting pillage; Article 46 of the Hague Regulations, prohibiting confiscation of private property.

187 *Kordić and Čerkez* Appeal Judgement, para. 84.

188 *Kordić and Čerkez* Appeal Judgement, para. 79. *See also Blaškić* Appeal Judgement, para. 147. Acts of unjustified appropriation of property range from isolated acts of looting, theft or plunder committed by individuals for private gain, to organised seizure of property in violation of the rights of the owners, undertaken within the framework of a systematic economic exploitation of the targeted area, *Čelebići* Trial Judgement, para. 590; *Jelišić* Trial Judgement, para. 48; *Kordić and Čerkez* Trial Judgement, para. 352.

189 *Kordić and Čerkez* Appeal Judgement, para. 79.

190 *Naletilić and Martinović* Trial Judgement, para. 616; *Hadžihasanović and Kubura* Trial Judgement, para. 51.

191 *Hadžihasanović and Kubura* Trial Judgement, para. 51. *See also* Lieber Code, Article 45; Hague Regulations, Article 4; Geneva Convention III, Article 18 (1).

192 Hague Regulations, Articles 51–53. Article 52 provides that "Requisitions in kind and services shall not be demanded from municipalities or inhabitants except for the needs of the army of occupation. They shall be in proportion to the resources of the country, and of such a nature as not to involve the inhabitants in the obligation of taking part in military operations against their own country. Such requisitions and services shall only be demanded on the authority of the commander in the locality occupied. Contributions in kind shall as far is possible be paid for in cash; if not, a receipt shall be given and the payment of the amount due shall be made as soon as possible". *See also* Geneva Convention IV, Articles 55(2) and 57; *Naletilić and Martinović* Trial Judgement, para. 616; *Simić et al.* Trial Judgement, para. 100. Article 4(2)(g) of Additional Protocol II prohibits pillage in non-international armed conflicts, *see Hadžihasanović and Kubura* Trial Judgement, para. 52; *Customary International Humanitarian Law*, ICRC, Volume I, pp 181–182.

193 *Čelebići* Trial Judgement, para. 1154, *referred to by Kordić and Čerkez* Trial Judgement, para. 352 and later upheld by *Kordić and Čerkez* Appeal Judgement, para. 82.

194 *Kordić and Čerkez* Appeal Judgement, para. 82; *Hadžihasanović and Kubura* Trial Judgement, para. 55.

people, even though they do not lead to grave consequences for each individual.[195] What needs to be considered here is "the overall effect on the civilian population and the multitude of offences committed".[196]

104. With respect to the *mens rea* of this crime, the unlawful appropriation of property must have been perpetrated with either direct or indirect intent.[197]

M. Deportation and other inhumane acts (forcible transfer)

105. Milan Martić is charged with deportation and other inhumane acts (forcible transfers) under Article 5(d) and (i), respectively (Counts 10 and 11).[198]

106. The protected interests underlying the prohibitions against deportation and forcible transfer "include the right of the victim to stay in his or her home and community and the right not to be deprived of his or her property by being forcibly displaced to another location."[199] **[page 39]**

107. The *actus reus* of deportation is "the forced displacement of persons by expulsion or other forms of coercion from the area in which they are lawfully present, across a *de jure* border or, in certain circumstances, a *de facto* border, without grounds permitted under international law."[200] The *actus reus* of forcible transfer is the forced displacement of persons within national boundaries.[201]

108. The element that the displacement be forced requires that the victims had no genuine choice in their displacement.[202] In situations where the victims have consented, or even requested, their removal, that consent "must be real in the sense that it is given voluntarily and as a result of the individual's free will, assessed in the light of surrounding circumstances."[203]

109. International law permits involuntary displacements on humanitarian grounds.[204] Thus, in cases where displacements are permitted on humanitarian grounds, the act of displacement cannot constitute the *actus reus* of deportation or forcible transfer.[205] However, displacements for humanitarian reasons are not justifiable where the humanitarian crisis that caused the displacement is itself the result of the accused's own unlawful activity.[206]

110. With regard to deportation, the *Stakić* Appeals Chamber found that "the default principle under customary international law [...] is that there must be expulsion across a *de jure* border to another country."[207] The Appeals Chamber has also held that under certain circumstances displacement across a *de facto* border may be sufficient to amount to deportation.[208]

---

195 *Kordić and Čerkez* Appeal Judgement, para. 83; *Naletilić and Martinović* Trial Judgement, para. 614; *Hadžihasanović and Kubura* Trial Judgement, para. 55.

196 *Kordić and Čerkez* Appeal Judgement, para. 83.

197 *Hadžihasanović and Kubura* Trial Judgement, para. 50; *Orić* Decision on the Motion for Acquittal pursuant to Rule 98 *bis*, Hearing, 8 Jun 2005, T. 9027.

198 In this judgement, the term "forcible transfer" will be used concerning displacement charged in Count 11.

199 *Stakić* Appeal Judgement, para. 277, *accepting Stakić* Trial Judgement, para. 681.

200 *Stakić* Appeal Judgement, para. 278.

201 *Stakić* Appeal Judgement, para. 317.

202 *Stakić* Appeal Judgement, para. 279. The absence of genuine choice has been interpreted to include displacement as a result of threats or the use of force, fear of violence, and illegal detention, *Krnojelac* Appeal Judgement, para. 229. The Appeals Chamber has held that factors other than force may render an act involuntary, such as taking advantage of coercive circumstances, *Kunarac et al.* Appeal Judgement, para. 129 (in the context of rape).

203 *Stakić* Appeal Judgement, para. 279, referring to *Krnojelac* Appeal Judgement para. 299 and *Kunarac et al.* Appeal Judgement, paras 127–128 (the latter in the context of rape).

204 Article 49(2) of Geneva Convention IV, which is applicable to international armed conflict, provides that "the Occupying Power may undertake total or partial evacuation of a given area if the security of the population or imperative military reasons so demand." Similarly, Article 17 of Additional Protocol II, which is applicable to non-international armed conflict, provides that "[t]he displacement of the civilian population shall not be ordered for reasons related to the conflict unless the security of the civilians involved or imperative military reasons so demand." While Article 17 of Additional Protocol II does not use the term "evacuation" it is clear from reading the provision that the same temporary measure as described in Article 49(2) of Geneva Convention IV is intended.

205 *Stakić* Appeal Judgement, para. 286, noting that "the participation of an NGO in facilitating displacements does not in and of itself render an otherwise unlawful transfer lawful", *ibid.*

206 *Stakić* Appeal Judgement, para. 287.

207 *Stakić* Appeal Judgement, para. 300.

208 In general, the question whether a particular *de facto* border is sufficient for the purposes of the crime of deportation should be examined on a case by case basis in light of customary international law, *Stakić* Appeal Judgement, para. 300, (footnotes omitted).

111. The *mens rea* of deportation is that the perpetrator must intend to displace the victims across the border.[209] The *mens rea* of forcible transfer is that the perpetrator must intend to displace the **[page 40]** victims within the relevant national border.[210] It is not necessary for either crime that the perpetrator intends the displacement to be permanent.[211]

N. Persecution

112. Milan Martić is charged with persecution, as a crime against humanity pursuant to Article 5(h) of the Statute (Count 1).

113. The crime of persecution consists of an act or omission, which:

1. discriminates in fact and which denies or infringes upon a fundamental right laid down in international customary or treaty law; and
2. was carried out deliberately with the intention to discriminate on political, racial or religious grounds.[212]

114. Each of the three grounds listed is in itself sufficient to qualify conduct as persecution, notwithstanding the conjunctive "and" in the text of Article 5(h).[213]

115. What distinguishes persecution from other crimes against humanity is that the underlying act is committed on discriminatory grounds.[214] There is no comprehensive list of the acts which may constitute persecution.[215] Such acts may be one of those listed under Article 5 of the Statute, or one of the acts constituting a crime under other articles of the Statute.[216] Furthermore, a persecutory act need not be prohibited explicitly either in Article 5 or elsewhere in the Statute.[217]

116. It is not the case, however, that *any* act, if committed with the requisite discriminatory intent, amounts to persecutions as a crime against humanity.[218] There must be clearly defined limits on the expansion of the types of acts which qualify as persecution.[219] In order to amount to persecutions, the act must constitute a denial or infringement of a fundamental right laid down in **[page 41]** customary international law.[220] Furthermore, not every act which constitutes a denial or infringement of a fundamental right is serious enough to constitute persecution. Acts of persecution must be of equal gravity to the acts enumerated under Article 5.[221]

117. A single act or omission may be sufficient to constitute persecution "as long as this act or omission discriminates in fact and was carried out deliberately with the intention to discriminate on one of the listed grounds."[222] Therefore, the act or omission itself must have discriminatory consequences and not just be carried out with discriminatory intent.[223]

---

209 *Stakić* Appeal Judgement, para. 278.
210 *Stakić* Appeal Judgement, para. 317.
211 *Stakić* Appeal Judgement, paras 278, 317.
212 *Kvočka et al.* Appeal Judgement, para. 320; *Krnojelac* Appeal Judgement para. 185; *Vasiljević* Appeal Judgement para. 113; *Blaškić* Appeal Judgement, para. 131; *Kordić and Čerkez* Appeal Judgement para. 101; *Stakić* Appeal Judgement, para. 327.
213 *Tadić* Trial Judgement, para. 713. *See e.g. Krnojelac* Appeal Judgement, para. 184.
214 *Kupreškić et al.* Trial Judgement, para. 607.
215 *Vasiljević* Trial Judgement, para. 246, citing *Tadić* Trial Judgement, para. 694; *Kupreškić et al.* Trial Judgement, paras 567–568, 614; *Blaškić* Trial Judgement, 218–219; *Kordić and Čerkez* Trial Judgement, para. 192; *Krnojelac* Trial Judgement, para. 433.
216 *Krnojelac* Appeal Judgement, para. 219.
217 *Kupreškić et al.* Trial Judgement, para. 614. The Trial Chamber in *Tadić* held that "the persecutory act must be intended to cause, and result in, an infringement on an individual's enjoyment of a basic or fundamental right", *Tadić* Trial Judgement, para. 715. Furthermore, it has been held that the acts themselves do not have to be inherently criminal, but they may become criminal and persecutory if committed with discriminatory intent, *Kvočka et al.* Trial Judgement, para. 186. *See also Tadić* Trial Judgement, para. 710.
218 *Blaškić* Appeal Judgement, para. 139.
219 *Kupreškić et al.* Trial Judgement, para. 618; *Kordić and Čerkez* Trial Judgement para. 194.
220 *Kordić* Appeal Judgement, para. 103; *Blaškić* Appeal Judgement, para. 139.
221 *Blaškić* Appeal Judgement, para. 160; *Kupreškić et al.* Trial Judgement para. 619.
222 *Vasiljević* Appeal Judgement, para. 113. *See also Kordić and Čerkez* Appeal Judgement, para. 102.
223 *Blaškić* Appeal Judgement, para. 135. *See also Blagojević and Jokić* Trial Judgement, para. 583; *Stakić* Trial Judgement, para. 733.

118. It has been held that an act is discriminatory when a victim is targeted because of membership of a "group defined by the perpetrator on a political, racial or religious basis".[224] However, it is not necessary that a victim actually *be* a member of the targeted group. Thus, a Serb mistaken for a Muslim may still be the victim of the crime of persecution.[225]

119. The jurisprudence holds that the following acts, which the Prosecution has charged under Count 1 of the Indictment, may constitute the underlying acts of the crime of persecution: extermination and murder; imprisonment, inhumane living conditions, torture, beatings, sexual assault, unlawful attacks on civilians, restrictive and discriminatory measures, robbery, deportation or forcible transfer, destruction of homes, other public and private property, cultural institutions, historic monuments and sacred sites.[226] **[page 42]**

120. The crime of persecution requires evidence of a specific intent to discriminate on political, racial or religious grounds.[227] This intent must be aimed at a group, rather than an individual; thus the *mens rea* "is the specific intent to cause injury to a human being because he belongs to a particular community or group."[228]

121. Discriminatory intent may be inferred, for example from the discriminatory nature of an attack characterised as a crime against humanity provided that the circumstances surrounding the commission of the alleged acts substantiate the existence of such intent.[229] However, discriminatory intent may not be inferred directly from the *general* discriminatory nature of such an attack, that is such a context may not in and of itself amount to evidence of discriminatory intent.[230]

122. Circumstances which may be taken into consideration when inferring discriminatory intent include "the systematic nature of the crimes committed against a racial or religious group and the general attitude of the alleged perpetrator as demonstrated by his behaviour".[231] Generally, such specific intent can only be inferred from "objective facts and the general conduct of an accused seen in its entirety."[232]

---

224 *Blagojević and Jokić* Trial Judgement, para. 583.

225 *Krnojelac* Appeal Judgement para. 185.

226 *Blaškić* Appeal Judgement, paras 143, 153, 155, 159; *Kordić and Čerkez* Appeal Judgement paras 104–106, 108, 672; *Krnojelac* Appeal Judgement, paras 221–222; *Brđanin* Trial Judgement, paras 999, 1029 *et seq*; *Krnojelac* Trial Judgement, paras 438–443; *Kupreškić et al.* Trial Judgement, para. 615; *Stakić* Trial Judgement, para. 757 (holding that "not only rape, but also any other sexual assault falling short of actual penetration is punishable [as persecution]"); *Tadić* Trial Judgement, para. 717. While robbery has not previously been expressly considered as a crime which may constitute an underlying act of persecutions, the Trial Chamber notes that the fundamental right to property is recognised in the Tribunal's jurisprudence, *see e.g. Blaškić* Appeal Judgement, para. 145, *Blagojević* Trial Judgement, paras 593–594; *Naletelić and Martinović* Trial Judgement, para. 699 (and authorities cited therein); *Kordić and Čerkez* Appeal Judgement, para. 81. The Trial Chamber further notes that destruction of property may constitute an underlying act of the crime of persecutions, *see e.g. Blaškić* Appeal Judgement, para. 146 (and authorities cited therein); *Kordić and Čerkez* Appeal Judgement, para. 108. Aggravated forms of crimes against property in the context of plunder under Article 3 of the Statute have been recognised as acts of persecutions, *see e.g. Kupreškić et al.* Trial Judgement, para. 631; *Kordić and Čerkez* Trial Judgement, para. 205. Moreover, theft and robbery have been considered in the context of a persecutory campaign, *see e.g. Kvočka et al.* Trial Judgement, para. 496, in which the Trial Chamber held "[the Accused] was involved in the extortion of detainees and stealing money from detainees in Omarska camp, which in this context can be characterized as part of the harassment inflicted upon detainees in the camp and thus a part of the persecutory campaign". *See also Kvočka et al.* Trial Judgement, para. 731, *Kordić and Čerkez* Trial Judgement, paras 514–520. The Trial Chamber is therefore satisfied that the appropriation of property with violence in the form of robbery may constitute an underlying act of the crime of persecution if perpetrated with the requisite intent. In relation to destruction, the Trial Chamber in *Kupreškić et al.* found that the comprehensive destruction of homes and property, which constituted the destruction of the livelihood of a certain population, may constitute a gross or blatant denial of fundamental rights, and if committed on discriminatory grounds, could amount to persecutions, *Kupreškić et al.* Trial Judgement, para. 631. The Trial Chamber in *Kordić and Čerkez* held that the destruction and damage of religious or educational institutions may constitute persecution, *Kordić and Čerkez* Trial Judgement, para. 207. In relation to plunder, the Appeals Chamber in *Kordić and Čerkez* held that it must be considered whether an act of plunder, committed separately or cumulatively, with discriminatory intent *in concreto* amounts to persecutions being of an equal gravity as the other crimes against humanity listed in Article 5 of the Statute, *Kordić and Čerkez* Appeal Judgement para. 109. *See also Blaškić* Trial Judgement, para. 227; *Kordić and Čerkez* Trial Judgement para. 205; *Kupreškić et al.* Trial Judgement para. 631; *Tadić* Trial Judgement paras 707, 710.

227 *Kvočka et al.* Appeal Judgement, para. 460; *Blaškić* Appeal Judgement, para. 165.

228 *Kordić and Čerkez* Appeal Judgement, para. 111.

229 *Blaškić* Appeal Judgement, para. 164, citing *Krnojelac* Appeal Judgement, 184. *See also Kordić and Čerkez* Appeal Judgement paras 110, 950; *Kvočka et al.* Appeal Judgement para. 366; *Naletelić and Martinović* Appeal Judgement, paras 131, 146, 572.

230 *Kvočka et al.* Appeal Judgement, para. 460 (emphasis added).

231 *Kvočka et al.* Appeal Judgement, para. 460.

232 *Kordić and Čerkez* Appeal Judgement, para. 715.

O. The Defence's challenge to the concept of JCE

123. In its closing arguments, the Defence submitted that JCE is not envisaged in the Statute as a mode of liability and that its existence and applicability can only be established by the United Nations Security Council.[233] The Defence therefore submits that the application of JCE in the instant case is beyond the competence of the Trial Chamber.[234] This conclusion, in the Defence's view, is not affected by the consideration that JCE has been applied in previous cases.[235] **[page 43]**

124. The Trial Chamber will discuss JCE as a mode of liability later in the judgement.[236] However, as the Defence has effectively raised a jurisdictional challenge in relation to the application of JCE to the instant case, the Trial Chamber considers it necessary to deal with the Defence submission in the present section.

125. The principle of individual criminal responsibility is laid down in Article 7(1) of the Statute, which provides as follows:

> A person who planned, instigated, ordered, committed or otherwise aided and abetted in the planning, preparation or execution of a crime referred to in articles 2 to 5 of the present Statute, shall be individually responsible for the crime.

126. The Appeals Chamber found that the Statute does not confine itself to providing for jurisdiction over those persons who plan, instigate, order, physically perpetrate a crime or otherwise aid and abet in its planning, preparation or execution.[237] This is established jurisprudence. In other words, the Statute does not exclude other modes of liability such as JCE, which are based in customary international law. After reviewing relevant treaties and national legislation, as well as several post-World War II war-crimes cases, the Appeals Chamber held that JCE existed as a mode of individual criminal responsibility in customary international law at the time of the events in the former Yugoslavia.[238] The Appeals Chamber therefore found that JCE is a form of "commission" under Article 7(1) of the Statute for which the Tribunal has jurisdiction *ratione personae*. The Defence argument is therefore dismissed.

III. FACTUAL FINDINGS

A. Background

127. In April and May 1990, multi-party elections were held in the Socialist Republic of Croatia.[239] The Croatian Democratic Union ("HDZ") won 41.5% of the votes and two-thirds of the seats in the Parliament.[240] On 30 May 1990, the HDZ candidate Franjo Tuđman was elected President of the Presidency of the Socialist Republic of Croatia.[241] As a result of the elections, the **[page 44]** Serbian Democratic Party ("SDS") gained power in the municipalities of Benkovac, Donji Lapac, Gračac, Glina, Korenica, Knin, Obrovac, and Vojnić.[242]

---

233 Defence Closing Argument, 11 Jan 2007, T. 11325–11327.

234 *Ibid.*

235 *Ibid.*

236 *See infra* Section IV, B 1.

237 *Tadić* Appeal Judgement, para. 190.

238 *Tadić* Appeal Judgement, para. 226. *See also Brđanin* Appeal Judgement, paras 363–365.

239 Ex. 820, Agreed Facts, para. 3. *See also* Veljko Džakula, 16 Jan 2006, T. 344; Milan Babić, 3 Mar 2006, T. 1852; Vlado Vuković, 27 Mar 2006, T. 2681; Witness MM-036, 4 Apr 2006, T. 3198; Ratko Ličina, 14 Aug 2006, T. 6370.

240 Ex. 820, Agreed Facts, para. 3. *See also* Milan Babić, 15 Feb 2006, T. 1358, 21 Feb 2006, T. 1720; Witness MM-022, 20 Mar 2006, T. 2321; Vlado Vuković, 27 Mar 2006, T. 2681; Witness MM-078, 25 May 2006, T. 4481; Witness MM-096, 18 Aug 2006, T. 6728.

241 Ex. 820, Agreed Facts, para. 3. *See also* Veljko Džakula, 17 Jan 2006, T. 453–454; Milan Babić, 21 Feb 2006, T. 1720.

242 Veljko Džakula, 16 Jan 2006, T. 344; Milan Babić, 15 Feb 2006, T. 1359; Witness MM-037, 28 Mar 2006, T. 2767–2668; Ratko Ličina, 14 Aug 2006, T. 6381–6382, 6403–6404; Branko Popović, 8 Sep 2006, T. 7996–7997. The SDS' aims and goals included "creating conditions for the full self-confirmation of the spiritual and cultural identity of each Yugoslav people by itself, independently of which federal unit it belonged to; ensuring constitutional possibility for establishing territorial autonomies inside the federal units, if the population on the territories with a special ethnic composition or cultural and historical identity decides so on a referendum", Ex. 138. *See also* Veljko Džakula, 16 Jan 2006, T. 344; Ratko Ličina, 14 Aug 2006, T. 6371; Ex. 23, pp 20, 24–25.

128. On 25 July 1990, a Serbian Assembly was established in Srb, north of Knin, as the political representation of the Serbian people in Croatia.[243] The Serbian Assembly declared sovereignty and autonomy of the Serb people in Croatia.[244] On 31 July 1990, Milan Babić became president of the Serbian National Council ("SNC"), the executive body of the Serbian Assembly.[245] On 16 August 1990, the SNC called for a referendum on the autonomy of Serbs in Croatia to be held between 19 August and 2 September 1990.[246] The following day, 17 August 1990, the Government of Croatia declared the referendum illegal. The Croatian police moved towards several Serb-majority towns in the Krajina region and removed weaponry from the SJBs.[247] Serbs responded by putting up barricades in Knin and surroundings.[248] The referendum was held between 19 August and 2 September 1990: 97.7% voted in favour of autonomy.[249]

B. The SAO Krajina

1. Development of the SAO Krajina

129. On 21 December 1990, the SAO Krajina was proclaimed by the municipalities of the regions of Northern Dalmatia and Lika, in south-western Croatia.[250] Article 1 of the Statute of the SAO Krajina defined the SAO Krajina as "a form of territorial autonomy within the Republic of Croatia" on which the Constitution of the Republic of Croatia, state laws and the Statute of the SAO Krajina were applied.[251] **[page 45]**

130. On 22 December 1990, the Parliament of Croatia adopted a new constitution, wherein Croatia was defined as "the national state of the Croatian nation and a state of members of other nations and minorities who are citizens: Serbs [...] who are guaranteed equality with citizens of Croatian nationality [...]".[252] The Serb population in the Krajina region considered that by the adoption of the new constitution, they had been deprived of the right to be a constituent nation in Croatia, which would include the right of self-determination.[253]

131. On 4 January 1991, the Executive Council of the SAO Krajina established the Regional Secretariat for Internal Affairs ("SUP") in Knin.[254] On the same date, Milan Martić was appointed the Secretary for Internal Affairs of the SAO Krajina.[255] On 5 January 1991, the Executive Council informed the MUP of Croatia that the establishment of the SUP revoked the authority of the MUP of Croatia in the SAO Krajina territory.[256]

---

243 Ex. 820, Agreed Facts, para. 4. *See also* Ex. 23, p. 25.

244 Ex. 820, Agreed Facts, para. 4. *See also* Veljko Džakula, 16 Jan 2006, T. 385, 18 Jan 2006, T. 507; Milan Babić, 21 Feb 2006, T. 1743–1744; Ratko Ličina, 15 Aug 2006, T. 6497, 17 Aug 2006, T. 6693–6696; Lazar Macura, 13 Sep 2006, T. 8272; Ex. 141.

245 Milan Babić, 15 Feb 2006, T. 1327.

246 Ex. 820, Agreed Facts, para. 5. *See also* Ex. 179.

247 Witness MM-096, 18 Aug 2006, T. 6755, 6761–6762, 6769. *See also* Ex. 22; Ex. 23.

248 This is also referred to as the "Log Revolution", Ex. 820, Agreed Facts, para. 6. *See also* Ex. 496, p. 6; Ex. 497; Witness MM-003, 8 Mar 2006, T. 1968–1969; Witness MM-078, 25 May 2006, T. 4475; Ratko Ličina, 14 Aug 2006, T. 6397, 6400; Witness MM-096, 18 Aug 2006, T. 6777–6778.

249 Ex. 820, Agreed Facts, para. 7. *See also* Veljko Džakula, 18 Jan 2006, T. 508; Milan Babić, 21 Feb 2006, T. 1746–1747, 2 Mar 2006, T. 1771; Ex. 142.

250 Ex. 820, Agreed Facts, para. 9. *See also* Milan Babić, 21 Feb 2006, T. 1747; Ex. 143.

251 Ex. 820, Agreed Facts, para. 9. *See also* Milan Babić, 21 Feb 2006, T. 1747–1748. Art 4 of the Statute provided that "[t]he Serbian Autonomous District of Krajina shall have territory that is comprised of territories of the present Union of Municipalities of Northern Dalamatia and Lika, territories of municipalities with majority Serbian populations which adopt decisions to joint the Serbian Autonomous District of Krajina, and settlements in which Serbian people comprise the majority of the population and which have voted at a referendum in favour of joining one of the existing or newly established municipalities with a majority Serbian population", Ex. 143.

252 Ex. 910, p. 9; Veljko Džakula, 18 Jan 2006, T. 513.

253 Ratko Ličina, 14 Aug 2006, T. 6386, 16 Aug 2006, T. 6542–6543; Witness MM-090, 1 Sep 2006, T. 7563–7573.

254 Ex. 183. The SUP in Knin included SJBs of Obrovac, Benkovac, Knin, Gračac, Titova Korenica, Donji Lapac, Dvor na Uni, Glina, Kostajnica, Vojnić, *ibid.*; Witness MM-096, 21 Aug 2006, T. 6829, 6831–6832. *See also* Ex. 182; Ex. 181; Reynaud Theunens, 26 Jan 2006, T. 686–687; Ex. 1042, Tab 2; Ex. 1043, Tab 2, DVD 3, pp 10–16; Ex. 1044.

255 Ex. 820, Agreed Facts, para. 10. *See also* Milan Babić, 15 Feb 2006, T. 1397–1398, 1406, 2 Mar 2006, T. 1800; Reynaud Theunens, 3 Feb 2006, T. 1013; Ex. 33.

256 Ex. 183. *See also* Ex. 485, Decree on Internal Organisation and Operation of the Ministry of the Interior, providing that there were two services within the MUP, the Public Security Service and the State Security Service (Art. 7), and that in the event of a state of war or imminent threat of war "special police units" would be formed (Art. 6a).

132. In March 1991, there were armed clashes in Pakrac in Western Slavonia and in Plitvice between Titova Korenica and Saborsko between Croatian MUP special police forces and the police of the SAO Krajina. In both of these clashes, the JNA intervened to separate the two sides.[257]

133. On 1 April 1991, Milan Babić as President of the Executive Council of the SAO Krajina ordered mobilisation of the TO and volunteer units of the SAO Krajina.[258] However, the evidence shows that between January and August 1991 the municipal TO staffs and units only existed on paper.[259] In the same order, Milan Babić requested the MUP of Serbia to provide technical and **[page 46]** personnel support to the SUP of the SAO Krajina.[260] Also on 1 April 1991, the Executive Council of the SAO Krajina passed a decision joining the SAO Krajina to Serbia, wherein it was stipulated that the constitution and laws of Serbia, as well as the constitutional-legal system of the SFRY, were to apply in the SAO Krajina.[261] It was also decided that a referendum was to be held on the question: "[a]re you in favour of the annexation of the SAO Krajina to the Republic of Serbia on the 30th of April?"[262] The President of Serbia, Slobodan Milošević, publicly opposed the referendum on joining the SAO Krajina with Serbia, stating that the ballot would have to read instead "in favour of remaining in Yugoslavia"; moreover, he asked that the decision on the annexation of the SAO Krajina to Serbia, be withdrawn.[263]

134. On 12 May 1991, after the intervention of Slobodan Milošević, the referendum was held on the following question: "[a]re you in favour of the SAO Krajina joining the Republic of Serbia and staying in Yugoslavia with Serbia, Montenegro and others who wish to preserve Yugoslavia?" with 99.8% voting in favour.[264] On 16 May 1991, the Assembly of the SAO Krajina approved the outcome of the referendum and stated that "the territory of the SAO Krajina is a constitutive part of the unified state territory of the Republic of Serbia".[265] Both Milan Babić and Milan Martić publicly expressed views that SAO Krajina belonged with Serbia.[266] On 19 May 1991, a referendum was held in Croatia, except in predominantly Serb areas, concerning independence of Croatia from Yugoslavia. 94.1% of those voting came out in favour of independence.[267]

135. On 29 May 1991, the SAO Krajina government was established with Milan Babić as President.[268] Milan Babić appointed Milan Martić as Minister of Defence.[269] On the same day, the Assembly of the SAO Krajina established "special purpose police units" named *Milicija Krajine*, in addition to the previously established Public Security Service police and State Security Service police.[270] The *Milicija Krajine* was

---

257 Veljko Džakula, 18 Jan 2006, T. 516–517; Milan Babić, 17 Feb 2006, T. 1506–1507, 1510–1513, (also testifying that a Croat and a Serb policeman were killed), 20 Feb 2006, T. 1600; Marko Vuković, 24 Mar 2006, T. 2571; Vlado Vuković, 27 Mar 2006, T. 2651, 2686–2688, 28 Mar 2006, T. 2722, 2729; Witness MM-037, 28 Mar 2006, T. 2758; Ex. 268, T. 11621; Slobodan Perić, 7 Sep 2006, T. 7908–7910; Lazar Macura, 12 Sep 2006, T. 8208; Stevo Plejo, 20 Sep 2006, T. 8676–8677; Nikola Medaković, 9 Oct 2006, T. 8957–8958; Ex. 476, p. 251.

258 Ex. 29. In the SFRY, the TO was organised, funded and equipped on the level of the Republics of the SFRY, Reynaud Theunens, 26 Jan 2006, T. 656; Ex. 6, p. 6. *See also* Ex. 147.

259 Milan Babić, 15 Feb 2006, T. 1393–1395, testifying that the only armed units of the SAO Krajina during this time period were the *Milicija Krajine* and volunteer units, *see also* Radoslav Maksić, 6 Feb 2006, T. 1154–1155, 1171. Ex. 30 providing (p. 1) that the Benkovac municipality TO staff, following a decision by the SAO Krajina Government of 15 July 1991, began "forming and arming the TO units of Benkovac Municipality on 17 July 1991". It is also stated (p. 1) that "the most difficult problem during the beginning of the formation of TO units was that there was a very small quantity of weapons available."

260 Ex. 29.

261 Ex. 820, Agreed Facts, para. 11. *See also* Milan Babić, 16 Feb 2006, T. 1511; Ex. 144; Ex. 145.

262 Milan Babić, 2 Mar 2006, T. 1824, 1830–1832; Ex. 148.

263 Ex. 235. *See also* Ex. 201, p. 3; Mile Dakić, 25 Oct 2006, T. 10025–10026; Milan Babić, 16 Feb 2006, T. 1476–1477, 2 Mar 2006, T. 1830–1831; Lazar Macura, 14 Sep 2006, T. 8326.

264 Ex. 820, Agreed Facts, para. 13. *See also* Milan Babić, 2 Mar 2006, T. 1830; Ex. 146; Ex. 148; Ex. 234.

265 Ex. 613, Art. 3, p. 45. *See also* Ex. 149. Following this decision, an SAO Krajina delegation went to Belgrade to present the results of the referendum as well as the request on the annexation of the SAO Krajina to Serbia, however the delegation was not received by the Serbian Assembly, Lazar Macura, 12 Sep 2006, T. 8201–8203. *See also* Ljubica Vujanić, 15 Sep 2006, T. 8479–8480, 18 Sep 2006, T. 8535–8538; Ex. 956.

266 Ex. 973; Ex. 955, pp 3–4. *See also* Witness MM-105, 1 Nov 2006, T. 10496–10497. On 29 May 1991, the Assembly of the SAO Krajina passed the Constitutional Law of the SAO Krajina which defined the SAO Krajina as part of the federative Yugoslavia, Ex. 820, Agreed Facts, para. 13.

267 Ex. 820, Agreed Facts, para. 14. *See also* Ex. 1019, p. 5.

268 Milan Babić, 15 Feb 2006, T. 1328.

269 Milan Babić, 15 Feb 2006, T. 1405–1407. *See also* Ex. 154.

270 Ex. 820, Agreed Facts, para. 15. *See also* Ex. 485. The Public Security Service was responsible for maintaining law and order. The SDB handled political crime, terrorism, extremism, and intelligence work. The *Milicija Krajine* units defended the territorial

established within the MUP, but was put under the authority of **[page 47]** the Ministry of Defence.[271] The *Milicija Krajine* units wore patches on the sleeves of their uniforms reading in Cyrillic "Milicija Krajine".[272] On 27 June 1991, Milan Martić was appointed Minister of Interior.[273] According to Milan Babić, on this day Milan Martić withdrew from his position as Minister of Defence.[274]

136. On 25 June 1991, Croatia and Slovenia declared independence from Yugoslavia.[275] However, on 8 July 1991, an international agreement was reached that Croatia and Slovenia would suspend implementation of their independence until 8 October 1991.[276]

137. On 1 August 1991, the SAO Krajina government decided to apply the Law on Defence of Serbia in the SAO Krajina. Accordingly, the *Milicija Krajine* units together with the TO made up the armed forces of the SAO Krajina.[277] The evidence shows that the TO used JNA solid-colour uniforms with patches reading "SAO Krajina" in Cyrillic, on the sleeve.[278] Milan Babić, as President, was the Commander of the TO of the SAO Krajina.[279] On 8 August 1991, Milan Martić was appointed Deputy Commander of the TO of the SAO Krajina, in which position he remained **[page 48]** until 30 September 1991.[280] He continued to hold the position of Minister of the Interior while he was Deputy Commander of the TO.[281]

138. As will be discussed below, there were several ongoing clashes between Croatian armed forces and formations and the forces of the SAO Krajina from the spring of 1991, including in Kijevo, Drniš, Hrvatska Dubica, Saborsko, and Škabrnja.[282] During the second half of 1991, there were numerous cease-fire agreements and agreements on the withdrawal of the JNA from Croatia.[283] On 23 November, the Vance Plan was signed

integrity of the [SAO Krajina], secured vital facilities, infiltrated sabotage groups, and could also be used in military operations, Radoslav Maksić, 6 Feb 2006, T. 1169–1170; Witness MM-079, 31 Mar 2006, T. 3030–3031; Nikola Medaković, 10 Oct 2006, T. 9054; Witness MM-117, 18 Oct 2006, T. 9674; Ex. 32.

271 Ex. 820, Agreed Facts, para. 15. The Trial Chamber notes the evidence that a clash occurred between Milan Babić and Milan Martić as a result of the former's decision to appoint Dušan Vještika as Minister of Interior, and that according to Milan Babić, Milan Martić only accepted the appointment as Minister of Defence on condition that he "could still maintain his control over the special police units which were being trained at Golubić", Milan Babić, 15 Feb 2006, T. 1406, 1408; Ex. 44; Ex. 544; Ex. 1028, Group 2, p. 13. *See also* Ex. 485, Art. 6b, according to which the "leader" of the future *Milicija Krajine* Service would be accountable to the Minister of the Interior.

272 Vlado Vuković, 27 Mar 2006, T. 2701–2703; Nikola Medaković, 10 Oct 2006, T. 9052; Ex. 266.

273 Ex. 820, Agreed Facts, para. 16. *See also* Milan Babić, 15 Feb 2006, T. 1408, 2 Mar 2006, T. 1803–1804; Ex. 34. With the establishment of the government in May 1991, the SUP of the SAO Krajina was changed into the MUP of the SAO Krajina, Milan Babić, 15 Feb 2006, T. 1406–1407; Ex. 44. On 1 August 1991, a decision was reached about the application of the law on internal affairs of the Republic of Serbia on the territory of Krajina, Milan Babić, 15 Feb 2006, T. 1403–1404.

274 Milan Babić, 15 Feb 2006, T. 1407. The Trial Chamber notes that while Ex. 582, dated 23 July 1991 and Ex. 215, dated 19 August 1991, refer to Milan Martić as Minister of Defence, it however accepts the evidence of Milan Babić.

275 Ex. 820, Agreed Facts, para. 14.

276 Ex. 820, Agreed Facts, para. 17. *See also* Milan Babić, 2 Mar 2006, T. 1836, 3 March 2006, T. 1882, 1887, 1923.

277 Ex. 31, Art. 5.

278 Witness MM-037, 28 Mar 2006, T. 2787–2788, 29 Mar 2006, T. 2813; Ex. 188. Regarding JNA uniforms, *see infra* fn 283.

279 Ex. 31, Art. 6. The Trial Chamber notes that the *Milicija Krajine* is not mentioned in this provision, Milan Babić, 16 Feb 2006, T. 1422–1424. *See also* Ex. 189; Radoslav Maksić, 6 Feb 2006, T. 1154.

280 Ex. 820, Agreed Facts, para. 19. *See also* Milan Babić, 15 Feb 2006, T. 1395–1396, 16 Feb 2006, T. 1435–1437, testifying that in early August 1991 Slobodan Milošević requested him to appoint Milan Martić as Commander of the TO, however he refused to do this because Milan Martić "was not qualified to hold that position, that this was something that a general of the army should do", and that Milan Martić was instead appointed Deputy Commander of the TO to prevent him from becoming "independent of the government"; Radoslav Maksić, an officer in the SAO Krajina TO and subsequently TO Commander, testifying that he had numerous meetings with Milan Babić as Supreme Commander and only rarely with Milan Martić, Radoslav Maksić, 7 Feb 2006, T. 1230–1231; Reynaud Theunens, 6 Feb 2006, T. 1128–1129; Ex. 37.

281 Milan Babić, 15 Feb 2006, T. 1395–1396, 16 Feb 2006, T. 1436. *See also* Ex. 121; Reynaud Theunens, 6 Feb 2006, T. 1128–1129.

282 *See infra* paras 161–171, 173–175, 220–224, 236–243.

283 These cease-fire agreements included the Brioni Moratorium, Ex. 820, Agreed Facts, para. 17. *See also* Veljko Džakula, 18 Jan 2006, T. 527–528; Milan Babić, 2 Mar 2006, T. 1834–1835, 3 Mar 2006, T. 1871–1872; the Carrington Plan, Milan Babić, 20 Feb 2006, T. 1614–1615, 1634–1635; Lazar Macura, 14 Sep 2006, T. 8328. On 8 October 1991, the JNA and the Croatian armed forces signed an agreement, under the auspices of the European Community, concerning the withdrawal of JNA units from Croatia, Ex. 240; Milan Babić, 3 March 2006, T. 1922–1923. In the SFRY, JNA was a federal institution, Reynaud Theunens, 26 Jan 2006, T. 656; Ex. 6, p. 6. The evidence shows that JNA soldiers wore solid-colour uniforms, which witnesses described as olive-grey or olive-green in colour. The evidence also shows that from 1992 or 1993 camouflage uniforms were introduced for JNA units. The caps had a five-pointed star and the officers had shoulder patches to denote rank, Vlado Vuković, 27 Mar 2006, T. 2706; Lazar Macura, 15 Sep 2006, T. 8401, 8405.

by the President of Croatia Franjo Tuđman, the President of Serbia Slobodan Milošević and the SFRY Federal Secretary for Defence General Veljko Kadijević.[284] The Vance Plan made provision for the deployment of a United Nations Protection Force ("UNPROFOR") in the Krajina, Western Slavonia and Eastern Slavonia, for demilitarisation, and eventual return of refugees and displaced persons.[285] Importantly, the Vance Plan stated that "[t]he role of the United Nations troops would be to ensure that the areas remained demilitarised and that all persons residing in them were protected from fear of armed attack."[286]

139. On 30 November 1991, the SAO Krajina adopted its own Law on Defence, whereby the Law on Defence of Serbia ceased to apply in the SAO Krajina.[287] According to the new law, the TO **[page 49]** was "part of the unified armed forces of the [SFRY]" and the President of the SAO Krajina led "the armed forces in times of peace and in times of war."[288]

2. Support provided to the SAO Krajina

140. As early as August 1990 and through the summer of 1991, officials of the MUP of Serbia, including the Chief of the SDB, Jovica Stanišić, and an official thereof, Franko "Frenki" Simatović, met with the SAO Krajina leadership, in particular with Milan Martić, concerning the provision of financial, logistical and military assistance.[289] From January 1991, Milan Martić went on occasion to Belgrade to meet with these officials and with Radmilo Bogdanović, the Minister of the Interior of Serbia, concerning the provision of support to the SAO Krajina.[290]

141. The SAO Krajina budget was very small as a result of Croatia having ceased to provide budget allocations to Serb municipalities in May 1991.[291] The SAO Krajina government, including Milan Martić, sent requests to

[284] Ex. 820, Agreed Facts, para. 22. *See also* Milan Babić, 20 Feb 2006, T. 1639, 3 March 2006, T. 1914, 1923–1924; Lazar Macura, 14 Sep 2006, T. 8329; Ex. 948.

[285] Veljko Džakula, 16 Jan 2006, T. 406–407; Milan Babić, 20 Feb 2006, T. 1635; Charles Kirudja, 30 May 2006, T. 4787–4788, 1 Jun 2006, T. 4901–4902; Lazar Macura, 13 Sep 2006, T. 8225–8231, 14 Sep 2006, T. 8337; Ex. 115; Ex. 478, p. 1. A cease-fire agreement was subsequently signed on 2 January 1992, Ex. 820, Agreed Facts, para. 24. *See also* Veljko Džakula, 18 Jan 2006, T. 559; Charles Kirudja, 31 May 2006, T. 4888; Slobodan Jarčević, 13 Jul 2006, T. 6196–6197; Ex. 766.

[286] Ex. 115, paras 7, 10–11.

[287] Ex. 36.

[288] Ex. 36, Articles 6 and 31.

[289] Milan Babić, 17 Feb 2006, T. 1524–1526; Witness MM-003, 8 Mar 2006, T. 1987–1988, 1991–1992. *See also* Radoslav Maksić, 6 Feb 2006, T. 1179–1180.

[290] Milan Babić, 17 Feb 2006, T. 1525; Witness MM-003, 8 Mar 2006, T. 1994–1995; 10 Mar 2006, T. 2134. *See also* Milan Babić, 15 Feb 2006, T. 1392, 16 Feb 2006, T. 1426–1427; Witness MM-079, 3 Apr 2006, T. 3061; Rade Rašeta, 2 May 2006, T. 3921–3924; Witness MM-018, 9 Jun 2006, T. 5354; Ex. 460; Ex. 619. Milan Babić testified that on Slobodan Milošević's recommendation he met the Ministry of Defence of Serbia to discuss the need to finance and equip the TO "a couple of times" in September of 1991 and in November 1991 in Belgrade, Milan Babić, 16 Feb 2006, T. 1461–1462, 1464. On 1 August 1991, Milan Babić, as President of the SAO Krajina, abolished the SDB of the SAO Krajina, and thereby the SDB of Serbia, on the territory of the SAO Krajina. Milan Babić testified that this was done in order to establish government control over Ministry of Defence of the SAO Krajina. However, the decision was ultimately unsuccessful, which Milan Babić claimed was due to the close ties between the SDB of Serbia and the MUP of the SAO Krajina, Ex. 187; Milan Babić, 16 Feb 2006, T. 1417, 1420 onwards, 2 Mar 2006, T. 1802; Ex. 523 (confirming that the SDB of Serbia was still active and operating in the SAO Krajina in November 1991). *See also* Witness MM-079, 3 Apr 2006, T. 3078–3079. Milan Babić also testified that he asked Slobodan Milošević to remove Franko Simatović from the SAO Krajina, which eventually happened, however by the time of the attack on Lovinac, Franko Simatović had returned, Milan Babić, 16 Feb 2006, T. 1431. Furthermore, Milan Babić testified that Milan Martić was controlled by the SDB of Serbia and by Slobodan Milošević to such an extent that a "parallel structure" was created to the SAO Krajina government and authorities. According to Milan Babić, this parallel structure included the Minister of the Interior of Serbia, Radmilo Bogdanović, officials of the SDB of Serbia, in particular Jovica Stanišić, Franko Simatović, and Captain Dragan Vasiljković, and some representatives of the SDS and of the police in the Serb municipalities in the Krajina, Milan Babić, 15 Feb 2006, T. 1390–1393, 20 Feb 2006, T. 1601–1602. The Trial Chamber notes that Milan Babić characterised Milan Martić as "the most powerful man within the [parallel] structure in the SAO Krajina" and that he was unable to give orders to Milan Martić, Milan Babić, 15 Feb 2006, T. 1390–1392; Ex. 1037, Group 11, pp 4–6 where Milan Babić defines himself as a "spokesman" of the people in Krajina who was incapable of ordering Milan Martić. Contrary to this, Mile Dakić, testified that Milan Martić "was a clerk, an administrator in the SAO government [who] was far below Milan Babić." Mile Dakić recognised that Milan Martić "may have out-topped Babić in terms of popularity, the press coverage he received and so on and so forth. However, Milan Babić was the political figure at the head of the SAO Krajina leadership", Mile Dakić, 25 Oct 2006, T. 10021–10022.

[291] Milan Babić, 16 Feb 2006, T. 1454–1455, testifying that also the SAO Krajina ceased payments to Croatia, T. 1458–1459; Witness MM-003, 9 Mar 2006, T. 2086–2087.

the government of Serbia for military assistance and the evidence shows that these requests were frequently met.[292] The police of the SAO Krajina were mainly **[page 50]** financed with funds and material from the MUP and SDB of Serbia.[293] Moreover, there is evidence that weapons were sent from Serbia by Radmilo Bogdanović via Bosanski Novi, BiH, to the SAO Krajina.[294] Beginning at the end of April 1991, Dušan Smiljanić, Chief of Security of the JNA 10th Zagreb Corps, made contact with leading figures in the SDS in the SAO Krajina and provided large amounts of infantry and artillery weapons to Serbs in Krajina from JNA depots.[295]

142. The SFRY Federal Secretariat of National Defence of the JNA ("SSNO") made unit and personnel changes within the SAO Krajina armed forces.[296] There is evidence that beginning after the summer of 1991, the SAO Krajina TO was subordinate to the JNA.[297] There is also evidence of operational cooperation between the JNA and the armed forces of the SAO Krajina. Any resubordination of MUP units to the JNA for temporary assignment required prior approval of the Minister of Interior of the SAO Krajina.[298] When resubordinated, the MUP unit would be under the command of the JNA unit commander. However, if the MUP unit was merely acting in cooperation or concert with the JNA unit, it would remain under the command of the MUP commander.[299] After **[page 51]** the completion of a mission where it had been resubordinated, the MUP unit would return into the structure of the MUP.[300] For the purpose of combat operations, TO units could also be resubordinated to JNA units.[301] When resubordinating, the largest unit of either the TO or the JNA would command, which would normally be the JNA unit in a given area. Such resubordination of TO units would be carried out by the JNA.[302]

---

292 Milan Babić, 16 Feb 2006, T. 1460; Radoslav Maksić, 7 Feb 2006, T. 1243–1244; Ex. 41; Ex. 129; Ex. 190; Ex. 193. *See also* Ex. 204; Milan Dragišić, 19 Sep 2006, T. 8644, testifying that Milan Babić desired to create a Serb army of the SAO Krajina, something which Milan Martić opposed, instead advocating cooperation with the JNA.

293 Milan Babić, 16 Feb 2006, T. 1458–1460; Radoslav Maksić, 6 Feb 2006, T. 1179–1180; Witness MM-003, 8 Mar 2006, T. 1982–1984, 1987–1988, 9 Mar 2006, T. 2086–2087; Lazar Macura, 14 Sep 2006, T. 8339; Ex. 213. The Krajina was a poor area with few indigenous resources and it was dependent on the life-line that came through BiH from Serbia, Peter Galbraith, 25 Apr 2006, T. 3756. *See also* Ex. 498.

294 Milan Babić, 17 Feb 2006, T. 1527, 1575. *See also* Milan Babić, 17 Feb 2006, T. 1544–1545, 20 Feb 2006, T. 1603. Ex. 476, p. 283, wherein Borisav Jović, a member of the SFRY Presidency, describes a meeting with Slobodan Milošević, Veljko Kadijević and Blagoje Adžić on 5 April 1991 and stating that the "Serb nation in Croatia" had not armed itself but was counting on protection by the JNA.

295 Ex. 206. Milan Babić testified to meeting with Dušan Smiljanić during the summer of 1991, Milan Babić, 17 Feb 2006, T. 1531–1532. *See also* Ex. 24, p. 77, wherein Veljko Kadijević stated that "the future army of the Serbian Krajina was actually built up in the course of fighting, and equipped by the JNA with corresponding arms and material"; Ex. 857, p. 5, wherein Željko "Arkan" Raznjatović stated that he provided weapons and money to "Knin".

296 Witness MM-037, 28 Mar 2006, T. 2782–2783, 29 Mar 2006, T. 2823–2825, Ex. 268, T. 11579–11580; Ex. 120; Ex. 122; Ex. 124.

297 Nikola Medaković, 9 Oct 2006, T. 8991; Borislav Đukic, 19 Oct 2006, T. 9771–9772; Ex. 26. Milan Babić encountered resistance from the JNA concerning the appointments to TO positions which he made during the spring and summer of 1991. However, the resistance ceased in September 1991 when Milan Babić began signing appointments of officers who had been sent from Belgrade. In this respect, the Trial Chamber notes that on 28 November 1991 Radoslav Maksić succeded Ilija Đujić as TO Commander and that Radoslav Maksić testified that only the SSNO could appoint him as TO commander, Milan Babić, 16 Feb 2006, T. 1445–1447, 17 Feb 2006, T. 1568, 20 Feb 2006, T. 1588–1590; Radoslav Maksić, 6 Feb 2006, T. 1153–1155, 1186, 7 Feb 2006, T. 1197; Ex. 121; Ex. 128; Ex. 219. The SAO Krajina TO Staff in Knin was subordinated to the 9th Corps of the JNA, headquartered in Knin. The 9th Corps was subordinated to the JNA Naval Military District, headquartered in Split. The 9th Corps was composed, *inter alia*, of the 221st Motorised Brigade, commanded by Borislav Đukić until April 1992, the 180th Motorised Brigade (headquartered at the barracks in Benkovac), the 2nd TO Brigade, 1st TO Partisan Brigade, and a military police battalion, Milan Babić, 16 Feb 2006, T. 1448–1449, 17 Feb 2006, T. 1568, 20 Feb 2006, T. 1583, 1593; Radoslav Maksić, 6 Feb 2006, T. 1153–1155, 1160–1161, 7 Feb 2006, T. 1254–1255; Witness MM-080, 8 Jun 2006, T. 5245–5246, 5279–5280; Borislav Đukić, 18 Oct 2006, T. 9684–9686; Ex. 49.

298 Radoslav Maksić, 6 Feb 2006, T. 1166–1167. The Minister of the Interior and the MUP would be copied on the resulting order, or at least the parts relating to the MUP units participating in the operation. When resubordinated, regular police units would normally be employed to secure the implementation of the operation, by securing roads, buildings or areas from ambushes and sabotage actions. They could also provide personal security. However, in view of their strength and level of training for combat activities these units could not really participate in combat operations. If regular police units of a company or higher strength were involved, they could however take part in combat activities but this happened rarely, Radoslav Maksić, 6 Feb 2006, T. 1166–1167, 1171–1174. In this respect, the Trial Chamber recalls the evidence that in August and September 1991, Milan Martić cooperated with the 9th JNA Corps concerning coordination between JNA and MUP units, Milan Babić, 16 Feb 2006, T. 1445–1446.

299 Radoslav Maksić, 6 Feb 2006, T. 1173–1174.

300 Radoslav Maksić, 7 Feb 2006, T. 1188.

301 Witness MM-080, 8 Jun 2006, T. 5303.

302 Radoslav Maksić, 6 Feb 2006, T. 1160–1161, 1167, 7 Feb 2006, T. 1262, also testifying that if a MUP unit was the largest unit in an operation then any participating TO units would be resubordinated to the MUP unit. Ex. 47 gives an example of a JNA platoon of T-34 tanks, which was resubordinated to the 1st TO Brigade (p. 2). *See also* Reynaud Theunens, 26 Jan 2006, T. 718; Ex. 130.

143. In early September 1991, Milan Martić was arrested and detained for one to two days by the police in Otoka, close to Bosanska Krupa in BiH, which was a mostly Muslim area.[303] The evidence shows that there was strong coordination between the leaderships of the SAO Krajina, Serbia and BiH, through Milan Babić, Slobodan Milošević, Radovan Karadžić, and Jovica Stanišić, in securing Milan Martić's release.[304]

3. Training camp in Golubić and "Martić's Police"

144. In early 1991, the SUP in Knin established a training camp in Golubić, a small village located approximately 9 kilometres north of Knin, because Milan Martić wanted properly trained police officers.[305] There is evidence that this training camp still existed in 1993.[306] The training camp was run and funded by the MUP of the SAO Krajina and by the MUP and SDB of Serbia.[307] Furthermore, there is evidence that Milan Martić visited the camp.[308] Captain Dragan Vasiljković **[page 52]** from the SDB of Serbia trained special purpose units at the Golubić camp and was paid for this service by the SDB of Serbia.[309]

145. The training in Golubić included: drill practice, ambush training, ideological training geared towards loyalty to the state, not political parties, weapons training (including artillery training, mining training, sniper shooting and target practice), physical exercise, training in the securing of persons, self-protection and abseiling.[310] On average the training lasted for approximately 20 days.[311] Some witnesses testified that the training was classical police training,[312] whereas other witnesses testified that the training was of a military nature.[313] Based on the elements of the training described above, the Trial Chamber finds that the training in Golubić was predominantly military in character.

146. The trainees wore blue camouflage uniforms, which were different from ordinary police uniforms.[314] There is evidence that some trainees wore a patch on their sleeve, which was semi-circular with the words *Milicija Krajine* and the Serbian tricolour.[315] The training groups consisted of between 40 and 100

303 Milan Babić, 16 Feb 2006, T. 1441–1442, 20 Feb 2006, T. 1616–1618; Ex. 206.

304 Ex. 223; Ex. 224; Ex. 225; Ex. 226; Ex. 227.

305 Milan Babić, 16 Feb 2006, T. 1426–1427, 17 Feb 2006, T. 1539–1541, 1543–1544; Witness MM-003, 8 Mar 2006, T. 1999–2000, 2002, 10 Mar 2006, T. 2149–2150, 2195–2196; Ex. 268, T. 11569–11570, 11572; Witness MM-078, 24 May 2006, T. 4435–4437, 25 May 2006, T. 4538–4539; Witness MM-096, 22 Aug 2006, T. 6948, 23 Aug 2006, T. 6955, 25 Aug 2006, T. 7194; Witness MM-090, 4 Sep 2006, T. 7636; Lazar Macura, 14 Sep 2006, T. 8318; Stevo Plejo, 20 Sep 2006, T. 8692–8694, 8705; Nikola Medaković, 9 Oct 2006, T. 8965–8966, 10 Oct 2006, T. 9051, 9054; Borislav Đukić, 20 Oct 2006, T. 9815–9816, 23 Oct 2006, T. 9946, 9949; Dragan Knežević, 3 Nov 2006, T. 10698–10699; Ex. 244; Ex. 464; Ex. 619; Ex. 623; Ex. 627; Ex. 674; Ex. 675. *See also* Witness MM-037, 28 Mar 2006, T. 2804; Ex. 1042, Tab 2; Ex. 1043, Tab 2, DVD 4, pp 19–27; Ex. 1044.

306 Dragan Knežević, 3 Nov 2006, T. 10723; Ex. 674; Ex. 675. There is also evidence that training camps were established in Šamarica, Bruška and Korenica and that the SDB of Serbia was involved in the training in Bruška and Korenica, Milan Babić, 17 Feb 2006, T. 1541–1542, 1546–1547; Witness MM-003, 8 Mar 2006, T. 2002–2003, 10 Mar 2006, T. 2205; Ante Marinović, 23 Mar 2006, T. 2510; Rade Rašeta, 2 May 2006, T. 3922; Witness MM-078, 24 May 2006, T. 4435–4436; Ex. 565; Ex. 567; Ex. 568; Ex. 613, p. 25 (ERN 02011443).

307 Milan Babić, 16 Feb 2006, T. 1459, 17 Feb 2006, T. 1539–1543 (testifying that Milan Martić's assistant "was in charge of the administration of the camp" and "was overseeing the whole camp"), 2 Mar 2006, T. 1822; Witness MM-003, 8 Mar 2006, T. 1999, 2001–2004, 9 Mar 2006, T. 2086; Witness MM-079, 31 Mar 2006, T. 3050; Witness MM-078, 24 May 2006, T. 4436–4438; Lazar Macura, 14 Sep 2006, T. 8327–8328; Borislav Đukić, 23 Oct 2006, T. 9949–9950. *See also* Witness MM-078, 25 May 2006, T. 4539, 4547–4548; Ex. 244; Ex. 620; Ex. 621; Ex. 622; Ex. 623; Ex. 624; Ex. 677.

308 Witness MM-078, 24 May 2006, T. 4436–4437, 25 May 2006, T. 4547–4548.

309 Witness MM-003, 10 Mar 2006, T. 2209–2210; Milan Babić, 16 Feb 2006, T. 1427, 1429–1430, 17 Feb 2006, T. 1543; Ex. 478, p. 2; Ex. 626.

310 Milan Babić, 17 Feb 2006, T. 1541–1544, 2 Mar 2006, T. 1822; Witness MM-003, 8 Mar 2006, T. 2002–2005; Witness MM-078,24 May 2006, T. 4412, 25 May 2006, T. 4539; Stevo Plejo, 20 Sep 2006, T. 8693–8695, 21 Sep 2006, T. 8782; Nikola Medaković, 9 Oct 2006, T. 8968–8969, 10 Oct 2006, T. 9074–9075, 12 Oct 2006, T. 9281, 9284, 9286; Borislav Đukić, 20 Oct 2006, T. 9815–9816; Dragan Knežević, 03 Nov 2006, T. 10699–10700; Ex. 622.

311 Stevo Plejo, 20 Sep 2006, T. 8693–8695; Nikola Medaković, 9 Oct 2006, T. 8968; Borislav Đukić, 23 Oct 2006, T. 9946; Dragan Knežević, 3 Nov 2006, T. 10698; Ex. 620.

312 Stevo Plejo, 20 Sep 2006, T. 8694. *See also* Witness MM-078, 25 May 2006, T. 4506; Dragan Knežević, 3 Nov 2006, T. 10703.

313 Witness MM-003, 9 Mar 2006, T. 2100; Witness MM-096, 25 Aug 2006, T. 7196. *See also* Milan Babić, 15 Feb 2006, T. 1382, 2 Mar 2006, T. 1769–1770.

314 Dragan Knežević, 3 Nov 2006, T. 10723–10724.

315 Nikola Medaković, 9 Oct 2006, T. 8969, 10 Oct 2006, T. 9052–9053, 12 Oct 2006, T. 9289; Ex. 266, *Milicija Krajine* patch. Dragan Knežević testified that the only emblems the trainees had was the Yugoslav tricolour on the beret, Dragan Knežević, 3 Nov 2006, T. 10724.

trainees per group.[316] The men who had trained at Golubić set up further units and trained people in their municipalities.[317]

147. There is evidence of groups referred to as "Martić's Police" and "Martić's Men (*Martićevci*)" who were active in the territory of the SAO Krajina and the RSK during the Indictment period. Some witnesses testified that the term Martić's Police or Martić's men (*Martićevci*) referred to all those who had completed the training at the Golubić camp and were **[page 53]** employed in the SJBs.[318] One witness testified that the reason for that name was that Milan Martić established the Golubić training camp.[319] Other witnesses testified that these terms referred generally to the police force of the SAO Krajina and the RSK.[320] Nikola Medaković, who was the commander of the *Milicija Krajine* unit in Plaški in 1991, testified that the members of that unit were trained at the Golubić training camp and that they were referred to as "Martić's men".[321] Witness MM-037 called all of those who were led by Nikola Medaković "Martić's police".[322]

148. The evidence shows that groups trained in Golubić were, in some instances, referred to as Martić's Men or Martić's Police (*Martićevci*). However, the evidence is insufficient to conclude that all groups that were referred to by these names, or referred to themselves by these names, were trained in Golubić. The evidence also shows that members of the *Milicija Krajine* were trained in Golubić. The evidence is insufficient to conclude that all members of the police of the SAO Krajina were referred to as Martić's Men or Martić's Police (*Martićevci*).

C. The RSK

1. Development of the RSK

149. On 19 December 1991, the RSK was proclaimed by the Assembly of the SAO Krajina with Milan Babić as its President, and the RSK Constitution was passed.[323] The TO constituted the **[page 54]** armed forces of the

---

316 Borislav Đukić, 20 Oct 2006, T. 9817. *See also* Witness MM-003, 10 Mar 2006, T. 2195; Stevo Plejo, 20 Sep 2006, T. 8694, 8696–8697; Ex. 625, selection of JNA operative intelligence reports, p. 1, mentioning that 150 people were being trained at Golubić before 12 May 1991; Ex. 464, List of persons from Knin municipality region who finished training in Golubić settlement, listing 190 people who finished training at Golubić. Ex. 625, selection of JNA operative intelligence reports, p. 1.

317 Milan Babić, 17 Feb 2006, T. 1542–1543; Witness MM-003, 8 Mar 2006, T. 2006; Stevo Plejo, 20 Sep 2006, T. 8696–8697, 9704–9705, 21 Sep 2006, T. 8793–8794; Nikola Medaković, 10 Oct 2006, T. 9051; Dragan Knežević, 3 Nov 2006, T. 10698–10699, 10722; Ex. 568; Ex. 600; Ex. 620; Ex. 1028, L0079797. *See also* Ex. 471.

318 Witness MM-078, 24 May 2006, T. 4439. According Witness MM-078, these policemen were called Martić's Men or the *Martićevci*, and considered by the citizens to be specialists or an elite, more capable, trained "and even more loyal to the system", as compared to the other policemen in the SJBs. The reason for the name was that "Martić set up the whole thing and [...] it was after him that [...] they were named", Witness MM-078, 24 May 2006, T. 4439. Hamdija Krupić testified that there were also policemen in the municipality Bosanski Novi, BiH, who had undergone the training in Golubić "to carry out special tasks" and were called "Martić's Police". These men were from the Bosnian Krajina, Hamdija Krupić, 30 Mar 2006, T. 2958–2960. According to Witness MM-037, younger policemen at the Plaški SJB were sent to Golubić for training, and when they returned, they started to call themselves "Martić's police", Witness MM-037, 28 Mar 2006, T. 2749, 2804, Ex. 268, T. 11569–11570. The Trial Chamber notes that the units that had been trained at Golubić were also called the Special Police, Specials, Specialists or Special Purpose Units of the Krajina police, Witness MM-003, 8 Mar 2006, T. 2006–2007, 10 Mar 2006, T. 2195–2196; Milan Babić, 17 Feb 2006, T. 1539–1541; Ex. 1028, L0079768.

319 Witness MM-078, 24 May 2006, T. 4439.

320 Radoslav Maksić testified that the term *Martićevci* or Martić's Men was a colloquial term which referred "to the police force of the [SAO Krajina MUP]", Radoslav Maksić, 7 Feb 2006, T. 1191. Witness MM-096 also testified that the term was used to refer to the entire police force in the SAO Krajina and the RSK "or even something much broader, sometimes even all the citizens who were wearing uniforms", Witness MM-096, 25 Aug 2006, T. 7194. Witness MM-003 testified that the term Martić's police, the abbreviated name of which was *Martićevci* and Martić's Men, "applied to the overall police" of the SAO Krajina, Witness MM-003, 10 Mar 2006, T. 2194 –2195.

321 Nikola Medaković, 9 Oct 2006, T. 8965–8966, 8999, 10 Oct 2006, T. 9051, 9056, also testifying that in May 1991, he met with Milan Martić in Knin to request weapons to reinforce the Plaški municipality police, and that Milan Martić replied that long-barrelled weapons could only be given to persons who had been trained in Golubić. *See also* Ex. 507, p. 2, providing that Nikola Medaković was commander of the *Martićevci* or "Martić's men" and that this unit was part of the regular police commanded by Dušan Latas.

322 Witness MM-037, 28 Mar 2006, T. 2795.

323 Ex. 820, Agreed Facts, para. 23. *See also* Reynaud Theunens, 27 Jan 2006, T. 759; Witness MM-090, 29 Aug 2006, T. 7373; Witness MM-090, 5 Sep 2006, T. 7777–7779. The RSK was defined as a national state of the Serbian people and of all the citizens residing therein, Ex. 820, Agreed Facts, para. 23.

RSK.[324] On 16 February 1992, the government fell as Milan Babić was removed from the office of President of the RSK by the RSK Assembly due to his opposition to Slobodan Milošević in respect of the Vance Plan.[325] Milan Martić, who had previously opposed the Vance Plan, now publicly supported the adoption of the Vance Plan.[326] After Milan Babić was removed from office, the Vance plan was adopted by the Assembly of the RSK.[327]

150. On 21 February 1992, the UN Security Council adopted Resolution 743 implementing the Vance Plan and establishing UNPROFOR in certain areas of Croatia designated as "United Nations Protected Areas" ("UNPAs").[328] The UNPAs were areas where Serbs constituted the majority or a substantial minority of the population and where inter-communal tensions had previously led to armed conflict.[329] The Vance Plan defined three UNPAs, which covered four sectors: UNPA Krajina, covering Sector South (Lika and Dalmatia) and Sector North (Banija and Kordun), UNPA Western Slavonia, covering Sector West, and UNPA Eastern Slavonia, covering Sector East.[330] The UNPAs were to be demilitarised, with all armed forces to be either withdrawn or disbanded.[331] However, the plan foresaw maintaining the local police who could carry weapons and wear uniforms.[332] UN police monitors, UNCIVPOL, were to ensure that the local police carried out their duties without discriminating or violating human rights.[333] UNCIVPOL reported any incidents both **[page 55]** within its own chain of command, as well as to the relevant Croatian or RSK local police, however in serious cases reports were also sent directly to the relevant government.[334]

151. On 26 February 1992, the SAO Western Slavonia and the SAO Eastern Slavonia, Baranja and Western Šrem joined the RSK.[335] In the new RSK government, Zdravko Zečević became Prime Minister, Goran Hadžić was elected President, and Milan Martić was re-elected Minister of the Interior.[336] In April 1992, UNPROFOR troops started arriving in the UNPAs.[337] In addition, UNPROFOR was also mandated to patrol the so-called "pink zones" outside the UNPAs, which were areas under JNA control, in many instances with a significant Serb presence.[338]

---

324 Ex. 166, Art. 102. *See also* Ex. 6, p. 123.

325 Milan Babić, 20 Feb 2006, T. 1639–1642, 1644 (testifying that he wanted a change in the Vance Plan to the effect that the JNA would remain in the Krajina as a military force that would protect the Krajina until a political solution [was] found for the status); Lazar Macura, 12 Sep 2006, T. 8206. *See also* Ex. 657; Charles Kirudja, 31 May 2006, T. 4888; Slobodan Jarčević, 13 Jul 2006, T. 6196–6197; Lazar Macura, 13 Sep 2006, T. 8226–8231, 14 Sep 2006, T. 8337, 8396–8397.

326 Milan Babić, 20 Feb 2006, T. 1644–1645; Mile Dakić, 25 Oct 2006, T. 10044; Ex. 230. *See also* Lazar Macura, 14 Sep 2006, T. 8347.

327 Veljko Džakula, 16 Jan 2006, T. 405–406; Borislav Đukić, 23 Oct 2006, T. 9936.

328 Ex. 820, Agreed Facts, para. 25. *See also* Veljko Džakula, 18 Jan 2006, T. 559; Peter Galbraith, 25 Apr 2006, T. 3744; John McElligott, 26 May 2006, T. 4553–4554; Charles Kirudja, 30 May 2006, T. 4785–4786, 1 Jun 2006, T. 4901–4905; Ratko Ličina, 15 Aug 2006, T. 6435, 17 Aug 2006, T. 6629–6630; Lazar Macura, 14 Sep 2006, T. 8332; Borislav Đukić, 23 Oct 2006, T. 9903–9904; Ex. 115.

329 Ex. 820, Agreed Facts, para. 25. *See also* Veljko Džakula, 18 Jan 2006, T. 559; Ex. 864.

330 Veljko Džakula, 18 January 2006, T. 559, 19 Jan 2006, T. 610; Ex. 115; Ex. 61; Ex. 724. Charles Kirudja, 31 May 2006, T. 4805. The Croats and the Serbs differed in their interpretation of the borders of the UNPAs, with the Croats seeing the borders of municipalities as borders of the UNPAs and the Serbs seeing the confrontation line as the border of the UNPAs, Charles Kirudja, 31 May 2006, T. 4805–4809; Ex. 746.

331 Ex. 820, Agreed Facts, para. 25, providing that as UNPROFOR assumed its responsibilities, all JNA forces deployed in Croatia would be relocated outside Croatia. *See also* Veljko Džakula, 16 Jan 2006, T. 407; John McElligott, 26 May 2006, T. 4553; Charles Kirudja, 30 May 2006, T. 4788, 31 May 2006, T. 4810, 1 Jun 2006, T. 4902–4903; Slobodan Jarčević, 13 Jul 2006, T. 6197–6198, 6245; Slobodan Perić, 6 Sep 2006, T. 7837–7838; Witness MM-117, 13 Oct 2006, T. 9353; Borislav Đukić, 19 Oct 2006, T. 9721–9722, 23 Oct 2006, T. 9904; Ex. 115.

332 Borislav Đukić, 19 Oct 2006, T. 9723. The weapons were to be placed under a double-key system; one key for UNPROFOR and one key for the RSK authorities, Charles Kirudja, 31 May 2006, T. 4818–4819, 4821–4822; Slobodan Jarčević, 13 Jul 2006, T. 6198–6199, 6244; Ratko Ličina, 15 Aug 2006, T. 6436–6437; Witness MM-096, 22 Aug 2006, T. 6879; Slobodan Perić, 6 Sep 2006, T. 7838; Borislav Đukić, 23 Oct 2006, T. 9904; Ex. 748.

333 Ex. 115; John McElligott, 26 May 2006, T. 4553, 4555–4557, 29 May 2006, T. 4660–4662, 4669–4673, 30 May 2006, T. 4770–4771; Witness MM-096, 22 Aug 2006, T. 6880–6882; Ex. 721; Ex. 722; Ex. 723; Ex. 725. Milan Martić issued instructions regulating in detail the mode of cooperation with UNPROFOR and UNCIVPOL, Witness MM-117, 18 Oct 2006, T. 9648–9649.

334 John McElligott, 26 May 2006, T. 4565–4567, 29 May 2006, T. 4669–4671, 4676–4679, 30 May 2006, T. 4731, 4733; Witness MM-096, 22 Aug 2006, T. 6881–6882, 6929–6931, 24 Aug 2006, T. 7106.

335 Ex. 820, Agreed Facts, para. 26. *See also* Veljko Džakula, 16 Jan 2006, T. 347-348 (testifying that the SAO Western Slavonia had been declared on 12 August 1991), 358; Ratko Ličina, 15 Aug 2006, T. 6493.

336 Ex. 820, Agreed Facts, para. 26. Slobodan Jarčević was Minister of Foreign Affairs of the RSK from October 1992 to April 1994, when he was replaced by Milan Babić, Slobodan Jarčević, 12 Jul 2006, T. 6133, T. 6169; Ex. 191. *See also* Veljko Džakula, 16 Jan 2006, T. 358, 19 Jan 2006, T. 621.

337 Charles Kirudja, 30 May 2006, T. 4781, 4789, 31 May 2006, T. 4804–4805; Witness MM-096, 22 Aug 2006, T. 6873.

338 Veljko Džakula, 19 Jan 2006, T. 610–611; John McElligott, 26 May 2006, T. 4569, 29 May 2006, T. 4629–4630. *See also* Charles Kirudja, 31 May 2006, T. 4805–4809.

152. The evidence shows that the RSK was not demilitarised in its entirety in accordance with the Vance Plan.[339] On 28 April 1992, Special Police ("PJM") Brigades and a PJM Administration were established within the RSK Ministry of Defence by the SSNO of Serbia.[340] General Borislav Đukić, a JNA officer, was appointed Chief of the PJM Administration.[341] The PJM Brigades were connected both to the Ministry of Defence and to the MUP of the RSK.[342] The members of PJM units wore blue uniforms and used the side arms and the equipment of the TO.[343] There is also evidence that TO vehicles were repainted in blue and used by the PJM.[344] On 18 May 1992, the **[page 56]** SVK was established.[345] In peacetime, the SVK was to consist of TO units, however in the event of imminent threat of war and during wartime the PJM units would join the SVK.[346]

153. The RSK leadership was against the demilitarisation of the RSK, asserting it would be unable to defend itself in the event of Croatian attacks.[347] Thus, the Vance Plan was interpreted by the RSK authorities to mean that UNPROFOR was to protect the population in the areas of deployment.[348] In this context, the Trial Chamber notes that Croatian forces carried out several armed incursions into the UNPAs between 1992 and 1995, including on the Miljevac plateau on 21 June 1992, Maslenica on 22 January 1993, Medak pocket on 9 and 12 September 1993, and Operation Flash from 1 May 1995.[349]

154. During the spring of 1992, the road which went through the so-called Posavina Corridor, a predominantly Bosnian Croat strip of land in north-eastern BiH, had been blocked in the region of Doboj by Croatian forces in alliance with the forces of BiH.[350] The area was of strategic importance as it linked the Croatian and Bosnian Krajina regions with Serbia.[351] In two phases, during the summer and late autumn of 1992, a military operation known as "*Koridor 92*" was carried out in the Posavina Corridor. While there is evidence that the objective of the operation was to resolve a humanitarian situation which had arisen as a result of the blocking of the road near Doboj, there is significant evidence that the main objective was to link Serb lands.[352]

---

339 Veljko Džakula, 16 Jan 2006, T. 406–407; Milan Babić, 20 Feb 2006, T. 1645; Slobodan Jarčević, 13 Jul 2006, T. 6245, 6248; Ex. 75, pp 2–4. *See also* Borislav Đukić, 19 Oct 2006, T. 9722.

340 Ex. 978. The PJM brigades were subordinated to the PJM Administration in both peacetime and wartime, Ex. 978, p. 2, item 10; Borislav Đukić, 19 Oct 2006, T. 9723–9724, 9730.

341 Ex. 71; Borislav Đukic, 19 Oct 2006, T. 9740–9741; Ex. 633. *See also* Ex. 978; Witness MM-117, 18 Oct 2006, T. 9676–9677.

342 Borislav Đukić, 19 Oct 2006, T. 9793–9794, also testifying that "[t]he professional part of the execution of the task was connected to the [MUP]" that the PJM Brigades "carried out tasks from within the police force and were linked to the Minister of the Interior", 23 Oct 2006, T. 9911–9913; Ex. 72.

343 Charles Kirudja, 31 May 2006, T. 4816; Ex. 747; Slobodan Perić, 7 Sep 2006, T. 7942–7943.

344 Slobodan Perić, 7 Sep 2006, T. 7942–7943. *See also* Ex. 68; Ex. 696. In Ex. 747, p. 4, Charles Kirudja wrote:

> The recent emergence of a newly fortified militia is hard not to notice. Former military vehicles have been repainted from green to blue – the colors of the present police force. Many of the militiamen have begun to sport new blue uniforms and appear to be deployed along the front line.

See further Ex. 73; Ex. 74; Ex. 75; Ex. 730; Ex. 864; Ex. 985.

345 Ex. 6, p. 141, citing Constitutional Amendment No. VIII.

346 Law on Defence as amended, cited in Ex. 6, p. 142.

347 Veljko Džakula, 16 Jan 2006, T. 405–406; Milan Babić, 20 Feb 2006, T. 1644; John McElligott, 29 May 2006, T. 4631; Slobodan Jarčević, 13 Jul 2006, T. 6199–6200; Ratko Ličina, 15 Aug 2006, T. 6439–6440; Ex. 574, p. 1; Ex. 750. *See also* Charles Kirudja, 31 May 2006, T. 4837–4838, 1 Jun 2006, T. 4981–4982; Borislav Đukić, 19 Oct 2006, T. 9721–9722.

348 Ratko Ličina, 15 Aug 2006, T. 6439; Witness MM-096, 22 Aug 2006, T. 6880; Witness MM-090, 31 Aug 2006, T. 7484–7485.

349 John McElligott, 29 May 2006, T. 4631–4632, 4641, 4648–4649; Charles Kirudja, 1 Jun 2006, T. 4921–4922, 4928, 4942–4943; Ratko Ličina, 15 Aug 2006, T. 6450–6453, 6462–6464; Witness MM-096, 22 Aug 2006, T. 6880; Witness MM-090, 4 Sep 2006, T. 7706–7707; Slobodan Perić, 6 Sep 2006, T. 7841; Witness MM-117, 13 Oct 2006, T. 9383–9384, 9388; Patrick Barriot, 9 Nov 2006, T. 10764; Ex. 75, pp 1–2; Ex. 885. After the incursions on Maslenica and Medak pocket, the RSK removed weapons from storage depots, Charles Kirudja, 31 May 2006, T. 4819–4822, 1 Jun 2006, T. 4981–4982; Ratko Ličina, 17 Aug 2006, T. 6635. *See also* Peter Galbraith, 25 Apr 2006, T. 3795–3796; Slobodan Perić, 7 Sep 2006, T. 7945–7946.

350 Veljko Džakula, 17 Jan 2006, T. 432, 19 Jan 2006, T. 588; Charles Kirudja, 1 Jun 2006, T. 4966; Slobodan Jarčević, 13 Jul 2006, T. 6192; Borislav Đukić, 19 Oct 2006, T. 9778–9779, 9788–9789, 23 Oct 2006, T. 9918 (testifying that as a result of the blocking of the road a difficult humanitarian situation arose in Krajina and Bosanska Krajina); Witness MM-105, 2 Nov 2006, T. 10610; Ex. 6, p. 169; Ex. 103. *See also* Reynaud Theunens, 27 Jan 2006, T. 796–797.

351 The importance of this area was stated by Milan Martić in an article in *Vojska Krajine*, 3 Jun 1993, p. 3, *see* Ex. 6, p. 169. *See also* Reynaud Theunens, 27 Jan 2006, T. 797. Moreover, on 12 May 1992, at a session of the Assembly of the Serbian People in BiH, the President of the RS Radovan Karadžić announced as a strategic goal of the Serb people to establish a corridor between the Krajina region and Semberija in Serbia in order to "[integrate] the Serbian lands", Ex. 45, pp 13–14; Veljko Džakula, 19 Jan 2006, T. 589; Slobodan Jarčević, 13 Jul 2006, T. 6192.

352 Regarding the humanitarian situation, *see* Borislav Đukić 19 Oct 2006, T. 9779, 9788–9789; Witness MM-105, 2 Nov 2006, T. 10609 (*see also* Veljko Džakula, 17 Jan 2006, T. 589; Ex. 6, p. 169; Reynaud Theunens, 27 Jan 2006, T. 813). The Trial Chamber

As part of the operation, the **[page 57]** whole of the Posavina area was devastated; many houses were torched and many civilians, including Croats, were killed.[353]

155. On 20 April 1993, the RSK Supreme Defence Council was established, which was composed of the President of the RSK, the Prime Minister, the Minister of Defence, the Minister of the Interior, and the Commander of the SVK.[354] The President of the RSK "[led] the [SVK] in times of peace and war, in accordance with the [RSK] Constitution and decisions adopted by the Supreme Defence Council, and [presided] over the Supreme Defence Council".[355] The Supreme Defence Council was mandated to "adopt decisions on the readiness, mobilisation and deployment of the [SVK] and on other matters in accordance with the Constitution and the law."[356]

156. On 25 January 1994, Milan Martić was elected President of the RSK, defeating Milan Babić.[357] On 21 April 1994, a new government was formed under Milan Martić, *inter alia*, with Borislav Mikelić as Prime Minister and Milan Babić as Foreign Minister.[358] The new government's aim was to achieve "sovereignty of the RSK and the right of the Serb people to self-determination and unification with other parts of the Serb people."[359]

157. Following on from the Zagreb Agreement, which had been signed on 29 March 1994,[360] in January 1995 the Z-4 Plan was presented, envisaging a high degree of autonomy within Croatia for the Krajina region and that Eastern Slavonia, Baranja, and Šrem, and Western Slavonia would be **[page 58]** reincorporated into Croatia with lesser forms of autonomy.[361] The Z-4 Plan provided for a five-year transition period for the restoration of full sovereignty for Croatia.[362] On 30 January 1995, Milan Martić, as President of the RSK, refused to accept the Z-4 Plan, as Croatia had announced that it would not accept an extension of UNPROFOR's mandate.[363] The mandate was eventually extended in March 1995 and focused on reconstruction and cooperation, however Milan Martić continued to refuse to negotiate the Z-4 Plan because the reshaped UNPROFOR, now called

notes that of these witnesses only Borislav Đukić testified to the existence of a grave humanitarian situation. Regarding the linking of Serb lands, *see* Ex. 944; Lazar Macura, 15 Sep 2006, T. 8412–8413; Ex. 45, pp 13–14; Slobodan Jarčević, 13 Jul 2006, T. 6192 (*see also* Witness MM-003, 9 Mar 2006, T. 2040–2041).

353 Veljko Džakula, 19 Jan 2006, T. 590–592, 613, also stating that he heard that "there was damage inflicted and destruction wrought in places where there was no direct fighting or combat", and that the Posavina Corridor was "razed to the ground, devastated and laid [to] waste".

354 Ex. 78, p. 3.

355 Ex. 78, p. 3. *See also* Ex. 79, Art. 40, p. 1.

356 Ex. 78, p. 4.

357 Ex. 820, Agreed Facts, para. 29.

358 The government also comprised Ilija Prijić as Minister of Interior and Rade Tanja as Minister of Defence, Milan Babić, 15 Feb 2006, T. 1328–1329; Witness MM-117, 18 Oct 2006, T. 9646; Ex. 970, p. 2. Milan Babić remained as Foreign Minister until 27 July 1995 when he became Prime Minister, Milan Babić, 15 Feb 2006, T. 1328–1329; Nikola Dobrijević, 10 Nov 2006, T. 10855, 10902.

359 Ex. 970, p. 2 (quoting Borislav Mikelić as saying that "our negotiating position is and will be territorial integrity and sovereignty of the Republic of Serb Krajina. The RSK will sooner or later unite with the Serb republic and Montenegro into a unified state"). *See also* Witness MM-117, 16 Oct 2006, T. 9494–9495, 9483–9484.

360 The Zagreb Agreement foresaw the creation of two cantons within Croatia and also regulated the withdrawal of all indirect weaponry and artillery from the border between Croatia and the RSK. Moreover, all weapons were to be under UN control, Slobodan Jarčević, 12 Jul 2006, T. 6167–6168; Charles Kirudja, 1 Jun 2006, T. 4935–4936; Ex. 929. Two economic agreements ensued, signed in November and early December 1994, and the RSK government undertook measures to abide by these agreements, Milan Babić, 21 Feb 2006, T. 1660; Peter Galbraith, 25 Apr 2006, T. 3743–3745, 3794, 3815, 3796–3797; Charles Kirudja, 1 Jun 2006, T. 4935–4936; Slobodan Jarčević, 12 Jul 2006, T. 6169, 6175; Ratko Ličina, 15 Aug 2006, T. 6451–6452; Slobodan Perić, 6 Sep 2006, T. 7841. Previously during 1993, several unsuccessful attempts had been made at concluding agreements between Croatia and the RSK: the Daruvar Agreement on 18 February 1993 (Veljko Džakula, 16 Jan 2006, T. 359–362; Milan Babić, 20 Feb 2006, T. 1653–1654; Witness MM-105, 1 Nov 2006, T. 10534–10535, 10573–10574, in April 1993, an agreement was negotiated in Geneva (Slobodan Jarčević, 14 Jul 2006, T. 6281–6282), the Erdut Agreement in July 1993 (Slobodan Jarčević, 12 Jul 2006, T. 6151–6153, T. 6162–6163; Ex. 876), the Oslo agreement on 4 November 1993 (Slobodan Jarčević, 12 Jul 2006, T. 6157–6160), the Dobanovci Negotiations in December 1993 (Peter Galbraith, 25 Apr 2006, T. 3741; Slobodan Jarčević, 12 Jul 2006, T. 6163–6165).

361 Veljko Džakula, 17 Jan 2006, T. 440–441, 19 Jan 2006, T. 596–597; Milan Babić, 20 Feb 2006, T. 1654; Peter Galbraith, 25 Apr 2006, T. 3742–3743, 3754–3755 (testifying that the Krajina area was to have the right to its own flag and language and competence to decide on legislature, housing, education, culture, public services, energy, business and many other aspects of its society); Slobodan Jarčević, 12 Jul 2006, T. 6177–6178; Slobodan Perić, 7 Sep 2006, T. 7944–7945; Lazar Macura, 13 Sep 2006, T. 8232; Ex. 381.

362 Veljko Džakula, 19 Jan 2006, T. 597; Peter Galbraith, 25 Apr 2006, T. 3803.

363 Milan Babić, 20 Feb 2006, T. 1654–1655; Peter Galbraith, 25 Apr 2006, T. 3749–3751, 3801–3802; Slobodan Jarčević, 14 Jul 2006, T. 6299–6300; Lazar Macura, 13 Sep 2006, T. 8233, 14 Sep 2006, T. 8349.

UNCRO, was not a protection force.[364] There is evidence that Milan Martić acted under the instruction of Slobodan Milošević to reject the Z-4 Plan.[365] The negotiations between the RSK and Croatia continued through the first half of 1995, with the RSK government appearing seemingly more amenable to the Z-4 plan.[366]

158. On 2 August 1995, Milan Babić, as Prime Minister of the RSK, accepted the Z-4 Plan "in substance".[367] On 4 August 1995, the Croatian Army and police forces launched a military operation, called Operation Storm, on the RSK and the UNPAs, which eventually resulted in them taking control of the territory of the RSK.[368]

2. Cooperation with and assistance from Serbia

159. Throughout 1992, 1993 and 1994, the RSK leadership, including Milan Martić, requested financial, logistical and military support from Serbia on numerous occasions, including directly from Slobodan Milošević.[369] Most of these requests were fulfilled, and support was given to the RSK MUP[370] and to the TO and the SVK.[371] In January 1992, Milan Martić stated that cooperation **[page 59]** with Serbia never ceased and was good.[372] There is evidence describing the relationship between the RSK and Serbia as one "between two states" although the RSK listened to "the opinions of our ally."[373] There was a representation office in Belgrade of the RSK Foreign Minister's office.[374] The RSK Minister of Foreign Affairs was paid by Serbia as a result of being employed by the Ministry of Foreign Affairs of Serbia.[375] As President of the RSK, Milan Martić enjoyed the full support of the VJ.[376]

160. In respect of the cooperation between the RSK and the RS, the Trial Chamber notes the evidence regarding operation *Koridor 92*.[377] Both phases of the operation included units of the RSK police, PJM and TO, and the operation was led by the VRS and RS police.[378] Milan Martić visited the Posavina Corridor on several occasions during the first phase of the operation in June and July 1992.[379] During the second

364 Peter Galbraith, 25 Apr 2006, T. 3750, 3801–3802; Slobodan Jarčević, 12 Jul 2006, T. 6181–6183. *See also* Lazar Macura, 14 Sep 2006, T. 8350.

365 Rade Rašeta, 2 May 2006, T. 3918–3919 (testifying that Slobodan Milošević told Milan Martić to reject the Z-4 Plan *a priori*); Mile Dakić, 25 Oct 2006, T. 10055–10056 (testifying that the RSK leadership was "awaiting a response from Belgrade [which] was a higher level that was deciding about [whether] the Z-4 Plan would be accepted or not"). *See also* Peter Galbraith, 25 Apr 2006, T. 3751–3753; Charles Kirudja, 1 Jun 2006, T. 4957; Ex. 769, p. 2.

366 Peter Galbraith, 25 Apr 2006, T. 3793; Witness MM-117, 16 Oct 2006, T. 9450–9451, 17 Oct 2006, T. 9596; Ex. 391.

367 Milan Babić, 20 Feb 2006, T. 1656–1657; Peter Galbraith, 25 Apr 2006, T. 3747–3749. *See also* Witness MM-117, 18 Oct 2006, T. 9623–9625.

368 Ex. 820, Agreed Facts, para. 32.

369 Ex. 11 (identical to Ex. 659); Ex. 12; Ex. 68; Ex. 69; Ex. 194; Ex. 707; Ex. 840; Peter Galbraith, 25 Apr 2006, T. 3756–3757.

370 The RSK MUP received support from Serbia and the JNA/VJ, in many cases pursuant to a standing SSNO order of 20 April 1992 concerning supply of ammunition to the RSK MUP: Ex. 67; Ex. 692; Ex. 694; Ex. 695; Ex. 697; Ex. 698; Ex. 699, Ex. 700, Ex. 701, Ex. 702, Ex. 703, and Ex. 704. Milan Babić testified that in 1992 the RSK police was financed in the same way as in 1991 with the SAO Krajina, Milan Babić, 16 Feb 2006, T. 1465.

371 Milan Babić, 16 Feb 2006, T. 1466–1467. The support from Serbia to the SVK covered all aspects of its functioning, including personnel, operational and logistical support, Rade Rašeta, 2 May 2006, T. 3894–3896 (between 150–200 VJ officers were seconded to the SVK to leading positions), T. 3903 (testifying that the SVK and the VJ "were actually one and the same organisation, but positioned at two different locations"), T. 3907–3910, 3953–3954, Rade Rašeta, 3 May 2006, T. 3978; Slobodan Perić, 7 Sep 2006, T. 7933; Lazar Macura, 14 Sep 2006, T. 8338–8339; Borislav Đukic, 23 Oct 2006, T. 9927–9928; Ex. 63, p. 2; Ex. 64; Ex. 65, Ex. 456. The SSNO continued to order organisational changes in the SAO Krajina TO, Ex. 62; Ex. 71; Ex. 978. *See also* Ex. 6, pp 161–68; Reynaud Theunens, 27 Jan 2006, T. 806.

372 Ex. 951, p. 1.

373 Slobodan Jarčević, 13 Jul 2006, T. 6254.

374 Slobodan Jarčević, 12 Jul 2006, T. 6139, 13 Jul 2006, T. 6253–6254.

375 Slobodan Jarčević, 12 Jul 2006, T. 6139, 13 Jul 2006, T. 6170, 6253–6254, 14 Jul 2006, T. 6322–6323.

376 Rade Rašeta, 2 May 2006, T. 3907–3908. The JNA became the VJ when the SFRY ceased to exist and Serbia and the Republic of Montenegro made up the Federal Republic of Yugoslavia, Lazar Macura, 15 Sep 2006, T. 8428.

377 *See supra* para. 154.

378 On 5 June 1992, Milan Martić ordered the SUPs and MUP Brigades in the RSK to form "volunteer police companies" of 120 men each and armed with automatic weapons and wearing Krajina police insignia "in order to carry out tasks of interest for the [RSK] and the Serbian people as a whole", Ex. 635. On 10 June 1992, Milan Martić ordered these units to march along certain axes into BiH, Ex. 461. The RSK MUP forces formed part of TG-2, commanded by Colonel Mile Novaković, and were deployed in BiH at least as of 24 June 1992, Ex. 634, pp 4, 9. On 19 June 1992, the Ministers' Cabinet of the RSK MUP announced that RSK MUP units were participating in Operation Corridor, Reynaud Theunens, 27 Jan 2006, T. 813; Ex. 646. *See also* Ex. 6, p. 170; Ex. 568.

379 Ex. 634, pp 14, 48, 63, 93, 123.

phase of Operation Corridor, two RSK PJM brigades participated.[380] Milan Martić and Borislav Đukić commanded a "strong" RSK police detachment during this phase of operation *Koridor 92*.[381] The evidence shows that following operation *Koridor 92*, Milan Martić's popularity in the RSK increased significantly.[382] **[page 60]**

D. Armed clashes between Serb and Croatian forces

1. During spring and summer of 1991

161. Several armed clashes occurred between Croatian and SAO Krajina armed forces in several locations during the spring and summer of 1991.[383]

162. As noted above, in March 1991 there were armed clashes in Pakrac and in Plitvice between Croatian MUP special police forces and the police of the SAO Krajina. On both occasions, the JNA intervened after these clashes to separate the two sides.[384]

163. In June 1991, there was a Croatian SJB in Lovinac, in Gračac municipality north-west of Knin, and as a consequence the village was attacked by the police of the SAO Krajina.[385] Witness MM-003 testified that Milan Martić was in command of this attack. The Trial Chamber recalls its finding that the evidence of Witness MM-003 requires corroboration and notes that this piece of evidence is uncorroborated. However, the Trial Chamber notes Milan Babić's testimony that Milan Martić "participated" in the attack together with Franko Simatović.[386] While the evidence does not support a finding that Milan Martić commanded the attack on Lovinac, the Trial Chamber finds it established beyond reasonable doubt that Milan Martić participated in the attack.[387]

164. On 2 July 1991, the village of Ljubovo, south-west of Titova Korenica, was attacked by the *Milicija Krajine* because members of the Croatian MUP had stationed themselves there following the conflict in Plitvice. In public statements, Milan Martić said that this attack was carried out because an ultimatum of the SAO Krajina government had expired which required that all members and units of the Croatian MUP withdraw from the SAO Krajina territory and because of arrests and mistreatment by Croats of Serbs in the area of Lika.[388] **[page 61]**

---

380 Ex. 87 (Order, dated 13 November 1992, for the two PJM brigades to participate "with the aim of expanding the corridor and liberating all Serbian Territories").

381 Veljko Džakula, 17 Jan 2006, T. 432–433. *See also* Witness MM-003, 9 Mar 2006, T. 2041, 10 Mar 2006, T. 2211. There is also evidence that on 22 November 1992 Milan Martić, Borislav Đukić and General Momir Talić of the VRS held a meeting to assess "the situation regarding the forthcoming combat operations" in the area of Gradačac and Orašje, *see* Ex. 6, p. 173.

382 Veljko Džakula, 16 Jan 2006, T. 404.

383 There is also evidence that there were several similar armed clashes and attacks in other villages during the spring and summer of 1991, including in Potkonje, Vrpolje, and Lički Osik: Potkonje and Vrpolje: Sometime before June 1991, about 60 members of the SAO Krajina police raided the small Croat villages of Potkonje and Vrpolje located in the municipality of Knin, allegedly to locate a radio transmitter. Nobody was killed in this action, however the incident caused the civilian population to leave the area, Witness MM-078, 24 May 2006, T. 4453, 25 May 2006, T. 4520–4521; Witness MM-096, 21 Aug 2006, T. 6846–6849 (testifying that 60 automatic rifles and ammunition were found with some persons, that criminal charges were brought against them but that they were eventually released), 24 Aug 2006, T. 7067–7068, 7072–7073; Ex. 1037, L0092049. Lički Osik: On 2 July 1991, Croatian police in the town of Lički Osik were attacked by "Krajina forces", Ex. 214, p. 3, wherein Milan Martić described this as "our first offensive action".

384 *See supra* para. 132.

385 Milan Babić, 16 Feb 2006, T. 1432–1433; Witness MM-003, 8 Mar 2006, T. 2010–2011; Ratko Ličina, 14 Aug 2006, T. 6408.

386 Witness MM-003, 8 Mar 2006, T. 2010–2011; Milan Babić, 16 Feb 2006, T. 1432–1433.

387 The Trial Chamber recalls its findings that Milan Babić's evidence, as well as that of Witness MM-003, requires corroboration, *see supra* section I D 2. The Trial Chamber considers, however, that where the evidence of one of these witnesses corroborates the evidence of the other, such corroboration is sufficient.

388 Ex. 211; Ex. 973; Ex. 975. *See also* MM-003, 8 Mar 2006, T. 2005-2006. Ratko Ličina testified that the SAO Krajina police only reacted to the establishment of Croatian SJBs in municipalities where the Serbs were in majority, as was the case in Plitvice (Titova Korenica municipality), in Lovinac (Gračac municipality), in Kijevo (Knin municipality), in Kruševo (Obrovac municipality), in Škabrnja (Benkovac municipality), in Vidusevac (Glina municipality), Ratko Ličina, 14 Aug 2006, T. 6428, 15 Aug 2006, T. 6507–6508.

165. In mid-July 1991, the town of Glina, located in the Banija area north-west of Dvor, was attacked by a unit under the command of Captain Dragan Vasiljković.[389] The JNA intervened after the attack by creating a buffer zone.[390] On 25 July 1991, the village of Struga, a few kilometres north of Dvor along the Una river, was attacked by units under the command of Captain Dragan Vasiljković and the Glina War Staff: 50 members of a "special forces" unit, 50 policemen and 700 civilians participated in the operation.[391] Following the attack, the JNA intervened and created a buffer zone.[392]

166. On 26 August 1991, the Croat village of Kijevo, situated 15 kilometres east of Knin, was attacked because the MUP of Croatia had established an SJB in the village.[393] The decision to attack Kijevo was taken by Milan Martić in coordination with the JNA and followed an ultimatum issued by him to the Croatian SJB, in which he stated that "[y]ou and your leadership have brought relations between the Serbian and Croatian populations to such a state that further co-existence in our Serbian territories of the SAO Krajina is impossible".[394] In relation to the civilian population in Kijevo, the ultimatum provided that:

> We also want to advise the population of Kijevo to find safe shelters on time so that there should be no casualties among them. We would like to stress that we want co-existence and understanding between the residents of the Serbian villages and the Croatian population in Kijevo, and we guarantee civil and human rights to everyone .[395]

167. Units of the JNA 9th Corps in Knin, the *Milicija Krajine* and the local TO participated in the attack.[396] The evidence establishes that there was coordination between the JNA and the MUP, and that the JNA was in command of the participating forces.[397] The evidence is inconsistent as to the strength of the Croatian forces present in Kijevo.[398] Prior to the attack, between 23 and 25 August **[page 62]** 1991, the commander of the Croatian SJB evacuated almost the entire civilian population of Kijevo.[399]

168 The attack on Kijevo on 26 August 1991 only lasted a few hours.[400] There is differing evidence as to the purpose of the attack. Witnesses testified that the purpose was "to cleanse Kijevo of its Croatian population", to link up the two Serb villages of Polace and Civljani on either side of Kijevo, to "liberate the area", and to provide for further advancement of the JNA.[401] Borislav Đukić, who at the time was commander of Tactical Group 1 ("TG-1") of the JNA 9th Corps in Knin, testified that the attack had not been planned beforehand but was provoked by a Croatian attack on 25 August 1991 on buffer zones previously established by TG-1. According to Borislav Đukić, the purpose of the attack was to lift the blockade along the Kijevo road, set up by the Croatian SJB in Kijevo.[402]

169. The Catholic church in Kijevo was damaged during the attack, and was later destroyed.[403] The evidence also shows that private houses were looted and torched.[404]

---

389 Aernout van Lynden, 2 Jun 2006, T. 5002, 5012–5014.

390 Aernout van Lynden, 2 Jun 2006, T. 4996–4999, 5007.

391 Ex. 587. *See also* Ex. 582 (stating that Milan Martić, Captain Dragan Vasiljković and Bogdan Vajagić met on 23 July 1991 to discuss the situation in the Banija area).

392 Aernout van Lynden, 2 Jun 2006, T. 5008. *See also* Ex. 587, p. 1.

393 Milan Babić, 17 Feb 2006, T. 1553–1556; Ex. 1037, L0079681.

394 Ex. 820, Agreed Facts, para. 20. *See also* Milan Babić, 16 Feb 2006, T. 1438-1439, 17 Feb 2006, T. 1555, Ex. 1037, Group 11, L0079292-3, L0079682; Ex. 212.

395 Ex. 212; Milan Babić, 17 Feb 2006, T. 1555. *See also* Ex. 496, p. 11; Ex. 1037, L0079294, L0079682.

396 Milan Babić, 17 Feb 2006, T. 1558-1559; Milan Dragišić, 19 Sep 2006, T. 8655–8656.

397 Ex. 45, p. 48; Ex. 496, p. 11. *See also* Witness MM-003, 09 Mar 2006, T. 2035.

398 Witness MM-078, 24 May 2006, T. 4443 (members of the Croatian MUP were billeted in the culture hall in Kijevo). Milan Dragišić, 19 Sep 2006, T. 8655–8656 (there were at least 300 armed men in Kijevo, including ZNG); Borislav Đukić, 20 Oct 2006, T. 9875 (there was a gradual reinforcement of the Croatian forces in Kijevo, which eventually numbered 1,000 men).

399 Borislav Đukić, 20 Oct 2006, T. 9872.

400 Borislav Đukić, 20 Oct 2006, T. 9880.

401 Witness MM-003, 9 Mar 2006, T. 2030, 2032–2035; Witness MM-078, 24 May 2006, T. 4443.

402 Borislav Đukić, 20 Oct 2006, T. 9871–9873, 9875–9876; Milan Dragišić, 19 Sep 2006, T. 8655–8656. Milan Babić testified that the residents of Kijevo had blocked the road, Milan Babić, 17 Feb 2006, T. 1551–1552. *See also* Ex. 105.

403 Milan Babić, 3 Mar 2006, T. 1931; Witness MM-078, 24 May 2006, T. 4444; Borislav Đukić, 19 Oct 2006, T. 9767, 20 Oct 2006, T. 9886; Ex. 106 (reporting that ZNG was deployed in the church).

404 Witness MM-078, 24 May 2006, T. 4434–4435; Borislav Đukić, 20 Oct 2006, T. 9885–9886. *See also* Ex. 496.

170. On 28 August 1991, TG-1 of the JNA 9th Corps also attacked the mixed Croat and Serb village of Vrlika, located south of Knin near Kijevo.[405] After the attack, an SJB of the SAO Krajina MUP was established in Vrlika.[406] Subsequently, members of this SJB indirectly participated in the widespread looting by allowing lorries carrying looted goods to proceed towards Knin.[407]

171. On 16 September 1991, Drniš, which is located near Knin and at the time was 75% Croat, was attacked by forces and artillery of TG-1 of the JNA 9th Corps.[408] During the attack, and the following days, the centre of Drniš was almost completely destroyed.[409] Widespread looting was **[page 63]** committed by members of the JNA and the MUP and by local citizens.[410] Approximately 10–15 days after the attack, an SJB of the SAO Krajina MUP was set up in Drniš.[411]

172. Following these attacks, several larger clashes and attacks occurred in predominantly Croat areas of the SAO Krajina. These will be more fully described below.

2. Hrvatska Dubica, Cerovljani and Baćin

(a) Take-over of Hrvatska Kostajnica and Hrvatska Dubica

173. In 1990, Hrvatska Dubica, Cerovljani and Baćin were mixed or predominantly Croat villages in the Hrvatska Kostajnica municipality situated in north-eastern Croatia.[412] In 1990, Hrvatska Dubica had around 2,000 to 2,500 inhabitants.[413] Cerovljani is situated about three to six kilometres north of Hrvatska Dubica and in 1990 its population was some 500 people.[414] Baćin is situated about three to five kilometres west of Hrvatska Dubica and in 1990 it had 200 to 500 inhabitants.[415]

174. In the area of Hrvatska Kostajnica, there was intensive fighting during August and September 1991, which lasted until the beginning of October.[416] In September 1991, Milan Martić went together with Colonel Dušan Smiljanić, Chief of Security of the JNA 10th Zagreb Corps, to coordinate combat activities in relation to the "liberation of Kostajnica".[417]

175. On 12 or 13 September 1991, Serb forces, including the SAO Krajina TO, took control over Hrvatska Kostajnica.[418] The special police unit of the SAO Krajina police at Dvor na Uni participated and cooperated with the TO.[419] Following the takeover of Hrvatska Kostajnica, the **[page 64]** operation continued in order to take over the rest

---

405 Milan Babić, 17 Feb 2006, T. 1567; Witness MM-078, 24 May 2006, T. 4444; Borislav Đukić, 20 Oct 2006, T. 9887.

406 Witness MM-078, 24 May 2006, T. 4445.

407 Witness MM-078, 24 May 2006, T. 4445; Borislav Đukić, 20 Oct 2006, T. 9887–9888 (testifying that the JNA lifted the Croatian siege of Vrlika and that the JNA did not participate in looting); Ex. 221.

408 Witness MM-078, 24 May 2006, T. 4446, 4450–4451; Borislav Đukić, 20 Oct 2006, T. 9888, 9894–9895; Ex. 984, pp 7–12. Two JNA military facilities were located outside of Drniš and were blocked by the Croatian forces, Borislav Đukić, 20 Oct 2006, T. 9888–9889. There was no Croatian SJB in Drniš, Witness MM-078, 24 May 2006, T. 4452.

409 Witness MM-078, 24 May 2006, T. 4450, 25 May 2006, T. 4542.

410 Witness MM-078, 24 May 2006, T. 4450; Borislav Đukić, 20 Oct 2006, T. 9889–9890.

411 Witness MM-078, 24 May 2006, T. 4452.

412 Villages surrounding Hrvatska Dubica are Baćin, Cerovljani, Predore (about eight kilometres from Hrvatska Dubica), Slabinja, Živaja. Directly adjacent to Hrvatska Dubica across the river Una on the side of BiH is Bosanska Dubica, which in 1990 had approximately 10,000 inhabitants (about 40% Serbs, 45% Muslims and 500 Croats). Živaja (situated slightly north of Cerovljani and about eight to fifteen kilometres from Hrvatska Dubica) and Slabinja (ten to fifteen kilometres west of Hrvatska Dubica) were predominantly Serb villages, Witness MM-022, 20 Mar 2006, T. 2278, 2361; Witness MM-025, 12 Jun 2006, T. 5410, 5422–5424; Ex. 265, pp 2–3; Nikola Dobrijević, 10 Nov 2006, T. 10883–10884; Mijo Ciprić, Ex. 274, p. 2; Ex. 23, Atlas p. 21. *See also* Ex. 301, p. 3; Ex. 1042, Tab 2; Ex. 1043, Tab 2, DVD 1, pp 42–59 and DVD 2, pp 1–7; Ex. 1044.

413 Ex. 265, p. 2; Ex. 301, p. 2, in 1991, the population was 50% Croat and 38% Serb.

414 Ex. 265, p. 2. In 1991, 52.9% were Croats, and 39.5% were Serbs, Ex. 301, p. 3.

415 Witness MM-022, 20 Mar 2006, T. 2278; Ex. 265, p. 3; Mijo Ciprić, Ex. 274, p. 2; Ex. 301, p. 1, also stating that 94.9% were Croat, and 1.5% were Serb.

416 Milan Babić, 20 Feb 2006, T. 1597–98; Ex. 1034, L0092283; Ex. 1042, Tab 2; Ex. 1043, Tab 2, DVD 2, pp 7–8; Ex. 1044.

417 Milan Babić, 16 Feb 2006, T. 1441–1442. *See also* Ex. 206; Milan Babić, 17 Feb 2006, T. 1532–1533.

418 Nikola Dobrijević, 10 Nov 2006, T. 10873, 10878, 10882–10883. Nikola Dobrijević testified that among 500 or 600 members of the TO, there were 111 Croats and a few percent of Muslims, Nikola Dobrijević, 10 Nov 2006, T. 10881–10882, 13 Nov 2006 T. 10980–10981; Antun Blažević, Ex. 273, p. 2.

419 Ex. 568, p. 3; Nikola Dobrijević, 13 Nov 2006, T. 10955. *See also* Ex. 957, p. 2, stating that as of 2 September 1991 "[t]here are strong MUP forces in Dubica and Šita".

of the villages along the axis between Kostajnica and Novska, including the villages of Hrvatska Dubica, Cerovljani and Baćin.[420] A front line between the SAO Krajina and Croatian forces was established from Sunja to Hrvatska Dubica and further towards Novska.[421] Following this operation, there were daily conflicts on the front line.[422]

(b) Hrvatska Dubica

176. In 1991, the Croatian MUP took over the SJB in Hrvatska Dubica.[423] From mid-1991, ZNG units were formed in Hrvatska Dubica.[424] Around the same time, the Serb inhabitants started to move out of Hrvatska Dubica.[425]

177. After the occupation of Hrvatska Kostajnica around 12 or 13 September, Hrvatska Dubica was shelled from Hrvatska Kostajnica and from Bosanska Dubica, BiH.[426] Subsequently, the ZNG and Croatian MUP withdrew from Hrvatska Dubica and the surrounding villages and the civilian inhabitants started to leave.[427] After 13 September 1991, only about 60 Croats, mainly elderly and women, remained in Hrvatska Dubica.[428]

178. An SAO Krajina TO force and a police force, including a unit of the *Milicija Krajine* consisting of 30 policemen from the area, were set up in Hrvatska Dubica.[429] Veljko "Velja" Rađunović, his son Stevo Rađunović and Momčilo Kovačević were in charge of the *Milicija Krajine* unit, which had a command post at the old school building in Hrvatska Dubica.[430] There **[page 65]** were "reservists" in Živaja under the command of Stevo Borojević.[431] The reservists wore old military olive-green-grey uniforms.[432]

179. On 15 September 1991, the JNA, the TO and the police surrounded Predore, approximately 8 kilometres from Hrvatska Dubica, and proceeded to search houses.[433] They rounded up people and took six or seven, including Josip Josipović, a ZNG member, to the Sava river to reconnoitre the area using them as a live shield, and then returned them to the village.[434] Josip Josipović and his cousin Mićo Ćorić were then taken to Dubička Brda where they were detained for one month.[435] Thereafter, they were transferred to the school building in Hrvatska Dubica, which was used as a command post by Serb forces, including the TO and the police.[436] Present

---

420 Nikola Dobrijević, 10 Nov 2006, T. 10883–10884; Antun Blažević, Ex. 273, pp 2–3; Mijo Ciprić, Ex. 274, pp 3–4; Ex. 568, p. 4; Ex. 599, p. 5.

421 Nikola Dobrijević, 10 Nov 2006, T. 10884–10886. According to Witness MM-022, the front line was between Jasenovac and Sunja along the Sava River, Witness MM-022, 20 Mar 2006, T. 2350–2351.

422 Nikola Dobrijević, 10 Nov 2006, T. 10886.

423 Josip Josipović, 6 Apr 2006, T. 3338.

424 Witness MM-022, 20 Mar 2006, T. 2281–2283, 2324. There were about four units, each made up of four to five men, who did not have uniforms. The units had one firearm between them and some carried personal hunting rifles. The headquarters was in Hrvatska Dubica, close to the bridge between Hrvatska Dubica and Bosanska Dubica, Ex. 265, p. 5; Josip Josipović, 6 Apr 2006, T. 3297–3298, 3348.

425 Witness MM-022, 20 Mar 2006, T. 2284, 2325, 2330; Ana Kesić, 21 Mar 2006, T. 2385; Josip Josipović, 6 Apr 2006, T. 3304–3305, 3333–3334; Witness MM-025, 12 Jun 2006, T. 5421.

426 Tomislav Kozarčanin, Ex. 828, p. 2. *See also* Antun Blažević, Ex. 273, p. 2.

427 Witness MM-022, 20 Mar 2006, T. 2281, 2286–2287, 2289; Josip Josipović, 6 Apr 2006, T. 3298, 3346–3347; Witness MM-025, 12 Jun 2006, T. 5414, 5421, Ex. 265, p. 4; Tomislav Kozarčanin, Ex. 828, p. 2.

428 Witness MM-022, 20 Mar 2006, T. 2292–2293; Ana Kesić, 21 Mar 2006, T. 2385–2386; Witness MM-025, 12 Jun 2006, T. 5421–5422, Ex. 265, p. 4.

429 Witness MM-022, 20 Mar 2006, T. 2289–2290, 2293, 2316, 2336, 2350; Josip Josipović, 6 Apr 2006, T. 3297–3298.

430 Witness MM-022, 20 Mar 2006, T. 2291, 2297–2298, 2308; Josip Josipović, 6 Apr 2006, T. 3309–3310, 3314. Other *Milicija Krajine* members were Mirko Sarac, Milan Petrović, Đorđe Ratković, Đuro Jerinić, Marjan Prvalo, Mladen Pozar, Rajko Pauković, Dubravko Pauković, Mico Tepić, and Branko Kotur, Josip Josipović, 6 Apr 2006, T. 3309, 3318.

431 Witness MM-022, 20 Mar 2006, T. 2289, 2293.

432 Witness MM-022, 20 Mar 2006, T. 2293. The Serb forces in the area at the time wore a variety of insignia, including the five-pointed star and emblems with the inscription "SAO Krajina", with "*Milicija Krajine*", with a double-headed eagle and crossed swords, with four Cyrillic "S". It was not possible to tell to which unit soldiers belonged. There is also evidence of soldiers with patches reading "Special Police Units", "Blue", and "Ugljevik", worn by Serbs who came from BiH, Josip Josipović, 6 Apr 2006, T. 3299–3300, 3300–3303, 3353, 7 Apr 2006, T. 3382–3383; Ex. 266; Ex. 288.

433 Josip Josipović, 6 Apr 2006, T. 3294, 3309, 3349–3350.

434 Josip Josipović, 6 Apr 2006, T. 3310, 3350.

435 Josip Josipović, 6 Apr 2006, T. 3310–3311. The Trial Chamber considers that the Defence has not been put on notice regarding a detention facility in Dubička Brda and will not consider this evidence for a conviction, *see supra* section I C.

436 Josip Josipović, 6 Apr 2006, T. 3311, 3314.

at the school building were Momčilo Kovačević and Veljko Radjunović, who issued orders and participated in the beatings of detainees at the school building.[437] Josip Josipović identified Momčilo Kovačević, Stevo Radjunović, Mirko Šarac, Milan Petrović, Djordje Ratković, Djuro Jerinić, Marjan Prvalo and Miša Pozar as the soldiers guarding them.[438] Josip Josipović testified that he overheard the soldiers discussing amongst themselves and understood them as saying that they were receiving orders from Milan Martić.[439]

180. After the take-over of Hrvatska Dubica until mid-October 1991, some houses were torched in Hrvatska Dubica: approximately eight belonged to Croats, two belonged to couples of mixed marriages, and one belonged to a Serb.[440] There was also widespread looting, committed by the JNA, the TO, the *Milicija Krajine*, and local Serbs.[441] Detained Croats were also forced to loot.[442] All the houses of people who had fled, both Croats and Serbs, were looted and cars, tractors, tools, **[page 66]** machinery, furniture and cattle were stolen.[443] Serbs who had withdrawn from the areas of Pakrac and Lipik moved into the houses of the people who had fled.[444]

181. In the morning on 20 October 1991, a truck bearing the insignia "Milicija SAO Krajina" with Veljko Rađunović, Radovan Šoša and a man nicknamed "Janjeta" came to Ana Kesić's house and told her and her sister-in-law Katarina to come with them and attend a meeting.[445] Thereafter the truck picked up several other civilians and brought them to the fire station in Hrvatska Dubica.[446] On the same date, Tomislav Kozarčanin was told by Branko Majstorović, who was wearing a JNA uniform, to go to the fire station to attend a meeting, which he did.[447] A second bus arrived at the fire station after ten minutes bringing another 20 people.[448] In total, there were then more than 40 people in the fire station but more people arrived later.[449] They were mostly Croats, although there were also Serbs and Muslims.[450]

182. The people in the fire station were guarded by Katarina "Kaća" Pekić and Stevo Rađunovic, who were armed and wore JNA uniforms, and a man with the last name Kovačević.[451] The detainees were not free to leave.[452] Every two or three hours there was a change of guard, and the detainees' names would be read out from a list to check no one was missing.[453] Over the course of the day, eleven of the detainees were released or managed to escape, including Tomislav Kozarčanin.[454]

183. Several witnesses testified to having heard, including from Serb soldiers in Hrvatska Dubica, that the people detained in the fire station on 20 October 1991 were taken the following day **[page 67]** to a place called Krečane near Baćin where they were killed.[455] The bodies of the following 32 civilians, who the evidence shows had been detained in the fire station on 20 October 1991, were subsequently exhumed from several graves,

437 Josip Josipović, 6 Apr 2006, T. 3314.
438 Josip Josipović, 6 Apr 2006, T. 3318, 7 Apr 2006, T. 3375.
439 Josip Josipović, 6 Apr 2006, T. 3356.
440 Witness MM-022, 20 Mar 2006, T. 2295–2296.
441 Witness MM-022, 20 Mar 2006, T. 2293–2295, 2336.
442 Josip Josipović, 6 Apr 2006, T. 3312–3313.
443 Witness MM-022, 20 Mar 2006, T. 2294–2296; Ana Kesić, 21 Mar 2006, T. 2383. *See also* Josip Josipović, 6 Apr 2006, T. 3313.
444 Witness MM-022, 20 Mar 2006, T. 2296.
445 Witness MM-022, 20 Mar 2006, T. 2298–2301; Ana Kesić, 21 Mar 2006, T. 2388–2390, Ex. 258, p. 2.
446 Those who were picked up included Vera Franković, Veronika Stanković, Pavle Kropf, Bara Kropf and her daughter, an 80-year old man nicknamed "Brico", Danica Krizmanović, Ruza Dikulić, Sofija Dikulić, and Nikola Lončar, Witness MM-022, 20 Mar 2006, T. 2299–2301; Ana Kesić, 21 Mar 2006, T. 2388–2389, Ex. 258, p. 2. The Trial Chamber considers that Vera Stanković, born 1915, is Veronika Stanković in Annex I to the Indictment, that Pavle Kropf, aged 60, is Pavao Kropf in Annex I, that Bara Kropf, aged 60, is Barbara Kropf in Annex I, and that Nikola Lončar is Nikola Lončarević in Annex I. *See also* Josip Josipović, 6 Apr 2006, T. 3324; Ex. 1042, Tab 2; Ex. 1043, Tab 2, DVD 1, pp 49–53.
447 Tomislav Kozarčanin, Ex. 828, p. 2.
448 Witness MM-022, 20 Mar 2006, T. 2301.
449 Witness MM-022, 20 Mar 2006, T. 2301–2302. *See also* Ex. 380, pp 10, 12.
450 Witness MM-022, 20 Mar 2006, T. 2303.
451 Witness MM-022, 20 Mar 2006, T. 2343–2344; Tomislav Kozarčanin, Ex. 828, p. 3; Ex. 380, pp 11–12.
452 Tomislav Kozarčanin, Ex. 828, p. 3
453 Witness MM-022, 20 Mar 2006, T. 2302, 2343–2344. Two Serbs, Mićo Kesonja and Đuro Kesonja, made a list of all the people who remained in Hrvatska Dubica during the period of their occupation, Tomislav Kozarčanin, Ex. 828, pp 3–4.
454 Those released were three Serbs, one Muslim and seven Croats whose Serb neighbours or friends contacted the guards, Witness MM-022, 20 Mar 2006, T. 2304–2306, 2360; Ana Kesić, 21 Mar 2006, T. 2390, 2393–2394, Ex. 258, pp 2–3; Tomislav Kozarčanin, Ex. 828, p. 3; Ex. 380, pp 11–12.
455 Witness MM-022, 20 Mar 2006, T. 2310–2311; Josip Josipović, 6 Apr 2006, T. 3324–3325, 3354; Ana Kesić, 21 Mar 2006, T. 2381–2382, Ex. 258, p. 3; Tomislav Kozarčanin, Ex. 828, p. 3. *See also* Ex. 265, p. 6; Ex. 257.

including one at Krečane near Baćin:[456] Katarina Alavančić, Terezija Alavančić, Josip Antolović,[457] Marija Batinović,[458] Mara Ćorić,[459] Mijo Ćović,[460] Marija Delić, Ana Dikulić, Ruža Dikulić, Sofija Dikulić, Antun Đukić, Marija "Maca" Đukić,[461] Ana Ferić, Juraj Ferić, Kata Ferić, Filip Jukić, Marija Jukić, Antun Krivajić, Barbara Kropf, Pavao Kropf, Ivan Kulišić,[462] Nikola Lončarić, Antun Mucavac,[463] Ivo Pezo, Sofija Pezo, Anka Piktaja,[464] Štjepan Sabljar, Veronika Stanković, Antun Švračić, Marija Švračić, Ana Tepić,[465] and Katarina Vladić.[466] Moreover, the evidence shows that the following 9 civilians, whose bodies have not been recovered, were detained in the fire station on 20 October 1991 and killed the following day at Krečane near Baćin: Štjepan Dikulić, Antun Đurinović, Jozo Karanović, Reza Krivajić, Dušan Tepić, Ivan Trninić, Ivo Trninić, Kata Trninić and Terezija Trninić.[467] Although their bodies have not been recovered, in light of the fact that they were detained in the fire station at the same time as the above-mentioned 32 persons who were subsequently killed, the Trial Chamber considers that it has been established beyond reasonable doubt that they were killed.[468] All of the above victims were Croats, except for Ana Tepić and Dušan Tepić, who were Serbs.[469]

184. After Tomislav Kozarčanin fled from the fire station, he hid for seven or eight days. When he returned to his house, he was picked up by Đuro Majstorović and two others with the same surname. They wore JNA uniforms and carried automatic rifles. He was handcuffed, blindfolded **[page 68]** and beaten, after which he was taken in their car to an abandoned house. He was beaten throughout the journey, which resulted in broken ribs, and his legs were cut with a knife. They then drove him to another location, removed his handcuffs and abandoned him. A Serb later took him to the SJB in Hrvatska Dubica, where he described what had happened to him.[470]

185. After Ana Kesić and her sister-in-law Katarina were released from the fire station, they heard from one of their relatives, Milan Šestić, that three neighbours had been killed and that he dug graves for them.[471] There is no other evidence as to these three persons.[472] The Trial Chamber finds that the evidence is insufficient to establish beyond reasonable doubt that these three persons were killed.[473]

---

456 In 1997, 56 bodies were exhumed from a mass grave in Krečane near Baćin, Davor Strinović, 12 Apr 2006, T. 3669; Ana Kesić, Ex. 258, p. 3; Tomislav Kozarčanin, Ex. 828, p. 3; Antun Blažević, Ex. 273, p. 4; Mijo Ciprić, Ex. 274, p. 4; Ex. 301, p. 1; Ex. 380; Ex. 1042, Tab 2; Ex. 1043, Tab 2, DVD 2, pp 5–7; Ex. 1044.

457 Ex. 315.

458 Ex. 316.

459 Ex. 310; Josip Josipović, 6 Apr 2006, T. 3324–3325.

460 Ex. 317.

461 Ex. 308.

462 There is evidence that an individual called "Ivo Kuliša" remained in Hrvatska Dubica, Tomislav Kozarčanin, Ex. 828, p. 2. However, the Trial Chamber cannot conclude that this person is the same person as Ivan Kulišić.

463 Ex. 307.

464 Ex. 314.

465 Ex. 306.

466 With respect to these 32 individuals, *see* Ex. 257 (listing all of them except for Marija Batinović); Witness MM-022, 20 Mar 2006, T. 2312–2313; Ex. 302, Ex. 323. Ex. 302 indicates that all of them except for Marija Delić and Ivo Pezo, were exhumed from a mass grave in Krečane near Baćin. Ex. 323 identifies their causes of death as either gunshot wounds, trauma wounds or blast wounds, except for Ivan Kulišić, for whom Ex. 323 states the cause of death as unknown. Ex. 257 also lists FNU Jukić, FNU Krnić and FNU Šestić as having been detained in the fire station. There is no further evidence concerning these persons and in view of this lack of evidence the Trial Chamber is unable to identify them. Having regard to the Trial Chamber's finding as to the interpretation of the Indictment (*see supra* section I C) the Trial Chamber will not make any further finding regarding these persons.

467 Ex. 257; Ex. 302; Ex. 323.

468 In this respect, the Trial Chamber notes the evidence of Mijo Ciprić that there is a possibility that bodies were washed away from the mass grave at Krečane near Baćin as that grave is on the bank of the river Una, Mijo Ciprić, Ex. 274, 7–8 Nov 2000, p. 4. *See also* Ex. 1042; Ex. 1043, DVD 2, pp 5–7.

469 Witness MM-022, 20 Mar 2006, T. 2313.

470 Tomislav Kozarčanin, Ex. 828, p. 3.

471 Ana Kesić, Ex. 258, p. 3.

472 These three were Luka Krnić, Štef Uska and FNU Batinović, Ana Kesić, 21 Mar 2006, T. 2381, Ex. 258, p. 3. Annex I to the Indictment contains two individuals with the last name Batinović, however the Trial Chamber cannot find that this individual is the same person as either of those mentioned in Annex I.

473 There is evidence that Milan Šestić disappeared from Hrvatska Dubica, Ana Kesić, 21 Mar 2006, T. 2381, Ex. 258, p. 3. *See also* Ex. 302, p. 4. Documentary evidence also shows that Mijo Mišić disappeared from Hrvatska Dubica, Ex. 302, p. 4. Milan Šestić and Mijo Mišić are mentioned in Annex I to the Indictment as victims killed in Baćin and surroundings. However, in view of the evidence regarding these persons provided to the Trial Chamber (Ex. 302, Ex. 323), the Trial Chamber cannot conclude that these individuals are dead or were killed. Maca Dikulić (age 86) is listed in Annex I to the Indictment. There is evidence that she

(c) Cerovljani

186. Following the advice of the Croatian police and ZNG, most of the residents of Cerovljani left the village in August and early September 1991, after which only elderly people remained.[474]

187. On 13 and 21 September 1991, Serbs came to Cerovljani and burnt Croat houses.[475] The Serbs who came on 21 September were armed and about fifty in number, the majority wearing civilian clothes, although a few wore military uniforms.[476] The commander was Nikola Begović from Babin Rijeka near Hrvatska Kostajnica and most of the members were from Živaja, Šaš and the surroundings of Hrvatska Dubica.[477] On 24 September, the armed Serbs came again in the afternoon and shooting could be heard; that night three dead bodies were found.[478] On the same date, the houses of Đuro Petrović, Nikola Dragocajać, Anka Barišić and Željko Blinja were torched **[page 69]** by the Serbs and rocket launchers were fired at the Catholic church which damaged the bell tower.[479] Some of the armed Serbs also stole the car of Antun Blažević.[480]

188. The evidence shows that some time in October 1991, unidentified armed Serbs gathered the remaining civilians in Cerovljani into the local community centre under the pretext of having a meeting, following which they were detained for the night. The next morning they were taken away.[481] The bodies of Marija Antolović,[482] Ana Blinja,[483] Josip Blinja,[484] Katarina Blinja,[485] Andrija Likić,[486] Ana Lončar,[487] and Kata Lončar (born 1906)[488] were subsequently discovered in the mass grave in Krečane near Baćin.[489] Another woman also by the name of Kata Lončar, who was a Croat, remained in the village throughout the occupation because she had "connections with the Serbs".[490] The bodies of Nikola Blinja, Antun Lončar and Nikola Zaočević, who were also rounded up, have not been recovered.[491] In relation to Nikola Zaočević, the Trial Chamber notes that he is not mentioned in Annex I to the Indictment and recalls its interpretation of the Indictment in this respect.[492] Moreover, the Trial Chamber considers that the Defence has not been on notice concerning this victim and the Trial Chamber is therefore unable to consider this victim further. With regard to Nikola Blinja and Antun Lončar, in light of the evidence that they were detained with the other persons named above, all of whom were subsequently killed, the Trial Chamber finds it established beyond reasonable doubt that also they were killed at the same time.

(d) Baćin and surroundings

189. Following the take-over of Baćin, all the inhabitants left, with the exception of around thirty mostly elderly civilians, among whom were the following 22 persons: Željko Abaza, Matija Barunović, Antun

---

remained in Hrvatska Dubica after the occupation, Ana Kesić, Ex. 258, p. 3; Tomislav Kozarčanin, Ex. 828, p. 2. However, no other information is provided to the Trial Chamber in relation to this person (Ex. 302, Ex. 303). The Trial Chamber cannot conclude that this individual is dead or was killed.

474 Antun Blažević, Ex. 273, p. 3.

475 Antun Blažević, Ex. 273, p. 3. On 13 September 1991, "the Serbs" burnt three Croatian houses which were on the Živaja side of Cerovljani. On 21 September, they burnt three more, Antun Blažević, Ex. 273, p. 3.

476 Antun Blažević, Ex. 273, p. 3.

477 Antun Blažević, Ex. 273, p. 3.

478 The victims were Barbara Blinja, Nikola Likić, and Đuro Petrović, Antun Blažević, Ex. 273, pp 3–4. The Trial Chamber finds that these victims were killed by armed Serbs from Živaja under the command of Nikola Begović. The Trial Chamber notes that Barbara Blinja Nikola Likić, and Đuro Petrović are not listed in Annex I to the Indictment. The Trial Chamber considers that the Defence has not been on notice regarding these killings and will therefore not enter a conviction based on them. *See supra* section I C.

479 Antun Blažević, Ex. 273, p. 3.

480 Antun Blažević, Ex. 273, p. 3.

481 Antun Blažević, Ex. 273, p. 4.

482 Antun Blažević, Ex. 273, p. 4; Ex. 302; Ex. 311; Ex. 323, p. 4.

483 Antun Blažević, Ex. 273, 23 Jun 2003, p. 1; Ex. 302; Ex. 323, p. 4.

484 Antun Blažević, Ex. 273, p. 4; Ex. 302; Ex. 323, p. 4.

485 Antun Blažević, Ex. 273, 23 Jun 2003, p. 1; Ex. 302; Ex. 323, p. 4.

486 Antun Blažević, Ex. 273, p. 4; Ex. 302; Ex. 309; Ex. 323, p. 5.

487 Antun Blažević, Ex. 273, p. 4; Ex. 302; Ex. 323, p. 5.

488 Antun Blažević, Ex. 273, p. 4; Ex. 302; Ex. 313; Ex. 323, p. 5.

489 Antun Blažević, Ex. 273, p. 4, 23 Jun 2003, p. 1; Ex. 302.

490 Antun Blažević, Ex. 273, p. 4.

491 Antun Blažević, Ex 273, p. 4; Ex. 302 (regarding Nikola Blinja and Antun Lončar).

492 *See supra* section I C.

Bunjevac, Tomo Bunjevac, Antun Čorić, Barica Čorić, Josip Čorić (30 years old), another man by the name of Josip Čorić (60 years old), Vera Čorić, Nikola Felbabić, Grga Glavinić, Anka Josipović, Ankica Josipović, Ivan Josipović, Josip Karagić, Kata Lončar (born 1931), Štjepan Lončar, Antun Ordanić, Luka Ordanić, Antun Pavić, Matija Pavić, and Nikola **[page 70]** Vrpoljac.[493] The evidence shows that Željko Abaza was detained in mid-October in a toilet in the old school building in Hrvatska Dubica, that he was later killed by members of the *Milicija Krajine*, and that his body was thrown into the Una river by those members.[494] The evidence further shows that the bodies of Antun Bunjevac and Tomo Bunjevac were exhumed from individual graves in Hrvatska Dubica.[495] There is no exhumation evidence concerning the other persons listed above. The Trial Chamber notes the evidence that in October 1991 all of the people who remained in the village were taken to Krečane near Baćin, where they were killed along with a number of others who were brought from Cerovljani and Hrvatska Dubica.[496]

190. In light of the evidence that Željko Abaza was killed in Hrvatska Dubica and not buried but thrown into the Una river, and that Antun Bunjevac and Tomo Bunjevac were buried in Hrvatska Dubica, the Trial Chamber cannot conclude that the above-named persons were killed as one group. However, the Trial Chamber takes particular note of the situation in the area in October 1991 and that there is no evidence of fighting going on in Baćin proper at this time. The Trial Chamber further recalls the evidence that numerous killings of persons from Hrvatska Dubica, Cerovljani and Baćin were committed in Krečane near Baćin around 21 October 1991. In this connection, the Trial Chamber recalls that it visited Baćin and Krečane during the site visit to Croatia, and notes that Krečane is on the outskirts of Baćin and less than a ten-minute walk from the Catholic church in Baćin.[497] In light of the above, and the totality of the evidence, the Trial Chamber therefore considers that the evidence proves beyond reasonable doubt that the above-named persons were killed around October 1991, albeit not necessarily on one occasion or at one and the same location.

191. Annex I to the Indictment lists Ivo Barunović, Nikola Barunović, Kata Bunjevac, Vera Jukić, Terezija Kramarić, Mijo Krnić, Marija Milašinović, Marija Šestić and Soka Volarević as having been killed in or around Baćin. The evidence shows that Vera Jukić, Terezija Kramarić, Mijo Krnić, Marija Milašinović, Marija Šestić and Soka Volarević were exhumed from the mass **[page 71]** grave in Krečane near Baćin.[498] Moreover, the evidence shows that Nikola Barunović was exhumed from the mass grave at Višnjevački Bok, where Ivo Pezo, who had previously been detained at the fire station in Hrvatska Dubica, was also exhumed.[499] Furthermore, Ivo Barunović was exhumed from an individual grave in Baćin.[500] With regard to Kata Bunjevac, the evidence shows that she went missing from Kostrićima, however there is no further evidence in relation to her.[501] The Trial Chamber concludes that the above-mentioned victims were killed, except for Ivo Barunović and Kata Bunjevac, in relation to whom the Trial Chamber finds that the evidence is insufficient to establish beyond reasonable doubt that they were killed.

192. With respect to the following 22 individuals listed in Annex I to the Indictment, no evidence has been provided to the Trial Chamber: Sofija Barić, Marija Barunović, Anka Batinović, Danica Đukić, Kata Đukić,

---

493 Mijo Ciprić, Ex. 274, p. 3.

494 Josip Josipović was detained together with Željko Abaza, Antun Knežević and Idriz Čaušević. Idriz Čaušević was killed by persons under Veljko Rađunović's and Momčilo Kovačević's command at the old school building in Hrvatska Dubica. Three days later, Željko Abaza and Ante Knežević had their throats slit and Josip Josipović and Mićo Ćorić were forced by Stevo Rađunović, Momčilo Kovačević, Mirko Sarac, Milan Petrović, Đorđe Ratković, Đuro Jerinić, Marjan Prvalo, and Mladen Pozar to load the dead bodies of Željko Abaza and Antun Knežević onto a truck. Subsequently, the truck drove the three of them and the two bodies to the river and the bodies were thrown into the water by the same Serbs, Josip Josipović, 6 Apr 2006, T. 3315–3320, 7 Apr 2006, T. 3375–3377. The Trial Chamber finds that these three individuals were killed. However, none of these victims are mentioned in Annex I to the Indictment. The Trial Chamber considers that the Defence has not been on notice with regard to these killings and will not consider this evidence for a conviction. In this regard, the Trial Chamber recalls its findings on the interpretation of the indictment, *see supra* section I C. *See also* Mijo Ciprić, Ex. 274, p. 3; Ex. 1042, Tab 2; Ex. 1043, Tab 2, DVD 1, pp 46–48.

495 Ex. 302; Ex. 323.

496 Mijo Ciprić, Ex. 274, p. 3.

497 *See* Ex. 1043, DVD 2, pp 5–6; Ex. 1044, pp 5, 8–9.

498 Ex. 302. Regarding Soka Volarević, *see also* Ex. 312; Ex. 323.

499 Ex. 302. Ex. 323 indicates that the cause of death of Nikola Barunović was a blast wound and that the cause of death of the other victims was gunshot wounds.

500 Ex. 302; Ex. 323, providing that the cause of death is unknown.

501 Ex. 302; Ex. 323.

Liza Đukić, Iva Jukić, Marija Juratović, Janja Jurić, Marija Krnić, Štefo Krnić, Ivica Kulišić, Mijo Lazić, Anka Likić, Antun Likić, Jelka Likić, Antun Lončarević, Janja Lujić, Dragica Matijević, Mara Mucavac, Jula Šestić and Pero Vuković.[502] The Trial Chamber therefore finds that there is insufficient evidence to establish beyond reasonable doubt that these individuals were killed. With regard to Nevenka Perković, Vlado Perković and Zoran Perković, who are also listed in Annex I to the Indictment, the evidence shows that they were found alive.[503]

(e) Destruction in Cerovljani, Hrvatska Dubica, and Baćin after December 1991[504]

193. Prior to August 1993, a Catholic church in Hrvatska Dubica was razed to the ground and its foundations were removed.[505] The Orthodox church remained intact and was still standing in 1995.[506] Towards the end of 1992 and beginning of 1993, looting and torching of houses was carried out by local Serbs.[507] By 1995, many houses in Hrvatska Dubica belonging to Croats had been destroyed.[508] The part of the village which contained both Serb and Croat houses remained intact.[509] By 1995, most houses had been looted.[510] **[page 72]**

194. There is evidence that by 1995, Croat houses in Cerovljani had been burnt or blown up, and that the Catholic church had been destroyed.[511]

195. There is evidence that by 1995, half of the houses in Baćin were destroyed or torched.[512] The Catholic church in Baćin had been completely destroyed.[513] Many houses in the surrounding villages suffered damage, and the village of Predore was razed to the ground.[514]

3. Saborsko area

196. Saborsko is located in north-western Croatia and stretches seven kilometres along the Korenica-Ogulin road, which goes through Plitvice, Poljanak, Saborsko, Lička Jasenica, Plaški, and Josipdol before reaching Ogulin.[515] Purely or predominantly Croat villages were located south of Saborsko near the Plitvice Lakes,[516] whereas Serb villages, such as Plaški and Lička Jasenica, were located to the north of Saborsko.[517]

(a) Municipality of Plaški

197. In 1990, Plaški was within the municipality of Ogulin.[518] Following a referendum, Plaški formed its own municipality and joined the SAO Krajina. Nikola Medaković became the first president of the new

502 Ex. 302, pp 2–4, indicating that there is no information on these individuals.

503 Ex. 302, p. 4; Ivan Grujić, 10 Apr 2006, T. 3476.

504 The Trial Chamber recalls that the period governing the Indictment as to Counts 12 to 14 is 1 August 1991-31 December 1992, Indictment, para. 47.

505 Witness MM-022, 20 Mar 2006, T. 2365; Ana Kesić, 21 Mar 2006, T. 2383. *See also* Mijo Ciprić, Ex. 274, p. 3; Ex. 1042, Tab 2; Ex. 1043, Tab 2, DVD 1, pp 53–54; Ex. 1044.

506 Ana Kesić, 21 Mar 2006, T. 2383. *See also* Ex. 1042, Tab 2; Ex. 1043, Tab 2, DVD 1, pp 54–59; Ex. 1044.

507 Tomislav Kozarčanin, Ex. 828, p. 4.

508 Ana Kesić, 21 Mar 2006, T. 2383, Ex. 258, p. 3; Witness MM-022, 20 Mar 2006, T. 2361; Mijo Ciprić, Ex. 274, p. 3.

509 Mijo Ciprić, Ex. 274, pp 3–4.

510 Witness MM-022, 20 Mar 2006, T. 2318; Tomislav Kozarčanin, Ex. 828, p. 4.

511 Witness MM-022, 20 Mar 2006, T. 2362–2363; Antun Blažević, Ex. 273, p. 4; Mijo Ciprić, Ex. 274, p. 3. *See also* Ex. 1042, Tab 2; Ex. 1043, Tab 2, DVD 2, pp 1–2; Ex. 1044.

512 Witness MM-022, 20 Mar 2006, T. 2362; Mijo Ciprić, Ex. 274, p. 3.

513 Mijo Ciprić, Ex. 274, p. 3.

514 Witness MM-022, 20 Mar 2006, T. 2362.

515 Ex. 22, Map 8; Ex. 23, p. 19; Marko Vuković, 24 Mar 2006, T. 2610; Vlado Vuković, 27 Mar 2006, T. 2655, 2710; Witness MM-037, 28 Mar 2006, T. 2797; Nikola Medaković, 9 Oct 2006, T. 8961; Ana Bićanić, Ex. 276, p. 2. *See also* Ex. 1042, Tab 2; Ex. 1043, Tab 2, DVD 2, pp 30–41 and DVD 3, pp 1–10; Ex. 1044.

516 Such as Sertić Poljana and Poljanak, Marko Vuković, 24 Mar 2006, T. 2568.

517 Other Serb villages in this area were Blata, Plavca Draga, Haski, Latin, and Vojnovac, Marko Vuković, 24 Mar 2006, T. 2568; Witness MM-037, 28 Mar 2006, T. 2747; Nikola Medaković, 9 Oct 2006, T. 8946. There were JNA barracks and a large fuel depot in Lička Jasenica, Vlado Vuković, 27 Mar 2006, T. 2655; Marko Vuković, 24 Mar 2006, T. 2574, 2605; Witness MM-037, 28 Mar 2006, T. 2751–2752; Nikola Medaković, 9 Oct 2006, T. 8972.

518 Witness MM-037, 28 Mar 2006, T. 2746–2747; Nikola Medaković, 9 Oct 2006, T. 8945–8947, 10 Oct 2006, T. 9086.

municipality.[519] Plaški municipality comprised *inter alia* the Serb villages of Vojnovac, Plaški, Blata and Lička Jasenica and was surrounded by Croat villages.[520]

198. Following the armed clash in Plitvice in March 1991, a split occurred in the Plaški SJB, whereby policemen of Croat origin left the SJB and were replaced with Serb policemen from the **[page 73]** area.[521] After this, the SJB consisted of 10 to 15 employees and the Chief of the SJB was Dušan Lataš.[522]

199. During the spring and early summer of 1991, a unit of the *Milicija Krajine* was set up in Plaški following training at Golubić. Nikola Medaković, who had also undergone the training, commanded the unit, which at its fullest capacity consisted of 50 policemen.[523] The members of the unit called themselves "Martić's Police".[524] In September 1991, a TO Brigade was established in Plaški into which members of the *Milicija Krajine* unit were transferred.[525]

200. Following the armed clash in Plitvice and through the summer of 1991, both Serb and Croat forces set up roadblocks on the road from Saborsko through Lička Jasenica to Ogulin.[526] After the summer 1991, the road was closed by the Croatian MUP which set up barriers in Josipdol to the north of Plaški and Saborsko to the south, which resulted in a blockade of Plaški as well as the JNA training grounds in Slunj.[527] There were neither telephone lines nor electricity, nor basic necessities, such as food or medicine.[528]

(b) Lipovača

201. Lipovača was in the municipality of Slunj, approximately 25 kilometres from Saborsko and 18 kilometres from the town of Slunj and the former training ground of the JNA 5th Military District **[page 74]** in Slunj.[529] In 1991, Lipovača was a predominantly Croat village with a total of 267 inhabitants.[530] The Croat inhabitants of Lipovača had guards with a few rifles mounted along the road that passed through

519 Witness MM-037, 28 Mar 2006, T. 2747–2748, Ex. 268, T. 11570, 11572; Nikola Medaković, 9 Oct 2006, T. 8948, 10 Oct 2006, T. 9055.

520 The Croat villages included Slunj, Ogulin, the area of Stajnica, Lipice, and Saborsko, Witness MM-037, 28 Mar 2006, T. 2746–2748, 2770–2771; Nikola Medaković, 9 Oct 2006, T. 8975–8976, 10 Oct 2006, T. 9046.

521 The reason for the split was that the policemen of Croat ethnicity refused to sign a pledge of allegiance to the SAO Krajina, Marko Vuković, 24 Mar 2006, T. 2570–2571; Vlado Vuković, 27 Mar 2006, T. 2653; Nikola Medaković, 10 Oct 2006, T. 9094; Witness MM-037, Ex. 268, T. 11569, 11616. Regarding the clash in Plitvice, *see supra* para. 132.

522 Witness MM-037, 28 Mar 2006, T. 2749, 2751, 29 Mar 2006, T. 2821, Ex. 268, T. 11568–11569; Nikola Medaković, 9 Oct 2006, T. 8959, 8971, 8973.

523 Nikola Medaković, 9 Oct 2006, T. 8965–8966, 8970, 10 Oct 2006, T. 9051, 9054; Witness MM-037, 28 Mar 2006, T. 2748, 2804, Ex. 268, T. 11569–11570, 11572.

524 Witness MM-037, 28 Mar 2006, T. 2749, Ex. 268, T. 11570; Ex. 507, p. 2.

525 Nikola Medaković, 10 Oct 2006, T. 9054. The evidence is unclear as to whether all members of the *Milicija Krajine* unit became part of the TO Brigade at this point in time. Nikola Medaković testified that 15–20 *Milicija Krajine* members refused to join the TO Brigade and established a group of their own under the command of Rade Milanović. Eventually, though it is unclear when, this group was subsumed "in other units", Nikola Medaković, 10 Oct 2006, T. 9054, 9058–9070. The TO had semi-automatic rifles, machine-guns and olive-drab uniforms, Nikola Medaković, 10 Oct 2006, T. 9112–9113; Witness MM-037, 28 Mar 2006, T. 2787–2788, Ex. 268, T. 11577–11579; Ana Bićanić, Ex. 276, p. 2. By the summer of 1991, there were Serb forces including police, TO and JNA, in both Plaški and in Plitvice, on both sides of the villages of Saborsko, Vukovići and Poljanak, Nikola Medaković, 10 Oct 2006, T. 9047.

526 Vehicles and passengers were searched and communications in the area were affected, Marko Vuković, 24 Mar 2006, T. 2569, 2571, 2630; Vlado Vuković, 27 Mar 2006, T. 2656, 28 Mar 2006, T. 2722; Witness MM-037, 28 Mar 2006, T. 2758–2759, Ex. 268, T. 11567–11568, 11588, 11617; Nikola Medaković, 9 Oct 2006, T. 8974, 10 Oct 2006, T. 9044, 9120; Ana Bićanić, Ex. 276, p. 2.

527 Vlado Vuković, 27 Mar 2006, T. 2694; Nikola Medaković, 9 Oct 2006, T. 8961, 8975–8977, 10 Oct 2006, T. 9097–9098 (testifying that after August, the JNA could not pass the road between Slunj and Plitvice, because the town of Slunj was under control of the Croatian MUP), 12 Oct 2006, T. 9273–9275; Witness MM-037, Ex. 268, T. 11567, 11588, 11633–11636. The JNA training grounds in Slunj stretched from Slunj towards Saborsko and Plaški, Marko Vuković, 24 Mar 2006, T. 2574, 2604–2605; Vlado Vuković, 27 Mar 2006, T. 2710–2711; Nikola Medaković, 10 Oct 2006, T. 9096; Witness MM-037, Ex. 268, T. 11585. *See also* Reynaud Theunens, 3 Feb 2006, T. 1051; Ex. 1042, Tab 2; Ex. 1043, Tab 2, DVD 2, pp 11–15.

528 Nikola Medaković, 9 Oct 2006, T. 8976.

529 Witness MM-036, 4 Apr 2006, T. 3183–3184, 3201; Nikola Medaković, 10 Oct 2006, T. 9096; Ex. 1042, Tab 2; Ex. 1043, Tab 2, DVD 2, pp 21–24; Ex. 1044.

530 Ivan Grujić, 12 Apr 2006, T. 3629. Ex. 301, p. 9. About 60 houses belonged to Croats and about 15 houses belonged to Serbs, Witness MM-036, 4 Apr 2006, T. 3183–3184; Ex. 301, p. 9, states that 83.15% were Croats, and 16.48% were Serbs. It is near the Croat villages of Drežnik, Rakovica, Selište, Čatrinja, Smaljanac and Nova Kršlja and the Serb villages of Stara Kršlja, Jamari, Mucila, Witness MM-036, 4 Apr 2006, T. 3184; Ivan Marjanović, Ex. 426, T. 25005, 25013; Ex. 23, p. 19; Ex. 1044.

the village in case the JNA troops would arrive.[531] There were a few ZNG forces in the nearby Drežnik Grad, Rakovica and Slunj.[532] In 1991, helicopters were used by the JNA to carry weapons and ammunition, which were distributed to local Serbs.[533]

202. At the end of September or in early October 1991, the JNA entered Lipovača and almost all civilian inhabitants fled, with the exception of about 20–50 people.[534] The JNA stayed for seven to eight days and fired from tanks at the Croatian police in Drežnik Grad and Rakovica and a Catholic church in Drežnik Grad.[535] During this stay, some JNA soldiers warned a witness that "[w]hen we leave, beware of the reserve forces of those paramilitary units "who would" beat the people, set houses on fire, loot "and who would kill" regardless of age."[536] When the JNA troops left, several of the people who remained in the village fled to the forest and spent the night there.[537]

203. Sometime in October 1991, after the JNA had left, armed units including "Serb paramilitary units" from the region and outside of the region arrived in Lipovača.[538] These forces were called "reserve forces, Martić's troops or Martić's army", and that they wore uniforms "like the ones that the army had".[539]

204. On 27 October 1991, a JNA Miltary Police unit led by Milan Popović, together with members of the TO and uniformed local Serbs, arrived in the village of Nova Kršlja adjacent to Lipovača.[540] The JNA soldiers wore JNA uniforms whereas the TO soldiers wore black uniforms.[541] They arrested all of the young Croat men, including Ivan Marjanović's son Marijan,[542] **[page 75]** and searched Ivan Marjanović's house for weapons.[543] On the next day, the soldiers returned to Ivan Marjanović's house and demanded that he surrender his rifle to them, even though he did not have one.[544] The soldiers then beat him severely, kicked him in the groin and broke his wrist.[545] They again returned the next day and told him he was not allowed to leave his house or its immediate surroundings.[546]

205. At the end of October 1991, some time after the arrival of the paramilitary units, the bodies of Franjo Brozinčević, Marija Brozinčević, Mira Brozinčević, and Katarina Cindrić were found in Franjo Brozinčević's house in Lipovača.[547] All four victims were dressed in civilian clothes and had been killed by gunshots.[548]

206. Between 29 and 31 October 1991, Neđo Kotur, a local Serb commander,[549] came to the house of Ivan Marjanović and told him that "the Serbs" had killed some Croats and told Ivan Marjanović to go with

531 Witness MM-036, 4 Apr 2006, T. 3200–3201.
532 Witness MM-036, 4 Apr 2006, T. 3204.
533 Witness MM-036, 4 Apr 2006, T. 3186–3187, T. 3189, 3206–3207.
534 Witness MM-036, 4 Apr 2006, T. 3190.
535 Witness MM-036, 4 Apr 2006, T. 3205, 3210.
536 Witness MM-036, 4 Apr 2006, T. 3191–3192, 3208.
537 Witness MM-036, 4 Apr 2006, T. 3207.
538 Witness MM-036, 4 Apr 2006, T. 3190–3191.
539 Witness MM-036, 4 Apr 2006, T. 3207, T. 3191. The Trial Chamber notes that Witness MM-036 testified that to him a paramilitary unit is the same thing as a reserve force or the TO, Witness MM-036, 4 Apr 2006, T. 3207.
540 Ivan Marjanović, Ex. 426, T. 25005–25006, 25035, Milan Popović wore a standard JNA uniform and a cap with the five pointed star; Ivan Marjanović, Ex. 427, p. 2.
541 Ivan Marjanović, Ex. 427, p. 2.
542 Ivan Marjanović's son was released after 15 days with bruises all over his body, Ivan Marjanović, Ex. 426, T. 25006, 25032, upon his return the JNA gave him the choice of joining the army or of performing forced labour.
543 Ivan Marjanović, Ex. 426, T. 25006, 25035.
544 Ivan Marjanović, Ex. 426, T. 25007.
545 Ivan Marjanović, Ex. 426, T. 25007, Ex. 427, p. 3.
546 Ivan Marjanović, Ex. 426, T. 25007.
547 Witness MM-036, 4 Apr 2006, T. 3192; Ex. 1042, Tab 2; Ex. 1043, Tab 2, DVD 2, pp 21-23.
548 Witness MM-036, 4 Apr 2006, T. 3193–3194; Ivan Marjanović, Ex. 426, T. 25007, 25009, Ex. 427, p. 4; Ex. 304, pp 8–12; Ex. 323, p. 2. *See also* Ex. 375, pp 5–8, indicating that the deaths of these four victims were violent.
549 The Trial Chamber notes that Ivan Marjanović's evidence is contradictory as to the uniform that Neđo Kotur was wearing. In his testimony in the *Milošević* trial, he testified that Neđo Kotur was dressed in the JNA uniform of a reserve officer and a JNA hat with a red star, Ivan Marjanović, Ex. 426, T. 25007, 25023–25037. In a statement given in 2001, Ivan Marjanović stated that Neđo Kotur was wearing a black police uniform, with a patch of the SAO Krajina on it and a knit cap with a cockade, Ivan Marjanović, Ex. 427, p. 3. The Trial Chamber cannot draw any conclusions on the basis of this evidence.

him to Lipovača to bury the victims.[550] Neđo Kotur, Ivan Marjanović, and three other Croat villagers, drove to Lipovača and passed a checkpoint manned by "Martić's men".[551]

207. The group of men arrived in Lipovača at 0900 hours and went to the house of Mate Brozinčević, where they found his body in the kitchen with several bullet holes in the stomach.[552] Mate's wife, Roža, had also been shot, and the body of their son Mirko was lying at the entrance to the bedroom with a bullet hole in the neck.[553] All victims wore civilian clothing.[554] **[page 76]**

208. In June 1996, the above-mentioned seven individuals, who are listed in the Indictment, were exhumed from mass graves in Lipovača Drežnička.[555]

209. Milan Babić travelled to Lipovača and villages in the surrounding area in 1993 and testified that he saw "villages which used to be populated by Croats and Croat houses were devastated and there were no Croat residents any more."[556] Upon returning to Lipovača in 1995, Witness MM-036 found Lipovača and other villages in the municipality looted and burnt.[557]

(c) Poljanak and Vukovići

210. Poljanak is located about 14 kilometres south-east of Saborsko and 8 km north-west of Plitvice.[558] In 1991, there were around 30-50 predominantly Croat households in Poljanak.[559] The Croat hamlet of Vukovići, which is less than one kilometre away from Poljanak, consisted of about six or seven houses.[560]

211. Poljanak was shelled for the first time on 28 August 1991 and was shelled daily after that.[561] A few families initially left but returned two to three days later.[562]

212. On 5 September 1991, women with small children and minors in Poljanak and the surrounding villages left for Kraljevica, south-east of the city of Rijeka on the Adriatic coast.[563] Vukovići was shelled at around noon on 8 October 1991, after which there was shooting in the village by unidentified armed Serbs.[564] The next morning, Tomo Vuković was found dead in front of his burnt down house and at least two more houses had burnt down.[565] Around 14 October 1991, Mile Lončar, an invalid man, and his father, Ivan Lončar, were found hanged in their house.[566] **[page 77]**

---

550 Ivan Marjanović, Ex. 426, T. 25007, Ex. 427, p. 3.

551 Ivan Marjanović, Ex. 426, T. 25007, Ex. 427, p. 3.

552 Ivan Marjanović, Ex. 426, T. 25007; Ex. 323, p. 2. *See also* Ex. 304, pp 6–7; Ex. 375, pp 3–4; Ex. 1042, Tab 2; Ex. 1043, Tab 2, DVD 2, pp 23–24.

553 Ivan Marjanović, Ex. 426, T. 25007; Ex. 323, p. 2. *See also* Ex. 304, pp 4–6; Ex. 375, pp 2–3; Witness MM-036, 4 Apr 2006, T. 3194.

554 Ex. 304, pp 4-7; Ex. 375, pp 2–4; Ivan Marjanović, Ex. 426, T. 25007, 25009, 25022, Ex. 427, p. 4; Ex. 375, pp 2–4.

555 Ex. 302. The Trial Chamber notes that also the following persons were killed in Lipovača: Ana Pemper, Barbara Vuković, Juraj Šebalj, Juraj Conjar, and Milan Smolčić, Ex. 304, pp 13–15; Ex. 375, pp 9–10. These victims are not listed in the Indictment. The Trial Chamber recalls its findings regarding the interpretation of the Indictment and concludes that the Defence has not been on notice regarding these victims, *see supra* paras section I C.

556 Milan Babić, 20 Feb 2006, T. 1600–1601.

557 Witness MM-036, 4 April 2006, T. 3195. *See also id* at T. 3211.

558 Marica Vuković, 22 Mar 2006, T. 2403–2404; Ex. 1042, Tab 2; Ex. 1043, Tab 2, DVD 2, pp 24–26; Ex. 1044.

559 Marica Vuković, 22 Mar 2006, T. 2403, 2438, 2451; Witness MM-038, 24 Mar 2006, T. 2563.

560 Witness MM-038, 24 Mar 2006, T. 2451, 2457, 2561; Ex. 1042, Tab 2; Ex. 1043, Tab 2, DVD 2, pp 26–29; Ex. 1044.

561 Marica Vuković, 22 Mar 2006, T. 2411.

562 Marica Vuković, 22 Mar 2006, T. 2414. The shelling usually came from Bigina Poljana, a Serb village, Plitvice and Rastovača, a Croat village that had been burnt down and occupied by Serbs, Marica Vuković, 22 Mar 2006, T. 2415–2416. These villages were about a kilometre away from Poljanak, Marica Vuković, 22 Mar 2006, T. 2442. Marica Vuković did not know which units were stationed in these villages, *ibid.*

563 Marica Vuković, 22 Mar 2006, T. 2408, 2414–2415.

564 Marica Vuković, 22 Mar 2006, T. 2417.

565 Marica Vuković, 22 Mar 2006, T. 2404, 2416–2417 (testifying that the houses were "Pero's house and Aunt Lucilja's house"); Ex. 261, p. 2; Ex. 376, pp 6–7, concluding that Tomo Vuković was killed by a gunshot to the thorax; Witness MM-038, 24 Mar 2006, T. 2561–2562. The Trial Chamber notes that although paragraph 27 of the Indictment refers to Poljanak, paragraph 29 refers to the hamlet of Vukovići near Poljanak. Moreover, the Rule 65 *ter* summaries of Marica Vuković and Witness MM-038 contain references to the killing of Tomo Vuković. The Trial Chamber considers that the reference in paragraph 27 to Poljanak includes the hamlet of Vukovići and that the Defence has therefore been on notice in relation to the killing of Tomo Vuković.

566 Marica Vuković, 22 Mar 2006, T. 2419–2420, 2445. It is not clear from the evidence whether these men committed suicide or were killed; *see also* Ex. 261, p. 3.

213. There were no Croatian military units in Poljanak in the summer and autumn of 1991.[567] However, there was a civilian protection force that would keep watch, but the members were either unarmed or had two to three hunting rifles at their disposal.[568]

214. On 7 November 1991, there was a large group of soldiers present in Vukovići. The soldiers were dressed in green camouflage uniforms and their commanders wore JNA caps with a red star.[569] There were local people among these troops and there was also a JNA special unit present from Niš, Serbia, who wore darker camouflage uniforms.[570] The soldiers came to Nikola "Šojka" Vuković's house in Vukovići and lined up and killed Dane Vuković (son of Poldin), Dane Vuković (son of Mate),[571] Lucija Vuković, Milka Vuković, Vjekoslav Vuković, Joso Matovina and Nikola Matovina.[572] Nikola "Šojka" Vuković (born 1926) was too sick to leave the house and was shot from the window while lying in his bed.[573] All killed individuals were Croat civilians.[574] The evidence shows that one or two houses were burnt in Vukovići on 7 November 1991 by members of these units.[575]

215. The Defence pointed out certain discrepancies in the evidence concerning how the killings in Vukovići on 7 November 1991 were carried out.[576] However, the Trial Chamber considers that these discrepancies are not material and therefore do not affect its finding that these killings were committed.

216. Also on 7 November 1991, 20 armed soldiers dressed in camouflage and olive-drab uniforms surrounded the house of Marica Vuković, a Croat, in Poljanak.[577] Marica Vuković did not know where the soldiers were from but concluded that some must be locals because they appeared well informed about Marica Vuković and her family.[578] As soon as they arrived, the soldiers **[page 78]** "captured" Marica Vuković and the others present in the house.[579] The soldiers tied the arms of Marica Vuković's husband Nikola Vuković (born 1938) and her father Ivan Vuković.[580] Marica Vuković, her daughter Mira Vuković, her mother-in-law Jelena Vuković and her neighbour Marija Vuković were put under a plum tree where they were slapped, insulted and interrogated.[581] One of the soldiers threatened Marica Vuković and also put a knife at her throat.[582] The soldier wore a glove and said that it was "so that I won't get my hand bloody when I slit the throats of Ustashas."[583]

217. The women were separated from Ivan Vuković and Nikola Vuković (born 1938) and taken to a nearby maize field whereupon two or three other soldiers came from the direction of Vukovići, together with a boy. The boy was put with the women.[584] Subsequently, shooting was heard from the house where Ivan Vuković and Nikola Vuković had been left.[585]

218. Soon thereafter, a soldier came to the women and told them to flee. The women and the boy hid in the woods for a few hours.[586] After having seen some cars move away from the village, Marica Vuković returned

---

567 Marica Vuković, 22 Mar 2006, T. 2412–2413.

568 Marica Vuković, 22 Mar 2006, T. 2414, 2423; Ex. 261, p. 3; Witness MM-038, 23 Mar 2006, T. 2555.

569 Ex. 261, p. 5. It is not clear how many soldiers there actually were in Vukovići on that day. One witness stated that there were between 90–100 soldiers, Witness MM-038, 23 Mar 2006, T. 2549–2551.

570 Witness MM-038, 23 Mar 2006, T. 2551–2552, 2560, 2563–2564 (also testifying that the local people wore the same uniforms and served as guides); Milan Babić, 20 Feb 2006, T. 1599–1600; Radoslav Maksić, 7 Feb 2006, T. 1253; Ex. 261, p. 5.

571 Ex. 262; Ex. 302, p. 6.

572 Ex. 261, p. 4; Witness MM-038, 23 Mar 2006, T. 2535–2542. *See also* Marica Vuković, 22 Mar 2006, T. 2432; Ex. 376; Ex. 302, p. 6; Ex. 323; Ex. 715; Ex. 1042, Tab 2; Ex. 1043, Tab 2, DVD 2, pp 26–29.

573 Ex. 261, p. 4; Ex. 376, p. 5; Ex. 302; Ex. 323.

574 Witness MM-038, 23 Mar 2006, T. 2519.

575 Witness MM-038, 23 Mar 2006, T. 2551, 24 Mar 2006, T. 2562, Ex. 261, p. 5.

576 Witness MM-038, 23 Mar 2006, T. 2535–2542; Ex. 262; Ex. 263; Ex. 264.

577 Marica Vuković, 22 Mar 2006, T. 2443–2444, 2455. *See also id.*at T. 2424, 2450; Ex. 1042, Tab 2; Ex. 1043, Tab 2, DVD 2, pp 24–26.

578 Marica Vuković, 22 Mar 2006, T. 2424, 2426, 2446–2447.

579 Marica Vuković, 22 Mar 2006, T. 2424–2425.

580 The Trial Chamber notes that both Marica Vuković's husband and her uncle were named Nikola Vuković, that her husband was born 1938, and that her uncle was nicknamed "Šojka" (born 1926), Marica Vuković, 22 Mar 2006, T. 2424–2425. Both Nikola Vuković and Ivan Vuković were Croat, Marica Vuković, 22 Mar 2006, T. 2405.

581 Marica Vuković, 22 Mar 2006, T. 2425, 2454.

582 Marica Vuković, 22 Mar 2006, T. 2426.

583 Marica Vuković, 22 Mar 2006, T. 2426–2427.

584 Marica Vuković, 22 Mar 2006, T. 2425–2426.

585 Ex. 261, p. 5.

586 Marica Vuković, 22 Mar 2006, T. 2427–2429.

to her house and then came across the bodies of her father and husband in the maize field.[587] She saw that her husband's "brains were shattered" and that her father's "skull wasn't in place any more".[588] On that day, neither her husband nor her father was armed or wearing a uniform, nor were they members of a military force or the police.[589]

219. The evidence shows that several houses, sheds and cars were burnt in Poljanak on 7 November 1991, by the soldiers present in the village. The evidence also shows that before the houses were burnt private property was looted or destroyed.[590] When torching the houses, some soldiers made comments, such as "Milošević built the house and Milošević is going to destroy it" and "what's Tuđman done for you? All you are going to get from him is a bullet in your head".[591] **[page 79]**

(d) Saborsko

220. In early 1991, there were 600 to 850 people, mostly Croats, living in the 300 households of Saborsko.[592] In the centre of Saborsko, there was a large church called the church of St. John. Slightly outside the centre, there was a smaller church, the church of the Mother of God.[593]

221. On 2 April 1991, the Croat members of the Ogulin SJB established an outpost in Saborsko.[594] There were around 30 policemen, armed with automatic rifles and pistols, who engaged in regular police work but also manned check-points in case of an attack on Saborsko.[595] Between April and August 1991, JNA armoured vehicles were allowed to pass through roadblocks and patrolled daily through Saborsko going between Plitvice and Lička Jasenica.[596] From around June 1991, about 20 or 30 local men were organised in Saborsko and patrolled the village at night carrying "hunting guns or some military rifles."[597] Between June and August 1991, Saborsko was fired upon with rifle and artillery fire. It was mostly one of the churches and the school that were shot at and the fire came from Lička Jasenica and from Pištenik hill.[598]

222. In the early morning of 5 August 1991, Saborsko was shelled by mortars from the direction of the Lička Jasenica JNA barracks.[599] Shells fell on the cemetery and central parts of the village.[600] At the time of the shelling, a Croatian special police unit from Duga Resa, numbering 20–30 policemen, had taken

587 Marica Vuković, 22 Mar 2006, T. 2429.

588 Marica Vuković, 22 Mar 2006, T. 2430, also testifying that she wrapped the bodies in blankets which were later found during the exhumation; Ex. 376, pp 2–5. *See also* Ex. 323; Ex. 302.

589 Marica Vuković, 22 Mar 2006, T. 2430.

590 Marica Vuković, 22 Mar 2006, T. 2428–2429, 2457, also testifying that the soldiers took people out of houses and cars and then set fire to them. Ex. 259, 11 photographs of houses and places described by Marica Vuković. *See also* Milan Babić, 20 Feb 2006, T. 1600–1601, testifying that in 1993 he found Poljanak devastated and there were no Croat residents there anymore.

591 Marica Vuković, 22 Mar 2006, T. 2428.

592 Vlado Vuković, 27 Mar 2006, T. 2648–2649, 2679, 28 Mar 2006, T. 2730; Marko Vuković, 24 Mar 2006, T. 2567–2568; Ana Bićanić, Ex. 276, p. 2; Milan Babić, 20 Feb 2006, T. 1600; In 1991, Saborsko had 852 inhabitants (93.9% were Croat, and 3.3% were Serbs), Ex. 301, p. 7.

593 Nikola Medaković, 9 Oct 2006, T. 9014; Ana Bićanić, Ex. 276, p. 5. *See also* Ex. 1042, Tab 2; Ex. 1043, Tab 2, DVD 2, pp 30–35, 38–39.

594 Vlado Vuković, 27 Mar 2006, T. 2651–2652; Marko Vuković, 24 Mar 2006, T. 2572–2573, 2598; Lazar Macura, 14 Sep 2006, T. 8321; Nikola Medaković, 9 Oct 2006, T. 8960.

595 Marko Vuković, 24 Mar 2006, T. 2572–2573, 2602–2603; Vlado Vuković, 27 Mar 2006, T. 2654, 2686, 2689; Nikola Medaković, 9 Oct 2006, T. 8962–8963, also testifying that the outpost in Saborsko consisted of about 60 men, *id.* at T. 8960.

596 Marko Vuković, 24 Mar 2006, T. 2574; Vlado Vuković, 27 Mar 2006, T. 2655; Nikola Medaković, 10 Oct 2006, T. 9095; Ana Bićanić, Ex. 276, p. 3.

597 Ana Bićanić, Ex. 276, p. 3.

598 Ana Bićanić, Ex. 276, p. 2. In July 1991, Croatian social workers evacuated several elderly persons, younger women and children, *ibid*, p. 3. As a result of the attacks in June and July 1991, 10 people were killed, including Ivica Krizmanić, Marko Krizmanić, Tomo Matovina, Ante Kovačić, Pere Matovina and Joso Matovina, and there was a large number of wounded, *id.* at p. 3.

599 Marica Vuković, 22 Mar 2006, T. 2412, 2441; Marko Vuković, 24 Mar 2006, T. 2574–2576, 2608; Vlado Vuković, 27 Mar 2006, T. 2657–2659, 28 Mar 2006, T. 2724; Nikola Medaković, 10 Oct 2006, T. 9122; Ana Bićanić, Ex. 276, p. 3. *See also* Marko Vuković, 24 Mar 2006, T. 2577–2578; Ex. 38; Ex. 1042, Tab 2; Ex. 1043, Tab 2, DVD 3, pp 5–8. Vlado Vuković also testified, in relation to who fired upon Saborsko, that "it's well-known who it is; it's the JNA and the local leaders, so-called Martić's men", Vlado Vuković, 27 Mar 2006, T. 2658. Based solely on this evidence, the Trial Chamber is unable to draw a conclusion as to who was responsible for this shelling.

600 Vlado Vuković, 27 Mar 2006, T. 2659, 2692.

up a defence line at the primary school in the centre of the village.[601] On the **[page 80]** night of 5 August 1991, most of the civilian population of Saborsko fled through Rakovica to Grabovac, where the Red Cross had arrived with three buses. About 100 to 150 civilians were evacuated to areas under Croatian control, whereas around 400 persons returned to Saborsko in the following days.[602]

223. After 5 August 1991, Saborsko was shelled almost every day from various directions, including from the direction of the barracks at Lička Jasenica.[603] After this date, the policemen stationed at the Saborsko outpost were no longer engaged in regular police work, but were deployed in combat positions.[604] On 6 August 1991, 15–20 policemen armed with rifles and pistols came from Slunj to support the Saborsko police.[605] When the unit from Slunj had left, further reinforcements arrived from Drežnik Grad.[606] The church of St. John was the most hit during the shelling, though many other buildings in Saborsko were also damaged.[607] Around this time, there was also an attempt by the Serb side to take Kušelj, a hamlet of Saborsko, in which some members of the Croatian forces were wounded and killed.[608]

224. Around 25 September 1991, a unit of the Croatian MUP reserve was deployed from Zagreb to support the defence of Saborsko. The unit consisted of between 100 and 200 persons who were armed with automatic rifles, sub-machine guns, two mortars and an anti-aircraft gun.[609] The unit took up positions around Saborsko, in the hamlets of Sivnik, Alan, Kušelj, Borik and Strk, and remained until Saborsko fell on 12 November 1991.[610] There is evidence that the Croatian MUP reserve unit was partly deployed in the church of St. John, which was used as an observation point, machinegun nest and ammunition store.[611] In early October, there was an armed clash in the area of Sertic Poljana.[612] In October 1991, a convoy carrying food and weapons arrived in Saborsko, escorted by between 20 and 50 reserve policemen armed with automatic and semi-automatic rifles. These policemen remained in Saborsko.[613] Beginning on 4 November 1991, Croatian MUP and ZNG forces, including from Saborsko, launched an attack on the barracks at Lička Jasenica and an **[page 81]** area called Glibodolski Križ nearby.[614] During the attack, Serb civilians were killed by the Croatian forces.[615] The Croatian attack was eventually repelled on 8 November 1991.[616]

---

[601] Marko Vuković, 24 Mar 2006, T. 2576 (also testifying that this unit fled towards Slunj at 2200 or 2300 hours in the evening), 2606-2607; Vlado Vuković, 27 Mar 2006, T. 2658, 2690–2692 (also testifying that the unit arrived in late July 1991 and that it was armed with side arms and long-barrelled weapons), 28 Mar 2006, 2732; Nikola Medaković, 9 Oct 2006, T. 8963. Nikola Medaković testified that less than 50 metres from the church of the Mother of God, there were fortified Croat positions which constituted a line of defence, Nikola Medaković, 9 Oct 2006, T. 9015–9016.

[602] Marica Vuković 22 Mar 2006, T. 2412; Marko Vuković, 24 Mar 2006, T. 2578–2579, 2607–2608, 2629; Vlado Vuković, 27 Mar 2006, T. 2659, 2693; Nikola Medaković, 10 Oct 2006, T. 9048; Ana Bićanić, Ex. 276, p. 3.

[603] Marko Vuković, 24 Mar 2006, T. 2584–2586 (also testifying about aerial attacks); Vlado Vuković, 27 Mar 2006, T. 2659; Ana Bičanić, Ex. 276, p. 3; Jure Vuković, Ex. 277, p. 2.

[604] Vlado Vuković, 27 Mar 2006, T. 2696–2697.

[605] This unit took up positions in some of the hamlets of Saborsko and stayed at least for 12 days, Marko Vuković, 24 Mar 2006, T. 2579–2580, 2608–2611; Vlado Vuković, 27 Mar 2006, T. 2692, 2694 (testifying that this reinforcement remained in Saborsko for "two or three days").

[606] Marko Vuković, 24 Mar 2006, T. 2609.

[607] Vlado Vuković, 27 Mar 2006, T. 2659–2660.

[608] Marko Vuković, 24 Mar 2006, T. 2585.

[609] Marko Vuković, 24 Mar 2006, T. 2580, 2588, 2597–2598; 2614–2615, 2620; Vlado Vuković, 27 Mar 2006, T. 2660–2662 (testifying at T. 2661 that the members of this unit wore green uniforms), 2695–2696; Nikola Medaković, 9 Oct 2006, T. 8964, 8981, 8983, 11 Oct 2006, T. 9134.

[610] Marko Vuković, 24 Mar 2006, T. 2584, 2618. *See also* Nikola Medaković, 9 Oct 2006, T. 8984.

[611] Nikola Medaković, 9 Oct 2006, T. 9028–9029.

[612] Marko Vuković, 24 Mar 2006, T. 2619–2620.

[613] Marko Vuković, 24 Mar 2006, T. 2586, 2621–2622; Ana Bićanić, Ex. 276, p. 3

[614] Nikola Medaković, 9 Oct 2006, T. 8984–8987, 9003–9004, 11 Oct 2006, T. 9173–9174; Ex. 108, items 3–9; Ex. 962. Fire was guided in from Saborsko because it was at a higher elevation than Lička Jasenica, *ibid.* The presence in Saborsko, between September and November 1991, of a small number of ZNG members is confirmed by Marko Vuković, 24 Mar 2006, T. 2612–2614, 2628; Ex. 52.

[615] Witness MM-037, 28 Mar 2006, T. 2754–2755, 2781–2783; Ex. 268, T. 11625–16266; Nikola Medaković, 9 Oct 2006, T. 8985–8987, 8993–8995, 11 Oct 2006, T. 9167, 9174–9177, 12 Oct 2006, 9268–9269; Ex. 108, item 13; Ex. 605, pp 1–2.

[616] Witness MM-037, 28 Mar 2006, T. 2752, 2780–2781; Nikola Medaković, 11 Oct 2006, T. 9180.

(i) Attack on Saborsko on 12 November 1991

225. Saborsko was attacked mid-morning on 12 November 1991 by Tactical Group 2 ("TG-2"), under the command of Colonel Čedomir Bulat, and the 5th Partisan Brigade, both of which were within the structure of the JNA 13th Corps.[617] A unit of the Plaški SDB,[618] the Plaški TO Brigade[619] and *Milicija Krajine* units participated in the attack.[620] Within the Plaški TO Brigade, a battalion consisting of three companies under the command of Bogdan Grba participated.[621]

226. The attack commenced with aerial bombing followed by an artillery attack.[622] Afterwards, ground units, including tanks, moved in on Saborsko from three axes.[623] During the attack, the church of St. John was hit by a tank shell but the tower remained standing.[624] The church of the **[page 82]** Mother of God was also shelled and damaged during the attack.[625] That church was used as an observation post because there was a clear view of the Lička Jasenica barracks from it.[626] The fighting went on until some point between 1400 hours and 1700 hours; the tanks withdrew around 1800 hours.[627] There were no casualties on the Serb side whereas "[o]n the Croatian [MUP] side" there were 50 dead.[628]

227. After the attack, there were many Serb soldiers and policemen in the centre of Saborsko.[629] The evidence shows that a shop was looted by Zdravko Pejić and individuals with the last names Cekić or Cvekić, and Momčilović, both of whom were members of Đuro "Snjaka" Ogrizović's company.[630] An individual identified as "Peić" together with Željko "Buba" Mudrić and Nedeljko "Kiča" Trbojević, as well as "other Martić's men" drove away in private cars they found in Saborsko.[631] Moreover, all the

---

617 Radoslav Maksić, 7 Feb 2006, T. 1235 (also testifying that the 13th Corps had a forward command post in the village of Mukinje in the vicinity of Saborsko); Milan Babić, 20 Feb 2006, T. 1599–1600; Witness MM-037, 28 Mar 2006, T. 2789–2790, 2798; Ex. 268, T. 11591; Nikola Medaković, 9 Oct 2006, T. 8988–8989, 8998–8999, 9009, 12 Oct 2006, T. 9225–9226; Imra Agotić, Ex. 398, T. 23315, 23402; Ex. 51, pp 2–3; Ex. 52, p. 3; Ex. 108, item 18; Ex. 422; Ex. 507, p. 4; Ex. 603; Ex. 605. p. 2. TG-2 was established on 23 October 1991 by the 5th Army District, Ex. 960; Ex. 507, p. 4.

618 Ex. 603; Ex. 605, p. 1.

619 The Plaški TO Brigade was subordinated to TG-2, Witness MM-037, 28 Mar 2006, T. 2751, 2789–2790; Ex. 51, pp 2–3; Ex. 52, p. 3.

620 Ex. 605, p. 1.

621 These companies were of an *ad hoc* nature and were extracted from the TO Brigade and the police in Plaški, Nikola Medaković, 10 Oct 2006, T. 9104; Ex. 607. Nikola Medaković testified that his company consisted of about 60 men, including former members of the *Milicija Krajine* unit in Plaški who had been transferred to the Plaški TO Brigade in September 1991, Nikola Medaković, 9 Oct 2006, T. 8988, 8990–8992, 8998–8999, 10 Oct 2006, T. 9055, 12 Oct 2006, T. 9287; Witness MM-037, 28 Mar 2006, T. 2751, 2794–2795, 29 Mar 2006, T. 2821; Ex. 607, p. 2; Ex. 507, p. 4. The company in the middle was commanded by Đuro Ogrizović, Nikola Medaković, 9 Oct 2006, T. 9018, 10 Oct 2006, T. 9103; Ex. 607, p. 3; Ex. 608, p. 3; Witness MM-037, 28 March 2006, T. 2803–2804. An armoured company with about ten tanks advanced in the centre of the three companies, along the asphalt road, Nikola Medaković, 9 Oct 2006, T. 9014, 9018; Jure Vuković, Ex. 277, p. 2.

622 Witness MM-037, 28 Mar 2006, T. 2798, stating that the attack started just after 0900 hours. *See also* Ex. 268, T. 11593–11594, 11627 (stating that the artillery consisted of mortars and tanks positioned on elevations surrounding Saborsko and in Slunj); Nikola Medaković, 9 Oct 2006, T. 9010–9011, 11 Oct 2006, T. 9160; Ana Bićanić, Ex. 276, p. 3; Jure Vuković, Ex. 277, p. 2; Imra Agotić, Ex. 398, T. 23314–23315; Ex. 422; Ex. 507, p. 4; Ex. 608, p. 2. One of the bombs from the airplanes fell on the house of a neighbour of Jure Vuković and three floors of the house collapsed, Jure Vuković, Ex. 277, p. 2.

623 Nikola Medaković, 9 Oct 2006, T. 9009 (testifying that his company started in the village of Momčilovići, went towards Vukelić Poljana and Borik), 9017–9019 (at T. 9018 testifying that one company went towards Sivnik, that Đuro Ogrizović led the company in the centre, including ten tanks, going towards Saborsko itself along the road). *See also* Witness MM-037, 28 Mar 2006, T. 2798, 29 Mar 2006, T. 2798, 2803, Ex. 268, T. 11595; Nikola Medaković, 12 Oct 2006, T. 9238; Jure Vuković, Ex. 277, p. 2; Ex. 607, p. 3. Ex. 608, p. 3.

624 Witness MM-037, 28 Mar 2006, T. 2753; Jure Vuković, Ex. 277, p. 2.

625 Nikola Medaković, 9 Oct 2006, T. 9015–9016.

626 Nikola Medaković, 9 Oct 2006, T. 9016, testifying that there was a clear line of sight between the church of the Mother of God and the Lička Jasenica barracks.

627 Nikola Medaković, 9 Oct 2006, T. 9017–9019; Ex. 108, item 18.

628 Ex. 605, p. 3. *See also* Witness MM-037, 29 Mar 2006, 2812, Ex. 268, T. 11596.

629 Witness MM-037, Ex. 268, T. 11599–11601; Nikola Medaković, 11 Oct 2006, T. 9188, 12 Oct 2006, T. 9236–9237; Ex. 507, p. 4.

630 Witness MM-037, 28 Mar 2006, T. 2803, 29 Mar 2006, 2808–2810; Ex. 268, T. 11597–11600.

631 Ex. 507, p. 4–5 (on p. 4 Nedeljko Trbojević's nickname is listed as "Kičin"), providing, *inter alia*, that Mate Matovina's car was taken by Željko "Buba" Mudrić, and that Jura Matovina's lorry was torched in Saborsko. Ex. 606 lists Miloš Momčilović and Željko Mudrić as members of the "Reconnaissance-sabotage squad (Special forces) in Plaški" within the DB. Nikola Medaković testified that both these individuals went to the training ground in Slunj and were mobilised in the JNA after the *Milicija Krajine* unit was merged into the TO Brigade, Nikola Medaković, 10 Oct 2006, T. 9106.

tractors in Saborsko were driven away, subsequently to be put up for auction, and household goods were stolen by plunderers.[632] There is also evidence that more than 50 cattle from Saborsko were brought to Plaški and that 17 sheep were taken to Kunić.[633] Many houses in Saborsko were set alight and burnt after the attack.[634] The evidence shows that the perpetrators, who were engaged in the burning of the houses included Nedeljko "Kiča" Trbojević, "Peić", Željko "Buba" Mudrić, as well as "other Martić's men".[635] Houses in the hamlets of Tuk and Dumenčići, and in the Serb hamlet of Solaje, were also set alight.[636] In Borik, both Croat and Serb houses were burned.[637] By mid-December 1991, both the church of St. John and the church of the Mother of God had been destroyed.[638] By 1995, the whole of Saborsko, including the school, **[page 83]** had been destroyed.[639] The only houses left standing were two Serb houses, which had been very badly damaged.[640]

228. Following the attack, most of the inhabitants of Saborsko fled to Karlovac, Zagreb, and Ogulin.[641] However, about 30 to 60 elderly villagers remained in the village and were brought to the Lička Jasenica barracks by the Plaški TO. After spending the night at the barracks, they were taken by bus towards Ogulin and released in territory controlled by the Croatian side.[642]

(ii) Killings in Saborsko on 12 November 1991

229. During the aerial bombing of 12 November 1991, Ana Bićanić and her husband Milan Bićanić, took shelter in the basement of Petar "Krtan" Bićanić's house, where around 20 people had gathered, including the young boy, Jure Vuković.[643] Once it became quiet outside in the afternoon, Milan Bićanić heard someone say "give me the matches" which led him to believe that soldiers, who had entered the village, were burning houses and that they were going to be burned inside.[644] In order to prevent this, they waved a white undershirt tied to a piece of wood through the basement door, shouting that they were civilians.[645] There were soldiers outside wearing camouflage and olive-grey uniforms, as well as two soldiers dressed in "Serbian dark grey uniforms and wearing helmets with a five pointed red star".[646] The soldiers told all of the villagers to come out of the basement.[647] The soldiers were armed and spoke in a Serbian dialect.[648] Some of the soldiers swore at them, saying "fuck your Ustaša mother" and that all of them should be slaughtered.[649]

---

632 Ex. 507, p. 4, also providing that nearly every household in Saborsko had a tractor.

633 Nikola Medaković, 9 Oct 2006, T. 9025; Ex. 507, p. 4; Ex. 963, p. 2, providing that Slavko Dumenčić saw a man in military uniform, recognised as Milan Grković, move 25 sheep.

634 Milan Babić testified that by 1993 Saborsko, Poljanak and Lipovača contained no Croat residents and that Croat houses were devastated, Milan Babić, 20 Feb 2006, T. 1600–1601.

635 Ex. 507, p. 5, also provides that "Nedeljko Trbojević [...] went from house to house [...], hurled grenades into cellars and set hay stacks on fire [burning] around 20 houses".

636 Vlado Vuković, 27 Mar 2006, T. 2714; Witness MM-037, 28 Mar 2006, T. 2803, Ex. 268, T. 11597–11598; Imra Agotić, Ex. 398, T. 23315–23316; Ex. 507, pp 4–5.

637 Vlado Vuković, 28 Mar 2006, T. 2730, 2733; Ex. 1042, Tab 2; Ex. 1043, Tab 2, DVD 3, pp 3–4.

638 Witness MM-037, 28 Mar 2006, T. 2753; Nikola Medaković, 12 Oct 2006, T. 9245.

639 Marko Vuković, 24 Mar 2006, T. 2590, 2631; Ana Bićanić, Ex. 276, p. 4; Vlado Vuković, 27 Mar 2006, T. 2674–2675.

640 Witness MM-039, Ex. 277, p. 4.

641 Vlado Vuković, 28 Mar 2006, T. 2727. *See also* Imra Agotić, Ex. 398, T. 23315–23316, testifying that in more or less all Croat villages in the area, including Vagnac, Drežnik Grad and Rakovica, civilians were displaced, after which the houses and all facilities were devastated.

642 Witness MM-037, 28 Mar 2006, T. 2801–2803, Ex. 268, T. 11603–11604, 11612–11613, 11637; Nikola Medaković, 9 Oct 2006, T. 9019–9020. *See also* Ex. 963, pp 2–3.

643 Ana Bićanić, Ex. 276, p. 3. The persons in the basement were: Petar Bićanić and his wife Kate Bićanić, Ana Bićanić and her husband, Ivan Vuković, Nikola Bićanić, Pero Bićanić, Jure Štrk and his wife Kate Štrk, Jure Vuković and his half brother whose name was also Jure Vuković (nicknamed Jura Zenkov), Kate Vuković and her son Jure Vuković (who was 8–10 years old), a second woman named Ana Bićanić, Bara Bićanić, Ana Vuković, Jeka Vuković, a third woman named Ana Bićanić (born 1924), Marija Hodak, Jeka Dumančić, and Marija Štrk, Ana Bićanić, Ex. 276, p. 3; Jure Vuković, Ex. 277, p. 2. *See also* Ex. 1042, Tab 2; Ex. 1043, Tab 2, DVD 3, pp 1–2.

644 Ana Bićanić, Ex. 276, p. 3; Jure Vuković, Ex. 277, pp 2–3

645 Ana Bićanić, Ex. 276, p. 3; Jure Vuković, Ex. 277, p. 3.

646 Ana Bićanić, Ex. 276, p. 4.

647 Ana Bićanić, Ex. 276, p. 4; Jure Vuković, Ex. 277, p. 3.

648 Ana Bićanić, Ex. 276, p. 4; Jure Vuković, Ex. 277, p. 3.

649 Ana Bićanić, Ex. 276, p. 4; Jure Vuković, Ex. 277, p. 3.

230. One of the soldiers threw a hand grenade into the empty basement.[650] The soldiers separated the men from the women and lined them up opposite each other.[651] The soldiers searched the men **[page 84]** and took their money and valuables.[652] While the men were being searched, one soldier hit Jure Štrk and Milan Bićanić.[653] After about 15 minutes, the men were taken around a corner of Ivan Bićanić's house.[654] Two soldiers wearing Serbian dark grey uniforms shot and killed the men with automatic rifle fire.[655] The following seven men were killed: Milan Bićanić, Nikola Bićanić, Petar Bićanić, Jure Štrk,[656] Ivan Vuković, Jure Vuković and his half brother also named Jure Vuković.[657]

231. After the killings, the two soldiers returned to the rest of the group.[658] One of the two soldiers pointed the gun at Ana Bićanić and told them that they had an hour to leave or they would be killed.[659] As they ran away the soldiers shot at them.[660] Jeka Vuković fell, and that was the last time that Jure Vuković saw her.[661] They fled towards Borik and after three days, on 15 November 1991, they came to the HVO barracks in Lipice, east of Saborsko.[662]

232. After the attack on Saborsko, Nikola Medaković, in his capacity as president of the municipality of Plaški, issued an order to bury human corpses after which he received a report that the bodies of more than 20 people had been buried, including civilian women and elderly men.[663] **[page 85]**

233. Beginning in October 1995, several grave sites were exhumed in Saborsko.[664] The biggest site was at Popov Šanac, located close to the church of St. John, where the following 14 victims were found: Ana Bičanić, Milan Bičanić, Nikola Bičanić, Petar Bičanić, Kata Dumenčić, Nikola Dumenčić, Mate Matovina (born 1895), Milan Matovina, Mate Špehar, Ivan Vuković, Jeka Vuković, Jure Vuković (born 1929), Jure Vuković (born 1930), and Petar Vuković.[665] In the grave site at Borik, the following three victims were found:

---

650 Ana Bićanić, Ex. 276, p. 4; Jure Vuković, Ex. 277, p. 3.

651 Ana Bićanić, Ex. 276, p. 4; Jure Vuković, Ex. 277, p. 3; Marko Vuković, 24 Mar 2006, T. 2588.

652 Ana Bićanić, Ex. 276, p. 4.

653 Ana Bićanić, Ex. 276, p. 4.

654 Ana Bićanić, Ex. 276, p. 4; Jure Vuković, Ex. 277, p. 3.

655 Ana Bićanić, Ex. 276, p. 4; Jure Vuković, Ex. 277, p. 3. *See also* Marko Vuković, 24 Mar 2006, T. 2588–2589.

656 Jure Vuković, Ex. 277, p. 3; Ana Bićanić, Ex. 276, p. 4 (mentioning him as "Juraj"). The Trial Chamber notes that Annex I to the Indictment lists a Josip Štrk but cannot conclude that this is the same individual. However, the Trial Chamber recalls its interpretation of the Indictment in this respect and will consider the killing of Jure Štrk for a conviction, *see supra* section I C.

657 Ana Bićanić, Ex. 276, p. 4; Jure Vuković, Ex. 277, p. 3. Witness MM-037 was told in the evening on 12 November 1991 by a Serb soldier that five or six soldiers had killed Petar "Krtan" Bićanić and two more men. Witness MM-037 believed that perpetrators were a group of "renegades", members of Martić's Police, who thought Petar Bićanić was carrying a lot of money on him, Witness MM-037, 28 Mar 2006, T. 2800–2801. Witness MM-037 further named Đuro "Snjaka" Ogrizović and individuals called Lecin, Cvekić and Pejić, Witness MM-037, 29 Mar 2006, T. 2814–2815; Ex. 268, T. 11602, 11608–11609, 11613–11614, 11638–11639. The Trial Chamber notes the evidence that a Peić or Pejić was "the worst of all Martić's men" and that he, together with Željko "Buba" Mudrić, boasted about having "shot dead eight people in front of the Centre in Saborsko", Ex. 507, p. 4. However, the Trial Chamber cannot conclude beyond reasonable doubt that this reference to killings in the centre of Saborsko refers to the killings at Petar "Krtan" Bićanić's house. Vlado Vuković knows of one family that was killed as well as his aunt and uncle who had gone to their Serb neighbours' house seeking protection but were nonetheless killed, Vlado Vuković, 28 Mar 2006, T. 2730, 2733. The Trial Chamber notes that victims with the last name "Bićanić" are listed as "Bičanić" in Annex I to the Indictment. *See also* Marko Vuković, 24 Mar 2006, T. 2588–2589. The Trial Chamber has also been furnished with evidence that during the attack on Saborsko, Kata Dumaničić and Nikola "Dika" Dumaničić were killed in front of their house, Ex. 963, p. 2. The Trial Chamber considers that similar names Kata Dumeničić and Nikola Dumeničić listed in Annex I to the Indictment refer to these victims, and will consider these persons for a conviction.

658 Ana Bićanić, Ex. 276, p. 4.

659 Ana Bićanić, Ex. 276, p. 4; Jure Vuković, Ex. 277, pp 3–4; Marko Vuković, 24 Mar 2006, T. 2588.

660 Jure Vuković, Ex. 277, p. 4.

661 Jure Vuković, Ex. 277, p. 4. Annex I to the Indictment lists a Jela Vuković and the Trial Chamber considers this to refer to Jeka Vuković.

662 Ana Bićanić, Ex. 276, p. 4; Jure Vuković, Ex. 277, p. 4.

663 Nikola Medaković, 9 Oct 2006, T. 9021–9022, 9027–9028, 10 Oct 2006, T. 9250. Nikola Medaković testified that the victims were to be buried as close as possible to where they had been killed and with everything found on them, including identification, Nikola Medaković, 9 Oct 2006, T. 9027.

664 Marko Vuković, 24 Mar 2006, T. 2590–2591; Vlado Vuković, 27 Mar 2006, T. 2676; Davor Strinović, 12 Apr 2006, T. 3667. *See also* Ex. 302.

665 Vlado Vuković, 27 Mar 2006, T. 2676; Marko Vuković, 24 Mar 2006, T. 2591; Ivan Grujić, 10 Apr 2006, T. 3477; Ex. 302; Ex. 323 (providing that the cause of death was gunshot wounds for Mate Matovina (born 1895), Mate Špehar, Ivan Vuković, Jela

Darko Dumenčić, Ivica Dumenčić, and Josip Štrk.[666] The following ten victims were found in individual graves in Saborsko: Leopold Conjar, Ante Dumenčić, Ivan Matovina, Kata Matovina (born 1920), Kata Matovina (born 1918), Lucija Matovina, Marija Matovina, Marta Matovina, Slavica Matovina, and Slavko Sertić.[667]

234. Considering in particular that there is direct evidence regarding the killing of eight of the victims exhumed from the mass grave in Popov Šanac, the Trial Chamber finds that all 14 victims exhumed from that mass grave were killed in Saborsko on 12 November 1991. Moreover, based on evidence indicating their causes of death, the Trial Chamber considers it established beyond reasonable doubt that also Ivica Dumenčić, Kata Matovina (born 1920) and Slavko Sertić were killed in Saborsko on 12 November 1991. Furthermore, considering that Darko Dumenčić and Josip Štrk were found in the same mass grave as Ivica Dumenčić, who was killed on 12 November 1991, the Trial Chamber considers it established beyond reasonable doubt that these two persons were killed on the same date. Lastly, while the body of Jure/Juraj Štrk has not been recovered, the direct evidence establishes that he was killed on 12 November 1991. The Trial Chamber therefore finds beyond reasonable doubt that 20 persons were killed on 12 November 1991. For the remaining victims (Leopold Conjar, Ante Dumenčić, Ivan Matovina, Kata Matovina (born 1918), Lucija Matovina, Marija Matovina, Marta Matovina, and Slavica Matovina), the evidence is insufficient to establish when, where and by whom they were killed. **[page 86]**

4. Škabrnja and Nadin

(a) Škabrnja, Nadin and surrounding villages

235. Škabrnja is located in south-western Croatia and in 1991 formed part of the municipality of Zadar, which bordered the Benkovac municipality to the south-east.[668] Škabrnja had about 2,000 inhabitants and was almost exclusively Croat.[669] There were three churches in and around Škabrnja, the church of the Assumption of the Virgin in the centre of Škabrnja, St. Mary's Church in the hamlet of Ambar, and St. Luke's Church to the west of the centre of Škabrnja.[670] In 1991, Nadin was located in the Benkovac municipality and was approximately three kilometres south-east of Škabrnja.[671] Nadin, which was also almost exclusively Croat, had between 300 and 660 inhabitants living in approximately 120 to 150 houses.[672] Croat villages were located to the south of Škabrnja, whereas predominantly Serb villages were located to the north and north-east of Škabrnja, towards Benkovac municipality.[673]

Vuković, Jure Vuković (born 1929), Jure Vuković (born 1930), and Petar Vuković); Ex. 963 (regarding Kata Dumenčić and Nikola Dumenčić). *See also* Nikola Medaković, 12 Oct 2006, T. 9244–9245. The Trial Chamber visited Popov Šanac during the site visit, Ex. 1042, Tab 2; Ex. 1043, Tab 2, DVD 2, pp 36–38.

666 Ex. 302; Ex. 323, providing that the cause of death for Ivica Dumenčić was "probably trauma wounds". *See also* Ex. 1042, Tab 2; Ex. 1043, Tab 2, DVD 2, pp 40–41.

667 Ex. 323 (providing that the cause of death of Slavko Sertić and Kata Matovina (born 1920) were gunshot wounds). Mate Matovina (in Annex I to the Indictment listed with birth date unknown) is listed as killed in the list of victims which was created by the Office for Detainees and Missing Persons of the Government of Croatia, Davor Strinović, 12 Apr 2006, T. 3667–3668. His body was not exhumed from any of the graves and there is no other evidence concerning his alleged death. Based on the evidence, therefore, the Trial Chamber is unable to find that this Mate Matovina is dead. *See also* Ex. 302.

668 Marko Miljanić, 30 Mar 2006, T. 2915; Zoran Lakić, 26 Oct 2006, T. 10151; Ex. 22, Map 8; Ex. 23, pp 24–25; Ex. 1042, Tab 2; Ex. 1043, Tab 2, DVD 4, pp 31–50 and DVD 5, pp 1–12.

669 Marko Miljanić, 29 Mar 2006, T. 2862; Zoran Lakić, 26 Oct 2006, T. 10164; Ex. 301, p. 4; Marko Miljanić, 29 Mar 2006, T. 2862; Jasna Denona, 9 Feb 2006, T. 1280; Tomislav Šegarić, Ex. 826, p. 2; Ex. 301, p. 4 (providing that 1991, 97.59% were Croats, and 2.15% were Serbs).

670 Neven Šegarić, 29 Mar 2006, T. 2848 (referring to Ex. 271, ERN 0468-7818); Luka Brkić, 7 Apr 2006, T. 3393–3394; Ex. 109, p. 1; Ex. 1042, Tab 2; Ex. 1043, Tab 2, DVD 4, pp 42–50 and DVD 5, pp 8–12; Ex. 1044.

671 Witness MM-083, 16 Jun 2006, T. 5730; Zoran Lakić, 26 Oct 2006, T. 10151; Nada Pupovac, 31 Oct 2006, T. 10366; Ex. 1042, Tab 2; Ex. 1043, Tab 2, DVD 5, pp 12–20; Ex. 1044.

672 Witness MM-083, 16 Jun 2006, T. 5730–5731; Marko Miljanić, 29 Mar 2006, T. 2862; Ex. 301 (97.6% were Croats and 1.95% were Serbs).

673 Marko Miljanić, 29 Mar 2006, T. 2862 (testifying that Biljane was an exclusively Serb village and that some Croat villages surrounding Škabrnja, including Donji Zemunik, had some Serb population); Zoran Lakić, 27 Oct 2006, T. 10229–10230.

(b) Situation in Škabrnja, Nadin and surroundings prior to 18 November 1991

236. In August 1991, running water and electricity to Nadin had been switched off from Benkovac.[674] Around September 1991, approximately 240 Croatian reserve police members and local volunteers were present in Škabrnja.[675] In September 1991, Škabrnja and Nadin were shelled and subjected to aerial bombings, including by cluster bombs.[676] On 2 October 1991, three villagers **[page 87]** were killed, and it was decided to evacuate the civilian population, following which only members of the reserve police force and the volunteers remained in Škabrnja to guard the village.[677] Around 2 October 1991, Nadin was attacked by the JNA, whereupon two men were killed.[678] This attack was conducted in order to deblockade the road from Benkovac to the airport in Zemunik.[679] On 9 October 1991, an agreement was concluded between, *inter alia*, the 9th Corps command located in Knin and representatives of the Zadar municipality on cessation of combat operations, raising of the blockade of Zadar, and a pull-out of JNA from the Zadar garrison and the Zemunik airport to Benkovac.[680]

237. On 10 October 1991, Marko Miljanić was appointed commander for the defence of Škabrnja, Nadin, Gornji Zemunik, Donji Zemunik, Prkos, Gorica, Galovac and Glavica.[681] This defence force was called the Škabrnja Independent Battalion and consisted of some 730 reserve police and volunteers from the local area.[682] The Škabrnja Independent Battalion placed minefields in and around Škabrnja.[683] On 6 November 1991, the villagers who had been evacuated on 2 October returned to Škabrnja.[684]

238. In 1991, units of the JNA 9th Corps, of the Benkovac TO and of the SAO Krajina police were active in the area of Northern Dalmatia, including in the areas around Škabrnja, Nadin and Bruška.[685] The 180th Motorised Brigade was located in Benkovac and was within the structure of **[page 88]** the 9th Corps in Knin.[686]

---

674 Witness MM-083, 16 Jun 2006, T. 5731.

675 Marko Miljanić, 29 Mar 2006, T. 2862–2864 (testifying that following an order from the Chief of the Zadar police administration, Marko Miljanić, a Croatian MUP member, placed road check-points near Biljane and Zemunik and erected two barricades in Škabrnja; there was also a manned check-point in the hamlet of Ambar, Luka Brkić, 7 Apr 2006, T. 3391–3392), 2864–2865 (testifying that they were armed with six light machine-guns, two hand-held launchers, automatic and semi-automatic rifles and pistols), Marko Miljanić, 30 Mar 2006, T. 2890–2891; Luka Brkić, 5 Apr 2006, T. 3224–3226 (testifying that the village guards wore second-hand uniforms from East Germany and that he was issued with a an automatic rifle three to five days prior to 18 November 1991). There were also mortars in Škabrnja, Witness MM-080, 8 Jun 2006, T. 5254–5255; Ex. 116, p. 2. In Nadin at this time, the only weapons were hunting rifles, Witness MM-083, 16 Jun 2006, T. 5731.

676 Marko Miljanić, 29 Mar 2006, T. 2863, 2871; Tomislav Šegarić, Ex. 826, p. 2. There is also evidence of snipers shooting at Škabrnja, Neven Šegarić, Ex. 251, p. 2. Nadin was shelled on 18 September 1991 from the direction of the Serb villages of either Biljane or Lišane, following which women and children went to the Croat village of Polača, Witness MM-083, 16 Jun 2006, T. 5732.

677 Marko Miljanić, 29 Mar 2006, T. 2863, 2865; Tomislav Šegarić, Ex. 826, p. 2; Neven Šegarić, Ex. 251, p. 2.

678 Witness MM-083, 16 Jun 2006, T. 5732–5733.

679 Nada Pupovac, 30 Oct 2006, T. 10342–10344 (testifying that the attack was ultimately unsuccessful due to minefields on the Benkovac side of Nadin), 10421–10422; Zoran Lakić, 27 Oct 2006, T. 10214–10216. According to Witness MM-080, from the direction of Škabrnja, some of the Croat forces opened fire on JNA vehicles that moved along the Benkovac-Zemunik road to Zemunik airport, where the JNA was based. According to information available to the JNA, an independent battalion located in Škabrnja and consisting of 250 to 300 men, opened fire upon the JNA vehicles, Witness MM-080, 8 Jun 2006, T. 5250, 5254–5255, 5260. *See also* Ex. 40, a report of the SAO Krajina TO, indicates that on 16 September 1991, Milan Martić ordered the Benkovac TO Staff to "provide as many men as possible for Lieutenant Colonel Živanović who would command the operation to lift the blockade of Zemunik".

680 Milan Babić, 20 Feb 2006, T. 1604–1605; Ex. 1030. The Trial Chamber is unable to conclude on the basis of the evidence whether this agreement was complied with, *see* Zoran Lakić, 26 Oct 2006, T. 10148–10152 (testifying that the pull-out of the JNA was obstructed by the ZNG and Croatian police), 27 Oct 2006, T. 10221–10222; Ex. 991 (providing that by 14 October 1991 there had been no major difficulties during the evacuation of the Zadar garrison). Witness MM-080 testified that during November 1991 the JNA convoys from Zadar garrison and Zemunik airport were shot at by Croatian forces before they reached Biljane Donje, Witness MM-080, 8 Jun 2006, T. 5251, 5253, 5260. S*ee also* Ex. 784; Nada Pupovac, 31 Oct 2006, T. 10443.

681 Marko Miljanić, 29 Mar 2006, T. 2885, 30 Mar 2006, T. 2895–2897; Luka Brkić, 7 Apr 2006, T. 3388.

682 Marko Miljanić, 29 Mar 2006, T. 2885, 30 Mar 2006, T. 2890–2891, 2908; Luka Brkić, 5 Apr 2006, T. 3227, 7 Apr 2006, T. 3388–3389; Witness MM-080, 8 Jun 2006, T. 5254–5255. *See also* Zoran Lakić, 26 Oct 2006, T. 10166, 27 Oct 2006, T. 10173.

683 Marko Miljanić, 30 Mar 2006, T. 2895; Luka Brkić, 7 Apr 2006, T. 3411–3412; Nada Pupovac, 30 Oct 2006, T. 10342–10343, 10349, 10368, 31 Oct 2006, T. 10368, 10448–10449; Zoran Lakić, 27 Oct 2006, T. 10173–10174.

684 Marko Miljanić, 29 Mar 2006, T. 2868 (testifying that this happened following the signature in The Hague of a truce); Tomislav Šegarić, Ex. 826, p. 2; Neven Šegarić, Ex. 251, p. 2.

685 Milan Babić, 20 Feb 2006, T. 1601; Ex. 1036.

686 Witness MM-080, 8 Jun 2006, T. 5246. *See also* Nada Pupovac, 30 Oct 2006, T. 10339.

In the autumn of 1991, the commander of the TO in Benkovac was Zoran Lakić.[687] The Chief of the SJB in Benkovac was Boško Dražić.[688]

(c) Attack on Škabrnja and Nadin on 18 and 19 November 1991

239. Between 0600 and 0700 hours in the morning of 18 November 1991, a JNA mechanised infantry unit of between 80 to 200 men with eight to nine APCs and three tanks advanced from the Serb village of Smilčić towards Škabrnja.[689] The TO, including members of the Benkovac TO, also participated in this operation and were resubordinated to the JNA.[690] This JNA force was under the command of Lieutenant-Colonel Momčilo Bogunović of the JNA 180th Motorised Brigade.[691] There is evidence that both the Croatian and the Serb sides had mortars and artillery.[692] From around 0700 hours, Nadin was shelled from the direction of the Serb villages of Biljane or Lišane, and the shelling continued throughout the day.[693] Most of the women and children left Nadin and went to Polaca, Zaton and Zadar, while only men and a few women remained in the village.[694] At around 0730 hours, Škabrnja was subjected to intensive shelling, also from the direction of Biljane or Lišane, which lasted until 1230 hours.[695] **[page 89]**

240. When the column reached the junction of the roads leading to Biljani Donji and Zadar, Lieutenant Miodrag Stevanović and a soldier were killed after having left their APC.[696] The evidence is conflicting as to the reason for their leaving the APC.[697] Thereafter, intensive fire commenced.[698] Croatian forces shot at the JNA tanks and soldiers including from some of the houses.[699] A ZNG unit fired rockets at the JNA column

---

687 Zoran Lakić, 26 Oct 2006, T. 10128–10130.

688 Witness MM-080, 8 Jun 2006, T. 5246. *See also* Ex. 959.

689 Luka Brkić, 5 Apr 2006, T. 3225–3227 (testifying that the Škabrnja village guard was deployed during the night between 17 and 18 November 1991, *see also* Luka Brkić, 5 Apr 2006, T. 3256, 7 Apr 2006, T. 3395, 3434–3435; Zoran Lakić, 26 Oct 2006, T. 10155–10156, 10159–10160, 10166 (testifying that about 110 men took part); Nada Pupovac, 30 Oct 2006, T. 10349 (testifying that "some 200 soldiers on the part of the JNA" participated); Neven Šegarić, Ex. 251, p. 4. Command posts were established in Gornji Biljani and in the hamlet of Trljuge, Luka Brkić, 5 Apr 2006, T. 3255). *See also* Ex. 285 (which makes reference to tanks and APCs (called "BOVs") in the areas of Ambar, west of Škabrnja and in Biljane Donje). There is also evidence that some of the column went through Gornji Zemunik and that before reaching Ambar some of the vehicles turned to the church of St. Luke, Luka Brkić, 7 Apr 2006, T. 3434; Ex. 285; Ex. 107, p. 1. Luka Brkić testified that Captain Dragan's White Eagles ("Beli Orlovi") participated in the attack on Škabrnja, however the Trial Chamber notes that it has not been furnished with any evidence that Captain Dragan commanded a unit by this name, Luka Brkić, 7 Apr 2006, T. 3427.

690 Nada Pupovac, 30 Oct 2006, T. 10345, 31 Oct 2006, T. 10399, 10425; Ex. 107, pp 1, 3–4 (indicating that the TO was to seal off the area and prevent intervention and that coordination between the TO and the JNA was initially poor but improved). Zoran Lakić testified that the Benkovac TO participated with a unit of 25–30 men, who were deployed in the hamlet Skorić in the Biljani Donji area and that 12 of these TO members relocated wounded civilians and soldiers to Biljani Donji using two minibuses and an ambulance, Zoran Lakić, 26 Oct 2006, T. 10158–10159, 10163, 10168, 27 Oct 2006, T. 10178, 10248, 30 Oct 2006, T. 10278; Nada Pupovac, 30 Oct 2006, T. 10345, 10347, 10356–10358, 31 Oct 2006, T. 10445. Some of the JNA tank crews were manned to full strength by TO members from other locations, Zoran Lakić, 26 Oct 2006, T. 10156 (*see also* Marko Miljanić, 30 Mar 2006, T. 2929, testifying that he was told that some tank crews included volunteers from Serbia; Ex. 616, regarding volunteers from Serbia and BiH who were joined with the Benkovac TO). The Trial Chamber notes that Ex. 116, Ex. 117, Ex. 118, Ex. 411 and Ex. 614 provide that members of TO were present in Škabrnja and Nadin on 18 and 19 November 1991. The Trial Chamber notes Zoran Lakić's testimony that no other units from the Benkovac TO, than those listed above, participated in the attack, Zoran Lakić, 27 Oct 2006, T. 10190–10192, 30 Oct 2006, T. 10277. On the participation of the TO in the attack *see also* Veljko Džakula, 17 Jan 2006, T. 417–418.

691 Witness MM-080, 8 Jun 2006, T. 5262; Ex. 107. *See also* Zoran Lakić, 26 Oct 2006, T. 10154.

692 Luka Brkić, 5 Apr 2006, T. 3256, Zoran Lakić, 26 Oct 2006, T. 10166, Ex. 285, Nada Pupovac, 30 Oct 2006, T. 10354–10355, 31 Oct 2006, T. 10369.

693 Witness MM-083, 16 Jun 2006, T. 5732, 5735, 5737.

694 Witness MM-083, 16 Jun 2006, T. 5734–5735.

695 Marko Miljanić, 29 Mar 2006, T. 2869; Neven Šegarić, Ex. 251, p. 4; Tomislav Šegarić, Ex. 826, pp 2–3.

696 Nada Pupovac, 30 Oct 2006, T. 10345–10346; Zoran Lakić, 26 Oct 2006, T. 1016, 27 Oct 2006, T. 10232–10233.

697 Neven Šegarić, 29 Mar 2006, T. 2835, testifying that no warning was given; Nada Pupovac, 30 Oct 2006, T. 10351–10353; Zoran Lakić, 26 Oct 2006, T. 10161, both testifying that a warning was given by Lieutenant Stevanović using a megaphone after they left the APC.

698 Marko Miljanić, 29 Mar 2006, T. 2869, testifying that fire was opened first by the JNA column and artillery at around 0730 hours; Luka Brkić, 5 Apr 2006, T. 3229–3231 (testifying that shells hit his brother's house), 3255 (testifying that the map in Ex. 285 accurately describes that fire was first opened on Škabrnja at 0730 hours from the direction of Ambar), 7 Apr 2006, T. 3397, 3417; Zoran Lakić, 26 Oct 2006, T. 10161–10162, 27 Oct 2006, T. 10174, 10233–10234; Nada Pupovac, 30 Oct 2006, T. 10347, 10354; Tomislav Šegarić, Ex. 826, p. 2; Ex. 984, Annex 9.

699 Marko Miljanić, 29 Mar 2006, T. 2876 (testifying that around 1400 hours he and Luka Škara were by the church of the Assumption of the Virgin and tried to hit the tanks which had entered the village centre using a hand-held rocket launcher, but they

from the elevation Ražovljeva Glavica.[700] Helicopters were also used by the JNA to deploy ground troops in the vicinity of Škabrnja.[701] Cluster bombs dropped from JNA aircraft were also used in the attack.[702]

241. The church of the Assumption of the Virgin in the centre of Škabrnja was shot at by a JNA tank.[703] At one point, tanks attempted to enter the church of the Assumption of the Virgin but were stopped by Captain Janković, a member of the JNA.[704] Following this, and without authorisation by Captain Janković, several soldiers entered the church and fired their weapons.[705] A tank opened fire in the direction of the school in Škabrnja.[706] There is evidence that fire was opened on private houses by tanks and using hand-held rocket launchers.[707] **[page 90]**

242. During the fighting, civilians fled south.[708] Civilians were also taken out of Škabrnja by JNA and TO forces and transported to territory under the control of Croatian forces.[709] Village guards Luka Brkić, Ante "Neno" Gurlica and Marin Gurlica were taken by bus to Benkovac, where they stayed overnight after which they were taken to Knin.[710] About half of Škabrnja was controlled by the Serb forces by 1400 hours.[711] The fighting in Škabrnja lasted until dusk.[712] There were two dead and several wounded on the Serb side, whereas the Croatian side suffered about 15 killed.[713]

243. At 0500 hours in the morning of 19 November 1991, the Croatian forces withdrew from Škabrnja.[714] Around 0700 hours, the JNA convoy left Škabrnja and advanced along the road towards Nadin,

---

stopped because civilians, including women, children and old men were around the tanks with their hands on their necks); Luka Brkić, 5 Apr 2006, T. 3232–3233, 3246, 3248; Nada Pupovac, 30 Oct 2006, T. 10356, 10358, 31 Oct 2006, T. 10392; Zoran Lakić, 27 Oct 2006, T. 10173–10174 *See also* Ex. 109.

700 Nada Pupovac, 30 Oct 2006, T. 10354–10355, 31 Oct 2006, T. 10369. *See also* Marko Miljanić, 30 Mar 2006, T. 2901–2902, confirming that a ZNG unit was present at this elevation.

701 Marko Miljanić, 29 Mar 2006, T. 2870, 2075 (testifying that helicopters arrived at a meadow called Jabuka three or four times and deployed troops about 30 troops each time, who wore "dark uniforms"). The Trial Chamber notes that Zoran Lakić testified (27 Oct 2006, T. 10239–10240) that he heard neither helicopters nor airplanes during the attack. However, the Trial Chamber does not find this evidence credible in light of the direct evidence, Marko Miljanić, 29 Mar 2006, T. 2870; Luka Brkić, 5 Apr 2006, T. 3230; Neven Šegarić, Ex. 251, p. 4.

702 Marko Miljanić, 29 Mar 2006, T. 2870, 30 Mar 2006, T. 2925; Luka Brkić, 5 Apr 2006, T. 3230; 7 Apr 2006, T. 3393–3394.

703 Luka Brkić, 7 Apr 2006, T. 3393, 3417; Ex. 984, Annex 9; Ex. 922, p. 7. Nada Pupovac testified that the bell tower was shot at by the tank because there was a Croatian machine-gun nest there, Nada Pupovac, 30 Oct 2006, T. 10355–10356, 31 Oct 2006, T. 10431–10433, 1 Nov 2006, T. 10458. The Trial Chamber does not find this evidence convincing in light of the contrary evidence.

704 Luka Brkić, 5 Apr 2006, T. 3242–3243.

705 Luka Brkić, 5 Apr 2006, T. 3242–3243.

706 Luka Brkić, 5 Apr 2006, T. 3239.

707 Luka Brkić, 5 Apr 2006, T. 3239, 3246 (testifying that sniper fire was opened from a private house which was subsequently targeted by a tank); Zoran Lakić, 27 Oct 2006, T. 10175; Ex. 117, p. 3; Ex. 984, Annex 9, Statement of Svetka Miljanić, Statement of Snježana Ferica.

708 Marko Miljanić, 29 Mar 2006, T. 2880; Zoran Lakić, 30 Oct 2006, T. 10311, testifying that more than 1,500 civilians of Škabrnja withdrew in the direction of Zadar; Boško Brkić, Ex. 275, p. 2, stating that around 100 villagers fled to a quarry in the forest, a pre-arranged meeting point should the village come under attack, after which they went by foot to Prkos where buses eventually picked them up.

709 Luka Brkić, 5 Apr 2006, T. 3251–3252. Nada Pupovac testified that over 150 uninjured civilians were taken by the TO, first to Benkovac and then to a junction near the Croat village of Pristeg and the Serb village of Ceranje Gornje where they crossed over to "Croatian territory", Nada Pupovac, 31 Oct 2006, T. 10364, 10370. Zoran Lakić testified that when he arrived in Škabrnja at 1700 hours on 18 November 1991, he saw 120 or 130 civilians put up at the primary school, and a nursery school, and that later that evening they were transported to "Croatian forces" using buses of the "transport company of Benkovac", Zoran Lakić, 26 Oct 2006, T. 10164.

710 Luka Brkić, 5 Apr 2006, T. 3233 (testifying that these three were members of the village guard but that they had removed their camouflage uniforms by the time they were captured), 3250–3253 (also testifying that Ante "Neno" Gurlica was beaten by a soldier before being transported away and that the three of them were beaten as they entered the bus taking them to Benkovac), 3264–3265. *See infra* paras 278, 281.

711 Marko Miljanić, 29 Mar 2006, T. 2880.

712 Marko Miljanić, 29 Mar 2006, T. 2869-2870 (also testifying that civilians were killed in the shelling); Luka Brkić, 7 Apr 2006, T. 3417; Zoran Lakić, 26 Oct 2006, T. 10162–10163; Neven Šegarić, Ex. 251, p. 5; Ivica Bilaver, Ex. 821, p. 2; Tomislav Šegarić, Ex. 826, p. 2; Ex. 984, Annex 9. *See also* Nada Pupovac, 30 Oct 2006, T. 10354–10355. At one point, the Croatian side blew up the reserve ammunition of the JNA, Marko Miljanić, 29 Mar 2006, T. 2870–2871, 30 Mar 2006, T. 2902.

713 Marko Miljanić, 29 Mar 2006, T. 2878; Zoran Lakić, 26 Oct 2006, T. 10170; Ex. 377.

714 Marko Miljanić, 30 Mar 2006, T. 2904–2905; Witness MM-083, 16 Jun 2006, T. 5736–5737; Nada Pupovac, 31 Oct 2006, T. 10365. *See also* Zoran Lakić, 26 Oct 2006, T. 10165. After the hostilities had ended, the JNA found automatic rifles, pistols, sniper rifles, mortars, anti-aircraft guns, and handheld rocket launchers, which were brought to the Benkovac barracks, Zoran Lakić, 26 Oct 2006, T. 10166–10167, 27 Oct 2006, T. 10173; Nada Pupovac, 31 Oct 2006, T. 10369. Luka Brkić testified that when he was taken from Škabrnja to Benkovac he saw a large pile of weapons which he believed were confiscated in Škabrnja, Luka Brkić, 7 Apr 2006, T. 3406–3407.

which was subsequently shelled.[715] The convoy passed through Nadin around 1400 hours after which it withdrew to the Benkovac barracks.[716] During the night of 19 September 1991, "everything was burning" in Nadin.[717]

(d) Evidence of units present in Škabrnja

244. The Trial Chamber has been furnished with evidence describing the units present in Škabrnja on 18 November 1991. The evidence shows that the JNA units were composed of soldiers of different ethnicities.[718] The JNA units were composed of regular soldiers and reservists from **[page 91]** neighbouring Serb villages.[719] In addition to the uniforms ordinarily worn by members of the JNA, officers of the JNA present in Škabrnja wore a mix of camouflage uniforms and ceremonial uniforms.[720]

245. The TO present in Škabrnja wore the same uniforms, caps and helmets as the JNA.[721] However, the TO also wore the Serbian flag on their uniforms and some members had a white band on the left shoulder.[722] There is evidence that some TO soldiers wore SAO Krajina patches on their uniforms.[723]

246. Paramilitary units, in the evidence often referred to simply as "Chetniks", were present in Škabrnja and wore various kinds of JNA uniforms, some with an insignia with four Cyrillic "S", and different kinds of hats, including berets, fur hats with cockades and hats.[724] Their faces were painted, however the evidence shows that at least some of them appeared to be local.[725]

247. The evidence is insufficient to conclude whether members of the SAO Krajina MUP participated in the attack on Škabrnja on 18 and 19 November 1991.[726] The Prosecution alleges that Goran Opačić was a member of the police and present in Škabrnja at the time of the operation in Škabrnja.[727] The Defence denies both allegations.[728] The Trial Chamber finds that the evidence establishes beyond reasonable doubt that Goran Opačić was a member of the Benkovac SJB special unit on 18 and 19 November 1991. However, while the evidence establishes beyond reasonable doubt that Goran Opačić was present in Škabrnja at some point on 18 November 1991, it is **[page 92]** insufficient to establish beyond reasonable doubt that he participated in events or crimes in Škabrnja or Nadin on 18 or 19 November 1991.[729]

---

715 Nada Pupovac, 31 Oct 2006, T. 10366–10367; Witness MM-083, 16 Jun 2006, T. 5738.

716 Nada Pupovac, 31 Oct 2006, T. 10366–10367; 10369–10370.

717 Witness MM-083, 16 Jun 2006, T. 5745–5746.

718 Luka Brkić, 5 Apr 2006, T. 3243–3245, 7 Apr 2006, 3405–3406, 3420, 3441–3442 (stating that he believed Captain Janković was a Serb).

719 Luka Brkić, 7 Apr 2006, T. 3419, 3421 (listing the villages of Zemunik Gornje, Veljane, Biljane, Gornje Biljane, Djevrske, Kistanje, Lišane, and Rastević), 3429–3430, 3440–3441.

720 Luka Brkić, 5 Apr 2006, T. 3236–3237; Nada Pupovac, 31 Oct 2006, T. 10452–10453. For a description of the JNA uniforms, *see supra* fn 283.

721 Nada Pupovac, 31 Oct 2006, T. 10452–10453. *See also* Ex. 117.

722 Nada Pupovac, 31 Oct 2006, T. 10453; Ex. 117, p. 3.

723 Luka Brkić, 5 Apr 2006, T. 3237, 7 Apr 2006, T. 3426–3427.

724 Marko Miljanić, 30 Mar 2006, T. 2918–2919; Tomislav Šegarić, Ex. 826, pp 3, 5–6; Ex. 118, p. 1.

725 Tomislav Šegarić, Ex. 826, pp 3–4.

726 Zoran Lakić, 27 Oct 2006, T. 10258; Nada Pupovac, 31 Oct 2006, T. 10396, 10428; Milan Babić, 20 Feb 2006, T. 1607, Ex. 1036, L0092006; Ex. 116; Ex. 614. *See also* Ex. 411.

727 Prosecution Final Trial Brief, paras 189–190. The Prosecution relies upon Witness MM-003, 8 Mar 2006, T. 2024 (testifying that Goran Opačić was a member of the "Benkovac special police" at the time of the operation in Škabrnja); Milan Babić, 20 Feb 2006, T. 1607 (testifying that he had heard "that it wasn't true that Goran Opačić [...] had been involved in the fighting all the time [but that he] had been there at the outset but later left"; *see also* Ex. 1036); Ex. 411 (identifying Goran Opačić as a member of the Benkovac police special unit and that he gives information that killings were committed in Škabrnja); Ex. 511, p. 18 (an undated typed list which provides that Goran Opačić was a member of the Benkovac police until 31 Oct 1991).

728 Defence Final Trial Brief, para. 19. The Defence relies upon Zoran Lakić, 27 Oct 2006, T. 10258, 10263–10264, 30 Oct 2006, T. 10272 (testifying that Goran Opačić was not a member of the Benkovac SJB and that he did not take part in the fighting, *see also* Nada Pupovac, 31 Oct 2006, T. 10396, 10428); Ex. 116 (providing that "according to unconfirmed data" members of "Opačić's group" carried out killings in Nadin); Ex. 511, p. 18.

729 Regarding membership in the Benkovac SJB "special unit", the Trial Chamber notes Ex. 411, Ex. 511 and Milan Babić, 20 Feb 2006, T. 1601, 1607 (*see also* Ex. 1036). The Trial Chamber notes that in this respect Witness MM-003's testimony is corroborated (Witness MM-003, 8 Mar 2006, T. 2024). Regarding his presence in Škabrnja and Nadin, the Trial Chamber notes Milan Babić's hearsay evidence that Goran Opačić was only present at the "outset" in Škabrnja on 18 November 1991, that Nada Pupovac, who was present in Škabrnja 18 November 1991, denies Goran Opačić's presence, and that Ex. 116 only refers

(e) Killings in Škabrnja and Nadin

(i) Killings at Slavko Šegarić's house in Ambar on 18 November 1991

248. In the morning of 18 November 1991, Neven Šegarić, Ivica Bilaver, Lucia Šegarić, Krsto Šegarić, Maja Grgica Šegarić, Željko Šegarić, Josip Miljanić and Stana Vicković were hiding in the cellar of Slavko Šegarić's house in Ambar.[730] Shortly after the first shelling, there was banging on the door and they heard a voice outside asking who was in the cellar.[731] They heard someone outside say "Come out you Ustase, we are going to slaughter you all".[732] When the people in the cellar opened the door, about ten JNA soldiers entered.[733] The soldiers' faces were painted, and they wore plain olive green uniforms with a red star on the buttons and on the epaulets.[734] After having taken a rifle and a pistol which were elsewhere in the house, some of the soldiers left.[735] Shortly thereafter five or six "Serb volunteers, who were from the neighbouring villages" arrived.[736] They threatened the people in the cellar and forced them out; everyone left the cellar except Lucia Šegarić.[737] Just as the people exited the cellar, Neven Šegarić saw a "Chetnik" fire a burst of gunfire into the cellar.[738] About five minutes later, when Neven Šegarić and Željko Šegarić were forced to enter the cellar to look for weapons, Neven Šegarić saw that Lucia Šegarić was lying dead **[page 93]** a few metres from the door.[739] As Neven Šegarić again left the cellar he saw Stana Vicković and Josip Miljanić being forced to kneel after which a soldier, wearing a camouflage uniform with a patch on his sleeve reading "SAO Krajina", shot them in the head.[740] After this, Krsto Šegarić was beaten by five or six soldiers wearing green camouflage uniforms with SAO Krajina patches on their sleeves and red stars on the buttons, including Đuro Kosović, whom Neven Šegarić recognised.[741] Đuro Kosović then shot Krsto Šegarić in the back of the head.[742] The soldiers standing around outside at this point in time were a mix of JNA soldiers and soldiers with SAO Krajina patches on their camouflage uniforms.[743]

to "unconfirmed data" that "Opačić's group" killed members of a family in Nadin and three unidentified captives from Škabrnja. The Trial Chamber considers that the contrary evidence of Witness MM-003 is not sufficiently credible in this respect. The Trial Chamber notes the hearsay evidence (Marko Miljanić, 29 Mar 2006, T. 2879–2880) that Goran Opačić, nicknamed "Klempa", was heard over the radio in Škabrnja on 18 November 1991, but cannot make any finding based on this evidence (*see also* Milan Babić, 20 Feb 2006, T. 1607; Ex. 1036).

730 Neven Šegarić stated that he was in the cellar with his grandmother Lucia Šegarić (age 62), his grandfather Krsto Šegarić (age 60 or 61), his cousin Željko Šegarić (age 14 or 15), his great grandmother Maja Grgica Šegarić (age 94), Ivo Bilaver (age 14 or 15), and Josip/Joso Miljanić. However, right before the attack, Maja Grgica Šegarić was brought back to Neven Šegarić's father Mile Šegarić's house, Neven Šegarić, 29 Mar 2006, T. 2836, 2841–2842, Ex. 251, pp 3, 5; Ivica Bilaver, Ex. 821, p. 2 (also stating that the house was close to St. Mary's church in Ambar); Ex. 270, F-2. Ivica Bilaver was 14 or 15 years old, Neven Šegarić, 29 Mar 2006, T. 2836; Ivica Bilaver, Ex. 821, p. 2. *See also* Ex. 1042, Tab 2; Ex. 1043, Tab 2, DVD 4, pp 32–38.

731 Neven Šegarić, Ex. 251, p. 3.

732 Neven Šegarić, Ex. 251, p. 3. There is also evidence that women and children were being called "Ustašas" and were insulted, Ex. 984, Annex 9, Statement of Svotka Miljanić, Statement of Snježana Ferica.

733 Neven Šegarić, 29 Mar 2006, T. 2855–2856, Ex. 251, p. 3.

734 Neven Šegarić, Ex. 251, p. 3.

735 Ivica Bilaver, Ex. 821, p. 2; Neven Šegarić, 29 Mar 2006, T. 2834–2835, 2855–2856, Ex. 251, p. 3.

736 Neven Šegarić, Ex. 251, p. 3; Neven Šegarić, 29 Mar 2006, T. 2856; Ivica Bilaver, Ex. 821, p. 2.

737 Neven Šegarić, Ex. 251, p. 3.

738 Neven Šegarić, Ex. 251, p. 3.

739 Neven Šegarić, Ex. 251, p. 3. The Trial Chamber notes that Ex. 305, autopsy report, p. 22, list a Luca Šegarić, born 1920, who was identified by *inter alia* her two sons Slavko Šegarić and Mile Šegarić (*see also* Ex. 323, p. 10; Ex. 302). The autopsy report indicates that she was shot multiple times but that she died from a shot at close range to the head. Ex. 377, p. 12, lists a Luca Šegarić, born 1922, who was killed by gunshot to the head. The Trial Chamber finds that this evidence refers to Lucia Šegarić. In this context, the Trial Chamber notes Ex. 270, F-14, which lists a Lucka Šegarić, however due to the discrepancies between Ex. 305 and Ex. 270, F-14, the Trial Chamber cannot conclude that Ex. 270, F-14 refers to Lucia Šegarić. Neven Šegarić testified that Ex. 270, F-14 does not show Lucia Šegarić, Neven Šegarić, 29 Mar 2006, T. 2840.

740 Neven Šegarić, Ex. 251, p. 3. Regarding Stana Vicković, Ex. 344; Ex. 825, ERN 0469-0704; Ex. 377, p. 13, listing him as a "Croat civilian"; Ex. 323, p. 9; Ex. 302. Regarding Josip Miljanić, Ex. 360; Ex. 825, ERN 0469-0706; Ex. 377, p. 9, listing him as a "Croat civilian"; Ex. 323, p. 9; Ex. 302. The Trial Chamber notes that Ivica Bilaver's statement (Ex. 821, p. 2) is less detailed than that of Neven Šegarić but does not find that the discrepancy between their evidence gives rise to reasonable doubt as to the killing of Stana Vicković and Josip Miljanić. At one point, either when Lucia Šegarić or the group of adults was shot, Ivica Bilaver was wounded in the leg by a ricochet, Ivica Bilaver, Ex. 821, p. 2; Neven Šegarić, Ex. 251, p. 3; Ex. 270, F-2, (Neven Šegarić, 29 Mar 2006, T. 2841–2842, correcting the identities of the bodies in this photo).

741 Neven Šegarić, 29 Mar 2006, T. 2857; Ex. 251, p. 3 (also stating that Đuro Kosović was from Smoković).

742 Neven Šegarić, Ex. 251, p. 3; Ex. 270, F-4 and F-5 (*see also* Neven Šegarić, 29 Mar 2006, T. 2841–2842); Ex. 350; Ex. 825, ERN 0469-0704; Ex. 377, p. 12, listing him as a "Croat civilian"; Ex. 323, p. 9; Ex. 302.

743 Neven Šegarić, Ex. 251, p. 3. Neven Šegarić testified that a few of them were from a neighbouring village, Neven Šegarić, 29 Mar 2006, T. 2856–2857.

249. After this, Đuro Kosović, using a list of inhabitants in the village, questioned Neven Šegarić about where some of the inhabitants lived and if they had weapons.[744] When Neven Šegarić said that he did not know, Đuro Kosović left.[745] Subsequently, the soldier who had killed Stana Vicković and Josip Miljanić forced Neven Šegarić and Željko Šegarić against the wall of the house, however a "JNA officer" intervened and prevented their killing.[746] The soldiers then took Ivica Bilaver, Neven Šegarić and Željko Šegarić to Smilčić.[747]

(ii) Killings at Petar Pavičić's house in Škabrnja on 18 November 1991[748]

250. When the attack on Škabrnja started, Tomislav Šegarić hid in the cellar of Petar "Pešo" Pavičić's house in Škabrnja together with about 25 to 30 civilians, including women, children and **[page 94]** elderly people.[749] Around 1230 hours the shelling ceased, and there was silence for around 20 minutes whereupon Eva Šegarić went outside the cellar.[750] Shortly thereafter, Tomislav Šegarić heard men shouting that everyone should come out of the cellar or they would throw in hand grenades.[751] The people in the cellar started to leave with their hands up. Outside near the entrance to the cellar, there was a group of more than ten armed "Chetniks" from the local area who wore camouflage uniforms and a variety of headgear.[752]

251. As they left the cellar, people were pulled to the side and killed by the "Chetniks". Some of these people were first beaten with rifle butts and then killed.[753] The following persons were killed outside Petar Pavičić's house:[754] Jozo Brkić,[755] Jozo Miljanić,[756] Slavka Miljanić,[757] Mile Pavičić,[758] Petar Pavičić,[759] Ilija

[744] The list included the names of Mile Šegarić, Slavko Miljanić, *see infra* para. 255. Branko Šegarić, Marko Bilaver, Marko Miljanić, and Stipe Miljanić, Neven Šegarić, Ex. 251, pp 3–4.

[745] Neven Šegarić, 29 Mar 2006, T. 2834, Ex. 251, p. 4.

[746] Neven Šegarić, 29 Mar 2006, T. 2832, 2834, Ex. 251, p. 4.

[747] Neven Šegarić, Ex. 251, p. 4; Ivica Bilaver, Ex. 821, pp 2–3 (also stating that he saw that the house of Stana Vicković was burning). Ivica Bilaver was taken to the hospital in Benkovac, Ivica Bilaver, Ex. 821, p. 3.

[748] The Trial Chamber notes that Ivan Jelić stated that Pešo was the nickname of Petar Pavičić, Ivan Jelić, Ex. 825, p. 3.

[749] Tomislav Šegarić, Ex. 826, p. 3 (at p. 4 explaining that the house was located in the centre of Škabrnja). Ex. 270, Photo F-9 depicts the basement of Petar "Pešo" Pavičić's house, Neven Šegarić, 29 Mar 2006, T. 2845. *See also* Ex. 1042, Tab 2; Ex. 1043, Tab 2, DVD 4, pp 39–42.

[750] Tomislav Šegarić, Ex. 826, p. 3.

[751] Tomislav Šegarić, Ex. 826, p. 3.

[752] Tomislav Šegarić, Ex. 826, pp 3–4, stating that he particularly remembers one called "Kosović" but stated that that was a common surname of people coming from the village of Zemunik.

[753] Tomislav Šegarić, Ex. 826, p. 3; Ex. 984, Annex 9, statement of Svetka Miljanić.

[754] Ex. 984, Annex 9, Statement of Svetka Miljanić. The Trial Chamber notes that Ex. 984, Annex 9, statement of Snježana Ferica, lists an "Iviša Ražov" and concludes that this refers to Ive Ražov. There is no further evidence regarding this person and the Trial Chamber cannot conclude beyond reasonable doubt that Ive Ražov was among those killed outside Petar Pavičić's house. In relation to this victim, the Trial Chamber recalls its findings on the interpretation of the Indictment, *see supra* paras section I C.

[755] Ex. 354, Autopsy report; Ex. 984; Annex 9, Statement of Svetka Miljanić; Ex. 270, F-6 (Neven Šegarić, 29 Mar 2006, T. 2844); Ex. 825, ERN 0469-0706; Ex. 323, p. 9; Ex. 302; Ex. 377, p. 6, listing him as a "Croat civilian". The Trial Chamber notes that Annex I to the Indictment lists a Joso Brkić as killed in Škabrnja and finds that this refers to the same victim.

[756] Ex. 984, Annex 9, Statement of Svetka Miljanić. The Trial Chamber notes that Annex I to the Indictment lists a Josip Miljanić and recalls its finding that this person was killed at Slavko Šegarić's house in Ambar. The Trial Chamber recalls that Petar Pavičić's house was located in the centre of Škabrnja and not in the hamlet of Ambar (Tomislav Šegarić, Ex. 826, p. 4). The Trial Chamber therefore considers that Jozo Miljanić, who was killed at Petar Pavičić's house, is a different person from Josip Miljanić who is listed in Annex I to the Indictment._

[757] Ex. 984, Annex 9, Statement of Svetka Miljanić, stating that her husband Jozo Miljanić and her mother-in-law Slavka Miljanić were killed at this house. The Trial Chamber notes that Annex I to the Indictment lists a Slavko Miljanić but considers in light of the information in this statement that this is a different person. In relation to this victim, the Trial Chamber recalls its findings on the interpretation of the Indictment, *see supra* section I C.

[758] Ex. 362, Autopsy report; Ex. 984; Annex 9, Statement of Svetka Miljanić; Ex. 270, F-10 and F-11 (Neven Šegarić, 29 Mar 2006, T. 2846); Ex. 825, ERN 0469-0708; Ex. 323, p. 9; Ex. 302; Ex. 377, p. 3, listing him as a "Croat defender". *See also* Ex. 377, pp 3–4.

[759] Tomislav Šegarić, Ex. 826, p. 3, stating that he saw the dead body of Petar "Pešo" Pavičić outside the house; Ex. 365, Autopsy report; Ex. 984; Annex 9, Statement of Svetka Miljanić; Ex. 825, ERN 0469-0708; Ex. 323, p. 9; Ex. 302; Ex. 377, p. 10, listing him as a "Croat civilian".

[759] Ex. 362, Autopsy report; Ex. 984; Annex 9, Statement of Svetka Miljanić; Ex. 270, F-10 and F-11 (Neven Šegarić, 29 Mar 2006, T. 2846); Ex. 825, ERN 0469-0708; Ex. 323, p. 9; Ex. 302; Ex. 377, p. 3, listing him as a "Croat defender".

Ražov,[760] Kata "Soka" Rogić,[761] Ivica Šegarić,[762] Rade Šegarić[763] **[page 95]** and Vice Šegarić.[764] After this, women and children were lined up and insulted and asked where their men were.[765] Subsequently, they were made to walk towards Ambar while being threatened by the "Chetniks".[766] There were many JNA officers and soldiers in the area and the JNA officers prevented the "Chetniks" from further killings.[767]

(iii) Killings at Pere Sopić's house in Nadin on 19 November 1991

252. On 19 November 1991, soldiers wearing JNA uniforms came to the house of Pere Sopić in Nadin where they found Novica Atelj, Stoja Brkić, Danka Brzoja, Ika Čirjak, Maša Čirjak, Jakov Šestan and Marija Šestan. After having taken Novica Atelj and killed him outside the house, the soldiers returned to the house and killed the remaining civilians.[768] **[page 96]**

(iv) Other killings in Škabrnja and Nadin

253. Grgica "Maja" Šegarić, who was between 80 and 96 years old and infirm as a result of a stroke, was killed in Mile Šegarić's house in Ambar on 18 November 1991.[769]

254. Ante Ražov was killed on 18 November 1991 in Škabrnja. The evidence shows that Ante Ražov was beaten and had one of his ears cut off before being shot in the head in front of his mother.[770] Ante Ražov is listed in Annex I to the Indictment as a civilian victim. However, the evidence shows that he was a member of the Croatian defence force in Škabrnja. Nevertheless, it is established beyond reasonable doubt that he was not taking an active part in the hostilities when he was killed. In this respect, the Trial Chamber considers that the Defence has been put on notice of this victim by virtue of Annex I to the Indictment. The evidence is insufficient to conclude who perpetrated this killing.

255. Slavko Miljanić was killed in Škabrnja on 18 November 1991. Slavko Miljanić is listed in Annex I to the Indictment as a civilian victim, however the evidence shows that he was a member of the Croatian defence force in Škabrnja.[771] The Trial Chamber finds that it has not been established beyond reasonable doubt that Slavko Miljanić was taking no active part in the hostilities at the time of his death.

---

760 Neven Šegarić, 29 Mar 2006, T. 2844, testifying that the person in Ex. 270, F-5, is Ilija Ražov. In relation to this victim, the Trial Chamber recalls its findings on the interpretation of the Indictment, *see supra* section I C.

761 Neven Šegarić, 29 Mar 2006, T. 2841–2843; Tomislav Šegarić, Ex. 826, p. 4; Ex. 270, F-3 (Neven Šegarić, 29 Mar 2006, T. 2841–2843); Ex. 338, Autopsy report; Ex. 984, Annex 9, Statement of Svetka Miljanić and statement of Snježana Ferica; Ex. 825, ERN 0469-0702; Ex. 323, p. 9; Ex. 302; Ex. 377, p. 11, listing her as a "Croat civilian".

762 Ex. 363, Autopsy report; Ex. 984; Annex 9, Statement of Svetka Miljanić; Ex. 825, ERN 0469-0708; Ex. 323, p. 9; Ex. 302; Ex. 377, p. 4, listing him as a "Croat defender". *See also* Ex. 377, pp 3–4.

763 Ex. 358, Autopsy report; Ex. 984, Annex 9, Statement of Svetka Miljanić and statement of Snježana Ferica; Ex. 270, F-8 (Neven Šegarić, 29 Mar 2006, T. 2845); Ex. 825, ERN 0469-0706; Ex. 323, p. 9; Ex. 302; Ex. 377, p. 12, listing him as a "Croat civilian".

764 Tomislav Šegarić, Ex. 826, p. 3, stating that he saw the dead body of Vice Šegarić outside the house; Ex. 359, Autopsy report, Ex. 984; Annex 9, Statement of Svetka Miljanić; Ex. 825, ERN 0469-0706; Ex. 323, p. 9; Ex. 302; Ex. 377, p. 12, listing him as a "Croat civilian".

765 Ex. 984, Annex 9, Statement of Svetka Miljanić, Annex 9, Statement of Snježana Ferica.

766 Tomislav Šegarić, Ex. 826, p. 4.

767 Tomislav Šegarić, Ex. 826, p. 4.

768 Witness MM-083, 16 Jun 2006, T. 5736–5745; Ex: 109, p. 3; Ex. 302; Ex. 323, p. 7; Ex. 324 to Ex. 330 (these autopsy reports show that each victim was shot in the head at point-blank range as well as between five and eleven times from a distance of more than one metre); Ex. 825 ERN 0469-0710, 0469-0712, 0469-0714 (indicating that all victims wore civilian clothes). *See also* Ex. 1042, Tab 2; Ex. 1043, Tab 2, DVD 5, pp 12–20.

769 Marko Miljanić, 30 Mar 2006, T. 2920; Neven Šegarić, Ex. 251, p. 5; Ex. 356, Autopsy report; Ex. 377, p. 12, listing her as a "Croat civilian"; Ex. 825, ERN 0469-0706. *See also* Ex. 323, p. 9; Ex. 302.

770 Marko Miljanić, 29 Mar 2006, T. 2871; Ex. 270, F-1 (Neven Šegarić, 29 Mar 2006, T. 2841); Ex. 364, Autopsy report; Ex. 825, ERN 0469-0708; Ex. 377, p. 3, listing him as a "Croat defender"; Ex. 323, p. 9; Ex. 302. *See also* Nada Pupovac, 31 Oct 2006, T. 10414, testifying that she heard that there had been a man without an ear, Ex. 117, p. 4 (a member of the military police battalion stated that a ZNG member had been shot behind a house and that members of the TO had cut off his ear); Ex. 411, Report on the murder of civilians in Škabrnja.

771 Slavko Miljanić is listed as a civilian in Annex I to the Indictment. Ex. 357, Autopsy report; Ex. 825, ERN 0469-0706; Ex. 377, p. 3, listing him as a "Croat defender"; Ex. 323, p. 9; Ex. 302. *See* also Tomislav Šegarić, Ex. 826, p. 5.

256. On 18 November 1991, several "Chetniks" beat on the road from the centre of Škabrnja towards Ambar. Thereafter, the "Chetniks" put Šime Šegarić and Bude Šegarić in a JNA APC, which drove away in the direction of Biljani. Subsequently, their bodies were handed over to their relatives. The evidence shows that Šime Šegarić and Bude Šegarić were members of the Croatian defence force in Škabrnja.[772] The evidence further shows that they were taken to Knin where they were killed.[773]

257. There is also evidence that the following persons were killed in Škabrnja and Nadin on 18 or 19 November 1991: Ivan Babić, Luka Bilaver, Marija Brkić (born 1943), Marko Brkić, Željko **[page 97]** Ćurković, Marija Dražina, Ana Jurić, Grgo Jurić, Petar Jurić, Niko Pavičići, Josip Perica, Ljubo Perica, Ivan Ražov, Jela Ražov, Branko Rogić, Nikola Rogić, Kljajo Šegarić, Lucka/Luca Šegarić, Mara Žilić, Pavica Žilić, Roko Žilić, Tadija Žilić and Marko Župan.[774]

---

[772] Tomislav Šegarić, Ex. 826, p. 4. The Trial Chamber notes that each is listed as a "Croat defender" in Ex. 377, p. 4.

[773] Ex. 825, ERN 0469-0702, ERN 0469-0722, 0469-0727. Regarding the injuries on Šime Šegarić, Ex. 333, Autopsy report, and Ex. 825, ERN 0469-0702. *See also* Ex. 323, p. 9; Ex. 302. The Trial Chamber notes that Bude Šegarić is not listed in Annex I of the Indictment and refers to the section on the interpretation of the Indictment, *see supra* section I C. The Trial Chamber has not been provided with an autopsy report concerning Bude Šegarić.

[774] The Trial Chamber notes that Kljajo Šegarić, Lucka/Luca Šegarić, Luka Bilaver, and Branko Rogić are not listed as civilian victims in Annex I to the Indictment but recalls its findings regarding the interpretation of the Indictment, para. 13. Regarding Ivan Babić, Ex. 305, Autopsy report, pp 24–25 (killed by shrapnel); Ex. 377, p. 5, listing him as a "Croat civilian"; Ex. 323, p. 10; Ex. 302. Regarding Luka Bilaver, Ex. 270, F-15 (on which photograph the victim is wearing civilian clothes). The Trial Chamber notes that Ex. 377, p. 5, and Ex. 825 ERN 0469-0718 contain a person with the same name who died of hypothermia on 1 December 1991. However, the Trial Chamber cannot conclude that this is the same person as Luka Bilaver in Ex. 270, F-15. Regarding Marija Brkić, Ex. 334, Autopsy report (killed by gunshot to the head inflicted from close range); Ex. 825, ERN 0469-0702; Ex. 377, p. 6, listing her as a "Croat civilian"; Ex. 323, p. 9; Ex. 302. Regarding Marko Brkić, Ex. 361, Autopsy report (killed by gunshots to the head inflicted at point-blank range); Ex. 825, ERN 0469-0708; Ex. 377, p. 7, listing him as a "Croat civilian"; Ex. 323, p. 9; Ex. 302. Regarding Željko Ćurković, Ex. 335, Autopsy report; Ex. 825, ERN 0469-0702 (killed by several gunshots including one inflicted at point-blank range to the head). The Trial Chamber notes that Ex. 270, F-17, contains a "Zoran Ćurković. In light of the details provided in the autopsy report and visible on F-17, the Trial Chamber concludes beyond reasonable doubt that this is Željko Ćurković. The Trial Chamber notes that on the photograph F-17 the victim is dressed in civilian clothes. Regarding Marija Dražina, Ex. 367, Autopsy report (killed by gunshot to the head inflicted at point-blank range); Ex. 825, ERN 0469-0710; Ex. 377, p. 7, listing her as a "Croat civilian"; Ex. 302; Ex. 323, p. 9. Regarding Ana Jurić, Ex. 332, Autopsy report (killed by blunt trauma to the head); Ex. 377, p. 8, listing "Anica Jurić" as a "Croat civilian"; Ex. 323, p. 9; Ex. 302. Regarding Grgo Jurić, Ex. 355, Autopsy report (killed by multiple gunshot wounds to the head inflicted at a distance of a maximum of one metre); Ex. 825, ERN 0469-0706; Ex. 377, p. 8, listing him as a "Croat civilian"; Ex. 323, p. 9; Ex. 302. Regarding Petar Jurić, Ex. 346, Autopsy report (killed by gunshots to the head inflicted from a point-blank to close range); Ex. 825, ERN 0469-0704; Ex. 377, p. 9, listing him as a "Croat civilian"; Ex. 323, p. 9; Ex. 302. Regarding Niko Pavičići, Autopsy report Ex. 343 (killed by gunshots to the head and thorax inflicted from close range); Ex. 825, ERN 0469-0704; Ex. 377, p. 9, listing him as a "Croat civilian"; Ex. 323, p. 9; Ex. 302. Regarding Josip Perica, Ex. 331, Autopsy report (killed by gunshots, including to the head at point-blank range); Ex. 825, ERN 0469-0702; Ex. 377, p. 10, listing him as a "Croat civilian"; Ex. 323, p. 9; Ex. 302 (listed as "Joso"). Regarding Ljubo Perica, Ex. 347, Autopsy report (killed by several gunshot wounds, including to the head at point-blank range); Ex. 825, ERN 0469-0704; Ex. 377, p. 10, listing him as a "Croat civilian"; Ex. 323, p. 9; Ex. 302. Regarding Ivan Ražov, Ex. 345, Autopsy report (killed by gunshots, including two shots to the neck inflicted from a relatively close range); Ex. 825, ERN 0469-0704; Ex. 377, p. 11, listing him as a "Croat civilian"; Ex. 323, p. 9; Ex. 302. Regarding Jela Ražov, Ex. 368, Autopsy report (killed by two gunshots to the head inflicted at point-blank range); Ex. 825, ERN 0469-0718; Ex. 377, p. 11, listing her as a "Croat civilian"; Ex. 323, p. 9; Ex. 302. Regarding Branko Rogić, Ex. 270, F-16. There is no further evidence of this victim. Regarding Nikola Rogić, Ex. 339, Autopsy report (killed by several gunshots, including one to the head inflicted at point-blank range); Ex. 825, ERN 0469-0702; Ex. 377, p. 11, listing him as a "Croat civilian"; Ex. 323, p. 9; Ex. 302. Regarding Kljajo Šegarić: Ex. 270, F-4 (on which photograph the victim is wearing civilian clothes); Neven Šegarić, 29 Mar 2006, T. 2840, 2843. Regarding Lucka/Luca Šegarić, Ex. 270, F- 14 (on which photograph the victim is wearing civilian clothes). There is no further evidence of this victim. Regarding Mara Žilić, Ex. 353, Autopsy report (killed by several gunshots inflicted from a distance of more than one metre); Ex. 825, ERN 0469-0706; Ex. 377, p. 13, listing her as a "Croat civilian"; Ex. 323, p. 9; Ex. 302. Regarding Pavica Žilić, Ex. 352, Autopsy report (killed by blast wounds); Ex. 825, ERN 0469-0706; Ex. 377, p. 13, listing her as a "Croat civilian"; Ex. 323, p. 9; Ex. 302. Regarding Roko Žilić, Ex. 342, Autopsy report (killed by gunshots, including two inflicted to the head at point-blank range); Ex. 825, ERN 0469-0704; Ex. 377, p. 14, listing him as a "Croat civilian"; Ex. 323, p. 9; Ex. 302. Regarding Tadija Žilić, Ex. 351, Autopsy report (killed by several gunshots, including to the head inflicted at point-blank range); Ex. 825, ERN 0469-0706; Ex. 377, p. 14, listing him as a "Croat civilian"; Ex. 323, p. 9; Ex. 302. Regarding Marko Župan, Ex. 366, Autopsy report (killed by two gunshots, including to the head inflicted at point-blank range); Ex. 825, ERN 0469-0710; Ex. 377, p. 14, listing him as a "Croat civilian"; Ex. 323, p. 9; Ex. 302. There is also evidence of killings of unidentified victims in Škabrnja and Nadin on 18 and 19 November 1991, Marko Miljanić, 29 Mar 2006, T. 2877–2878, 30 Mar 2006, T. 2914, 2920; Boško Brkić, Ex. 275, p. 2; Ex. 109; Ex. 116; Ex. 117; Ex. 614. The Trial Chamber is unable to make any further findings on the basis of this evidence, in particular whether it concerns any of the proven killings.

258. There is evidence that Petar Rogić and Miljenko Šegarić from Škabrnja were killed in Benkovac on 18 November 1991.[775] There is also evidence that Milka Žilić from Škabrnja was wounded by a shell and died in Zadar on 18 November 1991.[776] **[page 98]**

259. Annex I to the Indictment lists the following persons as civilian victims killed in Škabrnja on 18 November 1991, however the evidence shows that they were "Croat defenders": Vladimir Horvat, Nediljko Jurić, Gašpar Perica, Marko Rogić, Nediljko Škara and Stanko Vicković.[777]

260. Following the attack on Škabrnja, some civilians remained in the village.[778] In December 1991, there were JNA soldiers in the village and machine-gun nests in the houses along the roads.[779] The evidence shows that a TO brigade under JNA command was stationed in the village.[780] Boško Brkić returned numerous times in secret to Škabrnja to visit his parents, Mate Brkić and Josipa Brkić, who had remained in the village.[781] Kata Perica, Marija Bilaver, Anica Pavičic and Eva Pavičić would come to his parents' house every evening to sleep.[782] At some point after December 1991, Boško Brkić was unable to see his parents due to the situation in the village.[783] His parents told him that every day "Chetniks" would come to them and both threaten and pretend to protect them.[784] The "Chetniks" had long beards and wore uniforms with "Chetnik insignia".[785] By mid-January 1992, there were only a few JNA soldiers in the village, however about 50 to 70 soldiers with "SAO Krajina" and White Eagle insignia on their camouflage uniforms were guarding and patrolling the village.[786] On 11 March 1992, Anica Pavičić and Eva Pavičić **[page 99]** came to the house and found Marija Bilaver, Mate Brkić, Josipa Brkić and Kata Perica dead on the floor.[787]

---

775 Neither of these persons is listed in Annex I to the Indictment. The Trial Chamber recalls its findings regarding the interpretation of the Indictment, *see supra* section I C, and that it will consequently consider these victims for a conviction. Regarding Petar Rogić, Ex. 825, ERN 0469-0722 (listed as killed); Ex. 377, p. 12 (listed as tortured and beaten to death on 18 November 1991 in Benkovac). Regarding Miljenko Šegarić, Ex. 377, p. 4 (listed as a "Croat defender" and captured, tortured and beaten to death in Benkovac).

776 Milka Žilić is not listed in Annex I to the Indictment. The Trial Chamber recalls its findings regarding the interpretation of the Indictment, para. 13. Ex. 825, ERN 0469-0722; Ex. 377, p. 13, listing her as "Croat civilian".

777 Regarding Vladimir Horvat, Ex. 336, Autopsy report (killed by gunshots, including by a shot to the head inflicted at point-blank range); Ex. 825, ERN 0469-0702; Ex. 377, p. 2, listing him as a "Croat defender"; Ex. 323, p. 9; Ex. 323, p. 9; Ex. 302. Regarding Nediljko Jurić: Ex. 349, Autopsy report (killed by several gunshots from a distance of more than one metre); Ex. 825, ERN 0469-0704; Ex. 377, pp 2–3, listing him as a "Croat defender"; Ex. 323, p. 9; Ex. 302. Regarding Gašpar Perica: Ex. 348, Autopsy report (killed by several gunshot wounds, including two shots to the head inflicted from a close range); Ex. 825, ERN 0469-0704; Ex. 377, p. 3, listing him as a "Croat defender"; Ex. 302. Regarding Marko Rogić: Ex. 340, Autopsy report (killed by several gunshots, including one to the head inflicted at point-blank range); Ex. 825, ERN 0469-0702; Ex. 377, p. 4, listing him as a "Croat defender"; Ex. 323, p. 9; Ex. 302. Regarding Nediljko Škara: Ex. 341, Autopsy report (killed by several gunshots from a distance of more than one metre and by blast wounds); Ex. 825, ERN 0469-0704; Ex. 377, p. 5, listing him as a "Croat defender"; Ex. 323, p. 9; Ex. 302. Regarding Stanko Vicković: Ex. 337, Autopsy report (killed by several gunshot wounds from a distance of more than one metre, including by a shot to the head which was the fatal wound); Ex. 825, ERN 0469-0702; Ex. 377, p. 5, listing him as a "Croat defender"; Ex. 323, p. 9; Ex. 302.

778 Marko Miljanić, 29 Mar 2006, T. 2877; Boško Brkić, Ex. 275, p. 2.

779 Boško Brkić, Ex. 275, p. 3.

780 Zoran Lakić, 30 Oct 2006, T. 10289.

781 Mate Brkić was confined to a wheelchair as the result of a stroke, Boško Brkić, Ex. 275, pp 2–3.

782 Boško Brkić, Ex. 275, p. 3.

783 Boško Brkić, Ex. 275, p. 3.

784 Boško Brkić, Ex. 275, p. 3, also stating that his parents told him that the JNA soldiers had told them that they should be careful as "the Chetniks" would kill them.

785 Boško Brkić, Ex. 275, p. 3, also stating that his parents recognised two local Serbs among them.

786 Boško Brkić, Ex. 275, p. 3.

787 Boško Brkić, Ex. 275, pp 2–3, also stating that Anica Pavičić and Eva Pavičić immediately fled to Prkos where they told Boško Brkić what had happened. The Trial Chamber notes that the period listed in the Indictment for the killings in Škabrnja after 18 November 1991 is until and including February 1992, and that these killings took place in March 1992. However, the Trial Chamber finds that the Defence was put on notice through the inclusion of these names in Annex I to the Indictment and the summary of Boško Brkić's evidence in the Prosecution's 65 *ter* submission of 7 May 2004, which specifically describes this incident and connects it with Count 1 (Persecutions), Count 2 (Extermination), and Counts 3 and 4 (Murder). The Trial Chamber notes that Mate Brkić is listed as Mato Brkić in Annex I to the Indictment. The autopsy report of the victims provide that they wore civilian clothes at the time of their death (Mate Brkić, Ex. 373, body no. 6; Josipa Brkić, Ex. 374, body no. 7; Kata Perica, Ex. 374, body no. 9; Marija Bilaver, Ex. 373, body no. 8). Moreover, Ex. 377 also lists all four victims as civilians. *See also* Ex. 302; Ex. 323.

261. The evidence shows that killings occurred from 18 November 1991 until 11 March 1992.[788] In 1996, 26 bodies were exhumed from a mass grave site near the school in Škabrnja.[789] In addition to the four victims just mentioned, the exhumed bodies were identified as: Grgo Bilaver, Peka Bilaver, Šime Bilaver, Ana Brkić, Kata Brkić (born 1935), Kata Brkić (born 1939), Marija Brkić (born 1906), Mijat Brkić, Luka Čičak, Jure Erlić, Dumica Gospić, Ljubomir Ivković, Neđelko Ivković, Tereza Ivković, Jela Jurić, Simica Jurjević, Mirko Kardum, Grgica Ražov, Marko Ražov, Simo Ražov, Pera Škara, Božo Stura and Draginja Stura.[790] **[page 100]**

(f) Investigations into the events in Škabrnja and Nadin on 18 and 19 November 1991

262. On 20 November 1991, the JNA Naval Military District in Split, on the request of the European Community Monitoring Mission, asked the JNA 9th Corps command to provide a report by the following day on the killings in Škabrnja and Nadin on 18 and 19 November 1991.[791] There is evidence that an on-site investigation was carried out in cooperation with the Benkovac SJB.[792] The 180th Motorised Brigade conducted interviews, although not pursuant to superior orders.[793] Following the interviews, reports were sent to the JNA 9th Corps command.[794]

(g) Destruction in Škabrnja and Nadin

263. As noted above, during the attack on 18 and 19 November 1991 cluster bombs were dropped on Škabrnja with resulting damage to buildings. Moreover, private houses and the school were shot at by tanks and with

788 Ex. 305; Ex. 377. The Trial Chamber also notes that Ex. 107, p. 7, 16 provides for 10 December 1991 "in Škabrnja TO members kill one elderly person each day" and for 15 February 1992 "[a]nother dead body in the village of Škabrnja".

789 Ivan Grujić, 10 Apr 2006, T. 3477–3479; Davor Strinović, 12 Apr 2006, T. 3670–3671; Ex. 305; Ex. 373; Ex. 374; Ex. 1042, Tab 2; Ex. 1043, Tab 2, DVD 5, p. 1.

790 Grgo Bilaver, Ex. 305, pp 15–16, killed by a gunshot to the chest. *See also* Ex. 302; Ex. 323, p.10; Ex. 377, p. 5. Peka Bilaver, Ex. 305, pp 19–20, killed by gunshot. *See also* Ex. 302; Ex. 323, p. 10; Ex. 377, p. 6. Ana Brkić, Ex. 305, pp 21–22, killed by an explosion. *See also* Ex. 302; Ex. 323, p. 10; Ex. 377, p. 6. Kata Brkić (born 1935), Ex. 374, pp 3–4, killed by gunshot. *See also* Ex. 302; Ex. 323, p. 10. Kata Brkić (born 1939), Ex. 374, p. 6, killed by gunshot to the head. *See also* Ex. 302; Ex. 323, p. 10, Ex. 377, p. 6. Marija Brkić, Ex. 373, p. 2, killed by gunshot to the thorax and blunt trauma to the head. *See also* Ex. 302; Ex. 323, p. 10. Mijat Brkić, Ex. 305, pp 6–7, killed by gunshot. *See also* Ex. 302; Ex. 323, p. 10; Ex. 377, p. 7. Jure Erlić, Ex. 305, pp 8–9, killed by shrapnel but Ex. 377, p. 7, provides that he was shot. *See also* Ex. 302; Ex. 323, p.10. Dumica Gospić, Ex. 305, pp 18–19, killed by explosion but Ex. 377, p. 7, provides that she was shot. *See also* Ex. 302; Ex. 323, p. 10. Ljubomir Ivković, Ex. 374, pp 12–13, killed by shrapnel. *See also* Ex. 302; Ex. 323, p. 10; Ex. 377, p. 8. Neđelko Ivković, Ex. 305, pp 11–12, killed by gunshot wounds to the chest. The Trial Chamber notes that this victim is listed as a "Croat defender" in Ex. 377, p. 2, however his body when exhumed was dressed in civilian clothing. *See also* Ex. 302; Ex. 323, p. 10. Tereza Ivković, Ex. 373, pp 5–6, killed by a blow to the head with a sharp instrument. *See also* Ex. 302; Ex. 323, p. 10; Ex. 377, p. 8. Simica Jurjević, Ex. 305, p. 9, compression of the head and thorax. The Trial Chamber notes that Ex. 377, p. 9, provides that this victim was run over by a heavy vehicle. *See also* Ex. 302; Ex. 323, p. 10. Mirko Kardum, Ex. 305, pp 2–3, killed by shrapnel. *See also* Ex. 302; Ex. 323, p. 10, Ex. 377, p. 9. Simo Ražov, Ex. 305, pp 17–18, killed by gunshot to the head. The Trial Chamber notes that Ex. 377, p. 11, lists a victim called Šime Ražov born 1938, which is the same birth year as listed in Ex. 305 for Simo Ražov. The Trial Chamber notes that Annex I to the Indictment lists a Šime Ražov, born 1938, and concludes that this is the same person as listed in Ex. 305 and Ex. 377. *See also* Ex. 302; Ex 323, p. 10. Grgica Ražov, Ex. 305, pp 12–14, killed by gunshot to the head. *See also* Ex. 302; Ex. 323, p. 10; Ex. 377, p. 10. Marko Ražov, Ex. 305, pp 14–15, killed by gunshot to the head. *See also* Ex. 302; Ex. 323, pp 10; Ex. 377, p. 11. Pera Škara, Ex. 374, pp 10–11, killed by shrapnel. *See also* Ex. 302; Ex. 323, p. 10; Ex. 377, p. 13. Božo Stura, Ex. 374, pp 6–7, killed by blows to the head with a sharp instrument. *See also* Ex. 302; Ex. 323, p. 10. Draginja Stura, Ex. 373, p. 3, killed by multiple gunshot wounds. *See also* Ex. 302; Ex. 323, p. 10. Regarding Šime Bilaver, Luka Čičak, and Jela Jurić: The Trial Chamber notes that Šime Bilaver and Luka Čičak are recorded as having died of natural causes (Ex. 373, p. 5 and Ex. 305, pp 5–6 respectively). This evidence is therefore not relevant and will not be considered for a conviction. Jela Jurić is recorded as having been killed by shrapnel (Ex. 305, pp 4–5; Ex. 825, ERN 0469-0702). The Trial Chamber notes that this victim is not listed in Annex I to the Indictment, and recalls its findings regarding the interpretation of the Indictment, *see supra* section I C. The Trial Chamber concludes that the Defence has not been on sufficient notice regarding this victim.

791 Ex. 60. On 23 November 1991, the JNA handed over 35 bodies from Škabrnja to the Civilian Protection of the Zadar, Biograd, Benkovac and Obrovac municipalities. By 5 December 1991, a further 13 bodies from Škabrnja and Nadin had been received from the JNA, Ivan Jelić, Ex. 825, pp 2–3 and attached documents.

792 Zoran Lakić, 27 Oct 2006, T. 10254; Marko Miljanić, 29 Mar 2006, T. 2881, 30 Mar 2006, T. 2914, 2927; Ex. 270.

793 Ex. 109; Ex. 116; Ex. 117; Ex. 118; Ex. 411; Ex. 615. The Trial Chamber notes that Ex. 116, Ex. 117, Ex. 118, Ex. 411, Ex. 614, and Ex. 615 contain the names of alleged perpetrators of killings. However, the Trial Chamber finds that the evidence is insufficient to link any of the named persons to the above-mentioned killings in Škabrnja and Nadin on 18 and 19 November 1991.

794 Witness MM-080, 8 Jun 2006, T. 5270–5271, 5279–5280.

hand-held rockets, and the church of the Assumption of the Virgin was also shot at by a tank.[795] Marko Miljanić testified that by 19 November 1991, 30 to 40% of the houses in Škabrnja had been "destroyed" and that also the church of the Assumption of the Virgin and the school had been "destroyed".[796] The Trial Chamber notes that the only evidence of destruction of this church on 18 or 19 November 1991 is that a tank fired at the bell tower.[797] As noted above, "soldiers" entered this church and fired their weapons.[798] Furthermore, looting was committed by local Serbs and Serb paramilitaries.[799] There is also evidence that volunteers from Serbia and BiH, who were joined to the Benkovac TO, participated during the attack on Škabrnja and that they looted and robbed.[800]

264. After the attack on Škabrnja and until February 1992, Serb paramilitary forces and local Serbs looted and burnt houses in Škabrnja.[801] The evidence is inconclusive as to when Škabrnja was destroyed.[802] However, by 1994 about 90 to 95% of Škabrnja was destroyed and the church of St. **[page 101]** Mary in Ambar and the church of St. Luke near the centre of Škabrnja were badly damaged.[803] By October or November 1995, all the houses in Škabrnja and the church of the Assumption of the Virgin had been destroyed.[804] By 1996, the church as well as the houses in Nadin had been looted, destroyed and burnt down.[805]

5. Bruška

265. Bruška is located about 15 kilometres east of Benkovac.[806] In 1991, about 400 people lived there, and the village was predominantly Croat.[807] Marinovići is a hamlet in Bruška comprising of eight houses, which in 1991 was inhabited by Croats.[808]

266. From the spring of 1991, there was a Croatian reserve police force in Bruška, however, they did not have regular shifts, uniforms or weapons.[809] The "Militia Krajina, Martic's police" set up barricades which cut off the bus line between Zadar and Benkovac.[810] Armed men identifying themselves as "Martic's men" or "Martic's Militia" came to Bruška almost every day to scare the inhabitants.[811] The armed men called the villagers Ustašas and said that Bruška would be a part of a Greater Serbia and that the people of Bruška should leave.[812] However, as of December 1991 almost all of the inhabitants of Bruška were still living there.[813]

---

795 *See supra* paras 236, 241.

796 Marko Miljanić, 30 Mar 2006, T. 2925; Neven Šegarić, 29 Mar 2006, T. 2848 (describing the school as "blown up" and "torched"). The Trial Chamber recalls that a JNA tank fired in the direction of the school, *see supra* para. 241.

797 *See infra* para. 395.

798 *See supra* para. 241.

799 Ex. 107, p. 3; Ex. 922, p. 7; Boško Brkić, Ex. 275, p. 3.

800 Ex. 616, pp 2, 13–14. It is also alleged that these persons committed killings of unidentified individuals, *id* at p. 2.

801 Boško Brkić, Ex. 275, p. 3; Ex. 107, p. 3; Ex. 984, Annex 9.

802 Zoran Lakić, 30 Oct 2006, T. 10294–10295, 10303, testifying that in November 1992 Škabrnja was no more damaged than it had been one year earlier and that the damage was not as shown in Ex. 271 and Ex. 272 but that there was damage to roofs of houses from mortar shells and holes in the walls of buildings made by artillery and tank fire, *ibid.* Zoran Lakić testified that the kind of extensive damage to buildings in Škabrnja shown in the photographs may have occurred in 1993 or 1994 following Croatian attacks on the municipalities of Benkovac, Obrovac, Gracac and (partly) Knin, *ibid.* Boško Brkić stated that by December 1992 Škabrnja had been completely destroyed, Boško Brkić, Ex. 275, p. 4.

803 Marko Miljanić 30 Mar 2006, T. 2925 (testifying that houses had been blown up with explosives and razed to the ground, rather than having been hit by shells), 2926.

804 Neven Šegarić 29 Mar 2006, T. 2848, 2851; Luka Brkić, 5 Apr 2006, T. 3290.

805 Witness MM-083, 16 Jun 2006, T. 5747 (testifying to the taking of a tractor, and furniture and appliances).

806 Jasna Denona, 9 Feb 2006, T. 1293; Ex. 23, p. 25. *See also* Ex. 1042, Tab 2; Ex. 1043, Tab 2, DVD 5, pp 22–41; Ex. 1044.

807 Ex. 301, p. 6, states that there were 474 inhabitants in Bruška and that 89.54% were Croats, and 10.46% were Serbs; Jasna Denona, 9 Feb 2006, T. 1269; Ante Marinović, 23 Mar 2006. T. 2472.

808 Jasna Denona, 9 Feb 2006, T. 1269. The villages surrounding Bruška are Medviđa, Zelengrad, Karin, Brgud, Bjeline, and Kalanja Draga. Zelengrad, Karin, Brgud, and Kalanja Draga were Serb; Medviđa was half-Serb and half-Croat; and Bjeline was 20% Croat and 80% Serb, Ante Marinović, 23 Mar 2006. T. 2472–2473.

809 Ante Marinović, 23 Mar 2006. T. 2471, 2492.

810 Jasna Denona, 9 Feb 2006, T. 1270, 1305.

811 Ante Marinović, 23 Mar 2006. T. 2493, T. 2479–2480, 2498, also testifying that these men mostly came from Medviđa. Ante Marinović further testified that they would say "You have no business here. This is Serb. You can go away," and would call the people Ustašas, telling them that Bruška would be a part of a Greater Serbia, *ibid.*

812 Ante Marinović, 23 Mar 2006. T. 2480, testifying that the villagers of Bruška were not armed and thus could not protect themselves.

813 Ante Marinović, 23 Mar 2006. T. 2480.

267. On the evening of 21 December 1991, Ante Marinović was at home playing cards with his brother Dušan Marinović, his father Roko Marinović, his uncle Petar Marinović and Sveto Drača.[814] Ante Marinović's grandfather and Ljilja Marinović, the wife of Dušan Marinović, were upstairs with two children of theirs, Jure and Donja, and with the children of Sveto Drača and Soka **[page 102]** Drača.[815] The men were not armed and were dressed in civilian clothes, except Sveto Drača who was a Serb member of the JNA, and who was wearing an olive-drab uniform.[816] Although Ante Marinović was a reserve police officer at the time, he was not on active duty that night.[817]

268. At around 2000 or 2030 hours, three members of the *Milicija Krajine* barged into the house, took the men outside, lined them up against a wall and started shooting.[818] Dušan Marinović and Roko Marinović were killed and Ante Marinović was wounded.[819] Sveto Drača and Petar Marinović ran away but were chased and killed near the gate.[820]

269. The same evening Jasna Denona was in her family home, which was close to Roko Marinović's house, with her mother and her neighbours, Soka and Dragan Marinović.[821] Jasna Denona, her mother and Dragan Marinović were Croats, and Soka was a Serb.[822] At about the same time as the *Milicija Krajine* came to Roko Marinović's house, men identifying themselves as the *Milicija Krajine* and as "Martić's men" came to the door.[823] Dragan Marinović went to answer the door.[824] The women fled out into the garden and across a wall.[825] As they were running Jasna Denona heard one of the men shout "they got away", after which the men started shooting at them and Jasna Denona was hit.[826] Her mother came back and helped her move behind a wall in the vineyard, where they hid together with Jeka and Soka for about two hours.[827] Jeka then went to check what was happening in the house closest to them, which was the house of Roko Marinović.[828] They followed her and saw that at the gate of the yard she had found the dead body of her husband, **[page 103]** Petar Marinović, and of her neighbour, Sveto Drača.[829] In the front yard she had found the dead bodies of Roko Marinović and his son, Dušan Marinović.[830]

270. Joso Marinović came to the house and told them that both his son, Dragan Marinović, and his wife, Ika Marinović, had been killed.[831] Later that night Dusan Drača, the father of Sveto Drača, came and told them that there were four more dead bodies in Marinovići.[832] The following morning they discovered that the dead bodies belonged to Krsto Marinović, Draginja Marinović, his wife Stana Marinović, and her mother-in-law, Manda Marinović.[833] Jasna Denona's mother and neighbour Kata saw their bodies and told her that they had been shot and that their bodies were "bullet riddled".[834]

---

814 Ante Marinović, 23 Mar 2006. T. 2481–2483, 2498; Ex. 1042, Tab 2; Ex. 1043, Tab 2, DVD 5, pp 32–41.

815 Ante Marinović, 23 Mar 2006. T. 2481; Jasna Denona, 9 Feb 2006, T. 1291.

816 Ante Marinović, 23 Mar 2006. T. 2481–2482; Jasna Denona, 9 Feb 2006, T. 1290.

817 Ante Marinović, 23 Mar 2006. T. 2481–2482.

818 Ante Marinović, 23 Mar 2006. T. 2482–2484, (at T. 2483 testifying that they had "Milicija Krajine" on the sleeves of their uniforms).

819 Ante Marinović, 23 Mar 2006. T. 2484. Ante Marinović was shot seven times: twice in the left thigh, or above the left thigh, twice in the arm, twice above the right hip, and once in the hand, Ante Marinović, 23 Mar 2006. T. 2484. *See also* Ex. 370, p. 2; Jasna Denona, 9 Feb 2006, T. 1274–1275. With respect to Dušan Marinović and Roko Marinović, *see*, Ex. 370, also indicating that they wore civilian clothes; Ex. 323, p. 8, indicating that they were killed by gunshot. *See also* Ex. 302; Ex. 378.

820 Ante Marinović, 23 Mar 2006. T. 2484.

821 Jasna Denona, 9 Feb 2006, T. 1270–1271; Ex. 1042, Tab 2; Ex. 1043, Tab 2, DVD 5, pp 22–31.

822 Jasna Denona, 9 Feb 2006, T. 1271.

823 Jasna Denona, 9 Feb 2006, T. 1271–1272, 1281.

824 Jasna Denona, 9 Feb 2006, T. 1272, 1286, testifying that he was 23 years old.

825 Jasna Denona, 9 Feb 2006, T. 1272.

826 Jasna Denona, 9 Feb 2006, T. 1272–1273, 1276–1277. Today she has 50% disability, with her right arm being much weaker than her left arm as well as being disfigured, *id.* at T. 1279.

827 Jasna Denona, 9 Feb 2006, T. 1273.

828 Jasna Denona, 9 Feb 2006, T. 1273–1274.

829 Jasna Denona, 9 Feb 2006, T. 1274. With respect to Petar Marinović, Ex. 369, which also provides that he wore civilian clothes; Ex. 323, p. 8, providing that he was killed by gunshots. *See also* Ex. 302; Ex. 378. As regards Sveto Drača, Ex. 302. The Trial Chamber notes that no autopsy report has been provided concerning Sveto Drača.

830 Jasna Denona, 9 Feb 2006, T. 1274.

831 Jasna Denona, 9 Feb 2006, T. 1275; Ex. 372, also stating that they wore civilian clothes; Ex. 323, p. 8, stating that they were killed by gunshot. *See also* Ex. 302; Ex. 378.

832 Jasna Denona, 9 Feb 2006, T. 1275.

833 Jasna Denona, 9 Feb 2006, T. 1275.

834 Jasna Denona, 9 Feb 2006, T. 1275; Ex. 369 (regarding Krsto Marinović, Draginja Marinović); Ex. 371 (regarding Stana Marinović and Manda Marinović); Ex. 323, p. 8, providing that they were killed by gunshot. Ex. 369 and Ex. 371 also indicate that all the four victims wore civilian clothes. *See also* Ex. 302; Ex. 378.

271. The next day at 1800 hours an ambulance arrived with a policewoman from Benkovac who interviewed Jasna Denona about what had happened.[835]

272. There were investigations into the killings in Bruška. A JNA report from 11 March 1992 and one on 4 April 1992, confirmed that there were killings in Bruška on 21 December 1991 and indicate that the killings may have been motivated by revenge by a named individual.[836] There was also an on-site investigation team from Benkovac, an investigative judge and people from the SJB involved in the investigation at Bruška.[837]

273. By 1995, most of Bruška had been destroyed.[838] **[page 104]**

E. Detention-related crimes

1. SJB in Titova Korenica

274. The SJB in Titova Korenica, which was subordinated to the SUP in Knin, was used as a detention facility.[839] The facility consisted of three cells.[840] At the facility, there were *Milicija Krajine* as well as persons in camouflage uniforms and JNA uniforms.[841]

275. Vlado Vuković, a Croatian policeman, was detained at the SJB for approximately ten days together with Ignjac Ivanus, an SJB commander from Zagorje, and Nikola Pemper.[842] He was never informed why he was arrested and detained, rather his captors "would just say vulgar words and that the Republic of Croatia would cost us dearly".[843] On several occasions while detained at the SJB, Vlado Vuković was beaten by people who referred to themselves as "Martić's men" and by people wearing camouflage uniforms and by "the JNA in olive-drab uniforms".[844] During the beatings, members of the *Milicija Krajine* were present but did nothing to stop the beatings.[845] On one occasion, Vlado Vuković was cut on the face.[846]

276. The Trial Chamber has also received evidence of the detention of a Croat civilian named Milan Pavlić for about 15 days, and of Perica Bićanić and Ivica Bićanić, both members of the Poljanak civilian protection force, for nine months and one month, respectively. All three were severely mistreated at the SJB.[847] **[page 105]**

---

835 Jasna Denona, 9 Feb 2006, T. 1277–1278.

836 Ex. 403, dated 11 March 1992, pp 2–3, *see also* Imra Agotić, Ex. 398, T. 23277–23278; MM-096, 22 Aug 2006, T. 6901; Ex. 404, p. 2 (in the report, the author states that he believed this information to be true and that it was from a reliable source, *ibid*).

837 MM-080, 8 Jun 2006, T. 5281–5282, 5318. *See also* Ex. 617; Ex. 618. Jasna Denona was interviewed by Benkovac police, Ex. 134; Jasna Denona, 9 Feb 2006, T. 1281–1284. Witness MM-096 testified that there was information that the perpetrators were Serbs, but "Nobody said specifically the SAO Krajina Police.", Witness MM-096, 24 Aug 2006, T. 7092, 7095–7096. *See also* MM-080, 8 Jun 2006, T. 5318. Neither MM-080 nor Jasna Denona ever heard of anyone having been punished for the killings in Bruška on 21 December 1991, Jasna Denona, 9 Feb 2006, T. 1281; MM-080, 8 Jun 2006, T. 5318.

838 Ante Marinović, 23 Mar 2006, T. 2509; Jasna Denona, 9 Feb 2006, T. 1279–1280, 1307.

839 Vlado Vuković, 27 Mar 2006, T. 2669; MM-096, 21 Aug 2006, T. 6829, 6831–6832. The Trial Chamber notes that prior to his detention in Titova Korenica, Vlado Vuković had been detained in the Plaški SJB, where he was mistreated and beaten by men who referred to themselves as "Martić's men"(*see* Vlado Vuković, 27 Mar 2006, T. 2665–2667). However, the Trial Chamber notes that as the detention facility in Plaški SJB is not listed in paragraph 39 of the Indictment, it considers that the Defence was not put on notice of this detention. In this regard, the Trial Chamber recalls its finding regarding the interpretation of the Indictment. *See supra* section I C. *See also* Ex. 1042, Tab 2; Ex. 1043, Tab 2, DVD 2, pp 15–16; Ex. 1044, Map of Titova Korenica area.

840 Vlado Vuković, 27 Mar 2006, T. 2669–2670. Vlado Vuković was however not able to see whether there were other people detained in the other cells of the SJB, *ibid.*

841 Vlado Vuković, 27 Mar 2006, T. 2669, 2712.

842 Vlado Vuković, 27 Mar 2006, T. 2679, 2674. The Trial Chamber notes that there is no evidence that Nikola Pemper was mistreated at the Titova Korenica SJB.

843 Vlado Vuković, 27 Mar 2006, T. 2669, T. 2672, 2674.

844 Vlado Vuković, 27 Mar 2006, T. 2712–2713.

845 Vlado Vuković, 27 Mar 2006, T. 2671–2672.

846 Vlado Vuković, 27 Mar 2006, T. 2671–2672. Vlado Vuković was subsequently transferred to the Željeva military airport in Bihać where he was beaten by people wearing the uniforms of the Military Police. On 28 October 1991, Vlado Vuković was transferred to a hangar at the military training ground in Manjača, BiH. On 9 November 1991, he was exchanged in Slavonski and Bosanski Samac, Vlado Vuković, 27 Mar 2006, T. 2672–2674.

847 Marica Vuković, 22 Mar 2006, T. 2418–2419, 2422–2423, also testifying that Milan Pavlić sustained a broken nose and "a broken head", and that Perica Bićanić lost approximately half his body weight and was very traumatised. The Trial Chamber

2. Detention facilities in Benkovac[848]

277. On 14 October 1991, Ivan Atelj and Šime Čačić were arrested in Zagrad by a member of the "Martić's police" and taken to the SJB in Benkovac.[849] While being questioned they were threatened and beaten. After 19 days of detention, Ivan Atelj and Šime Čačić were moved to the old hospital in Knin, in the latter's case on the order of Milan Martić.[850]

278. Following the attack on Škabrnja on 18 November 1991, around 40 inhabitants, including the village guard Luka Brkić, the three children Tomislav Šegarić, Tomislav Gurlica and Marin Jurić, were taken to a kindergarten in Benkovac across the street from the JNA barracks.[851] During the night, more people were brought there.[852] They were interrogated by JNA soldiers.[853] The next morning, Tomislav Šegarić, Tomislav Gurlica and Marin Jurić were taken to the "communal store" in Biljani, northwest of Benkovac, where they were subjected to insults and threats all day by "Chetniks".[854] Toward the evening, they were driven back to the kindergarten; at that time the other detainees were gone.[855] On 20 November 1991, they were released a short distance from the Croat village of Pristeg.[856]

3. Detention facilities in Knin

279. There were two detention facilities in Knin, one at the barracks of the JNA 9th Corps and one at the old hospital.[857] The evidence shows that between 1991 and 1995, between 650 and 700 were detained in Knin.[858] **[page 106]**

(a) Detention at the JNA 9th Corps barracks

280. The barracks of the JNA 9th Corps is a large complex, which includes several buildings, a heliport and some warehouses.[859]

281. On 19 November 1991, Luka Brkić, Ante "Neno" Gurlica and Marin Gurlica were brought by truck to the JNA barracks in Knin by men wearing JNA uniforms.[860] While they were taken to the barracks, they were beaten and verbally abused.[861]

---

notes the evidence of Ivan Grujić that between 1991 and 1995 there were 22 prisoners detained in "Plaški-Korenica" and 5 persons detained at "Korenica", Ex. 300, p. 10. The Trial Chamber is unable to draw any conclusions based on Ivan Grujić's evidence in this respect.

848 The Indictment does not refer to detention facilities in Benkovac specifically. However, the Trial Chamber notes that the Prosecution Pre-Trial Brief (para. 50) contains a reference to detention of the non-Serb male population in Benkovac and Knin. Moreover, the Trial Chamber notes that the 65 *ter* summaries of Neven Šegarić, Tomislav Šegarić and Luka Brkić refer to detention in Benkovac. Lastly, the Trial Chamber notes that the Defence called Witness MM-096 who testified, *inter alia*, about detention in the Benkovac SJB.

849 Ex. 959, pp 1–4. Witness MM-090 testified that Šime Čačić was "taken prisoner as a prisoner of war", Witness MM-090, 4 Sep 2006, T. 7667. Immediately after their arrest, Ivan Atelj and Šime Čačić were beaten and a third person was shot in the leg. At the Benkovac SJB, Šime Čačić and Ivan Atelj were tied to a bench. They were questioned by Boško Dražić, the Chief of the Benkovac SJB, about Croatian army positions in Nadin and other places near Zadar, as well as weapons used by the Croatian army. Ivan Atelj was beaten after every question and he was also threatened with a knife to his throat. The detainees were beaten and kicked with boots, fists and wooden sticks in the face and other parts of the body. They were not allowed to wash despite their being covered in blood. Ivan Atelj named several persons as being involved in the beatings and interrogations, including Boško Dražić.

850 Ex. 959, p. 4; Ex. 529.

851 Luka Brkić, 5 Apr 2006, T. 3225–3226, 3252, 7 Apr 2006, T. 3390; Tomislav Šegarić, Ex. 826, p. 4. The Trial Chamber notes that it heard hearsay evidence that a man named Davor Lukić was detained at the barracks in Benkovac or at the Benkovac SJB, Witness MM-096, 25 Aug 2006, T. 7179–7180.

852 Tomislav Šegarić, Ex. 826, p. 4.

853 Tomislav Šegarić, Ex. 826, p. 4. Apart from the JNA soldiers, there were Serbs paramilitaries wearing different kinds of uniforms, including some with an insignia with four Cyrillic "S". Tomislav Šegarić believes that most of them were local Serbs, Tomislav Šegarić, Ex. 826, pp 4–6.

854 One person held a knife to Tomislav Šegarić's neck, Tomislav Šegarić, Ex. 826, pp 4–5.

855 Tomislav Šegarić, Ex. 826, p. 5.

856 Tomislav Šegarić, Ex. 826, p. 5.

857 Milan Babić, 20 Feb 2006, T. 1616; Ex. 8, p. 3; Mladen Lončar, 12 Jun 2006, T. 5435.

858 Ex. 300, p. 10; Ex. 008, p. 3. *See also* Mladen Lončar, 12 Jun 2006, T. 5435, Ex. 841, pp 92–93; Ex. 922, p. 15.

859 Luka Brkić, 5 Apr 2006, T. 3266–3267. *See also* Ex. 1042, Tab 2; Ex. 1043, Tab 2, DVD 4, pp 3–17.

860 Luka Brkić, 5 Apr 2006, T. 3264–3266.

861 Luka Brkić, 5 Apr 2006, T. 3264.

282. Luka Brkić was detained at various locations at the JNA barracks with between 8 and 17 people, ranging from 30 to 80 years old.[862] The detainees were severely beaten for at least twenty days.[863] The detainees did not receive medical treatment,[864] there was insufficient food and water,[865] and there were no sanitary facilities.[866]

283. Luka Brkić was also detained at the sports hall of the barracks with between 75 and 200 people, mostly Croats.[867] The detainees were occasionally severely beaten.[868] There were limited sanitary facilities and a 200-litre barrel next to the door that was used to urinate in.[869] Ratko Mladić, the then-Commander of the 9th Corps, twice visited the detainees at the sports hall.[870] Ratko Mladić taunted them, saying "if you don't do what you are told [...] your fate will be the same as the fate of the inhabitants from Škabrnja."[871] The detainees were "displayed as Ustashas" and made to "take an oath for the King and the fatherland, the Serbian fatherland".[872] **[page 107]**

284. While being detained in the JNA barracks, in addition to JNA soldiers, Luka Brkić saw soldiers wearing SAO Krajina insignia and the White Eagles ("*Beli Orlovi*") insignia.[873]

(b) Detention facility at the old hospital in Knin

285. In early 1991, a detention facility was established on the premises of the old hospital in the centre of Knin.[874] This facility was sometimes referred to as "Martić's prison" and the "District Prison".[875] A section of the hospital was used as a dormitory by "Captain Dragan's men and members of the JNA reserve force".[876] From the summer of 1991, the Ministry of Justice of the SAO Krajina took over control of the old hospital from the TO and hired professional guards.[877] On 28 September 1992, the Assembly of the RSK formally established the District Prison in Knin.[878]

286. On 2 October 1991, Stanko Erstić was arrested in Medviđa near Bruška by the *Milicija Krajine* and brought to the old hospital in Knin.[879] He was detained with another 120 prisoners, all non-Serbs from Croat

[862] Luka Brkić, 5 Apr 2006, T. 3251, 3264, 3268–3269, 3289, 7 Apr 2006, T. 3407; Ex. 286; Ex. 287. The Trial Chamber notes among others Ante "Neno" Gurlica, Marin Gurlica, a civilian named Petar Gurlica, and a man named Jero/Jere Misković, who was born 1912.

[863] Luka Brkić, 5 Apr 2006, T. 3271–3272: "In those rooms they beat us severely. I couldn't stand up. So somebody could help me stand up. If I was lying down, I couldn't stand up. If I was sitting, I couldn't get up from the chair. There was a vet who was there for 15 days. He couldn't sleep, so he helped me. For 20 days I slept standing up. If I lied down, I couldn't stand up. Everything was wet on the ground. It would freeze. So it was very difficult". Then they were taken to another location on the premises of the barracks, where they were beaten, Luka Brkić, 5 Apr 2006, T. 3267.

[864] Luka Brkić, 5 Apr 2006, T. 3269, 3272, testifying also that Jere Misković had a bad leg: "His leg was falling apart. He had thrombosis."

[865] Luka Brkić, 5 Apr 2006, T. 3270–3271, testifying that during the first three days, they did not receive any water, that the amount of drinking water they later received was limited, and that they did not have any water to wash themselves.

[866] Luka Brkić, 5 Apr 2006, T. 3270, testifying that they tore up a coat that belonged to Petar Gurlica and used it as toilet paper, that the detainees used a 30-litre bucket instead of a bathroom, and that some persons who were in a state of delirium defecated next to the door and other detainees had to clean up after them. The detained were provided with one blanket each and had to sleep on the concrete floor, *ibid.*

[867] Luka Brkić, 5 Apr 2006, T. 3272, 3274, 7 Apr 2006, T. 3430–3431.

[868] Luka Brkić, 5 Apr 2006, T. 3272, 3274–3275.

[869] Luka Brkić, 5 Apr 2006, T. 3274–3275.

[870] Luka Brkić, 5 Apr 2006, T. 3274–3275.

[871] Luka Brkić, 5 Apr 2006, T. 3275.

[872] Luka Brkić, 5 Apr 2006, T. 3264, 3267–3268.

[873] Luka Brkić, 5 Apr 2006, T. 3243–3244, 3273, 7 Apr 2006, T. 3407. Later on, Luka Brkić heard that "there were all sorts of people there; Martić's men and others", *id.* at T. 3407.

[874] Witness MM-090, 29 Aug 2006, T. 7382–7383, 30 Aug 2006, T. 7428–7429; Luka Brkić, 5 Apr 2006, T. 3277, 3283. The establishment took several months, Witness MM-090, 29 Aug 2006, T. 7381. *See also* Ex. 1042, Tab 2; Ex. 1043, Tab 2, DVD 3, pp 20–67 and DVD 4, pp 1–3.

[875] Luka Brkić, 5 Apr 2006, T. 3276–3277, 7 Apr 2006, T. 3408; Witness MM-90, 30 Aug 2006, T. 7428; Stevo Plejo, 20 Sep 2006, T. 8724.

[876] Stanko Erstić, Ex. 392, T. 24972; Stevo Plejo, 22 Sep 2006, T. 8900.

[877] Stevo Plejo, 20 Sep 2006, T. 8725; Witness MM-090, 4 Sep 2006, T. 7658–7659; Milan Babić, 20 Feb 2006, T. 1612–1613. *See also* Ex. 906. As of 17 August 1991, a total of 15 people were employed at the old hospital, Ex. 906, pp 10–19. By October 1992, approximately 30 people were listed as employees of the prison, Ex. 903. The 15 people who started work on 17 August 1991 were all still employed at that time, Ex. 923, pp 1–2, 7.

[878] Ex. 906, pp 10–19; Ex. 923, pp 1–2.

[879] Stanko Erstić, 26 Apr 2006, T. 3873, 3875–3877; Ex. 396, p. 3.

or mixed villages in the Krajina region.[880] Except for 20 members of the ZNG who had been captured during the fighting in Kijevo, all detainees were Croat civilians.[881] He was detained in a room with approximately 12 people.[882] In his view, "all the guards were paramilitary and part of 'Martić's militia'".[883] He testified to haing seen Ratko Mladić at the old hospital.[884] On 2 November, Stanko Erstić and approximately 100 non-Serb prisoners were exchanged for approximately 60 Serb prisoners.[885] Twenty Croats from Lika remained in the prison.[886] Members of "Special Military Police Unit", dressed in JNA uniforms, took them to the **[page 108]** JNA barracks in Knin, where they were loaded onto buses. Afterwards they were driven to Pakovo Selo where buses from the Croatian side picked them up.[887]

287. Luka Brkić was brought to the old hospital from the JNA barracks in Knin.[888] In his opinion, "it was the police or the army who operated there."[889] He also saw another 30 prisoners brought to the old hospital the day he arrived.[890] Luka Brkić was detained in a small room together with nine people.[891] After approximately 12 days, he was transferred to the ground floor of another wing of the old hospital, which was under the control of the JNA. There, he joined the people who had initially been detained with him at the JNA 9th Corps barracks.[892]

288. The detainees were threatened and beaten every day for long periods, often by several guards at a time using rifle butts, truncheons, and wooden staves.[893] The detainees were interrogated and also beaten by shift commanders.[894] The detainees also had cocked revolvers pressed against their temples, were beaten on their kidneys until they were swollen, and were denied the use of toilet facilities.[895] They were forced to drink urine and to clean toilets with their bare hands.[896] They had their heads forced into toilets.[897] They also had their personal belongings stolen.[898] There is evidence of sexual abuse of some detainees[899] and that detainees were subjected to sleep deprivation.[900] There was insufficient food.[901] The detainees were verbally abused by the guards, who said things like "the Croatian nation has to be destroyed", "all Croats have to be killed; Split and Zadar are burning, Šibenik will burn as well".[902] On one occasion, Vojislav Šešelj visited the old hospital and insulted the detainees, asking them "how many Serbian children they slaughtered, how many mothers".[903] **[page 109]**

---

880 Stanko Erstić, 26 Apr 2006, T. 3874; Stanko Erstić, Ex. 396, p. 4; Stanko Erstić, Ex. 392, T. 24996–24997.

881 Stanko Erstić, Ex. 396, p. 4; Stanko Erstić, Ex. 392, T. 24996. After the establishment of the Prisoner Exchange Commission, the JNA would bring prisoners of war to be temporarily held at the old hospital until the time of their exchange, Witness MM-090, 4 Sep 2006, T. 7674-7675. Ivan Atelj shared his cell with Denis Drča, a Serb who was beaten and accused of being a "Serbian traitor", Ex. 959, p. 5.

882 Stanko Erstić, Ex. 392, T. 24980.

883 Stanko Erstić, Ex. 396, p. 3.

884 Stanko Erstić, Ex. 396, p. 3; Stanko Erstić, Ex. 392, T. 24972.

885 Stanko Erstić, 26 Apr 2006, T. 3874–3875, Ex. 392, T. 24973; Ex. 959, pp 4–5. The Trial Chamber notes that Stevo Plejo has disputed the veracity of this document, Stevo Plejo, 22 Sep 2006, T. 8884. The Trial Chamber notes that this document contains an Official Note which was written on 3 May 1992 and that much of the information therein is corroborated by other evidence.

886 Stanko Erstić, Ex. 392, T. 24982.

887 Stanko Erstić, Ex. 392, T. 24972–24973, 26 Apr 2006, T. 3874–3875.

888 Luka Brkić, 5 Apr 2006, T. 3252, 3266, 3276–3277, 7 Apr 2006, T. 3390, 3408.

889 Luka Brkić, 7 Apr 2006, T. 3439.

890 Luka Brkić, 5 Apr 2006, T. 3279–3280, 3285. *See also* Ex. 518, p. 4; Ex. 286.

891 Luka Brkić, 5 Apr 2006, T. 3279, 7 Apr 2006, T. 3438.

892 Luka Brkić, 5 Apr 2006, T. 3282–3283.

893 Stanko Erstić, Ex. 392, T. 24971, 24980, 24983; Ex. 959, p. 5. Luka Brkić, 5 Apr 2006, T. 3280–3281, testifying that he was dragged into the hallway several times, where he was beaten by four or five men and that the beatings became more frequent as it became known that the detainees were going to be exchanged.

894 Ex. 959, p. 5. *See also* Ex. 919, under number 209 H; Ex. 286, p. 1; Ex. 287, p. 1.

895 Ex. 984, pp 23–24.

896 Ex. 984, pp 23–24.

897 Ex. 984, pp 23–24.

898 Ex. 984, pp 23–24.

899 Former detainees reported that detainees were sexually abused through forced mutual oral sex or oral sex with prison guards, and mutual masturbation, Ex. 984, p. 24. *See also* Luka Brkić 5 Apr 2006, T. 3283, testifying that he heard that there had been attempts to rape men in the room next to his.

900 Ex. 392, T. 24980, 24983; Ex. 959, p. 5; Ex. 984, pp 23–24.

901 Stanko Erstić, Ex. 392, T. 24980, 24983; Ex. 959, p. 5; Ex. 984, p. 23–24 (reporting that detainees had inadequate food, being fed only three eggs a day and that one former detainee lost over twenty kilograms during his detention).

902 Stanko Erstić, Ex. 396, p. 4.

903 Ex. 959, p. 7.

289. "Martić's police", wearing blue uniforms, carried out beatings together with people in camouflage uniforms.[904] Ivan Atelj, who was also detained and beaten at the old hospital, stated that while Stevo Plejo and Jovica Novaković were in charge of the old hospital prison, they "allowed beatings of prisoners by civilians, Serbian prisoners, 'Martić's Special Forces members' and all others who wanted to beat them."[905]

290. From his mistreatment in detention, Luka Brkić sustained permanent injuries to his stomach and contracted Hepatitis B. He is still receiving medical treatment.[906] Stanko Erstić sustained two broken ribs and one cracked rib, while Ivan Atelj sustained three broken ribs and injuries to his spine.[907]

291. On at least one occasion the leadership of the prison was informed that detainees had been mistreated by guards. Disciplinary measures were taken against the responsible guards.[908] However, the guards were not removed from the prison but were only suspended and reinstated later.[909]

292. The International Committee of the Red Cross ("ICRC") was allowed to visit the detainees at the old hospital.[910] During the visits, some prisoners did not dare to tell the ICRC representatives that they were being beaten, for fear of being "really beaten up". The detainees who had been badly beaten and seriously injured were transferred to other rooms where the ICRC representatives could not visit them.[911]

293. As of August 1991, any detainee held at the old hospital was supposed to be detained on the basis of a decision by a judge.[912] There is no evidence that Luka Brkić or Stanko Erstić were ever charged with any crime or that they were brought before a judge or military panel to assess the legality of their detention. However, Ivan Atelj stated that he was charged and that the indictment **[page 110]** was presented to him verbally, but he was not brought before a judge.[913] Denis Drča, the Serb cell-mate of Ivan Atelj, was released on 11 February 1992, by a decision of the Knin District Court.[914] Out of approximately 300 detainees at the old hospital between mid-1991 and mid-1992, only 13 people were released upon the decision of a court.[915]

294. In October 1991, Milan Martić was seen in the prison wearing a camouflage uniform with the insignia of the *Milicija Krajine*.[916]

F. Crimes of deportation and forcible transfer

295. In addition to evidence of displacement of the Croat population in the SAO Krajina and RSK discussed above, the Trial Chamber notes the following evidence concerning deportation and forcible transfer.[917]

---

904 Luka Brkić, 5 Apr 2006, T. 3280–3283, also testifying that a member of the "Martić's police" was the most violent during the beatings. Luka Brkić knew some of the members of the "Martić's police". He specifically mentions the "Grahovac brothers from Smiljčići", Djuro from Plavno and Momir Čupač, *ibid.* The Trial Chamber further notes that a Kazimir Graovac from Smiljčići is listed on Ex. 906, Employee list old hospital May 1993, p. 13. The Trial Chamber notes that Momo Čupač and Kazimir Grahovac are mentioned as guards at the prison by Ivan Atelj, Ex. 959, p. 6.

905 Ex. 959, p. 5. Although Stevo Plejo testified that as soon as professional guards started working in the old hospital, they were able to prevent anyone entering the prison, Stevo Plejo, 21 Sep 2006, T. 8811. The Trial Chamber does not find this piece of testimony credible in light of the surrounding evidence. *See also* Luka Brkić, 5 Apr 2006, T. 3280–3281, testifying that people came from outside of the old hospital to beat detainees.

906 Luka Brkić, 5 Apr 2006, T. 3291.

907 Stanko Erstić, Ex. 392, T. 24971; Ex. 959, p. 5.

908 Witness MM-090, 29 Aug 2006, T. 7386–7387, 30 Aug 2006, T. 7432; Stevo Plejo, 20 Sep 2006, T. 8735–8737.

909 Stevo Plejo, 22 Sep 2006, T. 8849–8850. Stevo Plejo testified that he had asked Risto Matković, the then-Minister of Justice, to replace Jovica Novaković because Novaković had been present when guards were "slapping [prisoners] about in his presence" and had done nothing about that. Jovica Novaković was suspended and later reinstated in a lower position. Stevo Plejo, 20 Sep 2006, T. 8730–8733, 8742; Ex. 905; Ex. 923.

910 Stanko Erstić, Ex. 392, T. 24981; Stevo Plejo, 20 Sep 2006, T. 8737–8738; Witness MM-090, 29 Aug 2006, T. 7386–7387.

911 Stanko Erstić, Ex. 392, T. 24981, 25000.

912 Witness MM-090, 4 Sep 2006, T. 7674–7675.

913 Ex. 959, p. 7.

914 Ex. 919, under no. 240 S.

915 Ex. 919, also providing that one detainee was handed over to the Military Police on orders of the Public Prosecutor, *ibid.*, under nr. 202 S. *See also* Ex. 895, pp 10–11, a Human Rights Watch Report, according to which in August 1991 the Knin prison held 51 prisoners to be exchanged and none of whom had been charged or provided with a defence attorney.

916 Stanko Erstić, 26 Apr 2006, T. 3869–3870. In this respect, the Trial Chamber recalls the evidence that on 12 December 1991, a meeting was held between Milan Martić and chiefs of SJBs during which it was mentioned that in "Krajina prisons in Korenica, Glina, Vrgin Most, Slunj and Knin" there were 128 persons detained, mostly members of the ZNG and the Croatian MUP, Ex. 518, p. 4 (report signed by Milan Martić).

917 *See supra* paras 167, 177, 180, 186, 189, 202, 209, 212, 222, 228, 236–237, 239, 242.

296. Beginning in 1990, Croat businesses and properties were blown up in Knin and there was constant pressure on the local Croat population.[918] From around April 1991, discriminatory policies were applied against Croats, and Croat houses in the Knin area were searched for weapons.[919] Following the fighting in the Hrvatska Kostajnica, Knin and Glina areas in August 1991, Croat civilians began to leave their homes to go to Zagreb, Sisak and other places.[920]

297. Due to the situation prevailing in the Knin area, the Croat population began to fear for their safety and began requesting authorisation from the RSK authorities to leave the RSK territory.[921] The insecurity of the Croats was also aggravated by speeches of Milan Martić on the radio that he could not guarantee their safety, particularly in the area of Knin.[922] As a result, in the period between 1992 and 1993 the RSK police directed the Croat population towards Croat settlements **[page 111]** near Knin, such as Vrpolje and Kninsko Polje.[923] In Vrpolje, which was five kilometres north of Knin, a cultural centre was used as a gathering point for Croats, who had requested authorisation to leave the RSK.[924] The Knin police secured the area at the cultural centre.[925] The conditions there were poor and the Croats were not free to leave but had to wait for an agreement to be reached between the RSK Government, international organisations and the Croatian authorities before they could be transferred.[926] The police from Knin organised and escorted bus convoys from Vrpolje to Šibenik and across Lika to Karlobag.[927]

298. A decision on the conditions upon which Croats and other nationalities could return to the RSK was adopted by the RSK government on 21 April 1992.[928] However, in September 1992, UNPROFOR reported that "it might be unrealistic to carry out any return [of displaced persons] in the forthcoming future" due to the likelihood of hostile acts being carried out against returning Croats.[929]

299. There is considerable evidence that similar displacement of the Croat population as a result of harassment and intimidation occurred elsewhere in the SAO Krajina, and subsequently RSK, territory and continued until the end of 1994.[930] The evidence shows that harrassment and **[page 112]** intimidation of the Croat population was

---

918 Witness MM-078, 24 May 2006, T. 4461–4462.

919 Milan Babić, 16 Feb 2006, T. 1418; Witness MM-078, 24 May 2006, T. 4461–4462, 25 May 2006, T. 4521; *See also* Witness MM-096, 24 Aug 2006, T. 7067, 7072–7073.

920 Nikola Dobrijević, 13 Nov 2006, T. 10977; Ex. 1017 (providing that in August 1991 there were 650 displaced people in Zagreb who were mostly from Glina and Knin, that most people from Glina had gone to Velica Gorica, that all of Kostajnica had been "evacuated" and some 2,500 had fled to Bosanski Novi and to Zagreb). *See also* Milan Babić, 17 Feb 2006, T. 1572–1574, 20 Feb 2006, T. 1598.

921 Witness MM-117, 13 Oct 2006, T. 9399.

922 Witness MM-078, 25 May 2006, T. 4518.

923 Milan Babić, 20 Feb 2006, T. 1646–1647; Ex. 897 (providing that "local Milicija" guarded residents of the village of Vrpolje, who had been forced to leave their homes and that the Milicija had three buses to transport the Croats to territories under Croatian control but that this had not been done as confirmation had not been received that the Croatian side was ready to receive them). *See also* Witness MM-096, 25 Aug 2006, T. 7153.

924 Milan Babić, 20 Feb 2006, T. 1647; MM-078, 24 May 2006, T. 4460–4461. Croats would travel to Vrpolje in their own vehicles and were accommodated at the cultural centre for up to three days, Witness MM-078, 24 May 2006, T. 4460–4461, 25 May 2006, T. 4545–4546, 4468; Ex. 729 (providing that Vrpolje was a "safe haven" for the Croats). *See also* Ex. 1042, Tab 2; Ex. 1043, Tab 2, DVD 4, pp 27–31; Ex. 1044.

925 Witness MM-078, 25 May 2006, T. 4465, 4519–4520 (also testifying that the police assisted the Croats in leaving the RSK, *ibid.*, T. 4465). *See also* Witness MM-117, 13 Oct 2006, T. 9399.

926 Witness MM-078, 25 May 2006, T. 4468 (testifying that the Croats were provided with blankets and only small quantities of food).

927 Witness MM-078, 25 May 2006, T. 4468.

928 Ex. 758; Charles Kirudja, 31 May 2006, T. 4872–4873.

929 Ex. 731, p. 3.

930 Witness MM-078, 24 May 2006, T. 4460–4461, 25 May 2006, T. 4466; Witness MM-096, 22 Aug 2006, T. 6914–6917 (testifying that Croats, who were afraid for their lives, were put up in schools and other public buildings in Benkovac by the municipality Crisis Staff which organised a convoy that was escorted by the RSK police until the confrontation line in Zemunik); Milan Babić, 20 Feb 2006, T. 1598; Ex. 551, p. 1 (providing that by April 1992 there were almost no Croats left in Glina); Ex. 726 (listing in summary form 497 crimes committed against the Croat population in Sector South and reporting on five instances of forced evictions of Croats and subsequent transfer to Croatia of one of the victims); Ex. 729, p. 1 (providing that over 100 Croats had left their homes in the Medvida area and were living in caves, fields and forests, that around 50 Croats had filed requests with the civil police in Drniš to leave); Ex. 736 (providing that 10 Croats were transferred from Medvida to the Croat side on 2 October 1992, that 16 Croats were transferred to the Croat side on 16 October 1992 from Medviđa Kruševo and Obrovac and that during one month 155 applications to leave the RSK territory had been received in Benkovac); Ex. 761 (reporting on the expulsion of 5 Croats from Ličko Petrovo Selo, dated 16 July 1992, *see also* Charles Kirudja, 31 May 2006, T. 4879–4880); Ex. 762, p. 3 (reporting the expulsion by "a

carried out on a large scale by the police and by local Serbs in the territory.[931] On 14 June 1993, Milan Martić met with Cedric Thornberry, the UNPROFOR Director of Civil Affairs, concerning, *inter alia*, the issue of Croats who wanted to leave the RSK. During the meeting, Milan Martić requested that Croats who wished to leave the RSK sign statements that no one had put pressure on them to leave and that these statements bear the signature of either Cedric Thornberry or another United Nations representative. Cedric Thornberry agreed to these requests.[932]

300. The RSK authorities cooperated with the authorities in Bosanski Novi, BiH, regarding the displacement of the non-Serb population from that municipality.[933] There is evidence that the RSK MUP was to be involved in providing security for an organised "safe departure" of Muslims and other non-Serbs in the direction of Croatia, Slovenia, Austria, and Germany in July 1992.[934]

301. In June 1993, the RSK population was 433,595 citizens, the ethnic break-down of which was 92% Serbs, 7% Croats and 2% others.[935] The Prosecution expert Ivan Grujić testified that 220,338 persons of non-Serb ethnicity were forcibly expelled "in the aggression against the Republic of Croatia".[936] Ivan Grujić was unable to explain with certainty how many of these persons were expelled from the territories which comprised the SAO Krajina and later the RSK.[937] The Trial Chamber therefore finds that it cannot rely on the evidence of Ivan Grujić to determine **[page 113]** the exact number of persons of Croat and other non-Serb ethnicities who left the territory of the SAO Krajina and RSK during the period of the Indictment.

G. Attacks on Zagreb on 2 and 3 May 1995

1. "Operation Flash"

302. In the early morning hours of 1 May 1995, armed forces of Croatia launched a military offensive known as Operation Flash.[938] The Trial Chamber has been provided conflicting evidence as to the purpose of

group of uniformed persons" of 12 Croats from the village Korana in the municipality of Korenica, *see also* Charles Kirudja, 31 May 2006, T. 4882–4883); Ex. 865, p. 25 (reporting that before being granted permission to leave Sector South the Croats were forced to sign a statement that their departure was voluntary); Ex. 971, p. 3 (providing that 16 persons from Podlapac had expressed a wish to be transferred to Croatia); Ex. 985, pp 4–5 (reporting that Croat families were gathered from their houses and transported by bus to areas outside the UNPAs). *See also* Ex. 75, p. 5 (reporting that the non-Serb population in Sector North was "very small").

931 Witness MM-079, 3 Apr 2006, T. 3111 (testifying that "[s]everal people said that Martić's policemen went door-to-door telling people to leave Knin, that is the SAO Krajina"); John McElligott, 26 May 2006, T. 4581, 4614–4615; Ex. 728, p. 3 (providing also that in the month of October 1992 five Croats were murdered and that houses vacated by Croats have been burned down); Ex. 731 (reporting that "the Serb side" is building up a climate of threat and fear of aggression out of ongoing incidents, that the "[Militia] is expanding ethnic cleansing systematically", and that the "Serb side" warned against returning Croats without RSK consent because "the recent acts against Croatians here can be considered as indication of what would happen on larger scale"); Ex. 732 (listing incidents of murder, destruction and intimidation of Croats in the Benkovac, Borovac, and Knin areas by the local police); Ex. 734 (letter reporting on beating and robbing of elderly and helpless people in the Vrlika area by members of the "Militia"); Ex. 736 (listing a number of incidents of violence, including murders, theft and destruction, aimed at Croats in Korenica, Zaluznica, Knin, Vrlika, Benkovac); Ex. 738 (providing that many Croats wanted to leave the UNPA due to not feeling safe); Ex. 757, p. 3 (providing that in Sector North by July 1992 about 22,000 Croats were listed as "Missing/Displaced"). *See also* Ex. 75; Ex. 866; Ex. 985.

932 Ex. 965, p. 8.

933 Ex. 752; Ex. 753; Ex. 754; Ex. 755; Ex. 756; Ex. 757, p. 7. Charles Kirudja testified that during the first organised convoy directed to Croatia, up to 8,000 Bosnian Muslims were expelled. He explained that the Muslims were not leaving voluntarily, Charles Kirudja, 31 May 2006, T. 4849, 4857–4863, 4871.

934 Ex. 754.

935 Ex. 178, ERN 0113-2359. This is further broken down by area (Eastern Slavonia, Western Srem and Baranja: 95% Serbs, 4% Croats, 1% others, Banija: 97% Serbs, 2% Croats, 1% others, Kordun: 98% Serbs, 2% Croats, Lika: 93% Serbs, 5% Croats, 2% others, Northern Dalmatia: 90% Serbs, 10% Croats, and Western Slavonia: 73% Serbs, 25% Croats, 2% others), *see* ERN 0113-2360. Witness MM-096 testified that by 1994 "quite a lot of inhabitants had left the territory of the RSK", 25 Aug 2006, T. 7139. *See also* Witness MM-090, 4 Sep 2006, T. 7703–7704.

936 Ex. 291, pp 18–19.

937 Ivan Grujić, 12 Apr 2006, T. 3597, testifying that he provided the Trial Chamber "with numbers that apply to the existing, current division into counties [in Croatia]" and "basically it covers [the SAO Krajina] municipalities as well. Counties were partly occupied, and the people recorded as expelled were expelled solely from these occupied territories."

938 Veljko Džakula, 16 Jan 2006, T. 381; Milan Babić, 21 Feb 2006, T. 1659; Peter Galbraith, 25 Apr 2006, T. 3805–3806; Mile Dakić, 26 Oct 2006, T. 10082.

this operation. There is evidence that the purpose was to take control over Western Slavonia (Sector West).[939] There is evidence that the operation was Croatia's response to Milan Martić's decision to close the Zagreb-Belgrade motorway.[940] There is also evidence that Croatia planned its attack long before the closure.[941] Two Croatian guard brigades, one regular HV brigade, and special police forces were involved in the operation.[942] Negotiations to find a peaceful settlement took place during the operation,[943] and agreements were reached on 3 May 1995.[944] Operation Flash ended around 4 May 1995 with the RSK losing control over Western Slavonia.[945] A large part of the Serb population fled the area of Western Slavonia.[946] **[page 114]**

2. Shelling of Zagreb

(a) 1 May 1995 – Preparation for attack

303. On 1 May 1995, a meeting was held between, *inter alia*, Milan Martić, the Chief of the SVK Main Staff General Milan Čeleketić, the Prime Minister and ministers of the RSK government. The meeting concerned the proposal of the Supreme Defence Council to deal with the situation which had arisen in Western Slavonia resulting from Operation Flash during the morning that day. The evidence shows that both peaceful solutions, involving negotiations and a surrender of parts of Western Slavonia, and non-peaceful solutions were discussed and that Milan Martić, Milan Čeleketić and the most senior officers of the SVK Main Staff were in favour of the latter.[947] At 1300 hours on 1 May 1995, Milan Čeleketić, in the presence of *inter alia* Milan Martić, ordered artillery fire on Sisak, south-east of Zagreb.[948] The evidence shows that the reason for the attack was "to retaliate against the HV who had carried out an aggression on the Western Slavonia."[949] Artillery fire was opened at 1700 on 1 May 1995.[950]

---

939 Peter Galbraith, 25 Apr 2006, T. 3805-3806; Mile Dakić, 25 Oct 2006, T. 10058. *See also* Ex. 99, p. 6.

940 Milan Babić, 21 Feb 2006, T. 1660–1661; Peter Galbraith, 25 Apr 2006, T. 3805–3806; Ex. 933, p. 5. On 28 April 1995, a Serb was killed at one of the rest areas on the motorway just outside Sector West, and in retaliation local Serbs fired on motorists inside that Sector and Milan Martić decided to close down the motorway. Peter Galbraith, 25 Apr 2006, T. 3805–3806; Mile Dakić, 25 Oct 2006, T. 10058; Ex. 933, p. 2; Ex. 99, p. 4. Milan Babić stated that during negotiations it was already agreed that the motorway would be reopened, but Milan Martić discarded that possibility and said he would not allow that to happen, Milan Babić, 21 Feb 2006, T. 1667. Documentary evidence presented to the Trial Chamber corroborated Milan Martić's refusal to open the motorway even though it was ready to be reopened, Ex. 789, p. 5; Ex. 233, intercepted telephone conversation, p. 5 (Ex. 789 and Ex. 233 are the same intercepted conversation); Ex. 99, p. 5.

941 In his book titled "All My Battles", Janko Bobetko, Chief of the Main Staff of the Croatian Army during Operation Flash, wrote that the initial operation was planned on 5 December 1994 and completed on 4 May 1995 as part of the overall plan of preparations for the final operations by the Croatian Army of what would later become "Operation Storm", Ex. 931, pp 8, 9–12, 17; Slobodan Perić, 6 Sep 2006, T. 7846–7847, 7849. *See also* Ex. 933, p. 27; Ex. 934, pp 1–3. The Croatian military command warned UNPROFOR in advance about the Operation, during the morning of 1 May 1995, Reynaud Theunens, 3 Feb 2006, T. 1087; Slobodan Perić, 6 Sep 2006, T. 7845; Ex. 930.

942 Reynaud Theunens, 3 Feb 2006, T. 1081.

943 Witness MM-117, 13 Oct 2006, T. 9402–9403. The Serb delegation asked for a cessation of hostilities to become effective immediately at midnight on 1 May 1995, but this was rejected by the Croatian side, Witness MM-117, 13 Oct 2006, T. 9406.

944 On 3 May 1995, members of the international community met in Knin to agree on the text of the agreement which was accepted by both the Serbs and the Croats that same day, Witness MM-117, 13 Oct 2006, T. 9408–9409. It was agreed that military activities would cease and thereafter UNPROFOR forces would be in a position to act in the area, Witness MM-117, 17 Oct 2006, T. 9596. On 3 May the Serbian delegation in Geneva accepted the entire offer of the international community for the resolution of the crisis in the relations between the Republic of the Serbian Krajina and Croatia, Witness MM-117, 18 Oct 2006, T. 9650–9651. *See also* Ex. 112; Ex. 935.

945 Milan Babić, 21 Feb, 2006, T. 1660–1661; Veljko Džakula, 18 Jan 2006, T. 568; Peter Galbraith, 25 Apr 2006, T. 3820; Slobodan Perić, 6 Sep 2006, T. 7848. *See also* Ex. 99, p. 14; Ex. 112.

946 Witness MM-117, 13 Oct 2006, T. 9401–9402; Reynaud Theunens, 3 Feb 2006, T. 1097; Ex. 99, p. 14. According to Witness MM-003 the entire Serb population was expelled from Western Slavonia, Witness MM-003, 10 Mar 2006, T. 2170–2171. Slobodan Perić stated that 20,000 people left the area, Slobodan Perić, 6 Sep 2006, T. 7866. *See also* Veljko Džakula, 18 Jan 2006, T. 571–572 (testifying that there were about 1,250 victims); Ivan Grujić, 12 Apr 2006, T. 3633 (that 168 persons were killed during Operation Flash); Rade Rašeta, 3 May 2006, T. 3970–3971 (testifying that there were about 100 victims); Slobodan Perić, 6 Sep 2006, T. 7866, 7 Sep 2006, T. 7947–7948 (testifying that the number of identified victims was 284, including 77 elderly, 30 women and 10 children but that the total number of killed during Operation Flash was 1,200).

947 Rade Rašeta, 2 May 2006, T. 3932–3933, 3940; Ex. 95.

948 Rade Rašeta, 2 May 2006, T. 3930–3931; Ex. 93 provides that "members of the Supreme Defence Council" were present when the order was given. However, Rade Rašeta, who was present, testified that it was a meeting of Milan Čeleketić and his closest associates, his "collegium", Rade Rašeta, 2 May 2006, T. 3930. Milan Čeleketić was appointed Commander of the Main Staff of the SVK by Milan Martić on 22 February 1994, Ex. 80; Ex. 83.

949 Ex. 93.

950 Ex. 93.

304. On 1 May 1995, Milan Čeleketić ordered the M-87 Orkan unit of the SVK to "be alert and ready for engagement on [his] order" and directed them to march from the Knin area to take up positions in Vojnić, 50 kilometres south of Zagreb, by 1400 hours that day.[951]

(b) 2 May 1995

305. In the mid-morning on 2 May 1995,[952] without warning,[953] Orkan rockets hit Zagreb.[954] Rockets struck the centre of the city, including: Strossmayer Square, Matica Hrvatska Street, **[page 115]** Petrinjska Street, Boškovićeva Street and Mrazovićeva Street as well as Draškovićeva Street, the intersection of Vlaška and Draškovićeva Streets and a school building in Križanićeva Street, the village of Plešo near Zagreb/Plešo airport,[955] and the airport itself.[956]

306. Five persons were killed during these rocket attacks. The body of Damir Dračić was found lying on the sidewalk at Vlaška Street.[957] Ana Mutevelić was killed when a tram was hit at the intersection of Draškovićeva and Vlaška Streets.[958] The body of Stjepan Krhen was found in the courtyard of No. 41 Vlaška Street.[959] Ivanka Kovač died at the trauma clinic in Draškoviceva Street from the injuries she sustained some 700 metres from the hospital.[960] Ivan Brodar was injured on Draškovićeva Street and died as a result of his injuries on 3 May 1995.[961]

307. A number of witnesses, who were injured during the shelling of Zagreb on 2 May 1995, testified before the Trial Chamber, many of whom still suffer from the injuries sustained on that day. Sanja Buntić was injured in Strossmayer Square.[962] She received injuries to her head and legs.[963] Aleksandra Szekely was

---

951 Ex. 92. The M-87 Orkan is a self-propelled long-range multiple rocket launching system, Ex. 7, p. 38; Jožef Poje, 6 Jun 2006, T. 5123. *See infra* section IV B 4 (b). In 1995, the Orkan rocket launchers were subordinated to Commander Lieutenant General Čeleketić, as Chief of the Main Staff of the SVK, Rade Rašeta, 2 May 2006, T. 3935; Jožef Poje, 6 Jun 2006, T. 5110–5111. The evidence also shows that the use of the Orkan was subject to the approval of the commander of the Main Staff of the SVK, Jožef Poje, 6 Jun 2006, T. 5112–5113; Ex. 781, p. 11, p. 25; Ex. 780, p. 13; Ex. 7, pp 62–63.

952 Peter Galbraith, 25 Apr 2006, T. 3769; Branko Lazarević, 14 Jun 2006, T. 5624; Aleksandra Szekely, Ex. 824, p. 2.

953 Branko Lazarević, 14 Jun 2006, T. 5623, 15 Jun 2006, T. 5715; Peter Galbraith, 25 Apr 2006, T. 3762; Sanja Risović, 14 Jun 2006, T. 5577; Rašeljka Grmoja, 19 Jun 2006, T. 5784; Mina Žunac, 20 Jun 2006, T. 5810–5811.

954 Ex. 95, p. 3, wherein on 2 May 1995, Rade Rašeta informed his counterparts in the VJ that the SVK fired eight rockets from "an *Orkan* multiple rocket launcher on the *Banski Dvori/* Presidential Palace/, the Ministry of Defence and *Pleso* airport"; Ex. 303; Ex. 94, p. 2, indicating that on 2 May 1995 UNPROFOR heard 5 rockets being fired from Glina and it was assessed that these were the Orkans which impacted in Zagreb.

955 Branko Lazarević, 15 Jun 2006, T. 5656–5657, 14 Jun 2006, T. 5629; Ivan Mikulčić, 14 Jun 2006, T. 5598, 5617–5618; Ex. 805; Ex. 1043, T. 3–11. Plešo village is around 500 meters from Zagreb/Plešo Airport, Ivan Mikulčić, 14 Jun 2006, T. 5597, 5608. *See also* Ex. 1042, Tab 2; Ex. 1043, Tab 2, DVD 1, pp 3–11, pp 12–16, pp 18–31.

956 Branko Lazarević, 14 Jun 2006, T. 5629. The Trial Chamber heard testimony that while the official name of the airport was "Zagreb" it was locally referred to as "Plešo", Ivan Mikulčić, 14 Jun 2006, T. 5607. Ex. 810 shows the damage inside the perimeter of Zagreb/Plešo Airport. *See also* Ex. 1042, Tab 2; Ex. 1043, Tab 2, DVD 1, pp 1–2.

957 Ex. 805, Plan 2, No. 2. *See also* Ex. 799, p. 46, p. 81; Branko Lazarević, 14 Jun 2006, T. 5634, 15 Jun 2006, T. 5700. His injuries were sustained while he was in his car, Ex. 805, Plan 2, marked with a number 3; Branko Lazarević, 15 Jun 2006, T. 5666–5667. An exhibit shows the body of Damir Dračić, Ex. 386, F-53 and F-54; Branko Lazarević, 15 Jun 2006, T. 5673–5674. *See also* Ex. 383, at 8 min. 8 sec.; Branko Lazarević, 14 Jun 2006, T. 5627.

958 Branko Lazarević, 15 Jun 2006, T. 5658. Ana Mutevelić was killed while on a tram, Branko Lazarević, 14 Jun 2006, T. 5634. *See also* Ex. 799, p. 81; Branko Lazarević, 15 Jun 2006, T. 5700. Ex. 805, Plan 2, marked with a number 1, indicates the location where the body of Ana Mutevelić was found, Branko Lazarević, 15 Jun 2006, T. 5666. Ex. 386, F-35 and F-36 show her body, Branko Lazarević, 14 Jun 2006, T. 5626, 15 Jun 2006, T. 5671. *See also* Ex. 383 at 7 min. 41 sec; Ex. 804, at the location marked in the map as number 1, Branko Lazarević, 15 Jun 2006, T. 5658. Ex. 386, F-1 shows Draškovićeva St., Mina Žunac, 20 Jun 2006, T. 5825. Ex. 386, F-30 shows the intersection of Vlaška and Draškovićeva streets, Mina Žunac, 20 Jun 2006, T. 5825.

959 Ex. 805, Plan 2, No. 3 marks the site where Stjepan Krhen was found during the on-site investigation, Branko Lazarević, 15 Jun 2006, T. 5667. *See also* Ex. 799, p. 81; Branko Lazarević, 15 Jun 2006, T. 5700. Stjepan Krhen had sustained several injuries on his body, on his chest, and on his legs, and had succumbed to his wounds "immediately", Branko Lazarević, 14 Jun 2006, T. 5634–5635; Ex. 799, p. 47. Ex. 386, F-98 and F-99 show Stjepan Krhen, Branko Lazarević, 15 Jun 2006, T. 5674.

960 Branko Lazarević, 14 Jun 2006, T. 5635. *See also* Ex. 799, p. 81; Branko Lazarević, 15 Jun 2006, T. 5700. The cause of her death is indicated as "[e]xplosive wounds of the head, of the body, and the extremities", Ex. 800; Branko Lazarević, 14 Jun 2006, T. 5639–5640.

961 Branko Lazarević, 14 Jun 2006, T. 5638–5639, 5641. He was aged 77 at the time of the shelling, and suffered multiple traumas of the head, chest, and lower extremities, Branko Lazarević, 14 Jun 2006, T. 5638–5639. *See also* Ex. 799, p. 71; Branko Lazarević, 14 Jun 2006, T. 5640–5641; Ex. 801.

962 Sanja Buntić, 19 Jun 2006, T. 5761–5763.

963 She received injuries to the upper part of both her legs from shrapnel and pellets, as well as two pellets which lodged in her head, one hitting the bone causing a splinter fracture, Sanja Buntić, 19 Jun 2006, T. 5776–5777. She still has pieces of shrapnel in

injured while waiting at the intersection of Boškovićeva-**[page 116]** Petrinjska, and received injuries to the left side of her body and her left leg.[964] Mina Žunac was injured in Vlaška Street.[965] She received injuries to her leg, hip, hand and head.[966] Rašeljka Grmoja was 17 years old at the time of the rocket attack on Zagreb and was in her school in Križanićeva Street[967] when she was injured in her shoulder and eye.[968] Ivan Mikulčić was injured at his house in Plešo village near Zagreb on 2 May 1995,[969] and received injuries in his back.[970] There is evidence that in total 160 people were injured during the attack on 2 May 1995.[971]

308. The Trial Chamber finds that as a result of the shelling on 2 May 1995, Ana Mutevelić, Damir Dračić, Stjepan Krhen, Ivanka Kovač and Ivan Brodar were killed, and at least 160 people were injured.

(c) 3 May 1995

309. At midday on 3 May 1995,[972] Zagreb was again shelled by Orkan rockets[973] on the following locations: Mažuranićeva Square, Marshall Tito Square where the Croatian National Theatre was located, and Klaićeva Street Children's Hospital.[974] **[page 117]**

310. Two people were killed in this attack. Luka Skračić was injured on 3 May 1995, and died in hospital on 6 June 1995.[975] Ivan Markulin, a bomb disposal technician and police officer, died when the bomblet he was trying to deactivate exploded outside Klaićeva Street Children's Hospital.[976]

---

her liver, which require considerable follow-ups; she also has constant headaches caused by the shrapnel in her head, Sanja Buntić, 19 Jun 2006, T. 5768–5769, 5777.

964 She had received approximately twelve pieces of shrapnel, six of which still remain in her body, Aleksandra Szekely, Ex. 824, p. 3.

965 Mina Žunac, 20 Jun 2006, T. 5811–5812, T. 5826; Ex. 819; Ex. 386, F-50, F-52.

966 Mina Žunac, 20 Jun 2006, T. 5819. She sustained serious injuries to her right leg, and one part of her foot was amputated, Mina Žunac, 20 Jun 2006, T. 5822. She also sustained injuries to her right hand, hip and head. She spent "all in all" about a year in the hospital, Mina Žunac, 20 Jun 2006, T. 5823–5824. Ex. 818, photographs showing injuries caused to Mina Žunac. She still has over 45 pieces of shrapnel in her leg and had seven surgeries during the first couple of months, and after that three more. Mina Žunac, 20 Jun 2006, T. 5824. She still suffers constant pain and has trouble walking, as well as problems with her hand and with writing, Mina Žunac, 20 Jun 2006, T. 5827–5830.

967 Križanićeva St. School is a ten-minute walk from Ban Jelačić square, Rašeljka Grmoja, 19 Jun 2006, T. 5780–5781.

968 Rašeljka Grmoja, 19 Jun 2006, T. 5781–5782. She received shrapnel in her left shoulder and glass in her left eye, Rašeljka Grmoja, 19 Jun 2006, T. 5781–5782, T. 5793; Ex. 813, Photograph of Križanićeva Street School marked by Rašeljka Grmoja, showing the window where she was injured. *See also* her explanation of this photo, Rašeljka Grmoja, 19 Jun 2006, T. 5785–5787. It took her a month to go back to school and she suffered psychological trauma for a year or two after the event, Rašeljka Grmoja, 19 Jun 2006, T. 5794–5795.

969 Ivan Mikulčić, 14 Jun 2006, T. 5598–5599.

970 He was injured in his spine and some of the shrapnel remains to this day, Ivan Mikulčić, 14 Jun 2006, T. 5600. *See also* Ex. 796, medical report; Ex. 797, granting him the status of civilian war invalid of group X with 20% permanent disability; Ivan Mikulčić, 14 Jun 2006, T. 5601. Ex. 798, map on which Ivan Mikulčić indicated his house and where cluster bombs had fallen. Ex. 809, indicates damage caused in Plešo village.

971 Ex. 799, pp 63–80; Branko Lazarević, 15 Jun 2006, T. 5700. Of the 146 victims listed as injured in the Indictment for 2 May 1995, Ex. 799 contains the names of 144 victims, Ex. 799, pp 63–80. The Trial Chamber does not find any reason to doubt that 160 people were injured. (Two persons listed as injured (Ines Malić and Stipe Miličević) in Annex II to the Indictment are found neither in this exhibit nor in other evidence). *See also* Ex. 303, listing 203 persons wounded and 5 persons killed on 2 and 3 May 1995, of which 7 wounded and 1 killed were "MUP.HV". The document states that all of these "MUP.HV" were "out of service", the Trial Chamber interprets this, in light of the principle of *in dubio pro reo* as meaning that they were off-duty and not that they were no longer enlisted in the army or police.

972 Božica Lisak, Ex. 822, p. 2; Sanja Risović, 14 Jun 2006, T. 5580.

973 Ex. 303; Ex. 94, p. 4, indicating that on 3 May 1995, UNMO heard the firing of rockets approximately from 5 kilometres northeast of Vrginmost and afterwards observed the movement of an M-87 "Orkan" rocket launcher during the same time as the attack against Zagreb.

974 Branko Lazarević, 15 Jun 2006, T. 5648–5649, 5659–5660; Ex. 805. Rockets also landed in the suburbs, Novi Zagreb (Čehi) and Žitnjak, but caused no damage, Branko Lazarević, 15 Jun 2006, T. 5649; Ex. 811. *See also* Ex. 1042, Tab 2; Ex. 1043, Tab 2, DVD 1, pp 32–36.

975 Branko Lazarević, 15 Jun 2006, T. 5652–5653, 5723. Ex. 803, containing the autopsy report for Ivan Brodar, shows that Luka Skračić had died a violent death as a result of a pneumonia which had developed after having suffered explosive wounds. The Exhibit establishes that there was a cause-effect relation between the injuries which Luka Skračić sustained on 3 May 1995, and his subsequent death, Branko Lazarević, 15 Jun 2006, T. 5653. Ex. 802, p. 53 indicates that Luka Skračić suffered a blast wound to the head with an alien object lodged in his brain and was in a coma on 3 May 1995. *See also* Sanja Risović, 14 Jun 2006, T. 5595.

976 Branko Lazarević, 15 Jun 2006, T. 5650–5651; Ex. 802, pp 40–41. Ex. 387, F-26, is the site where the bomblet exploded in the hands of Ivan Markulin, Branko Lazarević, 15 Jun 2006, T. 5687.

311. The Trial Chamber heard evidence from some of those who were injured on 3 May 1995. Sanja Risović was at Klaićeva Street Children's Hospital with her 4 month-old daughter when she was injured to her shoulders, stomach, right leg, foot and back.[977] Shortly after midday, 18 people, including Božica Lisak, were injured when bombs fell through the glass roof of the Croatian National Theatre.[978] Božica Lisak was severely injured by 27 pieces of shrapnel.[979] Milan Smoljan was injured in his knee by bomblets when he was at Mažuranićeva Square, near the Croatian National Theatre.[980]

312. In total, 54 persons were injured as a result of the shelling on Zagreb on 3 May 1995.[981]

313. The Trial Chamber finds that Luka Skračić and Ivan Markulin were killed and that 54 people were injured as a result of the shelling on 3 May 1995.

3. Involvement of the RSK leadership in the shelling of Zagreb

314. There is evidence that Milan Martić had considered shelling of Zagreb prior to 2 May 1995. Already in 1992 and 1993, Milan Martić, as Minister of the Interior, considered attacking Zagreb as **[page 118]** a response to Croatian attacks on RSK cities.[982] On 9 June 1993, Milan Martić, as Minister of the Interior, informed Slobodan Milošević that the P-65 LUNA rocket system had been moved to the area of Banija and Kordun in order to prevent aggression or to carry out possible attacks on Zagreb, should RSK towns come under attack.[983]

315. On 5 September 1994, Ratko Mladić, the Commander of the Main Staff of the VRS, requested Milan Martić to approve the loan of 15 Orkan rockets in order to manufacture such rockets for the VRS.[984]

316. In a meeting on 24 October 1994 with Peter Galbraith, the United States Ambassador to Croatia, Milan Martić threatened to shell Zagreb.[985] Milan Martić stated "in effect that attacking civilian targets in Zagreb, attacking the city itself was an option, a way in which the RSK could respond to [...] a Croatian attack on the RSK".[986] Peter Galbraith warned Milan Martić that a rocket attack on Zagreb would be a crime.[987]

317. On 10 February 1995, Milan Martić, in a speech to the commanding officers of the SVK stated emphatically that "[n]o one can stop us to fire at Zagreb, Osijek, Vinkovci, Zadar, Karlovac, Split".[988]

---

977 Sanja Risović, 14 Jun 2006, T. 5580–5584. She was wounded in her right shoulder blade, and one part of her back muscle had to be removed as well as her shoulder blade. Her ribs were fractured and her lungs injured. She had shrapnel wedged in her stomach muscle. She was also injured in her right leg and left foot, Sanja Risović, 14 Jun 2006, T. 5585; Ex. 794; Ex. 795. Sanja Risović was in hospital until 16 June 1995 and then at a rehabilitation centre until 10 August 1995. She has had a total of eleven surgical procedures because of her injuries. She still spends three weeks of every year in rehabilitation and suffers from rheumatoid arthritis which is aggravated by stress and shock. Sanja Risović, 14 Jun 2006, T. 5586–5588. Sanja Risović also testified that she saw three other injured persons at Klaićeva Street Hospital: Mirna Kostović, Zvonko Bakula and a pregnant lady, Sanja Risović, 14 Jun 2006, T. 5584, 5594–5595; Ex. 802, pp 57–58.

978 Božica Lisak, Ex. 822, pp 2–3, stating that Božica Lisak, Matea Pučko, Dubravko Kolšek, Barbara Novković, and Krištof Pastor were injured.

979 Božica Lisak, Ex. 822, p. 3. Božica Lisak was injured by 27 pieces of shrapnel in her body, mostly in her legs and feet and one in her neck. She spent four weeks in Vinogradska Hospital in Zagreb and had the casts removed in July and then spent a month in rehabilitation. As a result of her injuries Božica Lisak has 50% invalidity, *ibid.*

980 Milan Smoljan, Ex. 823, 28 Apr 2004, p. 2. He also saw other persons injured and bleeding, Milan Smoljan, Ex. 823, 28 Apr 2004, pp 2–3.

981 Ex. 802, pp 50–57, contains the names of all 48 victims listed in Annex II to the Indictment. *See also* Ex. 303, *see supra* fn 971.

982 The Trial Chamber also notes Milan Martić's statement on 18 July 1992 that "[I]t would be better [...] [for Tuđman and his soldiers] not to touch us again because that would compel us to head forcefully for Zagreb and to turn it into Vukovar," Ex. 119, p. 2.

983 Ex. 12, p. 2. *See also* Reynaud Theunens, 27 Jan 2006, T. 808. Further evidence that shelling of Zagreb was considered in 1993 can be seen from a report from the 51st Infantry Brigade Command, which states "[u]nless [Croatia] withdraws from occupied territories, the following operations will continue: hits on Zagreb with large missiles which have not been used yet and which the world does not know of", Ex. 89, p. 2.

984 Ex. 475.

985 Peter Galbraith, 25 Apr 2006, T. 3757–3759.

986 Peter Galbraith, 25 Apr 2006, T. 3778. Peter Galbraith also testified that he warned Milan Martić that the RSK would not be able to survive Croatian military action, to which Milan Martić responded that the RSK had the ability to defend itself and to attack Zagreb, Peter Galbraith, 25 Apr 2006, T. 3814–3815.

987 Peter Galbraith, 25 Apr 2006, T. 3759.

988 Ex. 90, p. 6.

318. In a newspaper article published in Serbia on 24 March 1995, Milan Čeleketić is reported as stating:

> In the case of the Ustasha aggression, we will certainly not miss the opportunity to hit them where it hurts the most. We know their weak spots and where it hurts the most. Weak points are city squares and we know who goes there – civilians. I have already said this and was criticised a little. Well now, they may ask which squares and in which cities. I shall reply that that's a military secret. We shall make a decision about it and I think we will be precise. It is hard to say these words because there are, as I said, civilians in the squares, innocent people. However, if we are in war (and we are waging a filthy war for which they are first and foremost to blame), then there will be no mercy. Not only will we be merciless but, as a commander, I shall decided [*sic*] where we will direct our attacks, when and where it hurts the most.[989] **[page 119]**

319. On 3 May 1995, Milan Martić stated:

> As a counter measure to what Tudjman did to you here, we have shelled all their cities: Sisak several times and Karlovac, Zagreb yesterday and today. This was done for you. [...] Today, an ultimatum followed if they continue to attack our besieged forces, we will continue to attack Zagreb and destroy their cities.[990]

In a conversation on 3 May 1995 between Slobodan Milošević and Borisav Mikelić, the Prime Minister of the RSK, Slobodan Milošević said that Milan Martić was "boasting about having shelled Zagreb."[991]

320. In a radio interview on 5 May 1995, Milan Martić stated:

> That order was given by me, personally, as a retaliation to Franjo Tuđman and his staff for the order he had given to commit aggression against the Western Slavonia [...].[992]

At a meeting in Knin on 5 May 1995 with UN Special Envoy, Yasushi Akashi, Milan Martić stated in response to Yasushi Akashi's condemnation of the rocket attacks on Zagreb that "[h]ad I not ordered the rocket attacks [...] they would have continued to bomb our cities".[993] Milan Martić threatened to resume the shelling of Zagreb if their conditions were not met, and spoke of "massive rocket attacks on Zagreb which would leave 100,000 people dead".[994] In an interview published on 16 May 1995, Milan Martić is reported as saying that he felt justified in ordering the rocket attacks because he was aiming at military installations.[995] Milan Martić also appeared on television admitting to having ordered the shelling.[996]

321. The RSK Commission charged with determining responsibility for the fall of Western Slavonia found that:

> [t]he course of events in Western Slavonia required of the SVK Main Staff to intervene in order to provide assistance to the 18th Corps [...] however, no opinions were sought from the commanding officers of the SVK Main Staff. Decisions were made by the Commander and the President and stances and orders were given on the telephone (there are no written orders).[997] **[page 120]**

Rade Rašeta, Chief of Security of the SVK Main Staff, confirmed that members of the Main Staff were not consulted about the decision to shell Zagreb.[998] The RSK Fact-Finding Commission on the Causes and Manner of the Fall of Western Slavonia found that among those responsible for the fall of Western Slavonia

989 Ex. 91, p. 6; Reynaud Theunens, 27 Jan 2006, T. 827. In this article, Milan Čeleketić refers to Milan Martić as "my supreme commander", Ex. 91, p. 4.

990 Ex. 388; *See also* Branko Lazarević, 15 Jun 2006, T. 5692–5693.

991 Ex. 233, p. 6, Transcript of intercepted telephone conversation between Slobodan Milošević and Borisav Mikelić. *See also* Milan Babić, 21 Feb 2006, T. 1666–1668.

992 Ex. 389. In an article in Agence France Presse published on 6 May 1995, Milan Martić is reported as saying "I personally gave the order to bombard Zagreb as a response to (Croatian President) Franjo Tuđman and the Croatian leadership behind the aggression on Western Slavonia and crimes on civilians", Ex. 1001. *See also* Ex. 98.

993 Ex. 97, para. 13. As regards the Defence's argument concerning reprisals, *see infra* section IV B 4 (c).

994 Ex. 97, paras 4, 15.

995 Ex. 390. *See infra* section IV B 4 (c), concerning the Defence's argument on reprisals. *See also* Patrick Barriot, 9 Nov 2006, T. 10780–10785; Witness MM-117, 17 Oct 2006, T. 9599–9600. *See* however Peter Galbraith, 25 Apr 2006, T. 3778.

996 Branko Lazarević, 15 Jun 2006, T. 5690–5691; Milan Babić, 21 Feb 2006, T. 1661. Peter Galbraith testified that in media statements Milan Martić "took credit" for this first day of attacks, Peter Galbraith, 25 Apr 2006, T. 3774.

997 Ex. 100, para. 9.

998 Rade Rašeta, 2 May 2006, T. 3943–3944, commenting on Ex. 100. General Čeleketić tried to transfer the order over the phone, however the decision "should have been collectively taken. We should all have been familiar with the order. In this case, this went through the closest associates of the commander." *Ibid.*

was "President of the RSK, Milan Martić, for exceeding his authority as set by the constitution by blocking and preventing the work of the Supreme Defence Council".[999]

322. Milan Čeleketić resigned on 15 May 1995, giving as a reason having failed to keep his promise "that not one milimetre of the territory of the [RSK]" would be lost.[1000] Peter Galbraith testified that following the shelling, there was a change in the SVK and that Milan Čeleketić was replaced. He believed that this was as a result of Slobodan Milošević's instructions.[1001]

H. Acts of persecution carried out against non-Serbs in the SAO Krajina and the RSK

323. The Trial Chamber has been presented with considerable evidence that acts of discrimination and intimidation were carried out against the non-Serb population in the SAO Krajina and the RSK during the Indictment period. Count 1 of the Indictment charges Milan Martić with a wide range of acts of persecution. Many of these are also charged as separate counts in the Indictment and have been dealt with above. In addition, however, the Trial Chamber notes below the following additional evidence.

1. 1991

324. There is evidence of Croats being killed in 1991,[1002] having their property stolen,[1003] having their houses burned,[1004] that Croat villages and towns were destroyed, including churches and religious buildings,[1005] and that Croats were arbitrarily dismissed from their jobs.[1006] **[page 121]**

325. A MUP report of 12 December 1991, signed by Milan Martić, reported on the collection of trucks, passenger vehicles and household items "as war booty from citizens in the war zones and stored in collection centres".[1007]

326. Following the fall of Slunj in November 1991, Marinko Mudrić reported seeing many burned houses, particularly in Rakovica and Slunj, including a department store, restaurants, an SJB and a hotel, as well as many private houses. He saw "uniformed men and members of the Krajina police in Slunj" as well as

---

999 Ex. 99, p. 21.

1000 Ex. 101. The Trial Chamber notes that in his letter of resignation, General Čeleketić specifically refers to "our doctrine of reprisal at the chosen vital targets of the combatant"; Rade Rašeta, 2 May 2006, T. 3944–3945. Rade Rašeta was present at a meeting of the Supreme Defence Council when General Milan Čeleketić informed of his resignation and confirmed the reason for the resignation, Rade Rašeta, 2 May 2006, T. 3930, 3 May 2006, T. 3973.

1001 Peter Galbraith, 25 Apr 2006, T. 3757.

1002 Ex. 922, reporting *inter alia* that between 5 and 14 August 1991 "Serbian paramilitary groups" reportedly killed five Croats from the village of Lovinac (Gracac), p. 3, and on 16 August 1991 four Croatian men were reported to have been killed when they returned to the village of Pečki (Vrginmost) to feed their livestock; the village had been occupied by "Serbian forces". On 13 October 1991, 13 people were reported to have been killed in Široka Kula (Gospić) by a mob led by a "Serbian police officer" and that the "Serbian leader of the local police" ordered the remaining Croats to assemble for evacuation, when they assembled "Serbian paramilitary groups" began looting the homes and shot at the villagers. The bodies of those who were killed were thrown into their homes which had been set on fire, p. 4–5. On 16 and 17 December 1991, five civilians were reportedly killed in the village of Jasenice (Obrovac) pp 10–11. Ex. 922, Helsinki Watch Report sent to Slobodan Milošević and General Blagoje Adžić, dated 21 January 1992; Marica Vuković, 22 Mar 2006, T. 2452–2453 testifying that around a hundred people were killed in the 10 or 15 villages around Vukovići. *See also* Ex. 133, an order from the Glina TO Staff dated 4 October 1991 ordering TO units "when mopping up the terrain in Glina, to spare Pajo Bubaš and his wife, who is a Serb, and their house: [t]hey have been verified as loyal people."

1003 Ex. 984, p. 19 reports that there was widespread looting around Drniš by 'reservists in JNA uniforms'. Borislav Đukić testified to requesting measures from the 9th Corps command in Knin to be taken against the looters and that seized looted property was sent to the JNA Knin logistics base, Borislav Đukić, 20 Oct 2006, T. 9890. Witness MM-078 testified that both the army and the police were involved in the looting and that the police would let the trucks with looted goods through check-points, Witness MM-078, 25 May 2006, T. 4533.

1004 Marica Vuković, 22 Mar 2006, T. 2411, 2442 (testifying that on 28 August 1991, the village of Rastovaca (Nova Gradiska) was set on fire by "Serbs"). Marko Vuković testified that after the attack on Grabovac some houses and a motel were torched and burnt, as well as the motel, Marko Vuković, 24 Mar 2006, T. 2634.

1005 Witness MM-078, 24 May 2006, T. 4450. During the attack in September 1991 the centre of Drniš was "completely" destroyed, Ex. 984, para. 5.3, p. 16; Borislav Đukić, 20 Oct 2006, T. 9896. Regarding damage to houses and churches and looting in Kijevo, *see* Witness MM-078, 24 May 2006, T. 4434–4435. Borislav Đukić testified that there were no JNA units in Kijevo on 27 August 1991, Borislav Đukić, 20 Oct 2006, T. 9885–9886; Witness MM-078, 24 May 2006, T. 4444, T. 4527–4528; Borislav Đukić, 19 Oct 2006, T. 9768–9769; Ex. 106, Report of Ratko Mladić, JNA 9th Corps, to General Staff of the SFRY concerning the attack on Kijevo, dated 4 October 1991; Milan Babić, 17 Feb 2006, T. 1559–1560.

1006 Ex. 895, pp 22–24.

1007 Ex. 518, p. 4, signed by Milan Martić as Minister of the Interior.

"Peić and [Željko 'Buba' Mudrić]" stealing cars.[1008] Police as well as Serb civilians were engaged in looting in the villages of Rakovica, Slunj, Saborsko and Poljanak.[1009] Attacks on Modruški Sabljaki and Medvedi and Plivelići were led by "Pejić and [Zelko 'Buba' Mudrić], accompanied by some 30 of Martić's men", who stole tractors and plundered houses before setting them on fire.[1010] On 21 November 1991, in Dabar a uniformed group led by Predrag Baklajić killed Stipe Brajković, raided Croat houses and stole property.[1011]

2. 1992

327. During 1992 on the territory of the RSK, there was a continuation of incidents of killings,[1012] harassment,[1013] robbery, beatings, burning of houses,[1014] theft,[1015] and destruction of churches[1016] carried out against the non-Serb population.[1017] **[page 122]**

3. 1993–1995

328. Throughout 1993, there were further reports of killings,[1018] intimidation,[1019] and theft.[1020] By 1995, several Croat villages had been attacked and destroyed, including Rakovica,[1021] Poljanak, Kuselj, Saborsko, Korana, Rastovaca, Celiste, Smoljanac, Dreznik, Rakovac, Lipovaca, Vaganac,[1022] Hrvatska Dubica[1023] and Medviđa.[1024]

1008 Ex. 507, Official Note on Saborsko Operation, dated 7 April 1992, p. 5. One of the cars they stole was afterwards in use by the Plaški SJB, *ibid.*

1009 Witness MM-037, 29 Mar 2006, T. 2821–2822.

1010 Ex. 507, Official Note on Saborsko Operation, dated 7 April 1992, p. 6.

1011 Ex. 561, Report of MUP concerning the activities of Predrag Baklajić, dated 14 July 1993. *See also* Ex. 43, a request of the commander of the 2nd Lika TO Brigade to Milan Martić to disband the unit of Predrag Baklajić, which had previously been trained in Golubić, because it was engaged in looting in November 1991 in Vrhovine near Dabar.

1012 On 18 January 1992, the Čengić family were killed in their house in Ervenik Village, Knin municipality by three members of the TO. The same three perpetrators also set fire to houses, sheds and barns in the village, Ex. 974; *see also* Witness MM-117, 17 Oct 2006, T. 9565, T. 9559–9560. Ex. 732. Ex. 75, dated 28 September 1992. Ex. 737, reporting that in Slunj a Croat was beaten to death and his father beaten into a coma by three persons in local "*Milicija*" uniforms, John McElligott, 26 May 2006, T. 4606–4607. *See also* Ex. 739; Ex. 732.

1013 Ex. 763, reporting on "a disturbing pattern of abuse, harassment and discriminatory treatment of Croats particularly in 7 villages south of Glina town" as well as murders, destruction of houses and terrorising of residents by "roaming gangsters". Also reporting on discriminatory distribution of humanitarian aid by the "local red cross" and that buses refused to stop at bus stops. *See also* Charles Kirudja, 31 May 2006, T. 4885–4886; Ex. 739; Ex. 728.

1014 Ex. 732, UNCIVPOL situation report for Sector South, dated 29 May 1992; John McElligott, 26 May 2006, T. 4579, T. 4606–4607; Ex. 728; Ex. 736.

1015 Ex. 733, reporting that local police officers wearing uniforms with "Serbian Krajina" or "policemen" based in the Vrlika [Sinj] area were consistently stealing from elderly Croatian people. *See also* Ex. 728.

1016 Ex. 735, dated 2 October 1992, reporting of the destruction by explosives of St Anna's Church in Zvjerinac, which is part of the village of Kosovo, south of Knin, on 1 October. *See also* John McElligott, 26 May 2006, T. 4601–4602, 4606–4607. Ex. 737, UNCIVPOL daily situation report for 6 and 7 November 1992, dated 8 November 1992.

1017 *See also* Ex. 75, dated 28 September 1992. UNCIVPOL's Report for October 1992 lists numerous incidents of killings, thefts, destruction and looting, Ex. 736. A United Nations Report on the Human Rights situation in the former Yugoslavia, dated 17 November 1992, reports from Sector South that United Nations staff were collecting evidence of murders, robberies, looting and other forms of criminal violence "often related to ethnic cleansing", Ex. 865, United Nations report on the situation of Human Rights in the territory of the former Yugoslavia dated 17 November 1992, paras 78–81. *See also* Ex. 728; Witness MM-117, 16 Oct 2006, T. 9472–9473, testifying that according to the Ministry of the Interior in 1992 there were 6,000 criminal reports which included looting and to a great extent that Croats were the victims of these crimes. Ex. 864, Further Report by the Secretary-General of the United Nations to the Security Council pursuant to UN resolution 743, dated 24 November 1992. Ex. 727. Ex. 726, Reporting on 497 crimes against Croats only in Sector South between August 1992 and May 1993. *See also* John McElligott, 26 May 2006, T. 4616–4617, 30 May 2006, T. 4731–4732.

1018 *See* Ex. 741. Ex. 726, Reporting on 497 crimes against Croats only in Sector South between August 1992 and May 1993; John McElligott, 26 May 2006, T. 4616–4617, 30 May 2006, T. 4731–4732. UNCIVPOL reported that the Benkovac police had reported between 11 and 17 Croats murdered and one woman raped "in the previous week", Ex. 729, Daily Situation Report from UNCIVPOL HQ Sector South, dated 22 February 1993. Concerning evidence of rape, *see also* Marica Vuković, 22 Mar 2006, T. 2453–2454. Ex. 743, reporting on the killing of an elderly Croat woman in Luka-Drage. Ex. 744, reporting on robbery and assault of Ivica Begić aged 69 by four men in "military uniforms", shooting of Kata Begić and murder of Ana Vracar, all being Croats living in Podlapača, Titova Korenica on 12 July 1993, and the shooting of Milka Bilusic on 16 Jun 1993 in Ljubotić by four men "dressed in uniforms of soldiers", as well as the beating and murder of Marija Sarić from Lukar Drage by "Serbian soldiers" on 7 June 1991. *See also* MM-117, 13 Oct 2006, T. 9358.

1019 *See also* Ex. 729, Ex. 743, reporting that "Captain Dragan's soldiers" harassed an elderly Croat near Bruška.

1020 Ex. 743, UNCIVPOL Report for Sector South for June and July 1993, dated July 1993.

1021 Vlado Vuković, 27 Mar 2006, T. 2675–2676.

1022 Marica Vuković, 22 Mar 2006, T. 2451. *See also* Ex. 1042, Tab 2; Ex. 1043, Tab 2, DVD 2, p. 17; Ex. 1044.

1023 Josip Josipović, 6 Apr 2006, T. 3325–3326.

1024 Stanko Erstić, Ex. 392, T. 24974.

I. The political objective of the Serb leadership

329. The President of Serbia, Slobodan Milošević, publicly supported the preservation of Yugoslavia as a federation of which, *inter alia*, the SAO Krajina would form a part.[1025] However, **[page 123]** Slobodan Milošević covertly intended the creation of a Serb state.[1026] Milan Babić testified that Slobodan Milošević intended the creation of such a Serb state through the establishment of paramilitary forces and the provocation of incidents in order to allow for JNA intervention, initially with the aim to separate the warring parties but subsequently in order to secure territories envisaged to be part of a future Serb state.[1027] In Milan Babić's view, Slobodan Milošević advocated this political objective from the summer of 1990 until the end of 1991.[1028]

330. Through the summer of 1991, the objective of the JNA was to protect the Serbs against attacks by Croatian armed formations and prevent occupation of cities under Serb control.[1029] At the end of the summer 1991 and coinciding with the attack on Kijevo, the JNA became an active participant in Croatia on the side of the SAO Krajina. According to the SFRY Federal Secretary for Defence, General Veljko Kadijević, the task of the JNA became one of protecting "the Serb people in Croatia in such a way that all regions with a majority Serb population would be completely freed from the presence of the Croatian army and the Croatian authorities".[1030] Veljko Kadijević also noted that among "the principal ideas" behind the deployment of the JNA during the second phase was "full co-ordination with Serb insurgents in the Serbian Krajina".[1031]

331. On 3 October 1991, Veljko Kadijević stated that the objective of the JNA in the conflict was "to restore control in crisis areas, to protect the Serbian population from persecution and annihilation".[1032] On 12 October 1991, General Blagoje Adžić, Chief of the General Staff of the JNA, stated that the main task of the JNA was to prevent "the spread of interethnic conflicts and the recurrence of genocide against the Serbian people in Croatia."[1033] On 25 October 1991, at a meeting of, among others, Slobodan Milošević, Veljko Kadijević and Blagoje Adžić, Slobodan Milošević stated that "we have helped [the Serbs in Croatia] abundantly and [we] will continue to do so until the end".[1034] **[page 124]**

332. Several witnesses explained that the JNA's role changed because Croatia considered the JNA a hostile army and in September 1991 had ordered the ZNG and police to block and seize JNA facilities across Croatia in order to immobilise the JNA.[1035] According to some witnesses, the JNA therefore intervened only to defend itself.[1036]

1025 Ex. 200; Ex. 201; Ex. 202; Ex. 979. *See also* Milan Babić, 16 Feb 2006, T. 1415–1416, (testifying that Slobodan Milošević endorsed a "firm type of federation" along with the preservation of the right of self-determination of people who were in majority in an area), T. 1488–1489, 15 Feb 2006, T. 1384–1385, 2 Mar 2006, T. 1781, 3 Mar 2006, T. 1925; Lazar Macura, 14 Sep 2006, T. 8326–8327. In this respect, the Trial Chamber recalls the evidence concerning the referendum held on 12 May 1991, *see supra* para. 134.

1026 Ex. 201; Milan Babić, 16 Feb 2006, T. 1415–1416, 21 Feb 2006, T. 1672; Witness MM-117, 16 Oct 2006, T. 9491–9497; Mile Dakić, 25 Oct 2006, T. 10025–10026; Ex. 1039, Group 13, pp 4–8.

1027 Milan Babić, 16 Feb 2006, T. 1416, 17 Feb 2006, T. 1572–1574.

1028 Milan Babić, 2 Mar 2006, T. 1806.

1029 Milan Babić, 17 Feb 2006, T. 1503–1506; Ex. 476, ERN: 03023105, noting that at a meeting on 4 April 1991, Slobodan Milošević, Veljko Kadijević, Blagoje Adžić and Borisav Jović agreed that "the military will not allow the Croatian police to occupy Knin and other Serb cities which are now under Serb control". Slobodan Perić, a lieutenant colonel in the 5th JNA Military District in Zagreb, testified that at his "operational level" he did not have the impression that the strategic goal of the JNA was to prepare the Serbs for a war against Croatia or that the JNA was "tasked with preparing the Serb people for their own defence", Slobodan Perić, 7 Sep 2006, T. 7913. However, the Trial Chamber is of the view that at his operational level, Slobodan Perić would not have been aware of the specific strategic goal. *See also* Ex. 24, p. 68, ERN: 00362704; Ex. 26.

1030 Ex. 24, p. 73, ERN: 00362709. *See also* Ex. 27, p. 3.

1031 Ex. 24, pp 73–74, 77, ERN: 00362709-00362710, 00362713. *See also* Ex. 214; Ex. 477; Ex. 973.

1032 Ex. 25, p. 3.

1033 Ex. 26.

1034 Ex. 476, p. 358, ERN: 03023174.

1035 Milan Babić, 17 Feb 2006, T. 1563, 3 Mar 2006, T. 1887, 1898; Radoslav Maksić, 7 Feb 2006, T. 1222; Slobodan Perić, 6 Sep 2006, T. 7871, 7 Sep 2006, T. 7922; Milan Dragišić, 19 Sep 2006, T. 8657; Borislav Đukić, 18 Oct 2006, T. 9694–9695, 20 Oct 2006, T. 9846-9847, 9850; Imra Agotić, Ex. 398, T. 23266; Ex. 238, p. 110.

1036 Slobodan Perić, 7 Sep 2006, T. 7923–7924, 7926–7928; Milan Dragišić, 19 Sep 2006, T. 8601.

333. The SAO Krajina, and subsequently the RSK, leadership endorsed Slobodan Milošević's vision to create a Serb-dominated state.[1037] In early July 1991, Milan Martić stated that the *Milicija Krajine* were "defending Serbian land and the Serbs' ethnic area".[1038] Similarly, on 19 August 1991 Milan Martić stated that he would accept no autonomy and that "the territories controlled by the police and the Territorial Defence of the Serbian Autonomous Region of Krajina will forever remain Serbian".[1039] Milan Babić embraced the same view, stating on 5 September 1991 that "the Serbs are recognised in every part of Yugoslav State territory as a nation, which they will continue to be [w]ithin the part of the state that remains as a whole following the secession of the former Socialist Republic of Croatia's real territory and all Slovenia."[1040] On 12 December 1991, Milan Martić stated that "nobody [...] has the right to deny the Serbian people the right to live in their own country".[1041]

334. On 14 May 1992, Mile Pašpalj, the President of the RSK Parliament, expressed the need to establish "the state of Serbian Krajina" in order to survive.[1042] On 3 July 1992, Milan Martić criticised the presidents of the Banija and Kordun municipal assemblies for their decision to form autonomous districts because the RSK had "paid in blood the corridor we won and [linked] up Serbian territories".[1043] At a meeting on 14 June 1993 with Cedric Thornberry, the UNPROFOR Director of Civil Affairs, Milan Martić stated that the "joint life of Croats and Serbs in one State is **[page 125]** impossible because of genocide politic [*sic*] of Croatia. We want to separate in 2 states [...] I am convinced that we will be good neighbors as separate states."[1044]

335. Efforts to unify the Croatian Krajina and the Bosnian Krajina continued throughout 1992 until 1995. The evidence shows that the RSK leadership sought an alliance, and eventually unification, with the RS in BiH and that Milan Martić was in favour of such unification.[1045] A letter dated 3 April 1993 from, *inter alia*, Milan Martić as Minister of the Interior to the Assembly of the RS, written on behalf of "the Serbs from the RSK", advocates a joinder of the "two Serbian states as the first stage in the establishment of a state of all Serbs".[1046] Moreover, in this regard, the Trial Chamber recalls the evidence concerning operation *Koridor 92*.[1047]

336. On 21 January 1994, during the election campaign for the RSK presidential elections, Milan Martić stated that he would "speed up the process of unification" and "pass on the baton to our all Serbian leader Slobodan Milošević."[1048]

J. Milan Martić's knowledge of and reactions to crimes committed

337. Several witnesses testified that in his capacity as Minster of the Interior, Milan Martić was *de jure* and *de facto* in control of the SAO Krajina and RSK police from 1991 through 1993.[1049] As Minister of the

---

1037 Veljko Džakula, 16 Jan 2006, T. 404–405, testifying that during 1991 and 1992, Milan Martić worked for the "recognition and joining the association of Serb lands, Republika Srpska, and Serbia"; Milan Babić, 16 Feb 2006, T. 1476–1477, 2 Mar 2006, T. 1830–1832; Ante Marinović, 23 Mar 2006, T. 2474; Witness MM-078, 25 May 2006, T. 4498; Witness MM-117, 16 Oct 2006, T. 9491–9496; Mile Dakić, 25 Oct 2006, T. 10025; Ex. 201, p. 3; Ex. 213; Ex. 474, p. 4; Ex. 912. According to the Constitutional Law of the SAO Krajina "[the SAO Krajina] shall represent a form of political and territorial autonomy within the Federative Yugoslavia [...].", *see* Ex. 151, Art. 1. Moreover, the header or the stamp of several official SAO Krajina documents in evidence show that the SAO Krajina was considered to form part of the SFRY, *see e.g.* Ex. 34; Ex. 35; Ex. 3; Ex. 42; Ex. 188; Ex. 190; Ex. 467. The Law on Defence of the RSK, adopted 23 March 1992, also provided that the RSK armed forces were a "composite part" of the armed forces of the SFRY, Ex. 6, p. 123.

1038 Ex. 498, p. 4. *See also* Ex. 205; Ex. 973; Ex. 975; Milan Babić, 17 Feb 2006, T. 1518; Witness MM-117, 17 Oct 2006, T. 9586–9587.

1039 Ex. 215.

1040 Ex. 236, p. 5.

1041 Ex. 518, p. 3.

1042 Ex. 750, p. 2. *See also* Slobodan Jarčević, 14 Jul 2006, T. 6292–6293; Ex. 861; Ex. 862.

1043 Ex. 77, p. 3. *See also* Slobodan Jarčević, 13 Jul 2006, T. 6192–6194.

1044 Ex. 965, p. 5.

1045 Veljko Džakula, 17 Jan 2006, T. 436; Rade Rašeta, 2 May 2006, T. 3925–3926, T. 3961–3962, testifying that in the summer of 1994 Radovan Karadžić met in Knin with the RSK leadership about the ways in which the RSK and the RS could come closer on political and military levels in view of possible future unification; Ex. 6, p. 168 describing the Prijedor Declaration of 31 October 1992; Ex. 110, paras 4–5; Ex. 475; Ex. 656, p. 3; Ex. 660; Ex. 868, p. 3.

1046 Ex. 976. The other signatories of the letter are the RSK General Staff Commander Mile Novaković, the Minister of Defence Stojan Španović, and the Chief of Staff of the RSK General Staff Borislav Đukić.

1047 *See supra* paras 154, 160.

1048 Ex. 14, p. 1; Ex. 660. *See also* Milan Babić, 16 Feb 2006, T. 1475–1476; Ex. 504; Ex. 868, p. 3, in which, in July 1994, Goran Hadžić, President of the RSK, stated that: "[o]ur aim is well known, and this is a unified Serbian state".

1049 Veljko Džakula, 16 Jan 2006, T. 400–403, also testifying that Milan Martić was "a person who had authority, who was obeyed, whose orders were complied with" and that "if someone failed to comply with an order of his, he could be quite rough. He could be

Interior, Milan Martić was kept informed concerning the activities of the SJBs and maintained "excellent communications" with the units subordinated to the MUP.[1050] The evidence shows that information concerning military activities during the autumn of 1991 was sent to Milan Martić.[1051] Moreover, information regarding crimes committed in the SAO Krajina and the RSK **[page 126]** was regularly reported to Milan Martić. In particular, police inspectors, who carried out investigations into crimes on the ground, reported to the MUP and Milan Martić during the time period of 1991 to 1995 pursuant to reporting regulations.[1052] Defence witness Slobodan Jarčević, who was the Foreign Minister of the RSK from October 1992 until April 1994, testified that crimes committed in the territory of the RSK, including those charged in the Indictment against Milan Martić, were discussed at government sessions.[1053] The evidence also shows that there were numerous contacts between UNPROFOR and the RSK government, including the SJBs, regarding crimes committed on the ground by members of the MUP.[1054]

338. There is evidence that Milan Martić stressed that the police should act in accordance with the law and that the police should never differentiate between citizens based on ethnic political, religious, or other affiliation.[1055] Moreover, the evidence shows that Milan Martić in some cases took measures to address the criminal behaviour of members of the MUP and of other units.[1056] At some point during 1991, there was

angry. He could threaten that they would be replaced"; Stevo Plejo, 20 Sep 2006, T. 8702–8703, 21 Sep 2006, T. 8797–8798, *see also* Aernout van Lynden, 2 Jun 2006, T. 5017–5018; Nikola Medaković, 9 Oct 2006, T. 8965–8966, 8968; Mile Dakić, 25 Oct 2006, T. 10023. *See also* Milan Babić, 15 Feb 2006, T. 1407, Ex. 1028, ERN: L0079770, p. 24; Stevo Plejo, 20 Sep 2006, T. 8703; Ex. 44. On 23 August 1993, Milan Martić suspended the work of the RSK SDB, pending restructuring of the SDB, because "the political and security situation has deteriorated and the work of certain ministry departments has been blocked", Ex. 525.

1050 Radoslav Maksić, 6 Feb 2006, T. 1177–1178. *See also* Witness MM-003, 8 Mar 2006, T. 1979–1981, testifying about meetings with chiefs of SJBs.

1051 Ex. 957, dated 1 to 2 September 1991, provides that information had been received from, *inter alia*, Kistanje, Plaški, Gračac, Glina, Kostajnica, and Dubica Štica, concerning fighting and "mopping up" activities. It is unclear in which capacity Milan Martić received this information, Minister of the Interior or Deputy Commander of the TO. *See also* Radoslav Maksić, 6 Feb 2006, T. 1177, testifying that the TO sent reports to the MUP.

1052 Witness MM-096, 25 Aug 2006, T. 7188–7189. Pursuant to an SFRY Regulation of 1974, the SJBs had a reporting obligation to the SUP and to the MUP, and these obligations were complied with. On 20 May 1992, this regulation was superseded by the "Mandatory Instruction on Implementation and Information in Internal Affairs Organs in the Republic of Serbian Krajina", which was issued by Milan Martić in his capacity as Minister of the Interior, Ex. 893, Witness MM-096, 23 Aug 2006, T. 6971–6974. Pursuant to this very detailed Instruction (item 9), "[t]he internal affairs organ shall urgently inform the [MUP] about all important incidents and trends, and measures undertaken". Moreover, the MUP's "permanent duty service" was under an obligation to "compile daily information about incidents, trends and measures undertaken" (item 11), regarding the permanent duty service, *see also* Witness MM-096, 25 Aug 2006, T. 7172–7173. If a report contained information concerning two or more casualties, the SJB would not only report to the SUP but would immediately inform also the MUP in Knin, Witness MM-096, 25 Aug 2006, T. 7171–7172.

1053 Slobodan Jarčević, 13 Jul 2006, T. 6209–6210, also testifying that in his capacity as Foreign Minister, he sent a letter to the UN Security Council wherein he attempted to explain the situation attending those crimes. Moreover, Slobodan Jarčević testified that the RSK government "did not take any steps against the members of any other nation or ethnic group", Slobodan Jarčević, 13 Jul 2006, T. 6212. In his view, it was difficult for the RSK government to protect the Croats who remained in the RSK because many of the crimes were committed out of revenge for losing family members, Slobodan Jarčević, 13 Jul 2006, T. 6209.

1054 Witness MM-096, 25 Aug 2006, T. 7185. On 24 August 1992, Cedric Thornberry, the Director for Civil Affairs of UNPROFOR, sent a letter to the RSK Ilija Prijić concerning crimes in the Vrlika area committed by the police, requesting the policemen who were engaging in such crimes be removed from the force, Ex. 734. *See also* Ex. 733; Ex. 735; Ex. 736; Ex. 737; Ex. 739; Ex. 740. Milan Martić issued instructions regulating in detail the mode of cooperation with UNPROFOR and UNCIVPOL, according to which all organs of the RSK MUP should be at the disposal of UNCIVPOL, which was permitted to observe at the SJBs and to act in response to complaints by RSK citizens, Witness MM-117, 18 Oct 2006, T. 9647–9649. The Trial Chamber notes that in the Secretary-General's report of 28 September 1992, it was reported that "the overall failure to cooperate with UNPROFOR has undermined UNPROFOR's ability to fulfil its police monitoring functions, Ex. 75, para. 17 (*see also* para. 18). Charles Kirudja testified about interference by RSK authorities with UNPROFOR's mission, Charles Kirudja, 31 May 2006, T. 4828 (*see also* T. 4832–4833 regarding arrests of UNPROFOR members). *See also* Ex. 757.

1055 Radoslav Maksić, 7 Feb 2006, T. 1231; Witness MM-096, 21 Aug 2006, T. 6845–6846; Witness MM-117, 13 Oct 2006, T. 9339, 9346, 17 Oct 2006, T. 9580–9582. There is evidence that in August 1991, Milan Martić was aware that prisoners were taken from Kijevo to the Knin SJB. On one occasion he told the police transferring prisoners to "[p]lease make sure that none of the people are harmed or killed". When asked why, by police officer Bozo Ceko, Milan Martić answered "these people have to be exchanged. They are prisoners", Dragan Knežević, 3 Nov 2006, T. 10674. The Trial Chamber also notes that some measures were taken by the JNA 9th Corps to prevent crimes, including to carry out investigations by military prosecutors, Borislav Đukić, 23 Oct 2006, T. 9920–9921. *See also* Ex. 27; Ex. 965, p. 5.

1056 Witness MM-003, 8 Mar 2006, T. 2025, testifying that Milan Martić was informed that looting was perpetrated by the police in areas where fighting had occurred and that he disapproved of this and changed the commanders of the police in the villages "where there were major problems and where he had indications of things like that going on".

an incident where Croat prisoners were mistreated by "a **[page 127]** commanding officer" at the training camp in Golubić wherefore Captain Dragan Vasiljković requested Milan Martić take measures.[1057] Milan Martić expelled the commanding officer, but eventually this person was allowed to stay on at Golubić.[1058] In November 1991, an attempt was made by Veljko Rađunović and Mile Mišljenović to secede, *inter alia*, Hrvatska Dubica from the Hrvatska Kostajnica municipality and annex it to Bosanska Dubica.[1059] The evidence shows that Milan Martić visited the area after the president of the Hrvatska Kostajnica municipality had requested assistance and that Milan Martić disbanded Veljko Rađunović's police unit and replaced it with a military police unit of the JNA Banja Luka Corps.[1060] In January 1992, SJBs were set up in Hrvatska Kostajnica and Šaš, after which some of the renegade groups were imprisoned or entered the legal formations of the SAO Krajina.[1061] However, the Trial Chamber also heard evidence that after a certain period the JNA unit was expelled and the previously disbanded unit was re-installed.[1062]

339. On 19 February 1992, Milan Martić ordered the disbandment of an RSK MUP Special Purpose unit commanded by Predrag Baklajić due to information that this unit had been involved in criminal activities, including several murders, and incidents of robbery, theft and destruction.[1063] This disbandment was ultimately not carried through and the unit continued with criminal activities in 1992.[1064] On 1 April 1993, Milan Martić requested the MUP of Serbia to provide 20–30 inspectors to deal with homicides and property offences which were "rapidly increasing recently in the RSK".[1065] On 7 September 1993, Milan Martić ordered the arrest of members of certain paramilitary groups, who were suspected of committing organised crimes.[1066] There is evidence that the unit Arkan's Tigers, under the command of Željko "Arkan" Raznjatović, left the territory of the RSK in 1993 after an order had been issued by the SVK commander Mile Novaković and Milan **[page 128]** Martić as Minister of the Interior.[1067] Lastly, there is some evidence that criminal investigations were carried out and that perpetrators were brought to justice.[1068]

340. There is no further evidence that measures were taken to address the widespread criminal activities which the evidence shows occurred in the SAO Krajina and the RSK from 1991 through 1995.[1069] Rather,

---

1057 Stevo Plejo, 20 Sep 2006, T. 8702.

1058 Stevo Plejo, 20 Sep 2006, T. 8702–8703, 21 Sep 2006, T. 8796–8798.

1059 Witness MM-022, 20 Mar 2006, T. 2315–2317, 2352–2353.

1060 Witness MM-022, 20 Mar 2006, T. 2316–2318, 2352–2353; Josip Josipović, 6 Apr 2006, T. 3322; Nikola Dobrijević, 10 Nov 2006, T. 10890–10901, 10895–10896. *See also* Ex. 290, p. 2, stating that the "local Chetniks", including Momčilo Kovačević and Stevo Rađun, controlled the area, and were in conflict with "Martić's men"; Ex. 600, indicating that in September 1991 Stevan Borojević requested that he and his unit remain under the command of Milan Martić; Ex. 601, indicating that on 13 January 1992 Stevan Borojević was under the command of Milan Martić; Ex. 602. *See further* Nikola Dobrijević, 13 Nov 2006, T. 10983–10985, 10112–10113.

1061 Nikola Dobrijević, 10 Nov 2006, T. 10889–10890, 10892–10893, 10896–10897, 13 Nov 2006, T. 10943, 10989.

1062 Josip Josipović, 6 Apr 2006, T. 3322.

1063 Ex. 43; Ex. 563; Ex. 566, providing that the arrest, in February 1992, of the leaders and several members of this unit only temporarily stopped its activities and that as a result of "inadequate judicial measures" and a "poor political situation in Krajina" this unit could resume its criminal activities. *See further* Ex. 561, which reports on murders in Dabar of seven civilians; Ex. 560, which provides that the "Minister of [the] Interior be informed about the content of this Information, since Baklajić refers to him as his order issuing authority and the only one he is subordinated to."

1064 Ex. 563.

1065 Ex. 665.

1066 Ex. 541. *See also* Witness MM-096, 22 Aug 2006, T. 6919, 25 Aug 2006, T. 7173–7174, testifying that sometime between 1993 and 1994 Milan Martić ordered that perpetrators of serious crimes, particularly murders, be arrested.

1067 Witness MM-096, 22 Aug 2006, T. 6921–6922, 6925, 24 Aug 2006, T. 7038–7039. The Trial Chamber notes that there is no evidence that this unit was suspected of having committed crimes.

1068 Witness MM-117, 13 Oct 2006, T. 9346–9347, 9351, concerning the murder of the Čengić family in 1992 near Knin, T. 9392–9393, concerning incidents in 1993, including murders, which may have been motivated by revenge by Serbs, and that the police identified several perpetrators and filed criminal reports for further judicial proceedings. Further, in relation to Milan Martić's authority to take measures, *see* Ex. 38, Report to the SAO Krajina TO Staff, dated 6 August 1991, providing that Milan Martić issued a cease-fire order due to the visit of the SFRY Vice-President Branko Kostić; Ex. 40, reporting that Milan Martić issued an order to the Benkovac TO staff on 16 September 1991 re-subordinating TO members of the Benkovac TO to a unit of Lieutenant Colonel Živanović for lifting the blockade of the Zemunik airport; Ex. 521; Ex. 602, order of Milan Martić, dated 26 Nov 1991, that "all persons wearing camouflage uniforms who are not members of the SAO Krajina police [...] have to return the insignia of police members and report to the recruiting office in Kostajnica in order to join [JNA]". *See also* Nikola Dobrijević, 13 Nov 2006, T. 11013.

1069 *See supra* section III H. In this respect, the Trial Chamber recalls the testimony of Josip Josipović that neither Momčilo Kovačević nor Stevo Rađunović were investigated or prosecuted concerning crimes committed in the Hrvatska Dubica area, Josip Josipović, 7 Apr 2006, T. 3373.

there is evidence which shows the contrary. After the attack on Struga, Captain Dragan Vasiljković arrested ten members of the TO in Dvor, who were allegedly responsible for killing several civilians. Subsequently, Milan Martić arrived in Dvor and ordered Captain Dragan Vasiljković to release the ten men, which he did.[1070]

341. Rade Rašeta testified that on one occasion Milan Martić told him that "he could not make himself hate Croats" and "whoever was saying that [he] was a nationalist and hated Croats was wrong".[1071] Witness MM-003 testified that Milan Martić did not express hatred towards the Croat population, but rather that "[h]e hated the chequerboard emblem" and that "[h]e hated Tudjman most of all".[1072] The Trial Chamber heard evidence that during the summer and autumn of 1991 Milan Martić instructed persons involved in humanitarian assistance to treat both Croat and Serb refugees arriving from Drniš equally.[1073] Slobodan Jarčević testified that Milan Martić "demonstrated the nobility of his character" by looking after refugees who arrived from BiH in 1994 despite the difficulties that the RSK was facing due to international sanctions.[1074] However, the Trial Chamber notes the evidence concerning the return of Croat refugees, which was a condition of the Vance Plan and which Milan Martić was clearly against and in fact obstructed.[1075] **[page 129]**

342. The evidence shows that Milan Martić actively advocated and pursued the goal of creating an ethnically Serb state in spite of his awareness of the serious and widespread crimes, which were being perpetrated against the Croat and other non-Serb civilian population as a result of this policy. While the Trial Chamber notes the evidence presented above that Milan Martić did not personally express hatred towards Croats or other non-Serbs, and on one occasion instructed that Serb and Croat refugees be treated equally, this evidence does not serve to outweigh the substantial evidence of Milan Martić's conscious disregard for the fate of the Croat and other non-Serb population and persistent pursuance of the goal to create a Serb state.

IV. RESPONSIBILITY OF MILAN MARTIĆ

A. Findings on the crimes charged

1. General requirements of Article 3 of the Statute

343. The Defence submitted that an armed rebellion organised by Croatian authorities existed in the territory of Croatia from 1990 to 1992 "when Yugoslavia *de facto* ceased to exist".[1076] It is alleged

1070 Aernout van Lynden, 2 Jun 2006, T. 5017–5019, 5038–5039; Ex. 587; Ex. 588. *See also* Ex. 1042, Tab 2; Ex. 1043, Tab 2, DVD 2, pp 8–11; Ex. 1044.

1071 Rade Rašeta, 2 May 2006, T. 3901. *See also* Charles Kirudja, 1 Jun 2006, T. 4961; Witness MM-096, 21 Aug 2006, T. 6846; Witness MM-090, 31 Aug 2006, T. 7482, 7522; Witness MM-117, 13 Oct 2006, T. 9336, 9339; Witness MM-105, 2 Nov 2006, T. 10623; Ex. 966, p. 1.

1072 Witness MM-003, 9 Mar 2006, T. 2105–2106.

1073 Ljubica Vujanić, 18 Sep 2006, T. 8499–8501. *See also* Ljubica Vujanić, 18 Sep 2006, T. 8498–8499.

1074 Slobodan Jarčević, 12 Jul 2006, T. 6172–6173.

1075 *See supra* para. 138. Milan Babić, 20 Feb 2006, T. 1645–1647, 1651–53, testifying that Milan Martić never stated that the right conditions existed for the return of refugees. *See also* Veljko Džakula, 16 Jan 2006, T. 405, 407, 17 Jan 2006, T. 410–411; John McElligott, 29 May 2006, T. 4707–4708; Charles Kirudja, 31 May 2006, T. 4881; Ex. 232; Ex. 761, a message concerning the expulsion of 5 Croats from Ličko Petrovo Selo, which was copied to Milan Martić but to which he never replied, Charles Kirudja, 31 May 2006, T. 4879–4881. However, according to Slobodan Jarčević Milan Martić was of the view that both Serbs and Croats should be allowed to return, Slobodan Jarčević, 14 Jul 2006, T. 6331, 6333. *See also* Witness MM-105, 2 Nov 2006, T. 10620–10621. The Trial Chamber notes Milan Martić's reaction to information received in June 1991 that Croat refugees in Šibenik from the Knin area had been beaten and harassed by the SAO Krajina police. As for the injuries, Milan Martić said "Well, they can injure themselves, inflict injuries on themselves and then show this and say that somebody had beaten them" and that Martić's Police beat no one without a reason. Moreover, Milan Martić said that he had "told [the refugees that] if they wanted to stay they could stay, but [they] had to respect the laws of the SAO Krajina", something which they rejected and therefore left, Witness MM-079, 3 Apr 2006, T. 3112–3113. Lastly, the Trial Chamber notes that on 23 November 1994 Charles Kirudja met with Slobodan Milošević and Milan Martić in Belgrade during which meeting Milan Martić was not amenable to letting humanitarian assistance go to the Muslim population in the Bihać pocket in BiH according to a plan devised by Charles Kirudja and Yasushi Akashi. Milan Martić had to be ordered by Slobodan Milošević to let the assistance go through, Charles Kirudja, 1 Jun 2006, T. 4897, 4962, 4965; Ex. 765. *See also* Ex. 85.

1076 Defence Closing Statement, T. 11257–11258; T. 11264–11267

that this rebellion was aimed at achieving the independence of Croatia. The Defence claims that the federal authorities of the SFRY in Belgrade, including the Presidency, the federal Defence Ministry, the SSNO and the JNA lawfully acted with the aim to suppress this armed rebellion.[1077] The Defence further claims that the SAO Krajina leadership, the police and the TO had a duty to comply with the order and instructions of the federal authorities.[1078] The Prosecution submits that an armed conflict existed during the Indictment period and that the SAO Krajina leadership, including Milan Martić, directly participated in the armed conflict.[1079] **[page 130]**

344. Armed clashes erupted between Serbs and Croats from April 1991 in the territory of Croatia. The police and local people from both sides participated in the hostilities. Following these armed clashes, the JNA intervened to separate the sides by establishing buffer zones. From August 1991, the hostilities intensified with the direct involvement of the JNA and the Serb forces of the SAO Krajina. During the summer and autumn of 1991, numerous attacks were carried out on Croat majority villages by the JNA acting in coordination with the TO and the *Milicija Krajine*.[1080] The evidence further shows that throughout 1991, the SAO Krajina leadership, including Milan Martić, played an active role in the conflict. During the conduct of the hostilities, the SAO Krajina leadership requested and obtained military assistance from Serbia.[1081] The leadership participated in the establishment of a training camp, which was predominantly military in character where members of the *Milicija Krajine* were trained. These units subsequently directly participated in the hostilities.[1082] Furthermore, evidence shows that the leadership established the armed forces of the SAO Krajina, made up of the TO and the *Milicija Krajine,* and cooperated with the JNA in organising operations on the ground.[1083] During this period, Croatian authorities organised the Croatian army, *inter alia*, by forming a special military unit, the ZNG, which was employed in the hostilities.[1084]

345. From the end of 1991, several cease-fire agreements and agreements on the withdrawal of the JNA from Croatia were adopted.[1085] In particular, the Trial Chamber notes the adoption on 21 February 1992 of the UN Security Council Resolution 743 implementing the Vance Plan and establishing UNPROFOR in the UNPAs.[1086] However, the peace plan did not end the conflict, which continued in Croatia and also extended into northern BiH, and which continued through 1995 with several attacks and incursions from both sides.[1087]

346. The Trial Chamber finds that the crimes which Milan Martić is charged with were closely related to the conflict. In this regard, the Trial Chamber notes that the perpetrators of the crimes included members of the JNA, the TO and the *Milicija Krajine*, who were involved in the conduct of hostilities. **[page 131]**

347. The Trial Chamber finds that a state of armed conflict existed in the relevant territories of Croatia and BiH during the time relevant to the crimes charged in the Indictment. The Defence's argument concerning an armed rebellion is therefore dismissed. Moreover, the Trial Chamber finds that the crimes charged were committed in the context of the armed conflict. Consequently, the Trial Chamber has jurisdiction over all crimes charged in the Indictment and general requirements of Article 3 of the Statute have been fully satisfied.

[1077] Defence Closing Statement, T. 11262–11268.

[1078] Defence Closing Statement, T. 11264–11267. In addition, the Defence submits that during the hostilities a violation of Article 3 of Additional Protocol II was carried out by foreign states, *see ibid.* at T. 11260–11262. The Trial Chamber does not find it necessary to consider this argument.

[1079] Prosecution Rebuttal, T. 11375–11378. *See also* Prosecution Final Trial Brief, paras 356–357.

[1080] *See supra* section III D.

[1081] *See supra* section III B 2.

[1082] *See supra* section III B 3; section III D.

[1083] The Trial Chamber notes that the SAO Krajina leadership had meetings with JNA commanders in order to plan operations on the ground. *See,* for example, *supra* para. 174, referring to a meeting between Milan Martić and Colonel Dusan Smiljanić, Chief of Security of the JNA 10th Zagreb Corps in relation to the take-over of the Kostajnica area.

[1084] The Trial Chamber notes that ZNG were found in areas such as Kijevo, Hrvatska Dubica, Saborsko and Škabrnja where attacks were carried out by the JNA and the Serb forces.

[1085] *See supra* para. 138.

[1086] *See supra* para. 150.

[1087] *See supra* paras 153–154, 158, 303–313, 327–328.

2. General requirements under Article 5 of the Statute

348. The Trial Chamber recalls its finding regarding the existence of an armed conflict and finds that crimes with which Milan Martić has been charged were linked geographically and temporally with the armed conflict.

349. From around June 1991 through December 1991, military operations and raids were carried out against predominantly Croat villages in the SAO Krajina, including by the *Milicija Krajine*, the JNA and the TO.[1088] The attacked villages included Potkonije, Vrpolje, Glina, Kijevo, Drniš, Hrvatska Kostajnica, Cerovljani, Hrvatska Dubica, Baćin, Saborsko, Poljanak, Lipovača, Škabrnja, Nadin and Bruška. Villagers were left with no choice but to flee. During or immediately after the attacks, villagers who stayed behind were killed and beaten. Private and public property, including churches and schools, were destroyed and looted. Hundreds of Croat and other non-Serb civilians and members of Croatian armed forces and formations were captured during and after the attacks and were detained in Knin and other locations, where they were subjected to severe mistreatment.[1089] Moreover, grave discriminatory measures were taken against the Croat population throughout 1991.[1090]

350. There is evidence that there were unarmed or poorly armed Croatian protection forces in the villages of Lipovača, Poljanak and Bruška.[1091] The Trial Chamber considers that this does not alter the civilian nature of the attacked population.[1092] Croatian armed forces and formations, consisting of several hundred men, were present in Škabrnja and in Saborsko and fought against the JNA, the TO and the police forces of the SAO Krajina.[1093] However, considering the size of the civilian population in these areas, the Trial Chamber finds that the presence of Croatian armed forces and formations in the Škabrnja and Saborsko areas does not affect the civilian character of the attacked population. **[page 132]**

351. Acts of violence and intimidation against the Croat and other non-Serb population, including killings, beatings, robbery, theft, harassment and destruction of houses and Catholic churches, were prevalent in the RSK during the period between 1992 and 1995, and resulted in an exodus of the Croat and other non-Serb population from the territory of the RSK.[1094] The Trial Chamber also recalls the evidence regarding operation "*Koridor 92*". As a result of this operation, the Posavina area was devastated, and many civilians, including Croats, were killed.[1095] There is also evidence that in July 1992, the RSK authorities cooperated with the authorities of Bosanski Novi, BiH, in the displacement of the non-Serb population from Bosanski Novi to Croatia and other countries.[1096]

352. The Trial Chamber finds that there was a widespread and systematic attack directed against the Croat and other non-Serb civilian population in the relevant territories of Croatia and BiH during the time relevant to the crimes charged in the Indictment.

353. The evidence presented establishes beyond reasonable doubt that the perpetrators of the crimes charged in the Indictment knew about the attack on the civilian population and that their acts were part thereof.

3. Counts 1, 3 to 4, and 12 to 14 – Persecution, murder, destruction and plunder (Articles 3 and 5)

(a) Hrvatska Dubica[1097]

354. The Trial Chamber finds that the following 41 persons were detained in the fire station in Hrvatska Dubica on 20 October 1991 and intentionally killed the following day at Krečane near Baćin:

1088 *See supra* section III D.
1089 *See supra* section III D; section III E.
1090 *See supra* paras 324–326.
1091 *See supra* paras 201, 213, 266. There were ZNG and Croatian police forces in Hrvatska Dubica and the surrounding villages. However, they withdrew from the villages around 13 September 1991, *see supra* para. 177.
1092 Article 50 of Additional Protocol I; *Blaškić* Appeal Judgement, para. 115. *See supra* fn 95.
1093 *See supra* paras 224 (regarding Saborsko), 236–237 (regarding Škabrnja).
1094 *See supra* section III F; section III H 2–3.
1095 *See supra* para. 154.
1096 *See supra* para. 300.
1097 *See supra* section III D 2 (b).

Katarina Alavančić, Terezija Alavančić, Josip Antolović, Marija Batinović, Mara Ćorić, Mijo Ćović, Marija Delić, Ana Dikulić, Ruža Dikulić, Sofija Dikulić, Štjepan Dikulić, Antun Đukić, Marija Đukić, Antun Đurinović, Ana Ferić, Juraj Ferić, Kata Ferić, Filip Jukić, Marija Jukić, Jozo Karanović, Antun Krivajić, Reza Krivajić, Barbara Kropf, Pavao Kropf, Ivan Kulišić, Nikola Lončarić, Antun Mucavac, Ivo Pezo, Sofija Pezo, Anka Piktaja, Štjepan Sabljar, Veronika Stanković, Antun Švračić, Marija Švračić, Ana Tepić, Dušan Tepić, Ivan Trninić, Ivo Trninić, Kata Trninić, Terezija Trninić, and Katarina Vladić. The Trial Chamber finds that it has been proven beyond reasonable doubt that all victims were civilians and that they were taking no active part in the hostilities at the time of their deaths. Based on the evidence concerning the organised rounding up, detention and guarding of the civilians at the fire station by the *Milicija Krajine*, and the evidence that the victims were killed only one day subsequent to their detention, the Trial Chamber **[page 133]** considers it established beyond reasonable doubt that the *Milicija Krajine* was responsible for these killings. The Trial Chamber finds that all the elements of murder as a crime against humanity (Count 3) and as a violation of the laws or customs of war (Count 4) have been established.

355. The Trial Chamber heard evidence that between mid-September 1991 and mid-October 1991, approximately ten Croat or mixed ethnicity houses were destroyed in Hrvatska Dubica.[1098] There is evidence that "reservists" were involved in these acts. The Trial Chamber notes in particular that by mid-September 1991 there were only some 60 mainly elderly people remaining in the village and considers that this destruction was not justified by military necessity. However, the Trial Chamber considers that the destruction of 10 houses in a village of some 400 to 500 households gives rise to doubt as to whether this destruction can be considered as destruction on a large scale. The Trial Chamber therefore finds that the elements of wanton destruction of villages or devastation not justified by military necessity (Count 12) have not been met.

356. In relation to the destruction of the Catholic church in Hrvatska Dubica, the Trial Chamber considers that the evidence does not establish beyond reasonable doubt that it was destroyed before December 1991.[1099] For these reasons, the Trial Chamber concludes that the elements of the crime of destruction or wilful damage done to institutions dedicated to education or religion (Count 13) have not been met.

357. The Trial Chamber heard evidence that the JNA, TO and *Milicija Krajine* took part in looting of Croat houses in Hrvatska Dubica from mid-September 1991 and stole cars, tractors, tools, machinery, furniture and cattle.[1100] The Trial Chamber finds that this intentional appropriation of property was carried out without lawful basis or legal justification. Furthermore, given the scale of the looting, the Trial Chamber finds that it resulted in grave consequences for the victims, having regard to the overall effect on the civilian population and the multitude of offences committed. The Trial Chamber finds that all the elements of the crime of plunder of public or private property (Count 14) have been established.

358. The Trial Chamber recalls that among the persons rounded up in the fire station in Hrvatska Dubica, the clear majority were Croats. The Trial Chamber notes that there were also Serbs among those rounded up. However, the evidence shows that three Serbs managed to leave the fire station and that seven Croats managed to leave the fire station after their Serb neighbours or friends had contacted the guards. The Trial Chamber finds that the killings of the above-mentioned 41 victims **[page 134]** were carried out with intent to discriminate on the basis of Croat ethnicity. The elements of the crime of persecutions (Count 1) have therefore been met in relation to these killings.

(b) Cerovljani[1101]

359. The Trial Chamber finds that the following persons from Cerovljani were intentionally killed: Marija Antolović, Ana Blinja, Josip Blinja, Katarina Blinja, Nikola Blinja, Andrija Likić, Ana Lončar, Antun Lončar, and Kata Lončar (born 1906). The Trial Chamber recalls the manner in which the victims from Hrvatska Dubica were rounded up and detained in the fire station on 20 October 1991 and that they were

1098 *See supra* para. 180.
1099 *See supra* para. 194.
1100 *See supra* para. 180.
1101 *See supra* section III D 2 (c).

subsequently killed on 21 October 1991 at Krečane near Baćin and buried in the mass grave at that location. Furthermore, the Trial Chamber recalls its finding that the *Milicija Krajine* was responsible for the killing of the victims detained in the fire station. The Trial Chamber considers that the rounding up, detention and killing of the above-named victims from Cerovljani is almost identical to the events in Hrvatska Dubica, including that most of the victims were buried at the mass grave in Krečane. It is therefore established beyond reasonable doubt that the above-mentioned victims from Cerovljani were killed on or around 20 or 21 October 1991 either by the *Milicija Krajine*, or units of the JNA or the TO, or a combination of some of them that the Trial Chamber has found were present in the area at this time. The Trial Chamber considers it proven beyond reasonable doubt that these victims were civilians and that they were not taking an active part in the hostilities at the time of their deaths. The Trial Chamber therefore concludes that all the elements of murder as a crime against humanity (Count 3) and as a violation of the laws or customs of war (Count 4) have been established.

360. The Trial Chamber finds that on 13, 21 and 24 September 1991, armed Serbs from Živaja under the command of Nikola Begović burnt 10 houses in Cerovljani.[1102] The Trial Chamber finds that in a small village of some 500 people, the destruction of 10 houses must be regarded as destruction on a large scale. The Trial Chamber finds that there is evidence that this destruction was not carried out for reasons of military necessity. In this regard, the Trial Chamber notes in particular the evidence that only elderly persons remained in Cerovljani and that the armed Serbs came on three separate occasions. Finally, the intent of the perpetrators may be inferred from the repeated and deliberate nature of the attacks, as well as from the absence of any military necessity. The Trial Chamber therefore finds that the elements of wanton destruction of villages or devastation not justified by military necessity (Count 12) have been met. **[page 135]**

361. The Trial Chamber finds that on 24 September 1991 the same armed Serbs damaged the Catholic church in Cerovljani.[1103] The Trial Chamber finds that it has been proven that the church was not used for military purposes at the time it was damaged. The intent of the perpetrators to cause damage may be inferred from the fact that it occurred without any military necessity and as part of a series of repeated attacks targeting property in Cerovljani. The Trial Chamber therefore concludes that the elements of the crime of destruction or wilful damage done to institutions dedicated to education or religion (Count 13) have been met.

362. The Trial Chamber heard evidence that the car of Antun Blažević was stolen by the same armed Serbs mentioned above.[1104] Given the circumstances of this appropriation, the Trial Chamber considers that it was done without any lawful basis or legal justification. However, it is required that the property be of "sufficient monetary value" for its appropriation to involve grave consequences for the victim. While the Trial Chamber finds that a personal vehicle is an item of some value, the evidence is insufficient to establish that this particular appropriation resulted in grave consequences for the victim. The elements of the crime of plunder of public or private property under Article 3 (Count 14) have therefore not been met.

363. The Trial Chamber considers the totality of the evidence in relation to the events in Cerovljani in September and October 1991 to establish that the Croat civilian population and Croat property, including the Catholic church, were the objects of attack. In this respect, the Trial Chamber recalls the systematic and repeated incursions into the village by armed Serbs with resulting killings and destruction. Moreover, the Trial Chamber recalls that a Croat civilian, Kata Lončar, survived the occupation because she had connections with the Serbs.[1105] The Trial Chamber therefore finds it established beyond reasonable doubt that the killings of the ten victims referred to above were carried out with intent to discriminate on the basis of Croat ethnicity. Moreover, the Trial Chamber considers the evidence to establish beyond reasonable doubt that the destruction of private houses and of the Catholic church was carried out with the same discriminatory intent. The elements of the crime of persecutions (Count 1) have therefore been met in relation to the killings and the destruction in Cerovljani.

1102 *See supra* para. 187.
1103 *Ibid.*
1104 *Ibid.*
1105 *See supra* para. 188.

(c) Baćin and surroundings[1106]

364. The Trial Chamber recalls that Vera Jukić, Terezija Kramarić, Mijo Krnić, Marija Milašinović, Marija Šestić and Soka Volarević were exhumed from the mass grave at Krečane near **[page 136]** Baćin, and that Nikola Barunović was exhumed from the mass grave at Višnjevački Bok, where Ivo Pezo, who had previously been detained at the fire station in Hrvatska Dubica, was also exhumed. On the basis of this evidence, the Trial Chamber considers it established beyond reasonable doubt that these seven victims were killed at or around the same time as the victims from Hrvatska Dubica and Cerovljani were killed. Moreover, the Trial Chamber considers it established beyond reasonable doubt that these victims were intentionally killed either by the *Milicija Krajine*, or units of the JNA or the TO, or a combination of some of them which the Trial Chamber has found were present in the area from mid-October 1991. The Trial Chamber finds it established beyond reasonable doubt that the victims were civilians and that they were taking no active part in the hostilities at the time of their deaths. The Trial Chamber concludes that the elements of murder as a crime against humanity (Count 3) and as a violation of the laws or customs of war (Count 4) have been established.

365. The Trial Chamber finds that the following 21 persons from Baćin were intentionally killed around October 1991: Matija Barunović, Antun Bunjevac, Tomo Bunjevac, Antun Ćorić, Barica Ćorić, Josip Ćorić, Josip Ćorić, Vera Ćorić, Nikola Felbabić, Grga Glavinić, Anka Josipović, Ankica Josipović, Ivan Josipović, Josip Karagić, Kata Lončar (born 1931), Štjepan Lončar, Antun Ordanić, Luka Ordanić, Antun Pavić, Matija Pavić and Nikola Vrpoljac.[1107] The Trial Chamber finds it established beyond reasonable doubt that the victims were civilians and that they were taking no active part in the hostilities at the time of their deaths. Based on the totality of the evidence, the Trial Chamber finds it established beyond reasonable doubt that the above-mentioned victims from Baćin were killed around October 1991 either by the *Milicija Krajine*, or units of the JNA or the TO, or a combination of some of them which the Trial Chamber has found were present in the area at this time. The Trial Chamber finds that the elements of crimes of murder as a crime against humanity (Count 3) and of murder as a violation of the laws or customs of war (Count 4) have been established.

366. In relation to the destruction of houses and the Catholic church in Baćin, it has not been proven beyond reasonable doubt that the destruction occurred before December 1991.[1108] For these reasons, the Trial Chamber concludes that the elements of the crime of wanton destruction of villages or devastation not justified by military necessity (Count 12) and of the crime of destruction or wilful damage done to institutions dedicated to education or religion (Count 13) have not been met. **[page 137]**

367. The Trial Chamber recalls that in 1991 the population in Baćin was 95% Croat and 1.5% Serb. Even making allowance for the possibility that there may have been a few Serbs among the 21 victims referred to above, this does not affect the Trial Chamber's assessment that these killings were carried out with intent to discriminate on the basis of Croat ethnicity. With regard to the six victims exhumed from the mass graves in Krečane near Baćin and in Višnjevački Bok, the Trial Chamber recalls its findings regarding the killing of persons from Cerovljani and Hrvatska Dubica and finds that also these six killings were carried out with intent to discriminate on the basis of Croat ethnicity. The Trial Chamber therefore finds that all the elements of the crime of persecution (Count 1) have been met.

(d) Lipovača and neighbouring hamlets[1109]

368. The Trial Chamber recalls that Franjo Brozinčević, Marija Brozinčević, Mate Brozinčević, Mira Brozinčević Mirko Brozinčević, Roža Brozinčević and Katarina Cindrić were killed in Lipovača towards the end of October 1991. The evidence shows beyond reasonable doubt that the victims were civilians and were not taking an active part in the hostilities at the time of their deaths. The Trial Chamber recalls the warning given by the JNA to the inhabitants of Lipovača to beware of paramilitary forces who followed after the JNA. The Trial Chamber further recalls that after the departure of the JNA, paramilitary

---

[1106] *See supra* section III D 2 (d).
[1107] The Trial Chamber recalls that it will not consider the killing of Željko Abaza for a conviction, *see supra* fn 494. *See also supra* section I C.
[1108] *See supra* para. 195.
[1109] *See supra* section III D 3 (b).

forces arrived in Lipovača and Nova Kršlja from mid-October and that after their arrival the dead bodies of the above-mentioned victims were discovered. The Trial Chamber therefore considers it established beyond reasonable doubt that these intentional killings were perpetrated by Serb paramilitary forces. The Trial Chamber concludes that the elements of murder as a crime against humanity (Count 3) and as a violation of the laws or customs of war (Count 4) have been established.

369. The Trial Chamber heard evidence that at the end of September or early October 1991, the JNA arrived in Lipovača and fired its tanks at and damaged the Catholic church in Drežnik Grad nearby.[1110] The Trial Chamber has not been furnished with evidence that the church was not being used for military purposes at the time it was damaged. In this respect, the Trial Chamber notes that the Croatian police were also present in Drežnik Grad at the time. The Trial Chamber therefore concludes that the elements of the crime of destruction or wilful damage done to institutions dedicated to education or religion (Count 13) have not been met.

370. The Trial Chamber recalls that in 1991 the population in Lipovača was 83% Croat and 16% Serb. Moreover, the Trial Chamber recalls the warning to the villagers by members of the JNA to **[page 138]** beware of Serb paramilitary units who followed after the JNA and that such paramilitary units arrived after the JNA had left.[1111] The evidence shows that after their arrival, Mate Brozinčević, Roža Brozinčević, and Mirko Brozinčević, all Croats, were killed.[1112] The Trial Chamber finds the evidence to establish beyond reasonable doubt that these killings were carried out with intent to discriminate on the basis of Croat ethnicity. Moreover, in light of the totality of the evidence, the Trial Chamber also finds that the killings of Franjo Brozinčević, Mira Brozinčević, Marija Brozinčević, and Katarina Cindrić were carried out with the same discriminatory intent. The Trial Chamber therefore finds that all the elements of the crime of persecution (Count 1) have been met.

(e) Vukovići and Poljanak[1113]

371. The Trial Chamber finds that Tomo Vuković was intentionally killed by unidentified armed Serbs in Vukovići on 8 October 1991. The Trial Chamber considers it proven beyond reasonable doubt that Tomo Vuković was a civilian and that he was not taking an active part in the hostilities at the time of his death.[1114] Moreover, the Trial Chamber finds that Joso Matovina, Nikola Matovina, Dane Vuković (son of Poldin), Dane Vuković (son of Mate), Lucija Vuković, Milka Vuković, Nikola "Šojka" Vuković (born 1926) and Vjekoslav Vuković were intentionally killed on 7 November 1991. The Trial Chamber finds that all victims were civilians and that none of them were taking an active part in the hostilities at the time of their deaths. The Trial Chamber finds that on 7 November 1991 there was a mixture of JNA soldiers, including members of a JNA special unit from Niš, as well as local armed men present in Vukovići. The Trial Chamber finds it proven beyond reasonable doubt that these groups of soldiers were responsible for the killings of these victims.

372. In relation to the killings in Poljanak, the Trial Chamber finds that Ivan Vuković and Nikola Vuković (born 1938) were intentionally killed on 7 November 1991. The Trial Chamber finds that these victims were civilians and that neither of them was taking an active part in the hostilities at the time of their deaths. The evidence shows beyond reasonable doubt that the killings were perpetrated by around 20 armed soldiers present in Poljanak on 7 November 1991, who wore camouflage and olive-green uniforms and some of whom had arrived from the direction of Vukovići just before the killing of Ivan Vuković and Nikola Vuković. **[page 139]**

373. The Trial Chamber concludes that the elements of murder as a crime against humanity (Count 3) and as a violation of the laws or customs of war (Count 4) have been established for the killings in Vukovići and Poljanak.

374. The Trial Chamber finds that at least three houses were destroyed in Vukovići as a result of the shelling on 8 October 1991 and that one or two further houses were burnt in Vukovići on 7 November 1991.[1115] The

1110 *See supra* para. 202.
1111 *Ibid.*
1112 *See supra* para. 207.
1113 *See supra* section III D 3 (c).
1114 The Trial Chamber notes in particular Ex. 376, pp 6–7 which provides that Tomo Vuković was killed as he tried to escape from his house which had been set on fire.
1115 *See supra* para. 214.

Trial Chamber finds beyond doubt that in a village consisting of some six or seven houses, the burning of four or five houses constitutes destruction on a large scale. The evidence is insufficient to identify the perpetrators of the destruction on 8 October 1991. With regard to the destruction on 7 November 1991, the Trial Chamber recalls its finding regarding the presence in Vukovići on this date of a large group of soldiers.[1116] The Trial Chamber concludes that the destruction was perpetrated by members of these units. The circumstances of the destruction on 7 November 1991 show beyond reasonable doubt that the destruction was not justified by military necessity and that the destruction was carried out intentionally. The Trial Chamber concludes that all the elements of the crimes of wanton destruction of villages or devastation of villages not justified by military necessity (Count 12) have been met.

375. With regard to Poljanak, the evidence establishes that several houses, sheds and cars were burnt on 7 November 1991 by the soldiers present in the village.[1117] The Trial Chamber considers that the evidence establishes beyond reasonable doubt that the destruction occurred on a large scale. The Trial Chamber is satisfied that the destruction was not carried out for reasons of military necessity and that it was perpetrated intentionally. The Trial Chamber therefore finds that the elements of destruction of villages or devastation not justified by military necessity (Count 12) have been met.

376. The Trial Chamber also heard evidence that some private property was looted in Poljanak.[1118] However, the Trial Chamber was not presented with evidence which would enable it to conclude that the property appropriated was of sufficient monetary value to involve grave consequences for the relevant victims. The Trial Chamber therefore finds that the elements of plunder of public or private property (Count 14) have not been met.

377. The Trial Chamber recalls that all victims from Vukovići and Poljanak were Croats. The Trial Chamber also recalls that one of the soldiers in Poljanak boasted that he slit the throats of **[page 140]** Ustašas.[1119] The Trial Chamber finds that the above-mentioned killings in Vukovići and Poljanak were carried out with intent to discriminate on the basis of Croat ethnicity. The Trial Chamber therefore finds that all the elements of the crime of persecution (Count 1) have been met.

378. The Trial Chamber recalls that all the houses that were destroyed in Vukovići and Poljanak belonged to Croats. Moreover, the evidence shows that while burning houses in Poljanak the soldiers made comments, such as "Milošević built the house and Milošević is going to destroy it" and "what's Tuđman done for you? All you are going to get from him is a bullet in your head".[1120] The Trial Chamber finds it established beyond reasonable doubt that the destruction in Vukovići and Poljanak was carried out with intent to discriminate on the basis of Croat ethnicity. The Trial Chamber therefore concludes that all the elements of the crime of persecution (Count 1) have been met.

(f) Saborsko[1121]

379. The Trial Chamber finds that 20 persons were intentionally killed in Saborsko on 12 November 1991: Ana Bičanić, Milan Bičanić, Nikola Bičanić, Petar Bičanić, Darko Dumenčić, Ivica Dumenčić, Kata Dumenčić, Nikola Dumenčić, Kata Matovina (born 1920), Mate Matovina (born 1895), Milan Matovina, Slavko Sertić, Mate Špehar, Josip Štrk, Jure/Juraj Štrk, Ivan Vuković, Jeka/Jela Vuković, Jure Vuković (born 1929), Jure Vuković (born 1930), and Petar Vuković. With regard to the killings at Petar Bićanić's house, the evidence establishes that the two perpetrators wore Serbian dark grey uniforms and helmets with a five pointed red star. The Trial Chamber finds that they were members of units present in Saborsko after the attack on 12 November 1991. With regard to the other twelve victims, the Trial Chamber finds it established beyond reasonable doubt that they were killed by members of units present in Saborsko after the attack on 12 November 1991. The evidence proves that the eight persons killed at Petar "Krtan" Bičanić's house were

---

1116 *Ibid.*
1117 *See supra* para. 219.
1118 *Ibid.*
1119 *See supra* para. 216.
1120 *See supra* para. 219.
1121 *See supra* Section III D 3.

civilians and that they were not taking an active part in the hostilities at the time of their deaths. Furthermore, the Trial Chamber concludes, based on the totality of the evidence, that Ana Bičanić, Kata Dumenčić, Nikola Dumenčić, Kata Matovina, and Mate Matovina were civilians and that they were not taking an active part in the hostilities at the time of their deaths. With regard to Darko Dumenčić, Ivica Dumenčić, Milan Matovina, Slavko Sertić, Mate Špehar, Josip Štrk, and Petar Vuković, the Trial Chamber finds that the evidence is insufficient to establish beyond reasonable doubt whether they were civilians or taking no active part in the **[page 141]** hostilities at the time of their deaths.[1122] In conclusion, the Trial Chamber finds that the elements of murder as a crime against humanity (Count 3) and as a violation of the laws or customs of war (Count 4) have been established for the killings of the following 13 victims: Ana Bičanić, Milan Bićanić, Nikola Bićanić, Petar Bićanić, Kata Dumenčić, Nikola Dumenčić, Kata Matovina, Mate Matovina, Jure Štrk, Ivan Vuković, Jela Vuković, Jure Vuković, and his half brother also named Jure Vuković.

380. The Trial Chamber finds that during the shellings of Saborsko from August 1991 until the attack on 12 November 1991, the church of St. John and civilian buildings and homes were damaged. The evidence shows that there was a significant armed presence in and around Saborsko during this time period and that from at least September 1991 until the fall of Saborsko on 12 November 1991 a Croatian MUP reserve force was deployed in the church of St. John, which was used as an observation post, machinegun nest and for ammunition storage.[1123] While the evidence establishes that the shelling of Saborsko was carried out from several directions, including from the direction of the JNA barracks at Lička Jasenica, it is insufficient to conclude which units were responsible for the shelling. The Trial Chamber further finds that both the church of St. John and the church of the Mother of God were hit during the attack on 12 November 1991. With regard to the latter church, the evidence establishes that it was used as a military observation post on 12 November 1991. The Trial Chamber therefore finds prior to the attack on 12 November 1991 the church of St. John was used for a military purpose and that during the attack on 12 November both churches were used for military purposes. The Prosecution has thus failed to meet its burden of proof in this respect. There is further evidence that the two churches were destroyed by mid-December 1991. However, the evidence is insufficient to establish who carried out this destruction. The Trial Chamber therefore finds that the elements of destruction or wilful damage done to institutions dedicated to education or religion (Count 13) have not been met.

381. The Trial Chamber finds that after the attack on Saborsko, civilian houses and property were burnt on a large scale by the Serb forces which entered the village.[1124] The Trial Chamber finds that this burning was carried out deliberately and was not justified by military necessity, noting in particular the evidence that the attack had ceased at the time this destruction took place. Consequently, the elements of the crime of wanton destruction of villages or devastation not justified by military necessity (Count 12) have been met. **[page 142]**

382. The Trial Chamber heard evidence that Serb soldiers and policemen who participated in the attack looted shops and businesses and took tractors, cars and livestock.[1125] The Trial Chamber finds that this looting was done on a large scale, noting in particular the evidence that nearly every household in Saborsko had a tractor stolen.[1126] The Trial Chamber finds that this appropriation resulted in grave consequences for the victims, taking into account the overall effect on the civilian population and the multitude of offences committed. Furthermore, the evidence establishes that this appropriation was done intentionally and without lawful basis or legal justification. The elements of the crime of plunder of public or private property under Article 3 (Count 14) have therefore been met.

383. The Trial Chamber recalls that some of the soldiers present in Saborsko abused the inhabitants with profanities such as "Fuck your Ustasha mother" and that all Croat villagers should be slaughtered.[1127] The Trial Chamber further recalls that Saborsko was 93.9% Croat and 3.3% Serb.[1128] Even making allowance for the possibility that there may have been a few Serbs among the 13 victims referred to above, this does not

---

1122 In this regard, the Trial Chamber has taken into account the evidence that 20 to 30 villagers were organised into armed patrols from June 1991 (*see supra* para. 221) and the range of the ages of the male victims referred to at the time of their death (between 19 and 59 years old).

1123 *See supra* para. 224.

1124 *See supra* para. 227.

1125 *Ibid.*

1126 *See supra* fn 632.

1127 *See supra* para. 229.

1128 *See supra* fn 592.

affect the Trial Chamber's overall assessment that these killings were carried out with intent to discriminate on the basis of Croat ethnicity. The Trial Chamber therefore concludes that all the elements of the crime of persecution (Count 1) have been met.

384. The Trial Chamber recalls that the crime of wanton destruction of villages or devastation not justified by military necessity was committed. The evidence shows that houses were burnt in Tuk, Dumenčići, Solaje and Borik.[1129] The evidence further shows that Solaje was a Serb hamlet and that in Borik both Serb and Croat houses were burnt. Therefore, the Trial Chamber does not find it established beyond reasonable doubt that these acts of destruction were carried out with intent to discriminate on the basis of Croat ethnicity. The Trial Chamber therefore concludes that the elements of the crime of persecution (Count 1) have not been met.

(g) Vaganac

385. The Indictment charges that destruction and looting was committed in Vaganac, however the Trial Chamber has not been furnished with evidence supporting these charges. For these reasons, the Trial Chamber concludes that the elements of the crime of wanton destruction of villages or devastation not justified by military necessity (Count 12), of the crime of destruction or **[page 143]** wilful damage done to institutions dedicated to education or religion (Count 13) and of the crime of plunder of public or private property under Article 3 (Count 14) have not been met.

(h) Škabrnja[1130]

386. The Trial Chamber recalls that Josip Miljanić, Krsto Šegarić, Lucia Šegarić and Stana Vicković were killed at Slavko Šegarić's house in Ambar on 18 November 1991. The Trial Chamber finds that Krsto Šegarić was intentionally killed by Đuro Kosović, a local paramilitary soldier wearing a camouflage uniform with an SAO Krajina patch and who participated together with other SAO Krajina forces in the attack on Škabrnja. The Trial Chamber further finds that the evidence establishes beyond reasonable doubt that Josip Miljanić, Stana Vicković, and Lucia Šegarić were intentionally killed by other members of such paramilitary soldiers. The Trial Chamber finds that all four victims were civilians and that none of them were taking an active part in the hostilities at the time of their deaths. The Trial Chamber concludes that all of the elements of murder as a crime against humanity (Count 3) and as a violation of the laws or customs of war (Count 4) have been established for the above-mentioned killings.

387. The Trial Chamber finds that Jozo Brkić, Jozo Miljanić, Slavka Miljanić, Petar Pavičić, Mile Pavičić, Ilija Ražov, Kata "Soka" Rogić, Ivica Šegarić, Rade Šegarić and Vice Šegarić were intentionally killed outside Petar Pavičić's house in Škabrnja on 18 November 1991. The perpetrators of these killings were members of local paramilitary units, who participated, together with other SAO Krajina forces, in the attack on Škabrnja and who wore camouflage uniforms and different sorts of headgear. Mile Pavičić and Ivica Šegarić are listed in Annex I to the Indictment as civilian victims, however the evidence shows that both were members of the Croatian defence force in Škabrnja. The evidence shows that neither of them were taking an active part in the hostilities at the time of their deaths. The Trial Chamber concludes that the remainder of the victims were civilians and were not taking an active part in the hostilities at the time of their deaths. The Trial Chamber finds that the elements of murder as a crime against humanity (Count 3) and as a violation of the laws or customs of war (Count 4) have been established for the killings of Jozo Brkić, Jozo Miljanić, Slavka Miljanić, Petar Pavičić, Ilija Ražov, Kata "Soka" Rogić, Rade Šegarić, and Vice Šegarić. With regard to Mile Pavičić and Ivica Šegarić, the Trial Chamber finds that the elements of murder, as a violation of the laws or customs of war (Count 4), have been established.

388. The Trial Chamber finds that Novica Atelj, Stoja Brkić, Danka Brzoja, Ika Čirjak, Maša Čirjak, Marija Šestan and Jakov Šestan were intentionally killed at Pere Sopić's house in Nadin on 19 November 1991 by soldiers wearing JNA uniforms. The Trial Chamber finds that these victims **[page 144]** were civilians and were not taking an active part in the hostilities at the time of their deaths. The Trial Chamber finds that

1129 *See supra* para. 227.
1130 *See supra* section III D 4.

the elements of murder as a crime against humanity (Count 3) and as a violation of the laws or customs of war (Count 4) have been established for these killings.

389. The Trial Chamber finds that the following civilians were killed in Škabrnja, Nadin or Benkovac on 18 and 19 November 1991: Ivan Babić, Luka Bilaver, Marija Brkić (born 1943), Marko Brkić, Željko Ćurković, Marija Dražina, Ana Jurić, Grgo Jurić, Petar Jurić, Niko Pavičići, Josip Perica, Ljubo Perica, Ivan Ražov, Jela Ražov, Branko Rogić, Nikola Rogić, Petar Rogić, Kljajo Šegarić, Lucka/Luca Šegarić, Grgica "Maja" Šegarić, Mara Žilić, Milka Žilić, Pavica Žilić, Roko Žilić, Tadija Žilić and Marko Župan. The Trial Chamber further finds that these victims were taking no active part in the hostilities at the time of their deaths. The Trial Chamber finds that it has been proven beyond reasonable doubt that these victims, with the exception of Petar Rogić, were intentionally killed by members of the units, including JNA and TO units, which took part in the attack on Škabrnja and Nadin on 18 and 19 November 1991. With regard to Petar Rogić, the Trial Chamber finds that he was intentionally killed in Benkovac by unidentified perpetrators after having been taken from Škabrnja. The Trial Chamber finds that the elements of murder as a crime against humanity (Count 3) and as a violation of the laws or customs of war (Count 4) have been established for these killings, except for the killing of Petar Rogić.

390. The Trial Chamber finds that the following members of the Croatian defence forces present in Škabrnja and Nadin were killed on 18 and 19 November 1991: Vladimir Horvat, Nediljko Jurić, Slavko Miljanić, Gašpar Perica, Ante Ražov, Marko Rogić, Bude Šegarić, Miljenko Šegarić, Šime Šegarić, Nediljko Škara and Stanko Vicković. The evidence as to cause of death establishes beyond doubt that Ante Ražov, Šime Šegarić and Miljenko Šegarić were not taking an active part in the hostilities at the time of their deaths. The evidence further establishes beyond reasonable doubt that Vladimir Horvat, Gašpar Perica, and Marko Rogić were not taking an active part in the hostilities at the time of their deaths. The Trial Chamber finds that it has been proven beyond reasonable doubt that these victims, with the exception of Šime Šegarić and Miljenko Šegarić, were intentionally killed by members of the units, including JNA and TO units, which took part in the attack on Škabrnja and Nadin on 18 and 19 November 1991. With regard to Miljenko Šegarić, the Trial Chamber finds that he was intentionally killed in Benkovac by unidentified perpetrators after having been taken from Škabrnja. With regard to Šime Šegarić, the evidence establishes beyond reasonable doubt that he was taking no active part in the hostilities when he was intentionally killed in Knin by unidentified perpetrators after having been put by paramilitary soldiers in a JNA APC in Škabrnja. With regard to Slavko Miljanić, Bude Šegarić, Nediljko Jurić, Nediljko Škara, and Stanko Vicković the evidence is insufficient to establish that at the time of their deaths they were taking no active part in the hostilities. **[page 145]**

391. The Trial Chamber finds that the elements of murder as a violation of the laws or customs of war (Count 4) have been established for Ante Ražov, Vladimir Horvat, Gašpar Perica, Marko Rogić and Šime Šegarić, but not for Miljenko Šegarić.

392. The Trial Chamber finds that Marija Bilaver, Josipa Brkić, Mate Brkić and Kata Perica were killed in Škabrnja on 11 March 1992. Moreover, the Trial Chamber finds that the following persons were killed between 18 November 1991 and 11 March 1992: Grgo Bilaver, Peka Bilaver, Ana Brkić, Mijat Brkić, Jure Erlić, Dumica Gospić, Ljubomir Ivković, Neđelko Ivković, Tereza Ivković, Simica Jurjević, Mirko Kardum, Simo Ražov, Grgica Ražov, Marko Ražov, and Pera Škara. The Trial Chamber finds all of these victims, except Neđelko Ivković, were civilians and were taking no active part in the hostilities at the time of their deaths. The Trial Chamber finds that it has been proven beyond reasonable doubt that these victims were intentionally killed by members of the units that took part in the attack on Škabrnja and Nadin on 18 and 19 November 1991, or which were subsequently present in the area of Škabrnja following the attack and until March 1992. These units included JNA units, units from a TO brigade under JNA command, and paramilitary units. The Trial Chamber finds that the elements of murder as a crime against humanity (Count 3) and as a violation of the laws or customs of war (Count 4) have been established, except with regard to Neđelko Ivković, who the evidence establishes was a "Croat defender". However, it has not been established beyond reasonable doubt that he was not taking an active part in the hostilities at the time of his death.

393. With regard to Kata Brkić (born 1935), Kata Brkić (born 1939), Marija Brkić (born 1906), Božo Stura, and Draginja Stura, the evidence is insufficient to conclude whether they were killed between 18 November 1991 and 11 March 1992. With regard to Neđelko Ivković, the evidence shows that he was a member of the Croatian defence forces and that he was killed on 19 November 1991. The evidence is insufficient to conclude that he was not taking active part in the hostilities at the time of his death. The Trial Chamber finds

that the elements of murder as a crime against humanity (Count 3) and as a violation of the laws or customs of war (Count 4) have not been established for these killings.

394. The Trial Chamber recalls the evidence that there was intensive shelling in Škabrnja on the morning of the attack.[1131] Moreover, there is evidence that fire was opened on private houses by JNA tanks and using hand-held rocket launchers.[1132] The Trial Chamber recalls the evidence that members of Croatian forces were in some of the houses in Škabrnja.[1133] In the Trial Chamber's **[page 146]** opinion, this gives rise to reasonable doubt as to whether the destruction resulting from these actions was carried out for the purposes of military necessity. The elements of wanton destruction of villages or devastation not justified by military necessity (Count 12) have therefore not been met.

395. There is evidence that during the attack, the church of the Assumption of the Virgin in the centre of Škabrnja was shot at by a JNA tank. Furthermore, several soldiers entered the church and fired their weapons.[1134] The Trial Chamber finds that the church of the Assumption of the Virgin was not used for military purposes at the time of this damage and furthermore that the circumstances surrounding this damage establishes the intent of the perpetrators to cause such damage. The Trial Chamber notes the evidence that on 18 November 1991 a JNA tank opened fire in the direction of the school in Škabrnja and that by 19 November 1991 the school had been destroyed. However, the Trial Chamber considers the evidence to be insufficient to show that the school was not being used for military purposes at the time it was damaged. The Trial Chamber finds that the elements of the crime of destruction or wilful damage done to institutions dedicated to education or religion (Count 13) have been met in relation to the church of the Assumption of the Virgin.

396. The Trial Chamber heard evidence that looting was committed in Škabrnja by soldiers under the command of the Benkovac TO, by Serb paramilitaries, and by local Serbs after the attack.[1135] However, the Trial Chamber was not presented with sufficient evidence as to the nature or scale of such looting in order to enable it to establish whether the property appropriated was of sufficient monetary value to result in grave consequences for the victims. The Trial Chamber therefore finds that the elements of the crime of plunder of public or private property (Count 14) have not been met.

397. The Indictment charges that destruction and looting was committed in Nadin, however the Trial Chamber has not been furnished with evidence supporting these charges. For these reasons, the Trial Chamber concludes that the elements of the crime of wanton destruction of villages or devastation not justified by military necessity (Count 12), of the crime of destruction or wilful damage done to institutions dedicated to education or religion (Count 13) and of the crime of plunder of public or private property under Article 3 (Count 14) have not been met.

398. The Trial Chamber recalls that the majority of the victims in Škabrnja and Nadin, referred to above, were of Croat ethnicity. The evidence shows that soldiers present in Škabrnja threatened villagers hiding in the basements, saying "Come out you Ustaše, we are going to slaughter you all" **[page 147]** and that even women and children were being called "Ustašas" and were insulted by soldiers.[1136] The Trial Chamber further recalls that Škabrnja and Nadin were almost exclusively Croat villages.[1137] Even making allowance for the possibility that there may have been a few Serbs among the victims referred to above, this does not affect the Trial Chamber's overall assessment that these killings were carried out with intent to discriminate on the basis of Croat ethnicity. The Trial Chamber therefore concludes that all the elements of the crime of persecution (Count 1) have been met.

399. The Trial Chamber recalls that the church of the Assumption of the Virgin was destroyed and that it was not used for military purposes at the time of the destruction. The Trial Chamber recalls the manner in which the church was destroyed and concludes that this destruction was carried out with the same discriminatory intent as referred to above. The Trial Chamber therefore concludes that the elements of the crime of persecution (Count 1) have been met.

1131 *See supra* para. 239.
1132 *See supra* para. 241.
1133 *See supra* para. 240.
1134 *See supra* para. 241.
1135 *See supra* para. 263.
1136 *See supra* para. 248.
1137 *See supra* para. 235.

(i) Bruška[1138]

400. The Trial Chamber finds that Sveto Drača, Dragan Marinović, Draginja Marinović, Dušan Marinović, Ika Marinović, Krsto Marinović, Manda Marinović, Petar Marinović, Roko Marinović and Stana Marinović were intentionally killed in Bruška on 21 December 1991 by the *Milicija Krajine*. The Trial Chamber considers that the JNA reports which indicate that these killings were carried out in revenge do not disturb this finding.[1139] With the exception of Sveto Drača, all victims were civilians and were not taking an active part in the hostilities at the time of their deaths. The Trial Chamber finds that the elements of murder as a crime against humanity (Count 3) and as a violation of the laws or customs of war (Count 4) have been established for these victims.

401. With regard to Sveto Drača, the Trial Chamber concludes that he was a member of the JNA and that he was wearing an olive-drab uniform when he was killed. The Trial Chamber recalls that the JNA fought on the same side as the *Milicija Krajine*. For these reasons, the Trial Chamber concludes that the elements of the crime of murder as a violation of the laws or customs of war (Count 4) have not been met.

402. The evidence presented to the Trial Chamber is insufficient to establish when the destruction occurred in Bruška and who carried out this destruction.[1140] For these reasons, the Trial Chamber **[page 148]** concludes that the elements of wanton destruction of villages or devastation not justified by military necessity (Count 12) have not been met.

403. The Trial Chamber recalls that prior to the above-mentioned killings in Bruška, armed men identifying themselves as "Martic's men" or "Martic's Militia" would come to Bruška daily to intimidate the inhabitants, calling them "Ustašas", and telling them that Bruška would be a part of a Greater Serbia and that they should leave.[1141] The Trial Chamber further recalls that the victims, with the exception of Sveto Drača, were Croats. The Trial Chamber therefore finds it established beyond reasonable doubt that these killings were carried out with intent to discriminate on the basis of Croat ethnicity. Trial Chamber therefore concludes that the elements of the crime of persecution (Count 1) have been met for all victims except Sveto Drača.

4. Count 2 – Extermination

404. The Trial Chamber recalls that the crime of extermination does not require a minimum number of victims and that it may be established by an accumulation of separate and unrelated killings. However, the Trial Chamber stresses that it is nevertheless a requirement that the evidence supports a finding that the killings occurred on a large scale. In the present case, the Trial Chamber has examined the killing incidents charged under Count 2 and has, in particular, considered the evidence that the crimes were committed within a limited period of time and within a limited territory. Having considered these factors, as well as the totality of the evidence surrounding the killing incidents charged as extermination, the Trial Chamber finds that the evidence is insufficient to establish that the crime of extermination was committed on an accumulated basis. Thus, the element that the killings be committed on large scale has not been met.

405. The Prosecution has argued in the alternative that, should the Trial Chamber not find extermination on the basis of an accumulation of all the killings charged, the killings committed "at Baćin" would amount to extermination in and of themselves.[1142] The Trial Chamber understands this to refer to the killings carried out at Krečane near Baćin. The killings committed at Krečane were without doubt grave, particularly considering the organised and callous manner in which the evidence shows that they were carried out. However, the Trial Chamber cannot agree with the Prosecution. These killings, even taken together, cannot be considered as having been committed on a large scale. In other words, the killings at Krečane near Baćin do not meet the element of massiveness required for extermination. **[page 149]**

1138 *See supra* section III D 5.
1139 *See supra* para. 272.
1140 *See supra* para. 273.
1141 *See supra* para. 266.
1142 Prosecution Final Trial Brief, para. 397.

406. In conclusion, the Trial Chamber finds that the elements of the crime of extermination as a crime against humanity (Count 2) have not been met.

5. Counts 1 and 5 to 9 – Detention-related crimes and persecution

(a) Detention facility at the JNA 9th Corps barracks in Knin[1143]

407. The Trial Chamber finds that between 75 and 200 persons were detained at several locations at the premises of the JNA 9th Corps barracks in Knin. Among the detainees were both Croat and other non-Serb civilians, and members of Croatian armed forces and formations. The Trial Chamber finds that the former category of detainees were deprived of their liberty without due process of law.

408. The Trial Chamber heard evidence of many instances of beatings and mistreatment of the detainees at the JNA 9th Corps barracks. The Trial Chamber finds, in light of all the circumstances in which beatings and mistreatment were carried out, that such acts caused serious physical and/or mental suffering to the detainees. The Trial Chamber further finds that in some instances the mistreatment was carried out intentionally for the prohibited purpose of intimidating the victims.[1144]

409. The Trial Chamber finds that the detainees at the JNA 9th Corps barracks were detained by the JNA. Moreover, while the evidence is insufficient to establish who carried out the beatings and the mistreatment at the premises of the JNA 9th Corps barracks, the Trial Chamber concludes that the beatings and mistreatment were carried out at locations under the control of the JNA.

410. The Trial Chamber finds that the elements of the crimes of imprisonment (Count 5), torture (Counts 6 and 8), other inhumane acts (Count 7), and cruel treatment (Count 9) have been met in relation to the civilian detainees at the JNA 9th Corps barracks, including Petar Gurlica and Jere Misković. With regard to the detainees who were not civilian, including Luka Brkić, Ante "Neno" Gurlica and Marin Gurlica, the Trial Chamber finds that the elements of the crimes of torture (Count 8) and cruel treatment (Count 9) have been established.

411. The Trial Chamber recalls that most of those imprisoned in the JNA barracks in Knin were not of Serb ethnicity. Moreover, the Trial Chamber recalls the discriminatory remarks of Ratko Mladić when he visited the sports hall at the JNA barracks premises and that he threatened the detainees, saying that their fate would be the same as that of the people from Škabrnja.[1145] Furthermore, the Trial Chamber recalls that the detainees were forced to take oaths "for the King **[page 150]** and the fatherland, the Serbian fatherland".[1146] The Trial Chamber finds the evidence to establish beyond reasonable doubt that the crimes of imprisonment, torture, inhumane acts, and cruel treatment were carried out with intent to discriminate on the basis of ethnicity. The Trial Chamber therefore concludes that all the elements of the crime of persecution (Count 1) have been met in relation to the civilians who were detained at the JNA barracks.

(b) Detention facility at the old hospital in Knin[1147]

412. The Trial Chamber finds that from mid-1991 to mid-1992 between 120 and 300 persons were detained in the old hospital in Knin. Among the detainees were both Croats and other non-Serb civilians and members of Croatian armed forces and formations. The Trial Chamber finds that the majority of the former category of detainees were deprived of their liberty without due process of law. The Trial Chamber concludes that the elements of the crime of imprisonment under Count 5 have been met.

413. The Trial Chamber heard evidence of many instances of beatings and mistreatment of detainees at the old hospital.[1148] The Trial Chamber finds, in light of all the circumstances in which beatings and mistreatment

1143 *See supra* section III E 3 (a).
1144 *See supra* para. 283.
1145 *Ibid.*
1146 *Ibid.*
1147 *See supra* section III E 3 (b).
1148 *See supra* paras 288–289.

were carried out, that such acts caused serious physical and/or mental suffering to the detainees. The Trial Chamber further finds that in some instances the mistreatment was carried out intentionally for the prohibited purposes of obtaining information and/or to discriminate against them because of their ethnicity.[1149]

414. The Trial Chamber finds that as of the summer of 1991, the detention facility at the old hospital in Knin was run by the Ministry of Justice of the SAO Krajina. The evidence establishes beyond reasonable doubt that the beatings, mistreatment and torture of the detainees was carried out, *inter alia*, by members of the MUP, referred to by witnesses as "Martić's police", wearing blue police uniforms, by the *Milicija Krajine* and by persons wearing camouflage uniforms.[1150] Moreover, the evidence shows beyond reasonable doubt that the leadership permitted civilians from outside the old hospital and Serb detainees to beat and mistreat the non-Serb detainees.

415. The Trial Chamber finds that the elements of the crimes of torture (Counts 6 and 8), other inhumane acts (Count 7), and cruel treatment (Count 9) have been met in relation to the civilian **[page 151]** detainees. With regard to the detainees who were not civilian, the Trial Chamber finds that the elements of the crimes of torture (Count 8) and cruel treatment (Count 9) have been met.

416. The Trial Chamber recalls that at the old hospital in Knin there were Croat and other non-Serb detainees. The evidence shows that detainees were insulted by the guards, saying that "the Croatian nation has to be destroyed" and that "all Croats have to be killed".[1151] On one occasion, Vojislav Šešelj, from the Serbian Radical Party, visited the old hospital and asked the detainees "how many Serbian children they slaughtered, how many mothers".[1152] The Trial Chamber finds the evidence to establish beyond reasonable doubt that the crimes of imprisonment, torture, inhumane acts, and cruel treatment were carried out with intent to discriminate on the basis of ethnicity. The Trial Chamber therefore concludes that all the elements of the crime of persecution (Count 1) have been met in relation to the civilians who were detained at the old hospital in Knin.

(c) Detention facility at the SJB in Titova Korenica[1153]

417. The Trial Chamber heard evidence that the following persons were detained in the SJB in Titova Korenica for periods ranging between 10 days and 9 months: Vlado Vuković, Ignjac Ivanus, Nikola Pemper, Milan Pavlić, Perica Bićanić and Ivica Bićanić. The Trial Chamber recalls that they were all Croats. However, the Trial Chamber notes that Vlado Vuković and Ignjac Ivanus were Croatian policemen and that Perica Bićanić and Ivica Bićanić were members of the civilian protection force of Poljanak. Therefore, at the moment of their detention these persons did not hold the status of civilians, as opposed to Milan Pavlić, who the evidence shows was a civilian. The Trial Chamber has not received evidence as to whether Nikola Pemper was a civilian. Furthermore, the Trial Chamber has not received evidence that he was mistreated at the Titova Korenica SJB. With regard to the other the persons detained at the Titova Korenica SJB, the Trial Chamber finds that the evidence is insufficient to establish that they were civilians. With regard to Milan Pavlić, the Trial Chamber cannot establish beyond reasonable doubt he was detained without due process of law, and the Trial Chamber therefore finds that the elements of the crime of imprisonment (Count 5) have not been met.

418. The Trial Chamber heard evidence that while detained, Vlado Vuković was subjected to beatings and mistreatment, *inter alia*, by members of the MUP, who called themselves "Martić's men", and by persons in camouflage uniforms. The evidence shows that members of the *Milicija Krajine* were present during the beatings but did nothing to stop the beatings. Moreover, the Trial Chamber notes the evidence that Milan Pavlić and Perica Bićanić were severely mistreated. The **[page 152]** Trial Chamber finds, in light of all the circumstances in which the beatings and mistreatment were carried out, that they caused serious physical

1149 *See supra* para. 288.

1150 In this respect, the Trial Chamber notes in particular the evidence that members of the *Milicija Krajine* brought Stanko Erstić to the old hospital, that members of "Martić's Special Forces" carried out beatings, and that Milan Martić was present on one occasion wearing camouflage uniform with the *Milicija Krajine* patch on the sleeve, *see supra* para. 286.

1151 *See supra* para. 288.

1152 *Ibid.*

1153 *See supra* section III E 1.

and/or mental suffering to the detainees. The Trial Chamber further finds that the mistreatment of Vlado Vuković was carried out intentionally for the prohibited purpose of intimidating him.[1154]

419. With regard to Milan Pavlić, the Trial Chamber finds that the elements of the crime of inhumane acts (Count 7) have been met. However, the Trial Chamber has not received evidence to establish the elements of torture (Count 6) or persecutions (Count 1). With regard to the other detainees at the SJB, the Trial Chamber finds that the elements of the crimes of cruel treatment (Count 9), and, in relation to Vlado Vuković, also torture (Count 8), have been met.

(d) Detention facilities in Benkovac[1155]

420. The Trial Chamber finds that two Croats, Ivan Atelj and Šime Čačić, were detained in the SJB in Benkovac for 19 days. There is insufficient evidence to conclude that these persons were civilians. However, the evidence establishes that they were taking no active part in the hostilities.

421. During interrogations at the Benkovac SJB, Ivan Atelj and Šime Čačić were threatened and subjected to severe beatings by the policemen. The Trial Chamber finds that the beatings caused serious physical and mental suffering to the detainees. The Trial Chamber also finds that the mistreatment was carried out intentionally in order to obtain information.

422. The Trial Chamber concludes that the elements of the crimes of imprisonment (Count 5), torture (Count 6), inhumane acts (Count 7), and persecutions (Count 1) have not been met. However, the elements of the crimes of torture (Count 8) and cruel treatment (Count 9) have been met.

423. The Trial Chamber finds that at least 40 non-Serb civilians and members of the Croatian armed forces and formations, including Luka Brkić, Tomislav Šegarić, Tomislav Gurlica and Marin Jurić, were detained by the JNA at the kindergarten in Benkovac following the attack on Škabrnja. While the Trial Chamber considers that these persons were detained without due process of law, the Trial Chamber finds that this detention is more appropriately described as part of the crime of deportation to which these persons were later subjected. The Trial Chamber therefore finds that the elements of the crime of imprisonment (Count 5) have not been established. **[page 153]**

424. The evidence is insufficient as to whether the detainees at the kindergarten in Benkovac were mistreated. Thus, the Trial Chamber concludes that the elements of the crimes of inhumane acts (Count 7), torture (Counts 6 and 8), and cruel treatment (Count 9) have not been met. The evidence shows that Tomislav Šegarić, Tomislav Gurlica and Marin Jurić were taken from the kindergarten to the communal store in Biljani by the same individuals who detained them at the kindergarten. In Biljani, they were threatened and insulted after which they were brought back to the kindergarten.[1156] The Trial Chamber concludes, considering in particular the age of the three victims, that they were subjected to inhumane acts and cruel treatment in Biljani. The elements of these crimes (Counts 7 and 9) have therefore been met. However, the elements of torture (Counts 6 and 8) have not been met.

425. With regard to the mistreatment of Tomislav Šegarić, Tomislav Gurlica and Marin Jurić, the Trial Chamber finds that the evidence is insufficient to establish that these acts were carried out with intent to discriminate on the basis of Croat ethnicity. The Trial Chamber therefore concludes that the elements of the crime of persecution (Count 1) have not been met.

6. Counts 1, 10 and 11 – Persecution, deportation and forcible transfer[1157]

426. From 1990 through the spring of 1991, the Croat and non-Serb population in the Knin area was subjected to increasingly severe forms of discriminatory treatment.[1158] From June 1991, military operations

[1154] *See supra* para. 275.
[1155] *See supra* section III E 2.
[1156] *See supra* para. 278.
[1157] *See supra* section III F.
[1158] *See supra* para. 296.

were carried out by the SAO Krajina police, including the *Milicija Krajine,* the JNA and the TO against predominantly Croat villages, including Lovinac, Ljubovo, Glina, and Struga.[1159] This further raised the tensions. Following Milan Martić's ultimatum to the inhabitants of Kijevo, most of the Croat population was evacuated after which the JNA 9th Corps, the *Milicija Krajine* and the local TO attacked the village.[1160] The attack resulted in destruction of houses, damage to the church and looting. In August 1991, Croat civilians were displaced from the areas of Knin and Glina to areas under Croatian control.[1161] After the attack on Kijevo, the villages of Vrlika and Drniš were attacked. Destruction and looting were carried out following these attacks.[1162] There is further evidence that in 1991 Croats were killed by Serb forces in various locations in the SAO Krajina.[1163] **[page 154]**

427. From August 1991 and into early 1992, forces of the TO and the police of the SAO Krajina and of the JNA attacked Croat-majority villages and areas, including the villages of Hrvatska Kostajnica, Cerovljani, Hrvatska Dubica, Baćin, Saborsko, Poljanak, Lipovača, Škabrnja and Nadin. The displacement of the non-Serb population which followed these attacks was not merely the consequence of military action, but the primary objective of it. This conclusion is supported by the evidence of a generally similar pattern to the attacks. The area or village in question would be shelled, after which ground units would enter. After the fighting had subsided, acts of killing and violence would be committed by the forces against the civilian non-Serb population who had not managed to flee during the attack. Houses, churches and property would be destroyed in order to prevent their return and widespread looting would be carried out. In some instances the police and the TO of the SAO Krajina organised transport for the non-Serb population in order to remove it from SAO Krajina territory to locations under Croatian control. Moreover, members of the non-Serb population would be rounded up and taken away to detention facilities, including in central Knin, and eventually exchanged and transported to areas under Croatian control.[1164]

428. The Trial Chamber considers the evidence to establish beyond reasonable doubt that the systematic acts of violence and intimidation carried out, *inter alia*, by the JNA, the TO and the *Milicija Krajine* against the non-Serb population in the villages created a coercive atmosphere in which the non-Serb population did not have a genuine choice in their displacement. Based on this evidence, the Trial Chamber concludes that the intention behind these acts was to drive out the non-Serb population from the territory of the SAO Krajina. In this respect, the Trial Chamber recalls that the forces in question also undertook direct actions to remove those who had not fled to territories under Croatian control. The Trial Chamber also recalls that in spite of this intention to remove the non-Serb population from the territory of the SAO Krajina, in some instances the non-Serb population left their homes temporarily as a result of the acts of violence and intimidation and subsequently returned.

429. Based on the above, the Trial Chamber concludes that by the end of 1991 large numbers of the non-Serb population had been forcibly removed from the territory of the SAO Krajina to territories under the control of Croatia. The elements of the crime of deportation (Count 10) have therefore been met. Moreover, the Trial Chamber concludes that in some instances, due to the existing coercive atmosphere existing during this time period, members of the non-Serb population **[page 155]** fled their homes without going to territories under Croatian control.[1165] In such instances, the elements of the crime of other inhumane acts (forcible transfer) (Count 11) have been met.

430. With regard to the period from 1992 to 1995, the Trial Chamber has been furnished with a substantial amount of evidence of massive and widespread acts of violence and intimidation committed against the non-Serb population, which were pervasive throughout the RSK territory.[1166] The Trial Chamber notes, in particular, that during this time period there was a continuation of incidents of killings, beatings, robbery and theft, harassment, and extensive destruction of houses and Catholic churches carried out against the non-Serb

---

[1159] *See supra* paras 163–165.

[1160] *See supra* paras 166–168.

[1161] *See supra* para. 296.

[1162] *See supra* paras 170–171.

[1163] *See supra* para. 324.

[1164] In relation to Hrvatska Kostajnica, *see* section III D 2 (a), Hrvatska Dubica, *see* section III D 2 (b), Cervoljani, *see* section III D 2 (c), Baćin, *see* section III D 2 (d) *see also* section III D 2 (e). In relation to Lipovača, *see* section III D 3 (b). Poljanak and Vukovići, *see* section III D 3 (c). Saborsko, *see* section III D 3 (d). Škabrnja, *see* section III D 4.

[1165] *See supra* paras 202, 211, 222.

[1166] *See supra* paras 327–328.

population.[1167] These acts created a coercive atmosphere which had the effect of forcing out the non-Serb population from the territory of the RSK. As a consequence, almost the entire non-Serb population left the RSK. Moreover, in some instances the RSK authorities provided transportation and escorts in order to remove the non-Serb population to territories under Croatian control. Furthermore, the Trial Chamber recalls that in July 1992 the RSK authorities cooperated with the authorities in Bosanski Novi, BiH, in the displacement of the non-Serb population from that municipality to Croatia, Slovenia, Austria and Germany.[1168]

431. Based on the substantial evidence referred to above, the Trial Chamber finds that due to the coercive atmosphere in the RSK from 1992 through 1995, almost the entire non-Serb population was forcibly removed to territories under the control of Croatia. The elements of the crime of deportation (Count 10) have therefore been met.

432. In light of the evidence referred to above, which establishes that acts of killing, mistreatment, deportation, forcible transfer, destruction and other acts of intimidation were carried out with the intent to discriminate on the basis of ethnicity, the Trial Chamber finds that all the elements of persecution (Count 1) have been met for the period from August 1991 through 1995.

7. Counts 1 and 15 to 19 – Shelling of Zagreb on 2 and 3 May 1995[1169]

433. The Trial Chamber will consider Counts 15 to 19 in the following section.[1170] **[page 156]**

B. Findings on the individual criminal responsibility of Milan Martić

434. Milan Martić is charged with individual criminal responsibility pursuant to Article 7(1) in its entirety in relation to each Count. Article 7(1) of the Statute provides:

> A person who planned, instigated, ordered, committed or otherwise aided and abetted in the planning, preparation or execution of a crime referred to in articles 2 to 5 of the present Statute, shall be individually responsible for the crime.

With regard to Counts 3 to 14, and Count 1 insofar as it relates to these counts, the Trial Chamber finds that the individual criminal responsibility of Milan Martić is one of JCE pursuant to Article 7(1) of the Statute. With regard to Counts 15 to 19, and Count 1 insofar as it relates to these counts, the Trial Chamber finds that the individual criminal responsibility of Milan Martić is one of ordering pursuant to Article 7(1) of the Statute. Other modes of liability pursuant to Article 7(1) and 7(3) of the Statute will not be considered.

1. JCE pursuant to Article 7(1) of the Statute

435. JCE is established as a form of liability within the meaning of "commission" under Article 7(1) of the Statute.[1171] The Appeals Chamber found that "whoever contributes to the commission of crimes by [a] group of persons or some members of [a] group, in execution of a common criminal purpose, may be held to be criminally liable, subject to certain conditions".[1172] Three categories of JCE have been identified in customary international law.[1173] The Prosecution charges Milan Martić pursuant to the "first" and "third" categories of JCE.[1174] As stated by the Appeals Chamber, regardless of the categories of JCE, a conviction requires a finding

1167 *Ibid.*
1168 *See supra* para. 300.
1169 *See supra* section III G.
1170 *See infra* section IV B 4.
1171 *Tadić* Appeal Judgement, para. 190. *See also Prosecutor v. Milan Milutinović, Nikola Šainović and Dragoljub Ojdanić*, Case No. IT-99-37-AR72, Decision on Dragoljub Ojdanić's Motion Challenging Jurisdiction – Joint Criminal Enterprise, 21 May 2003, paras 20, 31; *Stakić* Appeal Judgement, para. 62 and the jurisprudence cited therein.
1172 *Tadić* Appeal Judgement, para. 190.
1173 *Tadić* Appeal Judgement, para. 220.
1174 Indictment, para. 5. The first form of JCE is described by the Appeals Chamber as follows: "all-co-defendants, acting pursuant to a common design, possess the same criminal intention; for instance, the formulation of a plan among the co-perpetrators

that the accused participated in a JCE. There are three requirements for such a finding: a plurality of persons, the existence of a **[page 157]** common purpose (or plan) which amounts to or involves the commission of a crime provided for in the Statute and the participation of the accused in this common purpose.[1175]

436. A JCE exists when a plurality of persons participate in the realisation of a common criminal purpose. However, they need not be organised in a military, political or administrative structure.[1176]

437. The first form of JCE requires the existence of a common purpose, which amounts to, or involves the commission of one or more crimes provided for in the Statute.[1177] The common purpose need not be previously arranged or formulated and may materialise extemporaneously.[1178]

438. It is not required that the principal perpetrators of the crimes which are part of the common purpose be members of a JCE.[1179] An accused or another member of a JCE may use the principal perpetrators to carry out the *actus reus* of a crime. However, "an essential requirement in order to impute to any accused member of the JCE liability for a crime committed by another person is that the crime in question *forms part of the common criminal purpose*."[1180] This may be inferred, *inter alia,* from the fact that "the accused or any other member of the JCE closely cooperated with the principal perpetrator in order to further the common criminal purpose."[1181]

439. For the first form of JCE, it is also required that the accused must both intend the commission of the crime and intend to participate in a common plan aimed at its commission.[1182] For the third form of JCE, the accused is held responsible for a crime outside the common purpose if, under the circumstances of the case, (i) it was *foreseeable* that such a crime might be perpetrated by one or other members of the group and (ii) the accused *willingly took that risk* (*dolus eventualis*). The crime must be shown to have been foreseeable to the accused in particular.[1183]

440. The requirement of participation for both forms of JCE is satisfied when the accused assisted or contributed to the execution of the common purpose. The accused need not have **[page 158]** performed any part of the *actus reus* of the perpetrated crime.[1184] It is also not required that his participation be necessary or substantial to the crimes for which the accused is found responsible.[1185] Nevertheless, it should at least be a significant contribution to the crimes for which the accused is to be found responsible.[1186]

---

to kill, where, in effecting this common design (and even if each co-perpetrator carries out a different role within it), they nevertheless all possess the intent to kill. The objective and subjective prerequisites for imputing criminal responsibility to a participant who did not, or cannot be proven to have, effected the killing are as follows: (i) the accused must voluntarily participate in one aspect of the common design (for instance, by inflicting non-fatal violence upon the victim, or by providing material assistance to or facilitating the activities of his co-perpetrators); and (ii) the accused, even if not personally effecting the killing, must nevertheless intend this result," *Tadić* Appeal Judgement, para. 196; the third is characterized as follows: "a common design to pursue one course of conduct where one of the perpetrators commits an act which, while outside the common design, was nevertheless a natural and foreseeable consequence of the effecting of that common purpose. An example of this would be a common, shared intention on the part of a group to forcibly remove members of one ethnicity from their town, village or region (to effect 'ethnic cleansing') with the consequence that, in the course of doing so, one or more of the victims is shot and killed," *Tadić* Appeal Judgement, para. 204.

1175 *Brđanin* Appeal Judgement, para. 364.

1176 *Vasiljević* Appeal Judgement, para. 100, referring to *Tadić* Appeal Judgement, para. 227.

1177 *Brđanin* Appeal Judgement, para. 418. The Appeals Chamber stated that the Trial Chamber should make a finding that the criminal purpose is not "merely the same, but also common to all of the persons acting together within a joint criminal enterprise", *Brđanin* Appeal Judgement, para. 430.

1178 *Brđanin* Appeal Judgement, para. 418.

1179 *Brđanin* Appeal Judgement, para. 410.

1180 *Brđanin* Appeal Judgement, para. 418.

1181 *Brđanin* Appeal Judgement, para. 410. *See also* paras 413, 418, noting that the requirement that the crime be part of a common purpose is a matter of evidence.

1182 *Brđanin* Appeal Judgement, para. 365. The Appeals Chamber also noted that "a Chamber can only find that the accused has the requisite intent if this is the only reasonable inference on the evidence", *id.* para. 429.

1183 *Brđanin* Appeal Judgement, para. 365. The Appeals Chamber has clarified that it is not a requirement that the crime which was foreseeable was carried out by a member of the JCE, but that it may be perpetrated also by one or more persons used by a member of the JCE in order to carry out the *actus reus* of the crimes forming part of the common purpose, *id.* para. 411.

1184 *Kvočka et al.* Appeal Judgement, para. 99; *Stakić* Appeal Judgement, para. 64.

1185 *Brđanin* Appeal Judgement, para. 430; *Kvočka et al.* Appeal Judgement, para. 98.

1186 *Brđanin* Appeal Judgement, para. 430.

2. Ordering pursuant to Article 7(1) of the Statute

441. Ordering requires that a person in a position of authority instructs another person to commit a crime.[1187] It is required that the crime in question was actually committed by the principal perpetrators.[1188] It is sufficient that the person ordering the crime possesses authority, whether *de jure* or *de facto*.[1189] This authority may be proved expressly or may be reasonably implied from the evidence.[1190] The mens rea is either direct intent in relation to the perpetrator's own ordering or indirect intent, that is, a person, who orders with the awareness of the substantial likelihood that a crime will be committed in the execution of that order, has the requisite mens rea for this mode of liability under Article 7(1) of the Statute.[1191]

3. Findings on Counts 1 to 14

(a) Common purpose

442. The Prosecution alleges that the common purpose of the JCE was "the forcible removal of a majority of the Croat, Muslim and other non-Serb population from approximately one-third of the territory of the Republic of Croatia ["Croatia"] and large parts of the Republic of Bosnia and Herzegovina ["BiH"], in order to make them part of a new Serb-dominated state."[1192] The evidence establishes the existence, as of early 1991, of a political objective to unite Serb areas in Croatia and in BiH with Serbia in order to establish an unified territory.[1193] Moreover, the evidence establishes that the SAO Krajina, and subsequently the RSK, government and authorities fully embraced and advocated this objective, and strove to accomplish it in cooperation with the Serb leaderships in Serbia and in the RS in BiH.[1194] The Trial Chamber considers that such an objective, that is to unite with other ethnically similar areas, in and of itself does not amount to a common purpose within the **[page 159]** meaning of the law on JCE pursuant to Article 7(1) of the Statute. However, where the creation of such territories is intended to be implemented through the commission of crimes within the Statute this may be sufficient to amount to a common criminal purpose.

443. The Trial Chamber recalls that several armed clashes occurred during the spring and early summer of 1991 between SAO Krajina and Croatian armed forces and formations.[1195] Initially, these clashes were the result of tensions between the Croatian and SAO Krajina police and the climate of fear and mistrust between the Serb and Croat inhabitants. The evidence shows that beginning with the armed attack on the predominantly Croat village of Kijevo in August 1991, the SAO Krajina MUP and TO forces cooperated with the JNA. As of this point in time, the JNA was firmly involved on the side of the SAO Krajina authorities in the struggle to take control of territory in order to unite predominantly Serb areas.[1196] The Trial Chamber recalls the ultimatum given by Milan Martić on 26 August 1991 in relation to the imminent attack on Kijevo that "[y]ou and your leadership have brought relations between the Serbian and Croatian populations to such a state that further co-existence in our Serbian territories of the SAO Krajina is impossible".[1197] From at least this point in time until early 1992, several other predominantly Croatian villages were attacked by forces of the TO and the police forces of the SAO Krajina and of the JNA acting in cooperation.[1198] The Trial Chamber recalls that these attacks followed a generally similar pattern, which involved the killing and the removal of the Croat population.[1199] Furthermore, after these attacks, widespread crimes of violence and intimidation and crimes against private and public property were perpetrated against the Croat population, including

---

1187 *Kordić and Čerkez* Appeal Judgement, para. 28; *Gacumbitsi* Appeal Judgement, para. 182.
1188 *Brđanin* Trial Judgement, para. 267 (with further references).
1189 *Brđanin* Trial Judgement, para. 270. *See also Kordić and Čerkez* Appeal Judgement, para. 28, in which it is held that a formal superior-subordinate relationship is not required.
1190 *Brđanin* Trial Judgement, para. 270; *Limaj et al.* Trial Judgement, para. 515.
1191 *See Kordić and Čerkez* Appeal Judgement, paras 29–30; *Blaškić* Appeal Judgement, para. 42.
1192 Indictment, para. 4.
1193 *See supra* Section III I.
1194 *Ibid.*
1195 *See supra* Section III D 1.
1196 *See supra* paras 166–168, 170–171; section III I.
1197 *See supra* para. 166.
1198 *See supra* section III D 2–5 (*see also* paras 170–171); section IV A 6.
1199 *See supra* section IV A 6.

detention in facilities run by MUP forces of the SAO Krajina and the JNA.[1200] The threat clearly expressed in Milan Martić's ultimatum was therefore carried out throughout the territory of the SAO Krajina in this period through the commission of widespread and grave crimes which created an atmosphere of fear in which the further presence of Croats and other non-Serbs in these territories was made impossible. In this respect, the Trial Chamber has concluded that the displacement of the non-Serb population was not a mere side-effect but rather a primary objective of the attacks.[1201]

444. Widespread acts of violence and intimidation intensified against the non-Serb population and became pervasive throughout the RSK territory from 1992 to 1995.[1202] These acts were committed by members of the TO and the police of the RSK, and of the JNA, as well as members **[page 160]** of the local Serb population, and created such a coercive atmosphere that the Croat and other non-Serb inhabitants of the RSK were left with no option but to flee.[1203]

445. From at least August 1991, the political objective to unite Serb areas in Croatia and in BiH with Serbia in order to establish a unified territory was implemented through widespread and systematic armed attacks on predominantly Croat and other non-Serb areas and through the commission of acts of violence and intimidation. In the Trial Chamber's view, this campaign of violence and intimidation against the Croat and non-Serb population was a consequence of the position taken by the SAO Krajina and subsequently the RSK leadership that co-existence with the Croat and other non-Serb population, in Milan Martić's words, "in our Serbian territories of the SAO Krajina", was impossible.[1204] Thus, the implementation of the political objective to establish a unified Serb territory in these circumstances necessitated the forcible removal of the non-Serb population from the SAO Krajina and RSK territory. The Trial Chamber therefore finds beyond reasonable doubt that the common purpose of the JCE was the establishment of an ethnically Serb territory through the displacement of the Croat and other non-Serb population, as charged in Counts 10 and 11.

(b) Plurality of persons

446. The Trial Chamber has been furnished with a substantial amount of evidence that the objective to unite Serb territories was espoused by the leaderships in Serbia, in the RS in BiH, and in the SAO Krajina and the RSK.[1205] The SAO Krajina, and later the RSK, government which included Milan Babić and Milan Martić, sought and received significant financial, logistical and military support from Serbia, including from the MUP and SDB of Serbia, and from the RS in BiH.[1206] Milan Martić also admitted that he had himself "personally never ceased this cooperation" and that there was "good cooperation with the leadership of Serbia, notably the [MUP]."[1207] In fact, the evidence shows that the police of the SAO Krajina were mainly financed with funds and material from the MUP and the SDB of Serbia.[1208] This support continued from 1991 to 1995 and even included modifications regarding units and personnel within the armed forces of the SAO Krajina and of the RSK.[1209] There is evidence that the cooperation between the armed forces of the SAO Krajina, and later the RSK, and the JNA was extensive and covered such major military actions as those carried out in Kijevo, Hrvatska Kostajnica, Saborsko and in Škabrnja, as well as **[page 161]** operation *Koridor 92*.[1210] In this respect, the Trial Chamber recalls the evidence that the SVK and the VJ were in reality one and the same organisation, only located at two separate locations.[1211] Moreover, the evidence of Milan Martić's arrest in 1991 gives a clear example of joint

1200 *Ibid.*
1201 *Ibid.*
1202 *See supra* section III H 2–3; section IV A 6.
1203 *See supra* section IV A 6.
1204 *See supra* para. 166.
1205 *See supra* section III I
1206 *See supra* section III B 2; section III C 2.
1207 *See supra* section III C 2, referring to Ex. 951, p. 1.
1208 *See supra* section III B 2.
1209 *See supra* section III B 2; section III C 2. *See also* para. 142.
1210 *See supra* section III C 1; section III D 1–5. With regard to Kijevo, the Trial Chamber notes in particular Ex. 45, p. 48, *see supra* fn 397.
1211 *See supra* fn 371.

cooperation between political leaders in the SAO Krajina, in the RS in BiH and in Serbia.[1212] The Trial Chamber has been furnished with evidence that this type of cooperation continued until 1995.[1213] The Trial Chamber therefore finds that at least Blagoje Adžić, Milan Babić, Radmilo Bogdanović, Veljko Kadijević, Radovan Karadžić, Slobodan Milošević, Ratko Mladić, Vojislav Šešelj, Franko "Frenki" Simatović, Jovica Stanišić, and Captain Dragan Vasiljković participated in the furtherance of the above-mentioned common criminal purpose.

(c) Milan Martić's participation in the JCE

447. As noted above, the Prosecution alleges that Milan Martić participated in the JCE in a number of ways.[1214]

448. Milan Martić's contacts with other members of the JCE had already begun during the autumn of 1990 and intensified during 1991 and onwards.[1215] The evidence shows that these contacts were close and direct and that as a result, substantive financial, logistical and military support was rendered to the SAO Krajina and the RSK.[1216] The evidence is clear that Milan Martić actively worked together with the other JCE participants to fulfil the objective of a united Serb state, something which he expressed publicly on several occasions between 1991 and 1995.[1217]

449. Milan Martić was considered one of the most important and influential political figures in the SAO Krajina and the RSK governments.[1218] During his tenure as Minister of the Interior of the SAO Krajina and RSK, Milan Martić exercised absolute authority over the MUP, including the power to intervene on an individual level by appointing and removing chiefs of the SJBs as well as the authority to disband units within the MUP.[1219]

450. The evidence shows that the displacement of the non-Serb population had commenced in and around Knin already in 1991. The ultimatum issued by Milan Martić to the Croatian SJB and the inhabitants of Kijevo at the end of August 1991 is indicative of Milan Martić's mindset in **[page 162]** relation to the Croat population of the SAO Krajina.[1220] Furthermore, Milan Martić contributed to this displacement by fuelling the atmosphere of insecurity and fear through radio speeches wherein he stated he could not guarantee the safety of the non-Serb population.[1221]

451 There is no doubt that Milan Martić was aware that the non-Serb population was being driven out as a result of the coercive atmosphere in the SAO Krajina and the RSK. The sheer scale of the widespread and pervasive crimes against the non-Serb population of the SAO Krajina and the RSK must have made such crimes common knowledge.[1222] The Trial Chamber recalls that crimes committed within the territory of the RSK were discussed at RSK government sessions.[1223] Furthermore, Milan Martić and the MUP were informed by UNCIVPOL of the multitude of crimes which were being committed against the non-Serb population.[1224] Here, the Trial Chamber recalls that Milan Martić himself issued detailed instructions concerning the cooperation of the MUP with UNPROFOR and UNCIVPOL, and concerning reporting obligations within the MUP. The evidence shows that these instructions were adhered to.[1225]

1212 *See supra* section III B 2.
1213 *See supra* section III C 2.
1214 Indictment, para. 7. *See supra* para. 6.
1215 *See supra* section III B 2.
1216 *See supra* section III B 2; section III C 2.
1217 *See supra* section III B; section III C.
1218 *See supra* section III J.
1219 *Ibid.*
1220 *See supra* para. 166.
1221 *See supra* section III F.
1222 The Trial Chamber recalls the testimony of Slobodan Jarčević, the Foreign Minister of the RSK, that the RSK government "did not take any steps against the members of any other nation or ethnic group" and that it was difficult for the RSK government to protect the Croats who remained in the RSK because many of the crimes were committed out of a revenge for losing family members, *see supra* fn 1053. In view of the pervasive nature of the crimes committed against the non-Serb population, the Trial Chamber does not find this evidence credible. In this respect, the Trial Chamber also recalls the evidence that Milan Martić was aware of the various detention facilities, which existed in the SAO Krajina and the RSK, *see supra* para. 294; Ex. 518; Ex. 919.
1223 *See supra* section III J.
1224 *Ibid.*
1225 *Ibid.*

Moreover, the Trial Chamber recalls that Milan Martić disbanded both Predrag Baklajić's unit and Veljko Rađunović's police unit due to criminal activities. However, despite the substantial evidence concerning ongoing crimes committed by the MUP throughout the territory of the SAO Krajina and the RSK, the Trial Chamber has only been presented with evidence of a few examples where Milan Martić intervened to punish members of the MUP who had behaved in a criminal manner.[1226] The Trial Chamber cannot but conclude that Milan Martić deliberately refrained from intervening against perpetrators who committed crimes against the non-Serb population.

452. The evidence establishes that Milan Martić actively participated in the forcible removal of the non-Serb population both through his own actions and those of the members of the MUP. There is evidence of direct acts of deportation perpetrated by MUP forces, which resulted in the removal from the SAO Krajina and RSK territory of the non-Serb population.[1227] In this respect, the Trial Chamber recalls in particular the collection centre at Vrpolje, only a few kilometres north of Knin, **[page 163]** which was secured by members of the Knin SJB and to which they directed the non-Serb population, who desired to leave the RSK territory. Members of the Knin SJB organised bus transport of the non-Serb population to areas under Croatian control. During a meeting with Cedric Thornberry on 14 June 1993, Milan Martić requested that Croats who wished to leave the RSK sign statements that no one had put pressure on them to leave.[1228] Milan Martić was aware of the persecutory and coercive atmosphere which existed and had existed in the SAO Krajina and RSK territory for a long time and that those non-Serbs who expressed a desire to leave the territory did so without having a genuine choice in their displacement. Moreover, there is evidence that Milan Martić repeatedly and publicly opposed the return of refugees.[1229]

453. The Trial Chamber therefore concludes that Milan Martić intended to forcibly displace the non-Serb population from the territory of the SAO Krajina, and subsequently the RSK, and actively participated in the furtherance of the common purpose of the JCE.

454. The Trial Chamber finds that the crimes found to have been perpetrated against the non-Serb population under Counts 3 to 9, Counts 12 to 14, and Count 1 insofar as it relates to these counts, were outside of the common purpose of the JCE. However, the Trial Chamber recalls that Milan Martić was aware that the non-Serb population was being subjected to widespread and systematic crimes, including killings, unlawful detentions, beatings while detained, and crimes against property, as a result of the coercive atmosphere in the SAO Krajina and the RSK. The Trial Chamber considers that this atmosphere was created and sustained by the actions of Milan Martić and other members of the JCE. The Trial Chamber therefore finds that the crimes which have been found to be outside the common purpose were foreseeable to Milan Martić. Furthermore, the evidence includes only scarce reference to Milan Martić acting to take measures to prevent or punish such crimes. Moreover, despite the overwhelming evidence of the scale and gravity of the crimes being committed against the non-Serb population, Milan Martić persisted in pursuing the common purpose of the JCE. Thus, the Trial Chamber considers it proven beyond reasonable doubt that Milan Martić willingly took the risk that the crimes which have been found to be outside the common purpose might be perpetrated against the non-Serb population.

455. The Trial Chamber finds that Milan Martić incurs individual criminal responsibility pursuant to Article 7(1) of the Statute for Counts 3 to 14, and Count 1, insofar as it relates to these counts. **[page 164]**

4. Findings on Counts 1 and 15 to 19

(a) Milan Martić's ordering of the shelling of Zagreb on 2 and 3 May 1995

456. The Trial Chamber recalls that Milan Martić repeatedly admitted in media statements that he had ordered the shelling of Zagreb on 2 and 3 May 1995. In this Trial Chamber's view, this is persuasive evidence, which is further supported by circumstantial evidence.

1226 *Ibid.*
1227 *See supra* section III D 2–5; section III F.
1228 *See supra* para. 299.
1229 *See supra* para. 341.

457. The evidence shows that already in 1992 and 1993 Milan Martić, as Minister of the Interior, considered attacking Zagreb as a response to Croatian attacks on RSK cities.[1230] Moreover, as President of the RSK on 24 October 1994, Milan Martić threatened to strike Zagreb with rockets if the situation deteriorated.[1231]

458. The Trial Chamber recalls that following the start of Operation Flash in the early morning hours on 1 May 1995, the Chief of the SVK Main Staff General Milan Čeleketić deployed the M-87 Orkan unit to Vojnić 50 kilometres south of Zagreb. The Trial Chamber further recalls that during a meeting which was held on 1 May 1995, Milan Martić and Milan Čeleketić were in favour of a non-peaceful solution. Following this meeting, at 1300 hours and in the presence of Milan Martić, Milan Čeleketić issued an order to several military commanders to shell Sisak.[1232] The evidence shows that Sisak was shelled at 1700 hours on 1 May 1995. The Trial Chamber finds that the above-mentioned evidence establishes that Milan Martić was involved from the beginning in the RSK's military response to Operation Flash. The Trial Chamber notes the evidence of Patrick Barriot that Milan Martić merely took responsibility for the ordering of the shelling of Zagreb, and that Patrick Barriot came to this conclusion on "an analysis of his personality".[1233] In light of the significant evidence to the contrary presented above, the Trial Chamber finds his testimony unconvincing.

459. The Trial Chamber recalls that according to the RSK Constitution, the President led the SVK in times of peace and war in accordance with the Constitution and the decisions of the Supreme Defence Council.[1234] Accordingly, any decision to shell Zagreb should have been taken by the collegiate body of the Supreme Defence Council. However, the evidence establishes that Milan Martić and Milan Čeleketić circumvented the Supreme Defence Council. The Trial Chamber recalls the evidence of Rade Rašeta, Chief of Security of the SVK Main Staff, that the decisions to shell Zagreb on 2 and 3 May 1995 were not taken by the Supreme Defence Council but by the SVK **[page 165]** Commander and the President of the RSK.[1235] This is further supported by reports of the two RSK commissions referred to above.[1236]

460. In light of the totality of the evidence, the Trial Chamber finds beyond reasonable doubt that Milan Martić ordered the shelling of Zagreb on 2 and 3 May 1995.

(b) Military targets in Zagreb and the nature of the M/87 Orkan

461. The Defence argues that there were military targets in Zagreb at the time of the attacks on 2 and 3 May 1995, including the Ministry of Interior, Ministry of Defence, Zagreb/Plešo airport which had a military purpose, and the Presidential Palace.[1237] The Trial Chamber notes the report of 2 May 1995 from the SVK Main Staff to the VJ General Staff, which provides that the following targets in Zagreb were fired at by Orkan rockets on that day: the Ministry of Defence, the Presidential Palace and Zagreb/Plešo airport.[1238] The Trial Chamber notes that of these targets, the only one that was hit was Zagreb/Plešo airport, where one bomblet landed in a parking lot.[1239] The report also provides that "[a]ccording to our source, the Ministry of Defence in Križanićeva Street was hit." However, the Trial Chamber notes that the Ministry of Defence is not located in this street but in the nearby Baureova Street.[1240] The Trial Chamber notes that two police buildings in Matica Hrvatska Street also received damage, to the roof and upper floors, on 2 May 1995.[1241] However, as will be shown below, the presence or otherwise of military targets in Zagreb is irrelevant in light of the nature of the M-87 Orkan.

1230 *See supra* section III G 3.
1231 *Ibid.*
1232 *Ibid.*
1233 Patrick Barriot, 9 Nov 2006, T. 10773–10774, 10777–10778, 10 Nov 2006, T. 10841.
1234 *See supra* para. 155.
1235 *See supra* para. 321.
1236 *Ibid.*
1237 Defence Final Trial Brief, paras 90, 147. *See also* Ex. 1042, Tab 2; Ex. 1043, Tab 2, DVD 1, pp 31, 37, 42.
1238 Ex. 95, p. 3.
1239 Branko Lazarević, 14 Jun 2006, T. 5629; Ex. 810; Ex. 1042, Tab 2; Ex. 1043, Tab 2, DVD 1, pp 1–2.
1240 Branko Lazarević, 15 Jun 2006, T. 5663–5664 (testifying that the Ministry complex is 300 by 400 metres and includes military facilities and institutions); Ex. 1042, Tab 2; Ex. 1043, Tab 2, DVD 1, pp 30–31; Ex. 814; Jožef Poje, 7 Jun 2006, T. 5211.
1241 Ex. 808, F-86 to F-89; Ex. 807, F-34 to F-68; Ex. 806; Branko Lazarević, 14 Jun 2006, T. 5628, 15 Jun 2006, T. 5676, 5678.

462. The M-87 Orkan is a non-guided projectile, the primary military use of which is to target soldiers and armoured vehicles.[1242] Each rocket may contain either a cluster warhead with 288 so-called bomblets or 24 anti-tank shells.[1243] The evidence shows that rockets with cluster warheads containing bomblets were launched in the attacks on Zagreb on 2 and 3 May 1995.[1244] Each bomblet contains 420 pellets of 3mm in diameter.[1245] The bomblets are ejected from the rocket at a **[page 166]** height of 800–1,000m above the targeted area and explode upon impact, releasing the pellets.[1246] The maximum firing range of the M-87 Orkan is 50 kilometres.[1247] The dispersion error of the rocket at 800–1,000m in the air increases with the firing range. Fired from the maximum range, this error is about 1,000m in any direction.[1248] The area of dispersion of the bomblets on the ground is about two hectares.[1249] Each pellet has a lethal range of ten metres.[1250]

463. The evidence shows that the M-87 Orkan was fired on 2 and 3 May 1995 from the Vojnić area, near Slavsko Polje, between 47 and 51 kilometres from Zagreb. However, the Trial Chamber notes in this respect that the weapon was fired from the extreme of its range. Moreover, the Trial Chamber notes the characteristics of the weapon, it being a non-guided high dispersion weapon. The Trial Chamber therefore concludes that the M-87 Orkan, by virtue of its characteristics and the firing range in this specific instance, was incapable of hitting specific targets. For these reasons, the Trial Chamber also finds that the M-87 Orkan is an indiscriminate weapon, the use of which in densely populated civilian areas, such as Zagreb, will result in the infliction of severe casualties. By 2 May 1995, the effects of firing the M-87 Orkan on Zagreb were known to those involved.[1251] Furthermore, before the decision was made to once again use this weapon on Zagreb on 3 May 1995, the full impact of using such an indiscriminate weapon was known beyond doubt as a result of the extensive media coverage on 2 May 1995 of the effects of the attack on Zagreb.

(c) Defence argument on reprisals

464. The Defence submits that the shelling of Zagreb may be considered lawful reprisal, carried out with the aim of putting an end to violations of international humanitarian law committed by "the Croatian military and police forces".[1252] In particular, the Defence submits that the shelling of **[page 167]** Zagreb was a reaction to Operation Flash, which was in breach of the cease fire agreement, and "conducted without any respect to the norms of international humanitarian law".[1253]

465. In the law of armed conflict, belligerent reprisals are acts resorted to by one belligerent which would otherwise be unlawful, but which are rendered lawful by the fact that they are taken in response to a violation

[1242] Jožef Poje, 6 Jun 2006, T. 5067–5068, 5136; Ex. 7, p. 38.

[1243] Ex. 7, pp 23, 44; Jožef Poje, 6 Jun 2006, T. 5068–5069. *See also* Ex. 94, p. 8; Jožef Poje, 6 Jun 2006, T. 5103, 5129–5130, 5133–5134.

[1244] Jožef Poje, 7 Jun 2006, T. 5159; Reynaud Theunens, 27 Jan 2006, T. 824–825; Ex. 772; Ex. 775; Branko Lazarević, 15 Jun 2006, T. 5689; Ex. 809, F-65, F-66.

[1245] Jožef Poje, 6 Jun 2006, T. 5133; Ex. 7, p. 23; Ex. 94, p. 8.

[1246] Jožef Poje, 6 Jun 2006, T. 5129-5130, 5133; Ex. 7, pp 23, 44; Ex. 94, p. 8.

[1247] Jožef Poje, 6 Jun 2006, T. 5066-5067; Ex. 7, p. 47.

[1248] Firing a rocket from a distance of 49 kilometres results in an elliptical area of dispersion of 972m by 1032m, Jožef Poje, 6 Jun 2006, T. 5100–5103; Ex. 776; Ex. 778; Ex. 779. *See also* Ex. 777 (showing the area of dispersion for the distance of 40 kilometres). Rade Rašeta, 2 May 2006, T. 3939, testified that "persons who are familiar with these artillery pieces knew that they were intended for targeting wider areas and not points, and that as such they could entail a lot of casualties". In this respect, Jožef Poje testified that it would have been easy to conclude what the consequences of using the Orkan would be, however allowed for the possibility that not everyone is familiar with the consequences of using this weapon, Jožef Poje, 6 Jun 2006, T. 5113–5114. *See also* Jožef Poje, 6 Jun 2006, T. 5064–5065, 5108, 5118, 7 Jun 2006, T. 5155–5156, 5190–5192, 5233–5234; Ex. 7, pp 19, 38, 61, 66–68.

[1249] Ex. 7, p. 23; Jožef Poje, 6 Jun 2006, T. 5069; Ex. 94, p. 8; Ex. 771. If the warhead opens along the edge of the dispersion ellipse, it is possible that part of the bomblets fall outside of the ellipse, by approximately 100 m (since the surface area on which the bomblets drop is two hectares), Jožef Poje, 6 Jun 2006, T. 5103.

[1250] Ex. 7, pp 23, 44.

[1251] *See supra* section III G 2.

[1252] Defence Final Trial Brief, paras 86–93. *See also* paras 114–136. This argument was contested by the Prosecution, *see* Prosecution Closing Argument, 10 Jan 2006, T. 11221–11223.

[1253] Defence Final Trial Brief, para. 125.

of that law committed by the other belligerent.[1254] Reprisals are therefore drastic and exceptional measures employed by one belligerent for the sole purpose of seeking compliance with the law of armed conflict by the opposite party. It follows that reprisals, in order to be considered lawful, are subject to strict conditions. These conditions are well-established in customary law and are set forth below.[1255]

466. Reprisals may be used only as a last resort and only when all other means have proven to be ineffective.[1256] This limitation entails that reprisals may be exercised only after a prior and formal warning has been given, which has failed to put an end to the violations committed by the adversary.[1257] In addition, reprisals may only be taken after a decision to this effect has been made at the highest political or military level. [1258]

467 A further requirement is that the measures taken must be proportionate to the initial violation of the law of armed conflict of the opposite party.[1259] According to this condition, the reprisals must cease as soon as they have achieved their purpose of putting an end to the breach which provoked them.[1260] Finally, acts of reprisal must respect the "laws of humanity and dictates of public conscience".[1261] The Trial Chamber interprets this condition to mean that reprisals must **[page 168]** be exercised, to the extent possible, in keeping with the principle of the protection of the civilian population in armed conflict and the general prohibition of targeting civilians.[1262]

468. The Trial Chamber finds that the evidence presented to the Trial Chamber regarding the shelling of Zagreb fails to show that the conditions for lawful reprisals have been met. First, even if the Trial Chamber was to assume that the Croatian forces had engaged in serious violations of international humanitarian law during Operation Flash, the evidence shows that the shelling was not carried out as a last resort, after having exhausted all other means. Indeed, the Trial Chamber has been provided with evidence that peace negotiations were ongoing during Operation Flash, until 3 May 1995.[1263] Furthermore, no formal warning was given prior to the shelling that acts of reprisals would be carried out in reaction to the alleged violations conducted during Operation Flash.[1264] The Trial Chamber cannot therefore find that the shelling of Zagreb constituted a lawful reprisal and does not consider it necessary to analyse the issue of reprisal any further. The Defence argument, in this regard, is consequently dismissed.

(d) General requirements of Article 3 and Article 5 of the Statute

469 The Trial Chamber recalls its findings concerning the existence of an armed conflict in the territories relevant to the crimes charged in the Indictment. The Trial Chamber considers the shelling of Zagreb on

---

1254 Commentary ICRC, para. 3427, citing the definition of reprisal adopted by the Institut de droit international in Annuaire 708-11, 1934 and defining reprisal as follows: "compulsory measures, derogating from the ordinary rules of such law, taken by a belligerent following unlawful acts to its detriment committed by another belligerent and which intend to compel the latter, by injuring it, to observe the law".

1255 *See* Commentary ICRC on Additional Protocols, para. 3457, which reports that the discussion about the issue of reprisal at the Diplomatic Conference on the adoption of the Additional Protocols to the Geneva Conventions showed agreement among the States on some minimum restrictions, as spelled out in the main text. *Kupreskić et al.* Trial Judgement, para. 535.

1256 *Ibid.* For example, the YPA Military Manual of the SFRY (FRY) (1988), para. 29 states that "before they undertake reprisals, the armed forces of the SFRY shall try to force the enemy to respect the laws of war by means of other methods for preventing violations of such laws". A similar wording is contained in the military manuals of numerous States, including, *inter alia*, Canada, LOAC Manual (1999), p. 15–3, para. 17; United States, Field Manual (1956), para. 497(b); Germany, Military Manual (1992), para. 478; Netherlands, Military Manual (1993), p. IV-5; United Kingdom Military Manual (1958), para. 646; Ecuador's Naval Manual (1989), para. 6.2.3.1; New Zealand, Military Manual (1992), para. 1606(4)(c) and (d); Spain, LOAC Manual (1996), Vol. I, para.2.3.b. (6). Several of the above references to military manuals were extracted from *Customary International Humanitarian Law*, Volume II, pp 3328–3337.

1257 Commentary ICRC on Additional Protocols, para. 3457; *Kupreskić et al.* Trial Judgement, para. 535.

1258 *Ibid.*

1259 Commentary ICRC on Additional Protocols, para. 3457; *Kupreskić et al.* Trial Judgement, para. 535.

1260 *Ibid.*

1261 *Ibid.*

1262 *See supra* section II E.

1263 *See supra* para. 302.

1264 *See supra* section III G 1–2. In this regard, the Trial Chamber notes that the threat to shell Zagreb given by Milan Martić to Ambassador Peter Galbraith on 24 October 1994 cannot be considered a warning for the purpose of reprisal for at least three reasons: it was given long before Operation Flash commenced, it was not addressed directly to the Croatian authorities, and it lacked any elements of formality. The same is true for the speech given by Milan Martić on 10 February 1995 to the SVK commanding officers and for the interview of Milan Čeleketić reported in a newspaper article on 24 March 1995. The Trial Chamber notes also that with regard to the interview of Milan Čeleketić, it could not be considered as a warning for the purpose of reprisal since it was not given by the highest political or military authority.

2 and 3 May 1995, and the crimes in relation to this shelling with which Milan Martić has been charged, were related to the armed conflict in such a way as to meet the relevant general requirements of Article 3 and Article 5 of the Statute. Moreover, in particular due to the characteristics of the M-87 Orkan and due to the large-scale nature of the attack, the Trial Chamber finds that the shelling constituted a widespread attack directed against the civilian population of Zagreb. Furthermore, the Trial Chamber considers it proven beyond doubt that Milan Martić was aware of this attack on the civilian population and that his ordering of the shelling formed part of the attack. The Trial Chamber therefore concludes that the general requirements of Article 3 and Article 5 of the Statute have been met. **[page 169]**

(e) Counts 15 and 16 – Murder

470. The Trial Chamber finds that the deaths of Ana Mutevelić, Damir Dračić, Stjepan Krhen, Ivanka Kovač, Ivan Brodar, Luka Skračić and Ivan Markulin were caused as a result of the rocket attacks on Zagreb, which were ordered by Milan Martić. Having regard in particular to the Trial Chamber's findings concerning the nature of the M-87 Orkan and that Milan Martić, who ordered the use of the M-87 Orkan, was aware that death was a probable consequence of this attack, the Trial Chamber finds that the mental element of the crime of murder is established. The Trial Chamber recalls that Ivan Markulin was a member of the Croatian MUP and that he was in the process of deactivating a bomb at the time of his death and was not taking an active part in the hostilities. The Trial Chamber therefore finds that Milan Martić bears individual criminal responsibility under Article 7(1) of the Statute for Counts 15 and 16 for the murder of Ana Mutevelić, Damir Dračić, Stjepan Krhen, Ivanka Kovač, Ivan Brodar, and Luka Skračić. The Trial Chamber further finds that Milan Martić bears individual criminal responsibility under Article 7(1) of the Statute for Count 16 for the murder of Ivan Markulin.

(f) Counts 17 and 18 – Inhumane acts under Article 5(i) and cruel treatment under Article 3

471 The Trial Chamber finds that the evidence from persons injured during the shelling of Zagreb is representative of the injuries and suffering caused to the 214 persons who were injured on 2 and 3 May 1995. The Trial Chamber therefore concludes that the shelling caused serious mental and/or physical suffering to those injured. The Trial Chamber considers that Milan Martić knew that the shelling was likely to cause such suffering, and thus intentionally committed acts which amount to cruel treatment under Article 3 and inhumane acts under Article 5 against these persons. The Trial Chamber recalls that of the persons injured, 7 were not civilians. The Trial Chamber therefore finds Milan Martić incurs individual criminal responsibility under Article 7(1) of the Statute for Count 17, other inhumane acts under Article 5(i), and for Count 18 for cruel treatment under Article 3 in relation to 207 victims and for Count 18, cruel treatment under Article 3, in relation to the other 7 victims.

(g) Count 19 – Attacks on civilians under Article 3

472. In examining the responsibility of Milan Martić for the crime of attacks on civilians under Article 3, the Trial Chamber recalls that a direct attack on civilians may be inferred from the indiscriminate character of the weapon used. The Trial Chamber has previously found that the M-87 Orkan was incapable of hitting specific targets.[1265] The Trial Chamber has also found that these **[page 170]** attacks resulted in death and serious injury to the civilian population. Having regard in particular to the nature of the M-87 Orkan and the finding that Milan Martić knew of the effects of this weapon, the Trial Chamber finds that Milan Martić wilfully made the civilian population of Zagreb the object of this attack. Milan Martić therefore incurs individual criminal responsibility under Article 7(1) of the Statute for Count 19, attacks on civilians under Article 3.

(h) Count 1 – Persecution

473. The Trial Chamber recalls the situation prevailing prior to the shelling of Zagreb, including the launch of Operation Flash by Croatian armed forces. Moreover, the Trial Chamber recalls that prior to the shelling

---

[1265] *See supra* section IV B 4 (b).

of Sisak and Zagreb, Milan Martić considered the shelling of Croatian cities as a response to Croatian attacks on RSK cities. However, the Trial Chamber has not found any evidence which would persuade it beyond reasonable doubt that Milan Martić intended to commit such attacks, including the attacks which were eventually carried out on Zagreb on 2 and 3 May 1995, with discriminatory intent on the basis of ethnicity. Rather, the evidence shows that Milan Martić intended to shell the city of Zagreb in order to retaliate on Croatia and to stop further Croatian attacks on the RSK. While an attack on a city, such as in this case, is without doubt grave, the Trial Chamber cannot find that it establishes in and of itself that it was carried out with the requisite intent. The Trial Chamber therefore concludes that the elements of the crime of persecution (Count 1) have not been established.

C. Cumulative convictions

474. Cumulative convictions, that is multiple convictions entered under different statutory provisions in relation to the same conduct, are permissible only if each statutory provision involved has a materially distinct element not contained in the other. An element is materially distinct from another if it requires proof of a fact not required by the other element. Where this test is not met, the Trial Chamber will enter a conviction only under the more specific provision.[1266]

475. Milan Martić has been found criminally responsible for the crime of persecution (Count 1) and for the crimes charged in Counts 3 to 19.[1267] The acts underlying the findings of persecution include the acts underlying the findings of the crimes under Counts 3 to 14. Persecution requires a **[page 171]** materially distinct element that is not present as an element in any of the other crimes, that is proof that the act or omission discriminated in fact and that the act or omission was committed with the specific intent to discriminate on the basis of one of the grounds listed in Article 5.[1268] The other crimes under Counts 3 to 14 require proof of materially distinct elements, which are not present in the crime of persecution. As a result, cumulative conviction is permissible for persecution and for the crimes found to have been committed under Counts 3 to 14.

476. Milan Martić has been found criminally responsible for the following crimes, charged under Article 3 and Article 5 of the Statute, which are based on the same conduct: murder as a crime against humanity (Count 3) and murder as a violation of the laws and customs of war (Count 4),[1269] torture as a crime against humanity (Count 6) and torture as a violation of the laws or customs of war (Count 8),[1270] inhumane acts as a crime against humanity (Count 7) and cruel treatment as a violation of the laws or customs of war (Count 9),[1271] murder as a crime against humanity (Count 15) and murder as a violation of the laws and customs of war (Count 16),[1272] and inhumane acts as a crime against humanity (Count 17) and cruel treatment as a violation of the laws or customs of war (Count 18).[1273] Crimes under Article 3 of the Statute require a materially distinct element to be proven which is not required for the crimes under Article 5 of the Statute, that is the nexus between the acts of the accused and the armed conflict. Crimes under Article 5 of the Statute require a materially distinct element that is not required for the crimes under Article 3 of the Statute, a widespread or systematic attack directed against any civilian population. Therefore, cumulative convictions are permissible under Article 3 and Article 5.[1274]

1266 *Čelebići* Appeal Judgement, paras 412–413. This test has been further clarified by the Appeals Chamber in *Kordić and Čerkez* as follows: "[w]hen applying the *Čelebići* test, what must be considered are the legal elements of each offence, not the acts or omissions giving rise to the offence. What each offence requires, as a matter of law, is the pertinent inquiry. The Appeals Chamber will permit multiple convictions for the same act or omission where it clearly violates multiple distinct provisions of the Statute, where each statutory provision contains a materially distinct element not contained in the other(s), and which element requires proof of a fact which the elements of the other statutory provision(s) do not. [...]", *Kordić and Čerkez* Appeal Judgement, para. 1033 (footnotes omitted). *See also Kunarac et al.* Appeal Judgement, para. 177; *Stakić* Appeal Judgement, paras 355–358.

1267 *See supra* section IV A, B.

1268 *Stakić* Appeal Judgement, paras 359–364; *Kordić and Čerkez* Appeal Judgement, para. 1041.

1269 *See supra* paras 354, 359, 364, 365, 368, 373, 379, 386–389, 392, 400.

1270 *See supra* paras 410, 415.

1271 *See supra* paras 410, 415, 419, 424.

1272 *See supra* para. 471.

1273 *See supra* para. 472.

1274 *Jelišić* Appeal Judgement, para. 82.

477. Milan Martić has been found criminally responsible for the crimes of torture (Count 6) and inhumane acts (Count 7) as crimes against humanity, in relation to the same conduct.[1275] The crime of torture has a materially distinct element, that is, the act or omission must have been carried out for a prohibited purpose. This element is not required for the crime of inhumane acts. However, the crime of inhumane acts does not require proof of a materially distinct element.[1276] Accordingly, a cumulative conviction for the two crimes is not permissible and the Trial Chamber will enter a conviction for the crime of torture only. The same reasoning applies to the crime of torture and the **[page 172]** crime of cruel treatment as violations of laws and customs of war, for which Milan Martić has been found criminally responsible in relation to the same conduct.[1277]

478. In relation to the shelling of Zagreb, Milan Martić has been found criminally responsible for the crimes of murder (Count 16), cruel treatment (Count 18), and attacks on civilians (Count 19), all violations of laws and customs of war under Article 3.[1278] These crimes are based on the same conduct. The crime of attacks on civilians requires the existence of an attack directed against a civilian population, the killings of, or infliction of serious bodily injury to, civilians as a consequence of the attack, and the intent to make the civilian population the object of attack. As the crime of attacks on civilians requires materially distinct elements not required for murder or cruel treatment, the latter crimes are absorbed by the crime of attacks on civilians. As a result, cumulative conviction for these crimes is not permissible and the Trial Chamber will only enter a conviction for the crime of attacks on civilians.[1279]

D. Summary of the Trial Chamber's findings in relation to each count

479. The Trial Chamber finds Milan Martić **NOT GUILTY** of:

Count 2: Extermination, a crime against humanity

480. The Trial Chamber finds Milan Martić **GUILTY** pursuant to Article 7(1) of the Statute on the following counts:

Count 1:	Persecutions, a crime against humanity;[1280]
Count 3:	Murder, a crime against humanity;[1281]
Count 4:	Murder, a violation of the laws or customs of war;[1282]
Count 5:	Imprisonment, a crime against humanity;[1283]
Count 6:	Torture, a crime against humanity;[1284]
Count 7:	Inhumane acts, a crime against humanity;[1285] **[page 173]**
Count 8:	Torture, a violation of the laws or customs of war;[1286]
Count 9:	Cruel treatment, a violation of the laws or customs of war;[1287]

1275 *See supra* paras 410, 415.

1276 *Kunarac et al.* Appeal Judgement, paras 142, 144, confirming *Kunarac et al.* Trial Judgement, para. 497. *See also Brđanin* Trial Judgement, para. 481; *Krnojelac* Trial Judgement, para. 181.

1277 *See supra* paras 410, 415, 419, 422.

1278 *See supra* paras 471, 472, 473.

1279 *Strugar* Trial Judgement, para. 449.

1280 *See supra* paras 358, 363, 367, 370, 377–378, 383, 398–399, 403, 411, 416, 432. Hence acquitting Milan Martić as to the rest of the charges under Count 1, *see supra* paras 384, 403, 419, 422, 425,474.

1281 *See supra* paras 354, 359, 364–365, 368, 373, 379, 386–389, 392, 400. Hence acquitting Milan Martić as to the rest of the charges under Count 3, *see supra* paras 387, 389–393, 401.

1282 *See supra* paras 354, 359, 364–365, 368, 373, 379, 386–389, 391–392, 400. Hence acquitting Milan Martić as to the rest of the charges under Count 4, *see supra* paras 389–393, 401.

1283 *See supra* paras 410, 412. Hence acquitting Milan Martić as to the rest of the charges under Count 5, *see supra* paras 417, 422, 423.

1284 *See supra* paras 410, 415. Hence acquitting Milan Martić as to the rest of the charges under Count 6, *see supra* paras 419, 422, 424.

1285 *See supra* paras 410, 415, 419, 424. Hence acquitting Milan Martić as to the rest of the charges under Count 7, *see supra* para. 422, 424.

1286 *See supra* paras 410, 415, 419, 422. Hence acquitting Milan Martić as to the rest of the charges under Count 8, *see supra* paras 424.

1287 *See supra* paras 410, 415, 419, 422, 424. Hence acquitting Milan Martić as to the rest of the charges under Count 9, *see supra* para. 424.

Count 10:	Deportation, a crime against humanity;[1288]
Count 11:	Forcible transfer, a crime against humanity;[1289]
Count 12:	Wanton destruction of villages, or devastation not justified by military necessity, a violation of the laws or customs of war;[1290]
Count 13:	Destruction or wilful damage done to institutions dedicated to education or religion, a violation of the laws or customs of war;[1291]
Count 14:	Plunder of public or private property, a violation of the laws or customs of war;[1292]
Count 15:	Murder, a crime against humanity;[1293]
Count 16:	Murder, a violation of the laws or customs of war;[1294]
Count 17:	Inhumane acts, a crime against humanity;[1295]
Count 18:	Cruel treatment, a violation of the laws or customs of war;[1296]
Count 19:	Attacks on civilians, a violation of the laws or customs of war.[1297]

While the Trial Chamber has found that the elements have been established for the crimes charged under Count 16 and Count 18, in view of the fact that these crimes are absorbed by the crime of attacks on civilians under Count 19, the Trial Chamber will only enter a conviction with respect to the crime of attacks on civilians.

V. SENTENCING LAW AND FACTS

A. Applicable law

481. The relevant provisions covering sentencing are set out in Article 24 of the Statute and Rule 101 of the Rules of Procedure and Evidence. Article 24 of the Statute provides: **[page 174]**

> 1. The penalty imposed by the Trial Chamber shall be limited to imprisonment. In determining the terms of imprisonment, the Trial Chambers shall have recourse to the general practice regarding prison sentences in the courts of the former Yugoslavia.
>
> 2. In imposing the sentences, the Trial Chambers should take into account such factors as the gravity of the offence and the individual circumstances of the convicted person.
>
> 3. In addition to imprisonment, the Trial Chambers may order the return of any property and proceeds acquired by criminal conduct, including by means of duress, to their rightful owners.

Rule 101 of the Rules of Procedure and Evidence provides:

> (A) A convicted person may be sentenced to imprisonment for a term up to and including the remainder of the convicted person's life.

[1288] *See supra* para. 431.
[1289] *See supra* para. 429.
[1290] *See supra* paras 360, 374–375, 381. Hence acquitting Milan Martić as to the rest of the charges under Count 12, *see supra* paras 355, 366, 385, 394, 397, 402.
[1291] *See supra* paras 361, 395. Hence acquitting Milan Martić as to the rest of the charges under Count 13, *see supra* paras 356, 366, 369, 380, 385, 397.
[1292] *See supra* paras 357, 382. Hence acquitting Milan Martić as to the rest of the charges under Count 14, *see supra* paras 362, 376, 385, 396–397.
[1293] *See supra* para. 471.
[1294] *See supra* para. 471.
[1295] *See supra* para. 472.
[1296] *See supra* para. 472.
[1297] *See supra* para. 473.

(B) In determining the sentence, the Trial Chamber shall take into account the factors mentioned in Article 24, paragraph 2, of the Statute, as well as such factors as:

(i) any aggravating circumstances;

(ii) any mitigating circumstances including the substantial cooperation with the Prosecutor by the convicted person before or after conviction;

(iii) the general practice regarding prison sentences in the courts of the former Yugoslavia;

(iv) the extent to which any penalty imposed by a court of any State on the convicted person for the same act has already been served, as referred to in Article 10, paragraph 3, of the Statute.

(C) Credit shall be given to the convicted person for the period, if any, during which the convicted person was detained in custody pending surrender to the Tribunal or pending trial or appeal.

These provisions set forth factors to be taken into consideration by the Trial Chamber when deciding a sentence.[1298] They do not constitute binding limitations on the Trial Chamber's discretion to impose a sentence,[1299] which must always be decided based on the facts of each particular case.[1300]

482. The Appeals Chamber has held that the sentencing practice of the Tribunal in cases involving similar circumstances is but one factor which a Chamber must consider when exercising its discretion in imposing a sentence.[1301] The Appealś Chamber has held that comparisons between cases as regards sentencing are not reliable as the sole basis for sentencing.[1302] On the other hand, "[a] previous decision on sentence may indeed provide guidance if it relates to the same offence and was committed in substantially similar circumstances".[1303] However, this assistance may be limited,[1304] as "when comparing a case to the same offence committed in substantially similar circumstances, the Trial Chamber still has an overriding obligation to tailor a penalty to fit the **[page 175]** gravity of the crime and the individual circumstances of the accused, which include the consideration of both aggravating and mitigating circumstances."[1305]

483. The Prosecution recalls the sentencing judgement of Milan Babić, who was sentenced by the Tribunal to a period of 13 years' imprisonment for his criminal conduct, to which he pled guilty. The Prosecution submits that the culpability of Milan Martić should be compared with that of Milan Babić, whose conduct occurred within a more limited time (1 August 1991 to 15 February 1992), who cooperated with the Tribunal, and who testified in three trials and therefore received a lower sentence than he otherwise might have.[1306] The Trial Chamber considers that guidance may be had from the *Babić* case, however such guidance will necessarily be limited.

1. Principles and purposes of sentencing

484. The jurisprudence of the Tribunal has consistently held that the main purposes of sentencing for crimes within the jurisdiction of the Tribunal are deterrence and retribution.[1307] The penalties imposed by the Tribunal must, in general, have sufficient deterrent value to dissuade those who would consider committing similar crimes from doing so.[1308] However, deterrence "must not be accorded undue prominence in the overall

---

[1298] Rule 101(B) of the Rules. *See also Krstić* Appeal Judgement, para. 241; *Čelebići* Appeal Judgement, para. 716.

[1299] *Krstić* Appeal Judgement, paras 241–242; *Čelebići* Appeal Judgement, paras, 715, 718, 780. *See also Kambanda* Appeal Judgement, para. 124; *Furundžija* Appeal Judgement, para. 238.

[1300] *Krstić* Appeal Judgement, para. 241; *Jelisić* Appeal Judgement, para. 101; *Čelebići* Appeal Judgement, para. 717.

[1301] *Krstić* Appeal Judgement, para. 248; *Čelebići* Appeal Judgement, para. 757.

[1302] *Čelebići* Appeal Judgement, para. 719.

[1303] *Momir Nikolić* Sentencing Appeal Judgement, para. 38, citing *Furundžjia* Appeal Judgement, para. 250; *Čelebići* Appeal Judgement, para. 720.

[1304] *Čelebići* Appeal Judgement, para. 721.

[1305] *Momir Nikolić* Sentencing Appeal Judgement, para. 38, citing *Čelebići* Appeal Judgement, paras 717, 719.

[1306] Prosecution Closing Argument, 10 Jan 2007, T. 11231.

[1307] *Čelebići* Appeal Judgement, para. 806; Aleksovski Appeal Judgement, para. 185. *See also Furundžija*, Trial Judgement, para. 288; Tadić Sentencing Judgement, paras 7–9; *Kupreškić et al.* Trial Judgement, para. 848. As regards deterrence, *see also Čelebići* Appeal Judgement, para. 800, citing *Tadić* Jurisdiction Decision, para. 72.

[1308] *Kordić and Čerkez* Appeal Judgement, para. 1078.

assessment of the sentences to be imposed on persons convicted by the International Tribunal".[1309] Moreover, "unlike vengeance, retribution incorporates a principle of restraint; retribution requires the imposition of a just and appropriate punishment, and nothing more".[1310] However, a sentence imposed "should make plain the condemnation of the international community of the behaviour in question."[1311] A third purpose of sentencing is rehabilitation which, while it may be considered a relevant factor, "is not one which should be given undue weight".[1312]

2. Gravity and individual circumstances of the convicted person

485. Article 24(2) of the Statute provides that in imposing sentences Trial Chambers should take into account such factors as the gravity of the offence and the individual circumstances of the convicted person. The Appeals Chamber has held that the gravity of the offence is a primary **[page 176]** consideration in imposing a sentence.[1313] There is no hierarchy of crimes within the jurisdiction of the Tribunal.[1314] Sentences must reflect the inherent gravity or totality of the criminal conduct of the accused, requiring a consideration of the particular circumstances of the case, as well as the form and degree of the participation of the accused in the crime.[1315]

486. The Appeals Chamber has found that factors to be considered include the discriminatory nature of the crimes where this is not considered as an element of a conviction,[1316] and the vulnerability of the victims.[1317] The Appeals Chamber has also held that the consequences of the crime upon the victim directly injured is always relevant to sentencing;[1318] further factors, such as the effects of the crime on relatives of the immediate victims, may also be considered.[1319]

487. The Prosecution submits that the crimes with which Milan Martić is charged are of serious gravity and directs the Trial Chamber's attention to persecutions as a crime against humanity and crimes involving the intentional deprivation of life.[1320] The Prosecution further submits that the targeted group in this case was predominantly civilian and included women, children and the elderly.[1321]

488. Milan Martić has been found responsible for, *inter alia,* the crimes of murder, imprisonment, torture, cruel treatment, destruction, including of buildings dedicated to religion as well as plunder, directed against people of Croat ethnicity. Many of these crimes were committed with discriminatory intent. The Trial Chamber agrees with the Prosecution that the fact that the crimes were committed with discriminatory intent is a factor to be taken into consideration when assessing the gravity of the criminal conduct of Milan Martić.

489. Milan Martić has also been found guilty of the crimes of deportation and other inhumane acts (forcible transfer). The Trial Chamber particularly notes that the non-Serb population was subjected to widespread and systematic crimes, including killings, beatings, and crimes against **[page 177]** property, as a result of the

1309 *Kordić and Čerkez* Appeal Judgement, para. 1078; *Čelebići* Appeal Judgement, para. 801; *Aleksovski* Appeal Judgement, para. 185; *Tadić* Sentencing Appeal Judgement, para. 48.

1310 *Kordić and Čerkez* Appeal Judgement, para. 1075 (emphasis in original). *See also Aleksovski* Appeal Judgement, para. 185; *Dragan Nikolić* Sentencing Judgement, para. 140.

1311 *Aleksovski* Appeal Judgement, para. 185, citing *Erdemović* Sentencing Judgement, paras 64–65.

1312 *Čelebići* Appeal Judgement, para. 806. *See also Deronjić* Sentencing Appeal Judgement, paras 135–137; *Stakić* Appeal Judgement, paras 400–402.

1313 *Blaskić* Appeal Judgement, para. 683; *Čelebići* Appeal Judgement, para. 731; *Kupreškič et al.* Appeal Judgement, para. 442. *See also Aleksovski* Appeal Judgement, para. 182.

1314 *Stakić* Appeal Judgement, para. 375.

1315 *Blaškić* Appeal Judgement, para. 683, citing *Furundžija* Appeal Judgement, para. 249. *See also Èelebiæi* Appeal Judgement para. 731, citing *Kupreškić et al.* Trial Judgement, para. 852, cited in the *Aleksovski* Appeal Judgement at para. 182. *See also Čelebići* Appeal Judgement, para. 769; *Stakić* Trial Judgement, para. 903.

1316 *Kvočka et al.* Trial Judgement, para. 702.

1317 *Blaškić* Appeal Judgement, para. 683; *Kunarac et al.* Appeal Judgement, para. 352.

1318 *Blaškić* Appeal Judgement, para. 683; *Krnojelac* Trial Judgement, para. 512.

1319 *Blaškić* Appeal Judgement, para. 683; *Krnojelac* Appeal Judgement, para. 260. The Trial Chamber in *Čelebići* held that: "The gravity of the offences of the kind charged has always been determined by the effect on the victim or, at the most, on persons associated with the crime and nearest relations. Gravity is determined *in personam* and is not one of a universal effect," *Čelebići* Trial Judgement, para. 1226.

1320 Prosecution Final Trial Brief, para. 478.

1321 Prosecution Final Trial Brief, para. 480; Prosecution Closing Argument, 10 Jan 2007, T. 11234.

coercive atmosphere in the SAO Krajina and the RSK between 1991 and 1995, and that as a result almost all of the Croat and other non-Serb population were forcibly displaced. The scale and systematic nature of these crimes are factors which the Trial Chamber considers to be of particular gravity.

490. The Trial Chamber recalls that the majority of the crimes for which Milan Martić has been found guilty were committed against elderly persons or against people held in detention. Furthermore, the majority of the victims were civilians. The special vulnerability of these groups of victims adds to the gravity of the crimes for which Milan Martić has been found guilty.

491. The Trial Chamber recalls the effects of the crimes committed on victims and their families. Virtually the entire Croat and other non-Serb population was expelled and many had their houses and property burnt and looted. Appalling acts of inhumane treatment, including torture, were committed in detention facilities against Croat and other non-Serb detainees. The Trial Chamber recalls in particular the testimony of some victims of these crimes concerning the suffering they endured and continue to endure as a result of these crimes. Moreover, the Trial Chamber recalls the horrific injuries and the serious suffering inflicted on civilians as a consequence of the indiscriminate attacks on Zagreb ordered by Milan Martić. The impact and long-lasting effects of these crimes, for which Milan Martić is individually criminally responsible, including as a direct perpetrator, render them especially grave.

492. In relation to "the individual circumstances of the convicted person", the Appeals Chamber has held that while such circumstances can be either mitigating or aggravating, family concerns should, in principle, be a mitigating factor.[1322] The Trial Chamber will consider this factor in the following section.

3. Aggravating and mitigating factors

493. The Statute and the Rules require the Trial Chamber to take account of both aggravating and mitigating circumstances when imposing a sentence.[1323] The Appeals Chamber has held that the weight to be attached to such circumstances is a matter within the Trial Chamber's discretion.[1324] **[page 178]** Factors which a Trial Chamber takes into account as aspects of the gravity of the crime cannot additionally be taken into account as separate aggravating circumstances, and *vice versa*.[1325]

494. While mitigating circumstances not directly related to the offence may be considered, with regard to aggravating circumstances only those relating directly to the commission of the offence may be considered.[1326] Furthermore, the absence of a mitigating factor can never serve as an aggravating factor.[1327]

(a) Aggravating circumstances

495. Aggravating circumstances must be proved by the Prosecution beyond reasonable doubt.[1328] Such factors include: (i) the position of the accused, that is, his position of leadership, his level in the command structure, or his role in the broader context of the conflict of the former Yugoslavia;[1329] (ii) the discriminatory

1322 *Kunarac et al.* Appeal Judgement, para. 362; *Erdemović* Second Sentencing Judgement, para. 16; *Tadić* Sentencing Judgement, para. 26.

1323 *See above* Article 24 of the Statute and Rule 101 of the Rules; *Čelebići* Appeal Judgement, para. 717.

1324 *Čelebići* Appeal Judgement, paras 718, 777, 780; *Blaškić* Appeal Judgement, para. 696.

1325 *Deronjić* Sentencing Appeal Judgement, para. 106, citing *Krnojelac* Trial Judgement, para. 517; *Plavšić* Sentencing Judgement, para. 58; *Banović* Sentencing Judgement, para. 53. *See also Momir Nikolić* Sentencing Appeal Judgement, para. 58; *Obrenović* Sentencing Judgement, para. 101; *Češić* Sentencing Judgement, para. 53.

1326 *Kunarac et al.* Trial Judgement, para. 850.

1327 *Blaškić* Appeal Judgement, para. 687, citing *Čelebići* Appeal Judgement, paras 763, 783; *Plavšić* Sentencing Judgement, para. 64; *Kunarac et al.* Trial Judgement, para. 847.

1328 *Blaškić* Appeal Judgement, para. 686, citing *Čelebići* Appeal Judgement, para. 763.

1329 *Ibid.*, citing *Jokić* Sentencing Judgement, paras 61–62. *See also Tadić* Sentencing Appeal Judgement, paras 55–56. The Appeals Chamber in *Stakić* noted that "in considering the superior position in connection with Article 7(1), the Appeals Chamber recalls that it is settled in the jurisprudence of the Tribunal that superior position itself does not constitute an aggravating factor. Rather it is the abuse of such position which may be considered an aggravating factor," *Stakić* Appeal Judgement, para. 411, citing *Kayishema and Ruzindana* Appeal Judgement, paras 358-359; *Babić* Sentencing Appeal Judgement, para. 80; *Kamuhanda* Appeal Judgement, para. 347.

intent[1330] or the discriminatory state of mind for crimes for which such a state of mind is not an element or ingredient of the crime;[1331] (iii) the length of time during which the crime continued;[1332] (iv) active and direct criminal participation, if linked to a high-rank position of command,[1333] the accused's role as fellow perpetrator,[1334] and the active participation of a superior in the criminal acts of subordinates;[1335] (v) the informed, willing or enthusiastic participation in crime;[1336] (vi) premeditation and motive;[1337] (vii) the sexual, violent, and humiliating nature of the acts and the vulnerability of the victims;[1338] (viii) the status of the **[page 179]** victims, their age and number, and the effect of the crimes on them;[1339] (ix) civilian detainees;[1340] (x) the character of the accused;[1341] and (xi) the circumstances of the offences generally.[1342]

496. Furthermore, it has also been held that the refusal of an accused to testify cannot be taken into account in the determination of the sentence.[1343]

497. The Prosecution submits that the fact that the criminal conduct lasted from 1991 to 1995 throughout the Krajina region should be treated as an aggravating factor in sentencing.[1344] Moreover, the Prosecution submits that the following additional factors are relevant as aggravating circumstances: the discriminatory intent with which the crimes were committed (except for the crime of persecution where discriminatory intent is an element of the crime); the scale of the crimes (except for the crime of extermination where scale is an element); premeditation of the crimes; the willing and enthusiastic participation of the accused; and that crimes were committed against civilian detainees.[1345]

498. The Trial Chamber recalls that throughout the period relevant for the Indictment, Milan Martić held high positions within the SAO Krajina, and subsequently the RSK, including Minister of Interior and President of the RSK. The evidence shows that Milan Martić was one of the most important and influential political figures in the SAO Krajina and the RSK governments and that as Minister of the Interior he exercised absolute authority over the MUP. As President of the RSK, Milan Martić held the highest political office and controlled the armed forces of the RSK. The Trial Chamber considers that in holding such positions, Milan Martić was obligated to prevent the commission of crimes and to ensure that all inhabitants of the territories under his authority enjoyed respect for human rights. However, the evidence presented to the Trial Chamber proves beyond reasonable doubt that Milan Martić abused his positions and that he, through continuous and systematic efforts to create an ethnically Serb territory, promoted an atmosphere of mistrust and fear between Serbs and non-Serbs, in particular Croats. In doing so, Milan Martić contributed significantly to the furtherance of the common purpose of the JCE, of which he was a key member in the SAO Krajina and the RSK. The Trial Chamber considers that these factors are aggravating circumstances when determining Milan Martić's sentence. **[page 180]**

1330 *Ibid.*, citing *Vasiljević* Appeal Judgement, paras 172–173. *See also Vasiljević* Trial Judgement, para. 277, holding that "the discriminatory purpose of the crimes and the selection of victims based on their ethnicity [...] can only Šconstitute an aggravating factor] where the crime for which an accused is convicted does not include a discriminatory state of mind as an element. The crime of persecution in Article 5(h) of the Statute already includes such an element. Such a discriminatory state of mind goes to the seriousness of the offence, *but it may not additionally aggravate that offence*." (Emphasis added). *See also Kunarac et al.* Appeal Judgement, para. 357.

1331 *Blaškić* Appeal Judgement, para. 686, referring to *Kunarac et al.* Appeal Judgement, para. 357, citing *Tadić* Appeal Judgement, para. 305. *See also Todorović* Sentencing Judgement, para. 57.

1332 *Ibid.*, referring to *Kunarac et al.* Appeal Judgement, para. 356; *Todorović* Sentencing Judgement, para. 65.

1333 *Ibid.*, referring to *Krstić* Trial Judgement, para. 708.

1334 *Ibid.*, referring to *Furundžija* Trial Judgement, para. 281.

1335 *Ibid.*, referring to *Čelebići* Appeal Judgement, paras 736–737.

1336 *Ibid.*, referring to *Jelisić* Appeal Judgement, para. 86; *Kayishema and Ruzindana* Appeal Judgement, para. 351.

1337 *Ibid.*, referring to *Krstić* Trial Judgement, paras 711–712. *See also Krstić* Appeal Judgement, para. 258.

1338 *Ibid.*, referring to *Kunarac et al.* Trial Judgement, para. 867; *Kunarac et al.* Appeal Judgement, para. 352.

1339 *Ibid.*, referring to *Kunarac et al.* Trial Judgement, paras 864, 866; *Kunarac et al.* Appeal Judgement, para. 355.

1340 *Ibid.*, referring to *Furundžija* Trial Judgement, para. 283.

1341 *Ibid.*, referring to *Čelebići* Appeal Judgement, para. 788.

1342 *Ibid.*, referring to *Tadić* Sentencing Judgement, para. 19.

1343 *Čelebići* Appeal Judgement, para. 783; *Blaškić* Appeal Judgement, para. 687; *Plavšić* Sentencing Judgement, para. **64**. *See also Čelebići* Appeal Judgement, para. 763; *Kunarac et al.* Trial Judgement, para. 847, cited in *Blaškić* Appeal Judgement, *ibid.*

1344 Prosecution Closing Argument, 10 Jan 2007, T. 11231, 11234, 11236.

1345 Prosecution Closing Argument, 10 Jan 2007, T. 11231; Prosecution Final Trial Brief, para. 482.

499. Furthermore, the Trial Chamber considers that the widespread criminal conduct which covered the entire territory of the SAO Krajina and the RSK during a period of more than four years serves as an aggravating circumstance.

500. The Trial Chamber recalls that the vulnerability and status of the victims, as well as the discriminatory intent associated with the crimes were taken into account in assessing the gravity of the crimes for which Milan Martić has been found guilty. Therefore, these factors cannot be additionally considered as aggravating circumstances.

(b) Mitigating circumstances

501. Mitigating factors have to be proven "on a balance of probabilities", that is "the circumstance in question must have existed 'more probably than not'."[1346] Factors to be taken into account may include the following: (i) co-operation with the Prosecution;[1347] (ii) the admission of guilt or a guilty plea;[1348] (iii) an expression of remorse;[1349] (iv) voluntary surrender;[1350] (v) good character with no prior criminal convictions;[1351] (vi) comportment in detention;[1352] (vii) personal and family circumstances;[1353] (viii) the character of the accused subsequent to the conflict;[1354] (ix) duress[1355] and indirect participation;[1356] (x) diminished mental responsibility;[1357] (xi) age;[1358] and (xii) assistance to detainees or victims.[1359] Poor health is to be considered only in exceptional or rare cases.[1360]

502. The Prosecution submits that it cannot identify any mitigating circumstances warranting a reduction in sentence. Furthermore, the Prosecution submits that Milan Martić has failed to demonstrate any remorse.[1361] **[page 181]**

503. The Defence submits that before the indictment period Milan Martić had a reputation of being a professional and successful police inspector in Knin and that he was considered a person of broad-minded views and moral integrity.[1362] Moreover, the Defence relies on the testimony of MM-078 who stated that "he was not aware of any such case where Mr. Martić ordered someone to do something harmful to someone else".[1363]

504. The Trial Chamber notes, in this respect, the Prosecution submission that Witness MM-078 also testified that Milan Martić abused his position as a police inspector in Knin by using coercive means on suspects, forcing them to make statements or admissions against their will, beating prisoners and detaining persons without sufficient evidence.[1364] As a consequence, Milan Martić was suspended from his position.[1365]

505. The Trial Chamber finds that the direct and specific evidence given by Witness MM-078 concerning examples of Milan Martić's abuse of position is credible and outweighs the Witness MM-078's evidence

1346 *Babić* Sentencing Appeal Judgement, para. 43.

1347 *Blaškić* Appeal Judgement, para. 696. *See also Jokić* Sentencing Judgement, paras 95–96; *Todorović* Sentencing Judgement, para. 88; *Kvočka et al.* Appeal Judgement, para. 722.

1348

1349 *Ibid.*, referring to *Jokić* Sentencing Judgement, para. 89; *Erdemović* Second Sentencing Judgement, para. 16(iii).

1350 *Ibid.*, referring to *Jokić* Sentencing Judgement, para. 73.

1351 *Ibid.*, referring to *Erdemović* Second Sentencing Judgement, para. 16(i); *Kupreškić et al.* Appeal Judgement, para. 459.

1352 *Ibid.*, referring to *Jokić* Sentencing Judgement, para. 100; *Dragan Nikolić* Sentencing Judgement, para. 268.

1353 *Ibid.*, referring to *Kunarac et al.* Appeal Judgement, paras 362, 408.

1354 *Ibid.*, referring to *Jokić* Sentencing Judgement, paras 90–91, 103.

1355 *Ibid.*, referring to *Erdemović* Second Sentencing Judgement, para. 17.

1356 *Ibid.*, referring to *Krstić* Appeal Judgement, para. 273.

1357 *Ibid.*, referring to *Čelebići* Appeal Judgement, para. 590.

1358 *Ibid.*, referring to *Jokić* Sentencing Judgement, para. 100.

1359 *Ibid.*, referring to *Sikirica et al.* Sentencing Judgement, paras 195, 229.

1360 *Ibid.*, referring to *Krstić* Appeal Judgement, para. 271; *Milan Simić* Sentencing Judgement, para. 98.

1361 Prosecution Final Trial Brief, para. 483.

1362 Witness MM-096, 21 Aug 2006, T. 6825–6826; Witness MM-116, 28 Aug, T. 7257.

1363 Witness MM-078, 25 May 2006, T. 4499. Defence's Submission Concerning Individual Circumstances of the Accused Milan Martić, 30 May 2007, para. 9.

1364 Witness MM-078, 24 May 2006, T. 4393–4395; Prosecution Submission Regarding Individual Circumstances of the Accused, 30 May 2007, para. 3.

1365 Witness MM-078, 24 May 2006, T. 4396; Prosecution Submission Regarding Individual Circumstances of the Accused, 30 May 2007, para. 3.

referred to by the Defence, as well as other similarly general statements concerning Milan Martić's character. The Trial Chamber therefore finds that the conduct of Milan Martić prior to the indictment period cannot serve as a mitigating factor.

506. The Defence argued in its closing arguments that Milan Martić was not driven by "chauvinism, intolerance, ruthlessness in relation to members of a certain religion or ethnic group: Muslims and Croats". The Defence recalled the testimonies of witnesses who stated that they never observed any traces of hatred or any kind of intolerance in Milan Martić against members of Croat community.[1366] The Defence further referred to the testimony of Charles Kirudja, who testified that during his meetings with Milan Martić he did not get the impression that Milan Martić wanted to expel or destroy any other peoples or to mistreat them in any way.[1367]

507. The Trial Chamber recalls that during the summer and autumn of 1991, Milan Martić instructed persons involved in humanitarian assistance to treat both Croat and Serb refugees arriving from Drniš equally.[1368] The Trial Chamber further recalls Slobodan Jarčević's testimony that Milan Martić "demonstrated the nobility of his character" by looking after refugees who **[page 182]** arrived from BiH in 1994, despite the difficulties which the RSK was facing due to international sanctions.[1369]

508. The Trial Chamber considers that even though there is evidence showing positive traits in the character of Milan Martić and that sporadic help was given by him to Croats and other non-Serbs, the effect thereof is diminished by the fact that Milan Martić at all times relevant for the crimes for which he has been found guilty, held positions in which he was able and obliged to take measures to prevent or punish acts of violence.[1370] The Trial Chamber recalls that in such a case, sporadic benevolent acts or ineffective assistance may be disregarded.[1371] The Trial Chamber finds that neither the personality of Milan Martić nor any sporadic acts of assistance given to Croats and other non-Serbs can be treated as mitigating circumstances in this case. The Trial Chamber also finds that neither the age of Milan Martić, nor his family situation at the time of the commission of the crimes can be treated as mitigating circumstances in this case.[1372]

509. As to Milan Martić's situation since the commission of the crimes for which he has been found guilty, the Defence submits that Milan Martić and his family were expelled and displaced following "Operation Storm".[1373] The Trial Chamber considers this to be a mitigating circumstance of limited weight.

510. The Trial Chamber notes that the first Indictment against Milan Martić was confirmed on 25 July 1995 and made public on 23 January 1996.[1374] According to Milan Martić's own admission on the last day of the trial, he was aware of the first Indictment issued against him.[1375] In this respect, the Trial Chamber recalls the decision taken during the pre-trial phase in this case wherein it was considered that Milan Martic's surrender on 15 May 2002 was not necessarily fully voluntary.[1376] The Trial Chamber notes that Milan Martić evaded justice for around seven years in the knowledge that an indictment was issued against him. Rather than surrender in order to respond to the charges brought against him, he chose to publicly make disparaging remarks about the Tribunal.[1377] The **[page 183]** Trial Chamber finds that the fact that Milan Martić surrendered to the Tribunal in 2002, although constituting a mitigating factor in this case, will be given only minimal weight.

1366 Defence Closing Argument, 10 Jan 2007, T. 11241. *See also* Defence's Submission Concerning Individual Circumstances of the Accused Milan Martić, 30 May 2007, paras 11–12.

1367 Charles Kirudja, 1 Jun 2006, T. 4961; Defence's Submission Concerning Individual Circumstances of the Accused Milan Martić, 30 May 2007, para. 10.

1368 Ljubica Vujanić, 18 Sep 2006, T. 8498–8501.

1369 Slobodan Jarčević, 12 Jul 2006, T. 6172–6173.

1370 *See supra* section III J.

1371 *Čelebići* Appeal Judgement, para. 776; *Češić* Sentencing Judgement, para. 79. *See also Krajišnik* Trial Judgement, para. 1162.

1372 Ex. 494, L0107131.

1373 Defence's Submission Concerning Individual Circumstances of the Accused Milan Martić, 30 May 2007, para. 3.

1374 Review of the Indictment, 25 Jul 1995; Advertisement of Indictment, 23 Jan 1996.

1375 Statement of the Accused, 12 Jan 2007, T. 11441.

1376 The Trial Chamber considered that Milan Martić's surrender to the Tribunal in 2000 was at least partially caused by the enactment of the Law on Co-operation by the FRY, making his further hiding almost impossible, *see* Decision on the Motion for Provisional Release, 10 Oct 2002, pp 3–4.

1377 Prosecution's Response to Motion for Provisional Release Filed by the Accused Milan Martić, 18 July 2002, para. 14 and Addendum; Prosecution Submission Regarding Individual Circumstances of the Accused, 30 May 2007, para 4.

511. The Trial Chamber notes the Defence's submission of the neuropsychiatrist's opinion describing Milan Martić as having "a stable personality structure with a dominating quantum of emotions" and finding him to be "socially integrated, non-conflictive [and] conciliatory".[1378] However, in light of Milan Martić's conduct demonstrated during the trial, especially the fact that he did not express any remorse for any of the crimes for which he has been found guilty, the Trial Chamber rejects this opinion.

4. General practice regarding sentencing in the former Yugoslavia

512. Article 24(1) of the Statute provides that "Trial Chambers shall have recourse to the general practice regarding prison sentences in the courts of the former Yugoslavia". The jurisprudence of the Tribunal has consistently held that this does not require the Trial Chambers to conform to the practice regarding prison sentences in the courts of the Former Yugoslavia; it only requires that the Trial Chambers take that practice into account.[1379]

513. The Trial Chamber reviews this practice only as an aid in determining the appropriate penalty and may impose a sentence less than or in excess of the punishment that would be applicable under the sentencing law of the former Yugoslavia.[1380]

514. The Criminal Code of the Socialist Federal Republic of Yugoslavia ("SFRY Criminal Code") regulated sentencing law in the territory at issue during the Indictment period.[1381] Article 41 of that Code provides the various factors to be taken into account in determining the sentence, including mitigating and aggravating circumstances, the degree of criminal responsibility, the motives of the accused, his personal circumstances, and his conduct after the commission of the crime.

515. In terms of punishment, Article 34 of the SFRY Criminal Code provides that the court could impose capital punishment, imprisonment, a fine, and confiscation of property. Article 38 of the SFRY Criminal Code provides further that prison sentences could not exceed 15 years unless the crime was eligible for the death penalty, in which case the term of imprisonment could not exceed **[page 184]** 20 years.[1382] The Trial Chamber recalls that Article 24 of the Statute limits it to imposing a sentence of imprisonment. In this context, the Appeals Chamber has held that it does not violate the principle of *nulla poena sine lege* to impose sentences in excess of 20 years.[1383]

516. Having considered all of the evidence and the arguments of the Parties, and based upon the factual and legal findings as determined in this judgement, the Trial Chamber decides as follows: **[page 185]**

VI. DISPOSITION

517. The Trial Chamber finds Milan Martić **NOT GUILTY** of:

Count 2: Extermination, a crime against humanity

1378 Defence's Submission Concerning Individual Circumstances of the Accused Milan Martić, 30 May 2007, para. 13.

1379 *Čelebići* Appeal Judgement, para. 813, citing *Serushago* Sentencing Appeal Judgement, para. 30. *See also Tadić* Sentencing Appeal Judgement, para. 21; *Kunarac et al.* Appeal Judgement, para. 377; *Jelisić* Appeal Judgement, paras 116–117; *Stakić* Appeal Judgement, para. 398.

1380 *Stakić* Appeal Judgement, para. 398.

1381 Adopted by the SFRY Assembly at the Session of Federal Council held on 28 September 1976; declared by decree of the President of the Republic on 28 September 1976; published in the Official Gazette SFRY No. 44 of 8 October 1976; took effect on 1 July 1977.

1382 Due to the gravity of the crimes at issue, the accused would have been aware that such actions constituted serious violations of international humanitarian law, punishable by the harshest of penalties, *see Čelebići* Appeal Judgement, paras 816–817; *Blaškić* Appeal Judgement, para. 681. Furthermore, the Trial Chamber notes that violations of Articles 142 ("War crime against the civilian population"), 148 ("Making use of forbidden means of warfare") provide for a minimum sentence of five years imprisonment with a maximum sentence of death; Article 151 ("Destruction of cultural and historical monuments") mandates a sentence of at least one year imprisonment; and Article 154 ("Racial and other discrimination") allows for a sentencing range of 6 months to five years of imprisonment.

1383 *Stakić* Appeal Judgement, para. 398.

518. The Trial Chamber finds Milan Martić **GUILTY** pursuant to Article 7(1) of the Statute on the following counts:

Count 1:	Persecutions, a crime against humanity
Count 3:	Murder, a crime against humanity
Count 4:	Murder, a violation of the laws or customs of war
Count 5:	Imprisonment, a crime against humanity
Count 6:	Torture, a crime against humanity
Count 7:	Inhumane acts, a crime against humanity
Count 8:	Torture, a violation of the laws or customs of war
Count 9:	Cruel treatment, a violation of the laws or customs of war
Count 10:	Deportation, a crime against humanity
Count 11:	Forcible transfer, a crime against humanity
Count 12:	Wanton destruction of villages, or devastation not justified by military necessity, a violation of the laws or customs of war
Count 13:	Destruction or wilful damage done to institutions dedicated to education or religion, a violation of the laws or customs of war
Count 14:	Plunder of public or private property, a violation of the laws or customs of war
Count 15:	Murder, a crime against humanity
Count 17:	Inhumane acts, a crime against humanity
Count 19:	Attacks on civilians, a violation of the laws or customs of war

519. The Trial Chamber sentences Milan Martić to a single sentence of **thirty-five (35) years** of imprisonment. **[page 186]**

520. Milan Martić has been detained since 15 May 2002. Pursuant to Rule 101(C) of the Rules, Milan Martić is entitled to credit for time spent in detention, which as of the date of this judgement amounts to 1,855 days, and for such additional time he may serve pending the determination of any appeal. Pursuant to Rule 103(C) of the Rules, Milan Martić shall remain in the custody of the Tribunal pending finalisation of arrangements for his transfer to the State where he shall serve his sentence.

Done in English and French, the English version being authoritative.

Janet Nosworthy **Judge**	**Bakone Justice Moloto** **Presiding Judge**	**Frank Höpfel Judge**

Dated this twelfth day of June 2007

At The Hague

The Netherlands

[Seal of the Tribunal] [page 187]

ANNEX A – PROCEDURAL HISTORY

A. Pre-trial proceedings

521. The Initial Indictment against Milan Martić was confirmed on 25 July 1995, with corrected or amended versions subsequently filed on 26 August 2002, 18 December 2002 and 14 July 2003, and the Second Amended Indictment being filed on 9 September 2003.[1384]

522. On 8 March 1996, an international arrest warrant was issued for Milan Martić.[1385] On 15 May 2002, Milan Martić surrendered and was transferred to the Tribunal, and ordered to be detained at the UNDU in The Hague.[1386] At the initial appearance on 21 May 2002, Milan Martić pled not guilty to all charges, and on 28 January 2003, Milan Martić pled not guilty to all additional charges and allegations of the Amended Indictment.[1387]

523. During his initial appearance, Milan Martić was represented by Strahinja Kastratović, temporarily assigned by the Registrar from 31 May 2002 until 13 June 2002.[1388] On 13 December 2002, in light of Milan Martić's request for the withdrawal of Strahinja Kastratović and of the communication from the latter stating unwillingness to represent Milan Martić, the Registrar assigned Predrag Milovančević as counsel for Milan Martić.[1389]

524. On 10 October 2002, the Trial Camber denied the Defence requests for provisional release of Milan Martić, and on 12 September 2005, the Trial Chamber denied a further motion for provisional release.[1390] **[page 188]**

525. The Prosecution disclosed supporting material to the Defence pursuant to Rule 66(A)(i) and (ii) on 21 May 2002, and 26 August 2002.[1391] On 7 May 2004, the Prosecution disclosed material previously undisclosed to the Defence pursuant to Rule 65 *ter* (E)(iii). On 22 January 2004, the Prosecution assured the Trial Chamber that it had disclosed all Rule 66 (A) material, except for that which the Trial Chamber had agreed to delay disclosure.[1392] On 5 March 2004, the Prosecution disclosed to the Defence exculpatory material relative to Rule 68. On 2 November 2004, the Prosecution recognised that the "Statement of Matters that are not in Dispute", which was attached to the Defence's Pre-Trial Brief, accurately reflected the agreement between the Parties.[1393]

1384 Review of the Indictment, 25 Jul 1995; Motion to Request Leave to File an Amended Indictment, 26 Aug 2002; Decision on the Prosecution; Motion to file a Corrected Amended Indictment, 13 Dec 2002; Prosecution Motion to file Amended Indictment pursuant to Trial Chamber's Decision on Preliminary Motion against the Amended Indictment, 14 Jul 2003. In relation to the Amended Indictment, on 2 Jun 2003 the Trial Chamber granted in part the Defence Preliminary Motion pursuant to Rule 72A (ii) of the Rules on Procedure and Evidence against the Amended Indictment dated 18 Dec 2002, and 17 Mar 2003, and ordered the Prosecution to file a new Amended Indictment clarifying inconsistencies, *see* Decision on Preliminary Motion against the Amended Indictment, 2 Jun 2003. On 5 Sep 2003, the Trial Chamber denied a further preliminary motion filed by the Defence against the Amended Indictment, declaring it as frivolous, and ordered the Prosecution to file the Amended Indictment, to be known as the Second Amended Indictment, which the Prosecution did on 9 Sep 2003. On 9 Dec 2005, the Second Amended Indictment was re-filed due to a numbering mistake.

1385 Decision of the Registrar, 8 Mar 1996.

1386 Order for Detention, 15 May 2002.

1387 Initial Appearance, 21 May 2002, T. 11–13. Further Appearance and Status Conference, 28 Jan 2003, T. 74–80.

1388 Decision of the Registrar, 31 May 2002. On 14 June 2002, the Registrar assigned Gert-Jan Knoops as counsel for a period of 100 days, Decision of the Registrar, 14 Jun 2002. Following an appeal by Strahinja Kastratović and order by the Trial Chamber, on 16 August 2002, the Registrar withdrew the assignment of Gert-Jan Knoops and assigned Strahinja Kastratović, Defence's Appeal against the Decision of Registry, 18 Jun 2002; Decision on Appeal against Decision of Registry, 2 Aug 2002; Decision of the Registrar, 16 Aug 2002.

1389 Decision of the Registrar, 13 Dec 2002.

1390 The Trial Chamber noted several factors which substantially weighed against the Defence's contention that there was no risk of flight: Milan Martić had shown capacity for evading arrest for a prolonged period of time, he had used false names, had the means and know-how to obtain false documents, had publicly and repeatedly displayed disregard for the Tribunal, and had publicly announced his willingness to resort to violence in the case of forcible apprehension. Moreover, the Trial Chamber noted that Milan Martić's surrender was not necessarily fully voluntary. On 13 October 2002, the Defence applied for leave to appeal the Trial Chamber's Decision of 10 October 2002. The Appeals Chamber dismissed the application on 18 Dec 2002. *See also* Milan Martić's Request for Provisional Release until Beginning of Trial, dated 21 June 2002, and filed on 10 July 2002; Motion for Provisional Release, 9 Jul 2002; Second Motion for Provisional Release, 25 Apr 2005.

1391 Initial Appearance, 21 May 2002, T. 13. Prosecution's Material in Support of the Amended Indictment, 26 Aug 2002. An addendum of supporting materials for the Amended Indictment being submitted on 18 November 2002, Prosecution's Addendum of Supporting Materials in Support of Amended Indictment.

1392 Status Conference, 22 January 2004, T. 105–106.

1393 Defence Pre-Trial Brief Pursuant to Rule 65 *ter* (F) with a Confidential Annex, 1 Nov 2004. *See* Prosecution Pre-Trial Brief, 7 May 2004. Prosecution's Submission to Defence's Pre-Trial Brief, 2 Nov 2004; at the Rule 65*ter* conference on 14 Sep 2005, both

526. Status Conferences were held on 23 September 2002, 28 January 2003, 29 May 2003, 29 September 2003, 22 January 2004, 21 September 2004, 19 May 2005, 15 September 2005, and 22 November 2005.

527. The Prosecution filed its Pre-Trial Brief on 7 May 2004. On 1 November 2004, after having been given an extension of 47 days, the Defence submitted its Pre-Trial Brief.

528. On 10 November 2005, the Trial Chamber denied a Prosecution Motion for Joinder of the cases of Milan Martić, Jovica Stanišić, Franko Simatović and Vojislav Šešelj on the basis that the case against Milan Martić had been ready for trial for some time and that Milan Martić had been in detention for over three years and four months, and therefore the trial should commence with the shortest possible delay.[1394]

529. On 15 December 2005, the Trial Chamber granted in part the Prosecution Motion for Leave to Amend its Rule 65 *ter* Exhibits List by adding 719 documents and video footage to the Prosecution exhibit list.[1395] The Trial Chamber denied the motion insofar as it sought the addition **[page 189]** of material pertaining to the charges concerning Prnjavor, Šipovo and Bosanska Gradiška, regarding which areas the Prosecution had previously stated that it would not lead evidence.[1396]

530. On 18 November 2005, the President of the Tribunal assigned Judge Bakone Justice Moloto (South Africa) to the present case, and on 1 December 2005, the President of the Tribunal ordered that the Bench be composed of Judge Bakone Justice Moloto, presiding, Judge Janet Nosworthy (Jamaica) and Judge Frank Höpfel (Austria).[1397] The Pre-Trial Conference was held on 12 December 2005 and the Pre-Defence Conference was held on 7 July 2006.

B. Trial proceedings

1. Overview

531. Pursuant to Rule 84 *bis* of the Rules, Milan Martic made an opening statement on 13 December 2005 and in-court statements on 13 March 2006 and 12 January 2007.[1398] The Prosecution case started on 13 December 2005 and concluded on 20 June 2006.[1399] Guidelines on the Standards Governing the Admission of Evidence, and Guidelines Governing the Presentation of Evidence and the Conduct of Counsel in Court, were adopted on 19 January 2006, and 13 April 2006, respectively.[1400]

532. The Prosecution called 45 *viva voce* witnesses, four of whom testified pursuant to Rule 89 (F), and 12 of whom testified pursuant to former Rule 92 *bis* (E).[1401] 16 witness statements were admitted into evidence

---

the Prosecution and the Defence stated that they could not go further than the already agreed facts, Rule 65 *ter* Conference, 14 Sep 2005.

[1394] Decision on Prosecution Motion for Joinder, 10 Nov 2005. Prosecution Motion for Joinder, 30 May 2005. Response to the Prosecution's Motion for Joinder, 13 Jun 2005.

[1395] Prosecution's Motion for Leave to Amend Its Rule 65 *ter* Exhibit List, 17 Aug 2005; Decision on Prosecution's Motion to Amend Its Rule 65 *ter* Exhibit List, 15 Dec 2005.

[1396] Prosecution Notification Regarding Certain Witnesses on its Rule 65 *ter* List, 24 Nov 2005.

[1397] Order Replacing a Judge in a Case before a Trial Chamber, 18 Nov 2005. Order Assigning Judges to a Case in a Trial Chamber, 1 Dec 2005. During the pre-Trial phase, on 15 May 2002, the President of the Tribunal transferred the case to Trial Chamber I, consisting of Judge Liu Daqun (China), presiding, Judge Amin El Mahdi (Egypt) and Judge Alphonsus Orie (The Netherlands). Order of the President Assigning a Case to a Trial Chamber, 15 May 2002. On 30 May 2003, the President of the Tribunal ordered the composition of the Trial Chamber as Judge Amin El Mahdi, Judge Alphonsus Orie and Judge Joaquín Martín Canivell (Spain). Order Assigning a Case to a Trial Chamber, 30 May 2003. On 2 June 2003, Judge Liu Daqun, as Presiding Judge of Trial Chamber I, designated Judge Alphonsus Orie as Presiding Judge in the case. Order Designating a Presiding Judge for the Case, 2 Jun 2003. On 7 June 2005, the President of the Tribunal assigned the case to Trial Chamber III. Order Reassigning a Case to a Trial Chamber, 7 Jun 2005. The case was reassigned to Trial Chamber I on 4 July 2005. Order Reassigning a Case to a Trial Chamber and Referring the Joinder Motion, 4 Jul 2005.

[1398] Hearing, 13 Dec 2005, T. 296–318. Hearing, 13 March 2006, T. 2222–2224. Hearing, 12 Jan 2007, T. 11441–11442.

[1399] Hearing, 13 Dec 2005, T. 261; Hearing, 20 Jun 2006, T. 5835–5836.

[1400] Decision Adopting Guidelines on the Standards Governing the Admission of Evidence, 19 Jan 2006 (with Annex A). Decision Adopting Guidelines on the Standards Governing the Presentation of Evidence and the Conduct of Counsel in Court, 13 Apr 2004 (with Annex A). The Guidelines were revised on 19 May 2006; Revised Version of the Decision Adopting Guidelines on the Standards Governing the Presentation of Evidence and the Conduct of Counsel in Court, 19 May 2006.

[1401] Decision on Prosecution's Motion for Admission of Statement of Witness Milan Babić Pursuant to Rule 89 (F), 10 Feb 2006; Decision on the Prosecution Motion for the Admission of a Statement of a Witness Pursuant to Rule 89(F), with Confidential Annex

pursuant to former Rule 92 *bis* (B), two witness statements were admitted pursuant to former Rule 92 *bis* (C), and transcripts of nine witnesses were admitted pursuant to **[page 190]** former Rule 92 *bis* (D).[1402] The testimonies of three witnesses of the Prosecution were heard via videoconference link.[1403] On 13 January 2006, the Trial Chamber granted the Defence's request for cross-examination of five Prosecution experts but dismissed the Defence's objections that the individuals could not, based on their qualifications, be considered as experts, and the objections concerning the impartiality of the experts, and the reliability of the reports.[1404] One subpoena was issued by the Trial Chamber for one witness at the request of the Prosecution.[1405] The Trial Chamber also issued one order for the temporary transfer of a detained witness.[1406] The Trial Chamber admitted 901 exhibits tendered into evidence by the Prosecution.

533. On 26 June 2006, the Defence presented oral submissions pursuant to Rule 98 *bis* of the Rules, moving for an acquittal on all counts.[1407] The Prosecution responded on the same day and opposed the Defence submissions in their entirety.[1408] On 3 July 2006, the Trial Chamber rejected the Defence motion in all respects.[1409]

534. The Defence case began on 11 July 2006 and ended on 16 November 2006.[1410] The Trial Chamber heard 22 *viva voce* witnesses, two of whom testified pursuant to Rule 92 *ter*.[1411] The testimony of one Defence witness was heard via video-conference link.[1412] On 13 January 2006, the Trial Chamber granted a Prosecution motion requesting assignment of pseudonyms to certain witnesses, that certain witnesses would testify in closed session, and that certain confidential material would not be disclosed to the public.[1413] On 18 August 2006, the Trial Chamber granted a Defence motion requesting the assignment of a pseudonym to a witness and closed session **[page 191]** testimony.[1414] Additional protective measures for witnesses were granted orally during the trial.[1415] The Trial Chamber issued 20 orders for safe conduct at the request of the Defence. In total, the Trial Chamber admitted 90 Defence exhibits into evidence. The Trial Chamber also admitted 24 exhibits as Chambers exhibits.

535. On 28 November 2006, the Trial Chamber denied the Prosecution's motion to admit evidence in rebuttal on the basis that it did not meet the standard for admission as rebuttal evidence pursuant to Rule 85(A)(iii).[1416]

A, 28 Apr 2006; Oral Decision on Prosecution's Motion for Admission of Statements of Witnesses MM-016 and MM-018 Pursuant to Rule 89 (F), 9 May 2006, T. 4151–4152.

[1402] Decision on Prosecution's Motions for the Admission of Written Evidence Pursuant to Rule 92 *Bis of* the Rules, 16 Jan 2006; Decision on Prosecution Motions on Admission of Written Statements Pursuant to Rule 92 *Bis* (C), 15 Jun 2006; Decision on Prosecution's Motions for Admission of Transcripts Pursuant to Rule 92 bis (D) and of Expert Reports Pursuant to Rule 94 bis, 13 Jan 2006; Oral Decisions on Prosecution's Second Rule 92 *bis* Motion of 25 January 2006, 15 Feb 2006, T. 1322–1323, and 2 May 2006, T. 3889–3890; Oral Decision to Admit the Statement of Witness MM-038, 23 Mar 2006, T. 2464.

[1403] Hearing, 2 Mar 2006, T. 1751–1752.

[1404] Decision on the Prosecution's Motions for Admission of Transcripts Pursuant to Rule 92 *bis* (d) and of Expert Reports Pursuant to Rule 94 *bis*, 13 Jan 2006.

[1405] Subpoena to a Witness to Appear for a Meeting with the Prosecution, 16 Sep 2005.

[1406] Order for Transfer of a Detained Witness, 13 Jan 2006.

[1407] Hearing, 26 Jun 2006, T. 5841–5886.

[1408] Hearing, 26 Jun 2006, T. 5886–5925, Hearing, 27 Jun 2006, T. 5927–5939.

[1409] Hearing, 3 Jul 2006, T. 5959–5971.

[1410] Hearing, 11 Jul 2006, T. 6024–6025; Hearing, 16 Nov 2006, T. 11142–11143.

[1411] Rule 92 *ter* was adopted at the Extraordinary Plenary Session on 13 Sep 2006 and codifies the procedure, which had developed pursuant to Rule 89(F), *see Milošević Decision*. According to the Rule 92 *bis* (C), Rule 92 *ter* also applies to witnesses who appear for cross-examination, *i.e.* witnesses who were formerly called pursuant to Rule 92 *bis* (E). Before the introduction of Rule 92 *ter*, Rule 89 (F) was applied in determining the admission of such evidence.

[1412] Decision on Defence Motion for the Testimony of Professor Simlja Avramov Via Video-Conference Link, 10 Nov 2006.

[1413] Decision on Prosecution Second Motion for Protective Measures with Confidential Annexes A, C and E, and Confidential and *Ex-Parte* Annexes B, D, and F, 13 Jan 2006. A previous Prosecution request for protective measures had been granted on 18 December 2003, Order on Prosecution Motion for Non-Disclosure of Materials Provided Pursuant to Rules 66(A)(Ii) and 68 and for Protective Measures for Witnesses During the Pre-Trial Phase. *See also* Decision on Prosecution's Motion for Variation of Protective Measures, 17 Mar 2006.

[1414] Decision on Defence Motion for Protective Measures for Witnesses MM-096, MM-116 and MM-090, 18 Aug 2006.

[1415] Hearing, 8 Mar 2006, T. 1943; Hearing, 15 Mar 2006, T. 2265–2267; Hearing, 4 Apr 2006, T. 3178–3179; Hearing, 23 Mar 2006, T. 2467; Hearing, 5 May 2006, T. 4073–4075; Hearing, 14 Aug 2006, T. 6430; Hearing, 11 Oct 2006, T. 9129–9130; Hearing, 31 Oct 2006, 10388–10389.

[1416] Decision on Prosecution Motion to Admit Evidence in Rebuttal Pursuant to Rule 92 *bis*, with Annexes A, B and C, 28 Nov 2006. *See* Prosecution Motion to Admit Evidence in Rebuttal Pursuant to Rule 92 *bis*, with Annexes A, B and C, 16 Nov 2006.

536. On 5 January 2007, the final trial briefs of the Prosecution and the Defence were filed. Closing arguments were heard on 10, 11 and 12 January 2007. On 9 April 2007, the Prosecution sent a letter to the Defence disclosing details of its assistance provided to Witness MM-003 in his asylum case.[1417] On 24 May 2007, the Trial Chamber ordered the Parties to make written submissions regarding the individual circumstances of Milan Martić because the Trial Chamber considered that the Parties had not adequately addressed this in their final trial briefs or closing arguments as was their duty under the Statute and under the Rules.[1418]

2. Testimony and evidence of Milan Babić

537. On 6 March 2006, the trial was adjourned until 8 March 2006 on account of the death of Milan Babić on 5 March 2006 at the United Nations Detention Unit, where he was being detained for the duration of his testimony as a Prosecution's witness.[1419] On 8 March 2006, the question of whether Milan Babić's death affected his evidence was raised in court and the Trial Chamber ordered the Parties to address the matter of Milan Babić's evidence "at an appropriate moment", and that the trial proceed in the meantime.[1420] On 9 June 2006, having heard the submissions of the Parties, the Trial Chamber rejected the Defence's arguments, determining that, pursuant to Rule 89 **[page 192]** (D) of the Rules, in spite of the incomplete cross-examination the need to ensure a fair trial did not outweigh the probative value of the evidence of Milan Babić.[1421]

538. On 20 June 2006, the Trial Chamber granted certification for appeal of the Trial Chamber's decision of 9 June 2006 to the Defence.[1422] On 10 July 2006, after being given an enlargement of time by the Appeals Chamber, the Defence filed its interlocutory appeal.[1423] The Appeals Chamber dismissed the Defence's appeal on 14 September 2006.[1424] On 30 September 2006, the Trial Chamber denied the Defence's motion for reconsideration and modification of the Trial Chamber's order of 9 June 2006.[1425]

539. On 17 November 2006, the Trial Chamber admitted into evidence excerpts of Milan Babić's Prosecution Interviews submitted by the Defence to it pursuant to the Trial Chamber's order of 9 June 2006.[1426]

1417 Letter from Alex Whiting to Predrag Milovančević, 9 Apr 2007. The Trial Chamber was copied on this letter.

1418 Order for submissions, 24 May 2006; Prosecution Submission Regarding Individual Circumstances of the Accused, 30 May 2007;Defence's Submission Concerning Individual Circumstances of the Accused Milan Martić, 30 May 2007. Each Party filed a response on 1 Jun 2007.

1419 Hearing, 6 Mar 2006, T. 1935–1936.

1420 Hearing, 8 Mar 2006, T. 1945–1948.

1421 Decision on Defence Motion to Exclude Testimony of Witness Milan Babić, Together with Associated Exhibits, from Evidence, 9 June 2006. *See supra* para. 33. Prosecution's Submissions Regarding the Evidence of Witness Milan Babić, 6 April 2006. The Prosecution submitted that Milan Babić's evidence bore numerous indicia of reliability, such as the fact that the testimony was given under oath, in open session, in the presence of the Accused, was subject to three days of cross-examination and was in large part corroborated by other evidence, both documentary and testimonial. Motion to Exclude Testimony of Witness Milan Babić, Together with Associated Exhibits, from Evidence, 2 May 2006. In its motion filed on 2 May 2006, the Defence requested the Trial Chamber to exclude the testimony of Milan Babić from the trial record on the basis that it was so lacking in indicia of reliability that it had no probative value, and in any case that it was substantially outweighed by the need to ensure a fair trial. On 8 May 2006, the Prosecution filed its Response to the Defence Motion to Exclude Testimony of Witness Milan Babić, Together with Associated Exhibits, from Evidence. The Defence replied on 15 May 2006.

1422 Decision on Defence Application for Certification of Appeal Pursuant to Rule 73 (B), 20 June 2006. *See also* Prosecution's Response to Defence Application for Certification of Appeal Pursuant to Rule 73 (B), 19 June 2006. Appeal against the Trial Chamber's Decision on the Evidence of Witness Milan Babić, 10 July 2006. On 20 July 2006, the Prosecution filed its Response to Defence Interlocutory Appeal against the Trial Chamber's Decision on the Evidence of Witness Milan Babić.

1423 Decision on Motion for Enlargement of Time, 23 Jun 2006.

1424 Decision on Appeal against the Trial Chamber's Decision on the Evidence of Witness Milan Babić, 14 September 2006. The Appeals Chamber found that the Defence had failed to demonstrate any of the discernible errors allegedly committed by the Trial Chamber that would result in prejudice.

1425 Decision on Defence Motion for Reconsideration and Modification of the Trial Chamber's Order of 9 June 2006, 30 Sep 2006. The Defence Motion was rejected, *inter alia*, on the basis that it was not shown by the Defence that there had been a change of circumstances, which would require the Trial Chamber to reconsider its decision *See* Defence Motion for Reconsideration and Modification of the Trial Chamber's Order of 9 June 2006, 24 September 2006. Prosecution's Response to the Defence Motion for Reconsideration and Modification of the Trial Chamber's Order of 9 June 2006, 28 September 2006.

1426 Decision on Defence's Submission Pursuant to the Trial Chamber's Order of 9 June 2006, 17 Nov 2006. *see* Defence's Submission Pursuant to the Trial Chamber's Order of 9 June 2006, 4 Oct 2006. Prosecution's Response to the Defence's Submission Pursuant to the Trial Chamber's Order of 9 June 2006, 16 October 2006.

540. On 28 November 2006, the Trial Chamber dismissed the Defence Motion requesting the Trial Chamber to order Judge Kevin Parker, the Vice-President of the Tribunal, to disclose to the Defence the full statements obtained during the inquiry on Milan Babić'c death, having found that it **[page 193]** was not the proper forum before which a request for review of the decision taken by Judge Parker could be brought.[1427]

3. Site visit

541. The Trial Chamber and the Parties carried out a site visit between 25 and 30 September 2006, pursuant to the Trial Chamber's Order of 16 May 2006 on Site visit.[1428] An audiovisual record was made of the site visit. The record was subsequently transcribed and both the record and the transcripts thereof were admitted into evidence by the Trial Chamber.[1429] **[page 194]**

ANNEX B – LIST OF CASES, SOURCES AND SHORT CITES

C. ICTY

Aleksovski Appeal Judgement	*Prosecutor v. Zlatko Aleksovski, Case No. IT-95-14/1-A, Judgement, 24 Mar 2000*
Babić Sentencing Appeal Judgement	*Prosecutor v. Milan Babić, Case No. IT-03-72, Judgement on Sentencing Appeal, Judgement, 18 Jul 2005*
Banović Sentencing Judgement	*Prosecutor v. Predrag Banović, Case No. IT-02-65/1-S, Sentencing Judgement, 28 Oct 2003*
Blagojević and Jokić Trial Judgement	*Prosecutor v. Vidoje Blagojević and Dragan Jokić, Case No. IT-02-60-T, Judgement, 17 Jan 2005*
Blaškić Appeal Judgement	*Prosecutor v. Tihomir Blaškić, Case No. IT-95-14-A, Judgement, 29 Jul 2004*
Brđanin Appeal Judgement	*Prosecutor v. Radoslav Brđanin, Case No. IT-99-36-A, Judgement, 3 Apr 2007*
Brđanin Trial Judgement	*Prosecutor v. Radoslav Brđanin, Case No. IT-99-36-T, Judgement, 1 Sep 2004*
Čelebići Appeal Judgement	*Prosecutor v. Zejnil Delalić, Zdravko Mucić (a.k.a. "Pavo"), Hazim Delić and Esad Landzo (a.k.a. "Zenga"), Case No. IT-96-21-A, Judgement, 20 Feb 2001*
Čelebići Trial Judgement	*Prosecutor v. Zejnil Delalić, Zdravko Mucić (a.k.a. "Pavo"), Hazim Delić and Esad Landzo (a.k.a. "Zenga"), Case No. IT-96-21-T, Judgement, 16 Nov 1998*
Češić Sentencing Judgement	*Prosecutor v. Ranko Češić, Case No. IT-95-10-1, Sentencing Judgement, 11 Mar 2004*

[1427] Decision on Defence's Motion for Access to Full Statements Obtained in the Inquiry of the Death of Milan Babić, 28 Nov 2006. *See* Defence's Motion for Access to Full Statements Obtained in the Inquiry of the Death of Milan Babić, 13 Nov 2006.

[1428] The locations visited were Zagreb, Hrvatska Dubica, Cerovljani, Baćin, Slunj, Hrvatska Kostajnica, Dvor na Uni, Saborsko, Poljanak (including the hamlet of Vukovići), Lipovača, Vaganac, Hrvatska Korenica, Škabrnja, Nadin, Bruška (including the hamlet of Marinovići), Knin, Vrpolje and Golubić.

[1429] Order On Site Visit, 16 May 2006. Order on Itinerary for the Site Visit, 23 Jun 2006. Decision on Admission into Evidence of Record of Site Visit, 28 Nov 2006. Ex. 1042: video record; Ex. 1043: transcript. *See also* Prosecution's Proposal of Locations to Visit During Proposed Site Visit, filed confidentially on 6 Apr 2006. Defence Submission Regarding sites to be Visited during the Proposed Site Visit, filed confidentially on 9 May 2006. Prosecution Response to Defence Submission Regarding Sites to be Visited During the Proposed Site Visit, 10 May 2006. *See also* Order to Redact Site Visit Record, 6 June 2007.

Deronjić Sentencing Appeal Judgement	*Prosecutor v. Miroslav Deronjić, Case No. IT-02-61, Judgement on Sentencing Appeal, 29 Jul 2005*
Dragan Nikolić Sentencing Judgement	*Prosecutor v. Dragan Nikolić, Case No. IT-94-02, Sentencing Judgement, 18 Dec 2003*
Erdemović Sentencing Judgement	*Prosecutor v. Drazan Erdemović, Case No. IT-96-22, Sentencing Judgement, 29 Nov 1996*
Erdemović Second Sentencing Judgement	*Prosecutor v. Dražen Erdemović, Case No. IT-96-22-Tbis, Sentencing Judgement, 5 Mar 1998*
Furundžija Appeal Judgement	*Prosecutor v. Anto Furundžija, Case No. IT-95-17/1-A, Judgment, 21 Jul 2000*
Furundžija Trial Judgement	*Prosecutor v. Anto Furundžija, Case No. IT-95-17/1-T, Judgement, 10 Dec 1998*
Galić Appeal Judgement	*Prosecutor v. Stanislav Galić, Case No. IT-98-29-A, Judgement, 30 Nov 2006*
Galić Trial Judgement	*Prosecutor v. Stanislav Galić, Case No. IT-98-29-T, Judgement, 14 Dec 2003*
Hadžihasanović and Kubura Rule 98 bis Appeal Decision	*Prosecutor v. Enver Hadžihasanović and Amir Kubura, Case No. IT-01-47-AR 73.3, Decision on Joint Defence Interlocutory Appeal of Trial Chamber Decision on Rule 98 bis Motions for Acquittal, 11* **[page 195]** *Mar 2005*
Halilović Trial Judgement	*Prosecutor v. Sefer Halilović, Case No. IT-01-48-T, Judgement, 16 Nov 2005*
Jelisić Appeal Judgement	*Prosecutor v. Goran Jelisić, Case No. IT-95-10-A, Judgement, 5 Jul 2001*
Jokić Sentencing Judgement	*Prosecutor v. Miodrag Jokić, Case No. IT-01-42-1-T, Sentencing Judgement, 18 Mar 2004*
Kordić and Čerkez Appeal Judgement	*Prosecutor v. Dario Kordić and Mario Čerkez, Case No. IT- 95-14/2-A, Judgement, 17 Dec 2004*
Kordić and Čerkez Trial Judgement	*Prosecutor v. Dario Kordić and Mario Čerkez, Case No. IT- 95-14/2-T, Judgement, 26 Feb 2001*
Krajišnik Trial Judgement	*Prosecutor v. Momčilo Krajišnik, Case No. IT-00-39-T, 27 Sep 2006*
Krnojelac Appeal Judgement	*Prosecutor v. Milorad Krnojelac, Case No. IT-97-25-A, Judgement, 17 Sep 2003*
Krnojelac Trial Judgement	*Prosecutor v. Milorad Krnojelac, Case No. IT-97-25-T, Judgement, 15 Mar 2002*
Krstić Appeal Judgement	*Prosecutor v. Radislav Krstić, Case No. IT-98-33-A, Judgement, 19 Apr 2004*
Krstić Trial Judgement	*Prosecution v. Radislav Krstić, Case No. IT -98-33-T, Judgement, 2 Aug 2001*
Kunarac et al. Appeal Judgement	*Prosecutor v. Dragoljub Kunarac et al., Case No. IT-96-22&23-/1-A, Judgement, 12 Jun 2002*
Kunarac et al. Trial Judgement	*Prosecutor v. Dragoljub Kunarac, Radomir Kovac and Zoran Vuković, Case No. IT-96-22&23-/1-T, Judgement, 21 February 2001*
Kupreškić et al. Appeal Judgement	*Prosecutor v. Zoran Kupreškić, Mirjan Kupreškić, Vlatko Kupreškić, Drago Josipović and Vladimir Šantić (aka "Vlado"), Case No. IT-95-16-A, Judgement, 23 Oct 2001*

Kupreškić et al. Trial Judgement	*Prosecutor v. Zoran Kupreškić, Mirjan Kupreškić, Vlatko Kupreškić, Drago Josipović, Dragan Papić and Vladimir Šantić (aka "Vlado"), Case No. IT-95-16-T, Judgement, 14 Jan 2000*
Kvočka et al. Appeal Judgement	*Prosecutor v. Miroslav Kvočka, Milojica Kos, Mlađo Radić, Zoran Žigić and Dragoljub Prcać, Case No. IT-98-30/1-A, Judgement, 28 Feb 2005*
Kvočka et al. Trial Judgement	*Prosecutor v. Miroslav Kvočka, Milojica Kos, Mlađo Radić, Zoran Žigić and Dragoljub Prcać, Case No. IT-98-30/1-T, Judgement, 2 Nov 2001*
Limaj et al. Trial Judgement	*Prosecutor v. Fatmir Limaj, Haradin Bala and Isak Musliu, Case No. IT-03-66-T, Judgement, 30 Nov 2005*
Milan Simić Sentencing Judgement	*Prosecutor v. Milan Simić, Case No. IT-95-9/2, Sentencing Judgement, 17 Oct 2002*
Milošević Decision	*Prosecutor v. Slobodan Milošević, Decision on Interlocutory Appeal on the Admissibility of Evidence-in-Chief in the Form of Written Statements, 30 Sep 2003*
Milutinović et al. Decision	*Prosecutor v. Milan Milutinović et al., Case No. IT-* **[page 196]** *05-87-T, Decision on Prosecution Request for Certification of Interlocutory Appeal of Decision on Admission of Witness Philip Coo's Expert Report, 30 Aug 2006*
Momir Nikolić Sentencing Appeal Judgement	*Prosecutor v. Momir Nikolić, Case No. IT-02-60/1-A, Judgement on Sentencing Appeal, 8 Mar 2006*
Mrkšić et al. Decision	*Prosecutor v. Mile Mrkšić et al., Case No. IT-95-13/1-T, Decision on Motion Seeking Clarification with Regard to Count 1 of the Indictment, 19 May 2006*
Naletilić and Martinović Appeal Judgement	*Prosecutor v. Mladen Naletilić (a.k.a. "Tuta") and Vinko Martinović (a.k.a. "Štela"), Case No. IT-98-34-A, Judgement, 3 May 2006*
Naletilić and Martinović Trial Judgement	*Prosecutor v. Mladen Naletilić (a.k.a. "Tuta") and Vinko Martinović (a.k.a. "Stela"), Case No. IT-98-34-T, Judgement, 31 Mar 2003*
Obrenović Sentencing Judgement	*Prosecutor v. Dragan Obrenović, Case No. IT-02-60/2, Sentencing Judgement, 10 December 2003*
Orić Trial Judgement	*Prosecutor v. Naser Orić, Case No. IT-03-68, Judgement, 30 Jun 2006*
Plavšić Sentencing Judgement	*Prosecutor v. Biljana Plavšić, Case No. IT-00-39&40/1-S, Sentencing Judgement, 27 Feb 2003*
Prlić Decision	*Prosecutor v. Jadranko Prlić et al., Case No. IT-04-74-PT, Decision on Defence Preliminary Motions Alleging Defect in the Form of the Indictment, 22 Jul 2005*
Sikirica et al. Sentencing Judgement	*Prosecutor v. Duško Sikirica et al., Case No. IT-95-8, Sentencing Judgement, 13 November 2001*
Simić et al. Trial Judgement	*Prosecutor v. Blagoje Simić, Miroslav Tadić, and Simo Zarić, Case No. IT-95-9, Judgement, 17 Oct 2003*
Stakić Appeal Judgement	*Prosecutor v. Milomir Stakić, Case No. IT-97-24-A, Judgement, 22 Mar 2006*

Stakić Trial Judgement	*Prosecutor v. Milomir Stakić, Case No. IT-97-24-T, Judgement, 29 Oct 2003*
Strugar Trial Judgement	*Prosecutor v. Pavle Strugar, Case No. IT- 01-42-T, Judgement, 31 Jan 2005*
Tadić Sentencing Appeal Judgement	*Prosecutor v. Duško Tadić (a.k.a. "Dule"), Case No. IT-94-1-A and IT-94-1-Abis, Judgement in Sentencing Appeals, 26 Jan 2000*
Tadić Appeal Judgement	*Prosecutor v. Duško Tadić (a.k.a. "Dule"), Case No. IT-94-1-A, Judgement, 15 Jul 1999*
Tadić Sentencing Judgement	*Prosecutor v. Duško Tadić (a.k.a. "Dule"), Case No. IT-94-1-Tbis-R117, Sentencing Judgement, 11 Nov 1999*
Tadić Trial Judgement	*Prosecutor v. Duško Tadić, Case No. IT-94-1-T, Judgement, 14 Jul 1997*
Tadić Jurisdiction Decision	*Prosecutor v. Duško Tadić, Case No. IT-94-1-AR72, Decision on the Defence Motion for Interlocutory Appeal on Jurisdiction, 2 Oct 1995* **[page 197]**
Todorović Sentencing Judgement	*Prosecutor v. Stevan Todorović, Case No. IT-95-9-1, Sentencing Judgement, 31 Jul 2001*
Vasiljević Appeal Judgement	*Prosecutor v. Mitar Vasiljević, Case No. IT-98-32-A, Judgement, 25 Feb 2004*
Vasiljević Trial Judgement	*Prosecutor v. Mitar Vasiljević, Case No. IT-98-32-T, Judgement, 29 Nor 2002*

D. ICTR

Akayesu Trial Judgement	*Prosecutor v. Jean-Paul Akayesu, Case No. ICTR-96-4-T, Judgement, 2 Sep 1998*
Gacumbitsi Appeal Judgement	*Prosecutor v. Sylvestre Gacumbitsi, Case No. ICTR-2001-64-A, Judgement, 7 Jul 2006*
Kambanda Appeal Judgement	*Prosecutor v. Jean Kambanda, Case No. ICTR-97-23-A, Judgement, 19 Oct 2000*
Kamuhanda Appeal Judgement	*Prosecutor v. Jean de Dieu Kamuhanda, Case No. ICTR-99-54A-A, Judgement, 19 Sept 2005*
Kayishema and Ruzindana Appeal Judgement	*Prosecutor v. Clément Kayishema and Obed Ruzindana, Case No. ICTR-95-1-A, Judgement, 1 Jun 2001*
Kayishema and Ruzindana Trial Judgement	*Prosecutor v. Clement Kayishema and Obed Ruzindana, Case No. ICTR-95-1-T, Judgement, 21 May 1991*
Musema Trial Judgement	*Prosecutor v. Alfred Musema, Case No. ICTR-96-13-T, Judgement, 27 Jan 2000*
Nahimana et al. Trial Judgement	*Prosecutor v. Ferdinand Nahimana et al., Case No. ICTR-99-52-T, Judgement, 3 Dec 2003*
Niyitegeka Appeal Judgement	*Prosecutor v. Eliézer Niyitegeka, Case No. ICTR-96-14-A, Judgement, 9 Jul 2004*
Ntakirutimana Appeal Judgement	*Prosecutor v. Elizaphan Ntakirutimana and Gérard Ntakirutimana, Cases Nos. ICTR-96-10-A and ICTR-96-17-A, Judgement, 13 Dec 2004*

Rutaganda Trial Judgement	*Prosecutor v. Georges Anderson Nderubumwe Rutaganda, Case No. ICTR-96-3-T, Judgement, 6 Dec 1999*
Serushago Sentencing Appeal Judgement	*Prosecutor v. Omar Serushago, Case No. ICTR-98-39-A, Judgement (Reasons), 6 Apr 2000*

E. <u>ICJ</u>

ICJ Advisory Opinion	*Legality of the Threat or Use of Nuclear Weapons, ICJ Advisory Opinion of 8 Jul 1996, I.C.J. Reports 1996*

F. <u>Other</u>

ICRC Commentary on Geneva Convention III	*Jean S. Pictet, ed., Commentary: Geneva Convention III Relative to the Treatment of Prisoners of War (Geneva: ICRC, 1960)*
ICRC Commentary on Geneva Convention IV	*Jean S. Pictet, ed., Commentary: Geneva Convention IV Relative to the Protection of Civilian Persons in Time of War (Geneva: ICRC, 1958)* **[page 198]**
ICRC Commentary on Additional Protocols	*Yves Sandoz, Christoph Swinarski and Bruno Zimmernmann, eds., Commentary on the Additional Protocols of 8 June 1977 to the Geneva Convention of 12 August 1949 (Dordrecht: Martin Nijhoff Publishers, 1987)*
Customary International Humanitarian Law, ICRC	*Jean-Marie Henckaerts and Louise Doswald-Beck, eds., International Committee of the Red Cross: Customary International Humanitarian Law, Volume I: Rules and Volume II: Practice (Cambridge: Cambridge University Press, 2005)*

Commentary

1. Introduction

Milan Martić, the former president and then minister of the interior of the self-proclaimed Republic of Serbian Krajina (RSK), located in north-eastern Croatia, was convicted by the ICTY in 2007 for his responsibility in crimes committed against the non-Serbian population of Croatia between 1991 and 1995. The initial indictment against Martić was confirmed by the judges on 25 July 1995. An international arrest warrant had been issued in March 1996; Martić surrendered and was transferred to the ICTY on 15 May 2002.

A first and second amended indictments followed, the latter one filed on 9 September 2003.[1] According to the indicting document, during the relevant period, Milan Martić held various leadership positions in the RSK (previously called Serbian Autonomous District – SAO - Krajina) and, as such, he committed a number of war crimes and crimes against humanity, acting in concert with other individuals in pursuance of a common criminal plan. Such a common plan consisted of the forcible removal of the majority of Croat, Muslim and other non-Serbian populations from the area.

According to the ICTY prosecutor, Martić was regarded as one of the most important and influential political figures in the RSK government, and he exercised absolute authority over the police units. From 1991 onwards, he actively worked to pursue a united Serb State; an aim that was pursued also through criminal means and policies. In particular, according to the allegations conveyed by the prosecutor, the accused: (i) participated in the creation, funding, supplying, training and direction of the so-called "Martić's police" – *i.e.* police forces created to support the plan of removing the Croat, Muslim and non-Serbian populations - and other military defence forces; (ii) personally participated in the military actions and subsequent crimes committed by these police and military forces, including the planning and execution of the forcible removal of the non-Serbian populations; (iii) openly espoused and encouraged creation bythe violence of a purely Serbian State in the Croat territories, and directed his troops to achieve this aim; and (iv) planned and ordered the shelling on Zagreb in May 1995.

The judgment commented upon here presents some interesting aspects, in particular with regard to the Trial Chamber's findings on specific elements of crimes against humanity, war crimes and on the individual liability of the accused for his participation in a "joint criminal enterprise". However, before turning to the specific analysis of these elements, we shall first have a brief look at the generality of the judgment and its findings.

2. The Trial Chamber Judgment

Following a year and a half-long trial (commencing in December 2005), in the judgement dated 12 June 2007 the accused was convicted and sentenced to 35 years imprisonment. Milan Martić was found guilty in 18 out of the 19 counts brought against him, and in particular of the following charges: persecution as a crime against humanity; murder as a crime against humanity and as a violation of the law and customs of war; imprisonment as a crime against humanity; torture as a crime against humanity and as a violation of the laws and customs of war; inhumane acts as a crime against humanity; cruel treatment as a violation of the laws and customs of war; deportation as a crime against humanity; forcible transfer as a crime against humanity; wanton destruction of villages, or devastation not justified by military necessity as violations of the laws and customs of war; destruction or wilful damage done to institutions dedicated to education or religion as violations of the laws and customs of war; plunder of public or private property as a violation of the laws and customs or war; and finally, attacks on civilians as a violation of the laws and customs of war.

The only count that Martić was acquitted from, number 2 of the indictment, regarded the charge of extermination as a crime against humanity, which the Trial Chamber found not proven due to the lack of one of that crime's elements – the massiveness of the killings. The reasoning of the chamber in this regard focused on the "large scale" requirement of the crime; although acknowledging that the crime of extermination does not require a minimum number of victims, and that it may be established by "an accumulation of separate and

1 On 9 December 2005, the second amended indictment was re-filed due to a mistake in the numbering of the previous one.

unrelated killings",[2] the judges found that the killing incidents charged under count 2 were committed "within a limited period of time and within a limited territory", and that the evidence was insufficient to establish that "the crime of extermination was committed on an accumulated basis".[3]

Martić was also convicted for the shelling of Zagreb in May 2005, where several people died and were injured, which he was found to have ordered as a direct response to "Operation Flash", launched on 1 May 2005 by the armed forces of Croatia.[4] In reality, the chamber considered that, already in 1992 and 1993, Martić, as minister of the interior, had in mind to attack Zagreb as a response to Croatian attacks on RSK cities,[5] and that he expressly threatened to attack the civilians in Zagreb during a meeting with the US Ambassador in 2004.[6]

On 8 October 2008, Martić's conviction to 35 years imprisonment was confirmed by the ICTY Appeals Chamber, with minor changes.[7]

3. The overlapping of war crimes and crimes against humanity: the issue of cumulative convictions

It is common practice in the case law of the *ad hoc* Tribunals – and in particular of the ICTY – to have cumulative convictions. The term 'cumulative conviction' indicates when an accused is convicted under different provisions (of the ICTY statute) on the basis of the same underlying conduct. As in the case of Martić, an accused can therefore be found guilty at the same time of both murder as a crime against humanity and murder as a violation of the law and customs of war, for the same underlying conduct, provided that some circumstances are satisfied. As the Trial Chamber stated in Martić: "Cumulative convictions that is multiple convictions entered under different statutory provisions in relation to the same conduct, are permissible only if each statutory provision involved has a materially distinct element not contained in the other."[8] As for the definition of "materially distinct element", the judges clarified that "an element is materially distinct from another if it requires proof of a fact not required by the other element."[9]

This test had been already established by the Appeals Chamber in the Čelebići case[10] and further clarified in the Kordić and Čerkez case, in the sense that what must be considered for the purpose of the cumulative convictions are the *legal elements* of each offence, and not the factual acts or omissions giving rise to the offence. If the test is not met, the chamber shall enter a conviction only under the more specific provision, – *i.e.* the one that contains all the elements of the other plus any additional ones (the so called "specialization element" in criminal law doctrine). Thus, multiple convictions for the same act or omission are permitted only where the conduct clearly violates multiple distinct provisions of the statute, "where each statutory provision contains a materially distinct element not contained in the other(s), and which element requires proof of a fact which the elements of the other statutory provision(s) do not." [11]

The Trial Chamber in the Martić case found that the accused was criminally responsible for the crime of persecution as a crime against humanity (as detailed in count 1 of the indictment). Such crime comprises the same acts that constitute other crimes against humanity or war crimes according to the statute. In fact, each of the underlying conduct that amounts to persecution – such as killings, wanton destruction of property, devastation – involves a criminal offence *per se* under the ICTY statute.[12] Persecution, however, is characterised by a specific discriminatory intent, which is based on political, racial or religious grounds (compare Article 5 ICTY statute). The chamber indeed found that most of the destruction and killings, carried

---

2 ICTY, Judgement, *Prosecutor v. Martić*, Case No. IT-95-11-T, T. Ch. I, 12 June 2007 in this volume, p. 481, par. 404.

3 *Ibid.*

4 *Ibid.*, par. 302.

5 *Ibid.*, par. 214.

6 *Ibid.*, par. 316, 317 and 318.

7 ICTY, Judgement, *Prosecutor v. Martić*, Case No. IT-95-11-A, A. Ch., 8 October 2008, to be published in volume XXXVII.

8 Judgement, *Prosecutor v. Martić*, T. Ch. I, *supra* note 1, par. 474; see also ICTY, Judgment on Sentence Appeal, *Prosecutor v. Mucić, Delić and Landžo*, Case No. IT-96-21-A *bis*, A. Ch., 8 April 2003, Klip/ Sluiter, ALC-XIV-847, par. 412.

9 *Ibid.*

10 Judgment on Sentence Appeal, *Prosecutor v. Mucić, Delić and Landžo*, A. Ch., *supra* note 8, par. 412 and 413.

11 ICTY, Judgement, *Prosecutor v. Kordić and Čerkez*, Case No. IT-95-14/2-A, A. Ch., 17 December 2004, Klip/ Sluiter, ALC-XXVI-19, par. 1033.

12 A crime against humanity, genocide or a war crime, depending on the actual elements present in the case.

out by the armed forces controlled by Martić in the various villages attacked, were committed with the "intent to discriminate on the basis of Croat ethnicity", therefore concluding that all the elements of the crime of persecution had been met.[13] As a consequence, the accused was convicted for the same acts under different counts corresponding to different crimes, as for instance - in the case of the attacks against Vojkovići and Poljanak - murder (counts 3 and 4), wanton destruction and devastation of villages (count 12), *and* persecution (count 1).

In the opinion of the judges, persecution would require a "materially distinct element that is not present as an element in any other crime, that is proof that the act or omission discriminated in fact and that the act or omission was committed with the specific intent to discriminate on the basis of one of the grounds listed in Article 5".[14] On the other hand the crimes listed under the other counts would require proof of "materially distinct elements", which are not present in the crime of persecution.[15]

Moreover, with regard to several criminal acts underlying the crime of persecution (such as killings, torture or inhumane acts), the Trial Chamber found that Martić's responsibility had to be cumulatively affirmed under both Article 3 (violations of laws and customs of war) and Article 5 (crimes against humanity) of the ICTY statute. Crimes under Article 3 require a "materially distinct element", which is not required for the crimes against humanity under Article 5 of the statute that is the "nexus between the acts of the accused and the armed conflict".[16]

Regarding the contextual element[17] of Article 5 of the ICTY statute, for some time already jurisprudence has established that – although the letter of the statute requires that the crime must occur "in armed conflict, whether international or internal in character" – this would not mean that the drafters aimed at reintroducing into the notion of crimes against humanity the "armed conflict nexus", a long abandoned supplementary requirement of the Nuremberg Charter.[18] The formulation of Article 5 of the statute is therefore interpreted as simply drawing a connection in place and time between the facts that occurred within the Yugoslav conflict,[19] by introducing a "purely jurisdictional prerequisite".[20]

Conversely, crimes against humanity under Article 5 of the statute do require proof of an element not included under Article 3, which is the widespread or systematic attack directed against any civilian population.[21] Therefore, in the words of the Trial Chamber, "cumulative convictions are permissible". It can be noted, however, that the issue of "cumulative convictions" remains problematic, despite the developments in the international criminal law jurisprudence over the last two decades and despite also the apparent lack of uncertainty on the part of the Trial Chamber in the present case, which dedicates little reasoning on the issue, which is presented as an apparently clear cut one.[22]

As already noted, the principle had been previously "settled" by the Appeal Chamber in the Čelebići case, which also fixed the test to apply in order to distinguish cases of cumulative convictions from the others (when only one legal count applies). In reality, the "Čelebići test" has been put into question by several commentators, as it is deemed "not sufficiently nuanced to account for the unique nature of international crimes or the inherent hierarchy which exists between these crimes".[23] No consistency has been achieved

[13] *Cf.* Judgement, *Prosecutor v. Martić*, T. Ch. I, supra note 1, par. 378, 383, 389 and 403.

[14] *Ibid.*, par. 475.

[15] *Ibid.*

[16] *Ibid.*, par. 476.

[17] See G. Werle, Principles of International Criminal Law, 2nd Edition, T.M.C. Asser, The Hague 2005, p. 293.

[18] In this sense, *ibid.*, p. 291. It is interesting to note that, in fact, Article 3 of the ICTR statute does not require or mentions any link to armed conflict for crimes against humanity.

[19] See ICTY, Judgement, *Prosecutor v. Tadić*, Case No. IT-94-1-A, A. Ch., 15 July 1999, Klip/ Sluiter, ALC-III-761, par. 249 and 251.

[20] ICTY, Judgement, *Prosecutor v. Kunarac, Kovač and Vuković*, Case No. IT-96-23&IT-96-23/1-A, A. Ch., 12 June 2002, Klip/ Sluiter, ALC-VIII-911, par. 83. See also R. Cryer, H. Friman, D. Robinson and E. Wilmshurst, An Introduction to International Criminal Law and Procedure, 2nd Edition, Cambridge University Press, Cambridge 2010, p. 237 and related footnotes.

[21] Judgement, *Prosecutor v. Martić*, T. Ch. I, supra note 1, par. 476.

[22] *Ibid.*, par. 474–478.

[23] See I. Erdei, Cumulative convictions in international criminal law: reconsideration of a seemingly settled issue, 34 Suffolk Transnational Law Review 2011, p. 317. The test in fact had been mutuated by the ICTY judges from a U.S. Supreme Court case (United States Supreme Court, *Blockburger v. United States*, 4 December 1931, 284 U.S. 299 (1932)), by failing to appreciate that the crimes underlying the two cases are not analogous, in particular with regard to the 'actus reus' element, which is much more

through the application of this test in the jurisprudence of the *ad hoc* Tribunals on cumulative convictions. In particular, whereas in some cases the ICTY rejected cumulative convictions for murder and persecution as crimes against humanity, on the rationale that murder was subsumed by persecution, which had the materially distinct element of discriminatory intent,[24] in other cases (as the one here), the judges have imposed cumulative convictions for persecution and murder on the basis that persecution had a materially distinct element (the specific intent to discriminate).[25]

The correctness of the application of the "Čelebići test" made by the Appeals Chamber of the ICTY in the Kordić and Stakić cases, and followed by the judges of the Trial Chamber in Martić, is very doubtful: as it was noted, "the test does not simply require that one of the two offenses have a materially distinct element requiring proof of an additional fact – both offences must require proof of different facts".[26]

4. Attacks on civilians: the notion of civilians and persons *hors de combat*

Milan Martić was charged and convicted, *inter alia*, of the crime of attacks on civilians, both as (i) a war crime under Article 3 ICTY statute, and (ii) as a crime against humanity under Article 5; the Trial Chamber had to deal with the notion of civilians for the purposes of the ICTY statute and, as we shall see, some of its findings in this regard are remarkable or appear to raise some questions and doubts.

(i) Analysing the crime of attacks on civilians as a violation of laws and customs of war punishable under Article 3 ICTY statute,[27] the chamber correctly noted that the offence is based on Article 51, paragraph 2 of Additional Protocol (AP) I and Article 13, paragraph 2 of Additional Protocol II to the Geneva Conventions, which provide that: "the civilian population as such, as well as individual civilians, shall not be made the object of attack". Such provisions have attained the status of customary international law according to the jurisprudence of the ICTY,[28] and "customary international law establishes that a violation of these principles entails individual criminal responsibility".[29]

The prohibition of attacks against civilians cannot be derogated even in the case of military necessity.[30] International humanitarian law clearly establishes the principle that only military objectives may be lawfully attacked,[31] meaning "those objects which by their nature, location, purpose or use make an effective contribution to military action and whose total or partial destruction, capture or neutralisation, in the circumstances ruling at the time, offers a definite military advantage".[32]

The Trial Chamber found that the absolute prohibition against targeting civilians does not exclude the possibility that civilian casualties may occur as an incidental, unintentional effect of an attack aimed at military targets (so-called "collateral damage"). However, in order not to incur criminal liability, such casualties must not be "disproportionate to the concrete and direct military advantage anticipated before the attack".[33]

complex in the international context; in this sense and for further analysis see, I. Erdei, Cumulative convictions in international criminal law: reconsideration of a seemingly settled issue, *ibid.*

24 See ICTY, Judgement, *Prosecutor v. Vasiljević*, Case No. IT-98-32-A, A. Ch., 25 February 2004, Klip/ Sluiter, ALC-XIX-465, par. 146; ICTY, Judgement, *Prosecutor v. Krstić*, Case No. IT-98-33-A, A. Ch., 19 April 2004, Klip/ Sluiter, ALC-XIX-539, par. 231 and 232. For a comment, see I. Erdei, Cumulative convictions in international criminal law: reconsideration of a seemingly settled issue, *supra* note 23 with related references.

25 The Trial Chamber in Martić refers to the following cases: Judgement, *Prosecutor v. Kordić and Čerkez*, A. Ch., *supra* note 11, par. 1038–1041; and Decision on Ojdanić's motion challenging jurisdiction: indirect co-perpetration, *Prosecutor v. Milutinović et al.*, Case No. IT-05-87, T. Ch. III, 22 March 2006, Klip/ Sluiter, ALC-XXIX-11, par. 359-364. For a critical assessment of these judgments' findings on the point, see again I. Erdei, Cumulative convictions in international criminal law: reconsideration of a seemingly settled issue, *supra* note 23.

26 *Ibid.*

27 *Cf.* count 19 of the indictment.

28 *Cf.* ICTY, Decision on Interlocutory Appeal, *Prosecutor v. Strugar, Jokić and others*, Case No. IT-01-42-AR72, A. Ch., 22 November 2002, Klip/ Sluiter, ALC-XI-67, par. 9.

29 Ibid., par. 10. See also ICTY, Judgement, *Prosecutor v. Blaškić*, Case No. IT-95-14-A, A. Ch., 29 July 2004, Klip/ Sluiter, ALC-XX-295, par. 90; and ICTY, Judgement, *Prosecutor v. Galić*, Case No. IT-98-29-A, A. Ch., 30 November 2006, Klip/ Sluiter, ALC-XXXIII-809, par. 190.

30 See Judgement, *Prosecutor v. Kordić and Čerkez*, A. Ch., *supra* note 11, par. 54.

31 *Cf.* Article 52, paragraph 2, Additional Protocol I.

32 See Judgement, *Prosecutor v. Kordić and Čerkez*, A. Ch., *supra* note 11, par. 53.

33 See Judgement, *Prosecutor v. Martić*, T. Ch. I, *supra* note 1, par. 69, referring to Judgement, *Prosecutor v. Galić*, A. Ch.,

The difficulties related to the principle of proportionality, i.e. on how to measure whether an attack was 'proportionate' in terms of military advantage expected *vis-á-vis* the damages caused, are well known.[34] However, the standards set by the jurisprudence so far are not very helpful in this regard: how to identify the "reasonably well-informed person in the circumstances of the actual perpetrator, making a reasonable use of the information available to him or her" in order to evaluate if "excessive civilian causalities [could] result from the attack".[35] In fact, the judges tend to follow a case-by-case approach on this issue, where the proportionality of the attack must be determined in light of the available evidence and applied in conjunction with the prohibition of indiscriminate attacks.[36]

Significantly, the Trial Chamber in Martić found that indiscriminate attacks, affecting military and civilian objects (or individuals) without distinction, may also amount to direct attacks on civilians, and that in this case "a direct attack against civilians can be inferred from the indiscriminate character of the weapon used".[37] To draw such a conclusion, the court relied also on the finding of the ICJ in its Advisory Opinion on the Legality of the Threat of Nuclear Weapons in Armed Conflicts of 1996, as well as previous case law of the Appeals Chamber of the ICTY.[38] The fact that indiscriminate attacks may amount to direct attacks on civilians implies, as was noted, that indiscriminate attacks generally do not need to be disproportionate in order to be unlawful.[39]

In its application of the above mentioned findings, the Trial Chamber in Martić held that the attacks on Zagreb of 2 and 3 May 1995 were unlawful. In those days, the centre of the city was hit by Orkan rockets, which were launched with no prior warnings, causing the death of seven civilians, with at least 214 people injured. The Orkan rocket, a long range weapon, can be fitted with different warheads to accomplish different tasks: when it is fitted with a cluster bomb, the Orkan rocket becomes an anti-personnel weapon designed to kill people. The rockets fired on 2 and 3 May 1995 on central Zagreb were of this kind, fitted with cluster bombs.[40] The judges established the personal responsibility of the accused in this regard, for having ordered the attacks and the employment of such weapons on the civilian population.

(ii) With regard to the charges of attacks against civilians as a crime against humanity, one aspect of the Trial Chamber's judgment needs to be highlighted in particular, that is the notion of civilians under Article 5 ICTY statute.

As acknowledged by the court, the term "civilian population" contained in Article 5 of the statute, should be given a broad definition: thus, "the presence of combatants within a civilian population does not necessarily alter its characterisation as such".[41] Nevertheless, the status of the victim as a civilian is considered as one of the characterizing elements of crimes against humanity, and as such it is to be carefully defined.[42] In doing so, the chamber referred to the previous jurisprudence of the ICTY, and in particular to Blaškić case,[43] where the Appeals Chamber relied upon the provision of Article 50 Additional Protocol I in order to find a definition of civilian. The provision states that:

> "A civilian is any person who does not belong to on of the categories of persons referred to in Article 4 A (1), (2), (3) and (6) of the Third [Geneva] Convention and in Article 43 of this Protocol. In case of doubt whether the person is a civilian, that person shall be considered to be a civilian".

---

supra note 29, par. 190 *et seq.*

34 See W.J. Fenrick, The Rule of Proportionality and Protocol I in Conventional Warfare, 98 Military Law Review 1981, p. 91 *et seq.*

35 ICTY, Judgement and Opinion, *Prosecutor v. Galić*, Case No. IT-98-29-T, T. Ch. I, 5 December 2003, Klip/ Sluiter, ALC-XV-413, par. 58. For a comment, see C. Wuerzner, Mission Impossible? Bringing charges for the crime of attacking civilians or civilian objects before international criminal tribunals, 90 International Review of the Red Cross 2008, p. 907 *et seq.*, in particular p. 922. See also W.J. Fenrick, Attacking the enemy civilian as a punishable offense, 7 Duke Journal of Comparative and International Law 1997, p. 545–549.

36 See ICTY, Judgement, *Prosecutor v. Kupreškić, Kupreškić, Kupreškić, Josipović, Papić and Šantić*, Case No. IT-95-16-T, T. Ch. II, 14 January 2000, Klip/ Sluiter, ALC-IV-703, par. 524.

37 Judgement, *Prosecutor v. Martić*, T. Ch. I, *supra* note 1, par. 69.

38 See in particular Judgement, *Prosecutor v. Galić*, A. Ch., *supra* note 29, par. 132.

39 See C. Wuerzner, Mission Impossible? Bringing charges for the crime of attacking civilians or civilian objects before international criminal tribunals, supra note 35, p. 907 *et seq.*, in particular p. 920 and 921.

40 See ICTY, Initial Indictment, *Prosecutor v. Martić*, Case No. IT-95-11-T, T. Ch. I, 25 July 1995, par. 7–8; Judgement, *Prosecutor v. Martić*, T. Ch. I, supra note 1, par. 461, 462 and 463.

41 Judgement, *Prosecutor v. Martić*, T. Ch. I, *supra* note 1, par. 50.

42 *Ibid.*, par. 51.

43 See ICTY, Judgement, *Prosecutor v. Blaškić*, Case No. IT-95-14-A, A. Ch., 29 July 2004, Klip/ Sluiter, ALC-XX-295, par. 110.

If the recourse, in general, to Article 50 Additional Protocol I to define the notion of civilians under Article 5 ICTY statute does not seem *prima facie* particularly problematic, the problems start to appear on the surface when one tries to draw more precise lines in order to frame the concepts of "member of armed forces", "member of a militia" or "member of a resistance group" as contained in Article 4 of the Third Geneva Convention (GC) and Article 43 Additional Protocol I. Particularly doubtful is whether a person *hors de combat* shall be considered as a "civilian" for the purposes of Article 5 ICTY statute.[44] In this regard, the Trial Chamber in Martić expressly adopted the notion of civilian as elaborated further by the Appeal Chamber in Blaškić, which stated that:

> "the specific situation of the victim at the time the crimes are committed may not be determinative of his civilian or non-civilian status. If he is indeed a member of an armed organisation, the fact that he is not armed or in combat at the time of the commission of the crimes, does not accord him a civilian status".[45]

Thus, according to the Trial Chamber in Martić, since a person *hors de combat* shall not be regarded as a civilian in the context of international humanitarian law,[46] that person shall not equally qualify as a civilian for the purposes of Article 5 of the ICTY statute, and thus cannot be considered a victim of crimes against humanity.[47]

In the view of the judges, it is a consequence of the principle of distinction between civilians and combatants that permeates the laws of war and international humanitarian law that Article 5 only applies to civilians, and that this notion shall be narrowly interpreted.[48] In its application of such reasoning, several charges of crimes against humanity brought by the prosecutor against Martić under Article 5 ICTY statute with regard to the killings of individuals considered to be combatants, but *hors the combat* at the moment of the attack, were dismissed by the Trial Chamber.

Such a conclusion by the Trial Chamber in this case, which was later reversed by the Appeals Chamber,[49] is doubtful. As was noted, "what is crucial is not formal status, such as membership in specific military forces or units, but the person's actual role at the time of the commission of the crime".[50] It should be noted that the jurisprudence of the ICTY is not consistent on the point. The Appeals Chamber in Kordić – which at first follows the Blaškić decision's findings on the point[51] – seems to have then taken a different approach by expanding the concept of civilians as to also include soldiers who were killed after their arrest, thus when they were *hors de combat*: "these persons, wilfully killed by Croat forces, were without doubt [...] "civilians" in the sense of Article 5 of the statute".[52]

When reversing the Trial Chamber's findings on this point, the Appeals Chamber noted that the relevance of the "civilian population" in Article 5 of the ICTY statute is limited to the contextual element of crimes against humanity (the *chapeau* of the provision), that there be a *widespread or systematic attack against the civilian population*. On the contrary, there is nothing in the text of Article 5 that would require that the individual victims of crimes against humanity to be civilians.[53] In this sense, the Appeals Chamber did not agree with the interpretation submitted by the prosecutor, that the definition of "civilians" when used in the context of crimes against humanity should not be limited to its definition under international humanitarian law, but could also include other categories of people: on the contrary, in the view of the Appeals Chamber, Article 50 Additional Protocol I would still reflect the definition of "civilian" for the purposes of Article 5 ICTY statute (but, as seen above, limited to its *chapeau*).[54]

---

44 *Cf.*, Judgement, *Prosecutor v. Martić*, T. Ch. I, supra note 1, par. 52 ff.

45 Judgement, *Prosecutor v. Blaškić*, A. Ch., *supra* note 43, par. 114, quoted in Judgement, *Prosecutor v. Martić*, T. Ch. I, supra note 1, par. 52.

46 See in this sense also Judgement, *Prosecutor v. Galić*, A. Ch., *supra* note 29, footnote 437, quoted in Judgement, *Prosecutor v. Martić*, T. Ch. I, *supra* note 1, par. 54.

47 Judgement, *Prosecutor v. Martić*, T. Ch. I, *supra* note 1, par. 55.

48 *Ibid.*, par. 56.

49 See Judgement, *Prosecutor v. Martić*, A. Ch., *supra* note 7, par. 272 *et seq.*

50 In this sense G. Werle, Principles of International Criminal Law, *supra* note 17, p. 294.

51 See : Judgement, *Prosecutor v. Kordić and Čerkez*, A. Ch., *supra* note 11, par. 97.

52 *Ibid.*, par. 458.

53 See Judgement, *Prosecutor v. Martić*, A. Ch., *supra* note 7, par. 291 ff.

54 As a consequence, the Appeals Chamber in Martić found that the Trial Chamber erred in law in this respect and reversed

5. The individual responsibility of Milan Martić

In his position as the former president and minister of the interior of the RSK, Milan Martić was charged with individual criminal responsibility pursuant to Article 7, paragraph 1 ICTY statute in relation to each count of the indictment. The provision reads as follows:

> "A person who planned, instigated, ordered, committed or otherwise aided and abetted in the planning, preparation or execution of a crime referred to in articles 2 to 5 of the present Statute, shall be individually responsible for the crime".

It is self-evident that Article 7, paragraph 1 contains several distinct modes of liability, which also imply a different level of culpability and grade of the individual responsibility;[55] Martić in particular was found responsible for his participation in most of the imputed crimes pursuant to the mode of liability indicated as "joint criminal enterprise" (JCE). Only with regard to the crimes committed in the context of the shelling of Zagreb (counts 1, 15 and 19), his responsibility was framed as "ordering".[56] The Trial Chamber found in this regard that there was sufficient evidence to conclude that Martić personally ordered the attacks on Zagreb of 2 and 3 May 1995, in circumvention of the procedures and the RSK Constitution that would have assigned this kind of decision to the Supreme Defence Council.[57]

The chamber found that "Milan Martić intended to shell the city of Zagreb in order to retaliate on Croatia and to stop further Croatian attacks on the RSK".[58] However the judges were not persuaded that the attacks were ordered and carried out by the accused "with discriminatory intent on the basis of ethnicity", and therefore concluded that the crime of persecution, in the specific context of the shelling of Zagreb, was not proven.[59] The chamber on the contrary found Martić's individual criminal responsibility established under Article 7, paragraph 1 ICTY statute for murder, inhumane acts, cruel treatment and attacks on civilians committed in Zagreb as a consequence of his order to shell the city.

Whereas the above-mentioned findings related to the responsibility of Martić for ordering are not particularly problematic (although not always thoroughly reasoned),[60] some problems arise with regard to the other mode of liability upon which the judges established the responsibility of the accused, that is the JCE doctrine, and in particular the so-called "extended form" of JCE.

6. The "extended form" of JCE

Martić was charged and convicted pursuant to Article 7, paragraph 1 ICTY statute for his participation in a "joint criminal enterprise" by, *inter alia*, creating, financing, supplying, training, and directing the "Martić's Police" and other Serbian "Territorial Defence" forces of the Socialist Federal Republic of Yugoslavia (SFRY), and by creating, training and directing special police forces of the Serbian security service. The prosecutor also alleged that Martić participated in the planning, preparation and execution of the takeover of territories in the RSK, and that he personally participated in military action and subsequent crimes by these forces, including the removal of the non-Serb populations.[61]

---

the acquittal of the accused from crimes against humanity with regard to the individual victims *hors the combat* at the time of the commission of the offences, thus entering convictions under Article 5 ICTY Statute for murder, torture, inhumane acts and persecution for acts committed against these victims.

[55] On the different modes of liability, see E. van Sliedregt, The criminal responsibility of individuals for violations of International Humanitarian Law, T.M.C. Asser, The Hague 2003.

[56] See Judgement, *Prosecutor v. Martić*, T. Ch. I, supra note 1, par. 456–473.

[57] *Ibid.*, par. 459.

[58] *Ibid.*, par. 473.

[59] *Ibid.*

[60] There seems to be a lack of reasoning to the extent that the Chamber did not elaborate on the responsibility of Martić for having actually ordered the specific crimes: it could be argued in fact that it is one thing to have ordered the shelling of Zagreb, and thus the attacks on civilians, and a different one is to have personally ordered the murders and the inhumane or cruel treatment. The legal findings about 'ordering' are limited to one paragraph (*cf.* Judgement, *Prosecutor v. Martić*, T. Ch. I, *supra* note 1, par. 441).

[61] *Ibid.*, par. 6.

The ICTY introduced the joint criminal enterprise doctrine as a mode of liability to regulate the cases of commission of a crime (falling under the jurisdiction of the Tribunal) by a group of persons in execution of a common criminal purpose.[62] Although the statute does not expressly provide for such mode of liability, the jurisprudence found that the participation in a joint criminal enterprise is implicitly recognised in Article 7, paragraph 1 of the statute.[63] The ICTY has consistently interpreted the participation in a joint criminal enterprise as a form of (joint) commission to which principal liability for the crime is attached.[64] However, the Appeals Chamber in the Brđanin case has questioned this conclusion, with specific regard to such cases where the crimes are actually committed by individuals who are not members of the JCE (see *infra*).

This doctrine is based on a mutual attribution of acts among a plurality of persons acting in pursuance of a common plan (also referred to as a common design or purpose). It follows that JCE members are responsible not only for their personal contribution, but also for the behaviour of the other individuals who participated in the common criminal plan. The jurisprudence of the *ad hoc* tribunals recognised three forms of JCE (the so-called JCE 1, 2 and 3 – the latter also referred to as the "extended form"), which present common features and some differences.[65] The differences between the three forms are found in particular at the *mens rea* level, whereas at the *actus reus* level, the JCE doctrine is based on the following common elements: a plurality of persons, the common plan between the co-perpetrators amounting to or involving the commission of a crime, and the contribution of the accused to the common plan.[66]

The various forms of JCE may actually differ significantly from each other, leading to quite different results.[67] Intent and knowledge are always required with regard to the first form of JCE, so that every member of the enterprise must have intended to commit the crimes included in the common plan, in order to be responsible thereof as a co-perpetrator. The jurisprudence of the ICTY has established that the accused must share the "purpose of the joint criminal enterprise": merely knowing about it is not sufficient to be responsible as a member of the JCE. The same applies also to the other two categories of JCE, but the latter form ("JCE 3" or "extended JCE") broadens the possibility of attributing responsibility to the members of the criminal enterprise for crimes that fall outside of the common plan.

The scope of the application of this form of liability consists of cases where one member of the JCE commits acts extending beyond the framework of the common plan that was agreed upon among the enterprise members. On the basis of this extended form, all the participants to the criminal enterprise are responsible also for the crime falling outside of the common plan if it represents a "natural and foreseeable" consequence of the common plan.[68] *Dolus eventualis* or advertent recklessness suffice as a mental element with regard to the unplanned crime: in this sense it is enough that the accused "willingly took that risk".[69]

Martić was charged under the first and third categories of JCE.[70] The common purpose of the JCE had been identified in this case as "the forcible removal of a majority of the Croat, Muslim and other non-Serb

---

62 See the findings of the Trial Chamber on JCE, *ibid.*, par. 434–455.

63 See Judgement, *Prosecutor v. Tadić*, A. Ch., *supra* note 19, par. 194 *et seq.*

64 ICTY, Judgement, *Prosecutor v. Krnojelac*, Case No. IT-97-25-A, A. Ch., 17 September 2003, Klip/ Sluiter, ALC-XIV-753, par. 73; Judgement, *Prosecutor v. Kvočka et al*, Case No. IT-98-30/I-A, A. Ch., 28 February 2005, Klip/ Sluiter, ALC-XXVI-669, par. 91. See K. Gustafson, Joint Criminal Enterprise, in A. Cassese (ed.), The Oxford Companion to International Criminal Justice, Oxford 2009, p. 395.

65 Most recently see V. Haan, Joint criminal enterprise. Die Entwicklung einer Mittäterschaftlichen Zurechnungsfigur im Völkerstrafrecht, 179 Schriften zum Völkerrecht 2008. See also the contributions of J.D. Ohlin, H. van der Wilt, A. Cassese, K. Gustafson, K. Ambos, E. van Sliedregt and K. Hamdorf, in Symposium on JCE, G. Sluiter (ed.), 5 Journal International Criminal Justice 2007. For a comprehensive analysis of JCE in the framework of the co-perpetration model, see E. Amati and M. Costi, Autoria e Forme di Compartecipazione Criminosa, in E. Amati et al., Introduzione al Diritto Penale Internazionale, Giuffré, Milano 2010.

66 To establish responsibility for JCE, it is necessary that an individual has made a significant contribution to the common plan, but that does not need to amount to a causal contribution to the specific crime, and can also consist of any kind of assistance, even at the planning stage. See Judgement, *Prosecutor v. Tadić*, A. Ch., *supra* note 19, par. 227. G. Werle, Principles of International Criminal Law, *supra* note 17, p. 122.

67 In particular, this can be said with regard to the first and the third form, since JCE 2, the so-called concentration camp cases, should be considered just as a sub-category of the first one.

68 See Judgement, *Prosecutor v. Martić*, T. Ch. I, supra note 1, par. 439. See also ICTY, Judgement, *Prosecutor v. Tadić*, Case No. IT-94-1-A, A. Ch., 15 July 1999, Klip/ Sluiter, ALC-III-761, par. 436.

69 *Ibid.*, and related references.

70 Initial Indictment, *Prosecutor v. Martić*, T. Ch. I, *supra* note 40, par. 5.

population from parts of the territory of Croatia and Bosnia and Herzegovina, designated to become part of a new Serb-dominated state."[71]

The Trial Chamber found that several of the crimes perpetrated against the non-Serb populations were outside the common purpose of the JCE;[72] however, it considered that Martić was aware that the non-Serb populations were being subjected to widespread and systematic crimes and, therefore, "the crimes which have been found to be *outside the common purpose* were *foreseeable* to Milan Martić. [...] Thus the Trial Chamber considers it proven beyond reasonable doubt that Milan Martić *willingly took the risk* that the crimes which have been found to be outside the common purpose might be perpetrated against the non-Serbian population."[73]

The JCE approach, in general, has been the subject of several controversies[74] and its extended form, in particular, raises relevant doubts and criticisms.[75] Such difficulties in accepting the JCE approach should not surprise when one bears in mind that the JCE doctrine is intended to be a form of *commission*, and thus gives rise to principal liability for intentional crimes. The effects of JCE are the mutual attribution of responsibility between JCE members: the crime committed by one member is attributed also to the others, which are considered as co-perpetrators (principals). As was noted, "the central element of this concept is the participant's "common criminal purpose" and it is from this common purpose that, in the last resort, their liability derives, regardless of the weight of their individual objective contribution or of its proximity to the occurrence of the offence".[76]

Given this subjective approach, it is clear that particular problems arise when, pursuant to JCE 3, a member of the criminal enterprise is considered as the co-perpetrator of a crime falling outside of the scope of the common plan, without having the intent that such crime was committed and without any "substantial contribution" to its execution.[77]

The jurisprudence went as far as recognising the possibility of imputing crimes to members of the JCE even in cases where the principal perpetrator (the one that committed the *actus reus*) was not sharing the common criminal purpose of the enterprise and therefore was not a member of the JCE.[78] This can be in the case where one member of the JCE 'uses' the perpetrator in order to carry out the *actus reus* of a crime.[79] It can be noted, however, that it is not always clear what kind of link must exist between the member(s) of the JCE and the actual perpetrator (non-JCE member), in order to attribute the responsibility for the crime committed by the latter (also) to the former and, as a consequence, (also) to the other members of the JCE.

In sum, not only are the above-mentioned categories of JCE quite different from one another as regards their "structural features", but they can also lead to critically different results, as the jurisprudence of the ICTY shows.[80] While the first form of JCE (similarly to the second form, which is a variation of the first) can be framed as a form of co-perpetration recognized in customary international law,[81] the so-called extended form

71 Judgement, *Prosecutor v. Martić*, T. Ch. I, supra note 1, par. 442.

72 In particular insofar as they related to counts 3 to 9, 12 to 14 and in part count 1, see Judgement, *Prosecutor v. Martić*, T. Ch. I, supra note 1, par. 454.

73 Judgement, *Prosecutor v. Martić*, T. Ch. I, supra note 1, par. 545 (emphasis added).

74 See E. van Sliedregt, 19 Joint Criminal Enterprise as a Pathway to Convicting Individuals for Genocide, Journal International Criminal Justice 2007, p. 187–191.

75 See J.D. Ohlin, Three Conceptual Problems with the Doctrine of Joint Criminal Enterprise, 5 Journal International Criminal Justice 2007, p. 69 *et seq.* In defense of JCE, see A. Cassese, The Proper Limits of Individual Responsibility under the Doctrine of Joint Criminal Enterprise, 5 Journal International Criminal Justice 2007, p. 109 *et seq.*

76 *Cf.* T. Weigend, Intent, Mistake of Law, and Co-Perpetration in the Lubanga Decision on Confirmation of Charges, 6 Journal International Criminal Justice 2008, p. 477.

77 The jurisprudence has established that "it is also not required that [the] participation be necessary or substantial to the crime for which the accused is found responsible", it suffices a "significant contribution", see Judgement, *Prosecutor v. Martić*, T. Ch. I, supra note 1, par. 440 and related references.

78 ICTY, Judgement, *Prosecutor v. Brđanin*, Case No. IT-99-36-A, A. Ch., 3 April 2007, Klip/ Sluiter, ALC-XXXIII-609, par. 413 and 891.

79 See Judgement, *Prosecutor v. Martić*, T. Ch. I, supra note 1, par. 438 ff.

80 For a detailed analysis of the ICTY jurisprudence on JCE which reveals the different interpretation of the concept in the various judgments, see V. Haan, Joint criminal enterprise. Die Entwicklung einer Mittäterschaftlichen Zurechnungsfigur im Völkerstrafrecht, *supra* note 65, p. 73–191 and p. 198–200. *Cf.* for instance ICTY, Judgement, *Prosecutor v. Stakić*, Case No. IT-97-24-7, T. Ch. II, 31 March 2003, *vis-á-vis* the Judgement, *Prosecutor v. Brđanin*, Case No. IT-99-36-A, A. Ch., *supra* note 78.

81 For the arguments in this sense, see V. Haan, Joint criminal enterprise. Die Entwicklung einer Mittäterschaftlichen Zurechnungsfigur im Völkerstrafrecht, *supra* note 65, at. 248 *et seq.*

of JCE - because of the lower *mens rea* required - does not appear to be rooted in customary international law.[82]

Also with regards to the cases where the actual perpetrator is not part of the JCE, it can become very questionable whether commission (perpetration) is the right mode of liability in which to impute the crime to the JCE members. In this regard, one ICTY judge has noted that, if the mode of liability that links the JCE member to the actual perpetrator – non-JCE member – is for instance "ordering", the same mode of liability should apply to all JCE members for that crime.[83]

It is doubtful as to what is the true value of the JCE doctrine in international criminal law.[84] Certainly this doctrine has played a crucial role in international criminal law, and in particular in the jurisprudence of the ICTY, which recognized JCE as "firmly established in customary international law".[85] The future value of the JCE doctrine, however, depends mostly on its applicability before the ICC, which in fact has rejected it from the outset, on the basis of the different sources of applicable law before the court under Article 21, paragraph 1, sub a of the Rome Statute,[86] which therefore makes the circumstance that the ICTY declared JCE as being firmly established in customary law not relevant to the court.[87]

7. No conviction for "command responsibility", and the position of superior as an aggravating factor

The prosecutor had also charged Martić pursuant Article 7, paragraph 3 of the ICTY statute, for his failing – as a superior - to prevent or punish the crimes allegedly committed by his forces.[88] The Trial Chamber however found that the individual responsibility of the accused had to be established on the basis of "ordering" and a "JCE" pursuant to Article 7, paragraph 1 ICTY, and therefore other modes of liability "will not be considered".[89]

Article 7, paragraph 3 of the ICTY statute expressly provides for superior responsibility in the following terms:

> "The fact that any of the acts referred to in Articles 2 to 5 of the present statute was committed by a subordinate does not relieve his superior of criminal responsibility if he knew or had reason to know that the subordinate was about to commit such acts or had done so and the superior failed to take the necessary and reasonable measures to prevent such acts or to punish the perpetrators thereof."

The ICTY jurisprudence elaborated on this provision for the first time in the Čelebići case, undoubtedly the leading case on the issue. On that occasion the judges affirmed the existence of three elements of command responsibility: (i) the existence of a superior-subordinate relationship; (ii) the subordinate knew or had reason to know that the criminal act was about to be or had been committed; (iii) the superior failed to take the necessary and reasonable measures to prevent the criminal act or to punish the perpetrators thereof.[90]

---

82 *Ibid.*, at 303 and 304. See also G. Werle, Principles of International Criminal Law, *supra* note 17, p. 172–175.

83 See the ICTY, Separate opinion of Judge Meron, *Prosecutor v. Brđanin*, Case No. IT-99-36-A, A. Ch., 3 April 2007, Klip/ Sluiter, ALC-XXXIII-718, par. 6. See the comments of K. Gustafson, Joint Criminal Enterprise, *supra* note 64, p. 395, regarding the contrasting *mens rea* standards that would come out of a situation as the one described above.

84 Doubts have arisen *vis-á-vis* the JCE approach, which would put at risk the principle of individual responsibility by introducing a form of collective responsibility and guilt by association, connoted by negligent contribution and common plan. The principle of culpability would be at risk in particular by the extended form of JCE, because of its lower *mens rea* standard. *Contra* see K. Gustafson, Joint Criminal Enterprise, *supra* note 64, p. 395 and 396.

85 Judgement, *Prosecutor v. Tadić*, A. Ch., *supra* note 19, par. 220.

86 The Rome Statute, the Rules of Procedure and Evidence and the Elements of Crimes, while customary law only comes into account in the second place.

87 See further S. Manacorda and C. Meloni, Direct Perpetration versus Joint Criminal Enterprise: Concurring Approaches in the Practice of International Criminal Law?, 9 Journal of International Criminal Justice 2011.

88 Judgement, *Prosecutor v. Martić*, T. Ch. I, *supra* note 1, par. 8.

89 *Ibid.*, par. 434.

90 ICTY, Judgement, *Prosecutor v. Delalić, Mucić, Delić and Landžo*, Case No. IT-96-21-T, T. Ch. II*quater*, 16 November 1998, Klip/ Sluiter, ALC-III-363, par. 346, later confirmed by the Judgment on Sentence Appeal, *Prosecutor v. Mucić, Delić and Landžo*, A. Ch., *supra* note 8, par. 189-198. For an in depth analysis of this mode of liability I refer to C. Meloni, Command Responsibility in International Criminal Law, T.M.C. Asser, The Hague 2010, in particular with regard to the ICTY provision and jurisprudence under Chapter 3, p. 77–137.

From the findings of Trial Chamber, it is indeed possible to infer that each of these three elements of command responsibility were satisfied with regard to Martić. As for the first element, the chamber in Martić found that: the accused "exercised absolute authority over the MUP [the Minister of Interior], including the power to intervene on an individual level by appointing and removing chiefs of the SJBs [the police and security forces] as well as the authority to disband units within the MUP".[91]

With regard to the accused's knowledge of the crimes, in the words of the judges: "there is no doubt that Milan Martić was aware that the non-Serbian population was being driven out as a result of the coercive atmosphere in the Republic of Serbian Krajina."[92]

Moreover, as to the third element: "the Trial Chamber cannot but conclude that Milan Martić deliberately refrained from intervening against perpetrators who committed crimes against the non-Serb population."[93]

Although, regrettably, the judges did not elaborate on the issue, the Trial Chamber correctly declined to convict Martić for the same crimes under two different modes of liability: even though the prosecution tends to use command responsibility under Article 7, paragraph 3 ICTY statute as an additional charging criterion with regard to individuals holding a position of authority, the jurisprudence has progressively ruled out the possibility of convicting a defendant for different modes of liability in relation to the same crimes.[94] Thus, normally if there is enough evidence of the defendant's direct participation or active contribution in the crime, the conviction will be based on Article 7, paragraph 1 rather than on Article 7, paragraph 3 of the ICTY statute.[95]

This resulted in the end in the "erosion" of command responsibility under Article 7, paragraph 3 in favour of JCE under Article 7, paragraph 1 ICTY statute, a mode of liability that "offers advantages" from the probative point of view, and pursuant to which it is generally easier to convict the defendant.[96]

Having established the responsibility of the accused under Article 7, paragraph 1 ICTY statute, the position of superior becomes simply an aggravating factor for the purpose of sentencing.[97] As the Trial chamber found in Martić, one of the aggravating circumstances in this case was: "the position of the accused, that is, his position of leadership, his level in the command structure, or his role in the broader context of the conflict of the former Yugoslavia."[98]

Significantly, although only in a footnote, the Trial Chamber also recalled what was affirmed by the Appeals Chamber: when considering the superior position in connection with Article 7, paragraph 1, the superior position itself does not constitute an aggravating factor; rather it is *the abuse of such position* that may be considered an aggravating factor.[99]

Chantal Meloni

---

91 Judgement, *Prosecutor v. Martić*, T. Ch. I, supra note 1, par. 449.

92 *Ibid.*, par. 451.

93 *Ibid.*

94 See ICTY, Judgment, *Prosecutor v. Krnojelac*, Case No. IT-97-25-T, T. Ch. II, 15 March 2002, Klip/ Sluiter, ALC-VIII-755, par. 173.

95 See ICTY, Judgement, *Prosecutor v. Krstić*, Case No. IT-98-33-T, T. Ch. I, 2 August 2001, Klip/ Sluiter, ALC-VII-575, par. 605. For further elaboration, please see C. Meloni, Command Responsibility, *supra* note 90, p. 209 *et seq.*

96 In this sense and for more in depth analysis, C. Meloni, Command Responsibility, *supra* note 90, p. 244 *et seq.*

97 See ICTY, Judgement, *Prosecutor v. Kordić and Čerkez*, Case No. IT-95-14/2-T, T. Ch. III, 26 February 2001, Klip/ Sluiter, ALC-VII-249, par. 371.

98 Judgement, *Prosecutor v. Martić*, T. Ch. I, supra note 1, par. 495.

99 *Ibid.*, footnote 1329 and related references.

UNITED NATIONS

International Tribunal for the Prosecution of Persons Responsible for Serious Violations of International Humanitarian Law Committed in the Territory of the Former Yugoslavia since 1991	Case No.:	IT-01-48-A
	Date:	16 October 2007
	Original:	English

IN THE APPEALS CHAMBER

Before: **Judge Mehmet Güney, Presiding**
Judge Mohamed Shahabuddeen
Judge Andrésia Vaz
Judge Theodor Meron
Judge Wolfgang Schomburg

Registrar: **Mr. Hans Holthuis**

Judgement of: **16 October 2007**

PROSECUTOR

v.

SEFER HALILOVIĆ

PUBLIC

JUDGEMENT

The Office of the Prosecutor:

Mr. Peter Kremer
Mr. Arthur Buck
Ms. Laurel Baig
Mr. Xavier Tracol
Mr. Matteo Costi

Counsel for Sefer Halilović:

Mr. Peter Morrissey
Mr. Guénaël Mettraux

[page 1] Contents

[page 1] I. INTRODUCTION

1. The Appeals Chamber of the International Tribunal for the Prosecution of Persons Responsible for Serious Violations of International Humanitarian Law Committed in the Territory of the Former Yugoslavia since 1991 ("International Tribunal") is seized of an appeal from the judgement rendered by Trial Chamber I ("Trial Chamber") on 16 November 2005 in the case of *Prosecutor v. Sefer Halilović*, Case No. IT-01-48-T ("Trial Judgement").

A. Background

2. Sefer Halilović was born in Prijepolje (Serbia) in 1952. He had attained the rank of Major by the time he left the Yugoslav Peoples' Army ("JNA") in 1991 to join the Patriotic League in Bosnia and Herzegovina. On 25 May 1992, he was appointed Commander of the Territorial Defence ("TO") by the Presidency of Bosnia and Herzegovina ("BiH"). Halilović was Supreme Commander, with the title of "Chief" of the Main Staff of the Army of the Republic of Bosnia and Herzegovina ("ABiH") until 8 June 1993, when the new position of ABiH "Commander of the Main Staff" was established. On 8 June 1993, the President of BiH, Alija Izetbegović, appointed Rasim Delić to the position of ABiH Commander and provided that Halilović would retain the position of ABiH "Chief of the Main Staff". By order of 1 November 1993, Alija Izetbegović then relieved Halilović from his duties as "Chief of the Main Staff". At the time of his voluntary surrender to the International Tribunal, on 25 September 2001, Halilović was Minister for Refugees, Social Affairs and Displaced People in the Government of BiH.[1]

3. The events underlying the Trial Judgement took place in 1993 in BiH, specifically in the Bosnian Croat village of Grabovica,[2] part of the Drežnica commune, and in the Bosnian Croat village of Uzdol, in Prozor municipality (Herzegovina).[3] The Trial Chamber found that seven persons taking no active part in hostilities were killed in Grabovica by members of the 9th Brigade on 8 or 9 September 1993 and that six persons taking no active part in the hostilities were killed in Grabovica by unidentified members of the ABiH between 8 and 9 September 1993.[4] The Trial Chamber further found that 25 persons taking no active part in the hostilities were killed in Uzdol by members of units under ABiH command on 14 September 1993.[5] The Trial Chamber also found that these killings amounted to murder as a violation of the laws or customs of war.[6] Having established the commission of the crimes and the nexus between the existing armed conflict and the **[page 2]** crimes,[7] the Trial Chamber went on to determine whether Halilović bore responsibility for these crimes. The Prosecution alleged that senior commanders of the ABiH, including its Commander Rasim Delić, attended a meeting held in Zenica from 21 to 22 August 1993 and decided to conduct a military operation called "Neretva-93" in order to end the blockade of Mostar (Herzegovina) by the Croatian Defence Council ("HVO"). According to the Prosecution, Halilović was the commander of this operation and, therefore, the troops involved in the operation were under his command and control.[8] The Trial Chamber however found that the Prosecution failed to prove beyond reasonable doubt that Halilović was either *de jure* or *de facto* commander of "Operation Neretva-93".[9] The Trial Chamber further found that the Prosecution failed to prove beyond reasonable doubt that Halilović had effective control over the troops who committed the crimes in Grabovica and Uzdol.[10]

1 Trial Judgement, para. 1.
2 Trial Judgement, paras 373–377.
3 Trial Judgement, paras 526–527.
4 Trial Judgement, para. 728.
5 Trial Judgement, paras 730 and 734.
6 Trial Judgement, paras 728 and 734.
7 Trial Judgement, paras 722 and 727.
8 Trial Judgement, para. 2, citing *Prosecutor v. Sefer Halilović,* IT-01-48-I, Indictment, 10 September 2001 ("Indictment"), para. 4. *See* also Trial Judgement, para. 9.
9 Trial Judgement, para. 752. While the Trial Chamber was not convinced that the combat operations conducted in Herzegovina to lift the HVO blockade of Mostar were called "Operation Neretva" (or "Operation Neretva-93"), it stated that it would use the term "Operation Neretva" to refer to the combat operations which took place in Herzegovina at the relevant time, since this was the description used in the Indictment and the Prosecution had charged Halilović as commander of "Operation Neretva" (Trial Judgement, para. 175). The parties on appeal often referred to this operation simply as "the Operation". The Appeals Chamber will use both the expressions "Operation Neretva" and "Operation Neretva-93" to refer to these military activities.
10 Trial Judgement, paras 747 and 751–752.

4. As a result of its findings, on 16 November 2005, the Trial Chamber acquitted Halilović of the sole count charged against him: murder as a violation of the laws or customs of war, punishable under Article 3 and Article 7(3) of the Statute of the International Tribunal ("Statute").[11]

B. The Appeal

5. On 16 December 2005, the Prosecution filed a notice of appeal against the Trial Judgement, seeking the reversal of the acquittal for the charge of murder with respect to the killings perpetrated in Grabovica, the entering of a conviction pursuant to Articles 3 and 7(3) of the Statute for murder as a violation of the laws or customs of war, and the imposition of an appropriate sentence.[12] More specifically, the Prosecution's appeal consists of four grounds. At the heart of the first ground of appeal, which comprises six sub-grounds, lies the issue of effective control.[13] Since all grounds of appeal are intertwined, the other grounds hinge upon the outcome of the first ground of appeal: the second and third grounds concern the other two requirements of superior responsibility under Article 7(3) of the Statute: *mens rea* of Halilović and failure to prevent or punish, respectively.[14] **[page 3]** The fourth ground of appeal concerns the admission into evidence of the report and proposed testimony of an expert witness relating to Halilović's alleged failure to prevent or punish.[15] The Prosecution has not appealed Halilović's acquittal for the murders committed in Uzdol.[16] **[page 4]**

II. STANDARD FOR APPELLATE REVIEW

6. On appeal, the parties must limit their arguments to legal errors that invalidate the decision of the Trial Chamber and to factual errors that result in a miscarriage of justice. These criteria are set forth in Article 25 of the Statute and are well established by the Appeals Chambers of the International Tribunal and the ICTR.[17] In exceptional circumstances, the Appeals Chamber will also hear appeals where a party has raised a legal issue that would not lead to the invalidation of the judgement but that is nevertheless of general significance to the jurisprudence of the International Tribunal.[18] Article 25 of the Statute also states that the Appeals Chamber may affirm, reverse or revise the decisions taken by the Trial Chamber.

7. Any party alleging an error of law must identify the alleged error, present arguments in support of its claim and explain how the error invalidates the decision. An allegation of an error of law, which has no chance of changing the outcome of a decision, may be rejected on that ground. Even if the party's arguments are insufficient to support the contention of an error, however, the Appeals Chamber may conclude for other reasons that there is an error of law.[19] It is necessary for any appellant claiming an error of law based on the lack of a reasoned opinion to identify the specific issues, factual findings, or arguments, which the appellant submits the Trial Chamber omitted to address and to explain why this omission invalidated the decision.[20]

8. The Appeals Chamber reviews the Trial Chamber's impugned findings of law to determine whether or not they are correct.[21] Where the Appeals Chamber finds an error of law in the Trial Judgement arising

---

11 Trial Judgement, para. 753.

12 Prosecution's Notice of Appeal, 16 December 2005 ("Prosecution Notice of Appeal"), para. 12.

13 Prosecution Notice of Appeal, paras 4(i)–4(vi).

14 Prosecution Notice of Appeal, paras 5–8.

15 Prosecution Notice of Appeal, para. 9.

16 Prosecution Appellant's Brief, 1 March 2006 ("Prosecution Appeal Brief"), fn. 1.

17 *Blagojević and Jokić* Appeal Judgement, para. 6; *Brđanin* Appeal Judgement para. 8; *Galić* Appeal Judgement, para. 6; *Simić* Appeal Judgement, para. 7; *Stakić* Appeal Judgement, para. 7; *Kvočka et al.* Appeal Judgement, para. 14; *Vasiljević* Appeal Judgement, para. 5; *see* also *Kunarac et al.* Appeal Judgement, paras 35–48; *Kupreškić et al.* Appeal Judgement, paras 21–41; *Čelebići* Appeal Judgement, paras 434–435; *Furundžija* Appeal Judgement, paras 34–40. For jurisprudence under Article 24 of the ICTR Statute, *see Ndindabahizi* Appeal Judgement, paras 8–10; *Ntagerura et al.* Appeal Judgement, paras 11–12; *Gacumbitsi* Appeal Judgement, paras 6–9; *Kajelijeli* Appeal Judgement, para. 5; *Semanza* Appeal Judgement, paras 7–8; *Musema* Appeal Judgement, para. 15; *Kayishema and Ruzindana* Appeal Judgement, para. 177; *Akayesu* Appeal Judgement, paras 178–179.

18 *See*, for example, *Blagojević and Jokić* Appeal Judgement, para. 6; *Brđanin* Appeal Judgement, para. 8; *Galić* Appeal Judgement, para. 6. *See* also *Akayesu* Appeal Judgement, para. 24; *see* also *Krnojelac* Appeal Judgement, para. 8.

19 *See*, for example, *Limaj et al.* Appeal Judgement, para. 9, *Blagojević and Jokić* Appeal Judgement, para. 7; *Brđanin* Appeal Judgement, para. 9. *See* also *Ntagerura et al.* Appeal Judgement, para. 11; *Semanza* Appeal Judgement, para. 7.

20 *Brđanin* Appeal Judgement, para. 9; *Kvočka et al.* Appeal Judgement, para. 25.

21 *See*, for example, *Blagojević and Jokić* Appeal Judgement, para. 8; *Brđanin* Appeal Judgement, para. 10; *Galić* Appeal

from the application of the wrong legal standard, the Appeals Chamber will articulate the correct legal standard and review the relevant factual findings of the Trial Chamber accordingly.[22] In so doing, the Appeals Chamber not only corrects the legal error, but applies the correct legal standard to the evidence contained in the trial record, where necessary, and determines **[page 5]** whether it is itself convinced beyond reasonable doubt as to the factual findings challenged by the appellant before that finding may be confirmed on appeal.[23]

9. When considering alleged errors of fact, the Appeals Chamber will apply a standard of reasonableness. Only an error of fact which has occasioned a miscarriage of justice will cause the Appeals Chamber to overturn a decision by the Trial Chamber.[24] In reviewing the findings of the Trial Chamber, the Appeals Chamber will only substitute its own finding for that of the Trial Chamber when no reasonable trier of fact could have reached the original decision.[25]

10. The Appeals Chamber bears in mind that, in determining whether or not a Trial Chamber's finding was reasonable, it "will not lightly disturb findings of fact by a Trial Chamber".[26] The Appeals Chamber reiterates that an appeal is not a trial *de novo*[27] and recalls, as a general principle, the approach adopted in *Kupreškić et al.,* wherein it was stated that:

> Pursuant to the jurisprudence of the ₣Internationalğ Tribunal, the task of hearing, assessing and weighing the evidence presented at trial is left primarily to the Trial Chamber. Thus, the Appeals Chamber must give a margin of deference to a finding of fact reached by a Trial Chamber. Only where the evidence relied on by the Trial Chamber could not have been accepted by any reasonable tribunal of fact or where the evaluation of the evidence is "wholly erroneous" may the Appeals Chamber substitute its own finding for that of the Trial Chamber.[28]

11. The same standard of reasonableness and the same deference to factual findings of the Trial Chamber apply when the Prosecution appeals against an acquittal. Thus, when considering an appeal by the Prosecution, the Appeals Chamber will only hold that an error of fact was committed when it determines that no reasonable trier of fact could have made the impugned finding.[29] However, since the Prosecution must establish the guilt of the accused at trial, the significance of an error of fact occasioning a miscarriage of justice takes on a specific character when alleged by the Prosecution.[30] In this context, the Appeals Chamber has endorsed the following holding by the ICTR Appeals Chamber: **[page 6]**

> [b]ecause the Prosecution bears the burden at trial of proving the guilt of the accused beyond a reasonable doubt, the significance of an error of fact occasioning a miscarriage of justice is somewhat different for a Prosecution appeal against acquittal than for a defence appeal against conviction. An accused must show that the Trial Chamber's factual errors create a reasonable doubt as to his guilt. The Prosecution faces a more difficult task. It must show that, when account is taken of the errors of fact committed by the Trial Chamber, all reasonable doubt of the accused's guilt has been eliminated.[31]

Judgement, para. 8; *Simić* Appeal Judgement, para. 9.

22 *See*, for example, *Blagojević and Jokić* Appeal Judgement, para. 8; *Brđanin* Appeal Judgement, para. 10; *Galić* Appeal Judgement, para. 8; *Simić* Appeal Judgement, para. 9.

23 *See*, for example, *Blagojević and Jokić* Appeal Judgement, para. 8; *Brđanin* Appeal Judgement, para. 10; *Galić* Appeal Judgement para. 8; *Simić* Appeal Judgement, para. 9; *Blaškić* Appeal Judgement, para. 15; *see* also *Ntagerura et al.* Appeal Judgement, para. 136.

24 *See*, for example, *Simić* Appeal Judgement, para. 10; *Kvočka et al.* Appeal Judgement, para. 18; *Vasiljević* Appeal Judgement, para. 8.

25 *See Kvočka et al.* Appeal Judgement, para. 18. *See* also *Vasiljević* Appeal Judgement, para. 7; *Stakić* Appeal Judgement, para. 10; *Bagilishema* Appeal Judgement, para. 13.

26 *See*, for example, *Blagojević and Jokić* Appeal Judgement, para. 9; *Galić* Appeal Judgement, para. 9; *Simić* Appeal Judgement, para. 11; *Bagilishema* Appeal Judgement, para. 11; *Musema* Appeal Judgement, para. 18.

27 *Brđanin* Appeal Judgement, para. 15; *Blaškić* Appeal Judgement, para. 13; *Bagilishema* Appeal Judgement, para. 11.

28 *Kupreškić et al.* Appeal Judgement, para. 30. *See* also *Blagojević and Jokić* Appeal Judgement, para. 9; *Galić* Appeal Judgement, para. 9; *Simić* Appeal Judgement, para. 11; *Stakić* Appeal Judgement, para. 10.

29 *Blagojević and Jokić* Appeal Judgement, para. 9; *Brđanin* Appeal Judgement, para. 14; *Bagilishema* Appeal Judgement, para. 13.

30 *Krnojelac* Appeal Judgement, para. 14.

31 *Bagilishema* Appeal Judgement, para. 14, cited with approval in *Limaj et al.* Appeal Judgement, para. 13.

12. The Appeals Chamber recalls that it has inherent discretion to determine which of the parties' submissions merit a reasoned opinion in writing, and may dismiss arguments which are evidently unfounded without providing detailed reasoning.[32] A party may not merely repeat on appeal arguments that did not succeed at trial, unless the party can demonstrate that the Trial Chamber's rejection of them constituted an error warranting the intervention of the Appeals Chamber.[33] Moreover, submissions will be dismissed without detailed reasoning where: the appealing party's argument does not have the potential to cause the impugned decision to be reversed or revised;[34] the appealing party's argument unacceptably seeks to substitute its own evaluation of the evidence for that of the Trial Chamber; or where it is evident that a reasonable trier of fact could have come to the conclusion challenged by the appealing party.[35]

13. The Appeals Chamber's mandate cannot be effectively and efficiently carried out without focused contributions by the parties. In order for the Appeals Chamber to assess a party's arguments on appeal, the party is expected to present its case clearly, logically and exhaustively.[36] The Appeals Chamber recalls that the formal criteria require an appealing party to provide the Appeals Chamber with exact references to the parts of the records, transcripts, judgements and exhibits to which reference is made.[37] Further, submissions that are obscure, contradictory, vague or suffer from other formal and obvious insufficiencies will not be considered by the Appeals Chamber in detail.[38] **[page 7]**

III. REQUEST FOR SUMMARY DISMISSAL OF THE ENTIRE APPEAL

14. Halilović generally submits that the Prosecution's appeal should be summarily dismissed because it fails to meet the requisite standard of appellate review, it suffers from "grave, widespread and systematic procedural/formal shortcomings", or it raises matters that had previously been waived.[39] These arguments are then developed by Halilović in relation to each ground or sub-ground of appeal. With respect to those instances where a brief discussion is warranted, the Appeals Chamber will address the requests in more detail in the corresponding section of this judgement. However, when it is clear that a request for summary dismissal cannot possibly prosper, it will be rejected without addressing the arguments advanced in detail.

15. Halilović also urges the Appeals Chamber to recognise the Prosecution's "exceptional statutory entitlement" to appeal an acquittal, which should only be exercised "with the greatest of diligence, in compliance with the fundamental rights of the accused and only where such an appeal would serve one of the purposes for which th[e] [International] Tribunal has been created".[40] This, in his view, is all the more appropriate at a time when the International Tribunal is scaling down its operations and resources "must be allocated only where they are absolutely needed and justified".[41] He submits that "this appeal falls far short of a situation where the Prosecutor could legitimately claim to have been exercising her statutory entitlement to appeal within the limits mentioned above".[42] Halilović concludes that, in this case, the Prosecution's appeal should be dismissed *in toto* without further consideration.[43]

---

[32] *See*, for example, *Brđanin* Appeal Judgement, para. 16; *Galić* Appeal Judgement, para. 12; *Simić* Appeal Judgement, para. 14; *Stakić* Appeal Judgement, para. 13; *Gacumbitsi* Appeal Judgement, para. 10; *Kamuhanda* Appeal Judgement, para. 10.

[33] *See*, for example, *Blagojević and Jokić* Appeal Judgement, para. 10; *Brđanin* Appeal Judgement, para. 16; *Galić* Appeal Chamber, para. 10; *Simić* Appeal Judgement, para. 12; *Gacumbitsi* Appeal Judgement, para. 9.

[34] *See Blagojević and Jokić* Appeal Judgement, para. 10; *Galić* Appeal Judgement, para. 10; *Simić* Appeal Judgement, para. 12; *Stakić* Appeal Judgement, para. 11; *Gacumbitsi* Appeal Judgement, para. 9; *Ntagerura* Appeal Judgement para. 13.

[35] *See Kunarac et al.* Appeal Judgement, para. 48. *See* also *Blagojević and Jokić* Appeal Judgement para. 11; *Brđanin* Appeal Judgement, paras 17–31.

[36] *See Kunarac et al.* Appeal Judgement, para. 43.

[37] *See* Practice Direction on Formal Requirements for Appeals from Judgement, paras 1(c)(iii), 1(c)(iv), and 4(b)(ii). *See* also *Blagojević and Jokić* Appeal Judgement, para. 11; *Brđanin* Appeal Judgement, para. 15; *Gacumbitsi* Appeal Judgement, para. 10.

[38] *Blagojević and Jokić* Appeal Judgement, para. 11; *Simić* Appeal Judgement para. 13; *Naletilić and Martinović* Appeal Judgement, para. 14; *Gacumbitsi* Appeal Judgement para. 10.

[39] Respondent's Brief, paras 1–5.

[40] Respondent's Brief, para. 6.

[41] Respondent's Brief, para. 6 (emphasis omitted).

[42] Respondent's Brief, para. 7.

[43] Respondent's Brief, para. 8.

16. The Appeals Chamber notes that Halilović does not identify any authority for his assertion that the Prosecution's right to appeal against acquittals should be exercised only exceptionally, nor does he provide support for his claim that such an appeal would have to reach a higher threshold of "diligence" to be exercised by the appellant in such a case.[44] Similarly, Halilović fails to specify on what ground he bases his assertion that an appeal against acquittal by the Prosecution would have, as a pre-condition, to serve the "purposes for which th[e] [International] Tribunal has been created",[45] in a manner different from all other appeals against judgements rendered by the International Tribunal. The Appeals Chamber also stresses that it is not its task, as suggested by **[page 8]** Halilović, to ascertain whether the Prosecutor has fulfilled her responsibilities in accordance with the Completion Strategy laid out in Security Council Resolution 1503 (2003).[46] The Appeals Chamber further considers that Halilović has failed to point to any element suggesting that the Prosecution abused its discretion in appealing his acquittal. It should also be recalled that the Appeals Chamber has already dismissed Halilović's request to dismiss the appeal without hearing the parties' arguments.[47] Thus, Halilović's request for summary dismissal of the entire appeal is denied. **[page 9]**

IV. FIRST GROUND OF APPEAL: WHETHER HALILOVIĆ WAS THE SUPERIOR OF THE PERPETRATORS OF THE CRIMES COMMITTED IN GRABOVICA

A. Overview of the first ground of appeal

17. The Prosecution submits that the Trial Chamber erred in law and in fact in finding that the Prosecution had not proven beyond reasonable doubt that Halilović was the superior of subordinates who committed crimes in Grabovica and in consequently entering an acquittal.[48] The Prosecution alleges six "sub-errors" ("sub-grounds") under this ground of appeal: (i) the Trial Chamber erred in law in applying the legal standard required to demonstrate effective control;[49] (ii) the Trial Chamber erred in law in requiring the Prosecution to prove not only that a military operation existed, but also its name, and it erred in fact in finding that the Prosecution had not established that the operation was called "Neretva";[50] (iii) the Trial Chamber erred in law in requiring the Prosecution to prove that the location where the Inspection Team was accommodated was a forward command post ("IKM") from which the operation in Herzegovina was commanded;[51] (iv) the Trial Chamber erred in using evidence that Halilović had not taken necessary and reasonable measures to punish the perpetrators of the crimes committed in Grabovica to support its finding that he did not have the material ability to punish these perpetrators;[52] (v) the Trial Chamber erred in its application of the standard of proof beyond reasonable doubt;[53] and (vi) the Trial Chamber erred in refusing to admit a statement by Halilović given to the Prosecution in 1996 ("1996 Statement" or "Statement").[54] The Prosecution asks the Appeals

[44] In this context, the Appeals Chamber recalls (*see supra*, para. 11) that the Prosecution's task in the case of appealing an acquittal is "more difficult", in as much as it has "to show that, when account is taken of the errors of fact committed by the Trial Chamber, all reasonable doubt of the accused's guilt has been eliminated" (*Bagilishema* Appeal Judgement, para. 14).

[45] Respondent's Brief, para. 6.

[46] *See*, in particular, Security Council Resolution 1503, S/RES/1503 (2003), adopted on 28 August 2003, para. 6, as well as Security Council Resolution 1534, S/RES/1534 (2004), adopted on 26 March 2004, paras 4 and 6, requesting the Prosecutor to review the case load of the International Tribunal and to explain, in its progress reports *submitted to the Security Council* every six months, "what measures have been taken to implement the Completion Strategy and what measures remain to be taken".

[47] *See* Decision on Defence Motion for Prompt Scheduling of Appeals Hearing, 27 October 2006, paras 8–9, where the Appeals Chamber found that, since the Prosecution opposed the request for summary disposition of the appeal, the question of whether or not it was open to the parties to waive their entitlement to an oral hearing did not arise.

[48] Prosecution Notice of Appeal, para. 3.

[49] Prosecution Notice of Appeal, para. 4(i); Prosecution Appeal Brief, paras 2.6–2.40; Prosecution Reply Brief, paras 3.1–3.7.

[50] Prosecution Notice of Appeal, para. 4(ii); Prosecution Appeal Brief, paras 2.41–2.82; Prosecution Reply Brief, paras 3.8–3.14. The Prosecution refers to the operation as "Neretva" in the Notice of Appeal, but uses both "Neretva" and "Neretva-93" in the Prosecution Appeal Brief.

[51] Prosecution Notice of Appeal, para. 4(iii); Prosecution Appeal Brief, paras 2.83–2.106; Prosecution Reply Brief, paras 3.15–3.18.

[52] Prosecution Notice of Appeal, para. 4(iv); Prosecution Appeal Brief, paras 2.107–2.120; Prosecution Reply Brief, paras 3.19–3.25.

[53] Prosecution Notice of Appeal, para. 4(v); Prosecution Appeal Brief, paras 2.121–2.136; Prosecution Reply Brief, paras 3.26–3.30.

[54] Prosecution Notice of Appeal, para. 4(vi); Prosecution Appeal Brief, paras 2.137–2.155; Prosecution Reply Brief, paras 3.31–3.35.

Chamber to apply the correct legal standards, admit evidence erroneously excluded and to proceed by making its own findings of fact regarding the existence of a superior-subordinate relationship between Halilović and the perpetrators of the crimes committed in Grabovica.[55] **[page 10]**

18. The six sub-grounds of appeal advanced under the Prosecution's first ground of appeal are deeply intertwined, in that they all go to the issue of whether Halilović was the superior of the troops that committed the crimes in Grabovica. The discussion on the arguments raised under the first ground of appeal, however, will not conform to the order followed by the Prosecution in the presentation of these sub-grounds of appeal. The Appeals Chamber will first address sub-ground 6, since a reversal of the Trial Chamber's decision on this matter could have an impact upon the evidence to be considered. The Appeals Chamber will then turn to address sub-ground 1, for its resolution will delimit the scope of the Prosecution's appeal, and then sub-grounds 5, 2 and 3 related to the standard of proof applied by the Trial Chamber. Finally, the Appeals Chamber will conclude its analysis of the first ground of appeal by addressing sub-ground 4, which concerns the material ability to punish in order to establish effective control. **[page 11]**

B. Sub-Ground 6: Denial of Admission of 1996 Statement

1. Introduction

19. On 8 July 2005, pursuant to a motion filed by Halilović,[56] the Trial Chamber issued its "Decision on Motion for Exclusion of Statement of Accused" ("Decision of 8 July 2005") effectively denying admission of the 1996 Statement, a 25-page statement tendered by the Prosecution from the bar table. The Statement had been given voluntarily by Halilović to the Prosecution during the course of various interviews between February and May 1996, about five years before the Indictment in this case was confirmed.[57] On 25 July 2005, the Trial Chamber denied certification when the Prosecution sought to appeal the Decision of 8 July 2005.[58]

20. Rule 42 of the Rules ("Rights of Suspects During Investigations") reads:

(A) A suspect who is to be questioned by the Prosecutor shall have the following rights, of which the Prosecutor shall inform the suspect prior to questioning, in a language the suspect understands:

(i) the right to be assisted by counsel of the suspect's choice or to be assigned legal assistance without payment if the suspect does not have sufficient means to pay for it;

(ii) he right to have the free assistance of an interpreter if the suspect cannot understand or speak the language to be used for questioning; and

(iii) the right to remain silent, and to be cautioned that any statement the suspect makes shall be recorded and may be used in evidence.

(B) Questioning of a suspect shall not proceed without the presence of counsel unless the suspect has voluntarily waived the right to counsel. In case of waiver, if the suspect subsequently expresses a desire to have counsel, questioning shall thereupon cease, and shall only resume when the suspect has obtained or has been assigned counsel.

21. Rule 43 of the Rules ("Recording Questioning of Suspects") reads:

Whenever the Prosecutor questions a suspect, the questioning shall be audio-recorded or video-recorded, in accordance with the following procedure:

---

55 Prosecution Notice of Appeal, para. 11; Prosecution Appeal Brief, para. 6.1.

56 *Prosecutor v. Sefer Halilović*, Case No. IT-01-48-T, Defence Motion for Exclusion of Statement of Accused, 6 June 2005 ("Motion for Exclusion of Statement").

57 Decision of 8 July 2005, para. 2. *See* also Trial Judgement, Part VII (Procedural History), paras 29–30. A different interview by Halilović had been originally admitted by the Trial Chamber on 20 June 2005 (*Prosecutor v. Sefer Halilović*, Case No. IT-01-48-T, Decision on Admission into Evidence of Interview of the Accused), but later rendered inadmissible by an interlocutory decision of the Appeals Chamber (*Prosecutor v. Sefer Halilović*, Case No. IT-01-48-AR73.2, Decision on Interlocutory Appeal Concerning Admission of Record of Interview of the Accused from the Bar Table, 19 August 2005 ("Decision on Appeal Concerning Admission of Record of Interview")).

58 *Prosecutor v. Sefer Halilović*, Case No. IT-01-48-T, Decision on Prosecution Request for Certification for Interlocutory Appeal of 'Decision on Motion for Exclusion of Statement of Accused', 25 July 2005 ("Certification Decision of 25 July 2005"), p. 4.

(i) the suspect shall be informed in a language the suspect understands that the questioning is being audio-recorded or video-recorded;

(ii) in the event of a break in the course of the questioning, the fact and the time of the break shall be recorded before audio-recording or video-recording ends and the time of resumption of the questioning shall also be recorded;

(iii) at the conclusion of the questioning the suspect shall be offered the opportunity to clarify anything the suspect has said, and to add anything the suspect may wish, and the time of conclusion shall be recorded;

(iv) a copy of the recorded tape will be supplied to the suspect or, if multiple recording apparatus was used, one of the original recorded tapes; **[page 12]**

(v) after a copy has been made, if necessary, of the recorded tape, the original recorded tape or one of the original tapes shall be sealed in the presence of the suspect under the signature of the Prosecutor and the suspect; and

(vi) the tape shall be transcribed if the suspect becomes an accused.

22. There is no disagreement among the parties that the procedure for questioning suspects provided for in Rules 42 and 43 of the Rules was not followed in the case of Halilović's interviews because the Prosecution did not consider him a suspect at the time.[59] However, the Prosecution did inform Halilović of his rights to counsel and to remain silent.[60]

23. After having been made aware by the Prosecution of its intention to tender this Statement at trial, once the proceedings against him had started, Halilović asked the Prosecution on six separate occasions (between the months of February and April 2005) to indicate how and through which witness the Prosecution intended to tender the 1996 Statement.[61] In the course of a meeting with Defence Counsel, the Prosecution indicated that it intended to tender the 1996 Statement from the bar table. During a status conference held on 28 April 2005, the Prosecution formally offered to tender the 1996 Statement.[62] Upon objection by the Defence, the Presiding Judge invited Halilović to file submissions in writing.[63] On 30 May 2005, Halilović requested details on the modalities of the interviews and enquired whether records of these interviews existed.[64] On 1 June 2005, the Prosecution submitted that there were no records of the interviews other than the Statement itself.[65] On 6 June 2005, four days after the Prosecution had rested its case,[66] Halilović filed the Motion for Exclusion of Statement.[67] On 8 July 2005, the Trial Chamber decided that the 1996 Statement was inadmissible. It stated, *inter alia*:

> [T]he Trial Chamber is not satisfied that the Statement represents a full and complete record of what Sefer Halilović said. It is more probable than not that not every detail or nuance of the interview was included in the Statement, which affects its reliability. Because the Statement was not audio or video recorded, the Defence at present is incapable to verify the accuracy of the Statement. The only effective way to challenge the content of the statement at this moment in time would be for Sefer Halilović to waive his right to remain silent and testify before this Tribunal.[68] **[page 13]**

---

59 *See*, for example, Prosecution Appeal Brief, paras 2.139 and 2.145 (referring to the declarations of two investigators, Gamini Wijeyesinghe and Robert William Reid). *See* also Motion for Exclusion of Statement, para. 29.

60 Prosecution Appeal Brief, para. 2.146; *see* also Prosecution Reply Brief, para. 3.32, citing Decision of 8 July 2005, paras 22–23.

61 Motion for Exclusion of Statement, para. 5, cited in Respondent's Brief, para. 218.

62 Motion for Exclusion of Statement, para. 7, cited in Respondent's Brief, para. 218.

63 Prosecution Appeal Brief, para. 2.140. *See* also T. 26–27 (28 April 2005): "I believe that the ball is in the court of the Defence and the Defence will file its submission to express [its] views on that. And after that, the Prosecution [will] also have an opportunity to make a reply".

64 Motion for Exclusion of Statement, para. 8, cited in Respondent's Brief, para. 218.

65 Motion for Exclusion of Statement, para. 9, cited in Respondent's Brief, para. 218.

66 Prosecution Appeal Brief, para. 2.140.

67 *See* Respondent's Brief, para. 218 (referring to the "Motion for Exclusion of Statement" for the relevant procedural background).

68 Decision of 8 July 2005, para. 25.

On 13 July 2005, the Prosecution requested certification to appeal the Decision of 8 July 2005, a request denied by the Trial Chamber on 25 July 2005 on the ground that "a resolution by the Appeals Chamber at this moment in time would not materially advance the proceedings".[69] In the meantime, on 14 July 2005, the Defence had also rested its case.[70]

24. Under this sub-ground, the Prosecution submits that the Trial Chamber abused its discretion by not admitting the 1996 Statement into evidence.[71]

2. Halilović's request for summary dismissal

25. As part of his response, Halilović requests the summary dismissal of this sub-ground of appeal on the grounds that it was impermissibly varied and that the Prosecution failed to meet the required burden of argument or persuasion, in particular with respect to the alleged effect of the error on the verdict.[72] This request is mainly premised on the alleged abandonment of the Prosecution's allegation of abuse of discretion by the Trial Chamber. According to Halilović, there has been an impermissible variation of the sub-ground between the Notice of Appeal (where "abuse of discretion" is mentioned) and the Appeal Brief (where reference to misinterpretation of Rule 43 of the Rules is made).[73] Although it would have been preferable for the Prosecution to cite in its Notice of Appeal the Rule that was pivotal to this aspect of the appeal, the fact that the Prosecution did not explicitly refer to Rule 43 of the Rules does not amount to an impermissible variation or abandonment of this sub-ground of appeal. The Notice of Appeal states that the Trial Chamber abused its discretion when refusing to admit the Statement and that this amounts to an error of law.[74] This allegation of error is developed and explained in the Appeal Brief as the wrong interpretation of the law (specifically, of Rule 43 of the Rules), which the Trial Chamber identified as applicable to the exercise of its discretion.[75] Thus, the Appeals Chamber dismisses Halilović's arguments in this respect.

26. The Appeals Chamber finds that the issue of whether the Prosecution has failed to meet its burden of argument or persuasion regarding the impact of the admission of the Statement on the verdict[76] is best addressed in the analysis on the merits of the Prosecution's appeal. As to the effect of the alleged error, should the Prosecution establish that the Trial Chamber erred in law in refusing to admit the 1996 Statement into evidence, the verdict might indeed be affected. **[page 14]**

27. For the foregoing reasons, Halilović's request for summary dismissal of sub-ground 6 is dismissed.

3. Whether the Trial Chamber abused its discretion in denying admission of the 1996 Statement

28. The Appeals Chamber recalls that, when seized of the interlocutory appeal concerning the admission into evidence of the record of another interview by Halilović to the Prosecution, it acknowledged that "[a]n accused has the right to refuse to give statements incriminating himself prior to trial, and he ha[s] the right to refuse to testify at trial".[77] However, the Appeals Chamber qualified this statement by holding that "where the accused has freely and voluntarily made statements prior to trial, he cannot later on choose to invoke his right against self-incrimination retroactively to shield those statements from being introduced, provided he was informed about his right to remain silent before giving his statement".[78]

29. In the instant case, Halilović voluntarily consented to be interviewed by the Prosecution and waived his right to be assisted by counsel. However, Halilović argues that he should not be considered an accused

---

69 Prosecution Appeal Brief, para. 2.141, citing Certification Decision of 25 July 2005, p. 4.

70 T. 4 (14 July 2005).

71 Prosecution Notice of Appeal, para. 4(vi).

72 Respondent's Brief, paras 215–217.

73 Respondent's Brief, paras 215–216. The Prosecution replied to these claims in Prosecution Reply Brief, para. 3.31.

74 Prosecution Notice of Appeal, para. 4(vi).

75 Prosecution Appeal Brief, 2.137–2.139.

76 Respondent's Brief, heading (B) after para. 217, p. 70.

77 Decision on Appeal Concerning Admission of Record of Interview, para. 15.

78 Decision on Appeal Concerning Admission of Record of Interview, para. 15 (footnote omitted); *see* also *Niyitegeka* Appeal Judgement, paras 30–36.

who "freely and voluntarily made statements prior to trial" if, in 1995, his status was that of a witness. Thus, according to him, the admission of a statement into evidence under these circumstances would be unfair.[79] The Prosecution submits that, since Halilović was not a suspect at the time of the interview, its investigators were not obliged to follow all of the procedures set out in Rules 42 and 43 of the Rules.[80] In its view, the fact that Halilović later became a suspect and an accused does not retroactively turn the 1996 Statement into a "suspect interview" nor can it affect the waiver of his procedural rights.[81]

30. The Prosecution submits that the Trial Chamber erred in law in refusing to admit into evidence the 1996 Statement on the grounds that it was not audio- or video-recorded in accordance with Rule 43 of the Rules,[82] since the Trial Chamber found that all safeguards in Rule 43 of the Rules, meant to protect rights of a suspect, were met,[83] and since the accuracy of the Statement is confirmed by Halilović's own signature and by the interpreter's certification.[84] Any concern that **[page 15]** Halilović might have harboured at trial should have been addressed through a *voir dire* at that stage.[85]

31. The Prosecution further submits that, in the 1996 Statement, Halilović makes a number of admissions that would have affected the Trial Chamber's ultimate findings regarding his effective control over the soldiers responsible for the killings in Grabovica, his knowledge of the crimes in Grabovica and his failure to prevent or punish the perpetrators.[86] The Prosecution maintains that the admission of the 1996 Statement would not require a retrial, since the Appeals Chamber is entitled to review and consider it in the context of all the evidence on the record.[87]

32. Halilović observes that the purpose of Rule 43 of the Rules is not limited to ensuring the voluntary nature of a suspect's interview, but also the reliability of the statements derived from such an interview.[88] When a Trial Chamber assesses the admissibility of statements of an accused, it is required to consider whether the evidence was obtained in a manner which casts doubts on its reliability or whether no proper record of the interview exists.[89]

33. Halilović submits that it is not necessary to show that the evidence "was or may" actually be unreliable, but only that the circumstances surrounding the taking of the Statement made it likely to be unreliable.[90] Halilović argues that the 1996 Statement is clearly unreliable on the basis of twelve specific grounds, ranging from language issues to the fact that Halilović was not represented by counsel at the time and, additionally, that the Statement was compiled from undisclosed notes taken by an investigator during seven meetings over a ten-week period.[91]

34. Moreover, Halilović argues that an individual is not entitled to the protection granted under Rules 42 and 43 of the Rules because the Prosecution regards him as a suspect.[92] Rather, this protection applies to this individual "because, *as a suspect* [a person concerning whom the Prosecutor possesses reliable information which tends to show that the person may have committed a crime over which the International Tribunal has jurisdiction][93] these guarantees will apply to him automatically so as to ensure that his rights are being preserved".[94] Halilović submits that the issue **[page 16]** of whether he was a suspect at the time of the

79 Halilović's Respondent Brief, paras 231–235.
80 Prosecution Appeal Brief, paras 2.142–2.148 and 2.154.
81 Prosecution Appeal Brief, paras 2.151 and 2.154.
82 Prosecution Appeal Brief, paras 2.137–2.139 and 2.142–2.144.
83 Prosecution Appeal Brief, paras 2.138 and 2.154–2.155.
84 Prosecution Appeal Brief, paras 2.147–2.148 and 2.152. *See* also Prosecution Reply Brief, paras 3.32–3.33.
85 Prosecution Reply Brief, para. 3.32, citing Respondent's Brief, paras 225–230.
86 Prosecution Notice of Appeal, para. 4(vi); Prosecution Appeal Brief, paras 2.138 and 2.149–2.150; Prosecution Reply Brief, para. 3.34.
87 Prosecution Reply Brief, para. 3.35.
88 Respondent's Brief, para. 236, citing Prosecution Appeal Brief, paras 2.143–2.144 and 2.148.
89 Respondent's Brief, paras 225 and 236.
90 Respondent's Brief, para. 225.
91 Respondent's Brief, para. 226. *See* also Respondent's Brief, paras 227–229 (detailing examples of complaints by witnesses on how some of these statements were taken, and of inaccuracies in translations by the Prosecution during the trial).
92 Respondent's Brief, para. 238.
93 Rule 2 of the Rules.
94 Respondent's Brief, para. 238.

interview is irrelevant,[95] since "treating the accused as a witness at any stage of the investigation compromises the right of the accused not to be forced to testify against himself or to confess guilt".[96] He considers that, in application of this principle, the guarantees provided for in the Rules must be applied retroactively, at least where the Prosecution seeks to tender evidence obtained from an accused.[97]

35. Finally, Halilović recalls that the Trial Chamber did not deny admission of the 1996 Statement pursuant to Rule 43 of the Rules, but rather pursuant to Rule 89(D) of the Rules.[98] It is not the usefulness or significance of the evidence that should be weighed against the requirement for a fair trial, but rather the "probative value" of that evidence.[99] The Statement was excluded because, in the absence of records of the interview proper, it was impossible to verify the Statement's accuracy and to challenge its content without sacrificing Halilović's rights to remain silent and to a fair trial.[100] Halilović submits that the non-admission of the 1996 Statement fell within the Trial Chamber's discretionary powers under Rule 89(D) of the Rules. He asserts that the Trial Chamber's discretion to exclude evidence should be applied with particular "vigour" where the fundamental right of the accused to remain silent is at stake. It need not be shown that the defendant was in fact treated unfairly.[101]

36. The Trial Chamber found that:

> in order to protect the right of the Accused to a fair trial, in accordance with Article 21 of the Statute, it should be taken into account whether the safeguards of Rules 42, 43 and 63 of the Rules have been fully respected when deciding on the admission of *any* former statement of an accused irrespective of the status of the accused at the time of taking the statement.[102]

The Trial Chamber's understanding of the protections afforded by the Statute and the Rules is consistent with the principles expressed in the case law of the International Tribunal and the ICTR[103] as well as the law of other jurisdictions.[104] **[page 17]**

37. The Decision of 8 July 2005 dealt with the issue of whether the Statement had been taken in accordance with Rules 42, 43, 63, 89 and 95 of the Rules.[105] The Trial Chamber reasoned that the main question at issue was "what safeguards should have been applied by the Prosecution in order for a former statement of a now accused person to be admissible into evidence".[106] The Trial Chamber concluded that:

> ...the Statement was read out to Sefer Halilović in his own language before he signed each page of the document. The Trial Chamber finds that the content of the Statement is a general reflection of what Sefer Halilović said during the interview. However, the fact is that the Statement is but a summary of seven days of interviews, taken over a period of four months. Considering that according to the interpreter Sefer Halilović gave 'very detailed answers to the questions,' the Trial Chamber is not satisfied that the Statement represents a full and complete record of what Sefer Halilović said. It is more probable than not that not every detail or

95 Respondent's Brief, para. 240.
96 Respondent's Brief, para. 240. *See* also Respondent's Brief, paras 225 and 243.
97 Respondent's Brief, para. 245.
98 Respondent's Brief, para. 246.
99 Respondent's Brief, para. 221. *See* also Respondent's Brief, paras 249 and 251–252.
100 Respondent's Brief, para. 222. *See* also Respondent's Brief, paras 231–232.
101 Respondent's Brief, para. 233 and fn. 424. *See* also Respondent's Brief, para. 232.
102 Decision of 8 July 2005, para. 21.
103 *See*, for example, *Prosecutor v. Jean-Paul Akayesu*, Case No. ICTR-96-4-T, Decision on Defendant's Motion for Summonses and Protection of Witnesses called by the Defence, 17 February 1998; *Prosecutor v. Zejnil Delalić et al.*, Case No. IT-96-21-T, Decision on Zdravko Mucić's Motion for the Exclusion of Evidence, 2 September 1997.
104 The European Court of Human Rights ("ECtHR") has dealt with this issue mostly in the context of punishment (in a broad sense) of accused persons relying on their right to remain silent. However, the Appeals Chamber finds the ECtHR case law to be informative of the principles that "[t]he right not to incriminate oneself is primarily concerned ... with respecting the will of an accused person to remain silent" (*Heaney and McGuinness v. Ireland*, Reports of Judgments and Decisions 2000-XII, para. 40) and that the status of a person (not yet formally charged) is modified when that individual's situation has been "substantially affected" therefore anticipating the right to remain silent, the right against self-incrimination and the related warnings (*Id.*, 41-42, 45). *See* also *Serves v. France*, Reports 1997-VI, para. 42; *Saunders v. the United Kingdom*, Reports 1996-VI, para. 74; *Shannon v. United Kingdom*, no. 6563/03, judgement of 4 October 2005 (consulted in the Internet).
105 Decision of 8 July 2005, paras 21 and 24.
106 Decision of 8 July 2005, para. 19.

> nuance of the interview was included in the Statement, which affects its reliability. Because the Statement was not audio or video recorded, the Defence at present is incapable to verify the accuracy of the Statement. The only effective way to challenge the content of the statement at this moment in time would be for Sefer Halilović to waive his right to remain silent and testify before this Tribunal.[107]
>
> In the present case, Rule 43 [of the Rules] was not applied at the time of taking the Statement. Sefer Halilović has not chosen to waive his right to remain silent during trial. Thus, the Trial Chamber finds that the admission of the Statement would infringe upon the Accused's right to a fair trial.[108]

38. Whether the statement would also be inadmissible due to a retroactive reading of Rule 43 of the Rules was not a decisive consideration in the Trial Chamber's reasoning.[109] It is clear that the Trial Chamber instead excluded the Statement because, in accordance with Rule 89(D) of the Rules, it did not deem the statement reliable enough, so that it could have threatened the fairness of the proceedings.[110] The Appeals Chamber is only called to decide on whether this specific decision was unreasonable.

39. The language used by the Trial Chamber throughout its decision shows that, with no way to test the accuracy of the Statement or its interpretation, its reliability was in doubt.[111] The circumstances of the case, which included the fact that the Statement was being tendered from the bar table, the summary format of the document and the fact that no record of any kind was offered to show its reliability, had an impact upon Halilović's ability to challenge the content of the Statement and prepare an effective defence without forfeiting his right to remain silent. In this respect, the Appeals Chamber emphasizes the large measure of discretion afforded under the Rules **[page 18]** to Trial Chambers in establishing the authenticity of a document.[112] Considering that Trial Chambers' decisions on issues of evaluation of evidence must generally be given a margin of deference,[113] it is only where an abuse of such discretion can be established that the Appeals Chamber should reverse such decisions.[114]

40. The Appeals Chamber is not satisfied that the Prosecution has shown that the Trial Chamber in this instance abused its discretion.[115] The issue of whether the Statement contained relevant and probative evidence, in the sense of Rule 89(C) of the Rules, is therefore moot.

41. For the foregoing reasons, the Appeals Chamber dismisses sub-ground 6. **[page 19]**

C. Sub-ground 1: Requirement of effective control

1. Introduction

42. The Prosecution avers that the Trial Chamber erred in law in paragraphs 38 to 54, 363 to 372, 736 to 747 and 752 of the Trial Judgement in applying the legal standard required to demonstrate effective control.[116] It submits that the Trial Chamber committed three errors in finding that Halilović was not the superior of

---

107 Decision of 8 July 2005, para. 25 (footnote omitted).

108 Decision of 8 July 2005, para. 26.

109 *See*, in this respect, *Čelebići* Appeal Judgement, para. 533 and *Kvočka* Appeal Judgement, para. 128.

110 Decision of 8 July, in particular paras 17 and 27, referring to Rule 89(D) of the Rules.

111 Decision of 8 July 2005, para. 25.

112 *See* Decision on Appeal Concerning Admission of Record of Interview, para. 19.

113 *Čelebići* Appeal Judgement, para. 533, where the Appeals Chamber stated that "a Trial Chamber exercises considerable discretion in deciding on issues of admissibility of evidence" and that, as a result, "a Trial Chamber should be afforded [...] deference in making decisions based on the circumstances of the case before it".

114 *See*, for example, *Prosecutor v. Dario Kordić and Mario Čerkez,* Case No. IT-95-14/2-AR73.5, Decision on Appeal Regarding Statement of a Deceased Witness, 21 July 2000; *Prosecutor v. Dario Kordić and Mario Čerkez,* Case No. IT-95-14/2-AR73.6, Decision on Appeal Regarding the Admission into Evidence of Seven Affidavits and One Formal Statement, 18 September 2000.

115 *Cf. Naletilić and Martinović* Appeal Judgement, paras 530 and 544; *Čelebići* Appeal Judgement, para. 533 (concerning the Appeals Chamber's power to intervene to exclude evidence when it finds that a Trial Chamber committed a discernible error in the exercise of its discretion to admit evidence and that this error resulted in unfair prejudice to the appellant, thereby rendering his trial unfair). *See* also *Gacumbitsi* Appeal Judgement, para. 19 (concerning a Trial Chamber's abuse of discretion in relation to a scheduling decision).

116 Prosecution Notice of Appeal, para. 4(i). *See* also AT. 8–9.

subordinates who committed the crimes in Grabovica. First, it argues that the Trial Chamber erred in law by requiring the Prosecution to prove that Halilović had "command" and "overall control of combat operations in Herzegovina" rather than effective control over the perpetrators of the crimes committed in Grabovica.[117] Second, the Trial Chamber erred in law in failing to consider whether Halilović had effective control over the perpetrators of the crimes because he was the Team Leader of the Inspection Team, or because he was the most senior ranking ABiH officer in Herzegovina at the time.[118] Third, the Prosecution submits that the Trial Chamber erred in fact in finding that Halilović was not the superior of those perpetrators, notwithstanding the factual findings that establish his material ability to prevent, punish and initiate measures leading to proceedings against the perpetrators.[119]

2. Halilović's request for summary dismissal

43. As part of his response to the Prosecution's arguments, Halilović requests the summary dismissal of this sub-ground of appeal on the grounds that the Prosecution has abandoned or impermissibly varied many of its arguments within this sub-ground of appeal,[120] and that it has failed to meet the burden of argument or persuasion.[121]

44. The Appeals Chamber recalls that in addition to identifying the order, decision or ruling challenged, the Notice of Appeal must set forth the grounds of appeal and "indicate the substance of the alleged errors and the relief sought".[122] An Appellant's brief will thereafter be filed, containing **[page 20]** all the arguments and authorities in support of the grounds outlined in the notice of appeal.[123] Accordingly, the mere fact that an Appellant's brief contains more arguments which elaborate upon an allegation of error raised in a notice of appeal does not necessarily imply that the grounds of appeal were impermissibly varied. With these principles in mind, and as noted in section III of the present judgement,[124] the Appeals Chamber will address in detail only those arguments advanced in support of Halilović's requests for summary dismissal that warrant discussion.

(a) Failure to find that Halilović was *de facto* commander of the operation

45. In its Notice of Appeal, the Prosecution alleges that "the Trial Chamber erred in law at paragraphs 372 and 752 [of the Trial Judgement] in finding that the Prosecution had failed to prove beyond reasonable doubt that Sefer Halilović was *de facto* commander of an operation called 'Operation Neretva'".[125] Halilović argues that since this allegation was not reiterated in the Prosecution Appeal Brief, it has been abandoned and does not form part of the appeal.[126]

46. In the introduction to its first ground of appeal, the Prosecution states that:

---

117 Prosecution Appeal Brief, paras 2.6–2.15. *See* also AT. 9–10 and 12. The Appeals Chamber notes that, during the Appeal Hearing, the Prosecution submitted, on the one hand, that the Trial Chamber examined whether Halilović was commanding and controlling combat activities and whether "Halilović [was] either *de jure* or *de facto* commander of the alleged Operation Neretva [...] Again, *with emphasis on de facto commander"* (AT. 10 (emphasis added)). On the other hand, it argued that "the Trial Chamber looked again and again for combat -- command responsibility *in a formal military sense*. It looked for *formal appointment, it looked for formal military title,* and it looked for defined military command roles" (AT. 13 (emphasis added)).

118 Prosecution Appeal Brief, paras 2.6–2.7 and 2.16–2.27. *See* also AT. 14: "The Trial Chamber overlooked that the case pleaded in the [I]ndictment rested on the authority and power vested in Halilović through his role and function as *de facto* superior, as senior officer in Herzegovina for the operation, and as a team leader of the inspection team".

119 Prosecution Appeal Brief, para. 2.7. *See* also Prosecution Appeal Brief, paras 2.28–2.40.

120 Respondent's Brief, paras 10–18, 45, 53, 60, 90–91 and 96.

121 Respondent's Brief, paras 19–23.

122 Rule 108 of the Rules. *See* also Practice Direction on Formal Requirements for Appeals from Judgement, para. 1.

123 Rule 111 of the Rules. *See* also Practice Direction on Formal Requirements for Appeals from Judgement, para. 4.

124 *See supra,* para. 14.

125 Prosecution Notice of Appeal, para. 4(i). This allegation is raised under sub-grounds 2 and 3, where the Prosecution claims that "the Trial Chamber erred in law and fact at paragraphs 372 and 752 in finding that the Prosecution had failed to prove beyond reasonable doubt that Sefer Halilović was *de facto* commander of an operation called 'Operation Neretva'" (Prosecution Notice of Appeal, paras 4(ii) and 4(iii)).

126 Respondent's Brief, para. 10.

> [t]hus, according to Halilović's superior, to Halilović's subordinate, to Halilović's "Inspection Team", and to Halilović himself, Halilović was the *de jure or de facto commander* of an operation called "Neretva" carried out from an IKM in Jablanica. At the very least, Halilović had "effective control" over the troops that committed the crimes in Grabovica.[127]

However, the specific allegation that the Trial Chamber erred in failing to find that Halilović was the *de facto* commander of Operation Neretva was not reiterated or elaborated upon in the Prosecution Appeal Brief. The allegation of errors of law concerns paragraphs 372 and 752 of the Trial Judgement. The only other instance where the Prosecution makes express reference to paragraph 372 of the Trial Judgement within the context of sub-ground 1, however, is in an introductory line before quoting the paragraph in question:

> The Trial Chamber's legally incomplete findings on effective control end with the conclusion that: [t]he Prosecution has failed to prove beyond reasonable doubt that Sefer Halilović was either *de jure* or *de facto* commander of the alleged operation called 'Operation Neretva' which the Prosecution submits was carried out in Herzegovina in September 1993.[128] **[page 21]**

47. Thus, the Prosecution Appeal Brief and the Prosecution Reply Brief do not appear, at first glance, to argue that the Trial Chamber erred in failing to find that Halilović was the *de facto* commander of the combat activities that took place in Herzegovina in September 1993 and which the Trial Judgement refers to as "Operation Neretva".[129] Rather, the substance of the Prosecution's argument seems to be that Halilović had effective control over the perpetrators of the crimes committed in Grabovica on other bases.[130]

48. In light of the foregoing, the Appeals Chamber invited the Prosecution to clarify during the Appeal Hearing whether the allegation in question had in fact been abandoned.[131] At the Appeal Hearing, the Prosecution asserted that the allegation in question is not abandoned[132] and referred to the following paragraphs of the Prosecution Appeal Brief in support: 2.3, 2.10, 2.11, 2.23, 2.47, 2.50, 2.52, 2.59, 2.83, 2.86, 2.94 and 2.98.[133]

49. At the Appeal Hearing, Halilović responded that the allegation in question was either abandoned or inadequately argued and supported.[134] Considering that paragraph 2.16 of the Prosecution Appeal Brief only states that the Trial Chamber had the duty to enquire whether Halilović had superior authority over the perpetrators because he was the most senior ABiH officer or because he was the Team Leader of the Inspection Team, Halilović argued that this effectively amounted to an explicit abandonment of the allegation that the Trial Chamber erred in failing to find that Halilović was the *de facto* commander of Operation Neretva.[135] Further, Halilović argued that although the Prosecution "skilfully constructs an argument that *de facto* command is just one of the small parts of effective control, [i]t's inconsistent with the criticisms levelled at the Trial Chamber for its focus on command and it's inconsistent with the argument that there was a case beyond command".[136] **[page 22]**

50. With respect to paragraph 2.3 of the Prosecution Appeal Brief, the Appeals Chamber has already noted that the specific allegation that the Trial Chamber erred in failing to find that Halilović was the *de facto*

---

127 Prosecution Appeal Brief, para. 2.3 (emphasis added).

128 Prosecution Appeal Brief, para. 2.17. Paragraph 372 of the Trial Judgement is further quoted in the Prosecution Appeal Brief, para. 2.41, where the Prosecution submits that the Trial Chamber required it to prove not only that the military operation took place, but also that the name of this operation was "Neretva".

129 *See* Trial Judgement, para. 175.

130 Prosecution Appeal Brief, paras 2.6–2.40.

131 The Appeals Chamber put the following question to the Prosecution: "1. In its Notice of Appeal, the Prosecution alleges that 'the Trial Chamber erred in law and in fact at paragraphs 372 and 752 Fof the Trial Judgementğ in finding that the Prosecution had failed to prove beyond reasonable doubt that Sefer Halilović was de facto commander of an operation called 'Operation Neretva''. Given that it is not explicitly reiterated in the Prosecution Appeal Brief, could this claim be deemed as having been abandoned? If not, can the Prosecution point at specific paragraphs in its Appeal Brief where this claim is substantiated?" (footnote omitted). Addendum to Scheduling Order for Appeal Hearing (Questions to the Parties), 19 June 2007, p. 2.

132 AT. 6.

133 AT. 6–7. The Prosecution also stated that: "[*d*]*e facto* superior is [...] implicit in [paragraph 2.15 of the Prosecution Appeal Brief]". Paragraph 2.15 reads as follows: "Annex A to this brief contains thirteen other excerpts from the Judgement which further illustrate that the Trial Chamber's main line of inquiry was erroneously focused on command instead of effective control".

134 AT. 74–77.

135 AT. 76.

136 AT. 76–77.

commander of Operation Neretva is not reiterated; no allegation of error was raised, and the Prosecution simply stated that "Halilović was the *de jure or de facto commander* of an operation called 'Neretva'".[137] Paragraph 2.10 states that the term "superior" includes (but is not limited to) military commanders. Paragraph 2.11 then goes on to state that "superior responsibility" extends to *de facto* superiors, as well as to non-military or civilian superiors who cannot be described as being "commanders"; in paragraph 2.23, the Prosecution suggested that the Trial Chamber failed to ask itself whether Halilović had "command authority" by virtue of his senior position; paragraph 2.47 states that formal designation as a commander is not a prerequisite and a *de facto* position as a "superior" is sufficient. Finally, paragraphs 2.50, 2.52, 2.59, 2.83, 2.86, 2.94 and 2.98 refer generally to Halilović being the *de facto* "superior" of "those who committed the crimes in Grabovica" during the military operation.

51. The review of these paragraphs shows that the terms "superior", "superior responsibility" and "command authority" are used interchangeably by the Prosecution in its Appeal Brief and are also intended to encompass "command" of Operation Neretva. During the Appeal Hearing, the Prosecution also clarified that "every time the Appeal Brief refers to Halilović's *de facto* superior position, it includes *de facto* command".[138] Finally, the Appeals Chamber emphasizes the Prosecution's concluding remarks on this issue:

> [T]he core of the Prosecution's argument is on effective control and superior position instead of *de facto* command. And this is reflected in the notice of appeal at paragraphs 3 and 4(i). In conclusion, the Prosecution's position is that Halilović was the *de facto* commander of the operation, but in any event he had effective control over those who committed the crimes. The Prosecution has not abandoned this position.[139]

52. In light of the foregoing, the Appeals Chamber denies Halilović's request for summary dismissal of the allegation that the Trial Chamber erred in law at paragraphs 372 and 752 of the Trial Judgement in finding that the Prosecution had failed to prove beyond reasonable doubt that Halilović was *de facto* commander of Operation Neretva.

(b) Failure to find that Halilović had effective control

53. The Prosecution Notice of Appeal states that the Trial Chamber's failure to find that Halilović was *de facto* commander of Operation Neretva "led to the further erroneous findings at paragraphs 747 and 752 that Sefer Halilović did not have effective control over the offending **[page 23]** troops".[140] Halilović argues that this last allegation must be considered to have been abandoned since it "derived or resulted" from the abandoned allegation that the Trial Chamber erred in failing to find that he was *de facto* commander of Operation Neretva.[141] Halilović also avers that the following allegations contained in the Notice of Appeal have been abandoned: (1) that the Trial Chamber erred in law through a misapplication of the effective control test in a number of paragraphs in the Trial Judgement[142] and (2) that the Trial Chamber erred in law in concluding that a person tasked with "coordinating combat activities" could not, by virtue of this position, have had effective control over the offending troops.[143]

54. The Appeals Chamber finds that the Prosecution did not abandon these allegations of error. Paragraphs 2.6 to 2.40 of the Prosecution Appeal Brief seek to demonstrate that the Trial Chamber erred in its application of the effective control standard and in its conclusion that Halilović did not have effective control over the offending troops. Moreover, the Prosecution also argues that Halilović's coordinating role as Team Leader of the Inspection Team warrants a conclusion of effective control.[144] The Prosecution Notice of Appeal states that "the Trial Chamber erroneously required Sefer Halilović to have the position of a military 'commander'

137 *See supra,* para. 45.
138 AT. 7.
139 AT. 7.
140 Prosecution Notice of Appeal, para. 4(i).
141 Halilović Respondent's Brief, paras 11 and 90.
142 Respondent's Brief, paras 12 and 45.
143 Respondent's Brief, para. 55.
144 Prosecution Appeal Brief, paras 2.16, 2.24–2.26, 2.29 *et seq.*

for him to have effective control over the offending troops".[145] This issue is intrinsically connected to the allegations made in the Prosecution Appeal Brief to the effect that the Trial Chamber erroneously focused on command and the Prosecution's general arguments on a "case beyond command". The Appeals Chamber finds that the Prosecution Appeal Brief does not vary the allegations of error made in the Prosecution Notice of Appeal, but merely develops arguments in support of these allegations. Thus, Halilović's request for summary dismissal regarding the alleged abandonment of the Prosecution's allegation is denied.

(c) Failure to meet burden of argument or persuasion

55. Halilović submits that, since the Prosecution has put forth unsubstantiated allegations that fall short of the required burden of persuasion, summary dismissal is justified.[146] The Appeals Chamber finds that the arguments advanced by Halilović in this respect are unconvincing. As a result, Halilović's request for summary dismissal on the basis of the alleged failure of the Prosecution to meet its burden of argument or persuasion is denied. **[page 24]**

(d) New allegation which did not form part of the Prosecution's case at trial

56. Halilović claims that a case of effective control beyond Halilović's role as commander of Operation Neretva was never pleaded at trial. He submits that therefore, since this is a new argument which did not form part of the Prosecution's case, no notice thereof was given and, therefore, summary dismissal of this argument is warranted.[147] The Appeals Chamber considers that a determination on the issue of whether the Prosecution pleaded a case of effective control beyond Halilović's role as commander of Operation Neretva at trial, and consequently the issue as to whether the Trial Chamber "erred in law in failing to make necessary findings concerning effective control beyond 'command'",[148] require a detailed analysis of the Indictment and the relevant submissions of the parties at trial. It would therefore not be appropriate to dismiss this sub-ground of appeal without considering its merits. Accordingly, Halilović's request for summary dismissal on the basis that the Prosecution raises a new allegation which did not form part of its case at trial is denied.

3. Whether the Trial Chamber required proof of command in determining superior responsibility

57. The Prosecution submits that the Trial Chamber erred in law in treating "command" as a legal requirement of superior responsibility pursuant to Article 7(3) of the Statute[149] and, as a consequence, in erroneously focusing on Halilović's role as commander of Operation Neretva and on his control of combat operations to determine his effective control over the offending troops.[150]

58. Halilović responds that the Trial Chamber correctly identified the three elements of superior responsibility; there is no indication that it regarded the position of "commander" as an element or condition of effective control.[151] He submits that the Trial Chamber found on the evidence that the Prosecution had failed to establish that he was the commander of an operation and consequently unable to exercise effective control over the perpetrators, as expressly pleaded in the Indictment.[152] Halilović argues alternatively that, even if the Trial Chamber erred, the Prosecution has failed to establish that the alleged error would invalidate the Trial Judgement, for the Trial Chamber thoroughly assessed all evidence relevant to Halilović's alleged effective control, including **[page 25]** evidence concerning his high-ranking position in the ABiH and his position as Team Leader of the Inspection Team.[153]

---

145 Prosecution Notice of Appeal, para. 4(i).

146 *See* Respondent's Brief, paras 19–23.

147 *See* Respondent's Brief, paras 24 and 40.

148 Prosecution Appeal Brief, heading (B) p. 13. *See*, in particular, Prosecution Appeal Brief, paras 2.16–2.18.

149 Prosecution Appeal Brief, paras 2.8–2.9. The Prosecution submits that the Trial Chamber erred in law by requiring "Halilović to have the position of a military 'commander' for him to have effective control over the offending troops". (Prosecution Notice of Appeal, para. 4(i)).

150 Prosecution Appeal Brief, para. 2.12. *See also* AT. 8–10.

151 Respondent's Brief, paras 46 (citing Trial Judgement, paras 57 *et seq.*) and 47–50; AT. 64 and 75.

152 Respondent's Brief, paras 47–49. *See* also AT. 65–66.

153 Respondent's Brief, paras 51–52; *see* also Respondent's Brief, paras 57–58.

59. As a preliminary matter, the Appeals Chamber notes that, in paragraph 56 of the Trial Judgement, the Trial Chamber correctly set out the elements that must be satisfied to hold a superior responsible under Article 7(3) of the Statute:

i. The existence of a superior-subordinate relationship;

ii. the superior knew or had reason to know that the criminal act was about to be or had been committed; and

iii. the superior failed to take the necessary and reasonable measures to prevent the criminal act or punish the perpetrator thereof.

Regarding the first of these elements, the Appeals Chamber recalls that the concept of effective control over a subordinate – in the sense of a material ability to prevent or punish criminal conduct, however that control is exercised – is the threshold to be reached in establishing a superior-subordinate relationship for the purpose of Article 7(3) of the Statute.[154] Against this backdrop, the Appeals Chamber recalls that the necessity of proving that the perpetrator was the "subordinate" of the accused (against whom charges have been brought under Article 7(3) of the Statute) does not require direct or formal subordination. Rather, the accused has to be, by virtue of his position, senior in some sort of formal or informal hierarchy to the perpetrator. The ability to exercise effective control in the sense of a material power to prevent or punish, which the Appeals Chamber considers to be a minimum requirement for the recognition of a superior-subordinate relationship for the purpose of superior responsibility, will almost invariably not be satisfied unless such a relationship of subordination exists.[155] The Appeals Chamber considers that a material ability to prevent and punish may also exist outside a superior-subordinate relationship relevant for Article 7(3) of the Statute. For example, a police officer may be able to "prevent and punish" crimes under his jurisdiction, but this would not as such make him a superior (in the sense of Article 7(3) of the Statute) vis-à-vis any perpetrator within that jurisdiction. The Trial Chamber's analysis of the law on the first element of superior responsibility is consistent with this approach.[156]

60. At paragraph 57 of the Trial Judgement, the Trial Chamber stated that "[i]t is the position of command over the perpetrator which forms the legal basis for the superior's duty to act, and for his **[page 26]** corollary liability for a failure to do so".[157] In the following paragraphs,[158] the Trial Chamber correctly described the jurisprudence of the International Tribunal with respect to superior responsibility, particularly by identifying the threshold test as that of "effective control" and recognising the broad definition given to the term "command" so that *de facto* superiors may be found liable under Article 7(3) of the Statute.[159] The Trial Chamber therefore correctly articulated the law[160] and, contrary to the Prosecution's submissions,[161] did not consider a position of military command as a requirement for establishing superior responsibility.

61. The Appeals Chamber will now consider the Prosecution's submissions that the Trial Chamber erred in restating the law on the third element of superior responsibility.[162] According to the Prosecution, in paragraphs 81 to 90 of the Trial Judgement, the Trial Chamber created an unnecessary and unwarranted distinction between a general obligation and a specific obligation to prevent crimes.[163] **[page 27]**

---

154 *Čelebići* Appeal Judgement, para. 256.

155 *Čelebići* Appeal Judgement, para. 303.

156 *See* Trial Judgement, paras 57–63.

157 Trial Judgement, para. 57, citing *Aleksovski* Appeal Judgement, para. 76; ICRC Commentary, p. 1010; ILC Commentary, p. 36.

158 Trial Judgement, paras 58–63.

159 Trial Judgement, para. 60, citing *Čelebići* Appeal Judgement, paras 193, 195 and 303.

160 The Appeals Chamber notes that the Prosecution acknowledged this during the Appeal Hearing (AT. 8–9).

161 Prosecution Appeal Brief, paras 2.8–2.12.

162 Prosecution Appeal Brief, paras 4.2–4.17. *See* also Halilović Respondent's Brief, paras 286–294; Prosecution Reply Brief, paras 5.1–5.4; AT. 53–55.

163 Prosecution Notice of Appeal, para. 7 (which concerns the Prosecution's third ground of appeal). *See*, in particular, the following excerpts of the Trial Judgement (footnotes omitted):

81.The existence of a general obligation to prevent the commission of crimes stems from the duty of a commander, arising from his position of effective control, which places him in the best position to prevent serious violations of international humanitarian law. This obligation can be seen to arise from the importance which international humanitarian law places on the prevention of violations.

87.The Trial Chamber notes that it is well established that international humanitarian law intends to bar not only actual breaches of its norms, but aims also at preventing its potential breaches. As noted above, international humanitarian law

62. The Appeals Chamber acknowledges that the Trial Chamber's reference to both types of obligations – "general" and "specific" – under its analysis on the duty to prevent fosters confusion.[164] Hence, the Prosecution understood this distinction between general and specific obligation as being "an unhelpful addition to the correct legal standard".[165]

63. In discussing the "duty to prevent" in paragraphs 79 through 90 of the Trial Judgement, the Trial Chamber described what it termed a "general obligation" of each commander to maintain order and control of his own troops. The general duty of commanders to take the necessary and reasonable measures is well rooted in customary international law and stems from their position of authority.[166] The Appeals Chamber stresses that "necessary" measures are the measures appropriate for the superior to discharge his obligation (showing that he genuinely tried to prevent or punish) and "reasonable" measures are those reasonably falling within the material powers of the superior.[167] What constitutes "necessary and reasonable" measures to fulfil a commander's duty is not a matter of substantive law but of evidence.[168]

64. The Appeals Chamber holds that the Trial Chamber erred when giving the impression that there is an additional requirement to the third element of superior responsibility and agrees with the Prosecution that the correct legal standard is solely whether the superior failed to take the necessary and reasonable measures to prevent the criminal act or punish the perpetrator thereof.[169] Of course, this single standard will have to be applied differently in different circumstances; however, the **[page 28]** artificial distinction between "general" and "specific" obligations creates a confusing and unhelpful dichotomy.

65. Having solved this preliminary matter, the Appeals Chamber will now discuss whether the Trial Chamber erroneously required proof of command in determining Halilović's superior responsibility, as submitted by the Prosecution under the present sub-ground of appeal.

---

entrusts commanders with a role of guarantors of laws dealing with humanitarian protection and war crimes, and for this reason they are placed in a position of control over the acts of their subordinates, and it is this position which generates a responsibility for failure to act. It is a natural element of the *preventative* constituent of command responsibility that a commander must make efforts to ensure that his troops are properly informed of their responsibilities in international law, and that they act in an orderly fashion.

88. While it is evident that no criminal liability may attach to the commander for failure in this duty *per se*, it may be an element to be taken into consideration when examining the factual circumstances of the case. However, the adherence to this general obligation does not suffice by itself to avoid the commanders [sic] criminal liability in case he fails to take the necessary appropriate measure under his specific obligation.

89. As noted above, what the duty to prevent entails in a particular case will depend on the superior's material ability to intervene in a specific situation. In establishing individual responsibility of superiors military tribunals set up in the aftermath of World War II have considered factors such as the superior's failure to secure reports that military actions have been carried out in accordance with international law, the failure to issue orders aiming at bringing the relevant practices into accord with the rules of war, the failure to take disciplinary measures to prevent the commission of atrocities by the troops under their command, the failure to protest against or to criticise criminal action, and the failure to insist before a superior authority that immediate action be taken. The Tokyo Trial held that a superior's duty may not be discharged by the issuance of routine orders and that more active steps may be required.

164 *See*, in particular, paragraph 88 of the Trial Judgement: "While it is evident that no criminal liability may attach to the commander for failure in this duty *per se*, it may be an element to be taken into consideration when examining the factual circumstances of the case. However, the adherence to this general obligation does not suffice by itself to avoid the commanders [*sic*] criminal liability in case he fails to take the necessary appropriate measure under his specific obligation" (footnote omitted).

165 Prosecution Appeal Brief, para. 4.9.

166 *See,* for example, *Aleksovski* Appeal Judgement, para. 76.

167 Article 86 of Additional Protocol I provides that superiors are responsible if, *inter alia* "[t]hey did not take all feasible measures within their power to prevent or repress the breach"; in this respect, the ICRC Commentary explains that, for a superior to be found responsible, it must be demonstrated that the superior "did not take the *measures within his power* to prevent it" and elaborates that these measures must be "'feasible' measures, since it is not always possible to prevent a breach or punish the perpetrators" (ICRC Commentary, paras 3543 and 3548, emphasis added); Article 87 adds the duty to "initiate such steps as are necessary to prevent such violations [...] and, where appropriate, to initiate disciplinary or penal action against violators thereof." *See* also the US Supreme Court's holding in *In re Yamashita*, 327 US 1 (1945), at 16 ("such measures [...] within his power and appropriate in the circumstances") and *US v. Karl Brandt et al.*, in TWC, Vol. II, p. 212 ("The law of war imposes on a military officer in a position of command an affirmative duty to take such steps as are within his power and appropriate to the circumstances to control those under his command...").

168 *Blaškić* Appeal Judgement, para. 72.

169 *See* Prosecution Appeal Brief, para. 4.9.

66. In determining whether a superior-subordinate relationship existed between Halilović and the perpetrators of the crimes committed in Grabovica, the Trial Chamber was obliged to assess, as it did, all the evidence presented. In doing so, the Trial Chamber must have determined whether the evidence contained indicators which showed, *inter alia,* that Halilović had the power to prevent, punish, or initiate measures leading to proceedings against the alleged perpetrators where appropriate.[170] Some factors indicative of effective control, such as the accused's position, his capacity to issue orders, his position within the military or political structure, the procedure for appointment and the actual tasks performed, were specifically identified in the Trial Judgement and considered by the Trial Chamber in reaching a determination as to whether the evidence presented established Halilović's effective control over the perpetrators of the crimes committed in Grabovica.[171]

67. In support of the contention that "[t]he Trial Chamber's ultimate conclusion was that 'command' is legally required for superior responsibility"[172] the Prosecution quotes part of paragraph 752 of the Trial Judgement:

> It is a principle of international criminal law that a commander cannot be held responsible for the crimes of persons who were not *under his command* at the time the crimes were committed. The Trial Chamber finds that the Prosecution has failed to prove beyond reasonable doubt that Sefer Halilović was either *de jure* or *de facto* commander of an operation called "Operation Neretva", which the Prosecution alleges was carried out in Herzegovina.[173]

Nonetheless, when read in its entirety, paragraph 752 of the Trial Judgement does not support this contention. The Prosecution emphasizes the expression "under his command" and selectively omits this paragraph's first two sentences, thereby taking the excerpt cited in the Prosecution Appeal Brief out of context.[174] However, the Trial Chamber rightly relied here upon a principle laid down in the *Hadžihasanović* case, where the Appeals Chamber held that an accused cannot be charged under Article 7(3) of the Statute for crimes committed by a subordinate before the accused assumed **[page 29]** command over this subordinate.[175] By taking the Trial Chamber's reference to "command" in paragraph 752 of the Trial Judgement out of context, the Prosecution ignores the Trial Chamber's explicit consideration of Halilović's influence as falling short of the standard required to establish effective control. Contrary to the Prosecution's allegation, this paragraph does not focus on the term "command" as a requirement to establish superior responsibility.

68. The Appeals Chamber notes that, at trial, the Prosecution pleaded Halilović's role of military commander as a material fact underlying the allegation of Halilović's effective control over the perpetrators.[176] Paragraph 38 of the Indictment states that "[a]t all times relevant to the charges in the [I]ndictment, by virtue of his position and authority as Commander of the Operation [Halilović] had effective control over the units subordinated to him".[177] This is the only paragraph of the Indictment which explicitly pleads effective control. It is also a clear allegation that Halilović possessed effective control at the time of the crimes over the 9th Motorised Brigade, the 10th Mountain Brigade, the 2nd Independent Battalion and the Prozor Independent Battalion, *by reason* of his position and authority as Commander of Operation Neretva. The Appeals Chamber notes that Halilović was not alleged to be a civilian leader, but rather a commander of the troops participating in Operation Neretva, exercising both *de jure* and *de facto* "power" over the relevant units "by his control in military matters".[178] The Trial Chamber therefore did not err, as claimed by the Prosecution,[179] in assessing whether Halilović was indeed "commander" of Operation Neretva.

---

170 *Cf. Blaškić* Appeal Judgement, para. 69.

171 Trial Judgement, para. 58.

172 Prosecution Appeal Brief, para. 2.12.

173 Trial Judgement, para. 752, quoted in Prosecution Appeal Brief, para. 2.12 (emphasis added by the Prosecution).

174 "The Trial Chamber recalls its finding that Sefer Halilović possessed a degree of influence as a high ranking member of the ABiH and as one of its founders. However, the Trial Chamber considers that Sefer Halilović's influence falls short of the standard required to establish effective control." (Trial Judgement, para. 752).

175 *Prosecutor v. Enver Hadžihasanović and Amir Kubura*, Case No. IT-01-47-AR72, Decision on Interlocutory Appeal Challenging Jurisdiction in Relation to Command Responsibility, 16 July 2003 ("*Hadžihasanović* Interlocutory Decision"), para. 51.

176 On appeal, the Prosecution does not dispute that it pleaded Halilović's position of command as a basis for the charge of superior responsibility (Prosecution Appeal Brief, para. 2.20).

177 *See* also Indictment, para. 4: "Sefer Halilović was the commander of the Operation and as such the troops involved in the 'NERETVA-93' Operation were under his command and control'".

178 *See* Indictment, paras 38 and 39. *See* also Prosecution Pre-Trial Brief, para. 24; Prosecution Final Trial Brief, para. 186.

179 Prosecution Notice of Appeal, para. 4(i).

69. Similarly, while being in "overall control of combat operations" is not an express requirement under Article 7(3) of the Statute, the Trial Chamber is expected to make a finding in this respect if such a fact is pleaded as underlying one of the requirements of superior responsibility. In the present case, although the Prosecution did not explicitly allege "control of combat operations", it argued that Halilović had authority to "command combat activities"[180] and that he issued combat orders "consistent with those a commander of an operation would normally issue",[181] as a way of showing that a superior-subordinate relationship existed. The Trial Chamber was therefore expected to rule on this allegation as part of its overall analysis regarding Halilović's **[page 30]** authority to issue orders which would, in turn, assist in assessing whether a superior-subordinate relationship existed.[182]

70. The Prosecution further claims that the Trial Chamber erroneously focused on the existence of combat orders and evidence of formal subordination to establish Halilović's *command* instead of assessing whether Halilović had effective control over the perpetrators.[183] The Appeals Chamber considers that, in light of the Prosecution's pleadings at trial outlined above,[184] the Trial Chamber did not err in assessing Halilović's "command". In particular, the Prosecution itself pleaded the issuing of orders to demonstrate that Halilović had "both formal *de jure* and *de facto* power".[185] The capacity to issue orders can amount to a factor indicative of effective control.[186] The Trial Chamber did not err, as submitted by the Prosecution,[187] in examining the context in which Halilović issued his orders as a means to assess whether these orders could establish Halilović's effective control.[188] Indeed, the evidence indicated that the orders issued by Halilović were within the ambit of Rasim Delić's authority and not Halilović's.[189] The Trial Chamber did also find that some orders issued by Halilović were not followed[190] or were followed only after confirmation by Rasim Delić.[191]

71. Moreover, the issue of the 9th Brigade's subordination was relevant as an element to ascertain whether Halilović was able to control the troops in question.[192] Indeed, considering that the 9th Brigade was under the command of Zulfikar Ališpago,[193] any military chain of command might legitimately be considered as going through Ališpago. It was for the Prosecution to prove the existence of other indicators establishing effective control outside Ališpago's subordination to Halilović. Indeed, as the Trial Chamber correctly noted, command can also be "based on the **[page 31]** existence of *de facto* powers of control".[194] Therefore the Trial Chamber did not err in assessing the subordination of the 9th Brigade and its commander Ališpago to Halilović.

72. The Prosecution also submits that the Trial Chamber erred in assessing Halilović's actions as Team Leader of the Inspection Team only in view of his position as "commander" and in failing to consider whether these actions established that he had "effective control".[195] However, the Prosecution specifically pleaded that the Inspection Team had a "commanding role and function" and that Halilović was "its *commander*"[196] when alleging Halilović's effective control. The Trial Chamber was therefore expected to address this issue

180 Prosecution Pre-Trial Brief, para. 27.
181 Prosecution Pre-Trial Brief, para. 43.
182 Trial Judgement, para. 371.
183 Prosecution Appeal Brief, paras 2.13 and 2.14, citing Trial Judgement, paras 735–752. *See* also AT. 13–14 and 16.
184 *See supra*, para. 68.
185 Indictment, para. 39.
186 Trial Judgement, para. 58.
187 Prosecution Appeal Brief, para. 2.14.
188 Trial Judgement, paras 244 and 350; *see* also Trial Judgement, para. 741.
189 *See* Trial Judgement, para. 370, where the Trial Chamber found that "an analysis of the evidence concerning orders issued by Sefer Halilović and information sent to him from the field indicates that the orders issued by Sefer Halilović were issued under the overall authority of Rasim Delić as Commander of the ABiH, and that orders issued by Sefer Halilović were, in general, implementing the instructions of the Commander". *See* also Trial Judgement, paras 199, 201 and 369.
190 *See* Trial Judgement, paras 351 and 744, concerning the disobedience of Zulfikar Ališpago.
191 *See* Trial Judgement, paras 233 and 743, concerning Vahid Karavelić's failure to carry out an order issued by Halilović on 2 September 1993 until it was confirmed by Delić.
192 The Appeals Chamber notes the Prosecution's submissions to the effect that: "Halilović's orders flowed down to the corps and unit commanders. The corps and unit commanders followed these orders with the corps and unit command orders cascading down to brigade commanders and so on" (AT. 15).
193 Trial Judgement, paras 345 and 744. *See* also Trial Judgement, para. 302, referring to Exhibit 503.
194 Trial Judgement, para. 60, quoting *Čelebići* Appeal Judgement, para. 195.
195 Prosecution Appeal Brief, para. 2.14. *See* also AT. 14.
196 Prosecution Pre-Trial Brief, para. 27 (emphasis added).

when assessing Halilović's role as Team Leader of the Inspection Team.[197] Indeed, the Trial Chamber heard evidence to the effect that the order appointing Halilović as Team Leader did not appoint him as commander of "Operation Neretva",[198] a position, as noted above, pleaded in the Indictment as the basis for Halilović's effective control over the troops in question.[199] The Appeals Chamber considers that the Prosecution, in its submissions at trial, did not substantiate how Halilović's role as Team Leader allegedly gave him "effective control" other than through his alleged position as commander.

73. Nevertheless, and contrary to the Prosecution's claim on appeal,[200] the Trial Chamber's analysis of Halilović's role as Team Leader of the Inspection Team was not confined to his alleged position as commander. In fact, the Trial Chamber first considered in detail evidence regarding the establishment and specific functions of the Inspection Team,[201] as well as Halilović's role as its Team Leader.[202] The Trial Chamber found that the Inspection Team was charged with inspection, coordination and cooperation among units,[203] and had to submit reports to Rasim Delić, who would then give the order to use or replace a unit.[204] The Trial Chamber also found that Halilović implemented Rasim Delić's orders in keeping with his role as Team Leader responsible for coordinating and monitoring units.[205] It is against this background that the Trial Chamber found that the documents sent by Halilović during the relevant time were consistent with his coordination role as Team Leader of the Inspection Team and that the orders he issued were all within the framework **[page 32]** of the orders issued by Rasim Delić.[206] Similarly, the Appeals Chamber notes that, at trial, the Prosecution specifically pleaded Halilović's organisation regarding the redeployment of units in the context of his position as a commander, since this redeployment began upon his "appointment as commander of the operation by Delić and [is] demonstrative of the Accused's command responsibilities related to Operation-93".[207] In fact, contrary to the Prosecution's arguments on appeal,[208] the Trial Chamber assessed the reorganisation and resubordination of troops as such,[209] before making a finding on Halilović's role. The Trial Chamber concluded, in this context, that Halilović implemented the orders of Rasim Delić "in keeping with his role as Team Leader of the Inspection Team charged with coordinating and monitoring functions".[210] The Appeals Chamber therefore considers that the Trial Chamber analysed Halilović's coordinating functions in the context of indicators of effective control, finding that the functions bestowed upon Halilović and the restrictions within which he was bound to act[211] were not sufficient to establish his effective control beyond reasonable doubt.

74. Thus, the Trial Chamber did ascertain whether Halilović held the position of military commander because this fact was pleaded by the Prosecution as a material fact in support of the allegation that he had effective control over the units subordinated to him.[212] However, this does not mean that, upon concluding that Halilović was not the *de jure* military commander of Operation Neretva, the Trial Chamber failed to further address other indicators of effective control. For the foregoing reasons, the Appeals Chamber finds that the Trial Chamber did not treat military command as a necessary element of superior responsibility,

---

197 Trial Judgement, paras 202–210 and 369.
198 Trial Judgement, paras 210 and 364.
199 Indictment, para. 38. *See supra*, para. 68.
200 Prosecution Appeal Brief, para. 2.14.
201 Trial Judgement, paras 193–205. The Trial Chamber concluded that the Inspection Team had been set up by the order issued by the Commander of the Supreme Command Staff, Rasim Delić, dated 30 August 1993 "to *coordinate* the work and tasks of units in the zones of responsibility of the 4th and 6th Corps" (Trial Judgement, para. 210 (emphasis added)).
202 Trial Judgement, paras 199 and 202–205. S*ee* also Trial Judgement, paras 355–364, concerning Halilović's role as Team Leader of the Inspection Team.
203 Trial Judgement, paras 350 and 364.
204 Trial Judgement, para. 350.
205 Trial Judgement, para. 244. *See* also Trial Judgement, para. 741.
206 Trial Judgement, para. 742. *See* also Trial Judgement, para. 359, for evidence that Halilović had issued orders but that they had to remain within the limits of the order issued by Rasim Delić.
207 Prosecution Pre-Trial Brief, para. 31.
208 Prosecution Appeal Brief, para. 2.14.
209 Trial Judgement, paras 222–244.
210 Trial Judgement, para. 244. *See* also Trial Judgement, para. 741.
211 *See*, for example, Trial Judgement, para. 743, where the Trial Chamber notes that Vahid Karavelić did not carry out an order from Halilović until it had been confirmed by Rasim Delić.
212 The Prosecution conceded that at trial it failed to prove that Halilović was the *de jure* commander of Operation Neretva (AT. 141).

thereby committing an error of law and, as the Prosecution suggests, "shift[ing] the focus of the [Trial] Judgement away from a determination of effective control".[213]

4. Whether the Trial Chamber erred in failing to consider a case beyond command

75. The Trial Chamber considered that the Prosecution based its charge of Halilović's individual criminal responsibility solely on his alleged position as Commander of Operation **[page 33]** Neretva-93.[214] It found on the evidence that (i) the Prosecution had not established beyond reasonable doubt that Halilović was *de jure* or *de facto* commander of Operation Neretva[215] and that (ii) the Prosecution had not proven beyond reasonable doubt that Halilović had effective control over the troops which committed the crimes in Grabovica and Uzdol.[216]

76. The Prosecution submits that, after having reached the conclusion that Halilović was not a formal or *de jure* commander of Operation Neretva, the Trial Chamber was under a duty to continue its inquiry and to determine whether he nevertheless had superior authority over the perpetrators of the crimes by virtue of the other factual bases pleaded at trial.[217] These alternative bases were Halilović's position as the most senior ranking ABiH officer in Herzegovina at the time[218] and his position as Team Leader of the Inspection Team.[219] The Prosecution claims that the Trial Chamber erred in law in failing to make "necessary" findings concerning effective control beyond command[220] and in assuming that the Prosecution's case was limited to Halilović's command over Operation Neretva.[221] The Prosecution requests the Appeals Chamber to intervene and correct this error by entering its own findings on the other bases of superior responsibility pleaded in the Indictment.[222]

77. Halilović responds that the Prosecution has waived its right to invoke these allegations on appeal, since it did not plead them at trial or pleaded them so inadequately that the Defence could not be said to have received adequate and timely notice.[223] He further argues that the Trial Chamber was under no obligation to consider a case beyond command, a case that was not clearly pleaded or argued at trial.[224] In particular, Halilović contends that the Prosecution alleged his role as Team Leader of the Inspection Team and his senior status in the ABiH only in order to demonstrate his command of the operation and not as alternative bases for a conclusion of effective control.[225] Halilović also submits that the Trial Chamber did consider all matters and evidence relevant to the issue of effective control, including the evidence pertaining to his senior status and his coordinating role as Team Leader of the Inspection Team, but found that this evidence did not show that he had **[page 34]** effective control over the perpetrators.[226] The Prosecution reiterates in its Reply Brief that "a case beyond command" was pleaded at trial.[227]

78. The Appeals Chamber deems it useful at this juncture to recall the material facts which must be pleaded in the indictment where criminal responsibility pursuant to Article 7(3) of the Statute is alleged:

> (1) that the accused is the superior of certain persons sufficiently identified, over whom he had effective control – in the sense of a material ability to prevent or punish criminal conduct – and for whose acts he is alleged to be responsible;

213 Prosecution Appeal Brief, para. 2.8.
214 Trial Judgement, para. 111 and fn. 267, citing Indictment, para. 38; Prosecution Final Brief, para. 186; Prosecution Pre-Trial Brief, paras 203 and 207–208. *See* also Trial Judgement, paras 342 and 735.
215 Trial Judgement, para. 372. *See* also Trial Judgement, para. 752.
216 Trial Judgement, paras 747 and 752.
217 Prosecution Appeal Brief, paras 2.16, 2.18–2.19 and 2.21. *See* also AT. 12, 14 and 17–18.
218 Prosecution Appeal Brief, paras 2.16, 2.19 and 2.21–2.23, citing, *inter alia*, para. 36 of the Indictment.
219 Prosecution Appeal Brief, paras 2.16, 2.19, 2.21 and 2.24–2.26, citing paras 1, 3, 31 and 39 of the Indictment.
220 Prosecution Appeal Brief, heading (B) p. 13. *See*, in particular, Prosecution Appeal Brief, paras 2.16–2.18.
221 Prosecution Appeal Brief, paras 2.19–2.20, citing Trial Judgement, paras 111, 342 and 735. Prosecution Reply Brief, paras 2.5–2.11. *See* also AT. 12.
222 Prosecution Appeal Brief, para. 2.27. *See* also AT. 17.
223 Respondent's Brief, paras 24–44, 54, 60, 71 and 92. *See* also AT. 112: "The case beyond command we say was waived and it's no error to ignore it".
224 Respondent's Brief, paras 61 and 63. *See* also AT. 68–69.
225 Respondent's Brief, paras 66, 73–74 and 78.
226 Respondent's Brief, paras 65 and 67–70. *See* also AT. 112: "The Trial Chamber at 752 and 746 still dealt with effective control and found that it was not established".
227 *See* Prosecution Reply Brief, paras 2.5–2.11.

(2) the criminal acts of such persons, for which he is alleged to be responsible;

(3) the conduct of the accused by which he may be found to have known or had reason to know that the crimes were about to be committed or had been committed by his subordinates; and

(4) the conduct of the accused by which he may be found to have failed to take the necessary and reasonable measures to prevent such acts or to punish the persons who committed them.[228]

Bearing in mind these principles of pleading settled in the jurisprudence of the Appeals Chambers of the International Tribunal and the ICTR, the present judgement turns to analyse the Indictment in conjunction with the Prosecution's submissions on appeal.

79. Paragraph 38 of the Indictment states that "[a]t all times relevant to the charges in the [I]ndictment, by virtue of his position and authority as Commander of the Operation [Halilović] had effective control over the units subordinated to him". As noted above, this is the only paragraph of the Indictment which explicitly pleads effective control.[229] Nevertheless, the Prosecution submits on appeal that the Trial Chamber failed to fully address two further factual bases pleaded in the Indictment.

80. The first such factual basis is Halilović's position as the most senior ranking ABiH officer in Herzegovina,[230] as set out in paragraph 36 of the Indictment: **[page 35]**

> **Sefer HALILOVIĆ** was Chief of the Supreme Command Staff, one of Rasim Delic's [sic] deputies and was the most senior ranking Commander in Herzegovina at that time for the Operation. The ABiH Disciplinary Regulations, in particular those gazetted on 13 August 1992, as amended, to implement the rules relating to the investigation of war crimes, also bound him.

The other factual basis is the fact that "Halilović was a superior because he was the Team Leader of the Inspection Team".[231] The Prosecution relies on paragraphs 1, 3, 31 and 39 of the Indictment to support this contention:[232]

> 1. **Sefer HALILOVIĆ**: the son of Rustem, born on 6 January 1952 in Prijepolje in the region of Serbia known as Sandžak. He attended the military academy in Belgrade in 1971 for 3 years. In 1975 he went to the military school in Zadar where he became an Officer in the Yugoslav People's Army (JNA). On 31 August 1990 he went to Belgrade and attended a two-year course at the school for commanders.
>
> When **Sefer HALILOVIĆ** left the JNA in September 1991 he was a professional military officer who had attained the rank of Major. He returned to Bosnia-Herzegovina in September 1991, joined the Patriotic League and planned the defence of Bosnia-Herzegovina. On 25 May 1992 he was appointed by the Presidency of the Republic of Bosnia and Herzegovina (RBiH) as Commander of the Territorial Defence (TO) Staff of the RBiH, replacing Hasan Efendić.
>
> Consequently he became the most senior Military Commander of the armed forces of the RBiH.
>
> During the period 25 May 1992 until early July 1992, whilst the TO evolved into the Army, as per the Law of the Army of the Republic of Bosnia and Herzegovina dated 20 May 1992, **Sefer HALILOVIĆ** performed the function of the Commander of the TO Staff of the RBiH. His function meant he was also a member of the

---

228 *Ntagerura et al.* Appeal Judgement, para. 26 (regarding the corresponding provision under Article 6(3) of the ICTR Statute), referring to *Blaškić* Appeal Judgement, para. 218 and *Naletilić and Martinović* Appeal Judgement, para. 67. The Appeals Chamber notes that "the facts relevant to the acts of those others for whose acts the accused is alleged to be responsible as a superior, although the Prosecution remains obliged to give all the particulars which it is able to give, will usually be stated with less precision, because the detail of those acts are often unknown, and because the acts themselves are often not very much in issue" (*Blaškić* Appeal Judgement, para. 218 and accompanying references).

229 *See supra*, para. 68.

230 *See* Prosecution Appeal Brief, paras 2.19 and 2.22–2.23. At paragraph 2.21 of its Appeal Brief, the Prosecution only adds that paragraphs 1, 4, 36, 37 and 39 of the Indictment pleaded facts relating to Halilović's superior responsibility as the most senior ranking officer in Herzegovina at the time.

231 Prosecution Appeal Brief, heading (b) p. 15.

232 *See* Prosecution Appeal Brief, paras 2.19 and 2.24–2.25. At paragraph 2.21 of its Appeal Brief, the Prosecution states that paragraphs 1, 3, 4, 5 and 39 of the Indictment pleaded information relating to Halilović's superior responsibility as Team Leader of the Inspection Team, but it does not discuss paragraphs 4 and 5 of the Indictment further.

War Presidency. After July 1992, he functioned as the Chief of the General Staff of the Army of the Republic of Bosnia and Herzegovina (ABiH).

On 18 August 1992 the Presidency formed five corps of the ABiH with **Sefer HALILOVIĆ** as Chief of the Supreme Command Staff/Chief of the Main Staff.

On 8 June 1993 a new position was created, Commander of the Supreme Command Staff. Rasim Delić filled this post. **Sefer HALILOVIĆ** retained the post of Chief of the Supreme Command Staff of the ABiH until November 1993.

Between 18 July 1993 to November 1993 **Sefer HALILOVIĆ** held the post of Deputy Commander of the Supreme Command Staff of the ABiH as well as Chief of the Supreme Command Staff.

After a meeting in Zenica on 20–21 August 1993 **Sefer HALILOVIĆ** was appointed Head of an Inspection Team and commander of an Operation called "NERETVA-93".

He is now a retired General of the ABiH and is a Minister in the Government of Bosnia-Herzegovina.

3. At a meeting on 21 to 22 August 1993 in Zenica, attended by most of the senior military commanders of the ABiH including Rasim Delić, it was decided that the ABiH would conduct a military Operation in Herzegovina. It was called "NERETVA-93". The main purpose of the Operation was to capture territory held by the Bosnian Croat forces (HVO) from Bugojno to Mostar thereby ending the blockade of Mostar. In order to achieve these aims the ABiH would launch offensives within this area. At the meeting an Operational plan which had been prepared and tabled by **Sefer HALILOVIĆ** was discussed. The Commander of the Supreme Command Staff, Rasim Delić, who was also present, agreed that an Inspection Team headed by his Deputy, **Sefer HALILOVIĆ** who was then also Chief of the Supreme Command Staff, would go to Herzegovina to command and co-ordinate the Operation. Units from the 1st, 3rd, 4th and 6th Corps including a unit which was commanded by Zulfikar Ališpago were to be subordinated to **Sefer HALILOVIĆ** for the Operation.

31. On 20 September 1993 **Sefer HALILOVIĆ** and the other members of his Inspection Team signed a report about their mission in Herzegovina. The report recommends criminal procedures be instituted against certain military officers and civilian officials yet makes no mention about the Grabovica or Uzdol incidents. **[page 36]**

39. **Sefer HALILOVIĆ** demonstrated both formal *de jure* and *de facto* power, by his command and control in military matters in a manner consistent with the exercise of superior authority, by issuing orders, instructions and directives to the units, by ensuring the implementation of these orders, instructions and directives and bearing full responsibility for their implementation. He also assigned lines of attack and coordinated the combat activities of the units. He planned and was instrumental in the implementation of the military operations carried out by the units which took part in the "NERETVA-93" Operation.

81. The Appeals Chamber considers that the paragraphs quoted above do not demonstrate that the Indictment clearly pleaded a "case beyond command". On the contrary, paragraph 38 of the Indictment is an unambiguous allegation that Halilović possessed effective control at the time of the crimes over the 9th Motorised Brigade, the 10th Mountain Brigade, the 2nd Independent Battalion and the Prozor Independent Battalion *by reason* of his position and authority as Commander of Operation Neretva-93.

82. In light of this specificity, the Defence was entitled to understand that this was the only basis advanced by the Prosecution to demonstrate Halilović's effective control over the perpetrators of the crimes. While other paragraphs in the Indictment refer to Halilović's high rank in the ABiH and his role as Team Leader of the Inspection Team, these facts are not clearly presented or pleaded as alternative bases for a finding of effective control. In other words, the Prosecution did not clearly allege that, even if Halilović was not in command of Operation Neretva-93, he still had effective control over the troops in question by means of his position as Team Leader of the Inspection Team or of his high rank in the ABiH.

83. This conclusion is further supported by the following paragraphs in the Indictment. Paragraph 1 provides background information concerning Halilović's career and lists his titles and appointments. The gist of paragraphs 3, 4 and 5 is that Halilović was commander of a military operation called Operation Neretva-93. The Prosecution referred to the fact that the Commander of the Supreme Command Staff, Rasim Delić, agreed that Halilović would head the Inspection Team and to the fact that Halilović was the most senior military commander for Operation Neretva-93. The Prosecution used this fact to support its allegation that Halilović was the Commander of the operation and, therefore, the troops involved in Operation Neretva-93 were under his command and control.

84. Paragraph 31 of the Indictment, which concerns the report authored by the Inspection Team, suggests that Halilović failed to take necessary and reasonable measures to initiate criminal proceedings against officials responsible for the crimes committed in Grabovica and Uzdol. This paragraph cannot be read as an allegation that, even if Halilović was not a commander of Operation Neretva-93, he nonetheless had the material ability to initiate proceedings against the perpetrators of the crimes committed in Grabovica by reason of his position as Team Leader of the Inspection Team. Paragraph 36 of the Indictment states that Halilović "was Chief of the Supreme Command **[page 37]** Staff, one of [ABiH Commander] Rasim Delić's deputies and was the most senior ranking Commander [as opposed to officer] in Herzegovina at that time for the Operation". A plain reading of this sentence leads to the conclusion that this paragraph may not be read as an alternative basis for the allegation that Halilović had effective control over the units subordinated to him (the allegation expressed in paragraph 38 of the Indictment), but rather as a mere argument in support of this allegation. The same is true for paragraph 37 of the Indictment.

85. Paragraph 39 of the Indictment further elaborates on paragraph 38 and sets out examples of how Halilović "demonstrated both formal *de jure* and *de facto* power, by his command and control in military matters". There is no clear indication in this paragraph that Halilović's role as Team Leader of the Inspection Team constitutes an alternative basis for a finding of effective control. In fact, paragraph 39 of the Indictment does not even refer to his role as Team Leader of the Inspection Team. Moreover, the exercise of effective control by reason of Halilović's position as the most senior ranking officer in Herzegovina cannot be said to have been pleaded implicitly in this paragraph either, mainly because, for the purposes of criminal responsibility as a superior, *de jure* power is not synonymous with effective control. In fact, the former may not in itself amount to the latter. The same applies with respect to *de facto* power: a *de facto* superior must be found to wield substantially similar powers of control as *de jure* superiors who exercise effective control over subordinates to be held criminally responsible for their acts. It therefore cannot be said that pleading the exercise of both *de jure* and *de facto* power amounts to pleading effective control.[233]

86. A decisive factor in determining the degree of specificity with which the Prosecution is required to particularise the facts of its case in an indictment is the nature of the alleged criminal conduct charged.[234] In this respect, in line with the principles of pleading recognised by the Appeals Chambers of the International Tribunal and the ICTR set out above, the Indictment pleads that Halilović had effective control over the units subordinated to him. The manner in which such control was exercised might encompass facts which are not required to be alleged as long as there is a clear indication that he possessed effective control at the time of the crimes.[235] With respect to the degree of specificity with which the material facts must be pleaded, Chambers of the International Tribunal have held that each of the material facts must usually be pleaded expressly, although in **[page 38]** some circumstances it may suffice if they are expressed by necessary implication[236] and that, in any case, an indictment "is to be read as a whole, not as a series of paragraphs existing in isolation".[237] The allegation in paragraph 38 of the Indictment states that Halilović possessed effective control at the time of the crimes over the 9th Motorised Brigade, the 10th Mountain Brigade, the 2nd Independent Battalion and

---

233 Prosecutor v. Enver Hadžihasanović and Amir Kubura, Case No. IT-01-47-PT, Decision on Form of Indictment, 7 December 2001, para. 17 (footnotes omitted), citing and elaborating on the principle enshrined in *Čelebići* Appeal Judgement, paras 196–198 and 266.

234 *Ntagerura et al.* Appeal Judgement, para. 121; *Krnojelac* Appeal Judgement, para. 132; *Kupreškić et al.* Appeal Judgement, para. 89.

235 *Cf. Prosecutor v. Rasim Delić,* Case No. IT-04-83-AR72, Decision on Interlocutory Appeal Challenging the Jurisdiction of the Tribunal, 8 December 2005, para. 10.

236 *Blaškić* Appeal Judgement, para. 219; *Prosecutor v. Mitar Rasević,* Case No. IT-97-25/1-PT, Decision Regarding Defence Preliminary Motion on the Form of the Indictment, 28 April 2004, para. 18; *Prosecutor v. Mile Mrkšić,* Case No. IT-95-13/1-PT, Decision on Form of the Indictment, 19 June 2003, para. 12; *Prosecutor v. Enver Hadžihasanović and Amir Kubura,* Case No. IT-01-47-PT, Decision on Form of Indictment, 7 December 2001, para. 10; *Prosecutor v. Radoslav Brđanin and Momir Talić,* Case No. IT-99-36-PT, Decision on Form of Fourth Amended Indictment, 23 November 2001, para. 12; *Prosecutor v. Radoslav Brđanin and Momir Talić,* Case No. IT-99-36-PT, Decision on Objections by Momir Talić to the Form of the Indictment, 20 February 2001, para. 48.

237 *Enver Hadžihasanović and Amir Kubura* Trial Judgement, para. 266; *Prosecutor v. Jadranko Prlić et al.,* Case No. IT-04-74-PT, Decision on Prosecution Application for Leave to Amend the Indictment and on Defence Complaints on Form of Proposed Amended Indictment, 18 October 2005, para. 78; *Prosecutor v. Jadranko Prlić et al.,* Case No. IT-04-74-PT, Decision on Defence Preliminary Motions Alleging Defect in the Form of the Indictment, 22 July 2005, paras 13 and 50; *Prosecutor v. Mile Mrkšić,* Case No. IT-95-13/1-PT, Decision on Form of the Indictment, 19 June 2003, para. 28; *see* also *Prosecutor v. Enver Hadžihasanović and Amir Kubura*, Case No. IT-01-47-PT, Decision on Form of Indictment, 7 December 2001, para. 38.

the Prozor Independent Battalion, "by virtue of his position and authority as Commander of the Operation". These were the military units, which, according to the Prosecution, were involved in Operation Neretva-93[238] and responsible for killing 33 Bosnian Croat civilians in Grabovica.[239] If one is to consider these facts as a whole, a reasonable conclusion is that they plainly allege that Halilović had effective control over the units in question at the time of the relevant events *by reason* of his position as Commander of Operation Neretva-93. Accordingly, when read as a whole, the Indictment does not unambiguously plead that Halilović had effective control by means *other* than his alleged position as commander of Operation Neretva-93. Nor can it be said that Halilović's effective control by virtue of his position as the most senior ranking officer in Herzegovina or by virtue of his position as Team Leader of the Inspection Team are implicitly pleaded in the Indictment when read as a whole.

87. The Appeals Chamber now turns to determine whether, as argued by the Prosecution,[240] timely, clear and consistent information might have put Halilović on notice throughout the proceedings that effective control beyond command was part of the Prosecution case.[241]

88. While Halilović asserts that a case of effective control beyond command was never pleaded or argued at trial,[242] the Prosecution replies that "[t]he trial record proves the contrary" and refers to the Prosecution Appeal Brief for relevant references in support.[243] However, the references in **[page 39]** question only concern paragraphs 1, 3 to 5, 36 to 37 and 39 of the Indictment, which have already been addressed above.[244]

89. The Prosecution also avers that "[r]eferences to the case theory and facts in support of effective control are found in the Indictment, Prosecution and Defence Pre-trial Briefs, Prosecution and Defence Final Trial Briefs and the Judgement".[245] However, on the basis of the submissions before it, the Appeals Chamber concludes that the Prosecution's contention throughout the pre-trial and trial proceedings was that Halilović's effective control was exercised by virtue of his position and authority as Commander of Operation Neretva-93, not by means of his senior rank in the ABiH or his role as Team Leader of the Inspection Team, the "alternative bases" mentioned above.

90. Among the paragraphs in the Pre-Trial Brief cited by the Prosecution, paragraph 4 states that "[t]he Accused had effective control over the units [in question] by virtue of being the commander of an operation called 'NERETVA-93' (the Operation)". Paragraph 5 states that "as the most senior commander [as opposed to officer] in charge in the theatre of operation, the Accused had effective control over the troops and was considered by them to be the supreme commander in the field". Paragraph 16 does state that Halilović was appointed commander of the TO on 25 May 1992 becoming "the most senior military commander". However, the Appeals Chamber notes that he held a different position at the time relevant to the Indictment (September 1993). Paragraph 42 states that "the Accused was the most senior member of the ABiH in the area. He had been its supreme commander up until July 2003". Nonetheless, this statement is made to support the allegation that he *commanded* Operation Neretva.[246] In paragraph 172, the Prosecution contends that "the Accused had effective control over the troops subordinated to him *for the Operation,* as evidenced both by his *de jure* authority and the cumulative effect of the facts, which establish that he was a *de facto* commander who was able to exercise effective control over the troops who committed the crimes referred to in the [I]ndictment".[247]

---

238 Indictment, para. 4.

239 Indictment, para. 21; *see* also Prosecution Pre-Trial Brief, paras 3 and 9.

240 Prosecution Reply Brief, para. 2.5. *See* also AT. 12.

241 *Simić* Appeal Judgement, paras 23–24; *Ntagerura et al.* Appeal Judgement, paras 28 and 30; *Naletilić and Martinović* Appeal Judgement, para. 26; *Kvočka et al.* Appeal Judgement, para. 33; *Kupreškić et al.* Appeal Judgement, para. 114.

242 *See* Halilović Respondent's Brief, para. 24.

243 Prosecution Reply Brief, para. 2.9, citing Prosecution Appeal Brief, para. 2.21.

244 In response to a question posed by the Bench regarding the way in which it pleaded its case at trial, the Prosecution submitted during the Appeal Hearing that: "the Defence was always aware [...] that the Prosecution's case was based on an allegation that Halilović was the superior over subordinates who committed the crime and not solely on whether he was the commander of the operation" (AT. 138). In support of its position, the Prosecution again relied upon paragraphs 1, 3, 4, 35–39 and 43 of the Indictment (AT. 139–140).

245 Prosecution Reply Brief, para. 2.9 (footnote omitted).

246 The emphasis in this paragraph is on the fact that Halilović was regarded as the commander of Operation Neretva-93 by the members of the Inspection Team, by the troops and by civilian authorities.

247 Emphasis added. *See* also AT. 140–142 where the Prosecution relies, *inter alia*, on paragraph 172 of the Prosecution Pre-Trial Brief in support of its argument that "the Defence [...] were fully aware of the fact that the [Prosecution's] case was not based solely on the *de facto* commander position, but went beyond that to include superior authority" (AT.140).

91. These paragraphs support the conclusion that the Prosecution's case was that Halilović had effective control over the units subordinated to him solely by virtue of his command of Operation **[page 40]** Neretva-93.[248] In fact, the section of the Prosecution Pre-Trial Brief entitled "Effective Control of the Accused" is premised on Halilović's command of Operation Neretva.[249] The following portions of the Prosecution Pre-Trial Brief illustrate this point:

> The Prosecution avers that the evidence will demonstrate that [Halilović] was commander both in law and in fact and as such had effective control to prevent the killings in Grabovica and Uzdol, initiate investigations to identify the perpetrators and thereafter punish them.[250]
>
> On 30 August 1993 Commander Delić appointed the Accused to be *de jure* commander of Operation Neretav-93 [*sic*].[251]
>
> Commander Delić's order dated 30 August 1993 gave the Team, under the command of the Accused, the authority to, *inter alia,* co-ordinate and command combat activities in the area [...] Although the team was called an Inspection Team, it had authority that exceeded mere preparation and conduct of the operation. It had a commanding role and function and the Accused was its commander.[252]
>
> Upon the appointment as commander of the operation by Delić and demonstrative of the Accused's command responsibilities related to Operation-93 in the Neretva Valley, HALILOVIĆ deployed in the area of operations and began to organise the redeployment of units required for the task.[253]
>
> ...The members of the Team that were with [Halilović] regarded him as commander of the Operation, as did the troops and their commanders in the area in which the Team operated. Even the military commander of the 6th Corps who ordinarily was the *de jure* commander in the territory that included Grabovica stated that once the Operation commenced the area fell under the command and control of the commander of the operation, that being the Accused. The civilian authorities also regarded him as commander of the Operation.[254]

The Prosecution's opening statement confirms that the Prosecution sought to establish that Halilović exercised effective control over the units in question *only* by virtue of Halilović's command of Operation Neretva-93.[255]

92. The Prosecution also relies upon its submissions in the Prosecution Final Trial Brief.[256] However, these submissions cannot constitute timely notice that "effective control beyond command was always part of the Prosecution's case"[257] and that the Prosecution was seeking to establish effective control also through the other two factual bases. The thesis proposed in the **[page 41]** Prosecution Final Trial Brief is that Halilović was in command of Operation Neretva-93 and that therefore he had effective control over the perpetrators of the crimes charged: the Prosecution did not clearly argue that, even if Halilović was not in command of this operation, he nevertheless had effective control over the perpetrators for other reasons.[258] It appears that, when the Prosecution referred to Halilović's position in the ABiH or his role as Team Leader of the Inspection Team, this was done in support of its argument that Halilović was the commander of Operation Neretva-93.[259] The following paragraphs sum up the Prosecution's position:

248 *See* also Prosecution's Supplementary Explanation to its Pre-Trial Brief, 22 December 2004, paras 7–8.
249 *See* Prosecution Pre-Trial Brief, paras 24–45.
250 Prosecution Pre-Trial Brief, para. 24.
251 Prosecution Pre-Trial Brief, para. 26.
252 Prosecution Pre-Trial Brief, para. 27.
253 Prosecution Pre-Trial Brief, para. 31.
254 Prosecution Pre-Trial Brief, para. 42.
255 *See*, in particular, T. 15–17 (31 January 2005). The Prosecution argued that, although the team headed by Halilović was called an "inspection team", it had a command function and Halilović did in fact command Operation Neretva-93 and had full authority over the troops to be deployed in that operation (T. 15). The Prosecution argued that Halilović's seniority in the ABiH invested him with the "gravitas" that ensured respect for his command authority (T. 16).
256 Prosecution Appeal Brief, para. 2.16, citing Prosecution Final Trial Brief, paras 142–186. *See* also AT. 17–18 and Prosecution Reply Brief, paras 2.5–2.6.
257 Prosecution Reply Brief, para. 2.5.
258 *See* Prosecution Final Trial Brief, paras 148–186.
259 *See* Prosecution Final Trial Brief, para. 187.

> The Prosecution submits that the evidence adduced at trial has proved beyond a reasonable doubt that Halilović planned, organized, commanded, coordinated and inspected Operation Neretva. Halilović had command authority over the units that participated in Operation Neretva. The evidence also establishes that this command authority was effective, and that Halilović's command was obeyed in practice. Therefore he had effective control of the troops who participated in this military Operation.[260]
>
> As shown above Halilović had effective control over the units subordinated to him as the leader of the inspection team *commanding combat operations* in Operation Neretva 93.[261]

93. The Prosecution also points to a number of paragraphs from the Defence Pre-Trial Brief and the Defence Final Trial Brief in support of the argument that a "case beyond command" had been clearly pleaded at trial.[262] The Appeals Chamber recalls that such submissions "may in some instances assist in assessing to what extent the accused was put on notice of the Prosecution's case and was able to respond to the Prosecution's allegations".[263]

94. However, an analysis of the Defence Pre-Trial Brief and of the Defence Final Trial Brief shows that these documents do not support the argument advanced by the Prosecution. On the contrary, they indicate Halilović's understanding that the allegations made against him hinged on his position as commander of Operation Neretva-93.[264] The following examples illustrate this point: **[page 42]**

> We point out again that there was no separate command for carrying out Operation *Neretva 93*. BH Army GŠ Commander Rasim DELIĆ commanded all units of the BH Army through the corps commanders, including the units which carried out Operation *Neretva 93*.[265]
>
> The Defence further points out [that] even when a commander transfers command rights to another person, he cannot transfer responsibility for the consequences of exercising command.
>
> Operation *Neretva 93* was planned and approved by the BH Army GŠ Commander [Rasim Delić], so he was the commander of the operation. The highest military experts of the BH Army took part in planning this operation. During the planning of Operation *Neretva 93*, they worked out the following in detail: the command and control system, the assignment of combat zones to specific units and commands, the axes of attack for lower-ranking units, etc. Therefore, it was precisely known which commander in which zone of responsibility was in charge of carrying out which task. In this operation, the Accused was not in charge of any of the operations zones, nor of the operation as a whole, nor did he have any command rights over any units.[266]

95. The Prosecution also argues that a pre-trial decision issued on 17 December 2004 put the Defence on notice "that the charges of superior responsibility were based on a broad range of facts",[267] and not just on command of the military operation. The Prosecution's choice of words is interesting in this respect, as it refers to the broader term of "superior responsibility", rather than to "effective control". In any event, and regardless of the language

260 Prosecution Final Trial Brief, para. 186 (footnotes omitted).

261 Prosecution Final Trial Brief, para. 187 (emphasis added).

262 *See* Prosecution Reply Brief, paras 2.8–2.9 and fns 9–11. *See* also AT. 143, where the Prosecution refers to the "Response to Prosecution's Application pursuant to Rule 92*bis* (A), filed on 2 February 2004, and paragraphs 163, 164, 169, 199 and 200 of the Defence Pre-Trial Brief, as clarifying "that there was no misunderstanding as to the scope of the allegations in the [I]ndictment and that they included, indeed, *superior responsibility*" (emphasis added).

263 *Naletilić and Martinović* Appeal Judgement, para. 27. *See* also *Simić* Appeal Judgement, para. 24; *Kvočka et al.* Appeal Judgement, paras 52-53 and *Kordić and Čerkez* Appeal Judgement, para. 148.

264 *See*, in particular, Defence Pre-Trial Brief, paras 161–164, pp. 31–32 (where the Defence argues that Halilović was not the commander of Operation Neretva-93) and Defence Final Trial Brief, paras 162 ff. (where the Defence argues that the relevant question is whether Halilović was *de jure* or *de facto* commander of the troops), 329–353 (where the Defence argues that there was no chain of command between Halilović and the perpetrators).

265 Defence Pre-Trial Brief, para. 62, pp. 9–10 (Section entitled: "1. Effective Control Over the Combat Units Assigned to the Operation").

266 Defence Pre-Trial Brief, paras 163–164, p. 33 (Section entitled: "i. Superior-Subordinate Relationship").

267 Prosecution Appeal Brief, para. 2.21, citing Decision on Prosecutor's Motion Seeking Leave to Amend the Indictment, 17 December 2004 ("Decision of 17 December 2004"), para. 15, fn. 31. *See* also AT. 139, lines 20–23. The Appeals Chamber notes that the transcript of the Appeal Hearing refers to "the decision of 17 February 2004"; however, it is clear from the context of the Prosecution's submissions that it was, in fact, citing fn. 31 of the Decision of 17 December 2004.

used by the Prosecution, the decision in question states that "[a]ll the material facts listed in paragraph (a) quoted above – the superior-subordinate relationship, effective control, and the Accused's responsibility for the crimes of his subordinates – are explicitly included in the Current Indictment". [268] The Trial Chamber then referred in a footnote to paragraphs 1, 3 to 5, 35 to 39 and 43 of the Indictment.[269] The Appeals Chamber finds that this decision could not have put the Defence on notice that the Prosecution sought to establish effective control on bases other than Halilović's command of Operation Neretva-93 as pleaded in paragraph 38 of the Indictment.

96. The fact that the Indictment, the Prosecution Pre-Trial Brief and the evidence adduced at trial by the Prosecution showed the Prosecution's attempt to establish effective control through *command* is further illustrated by the way in which the Prosecution closed its case:

> In fact [in] all our pleadings, pre-trial brief, opening statement, we have consistently maintained this position. The accused went to Herzegovina to command Operation Neretva by the authority of Commander Delić. That is our position. A huge section of the Defence brief is similarly devoted to the duties of a Chief of Staff, which are not denied and they are correctly stated, but it has never been our case that the accused was in Herzegovina within his duties and capacity as Chief of Staff. **[page 43]** The accused went to Herzegovina to command Operation Neretva by the authority of Commander Delić. That is our position.[270]
>
> All the evidence adduced in this case viewed as a whole, the only reasonable inference which can be drawn from this evidence is that the accused was the commander of Operation Neretva and the superior of -- superior of the perpetrators who committed the crimes. And the Prosecution invites the Trial Chamber to so hold.[271]

97. On the basis of the foregoing, the Appeals Chamber finds that no timely, clear and consistent information was provided during the trial proceedings to put the Defence on notice that, even if Halilović was not *de jure* or *de facto* commander of Operation Neretva-93, he allegedly still had effective control over the perpetrators of the crimes charged in the Indictment, on the basis of his position as the most senior ranking ABiH officer in Herzegovina or due to his position as Team Leader of the Inspection Team. Accordingly, the Prosecution cannot argue on appeal that "the Trial Chamber failed to address the additional ways in which Halilović could have exercised effective control".[272]

98. For these reasons, the Appeals Chamber finds that the Prosecution has failed to show that the Trial Chamber "erred in law in failing to make the necessary findings concerning effective control beyond command".[273] The Appeals Chamber considers that the Trial Chamber committed no error of law invalidating its decision in: (1) failing to consider whether Halilović had effective control over the perpetrators of the crimes charged in the Indictment by reason of his position as Team Leader of the Inspection Team or by virtue of his position as the most senior ranking officer in Herzegovina at the time;[274] and in (2) "confining its consideration of effective control to evaluating the evidence of whether Halilović was the military commander over the offending troops".[275] The Trial Chamber has not failed to make the necessary legal findings relating to Halilović's position as the most senior ranking officer in the ABiH and his position as Team Leader of the Inspection Team.

99. This part of sub-ground 1 is therefore dismissed.

5. Whether the Trial Chamber erred in fact in concluding that Halilović was not the superior of the perpetrators of the crimes

100. The Prosecution submits that the Trial Chamber erred in fact in reaching the conclusion that Halilović was not the superior of the perpetrators of the crimes committed in Grabovica. It suggests **[page 44]** that the factual findings

268 Decision of 17 December 2004, para. 15 (footnote omitted).
269 Decision of 17 December 2004, fn. 31.
270 Prosecution's closing argument, T. 20 (30 August 2005).
271 Prosecution's closing argument, T. 35 (30 August 2005).
272 Prosecution Appeal Brief, para. 2.18.
273 Prosecution Appeal Brief, heading (B), p. 13. *See*, in particular, Prosecution Appeal Brief, paras 2.16–2.18 and 2.27.
274 *See* Prosecution Appeal Brief, paras 2.19 and 2.21–2.26. *See* also AT.14.
275 Prosecution Brief in Reply, para. 3.1.

in the Trial Judgement do establish Halilović's material ability to prevent, punish and initiate measures leading to proceedings against the perpetrators.[276] The Prosecution avers that, in light of the totality of those findings, the Trial Chamber's conclusion that Halilović did not have effective control should be reversed as unreasonable.[277]

101. In light of its previous findings on the alleged errors of law, the Appeals Chamber need not address the Prosecution's claim whether the Trial Chamber's misplaced focus on determining whether Halilović was the commander of Operation Neretva caused the Trial Chamber to ignore or underestimate the importance of its findings regarding his material ability to prevent, punish or initiate proceedings against the perpetrators in order to determine whether Halilović had effective control.[278]

102. The analysis of sub-ground 1 has led the Appeals Chamber to conclude that, given that the Prosecution did not plead a "case beyond command" at trial, the Trial Chamber committed no error of law in not considering whether Halilović had effective control over the perpetrators of the crimes charged in the Indictment by reason of his positions as Team Leader of the Inspection Team or as the most senior ranking ABiH officer in Herzegovina beyond his alleged position as commander of Operation Neretva.

103. However, it still falls upon the Appeals Chamber to consider the remainder of the sub-grounds alleged under the Prosecution's first ground of appeal in light of Halilović's alleged position as the *de facto* commander of Operation Neretva. Only by considering the arguments advanced under these sub-grounds as a whole, will the Appeals Chamber be in a position to assess whether the Trial Chamber erred "in finding that the Prosecution had not proven beyond reasonable doubt that Sefer Halilović was the superior of subordinates who committed the crimes in Grabovica, and in entering an acquittal".[279] **[page 45]**

D. Standard of proof (Sub-grounds 5, 2 and 3)

104. Under sub-ground 5, the Prosecution submits that the Trial Chamber erred in law in misapplying the standard of proof throughout the Trial Judgement.[280] Under sub-grounds 2 and 3, the Prosecution raises two specific allegations of errors of law also concerned with the alleged misapplication of the standard of proof.[281] Considering the way in which the arguments of the Prosecution are presented, the Appeals Chamber deems it useful to analyse these sub-grounds in conjunction with each other, starting with the general allegation raised under sub-ground 5 and then applying its conclusions to sub-grounds 2 and 3.

1. Sub-ground 5: Standard of proof beyond reasonable doubt

(a) Introduction

105. In submitting that the Trial Chamber erred in misapplying the standard of proof throughout the Trial Judgement, the Prosecution raises two distinct points: (i) the Trial Chamber's interpretation of the *in dubio pro reo* principle;[282] and (ii) the Trial Chamber's application of the "beyond reasonable doubt" standard to its findings.[283] The Appeals Chamber will first examine Halilović's request for summary dismissal of the Prosecution's arguments under sub-ground 5.

---

276 Prosecution Appeal Brief, para. 2.7. *See* Prosecution Appeal Brief, paras 2.28–2.40 for detailed arguments in support of this allegation.

277 Prosecution Appeal Brief, para. 2.28.

278 Prosecution Appeal Brief, para. 2.28.

279 Prosecution Notice of Appeal, para. 3, concerning the general allegations raised under the first ground of appeal.

280 In its Notice of Appeal, the Prosecution alleges that the Trial Chamber erred in law, at paragraph 433 of the Trial Judgement, in requiring the Prosecution to prove beyond reasonable doubt even those facts, allegations or events that were not an element of the crime or of the mode of liability. It further submits that, although this standard was applied throughout the Trial Judgement, the error was made manifest in paragraphs 189 and 221. *See* Prosecution Notice of Appeal, para. 4(v). *See* also Prosecution Appeal Brief, para. 2.127.

281 Prosecution Appeal Brief, paras 2.41–2.82 (sub-ground 2) and paras 2.83–2.106 (subground 3). *See* also AT. 11.

282 This principle provides that any ambiguity must accrue to the defendant's advantage (*Tadić* 1999 Sentencing Judgement, para. 31). The principle of *in dubio pro reo* is one of the foundational precepts of contemporary criminal law recognised in the jurisprudence of the International Tribunal (*Čelebići* Trial Judgement, para. 601, *Jelisić* Trial Judgement, para. 108 and *Limaj* Appeal Judgement, para. 21. *See* also *Akayesu* Trial Judgment, para. 319).

283 Prosecution Appeal Brief, paras 2.121–2.123.

(b) Halilović's request for summary dismissal

106. Halilović requests that sub-ground 5 be summarily dismissed for various reasons: (i) the vagueness and oppressiveness of the Prosecution's arguments;[284] (ii) the impermissible variation and abandonment of this ground of appeal;[285] (iii) the Prosecution's failure to meet its burden of argument or persuasion;[286] (iv) the fact that this sub-ground of appeal is an attempt to turn appeal proceedings in this matter into a trial *de novo*;[287] and (v) the fact that in the *Ntagerura et al.* Appeal Judgement, the ICTR Appeals Chamber rejected similar arguments.[288] The Appeals Chamber finds **[page 46]** that none of these arguments warrant the summary dismissal of sub-ground 5, and, as a result, denies Halilović's request.

(c) The Trial Chamber's interpretation of the *in dubio pro reo* principle

107. The Prosecution first avers that the Trial Chamber erred in law in stating, at paragraph 12 of the Trial Judgement, that "[a]ny ambiguity or doubt has been resolved in favour of the Accused in accordance with the principle of *in dubio pro reo*",[289] rather than referring to any *reasonable* ambiguity or doubt.[290] Since this error, the Prosecution argues, calls into question *all* of the findings of the Trial Chamber,[291] the Appeals Chamber should re-evaluate all of the evidence at trial applying the correct standard of proof.[292] Halilović responds that, when read in its full context (including footnotes 24 and 25, to which the Prosecution fails to refer), the passage in paragraph 12 of the Trial Judgement clarifies that it is only *reasonable* doubts that will be considered in determining whether the Prosecution has proven its case.[293] Moreover, even if a legal error had been established, the Prosecution identified no instance where this standard was applied by the Trial Chamber. In practice, Halilović argues, in assessing whether he had effective control over the perpetrators of the crimes committed in Grabovica, the Trial Chamber did explicitly – at paragraph 747 of the Trial Judgement – set out the appropriate standard.[294]

108. Paragraph 12 of the Trial Judgement in its entirety reads as follows:

> Article 21(3) of the Statute provides that the Accused shall be presumed innocent until proven guilty. The Prosecution therefore bears the burden of establishing the guilt of the Accused, and, in accordance with Rule 87(A) of the Rules, the Prosecution must do so beyond reasonable doubt. In determining whether the Prosecution has done so with respect to the Count in the Indictment, the Trial Chamber has carefully considered whether there is any reasonable interpretation of the evidence admitted other than the guilt of the Accused Any [sic] ambiguity or doubt has been resolved in favour of the Accused in accordance with the principle of *in dubio pro reo*.[295]

109. When the portion of the Trial Judgement identified by the Prosecution as a basis for its allegation is read in context with the rest of the paragraph as a whole, including the footnote references to the jurisprudence of the International Tribunal and that of the ICTR,[296] it is clear that **[page 47]** the Trial Chamber considered only *reasonable* doubts as relevant in determining whether the Prosecution had proven its case. The reference

284 Halilović Respondent's Brief, paras 185–187 and 190–191.
285 Halilović Respondent's Brief, para. 183.
286 Halilović Respondent's Brief, para. 189.
287 Halilović Respondent's Brief, para. 184.
288 Halilović Respondent's Brief, para. 192.
289 Prosecution Appeal Brief, para. 2.133, quoting Trial Judgement, para. 12 (footnote omitted).
290 Prosecution Notice of Appeal, para. 4(v); Prosecution Appeal Brief, para. 2.122.
291 Prosecution Appeal Brief, paras 2.134–2.135.
292 Prosecution Appeal Brief, para. 2.136.
293 Respondent's Brief, paras 209–210, citing Trial Judgement, para. 12 and fns 24–25.
294 Respondent's Brief, para. 211. *See* also Respondent's Brief, para. 212.
295 Trial Judgement, para. 12 (footnotes omitted).
296 The Appeals Chamber notes the following statement in fn. 24 of the Trial Judgement: "The Trial Chamber interprets the standard 'beyond reasonable doubt' to mean a high degree of probability; it does not mean certainty or proof beyond the shadow of doubt". The Appeals Chamber further notes that the references in fn. 25, related to the last sentence in paragraph 12 of the Trial Judgement, include: *Prosecutor v. Duško Tadić*, Case No. IT-94-1-A, Decision on Appellant's Motion for the Extension of the Time-Limit and Admission of Additional Evidence, 15 October 1998 (filed 16 October 1998), para. 73; *Čelebići* Trial Judgement, para. 601; *Akayesu* Trial Judgement, para. 319.

to "[a]ny ambiguity or doubt" should be read in light of the caveat that "the Trial Chamber has carefully considered whether there is any reasonable interpretation of the evidence admitted other than the guilt of the Accused", which is a way to express the appropriate standard. In light of the foregoing, the Appeals Chamber finds that the Trial Chamber did not err in law at paragraph 12 of the Trial Judgement.

110. The fact that the Trial Chamber properly expressed the standard of proof in the section of the Trial Judgement containing its general considerations on the evaluation of evidence does not in principle prevent the Prosecution from raising this allegation of error of law with regard to specific factual findings. However, since in its submissions under sub-ground 5 the Prosecution does not provide specific reference to factual findings where the Trial Chamber allegedly misapplied the *in dubio pro reo* principle, the Appeals Chamber will address this allegation only insofar as it has been raised with regard to specific factual findings under other sub-grounds of appeal.

(d) The Trial Chamber's application of the "beyond reasonable doubt" standard

111. The second error alleged by the Prosecution under sub-ground 5 relates to the principle, enshrined in Rule 87(A) of the Rules, that guilt must be proven beyond reasonable doubt. According to the Prosecution, in application of this principle, all elements of the crime as well as all requirements for a specific mode of responsibility must be proven beyond reasonable doubt in order for an accused to be convicted.[297] The Prosecution explicitly refers to the *Ntagerura et al.* Appeal Judgement in this respect, which states that the beyond reasonable doubt standard is applicable to all facts "indispensable for entering a conviction".[298] However, the Prosecution submits that the Trial Chamber wrongly applied the standard of proof beyond reasonable doubt to "predicate facts".[299]

112. As a preliminary matter, the Appeals Chamber makes the following terminological observations. A predicate fact is a fact from which a presumption or inference arises, and it is also termed "foundational fact" or "evidentiary fact".[300] However, for the purposes of the present judgement and in light of the Prosecution's submissions,[301] the Appeals Chamber understands the expression "predicate facts" to encompass those factual allegations that are not essential to prove the elements of the crime or the mode of responsibility alleged. **[page 48]**

113. The Prosecution asserts that the beyond reasonable doubt standard does not apply to "predicate facts".[302] Moreover, "individual [facts] or factual allegations" contained in an indictment are subject to this standard only if they are essential to proving an element of the offence or mode of liability.[303] Consequently, it claims that the Trial Chamber erred in requiring the Prosecution to prove each factual allegation of the Indictment beyond reasonable doubt.[304] In doing so, the Trial Chamber in effect allegedly "created a two-stage application of the beyond reasonable doubt standard – applying it first to the evidence or proof of facts and then again to the ultimate issue of guilt".[305] Such a misapplication of the required standard, the Prosecution argues, permeates the whole Trial Judgement, thus affecting each disputed fact.[306]

114. According to the Prosecution, this error had an important impact on the Trial Chamber's assessment of the evidence. In the introduction to the first ground of appeal, the Prosecution submits that "[t]he requirement that the Prosecution prove *intermediate* facts 'beyond reasonable doubt', for example, led to the Trial Chamber's conclusion that the Prosecution had not proven the existence of an IKM and an operation called 'Neretva'".[307] The Prosecution further submits that "[t]he name of the operation, the exact meeting at which

---

297 Prosecution Appeal Brief, paras 2.124 and 2.126.

298 AT. 10–11.

299 Prosecution Appeal Brief, para. 2.121. *See* also Prosecution Notice of Appeal, para. 4(v) and AT. 11.

300 Black's Law Dictionary, 7th Edition (St. Paul, West Group, 1999).

301 Prosecution Notice of Appeal, para. 4(v); Prosecution Appeal Brief, para. 2.121, and heading (A), p. 46 and paras 2.124–2.125; Prosecution Reply Brief, heading (A), p. 18 and para. 3.26.

302 Prosecution Appeal Brief, heading (A) p. 46; Prosecution Reply Brief, heading (A), p. 18.

303 Prosecution Appeal Brief, para. 2.125. The quote actually reads: "individual factual or factual allegations".

304 Prosecution Appeal Brief, para. 2.127.

305 Prosecution Appeal Brief, para. 2.132.

306 Prosecution Appeal Brief, para. 2.127.

307 Prosecution Appeal Brief, para. 2.5 (emphasis added). The Appeals Chamber notes that this is the only instance where the Prosecution uses the expression "intermediate facts", without explicitly explaining what it means. Considering the context of the

it was planned, and the establishment of an IKM are merely factual allegations, not elements of the crimes charged",[308] thus appearing to suggest that they amount to "predicate facts". By subjecting these "predicate facts" to the beyond reasonable doubt standard, the Trial Chamber concluded that they had not been proven. Therefore, during its final analysis on Halilović's criminal responsibility, the Trial Chamber referred to its conclusions about these "predicate facts" and effectively excluded relevant evidence that should have been considered in its final analysis.[309] Instead, the Prosecution concludes, the Trial Chamber should have weighed the evidence *as a whole* to determine whether Halilović's superior responsibility had been proven beyond reasonable doubt.[310]

115. The Prosecution cites two specific paragraphs of the Trial Judgement where mere factual allegations are allegedly treated by the Trial Chamber as elements of the crimes charged and, as **[page 49]** such, requiring proof beyond reasonable doubt.[311] Paragraph 189 reads, in its relevant part, as follows:

> ... the Prosecution has not established beyond reasonable doubt that an "Operation Neretva" or the question who would be the commander of such an operation was discussed at the meeting in Zenica, nor that any specific and detailed operation to liberate Mostar was planned at that meeting.

Paragraph 221 reads, in its relevant part, as follows:

> ...the Prosecution has failed to prove beyond reasonable doubt that an IKM was established for the purpose of commanding an "Operation Neretva".

116. Halilović responds that the alleged error has not been properly argued or established,[312] since the Prosecution identified only three factual matters to which the beyond reasonable doubt standard was allegedly misapplied, but did not establish the significance of this alleged error in respect of all predicate facts, allegations or events.[313] Moreover, Halilović argues that the Trial Chamber correctly applied the "beyond reasonable doubt" standard in paragraphs 189 and 221 of the Trial Judgement, because these were all material facts pleaded in the Indictment as relevant and central to establishing Halilović's responsibility.[314] He adds that the findings at paragraphs 189 and 221 of the Trial Judgement, even if reversed, would not compel a finding of effective control by Halilović over the perpetrators of the crimes committed in Grabovica.[315]

117. The Prosecution appears to raise two distinct issues under the same heading.[316] First, it suggests that there is no legal authority to support the proposition that "individual pieces of evidence should be subjected to the beyond reasonable doubt standard".[317] This matter pertains to the evaluation of single items of evidence tendered and introduced into the trial record during the proceedings. Second, the Prosecution contends that "[t]he Trial Chamber erred by requiring the Prosecution to prove each factual allegation of the [I]ndictment beyond reasonable doubt, whether or not that factual allegation was necessary for conviction".[318] This matter relates to the way in which specific allegations are to be proven and will partly hinge on whether an allegation is supported by an individual piece of evidence or must be proven through the combined assessment of various pieces of evidence. The Appeals Chamber will deal with these two allegations in turn. **[page 50]**

Prosecution's submissions, the Appeals Chamber infers that the expressions "intermediate facts" and "predicate facts" are essentially equivalent.

308 Prosecution Appeal Brief, para. 2.129.

309 *See* Prosecution Appeal Brief, paras 2.129–2.131.

310 Prosecution Appeal Brief, paras 2.129 and 2.132; AT. 10–11.

311 Prosecution Appeal Brief, paras 2.127–2.129. At the Appeal Hearing, the Prosecution also suggested that sub-grounds 2 and 3 serve as examples of this erroneous approach (AT. 11). The Appeals Chamber will consider this issue *infra* in its discussion of those sub-grounds of appeal.

312 Respondent's Brief, paras 193–194.

313 *See* Respondent's Brief, paras 194, 196–200 and 204.

314 Respondent's Brief, paras 201–202 and 208.

315 Respondent's Brief, para. 205.

316 Prosecution Appeal Brief, heading (A), entitled: "The 'beyond reasonable doubt' standard does not apply to predicate facts'", p. 46.

317 Prosecution Appeal Brief, para. 2.126; *see* para. 2.132, which also appears to relate to this argument.

318 Prosecution Appeal Brief, para. 2.127. The following paragraphs (2.128–2.131) appear to relate to this argument.

(i) Whether the Trial Chamber properly evaluated individual pieces of evidence

118. The Prosecution submits that the Trial Chamber erred in suggesting in paragraph 15 of the Trial Judgement that "individual pieces of evidence should be subjected to the beyond reasonable doubt standard".[319] The relevant portion of paragraph 15 reads as follows:

> In some instances, the Trial Chamber has relied upon circumstantial evidence in order to determine whether or not a certain conclusion could be drawn. The Trial Chamber follows the Appeals Chamber when considering that "[s]uch a conclusion must be established beyond reasonable doubt. [...] It must be the *only* reasonable conclusion available. If there is another conclusion which is also reasonably open from that evidence, and which is [as] consistent with the [innocence of an accused as with his or her guilt], he or she must be acquitted."[320]

119. In the view of the Appeals Chamber, the concerns of the Prosecution in respect to this statement are misplaced. The paragraph in question has to be read as a whole. The sentences preceding the portion relied upon by the Prosecution concern the probative value of evidence and its reliability.[321] In light of this context, the Appeals Chamber understands the portion of paragraph 15 of the Trial Judgement quoted above as a statement made pursuant to the Appeals Chamber's holdings in *Čelebići*. The effect of this is that the Trial Chamber's overall conclusions, drawn from circumstantial evidence pointing to the guilt of the accused, must be drawn beyond reasonable doubt.[322] Further, the Appeals Chamber notes that, in accordance with the principle that the assessment of the credibility of relevant evidence cannot be undertaken by a piecemeal approach, individual items have to be analysed in light of the entire body of evidence.[323] The Trial Chamber stated that it had "carefully considered the charges against [Halilović] in light of the entire record, including all evidence put forth by the Prosecution and the Defence".[324] Another related matter raised under this sub-ground is the contention that the Trial Chamber excluded relevant evidence in reaching its final conclusions.[325]

120. The Appeals Chamber understands this last contention to suggest that the Trial Chamber, by applying the "beyond reasonable doubt" standard twice, to each piece of evidence and then again to **[page 51]** the ultimate issue of guilt, effectively dismissed relevant evidence that could have been relied upon to find Halilović commander of the operation in question. The Appeals Chamber recalls that a party alleging an error of law must identify the alleged error, present arguments in support of its claim and explain how the error invalidates the decision.[326] Where an error of law is found, it is open to the Appeals Chamber to review the relevant findings of the Trial Chamber according to the correct legal standard.[327] In cases like the instant one, however, where it is submitted that an error of law potentially impacts every single piece of evidence and, by implication, every finding made by the Trial Chamber, the appellate party is required to develop its arguments more precisely by referring to specific portions of the Trial Judgement, thus limiting the import of its allegations – lest the appeal procedure effectively becomes a trial *de novo*.[328] The Prosecution has failed

319 Prosecution Appeal Brief, para. 2.126.

320 Trial Judgement, para. 15 (footnote, referring to *Čelebići* Appeal Judgement, para. 458, omitted).

321 "In addition to direct evidence, the Trial Chamber has admitted hearsay and circumstantial evidence. Hearsay evidence is evidence of facts not within the testifying witness' own knowledge. In evaluating the probative value of hearsay evidence, the Trial Chamber has carefully considered indicia of its reliability and, for this purpose, it has evaluated whether the statement was 'voluntary, truthful and trustworthy' and has considered the content of the evidence and the circumstances under which it arose."(Trial Judgement, para. 15 (footnotes omitted)).

322 Footnote 30 in paragraph 15 of the Trial Judgement is a citation to *Čelebići* Appeal Judgement, para. 458: "A circumstantial case consists of evidence of a number of different circumstances which, taken in combination, point to the guilt of the accused person because they would usually exist in combination only because the accused did what is alleged against him – here that he participated in the second beating of Gotovac. Such a conclusion must be established beyond reasonable doubt". This finding was reached by the Appeals Chamber when dealing with the issue of the reliability of circumstantial evidence. *See*, generally, *Čelebići* Appeal Judgement, paras 450–457.

323 *Ntagerura et al.* Appeal Judgement, para. 174.

324 Trial Judgement, para. 14.

325 Prosecution Appeal Brief, paras 2.131–2.132.

326 *See supra*, paras 7 and 12–13.

327 *Blaškić* Appeal Judgement, para. 15.

328 *See supra*, para. 10.

to properly fulfill this requirement. Therefore, the Appeals Chamber dismisses the allegation that the Trial Chamber excluded probative evidence or subjected it to an inappropriate standard.

121. The contention by the Prosecution that the Trial Chamber excluded, and effectively dismissed, relevant evidence – in light of other arguments elsewhere by the Prosecution that the Trial Chamber *ignored* certain exhibits[329] – might also be interpreted as suggesting that, since the Trial Chamber dismissed the Prosecution's contentions on the Zenica meeting and on the IKM, it disregarded evidence relating to those issues when making its final determination on Halilović's guilt. It is a settled principle in the jurisprudence of the International Tribunal that a Trial Chamber need not refer to the testimony of every witness or every piece of evidence on the trial record. There is a presumption that a Trial Chamber has evaluated all the evidence presented to it, as long as there is no indication that the Trial Chamber completely disregarded any particular piece of evidence.[330]

122. The Appeals Chamber notes that the Trial Chamber explicitly stated, in paragraph 747 of the Trial Judgement that:

> [*h*]*aving examined all the evidence presented to it and in light of its factual findings,* the Trial Chamber finds that the Prosecution has not proven beyond reasonable doubt that Sefer Halilović had effective control over the troops that were in Grabovica on 8 and 9 September 1993, which the Trial Chamber has found committed the crimes.[331]

123. Such a statement does not, of course, establish an irrebuttable presumption that all of the evidence was indeed considered by the Trial Chamber.[332] It would have been preferable if the Trial Chamber had systematically analyzed and explicitly assessed the evidence in order to reach its **[page 52]** factual findings. The Prosecution, however, generally has not identified specific pieces of evidence that would have been wrongly evaluated by the Trial Chamber.

124. As the Prosecution points out, Exhibit 498 was not mentioned at all in the Trial Judgement.[333] Having carefully analysed the relevant portions of the Trial Judgement, the Appeals Chamber considers that the fact that this exhibit was not referred to by the Trial Chamber might be an indication that it disregarded relevant evidence.[334] This document is a letter written in 1995 by Halilović himself to BiH President Alija Izetbegović, where Halilović declared, among other things, that the Inspection Team headed by him carried out "Operation Neretva 93", thereby corroborating exhibits and testimonies that the Trial Chamber considered unreliable[335] and contradicting the final conclusions reached in the Trial Judgement.[336] The Appeals Chamber is however mindful that the Trial Chamber might legitimately have looked with extreme caution at a document written many months after the events by an accused who chose not to testify. It cannot be said that, even considering this piece of evidence, no reasonable trier of fact could have reached the conclusions that the Trial Chamber reached. In light of these considerations, and since the Prosecution has generally not identified specifically where the Trial Chamber might have erred, the Appeals Chamber will not entertain this contention further.

125. With respect to the process through which a trier of fact evaluates the evidence, the Appeals Chamber endorses the following considerations of the ICTR Appeals Chamber:

> - At the first stage, the Trial Chamber has to assess the credibility of the relevant evidence presented. This cannot be undertaken by a piecemeal approach. Individual items of the evidence, such as the testimony of different witnesses, or documents admitted into evidence, have to be analysed in the light of the entire

329 Prosecution Appeal Brief, para. 2.74.
330 *Kvoèka et al.* Appeal Judgement, para. 23.
331 Trial Judgement, para. 747 (emphasis added).
332 *Kvočka et al.* Appeal Judgement, para. 23.
333 Prosecution Appeal Brief, para. 2.1.
334 *Kvočka et al.* Appeal Judgement, para. 23.
335 *See*, for example: Bakir Alispahić, T. 62 (23 May 2005) and T. 33 (27 May 2005); Vahid Karavelić, T. 107 (19 April 2005) (cited in Trial Judgement, para. 183); Salko Gušić, T. 43 (7 February 2005) (cited in Trial Judgement, para. 191); Ramiz Delalić, T. 25 (18 May 2005) (cited in Trial Judgement, para. 219); Exhibit 131 (a map erroneously cited in Trial Judgement, para. 175, as the only exhibit mentioning "Operation Neretva"); Exhibit 281, p. 2 (the book "A Cunning Strategy" by Sefer Halilović cited, *inter alia*, in Trial Judgement, para. 258).
336 Trial Judgement, paras 189, 210 and 737.

body of evidence adduced. Thus, even if there are some doubts as to the reliability of the testimony of a certain witness, that testimony may be corroborated by other pieces of evidence leading the Trial Chamber to conclude that the witness is credible. Or, on the other hand, a seemingly convincing testimony may be called into question by other evidence which shows that evidence to lack credibility.

- Only after the analysis of all the relevant evidence, can the Trial Chamber determine whether the evidence upon which the Prosecution relies should be accepted as establishing the existence of the facts alleged, notwithstanding the evidence upon which the Defence relies. At this fact-finding stage, the standard of proof beyond a reasonable doubt is applied to establish the facts forming the elements of the crime or the form of responsibility alleged against the accused, as well as with respect to the facts which are indispensable for entering a conviction. **[page 53]**
- At the final stage, the Trial Chamber has to decide whether all of the constitutive elements of the crime and the form of responsibility alleged against the accused have been proven. Even if some of the material facts pleaded in the indictment are not established beyond reasonable doubt, a Chamber might enter a conviction provided that having applied the law to those material facts it accepted beyond reasonable doubt, all the elements of the crime charged and of the mode of responsibility are established by those facts.[337]

The ICTR Appeals Chamber also clarified that "'material facts' which have to be pleaded in the indictment to provide the accused with the information necessary to prepare his defence have to be distinguished from the facts which have to be proved beyond reasonable doubt".[338] Following this principle, the Appeals Chamber has acknowledged that not every factual finding in a Trial Judgement must be established beyond reasonable doubt and has unequivocally stated that "[t]he standard of proof at trial requires that a Trial Chamber may only find an accused guilty of a crime if the Prosecution has proved each element of that crime and of the mode of liability, *and any fact which is indispensable for the conviction*, beyond reasonable doubt".[339] With these considerations in mind, the Appeals Chamber turns to address the second part of the argument raised by the Prosecution under the heading "standard of proof".

(ii) Whether the Trial Chamber misapplied the standard of proof to its factual findings

126. With respect to the allegation that the Trial Chamber erred in requiring the Prosecution to prove each factual allegation in the Indictment beyond reasonable doubt regardless of whether this fact was necessary for conviction, the Appeals Chamber notes that the Prosecution only identified two paragraphs (189 and 221) in the Trial Judgement where the Trial Chamber allegedly committed such an error.[340] Apart from these examples, the Appeals Chamber was not provided with specific references to factual findings affected by the alleged error. Given that the alleged error of law potentially impacts on every finding made by the Trial Chamber, the Prosecution was required to develop its arguments more precisely by referring to specific paragraphs of the Trial Judgement. Indeed, the appealing party must explain how the alleged error invalidates the decision in practice; it is not enough to point to a general deficiency throughout the Trial Judgement and request review of unspecified factual findings.[341] The Appeals Chamber also notes that the paragraphs mentioned contain a total of four factual findings. In particular, paragraph 189 contains the finding that the Prosecution had not proven beyond reasonable doubt that, at the Zenica meeting, its participants: (i) discussed "Operation Neretva", (ii) discussed who would be commander of such an operation, and (iii) planned a specific and detailed operation to liberate Mostar. Paragraph 221 contains the finding **[page 54]** that the Prosecution had not proven beyond reasonable doubt that (iv) an IKM was established for the purpose of commanding an "Operation Neretva".[342]

337 *Ntagerura et al.* Appeal Judgement, para. 174 (footnote omitted).
338 *Ntagerura et al.* Appeal Judgement, fn. 356.
339 *Blagojević and Jokić* Appeal Judgement, para. 226 (emphasis added). *See* also *Ntagerura et al.* Appeal Judgement, para. 174; *Prosecutor v. Radoslav Brđanin*, Case No. IT-99-36-A, Order to File Table, 24 July 2006 ("*Brđanin* Order to File Table"), p. 1. For an application of this principle, *see Kupreškić et al.* Appeal Judgement, para. 226.
340 Prosecution Appeal Brief, paras 2.127–2.131.
341 *See supra*, para. 7; *see* also *supra*, para. 120.
342 For the relevant text of the two paragraphs in question, *see supra*, para. 115.

127. Sub-ground 5, as part of the first ground of the Prosecution's appeal, relates to Halilović's superior position over the soldiers who committed the crimes in Grabovica. Indeed, the Prosecution submits that the Trial Chamber's improper application of the standard of proof resulted in the erroneous conclusion – at paragraphs 372, 747 and 752 of the Trial Judgement – that Halilović did not have effective control over the subordinates in question.[343] The Prosecution alleges that by requiring it to prove "predicate facts" – paragraphs 189 and 221 of the Trial Judgement being highlighted as findings based on such facts – beyond reasonable doubt, the Trial Chamber removed these facts from the Trial Chamber's ultimate findings.[344] This legal error allegedly affected the Trial Chamber's ultimate findings on whether Halilović's superior responsibility had been established.[345]

128. The Appeals Chamber finds that it is not strictly relevant whether the Prosecution considers the factual allegations in question "central" to establishing responsibility or whether they are pleaded in a specific section of the Indictment.[346] The task of a trier of fact is that of assessing all the relevant evidence presented with a holistic approach; this is all the more necessary in cases as complex as the ones before the International Tribunal. According to the Statute and the Rules, a trier of fact should render a reasoned opinion on the basis of the entire body of evidence and without applying the standard of proof "beyond reasonable doubt" with a piecemeal approach.

129. The four findings in paragraphs 189 and 221 of the Trial Judgement were reached "beyond reasonable doubt", as the Trial Chamber evidently considered them material to reaching a conclusion on Halilović's form of responsibility.[347] As the Prosecution itself acknowledges,[348] a trier of fact is called upon to make findings beyond reasonable doubt based on all of the evidence on the trial record – direct or circumstantial – not only on facts which are essential to proving the elements of the crimes and the forms of responsibility. There might be other facts that need to be proven beyond reasonable doubt due to the way in which the case was pleaded in the indictment and presented during trial to the Defence and to the Trial Chamber. All facts underlying the **[page 55]** elements of the crime or the form of responsibility alleged as well as all those, which are indispensable for entering a conviction, must be proven beyond reasonable doubt.[349]

130. In *Vasiljević*, for example, the Appeals Chamber addressed very clearly the issue that a specific factual finding may or may not be necessary to reach a conclusion beyond reasonable doubt as to the element of a crime, depending on the specific circumstances of the case and on the way the case was pleaded.[350]

131. In the present case, the Prosecution specifically claims under this part of sub-ground 5 that the Trial Chamber erred in requiring the Prosecution to prove *each* factual allegation in the Indictment beyond

343 Prosecution Notice of Appeal, para. 4(v).

344 *See supra,* para. 114.

345 *See* Prosecution Appeal Brief, paras 2.129–2.130.

346 Respondent's Brief, paras 201 and 208.

347 It is, of course, irrelevant whether the Prosecution itself at trial considered these findings to have been proven beyond reasonable doubt. *See* Respondent's Brief, para. 197.

348 AT. 11.

349 *Ntagerura et al.* Appeal Judgement, para. 174; *Blagojević and Jokić* Appeal Judgement, para. 226.

350 The *Vasiljević* Trial Chamber had found that Mitar Vasiljević had forcibly transported seven Muslim men to the eastern bank of the Drina River, where they were shot. Despite not being satisfied that Vasiljević had personally killed any of the victims, the Trial Chamber considered other factual findings (reached beyond reasonable doubt) and concluded that Vasiljević indeed shared the intent to kill them (*Vasiljević* Trial Judgement, paras 112, 113 and 208). It convicted him for persecution pursuant to Article 5(h) of the Statute and for murder pursuant to Article 3 of the Statute (*Vasiljević* Appeal Judgement, paras 2 and 88). The Appeals Chamber subsequently reversed one of the findings underpinning Vasiljević's conviction, namely that "he had knowledge that the seven Muslim men were to be killed and not exchanged based on the information provided to him" (*Vasiljević* Appeal Judgement, para. 124). The Appeals Chamber then concluded that, since the Trial Chamber had found that Vasiljević knew that the seven men would be killed when he escorted them to the bank of the Drina River and stood behind them shortly before the shooting occurred, it had been able to establish his *mens rea* beyond reasonable doubt, despite the fact that he had not fired his weapon. However, after the Appeals Chamber overturned the finding that Vasiljević knew that the men were to be killed at the time he accompanied the group, the remaining factual findings did not suffice to reach the conclusion, as the only reasonable inference available on the evidence, that he had the intent to kill the seven Muslim men (*Vasiljević* Appeal Judgement, para. 131). In the circumstances of that case, that finding was necessary to reach a conclusion beyond reasonable doubt as to one element of the crime. Nonetheless, this was not strictly a finding on an element of the crime *in abstracto*; it had become indispensable for entering a conviction due to the way the case had developed on the basis of the pleadings and of the evidence presented.

reasonable doubt and that this error "permeates the [Trial] Judgement".[351] However, as explained above, the Appeals Chamber has only considered the Prosecution's challenges relating to paragraphs 189 and 221.[352] The Prosecution has not shown how the alleged misapplication of the standard of proof in paragraphs 189 and 132 of the Trial Judgement could impact the ultimate finding it is attempting to challenge, namely Halilović's effective control over the perpetrators.[353] This allegation is accordingly dismissed.

132 However, since the four factual findings contained in paragraphs 189 and 221 of the Trial Judgement are strictly related to sub-grounds 2 and 3, the Appeals Chamber will bear them in mind when dealing with these two other sub-grounds. This is so because, while the Prosecution itself recognizes that sub-grounds 2 and 3 are exemplary of the overall error alleged in sub-ground 5,[354] **[page 56]** the Appeals Chamber considers paragraphs 189 and 221 of the Trial Judgement as containing the only factual findings being properly appealed by the Prosecution under sub-ground 5.

133. For the foregoing reasons, sub-ground 5 is dismissed. **[page 57]**

2. Sub-Ground 2: The name of the operation

(a) Introduction

134. The Prosecution submits that the Trial Chamber erred in law at paragraph 175 of the Trial Judgement in requiring the Prosecution to prove not only the existence of combat operations in Herzegovina to lift the HVO blockade of Mostar, but also that the name of these operations was "Operation Neretva" as a prerequisite to find that Halilović had effective control over the troops who committed the crimes in Grabovica.[355] The Prosecution claims further that the Trial Chamber erred in fact in finding that the Prosecution had failed to prove that the operation in question was called "Operation Neretva".[356]

(b) Halilović's request for summary dismissal

135. Halilović requests that this sub-ground of appeal be summarily dismissed on the basis that (i) the Prosecution impermissibly varied this sub-ground of appeal; (ii) it failed to meet the requisite standard of review; (iii) it failed to meet the burden of argument or persuasion; and (iv) it failed to raise this argument at trial.[357] The Appeals Chamber finds that none of these arguments warrants the summary dismissal of this sub-ground of appeal, and thus denies Halilović's request.

(c) Whether the Trial Chamber erred in law by requiring proof beyond reasonable doubt of the name of the combat operations

136. The Prosecution claims that the Trial Chamber erred when requiring proof beyond reasonable doubt of the formal denomination of the military operation in question,[358] arguing that "the law on superior responsibility does not require the identification of the specific/official/formal name of the military operation during which crimes were committed".[359] Echoing its arguments under sub-ground 5 that not all facts in the Indictment need to be proven, the Prosecution further argues that the Trial Chamber erroneously considered that the name of

---

351 Prosecution Appeal Brief, para. 2.127.
352 *See*, *inter alia*, Prosecution Reply Brief, para. 2.19.
353 In fact, as part of its arguments concerning paragraphs 189 and 221 of the Trial Judgement, the Prosecution mainly limits itself to claiming that the Trial Chamber should have assessed the evidence relating to the name of the operation, the exact meeting at which it was planned, and the establishment of an IKM "together, along with the rest of the evidence adduced at trial, to determine whether the elements of the crimes were established beyond reasonable doubt" (Prosecution Appeal Brief, para. 2.129).
354 AT. 11.
355 Prosecution Notice of Appeal, para. 4(ii); Prosecution Appeal Brief, paras 2.41–2.42; AT. 10 and 137–138.
356 Prosecution Notice of Appeal, para. 4(ii).
357 Respondent's Brief, paras 110–115.
358 Prosecution Appeal Brief, paras 2.43 and 2.51. *See* also Prosecution Reply Brief, para. 3.14; AT. 10–11.
359 Prosecution Appeal Brief, para. 2.44. *See* also AT. 137–138.

the operation had to be established,[360] while only the operation's existence (as opposed to its denomination) might have an impact on the findings in relation to a superior-subordinate relationship.[361] It avers that the Trial **[page 58]** Chamber adopted an overly formalistic approach in appraising the evidence, implicitly requiring a *de jure* structure and erroneously excluding a *de facto* superior-subordinate relationship.[362]

137. Halilović responds that no error of law has been established by the Prosecution as the Trial Chamber did not require the Prosecution to prove the name of the operation as a pre-condition to establishing superior responsibility.[363] Moreover, he avers, even if the Trial Chamber had erred in requiring the Prosecution to prove the name of the operation, such an error could never invalidate the judgement as this was a "mere preliminary and peripheral matter".[364] At the Appeal Hearing, Halilović further suggested that the Trial Chamber, considering the military setting of the events and the chain of command described in the Indictment, adopted the right approach in assuming that proof of a formalized military structure within Operation Neretva-93 would have been pivotal for the Prosecution case. In this context, the name of the operation itself was an indispensable fact for the Trial Chamber when assessing whether Halilović's responsibility was proven.[365] He claimed that, having failed to prove at trial that Operation Neretva-93 was ever mounted by the ABiH, the Prosecution may not suggest an error of law to overcome its failure to provide evidence supporting its allegations.[366]

138. While clearly the formal denomination of a combat operation is not an express criterion under Article 7(3) of the Statute, if such a fact was pleaded in support of the allegation that one of the requirements for establishing superior responsibility was met, then the Trial Chamber is expected to make a finding on whether such a fact was proven.[367] In this respect, the Appeals Chamber recalls that "the Prosecution must always prove the existence of the facts charged as well as the accused's responsibility therefor".[368] In the present case, the Prosecution alleged in the Indictment that Halilović commanded a military Operation called "NERETVA-93" as a basis for its claim that a superior-subordinate relationship existed.[369] In order to address the Prosecution's allegation and to assess Halilović's role, the Trial Chamber was expected to make findings on the specificity of the pleaded military operation allegedly under Halilović's command. The Appeals Chamber therefore finds that the Trial Chamber did not err when considering the alleged name of the combat operation as one of the elements of the Prosecution's case.[370] **[page 59]**

139. The Trial Chamber detailed the elements of command responsibility to be taken into account when assessing the liability of a superior.[371] In particular, when outlining the elements necessary to establish a superior-subordinate relationship,[372] the Trial Chamber gave examples of factors it considered indicative of an accused's position of authority and effective control. These factors were: the official position held by the accused, his capacity to issue orders, the procedure for appointment, the position of the accused within the military or political structure and the actual tasks that he performed.[373] Nothing in this portion of the Trial Judgement indicates that the Trial Chamber required proof of a formal denomination of the military operation to establish a superior-subordinate relationship. In light of the examination of the relevant findings of the Trial Chamber, the Appeals Chamber finds that the Prosecution failed to substantiate how the Trial Chamber's

360 Prosecution Appeal Brief, para. 2.53.
361 Prosecution Appeal Brief, paras 2.45–2.46; Prosecution Reply Brief, para. 3.8. *See* also Prosecution Appeal Brief, paras 2.54–2.58.
362 Prosecution Appeal Brief, para. 2.47. *See* also Prosecution Appeal Brief, paras 2.48–2.50.
363 Respondent's Brief, para. 116, citing Trial Judgement, paras 174 and 737–739; AT. 114–115.
364 Respondent's Brief, para. 125.
365 AT. 112–115.
366 AT. 113–116.
367 *See* also *supra*, para. 69.
368 *Kayishema and Ruzindana* Appeal Judgement, para. 113. *See* also *Rutaganda* Appeal Judgement, para. 172.
369 Indictment, paras 3–4.
370 Indictment, paras 3–4. *See* also Prosecution Pre-Trial Brief, para. 4, where the Prosecution reiterated that the "Accused had effective control over both these units by virtue of being the commander of an operation called 'Neretva-93'". In the Prosecution Final Trial Brief, paras 142 and following, the Prosecution argued in detail the specifics of Operation Neretva, including its name (*see, inter alia*, Prosecution Final Trial Brief, para. 145: "Alispahić later learned that the Operation was code-named Neretva and that Halilović was to command the Operation.").
371 Trial Judgement, paras 55–100.
372 Trial Judgement, paras 57–63.
373 Trial Judgement, para. 58.

conclusion that it was "not convinced that these combat operations *were called* 'Operation Neretva'",[374] or any other finding relied upon,[375] showed that the Trial Chamber required the Prosecution to prove the name of the operation as an element necessary for establishing the existence of a superior-subordinate relationship between Halilović and the offending troops.

140. More specifically, when considering Halilović's role in the context of the military operations carried out in Herzegovina, the Trial Chamber made findings with regard to the existence of a military operation, which – according to the Prosecution – was called "NERETVA-93".[376] This is the first finding in the Trial Chamber's analysis of this military operation and Halilović's role therein.[377] The Trial Chamber concluded this analysis by finding that "the Prosecution has failed to prove beyond reasonable doubt that Sefer Halilović was either *de jure* or *de facto* commander of the alleged operation called 'Operation Neretva' which the Prosecution submit[s] was carried out in Herzegovina in September 1993".[378] Contrary to the Prosecution's arguments,[379] this finding does not demonstrate that the name of the operation was a requirement for the establishment of a superior-subordinate relationship between Halilović and the offending troops. Rather, this finding was aimed at assessing Halilović's responsibility within the context of his alleged command of one specific operation as charged in the Indictment. **[page 60]**

141. The Prosecution does concede that the "*existence* of a military operation may have an impact on the findings in relation to the superior-subordinate relationship".[380] When assessing Halilović's position as commander of the military operation Neretva-93, the Trial Chamber specifically focused on the *existence* of a military operation relevant in the context of the Indictment. Indeed, the Trial Chamber stated that it had been "presented with evidence that there were combat operations in Herzegovina to lift the HVO blockade of Mostar at the time relevant to the Indictment", and, although it was "not convinced that these combat operations were called 'Operation Neretva'", it chose to "use the term 'Operation Neretva' to refer to the combat operations which took place in Herzegovina at the relevant time".[381] The Trial Chamber further found that "combat operations were carried out by units, which included the 9th Brigade, the 10th Brigade, the 2nd Independent Battalion and the Prozor Independent Battalion, in the areas around Grabovica and Uzdol in September 1993".[382]

142. These findings do not show that the Trial Chamber gave undue weight to the formal denomination of such an operation. In fact, the Trial Chamber continued its analysis of Halilović's alleged position as commander, irrespective of its finding that the name "Operation Neretva" had not been established.[383] Considering that the establishment of the formal denomination of the operation was not essential to the Trial Chamber's findings concerning Halilović's position in that operation, it is therefore moot to consider the Prosecution's further claim that by requiring the Prosecution to prove the formal name, the Trial Chamber implicitly required a *de jure* structure and wrongly excluded a *de facto* superior-subordinate relationship.[384] In any event, the Prosecution failed to substantiate on appeal any argument that would allow the Appeals Chamber to conclude that the mere existence of a military operation "together with the entirety of the evidence presented at trial, would have [lead to the conclusion] that Halilović was at least the *de facto* superior of those who committed the crime in Grabovica during this military operation".[385]

143. In light of the foregoing, the Appeals Chamber dismisses the allegation that the Trial Chamber erroneously required the Prosecution to prove that the combat operations carried out in Herzegovina in September 1993 to lift the HVO blockade of Mostar were called "Operation Neretva" as a necessary precondition for a finding of effective control and, therefore, for Halilović's conviction. **[page 61]**

---

374 Prosecution Appeal Brief, para. 2.41, citing Trial Judgement, para. 175 (emphasis added by the Prosecution).
375 The Prosecution refers in particular to Trial Judgement, paras 372, 737 and 752 (Prosecution Appeal Brief, para. 2.41).
376 Trial Judgement, paras 174–175, quoting Indictment, para. 3.
377 Trial Judgement, paras 174–372 (Section IV.C., entitled "Operation Neretva").
378 Trial Judgement, para. 372.
379 *See* Prosecution Notice of Appeal, para. 4(ii). *See* also Prosecution Appeal Brief, paras 2.41–2.42.
380 Prosecution Appeal Brief, para. 2.46.
381 Trial Judgement, para. 175.
382 Trial Judgement, para. 737.
383 *See*, in particular, Trial Judgement, paras 363–372.
384 Prosecution Appeal Brief, para. 2.47. *See* also Prosecution Appeal Brief, paras 2.48–2.50.
385 Prosecution Appeal Brief, para. 2.52.

(d) Whether the Trial Chamber erred in fact in finding that the Prosecution did not prove that the operation was called "Operation Neretva"

144. The Appeals Chamber has found that the Trial Chamber did not require the establishment of the formal denomination of the military operation carried out in Herzegovina when assessing Halilović's alleged position as the *de jure* or *de facto* commander of this operation.[386] Moreover, it is not established that the Trial Chamber relied on the name of this operation in its final conclusion that Halilović was not responsible under Article 7(3) of the Statute for the crimes committed in Grabovica.[387] Therefore, notwithstanding the vast amount of evidence on the trial record suggesting that an "Operation Neretva" (or "Neretva-93") did indeed exist,[388] the Appeals Chamber finds it moot to consider whether the Trial Chamber erred in fact when concluding that it was not convinced that the name of the military operation in question was "Neretva". Such an error, even if proven, could not eliminate "all reasonable doubt of the accused's guilt".[389]

145. In light of this finding, the Appeals Chamber does not need to address the Prosecution's allegations – under sub-ground 5 of its appeal in relation to the finding of fact in paragraph 189 of the Trial Judgement[390] – that the Trial Chamber erred in requiring proof "beyond reasonable doubt" to establish that, at the Zenica meeting, the participants discussed an "Operation Neretva" as well as who would be the commander of such an operation, or that they planned a specific and detailed operation to liberate Mostar.[391] Due to their nature, these factual findings would only assist in establishing the formal denomination of the operation, the formal appointment of Halilović (or of somebody else) as a commander, or some aspects of the planning of a military operation. In other words, they would not by themselves be able to overturn the Trial Chamber's conclusion regarding Halilović's effective control as a commander over the perpetrators of the Grabovica murders.

146. For the foregoing reasons, sub-ground 2 is dismissed. **[page 62]**

3. Sub-Ground 3: The IKM

(a) Introduction

147. Paragraph 221 of the Trial Judgement reads as follows:

> The Trial Chamber finds that the Inspection Team was based in Jablanica. However, the Trial Chamber also finds that while that this [*sic*] location, on occasion, was referred to as an IKM, the evidence does not establish that this location was an IKM in the true sense of the rules applicable in the ABiH as explained to the Trial Chamber by witnesses. In this respect, the Trial Chamber notes that the expression IKM was also used for the Zulfikar Detachment's base in Donja Jablanica. The Trial Chamber therefore finds that the Prosecution has failed to prove beyond reasonable doubt that an IKM was established for the purpose of commanding an "Operation Neretva". For the purposes of this Judgement, for clarity, the Trial Chamber will however, continue to use the term IKM for the location of the Inspection Team in Jablanica.

148. The Prosecution submits that the Trial Chamber erred in law in requiring the Prosecution to prove as a pre-condition for conviction that the location where the Inspection Team was accommodated in Jablanica was

386 Trial Judgement, para. 372.
387 Trial Judgement, para. 752.
388 *See*, for example: Bakir Alispahić, T. 62 (23 May 2005) and T. 33 (27 May 2005); Vahid Karavelić, T. 107 (19 April 2005) (cited in Trial Judgement, para. 183); Salko Gušić, T. 43 (7 February 2005) (cited in Trial Judgement, para. 191); Ramiz Delalić, T. 25 (18 May 2005) (cited in Trial Judgement, para. 219). The Appeals Chamber notes that the Trial Chamber stated that it was not fully satisfied that the evidence from these witnesses was entirely reliable (Trial Judgement, fn. 34). Exhibit 131 (a map erroneously cited in Trial Judgement, para. 175, as the only exhibit mentioning "Operation Neretva"); Exhibit 281, p. 2 (the book "A Cunning Strategy" by Sefer Halilović cited, *inter alia*, in Trial Judgement, para. 258) and Exhibit 498 (letter from Sefer Halilović to Alija Izetbegović, dated 1 May 1995).
389 *Bagilishema* Appeal Judgement, para. 14. *See supra*, para. 11.
390 *See supra*, para. 126.
391 Prosecution Appeal Brief, para. 2.127.

a "forward command post" or IKM[392] from which a military "operation" in Herzegovina was commanded.[393] The Prosecution further argues that the Trial Chamber also erred in fact in concluding that the evidence presented at trial was insufficient to support a finding that the location where the Inspection Team was accommodated in Jablanica was an IKM from which the operation in question was directed.[394]

149. More specifically, the Prosecution asserts that the Trial Chamber's requirement to prove the existence of a "formal IKM" constituted an error in defining the law on superior responsibility,[395] particularly in the context of a *de facto* superior-subordinate relationship.[396] It submits that there was a command post in Jablanica from which military operations were coordinated and controlled, regardless of whether it met the formal military definition of IKM.[397] It notes that the Trial Chamber recognised that "the term IKM was used as 'jargon' to denote the location of senior officers".[398] The Prosecution further claims that, although a finding that an IKM was established in Jablanica could not by itself have led to the conclusion that Halilović was *de facto* superior, "the **[page 63]** existence of an IKM or operational command post used by Halilović is an indicator of effective control which can support a positive finding of *de facto* superior".[399]

150. Second, reiterating that only facts which are necessary to establish an element of the offence or mode of liability must be proven beyond reasonable doubt,[400] the Prosecution claims that the existence of an IKM was not such an "essential" fact.[401] It argues that, in any event, the Defence was clearly informed by the Indictment that the Prosecution's case was that a command post was established in Jablanica to command the combat operation, so that the absence of formal orders establishing a command post as an IKM did not affect in any way Halilović's rights to an informed and proper defence.[402]

151. Moreover, the Prosecution claims that, even if the existence of an IKM had to be proven beyond reasonable doubt, a reasonable trier of fact could only have concluded on the basis of the evidence presented at trial, that a "formal" forward command post[403] was established in Jablanica and that the operation at issue was directed from there.[404]

(b) Halilović's request for summary dismissal

152. Halilović requests that this sub-ground of appeal be summarily dismissed on three distinct grounds, namely (i) that it has been impermissibly varied; (ii) that it is incapable of meeting the relevant standard of review; and (iii) that the Prosecution has failed to meet its burden of argument or persuasion.[405] The Appeals Chamber finds that none of these arguments warrants the summary dismissal of this sub-ground. Moreover, the assertions regarding the existence of an IKM in Jablanica should be considered in light of the Prosecution's broader arguments on whether the Trial Chamber erred in defining and applying the law on superior responsibility.[406] Accordingly, Halilović's request for summary dismissal of sub-ground 3 is denied. **[page 64]**

---

392 "Forward command post" is a translation of "*Istureno komandno mesto*"; "IKM", the acronym of the expression in its original language, was used throughout the case (Trial Judgement, fn. 659).

393 Prosecution Notice of Appeal, para. 4(iii). *See* also Prosecution Appeal Brief, para. 2.83; Prosecution Reply Brief, paras 3.15 and 3.18; AT. 10.

394 Prosecution Notice of Appeal, para. 4(iii); Prosecution Appeal Brief, para. 2.106.

395 Prosecution Appeal Brief, para. 2.85, quoting Trial Judgement, para. 365.

396 Prosecution Appeal Brief, para. 2.86.

397 Prosecution Appeal Brief, para. 2.87.

398 Prosecution Appeal Brief, para. 2.87, quoting Trial Judgement, para. 365. *See* also Prosecution Appeal Brief, para. 2.91.

399 AT. 10. The Appeals Chamber notes that this appears to show a different focus than the Prosecution's arguments in the Prosecution Appeal Brief, para. 2.94: "The fact that a command post existed from which Halilović operated was sufficient. If the Trial Chamber, instead of focusing on the alleged failure to prove that the command post in Jablanica was a formal IKM [...] had focused on whether there was a *de facto* command post from which the military operation was directed by Halilović, it would have concluded that Halilović was at least the *de facto* superior of those who committed the crimes during the military operation he directed from the *de facto* IKM".

400 Prosecution Appeal Brief, para. 2.96. The Prosecution here refers to its arguments in the Prosecution Appeal Brief, paras 2.53–2.56, relating to the formal denomination of Operation Neretva.

401 Prosecution Appeal Brief, para. 2.95, citing Indictment, para. 4; Prosecution Reply Brief, para. 3.18; AT. 10.

402 Prosecution Appeal Brief, para. 2.97, citing Indictment, para. 4.

403 Prosecution Appeal Brief, para. 2.99.

404 Prosecution Appeal Brief, paras 2.99 and 2.106.

405 Respondent's Brief, paras 140–147.

406 Prosecution Appeal Brief, paras 2.85–2.94.

(c) Whether the Trial Chamber erred in law in requiring proof beyond reasonable doubt of the existence of an IKM

153. The Prosecution essentially claims that the Trial Chamber erred in law when, in order to enter a conviction under Article 7(3) of the Statute, it required proof beyond reasonable doubt that the command post from which the military operation was conducted was a formally established IKM.[407] Halilović responds that the Trial Chamber did not require proof of existence of an IKM as a legal "pre-condition for conviction" and that the impugned paragraphs of the Trial Judgement do not contain a legal finding, but a finding of fact.[408] While it is true that a finding on the existence of an IKM is in essence a factual finding, the Appeals Chamber considers that the Trial Chamber appears to have based its conclusion that Halilović was not *de jure* or *de facto* commander of Operation Neretva, *inter alia*, on the finding that "the evidence presented by the Prosecution [was] insufficient to support a finding that the location where the Inspection Team was accommodated in Jablanica was an IKM from which an 'operation' in Herzegovina was commanded".[409] The Trial Chamber therefore relied, *inter alia*, on such a factual finding to establish whether Halilović had effective control over the perpetrators of the crimes committed in Grabovica.

154. The Prosecution claims that the Trial Chamber erred in law in considering that the allegation in the Indictment that an operation was commanded from an IKM in Jablanica needed to be proven beyond reasonable doubt.[410] In this respect, the Appeals Chamber recalls that the establishment of an IKM was a fact not only alleged in the Indictment, where the Prosecution claimed that the "operation was commanded and co-ordinated from the Forward Command Post in Jablanica".[411] This fact was also pleaded by the Prosecution throughout the trial proceedings.[412] The Prosecution specifically highlighted the importance of an IKM's existence in Jablanica when it argued that "[a]nother piece of evidence proving that Halilović commanded Operation Neretva was that of the establishment of a forward command post [...] in Jablanica".[413] The Appeals Chamber considers that the qualification of a location as an IKM bears significance as "IKMs were used by commanders in order to exercise command when they were in the field"[414] and their establishment could as such amount to one of the "indicators of effective control" as outlined by the Trial **[page 65]** Chamber.[415] Accordingly, the Appeals Chamber finds that the Trial Chamber did not err in considering that the allegation in the Indictment that an operation was commanded from an IKM in Jablanica needed to be proven beyond reasonable doubt. The Appeals Chamber will now turn to address the parties' submissions concerning the distinction between a "formal" and a "*de facto*" IKM.

(d) Distinction between "formal" and "*de facto*" IKM

155. The Prosecution focuses its claim under this sub-ground of appeal on the allegation that the Trial Chamber erroneously required proof of a "*formal* IKM",[416] and proof that the "command post was *formally established* as an IKM for the operation",[417] in order to establish Halilović's superior responsibility. This allegation is based on the Trial Chamber's finding that "this location was [not] an IKM *in the true sense of the rules applicable in the ABiH*".[418] Halilović responds that the distinction between a "formal IKM" and a "*de facto* IKM" was

407 Prosecution Appeal Brief, paras 2.84 (citing Trial Judgement, para. 221) and 2.86; AT. 10 and 137–138.

408 Respondent's Brief, para. 148, citing Trial Judgement, paras 221, 365 and 375.

409 Trial Judgement, para. 365; *see* also Trial Judgement, para. 372. Although, as claimed by Halilović (Respondent's Brief, para. 154), proof of the existence of a "*de facto* IKM" would not by itself establish Halilović's authority over the perpetrators, the arguments raised under this sub-ground of appeal are to be read in conjunction with the other arguments advanced under the first ground of appeal in support of the contention that Halilović was the superior officer of subordinates who committed the crimes in Grabovica.

410 Prosecution Appeal Brief, paras 2.95–2.96.

411 Indictment, para. 4.

412 Prosecution Final Trial Brief, para. 177; Prosecution's closing argument, T. 69–70 (30 August 2005).

413 Prosecution Final Trial Brief, para. 177.

414 Trial Judgement, para. 212. *See* also Prosecution Final Trial Brief, para. 177.

415 Trial Judgement, para. 58 (citing *Blaškić* Appeal Judgement, para. 69) and paras 363–372 (making the findings based on the above-mentioned indicators).

416 Prosecution Appeal Brief, paras 2.84–2.86 (emphasis added).

417 Prosecution Appeal Brief, para. 2.94 (emphasis added).

418 Prosecution Appeal Brief, paras 2.93 (quoting Trial Judgement, para. 221, emphasis added by the Prosecution) and 2.94.

never advanced at trial[419] and that, in any event, a "*de facto* command post" was not a meaningful term which could impact upon the issue of effective control.[420] Indeed, the Prosecution did not draw a distinction between the existence of a "*de facto* IKM" and a "formal IKM" at trial. However, the Appeals Chamber considers that the Prosecution does not seek to argue that such a distinction was indeed pleaded at trial. On the contrary, its argument hinges on the contention that the Trial Chamber erroneously made this distinction, by allegedly requiring the *formal establishment* of a forward command post, instead of focusing on the existence of an IKM from which Halilović directed Operation Neretva.[421] Moreover, the Appeals Chamber considers that the Prosecution's submissions at trial do not show, contrary to Halilović's claim,[422] that the Prosecution actually argued that the "military expression IKM" was significant. Rather, it used the term "IKM" to refer to a "center established to command an operation",[423] and submitted that "an IKM in general terms is a centre from which a commander can issue commands while a commander is in the field".[424] **[page 66]**

156. In its analysis, the Trial Chamber first specifically considered testimonies to ascertain the military rules underlying the setting up of IKMs in general,[425] as it had "not [been] provided with any written rules or regulations concerning the establishment of IKMs".[426] Then, it proceeded to assess if the location where the Inspection Team had been accommodated in Jablanica could be considered an IKM pursuant to these rules.[427] The Appeals Chamber therefore considers that, when analysing the evidence regarding the existence of an IKM in Jablanica, the Trial Chamber indeed focused on the establishment of what the Trial Chamber itself called an "*official* IKM",[428] which – it found – needed to be set up by a specific order.[429] As Halilović suggests, this approach was probably prompted by the way in which the case was pleaded: formal establishment of an IKM would have assisted in determining whether Halilović was *de jure* commander of the military operation in question, the first logical step in assessing his effective control as a commander.[430]

157. While recognising that the expression "IKM" is a specific military term, the Appeals Chamber considers that the issue here is whether a forward command post existed in Jablanica, as claimed by the Prosecution at trial, and whether Halilović commanded Operation Neretva and issued orders from this command post. These findings, in the opinion of the Prosecution and of the Trial Chamber itself, are relevant in establishing whether Halilović had control over the perpetrators of the crimes committed in Grabovica.[431] In this respect, the focus by the Trial Chamber on the formal establishment of an IKM through an order was unreasonable. The Appeals Chamber therefore finds that the Trial Chamber erred when it required the establishment of an "official IKM" to be proven beyond reasonable doubt in order to ascertain whether the Prosecution had proven that Operation Neretva was commanded from this location.[432]

158. In light of this finding, the Appeals Chamber will now turn to determine whether the Prosecution did prove, as it contends,[433] that there was an IKM in Jablanica from which Operation Neretva was directed by Halilović. **[page 67]**

---

419 Respondent's Brief, paras 152 and 155.

420 Respondent's Brief, para. 152.

421 Prosecution Appeal Brief, para. 2.94.

422 Respondent's Brief, paras 150 and 155. Rather, it was Halilović who argued at trial that, in order for the location in Jablanica to function as an IKM, it had to be formally established by an order, which he claimed was not the case here (Defence Final Trial Brief, paras 257 and 260).

423 Prosecution Pre-Trial Brief, para. 28.

424 Prosecution's closing argument, T. 69 (30 August 2005).

425 Trial Judgement, paras 212–213.

426 Trial Judgement, para. 212.

427 Trial Judgement, paras 214–221.

428 Trial Judgement, para. 215: "The Trial Chamber heard testimony that there was no *official* IKM in Jablanica."

429 Trial Judgement, paras 213 and 217.

430 AT. 117–119. The Appeals Chamber notes that the Prosecution conceded that, at trial, it failed to prove that Halilović was the *de jure* commander of Operation Neretva (AT. 141).

431 In this context, Jusuf Jašarević (Chief of the Main Staff Security Administration), who made a distinction between an IKM according to the "rules" and those locations only defined as a "forward command post" (because of the presence of a group of superior officers), noted that elements of command and control were present even in the latter, non-official, IKMs. *See* Trial Judgement, para. 217.

432 Trial Judgement, paras 221 and 365.

433 *See* Prosecution Appeal Brief, para. 2.98. *See* also AT. 137–138 (requesting that the Appeals Chamber apply the correct legal standard to the evidence relating to this sub-ground and therefore, by implication, to make a finding on the existence of the IKM).

(e) Whether the Prosecution proved that an IKM was established for the purpose of commanding Operation Neretva

159. As noted earlier, the Prosecution argues that the Trial Chamber also erred in fact in concluding that the evidence presented at trial was insufficient to support a finding that the location where the Inspection Team was accommodated in Jablanica was an IKM from which Operation Neretva was directed.[434] In support of this allegation, the Prosecution submits that it proved at trial that an IKM was established in Jablanica for the purpose of commanding Operation Neretva.[435]

160. The Trial Chamber noted that the "term IKM was used as 'jargon' to denote the location of senior officers",[436] this being "the practice within the ABiH",[437] and quoted several witnesses stating that the location of the Inspection Team in Jablanica was referred to as "forward command post", although no official IKM was set up there on the basis of an order.[438]

161. In particular, Halilović himself wrote in the Final Report of the Inspection Team that an IKM was set up in Jablanica with the aim of coordinating and executing combat operations.[439] Moreover, Halilović's superior, Rasim Delić, also addressed an order to the "Forward Command Post of the Supreme Staff of the Armed Forces".[440] The Trial Chamber further noted that seven documents submitted as evidence were sent from the "IKM" in Jablanica,[441] including four orders issued by Halilović himself.[442] The Appeals Chamber considers that the reference to an IKM in these documents has a meaning beyond their qualification as "jargon" and points to the actual existence of an IKM. This language and the qualification of a forward command post, as noted above,[443] could in theory be an "indicator of effective control", as they might establish Halilović's capacity to issue orders.

162. Nevertheless, in light of the testimonies considered by the Trial Chamber, it remains unclear whether the IKM in Jablanica indeed had all the trappings of a real forward command post with **[page 68]** actual command and control functions. This uncertainty is reflected in paragraph 215 of the Trial Judgement:

> Vehbija Karić testified that [the IKM in Jablanica] was not an IKM or a temporary command post "in the traditional sense, with its prerogatives, with its communication centre, with all its organs and the commands." Reports were not submitted to them daily and they did not issue 'dozens' of orders every day, as is the case when commands have such authority. They used the communication system of another brigade as they did not have their own. Salko Gušić testified that the IKM did not have all the facilities of a proper command post, but had sufficient resources in terms of accommodation and communications. They had many of the elements that an IKM has to have, the essential ones such as a communications centre, and their security.[444]

163. The Trial Chamber itself noted a possible source of confusion, since the term IKM was also used with reference to the base of Zulfikar Ališpago in Donja Jablanica.[445] Ramiz Delalić's testimony, relied upon by the Prosecution to show that Operation Neretva was commanded from the Jablanica IKM,[446] actually refers to the

---

434 Prosecution Notice of Appeal, para. 4(iii); Prosecution Appeal Brief, para. 2.106.

435 Prosecution Appeal Brief, heading (B) p. 38 and paras 2.99–2.105.

436 Trial Judgement, para. 365.

437 Trial Judgement, para. 217, quoting the testimony of Namik Džanković.

438 Trial Judgement, fn. 696, quoting the testimonies of Namik Džanković, Bakir Alispahić and Jusuf Jašarević. *See* also testimony of Vehbija Karić, T. 19 (2 June 2005).

439 Trial Judgement, para. 214, citing Exhibit 130.

440 Exhibit 120, Order on organisational changes in the zone of responsibility of the 1st, 4th and 6th Corps, 1 September 1993 ("Reorganisation Order"), cited in Trial Judgement, para. 216. *See* also Trial Judgement, para. 225, quoting point 7 of the Reorganisation Order, which instructs the "Officers from the Forward Command Post – Staff of Supreme Command" to provide the necessary specialised assistance to the commands of the 4th and 6th Corps in the tasks set forth in the order.

441 Trial Judgement, para. 216. The Trial Chamber noted that four of these documents bore the heading "IKM Jablanica".

442 Trial Judgement, para. 216 and fns 683 and 686, citing Exhibits 118 (the only order sent by Halilović bearing the heading "IKM"), 161, 122 and 123.

443 *See supra*, para. 154.

444 Trial Judgement, para. 215 (footnotes omitted).

445 Trial Judgement, para. 219.

446 Prosecution Appeal Brief, para. 2.104.

base of the Zulfikar Detachment in Donja Jablanica.[447] The other witness clearly stating that "[t]he operation was coordinated and carried out from the Jablanica forward command post, and [that] General Halilović was in charge of it",[448] was Salko Gušić, whose evidence the Trial Chamber deemed not to be "entirely reliable" and, as such, required corroboration.[449]

164. In light of the foregoing, while agreeing with the Prosecution that a post described as "IKM" was indeed set up in Jablanica by the Inspection Team,[450] the Appeals Chamber finds that the finding that "the Prosecution ha[d] failed to prove beyond reasonable doubt that an IKM was established *for the purpose of commanding an 'Operation Neretva'*",[451] was not unreasonable. In other words, establishing that an IKM did exist does not suffice to show *why* it was established and, above all, *what role*, if any, this post played in practice with respect to Operation Neretva. While, as noted above,[452] the existence of an IKM *might* indicate that an operation was commanded from this location, the Prosecution has failed to establish how the "military documents, orders, requests, [and] reports" issued[453] would support not only the existence of a forward command post in Jablanica, but also the Prosecution's claim that Halilović commanded Operation Neretva from this IKM. **[page 69]**

165. The Appeals Chamber finds that the Prosecution failed to substantiate its claim that, had the existence of an IKM in Jablanica been established at trial, the Trial Chamber "would have concluded that Halilović was at least the *de facto* superior of those who committed the crimes during the military operation he directed from the *de facto* IKM".[454] In light of this finding, the Appeals Chamber does not need to address the Prosecution's allegation – under sub-ground 5 in relation to the finding of fact in paragraph 221 of the Trial Judgement[455] – that the Trial Chamber erred in requiring proof "beyond reasonable doubt" that an IKM was established for the purpose of commanding an "Operation Neretva".

166. For the foregoing reasons, sub-ground 3 is dismissed. **[page 70]**

E. Sub-ground 4: Material ability to punish

1. Introduction

167. Paragraph 746 of the Trial Judgement reads as follows:

> The Trial Chamber also notes that, in relation to the investigations of the crimes in Grabovica, Sefer Halilović, in the evening of 9 September, instructed Namik Džanković, a member of the Inspection Team and the UB ["Main Staff Security Administration"], to work together with the MUP, as well as with other members of the SVB ["Military Security Service"], and to keep "the Sarajevo command", rather than himself, informed. The evidence shows that at this point in time investigations were already under way. The evidence does not show that Sefer Halilović initiated the investigations or that the investigations were in any way carried forward through his actions. The evidence further shows that the 6th Corps SVB, the Military Police Battalion of the 6th Corps and the Military Police of the 44th Brigade were involved in the investigation into the events in Grabovica and that the Chief of the UB of the Main Staff, Jusuf Jašarević, was kept informed of the results of their investigations. The Trial Chamber finds that based on the evidence, it cannot be concluded that Sefer Halilović had the material ability to punish the perpetrators of the crimes committed in Grabovica.[456]

---

447 Trial Judgement, para. 219, citing Ramiz Delalić, T. 25 (18 May 2005).
448 Salko Gušić, T. 62 (3 February 2005).
449 Trial Judgement, para. 17 and fn. 34.
450 Exhibit 130, Final Report of the Inspection Team, p. 1: "With the aim of co-ordinating and executing combat operations, an IKM/forward command post/was set up in Jablanica, where the team planned the operation, […] and ensured logistic means for the operation".
451 Trial Judgement, para. 221 (emphasis added).
452 *See supra,* para. 154.
453 Prosecution Appeal Brief, para. 2.105.
454 Prosecution Appeal Brief, para. 2.94.
455 *See supra*, para. 126.
456 Footnote omitted.

168. The Prosecution submits that the Trial Chamber erred in law in concluding that Halilović did not have the material ability to punish the perpetrators of the crimes committed in Grabovica based, in large part, on its conclusion that the evidence did not show that he initiated or carried forward investigations.[457] It claims that the Trial Chamber's findings were unreasonable, submitting that "the fact that Halilović *did not* punish the perpetrators does not imply that he *could not*".[458]

2. Halilović's request for summary dismissal

169. Halilović requests that this sub-ground of appeal be summarily dismissed.[459] First, he submits that the Prosecution's claim that the error in paragraph 746 of the Trial Judgement "significantly affected" the finding on the existence of a superior-subordinate relationship relies on a standard that falls short of the applicable standard of review because the Prosecution does not argue that the alleged error had the effect of invalidating the Trial Judgement.[460] Regardless of the fact that the terminology used by the Prosecution is perhaps unfortunate, the Appeals Chamber finds that the relevant issue is whether the error of law alleged by the Prosecution invalidates the decision.[461] Second, the Prosecution contends that the Trial Chamber concluded that Halilović did not have the material ability to punish, based, *in large part,* on evidence that he did not initiate investigations, which shows that the Prosecution acknowledges that the Trial Chamber did not base **[page 71]** the challenged finding *solely* on evidence that he did not initiate the investigation.[462] The Appeals Chamber reiterates that the relevant issue is whether the Prosecution has demonstrated that the Trial Chamber's reliance on evidence that Halilović did not initiate the investigation into the Grabovica crimes was erroneous and that such an error invalidates the judgement.[463] Third, Halilović claims that this sub-ground of appeal is replete with "grave, un-substantiated, assertions and distortions of factual findings" in the Trial Judgement, which warrant summary dismissal as an abuse of process.[464] Halilović's arguments in support of this claim are without merit. While some of the identified statements from the Prosecution Appeal Brief do not always reflect the Trial Judgement's paragraphs in question with utmost clarity, this is not sufficient to compel a conclusion that the Prosecution significantly misrepresents the Trial Chamber's findings to the point that the Prosecution's arguments should not be addressed on the merits.

170. For the foregoing reasons, Halilović's request for summary dismissal of sub-ground 4 is denied.

3. Whether the Trial Chamber erred in basing its conclusion on Halilović's failure to punish

171. The Prosecution submits that "in seeming contradiction to its findings, the Trial Chamber concluded that Halilović did not have the material ability to initiate and conduct his own effective investigation".[465] It claims that Halilović's instruction to Namik Džanković to investigate, as well as Rasim Delić's order to Halilović to investigate, isolate the perpetrators and order the 9th Brigade back to Sarajevo, establish at least "that Halilović had the material ability to investigate, order an investigation, have the facts presented to him, and then prepare a report for his superiors".[466] The Prosecution asserts that the only reasonable conclusion is that he disobeyed Delić's order and failed to take the steps to punish the perpetrators who were within his power and responsibility.[467] Additionally, the Prosecution avers that the Trial Chamber apparently concluded that, since various persons were conducting some form of investigations, Halilović was exonerated from his duty

457 Prosecution Notice of Appeal, para. 4(iv); Prosecution Appeal Brief, para. 2.107.
458 Prosecution Appeal Brief, para. 2.108.
459 Respondent's Brief, paras 168–172.
460 Respondent's Brief, para. 170, citing Prosecution Appeal Brief, para. 2.118.
461 *See supra*, para. 7.
462 Respondent's Brief, para. 168 (emphasis added by Halilović).
463 *See supra*, para. 7.
464 Respondent's Brief, para. 172, citing Trial Judgement, paras 307–308, and Prosecution Appeal Brief, para. 2.111.
465 Prosecution Appeal Brief, para. 2.112, citing Trial Judgement, para. 746.
466 Prosecution Appeal Brief, para. 2.115. *See* also Prosecution Appeal Brief, para. 2.111, citing Trial Judgement, para. 521 and Exhibit 157.
467 Prosecution Appeal Brief, para. 2.112.

to investigate.[468] As a result, the Trial Chamber concluded that Halilović did not have the material **[page 72]** ability to punish,[469] implying that Halilović did not have the "material ability to investigate", either.[470]

172. The Prosecution submits that, while the Trial Chamber "correctly found that Halilović did not initiate or carry forward the investigations"[471] and that accordingly Halilović's "actions fell short of his obligation under the third element [of superior responsibility] to conduct an effective investigation",[472] it reached the erroneous conclusion that he did not have the material ability to punish the perpetrators.[473] According to the Prosecution, the Trial Judgement is premised on the assumption that Halilović's inactions demonstrate that he could not punish or investigate.[474] The finding in paragraph 746 of the Trial Judgement significantly affected the finding on the existence of a superior-subordinate relationship between him and the perpetrators.[475] This, in turn, led to the conclusion that Halilović did not have effective control, a conclusion that resulted in his acquittal.[476] Claiming that the Trial Chamber failed to apply a correct analysis, the Prosecution concludes by outlining the process by which a proper determination of Halilović's responsibility under Article 7(3) of the Statute should have been conducted.[477]

173. Halilović responds that the Trial Chamber did not err in law by using evidence of Halilović's role in the investigation of crimes to assess whether or not he had the material ability to prevent and punish the Grabovica crimes.[478] He adds that there is a close evidentiary nexus between the first and the third elements of superior responsibility, given that the "effective control" of a superior is based on his "material ability to prevent offences or punish the principal offenders".[479] Halilović asserts that, contrary to the Prosecution's suggestion, the Trial Chamber did not conclude that Halilović had no effective control "in large part" because he did not initiate or carry forward an investigation. Rather, he submits, the Trial Chamber simply found that the evidence of Halilović's role in the investigation process concerning the Grabovica crimes did not provide positive evidence of his effective control over the perpetrators.[480] **[page 73]**

174. The Prosecution argues in essence that, in reaching its conclusions in paragraph 746 of the Trial Judgement, "the Trial Chamber used evidence that the third element of command responsibility was satisfied to infer that the first element of command responsibility was not".[481] At the outset, the Appeals Chamber recalls that each of the three elements of superior responsibility, as set out above,[482] must be proven beyond reasonable doubt in order for a Trial Chamber to establish that an accused is responsible under Article 7(3) of the Statute. A Trial Chamber will first ascertain whether the superior had effective control over the persons committing crimes subject to the jurisdiction of the International Tribunal (in the sense of possessing the material ability to prevent or punish the commission of the crimes in question) and then proceed to determine whether the second and third elements of superior responsibility are met.[483] In the present case, the Appeals Chamber must therefore determine if the Trial Chamber erred when assessing whether a superior-subordinate relationship pursuant to Article 7(3) of the Statute existed between Halilović and the perpetrators of the crimes committed in Grabovica. In so doing, the Trial Chamber had to consider whether the evidence on the record contained indicators establishing beyond reasonable doubt that Halilović was the superior of the

468 Prosecution Appeal Brief, para. 2.114.

469 Prosecution Appeal Brief, para. 2.117. *See* also Prosecution Appeal Brief, para. 2.113, citing Trial Judgement, para. 746: "The evidence does not show that Sefer Halilović initiated the investigations or that the investigations were in any way carried forward through his actions."

470 Prosecution Appeal Brief, para. 2.117. *See* also Prosecution Appeal Brief, paras 2.112, 2.114, 2.118, 2.119 and fn. 188.

471 Prosecution Appeal Brief, para. 2.118, citing Trial Judgement, para. 746.

472 Prosecution Appeal Brief, para. 2.117.

473 Prosecution Appeal Brief, para. 2.118. *See* also Prosecution Reply Brief, para. 3.24, and AT. 61.

474 Prosecution Appeal Brief, para. 2.118.

475 Prosecution Appeal Brief, para. 2.118, citing Trial Judgement, para. 747.

476 Prosecution Appeal Brief, paras 2.118–2.119.

477 Prosecution Appeal Brief, para. 2.120. *See* also AT. 61.

478 Respondent's Brief, para. 173. *See* also AT. 100–101.

479 Respondent's Brief, para. 174, citing *Čelebići* Appeal Judgement, paras 196–198; *Bagilishema* Appeal Judgement, paras 49–55; *Kayishema and Ruzindana* Appeal Judgement, para. 294.

480 Respondent's Brief, para. 176.

481 Prosecution Appeal Brief, para. 2.107 (footnotes omitted).

482 *See supra*, para. 59.

483 *Blaškić* Appeal Judgement, para. 484.

alleged perpetrators and had effective control over them.[484] Considering the facts in this case, this essentially hinged on a finding about whether he had the power to punish criminal conduct or initiate measures leading to proceedings against the alleged perpetrators.

175. The Appeals Chamber notes that the Trial Chamber correctly outlined, in its analysis of the applicable law,[485] the need to establish the position of command of a superior over a subordinate by means of his effective control – in the sense of "the material ability to prevent and punish criminal conduct"[486] – (the first element enshrined in Article 7(3) of the Statute) before subsequently addressing the separate obligation to take necessary and reasonable measures to prevent the commission of crimes and to punish the perpetrators once crimes have been committed (the third element under Article 7(3) of the Statute).[487] Therefore, the Trial Chamber clearly distinguished the different elements of superior responsibility and addressed the need to prove whether each of these elements has been established. **[page 74]**

176. The Trial Chamber then went on to consider in detail the specific rules governing *in concreto* the ABiH investigations on military personnel suspected of killing civilians.[488] In particular, based on oral and written evidence, the Trial Chamber concluded that the ABiH and the MUP were competent to carry out investigations in these cases and noted that cooperation between military organs and civilian police was often required.[489] In light of this analysis, the Trial Chamber then proceeded to consider evidence on the authority to conduct investigations into the crimes committed in Grabovica[490] and finally set out and analysed the evidence regarding the actual measures taken to report and investigate those crimes.[491]

177. The Appeals Chamber considers that the conclusion reached in paragraph 746 of the Trial Judgement must be read in light of the totality of the Trial Chamber's findings regarding investigations into the crimes committed in Grabovica. The Appeals Chamber acknowledges that the statement that "[t]he evidence does not show that Sefer Halilović initiated the investigations or that the investigations were in any way carried forward through his actions"[492] could be misleading. The Appeals Chamber considers that such a statement, made within the context of the Trial Chamber's concluding remarks on Halilović's material ability to punish, may be confusing, since failure to initiate investigations is not, as such, an indication of lack of power to investigate.

178. However, even the Prosecution concedes that the Trial Chamber did not base its finding that Halilović did not have the material ability to punish *solely* on its conclusion that the evidence did not show that he had initiated investigations.[493] Rather, the Trial Chamber took into account the evidence relating to all investigations into the crimes committed in Grabovica, which it had previously analysed in the Trial Judgement.[494] This evidence included: (i) Halilović's instruction to Namik Džanković; (ii) the fact that other investigations were already underway at that time; and (iii) evidence of those investigations in which the

484 *Cf. Blaškić* Appeal Judgement, para. 69.

485 Trial Judgement, paras 55–100, section titled: "3. The Elements of Command Responsibility". During the Appeal Hearing, the Prosecution itself conceded that the Trial Chamber set out the correct legal standard with regard to the application of Article 7(3) of the Statute (AT. 8–9).

486 Trial Judgement, para. 58, quoting *Čelebići* Appeal Judgement, para. 256.

487 Trial Judgement, paras 72–78 and 91–100.

488 Trial Judgement, paras 653–659. The Trial Chamber specifically found that there was a "dual chain of command", considering that "[a]t the brigade level and higher up in the military structure, there were military police units specifically assigned with the task of carrying out investigations" and that the "military police acted on orders of the unit commander or of the chief of the [Military Security Service]" (Trial Judgement, para. 657). *See* also Trial Judgement, paras 112–114 on the role and the functioning of the Military Security Service.

489 Trial Judgement, paras 653 and 654.

490 *See*, in particular, Trial Judgement, paras 663–671 and 677.

491 Trial Judgement, paras 660–701.

492 Trial Judgement, para. 746.

493 The Appeals Chamber notes in this respect the Prosecution's use of the expression "based in large part" both in its Notice of Appeal, para. 4(iv) ("The Trial Chamber erred in law at paragraph 746 wherein it concluded that Sefer Halilović did not have the material ability to punish the perpetrators of the crimes committed in Grabovica *based, in large part,* on its conclusion that the evidence did not show that Sefer Halilović initiated investigations or that investigations were in any way carried forward through his actions." (emphasis added)) and in its Appeal Brief, para. 2.107 ("The Trial Chamber concluded that Halilović did not have the material ability to punish the perpetrators of the crimes committed in Grabovica *based in large part* on the lack of evidence that Halilović initiated investigations into the crimes or that investigations were carried forward through his actions." (emphasis added)).

494 Trial Judgement, paras 660–701.

6th Corps SVB, the Military Police Battalion of **[page 75]** the 6th Corps and the Military Police of the 44th Brigade were involved.[495] The Trial Chamber placed emphasis on the fact that the evidence demonstrated that "the Sarajevo command" and the "Chief of the UB of the Main Staff, Jusuf Jašarević", were kept informed of the results of the investigations by the 6th Corps SVB, the Military Police Battalion of the 6th Corps and the Military Police of the 44th Brigade.[496]

179. In light of the foregoing, the Appeals Chamber finds that the Trial Chamber did not erroneously rest its finding that Halilović did not have the material ability to punish the perpetrators of the crimes committed in Grabovica on its conclusion that the evidence failed to show either that he initiated the investigations or that the investigations were in any way carried forward through his actions.

180. Accordingly, the Appeals Chamber dismisses the Prosecution's allegation that the Trial Chamber improperly used evidence that Halilović did not take necessary and reasonable measures in order to support its finding that he was not the superior of the troops who committed the crimes in Grabovica.

4. Whether Halilović had the material ability to punish

181. The Prosecution claims that the evidence submitted at trial establishes that Halilović had the material ability to punish the perpetrators.[497] It specifically refers to Halilović's instruction given to Džanković on 9 September 1993, together with the order issued by Delić on 12 September 1993,[498] as well as the final report drawn up by the Inspection Team.[499] The Prosecution claims that, in contradiction with its own findings, the Trial Chamber concluded that Halilović did not have the "material ability to initiate and conduct his own effective investigation"[500] and stresses the importance of Halilović's material ability to punish, directly focusing on the "effective control test".[501] **[page 76]**

182. At the outset, the Appeals Chamber notes that, in the present case, the issue of Halilović's alleged material ability to punish the perpetrators in order to establish his effective control over them is not based on his ability to impose sanctions or take punitive actions, but rather on his capacity to initiate investigations leading to the criminal prosecution of the perpetrators.[502] On the one hand, the Appeals Chamber agrees with Halilović that the issue of the alleged failure to investigate has to be seen as an integral part of the assessment of a superior's duty to punish.[503] On the other hand, however, the ability to initiate criminal investigations against the perpetrators may be an indicator of effective control.[504] Therefore, Halilović's ability in this respect has to be carefully assessed in order to establish whether he had effective control over the perpetrators of the crimes committed in Grabovica. Indeed, as the Trial Chamber correctly outlined, "the duty to punish includes at least an obligation to investigate possible crimes or have the matter investigated, to establish the facts, and *if the superior has no power to sanction, to report them to the competent authorities*".[505] In this regard, the instruction Halilović gave Džanković "to collect as much information as possible and send it and

---

[495] Trial Judgement, para. 746.

[496] Trial Judgement, para. 746.

[497] Prosecution Brief in Reply, paras 3.23 and 3.25. *See* also Prosecution Appeal Brief, paras 2.115 and 2.117; AT. 33–34 and 42–43. During the Appeal Hearing, the Prosecution claimed that Halilović had accepted his material ability to punish his subordinates and his correspondent duty to investigate, but that he failed to take the corresponding measures (AT. 32–33).

[498] Prosecution Appeal Brief, paras 2.111–2.115 and fn. 189, where the Prosecution claimed that "Halilović ordering [Namik] Džanković to investigate is sufficient evidence of his material ability to investigate. So is Delić's order to Halilović to investigate". *See* also Prosecution Reply Brief, paras 3.23–3.25.

[499] AT. 40, citing Exhibit 130. The Prosecution claims that this report shows that criminal investigations were recommended with regard to "various members of the ABiH as well as other measures", but that Halilović did not make recommendations with regard to the crimes committed in Grabovica (AT. 40). *See* also AT. 51.

[500] Prosecution Appeal Brief, para. 2.112, citing Trial Judgement, para. 746.

[501] AT. 32.

[502] The arguments of both parties focus solely on Halilović's alleged material ability to take effective steps to initiate proceedings against the perpetrators. *See*, in particular, the submissions of the Prosecution (AT. 32–34 and 45–46) and Halilović's submissions (AT. 99 and 101–104).

[503] *Cf. Blaškić* Appeal Judgement, paras 68–69, relating to the duty of commanders to *report* to competent authorities, as well as paras 499 and 511. *See* AT. 97.

[504] *Cf. Blaškić* Appeal Judgement, paras 68–69.

[505] Trial Judgement, para. 97 (emphasis added), referring to *Kordić and Čerkez* Trial Judgement, para. 446. *See* also *Blaškić* Appeal Judgement, paras 68–69, 499 and 511.

inform the Sarajevo command about it",[506] read together with Delić's order to Halilović,[507] could suggest that Halilović had at least the ability to order an investigation and then prepare a report for his superiors.[508] The Appeals Chamber recalls in this regard that "reporting criminal acts of subordinates to appropriate authorities is eviden[ce] of the material ability to punish them in the circumstances of a certain case, albeit to a very limited degree".[509]

183. The Appeals Chamber notes that the Trial Chamber considered in detail the rules governing ABiH investigations on military personnel suspected of killing civilians, thereby setting out the framework of a commander's material ability to punish his subordinates.[510] According to the applicable ABiH rules,[511] reflected in the findings of the Trial Chamber,[512] it was the Military **[page 77]** Security Service or SVB which had to "take the necessary measures to find the perpetrator of the criminal offence" when there was "*reasonable suspicion* that a criminal offence triable by military courts ha[d] been committed".[513]

184. However, the evidence heard by the Trial Chamber, including the analysis of applicable ABiH regulations,[514] is ambiguous as to who would have had the duty and the ability to initiate an investigation into the killings committed in Grabovica: both the ABiH and the MUP were legally competent to initiate a criminal investigation in such a case.[515] In this context, the Appeals Chamber observes that contradictory evidence is reflected in the Trial Judgement. Such contradictions are exemplified in paragraph 677 of the Trial Judgement, which points out that, while Ramiz Delalić testified that "it was Sefer Halilović's duty to order Zulfikar Ališpago to undertake measures and conduct an investigation in order to find the perpetrators of the crime",[516] Vehbija Karić stated that "the Main Staff [Security Administration] was in charge of collecting all the information about the perpetrators and then handing them over to the military prosecutor",[517] and that "the Inspection Team did not have any authority to file criminal reports and initiate court proceedings".[518]

185. The Prosecution specifically claims that the fact that the Trial Chamber did not mention Delić's order of 12 September 1993 in paragraph 746 of the Trial Judgement constitutes an error.[519] However, Delić's order of 12 September 1993 was but one of the items of evidence properly considered by the Trial Chamber. Recalling that failure to list in the Trial Judgement each and every circumstance on the record does not necessarily mean that the Trial Chamber ignored or failed to evaluate the factor in question,[520] the Appeals Chamber considers that the Trial Chamber did not "fail" to mention Delić's order.

186. The Trial Chamber did indeed mention this order several times in the Trial Judgement, as illustrated by the following references: paragraph 7 (where the Trial Chamber noted the allegation that Halilović failed to implement Delić's order); paragraphs 307 and 308 (where the text of the order is quoted and the testimony of witness Hodžić is recounted); and paragraph 680 (in the section of the Trial Judgement entitled "Investigations into Murders committed in Grabovica"). **[page 78]** These references indicate that the Trial Chamber did take Delić's order of 12 September 1993 into account when assessing Halilović's material ability to punish.

---

506 Trial Judgement, paras 521 and 670, both quoting Namik Džanković, T. 28 (21 March 2005).

507 Trial Judgement, paras 307–308, quoting Exhibit 157 ("Check the accuracy of information regarding the genocide committed against the civilian population by the members of the 1st Corps 9th bbr/ Mountain Brigade/. If the information is correct, isolate the perpetrators and take energetic measures").

508 Prosecution Appeal Brief, para. 2.115. *See* also AT. 33 and 42.

509 *Blaškić* Appeal Judgement, para. 499.

510 *See supra,* para. 176.

511 Rules for the Military Security Service in the Armed Forces of the Republic of Bosnia and Herzegovina, Sarajevo 1992 ("Rules for the Military Security Service"), Exhibit 137, in particular Articles 39–41.

512 Trial Judgement, paras 653–659. *See* also Trial Judgement, paras 112–114 on the role and the functioning of the Military Security Service.

513 Rules for the Military Security Service, Article 40 (emphasis added).

514 Trial Judgement, paras 653–659. *See* also Trial Judgement, paras 112–114.

515 Trial Judgement, para. 653.

516 Ramiz Delalić, T. 10 (18 May 2005).

517 Trial Judgement, para. 677, citing Exhibit 444 (Transcript of the Deposition of Witness Vehbija Karić).

518 Trial Judgement, fn. 2424, citing Exhibit 444 (Transcript of the Deposition of Witness Vehbija Karić), T. 120–121.

519 Prosecution Appeal Brief, para. 2.114: after noting that the Trial Chamber stated that "(ineffectual) investigations were underway by [Namik] Džanković [and others]" and noted Halilović's order to Namik Džanković in paragraph 746 of the Trial Judgement, the Prosecution claims that the Trial Chamber "failed to mention Delić's order to Halilović to investigate".

520 *Kupreškić et al.* Appeal Judgement, para. 458.

187. Similarly, in the context of the Trial Chamber's analysis of the "Investigations into Murders committed in Grabovica",[521] Halilović's instruction of 9 September 1993 to Namik Džanković and the steps undertaken pursuant to such instruction were duly considered by the Trial Chamber in reaching its findings.[522] Indeed, the Trial Chamber took into account that, on the evening of 9 September 1993 (after having heard what had happened in Grabovica), Halilović instructed Džanković "to collect as much information as possible and send it and inform the Sarajevo command about it".[523] At this time, Džanković, as a member of the UB, had already sent a short report about the events to Jusuf Jašarević, Chief of the UB.[524] All further reports Džanković compiled about the events in Grabovica were likewise sent to Jašarević.[525]

188. The Appeals Chamber therefore finds that the Trial Chamber indeed took Halilović's instruction of 9 September 1993 to Džanković and Delić's order of 12 September 1993 into account. In this regard, the Appeals Chamber reiterates that where the evidence is discussed in a Trial Judgement, it must be presumed to have been considered for each finding that it affects.[526] More broadly, the Appeals Chamber recalls its previous holding to the effect that,

> [I]t is not necessary to refer to the testimony of every witness or every piece of evidence on the trial record. It is to be presumed that the Trial Chamber evaluated all the evidence presented to it, as long as there is no indication that the Trial Chamber completely disregarded any particular piece of evidence. There may be an indication of disregard when evidence which is clearly relevant to the findings is not addressed by the Trial Chamber's reasoning, but not every inconsistency which the Trial Chamber failed to discuss renders its opinion defective. Considering the fact that minor inconsistencies commonly occur in witness testimony without rendering it unreliable, it is within the discretion of the Trial Chamber to evaluate it and to consider whether the evidence as a whole is credible, without explaining its decision in every detail. If the Trial Chamber did not refer to the evidence given by a witness, even if it is in contradiction to the Trial Chamber's finding, it is to be presumed that the Trial Chamber assessed and weighed the evidence, but found that the evidence did not prevent it from arriving at its actual findings.[527]

Considering that the Trial Chamber specifically addressed the two orders in question in its factual findings, the Appeals Chamber concludes that there is no indication that the Trial Chamber disregarded this evidence. In particular, the instruction Halilović gave Džanković to initiate investigations was specifically mentioned in the impugned paragraph 746 of the Trial Judgement.[528] **[page 79]**

189. These considerations must be borne in mind when examining the issue of whether the Trial Chamber correctly analysed the relevant evidence (including Halilović's instruction of 9 September 1993 to Džanković and Delić's order of 12 September 1993 to Halilović) in order to ascertain (i) whether the evidence contained indicators showing that Halilović had the power to punish criminal conduct or initiate measures leading to proceedings against the alleged perpetrators of the crimes committed in Grabovica and (ii) whether the evidence established beyond reasonable doubt that Halilović had effective control over the perpetrators.[529]

190. With regard to Halilović's instruction to Džanković, of 9 September 1993, the Appeals Chamber recalls that Džanković was a member of the UB[530] and, as such, was a representative of the SVB within the Inspection Team.[531] This is particularly relevant because, as mentioned above, it fell in principle upon the SVB to investigate allegations of crimes committed by military personnel against civilians.[532] It is in his function

521 Trial Judgement, paras 660–701.
522 Trial Judgement, paras 670, 686, 694, 697 and 698. *See* also Trial Judgement, para. 521.
523 Trial Judgement, paras 521 and 670, both quoting Namik Džanković, T. 28 (21 March 2005).
524 Trial Judgement, paras 522 and 660–661.
525 Trial Judgement, paras 686, 694 and 697–698.
526 *Blagojević and Jokić* Appeal Judgement, para. 227.
527 *Kvoèka et al.* Appeal Judgement, para. 23 (footnotes omitted); *see* also *Kvoèka et al.* Appeal Judgement, para. 288.
528 *See* Trial Judgement, para. 746.
529 *Cf. Blaškić* Appeal Judgement, para. 69.
530 *See* Trial Judgement, paras 205 and 660 on the role of Namik Džanković within the Inspection Team. *See* also, in particular, Trial Judgement, fn. 2498, detailing the "dual line of responsibility" of Namik Džanković: "He had to obey commands of his superior officer, in that case, Sefer Halilović; but he had also an obligation to report up the professional line to Jusuf Jašarević".
531 "The [UB] was at the top of the SVB" (Trial Judgement, para. 112, footnotes omitted).
532 *See supra*, para. 176, fn. 488 and para. 183. *See* also Trial Judgement, para. 677, where the Trial Chamber considered the testimony of Vehbija Karić (senior officer in the Main Staff and member of the Inspection Team), that "the [UB] was in charge of

as member of the UB that Džanković sent his reports on the events in Grabovica to Jašarević, Chief of the UB.[533] In fact, it is noteworthy that Džanković had already sent his first short report to Jašarević regarding the events in question, indicating that more information would follow,[534] before being instructed by Halilović on the evening of 9 September 1993 to collect information about the events and inform the Sarajevo command.[535] As mentioned above, all further reports Džanković compiled about the events in Grabovica were also sent to Jašarević.[536] The Trial Chamber considered in detail the impact of Džanković's second report and the steps undertaken by Jašarević thereafter.[537] The Appeals Chamber also notes that, as mentioned above,[538] different high ranking officials initiated several investigations into the events in **[page 80]** Grabovica.[539] In particular, Jašarević issued a specific order to Nermin Eminović, Chief of the SVB of the 6th Corps, instructing him to undertake an investigation into the crimes committed in Grabovica.[540] In light of the foregoing, the Appeals Chamber finds that it cannot be concluded that the instruction Halilović issued to Džanković on 9 September 1993 was an order which only a commander could have issued. The Prosecution therefore failed to show how this instruction demonstrated Halilović's effective control over the perpetrators.

191. The Prosecution Appeal Brief states that the order issued by Delić to Halilović on 12 September 1993[541] is sufficient evidence of Halilović's material ability to investigate.[542] During the Appeal Hearing, the Prosecution further submitted that this order confirms that Halilović had effective control over the perpetrators of seven of the murders in Grabovica and that Halilović had the material ability to prevent and punish.[543] However, during its oral arguments in reply, the Prosecution stated that it did not rely on this order as a *basis* for Halilović's material ability to prevent and punish, but only as a *confirmation* of the effective control Halilović had over the troops at the relevant time.[544] The Prosecution now claims that this order's particular importance lies in the fact that it specifically identifies the alleged perpetrators of the crimes committed in Grabovica, namely the 9th Brigade,[545] and sets out all the reasonable and necessary measures that Halilović could have taken to punish the troops.[546]

192. Indeed, Delić's order is relevant especially in the assessment of the third element of superior responsibility under Article 7(3) of the Statute, which relates to the necessary and reasonable measures Halilović should have taken to punish the perpetrators of the crimes.[547] However, in light of the submissions

collecting all the information about the perpetrators and then handing them over to the military prosecutor", and Trial Judgement, para. 679, referring to the testimony of Salko Gusić (Commander of the 6th Corps) that "under the rules, investigations into the killings in Grabovica had to be a criminal investigation conducted by the SVB and the civilian police".

533 *See* Trial Judgement, fn. 2498: "Namik Džanković testified that in a matter such as the investigation of the killings in Grabovica, he was obliged by the rules to report to Jusuf Jašarević".

534 Trial Judgement, paras 522 and 660–661. Namik Džanković sent a first short report to Jusuf Jašarević on 9 September 1993, before being instructed to do so by Halilović (Trial Judgement, paras 522 and 660). He sent a second, detailed report to Jusuf Jašarević, dated 13 September 1993 (Exhibit 215), based on the instruction given by Halilović to investigate these events further (Trial Judgement, paras 521 and 686–689). Namik Džanković sent a third report to Jusuf Jašarević on 29 September 1993 (Exhibit 235), containing the information he had collected at the time (Trial Judgement, para. 697). The Prosecution itself acknowledged that Namik Džanković did not report to Halilović, but had to send his reports to the UB (AT. 34 and 45).

535 Trial Judgement, para. 521.

536 Trial Judgement, para. 686, fn. 2454, and para. 697.

537 Trial Judgement, paras 690–696.

538 *See supra*, para. 178.

539 In particular, the Trial Chamber considered that: (i) Bakir Alispahić, Minister of the Interior during the time relevant to the Indictment, had tasked Emin Zebić with collecting as much information as possible and subsequently informing the MUP (Trial Judgement, para. 669); (ii) Namik Džanković testified that he had always exchanged information with Emin Zebić (Trial Judgement, para. 673); and (iii) the instruction given by Nermin Eminović, Chief of the SVB of the 6th Corps, to Nusret Sahić (Commander of the 6th Corps military police battalion) to investigate the crime scene and report back to him (Trial Judgement, para. 675).

540 Trial Judgement, para. 683, quoting Jusuf Jašarević's order to Nermin Eminović (Exhibit 224) and para. 684, detailing the ensuing investigation led by Nermin Eminović.

541 Exhibit 157, quoted in Trial Judgement, para. 307.

542 Prosecution Appeal Brief, fn. 189.

543 AT. 42. *See* also Prosecution Reply Brief, para. 3.25, where the Prosecution states that "Delić's order is further evidence that Halilović had the material ability to punish".

544 AT. 147–148.

545 AT. 42–43.

546 AT. 148.

547 The Appeals Chamber notes the Prosecution's submissions in this respect: "More important, we rely on the order as listing all of the -- all of the reasonable measures and necessary measures that he could have taken to punish the troops. So we don't rely on it

noted above and considering, in particular, the fact that Delić's order, as stressed **[page 81]** by Halilović,[548] was only issued three days *after* the Grabovica murders were committed, the Appeals Chamber finds that it was not unreasonable for the Trial Chamber to assess the evidence as it did and conclude that the order in question was not sufficient to establish beyond reasonable doubt Halilović's effective control over the perpetrators at the time of the commission of crimes.[549]

193. Moreover, the Prosecution has neither demonstrated that Delić's order "confirms" a pre-existing material ability of Halilović to punish the perpetrators, nor has it shown that the Trial Chamber erred in its assessment of the order in question. The same holds true for the Final Report of the Inspection Team,[550] invoked by the Prosecution during the Appeal Hearing to demonstrate Halilović's "material ability to initiate measures" in order to punish the perpetrators.[551] Noting that the Trial Chamber examined this report in detail in the Trial Judgement,[552] the Appeals Chamber considers that it was duly taken into account by the Trial Chamber and finds that the Prosecution has not established any error in the Trial Chamber's assessment.

194. In light of the above, and considering in particular the Trial Chamber's findings that various officials had initiated investigations into the events in Grabovica,[553] the Appeals Chamber finds that the Prosecution has not shown any error in the Trial Chamber's assessment of the evidence as a whole with regard to Halilović's material ability to punish.[554] In particular, the Appeals Chamber considers that a reasonable trier of fact could have reached the conclusion that Halilović's ability to investigate and, more specifically, to draw up reports based on the information received did not necessarily amount to the threshold required to establish even a "very limited degree" of effective control over the perpetrators.[555] The Appeals Chamber therefore dismisses the Prosecution's arguments in this respect. **[page 82]**

195. Having found that the Prosecution has failed to prove that the Trial Chamber erred in holding that Halilović had no material ability to punish based on the evidence before it,[556] the Appeals Chamber need not address the question as to what the duty to punish would have entailed *in concreto* in the present case[557] and whether Halilović discharged this duty, in particular through his instruction to Džanković to investigate.

196. For the foregoing reasons, the Appeals Chamber dismisses sub-ground 4. **[page 83]**

F. <u>Conclusions on the first ground of appeal</u>

197. At the outset, the Appeals Chamber recalls that it has dismissed sub-ground 6 of the Prosecution's first ground of appeal, which sought the admission of the 1996 Statement into evidence.[558]

198. Under sub-ground 1 of its appeal, the Prosecution suggested that, although it had argued that the evidence regarding Halilović's role as a Commander was proffered with the aim of establishing his effective

---

for its purpose of establishing that Mr. Halilović was, in fact, commander on the 12th because we say that the order, in fact, confirms that he was the commander or superior of the troops prior to that date." (AT. 148).

548 *See* AT. 106 and 136. *See* also AT. 147–148, where the Prosecution submitted that: "We do not rely on the 12th September order as the basis for the material ability to prevent and punish. If it was, I would agree with Mr. Mettraux that it would be *ex post facto*".

549 *Cf. Hadžihasanović* Interlocutory Decision, para. 51.

550 Exhibit 130, Final Report of the Inspection Team, dated 20 September 1993.

551 AT. 40, where the Prosecution suggested that this report shows that the Inspection Team recommended criminal investigations and proceedings against various members of the ABiH, but that no recommendations were made with regard to the events in Grabovica.

552 *See* Trial Judgement, paras 206–210 (section entitled "Report of the Inspection Team"), and para. 331. *See*, in particular, Trial Judgement, para. 209 and fn. 656, referring to the recommendation to initiate criminal proceedings against individuals collaborating with the HVO and noting the fact that the events in Grabovica and Uzdol were not mentioned.

553 *See supra*, paras 178 and 190.

554 The Appeals Chamber also notes that, contrary to the Prosecution's claim, Halilović did not "accept[...] that he had the material ability to punish" (AT. 32; *see* also AT. 33). *See*, in particular, Trial Judgement, para. 519, quoting the testimony of Šefko Hodžić, T. 101 (24 March 2005): Hodžić declared that Halilović had told him that "there were people around whose duty it was to investigate these matters".

555 *Cf. Blaškić* Appeal Judgement, para. 499.

556 Trial Judgement, para. 746.

557 During the Appeal Hearing, the Prosecution submitted that the "duty to punish requires the superior to conduct an effective investigation and to take active steps to ensure that the perpetrators will be brought to justice" (AT. 49).

558 *See supra*, para. 41.

control over the troops responsible for the crimes in Grabovica, this did not foreclose the Trial Chamber from considering a "case beyond command" – "[I]n fact, the Trial Chamber was duty bound to consider the whole of the evidence of Halilović's role in determining the main issue of effective control".[559] Considering the way the Prosecution pleaded its case at trial, and in light of the fact that a trier of fact is necessarily bound by the theories of the case advanced by the Prosecution, the Appeals Chamber has dismissed the Prosecution's allegation that the Trial Chamber erred in failing to consider whether Halilović had effective control over the perpetrators of the crimes charged in the Indictment by reason of his position as Team Leader of the Inspection Team or by virtue of his position as the most senior ranking ABiH officer in Herzegovina at the time.[560]

199. As a result, the Appeals Chamber limited its analysis to the Prosecution's submissions regarding Halilović's effective control over the perpetrators of the crimes committed in Grabovica in light of his alleged position as commander of Operation Neretva. In so doing, the Appeals Chamber focused its assessment specifically on Halilović's alleged position as *de facto* commander.[561]

200. In this respect, the Appeals Chamber addressed the Prosecution's allegation raised under sub-ground 5 that the Trial Chamber erred in law in misapplying the standard of proof, as this general allegation of error was claimed to have had an impact on findings throughout the Trial Judgement. The Appeals Chamber found that the Prosecution did not properly identify any specific piece of evidence which would have been evaluated by the Trial Chamber according to an erroneous standard.[562] Since an alleged misapplication of the required standard of proof to factual allegations may only be considered in relation to specifically identified findings, the Appeals **[page 84]** Chamber also found that the Prosecution did not clearly show how the alleged misapplication of the standard of proof within the only two paragraphs in the Trial Judgement specifically identified by the Prosecution could impact on the issue of Halilović's effective control.[563] Since the four factual findings identified within these two paragraphs and appealed by the Prosecution are strictly related to sub-grounds 2 and 3, the Appeals Chamber bore them in mind for its assessment of these two sub-grounds.[564]

201. With respect to sub-ground 2, the Appeals Chamber found that it has not been shown that the Trial Chamber required the Prosecution to prove the formal denomination of the military operation as an element necessary to establish the existence of a superior-subordinate relationship between Halilović and the offending troops.[565] Accordingly, the Appeals Chamber has dismissed the allegation that the Trial Chamber erroneously required the Prosecution to prove that the combat operations carried out in Herzegovina in September 1993 to lift the HVO blockade of Mostar were called "Operation Neretva" as a necessary pre-condition for a finding of effective control and, therefore, for Halilović's conviction.[566]

202. With respect to sub-ground 3, and despite the fact that the Trial Chamber did erroneously focus on the formal establishment of an IKM, thereby disregarding the possible existence of a *de facto* IKM,[567] the Appeals Chamber found that, even assuming the existence of an IKM in Jablanica, this finding could not in itself eliminate all reasonable doubt about Halilović's position as *de facto* superior of the perpetrators of the crimes in Grabovica.[568]

203. Thus, the errors alleged by the Prosecution in these sub-grounds could not, on their own, possibly invalidate the Trial Judgement.[569] However, the Appeals Chamber will nevertheless take these allegations

559 Prosecution Reply Brief, para. 2.6.

560 *See supra,* paras 97–98.

561 The Prosecution itself conceded during the Appeal Hearing that Halilović "did not have the formal title of commander of Operation Neretva" (AT. 19. *See* also, *inter alia*, AT. 13, 21 and 23), and pleaded that Halilović was "*de facto* commander" of the operation (*see*, *inter alia*, AT. 7, 20 and 23).

562 *See supra*, para. 123.

563 *See supra*, para. 131.

564 The Prosecution recognized that sub-grounds 2 and 3 are exemplary of the overall error alleged in sub-ground 5 (AT. 11).

565 *See supra*, paras 139 and 140.

566 *See supra*, para. 143.

567 *See supra*, para. 157.

568 *See supra*, paras 164 and 165. *See* also *Bagilishema* Appeal Judgement, para. 14 and *supra*, para. 11.

569 The Prosecution itself acknowledged during the Appeal Hearing that a finding on the existence of an IKM alone would not lead to the conclusion that Halilović was a *de facto* superior, but that this was an "indicator of effective control which can support a positive finding of *de facto* superior" (AT. 10).

of error into account in its assessment of whether, when considering the first ground of appeal as a whole and in light of the discussion on the appropriate standard of proof, they are capable of eliminating all reasonable doubt as to Halilović's effective control over the perpetrators of the crimes committed in Grabovica. **[page 85]**

204. The Prosecution generally claimed that Halilović's effective control was grounded "in his exercise of material abilities to take all measures associated with the planned combat operation",[570] and more specifically "in his actions and the actions of those he controlled".[571] Underlying these submissions was the Prosecution's claim that Halilović "issued orders that certainly confirmed that he [was] in charge".[572] As the Trial Chamber correctly set out, the capacity to issue orders can indeed amount to an indicator of the effective control exercised by a superior.[573] However, such orders do not *per se* prove effective control; the orders in question will rather have to be carefully assessed in light of the rest of the evidence in order to ascertain the degree of control over the perpetrators.[574]

205. The Appeals Chamber first notes that the Prosecution's submissions relating to Halilović's orders were based on his role as Team Leader of the Inspection Team, which, the Prosecution claimed, performed functions of central control over combat operations.[575] As considered above,[576] the Trial Chamber assessed in detail the evidence regarding the establishment and the specific functions of the Inspection Team, as well as Halilović's role as Team Leader, and found that the Inspection Team was tasked with inspection, coordination and cooperation among units.[577] Within its analysis, the Trial Chamber assessed the orders given by Halilović, in particular with regard to the reorganisation and resubordination of units.[578] The Appeals Chamber considers that it was not unreasonable for the Trial Chamber, on the basis of the evidence before it, to conclude that the orders issued by Halilović were consistent with the monitoring and coordination functions of the Inspection Team. The Prosecution has failed to show that these orders demonstrate that Halilović had any disciplinary powers which might establish his material ability to prevent or punish the perpetrators of the crimes committed in Grabovica, since a trier of fact could legitimately consider them mere indicia of some degree of organizational authority. **[page 86]**

206. In this respect, the Appeals Chamber notes that Halilović's authority to issue orders was already limited by the order establishing the Inspection Team.[579] In particular, orders given by Halilović were all issued under the overall authority of Rasim Delić:[580] this is reflected in the fact that Inspection Team members would wait for Delić's decision, for example, as to the use of certain units in combat operations.[581] This is further evidenced by the fact that the addressees of Halilović's orders requested confirmation from Delić before following them.[582] Contrary to the Prosecution's arguments that such confirmations should be seen as Delić's

---

570 AT. 43.

571 AT.14.

572 AT. 20. *See* also AT. 8, 15–16, 30 and 43.

573 Trial Judgement, para. 58. *See* also *supra*, para. 69.

574 The Appeals Chamber agrees with Halilović that the "issuing of orders is not a matter that mathematically proves whether a person has effective control" (AT. 92). In this context, the Appeals Chamber also recalls that "the indicators of effective control are more a matter of evidence than of substantive law, and [that] those indicators are limited to showing that the accused had the power to prevent, punish, or initiate measures leading to proceedings against the alleged perpetrators where appropriate" (*Blaškić* Appeal Judgement, para. 69). As an example of the application of these principles to the circumstances of the case, the Appeals Chamber found, again in the *Blaškić* case, that "the issuing of humanitarian orders does not by itself establish that the Appellant had effective control over the troops that received the orders" (*Blaškić* Appeal Judgement, para. 485).

575 AT. 30.

576 *See supra*, para. 72.

577 *See*, in particular, the Trial Chamber's conclusions in paragraphs 210 and 364 of the Trial Judgement.

578 *See*, in particular, Trial Judgement, paras 222–244. *See* also *supra*, para. 72.

579 *See* Trial Judgement, para. 369, where the Trial Chamber noted Halilović's limitation to issue orders: "first in that for any 'drastic proposals' Sefer Halilović had to consult with Rasim Delić, and secondly, by this order Sefer Halilović only had the power to issue orders 'in keeping with his authority'". *See* also Trial Judgement, para. 198, quoting the 30 August 1993 order (Exhibit 146).

580 Trial Judgement, paras 369–370.

581 *See* Trial Judgement, para. 247, quoting a Report of the Inspection Team members Vehbija Karić, Rifat Bilajac and Zićro Suljević to Rasim Delić (Exhibit 406), and para. 369.

582 *See*, for example, Trial Judgement, paras 233 and 743, where the Trial Chamber notes evidence that Vahid Karavelić did not carry out an order from Halilović until it had been confirmed by Rasim Delić (Exhibit 161). Karavelić testified specifically that "he contacted Rasim Delić because Sefer Halilović as 'Chief of Staff' could only issue orders with authorisation from the Commander" (Trial Judgement, para. 233, referring to Vahid Karavelić, T. 2–3 (20 April 2005)).

assertion of Halilović's command authority,[583] the Appeals Chamber considers that this course of action by Delić and Halilović may legitimately be considered by a trier of fact as reflecting Halilović's limited ability to issue effective orders on his own.

207. In this context, the Appeals Chamber considers that proof that an accused is not only able to issue orders but that his orders are actually followed, provides another example of effective control.[584] In the present case, the Trial Chamber made specific findings with regard to the resistance – even disobedience – that the Inspection Team and Halilović as its Team Leader encountered from Corps and unit commanders.[585] The Prosecution has submitted that there was, "in each of these cases a following-up and a following through of the order".[586] Nonetheless, the Appeals Chamber considers that, as the Prosecution itself concedes,[587] in most of these cases only Delić's intervention led to the execution of Halilović's orders. The Appeals Chamber therefore finds that a reasonable trier of fact could have concluded that Halilović's orders were not followed and could have taken into account this important consideration in the overall assessment of Halilović's effective control over the perpetrators.

208. The Appeals Chamber therefore finds that a reasonable trier of fact could have reached the conclusion that the orders issued by Halilović as Team Leader of the Inspection Team were not by themselves sufficient to demonstrate Halilović's material ability to prevent or punish crimes, thereby establishing his effective control over the perpetrators. **[page 87]**

209. When submitting that Halilović exercised effective control over the perpetrators, the Prosecution relied specifically on Halilović's material ability to punish as "the most important discussion ... because it focuses directly on the effective control test".[588] In its analysis of sub-ground 4, the Appeals Chamber has found that it was not unreasonable for the Trial Chamber to conclude that Halilović lacked the material ability to punish the persons who committed the crimes in Grabovica.[589]

210. In any event, even assuming that Halilović had the ability to contribute to an investigation or to the punishment of the perpetrators of the crimes committed in Grabovica, these abilities can only amount to effective control relevant for Article 7(3) of the Statute if they are the consequence of a relationship of subordination between Halilović and these perpetrators.[590] Indeed, the Appeals Chamber recalls that the material ability to punish and its corresponding duty to punish can only amount to effective control over the perpetrators if they are premised upon a pre-existing superior-subordinate relationship between the accused and the perpetrators. In this regard, the ability to exercise effective control in the sense of a material power to prevent or punish necessitates a pre-existing relationship of subordination, hierarchy or chain of command.[591] Of course, the concepts of subordination, hierarchy and chains of command need not be established in the sense of formal organisational structures so long as the fundamental requirement of effective control over the subordinate, in the sense of material ability to prevent or punish criminal conduct, is satisfied.[592]

583 AT. 23 and 41–42.

584 *Cf. Blaškić* Appeal Judgement, para. 69.

585 *See*, in particular, Trial Judgement, paras 351 and 744.

586 AT. 147. *See* also AT. 15–16 and 43

587 AT. 147. *See* also AT. 23 and 41.

588 AT. 32.

589 *See supra*, para. 194.

590 *See supra*, para. 59.

591 *Čelebići* Appeal Judgement, para. 303, where the Appeals Chamber explained that the doctrine of command responsibility "developed with an emphasis on persons who, by virtue of the position which they occupy, have authority over others". This approach also underlies the reasoning in the *Blaškić* Appeal Judgement, paras 372ff: the Appeals Chamber first ascertained whether Blaškić had "command authority" over the Military Police (an authority it found he could have for *ad hoc* missions pursuant to specific requests, paras 375–381), before assessing whether he had effective control over said Military Police (paras 382 ff). In the *Kajelijeli* Appeal Judgement (paras 85–86), the ICTR Appeals Chamber first recalled that "a superior is one who possesses power or authority over subordinates either *de jure* or *de facto*" (para. 85), before outlining the threshold to be reached in establishing a superior-subordinate relationship, namely "that it be found beyond reasonable doubt that the accused was able to exercise effective control over his or her subordinates" (para. 86). *See* also *Blagojević and Jokić* Appeal Judgement, paras 301–303.

592 *Čelebići* Appeal Judgement, para. 254.

211. In the present case, the Prosecution has failed to show how Halilović's alleged position as *de facto* commander of Operation Neretva established a chain of command or a hierarchical relationship between him and the perpetrators amounting to a superior-subordinate relationship in which he could have exercised effective control over the perpetrators, in the sense of material ability to prevent or punish crimes. In particular, the Prosecution has failed to show how Halilović's **[page 88]** role as Chief of Staff of the Main Staff of the Supreme Command of the ABiH[593] (and allegedly the most senior ABiH officer in Herzegovina) or his functions within the Inspection Team created such a chain of command.[594]

212. In fact, the most relevant issue in relation to these two positions is the authority and responsibility broadly associated with the functions of Chief-of-Staff.[595] In this context, the Appeals Chamber refers to the findings of the Military Tribunal in *United States v. Wilhelm von Leeb et al.*[596] As a commander-in-chief of an Army group, "the duties imposed upon [von Leeb] were exclusively operational and his headquarters and staff were strictly operational in their functions".[597] Therefore, "his authority in th[e] field [of executive power] was more in the nature of a right to intervene than a direct responsibility".[598] The Military Tribunal found that, under the circumstances of the case, "it [was] not considered [...] that criminal responsibility attache[d] to him merely on the theory of subordination and over-all command".[599]

213. In the present case, the Appeals Chamber considers that the Prosecution has failed to show that no reasonable trier of fact could have reached the conclusion that the order establishing the Inspection Team did not create any type of subordination, hierarchy or chain of command between Halilović and the perpetrators going beyond Halilović's authority as Chief of Staff, or that Halilović had duties and responsibilities which were "exclusively operational".[600]

214. In particular, considering that criminal responsibility does not attach to a military official merely on the basis of his "over-all command", the Appeals Chamber finds that, even assuming Halilović was a *de facto* superior of the perpetrators of the murders in Grabovica, the Prosecution has failed to show that the Trial Chamber erred in finding that the mandate of the Inspection Team did not include duties or obligations related to the effective prevention or punishment of crimes (which would form the required basis for Halilović's effective control over the perpetrators).[601] The Appeals Chamber considers that, while it is true that the Inspection Team suggested the initiation of **[page 89]** some criminal proceedings in its Final Report,[602] a reasonable trier of fact could reach the conclusion that these mere "suggestions", in the context of an "estimate of the overall situation in the Neretva valley",[603] did not establish beyond reasonable doubt even a "very limited degree" of effective control of Halilović over the perpetrators.[604]

215. The Appeals Chamber therefore finds that, even assuming that (i) a *de facto* IKM was established, (ii) the name of the military operation in question was "Neretva", and (iii) the participants at the Zenica meeting discussed who would be commander of this operation and planned a specific and detailed operation to liberate Mostar,[605] the Prosecution has not shown that the Trial Chamber erred in concluding that the Prosecution did not prove beyond reasonable doubt that Halilović had the material ability to prevent or punish the crimes committed in Grabovica.

---

593 The Appeals Chamber notes that the Trial Chamber discussed extensively Halilović's role within the structure of the Main Staff, but made no ultimate finding as to his *de jure* or *de facto* position therein (Trial Judgement, paras 105 to 111). The Trial Chamber only held that Halilović's position "within the structure of the Main Staff was circumscribed as a result of the 8 June and 18 July Decisions" (Trial Judgement, para. 369).

594 *Cf. supra*, para. 70, regarding the alleged subordination of the 9th Brigade and its commander Ališpago to Halilović.

595 The Prosecution argued that the Inspection Team was appointed to perform a role of "central control" over the planned combat operation (AT. 30).

596 *United States v. Wilhelm von Leeb et al.* ("*High Command* Case"), in TWC, Vol. XI.

597 *High Command* Case, p. 554.

598 *High Command* Case, p. 554.

599 *High Command* Case, p. 555.

600 *See* Trial Judgement, paras 198–205, assessing Delić's order of 30 August 1993 to form an Inspection Team.

601 The Appeals Chamber notes that, of course, the distinction outlined above between a pre-existing *de facto* superior position, on the one side, and effective control, on the other, does not necessarily mean that findings on both these requirements will not be based in whole or in part, in certain cases, on the same evidence related to the ability to prevent and punish.

602 Trial Judgement, para. 209, referring to Exhibit 130, pp. 4–5.

603 Exhibit 130, p. 3.

604 *Cf. Blaškić* Appeal Judgement, para. 499.

605 *See supra*, para. 125, sub (ii) and (iii).

216. Therefore, the Prosecution failed to show that no reasonable trier of fact could have reached the conclusion that Halilović, as a commander of Operation Neretva, did not have the required degree of "effective control" over the perpetrators to establish his superior responsibility under Article 7(3) of the Statute. For the foregoing reasons, the first ground of appeal is dismissed.

217. Consequently, considering that the Prosecution has failed to show that the Trial Chamber erred in finding that the first element of superior responsibility had not been met, the Appeals Chamber need not address the Prosecution's arguments advanced under the remaining grounds of appeal.[606] These grounds, which concern the other two elements required to establish superior responsibility under Article 7(3) of the Statute, intrinsically hinge upon the outcome of the first ground of appeal.[607] **[page 90]**

V. DISPOSITION

For the foregoing reasons, **THE APPEALS CHAMBER,**

PURSUANT TO Article 25 of the Statute and Rules 117 and 118 of the Rules;

NOTING the respective written submissions of the Parties and the arguments they presented at the hearings of 10 and 11 July 2007;

SITTING in open session;

DISMISSES the Prosecution's appeal; and

AFFIRMS Halilović's acquittal.

Done in English and French, the English text being authoritative.

Judge Mehmet Güney Presiding	Judge Mohamed Shahabuddeenv	Judge Andrésia Vaz
Judge Theodor Meron		Judge Wolfgang Schomburg

Judge Theodor Meron appends a separate opinion.

Judge Wolfgang Schomburg appends a separate opinion.

Judge Mohamed Shahabuddeen appends a declaration.

Dated this 16th day of October 2007

At The Hague,

The Netherlands

[Seal of the International Tribunal] [page 91]

606 Likewise, the Trial Chamber was not required to enter a finding to the effect that Halilović had failed to *punish* the perpetrators of the crimes, since it had found that Halilović had no effective control based on a superior-subordinate relationship over the troops which committed the crimes in Grabovica.

607 The Appeals Chamber recalls that the Prosecution's second and third grounds of appeal concern the other two requirements of superior responsibility under Article 7(3) of the Statute, namely whether Halilović knew or had reason to know that a criminal act was about to be or had been committed and whether Halilović failed to prevent or punish the criminal conduct (Prosecution Notice of Appeal, paras 5–8). The fourth ground of appeal relates to the admission into evidence of a report by a military expert witness. The Prosecution Notice of Appeal, para. 9, argued under the fourth ground of appeal that the admission of the military expert's report and his proposed testimony would have affected the findings of the Trial Chamber on the existence of a superior-subordinate relationship (Trial Judgement, paras 363–372, 736–747 and 752) and on whether Halilović knew or had reason to know that the criminal act was about to be or had been committed (Trial Judgement, paras 485–525). These parts of the fourth ground of appeal were withdrawn in the Prosecution Appeal Brief, fn. 344. Consequently, according to the Prosecution, the admission of this evidence would only have affected the third element of superior responsibility under Article 7(3) of the Statute (Prosecution Notice of Appeal, para. 9, citing Trial Judgement, paras 97–100, 660–701 and 743–747).

VI. SEPARATE OPINION OF JUDGE MERON

1. I write separately on the issue of Sub-Ground 6. Although I agree with the majority that the Trial Chamber correctly excluded Halilović's 1996 Statement, I believe that such a conclusion necessarily derives from Rule 43 and is not, as the majority holds, a discretionary decision pursuant to Rule 89(D).

2. The majority holds that "[wğhether [Halilović's] statement would also be inadmissible due to a retroactive reading of Rule 43 of the Rules was not a decisive consideration in the Trial Chamber's reasoning."[1] I disagree. In reproducing the Trial Chamber's holding regarding the Statement, the majority omits a critical paragraph from the Trial Judgement:

> Rule 43 provides for audio and video-recording of the interview of suspects and aims at ensuring the integrity of the proceedings, *inter alia*, by providing for an instrument to ascertain the voluntariness of a statement and the adherence to other relevant safeguards as provided for in Rule 42 and Rule 95. The Trial Chamber finds that Rule 43 is a fundamental provision to protect the rights of a suspect and an accused. Moreover, it is a safeguard for a full and accurate reflection of the questions and answers during the interview and thus enables the parties and the Trial Chamber to verify the exact wording of what was said during the interview.[2]

The centrality of Rule 43 in the Trial Chamber's logic could hardly be more clear. Thus, the correct interpretation of Rule 43 is an issue that the Appeals Chamber should address.

3. Rule 43 provides:

> Whenever the Prosecutor questions a suspect, the questioning shall be audio-recorded or video-recorded . . . .

4. The Trial Chamber correctly recognized that two fundamental legal questions arise with respect to Rule 43 and Halilović's Statement: (1) What procedural safeguards applied to the Statement?; and (2) What is the remedy for violations of those safeguards?

5. The first legal question involves the scope of Rule 43, specifically whether it applies only when someone is already a suspect or whether it applies also to questioning that occurred before the person became a suspect. As the Trial Chamber correctly recognized, Rule 43 has a two-fold purpose—ensuring *voluntariness* and *reliability*. Precisely because of concerns about reliability, Rule 43 must apply to all statements by an accused to the Prosecutor. Notwithstanding that a Prosecutor might have acted in good faith by not applying Rule 43 when questioning someone who, at the time, was not a suspect, Rule 43 embodies a substantive policy judgment that only statements memorialized on a video or audio tape are sufficiently reliable to be admitted into evidence against **[page 92]** an accused. Therefore, the Trial Chamber correctly determined that Rule 43 was among the procedural safeguards that applied to the Statement.

6. Since Rule 43 applied to the Statement, and given that there is no question that the Statement was not recorded in compliance with the rule, the second question concerns the appropriate remedy. Rule 43 reflects a substantive judgment that unrecorded statements by the accused are, by definition, insufficiently reliable. A Trial Chamber normally assesses reliability on a case-by-case basis under Rule 95 and excludes evidence when there is "substantial doubt" about its reliability. Similarly, it determines probativeness under Rule 89(D). The discretion that a Trial Chamber normally exercises pursuant to these rules is inapposite, though, because an unrecorded statement by an accused is per se unreliable under Rule 43. As an unrecorded statement by an accused is never sufficiently reliable, the only appropriate remedy is exclusion of that statement.

7. My conclusion about the appropriateness of exclusion for violations of Rule 43 is bolstered by the precedents of the Tribunal. The *Čelebići* Appeal Judgement noted that the Appeals Chamber must seek to ensure (1) that procedural safeguards are respected and (2) that the evidence is reliable.[3] The Appeals Chamber there clearly contemplated that, despite scrupulous adherence to all procedural safeguards, some

---

1 Appeal Judgement, para. 38.
2 Decision of 8 July 2005, para. 24 (footnote omitted).
3 *Čelebići* Appeal Judgement, para. 533.

evidence might still be unreliable. It did not indulge the converse (*i.e.*, that despite procedural violations, some evidence might still be sufficiently reliable). A violation of Rule 43 thus incurably taints the evidence.[4]

8. In light of the foregoing analysis, the majority's holding fails to appreciate that a Trial Chamber exercises discretion in assessing probativeness under Rule 89(D), and in determining reliability under Rule 95, only *after* the Trial Chamber has established that the Prosecution respected certain procedural safeguards, including Rule 43. Once it is established that Rule 43 applied, and that it was violated, there is no room for discretion—the statement must be excluded.

9. Finally, I note that Judge Schomburg and I are largely in agreement on this issue. Although we disagree slightly as to the precise scope of Rule 43, we both agree that it applied here, that it was violated, and that exclusion is the only appropriate remedy.

10. Except for these observations, I am in full agreement with the majority opinion.

Done in English and French, the English text being authoritative. **[page 93]**

Dated this 16th day of October 2007
At The Hague,
The Netherlands

Judge Theodor Meron

[Seal of the International Tribunal] [page 94]

[4] *Cf. Prosecutor v. Delalić et al.*, Case No. IT-96-21-T, Decision on the Motion on the Exclusion and Restitution of Evidence and Other Material Seized From the Accused Zejnil Delalić, 9 October 1996, para. 15; *Prosecutor v. Delalić et al.*, Case No. IT-96-21-T, Decision on the Motions for the Exclusion of Evidence by The Accused, Zejnil Delalić, 25 September 1997, paras 44-46 (holding that the defendant carries the burden of demonstrating that a statement recorded in compliance with Rule 43 is otherwise unreliable).

VII. SEPARATE OPINION OF JUDGE SCHOMBURG

1. I agree with the majority that the Trial Chamber could decide not to admit Sefer Halilović's 1996 statement to the Prosecution into evidence. However, I concur with Judge Meron that the reasoning in the Judgement, solely based on Rule 89(D), is not sufficient. Indeed, Rule 89(D) can only be seen together with Rules 42 and 43, both of which work in tandem to protect fundamental rights of a suspect *de jure* and *de facto* when he later becomes an accused. Furthermore, a distinction has to be made between the admission of evidence and making use of this evidence at the end of the trial in the judgement. Only the later point in time is decisive because the assessment of evidence might vary in light of the entirety of the evidence before the Trial Chamber. The admission of evidence does not necessarily mean that it will be used as evidence at the end of the day.

2. Rule 42 and Rule 43 of the Rules aim at safeguarding fundamental rights of a suspect in the best possible way. Rule 42 protects a suspect against giving uninformed statements and in particular against involuntary self-incrimination. The rationale of Rule 43 is to translate these guarantees into reality using contemporary technical standards and at the same time to assure the precision and reliability of a suspect's statement in the language he used when answering the questions put to him by an interrogator.[1] It is a general observation in criminal proceedings that summaries, replacing the question/answer standard, and even the best translation or interpretation are among the most significant sources of error in the fact-finding process. This is of particular importance before international tribunals, which by their nature have to rely heavily on precise translation and interpretation. An accused must always be entitled to challenge the precision of the translation or interpretation of a statement he gave as a suspect, which is later used as evidence in a case against him. The only safeguard can be an audio recording or, even better, a video recording, which also shows the environment in which the statement was taken and other details like, *inter alia*, the body language of all the participants.

3. In the case at hand, of particular relevance, as the Trial Chamber appreciated, is Rule 43, which provides, in its relevant part: **[page 95]**

> Whenever the Prosecutor questions a suspect, the questioning *shall*[2] be audio-recorded or video-recorded . . . .

What has to be established in general is the rationale and precise scope of Rule 43, specifically whether *in concreto* it applies to Sefer Halilović's 1996 statement to the Prosecution.

4. At domestic level, different approaches are followed regarding the qualification of someone as a "suspect," in particular in determining at what point in time a person's status changes to being a suspect. Some legal systems rely on objective criteria.[3] Others follow a subjective approach mixed with objective criteria.[4] However, there is no need to enter into a comparative legal analysis as the International Tribunal's Rules contain a statutory definition of the term "suspect." Rule 2(A) prescribes that a suspect is a

> person concerning whom the Prosecutor possesses reliable information which tends to show that the person may have committed a crime over which the Tribunal has jurisdiction.

---

[1] In the jurisprudence of the International Tribunal, a distinction has been drawn between, on the one hand, the questioning or taking of statements by the Prosecution (specifically regulated in Rule 43 of the Rules), or persons or authorities mandated by the Prosecution, and the questioning, on the other hand, by authorities "who have no relevant connection with the ICTY Prosecutor" (*Prosecutor v. Mrkšić et al.* Case No. IT-95-13/1-T, Decision Concerning the Use of Statements Given by the Accused, 9 October 2006, paras 21–22 and 27). *See* also *Prosecutor v. Delalić et al.*, Case No. IT-96-21-T, Decision on Zdravko Mucić's Motion for the Exclusion of Evidence, 2 September 1997, para. 51. This also applies to statements taken in response to requests made within the framework of international cooperation in criminal matters pursuant to Article 29(2)(b) of the Statute.

[2] Italics added for emphasis.

[3] *E.g.* Switzerland, *see* Robert Hauser & Erhard Schweri, Schweizerisches Strafprozessrecht 140 (4th ed. 1999).

[4] *E.g.* France, *see* Gaston Stefani et al, Procédure Pénale 325 (16th ed. 1996); Germany, *see* Bundesgerichtshof [BGH] [Federal Supreme Court of Justice] 3 July 2007, 1 StR 3/07 (Germany), yet unpublished, *see* www.bundesgerichtshof.de, following Bundesgerichtshof [BGH] [Federal Supreme Court of Justice] 27 February 1992, Entscheidungen des Bundesgerichtshofs in Strafsachen [BGHSt] 38, 214 (218); *See also* in this context, however in relation to the right against self-incrimination alone: *Serves v. France*, ECtHR, App.No. 82/1996/671/893, 20 October 1997, paras 38, 42, on "the first complaint, based on Art. 6(1) [of the European Convention for the Protection of Human Rights and Fundamental Freedoms] alone."

This definition is unequivocally objective in nature. It is insignificant whether the Prosecution, or another authorized person, believes that the person is a suspect or not. Rather, as soon as there is reliable information which tends to show that the person may have committed a crime under the International Tribunal's Statute, the person automatically becomes a suspect. Whether this objective criterion was fulfilled has to be assessed by the Trial Chamber from an *ex post* perspective. In any event before *making use* of such a statement in the judgement, a Trial Chamber must be satisfied that, objectively, the accused before it was not a suspect at the time he gave the statement.

5. It could be argued that this requirement places an unduly harsh burden on the Prosecution. However, bearing in mind the aforementioned purpose of Rule 43, the use of audio or video recordings best reveals the circumstances in which a statement was given by a suspect, thus facilitating the assessment by a Trial Chamber of whether or not there were any obstacles that would impede the use of the statement as evidence and the reliability of its content. The difference between Judge Meron's opinion and mine is that under his approach the Prosecution would *de facto* feel obliged in its own interest to make audio or video recordings of all statements by all witnesses who could potentially become suspects. This would go beyond the ambit of Rule 43 and its clear wording. However, our joint strong opinion is that the very moment the Prosecution is in the **[page 96]** possession of reliable information which tends to show that a witness may have committed a crime, the technical guarantees of Rule 43 have to be implemented immediately.

6. On the question of whether Sefer Halilović was objectively a suspect, the incriminatory nature of the statement is self-evident. Halilović candidly acknowledged that the investigation "may subsequently bring out facts which might involve [his] own responsibility."[5] I note that the Prosecution gave warnings to Halilović similar to those that it has to give to suspects pursuant to Rule 42. However, today the Prosecution submits only that it did not regard Halilović as a suspect at the time.[6] This submission does not respond to the objective criterion set by the Rules for ascertaining as of when Halilović became a suspect.

7. The appropriateness of exclusion of evidence for violations of Rule 43 is already sufficiently discussed by Judge Meron in his Separate Opinion, based on the case-law of the International Tribunal.[7] Indeed, once it is established that the statement was not recorded in compliance with Rule 43, the appropriate remedy following non-compliance with Rule 43 must be determined. This question has never been squarely presented in a previous case. However, it is uncontested that statements of a suspect that were gained in violation of the requirements of Rule 42 cannot be used against him at trial. The same applies to Rule 43, which reflects the decision of the legislator that unrecorded statements by a suspect who later becomes an accused are, in principle, insufficiently reliable. Consequently, if a statement is taken in violation of Rule 43, there is no discretion vested in the Trial Chamber to assess its probative value pursuant to Rule 89(D) or its reliability pursuant to Rule 95. Thus, the only appropriate remedy is the exclusion of such an unrecorded statement. However, again slightly differing from the views expressed in Judge Meron's Separate Opinion, I interpret Rule 43 in such a way that these considerations only apply in cases like this one where use of the statement is sought in proceedings against the former suspect himself and against his will. Rule 43 does not apply in relation to the use of the statement in proceedings against other persons or if the accused irrevocably consents to the use of this statement because it might be in his favour.

8. In sum, with respect, I disagree with Judge Meron solely on the point where he interprets the scope of Rule 43 in such a way that it would also apply retroactively, so that the statement made by a witness at a point in time when he was objectively not a suspect could not be used at all if that witness *later* found himself in the role of an accused. In my view, such an interpretation of Rule 43 is not only too expansive but is also unpractical as it would effectively require the Prosecution to **[page 97]** record each and every witness statement. Thus, Rule 43 can only apply if the interrogated person objectively was a suspect pursuant to Rule 2 *at the time the statement was made.*

---

5 1996 Statement.

6 *See, e.g.*, Prosecution Response to Motion for Exclusion of Statement, paras 20, 24.

7 Separate Opinion of Judge Meron, para. 7.

9. In passing, I note that the Prosecution did not seek to call the Appellant's interrogator(s)[8] or the person(s) who provided interpretation at the time[9] as witnesses during the trial. The Prosecution did not attempt to do so on appeal either. The question of whether a violation of Rule 43 would still allow for the testimony of the person(s) involved in the interrogation at that time[10] therefore does not need to be addressed. However, if, as endorsed by the majority, the rejection of Halilović's statement is based solely on its lack of reliability and probative value pursuant to Rules 89 and 95, then it would have been mandatory to discuss whether the Trial Chamber erred when it did not exercise its discretion pursuant to Rule 98 at all and omitted to consider whether to summon these persons involved in the interrogation as they were obviously available.[11] Indeed, hearing these witnesses might have assisted the Trial Chamber in its determination of whether to exclude the statement pursuant to Rules 89 and 95.

10. In sum, the Trial Chamber correctly concluded that the exclusion of the statement is the proper remedy. I concur with the Appeals Chamber upholding that decision but with all due respect suggest that it should have done so with a complete reasoning.

Done in English and French, the English text being authoritative.

Dated this sixteenth day of October 2007
At The Hague, The Netherlands.

Judge Wolfgang Schomburg

[Seal of the International Tribunal] [page 98]

[8] *See* Annex II to the Prosecution Response to Defence Motion to Exclude the Statement of the Accused, 17 June 2005.
[9] *See* Annex I to the Prosecution Response to Defence Motion to Exclude the Statement of the Accused, 17 June 2005.
[10] This could be a substitute only; its probative value would have to be assessed with greatest caution.
[11] *See supra* notes 8 and 9.

VIII. DECLARATION OF JUDGE SHAHABUDDEEN

1. All members of the Appeals Chamber support its judgement, including its finding that the Trial Chamber was correct in holding that Halilović's written statement was inadmissible. There is however a difference of opinion as to the basis on which the statement was inadmissible. Before dealing with the matter, there is a preliminary question to be considered as to whether it is open to the Appeals Chamber to pronounce on the point.

2. The preliminary question turns on what the Trial Chamber did. One view is that the Trial Chamber held that the statement was inadmissible for simple non-compliance with the recording procedure prescribed by Rule 43 of the Rules of Procedure and Evidence of the Tribunal, which involved but foreclosed the issue of reliability (the first route). Another view is that the Trial Chamber took the position that, in the absence of a recording made under that Rule, it was not possible to remove from the statement an appearance of unreliability; the exclusion therefore rested on unreliability (the second route). I believe that all members of the Appeals Chamber are agreed that it was only if the Trial Chamber took the first route that the Appeals Chamber would be entitled to express its opinion as to whether the statement was inadmissible for simple non-compliance with the Rule.

3. As to which route was taken, opinion is divided, but, on balance, my interpretation of the Trial Chamber's reasoning leads me to conclude that it took the second route. While the Trial Chamber indeed referred to Rule 43, it really relied on the general concept of reliability; it used the unavailability of a recording as required by that Rule, not as an automatic bar, but merely to show that it had not the means of testing whether the *ex facie* unreliability of the statement was confirmed or removed by what in fact happened at the interview in the course of which the statement was given.

4. In other words, the Trial Chamber opted for the second route. It follows that the Trial Chamber's reference to Rule 43 is not a sufficient basis for entitling the Appeals Chamber to pronounce on the question whether simple non-compliance with the recording procedure of that Rule grounds inadmissibility of a statement made by a suspect to the Prosecutor.

5. However, if it becomes necessary to deal with the question, what is the position? The basic problem which I have with an affirmative answer is that such an answer assumes the answer – it assumes but does not prove that the statement is inadmissible for simple non-compliance with the recording procedure prescribed by Rule 43. It is hard not to admire the liberal underpinnings of that assumption. But, with respect, I do not think that the assumption is founded. **[page 99]**

6. I accept that whether the person giving the statement is referred to as a 'witness' is not decisive. The test is whether the person was objectively a suspect,[1] even though he may be called a witness. If objectively he was a suspect, his statement comes within Rule 43 operating on a current basis, without there being any need for the Appeals Chamber to trouble over the vexed question of retroactivity. Still that leaves open the question what is the effect of non-compliance with the recording procedure prescribed by the Rule: is the statement inadmissible simply because of the non-compliance?

7. I recognise that in the majority of cases non-compliance with the recording procedure prescribed by Rule 43 will contribute to exclusion, but the question is whether it is correct to proceed on the footing that exclusion is the simple result of such non-compliance. Rule 43 does not command any particular sanction of enforcement. As correctly observed by Jones and Powles,[2] speaking of the companion Rule 42, '[t]he Rules do not explicitly state what the remedy should be when a suspect's rights are violated'. The circumstances of *HMA v. Swift*[3] were slightly different, but the disposition read: 'Tape and oral evidence were equally primary evidence; Oral evidence admitted'. That case seems to be in keeping with what is mentioned below concerning confessions in the practice of the Tribunal. In this respect, there are various domestic models, but it is of course the Tribunal's model which is determinative.

8. In the case of a 'confession by an accused given during questioning by the Prosecutor', as referred to in Rule 92, non-compliance with the requirement of Rule 63 for audio-recording or video-recording in

1 *See Serves v. France*, ECtHR, 20 October 1997, para. 42, and *Heaney and Mc Guinness v Ireland*, ECtHR, 21 December 2000, para, 42.

2 *International Criminal Practice*, (Oxford, 2003), page 502.

3 [1983] SCCR, 204 at 207.

accordance with the procedure prescribed by Rule 43 does not lead to automatic exclusion of the confession. Rule 92 does say that the confession shall be presumed 'free and voluntary' if 'the requirements of Rule 63 were *strictly*[4] complied with', but Rule 92 goes on to make the sage addition, 'unless the contrary is proved'. So, even a 'confession by the accused' can be admitted though there has been non-compliance with the recording procedure of Rule 43.

9. That conforms to the test of inadmissibility of evidence obtained by certain methods. Obviously, a written statement obtained in compliance with the recording procedure prescribed by Rule 43 is admissible. But it does not follow that evidence not obtained in accordance with the prescribed procedure is inadmissible simply for non-compliance with that procedure. Such evidence was obtained by a method of one kind or another. Rule 95 provides that '[n]o evidence shall be admissible if obtained by methods which cast substantial doubt on its reliability or if its admission **[page 100]** is antithetical to, and would seriously damage, the integrity of the proceedings'. Some judicial judgement has to be exercised on whether the method followed has cast 'substantial doubt' on the reliability of the evidence. Evidence is not excluded simply because it has been obtained in non-compliance with an authorised method.

10. I would mention two situations in which inadmissibility is stipulated by the law itself. The first is a case in which a witness gives self-incriminating evidence under compulsion of the court. Rule 90(E) provides that '[t]estimony compelled in this way shall not be used as evidence in a subsequent prosecution against the witness for any offence other than false testimony'. Exclusion of the testimony is automatic. The second has to do with cases of sexual assault. Rule 96(iv) provides that 'prior sexual conduct of the victim shall not be admitted in evidence'; thus, even a statement by the victim is excluded if it bears on his or her prior sexual conduct.

11. In these cases, the law itself mandates exclusion of the evidence; nothing is left to the judgement of the court, except to find that there has been the precipitating event – compulsion by the court, or prior sexual conduct. As previously noted, Rule 43 does not provide for mandatory exclusion as an enforcement sanction: if there is non-compliance with the prescribed recording procedure, the court still has to make a judgement as to whether the method chosen casts 'substantial doubt' on the reliability of the unrecorded statement.

12. It remains to examine two of the cases decided by this Tribunal and the ICTR, respectively. It is true that, in this Tribunal, the Trial Chamber in *Delalić* excluded the statement for having been taken in non-compliance with Rule 42. But it is not clear that the exclusion rested on simple non-compliance. The Trial Chamber said:

> However violation of Sub-rules 42A(i) and 42(B) by themselves would be sufficient by virtue of Rule 5 to render the statements before the Austrian Police null and inadmissible in the proceedings before us and to be excluded.[5]

Rule 5, to which reference was made, provides that the Chamber 'shall grant relief if it finds that the alleged non-compliance is proved and that it has caused material prejudice to' the complaining party. So the Chamber did have to go an extra mile.

13. In *Bagosora*, an ICTR Trial Chamber said:

> As stated by the ICTY Chamber in Delalić, it is difficult to imagine a statement taken in violation of the fundamental right to the assistance of counsel which would not require its exclusion under Rule 95 as being 'antithetical to, and would seriously damage, the integrity of the proceedings'.[6] **[page 101]**

So, again, exclusion was not based simply on non-compliance with the prescribed procedure.

14. I concede, as recognised above, that the non-availability of a recording made under Rule 43 may lead to inadmissibility. But this is a far cry from saying that inadmissibility is the simple result of non-compliance with the Rule. That, I believe, is the proposition in issue; with respect, paragraph 9 of Judge Schomburg's

---

4 Emphasis added.
5 IT-96-21, 2 September 1997, para. 55.
6 ICTR-98-41-T, 14 October 2004. para. 21.

separate opinion does not help to establish it. The Trial Chamber chose to found inadmissibility on the general concept of unreliability. On the basis of this concept, it reached the correct conclusion: the statement was inadmissible. All members of the Appeals Chamber agree that it was inadmissible.

15. In conclusion, I regret that I cannot agree that simple non-compliance with the recording procedure grounds inadmissibility.

Done in English and French, the English text being authoritative.

Dated 16 October 2007
At The Hague
The Netherlands

Mohamed Shahabuddeen

[Seal of the International Tribunal] [page 102]

IX. ANNEX A – PROCEDURAL HISTORY

A. Trial proceedings

1. An initial indictment against Sefer Halilović was filed on 30 July 2001, modified by the Prosecution on 10 September 2001 and confirmed by Judge Patricia Wald on 12 September 2001. The Indictment charged Halilović with one count of murder, a violation of the laws or customs of war, under Articles 3 and 7(3) of the Statute.[1] In 2003, the Defence sought for particulars with respect to the Indictment and the charges filed against Halilović. Given that the particulars requested were contained in the Indictment, in the Pre-Trial Brief of the Prosecution or the discovery materials, or that the evidentiary matters for trial had not been affected, these motions were denied.[2]

2. Halilović voluntarily surrendered to the International Tribunal on 25 September 2001 and was transferred to the United Nations Detention Unit in The Hague ("UNDU"). His initial appearance before the Trial Chamber was held on 27 September 2001, when he entered a plea of not guilty to the charge against him. The trial commenced on 31 January 2005 and lasted 77 days. In the course of the proceedings, the Trial Chamber heard 41 live witnesses, two of whom testified by way of video-conference link and four of whom testified pursuant to Rule 89(F) of the Rules; one witness was heard by way of a deposition hearing supplemented by testimony received via video-conference link; 13 witness statements were admitted into evidence pursuant to Rule 92*bis* (B) of the Rules; and one statement of a deceased witness was admitted pursuant to Rule 92*bis* (C) of the Rules. The Trial Chamber additionally issued one subpoena and one order for safe conduct for two different witnesses, and one order for the temporary transfer of a detained witness. In all, the Trial Chamber admitted 287 Prosecution exhibits and 207 Defence exhibits into evidence.

3. The Trial Judgement was rendered on 16 November 2005. The Trial Chamber found Halilović not guilty, acquitting him of murder under Articles 3 and 7(3) of the Statute. As a result of the acquittal and pursuant to Rule 99(A) of the Rules, the Trial Chamber ordered Halilović's immediate release from the UNDU.[3] **[page 103]**

B. Appeal proceedings

1. Notice of Appeal

4. On 16 December 2005, in accordance with Article 25 of the Statute and Rule 108 of the Rules, the Prosecution filed its Notice of Appeal against the Trial Judgement.[4]

2. Composition of Appeals Chamber

5. On 11 January 2006, Judge Fausto Pocar, President of the International Tribunal, assigned the following judges to hear the present appeal: Judge Mohamed Shahabuddeen, Judge Mehmet Güney, Judge Andrésia Vaz, Judge Theodor Meron and Judge Wolfgang Schomburg.[5] On 3 February 2006, having been elected as Presiding Judge in the present appeal pursuant to Rule 22(B) of the Rules, Judge Mehmet Güney issued an order designating himself as the Pre-Appeal Judge, with responsibility for all pre-appeal proceedings in this case.[6]

---

1 Indictment, para. 34.

2 *Prosecutor v. Sefer Halilović*, Case No. IT-01-48-T, Defence Motion Pursuant to Rule 65*ter* (K) Requesting the Pre-Trial Judge to Grant Relief from Waiver and to Grant Relief Pursuant to Rule 72, 13 March 2003; Decision on Defence Motion Pursuant to Rule 65*ter* (K) Requesting the Pre-Trial Judge to Grant Relief from Waiver and to Grant Relief Pursuant to Rule 72, 1 April 2003; Decision on Defence Motion for Particulars, 16 December 2003; Motion for Certification, 23 December 2003; Decision on Motion for Certification, 28 January 2004.

3 Trial Judgement, paras 753–754 (Disposition).

4 Prosecution Notice of Appeal, para. 1.

5 Order Assigning Judges to a Case before the Appeals Chamber, 11 January 2006.

6 Order Designating a Pre-Appeal Judge, 3 February 2006.

3. Appeal Briefs

6. The Prosecution filed its Appeal Brief on 1 March 2006. The Appeal Brief was provided to Halilović in his language on 27 June 2006 and Halilović filed a draft of his Respondent's Brief on 12 July 2006.[7] The Appeals Chamber issued its decision on 14 July 2006, granting the motion in part.[8]

7. On 1 August 2006, the Prosecution filed its Brief in Reply and a motion to strike the annexes to the Respondent's Brief.[9] Pursuant to Rule 109 of the Rules and paragraph (C) of the Practice Direction on the Length of Briefs and Motions, the Appeals Chamber granted the motion in part, ordered Halilović to re-file his Respondent's Brief, and further ordered the Prosecution to re-file its Reply Brief, if necessary.[10] **[page 104]**

8. Halilović re-filed his Respondent's Brief on 20 September 2006. The Prosecution then re-filed its Brief in Reply on 22 September 2006.

4. Motion for Prompt Scheduling of Appeal Hearing

9. On 21 September 2006, Halilović filed a motion for prompt scheduling of the appeal hearing.[11]The Prosecution opposed this motion on 2 October 2006.[12] On 6 October 2006, Halilović filed his reply.[13] The Appeals Chamber dismissed the motion on 27 October 2006, on the basis that Article 21(4)(c) of the Statute provides for a right to be tried without undue delay and does not protect against *any* delay in the proceedings.[14]

5. Appeal Hearing

10. Pursuant to the Scheduling Order of 4 June 2007, the Appeal Hearing took place on 10 and 11 July 2007.[15] **[page 105]**

X. ANNEX B – TABLES OF AUTHORITIES AND DEFINED TERMS

A. Judgements and decisions

1. International Tribunal

ALEKSOVSKI
Prosecutor v. Zlatko Aleksovski, Case No. IT-95-14/1-A, Judgement, 24 March 2000 ("*Aleksovski* Appeal Judgement")

BLAGOJEVIĆ & JOKIĆ
Prosecutor v. Vidoje Blagojević and Dragan Jokić, Case No. IT-02-60-T, Decision on Prosecution's Motion for Clarification of Oral Decision Regarding Admissibility of Accused's Statement, 18 September 2003 ("*Blagojević* and *Jokić* Decision Concerning Clarification of Oral Decision")

---

7 On 21 March 2006, Halilović had filed a motion for an extension of time for the filing of his Response Brief (Motion for Extension of Time to File Respondent's Brief, 21 March 2006). This motion was granted on 23 March 2006 and the Appeals Chamber allowed Halilović an additional 20 days after the Trial Judgement was made available to him in his language to file his Respondent's Brief (Decision on Motion for Extension of Time to File Respondent's Brief, 23 March 2006).

8 Decision on Motion for Extension of Number of Words for Respondent's Brief, 14 July 2006.

9 Prosecution's Brief in Reply and Motion to Strike, 1 August 2006; Response to Motion to Strike, 11 August 2006.

10 Decision on Prosecution's Motion to Strike Annexes to the Respondent's Brief, 6 September 2006, p. 5. *See* also Decision on Prosecution's Motion for Clarification of the Appeals Chambers Decision of 6 September 2006, 22 September 2006.

11 Motion for Prompt Scheduling of Appeals Hearing, 21 September 2006.

12 Prosecution's Response to Halilović's Motion for Prompt Scheduling of Appeal Hearing, 2 October 2006.

13 Halilović's Reply *Re* Motion for Prompt Scheduling of Appeals Hearing – *Confidential Annexes,* 6 October 2006.

14 Decision on Defence Motion for Prompt Scheduling of Appeal Hearing, 27 October 2006, paras 17–19 and p. 8 (Disposition).

15 Scheduling Order for Appeal Hearing, 4 June 2007.

Prosecutor v. Vidoje Blagojević & Dragan Jokić, Case No IT-02-60-A, Judgement, 9 May 2007 ("*Blagojević & Jokić* Appeal Judgement")

BLAŠKIĆ
Prosecutor v. Tihomir Blaškić, Case No. IT-95-14-A, Judgement, 29 July 2004 ("*Blaškić* Appeal Judgement")

BRĐANIN
Prosecutor v. Brđanin and Talic, Case No. IT-99-36-PT, Decision on Objections by Momir Talić to the Form of the Indictment, 20 February 2001

Prosecutor v. Brđanin and Talic, Case No. IT-99-36-PT, Decision on Form of Fourth Amended Indictment, 23 November 2001

Prosecutor v. Radoslav Brđanin, Case No. IT-99-36-A, Order to File Table, 24 July 2006

Prosecutor v. Radoslav Brđanin, Case No. IT-99-36-A, Judgement, 3 April 2007 ("*Brđanin* Appeal Judgement)

"ČELEBIĆI"
Prosecutor v. Zejnil Delalić, Dravko Mucić a/k/a "Pavo", Hazim Delić, Esad Landžo a/k/a "Zenga", Case No. IT-96-21-T, Decision on Zdravko Mucić's Motion for the Exclusion of Evidence, 2 September 1997

Prosecutor v. Zejnil Delalić, Zdravko Mucić, a.k.a. "Pavo", Hazim Delić and Esad Landžo, a.k.a. "Zenga", Case No. IT-96-21-T, Judgement, 16 November 1998 ("*Čelebići* Trial Judgement")

Prosecutor v. Zejnil Delalić, Zdravko Mucić, a.k.a. "Pavo", Hazim Delić and Esad Landžo, a.k.a. "Zenga", Case No. IT-96-21-A, Judgement, 20 February 2001 ("*Čelebići* Appeal Judgement") **[page 106]**

DELIĆ
Prosecutor v. Rasim Delić, Case No. IT-04-83-AR72, Decision on Interlocutory Appeal Challenging the Jurisdiction of the Tribunal, 8 December 2005

FURUNDŽIJA
Prosecutor v. Anto Furundžija, Case No. IT-95-17/1-A, Judgement, 21 July 2000 ("*Furundžija* Appeal Judgement")

GALIĆ
Prosecutor v. Stanislav Galić, Case No. IT-98-29-A, Judgement, 30 November 2006 ("*Galić* Appeal Judgement")

HADZIHASANOVIĆ AND KUBURA
Prosecutor v. Enver Hadžihasanović et al., Case No. IT-01-47-PT, Decision on Form of Indictment, 7 December 2001

Prosecutor v. Enver Hadžihasanović et al., Case No. IT-01-47-AR72, Decision on Interlocutory Appeal Challenging Jurisdiction in Relation to Command Responsibility, 16 July 2003 ("*Hadžihasanović* Interlocutory Decision")

Prosecutor v. Enver Hadžihasanović and Amir Kubura, Case No. IT-01-47-T, Decision on Motions for Acquittal pursuant to Rule 98*bis* of the Rules of Procedure and Evidence, 27 September 2004 ("*Hadžihasanović* Rule 98*bis* Decision")

Prosecutor v. Enver Hadžihasanović and Amir Kubura, Case No. IT-01-47-T, Judgement, 15 March 2006 ("*Enver Hadžihasanović and Amir Kubura* Trial Judgement")

HALILOVIĆ
Prosecutor v. Sefer Halilović, Case No. IT-01-48-T, Judgement, 16 November 2005 ("Trial Judgement")

Prosecutor v. Sefer Halilović, Case No. IT-01-48-T, Decision on Prosecutor's Motion Seeking Leave to Amend the Indictment, 17 December 2004 ("Decision of 17 December 2004")

Prosecutor v. Sefer Halilović, Case No. IT-01-48-T, Decision on Motion for Exclusion of Statement of Accused, 8 July 2005 ("Decision of 8 July 2005")

Prosecutor v. Sefer Halilović, Case No. IT-01-48-T, Decision on Prosecution Request for Certification for Interlocutory Appeal of 'Decision on Motion for Exclusion of Statement of Accused', 25 July 2005 ("Certification Decision of 25 July 2005") **[page 107]**

Prosecutor v. Sefer Halilović, Case No. IT-01-48-AR73.2, Decision on Interlocutory Appeal Concerning Admission of Record of Interview of the Accused from the Bar Table, 19 August 2005 ("Decision on Appeal Concerning Admission of Record of Interview")

Prosecutor v. Sefer Halilović, Case No. IT-01-48-A, Addendum to Scheduling Order for Appeal Hearing (Questions to the Parties), 19 June 2007

JELISIĆ

Prosecutor v. Goran Jelisić, Case No. IT-95-10-T, Judgement, 14 December 1999 ("*Jelisić* Trial Judgement")

KORDIĆ AND ČERKEZ

Prosecutor v. Dario Kordić and Mario Čerkez, Case No. IT-95-14/2-AR73.5, Decision on Appeal Regarding Statement of a Deceased Witness, 21 July 2000

Prosecutor v. Dario Kordić and Mario Čerkez, Case No. IT-95-14/2-AR73.6, Decision on Appeal Regarding the Admission into Evidence of Seven Affidavits and One Formal Statement, 18 September 2000

Prosecutor v. Dario Kordić and Mario Čerkez, Case No. IT-95-14/2-A, Judgement, 17 December 2004 ("*Kordić and Čerkez* Appeal Judgement")

KRNOJELAC

Prosecutor v. Milorad Krnojelac, Case No. IT-97-25-A, Judgement, 17 September 2003 ("*Krnojelac* Appeal Judgement")

KUNARAC, KOVAČ AND VUKOVIĆ

Prosecutor v. Dragoljub Kunarac, Radomir Kovač and Zoran Vuković, Case No. IT-96-23 & IT-96-23/1-A, Judgement, 12 June 2002 ("*Kunarac et al.* Appeal Judgement")

Z. KUPREŠKIĆ, M. KUPREŠKIĆ, V. KUPREŠKIĆ, JOSIPOVIĆ, (PAPIĆ) AND SANTIĆ

Prosecutor v. Zoran Kupreškić, Mirjan Kupreškić, Vlatko Kupreškić, Drago Josipović and Vladimir Santić, Case No. IT-95-16-A, Appeal Judgement, 23 October 2001 ("*Kupreškić et al.* Appeal Judgement")

KVOČKA, KOS, RADIĆ, ŽIGIĆ AND PRCAĆ

Prosecutor v. Miroslav Kvoćka, Milojica Kos, Mlado Radić, Zoran Žigiè and Dragoljub Prcaè, Case No. IT-98-30/1-A, Judgement, 28 February 2005 ("*Kvoćka et al.* Appeal Judgement")

LIMAJ, BALA AND MUSLIU

Prosecutor v. Fatmir Limaj, Haradin Bala and Isak Musliu, Case No. IT-03-66-A, Judgement, 27 September 2007 ("*Limaj et al.* Appeal Judgement") **[page 108]**

MILOŠEVIĆ

Prosecutor v. Slobodan Milošević, Case Nos. IT-99-37-AR73, IT-01-50-AR73, and IT-01-51-AR73, Reasons for Decision on Prosecution Interlocutory Appeal from Refusal to Order Joinder, 18 April 2002

Prosecutor v. Slobodan Milošević, Case No. IT-00-54-AR73.7, Decision on Interlocutory Appeal of the Trial Chamber's Decision on the Assignment of Defence Counsel, 1 November 2004

MRKŠIĆ

Prosecutor v. Mile Mrkšić, Case No. IT-95-13/1-PT, Decision on Form of the Indictment, 19 June 2003

NALETILIĆ AND MARTINOVIĆ

Prosecutor v. Mladen Naletilić and Vinko Martinović, Case No. IT-98-34-A, Judgement, 3 May 2006 ("*Naletilić and Martinović* Appeal Judgement")

PRLIĆ, STOJIĆ, PRALJAK, PETKOVIĆ, ĆORIĆ AND PUŠIĆ

Prosecutor v. Jadranko Prlić, Bruno Stojić, Slobodan Praljak, Milivoj Petković, Valentin Ćorić and Berislav

Pušić, Case No. IT-04-74-PT, Decision on Defence Preliminary Motions Alleging Defect in the Form of the Indictment, 22 July 2005

Prosecutor v. Jadranko Prlić, Bruno Stojić, Slobodan Praljak, Milivoj Petković, Valentin Ćorić and Berislav Pušić, Case No. IT-04-74-PT, Decision on Prosecution Application for Leave to Amend the Indictment and on Defence Complaints on Form of Proposed Amended Indictment, 18 October 2005

RASEVIĆ
Prosecutor v. Mitar Rasević, Case No. IT-97-25/1-PT, Decision Regarding Defence Preliminary Motion on the Form of the Indictment, 28 April 2004

SIMIĆ
Prosecutor v. Blagoje Simić, Case No. IT-95-A, Judgement, 28 November 2006 ("*Simić* Appeal Judgement")

STAKIĆ
Prosecutor v. Milomir Stakić, Case No. IT-97-24-A, Judgement, 22 March 2006 ("*Stakić* Appeal Judgement")

TADIĆ
Prosecutor v. Duško Tadić, Case No. IT-94-1-A, Decision on Appellant's Motion for the Extension of the Time-Limit and Admission of Additional Evidence, dated 15 October 1998, filed 16 October 1998

Prosecutor v. Duško Tadić, Case No. IT-94-1-A, Judgement, 15 July 1999 ("*Tadić* Appeal Judgement") **[page 109]**

Prosecutor v. Duško Tadić, Case No. IT-94-1-T*bis*-R117, Sentencing Judgement, 11 November 1999 ("*Tadić* 1999 Sentencing Judgement")

VASILJEVIĆ
Prosecutor v. Mitar Vasiljević, Case No. IT-98-32-A, Judgement, 25 February 2004 ("*Vasiljević* Appeal Judgement")

2. ICTR

AKAYESU
Prosecutor v. Jean-Paul Akayesu, Case No. ICTR-96-4-T, Decision on Defendant's Motion for Summonses and Protection of Witnesses called by the Defence, 17 February 1998

Prosecutor v. Jean-Paul Akayesu, Case No. ICTR-96-4-T, Judgement, 2 September 1998 ("*Akayesu* Trial Judgement")

Prosecutor v. Jean-Paul Akayesu, Case No. ICTR-96-4-A, Judgment, 1 June 2001 ("*Akayesu* Appeal Judgement")

BAGILISHEMA
Prosecutor v. Ignace Bagilishema, Case No. ICTR-95-1A-A, Judgement, 3 June 2002 ("*Bagilishema* Appeal Judgement")

GACUMBITSI
Prosecutor v. Gacumbitsi, Case No. ICTR-01-64-A, Judgement, 7 July 2006 ("*Gacumbitsi* Appeal Judgement")

KAJELIJELI
Prosecutor v. Juvénal Kajelijeli, Case No. ICTR-98-44A-A, Judgement, 23 May 2005 ("*Kajelijeli* Appeal Judgement")

KAMUHANDA
Prosecutor v. Jean de Dieu Kamuhanda, Case No. ICTR-95-1-A, Judgement, 19 September 2005 ("*Kamuhanda* Appeal Judgement")

KAYISHEMA AND RUZINDANA
Prosecutor v. Clément Kayishema and Obed Ruzindana, Case No. ICTR-95-1-A, Judgement (Reasons), 1 June 2001 ("*Kayishema and Ruzindana* Appeal Judgement") **[page 110]**

MUSEMA *Prosecutor v. Alfred Musema*, Case No. ICTR-96-13-A, Judgement, 16 November 2001 ("*Musema* Appeal Judgement")

NDINDABAHIZI
Prosecutor v. Emmanuel Ndindabahizi, Case No. ICTR-01-71-A, Judgement, 16 January 2007 ("*Ndindabahizi* Appeal Judgement")

NIYITEGEKA
Prosecutor v. Eliézer Niyitegeka, Case No. ICTR-96-14-A, Judgement, 9 July 2004 ("*Niyitegeka* Appeal Judgement")

NTAGERURA ET AL
Prosecutor v. André Ntagerura, Emmanuel Bagambiki and Samuel Imanishimwe, Case No. ICTR-99-46-A, Judgement, 7 July 2006 ("*Ntagerura et al.* Appeal Judgement")

NTAKIRUTIMANA
Prosecutor v. Elizaphan and Gérard Ntakirutimana, Case No. ICTR-96-10-A & ICTR-96-17-A, Judgement, 13 December 2004 ("*Ntakirutimana* Appeal Judgement")

RUTAGANDA
Prosecutor v. Georges Anderson Nderubumwe Rutaganda, Case No. ICTR-96-3-A, Judgement, 26 May 2003 ("*Rutaganda* Appeal Judgement")

SEMANZA

Prosecutor v. Laurent Semanza, Case No. ICTR-97-20-A, Judgement, 20 May 2005 ("*Semanza* Appeal Judgement")

3. Judgements related to crimes committed during World War II

In re Yamashita, 327 US 1 (1945) (US Supreme Court)

US v. Karl Brandt et al., reprinted in Trials of War Criminals Before the Nuremberg Military Tribunals Under Control Council Law No. 10 (TWC), Voll I-II, Judgement of 19-20 August 1947

United States v. Wilhelm von Leeb et al. ("*High Command* Case"), reprinted in Trials of War Criminals Before the Nuremberg Military Tribunals Under Control Council Law No. 10 (TWC), Vol. XI, Judgement of 28 October 1948 **[page 111]**

4. Judgements of the European Court of Human Rights

Heaney and McGuinness v. Ireland, no. 34720/97, judgement of 21 December 2000, Reports of Judgments and Decisions 2000-XII

Saunders v. the United Kingdom, no. 19187/91, judgement of 17 December 1996, Reports 1996-VI

Shannon v. United Kingdom, no. 6563/03, judgement of 4 October 2005

Serves v. France, no. 20225/92, judgement of 20 October 1997, Reports 1997-VI

B. Other legal authorities

Black's Law Dictionary, 7th Edition (St. Paul, West Group, 1999)
Practice Direction on Formal Requirements for Appeals from Judgement, IT/201, 7 March 2002
Security Council Resolution 1503 (2003), 28 August 2003, S/RES/1503 (2003)
Security Council Resolution 1534 (2004), 26 March 2004, S/RES/1534 (2004) **[page 112]**

C. <u>Defined terms</u>

According to Rule 2 (B) of the Rules of Procedure and Evidence, the masculine shall include the feminine and the singular the plural (and vice-versa).

ABiH	Army of the Republic of Bosnia and Herzegovina (*Armija Bosne i Hercegovine*)
Additional Protocol I	Protocol Additional to the Geneva Conventions of 12 August 1949, and relating to the Protection of Victims of International Armed Conflicts
AT.	Transcript page from hearings on appeal in the present case.
BiH	Bosnia and Herzegovina (*Bosna i Herzegovina*)
Confidential Defence Final Trial Brief	*Prosecutor v. Sefer Halilović*, Case No. IT-01-48-T, Defence Final Brief (confidential), 25 August 2005
Defence Final Trial Brief	*Prosecutor v. Sefer Halilović*, Case No. IT-01-48-T, Defence Final Brief, public redacted version, 12 September 2005
Defence Pre-Trial Brief	*Prosecutor v. Sefer Halilović*, Case No. IT-01-48-PT, Defence Pre-Trial Brief filed in Accordance with Rule 65*ter* F(i)(ii)(iii), 26 March 2003
ECtHR	European Court of Human Rights
GC IV	Geneva Convention Relative to the Protection of Civilian Persons in Time of War of 12 August 1949, 75 UNTS 2
HVO	Croatian Defence Council (*Hrvatsko Vijeće Odbrane*)
ICRC	International Committee of the Red Cross
ICRC Commentary	Commentary on the Additional Protocols of 8 June 1977 to the Geneva Conventions of 12 August 1949, International Committee of the Red Cross, Geneva 1987
ICTR	International Criminal Tribunal for the Prosecution of Persons Responsible for Genocide and Other Serious Violations of International Humanitarian Law Committed in the Territory of Rwanda and Rwandan Citizens Responsible for Genocide and Other Such Violations Committed in the Territory of Neighbouring States between 1 January 1994 and 31 December 1994
IKM	Forward command post (*Istureno Komandno Mesto*)
ILC Commentary	ILC Commentary on the 1996 Draft Code of Crimes Against the Peace and Security of Mankind, Report of the International Law Commission on the work of its 48th session, UN doc. A/51/10.
Indictment	*Prosecutor v. Sefer Halilović*, Case No. IT-01-48-T, dated 10 September 2001 (confirmed on 12 September 2001)
International Tribunal	International Tribunal for the Prosecution of Persons Responsible for Serious Violations of International Humanitarian Law Committed in the Territory of the Former Yugoslavia since 1991
JNA	Yugoslav People's Army (*Jugoslovenska Narodna Armija*)
MUP	Ministry of Interior (*Ministarstvo Unutrašnjih Poslova*)
Prosecution	Office of the Prosecutor of the International Tribunal
Prosecution Appeal Brief	*Prosecutor v. Sefer Halilović*, Case No. IT-01-48-A, Prosecution Appellant's Brief, 1 March 2006 **[page 113]**

Prosecution Final Trial Brief	*Prosecutor v. Sefer Halilović*, Case No. IT-01-48-T, Prosecution's Final Trial Brief (with a confidential annex), 25 August 2005
Prosecution Notice of Appeal	*Prosecutor v. Sefer Halilović*, Case No. IT-01-48-A, Prosecution's Notice of Appeal, 16 December 2005
Prosecution Pre-Trial Brief	*Prosecutor v. Sefer Halilović*, Case No. IT-01-48-PT, Prosecutor's Pre-Trial Brief pursuant to Rule 65*ter* (E)(i), 13 October 2004
Prosecution Reply Brief	*Prosecutor v. Sefer Halilović*, Case No. IT-01-48-A, Re-filed Prosecution's Brief in Reply, 22 September 2006
Prosecution Supplementary Explanation	*Prosecutor v. Sefer Halilović*, Case No. IT-01-48-PT, Prosecution Supplementary Explanation to its Pre-trial Brief, 22 December 2004
Respondent's Brief	*Prosecutor v. Sefer Halilović*, Case No. IT-01-48-A, Re-Filed Respon[d]ent's Brief on Appeal, Partly Confidential, 20 September 2006.
Rules	Rules of Procedure and Evidence of the International Tribunal
SDB	State Security Service (*Služba Državne Bezbjednosti*)
SJB	Public Security Station (*Stanica Javne Bezbjednosti*)
SVB	Military Security Service (*Služba Vojne Bezbjednosti*)
Statute	Statute of the International Tribunal (unless otherwise specified), as amended by S/RES 1166 (1998), S/RES 1329 (2000), S/RES 1411 (2002), S/RES 1431 (2002), S/RES 1481 (2003), S/RES 1597 (2005), S/RES 1660 (2006).
SUP	Secretariat of Internal Affairs (*Sekretarijat za Unutrašnje Poslove*)
T.	Transcript page from hearings at trial in the present case. Since in the Halilović trial proceedings the pagination restarted every day, the date of each specific transcript referred to is added in parentheses.
TO	Territorial Defence (*Teritorijalna Odbrana*)
Trial Judgement	*Prosecutor v. Sefer Halilović*, Case No. IT-01-48-T, Judgement, 16 November 2005
UB	[Main Staff] Security Administration (*Uprava Bezbjednosti*)
UNDU	United Nations Detention Unit in The Hague
9th Brigade	9th Motorised Brigade
10th Brigade	10th Mountain Brigade

Commentary

1. Introduction

The accused in this case, Sefer Halilović, was a military commander, who by 1991, when he joined the Patriotic League in Bosnia and Herzegovina (BiH), had reached the rank of Major in the Yugoslav Peoples' Army. In the period relevant to this case, the accused held the position of "Chief of the Main Staff" of the Army of the Republic of Bosnia and Herzegovina (ABiH). The alleged crimes - the killing of tens of persons taking no active part in hostilities - took place in BiH. Allegedly, the accused was the commander of a military operation called "Operation Neretva" (or Operation Neretva-93), and that troops participating in this operation had committed these crimes. The Trial Chamber was not convinced that the relevant combat operations were called "Operation Neretva" and did not find that command responsibility of the accused had been established.[1]

At theeart of the appeal in the case *Prosecutor v. Halilović* lies the superior or command responsibility principle and the application of this doctrine. More specifically, the interpretation of the requirement of "effective control" - the most contested concept of the command responsibility doctrine - was at stake. The appeal was submitted by the prosecution against the acquittal of the accused by the Trial Chamber on one sole count charged against him: murder as a violation of the laws or customs of war. This crime is punishable under Article 3 of the Statute and was charged solely under Article 7, paragraph 3.[2]

The Appeals Chamber dismissed the argument by the defence, according to which the prosecution's right to appeal should be exercised only exceptionally where the accused had been acquitted on all charges by the Trial Chamber, and the appeal was thus allowed to proceed.[3] The appeal case concerned four grounds of appeal. The first ground was addressed in the judgement. Having concluded that the prosecution had failed to show that the Trial Chamber erred in finding that the first element of command responsibility had not been established, the Appeals Chamber dismissed this ground of appeal and did not find it necessary to address the other grounds of appeal.[4]

This commentary concentrates on those sub-grounds of appeal that are of direct relevance to the application of the command responsibility doctrine. Therefore, the sub-ground of appeal that concerned the admission into evidence of a certain report and testimony by an expert witness will not be elaborated.[5]

2. The superior-subordinate relationship between Halilović and the perpetrators

The first ground of appeal, under which several sub-errors were alleged, concerned – most importantly – the issue of effective control. While distinct sub-grounds of appeal were brought forward, they all concerned the fundamental question as to whether Halilović was the superior of the troops who committed the crimes concerned. Had the Trial Chamber required proof of "command" and "overall control of combat operations in Herzegovina", instead of "effective control" over the perpetrators?

The question that causes the majority of problems in command responsibility cases is: how do you establish the superior-subordinate relationship between the accused and the actual perpetrators of the crimes? While the case law recognizes that the superior needs to have exercised effective control over the subordinates in order to incur criminal liability, it proves far from easy to establish when such effective control has been exercised. With regard to the requirement of effective control, the prosecution alleged several errors by the Trial Chamber. The Appeals Chamber rightly acknowledged the importance of addressing these concerns by denying Halilović's request for summary dismissal of all the arguments presented by the prosecution.

1 ICTY, Judgement, *Prosecutor v. Halilović*, Case No. IT-01-48-A, A. Ch., 16 October 2007, in this volume, p. 633, par. 2–4.
2 *Ibid.*, par. 3–5.
3 *Ibid.*, par. 16.
4 *Ibid.*, par. 216 and 217.
5 *Ibid.*, par. 19–41.

3. The first element

The Appeals Chamber first addressed an alleged error concerning the requirement of a position of military command for establishing the superior-subordinate relationship. The discussion by the Appeals Chamber points to fundamental issues with regard to the perception of the command responsibility principle.[6] The Appeals Chamber recalled that it is the superior-subordinate relationship that constitutes the element that has to be established, and that the threshold to be reached is the "effective control" of the superior. In turn, there is only effective control on the part of the superior if he has the material ability to prevent or punish criminal conduct. As such, this was nothing new, but it stresses the fact that it is the superior-subordinate relationship that has to be established, and that the effective control is just a means to prove such a relationship. Consequently, this means that, for this first element, there has to be some kind of formal or informal hierarchy between the accused and the perpetrator.

The findings by the Appeals Chamber are useful when considering the question that may validly be asked in relation to present day conflicts - whether command responsibility can also be applied to those armed organisations that have a non-hierarchical structure and, thus, do not resemble traditional state armed forces. As the Appeals Chamber considered that the ability to exercise effective control for the purpose of command responsibility "will almost invariably not be satisfied unless such a relationship of subordination exists", the basis for criminal liability cannot be the command responsibility principle unless there is "some sort of formal or informal hierarchy". Horizontal "cells" operating independently would probably not qualify for this interpretation of effective control for the purpose of command responsibility. This is also in accordance with requirements of international humanitarian law, according to which organisations need some sort of formal or informal hierarchy, in order to qualify as an armed group belonging to a party to the conflict.[7]

Van der Wilt, in his most useful commentary to this judgement, found that the Appeals Chamber judgement had at least one strong asset, in that it clearly pointed to the intricate relationship between the superior-subordinate relationship and the third element of the command responsibility principle – the failure to take necessary and reasonable measures.[8] As pointed out by the Appeals Chamber, and as mentioned above, the threshold for effective control can only be reached where the superior had the material ability to prevent or punish his subordinates. However, while the ability to prevent or punish is a means to assess whether there was effective control, this should not be mixed up with the third element of the command responsibility principle – as defined by the Čelebići Trial Chamber – the failure to prevent and punish.

The Appeals Chamber clarified the matter by finding that "a material ability to prevent and punish may also exist outside a superior-subordinate relationship relevant for Article 7(3) of the Statute." The example used was that of a police officer. According to the Appeals Chamber, he or she "may be able to "prevent and punish" crimes under his jurisdiction, but this would not as such make him a superior (in the sense of Article 7(3) of the Statute) vis-à-vis any perpetrator within that jurisdiction."[9] The fact that someone may have the material ability to prevent or punish is a separate issue, and it is not this fact that constitutes the legal basis for the superior's duty to act. The duty to act rather stems from the position of the commander and from his relationship with the perpetrator.[10]

These findings are interesting in that they seem to give support to the thesis that the command responsibility principle – which originates in the military concept encompassing the responsibilities carried by any commander – should only be applied to civilian superiors in specific circumstances. In general, while for military commanders a duty to act in relation to any acts undertaken by their subordinates is inherent in their position, a similar duty of the civilian superior is more difficult to establish. The findings by the Appeals Chamber illustrate that, for the purpose of command responsibility, it is not justified to disregard the first element of the principle, the superior-subordinate relationship, and to solely consider the superior's ability to prevent or punish. To reiterate, even individuals who may have the ability to, most likely, prevent a crime

---

6 *Ibid.*, par. 57–74.

7 Article 4, paragraph 2, sub a, Geneva Convention Relative to the Treatment of Prisoners of War, 12 August 1949, 75 United Nations Treaty Series, p. 135.

8 H. Van der Wilt, Halilović on Appeal: The Intricate Concept of Effective Control, 2 Hague Justice Journal 2007, p. 8.

9 Judgement, *Prosecutor v. Halilović*, A. Ch., *supra* note 1, par. 59.

10 *Ibid.*, par. 59 and 60.

from happening – consider, in particular, civilian leaders – do not necessarily fulfil the requirements of a superior-subordinate relationship for the purpose of command responsibility.

The fact that someone may have had the ability to prevent a crime but did not do so may give support to the impression that the person is liable under the command responsibility principle. It is necessary to stress that any "mode of liability", command responsibility included, requires all the necessary elements to be fulfilled. The moral responsibility of the accused – or the criminal responsibility based on another mode of liability – should not be mixed up with command responsibility.

Having considered the role of the material ability to prevent or punish in the process of establishing effective control for the purposes of a superior-subordinate relationship, the Appeals Chamber found that, in relation to the first alleged error, the Trial Chamber had given a correct description of the jurisprudence of the tribunal and had not required a position of military command as a requirement for establishing command responsibility.

4. The third element

According to the prosecution, the Trial Chamber made another error in restating the law on the third element of command responsibility.[11] By doing this, the chamber allegedly "created an unnecessary and unwarranted distinction between a general obligation and a specific obligation to prevent crimes."[12] The Appeals Chamber agreed that the Trial Chamber created a "confusing and unhelpful dichotomy" by making an "artificial distinction" between general and specific obligations of the commander.[13] The Trial Chamber, indeed, addressed the general obligation and the specific obligation of the commander under separate headings. Whether this distinction is "artificial" may be disputed.

The present author disagrees with the finding that the Trial Chamber created a dichotomy, which would be confusing and unhelpful. In fact, there seems to be no reason to hold that the Trial Chamber created something new. The following analysis explains why more recognition could have been given to the Trial Chamber's findings.

In its discussion on the general obligation of the commander, the Trial Chamber held as follows:

"[I]nternational humanitarian law entrusts commanders with a role of guarantors of laws dealing with humanitarian protection and war crimes, and for this reason they are placed in a position of control over the acts of their subordinates, and it is this position which generates a responsibility for failure to act. It is a natural element of the *preventative* constituent of command responsibility that a commander must make efforts to ensure that his troops are properly informed of their responsibilities in international law, and that they act in an orderly fashion. While it is evident that no criminal liability may attach to the commander for failure in this duty *per se*, it may be an element to be taken into consideration when examining the factual circumstances of the case."[14]

With these findings, the Trial Chamber tried to pinpoint what may be called "general command responsibility",[15] or the responsibility that every commander has and which makes his position so unique in relation to the prevention of war crimes and to the command responsibility doctrine. This was an attempt to actually give some attention to what the command responsibility principle is all about, something that has been recognised as important in far too few of the judgements involving this doctrine. The Trial Chamber expressly stated that this criminal liability does not attach to the commander for failure in this duty *per se*, which is an accurate finding. If the discussion by the Trial Chamber should be criticised at all, then it is because of the chamber's use of the word "element", which could have been replaced by "factor". The general command responsibility of the commander should, indeed, be a factor to be taken into consideration when examining the factual circumstances of the case.

---

11 *Ibid.*, par. 61.

12 *Ibid.*

13 *Ibid.*, par. 64.

14 ICTY, Judgement, *Prosecutor v. Halilović*, Case No. IT-01-48, T. Ch. I, 16 November 2005, Klip/ Sluiter, ALC-XXVII-475, par. 87 and 88.

15 For this concept, see M. Nybondas, Command Responsibility and Its Applicability to Civilian Superiors, T.M.C. Asser Press, The Hague 2010, p. 53 *et seq*.

In fact, what the Trial Chamber attempted to clarify is directly related to what the Appeals Chamber tried to explain in relation to the first element, as discussed above. The Appeals Chamber found that the legal basis for the duty to act is formed by the position of command over the perpetrator – or the general obligation to prevent crimes (as discussed by the Trial Chamber) – not by the fact that someone may have the ability to prevent a crime on a certain occasion. This is related to the *first* element of command responsibility, and should not be confused with the material ability to prevent a crime for the purposes of the *third* element – or the specific obligation to prevent crimes.

As a last point related to this issue, one may add that the general and specific obligation to prevent crimes relate to each other as moral responsibility to criminal responsibility. Where a commander is a bad leader and does not fulfil his general obligation to prevent crimes – he does not "make efforts to ensure that his troops are properly informed of their responsibilities in international law, and that they act in an orderly fashion"[16] – he may be blamed for being a bad leader and for not fulfilling his moral responsibilities. Of course, his leadership will be a factor to be taken into account when assessing the facts of the case against him. However, only where he fails to fulfil his specific obligation to prevent crimes will he be held criminally responsible under the command responsibility principle.

5. A case beyond command

The prosecution raised two further issues, in relation to "command". First, it submitted that the Trial Chamber had required proof of command in determining command responsibility. The Appeals Chamber quite convincingly addressed those instances where the Trial Chamber allegedly erred in this respect, and showed that the Trial Chamber did not consider command as one of the elements, but rightly required effective control in order to establish the superior-subordinate relationship. For the purpose of clarification, the Appeals Chamber pointed out that "command", as well as "overall control of combat operations", may be pleaded as a fact "underlying one of the requirements of superior responsibility". If so pleaded, the Trial Chamber has to make a finding in this respect. This, however, does not mean that it considered "command" or any other underlying fact as one of the requirements of command responsibility.[17] The Appeals Chamber stressed that, after having found that Halilović was not the commander of the so called "Operation Neretva", the Trial Chamber had not failed to address other indicators of his effective control.[18]

Secondly, the prosecution submitted that, as Halilović was found not to have been the *de facto* or the *de jure* commander of "Operation Neretva", the Trial Chamber should have considered "a case beyond command". According to the prosecution, the Trial Chamber was under an obligation to inquire whether the accused had been in a position of superior "by virtue of the other factual bases pleaded at trial."[19] Halilović's position as the most senior ranking officer of the ABiH army in Herzegovina, and his position as Team Leader of a certain Inspection Team, should have been considered as alternative bases for establishing effective control.[20] As such, the argument is understandable. If the accused was not the commander of "Operation Neretva", then why not consider the other positions of authority that he held, for the purpose of establishing command responsibility.

The Appeals Chamber dismissed this argument. In its view, the indictment was built up around Halilović's position as commander of "Operation Neretva". The defence was entitled to understand this as being the only basis for demonstrating Halilović's effective control over the perpetrators.[21] In addition, the Trial Chamber had not failed to make findings in relation to the other positions held by the accused.[22]

The importance of this discussion lies in the clear rejection of command as one of the elements of command responsibility. The danger of this principle is that the accused is found liable because he held a certain command position (strict liability) and not on the basis of his personal liability. All indicators of effective control should be considered, including other positions of authority held by the accused.

---

16 See the discussion by the Trial Chamber above. Judgement, *Prosecutor v. Halilović*, T. Ch. I, *supra* note 14, par. 87–88.
17 Judgement, *Prosecutor v. Halilović*, A. Ch., *supra* note 1, par. 65–74.
18 *Ibid.*, par. 74.
19 *Ibid.*, par. 76.
20 *Ibid.*
21 *Ibid.*, par. 82.
22 *Ibid.*, par. 98.

6. Conclusion

The structure of the judgement in no way contributed to any clarification that the Appeals Chamber may have provided to the command responsibility discussion. The command responsibility principle as a doctrine in international criminal law will have benefited from the discussion relating to the superior-subordinate relationship and to the establishment of "effective control"'. By rejecting the discussion in the trial judgement on the general and specific obligations of a commander, the Appeals Chamber missed out on a great opportunity to elaborate on the meaning and role of command responsibility in international criminal law. That the Appeals Chamber judgement confirmed the acquittal of the accused shows the difficulties involved in applying and proving command responsibility.

Maria Nybondas

UNITED NATIONS

International Tribunal for the Prosecution of Persons Responsible for Serious Violations of International Humanitarian Law Committed in the Territory of the Former Yugoslavia since 1991	Case No.	IT-96-23/2-A
	Date:	31 October 2007
	Original:	English

IN THE APPEALS CHAMBER

Before: **Judge Liu Daqun, Presiding**
Judge Mohamed Shahabuddeen
Judge Mehmet Güney
Judge Andrésia Vaz
Judge Wolfgang Schomburg

Registrar: **Mr. Hans Holthuis**

Judgement of: **31 October 2007**

PROSECUTOR

v.

DRAGAN ZELENOVIĆ

PUBLIC

JUDGEMENT ON SENTENCING APPEAL

The Office of the Prosecutor:
Ms. Helen Brady
Ms. Julia Thibord

Counsel for the Accused:
Mr. Zoran Jovanović

CONTENTS

[page 1] I. INTRODUCTION

1. The Appeals Chamber of the International Tribunal for the Prosecution of Persons Responsible for Serious Violations of International Humanitarian Law Committed in the Territory of the Former Yugoslavia Since 1991 ("Appeals Chamber" and "International Tribunal", respectively) is seized of an appeal from the Sentencing Judgement rendered by Trial Chamber I on 4 April 2007 in the case *Prosecutor v. Dragan Zelenović*, Case No. IT-96-23/2-S ("Sentencing Judgement").

2. The events giving rise to this appeal took place in the Foča municipality and its surrounding villages, eastern Bosnia and Herzegovina, from April to October 1992. Dragan Zelenović ("Appellant") was born on 12 February 1961 in Foča. Prior to 1992, he worked as an electrician in Miljevina. The Appellant was a member of the "Dragan Nikolić Unit", a military unit in Foča which, in the beginning of the war, was part of the Bosnian-Serb Territorial Defence and, from the summer of 1992 onwards, part of the Bosnian-Serb army. The Appellant was a soldier and, *de facto*, a military policeman.[1]

3. The initial indictment against the Appellant was issued on 18 June 1996 and included seven other persons.[2] The indictment was amended on 5 October 1999 and a redacted version of the amended indictment ("Amended Indictment") was filed on 20 April 2001.[3] Following the initial indictment, a number of arrest warrants were issued against the Appellant,[4] who left Foča in 2000 or 2001 and travelled to Russia, where he lived until his arrest on 22 August 2005. He was subsequently transferred to Bosnia and Herzegovina on 8 June 2006 and to the International Tribunal on 10 June 2006.[5]

4. On 29 November 2004, the Office of the Prosecutor ("Prosecution") filed a motion for the referral of the case of the Appellant and Gojko Janković to the authorities of Bosnia and Herzegovina ("11*bis* Motion"). A Referral Bench was appointed by the President of the International Tribunal on 1 December 2004 and the case of Gojko Janković was referred to the authorities of Bosnia and Herzegovina in accordance with the decision of the Referral Bench issued on 22 July 2005.[6] On 14 December 2006, the Prosecution and the Defence filed a confidential Joint Motion for Consideration of Plea Agreement between Dragan Zelenović and the Office of the **[page 2]** Prosecutor pursuant to Rule 62*ter* ("Plea Agreement").[7] According to the Plea Agreement, the Appellant agreed to plead guilty to seven counts of crimes against humanity, three of which charged torture, as provided for by Article 5(f) of the Statute of the International Tribunal ("Statute") (counts 5, 13, and 41), and four of which charged rape, as provided for by Article 5(g) of the Statute (counts 6, 14, 42, and 49).[8] Because of the Appellant's guilty plea, no decision was taken on the 11*bis* Motion with regard to the Appellant.[9]

5. In the Sentencing Judgement, the Trial Chamber described the crimes committed by the Appellant as follows:

> The crimes which Mr. Zelenović has pleaded guilty to were part of a pattern of sexual assaults that took place over a period of several months, and in four different locations, and involved multiple victims. Mr. Zelenović took direct part in the sexual abuse of victims in a number of detention facilities, including the multiple rape of victims FWS-75 and FWS-87. Mr. Zelenović has been found guilty of personally committing nine rapes, eight of which were qualified as both torture and rape. He has also been found guilty of two instances of rape through co-perpetratorship, one of which was qualified as both torture and rape, and one instance of torture and rape through aiding and abetting. Four of the instances of sexual abuse were gang rapes, committed together with three or more other perpetrators. In one of those instances he participated as aider and abettor in the rape of FWS-75 by at least ten soldiers, which was so violent that the victim lost consciousness. He participated as co-perpetrator in an incident during which the victim was threatened with a gun to her head while being sexually abused.[10]

---

1 Sentencing Judgement, para. 17.

2 Sentencing Judgement, para. 1. The seven other accused were Dragan Gagović, Gojko Janković, Janko Janjić, Radomir Kovać, Zoran Vuković, Dragoljub Kunarac and Radovan Stanković.

3 Sentencing Judgement, para. 1.

4 Sentencing Judgement, para. 2.

5 Sentencing Judgement, para. 4.

6 Sentencing Judgement, para. 3. The decision was upheld on appeal, *see Prosecutor v. Gojko Janković*, Decision on 11*bis* Referral, 15 November 2005.

7 Sentencing Judgement, para. 10.

8 Sentencing Judgement, para. 10.

9 Sentencing Judgement, paras 9–13.

10 Sentencing Judgement, para. 38. For a more detailed description of the crimes for which the Appellant was convicted *see* Trial Judgement, paras 21–27.

6. On 4 April 2007, the Trial Chamber sentenced the Appellant to 15 years' imprisonment.[11] On 27 April 2007, the Appellant filed a Defence Notice for Leave to Appeal Sentencing Judgement ("Notice for Leave to Appeal"), which was considered by the Appeals Chamber, the Prosecution consenting, as the notice of appeal required under Rule 108 of the Rules of Procedure and Evidence of the International Tribunal ("Rules").[12]

7. The Appellant filed his Defence Appeal on Sentencing Judgement ("Appellant's Brief") on 25 May 2007. On 25 June 2007, the Prosecution filed its Response Brief ("Respondent's Brief") and on 3 July 2007, the Appellant filed its Reply to the Respondent's Brief ("Reply Brief").

8. In the Appellant's Brief, the Appellant submits that the Trial Chamber did not adequately assess the mitigating circumstances in the Sentencing Judgement, namely the Appellant's guilty plea which allowed psychological benefit for victims who would not be required to give evidence; **[page 3]** and the Appellant's cooperation with the Prosecution in general (first ground of appeal).[13] Furthermore, the Appellant submits that the final judgement of the State Court of Bosnia and Herzegovina in the case of *Prosecutor v. Radovan Stanković* should have been taken into consideration when determining the sentence (second ground of appeal).[14] **[page 4]**

II. STANDARD OF APPELLATE REVIEW

9. The provisions on sentencing are Articles 23 and 24 of the Statute and Rules 100 to 106 of the Rules. Both Article 24 of the Statute and Rule 101 of the Rules contain general sentencing guidelines for a Trial Chamber that amount to an obligation to take into account the following factors: the gravity of the offence or totality of the culpable conduct, the individual circumstances of the convicted person, the general practice regarding prison sentences in the courts of the former Yugoslavia, and aggravating and mitigating circumstances.[15]

10. Sentencing appeals, as appeals from a trial judgement, are appeals *stricto sensu* and not trials *de novo*.[16] The Appeals Chamber will, in principle, only take into account evidence referred to by the Trial Chamber in the body of the Judgement or in a related footnote; evidence contained in the trial record and referred to by the Parties; and additional evidence admitted on appeal.[17] Pursuant to Article 25 of the Statute, the role of the Appeals Chamber is limited to correcting errors of law invalidating a decision and errors of fact which have occasioned a miscarriage of justice.[18] These criteria are well established in the jurisprudence of the International Tribunal[19] and the International Criminal Tribunal for Rwanda ("ICTR").[20]

---

[11] Sentencing Judgement, para. 70.

[12] Prosecution Motion Concerning "Defence Notice for Leave to Appeal Sentencing Judgement", 3 May 2007 ("Prosecution Motion"), paras 1, 3 and 5. Scheduling Order, 24 July 2007.

[13] Appellant's Brief, para. 4.

[14] Appellant's Brief, para. 5. The Appeals Chamber notes that the Appellant fails to indicate whether the errors alleged are errors of law or of fact.

[15] *Blagojević and Jokić* Appeal Judgement, para. 320; *Bralo* Judgement on Sentencing Appeal, para. 7; *Galić* Appeal Judgement, para. 392; *Momir Nikolić* Judgement on Sentencing Appeal, para. 6; *Miodrag Jokić* Judgement on Sentencing Appeal, para. 6; *Deronjić* Judgement on Sentencing Appeal, para. 6; *Dragan Nikolić* Judgement on Sentencing Appeal, para. 7; *Čelebići* Appeal Judgement, paras 429 and 716.

[16] *Bralo* Judgement on Sentencing Appeal, para. 8; *Galić* Appeal Judgement, para. 393; *Momir Nikolić* Judgement on Sentencing Appeal, para. 7; *Miodrag Jokić* Judgement on Sentencing Appeal, para. 7; *Deronjić* Judgement on Sentencing Appeal, para. 7; *Dragan Nikolić* Judgement on Sentencing Appeal, para. 8; *Kupreškić et al.* Appeal Judgement, para. 408; *Mucić et al.* Judgement on Sentencing Appeal, para. 11; *Čelebići* Appeal Judgement, para. 724.

[17] *Bralo* Judgement on Sentencing Appeal, para. 8. *See also Naletilić and Martinović* Appeal Judgement, paras 11–12; *Blaškić* Appeal Judgement, paras 13 and 24.

[18] *Blagojević and Jokić* Appeal Judgement, para. 6; *Brđanin* Appeal Judgement, para. 8; *Bralo* Judgement on Sentencing Appeal, para. 8; *Momir Nikolić* Judgement on Sentencing Appeal, para. 7; *Miodrag Jokić* Judgement on Sentencing Appeal, para. 7; *Deronjić* Judgement on Sentencing Appeal, para. 7; *Dragan Nikolić* Judgement on Sentencing Appeal, para. 8; *Furundžija* Appeal Judgement, para. 40.

[19] *Kvočka et al.* Appeal Judgement, para. 14. *See also Vasiljević* Appeal Judgement, paras 4–12; *Kunarac et al.* Appeal Judgement, paras 35–48; *Kupreškić et al.* Appeal Judgement, para. 29; *Čelebići* Appeal Judgement, paras 434–435; *Furundžija* Appeal Judgement, para. 37; *Tadić* Appeal Judgement, para. 64.

[20] *Musema* Appeal Judgement, para. 15; *Akayesu* Appeal Judgement, para. 178; *Kayishema and Ruzindana* Appeal Judgement, para. 320.

11. Trial Chambers are vested with a broad discretion in determining an appropriate sentence, due to their obligation to individualise penalties to fit the circumstances of the accused and the gravity of the crime.[21] This discretion includes determining the weight given to mitigating or aggravating circumstances.[22] The conclusion as to whether a fact amounts to a mitigating **[page 5]** circumstance will be reached "on a balance of probabilities".[23] As a general rule, the Appeals Chamber will not revise a sentence unless the Trial Chamber has committed a discernible error in exercising its discretion or has failed to follow the applicable law.[24] It is for the Appellant to demonstrate how the Trial Chamber ventured outside its discretionary framework in imposing his sentence.[25] To show that the Trial Chamber committed a discernible error in exercising its discretion,

> the Appellant has to demonstrate that the Trial Chamber gave weight to extraneous or irrelevant considerations, failed to give weight or sufficient weight to relevant considerations, made a clear error as to the facts upon which it exercised its discretion, or that the Trial Chamber's decision was so unreasonable or plainly unjust that the Appeals Chamber is able to infer that the Trial Chamber must have failed to exercise its discretion properly.[26] **[page 6]**

III. FIRST GROUND OF APPEAL: WHETHER THE TRIAL CHAMBER ERRED BY FAILING TO GIVE PROPER WEIGHT TO SPECIFIC FACTORS IN MITIGATION OF SENTENCE

12. The Appellant submits that the Trial Chamber erred in failing to adequately assess the mitigating circumstances in the Sentencing Judgement, by giving insufficient weight to, first, the Appellant's admission of guilt and the resulting psychological benefit for victims who will not be required to give evidence; and, second, to the Appellant's cooperation with the Prosecution in general.[27]

A. The Appellant's Guilty Plea and its Effect in Relieving Victims from Testifying

13. The Appellant submits that his guilty plea is of "extraordinary importance", since it is the first guilty plea in the practice of the International Tribunal in connection with the massive rapes committed during the armed conflict in the Foča municipality.[28] In his view, his admission of guilt in this context is of such importance that it should have been given more weight than that given to guilty pleas in other cases.[29] Whilst recognising that the Trial Chamber took into account the beneficial effects of the guilty plea for the victims,[30] the Appellant argues that the Trial Chamber erred "in not providing a concrete appraisement of this particular

---

21 *Blagojević and Jokić* Appeal Judgement, para. 321; *Brdanin* Appeal Judgement, para. 500; *Bralo* Judgement on Sentencing Appeal, para. 9; *Galić* Appeal Judgement, para. 393; *Momir Nikolić* Judgement on Sentencing Appeal, para. 8; *Miodrag Jokić* Judgement on Sentencing Appeal, para. 8; *Deronjić* Judgement on Sentencing Appeal, para. 8; *Babić* Judgement on Sentencing Appeal, para. 7; *Dragan Nikolić* Judgement on Sentencing Appeal, para. 9; *Čelebići* Appeal Judgement, para. 717.

22 *Brđjanin* Appeal Judgement, para. 500.

23 *Bralo* Judgement on Sentencing Appeal, para. 8; *Babić* Judgement on Sentencing Appeal, para. 43; *Blaškić* Appeal Judgement, para. 697. *See also Čelebići* Appeal Judgement, para. 590.

24 *Blagojević and Jokić* Appeal Judgement, paras 137 and 321; *Brdanin* Appeal Judgement, para. 500; *Bralo* Judgement on Sentencing Appeal, para. 9; *Galić* Appeal Judgement, para. 393; *Momir Nikolić* Appeal Judgement on Sentencing Appeal, para. 8; *Miodrag Jokić* Judgement on Sentencing Appeal, para. 8; *Deronjić* Judgement on Sentencing Appeal, para. 8; *Blaškić* Appeal Judgement, para. 680; *Krstić* Appeal Judgement, para. 242; *Kupreškić et al.* Appeal Judgement, para. 408; *Jelisić* Appeal Judgement, para. 99; *Čelebići* Appeal Judgement, para. 725; *Furundžija* Appeal Judgement, para. 239; *Aleksovski* Appeal Judgement, para. 187; *Tadić* Judgement in Sentencing Appeals, para. 22.

25 *Brdanin* Appeal Judgement, para. 500; *Bralo* Judgement on Sentencing Appeal, para. 9; *Galić* Appeal Judgement, para. 393; *Momir Nikolić* Judgement on Sentencing Appeal, para. 8; *Miodrag Jokić* Judgement on Sentencing Appeal, para. 8; *Deronjić* Judgement on Sentencing Appeal, para. 8; *Dragan Nikolić* Judgement on Sentencing Appeal, para. 9; *Čelebići* Appeal Judgement, para. 725.

26 *Babić* Judgement on Sentencing Appeal, para. 44. *See also, Blagojević and Jokić* Appeal Judgement, paras 137 and 321; *Brdanin* Appeal Judgement, para. 500; *Bralo* Judgement on Sentencing Appeal, para. 9; *Galić* Appeal Judgement, para. 394; *Momir Nikolić* Judgement on Sentencing Appeal, para. 95.

27 Appellant's Brief, para. 4.

28 Notice for Leave to Appeal, para. 10; Appellant's Brief, para. 7. *See also*, AT. 10.

29 Appellant's Brief, para. 10. *See also* para. 12, where it is submitted that "it was necessary to accord a concrete and greater importance to this mitigating circumstance, particularly because it was for the first time to happen in the [practice of the International Tribunal]".

30 These beneficial effects are listed in paragraphs 10–11 of the Appellant's Brief.

circumstance and in not mentioning its significance" in determining the sentence.[31] Moreover, the Appellant submits that the Trial Chamber failed to assess "the expert's findings relating to the psychological benefit for the victims from their non-appearance before the Court and from avoidance of re-living their traumas".[32] In sum, the Appellant is of the view that the Trial Chamber erred in determining the penalty, since it "construed and assessed this circumstance in a generalized manner".[33]

14. The Prosecution responds that the Appellant did not identify any discernible error in the Trial Chamber's consideration of the guilty plea as a mitigating factor and that the Appellant's arguments "are contrary to the principle that the Chamber has discretion in attributing weight to a guilty plea".[34] In particular, the Prosecution submits that "the Trial Chamber was not obliged to separately specify the degree of mitigation arising from the beneficial effects for the victims" and **[page 7]** that in any event, the Trial Chamber expressly took into account the fact that victims were relieved from testifying.[35] The Prosecution contends that the Trial Chamber did not err by omitting to refer to the Expert Report, since it is not obliged "to set out in detail each and every factor it relied upon" and that, "the Trial Chamber's reasoning is consistent with the expert's conclusion".[36] Moreover, the Prosecution argues that the Trial Chamber did not err by not according more weight to the Appellant's guilty plea on the basis that it is the first one concerning the mass rapes which occurred during the armed conflict in Bosnia and Herzegovina.[37] According to the Prosecution, this assertion is overstated, since three other accused persons before the International Tribunal have pleaded guilty to charges of rape and a fourth admitted that they occurred in the Keraterm Camp.[38] The Prosecution concedes however that the Appellant's guilty plea is the first one concerning the rapes which occurred in the Foča region in 1992.[39] In addition, the Prosecution asserts that the beneficial effect of a guilty plea for the victims must be assessed against the inherent gravity of the offences[40] and that a "guilty plea does not deserve more weight because it admits particularly traumatising and humiliating crimes".[41]

15. In his Reply Brief, the Appellant restates his views on the weight that should be given to his guilty plea and submits that "precisely because of the nature of the crime the guilty plea has special importance in terms that victims will be relieved of the obligation to testify".[42] He further argues that the Trial Chamber did not attribute adequate importance to the Expert Report relating to the psychological benefit for the victims from their non-appearance before the Court and that this should be given more weight in the present case than in other cases where an accused pleaded guilty since "it needs to be particularly viewed in the light of the nature of emotional sufferings that victims of the rape would experience when testifying."[43]

16. The Appeals Chamber recalls at the outset that the mitigating weight to be attached to a guilty plea lies within the discretion of the Trial Chamber.[44] Therefore, the assessment of the beneficial effects resulting from that guilty plea also lies within such discretion. **[page 8]**

17. The parties agree on the fact that the guilty plea and the subsequent relieving effect on victims who will not have to testify before the International Tribunal have been considered as a mitigating factor by the Trial Chamber in the Sentencing Judgement.[45] The Trial Chamber stated in this respect that "the guilty plea can be given considerable weight in mitigation".[46] Moreover, it stated that the fact that a guilty plea involving serious

---

31 Appellant's Brief, para. 9.

32 Appellant's Brief, para. 9; AT. 11. The report of expert Ana Najman ("Expert Report") is included as Annex C to the Defence Sentencing Brief, 14 February 2007.

33 Appellant's Brief, para. 13; AT. 9–10.

34 Respondent's Brief, para. 10.

35 Respondent's Brief, para. 11.

36 Respondent's Brief, para. 12.

37 Respondent's Brief, para. 13.

38 Respondent's Brief, para. 13 and in particular, footnote 39.

39 AT. 24.

40 Respondent's Brief, para. 15.

41 Respondent's Brief, para. 16; AT. 24.

42 Reply Brief, para. 8.

43 Reply Brief, para. 10.

44 *Bralo* Judgement on Sentencing Appeal, para. 42. *See also Momir Nikolić* Judgement on Sentencing Appeal, para. 82. *Jelisić* Appeal Judgement, para. 121.

45 Appellant's Brief, paras 6, 8 and 12; Respondent's Brief, paras 10–13.

46 Sentencing Judgement, para. 46. *See also* para. 68, where the Trial Chamber states that it "has given considerable weight to Mr. Zelenović's guilty plea".

crimes such as torture and rape is likely to save the victims from reliving the trauma through testifying, is an effect that must be taken into consideration when determining the weight in mitigation the guilty plea should be given.[47] Further, the Trial Chamber was cognisant of the fact that the Appellant was the first accused person to admit responsibility for rapes which occurred in the Foča municipality in 1992 and took this factor into consideration, stressing that such an admission was contributing to "the establishment of truth and thereby to reconciliation in the region".[48]

18. The Appeals Chamber finds that the Appellant fails to show that the Trial Chamber gave insufficient weight to this mitigating circumstance. In addition, the Appeals Chamber recalls that, "upon finding that mitigating circumstances have been established, a decision as to the weight to be accorded thereto lies within the discretion of the Trial Chamber".[49] The Appeals Chamber holds that a Trial Chamber is not required to explicitly mention the extent of the mitigating value it grants to a guilty plea.[50] The Appeals Chamber therefore finds that, having considered and given "considerable weight"[51] to the Appellant's guilty plea and its beneficial effects for the victims as well as to the fact that this was the first guilty plea concerning the rapes that occurred "in the region", the Trial Chamber did not commit any discernible error when not specifying the degree of mitigation it accorded to the guilty plea.

19. With regard to the Appellant's submission that the Trial Chamber erred by failing to assess the Expert Report in relation to the psychological benefit for the victims from their non-appearance before the Court,[52] the Appeals Chamber recalls that Trial Chambers, although required to give a reasoned opinion,[53]

> [...] are not required to "articulate every step" of their reasoning in reaching particular findings, and failure to list in a judgement "each and every circumstance" placed before them and **[page 9]** considered "does not necessarily mean that [they] either ignored or failed to evaluate the factor in question.[54]

In any event, the transcript of the sentencing hearing held on 23 February 2007 shows that the Expert Report was discussed by the parties and duly taken into consideration by the Trial Chamber.[55] Furthermore, the Appeals Chamber finds that the Trial Chamber's reasoning according to which "a guilty plea is likely to save the victims from reliving the trauma through testifying"[56] is reflective of the Expert Report's conclusion that "by his admitting the committed offence the accused frees the victims from testifying, from painful confrontation and retraumatization".[57]

20. Consequently, this part of the Appellant's first ground of appeal is dismissed.

B. The Appellant's Cooperation with the Prosecution

21. The Appellant alleges that according to the Plea Agreement, the cooperation which he is obliged to only relates to "the proceedings against the co-accused or in other cases where charges encompass [...] known persons and events."[58] The Appellant submits that he nonetheless agreed to provide cooperation and information

---

47 Sentencing Judgement, para. 49.

48 Sentencing Judgement, para. 48.

49 *Miodrag Jokić* Judgement on Sentencing Appeal, para. 57; *Bralo* Judgement on Sentencing Appeal, para. 84. *See also Babić* Judgement on Sentencing Appeal, para. 44.

50 *See* for cooperation with the Prosecution as a mitigating factor, *Blaškić* Appeal Judgement, para. 702.

51 Sentencing Judgement, paras 46 and 68. *See also* para. 56, where the Trial Chamber held that the Appellant's guilty plea was one of the main mitigating circumstances in this case.

52 Appellant's Brief, para. 9; AT. 11.

53 Art. 23(2) of the Statute and Rule 98*ter*(C) of the Rules. *See also Kordić and Čerkez* Appeal Judgement, para. 383.

54 *Babić* Judgement on Sentencing Appeal, para. 43 (footnote omitted) quoting *Kupreškić et al.* Appeal Judgement, para. 458.

55 T. 500; T. 501; T. 512; T. 518.

56 Sentencing Judgement, para. 49.

57 Expert Report, p. 13.

58 Appellant's Brief, para. 17. The Appeals Chamber notes that a large portion of the Appellant's submissions with respect to his cooperation with the Prosecution has been filed confidentially. By motion filed on 11 October 2007, the Appellant requested that the Appeals Chamber maintain the confidentiality of paragraphs 18–21 of the Appellant's Brief, as well as allow the parties to discuss the issue of cooperation in private session during the appeals hearing of 15 October 2007. *See* Defence Response on "Questions to the Parties for Appeal Hearing on 15 October 2007" with Annex, 11 October 2007. The Prosecution agreed with the Appellant's request, AT. 25.

that went beyond the scope of the obligation he assumed.[59] Consequently, the Appellant submits that the Trial Chamber erred in the Sentencing Judgement, "when it characterized the cooperation offered by Mr. Zelenović [...] as 'some initial cooperation'" and gave this circumstance less importance than it deserved.[60]

22. The Prosecution responds that the Trial Chamber considered both the Appellant's commitment to cooperate and the cooperation he has already given and that the Appellant failed to show that the Trial Chamber discernibly erred in giving weight in mitigation to his cooperation with the Prosecution.[61] Moreover, the Prosecution contests the Appellant's interpretation of the extent of the obligation to cooperate contained in the Plea Agreement and submits that, "the Trial Chamber gave Zelenović credit for making a full commitment to co-operate and treated this as one of the 'main' mitigating circumstances".[62] Therefore, the Prosecution submits that the Appellant did not **[page 10]** demonstrate that the Trial Chamber underestimated the value of his promised or actual cooperation with the Prosecution.[63]

23. In his Reply Brief, the Appellant maintains that his "readiness to cooperate went beyond the scope of the established obligations".[64] Therefore, the Appellant upholds that the Trial Chamber erred when assessing his cooperation as "initial", rather than "substantial", and in not attributing it sufficient weight in mitigation of sentence.[65]

24. The Appeals Chamber recalls that substantial cooperation with the Prosecution is the only mitigating circumstance expressly mentioned in the Rules.[66] However, what constitutes "substantial cooperation" is not defined by the Rules. It is within the Trial Chamber's discretion to evaluate the extent and the nature of the accused's cooperation[67] and to determine the weight, if any, it should be accorded in mitigation.[68] As correctly noted by the Trial Chamber, an accused's cooperation does not need to be substantial[69] for it to be taken into account as a mitigating circumstance.[70]

25. The Appeals Chamber notes that the Plea Agreement does not specify the exact content of the Appellant's obligation to cooperate, but rather defines this obligation in broad terms.[71] According to the Plea Agreement, the Appellant agrees,

> to co-operate with, and to provide truthful and complete information to the Office of the Prosecutor whenever requested. In accordance with such co-operation, Dragan Zelenović agrees to meet as often as necessary with members of the Office of the Prosecutor in order to provide them with full and complete information and evidence that is known to him. Mr. Zelenović agrees to be truthful and candid, and to freely answer all questions put to him by members of the Office of the Prosecutor.[72]

Therefore, the Appeals Chamber finds that the Appellant did not prove that his cooperation with the Prosecution went "beyond the scope of the established obligations"[73] and "as such represents substantial co-operation".[74] **[page 11]**

26. In relation to the Appellant's submission that the Trial Chamber erred when considering his cooperation with the Prosecution as merely "some initial cooperation", the Appeals Chamber notes the Trial Chamber's finding that, regardless of the initial or substantial character of the cooperation,

59 Reply Brief, para. 14.
60 Appellant's Brief, para. 22.
61 Respondent's Brief, paras 18–19.
62 Respondent's Brief, para. 23.
63 Respondent's Brief, para. 24.
64 Reply Brief, para. 11.
65 Reply Brief, para. 14.
66 *See* Rule 101(B)(ii) of the Rules.
67 *Bralo* Judgement on Sentencing Appeal, para. 51. *See also Jelisić* Appeal Judgement, para. 124.
68 *Bralo* Judgement on Sentencing Appeal, para. 51; *Momir Nikolić* Judgement on Sentencing Appeal, para. 91. *See also Jelisić* Appeal Judgement, para. 126.
69 *See* Rule 101(B)(ii) of the Rules.
70 Sentencing Judgement, para. 52. *See also Bralo* Judgement on Sentencing Appeal, para. 51; *Dragan Nikolić* Judgement on Sentencing Appeal, para. 66; *Vasiljević* Appeal Judgement, para. 180.
71 Plea Agreement, para. 9.
72 Plea Agreement, para. 9, as quoted in the Sentencing Judgement, para. 52.
73 Reply Brief, para. 11.
74 Reply Brief, para. 14.

> it is the *commitment* to cooperate *as well as* actual cooperation, even if due to the particular experiences of the convicted person his or her full and sincere assistance is judged to be of little or no value to ongoing investigations or trials, that determines the weight that should be attached to this factor.[75]

The Trial Chamber further found that the Appellant's commitment to cooperate with the Prosecution was one of the "main mitigating circumstances in this case".[76] Hence, the Appeals Chamber is satisfied that the Trial Chamber did not commit a discernible error when considering the scope of the Appellant's cooperation with the Prosecution in mitigation of the sentence.

27. For the foregoing reasons, the Appellant's first ground of appeal is dismissed. **[page 12]**

IV. SECOND GROUND OF APPEAL: WHETHER THE STANKOVIĆ APPEAL JUDGEMENT RENDERED BY THE STATE COURT OF BOSNIA AND HERZEGOVINA SHOULD HAVE BEEN TAKEN INTO CONSIDERATION IN DETERMINING THE SENTENCE

28. This ground of appeal is based on the Appellant's contention that the Trial Chamber should have taken into account the appeal judgement in the case of *Prosecutor v. Radovan Stanković*[77] before the State Court of Bosnia and Herzegovina in determining the sentence against the Appellant. He argues that whilst it was possible for the Trial Chamber to learn about the *Stanković* Appeal Judgement, which was rendered on 28 March 2007 and "submitted to the first-instance court" on 17 April 2007, it did not take this judgement into account for the reason that the case was still under appeal.[78]

29. The Trial Chamber "refrained from taking guidance from [the *Stanković*] case",[79] having considered the arguments of the parties and "in particular the fact that the judgement in the *Stanković* case [was] under appeal."[80] The Appeals Chamber finds that the Appellant does not demonstrate that the Trial Chamber erred in this respect. Both parties agree that the *Stanković* Appeal Judgement was only made public on 17 April 2007,[81] which occured after the rendering of the Sentencing Judgement in the present case. Hence, the Appellant does not substantiate his allegation that it was possible for the Trial Chamber to learn about the *Stanković* Appeal Judgement prior to the rendering of the Sentencing Judgement.

30. For the foregoing reasons, the Appellant's second ground of appeal is dismissed. **[page 13]**

---

75 Sentencing Judgement, para. 52 (footnote omitted; emphases added).

76 Sentencing Judgement, para. 56.

77 Appellant's Brief, paras 25, 27; *Prosecutor v. Radovan Stanković* Case No. X-KRŽ-05/70, Panel of the Appellate Division, Appeal Judgement, 28 March 2007 (State Court of Bosnia and Herzegovina) ("*Stanković* Appeal Judgement").

78 Notice for Leave to Appeal, para. 15.

79 Trial Judgement, para. 69.

80 Trial Judgement, para. 69.

81 Confidential Defence Response on "Questions to the Parties for Appeal Hearing on 15 October 2007" with Public Annex, 11 October 2007, para. 9. For the Prosecution, *see* AT. 31. The Appeals Chamber notes that, during the appeal hearing, Counsel for the Appellant argued that the Trial Chamber should have taken into account the first instance Judgement in *Prosecutor v. Radovan Stanković* (AT. 46–47). The Appeals Chamber declines to consider this argument as it was raised for the first time during the appeal hearing and falls outside the scope of the arguments raised in the Appellant's Notice for Leave to Appeal. In any event, the Appeals Chamber is of the view that the first instance Judgement in *Stanković* would not have assisted the Appellant in making his case.

V. DISPOSITION

For the foregoing reasons, **THE APPEALS CHAMBER**, unanimously

PURSUANT to Article 25 of the Statute and Rules 117 and 118 of the Rules;

NOTING the respective written submissions of the Parties and the oral arguments they presented at the appeal hearing of 15 October 2007;

SITTING in open session;

DISMISSES the Appellant's grounds of appeal;

AFFIRMS the sentence of 15 (fifteen) years' imprisonment as imposed by the Trial Chamber, subject to credit being given under Rule 101(C) of the Rules for the time Dragan Zelenović has already spent in detention since 22 August 2005; and

ORDERS in accordance with Rule 103(C) and Rule 107 of the Rules, that the Appellant is to remain in the custody of the International Tribunal pending the finalisation of arrangements for his transfer to the State in which his sentence will be served.

Done in English and French, the English text being authoritative.

Dated this 31st day of October 2007 at The Hague, The Netherlands.

Liu Daqun Presiding Judge	Mohamed Shahabuddeen Judge	Mehmet Güney Judge
Andrésia Vaz Judge		Wolfgang Schomburg Judge

[Seal of the International Tribunal] [page 14]

VI. ANNEX A: PROCEDURAL BACKGROUND

A. Filing of the appeal submissions

31. The Appellant filed a "Defence Notice for Leave to Appeal Sentencing Judgement" on 27 April 2007.[82] The Appellant's Brief was filed on 25 May 2007[83] and the Respondent's Brief on 25 June 2007.[84] The Appellant filed his Reply Brief on 3 July 2007.[85]

B. Composition of the Appeals Chamber

32. By order of 2 May 2007, the President of the International Tribunal, Judge Fausto Pocar, designated the following Judges to hear the present appeal: Judge Mohamed Shahabuddeen, Judge Mehmet Güney, Judge Liu Daqun, Judge Andrésia Vaz and Judge Wolfgang Schomburg.[86] On 24 July 2007, having been elected as Presiding Judge in the present appeal pursuant to Rule 22(B) of the Rules, Judge Liu Daqun issued an order designating himself as the Pre-Appeal Judge with responsibility for all pre-appeal proceedings in this case, in accordance with Rules 65*ter* and 107 of the Rules.[87]

C. Substantive motions

33. On 3 May 2007, the Prosecution filed a motion requesting the Appeals Chamber to consider the Defence's Notice for Leave to Appeal[88] as the notice of appeal required under Rule 108 of the Rules and to consequently determine the deadlines for the remainder of the briefing in this appeal based on the date of the Notice for Leave to Appeal, namely 27 April 2007.[89] In the Appellant's Brief, the Appellant did not take a position regarding the request made to the Appeals Chamber in the Prosecution Motion. In the Scheduling Order of 24 July 2007, the Pre-Appeal Judge granted the Prosecution's request and confirmed that the Notice for Leave to Appeal constituted the notice of appeal required under Rule 108 of the Rules.[90]

34. On 18 July 2007, the Prosecution filed a confidential motion requesting the Appeals Chamber to strike out portions of the Reply Brief "because they are not supported by evidence in **[page 15]** the record and he has not sought to adduce additional evidence to support them under Rule 115"[91] of the Rules. The Appellant responded on 31 July 2007.[92] The Prosecution filed its reply on 6 August 2007.[93] On 6 September 2007, the Appeals Chamber issued its confidential Decision on Prosecution Motion to Strike Portions of the Appellant's Reply, partially granting the Prosecution's request and striking the last two sentences of paragraph 13 of the Reply Brief.

D. Status Conference

35. In accordance with Rule 65*bis*(B) of the Rules, a status conference was held on 27 August 2007.[94]

E. Appeal Hearing

36. Pursuant to the Scheduling Order of 20 September 2007, the hearing on the merits of the appeal took place on 15 October 2007. **[page 16]**

---

82 Defence Notice for Leave to Appeal Sentencing Judgment, 27 April 2007.
83 Defence Appeal on Sentencing Judgement, 25 May 2007.
84 Prosecution's Response Brief, 25 June 2007.
85 Defence Reply to "Prosecution Response Brief", 3 July 2007.
86 Order Assigning Judges to a Case Before the Appeals Chamber, 2 May 2007.
87 Order Designating Pre-Appeal Judge, 24 July 2007.
88 Prosecution Motion Concerning "Defence Notice for Leave to Appeal Sentencing Judgement", 3 May 2007.
89 Prosecution Motion, paras 1 and 5.
90 Scheduling Order, 24 July 2007.
91 Prosecution Motion to Strike Portions of Appellant's Reply (confidential), 18 July 2007, para. 1.
92 Defence Response to Prosecution Motion to Strike Portions of Appellant's Reply (confidential), 31 July 2007.
93 Prosecution Reply to Defence Response to Prosecution Motion to Strike Portions of Appellant's Reply (confidential), 6 August 2007.
94 Scheduling Order, 24 July 2007. During the status conference, the Pre-Appeal Judge asked the Appellant about his health condition during detention, AT. 3. In order for the information to be complete, the Appellant submitted the Defence Notice Regarding Health Condition of the Accused Dragan Zelenović with Confidential Annex, 11 October 2007. The issue was further mentioned by the Appellant in his final word at the end of the appeal hearing, AT. 49.

VII. ANNEX B: GLOSSARY OF TERMS

A. List of Cited Court Decisions

1. ICTY

ALEKSOVSKI

Prosecutor v. Zlatko Aleksovski, Case No. IT-95-14/1-A, Judgement, 24 March 2000 ("*Aleksovski* Appeal Judgement").

BABIĆ

Prosecutor v. Milan Babić, Case No. IT-03-72-A, Sentencing Judgement, 18 July 2005 ("*Babić* Judgement on Sentencing Appeal").

BLAGOJEVIĆ & JOKIĆ

Prosecutor v. Vidoje Blagojević & Dragan Jokić, Case No IT-02-60-A, Judgement, 9 May 2007 ("*Blagojević and Jokić* Appeal Judgement").

BLAŠKIĆ

Prosecutor v. Tihomir Blaškić, Case No. IT-95-14-A, Judgement, 29 July 2004 ("*Blaškić* Appeal Judgement").

BRALO

Prosecutor v. Miroslav Bralo, Case No. IT-95-17-A, Judgement on Sentencing Appeal, 2 April 2007 ("*Bralo* Judgement on Sentencing Appeal").

BRĐANIN

Prosecutor v. Radoslav Brđanin, Case No. It-99-36-A, Judgement, 3 April 2007 (*Brđanin* Appeal Judgement).

"ČELEBIĆI"

Prosecutor v. Zejnil Delalić, Zdravko Mucić, a.k.a. "Pavo", Hazim Delić and Esad Landžo, a.k.a. "Zenga", Case No. IT-96-21-A, Judgement, 20 February 2001 ("*Čelebići* Appeal Judgement").

DERONJIĆ

Prosecutor v. Miroslav Deronjić, Case No. IT-02-61-A, Judgement on Sentencing Appeal, 20 July 2005 ("*Deronjić* Judgement on Sentencing Appeal").

FURUNDŽIJA

Prosecutor v. Anto Furundžija, Case No. IT-95-17/1-A, Judgement, 21 July 2000 ("*Furundžija* Appeal Judgement").

GALIĆ

Prosecutor v. Stanislav Galić, Case No. IT-98-29-A, Judgement, 30 November 2006 ("*Galić* Appeal Judgement").

JELISIĆ

Prosecutor v. Goran Jelisić, Case No. IT-95-10-A, Judgement, 5 July 2001 ("*Jelisić* Appeal Judgement"). **[page 17]**

M. JOKIĆ

Prosecutor v. Miodrag Jokić, Case No. IT-01-42/1-A, Judgement on Sentencing Appeal, 30 August 2005 ("*Miodrag Jokić* Judgement on Sentencing Appeal").

KORDIĆ AND ČERKEZ

Prosecutor v. Dario Kordić and Mario Čerkez, Case No. IT-95-14/2-A, Judgement, 17 December 2004 ("*Kordić and Čerkez* Appeal Judgement").

KRSTIĆ

Prosecutor v. Radislav Krstić, Case No. IT-98-33-A, Judgement, 19 April 2004 ("*Krstić* Appeal Judgement").

KUNARAC, KOVAČ AND VUKOVIĆ

Prosecutor v. Dragoljub Kunarac, Radomir Kovač and Zoran Vuković, Case No. IT-96-23 & IT-96-23/1-A, Judgement, 12 June 2002 ("*Kunarac et al.* Appeal Judgement").

Z. KUPREŠKIĆ, M. KUPREŠKIĆ, V. KUPREŠKIĆ, JOSIPOVIĆ, (PAPIĆ) AND SANTIĆ

Prosecutor v. Zoran Kupreškić, Mirjan Kupreškić, Vlatko Kupreškić, Drago Josipović and Vladimir Santić, Case No. IT-95-16-A, Appeal Judgement, 23 October 2001 ("*Kupreškić et al.* Appeal Judgement").

KVOČKA, KOS, RADIĆ, ŽIGIĆ AND PRCAĆ

Prosecutor v. Miroslav Kvočka, Milojica Kos, Mlado Radić, Zoran Žigić and Dragoljub Prcać, Case No. IT-98-30/1-A, Appeal Judgement, 28 February 2005 ("*Kvočka et al.* Appeal Judgement").

MUCIĆ, DELIĆ AND LANDŽO

Prosecutor v. Zdravko Mucić, Hazim Delić and Esad Landžo, Case No. IT-96-21-A, Judgement on Sentence Appeal, 8 April 2003 ("*Mucić et al.* Judgement on Sentencing Appeal").

NALETILIĆ AND MARTINOVIĆ

Prosecutor v. Mladen Naletilić and Vinko Martinović, Case No. IT-98-34-A, Judgement, 3 May 2006 ("*Naletilić and Martinović* Appeal Judgement").

D. NIKOLIĆ

Prosecutor v. Dragan Nikolić, Case No. IT-94-02-A, Judgement on Sentencing Appeal, 4 February 2005 ("*Dragan Nikolić* Judgement on Sentencing Appeal").

M. NIKOLIĆ

Prosecutor v. Momir Nikolić, Case No. IT-02-60/1-A, Appeal Sentencing Judgement, 8 March 2006 ("*Momir Nikolić* Judgement on Sentencing Appeal").

D. TADIĆ

Prosecutor v. Duško Tadić, Case No. IT-94-1-A, Judgement, 15 July 1999 ("*Tadić* Appeal Judgement").

Prosecutor v. Duško Tadić, Case No. IT-94-1-A and IT-94-1-A*bis*, Judgement on Sentencing Appeal, 26 January 2000 ("*Tadić* Judgement in Sentencing Appeals").

VASILJEVIĆ

Prosecutor v. Mitar Vasiljević, Case No. IT-98-32-A, Judgement, 25 February 2004 ("*Vasiljević* Appeal Judgement"). **[page 18]**

ZELENOVIĆ

Prosecutor v. Dragan Zelenović, Case No. IT-96-23/2-S, Sentencing Judgement, 4 April 2007 ("Sentencing Judgement").

2. ICTR

AKAYESU

Prosecutor v. Jean-Paul Akayesu, Case No. ICTR-96-4-A, Judgement, 1 June 2001 ("*Akayesu* Appeal Judgement").

KAYISHEMA AND RUZINDANA

Prosecutor v. Clément Kayishema and Obed Ruzindana, Case No. ICTR-95-1-A, Judgement (Reasons), 1 June 2001 ("*Kayishema and Ruzindana* Appeal Judgement ").

MUSEMA

Prosecutor v. Alfred Musema, Case No. ICTR-96-13-A, Judgement, 16 November 2001 ("*Musema* Appeal Judgement").

NIYITEGEKA

Prosecutor v. Eliézer Niyitegeka, Case No. ICTR-96-14-A, Appeal Judgement, 9 July 2004 ("*Niyitegeka* Appeal Judgement").

3. Other courts

STANKOVIĆ

Prosecutor v. Radovan Stanković, Case No. X-KRŽ-05/70, First Instance Panel, Verdict, 14 November 2006 (State Court of Bosnia and Herzegovina) ("*Stanković* Judgement").

Prosecutor v. Radovan Stanković, Case No. X-KRŽ-05/70, Panel of the Appellate Division, Verdict, Appeal Judgement, 28 March 2007 (State Court of Bosnia and Herzegovina) ("*Stanković* Appeal Judgement").

B. List of Abbreviations

According to Rule 2(B) of the Rules of Procedure and Evidence, the masculine shall include the feminine and the singular the plural, and vice-versa.

Amended Indictment	*Prosecutor v. Gojko Janković, Dragan Zelenović and Radovan Stanković,* Case No. IT-96-23/2-1 Amended Indictment, 20 April 2001
Appellant	Dragan Zelenović
Appellant's Brief	*Prosecutor v. Dragan Zelenović,* Case No. IT-96-23/2-A, Defence Appeal on Sentencing Judgement (Confidential Version), 25 May 2007
AT.	Transcript page from hearings on appeal in the present case. All transcript page numbers referred to are from the unofficial, uncorrected version of the transcript, unless not specified otherwise. Minor differences may therefore exist **[page 19]** between the pagination therein and that in the final transcripts released to the public.
Defence	Counsel for Dragan Zelenović
ICTR	International Criminal Tribunal for the Prosecution of Persons Responsible for Genocide and Other Serious Violations of International Humanitarian Law Committed in the Territory of Rwanda and Rwandan Citizens responsible for genocide and other such violations committed in the territory of neighbouring States, between 1 January 1994 and 31 December 1994
International Tribunal	International Tribunal for the Prosecution of Persons Responsible for Serious Violations of International Humanitarian Law Committed in the Territory of the Former Yugoslavia since 1991
Notice for Leave to Appeal	*Prosecutor v. Dragan Zelenović,* Case No. IT-96-23/2-S, Defence Notice for Leave to Appeal Sentencing Judgement, 27 April 2007
Plea Agreement	*Prosecutor v. Dragan Zelenović,* Case No. IT-96-23/2-PT, Joint Motion for Consideration of Plea Agreement between Dragan Zelenović and the Office of the Prosecutor pursuant to Rule 62*ter*, 14 December 2006
Prosecution	Office of the Prosecutor

Prosecution Motion	*Prosecutor v. Dragan Zelenović,* Case No. IT-96-23/2-A, Prosecution Motion Concerning "Defence Notice for Leave to Appeal Sentencing Judgement", 3 May 2007
Reply Brief	*Prosecutor v. Dragan Zelenović,* Case No. IT-96-23/2-A, Defence Reply to "Prosecution Response Brief" (Confidential Version), 3 July 2007
Respondent's Brief	*Prosecutor v. Dragan Zelenović,* Case No. IT-96-23/2-A, Prosecution's Response Brief (Confidential Version), 25 June 2007
Rules	Rules of Procedure and Evidence
Sentencing Hearing	*Prosecutor v. Dragan Zelenović,* Case No. IT-96-23/2-S, Sentencing Hearing, 23 February 2007 ("Sentencing Hearing")
Sentencing Judgement	*Prosecutor v. Dragan Zelenović,* Case No. IT-96-23/2-S, Sentencing Judgement, 4 April 2007
Statute	Statute of the International Tribunal for the Former Yugoslavia established by Security Council Resolution 827 (1993) **[page 20]**
T.	Transcript page from hearings at trial in the present case. All transcript page numbers referred to are from the unofficial, uncorrected version of the transcript, unless specified otherwise. Minor differences may therefore exist between the pagination therein and in the final transcripts released to the public.
UN	United Nations

UNITED NATIONS

International Tribunal for the Prosecution of Persons Responsible for Serious Violations of International Humanitarian Law Committed in the Territory of Former Yugoslavia since 1991	Case No.	IT-96-23/2-S
	Date:	4 April 2007
	Original:	English

IN TRIAL CHAMBER I

Before: **Judge Alphons Orie, Presiding**
Judge Christine Van den Wyngaert
Judge Bakone Justice Moloto

Registrar: **Mr. Hans Holthuis**

Judgement of: **4 April 2007**

PROSECUTOR

v.

DRAGAN ZELENOVIĆ

SENTENCING JUDGEMENT

The Office of the Prosecutor:
Ms. Hildegard Uertz-Retzlaff
Mr. Vladimir Tochilovsky
Ms. Christina Moeller
Mr. Manoj Sachdeva

Counsel for the Accused:
Mr. Zoran Jovanović

Contents

General abbreviations

Bosnia-Herzegovina	Republic of Bosnia and Herzegovina
Bosnian-Serb Republic	Serbian Republic of Bosnia-Herzegovina; on 12 August 1992, the name of the republic was officially changed to *Republika Srpska*
Factual Statement	Joint Motion for consideration of Plea Agreement between Dragan Zelenović and the Office of the Prosecutor pursuant to Rule 62 *ter*, Tab 1 Factual Statement, 14 December 2006
JNA	*Jugoslovenska Narodna Armija* – Yugoslav People's Army
Plea Agreement	Joint Motion for Consideration of Plea Agreement between Dragan Zelenović and the Office of the Prosecutor pursuant to Rule 62 *ter*, 14 December 2006
SFRY	Socialist Federal Republic of Yugoslavia
SJB	*Stanica Javne Bezbjednosti* – Public Security Station
TO	*Teritorijalna Odbrana* – Territorial Defence
UNDU	United Nations Detention Unit
VRS	*Vojska Republike Srpske* – Army of the Bosnian-Serb Republic

[page 1] 1. Procedural history and plea

1. The initial indictment of 18 June 1996 against Dragan Zelenović was confirmed on 26 June 1996 and included seven other persons.[1] The indictment was amended on 5 October 1999.[2] A redacted version of the amended indictment ("Indictment") was filed on 20 April 2001.[3] The Indictment charged Mr. Zelenović with seven counts of torture and rape as crimes against humanity and seven counts of torture and rape as violations of the laws or customs of war.

2. Since the initial indictment, a number of warrants for the arrest of Mr. Zelenović have been issued, including one directed to Bosnia-Herzegovina on 26 June 1996 and one to the authorities of all member states of the United Nations on 12 January 2004.[4]

3. On 29 November 2004, the Prosecution requested the President of the Tribunal to appoint a Trial Chamber, in the case of *Prosecutor v. Dragan Zelenović and Gojko Janković*, to which a request under Rule 11 *bis* of the Rules of Procedure and Evidence ("Rules") could be filed for review.[5] On the same day, the Prosecution filed a motion for the referral of the case of Dragan Zelenović and Gojko Janković to the authorities of Bosnia-Herzegovina ("11 *bis* Motion").[6] On 1 December 2004, the President of the Tribunal appointed a Referral Bench to deal with the motion.[7] The case of Gojko Janković was referred to the authorities of Bosnia-Herzegovina in accordance with a decision of the Referral Bench on 22 July 2005.[8]

4. According to Mr. Zelenović, he had left Foča in 2000 or 2001 and travelled to Russia under a false name in order to avoid detection and arrest for the crimes charged in the indictment. His **[page 2]** family remained in Foča. Mr. Zelenović lived in Russia until he was arrested on 22 August 2005.[9] On 23 August 2005, the Acting Public Prosecutor of Khanti-Mansiysk, in the Russian Federation, ordered the detention of Mr. Zelenović. The detention was carried out pursuant to "the Decision of the [Tribunal]".[10] On 8 June 2006, Mr. Zelenović was transferred to Bosnia-Herzegovina, and two days later, on 10 June 2006, he was transferred to the Tribunal and detained at the United Nations Detention Unit (UNDU).[11]

5. On 9 June 2006, the case was assigned to Trial Chamber I,[12] and on 19 June 2006, Judge Alphons Orie was appointed pre-trial judge.[13]

---

[1] Indictment, 18 June 1996 (filed 19 June 1996) and Review of Indictment Pursuant to Article 19(1) of the Statute, 26 June 1996. The other seven accused were Dragan Gagović, Gojko Janković, Janko Janjić, Radomir Kovač, Zoran Vuković, Dragoljub Kunarac, and Radovan Stanković. The indictment was amended on 19 August 1998, consolidating the charges against Dragoljub Kunarac, and leaving out references to the seven other accused (Order Granting Leave to File an Amended Indictment and Confirming the Amended Indictment, 19 August 1998). On 30 July 1999, the Prosecutor withdrew the indictment against Dragan Gagović, who had died in the meantime (Order Granting Leave to Withdraw Indictment, 30 July 1999). A second amended indictment against Dragoljub Kunarac and Radomir Kovać was confirmed on 3 September 1999 (Order Granting Leave to File a Second Amended Indictment and Confirming the Second Amended Indictment, 3 September 1999).

[2] Amended Indictment, 5 October 1999 (filed 7 October 1999).

[3] Redacted version of the Amended Indictment, 5 October 1999 (filed 20 April 2001). Janko Janjić was excluded from this redacted version as he had died in the meantime. On 16 February 2000, the Trial Chamber had ordered the severance of the case against Zoran Vukovic (Order for Severance and Combined Case Number, 16 February 2000).

[4] See Warrant of Arrest and Order for Surrender, 26 June 1996; Warrant of Arrest and Order for Surrender, 29 May 2001; Warrant of Arrest and Order for Surrender, 6 September 2002; Warrant of Arrest and Order for Surrender, 12 January 2004.

[5] Motion by the Prosecutor under Rule 11 *bis* (A), 29 November 2004.

[6] Motion by the Prosecutor under Rule 11 *bis* (A) with Annexes I. II, II and Confidential Annexes IV and V, 29 November 2004.

[7] Order Appointing a Trial Chamber for the Purpose of Determining Whether an Indictment Should be Referred to Another Court Under Rule 11 *bis*, 1 December 2004.

[8] *Prosecutor v. Gojko Janković*, Decision on Referral of Case under Rule 11 *bis*, 22 July 2005. The decision was upheld on appeal (*Prosecutor v. Gojko Janković*, Decision on 11 *bis* Referral, 15 November 2005).

[9] Defence Sentencing Brief, Annex A (Detention Order by Acting Khanti-Mansiysk Inter-Municipal Public Prosecutor, 23 August 2005); T. 522–527.

[10] Defence Sentencing Brief, Annex A (Detention Order by Acting Khanti-Mansiysk Inter-Municipal Public Prosecutor, 23 August 2005); T. 552–554.

[11] Defence Sentencing Brief, Annex A (Order by the State Court in Bosnia-Herzegovina, 9 June 2006); Order for Detention on Remand, 12 June 2006.

[12] Order Assigning a Case to a Trial Chamber, 9 June 2006.

[13] Order Designating Pre-Trial Judge, 19 June 2006.

6. On 12 June 2006, Mr. Tjarda van der Spoel was appointed counsel for the initial appearance.[14] At his initial appearance on 13 June 2006, Mr. Zelenović requested 30 days to enter a plea to the Indictment as he did not have a permanent counsel at that time.[15] At the further initial appearance on 13 July 2006, the pre-trial judge granted Mr. Zelenović additional time to enter a plea since at this time he had still no assigned counsel.[16] At the second further initial appearance on 14 July 2006, after having discussed the Indictment with a lawyer who had been chosen by Mr. Zelenović but not been appointed as counsel, Mr. Zelenović entered a plea of not guilty.[17] On 16 August 2006, Mr. Zoran Jovanović was assigned as counsel for Mr. Zelenović.[18]

7. On 17 August 2006, the Referral Bench ordered the parties, and invited the Government of Bosnia-Herzegovina, to file submissions with regard to the 11 *bis* Motion and to submit responses to specific questions, including whether the gravity of the crime and the level of responsibility were compatible with the referral of the case to the War Crimes Chamber of the State Court in Bosnia-Herzegovina.[19] On 20 September 2006, the Government of Bosnia-Herzegovina filed its submission in response to the invitation of the Referral Bench.[20] On 21 and 22 September 2006, the Prosecution **[page 3]** and the Defence, respectively, filed their submissions in response to the order of the Referral Bench.[21]

8. On 14 September 2006, the Defence filed a preliminary motion alleging defects in the form of the Indictment, in particular that the Indictment was "not sufficiently particular to inform [Mr. Zelenović] clearly of the nature of the charges against him".[22] On 22 September 2006, the Prosecution responded that the motion of the Defence should be denied.[23] On 11 October 2006, the Trial Chamber denied the preliminary motion.[24]

9. On 13 October 2006, a hearing regarding the 11 *bis* Motion was held by the Referral Bench with the parties present, and a delegation of the Government of Bosnia-Herzegovina participating through video-conference link from Sarajevo.[25] Concluding this session, the Referral Bench informed the parties that its decision would be given in due course.[26] Because of subsequent events no decision was taken on the 11 *bis* Motion. The Prosecution has indicated to the Trial Chamber that it will withdraw the motion subsequent to the rendering of the present sentencing judgement.

10. On 14 December 2006, the Prosecution and the Defence jointly filed a Motion for Consideration of Plea Agreement between Dragan Zelenović and the Office of the Prosecutor pursuant to Rule 62 *ter*.[27] According to this Plea Agreement, Mr. Zelenović agreed to plead guilty to seven counts of crimes against humanity, three of which charge torture, as provided for by Article 5(f) of the Statute (counts 5, 13, and 41), and four of which charge rape, as provided for by Article 5(g) of the Statute (counts 6, 14, 42, and 49).[28] Mr. Zelenović declared his intention to plead guilty, as individually criminally responsible, for the crimes mentioned in relation to the incidents contained in the following paragraphs of the Indictment: 5.4, 5.5, 6.6, 6.8, 6.9, 6.10, 7.13, and 9.2.[29] He also agreed to cooperate with the Office of the Prosecutor, including testifying at any trial before the Tribunal.[30] The Prosecution agreed to withdraw the remaining charges against Mr. Zelenović at the time of the acceptance of the guilty plea by the Trial Chamber.[31] Finally, the Prosecution

[14] Decision by the Deputy Registrar, 12 June 2006.
[15] T. 370.
[16] T. 388–389.
[17] T. 392–397.
[18] Decision of Deputy Registrar, 16 August 2006.
[19] Order for Further Information in the Context of Prosecutor's Motion Pursuant to Rule 11 *bis*, 17 August 2006.
[20] Response by the Government of Bosnia-Herzegovina to Questions Posed by the Referral Bench in its Decision of 17 August 2006, 20 September 2006 (filed on 10 October 2006).
[21] Prosecutor's Further Submissions Pursuant to Referral Bench's Order of 17 August 2006, 21 September 2006; Defence Submissions Pursuant to Referral Bench's Order of 17 August 2006, 22 September 2006.
[22] Defence Preliminary Motion, 14 September 2006.
[23] Prosecution's Response to Defence Preliminary Motion, 22 September 2006.
[24] Decision on Defence Preliminary Motion, 11 October 2006.
[25] T. 404–425.
[26] T. 425.
[27] Joint Motion for Consideration of Plea Agreement between Dragan Zelenović and the Office of the Prosecutor pursuant to Rule 62 *ter*, 14 December 2006 ("Plea Agreement").
[28] Plea Agreement, para. 2.
[29] Ibid.
[30] Ibid., para. 9.
[31] Ibid., para. 3.

[page 4] recommended the Trial Chamber to impose a term of imprisonment within the range of 10 to 15 years, while the Defence recommended a term of imprisonment within the range of 7 to 10 years.[32]

11. During a hearing on 16 January 2007, the Trial Chamber requested the parties to clarify certain points of the Plea Agreement, in particular the relationship between the incidents which Mr. Zelenović admitted to and the counts he intended to plead guilty to, as well as why certain incidents were qualified as both torture and rape while one incident was qualified only as rape. In response to a question by the Trial Chamber, the Prosecution explained that the exclusion of certain victims, referred to in the Indictment, from the Plea Agreement was based on a consideration of the available evidence.[33] After having heard submissions from both parties, the Trial Chamber stated that it was "not satisfied with the plea agreement as a written basis for receiving pleas from Mr. Zelenović".[34] The Trial Chamber requested the parties to file, as an annex to the Plea Agreement, a copy of the Indictment in which the parties would strike out all parts to which Mr. Zelenović did not intend to plead guilty. This would include a clarification of the mode of liability and the number of victims under each count.[35]

12. On 16 January 2007, the parties filed an annex to the Plea Agreement, consisting of a redacted and revised copy of the Indictment reflecting the charges and underlying incidents Mr. Zelenović agreed to plead guilty to.[36]

13. On 17 January 2007, after the Trial Chamber had asked questions to clarify some outstanding matters concerning the aforementioned annex to the Plea Agreement,[37] the Prosecution requested leave to withdraw counts 7, 8, 15, 16, 43, 44, and 50 of the Indictment dealing with violations of the laws or customs of war.[38] The Trial Chamber granted the request.[39] The Trial Chamber further invited Mr. Zelenović to enter a plea to the counts of torture and rape as crimes against humanity.[40] Mr. Zelenović pleaded guilty to aiding and abetting the rape against FWS-75 and committing the rape against FWS-87 as torture and rape as crimes against humanity (counts 5 and 6),[41] and to co-perpetration of rape in relation to FWS-87 and two unidentified women and committing rape three times against FWS-75 and three times against FWS-87 as torture and rape as **[page 5]** crimes against humanity (counts 13 and 14).[42] Mr. Zelenović further pleaded guilty to committing rape against FWS-87 as torture and rape as crimes against humanity (counts 41 and 42),[43] and to co-perpetration of rape in relation to FWS-75 and two unidentified women and committing the rape against FWS-87 as rape as a crime against humanity (count 49).[44] The Trial Chamber accepted the guilty pleas, and found Mr. Zelenović guilty in accordance with his pleas.[45] The Prosecution proceeded to withdraw counts 7, 8, 15, 16, 43, 44, and 50.[46] Finally, the Trial Chamber lifted the confidentiality of the Plea Agreement.[47]

14. On 31 January 2007, the Prosecution filed its sentencing brief specifying the sentencing factors that should be taken into consideration and reiterating its recommendation that the Trial Chamber impose a term of imprisonment within the range of 10 to 15 years.[48] On 14 February 2007, the Defence filed its sentencing brief asking the Trial Chamber to take into account the gravity of the crime and certain mitigating circumstances and reiterating its recommendation that Mr. Zelenović should be sentenced to a term of imprisonment of between 7 and 10 years.[49]

---

[32] Ibid., para. 3.
[33] T. 464–465.
[34] T. 467.
[35] T. 467–473, 482.
[36] Joint Submission of Annex to Plea Agreement, 16 January 2007 ("Annex to Plea Agreement").
[37] T. 477–482.
[38] T. 483.
[39] T. 484.
[40] T. 484.
[41] T. 486.
[42] T. 488–489.
[43] T. 489–490.
[44] T. 490.
[45] T. 491–492.
[46] T. 493; Prosecution's Submission Regarding Withdrawal of Charges, 17 January 2007.
[47] T. 496.
[48] Prosecution's Sentencing Brief, 31 January 2007.
[49] Defence Sentencing Brief, 14 February 2007.

15. During the sentencing hearing on 23 February 2007, the parties emphasized the sentencing factors that the Trial Chamber, in their view, should take into consideration (as developed below). The Trial Chamber also sought the parties' submissions as to which case law would be of guidance in determining the sentence in the present case.[50] Accordingly, the parties filed additional submissions on the question of the extent to which the judgement of 14 November 2006 in the case of *Prosecutor v. Radovan Stanković* would be a suitable precedent.[51]

16. On 27 March 2007, the Prosecution provided notice to the Trial Chamber of cooperation of Mr. Zelenović with the Office of the Prosecutor.[52] On 29 March 2007, the Defence responded to this notice.[53] **[page 6]**

2. <u>Facts</u>

17. Dragan Zelenović was born on 12 February 1961 in Foča, eastern Bosnia-Herzegovina. Prior to 1992, he worked as an electrician in Miljevina.[54] Mr. Zelenović was a member of the "Dragan Nikolić Unit", a military unit in Foča which, in the beginning of the war, was part of the Bosnian-Serb TO and, from the summer of 1992 onwards, part of the Bosnian-Serb army (VRS). Mr. Zelenović was a soldier and, *de facto*, a military policeman.[55]

18. Foča municipality is located south-east of Sarajevo, in Bosnia-Herzegovina. According to the 1991 census, the population of Foča consisted of 40,513 persons of whom 52% were Muslim, 45.3% Serbian and 3.1% of other ethnicity. The political and military take-over of the municipality started with Serb forces shelling Foča town, with heavy artillery, on 8 April 1992. This attack was part of an armed conflict in Bosnia-Herzegovina between forces of the government of Bosnia-Herzegovina and Serb forces, comprised of the JNA, the TO (later the VRS), the Serb police and various irregular Serb military formations. By mid-April 1992, the take-over of the town of Foča by the Serb forces was completed. The attacks on the surrounding villages, most of which were undefended and had no military targets, lasted until mid-July 1992. The Serb forces effected the forcible removal of the majority of the non-Serb civilian population from Foča municipality through violence.[56]

19. During and after the take-over of Foča town and its surrounding villages and municipalities, Muslim and other non-Serb inhabitants were subjected to a widespread and systematic pattern of abuses, designed to remove the majority of them from the municipality. Muslim and other non-Serb inhabitants were methodically rounded up. In the course of their capture, civilians were frequently brutalized, beaten, and sometimes killed. Men and women were separated and transported to various detention facilities, such as school and community buildings and the Foča prison, where they were subjected to humiliating and degrading treatment. After extended periods of detention, the detainees were deported or forcibly transferred to Montenegro or locations controlled by the government of Bosnia-Herzegovina. The remaining non-Serb population outside the detention facilities was subjected to various discriminatory measures, such as restriction of movement, searching of homes, plunder and destruction of private as well as cultural and religious property, **[page 7]** beatings, and killings.[57] Mr. Zelenović was involved in the attack on Foča town and its surrounding villages and the subsequent arrest of civilians, between mid-April and mid-July 1992.[58]

---

50 T. 561.

51 Prosecution's Submission Regarding Use of Stanković Judgement, 27 February 2007; Defence Submission Regarding Use of Prosecutor v. Stanković Judgement, 28 February 2007. The case of Radovan Stanković was referred to the authorities of Bosnia-Herzegovina in accordance with a decision of the Referral Bench on 17 May 2005 (*Prosecutor v. Radovan Stanković*, Decision on Referral of Case under Rule 11 *bis*, 17 May 2005). The decision was upheld on appeal (*Prosecutor v. Radovan Stanković*, Decision on 11 *bis* Referral, 1 September 2005). On 14 November 2006, the State Court of Bosnia-Herzegovina convicted Stanković of crimes against humanity and sentenced him to 16 years of imprisonment. Both the Prosecution and the Defence have appealed the judgement.

52 Prosecution's Notice to Trial Chamber of Co-operation Pursuant to Plea Agreement, 27 March 2007.

53 Defence Response to Prosecution's Notice to Trial Chamber of Co-operation Pursuant to Plea Agreement, 29 March 2007.

54 Joint Motion for consideration of Plea Agreement between Dragan Zelenović and the Office of the Prosecutor pursuant to Rule 62 *ter*, Tab 1 Factual Statement, 14 December 2006 ("Factual Statement"), para. 2.

55 Factual Statement, paras 2, 6.

56 Factual Statement, para. 3.

57 Factual Statement, para. 4.

58 Factual Statement, para. 6.

20. As a consequence of the attack against the civilian population of Foča and its surrounding municipalities, Muslim civilians were to a very large extent expelled from the region. Out of the 52% of the population residing in Foča who were Muslims, only ten persons remained. In January 1994, Foča was renamed Srbinje for the reason that it was now almost exclusively inhabited by Serbs.[59]

21. On 3 July 1992, Mr. Zelenović, along with other men, arrested a group of about 60 Muslim women, children and elderly men from Tosanj and Mjesaja and took them to a temporary detention facility called Buk Bijela.[60] At the detention centre, Mr. Zelenović and other men separated the women from the children and interrogated the women about the hiding places of the male villagers and of weapons. The women were threatened with sexual assault and murder.[61] On or about 3 July 1992, Mr. Zelenović and another man interrogated FWS-75 about her village and whether the villagers had weapons. FWS-75 was warned by the other man that she would be raped by soldiers, and killed afterwards, if she did not answer truthfully. In the course of her interrogation she was taken by a soldier to another room where ten soldiers raped her in turn. Mr. Zelenović knew that his action in respect of the interrogation and his omission to act with regard to the threats of rape and death, and the eventual transfer of FWS-75 to the room where she was raped, substantially assisted in the commission of the crime.[62] Mr. Zelenović pleaded guilty to aiding and abetting this rape against FWS-75.[63]

22. On or about 3 July, Mr. Zelenović and three unidentified soldiers interrogated FWS-87, a 15-year-old girl, in a room at Buk Bijela. During the interrogation, Mr. Zelenović and the three soldiers accused the girl of not telling the truth and proceeded to rape her. During the rape one of the soldiers threatened FWS-87 by putting a gun to her head.[64] Mr. Zelenović pleaded guilty to committing this rape against FWS-87.[65]

23. Between 3 and 13 July 1992, the group of women, children, and elderly men who had been detained at Buk Bijela were transferred and detained together with other persons in two classrooms **[page 8]** at Foča high school.[66] On or about 6 or 7 July 1992, Mr. Zelenović, in concert with other men, selected four women and girls from the classrooms, among them FWS-75 and FWS-87. Mr. Zelenović led them to another classroom where soldiers were waiting. He then decided which woman should go with which soldier. Mr. Zelenović raped FWS-75, while the other co-perpetrators raped the other women and girls.[67] Mr. Zelenović pleaded guilty to committing the rapes against the four women, as principal perpetrator and as co-perpetrator.[68]

24. Between 8 and 13 July 1992, on three occasions, FWS-75 and FWS-87 were taken from Foča high school to various locations. On the first occasion, the women were taken to an apartment owned by Mr. Zelenović. There, Mr. Zelenović and three other men raped FWS-75. Mr. Zelenović also raped FWS-87 on that occasion.[69] On the second occasion, FWS-75 and FWS-87 were taken to another apartment, where Mr. Zelenović again raped them.[70] On the third occasion, Mr. Zelenović took FWS-75 and FWS-87 to an abandoned house in Gornje Polje where he raped FWS-87.[71] Mr. Zelenović pleaded guilty to committing the two rapes against FWS-75 and the three rapes against FWS-87.[72]

25. The physical and psychological health of many of the female detainees seriously deteriorated as a result of the sexual assaults. The detainees lived in constant fear and some of the sexually abused women became suicidal. Others became indifferent as to what happened to them and suffered from depression.[73]

---

59 Factual Statement, para. 5; T. 439.
60 Factual Statement, para. 7.
61 Factual Statement, para. 8.
62 Factual Statement, paras 8–9.
63 T. 486 (this refers to a part of counts 5 and 6).
64 Factual Statement, para. 10; Annex to Plea Agreement, para. 5.5.
65 T. 486 (this refers to a part of counts 5 and 6).
66 Factual Statement, para. 11.
67 Factual Statement, para. 12.
68 T. 488–489 (this refers to a part of counts 13 and 14).
69 Factual Statement, para. 13.
70 Factual Statement, para. 14.
71 Factual Statement, para. 15.
72 T. 488–489 (this refers to a part of counts 13 and 14).
73 Factual Statement, paras 10, 16.

26. On 13 July 1992, the detainees at Foča high school were transferred to Partizan Sports Hall where they were detained until 13 August 1992, after which most detainees were deported to Montenegro. The detainees, who numbered about 70, were all Muslim civilians from villages in Foča municipality.[74] Living conditions at Partizan Sports Hall were brutal and the detention was characterized by inhumane treatment, unhygienic conditions, overcrowding, starvation, and physical and psychological torture, including sexual assaults.[75] During July 1992, Mr. Zelenović and other men took FWS-87 away from Partizan Sports Hall and raped her.[76] Mr. Zelenović pleaded guilty to committing this rape against FWS-87.[77] **[page 9]**

27. On or about 3 August 1992, FWS-87 and FWS-75 were taken from Partizan Sports Hall and detained in a house close to Miljevina Hotel known as Karaman's house.[78] On or about 30 October 1992, Mr. Zelenović and two men took FWS-87, FWS-75, and two other women from that house to an apartment in Foča town. There, Mr. Zelenović raped FWS-87 while the other two men raped the other women.[79] The women remained detained at several houses and apartments, and continued to be subject to sexual assaults by various groups of soldiers.[80] Mr. Zelenović pleaded guilty to committing the rapes against the four women, as principal perpetrator and as co-perpetrator.[81]

28. The parties agree that an armed conflict existed in Bosnia-Herzegovina at all times relevant to the Indictment.[82] Furthermore, the parties agree that Mr. Zelenović's criminal acts and omissions were part of a widespread or systematic attack against the civilian population, especially the Muslim population of Foča municipality.[83] Finally, the parties agree that Mr. Zelenović was aware of the existence of the armed conflict and of the widespread or systematic attack against the non-Serb, primarily Muslim, civilian population and of the fact that his conduct occurred within and contributed to that attack.[84]

3. Law

3.1 Applicable law

29. The following provisions of the Tribunal's Statute and Rules are relevant to the present sentencing judgement:

Article 24

Penalties

1. The penalty imposed by the Trial Chamber shall be limited to imprisonment. In determining the terms of imprisonment, the Trial Chambers shall have recourse to the general practice regarding prison sentences in the courts of the former Yugoslavia.
2. In imposing the sentences, the Trial Chamber should take into account such factors as the gravity of the offence and the individual circumstances of the convicted person.
3. In addition to imprisonment, the Trial Chambers may order the return of any property and proceeds acquired by criminal conduct, including by means of duress, to their rightful owners. **[page 10]**

---

74 Factual Statement, paras 11, 17, 20.
75 Factual Statement, paras 18–19.
76 Factual Statement, para. 19.
77 T. 489–490 (this refers to counts 41 and 42).
78 Factual Statement, para. 21.
79 Factual Statement, para. 22.
80 Factual Statement, para. 23.
81 T. 490 (this refers to count 49).
82 Factual Statement, para. 24.
83 Factual Statement, para. 25.
84 Factual Statement, para. 26.

Rule 100

Sentencing Procedure on a Guilty Plea

A. If the Trial Chamber convicts the accused on a guilty plea, the Prosecutor and the defence may submit any relevant information that may assist the Trial Chamber in determining an appropriate sentence.

[…]

Rule 101

Penalties

A. A convicted person may be sentenced to imprisonment for a term up to and including the remainder of the convicted person's life.

B. In determining the sentence, the Trial Chamber shall take into account the factors mentioned in Article 24, paragraph 2, of the Statute, as well as such factors as:

i. any aggravating circumstances;

ii. any mitigating circumstances including the substantial cooperation with the Prosecutor by the convicted person before or after conviction;

iii. the general practice regarding prison sentences in the courts of the former Yugoslavia;

iv. the extent to which any penalty imposed by a court of any State on the convicted person for the same act has already been served, as referred to in Article 10, paragraph 3, of the Statute.

C. Credit shall be given to the convicted person for the period, if any, during which the convicted person was detained in custody pending surrender to the Tribunal or pending trial or appeal.

30. The following factors must be considered when imposing a sentence: (i) the gravity of the offences or the totality of the conduct; (ii) the individual circumstances of the convicted person, including aggravating and mitigating circumstances; (iii) the general practice regarding prison sentences in the courts of the former Yugoslavia; (iv) the credit to be given for time spent in detention pending transfer to the Tribunal and pending trial and appeal; and (v) the extent to which any penalty imposed by a court of any State on the convicted person for the same act has already been served.[85] The last factor is not applicable in this case.[86]

3.2 Purposes of sentencing

31. The case law of the Tribunal indicates two primary purposes of sentencing, namely retribution and deterrence.[87]

32. As a form of retribution, punishment expresses society's condemnation of the criminal act and of the person who committed it.[88] To fulfil the objective of retribution, the Trial Chamber must **[page 11]** therefore impose a punishment which properly reflects the personal culpability of the wrongdoer.[89] The Trial Chamber considers that this purpose is reflected in the obligation that the Trial Chamber has to take into account the gravity of the crime or the totality of the conduct.

85 *Blaškić* Appeal Judgement, para. 679.
86 T. 437–438.
87 *Aleksovski* Appeal Judgement, para. 185; *Čelebići* Appeal Judgement, para. 806; *Stakić* Appeal Judgement, para. 402.
88 *Jokić* Sentencing Judgement, para. 31; *Mrđa* Sentencing Judgement, para. 14.
89 *Kordić and Čerkez* Appeal Judgement, para. 1075.

33. Both special and general deterrence are important purposes of sentencing in criminal law.[90] The rationale of special deterrence is to dissuade the wrongdoer from recidivism in the future, whereas general deterrence aims at discouraging others from committing similar kinds of crime.[91] In the present case, and in view of the circumstances in which the crimes were committed, the Trial Chamber considers that the risk that Mr. Zelenović would commit the same kinds of crime in the future is small, which considerably reduces the relevance of special deterrence.

34. As far as general deterrence is concerned, persons who believe themselves to be beyond the reach of international criminal law must be warned that they have to abide by the norms underpinned by substantive criminal law or face prosecution.[92] The Trial Chamber is confident that an appropriate sentence for Mr. Zelenović in his case will have general deterrent effect.

35. Rehabilitation is also considered to be a relevant, though less important, purpose of sentencing.[93]

4. Sentencing factors

4.1 The gravity of the offences or the totality of the conduct

36. The gravity of the offences is the primary consideration in imposing a sentence.[94] Mr. Zelenović has pleaded guilty to torture and rape as crimes against humanity. Torture requires the intentional infliction of severe pain or suffering with the aim of obtaining information or a confession, or of punishing, intimidating or coercing the victim or a third person, or of discriminating against the victim or a third person.[95] Torture is among the most serious crimes in international criminal law and this must be properly reflected in the sentence. Moreover, torture by means of rape is a particularly grave form of torture.[96] Rape requires a sexual penetration of the **[page 12]** vagina or anus of the victim by the penis of the perpetrator or any other object used by the perpetrator, or of the mouth of the victim by the penis of the perpetrator, where such penetration occurs without the consent of the victim.[97] The violation of the moral and physical integrity of the victims makes rape a particularly serious crime.[98] Rape is an inherently humiliating offence, and humiliation is generally taken into account when assessing the gravity of a crime.[99]

37. The law on torture and rape as crimes against humanity requires that the crimes are committed as part of a widespread or systematic attack against a civilian population. This element is what distinguishes crimes against humanity from ordinary crimes. The targeting of a collective in the form of a civilian population, rather than the individual victim, places crimes against humanity among the gravest of crimes.

38. The determination of the gravity of the offences also requires consideration of the particular circumstances of the case and the form and degree of the participation of the convicted person in the crimes.[100] Of central concern when assessing the gravity of a crime is the scale of the crime, including the number of victims and its duration.[101] The crimes which Mr. Zelenović has pleaded guilty to were part of a pattern of sexual assaults that took place over a period of several months, and in four different locations, and involved multiple victims. Mr. Zelenović took direct part in the sexual abuse of victims in a number of detention

---

90 Ibid., para. 1076.

91 Ibid., paras 1077–1078; *Dragan Nikolić* Appeal Sentencing Judgement, para. 45.

92 *Kordić and Čerkez* Appeal Judgement, para. 1078.

93 *Čelebići* Appeal Judgement, para. 806; *Kordić and Čerkez* Appeal Judgement, para. 1079; *Stakić* Appeal Judgement, para. 402.

94 *Čelebići* Appeal Judgement, para. 731; *Kupreškić et al.* Appeal Judgement, para. 442; *Blaškić* Appeal Judgement, para. 683; *Momir Nikolić* Appeal Sentencing Judgement, para. 11; *Galić* Appeal Judgement, para. 442.

95 *Kunarac et al.* Appeal Judgement, paras 142, 144.

96 *Furundžija* Trial Judgement, para. 295.

97 *Kunarac et al.* Appeal Judgement, paras 127–128.

98 *Češić* Sentencing Judgement, para. 35.

99 Ibid., para. 53.

100 *Aleksovski* Appeal Judgement, para. 182; *Furundžija* Appeal Judgement, para. 249; *Čelebići* Appeal Judgement, para. 731; *Jelisić* Appeal Judgement, para. 101; *Blaškić* Appeal Judgement, para. 683; *Kordić and Čerkez* Appeal Judgement, para. 1061; *Dragan Nikolić* Appeal Sentencing Judgement, para. 18; *Babić* Appeal Sentencing Judgement, para. 39; *Galić* Appeal Judgement, para. 409.

101 *Plavšić* Sentencing Judgement, para. 52; *Češić* Sentencing Judgement, para. 32; *Mrđa* Sentencing Judgement, para. 21; *Babić* Sentencing Judgement, para. 47.

facilities, including the multiple rape of victims FWS-75 and FWS-87. Mr. Zelenović has been found guilty of personally committing nine rapes, eight of which were qualified as both torture and rape. He has also been found guilty of two instances of rape through co-perpetratorship, one of which was qualified as both torture and rape, and one instance of torture and rape through aiding and abetting. Four of the instances of sexual abuse were gang rapes, committed together with three or more other perpetrators. In one of those instances he participated as aider and abettor in the rape of FWS-75 by at least ten soldiers, which was so violent that the victim lost consciousness. He participated as co-perpetrator in an incident during which the victim was threatened with a gun to her head while being sexually abused. The Trial Chamber finds that the scale of the crimes committed was large and that Mr. Zelenović's participation in the crimes was substantial. **[page 13]**

39. An important factor when assessing the gravity of a crime is the vulnerability of the victims.[102] The victims in this case were arrested and detained under brutal conditions for long periods of time. They were unarmed and defenceless. The victims were therefore in a particularly vulnerable situation at the time of the commission of the crime. In addition, victim FWS-87, who was raped by Mr. Zelenović on numerous occasions, was about 15 years old at the time of the commission of the crimes. This further increases the gravity of the crimes committed against her.[103] Mr. Zelenović was aware, and took advantage of, this vulnerability of the victims.

40. Another important factor is the physical and mental trauma suffered by the victims, even long after the commission of the crime.[104] In 1992, FWS-75 and FWS-87 were 25 and 15 years old, respectively.[105] After their initial arrest, they were taken from one detention centre to another where they were repeatedly sexually abused by Mr. Zelenović and others. The victims of sexual abuse in the detention centres in Foča suffered the unspeakable pain, indignity, and humiliation of being repeatedly violated, without knowing whether they would survive the ordeal. As a result of the violent sexual assaults, the physical and psychological health of many of the victims was seriously damaged. The women and girls in the detention centres lived in constant fear of repeated rapes and sexual assaults. Some became suicidal and others became indifferent to what happened to them. The scars left from the crimes committed against them were deep and might never heal. This, perhaps more than anything, speaks about the gravity of the crimes in this case.

41. The Prosecution argued that the discriminatory grounds upon which the Accused committed the offences may be taken into account where discrimination is not an element of the offence.[106] An element of the crime cannot also constitute a separate factor for the purposes of sentencing.[107] However, when convictions for the same criminal conduct are properly entered, as in the present case, a factor taken into account as an element of the crime under one count does not prevent it from being considered as an aggravating factor in relation to the other count, where it is not an element of the crime, for the determination of the sentence.[108]

42. The Prosecution argued that all the incidents to which Mr. Zelenović has pleaded guilty are to be classified as torture because they were committed on discriminatory grounds.[109] As for the **[page 14]** incidents at Buk Bijela, the purpose of the rapes was to obtain information or a confession, which would be an additional reason to classify the incidents as torture.[110] As for the other instances of rape that occurred in July and August 1992, the Prosecution argued that they were committed for the purpose of punishing and intimidating or coercing the victim or a third person, which again would be a reason to classify the incidents as torture.[111] As for Count 49, according to which Mr. Zelenović is charged with rape, but not torture, as a crime against humanity, the parties agreed that also this act was committed on discriminatory grounds.[112] The Prosecution submits that, although it could have charged this act as torture, in its discretion it chose not to

---

102 *Kunarac et al.* Appeal Judgement, para. 352; *Blaškić* Appeal Judgement, para. 683; *Kordić and Čerkez* Appeal Judgement, para. 1088; *Deronjić* Appeal Sentencing Judgement, para. 124.

103 *Kunarac et al.* Trial Judgement, para. 864; *Deronjić* Appeal Sentencing Judgement, para. 124.

104 *Vasiljević* Appeal Judgement, para. 167; *Blaškić* Appeal Judgement, para. 683.

105 T. 510.

106 Prosecution's Sentencing Brief, para. 13.

107 *Vasiljević* Appeal Judgement, para. 173; *Blaškić* Appeal Judgement, paras 693, 695; *Kordić and Čerkez* Appeal Judgement, para. 1089; *Galić* Appeal Judgement, para. 408.

108 *Vasiljević* Appeal Judgement, para. 172.

109 T. 458.

110 T. 457–458.

111 T. 458.

112 T. 542.

do so.[113] Although permissible, the Trial Chamber will not consider the discriminatory grounds upon which Mr. Zelenović acted as a separate aggravating factor for the crime of rape but rather take them into account once when assessing the gravity of all the crimes to which Mr. Zelenović has pleaded guilty.

43. Mr. Zelenović has pleaded guilty to torture and rape as crimes against humanity. In addition to the inherent seriousness of these crimes, the Trial Chamber has considered the active and substantial participation of Mr. Zelenović as well as the scale and duration of the crimes. Furthermore, the Trial Chamber has considered the vulnerability of the victims and the physical and mental trauma suffered by them. All these factors make up the gravity of the offence and the totality of the conduct in this case.

4.2 Individual circumstances of the convicted person, including aggravating and mitigating circumstances

44. Any reduction of the penalty stemming from the application of mitigating circumstances does not diminish the gravity of the crime.[114] Both parties argued for a number of mitigating circumstances which relate to the behaviour of Mr. Zelenović after the commission of the crime, including the guilty plea. In particular, they emphasized that witnesses are relieved from giving evidence in court as a reason for giving the guilty plea considerable mitigating weight.[115]

45. A guilty plea may have a mitigating effect on the sentence since the admission of guilt may show honesty and readiness to take responsibility,[116] it may help establishing the truth and **[page 15]** contribute to reconciliation,[117] and, as mentioned above, because of the guilty plea victims are relieved from giving evidence in court and thereby potentially re-living their trauma.[118] The avoidance of a lengthy trial, and thereby the time and effort saved by the Tribunal, is also a factor to take into account in sentencing, although it should not be given undue weight.[119]

46. The timing of a guilty plea is among the aspects that determine the weight in mitigation that this factor should be given.[120] Mr. Zelenović did not voluntarily surrender to the Tribunal and he did not plead guilty at his initial appearance. His guilty plea therefore came late. However, it came before any trial proceedings in his case had commenced. The Trial Chamber therefore considers that the guilty plea can be given considerable weight in mitigation.

47. The fact that a perpetrator admits his guilt and steps forward to face the consequences of what he has done is the central aspect of a guilty plea, even if, as in the present case, it is done through a plea agreement with the Prosecution. The Trial Chamber is mindful of the fact that the agreement on the Prosecution's part in this case consisted of withdrawing cumulative counts of the violations of the laws or customs of war and some charges for which it considered that the evidence might have been insufficient.[121] The Trial Chamber therefore considers that the totality of Mr. Zelenović's conduct is well reflected in the counts to which he has pleaded guilty. The Trial Chamber recognizes that Mr. Zelenović's admission of guilt is complete and unconditional and shows that he is ready to take responsibility for what he has done.

48. The parties have argued that a guilty plea contributes to one of the objectives of the Tribunal, that is the establishment of truth. According to the Prosecution, this is the first time in the history of the Tribunal that a perpetrator admits to and confirms what happened to the female non-Serb population in

---

113 T. 458, 546.

114 *Erdemović* First Sentencing Judgement, para. 46; *Bralo* Sentencing Judgement, para. 42.

115 Prosecution's Sentencing Brief, para. 45; Defence Sentencing Brief, paras 26–31; T. 548.

116 *Dragan Nikolić* Sentencing Judgement, para. 237; *Jokić* Sentencing Judgement, para. 76; *Mrđa* Sentencing Judgement, para. 78.

117 *Sikirica et al.* Sentencing Judgement, para. 149; *Plavšić* Sentencing Judgement, para. 80; *Banović* Sentencing Judgement, para. 68; *Obrenović* Sentencing Judgement, para. 111; *Dragan Nikolić* Sentencing Judgement, para. 233; *Češić* Sentencing Judgement, para. 58; *Deronjić* Sentencing Judgement, para. 236.

118 *Todorović* Sentencing Judgement, para. 80; *Banović* Sentencing Judgement, para. 68; *Momir Nikolić* Sentencing Judgement, para. 150; *Češić* Sentencing Judgement, para. 58; *Deronjić* Sentencing Judgement, para. 134; *Mrđa* Sentencing Judgement, para. 78; *Bralo* Sentencing Judgement, para. 64.

119 *Dragan Nikolić* Appeal Sentencing Judgement, para. 51; *Bralo* Appeal Sentencing Judgement, para. 47.

120 *Sikirica et al.* Sentencing Judgement, paras 150, 228; *Milan Simić* Sentencing Judgement, para. 87; *Dragan Nikolić* Sentencing Judgement, para. 234; *Češić* Sentencing Judgement, para. 59; *Deronjić* Sentencing Judgement, para. 231.

121 T. 464–465.

Foča in 1992.[122] The Prosecution sees a possibility that Mr. Zelenović's guilty plea not only contributes to the establishment of the truth, but also to the reconciliation in the area.[123] Although neither party has presented any evidence concerning this, the Trial Chamber accepts that the admission of guilt, through a guilty plea, generally contributes to the establishment of truth and **[page 16]** thereby to reconciliation in the region. The Trial Chamber takes this into account when determining the weight in mitigation the guilty plea should be given.

49. As mentioned, both parties have emphasized that the guilty plea relieves victims from giving evidence in court and that this should afford Mr. Zelenović considerable mitigation.[124] In cases such as the present, involving serious crimes such as torture and rape, with severe consequences for the victims, a guilty plea is likely to save the victims from reliving the trauma through testifying about the crimes committed against them. The Trial Chamber considers that this is an effect that must be considered when determining the weight in mitigation the guilty plea should be given.

50. The Defence argued that the remorse of Mr. Zelenović should be considered a mitigating circumstance in the present case.[125] During the sentencing hearing on 23 February 2007, as well as in a separate written statement attached to the Defence sentencing brief, Mr. Zelenović expressed his remorse.[126] In order to take the expression of remorse of an accused into account in mitigation, the Trial Chamber must be satisfied that the remorse is sincere.[127]

51. Mr. Zelenović informed the Trial Chamber that he started to feel remorse when the indictment was issued against him in 1996.[128] However, he did not voluntarily surrender to the Tribunal at the time. In 2000 or 2001 he escaped from Foča to Russia, where he was arrested by Russian authorities in 2005. From there he was transferred to the Tribunal, via Bosnia-Herzegovina, on 10 June 2006. At the second further initial appearance on 14 July 2006 Mr. Zelenović pleaded not guilty. He then proceeded, as described in the procedural history above, to challenge the Indictment and to participate in the proceedings pursuant to the 11 *bis* motion.[129] Only on 14 December 2006, did the parties file the Plea Agreement, and on 17 January 2007, Mr. Zelenović formally pleaded guilty. Therefore, any expression of remorse by Mr. Zelenović came much later than the time which Mr. Zelenović himself identified as the moment when he began to feel remorse. Nevertheless, what is most important is that the remorse is sincere at the time it is expressed. The Trial Chamber accepts Mr. Zelenović's remorse as sincere and will therefore consider it as a mitigating circumstance.

52. Rule 101(B)(ii) of the Rules expressly provides that the Trial Chamber shall take into consideration the substantial cooperation with the Prosecutor by the convicted person before or after conviction. The Trial Chamber must assess the extent and nature of the cooperation, and therefore **[page 17]** the weight to be given to this mitigating circumstance.[130] Not only "substantial", but also more modest cooperation can be taken into account and be given weight in mitigation.[131] The Appeals Chamber has stressed that, when assessing a convicted person's cooperation, "special regard must be had to the [person's] willingness to cooperate as underlined by his actions and evidenced, in particular, by his earnestness when providing information to the Prosecution".[132] According to the Plea Agreement, Mr. Zelenović

> agrees to accept responsibility for his actions and to co-operate with, and to provide truthful and complete information to the Office of the Prosecutor whenever requested. In accordance with such co-operation, Dragan Zelenović agrees to meet as often as necessary with members of the Office of the Prosecutor in

122 T. 513, 551–552.

123 T. 513.

124 Prosecution's Sentencing Brief, para. 45; Defence Sentencing Brief, paras 26–31; T. 548.

125 Defence Sentencing Brief, para. 25.

126 T. 521.

127 *Vasiljević* Appeal Judgement, para. 177; *Blaškić* Appeal Judgement, paras 705, 728; *Kvočka et al.* Appeal Judgement, para. 715; *Momir Nikolić* Appeal Sentencing Judgement, para. 117.

128 T. 522.

129 T. 425, 533–534.

130 *Jelisić* Appeal Judgement, paras 124, 126; *Momir Nikolić* Appeal Sentencing Judgement, para. 91; *Bralo* Appeal Sentencing Judgement, para. 51.

131 *Vasiljević* Appeal Judgement, para. 180; *Dragan Nikolić* Appeal Sentencing Judgement, para. 66; *Bralo* Appeal Sentencing Judgement, para. 51.

132 *Bralo* Appeal Sentencing Judgement, para. 63.

> order to provide them with full and complete information and evidence that is known to him. Mr. Zelenović agrees to be truthful and candid, and to freely answer all questions put to him by members of the Office of the Prosecutor. If applicable, Mr. Zelenović agrees to testify truthfully at any trials, hearings, or other proceedings before the International Criminal Tribunal for the Former Yugoslavia (ICTY) as requested by the Office of the Prosecutor.[133]

During the sentencing hearing, the Defence noted that Mr. Zelenović had not had the opportunity to demonstrate his cooperation in practice, because of the short time period that had elapsed since the guilty plea. The Defence nevertheless asked the Trial Chamber to give full effect to this factor because of Mr. Zelenović's expressed intention.[134] Subsequent to this, the Prosecution and the Defence informed the Trial Chamber about some initial cooperation provided by Mr. Zelenović.[135] The Trial Chamber considers that it is the commitment to cooperate as well as actual cooperation, even if due to the particular experiences of the convicted person his or her full and sincere assistance is judged to be of little or no value to ongoing investigations or trials,[136] that determines the weight that should be attached to this factor. The Trial Chamber therefore considers Mr. Zelenović's commitment to cooperate with the Office of the Prosecutor, together with the cooperation he has provided so far, as a mitigating circumstance.

53. The Defence has also requested the Trial Chamber to take into account the personal circumstances of Mr. Zelenović, including his health and family situation, and the fact that he has **[page 18]** no criminal record to date.[137] Mr. Zelenović's medical conditions include diabetes mellitus type 2 and that he is disabled with 80% established disability.[138] Because of this, in the assessment of the medical officer at the UNDU, "it is important in the future that he receives adequate medical care".[139] Mr. Zelenović is married and has a 13-year-old son.[140] The Prosecution has conceded that this should be taken into account but, "in view of the number and severity of crimes committed by the accused", that this should only have a limited mitigating impact on the sentence.[141]

54. The Defence also argued that the behaviour of Mr. Zelenović in the UNDU should be considered in mitigation.[142] According to the Deputy Chief of the UNDU, Mr. Zelenović "has at all times shown respect for the staff and management of the unit. He has integrated well into the routine pattern of life in custody and interacts positively with his fellow detainees whilst participating fully in the program".[143]

55. The medical situation of a convicted person should be taken into account only "in exceptional or rare cases".[144] The family situation, the fact that the accused has no prior criminal record, and that a detainee behaves well in the UNDU are circumstances that have been accepted in mitigation in the case law of the Tribunal.[145] The Trial Chamber does not find that the fact that Mr. Zelenović has a wife and a son in itself constitutes a mitigating factor. The Trial Chamber will, however, take his family situation together with his health condition, the fact that he has no prior convictions and that he has behaved well in the UNDU and collectively assign to these factors some, although limited, weight in mitigation.

56. In conclusion, the Trial Chamber considers that the guilty plea of Mr. Zelenović, as well as the commitment that he has shown to cooperate with the Office of the Prosecutor, constitute the main mitigating circumstances in

---

133 Plea Agreement, para. 9.

134 T. 520.

135 Prosecution's Notice to Trial Chamber of Co-operation Pursuant to Plea Agreement, 27 March 2007; Defence Response to Prosecution's Notice to Trial Chamber of Co-operation Pursuant to Plea Agreement, 29 March 2007.

136 See *Bralo* Appeal Sentencing Judgement, para. 52.

137 Defence Sentencing Brief, Annex D (Certificate by Foča municipality, 26 September 2006) and F (Certificate of the Foča SJB, 6 February 2007).

138 Defence Sentencing Brief, Annex D (Certificate by Foča municipality, 26 September 2006).

139 Defence Sentencing Brief, Annex E (Memo by the Medical officer at the UNDU, 26 January 2007).

140 T. 527.

141 T. 514.

142 Defence Sentencing Brief, para. 33.

143 Defence Sentencing Brief, Annex E (Behaviour Report by Deputy Chief of Detention, 8 February 2007).

144 *Blaškić* Appeal Judgement, para. 696; *Babić* Appeal Sentencing Judgement, para. 43; *Galić* Appeal Judgement, para. 436.

145 *Kunarac et al.* Appeal Judgement, paras 362, 408; *Blaškić* Appeal Judgement, paras 696, 728; *Kordić and Čerkez* Appeal Judgement, paras 1090–1091; *Babić* Appeal Sentencing Judgement, para. 43; *Blagoje Simić et al.* Appeal Judgement, para. 266.

this case. The Trial Chamber has, however, also considered Mr. Zelenović's remorse, his family and health situation, the fact that he has no prior criminal record, and his good behaviour in the UNDU, in mitigation. **[page 19]**

4.3 The general practice regarding prison sentences in the courts of the former Yugoslavia

57. The Trial Chamber is required to consider "the general practice regarding prison sentences in the courts of the former Yugoslavia" in determining the appropriate penalty. This does not mean that the Trial Chamber is obliged to conform to that practice.[146] The Tribunal may impose a sentence in excess of that which would be applicable under the relevant law in the former Yugoslavia, and the Appeals Chamber has held that this sentencing practice does not violate the principle of *nulla poena sine lege* because a defendant would have been aware that the crimes for which he or she is indicted constitute serious violations of international humanitarian law, punishable by the most severe of penalties.[147] Moreover, the Trial Chamber may diverge from the sentencing practice of the former Yugoslavia if this practice is inadequate in light of international law.[148]

58. Article 24(1) of the Statute and Rule 101(B)(iii) of the Rules refer to actual practice in courts of the former Yugoslavia. It is however settled practice within the Tribunal that the sources to be consulted pursuant to these provisions are not limited to case law from the former Yugoslavia, but also include statutory provisions in force there at the time of the commission of the crimes in question.[149]

59. In 1991 and 1992, the sentencing law in Bosnia-Herzegovina was regulated by the Criminal Code of the SFRY, adopted by the Federal Assembly on 28 September 1976, and in force since 1 July 1977 (SFRY Criminal Code), and by the Criminal Code of the Socialist Republic of Bosnia-Herzegovina of 10 June 1977 (Bosnia-Herzegovina Criminal Code). The SFRY Criminal Code regulated the general aspects of criminal law and a few specific offences, such as crimes against the security of the SFRY, genocide, and war crimes, while the Bosnia-Herzegovina Criminal Code primarily regulated specific offences, and some general matters not addressed in the SFRY Criminal Code. Both criminal codes remained in force after Bosnia-Herzegovina declared independence in 1992.

60. Mr. Zelenović has pleaded guilty to torture and rape as crimes against humanity. Chapter 16 of the SFRY Criminal Code is entitled "Criminal acts against humanity and international law" and **[page 20]** covers crimes committed during armed conflict. It does not, however, codify crimes against humanity, with their specific actus reus and mens rea requirements. The punishment provided for specific crimes which do not require proof of these distinguishing elements does not take into account the seriousness of crimes against humanity. It is thus not an adequate basis for determining the punishment to be imposed for this category of crimes.[150]

61. The general provisions of the SFRY Criminal Code regarding punishment provide that the maximum term of imprisonment is 15 years,[151] but that for the most serious crimes the death penalty may be imposed,[152] or, instead of the death penalty, a prison sentence of 20 years.[153]

62. The Trial Chamber takes all of these factors relating to sentencing practices in the former Yugoslavia into consideration in making its determination of the sentence in this case.

---

146 *Tadić* Appeal Sentencing Judgement, para. 21; *Čelebići* Appeal Judgement, paras 813, 816 and 820; *Jelisić* Appeal Judgement, para. 117; *Kupreškić et al.* Appeal Judgement, para. 418; *Kunarac et al.* Appeal Judgement, paras 347–349; *Krstić* Appeal Judgement, para. 260; *Blaškić* Appeal Judgement, paras 681–682; *Kordić and Čerkez* Appeal Judgement, para. 1085; *Dragan Nikolić* Appeal Sentencing Judgement, paras 17, 69; *Jokić* Appeal Sentencing Judgement, para. 38; *Galić* Appeal Judgement, para. 398.

147 *Tadić* Appeal Sentencing Judgement, para. 21; *Čelebići* Appeal Judgement, para. 817; *Krstić* Appeal Judgement, para. 262; *Blaškić* Appeal Judgement, para. 681; *Stakić* Appeal Judgement, para. 398; *Blagoje Simić et al.* Appeal Judgement, para. 264.

148 *Kunarac et al.* Appeal Judgement, para. 377.

149 *Dragan Nikolić* Appeal Sentencing Judgement, para. 85.

150 *Erdemović* First Sentencing Judgement, para. 32.

151 Article 38 (1) of the SFRY Criminal Code.

152 Article 37 of the SFRY Criminal Code.

153 Article 38 (2) of the SFRY Criminal Code.

4.4 Credit to be given for time spent in detention pending transfer to the Tribunal and pending trial

63. According to Rule 101(C) credit shall be given to the convicted person for the period during which the convicted person was detained pending surrender to the Tribunal or pending trial. Mr. Zelenović was arrested on 22 August 2005, and formally detained the day after, by Russian authorities, pursuant to "the Decision of the [Tribunal]".[154] He remained in detention in Russia until his transfer to Bosnia-Herzegovina on 8 June 2006, from where he was transferred to the Tribunal two days later. Since 10 June 2006, Mr. Zelenović has been detained at the UNDU. Any time Mr. Zelenović has spent in custody for the purpose of this case must be taken into account,[155] regardless of the fact that he was not transferred directly from Russia to the Tribunal. Mr. Zelenović is therefore entitled to the credit of 591 days.

5. Determination of sentence

64. The Prosecution has recommended a term of imprisonment within the range of 10 to 15 years, while the Defence has recommended a term within the range of 7 to 10 years.[156] According to **[page 21]** Rule 62 *ter* (B) the Trial Chamber is not bound by these recommendations of the parties. The Prosecution has argued for a comparison with sentences in *Prosecutor v. Dragoljub Kunarac et al.*, while the Defence specifically referred to the cases of *Prosecutor v. Stevan Todorović* and *Prosecutor v. Biljana Plavšić*.[157]

65. The difficulty with comparing sentences imposed by the Tribunal is due to the fact that "any given case contains a multitude of variables, ranging from the number and type of crimes committed to the personal circumstances of the individual".[158] Moreover, a Trial Chamber must tailor the sentence to fit the individual circumstances of the convicted person and the gravity of the crime.[159] A previous judgement on sentence can nevertheless provide guidance "if it relates to the same offence and was committed in substantially similar circumstances".[160] The Trial Chamber is mindful of the fact that sentences of like individuals in like cases should be comparable.[161] The obvious case to compare the present case with is the *Kunarac et al.* case where the original indictment included Mr. Zelenović among the accused.

66. Dragoljub Kunarac was held responsible for committing seven instances of rape (some of them included multiple rapes) and aiding and abetting in three instances of rape. His conviction also included keeping two Muslim women in a house for several months, during which time he raped one of them several times. Kunarac was convicted of enslavement as a crime against humanity and of torture and rape as crimes against humanity and violations of the laws or customs of war. He was sentenced to 28 years of imprisonment.[162] Radomir Kovač was convicted of keeping four young girls in his apartment where they were raped, humiliated, degraded, and treated as "property" by Kovač, among others. On one occasion, three girls were forced to dance naked in front of him. Kovač was convicted of enslavement as a crime against humanity, outrages upon personal dignity as a violation of the laws or customs of war, and rape as a crime against humanity and a violation of the laws or customs of war. Kovač was sentenced to 20 years of imprisonment.[163] Finally, Zoran Vuković was held responsible for taking a Muslim woman from a detention centre to an apartment and raping her. He was convicted of torture and rape as crimes against humanity and violations of the laws or customs of war and was sentenced to 12 years of imprisonment.[164] **[page 22]**

---

154 Defence Sentencing Brief, Annex A (Detention Order by Acting Khanti-Mansiysk Inter-Municipal Public Prosecutor, 23 August 2005); T. 552–554.

155 See *Tadić* Appeal Sentencing Judgement, paras 38, 75; *Blaškić* Appeal Judgement, para. 709.

156 Plea Agreement, para. 3; Prosecution's Sentencing Brief, para. 50; Defence Sentencing Brief, para. 37.

157 T. 515, 520.

158 *Kvočka et al.* Appeal Judgement, para. 681.

159 *Čelebići* Appeal Judgement, para. 717; *Dragan Nikolić* Appeal Sentencing Judgement, para. 19; *Babić* Appeal Sentencing Judgement, para. 32; *Naletilić and Martinović* Appeal Judgement, para. 615; *Blagoje Simić et al.* Appeal Judgement, para. 157; *Bralo* Appeal Sentencing Judgement, para. 33.

160 *Furundžija* Appeal Judgement, para. 250. See also *Čelebići* Appeal Judgement, paras 721, 756–757; *Jelisić* Appeal Judgement, paras 96, 101; *Kvočka et al.* Appeal Judgement, para. 681.

161 *Kvočka et al.* Appeal Judgement, para. 681; *Blagoje Simić et al.* Appeal Judgement, para. 238.

162 *Kunarac et al.* Trial Judgement, paras 630–745.

163 *Kunarac et al.* Trial Judgement, paras 747–782.

164 *Kunarac et al.* Trial Judgement, paras 784–822.

67. The similarities between the present case and the *Kunarac et al.* case extend to the type of crime, how the crime was carried out, the duration of the criminal behaviour, and the characterization of the victims. The crime base in the present case is not only similar, but to a large extent identical to the one in the *Kunarac et al.* case. The participation of Mr. Zelenović in the crimes committed is comparable with that of at least some of the perpetrators in the aforementioned case. As mentioned, Mr. Zelenović has been found guilty of personally committing nine rapes, eight of which were qualified as both torture and rape. He has also been found guilty of two instances of rape through co-perpetratorship, one of which was qualified as both torture and rape, and one instance of torture and rape through aiding and abetting.

68. Despite the similarities, the Trial Chamber emphasizes that there are important factors distinguishing the present case from the *Kunarac et al.* case. One such important distinction is that Mr. Zelenović pleaded guilty, which none of the accused persons in the aforementioned case did. A guilty plea is in the case law of the Tribunal, including in the *Plavšić* and *Todorović* cases referred to by the Defence, considered an important mitigating factor. The Trial Chamber has given considerable weight to Mr. Zelenović's guilty plea.

69. Both parties considered that the judgement in the *Stanković* case before the State Court of Bosnia-Herzegovina gave little or no guidance to the Trial Chamber, although for different reasons. The Prosecution submitted that that judgement is under appeal, and that one of the grounds of appeal by the State Prosecutor is the sentence.[165] The Defence, on the other hand, considered that the scope of the two cases and the level of responsibility of the perpetrators differed, and that there were important differences in aggravating and mitigating circumstances.[166] Considering the arguments submitted by the parties, in particular the fact that the judgement in the *Stanković* case is under appeal, the Trial Chamber has refrained from taking guidance from that case.

70. The Trial Chamber has considered the circumstances referred to above and the recommendations for terms of imprisonment by the Prosecution and the Defence and finds the appropriate sentence in the present case to be a single sentence of 15 years of imprisonment. As mentioned above, Mr. Zelenović is entitled to credit for the time spent in detention, which as of the date of this judgement amounts to 591 days. **[page 23]**

6. Disposition

71. For the foregoing reasons, the **TRIAL CHAMBER**

having found Dragan Zelenović **GUILTY** of the following charges in the Indictment:

Count 5: torture as a crime against humanity;

Count 6: rape as a crime against humanity;

Count 13: torture as a crime against humanity;

Count 14: rape as a crime against humanity;

Count 41: torture as a crime against humanity;

Count 42: rape as a crime against humanity;

Count 49: rape as a crime against humanity.

here by **SENTENCES** Dragan Zelenović to a single sentence of 15 years of imprisonment.

72. Dragan Zelenović has been detained since 22 August 2005. Pursuant to Rule 101(C) of the Rules, he is entitled to credit for the time spent in detention, which as of the date of this judgement amounts to 591 days.

165 Prosecution's Submission Regarding Use of Stanković Judgement, 27 February 2007, paras 3, 5.

166 Defence Submission Regarding Use of Prosecutor v. Stanković Judgement, 28 February 2007, paras 5–9.

73. In accordance with Rule 103(C) of the Rules of Procedure, Mr. Zelenović is to remain in the custody of the Tribunal pending finalisation of arrangements for his transfer to the State where his sentence will be served.

Done in English and French, the English text being authoritative.

Dated this 4th day of April 2007
At The Hague
The Netherlands

Christine Van den Wyngaert **Judge**	**Alphons Orie** **Presiding Judge**	**Bakone Justice Moloto** **Judge**

[Seal of the Tribunal] [page 24]

Appendix I: Table of ICTY cases with abbreviations

Aleksovski	Appeal Judgement: *Prosecutor v. Zlatko Aleksovski*, Judgement (on appeal), 24 March 2000
Babić	Sentencing Judgement: *Prosecutor v. Milan Babić*, Sentencing Judgement, 29 June 2004 Appeal Sentencing Judgement: *Prosecutor v. Milan Babić*, Judgement on Sentencing Appeal, 18 July 2005
Banović	Sentencing Judgement: *Prosecutor v. Predrag Banović*, Sentencing Judgement, 28 October 2003
Blaškić	Appeal Judgement: *Prosecutor v. Tihomir Blaškić*, Judgement (on appeal), 29 July 2004
Bralo	Sentencing Judgement: *Prosecutor v. Miroslav Bralo*, Sentencing Judgement, 7 December 2005 Appeal Sentencing Judgement: *Prosecutor v. Miroslav Bralo*, Judgement on Sentencing Appeal, 2 April 2007
Čelebići	Appeal Judgement: *Prosecutor v. Zejnil Delalić, Zdravko Mucić, Hazim Delić, and Esad Landžo*, Judgement (on appeal), 20 February 2001
Češić	Sentencing Judgement: *Prosecutor v. Ranko Češić*, Sentencing Judgement, 11 March 2004
Deronjić	Sentencing Judgement: *Prosecutor v. Miroslav Deronjić*, Sentencing Judgement, 30 March 2004 Appeal Sentencing Judgement: *Prosecutor v. Miroslav Deronjić*, Judgement on Sentencing Appeal, 20 July 2005
Erdemović	First Sentencing Judgement: *Prosecutor v. Dražen Erdemović,* Sentencing Judgement, 29 November 1996 Second Sentencing Judgement: *Prosecutor v. Dražen Erdemović,* Sentencing Judgement, 5 March 1998
Furundžija	Trial Judgement: *Prosecutor v. Anto Furundžija*, Judgement, 10 December 1998 Appeal Judgement: *Prosecutor v. Anto Furundžija*, Judgement (on appeal), 21 July 2000
Galić	Trial Judgement: *Prosecutor v. Stanislav Galić,* Judgement, 5 December 2003 Appeal Judgement: *Prosecutor v. Stanislav Galić,* Judgement, 30 November 2006
Jelisić	Appeal Judgement: *Prosecutor v. Goran Jelisić*, Judgement, 5 July 2001
Jokić	Sentencing Judgement: *Prosecutor v. Miodrag Jokić,* Sentencing Judgement, 18 March 2004 Appeal Sentencing Judgement: *Prosecutor v. Miodrag Jokić,* Judgement, 30 August 2005 **[page 25]**
Kordić and Čerkez	Appeal Judgement: *Prosecutor v. Dario Kordić and Mario Čerkez*, Judgement (on appeal), 17 December 2004

Krajišnik	Trial Judgement: *Prosecutor v. Momčilo Krajišnik*, Judgement, 27 September 2006
Krstić	Trial Judgement: *Prosecutor v. Radislav Krstić*, Judgement, 2 August 2001 Appeal Judgement: *Prosecutor v. Radislav Krstić*, Judgement, 19 April 2004
Kunarac et al.	Trial Judgement: *Prosecutor v. Dragoljub Kunarac, Radomir Kovač, and Zoran Vuković*, Judgement, 22 February 2001 Appeal Judgement: *Prosecutor v. Dragoljub Kunarac, Radomir Kovač, Zoran Vuković*, Judgement (on appeal), 12 June 2002
Kupreškić et al.	Appeal Judgement: *Prosecutor v. Zoran Kupreškić, Mirjan Kupreškić, Vlatko Kupreškić, Drago Josipović, and Vladimir Šantić*, Judgement (on appeal), 23 October 2001
Kvočka et al.	Appeal Judgement: *Prosecutor v. Miroslav Kvočka, Mlađo Radić, Zoran Žigić, and Dragoljub Prcać*, Judgement (on appeal), 28 February 2005
Mrđa	Sentencing Judgement: *Prosecutor v. Darko Mrđa,* Sentencing Judgement, 31 March 2004
Naletilić and Martinović	Appeal Judgement: *Prosecutor v. Mladen Naletilić and Vinko Martinović*, 3 May 2006
Dragan Nikolić	Sentencing Judgement: *Prosecutor v. Dragan Nikolić,* Sentencing Judgement, 18 December 2003 Appeal Sentencing Judgement: *Prosecutor v. Dragan Nikolić,* Judgement, 4 February 2005
Momir Nikolić	Sentencing Judgement: *Prosecutor v. Momir Nikolić,* Sentencing Judgement, 2 December 2003 Appeal Sentencing Judgement: *Prosecutor v. Momir Nikolić*, Judgement of Sentencing Appeal, 8 March 2006
Obrenović	Sentencing Judgement: *Prosecutor v. Dragan Obrenović*, Sentencing Judgement, 10 December 2003
Plavšić	Sentencing Judgement: *Prosecutor v. Biljana Plavšić,* Sentencing Judgement, 27 February 2003
Sikirica et al.	Sentencing Judgement: *Prosecutor v. Dusko Sikirica, Damir Dosen, Dragan Kolundžija,* Sentencing Judgement, 13 November 2001
Blagoje Simić et al.	Appeal Judgement: *Prosecutor v. Blagoje Simić et al.*, Judgement, 28 November 2006
Milan Simić	Sentencing Judgement: *Prosecutor v. Milan Simić*, Sentencing Judgement, 17 October 2002
Stakić	Appeal Judgement: *Prosecutor v. Milomir Stakić,* Judgement (on appeal), 22 March 2006 **[page 26]**
Tadić	Appeal Sentencing Judgement: *Prosecutor v. Duško Tadić,* Judgement in Sentencing Appeals, 26 January 2000
Todorović	Sentencing Judgement: *Prosecutor v. Stevan Todorović,* Sentencing Judgement, 31 July 2001
Vasiljević	Appeal Judgement: *Prosecutor v. Mitar Vasiljević*, Judgement (on appeal), 25 February 2004

Commentary

1. Introduction

This commentary discusses the sentencing judgement,[1] and the judgement on sentencing appeal,[2] in the case of Prosecutor v. Zelenović. In 1992, Zelenović, a soldier in the Serb forces, was involved in taking over the municipality of Foča in Bosnia-Herzegovina and in forcibly removing the majority of the non-Serb civilian population in the area. The remaining non-Serb inhabitants were subjected 'to a widespread and systematic pattern of abuses'.[3] Separated groups of men, women and children were kept confined in various detention facilities. Zelenović was one of the soldiers supervising the detention facility Buk Bijela. Many of the women and girls detained there were raped, or were threatened by sexual assault and murder, as part of interrogations by Serb soldiers about the hiding places of male civilians and weapons.[4]

In the initial indictment, which included Janković and six other persons, Zelenović was charged with several counts of torture and rape as crimes against humanity and war crimes. In 2005, a Referral Bench referred the case against Janković to the national authorities of Bosnia-Herzegovina. A similar request under Rule 11*bis* was pending before the Referral Bench in the case against Zelenović.

Due to a plea agreement concluded between Zelenović and the prosecutor's office, a final decision on the 11*bis* Motion was never taken. Zelenović pleaded guilty to various counts of aiding and abetting and co-perpetrating rape 'as rape', and committing and co-perpetrating rape 'as rape and torture', all as crimes against humanity, and agreed to further cooperate with the prosecution.[5] The prosecution, in turn, withdrew the remaining charges in the initial indictment and recommended a sentence within the range of ten to fifteen years' imprisonment. The Trial Chamber accepted the guilty plea and found Zelenović guilty accordingly.

2. The sentencing judgement

The Trial Chamber in its sentencing judgement followed the usual order of things by first stating the applicable law and purposes of sentencing, and then addressing in more detail the gravity of the crimes and the mitigating and aggravating circumstances concerning the convicted person.

As to the gravity of the offences, the Trial Chamber underlined that 'torture is among the most serious crimes in international law', and stressed that 'torture by means of rape is a particularly grave form of torture'.[6] More specifically, it noted that '[r]ape is an inherently humiliating offence, and humiliation is generally taken into account when assessing the gravity of a crime'.[7] In line with earlier case law, the Trial Chamber also considered the form and degree of participation of Zelenović in the crimes,[8] the particular circumstances of the crimes, their duration, the number and vulnerability of the victims,[9] and the effects of the crimes on the victims.[10]

---

1 ICTY, Sentencing Judgement, *Prosecutor v. Zelenović*, Case No. IT-96-23/2-S, T. Ch. I, 4 April 2007, in this volume, p. 731.

2 ICTY, Judgement on Sentencing Appeal, *Prosecutor v. Zelenović*, Case No. IT-96-23/2-A, A. Ch., 31 October 2007, in this volume, p. 715.

3 Sentencing Judgement, *Prosecutor v. Zelenović*, T. Ch. I, *supra* note 1, par. 18 and 19.

4 *Ibid.*, par. 21.

5 *Ibid.*, par. 13.

6 *Ibid.*, par. 36.

7 *Ibid.*, par. 36.

8 ICTY, ICTY, Judgement, *Prosecutor v. Kupreškić, Kupreškić, Kupreškić, Josipović, Papić and Šantić*, Case No. IT-95-16-T, T. Ch. II, 14 January 2000, Klip/ Sluiter, ALC-IV-703, par. 852, cited in ICTY, Judgement, *Prosecutor v. Aleksovski*, Case No. IT-95-14/1-A, A. Ch., 24 March 2000, Klip/ Sluiter, ALC-IV-361, par. 182. ICTY, Judgement, *Prosecutor v. Delalić et al.*, Case No. IT-96-21-A, A. Ch., 20 February 2001, Klip/ Sluiter, ALC-V-369, par. 731; ICTY, Judgement, *Prosecutor v. Blaškić*, Case No. IT-95-14-A, A. Ch., 29 July 2004, Klip/ Sluiter, ALC-XX-295, par. 683. See also ICTY, Judgement, *Prosecutor v. Galić*, Case No. IT-98-29-A, A. Ch., 30 November 2006, Klip/ Sluiter, ALC-XXXIII-429, par. 409.

9 Judgement, *Prosecutor v. Blaškić*, A. Ch., *supra* note 8, par. 683 referring to ICTY, Judgement, *Prosecutor v. Kunarac, Kovač and Vuković*, Case No. IT-96-23 & IT-96-23/1-A, A. Ch., 12 June 2002, Klip/ Sluiter, ALC-VIII-911, par. 352.

10 ICTY, Appeal Judgement, *Prosecutor v. Kupreškić, Kupreškić, Kupreškić, Josipović and Šantić*, Case No. IT-95-16-A, A. Ch., 23 October 2001, Klip/ Sluiter, ALC-VIII-429, par. 442.

It is noted though, that in its case law, the tribunal has not been consistent in examining these elements under the heading of the gravity of the crime. In *Prosecutor v. Vasiljević*, for example, the impact of the crime upon the victims was taken into account as an aggravating factor.[11]

The Trial Chamber accepted Zelenović's guilty plea as mitigating, although it noted the late timing of the plea, and the fact that the convicted person had not surrendered voluntarily.[12] The convicted person's cooperation with the prosecution was also accepted in mitigation. Where Rule 101(B)(ii) of the RPE provides that the Trial Chamber must take into account the convicted person's substantial cooperation with the prosecutor, the judges stressed that 'also more modest cooperation can be taken into account and be given weight in mitigation'.[13] Cooperation, then, may consist both in 'the commitment to cooperate as well as actual cooperation, even if due to the particular experiences of the convicted person his or her full and sincere assistance is judged to be of little or no value to ongoing investigations or trials'.[14]

Finally, the Trial Chamber took into account Zelenović's health, his family situation as a married man with a 13-year old son, his good behaviour in the UNDU, and the fact that he had no criminal record. The Trial Chamber stated that the latter four factors were assigned only limited weight. Nonetheless, taking into account these factors *at all* may be considered ill-conceived, at least in respect to the latter three. The factor of not having a criminal record may be relevant in a domestic context, but is extraneous to sentencing systematic criminality.

Further, a person's family situation should be looked into when assessing a prisoner's potential for successful reintegration into society. It is thus appropriate to take this factor into account when deciding on a motion for early release. Apart from being prejudicial to childless and unmarried persons, attaching too much weight to this factor is misplaced in view of the insignificance of the rehabilitative aim in international sentencing.[15]

Moreover, intramural good or bad behaviour should not play a role in sentencing at all. First, it has been pointed out that 'adjusted social behaviour' - i.e. adjusted to the situation of detention - does not necessarily provide a reliable account of the convicted person's future behaviour after release,[16] and does not, therefore, contribute to the assessment of a person's fitness for reintegration into society (as said, a matter properly considered when deciding on motions for early release).

Secondly, taking into account detainees' and prisoners' behaviour while in confinement may undermine them exercising their intramural procedural rights. The Commanding Officer, by submitting reports on the inmate's behaviour, influences all kinds of extramural decisions, for example, on sentencing, early release and at some other tribunals also on the designation of States for the enforcement of sentences. The tribunal's rules of detention, and the administrative regulations adopted pursuant to those Rules, recognize the detainees' and prisoners' right to complain against, or appeal, the commanding officer's administrative or disciplinary decisions.[17] These procedural rights, which aim at preserving the rule of law inside the prison gates, are radically subverted where detention authorities are given the opportunity to get even with detainees or prisoners who may wish to take the first-line authorities' decisions up the chain of command. Detained and imprisoned persons may be deterred from making use of their procedural rights, out of fear of potentially harmful consequences.

Thirdly, the possible effect that the detainees' and prisoners' (mis)conduct has on the duration of their sentence may necessitate scrutinizing the UNDU's disciplinary system as to whether it is 'due process proof'. The European Court of Human Rights in Engel v. the Netherlands held that the concept of criminal charge

---

11 ICTY, Judgement, *Prosecutor v. Vasiljević*, Case No. IT-98-32-A, A. Ch., 25 February 2004, Klip/ Sluiter, ALC-XIX-465, par. 167. See, in a similar vein, Judgement, *Prosecutor v. Blaškić*, A. Ch., *supra* note 8, par. 686 and ICTY, Judgement, *Prosecutor v. Krnojelac*, Case No. IT-97-25-A, A. Ch., 17 September 2003, Klip/ Sluiter, ALC-XIV-753, par. 259.

12 Sentencing Judgement, *Prosecutor v. Zelenović*, T. Ch. I, *supra* note 1, par. 46.

13 *Ibid.*, par. 52.

14 *Idem.*

15 *Ibid.*, par. 35.

16 See D. Abels, Commentary, Klip/ Sluiter, ALC-XV-798, referring to Nijboer, Vervroegde Invrijheidsstelling onder voorwaarden [Conditional early release], Ars Aequi Libri, Nijmegen 2002, p. 17.

17 See the Rules 40–41 and 80–84 of the ICTY Rules of Detention. See, further, United Nations Detention Unit, Regulations for the Establishment of a Complaints Procedure for Detainees, issued April 1995, IT/96 and United Nations Detention Unit, Regulations for the Establishment of a Disciplinary Procedure for Detainees, issued April 1995, IT/97.

in article 6 ECHR has an autonomous meaning. The court established a three pronged test for discerning whether a charge falls within the article's ambit. First, one should see whether the 'provision(s) defining the offence charged belong, according to the legal system of the respondent State, to criminal law, disciplinary law or both concurrently'. Secondly, it is important to consider the nature of the offence. Finally, one must take into account 'the degree of severity of the penalty that the person concerned risks incurring'.[18]

In respect to the third criterion, it follows from the court's subsequent case law that, where loss of remission is at stake as a disciplinary sanction, it is likely that the "disciplinary charge" concerned must be properly viewed as a criminal charge in the meaning of Article 6, paragraph 1 ECHR,[19] which would entail the applicability of the whole gamut of due process rights to prison discipline.

In the case of Ezeh and Connors, the European Court of Human Rights left open the question of whether the Engel criteria would be applicable to a system based on principles of discretionary remission. The United Kingdom argued in Ezeh that it considered 'anomalous that the guarantees of Article 6 should apply because a State had introduced into its law a more transparent and legally certain system for the benefit of prisoners but which provided for the grant of awards of additional days' detention, whereas such guarantees would not be applicable to a less transparent system involving the grant and loss of discretionary periods of remission'.[20] One may argue that the latter kind of system does exist at the ICTY, where the (mis)conduct of detainees and prisoners is taken into account in sentencing decisions,[21] and in decisions on early release.[22]

The prosecution had recommended a term of imprisonment within the range of ten to fifteen years. The defence recommended a term within seven to ten years.[23] Although it underlined the importance of individualized sentencing and stressed the irrelevance, generally speaking, of comparing cases when trying to arrive at a proportionate sentence, the Trial Chamber also recalled that 'sentences of like individuals in like cases should be comparable'.[24] In this light, it held that the case against Kunarac was to a significant extent comparable to that against Zelenović.[25] It recognized that '[t]he similarities between the present case and the Kunarac *et al.* case extend to the type of crime, how the crime was carried out, the duration of the criminal behaviour, and the characterization of the victims. The crime base in the present case is not only similar, but to a large extent identical to the one in the Kunarac *et al.* case. The participation of Mr. Zelenović in the crimes committed is comparable with that of at least some of the perpetrators in the aforementioned case'.[26]

An important distinction between the two cases was that Zelenović had pleaded guilty. Where the sentences in the Kunarac *et al.* case had ranged from twenty-eight to twelve years' imprisonment, the Trial Chamber in Zelenović arrived at a term of imprisonment of fifteen years.

The significance accorded to the Kunarac case in the Trial Chamber's determination of an appropriate punishment for Zelenović is surprising from the viewpoint of the tribunal's poor opinion of ordinal proportionality.[27] To the detriment of transparency and 'foreseeability', the tribunal has consistently held

---

18 European Court of Human Rights, Judgement, *Engel and others v. The Netherlands*, Application nos. 5100/71;5101/71; 5102/71; 5354/72; 5370/72, 8 June 1976, par. 82.

19 See, for example, European Court of Human Rights, Judgement, *Campbell and Fell v. The United Kingdom*, Application nos. 7819/77; 7878/77, 28 June 1984; European Court of Human Rights, Judgement, *Ezeh and Connors v. The United Kingdom*, Application nos. 39665/98 and 40086/98, 9 October 2003; European Court of Human Rights, Judgement, *Ezeh and Connors v. The United Kingdom*, Application nos. 39665/98 and 40086/98, 15 July 2002; European Court of Human Rights, Judgement, *Young v. The United Kingdom*, Application no. 60682/00, 16 January 2007.

20 European Court of Human Rights, Judgement, *Ezeh and Connors v. The United Kingdom*, Application nos. 39665/98 and 40086/98, 9 October 2003, par. 89.

21 See, for example, Judgement, *Prosecutor v. Blaškić*, A. Ch., *supra* note 8, par. 696; ICTY, Sentencing Judgement, *Prosecutor v. Jokić*, Case No. IT-01-42/1-S, T. Ch. I, 18 March 2004, Klip/ Sluiter, ALC-XIX-779, par. 100; ICTY, Sentencing Judgement, *Prosecutor v. Nikolić*, Case No. IT-02-60/1-S, T. Ch. I, Section A, 2 December 2003, Klip/ Sluiter, ALC-XV-731, par. 268; ICTY, Judgement, *Prosecutor v. Kordić and Čerkez*, Case No. IT-95-14/2-A, A. Ch., 17 December 2004, Klip/ Sluiter, ALC-XXVI-19, par. 1090.

22 See, for example, ICTY, Order of the President on the Application for the Early Release of Milan Simić, Case No. IT-95/2, President, 27 October 2003; D. Abels, Commentary, Klip/ Sluiter, ALC-XV-798.

23 Sentencing Judgement, *Prosecutor v. Zelenović*, T. Ch. I, *supra* note 1, par. 64.

24 *Ibid.*, par. 65.

25 *Idem.*

26 *Ibid.*, par. 67. Emphasis in the original.

27 See, further, D. Abels, Commentary, Klip/ Sluiter, ALC-XIV-887.

that 'comparison with other cases is often of limited assistance', because 'often the differences are more significant than the similarities, and the mitigating and aggravating factors dictate different results'.[28] Admittedly, the cases of Zelenović and Kunarac et al. lent themselves rather well to compare, particularly since the original indictment against Kunarac had included that against Zelenović. One would wish, though, that the chamber's approach to ordinal proportionality in Zelenović sets an example for the tribunal's future sentencing judgements.

The sentencing judgement has been criticized by feminist legal scholars. Engle argues that it is unclear what the Trial Chamber meant by its statement that what makes rape particularly egregious is the 'violation of the moral and physical integrity of the victims'.[29] According to her, 'the Chamber's use of the term "moral" seems to imply a value judgment about the nature of sexual violence which the victims may not have shared'.[30] Admittedly, notwithstanding the fact that the Trial Chamber did not define 'moral integrity', where victims as a result of a guilty plea are not given the opportunity to testify in court, a reference to the moral harm done to them may very well be based on the Judges' preconception of the impact of such a crime on victims, which implies a culturally preconceived value judgement.

The Trial Chamber had awarded Zelenović a discount for pleading guilty. It is noted that the adduced justification for this – that the guilty plea was 'likely to save the victims from reliving the trauma through testifying about the crimes committed against them'[31] may augment the possibly already felt frustration among victims. In light of the foregoing, it is advisable for sentencing chambers, particularly when dealing with culturally sensitive gender-based crimes like (wartime) rape,[32] to proceed with caution when referring to the moral harm done to the victims, and when giving a voice to their suffering.

3. The judgement on sentencing appeal

On appeal, Zelenović complained that the Trial Chamber had not adequately assessed the mitigating circumstances, particularly his guilty plea and his cooperation with the prosecution. The Appeals Chamber, in line with earlier jurisprudence,[33] however, reiterated that the mitigating weight to be attached to a guilty plea, as to any mitigating circumstance, lies with the Trial Chamber. It also noted that Trial Chambers are 'not required to explicitly mention the extent of the mitigating value it grants to a guilty plea'.[34]

The Appeals Chamber has held previously that it is not incumbent upon Trial Chambers to specify the reduction of years of imprisonment in relation to each mitigating factor,[35] which reasoning fits in well with its general tendency to respect the Trial Chambers' discretionary powers in sentencing. In a similar vein, Trial Chambers are not obliged to set out in detail each factor relied upon, or to explain under exactly what heading a specific mitigating circumstance is taken into consideration - even if such a specific circumstance

---

28 ICTY, Judgement, *Prosecutor v. Delalić et al.*, Case No. IT-96-21-A, A. Ch., 20 February 2001, Klip/ Sluiter, ALC-V-369, par. 719 and 821. See also Judgement, *Prosecutor v. Kordić and Čerkez*, A. Ch., *supra* note 21, par. 1064; Judgement, *Prosecutor v. Kvočka et al*, Case No. IT-98-30/1-A, A. Ch., 28 February 2005, Klip/ Sluiter, ALC-XXVI-669, par. 681; ICTY, Judgement on Sentencing Appeal, *Prosecutor v. Nikolić*, Case No. IT-02-60/1-A, A. Ch., 8 March 2006, Klip/ Sluiter, ALC-XXVIII-901, par. 38; ICTY, Judgement, *Prosecutor v. Stakić*, Case No. IT-97-24-A, A. Ch., 22 March 2006, Klip/ Sluiter, ALC-XIX-213, par. 381; ICTY, Judgement, *Prosecutor v. Naletilić and Martinović*, Case No. IT-98-34-A, A. Ch., 3 May 2006, ALC-XIX-347, par. 615; ICTY, Separate and Partially Dissenting Opinion of Judge Meron, *Prosecutor v. Galić*, Case No. IT-98-29-A, A. Ch., 30 November 2006, Klip/ Sluiter, ALC-XXXIII-595, par. 8.

29 See http://intlawgrrls.blogspot.com/2010/08/torture-ban-cultural-relativism.html, last visited by the author on 10 August 2010.

30 *Idem.*

31 Sentencing Judgement, *Prosecutor v. Zelenović*, T. Ch. I, *supra* note 1, par. 49.

32 See, for example, E. M. Aswad, Torture by Means of Rape, 84 Georgetown Law Journal 1996, p. 1913-1943, footnote 104; J. Campanaro, Women, War, and International Law: The Historical Treatment of Gender-Based War Crimes, 89 Georgetown Law Journal 2001, p. 2557–2592, footnote 90. See, further, T. L. Tompkins, Prosecuting Rape as a War Crime: Speaking the Unspeakable, 70 Notre Dame Law Review 1995, p. 845–890; K. Engle, Feminism and Its (Dis)Contents: Criminalizing Wartime Rape in Bosnia and Herzegovina, 99 American Journal of International Law 2005, p. 778–816.

33 See, for example, ICTY, Judgement, *Prosecutor v. Delalić et al.*, Case No. IT-96-21-A, A. Ch., 20 February 2001, Klip/ Sluiter, ALC-V-369, par. 776 and 777; ICTY, Judgement, *Prosecutor v. Jelisić*, Case No. IT-95-10-A, A. Ch., 5 July 2001, Klip/ Sluiter, ALC-VII-513, par. 103.

34 ICTY, Judgement on Sentencing Appeal, *Prosecutor v. Zelenović*, Case No. IT-96-23/2-A, A. Ch., 31 October 2007, par. 18.

35 ICTY, Judgement, *Prosecutor v. Delalić et al.*, Case No. IT-96-21-A, A. Ch., 20 February 2001, Klip/ Sluiter, ALC-V-369, par. 841.

is mentioned in one of the parties' submissions.[36] This approach may, however, undermine important notions of (perceived) fairness, transparency and expressiveness.

Also, in connection with Zelenović's cooperation with the prosecutor's office, the Appeals Chamber concurred with the Trial Chamber's finding that it is within the latter's discretion 'to evaluate the extent and the nature of the accused's cooperation and to determine the weight, if any, it should be accorded in mitigation'.[37] It affirmed the Trial Chamber's ruling that cooperation by an accused need not be substantial for it to be considered in mitigation.[38] The sentence imposed by the Trial Chamber was affirmed on appeal.

Denis Abels

[36] ICTY, Appeal Judgement, *Prosecutor v. Kupreškić et al.*, Case No. IT-95-16-A, A. Ch., 23 October 2001, Klip/ Sluiter, ALC-VIII-429, par. 430; Judgement, *Prosecutor v. Kordić and Čerkez*, A. Ch., *supra* note 21, par. 1064, par. 1051; ICTY, Judgement on Sentencing Appeal, *Prosecutor v. Bralo*, A. Ch., IT-95-17-A, 2 April 2007, par. 29; ICTR, Judgement, *Prosecutor v. Musema*, Case No. ICTR-96-13-A, A. Ch., 16 November 2001, Klip/ Sluiter, ALC-X-863, par. 395.

[37] ICTY, Judgement on Sentencing Appeal, *Prosecutor v. Zelenović*, Case No. IT-96-23/2-A, A. Ch., 31 October 2007, par. 24 (footnotes omitted).

[38] *Idem.*

UNITED NATIONS

International Tribunal for the Prosecution of Persons Responsible for Serious Violations of International Humanitarian Law Committed in the Territory of the Former Yugoslavia since 1991	Case No.	IT-01-42-Misc.1
	Date:	7 June 2007
	Original:	English

<u>IN THE APPEALS CHAMBER</u>

Before: **Judge Theodor Meron, Presiding**
Judge Mohamed Shahabuddeen
Judge Mehmet Güney
Judge Andrésia Vaz
Judge Wolfgang Schomburg

Registrar: **Mr. Hans Holthuis**

Decision of: **7 June 2007**

PROSECUTOR

v.

PAVLE STRUGAR

PUBLIC

DECISION ON STRUGAR'S REQUEST TO REOPEN APPEAL PROCEEDINGS

<u>The Office of the Prosecutor:</u>
Ms. Carla Del Ponte
Ms. Helen Brady
Ms. Michelle Jarvis
Mr. Xavier Tracol

<u>Counsel for Mr. Strugar</u>
Mr. Goran Rodić
Mr. Vladimir Petrović

[page 2] 1. The Appeals Chamber of the International Tribunal for the Prosecution of Persons Responsible for Serious Violations of International Humanitarian Law Committed in the Territory of the Former Yugoslavia since 1991 ("Appeals Chamber" and "Tribunal", respectively) is seized of the "Defence Request Seeking the Re-Opening of Appeal Proceedings Before the Appeals Chamber" ("Defence Request"), filed confidentially on 26 March 2007. The Appeals Chamber also notes the "Prosecution Response to Defence Confidential 'Request Seeking the Re-Opening of Appeal Proceedings Before the Appeals Chamber' Dated 26 March 2007" ("Prosecution Response"), filed confidentially on 5 April 2007.[1]

I. Background

2. On 31 January 2005, Trial Chamber II found Pavle Strugar ("Strugar") guilty pursuant to Article 7(3) of the Statute of the Tribunal ("Statute") of certain crimes in connection with the attack by the Yugoslav Peoples' Army on the Old Town of Dubrovnik constituting violations of the Laws or Customs of war, under Article 3 of the Statute. He was acquitted of the other four counts in the Indictment. The Trial Chamber imposed a single sentence of eight years imprisonment.[2]

3. Both parties appealed. Strugar appealed the Trial Chamber's convictions, its chosen sentence, and its conclusion that Strugar was fit to stand trial.[3] The Prosecution appealed the Trial Chamber's treatment of command responsibility, its approach to cumulative convictions, and its chosen sentence.[4] Ultimately, however, both parties withdrew their appeals, and the Appeals Chamber accepted these withdrawals.[5]

4. At issue in the Defence Request is whether Strugar can reinstate his appeal. Before turning to the arguments of the parties, the Appeals Chamber will set forth in detail the events leading up to the withdrawals of the appeals. **[page 3]**

5. In the Trial Judgement, the Trial Chamber noted Strugar's "personal and family circumstances", including the fact that he was 71 years old (at the time of the Trial Judgement); that he was "in poor health [and] suffers in particular from some degree of vascular dementia and depression and experiences memory losses"; and that his wife, with whom he has been married for nearly half a century, would face significant hardship in his absence, particularly in light of her failing vision and need for assistance.[6] These circumstances continued to haunt Strugar during the course of his appeal. In addition, according to the Defence, Mr. Strugar's wife was "unable to visit him here because of, among other things, her eyesight difficulties. Her eyesight is impaired by 90 per cent. She is almost blind, and, for this reason, cannot visit him at the UNDU."[7] Finally, he developed other health concerns, including severe hip problems that required surgery.

6. With these humanitarian considerations in mind, and after the briefing in the appeal was completed, the Pre-Appeal Judge discussed with the parties the possibility of Strugar spending time in Montenegro. This occurred in a confidential meeting undertaken pursuant to Rule 65*ter*(I) of the Tribunal's Rules of Procedure and Evidence ("Rules") on 11 October 2005. The Pre-Appeal Judge explained that Strugar could not serve

---

1 Although these filings were made confidentially, the Appeals Chamber considers it appropriate to issue this decision publicly. In the course of the decision, the Appeals Chamber discusses and sometimes quotes from confidential materials (such as the minutes from Rule 65*ter* conferences). The Appeals Chamber deems this public use of confidential materials to be suitable, particularly since the references to these confidential materials generally pertain to an issue – the question of the withdrawals of the appeals – that was discussed subsequently in a public status conference and in public filings. *See generally* Transcript of Status Conference, 31 August 2006 (Open Session); Defence Notice of Withdrawing Appeal, 15 September 2006 ("Defence Withdrawal"); Withdrawal of Prosecution's Appeal Against the Judgement of Trial Chamber II Dated 31 January 2005, 15 September 2006 ("Prosecution Withdrawal"). The Appeals Chamber nonetheless declines to lift further the confidential status of the confidential sources referred to in this decision, since many of these sources make reference to specific medical details which, in the interest of the privacy of the accused, should be kept confidential.

2 Trial Judgement, 31 January 2005 ("Judgement"), para. 481.

3 *See generally* Defence Appeal Brief, 8 July 2005.

4 *See generally* Prosecution Appeal Brief, 17 May 2005.

5 Defence Withdrawal; Prosecution Withdrawal; Final Decision on "Defence Notice of Withdrawing Appeal" and "Withdrawal of Prosecution's Appeal Against the Judgement of Trial Chamber II Dated 31 January 2005", 20 September 2006 ("Decision Accepting Withdrawals").

6 Trial Judgement, para. 469 (finding these circumstances to be mitigating factors).

7 Transcript of Status Conference, 31 August 2006, p. 58 (Open Session).

his detention pending appeal in Montenegro, but suggested that there was a possibility that he could serve his final sentence in Montenegro. To this end, the Pre-Appeal Judge asked the parties to consider whether they were willing to mutually withdraw their appeals.[8]

7. At a Status Conference on 12 December 2005, the Pre-Appeal Judge returned to the issue of whether the parties might withdraw their appeals with an eye to letting Strugar serve his final sentence in Montenegro. The Pre-Appeal Judge explained that:

> One pre-requisite would be ... that a judgement becomes final, but then there is no obstacle at all that Mr. Strugar would, in this case – of course, we have not discussed it in the Chamber as such, but Mr. Strugar would undergo all these treatments in Montenegro. I can assure you once again that I would be prepared to convince the necessary persons in this Tribunal that a sentence could also be served in Montenegro.[9]

The Prosecution responded that it would give due consideration to this approach, if the Defence were interested.[10] Defence Counsel responded that Counsel and Strugar had engaged in "detailed discussions of all the options that were open to [Strugar]", but that Strugar was "still deeply convinced that the first-instance decision is unjust and is not justified by facts" and thus determined to maintain his appeal.[11] Around this time, the Appeals Chamber granted provisional release for **[page 4]** Strugar to go to Montenegro for the replacement of a hip, requiring however, that certain measures were in place in order to guarantee his presence for the continuation of the appellate hearings.[12]

8. In March 2006, the Pre-Appeal Judge held another Rule 65*ter*(I) conference. The Pre-Appeal Judge "invited the parties to further discuss ... in general terms the possibilities of the mutual withdrawal of appeals".[13] The Prosecution was willing, but the Defence remained hesitant.[14] The Pre-Appeal Judge stated "that transferring Mr. Strugar to serve sentence in his own country [Montenegro] should not be a problem".[15] The Pre-Appeal Judge further observed that there might be some difficulties in light of the absence of a bilateral agreement between Montenegro and the ICTY, and also that the detention facility in Montenegro would need to satisfy certain standards "and that it would no[t] be a kind of sham-detention. Applying Rule 11*bis* (B) *mutatis mutandis*, the detention center selected must comply with the conditions foreseen by the UN and the Council of Europe. In that sense, the authorities of Montenegro, for instance, should have to guarantee that a visit to the detention center can be done without notice, as stipulated by the European Committee for the Prevention of Torture and Inhumane or Degrading Treatment or Punishment (CPT)."[16] At the end of the meeting, the Defence agreed to look into whether Montenegro had an appropriate detention centre, and the Pre-Appeal Judge agreed to "talk with the President, the Registrar and the entire bench in order to find out whether it is possible to get an agreement with the competent authorities so that the Accused can serve his sentence in Montenegro."[17]

9. On 8 May 2006, the Defence filed a "Resolution of the Government of the Republic of Montenegro", which expressed the Government of Montenegro's willingness to work with the ICTY to enable Strugar to serve his sentence in Montenegro and which provided specifics on several possible detention facilities.[18] On 11 May 2006, another Rule 65*ter*(I) conference occurred. There, the Pre-Appeal Judge informed the parties that "the Appeals Chamber's position is that the Registrar and the President of the Tribunal have the last word in deciding whether or not Mr. Strugar can serve the sentence in Montenegro" and that the President "thinks positively about a transfer to Montenegro."[19] The Pre-Appeal Judge then "explain[ed] the legal

[8] Confidential Minutes of 65*ter*(I) Meeting, 11 October 2005, para. 4.
[9] Transcript of Status Conference, 12 December 2005, pp. 49–50 (Private Session).
[10] *Ibid.*, p. 50.
[11] *Ibid.*
[12] Decision on "Defence Motion: Defence Request for Provisional Release for Providing Medical Aid in the Republic of Montenegro", 16 December 2005.
[13] Confidential Minutes of 65*ter*(I) Meeting, 30 March 2006, para. 1.
[14] *Ibid.*, paras 2–3.
[15] *Ibid.*, para. 4.
[16] *Ibid.*, para. 4.
[17] *Ibid.*, para. 8.
[18] This document was filed confidentially.
[19] Confidential Minutes of 65*ter*(I) Meeting, 11 May 2006, para. 4.

reasoning behind a possible transfer of Mr. Strugar to serve sentence in Montenegro", referring to Article 27 of the **[page 5]** Statute of the Tribunal, Rules 102(a) and 103 of the Rules, and the Practice Direction on the Procedure for the International Tribunal's Designation of the State in which a Convicted Person is to Serve his/her Sentence of Imprisonment.[20] The Pre-Appeal Judge "stress[ed] yet again that he cannot guarantee that the sentence will be served in Montenegro," as the "preparations are for the Registry to be done, and the final word is for the President of the Tribunal."[21] The Pre-Appeal Judge recognized the hesitancy of the Defence to withdraw the appeal in the absence of a guarantee, but explained that "[f]ormal conversations between the Registry and the government of Montenegro will not start before a judgement has become final."[22] He urged the Defence to come to a speedy decision about whether it wished to withdraw its appeal.[23]

10. By a letter dated 22 May 2006, the Registry informed the Defence of its view that "[t]he enforcement of a sentence in Montenegro would currently be subject to a number of important legal and other obstacles, which would need to be removed."[24]

11. Several more months passed without clear resolution of the withdrawal issue. In the meantime, the oral hearings for the appeals were scheduled and then postponed.[25] Then, at a Status Conference on 31 August 2006, the parties further discussed Strugar's health and revisited the issue of withdrawal. With regard to his health, Strugar noted that, among other things, he would need a second hip operation.[26] Counsel for Strugar sought clarification from the Pre-Appeal Judge as to "whether, legally speaking, there is the possibility for such an option [of Strugar serving his sentence in Montenegro], which, in our opinion, would be the best solution for the situation in which Mr. Strugar currently finds himself."[27] The Pre-Appeal Judge responded that: **[page 6]**

> the Registrar, in consultation with the President, would first have to conclude agreement with the Republic of Montenegro ..., and the prison conditions in Montenegro would have to fulfil the standards required by the Statute, the Rules and the relevant United Nations provisions and principles. Thus, as a Pre-Appeal Judge, I'm not authorised to decide the matter.[28]

The Pre-Appeal Judge went on to observe, however, that:

> I have carefully reviewed the legal situation and, personally, I do not see any general obstacle to give a strong recommendation to both the Registrar and the President to grant, if there should be a mutual withdrawal of both appeals and therefore the sentence has become final, the conviction has become final, to grant such a motion for humanitarian reasons based on the health situation of Mr. Strugar.[29]

---

20 *Ibid.*, para. 5.

21 *Ibid.*, para. 11.

22 *Ibid.*, para. 12.

23 *Ibid.*, paras 12–13.

24 Letter from Hans Holthuis, Registrar, to Goran Rodić, Counsel for Strugar, 22 May 2006 ("Letter of 22 May 2006") (provided as Annex 5 to the Defence Request).

25 Scheduling Order for Appeals Hearing, 18 May 2006; Scheduling Order Temporarily Cancelling Appeals Hearing, 24 May 2006.

26 Transcript of Status Conference, 31 August 2006, p. 56 (Open Session).

27 *Ibid.*, p. 59. In full, the pertinent remarks read as follows:

> "In our view, [proper] medical care could be provided to General Strugar only if he were to serve his sentence in one of the institutions in Montenegro, the country he hails from. In this regard, the Defence respectfully appeals to this Chamber to be of assistance in this matter and, if possible, to inform Mr. Strugar's Defence of their view as to whether there is a possibility, in the context of this Tribunal's Statute, Rules of Procedure and Evidence and other legal acts, in view of the very specific circumstances of this case that are quite different from other cases that were before this Tribunal, for Mr. Strugar to serve his sentence in one of the relevant facilities in the territory of Montenegro. Furthermore, the Defence would like to hear the views of the pre-appeals Judge with regard to such a possibility. Finally, I would like to say that the Defence is aware of the fact that when it comes to the discussion about the facilities to be determined for such a purpose, the Defence would be prepared to withdraw their notice of appeal, or appeals brief, in order to make this sentence final; that this would be, of course, the precondition for such a discussion. Therefore, we would like to know first whether, legally speaking, there is the possibility for such an option, which, in our opinion, would be the best solution for the situation in which Mr. Strugar currently finds himself."

28 *Ibid.*, p. 61.

29 *Ibid.*

The Pre-Appeal Judge continued:

> I have to submit this to the entire Bench, which has to decide whether or not to accept such withdrawals as being informed, voluntary and unequivocal ones and to order, if need may be, final dispositions pursuant to Rules 101(C) and 103(C) of the Rules.[30]

The Pre-Appeal Judge further stressed "that [a withdrawal], under no circumstances, can be revoked. Therefore, I have to re-emphasise that I'm not able give any guarantees."[31]

12. Later on in the Status Conference, Strugar expressed his intent to withdraw the appeal. The Pre-Appeal Judge reminded Strugar that "your decision has to be an informed one. You have heard that neither I nor the Chamber as such can give any guarantees at this point in time because the power is clearly vested in the Registrar and finally the President. Once again, you have fully understood ... that once you have taken a decision, the decision cannot be revoked?"[32] Strugar responded "Yes. I have."[33]

13. On 15 September 2006, both parties filed withdrawals of their appeals. The Defence Withdrawal stated that "General Strugar has reached the aforesaid decision [to withdraw] after being informed that there exist no legal impediments which could prevent him from serving the remainder of his prison sentence in Montenegro."[34] A footnote to this statement cited remarks of the Pre-Appeal Judge quoted above from the 31 August 2006 Status Conference.[35] The Defence Withdrawal also attached a signed statement of Strugar as an Annex. This stated in part: "I hereby confirm that I am informed and aware of all of the legal consequences of my above decision, including the fact that, once the Appeal is withdrawn, there is no possibility of subsequent **[page 7]** reconsideration of the Judgement, pursuant to which I was convicted, in the Appellate proceedings, and having the same abolished or altered in my favor."[36] The Prosecution Withdrawal stated that "[o]n the basis that Pavle Strugar has withdrawn his appeal against the Judgement, the Prosecution hereby withdraws its own appeal in this case."[37] Both withdrawals also noted the "humanitarian circumstances" in relation to Strugar's age and health.[38]

14. On 20 September 2006, the Appeals Chamber issued the Decision Accepting Withdrawals. In this decision, the Appeals Chamber accepted the withdrawals and declared the appellate proceedings to be finished. It took into consideration the above-mentioned statement and the references to humanitarian circumstances.[39]

15. On 15 March 2007, Counsel for Strugar received a letter from the Registry stating that Mr. Strugar would not serve his sentence in Montenegro. The letter explained:

> The Republic of Montenegro was informed that agreements with respect to the enforcement of sentences of persons convicted before the Tribunal are negotiated by the Registrar. The facilities in which convicted persons of the International Tribunal serve their sentences must conform to international standards outline [*sic*] by various international treaties and non-governmental organizations. Further, the State in question must have legislation in relation to the implementation of the Tribunal's Statute.
>
> Pursuant to Article 4 of the Practice Direction on the Procedure for the International Tribunal's Designation of the State in Which a Convicted Person is to Serve His/Her Sentence of Imprisonment, the President decides in which of the States with which the Tribunal has an enforcement agreement a sentence is enforced. Moreover, we have verified with the Office of Legal Affairs at UN Headquarters that resolution 827 of the Security Council, accepting the Secretary General's report, S/25704, in which it is stated that 'the enforcement of sentences should take place outside the territory of the former Yugoslavia', places a geographic restriction.

---

30 *Ibid.*, p. 62.
31 *Ibid.*
32 *Ibid.*, p. 65.
33 *Ibid.*
34 Defence Withdrawal, para. 10.
35 *Ibid.*, fn. 3 (citing the text accompanying footnote 29, *supra*).
36 Annex to Defence Withdrawal.
37 Prosecution Withdrawal, para. 2.
38 Defence Withdrawal, paras 9, 12; Prosecution Withdrawal, para. 2.
39 Decision Accepting Withdrawals, p. 1 (quoting Annex to Defence Withdrawal, Defence Withdrawal, and Prosecution Withdrawal).

> As a result, the Tribunal is presently not in a position to conclude an agreement for enforcement of sentences within the Republic of Montenegro.[40]

This letter refers to paragraph 1 of the Security Council's Resolution 827 (adopted 25 May 1993), which "[a] pprove[d] the report of the Secretary General"; and to paragraph 121 of the report itself, which expressed the Secretary-General's view that "given the nature of the crimes in question and the international character of the tribunal, the enforcement of sentences should take place outside the territory of the former Yugoslavia." **[page 8]**

II. Arguments of the Parties

16. In the Defence Request, Strugar seeks to reopen his appeal.[41] He explains that one reason he sought to withdraw his appeal "was the fact that [he] was informed that there do not exist legal impediments that would prevent him from serving the remainder of his prison sentence in Montenegro".[42] In his view, the letter from the Registry of 15 March 2007 shows that there is in fact a clear legal impediment to his serving his sentence in Montenegro – namely, Security Council Resolution 827 (as interpreted by the Office of Legal Affairs at UN Headquarters).[43] Because he did not know of this legal impediment, he considers that his withdrawal was not an informed one.[44] Drawing a parallel to Rule 62*bis* of the Rules (which provides that guilty pleas must be found to be informed), he argues that an uninformed withdrawal cannot be deemed valid.[45] Strugar thus seeks revocation of the Decision Accepting Withdrawals. He also requests an oral hearing on this issue.

17. The Prosecution Response opposes the Defence Request. The Prosecution accepts the parallel to Rule 62*bis* of the Rules, but considers that Strugar's withdrawal was an informed one.[46] In the Prosecution's view, the question is not whether Strugar was informed of the existence of legal impediments; rather, it is whether Strugar was informed "that his withdrawal was not conditional upon him serving his sentence in Montenegro and that it was irrevocable".[47] The Prosecution submits that Strugar was indeed informed that his withdrawal was irrevocable and that he might not ultimately serve his sentence in Montenegro. The Prosecution also considers that in any event Strugar knew there were possible legal obstacles in light of the Registry's Letter of 22 May 2006 and the Pre-Appeal Judge's statements that he could make no guarantees.[48] The Prosecution considers that no oral hearing on this issue is necessary in light of the written submissions.[49] Finally, the Prosecution states that should the Appeals Chamber grant the Defence **[page 9]** Request, then it should also reinstate the Prosecution's appeal, as the Prosecution Withdrawal was conditional on the Defence Withdrawal.[50]

18. Strugar has not filed a reply to the Prosecution Response.

---

[40] Letter from Hans Holthius, Registrar, to Goran Rodić, Counsel for Strugar, 15 March 2007 ("Letter of 15 March 2007") (provided as Annex 8 to the Defence Request).

[41] The Appeals Chamber notes that Strugar has also sought other forms of relief. He asked the Appeals Chamber to allow him to return to Montenegro to receive medical treatment under detention conditions (a request this Chamber dismissed for lack of jurisdiction) and that the Appeals Chamber defer addressing the Defence Request until Strugar had received medical treatment (a request this Chamber denied). *See* Defence Request for Providing Medical Aid, 10 May 2007 (filed confidentially); Confidential Addendum, filed 14 May 2007; Defence Request Seeking the Postponement of the Decision to the 'Confidential Defence Request Seeking the Re-Opening of Appeal Proceedings before the Appeals Chamber', 10 May 2007 (filed confidentially); Prosecution Consolidated Response to the Defence Requests Dated 10 May 2007, 17 May 2007 (filed confidentially); Decision on Strugar's Requests Filed 10 May 2007, 23 May 2007 (filed confidentially). The Appeals Chamber also observes that Strugar filed a confidential "Defence Request Seeking Early Release" with the President of the Tribunal on 26 March 2007; and a confidential "Defence Submission" with the President of the Tribunal on 10 May 2007.

[42] Defence Request, para. 13.

[43] *Ibid.*, paras 35–39.

[44] Ibid., paras 39, 41–42.

[45] *See ibid.*, para. 38.

[46] Prosecution Response, para. 4.

[47] *Ibid.*, para. 7.

[48] *Ibid.*, para. 8.

[49] *Ibid.*, para. 10.

[50] *Ibid.*, para. 11.

III. Discussion

19. To begin with, the Appeals Chamber rejects Strugar's request for an oral hearing. No provision of the Rules so requires, and the Appeals Chamber considers that it can adequately dispose of the Defence Request on the basis of the written filings.[51]

20. The Appeals Chamber next turns to preliminary matters of some importance: namely, how to characterize the Defence Request procedurally and whether the Appeals Chamber has jurisdiction regarding it. The Decision Accepting Withdrawals terminated the appeal proceedings in Strugar's case.[52] It transformed him from an appellant into an individual with a final sentence. To reopen his case, Strugar must thus convince the Appeals Chamber to revisit the Decision Accepting Withdrawals. For the Appeals Chamber to revisit this Decision, however, it must have a jurisdictional basis for doing so.

21. One mechanism for reopening a case is to bring a successful motion for review under Article 26 of the Statute and Rules 119-120 of the Rules. The Decision Accepting Withdrawals can be considered a "final judgement" for purposes of Article 26 because it "terminates the proceedings".[53] Strugar nowhere suggests, however, that he is bringing a motion for review, and he fails to address how he satisfies the basic requirements for review. He nowhere explains, for example, how an apparent legal impediment constitutes a "fact"[54] or how it can be deemed "new" where the matter of legal impediments was plainly at issue in the earlier proceedings.[55] Accordingly, the Appeals Chamber does not consider the Defence Request to constitute a motion for review.

22. The Defence Request is more plausibly construed as a motion for reconsideration of the Decision Accepting Withdrawals. For one thing, Strugar specifically asks the Appeals Chamber to **[page 10]** "revoke[]" the Decision Accepting Withdrawals.[56] For another, his arguments closely resemble the kinds of arguments raised in motions for reconsiderations. In general, the Appeals Chamber has the power to reconsider past decisions, particularly "where it was realized that the previous decision was erroneous or where it has caused an injustice."[57] Here Strugar suggests an error and implies an injustice. He claims that the Decision Accepting Withdrawals erroneously accepted an uninformed withdrawal – a claim that, if true, would demonstrate a miscarriage of justice.[58] Given how closely his arguments track the sort of arguments relevant in motions for reconsideration, the Appeals Chamber considers that the Defence Request is properly viewed as such a motion.

23. This in turn raises the question of whether the Appeals Chamber has the power to consider such a motion. It is clear that the Appeals Chamber normally has the power to reconsider its prior decisions.[59] But matters are complicated by the fact that Strugar's case is now closed. While the Appeals Chamber once held that it has the inherent power to reconsider final judgements,[60] it has since taken a different position and held that there is no inherent power to reconsider final judgements.[61] Accordingly, the Appeals Chamber will consider whether, for purposes of a motion for reconsideration, the Decision Accepting Withdrawals constitutes a "final judgement".

---

[51] *See, e.g., Prosecutor v. Milan Lukić & Sredoje Lukić*, Case No. IT-98-32/1-AR65.1, Decision on Defence Appeal Against Trial Chamber's Decision on Sredoje Lukić's Motion for Provisional Release, 16 April 2007, para. 15.

[52] Decision Accepting Withdrawals, p. 2.

[53] *Jean-Bosco Barayagwiza v. Prosecutor*, Case No. ICTR-97-19-AR72, Decision (Prosecutor's Request for Review or Reconsideration), 31 March 2000 ("*Barayagwiza* Decision"), para. 49.

[54] *See Prosecutor v. Goran Jelisić,* Case No. IT-95-10-R, Decision on Motion for Review, 2 May 2002, p. 3 (rejecting the convicted person's argument that a change in the governing legal standard constituted a "new fact" of "an evidentiary nature").

[55] *See ibid.* (stating that the term "new fact" refers to "new information of an evidentiary nature of a fact that was not in issue during the trial or appeal proceedings").

[56] Defence Request, para. 43.

[57] *Prosecutor v. Stanislav Galić*, Case No. IT-98-29-AR73, Decision on Application by Prosecution for Leave to Appeal, 14 December 2001 ("*Galić* Decision"), para. 13.

[58] *See* Defence Request, para. 42.

[59] *Prosecutor v. Zdravko Mucić et al,* Case No. IT-96-21-Abis, Judgement on Sentence Appeal, 8 April 2003 ("*Čelebići* Decision"), para. 49; *Prosecutor v. Zoran Žigić*, Case No. IT-98-30/1-A, Decision on Zoran Žigić's 'Motion for Reconsideration of Appeals Chamber Judgement IT-98-30/1-A Delivered on 28 February 2005', 26 June 2006 ("*Žigić* Decision"), para. 9.

[60] *Čelebići* Decision, paras 49–53.

[61] *Žigić* Decision, para. 9; *see also Prosecutor v. Eliézer Niyitegeka*, Case No. ICTR-96-14-R, Decision on Request for Reconsideration of the Decision on Request for Review, 27 September 2006, pp. 1–2; *Prosecutor v. Timohir Blaškić*, Case No. IT-95-14-R, Decision on Prosecutor's Request for Review or Reconsideration, 23 November 2006, para. 79 (Public Redacted Version); *Georges Anderson Nderubumwe Rutaganda v. Prosecutor*, Case No. ICTR-96-03-R, Decision on Requests for Reconsideration, Review, Assignment of Counsel, Disclosure, and Clarification, 8 December 2006, para. 6.

24. In both the *Čelebići* Decision and the *Žigić* Decision, the Appeals Chamber appeared to presume that the "final judgements" on appeal were indeed appeal judgements in the classic sense of the word – namely, reviews on the merits of the trial judgements. The *Žigić* Decision, for example, emphasized that reconsideration was unwarranted with regard to "a person whose conviction has been confirmed on appeal".[62] It did not consider whether reconsideration was similarly unwarranted with regard to a person whose appeal terminated by another means and who thus did not receive full benefit of an appeal process that he had initiated. Similarly, in discussing **[page 11]** the special context of reconsideration of final judgements, the *Čelebići* Decision assumed that it spoke of a "final judgement" on the merits.[63]

25. The Appeals Chamber concludes that the Decision Accepting Withdrawals is fundamentally different from the kind of "final judgement" referred to in both the *Čelebići* Decision and the *Žigić* Decision. While the Decision Accepting Withdrawals may be a "final judgement" in the sense that it concluded the case,[64] it neither constitutes the kind of judgement envisioned in Article 25(2) of the Statute nor provides all the due process protections that naturally accompany a full judgement on the merits. It is essentially of a *sui generis* nature and is limited to procedure and process. It was adopted without any consideration of the merits of the Trial Chamber judgement. Were reconsideration prohibited in such circumstances, then substantive injustice might result. Accordingly, the Appeals Chamber concludes that it has the power to reconsider the Decision Accepting Withdrawals in the same way that it has the power to reconsider other decisions that do not constitute judgements on the merits.[65]

26. Having satisfied itself of its jurisdiction, the Appeals Chamber now turns to the merits. The Appeals Chamber will reconsider the Decision Accepting Withdrawals if it finds that the decision was erroneous or has led to a miscarriage of justice.[66]

27. As noted earlier, both parties suggest that a defendant's withdrawal of his appeal, like a guilty plea, must be informed.[67] The Appeals Chamber agrees. Where a defendant has invoked the legal right to appeal and now seeks to abandon this right, the Appeals Chamber should satisfy itself that this abandonment is informed. In the Decision Accepting Withdrawals, the Appeals Chamber did not explicitly discuss whether Strugar's withdrawal was an informed one. The Appeals Chamber will now consider this issue.

28. As the Prosecution points out, Strugar knew of the possibility that he might not serve his sentence in Montenegro and of the fact that withdrawal made his appeal final.[68] As the Defence observes, however, Strugar did not know that there was no legal possibility that he could serve his **[page 12]** sentence in Montenegro. Indeed, Strugar explicitly based his withdrawal on the assumption that it was legally possible for him to serve his sentence in Montenegro[69] – an assumption that is rejected in the Registry's Letter of 15 March 2007.[70] The Appeals Chamber is thus on notice of a "specific instance" where Strugar was confused.[71] It may be, of course, that Strugar's assumption in this respect was devoid of good sense in light of the Registry's Letter of 22 May 2006, which referenced "legal obstacles" although without specifically mentioning the Report of the Secretary General which accompanied the Statute, and in light of various caveats given by the Pre-Appeal Judge. But

---

62 *Žigić* Decision, para. 9.

63 *See Čelebići* Decision, para. 51 (considering a "judgement" of the Appeals Chamber to be one "which invalidates the Trial Chamber's decision or an error of fact which has occasioned a miscarriage of justice").

64 *See supra* note 53 and accompanying text.

65 This conclusion is supported by the *Barayagwiza* Decision. There, in considering a case that had been finalized through means other than a judgement on the merits, the Appeals Chamber neither indicated that reconsideration lay outside its power nor suggested that there was an unusually heightened standard for reconsideration. *Barayagwiza* Decision para. 73 (simply rejecting the motion for reconsideration on the merits).

66 *See Galić* Decision, para. 13; *see also Prosecutor v. Nahimana et al.*, Case No. ICTR-99-52-A, *Décision relative à la Requête de l'Appelant Jean-Bosco Barayagwiza demandant l'examen de la Requête de la Défense datée du 28 juillet 2000 et réparation pour abus de procédure*, 23 June 2006, para. 22.

67 Defence Request, para 38; Prosecution Response, para. 4.

68 Prosecution Response, para. 7. The Decision Accepting Withdrawals also noted Strugar's awareness that withdrawal would finalize his appeal. Decision Accepting Withdrawals, p. 1.

69 Defence Withdrawal, para. 12 ("General Strugar has reached the aforesaid decision [to withdraw] after being informed that there exist no legal impediments which could prevent him from serving the remainder of his prison sentence in Montenegro").

70 The Letter of 15 March 2007 clearly concludes that the Report of the Secretary General that accompanied the Statute precludes individuals convicted by the ICTY from serving their sentences within the former Yugoslavia.

71 *See Prosecutor v. Kambanda*, Case No. ICTR-97-23-A, Appeal Judgement, 19 September 2000, para. 77 (suggesting that for a Chamber to find that a defendant makes an uninformed decision, there should be clear indicia in the record of the defendant's lack of understanding).

an informed decision depends not just on the communication of information, but also on the decision-maker's comprehension of this information. Moreover, Strugar had some reason to be confused. The possibility of him serving his sentence in Montenegro had first been raised by the Pre-Appeal Judge; he had received assurances from the Pre-Appeal Judge over a period of many months that this could be done (albeit assurances of varying degrees of certainty); and at his final status conference he heard the personal opinion of the Pre-Appeal Judge (an opinion given with the caveat that it held no guarantees) that legally there was no general obstacle to the service of his sentence in Montenegro.

29. The Prosecution suggests that even assuming that Strugar was confused on the legal possibility of service of his sentence in Montenegro, this cannot justify reopening of his appeal. The Prosecution considers that Strugar needed to be informed only about the "general" consequences of his withdrawal and this is a rather specific issue. The Appeals Chamber agrees that a defendant need not be aware of all specific consequences of withdrawal for his withdrawal to be considered informed. But where it is clear that the defendant withdraws an appeal due to a misunderstanding of the options legally available in his situation, the Appeals Chamber cannot consider the withdrawal to be informed.[72] Here, Strugar's withdrawal was premised on such a misunderstanding, and he promptly sought reconsideration when informed in the Letter of 15 March 2007 that in fact he was legally barred from serving his sentence in Montenegro. In these **[page 13]** circumstances, the interests of justice plainly call for reconsideration of the Decision Accepting Withdrawals in order to avoid a miscarriage of justice.[73]

30. The Appeals Chamber accordingly reconsiders the Decision Accepting Withdrawals, reverses this decision, and reopens the appeals. It reopens not only the Defence Appeal, but also the Prosecution Appeal, since the Prosecution's withdrawal of its appeal was explicitly conditioned upon Strugar's withdrawing his own appeal.[74]

IV. Disposition

31. For the foregoing reasons, the Appeals Chamber **DISMISSES** the Defence Request to the extent that it requests an oral hearing on its contents; and otherwise **GRANTS,** Judge Schomburg dissenting, the Defence Request. The Appeals Chamber accordingly **RECONSIDERS,** Judge Schomburg dissenting, the Decision Withdrawing Appeals; **REVERSES**, Judge Schomburg dissenting, this Decision; and thus **REOPENS**, Judge Schomburg dissenting, both the Defence Appeal and the Prosecution Appeal in this case.

Done in English and French, the English text being authoritative.

Dated this 7th day of June 2007,At The Hague,
The Netherlands.

Judge Theodor Meron
Presiding Judge

Judge Mohamed Shahabuddeen appends a separate opinion.
Judge Wolfgang Schomburg appends a dissenting opinion.

[Seal of the International Tribunal] [page 1]

---

72 *See ibid.*, para 75 (noting the need, in the context of guilty pleas, for an accused to understand the "consequences of pleading guilty in general"); *see also Prosecutor v. Dražen Erdemović*, Case No. IT-96-22-A, Joint Separate Opinion of Judge McDonald and Judge Vohrah, 7 October 1997, para. 14 (finding that an accused must understand the general consequences of a guilty plea to be considered informed).

73 The Appeals Chamber need not address whether the legal impossibility of Strugar's serving his sentence in Montenegro existed at the time of his withdrawal or arose later in light of the legal position expressed in the Registry's Letter of 15 March 2007 (a position that Strugar does not ask the Appeals Chamber to review). Either way, the Appeals Chamber deems reconsideration to be in the interests of justice.

74 Prosecution Withdrawal, para. 2; Decision Accepting Withdrawals, p. 1; Prosecution Response, para. 11.

SEPARATE OPINION OF JUDGE SHAHABUDDEEN

1. I agree with today's decision. I have considered possible objections but, for the following reasons, conclude that they do not prevail.

A. The appellant was not informed

2. Enforcement of sentences is regulated by article 27 of the Statute of the Tribunal, Rule 103(A) of the Rules of Procedure and Evidence of the Tribunal ("Rules"), and the Practice Direction on the Procedure for the International Tribunal's Designation of the State in which a Convicted Person is to Serve his/her Sentence of Imprisonment. Article 27 of the Statute provides:

> Imprisonment shall be served in a State designated by the International Tribunal from a list of States which have indicated to the Security Council their willingness to accept convicted persons. Such imprisonment shall be in accordance with the applicable law of the State concerned, subject to the supervision of the International Tribunal.

Rule 103(A) of the Rules provides:

> Imprisonment shall be served in a State designated by the President of the Tribunal from a list of States which have indicated their willingness to accept convicted persons.

The Practice Direction sets out the procedure to be followed by the Registrar in assisting the President in making a designation.

3. Thus, as provided by Rule 103(A) of the Rules, the designation "by the International Tribunal", as visualised by article 27 of the Statute, is to be done by "the President of the Tribunal". The President of the Tribunal has not made a designation in favour of Montenegro as a state in which a sentence of imprisonment may be served. Absent such a designation, the appellant cannot serve his sentence of imprisonment in Montenegro. It is convenient to note that a designation is presupposed by Rule 103 (B) which provides: "Transfer of the convicted person to that State shall be effected as soon as possible after the time-limit for appeal has elapsed". The words "as soon as possible" do not dispense with the prior need for the designation of "that State" by the President; they are directed to the transferring of the convicted person to a state on the assumption that the state has been designated under the immediately preceding Rule.

4. The appellant told a bench of the Appeals Chamber, before which his appeal was pending, that, "after being informed that there exist no legal impediments which could prevent him from serving the remainder of his prison sentence in Montenegro",[1] he was withdrawing the appeal. That was not correct, because he had been warned by the Pre-Appeal Judge that the final say was with **[page 2]** the President and that there was no guarantee that the President would direct that he be sent to Montenegro. However, his attention was not drawn to the point later made in a letter from the Registrar of 15 March 2007 to his counsel to the effect that he could not be sent to a state which formed part of the territory of the former Yugoslavia. Nor was that point identified in an earlier letter from the Registrar to defence counsel of 22 May 2006, in which the Registrar broadly stated that the "enforcement of a sentence in Montenegro would currently be subject to a number of important legal and other obstacles, which would need to be removed". The appellant felt that the only problems were those arising from the President's discretion. In this respect, as recalled in paragraphs 7 and 11 of today's decision, the Pre-Appeal Judge indicated that he would make a recommendation that the appellant be sent to Montenegro. Thus, the appellant thought that the problems arising from the President's discretion could be resolved and that there was still a *possibility* of his being sent to Montenegro. His belief in that possibility was the basis on which he withdrew his appeal.

5. That basis was not correct: in the absence of a designation by the President in favour of Montenegro, there was no *possibility* of the sentence being served in that state. I believe that the problem in this appeal

---

1 Defence Notice Withdrawing Appeal, 15 September 2006, para. 10.

is the need to appreciate the importance attached by the appellant to the opposite view that the possibility existed. The possibility being non-existent, it appears that the appellant was misinformed. Justice requires that he be allowed to withdraw the withdrawal of his appeal, with the like liberty being given to the prosecution to withdraw its withdrawal of its own appeal.

B. The Appeals Chamber is not subordinating its views to those of an executive body

6. A concern is whether the Appeals Chamber is subordinating its views to those of an executive body. If the Appeals Chamber is doing that, it is doing what is plainly wrong. However, I do not believe that it is doing so.

7. The contrary view is based on the fact that the Secretary-General (through his Legal Counsel) has expressed the opinion that imprisonment in a state (such as Montenegro) which was part of the territory of the former Yugoslavia is barred. It is not clear what has led to Montenegro not being designated by the President, but, if the Secretary-General's views had anything to do with it, there is nothing to show that the President subordinated his own views to those of the Secretary-General; rather, absent evidence to the contrary, in accordance with the presumption of regularity it has to be presumed that the non-designation of Montenegro was due to the Secretary-General's opinion being considered by the President to be right and adopted by him on that account – and not because it possessed any overriding authority. **[page 3]**

C. The reasons given by the Secretary-General were correct

8. There could be a question as to whether the considerations on which the President acts in deciding whether a state is to be designated are open to review by the Appeals Chamber. The Appeals Chamber is a criminal court. What would seem to be important to it is whether there is in fact a designation, not the correctness of any reasons which led to there being a designation or none. In any event, however, if, in making no designation of Montenegro, the President acted on the views of the Secretary-General, those reasons are correct.

9. Paragraph 121 of the Secretary-General's report (on the basis of which the Security Council adopted the Statute of the Tribunal) reads:

> The Secretary-General is of the view that, given the nature of the crimes in question and the international character of the tribunal, the enforcement of sentences should take place outside the territory of the former Yugoslavia.

The Secretary-General's report does not have "the same binding authority" as if it formed part of the Statute itself.[2] But the Statute was adopted by the Security Council in the unaltered text in which it was submitted in draft to the Council in the report. And the Security Council did say it "[a]pprove[d]"[3] of the report when adopting the Statute. As was observed by the Appeals Chamber in *Tadić*:

> By "approving" the Report, the Security Council clearly intended to endorse its purpose as an explanatory document to the proposed Statute. Of course, if there appears to be a manifest contradiction between the Statute and the Report, it is beyond doubt that the Statute must prevail. In other cases, the Secretary-General's Report ought to be taken to provide an authoritative interpretation of the Statute.[4]

There is no "manifest" contradiction in this matter. It is incorrect to proceed on the basis that the Secretary-General's report lacks the authority of the Security Council. In the practice of the Tribunal, considerable weight has been given to the report.

10. Pausing there, it may be noticed that article 26 of the ICTR Statute expressly states that "[i]mprisonment shall be served in Rwanda or any of the States on a list of States which have indicated to the Security Council their willingness to accept convicted persons …". The provision was necessary because, in its absence, it

---

2 *Tadić*, IT-94-1-A, 15 July 1999, para. 295.
3 Paragraph numbered 1 of S/RES/827 (1993) of 25 May 1993.
4 IT-94-1-A, 15 July 1999, para. 295.

might be thought that Rwanda, being the state of conflict, was excluded as a possible place of imprisonment. Naturally, the ICTR still has a discretion whether to order imprisonment to be served in Rwanda, and how it is exercised is not a matter for present consideration. The important thing, however, is that, by comparison, there is the silence in **[page 4]** the Statute of the ICTY plus the express exclusionary language of paragraph 121 of the accompanying report of the Secretary-General.

11. It is obvious that paragraph 121 of the Secretary-General's report has to be regarded as conveying the intention of the Security Council that imprisonment in the case of the ICTY could only be done outside the territory of the former Yugoslavia. The Appeals Chamber cannot go behind that view. Accordingly, if the Appeals Chamber is competent to pass on the reasons why Montenegro has not been designated, it can only find in favour of the correctness of the reasons given in paragraph 121 of the Secretary-General's report.

D. Four possible objections

12. It is necessary to consider some objections. First, it is said that imprisonment in Montenegro would be possible if the appellant were sentenced by a court in that state under the referral procedure of Rule 11*bis* of the Rules as authorised by the Security Council. That is true. But I am not able to accept that the introduction of the referral procedure amounts to an implied modification by the Security Council of the procedure applicable where a sentence is imposed by the Tribunal itself. The appellant was not sentenced under the referral procedure. Whether the referral procedure could have been employed depended on a number of contingencies which are not pertinent to the procedure under which the appellant was in fact sentenced by the Tribunal.

13. Second, it is also said that there are international conventions which enjoin imprisonment in a convicted person's home state. But those conventions regulate relations as between states. The Tribunal is not a party to them. It can be bound by the principles of the conventions if these had the force of customary international law. But, though the conventions may represent the practice of many states, the status of customary international law is, correctly, not claimed for the conventions.

14. Third, it is argued that the Tribunal has to take account of the fact that the wartime conditions which gave birth to it have now ceased. It is not said that the exercise of the Tribunal's jurisdiction comes to an end with the restoration of peace. Peace may well require the continued exercise of jurisdiction to punish serious violations of international humanitarian law which previously occurred; and the conditions regulating the exercise of that jurisdiction need not be affected. Nothing in chapter 7 of the Charter (under which the Tribunal was established) or in Security Council resolution 827 (1993) (which established the Tribunal) supports the contention under reference. **[page 5]**

15. In *Erdemović* (decided in 1996), a Trial Chamber did seem to link imprisonment in a state outside the territory of the former Yugoslavia to "the situation prevailing in that region";[5] but the Trial Chamber did not suggest that imprisonment in a state forming part of the territory of the former Yugoslavia could be proper if, by itself, it was of the view that there was a change in "the situation prevailing in that region". The Trial Chamber said that it "share[d] the view of the Secretary-General that the sentences should be served outside of the former Yugoslavia".[6] I do not consider that it is the law that the Appeals Chamber can, on its own, say whether the security considerations underlying the Secretary-General's view (as, in my opinion, endorsed by the Security Council) have ceased to operate.

16. Fourth, it is also argued that the Tribunal may act on the basis of humanitarian considerations. Accepting the general influence of such considerations, yet it seems to me that they do not constitute an admissible ground for the particular action proposed in this case; they do not operate *in vacuo.* There must first be a designation by the President of the Tribunal of the state in question as a state in which a sentence of imprisonment may be served. In the absence of a designation of Montenegro, there cannot be imprisonment in that state – on any ground, humanitarian ones included.

5 IT-96-22-T, 29 November 1996, para. 70.

6 *Ibid.*

E. <u>Conclusion</u>

17. In the result, I am of opinion that today's decision is correct.

Done in English and in French, the English text being authoritative.

7 June 2007
The Hague
The Netherlands

Mohamed Shahabuddeen

[Seal of the International Tribunal] [page 1]

DISSENTING OPINION OF JUDGE SCHOMBURG

A. Introduction

1. With all due respect, I do not agree with the decision. The Trial Judgement has become final. Neither the Statute of the International Tribunal ("Statute") nor the Rules of Procedure and Evidence of the International Tribunal ("Rules") allow for a "reopening" of appellate proceedings. Moreover, an informed withdrawal of an appeal cannot be revoked. With respect to the enforcement of Mr. Strugar's sentence, there are no legal obstacles preventing him from serving the sentence in his home country Montenegro, especially when his request is based on exceptional humanitarian reasons.

2. When deciding to withdraw his appeal, Mr. Strugar was fully informed about the factual and legal situation which has not changed since then. He was well-aware that there could be obstacles to his transfer to Montenegro. It is regrettable that the President of the International Tribunal, who is pursuant to Rule 103 of the Rules the only competent authority to decide whether Mr. Strugar can be transferred to his home country, has not exercised his discretionary power to explicitly decide this matter. Thus, the case should have been first referred to the President for the sole purpose of letting him exercise his discretion "as soon as possible" (Rule 103(B)). Accordingly, there are no reasons allowing for a "reopening" of the appeal.

B. Finality of the Trial Judgement

3. Objectively and subjectively there are no new facts that might allow for a review of the Appeals Chamber's decision of 20 September 2006, which explicitly and unanimously accepted the mutual withdrawal of the appeals for extraordinary humanitarian reasons. Indeed, the decision provided that with the withdrawal of the parties' appeals "the sentence of eight years imposed on Pavle Strugar in the Trial Judgement has become final."[1] I recall the jurisprudence of the International Tribunal, which holds the following:

> The Appeals Chamber is satisfied that the existing appeal and review proceedings established under the Statute provide sufficient guarantees to persons convicted before this Tribunal that they have been tried fairly and in accordance with norms of due process. [...] This Appeals Chamber holds that there is no power to reconsider a final judgement.[2] **[page 2]**

There the Appeals Chamber considered, *inter alia*, that the interests of both the victims and the perpetrator entitle them to certainty and finality of legal judgements.[3] The only possibility to challenge a judgement that has become final is the review procedure as provided by the Statute and the Rules. However, in this case, the preconditions for the institution of review proceedings have not been met. There is no other legal basis on which the Appeals Chamber could base its decision resulting in a renewed challenge to the factual and legal findings of the Trial Judgement. By allowing the "reopening" of the appeals the Appeals Chamber circumvents the high threshold guaranteeing the finality of proceedings before the International Tribunal.

C. The legal situation with regard to Mr. Strugar serving his sentence in Montenegro for humanitarian reasons

4. The Appeals Chamber presumes that there is "no legal possibility that [Mr. Strugar] could serve his sentence in Montenegro."[4] The Appeals Chamber in this regard seems to defer to the view of the Registrar,

---

[1] Final Decision on "Defence Notice of Withdrawing Appeal" and "Withdrawal of Prosecution's Appeal Against the Judgement of Trial Chamber II Dated 31 January 2005," 20 September 2006 ("Decision Accepting Withdrawals"), p. 2.

[2] *Prosecutor v. Zoran Žigić*, Case No. IT-98-30/1-A, Decision on Zoran Žigić's 'Motion for Reconsideration of the Appeals Chamber Judgement IT-98-30/1-A Delivered on 28 February 2005', 26 June 2006, para. 9.

[3] *Id.*

[4] Decision, para. 28.

laid out in his letter of 15 March 2007.[5] In this letter, "verified with the Office of Legal Affairs at UN Headquarters," the Registrar claims that the Report of the Secretary-General of 1993[6] bars the transfer of sentenced person to one of the States on the territory of the former Yugoslavia.[7]

5. However, the independent judiciary of the International Tribunal is not bound by the legal opinion of the Registrar, which in this concrete case is apparently itself based on an opinion given by the executive. In particular, the view expressed in the Registrar's letter is a) not binding upon the President and b) not correct in substance. There certainly is a possibility to enforce Mr. Strugar's sentence in Montenegro, in particular in this case where all the decisions have been and should be based on exceptional humanitarian reasons. **[page 3]**

1. The judiciary is not bound by a legal opinion of the Registrar

6. Article 27 of the Statute solely stipulates that

> Imprisonment shall be served in a State designated by the International Tribunal from a list of States which have indicated to the Security Council their willingness to accept convicted persons. [...].[8]

Rule 103 of the Rules specifies that

> Imprisonment shall be served in a State designated by the *President of the Tribunal* from a list of States which have indicated their willingness to accept convicted persons.[9]

7. It is therefore plain that the authority to decide where a sentence handed down by the International Tribunal is enforced lies, pursuant to Rule 103(A) of the Rules, with the President of the Tribunal, *i.e.* a part of the judiciary. It is the President – not the Registrar – who has finally to determine the place of imprisonment. This is further supported by a more general consideration. The Registrar, pursuant to Article 17(1) of the Statute, is "responsible for the administration and servicing of the International Tribunal." He is thus expected to implement the decision of the Chambers or, in this case, of the President. The designation of where a convicted person shall serve his sentence touches on the fundamental rights of a convicted person at the end of the proceedings against him and must accordingly be made by the independent judiciary.

8. The legal advice provided by the Registrar is indispensable for the functioning of the Tribunal. However, this cannot mean that the Appeals Chamber or the President is bound by a legal opinion offered by the Registrar. In particular, if the Appeals Chamber or the President considers that the Registrar's legal views on a subject pertaining to the core functions of the judiciary, such as the designation of the State where the sentence is to be served, are at odds with the correct interpretation of the law, then the views of the Appeals Chamber or the President must prevail.

9. It is indeed the Registrar who concludes general enforcement agreements with States that are willing to accept convicted persons. The usual procedure is for States to enter into a general agreement with the Tribunal. It is true that there is no such general agreement with Montenegro. However, there have been cases in the past where convicted persons were transferred to a State without the existence of such a general enforcement agreement,[10] based on bilateral arrangements **[page 4]** concluded on a case-to-

---

5 *See* Annex 8 of the Defence Request Seeking the Re-Opening of Appeal Proceedings Before the Appeals Chamber, 26 March 2007 ("Defence Request").

6 The Secretary-General, *Report of the Secretary-General Pursuant to Paragraph 2 of Security Council Resolution 808 (1993)*, U.N. Doc. S/25704 (3 May 1993).

7 *See* Decision, para 27: "[...] an assumption that is rejected in the Registry's Letter of 15 March 2007."

8 It has to be noted that Article 27 does not exclude any country. The aforementioned Report of the Secretary-General has not found its way into the Statute.

9 Italics added for emphasis. Again, there is no limitation of States enforcing the sentence, and as will be explained later, practice shows that the International Tribunal has already in the past concluded enforcement agreements with States that are not on the Registrar's list.

10 The enforcement of the sentences of Duško Tadić and Dragoljub Kunarac is based on an *ad-hoc* enforcement agreement, concluded in the form of an exchange of letters by the Registrar and the German Ambassador to the Netherlands. *See* for Tadić, Exchange of Notes between the International Tribunal and Germany of 17 October 2000 and for Kunarac, Exchange of Notes between the International Tribunal and Germany of 14 November 2002.

case basis according to the practice in cooperation in criminal matters in general. Moreover, in this case Montenegro has explicitly expressed its willingness to conclude a bilateral arrangement with the Tribunal.[11] Consequently, the Registrar cannot be allowed to tie the hands of the judiciary by not trying to negotiate an agreement with Montenegro, even though it is the apparent wish of the Appeals Chamber, accepted by the Prosecution, that Mr. Strugar's sentence be enforced there for exceptional humanitarian reasons. Only the absence of detention facilities which meet the United Nations' standards[12] or a substantial likelihood that the sentence would be served in a sham prison could be an obstacle to such an arrangement.[13]

10. In sum, the Registrar's view, as expressed in its letter of 15 March 2007, may be considered by the President but does not have a binding effect on him. Furthermore, it is for the President to exercise the discretion vested in him and rule on the request of Mr. Strugar to be transferred to Montenegro.

2. The Registrar's assessment of the legal situation

11. In his letter of 15 March 2007, the Registrar referred to Security Council Resolution 827 "accepting the Secretary-General's report in which it is stated that 'the enforcement of sentences should take place outside the territory of the former Yugoslavia'".[14] The Registrar further explained that he had "verified with the Office of Legal Affairs at U.N. Headquarters that [this] places a geographical restriction" on the enforcement of sentences handed down by the International Tribunal and that therefore "the Tribunal is presently not in a position to conclude an agreement for enforcement of sentences with the Republic of Montenegro."[15]

12. I disagree with this assessment of the legal situation. The Report of the Secretary-General is not an impediment to the transfer of a person convicted by the International Tribunal to his home country for exceptional humanitarian reasons. Indeed, customary international law and a historical, systematic and teleological interpretation of the Secretary-General's Report do allow for the enforcement on the territory of the former Yugoslavia of sentences handed down by the **[page 5]** International Tribunal. Moreover, the Report of the Secretary-General does not bind the International Tribunal, or, in particular, its independent judiciary.

(a) Applicable international law

13. The recommendation that the enforcement of sentences should not take place on the territory of the former Yugoslavia does not reflect international law.[16] The treaty-based common State practice and international humanitarian law allow for a sentenced person, if he so wishes, to serve the sentence in his home country.

14. Several international conventions have provisions stipulating that sentences have to be enforced in the home country of the convicted persons. Those conventions and international treaties are ratified by a large number of States around the globe. It is the common practice of States to cooperate internationally when it comes to transferring convicted persons to their home countries.

15. I note that the International Tribunal is not party to any of those conventions. However, it cannot operate completely detached from the State practice of the international community which they reflect. Indeed, for humanitarian reasons, an accused who was charged and convicted elsewhere would obviously

---

11 *See* Decision, para. 9.

12 *See* United Nations Standard Minimum Rules for the Treatment of Prisoners, adopted by the First United Nations Congress on the Prevention of Crime and the Treatment of Offenders, held at Geneva in 1955, U.N. Doc. A/CONF/611, Annex 1

13 I note that Mr. Strugar was previously allowed to be medically treated in Montenegro, that though on provisional release he spent this time under detention conditions, and that he voluntarily returned to the seat of the Tribunal ahead of schedule.

14 Report of the Secretary-General, *supra* note 6, para. 121.

15 Letter of the Registrar of 15 March 2007 (Annex 8 of the Defence Request).

16 It is instructive to recall the rationale behind this recommendation. It reflects – as will be shown later – only the fact that at the time of the drafting of the Secretary-General's Report there was still war on the territory of the former Yugoslavia: no reasonable person would have sent convicted persons to the region at that time. However, time has passed, the war is over, and this exception to general State practice is no longer relevant.

benefit from the provisions of these conventions. He cannot be deprived of the rights granted therein solely because he was convicted by the International Tribunal.

16. The most important treaty in this context is the **Council of Europe's Convention on the Transfer of Sentenced Persons** of 21 March 1983.[17] Its relevant provisions read:

> **Preamble**
>
> [...] Considering that these objectives require that foreigners who are deprived of their liberty as a result of their commission of a criminal offence should be given the opportunity to serve their sentences within their own society; and [...]
>
> **Article 2:** General principles
>
> (1) The Parties undertake to afford each other the widest measure of cooperation in respect of the transfer of sentenced persons in accordance with the provisions of this Convention.
>
> (2) A person sentenced in the territory of a Party may be transferred to the territory of another Party, in accordance with the provisions of this Convention, in order to serve the sentence imposed on him. To that end, he may express his interest to the sentencing State or to the administering State in being transferred under this Convention.
>
> (3) Transfer may be requested by either the sentencing State or the administering State. **[page 6]**

This convention is an instrument whose application is not restricted to just Europe,[18] and it has been ratified by more than sixty countries around the world, *inter alia*, Australia, Bahamas, Bolivia, Canada, Chile, Costa Rica, Ecuador, Israel, Japan, Korea, Mauritius, Mexico, Panama, Tonga, Trinidad and Tobago, the United States of America, and Venezuela.[19] According to the convention's Explanatory Report, primary objectives of this convention are the following humanitarian reasons:

> As penal policy has come to lay greater emphasis upon the social rehabilitation of offenders, it may be of paramount importance that the sanction imposed on the offender is enforced in his home country rather than in the State where the offence was committed and the judgment rendered. This policy is also rooted in humanitarian considerations: difficulties in communication by reason of language barriers, alienation from local culture and customs, and the absence of contacts with relatives may have detrimental effects on the foreign prisoner. The repatriation of sentenced persons may therefore be in the best interests of the prisoners as well as of the governments concerned.[20]

17. On the basis of these objectives, the Committee of Ministers, the Council of Europe's decision-making body, adopted a recommendation to member States, which reads as follows:

> [...] Restating the importance of social rehabilitation of sentenced persons and to that end the transfer of such persons, where they do not have the nationality of the sentencing state, to the country where their own society is; [...]
>
> (1) Recommends the governments of member states:
>
> [...] (b) to proceed diligently and urgently in processing requests for transfer in such a way that the provisions of Article 5, paragraph 4, of the convention are entirely complied with; [...][21]

18. As regards the United Nations, only the most recent and important convention will be referred to, namely, the **United Nations Convention against Transnational Organized Crime** of 15 November 2000 (Palermo I). This convention was primarily drafted to promote international cooperation in order to prevent

---

17 CETS No. 112.

18 It should be noted that Montenegro has already acceded to this convention.

19 http://conventions.coe.int/Treaty/Commun/ChercheSig.asp?NT=112&CM=8&DF=5/25/2007&CL=ENG.

20 http://conventions.coe.int/Treaty/en/Reports/Html/112.htm, para. 9.

21 Recommendation No. R (92) 18 of the Committee of Minister of Member States Concerning the Practical Application of the Convention on the Transfer of Sentenced Persons (adopted on 19 October 1992).

and combat serious transnational organized crime. The Convention, ratified by more than 130 States, including Montenegro,[22] includes the following provisions:

> **Article 17:** Transfer of Sentenced Persons
>
> States Partied may consider entering into bilateral or multilateral agreements or arrangements on the transfer to their territory of persons sentenced to imprisonment or other forms of deprivation of liberty for offences covered by this Convention, in order that they may complete their sentences there.

19. Both the United Nations and the Council of Europe demand or at least encourage the repatriation of a convicted person to his home country. This standard of international humanitarian **[page 7]** law is also reflected in the Statutes and Rules of Procedure and Evidence of other international criminal courts and tribunals.

20. The Statute of the **International Criminal Tribunal for Rwanda** (ICTR), which was adopted by the Security Council about one year after the establishment of this Tribunal, reads:

> **Article 26:** Enforcement of Sentence
>
> Imprisonment shall be served *in Rwanda* or any of the States on a list of States which have indicated to the Security Council their willingness to accept convicted persons, as designated by the International Tribunal for Rwanda. Such imprisonment shall be in accordance with the applicable law of the State concerned, subject to the supervision of the International Tribunal for Rwanda.[23]

The ICTR Rules of Procedure and Evidence read:

> **Rule 103:** Place of Imprisonment
>
> (A) Imprisonment shall be served *in Rwanda* or any State designated by the Tribunal from a list of States which have indicated their willingness to accept convicted persons for the serving of sentences. Prior to a decision on the place of imprisonment, the Chamber shall notify the Government of Rwanda.
>
> (B) Transfer of the convicted person to that State shall be effected as soon as possible after the time limit for appeal has elapsed.

The ICTR's Statute and Rules explicitly envisage transfer to Rwanda, the home country of most of the accused in its jurisdiction. It is significant that the legal framework of the second international tribunal established by the Security Council encompasses this option. Indeed, in contrast to the situation in the former Yugoslavia in 1993, there was no ongoing war on the territory of Rwanda at the time of the ICTR's establishment which would have prevented the enforcement of sentences for safety reasons.

21. Although there is not yet an agreement in place with the Rwandan government on the transfer of persons sentenced by the ICTR to Rwanda,[24] this is primarily because of the risk that the death penalty could be executed for other crimes not contained in the ICTR Statute or not charged by the ICTR. It is not a reflection of the original intention of the drafters of the Statute and Rules.[25] **[page 8]**

22. The Statute of the **Special Court for Sierra Leone**,[26] attached to a special agreement between the United Nations and Sierra Leone, reads:

---

22 http://www.unodc.org/unodc/en/crime_cicp_signatures_convention.html.

23 Italics added for emphasis.

24 For the same reason, no case has yet been transferred to Rwanda pursuant to Rule 11*bis* of the ICTR's Rules of Procedure and Evidence as the abolition of the death penalty is still pending in Rwanda, the non-execution of the death penalty being one prerequisite under Rule 11*bis*(C) of the ICTR Rules as amended on 7 June 2005.

25 *See* The Secretary-General, *Report of the Secretary-General Pursuant to Paragraph 5 of Security Council Resolution 955 (1994)*, U.N. Doc. S/1995/134, 13 February 1995, at para. 19: "Unlike the former Yugoslavia, Rwanda is not excluded from the list of States where prison sentences pronounced by the International Tribunal for Rwanda may be served." As indicated already, a similar solution was not possible neither in 1993 nor in 1995 for the former Yugoslavia as there was, in contrast to Rwanda, still an ongoing war.

26 2178 U.N.T.S. 138.

Article 22: Enforcement of Sentences

(1) Imprisonment shall be served *in Sierra Leone*. If circumstances so require, imprisonment may also be served in any of the States which have concluded with the International Criminal Tribunal for Rwanda or the International Criminal Tribunal for the former Yugoslavia an agreement for the enforcement of sentences, and which have indicated to the Registrar of the Special Court their willingness to accept convicted persons. The Special Court may conclude similar agreements for the enforcement of sentences with other States.

(2) Conditions of imprisonment, whether *in Sierra Leone* or in a third State, shall be governed by the law of the State of enforcement subject to the supervision of the Special Court. The State of enforcement shall be bound by the duration of the sentence, subject to Article 23 of the present Statute.[27]

The Rules of Procedure and Evidence read:

Rule 103: Place of Imprisonment

(A) Imprisonment shall be served *in Sierra Leone*, unless circumstances require otherwise. The Special Court may conclude agreements with other countries willing to accept and imprison convicted persons.

(B) The place of imprisonment for each convicted person shall be designated by the *President*.

(C) Transfer of the convicted person to the place of imprisonment shall be effected as soon as possible after the time limit for appeal has lapsed. [28]

Indeed, the Report of the Secretary-General on the establishment of the Special Court explicitly mentioned that sentences should normally be served in Sierra Leone unless there are security issues.[29]

23. The **International Criminal Court**[30] can be seized of cases concerning individuals from an unpredictable number of States. Its Statute neither specifies nor excludes any specific country in which the sentences should be enforced. Rather, it sets out different factors that have to be taken into consideration when determining the State in which the sentence is to be enforced. Significantly, these include the views of the sentenced person and the nationality of the sentenced person. The respective provisions in the Statute read:

Article 103: Role of the States in enforcement of sentences of imprisonment **[page 9]**

(1) (a) A sentence of imprisonment shall be served in a State designated by the Court from a list of States which have indicated to the Court their willingness to accept sentenced persons. [...]

(3) In exercising its discretion to make a designation under paragraph 1, the Court shall take into account the following:

(a) The principle that States Parties should share the responsibility for enforcing sentences of imprisonment, in accordance with principle of equitable distribution, as provided in the Rules of Procedure and Evidence;

(b) *The application of widely accepted international treaty standards governing the treatment of prisoners*;

(c) *The views of the sentenced person*;

(d) *The nationality of the sentenced person*;

---

27 Italics added for emphasis.

28 Italics added for emphasis.

29 *See* The Secretary General, *Report of the Secretary-General on the Establishment of a Special Court for Sierra Leone*, U.N. Doc. S/2000/915, 4 October 2000, at para. 49: "While imprisonment shall normally be served in Sierra Leone, particular circumstances, such as the security risk entailed in the continued imprisonment of some of the convicted persons on Sierra Leonean territory, may require their relocation to a third State."

30 2187 U.N.T.S. 90.

(e) Such other factors regarding the circumstances of the crime or the person sentenced, or the effective enforcement of the sentence, as may be appropriate in designating the State of enforcement. [...][31]

24. In this context, it also has to be recalled that already in 1946, under the system in place before the first international criminal courts, the International Military Tribunals at Nuremberg and Tokyo, prison sentences were enforced in Germany and in Japan, respectively, *i.e.* the home countries of the perpetrators.[32]

(b) Political Situation in the territory of the former Yugoslavia in 1993

25. As was pointed out above, according to international humanitarian law, sentences should be enforced in the home country of the convicted person, wherever possible. The Report of the Secretary-General related to the ICTY has to be seen in light of the political situation in the former Yugoslavia at the time it was drafted, *i.e.* 1993, when armed conflict on the territory of the former Yugoslavia was still ongoing. It was indeed reasonable not to enforce the sentences handed down by the International Tribunal at a time when there was war, as this would have risked the lives of the sentenced persons. Moreover, there were serious doubts about the functioning of a regular prison regime and a judiciary supervising detention conditions, heightening the risk of interference with the enforcement of sentences if imprisonment were served on the territory of the former Yugoslavia.[33] However, the opinion of the Secretary-General has never found its way into the Statute, thus leaving the State of enforcement to a reasonable decision of the International Tribunal **[page 10]** when the circumstances so allowed, and indeed, the circumstances have changed fundamentally since 1993.[34]

26. Today's different political situation was also the prerequisite for the introduction of the current version of Rule 11*bis* of the Rules in 2002. According to this provision it is possible, *inter alia*, to refer a case to a State in whose territory the crime was committed "so that those authorities should forthwith refer the case to the appropriate court for trial within that State." Once a case is referred, it will be heard under the laws of the respective State. As a result, a sentence imposed by a court of that State is enforced on its territory. This mechanism is explicitly supported by the Security Council in its Resolution 1534 (2004) reads:

> *Commends* those States which have concluded agreements for the enforcement of sentences of persons convicted by the ICTY or the ICTR or have otherwise accepted such convicted persons to serve their sentences in their respective territories; *encourages other States in a position to so to act likewise*; and invites the ICTY and ICTR to continue and intensify their efforts to conclude further agreements for the enforcement of sentences or to obtain the cooperation of other States in this regard; [...]
>
> *Welcomes* in particular the efforts of the Office of the High Representative, ICTY, and the donor community to create a war crimes chamber *in Sarajevo*; encourages all parties to continue efforts to establish the chamber

31 Italics added for emphasis.

32 The only difference between both Tribunals was that in the case of the Nuremberg Tribunal it was the four occupying powers that shared the joint responsibility for the enforcement of the sentences. At Tokyo, this task was given to Japan itself.

33 *See* 1 Virginia Morris & Michael P. Scharf, An Insider's Guide to the International Criminal Tribunal for the Former Yugoslavia p. 304 (1995).

34 I also note that even when the creation of the ICTY was discussed, the Russian proposal to establish an international tribunal provided that "a judgement shall be executed in the State in whose territory the crime was committed, or in the State of which the perpetrator is a national." *Letter Dated 5 April 1993 from the Permanent Representative of the Russian Federation to the United Nations Addressed to the Secretary-General*, U.N. Doc. S/25537, p. 11. In a similar vein, Article 46(1) of the Conference on Security and Cooperation in Europe (CSCE) Draft Convention on an International War Crimes Tribunal for the former Yugoslavia, stipulated that "[p]enalties are to be enforced on behalf of the Court in a State party to this Convention which is a successor State to the former Yugoslavia." *See* Rapporteurs (Corell-Türk-Thune) under the CSCE Moscow Human Dimension Mechanism to Bosnia-Herzegovina and Croatia, *Proposal for an International War Crimes Tribunal for the Former Yugoslavia*, 9 February 1993, printed in 2 Morris & Scharf, *supra* note 33, p. 293. Indeed, in the explanatory section to the proposed convention, it was stated as follows: "A major issue is to decide where imprisonment is to be served. The Rapporteurs [to the CSCE] hold the view that the rule should be – subject to a narrow field of exception – that the sentences shall be served in the territory of the former Yugoslavia (cf. Article 46). This undoubtedly puts a heavy burden on the States in that territory. But unless they are prepared to take upon themselves to accept enforcement, the Rapporteurs see little possibility that justice can be done in the present case [...]." *Id.*, p. 264–265. It is thus clear that the Report of the Secretary-General was not based on normal State practice but followed strictly pragmatic considerations.

> expeditiously; and encourages the donor community to provide sufficient financial support to ensure the success of domestic prosecutions in Bosnia and Herzegovina and in the region; […].[35]

I note that the Security Council did not exclude any State from accepting convicted persons to serve their sentences in their territories according to international humanitarian law.

27. Rule 11*bis* of the Rules, which was implicitly endorsed by Security Council Resolution 1534 (2004), recognizes that the political situation on the territory of the former Yugoslavia has changed substantially. Moreover, if it is legally possible to refer an entire case to the territory of the former Yugoslavia, including the enforcement of the sentence in the event of a conviction, it can be concluded, *a maiore ad minus,* that the States on the territory of the former Yugoslavia can now be **[page 11]** entrusted with the enforcement of sentences. In particular, Resolution 1534 (2004) must be viewed in light of the *lex posterior derogat priori* principle, *i.e.* although the Security Council concurred with the Report of the Secretary-General in 1993, it later explicitly departed from the Report's suggestion not to send convicted persons to the territory of the former Yugoslavia.

(c) Separation of Powers

28. Furthermore, the 1993 Report of the Secretary-General, while providing guidance, does not have a binding force. I am aware that the principle of the separation of powers cannot yet be applied to international law in exactly the same way as it is applied in domestic systems. However, we are required to maintain and, where it is not yet recognized, to establish the independence of the judiciary in so far as possible.[36] This was already recognized by the Trial Chamber in the *Tadić* case:

> The International Tribunal has, as its Statutes and Rules attest, been constituted so as to ensure a fair trial to an accused and it is to be hoped that the way its Judges administer their jurisdiction will leave no room for complaints about lack of impartiality or want of independence.[37]

As judges we are bound only by the Statute and the Rules. The Report of the Secretary-General is of a *quasi* executive nature and it became with its approval by the Security Council a legislative source of guidance. It has to be reemphasized that the passage that considers that sentences may only be enforced outside the territory of the former Yugoslavia is not reflected in the wording of the Statute or the Rules. It may therefore only be taken into consideration as a non-binding opinion which facilitates interpretation of the applicable provisions under the prevailing circumstances at that time. However, it can never be obligatory for the independent judiciary to follow the Report's recommendations.

29. As already pointed out, the authority and hence the duty to decide where a sentence is enforced lies solely with the President of the Tribunal, acting as a body of the judiciary. This discretionary power has to be exercised as fundamental rights of the convicted person are at stake. If the convicted person wishes to have his sentenced enforced in his home country, humanitarian aspects have to be taken into consideration as well. In this context, the German Constitutional Court (*Bundesverfassungsgericht* – BVerfG) dealt with the question of legal protection and remedies of convicted persons who sought to have their sentences enforced in their home country. Significantly, **[page 12]** the Court emphasized the importance of safeguarding the dignity of the sentenced person when reaching the discretionary decision. The Constitutional Court held:

> The legal status of a person sentenced to a term of imprisonment is basically determined by his or her entitlement to rehabilitation […]. The objective of rehabilitation is in keeping with the image which a community subscribing to principles of human dignity and the social state has of itself. This ensures, when discretionary decisions are taken in the field of enforcement, that **the sentenced person is entitled to the**

35 S.C. Res. 1534, U.N. Doc. S/RES/1534 (26 March 2004), paras 8 and 10 (italics added for emphasis).

36 I refer to Montesquieu who stated as follows: "Il n'y a point encore de liberté, si la puissance de juger n'est pas séparée de la puissance législative & de l'exécutrice. Si elle étoit jointe à la puissance législative, le pouvoir sur la vie & la liberté des citoyens seroit arbitraire ; car le juge seroit législateur. Si elle étoit jointe à la puissance exécutrice, le juge pourroit avoir la force d'un oppresseur. Charles-Louis de Secondat, Baron de la Brède et de Montesquieu, L'Esprit des Loix, Livre XI, Chapitre VI (Nouvelle Edition, printed 1767).

37 *Prosecutor v. Duško Tadić*, Case No. IT-94-1, Decision on the Defence Motion on Jurisdiction, 10 August 1995, para. 32.

> **proper exercise of such discretion by the authorities**. This entitlement also encompasses the question from the point of view of enforcement legislation of whether the sentenced person is to be transferred to his or her homeland in order to serve sentence, which must be considered separately from the question of enforcement.
>
> If the sentenced person expresses the wish under the Convention on the Transfer of Sentenced Persons to be transferred to his or her homeland in order to serve the sentenced passed, the public prosecutor[38] must weigh the sentenced person's interest in social rehabilitation against the requirements of the administration of justice (including from the point of view of enforcement practice in the host state). This decision process allows the enforcement authorities to take account of the sentenced person's entitlement to probation when exercising its discretion. In this respect, the sentenced person is entitled to the proper exercise of their discretion by the enforcement authorities.[39]

30. Consequently, it is for the President to explicitly decide the matter of Mr. Strugar's possible transfer to Montenegro. Thus, the approach taken by the Appeals Chamber to declare Mr. Strugar's transfer to Montenegro legally impossible is premature because Mr. Strugar is first entitled to obtain an explicit decision by the only competent authority of the International Tribunal, *i.e.* the President.[40]

3. Preliminary conclusion: there is the legal possibility to transfer Mr. Strugar to Montenegro

31. It would have been legally possible to enforce Mr. Strugar's sentence in Montenegro. The Tribunal could have entered into a bilateral arrangement with Montenegro, as offered by Montenegro, and as it has been done on previous occasions with another State.[41]

32. Considering the exceptional humanitarian situation in the case at hand, a bilateral agreement would indeed have been warranted. While recognizing that the Registrar prefers to negotiate more general enforcement agreements, it is still possible to agree upon agreements relating to only one specific case. This has been the practice, for example, in the cases where Germany agreed to enforce sentences imposed by this Tribunal. As noted above, Montenegro has offered to enter into **[page 13]** such an agreement. Naturally, Montenegro would be required to offer detention conditions that comply with the demands of the United Nations;[42] and there could be no sham detention.

33. I therefore regret that the President of this Tribunal as the only competent authority has not taken a decision. In my view, a humanitarian solution tailor-made for this case only would have been an appropriate solution in Mr. Strugar's case, this being in line with the expressed opinions of the parties and the understanding of the Appeals Chamber at that time when it accepted the mutual withdrawal of the appeals.

34. It has to be noted that there is always a system of supervision in place. In particular, if the detention conditions do not meet the aforementioned standards of the United Nations or are revealed as a mere sham detention, the President is entitled to revoke a transfer decision and order the re-transfer of a convicted person to the seat of the Tribunal or to another State.

D. Mr. Strugar made an informed decision

35. The decision considers that Mr. Strugar's withdrawal of his appeal was not informed "due to a misunderstanding of the options *legally available* in his situation."[43] As stated before, in particular where exceptional humanitarian reasons exist, there were and are no legal obstacles to the transfer of Mr. Strugar

---

[38] The competent authority in the framework of the International Tribunal is the President.

[39] Bundesverfassungsgericht [BVerfG] [Federal Constitutional Court] 18 June 1997, 96 Entscheidungen des Bundesverfassungsgerichts [BVerfGE] 100, para. 87 (references omitted) bold for emphasis.

[40] I note that according to general legal practice a non-decision cannot be regarded as a decision if the law demands that an explicit decision is taken. Indeed, Rule 103 of the Rules presupposes such a decision. It is hardly conceivable that the State in which the convicted person will serve his sentence is designated in the absence of any decision on that matter.

[41] *See supra* note 10.

[42] *See* in particular, United Nations Standard Minimum Rules for the Treatment of Prisoners, *supra* note 12.

[43] Decision, para. 29 (italics added for emphasis).

to Montenegro. Consequently, there could not have been a misunderstanding of the legal options available to him. Mr. Strugar clearly and rightly so believed that *legally* it would be possible for him to serve his sentence in Montenegro.

36. Moreover, Mr. Strugar was informed of the *factual* obstacle that the Registrar adheres to a different legal opinion and accordingly would be unlikely to make efforts by his own volition to secure Mr. Strugar's transfer to Montenegro. It is clear from the Rule 65*ter* Meetings, the Status Conferences and the extensive communications between the parties, the Chamber, and the Registrar, that Mr. Strugar was well-aware of the fact that no guarantees on his transfer could be offered. I recall in particular the letter of the Registrar of 22 May 2006, in which he stated that "[t]he enforcement of a sentence in Montenegro would currently be subject to a number of important legal and other obstacles, which would need to be removed."[44] What Mr. Strugar believed was that the President (who at that time was the Presiding Judge in the appellate proceedings) as the competent authority would make every effort to facilitate his transfer to Montenegro. This hope unfortunately did not materialize. However, it cannot be said that Mr. Strugar was not put on notice **[page 14]** by the Appeals Chamber and the Registrar. Thus he was aware of the uncertainties in relation to a possible transfer to Montenegro.[45] Nevertheless, he made a voluntary and fully informed decision to withdraw his appeal, no doubt also with a view to the fact that the Prosecution withdrew its appeal as well.

37. Finally, I wonder with concern how a bench composed of four of the five judges that unanimously accepted the withdrawal of the appeal as an informed one[46] can come more than nine months later to the conclusion that neither Mr. Strugar[47] nor the former bench[48] was informed. Indeed, in light of the Registrar's letter of 22 May 2006, the entire bench was aware that the Registrar had expressed the opinion that the enforcement of Mr. Strugar's sentence in his home country faced "a number of important legal and other obstacles"[49] when it made its decision that unanimously accepted the mutual withdrawal of the parties' appeals. The legal and factual basis for Mr. Strugar's decision to withdraw his appeal and for the Appeals Chamber's acceptance of this decision has not changed since the decision accepting the withdrawal was rendered.

E. Conclusion

38. In sum, I respectfully disagree with the majority of the Appeals Chamber and would not have granted Mr. Strugar's request to "reopen" his appeal case and the corresponding request by the Prosecution. Mr. Strugar was sentenced by the Trial Chamber to eight years of imprisonment. For exceptional humanitarian reasons both Mr. Strugar and the Prosecution withdrew their appeals. With the acceptance of the parties' withdrawals of their appeals, the Trial Judgement has become final. Mr. Strugar was fully informed of any obstacles that could possibly prevent his transfer to Montenegro. The Chamber, also for humanitarian reasons in this exceptional case, accepted the mutual withdrawal of the parties' appeals. Consequently, Mr. Strugar was entitled to an explicit decision by the President. A convicted person like Mr. Strugar should not be left in limbo.[50] That is why Rule 103 provides that the decision by the President should be taken "as soon as possible." However, there is no legal basis for the Appeals Chamber to try to resolve the uncertainty by "reopening" the appeals. **[page 15]**

39. As a matter of principle, the withdrawal of the appeals cannot be revoked. This was emphasized during the Status Conference and explicitly accepted by Mr. Strugar.[51] The Appeals Chamber is not in a position to decide whether it is legally possible for Mr. Strugar to be transferred to Montenegro as this authority solely lies with the President. In my mind, the only correct course of action would have been to refer the matter to

---

[44] Letter of the Registrar of 22 May 2006, Annex 4 of the Defence Request. I note that Strugar's knowledge was also confirmed by his Counsel's e-mail to the Chamber of 26 May 2006 (Annex 7 of the Defence Request).

[45] *See* also the warnings given to Mr. Strugar in the Status Conference, Transcript pp. 61, 65 (31 August 2006).

[46] The at that time Presiding Judge has decided in his capacity as President not assign himself to the bench again.

[47] As quoted directly in footnote 39 of the Decision, it reads in the Decision Accepting Withdrawals, supra note 1, p. 1, that emphasizing that "Pavle Strugar [...] confirmed the following: 'I am aware of all the legal consequences of [the notice of withdrawal] including the fact that once the appeal is withdrawn there is no possibility of subsequent reconsideration of the judgment, pursuant to which I am convicted, and having the same abolished or altered in my favor.'"

[48] The transcripts of all Status Conferences and the minutes of all Rule 65*ter*(I) Meetings were served on all members of the bench by separate memoranda in compliance with Rules 65t*er*(J) and 107 of the Rules.

[49] Letter of the Registrar of 22 May 2006, Annex 4 of the Defence Request.

[50] Rule 103(B) of the Rules provides that "[t]ransfer of a convicted person […] shall be effected as soon as possible […]."

[51] Transcript, p. 62 (31 August 2006).

the President to exercise the power vested in him. The decision to "reopen" the case bars the President from any intervention[52] in this case until the judgement has again become "final."

40. It is for these reasons that with all due respect I dissent from the course of action taken by the Appeals Chamber.

Done in English and French, the English text being authoritative.

Dated this 7th day of June 2007,
At The Hague, The Netherlands.

Judge Wolfgang Schomburg

[Seal of the International Tribunal]

[52] This is also true for any possible request seeking early release.

Commentary

1. Introduction

Pavle Strugar's request to re-open appeal proceedings in the case against him forced the court to face an unusual predicament – one in which the members of the Appeals Chamber were not entirely without fault.[1] Strugar[2] had withdrawn his appeal on the basis of repeated statements by the Pre-Appeal Judge that there was a significant possibility that he would be able to serve his sentence in Montenegro, near his elderly and infirm wife.[3] The Appeals Chamber accepted the withdrawal of his appeal, and the prosecution's related withdrawal, in effect making the Trial Judgement final ("decision accepting withdrawals").[4] Shortly thereafter, however, Strugar was informed by the Registry that Security Council Resolution 827, passed in 1993, stipulates that ICTY sentences must be served *outside* the territory of the former Yugoslavia.[5] Strugar promptly requested that his appeal be reinstated.

The Appeals Chamber's decision in response to this request raises two principal legal issues.[6] First, the chamber addresses whether it has the jurisdictional ability to reconsider a decision accepting a defendant's withdrawal. Having concluded that it does, the chamber then considers whether Strugar's decision to withdraw had been "informed." The chamber ultimately finds that Strugar's withdrawal had not been properly informed, thereby entitling him to reinstate his appeal. The court's analysis of these two issues will be reviewed in turn.

2. Can the Appeals Chamber reconsider its decision accepting withdrawals?

Two venues exist for the Appeals Chamber to reconsider a previously issued decision or judgement – review and reconsideration. Article 26 of the Statute, and Rules 119 and 120 of the Rules, give the tribunal the authority to review its final judgements in the event that a new fact is discovered.[7] Because Strugar's request fails to satisfy the basic requirements for review – most notably, the post-conviction discovery of a "new fact" – it cannot be properly construed as a motion for review.[8] The Appeals Chamber thus finds that Strugar's request for his appeal to be reinstated is better construed as a motion for reconsideration.[9]

Reconsideration is not provided for in the Statute or the Rules, but the tribunal has held that it has an inherent power to reconsider past decisions, particularly "where it was realized that the previous decision was erroneous or where it has caused an injustice."[10] According to current case law, however, this inherent power is limited to the court's *decisions,* and does not extend to *final judgements.*[11] Therefore, the challenge

---

1 ICTY, Decision on Strugar's Request to Reopen Appeal Proceedings, *Prosecutor v. Strugar*, Case No. IT-01-42-Misc.1, A. Ch., 7 June 2007, in this volume, p. 757.

2 Strugar was convicted in 2005 of crimes relating to the 1991 attack on the Croatian city of Dubrovnik. ICTY, Judgement, *Prosecutor v. Strugar et al.*, Case No. IT-01-42, T. Ch. II, 31 January 2005, Klip/ Sluiter, ALC-XXVI-505.

3 F. Gaynor and B. Goy, Current Developments at the Ad Hoc International Criminal Tribunals, 5 Journal of International Criminal Justice 2007, p. 1204.

4 ICTY, Final Decision on "Defence Notice of Withdrawing Appeal" and "Withdrawal of Prosecution's Appeal Against the Judgement of Trial Chamber II Dated 31 January 2005," *Prosecutor v. Strugar,* Case No. IT-01-42-A, A. Ch., 20 September 2006.

5 Security Council Resolution 827 (adopted May 25, 1993), accepting the Secretary General's report, UN doc. S/25704, in which it is stated that "the enforcement of sentences should take place outside the territory of the former Yugoslavia."

6 Decision on Strugar's Request to Reopen Appeal Proceedings, *Prosecutor v. Strugar*, A. Ch., *supra* note 1.

7 "Where a new fact has been discovered which was not known at the time of the proceedings before the Trial Chambers or the Appeals Chamber and which could have been a decisive factor in reaching the decision, the convicted person or the Prosecutor may submit to the International Tribunal an application for review of the judgement." Article 26, ICTY Statute.

8 Decision on Strugar's Request to Reopen Appeal Proceedings, *Prosecutor v. Strugar*, A. Ch., *supra* note 1, par. 21.

9 Decision on Strugar's Request to Reopen Appeal Proceedings, *Prosecutor v. Strugar*, A. Ch., *supra* note 1, par. 22.

10 ICTY, Decision on Application by Prosecution for Leave to Appeal, *Prosecutor v. Galić,* Case No. IT-98-29-AR73, A. Ch., 14 December 2001, par. 13; see also ICTY, Judgment on Sentence Appeal, *Prosecutor v. Mucić, Delić and Landžo*, Case No. IT-96-21-A*bis*, A. Ch., 8 April 2003, Klip/ Sluiter, ALC-XIV-847, par. 49; ICTY, Decision on Zoran Žigić's Motion for Reconsideration of Appeals Chamber Judgement IT-98-30/1-A Delivered on 28 February 2005, *Prosecutor v. Žigić,* Case No. IT-98-30/1-A, A. Ch., 26 June 2006, par. 9.

11 In the Čelebići Decision, the Appeals Chamber held that it *did* have the inherent power to reconsider final judgements. Judgment on Sentence Appeal, *Prosecutor v. Mucić, Delić and Landžo*, A. Ch., *supra* note 10, par. 49–53. It subsequently took a different position, holding in the Žigić Decision that there is no inherent power to reconsider final judgements, Decision on Zoran Žigić's Motion for Reconsideration of Appeals Chamber Judgement IT-98-30/1-A Delivered on 28 February 2005, *Prosecutor v.*

in this case lay in the characterisation of the decision accepting withdrawals – was it a mere "decision" that is subject to reconsideration, or was it a "final judgement" that cannot be reconsidered? This was a case of first impression for the Appeals Chamber.

The court admits that the decision accepting withdrawals could be considered a final judgement for the purposes of Article 26 review, because it terminated the proceedings in Strugar's case.[12] It is also clear from the record that the defendant, the prosecution, and the court all deemed the decision accepting withdrawals equal to a final judgement in the case. In a signed annex to the defence withdrawal, Strugar stated that he was aware of the legal consequences of withdrawal, including that "once the Appeal is withdrawn, *there is no possibility of subsequent reconsideration* of the Judgement, pursuant to which [he] was convicted."[13]

Nonetheless, in deciding to allow for the reopening of Strugar's appeal, the Appeals Chamber reasons that "[w]hile the decision accepting withdrawals may be a 'final judgment' in the sense that it concluded the case, it neither constitutes the kind of judgement envisioned in Article 25(2) of the Statute nor provides all the due process protections that naturally accompany a full judgement on the merits."[14]

The Appeals Chamber thus distinguishes the Žigić decision, which established that final judgements cannot be reconsidered, by finding that a decision that does not consider the merits of a case cannot be deemed a "judgement."[15] Accordingly, the chamber concludes that it does have the power to reconsider the decision accepting withdrawals in the same way that it has the power to reconsider other decisions that do not constitute judgements on the merits.[16] Dissenting, Judge Schomburg opines that the decision accepting withdrawals had made the trial judgment final, and that neither the Statute nor the Rules allow for a reopening of appellate proceedings.

Behind the court's analytical struggle over the issue of reconsideration lies the principle of finality of judgment – an essential attribute of judicial power, which some describe as fundamental to the rule of law.[17] In both civil law and common law legal systems, finality is accomplished through the doctrine of *res judicata,* which bars further litigation when there has been a final judgment that is no longer subject to appeal.[18] The principle of finality serves several public policy goals, including conservation of judicial resources, certainty in the judicial process, and enforceability of judgements.[19] In the context of international tribunals, finality of judgements may also contribute to victims' sense of closure and, by extension, national reconciliation.

It is clear from the record in this case that this was the kind of finality that the Appeals Chamber intended to achieve by its decision accepting withdrawals.[20] In that Decision, the chamber noted that the defendant was aware of the unconditional and final nature of his withdrawal, and declared that "the sentence of eight years imposed on Pavle Strugar in the Trial Judgment has become final."[21] Nonetheless, less than a year later, three of the five judges who signed that Decision appear to have changed their minds. While the decision had

---

Žigić, A. Ch, *supra* note 10, par. 9; see also ICTR, Decision on Request for Reconsideration of the Decision on Request for Review, *Niyitegeka v. Prosecutor*, Case No. ICTR-96-14-R, A. Ch., 27 September 2006, Klip/ Sluiter, ALC-XXV-291, p. 1 and 2; ICTY, Decision on prosecutor's request for review or reconsideration (public redacted version), *Prosecutor v. Blaškić*, Case No. IT-95-14-R, A. Ch., 23 November 2006, Klip/ Sluiter, ALC-XXXIII-809, par. 79; ICTR, Decision on Requests for Reconsideration, review, Assignment of Counsel, Disclosure, and Clarification, *Rutaganda v. Prosecutor,* Case No. ICTR-96-03-R, A. Ch., 8 December 2006, par. 6.

12 Decision on Strugar's Request to Reopen Appeal Proceedings, *Prosecutor v. Strugar*, A. Ch., *supra* note 1, par. 21.

13 *Ibid.*, par. 13, emphasis added.

14 *Ibid.*, par. 25.

15 *Ibid.*, par. 24; see also Decision on Zoran Žigić's Motion for Reconsideration of Appeals Chamber Judgement IT-98-30/1-A Delivered on 28 February 2005, *Prosecutor v. Žigić,* A. Ch, *supra* note 10, par. 9.

16 Decision on Strugar's Request to Reopen Appeal Proceedings, *Prosecutor v. Strugar*, A. Ch., *supra* note 1, par. 25.

17 A. C. Freeman, A treaties on the law of judgments, Bancroft-Whitney Co., San Fransisco 1925, par. 305.

18 B. A. Garner, Black's Law Dictionary, 8th edition, Thomson West, St. Paul 2004, res judicata; see also Restatement (Second) of Judgments, American Law Institute, Philadelphia 1982, par. 17 and 24.

19 See, for example, Supreme Court of Louisiana, *State v. Watts,* 14 January 2003, 835 So. 2d 441, p. 453, "[t]he finality of judgments is an important judicial and societal goal. Those who have been victimized and the families of those who have been victimized desire closure, especially in a brutal and senseless crime against an innocent victim"; United States Courts of Appeal Eleventh Circuit, *Grayson v. King,* 18 August 2006, 460 F.3d 1328, p. 1342, stating that "the government has a strong interest in the finality of duly adjudicated criminal judgments".

20 Final Decision on "Defence Notice of Withdrawing Appeal" and "Withdrawal of Prosecution's Appeal Against the Judgement of Trial Chamber II Dated 31 January 2005," *Prosecutor v. Strugar,* A. Ch., *supra* note 4, p. 1.

21 *Ibid.*, p. 2.

concluded Strugar's case, it had not considered its merits, and was therefore not final in the same way that an appeals judgment is final.

The court's decision to reopen the appeal proceedings in effect establishes the rule that true finality cannot be attained in the absence of an appeals judgement on the merits. If a case is concluded in any other way, the possibility of reconsideration exists, and may result in the reopening of proceedings. The Appeals Chamber may not have wished or intended to set such a precedent, but likely found itself forced to do so, because the judges recognized that the decision accepting withdrawals had occasioned a genuine miscarriage of justice.

3. What constitutes an "informed" withdrawal of appeal?

On reconsideration, the Appeals Chamber can reverse a decision that it finds was erroneous, or has lead to a miscarriage of justice.[22] In his request to reinstate appellate proceedings, Strugar suggested that the decision accepting withdrawals occasioned a miscarriage of justice by erroneously accepting a withdrawal that was not properly "informed."[23] The court agrees that a defendant's withdrawal of his appeal, like a guilty plea, must be informed.[24] The question facing the judges is how to distinguish an informed decision from an uninformed one. In other words: Did Strugar's misunderstanding of the legal possibilities available to him render his decision uninformed, even though he was explicitly aware of its consequences?

The chamber cites prior case law to establish the standard that, in order to categorize a defendant's decision as uninformed, there should be clear indicia in the record of defendant's "lack of understanding."[25] The chamber finds such indicia in the defence withdrawal, which stated that "General Strugar has reached the aforesaid decision [to withdraw] after being informed that there exist no legal impediments which could prevent him from serving the remainder of his prison sentence in Montenegro."[26] Strugar expressly based his withdrawal on the assumption – flawed, as it turned out – that it was legally possible for him to serve his sentence in Montenegro.

In the prosecution's view, the court's inquiry should be limited to whether Strugar was informed that his withdrawal was irrevocable, and not conditional upon him serving his sentence in Montenegro.[27] In other words, the prosecution proposes that the defendant's decision was "informed," because he was aware of its consequences. From the court's statement, in the decision accepting withdrawals, that Strugar was "informed and aware of all the legal consequences of [his] informed decision, including the fact that [...] there is no possibility of subsequent reconsideration of the judgement," it plainly appears that this was also the definition of "informed" that the court had previously employed.[28] Where a defendant seeks to abandon his right to appeal, "the Appeals Chamber should satisfy itself that this abandonment is informed,"[29] and the court apparently felt that it had met this burden by ascertaining that Strugar knew that his withdrawal was irrevocable.

Because adhering to such a definition of "informed" would have disallowed the re-opening of appeals proceedings in Strugar's case, however, the chamber in this decision revises its previous standard for what constitutes an informed decision. It states that Strugar's withdrawal cannot be deemed informed, because he withdrew based on "a misunderstanding of the options legally available in his situation."[30] In effect, the court establishes the rule that a defendant must know and understand the full set of circumstances that bear on his

22 Decision on Strugar's Request to Reopen Appeal Proceedings, *Prosecutor v. Strugar*, A. Ch., *supra* note 1, par. 26.

23 Decision on Strugar's Request to Reopen Appeal Proceedings, *Prosecutor v. Strugar*, A. Ch., *supra* note 1, par. 22.

24 *Ibid.*, par. 27.

25 *Ibid.*, par. 28, citing ICTR, Judgement, *Kambanda v. Prosecutor*, Case No. ICTR-97-23-A, A. Ch., 19 October 2000, Klip/Sluiter, ALC-VI-659, par. 77.

26 Decision on Strugar's Request to Reopen Appeal Proceedings, *Prosecutor v. Strugar*, A. Ch., *supra* note 1, par. 13.

27 *Ibid.*, par. 17.

28 Final Decision on "Defence Notice of Withdrawing Appeal" and "Withdrawal of Prosecution's Appeal Against the Judgement of Trial Chamber II Dated 31 January 2005," *Prosecutor v. Strugar,* A. Ch., *supra* note 4, p. 1.

29 Decision on Strugar's Request to Reopen Appeal Proceedings, *Prosecutor v. Strugar*, A. Ch., *supra* note 1, par. 27. This matches the rule for guilty pleas, where the burden is generally on the court to ascertain that a plea is duly informed. See, generally, Benchbook for U.S. District Court Judges, Federal Judicial Center, Washington 2000, Section 2.01: Taking pleas of guilty or *nolo contendere*, Federal Rules of Criminal Procedure, Rule 11; see American Bar Association, 27 Standards for Criminal Justice 1999, Pleas of Guilty, available at http://www.abanet.org/crimjust/standards/pleasofguilty.pdf.

30 Decision on Strugar's Request to Reopen Appeal Proceedings, *Prosecutor v. Strugar*, A. Ch., *supra* note 1, par. 29.

decision to plead guilty or withdraw his appeal, in order for that decision to be truly informed. This standard places a heavy burden on the court. It also leaves the door open for a defendant to change his mind and force the court to reconsider, because his decision had been based on a flawed assumption.

Behind the Appeals Chamber's analysis of what constitutes an "informed" decision is an implicit recognition that the decision accepting withdrawals itself was not properly informed. The chamber was well aware that Strugar made the decision to withdraw his appeal based on the possibility that he could serve his sentence in Montenegro. Indeed, the defence withdrawal informed the court that "General Strugar has reached the aforesaid decision [to withdraw] after being informed that there exist no legal impediments which could prevent him from serving the remainder of his prison sentence in Montenegro."[31] The idea of such a conditional withdrawal had originated with, and been encouraged by, the pre-appeal judge.[32]

The judges who signed the decision accepting withdrawals did not notify Strugar that the possibility on which he based his withdrawal was legally moot. Perhaps they were unaware of the geographic limitations on sentence executions imposed by Security Council resolution 827, or perhaps they did not consider it an insurmountable obstacle. Notably, three of the judges that allowed Strugar's conditional withdrawal were on the panel that subsequently allowed the reopening of his appeal.

Whether in order to save face, or out of genuine concern for the wronged defendant, the court probably found itself forced to find a way to reinstate Strugar's appeal. Their solution – to revise the standard for what constitutes an "informed" decision – was unnecessary and ill advised. Why did the Appeals Chamber not go straight to the conclusion that "the interests of justice plainly call for reconsideration of the decision accepting withdrawals in order to avoid a miscarriage of justice,"[33] without the intermediary determination that Strugar's decision to withdraw his appeal had been "uninformed"? Ultimately, the legitimacy of the court's decision to reinstate Strugar's appeal was not rooted in the conclusion that his withdrawal had been uninformed, but rather in the court's inherent discretion to reverse decisions or review judgements that turn out to be unfair.

4. Conclusion

The court's analysis of Strugar's request is informed by two values crucial to the functioning of the tribunal – finality of judgement and the interests of justice. On the one hand, the Appeals Chamber implicitly recognizes that its decision accepting withdrawals was genuinely misinformed and that the interests of justice require that appeal proceedings be reinstated in Strugar's case. On the other hand, the chamber knows that reconsidering that decision undermines the finality with which decisions terminating proceedings are necessarily imbued. In its decision to reopen appeal proceedings, the court has a difficult time balancing these two competing values.

In most jurisdictions, the procedural norms that attach to a decision or judgment can be set aside if circumstances have transpired that render its execution unjust. In the incumbent case, the court probably would have been better off simply admitting that it had unintentionally mislead Strugar, that the decision accepting withdrawals had been misinformed, and that the interests of justice demand that the principle of finality yield to the defendant's due process rights. That way, it could have avoided unnecessarily revising the legal standard for "informed" decisions in a way that will likely have repercussions for future jurisprudence.

Anja Havedal-Ipp

---

[31] *Ibid.*, par. 13.

[32] Notably, the Pre-Appeals Judge had stated that, while no guarantees could be given, "I can assure you once again that I would be prepared to convince the necessary persons in this Tribunal that a sentence could also be served in Montenegro." *Ibid.*, par. 7. The incumbent decision describes in detail how the Pre-Appeals Judge encouraged Strugar's withdrawal. See *ibid.*, par. 5–15.

[33] *Ibid.*, par. 29.

INDEX

H

I

J

K

L

M

N

O

P

Q

R

S

T

U

V

W

Z

CONTRIBUTORS AND EDITORS

Denis Abels is Assistant Professor of Criminal Law at the University of Amsterdam and a Research Fellow at the Amsterdam Center for International Law. In 2012 he defended his PhD (cum laude) on the rights of persons detained at international criminal tribunals (Prisoners of the International Community, The Hague: T.M.C. Asser Press). He wrote several other commentaries for these series. He specializes in (international) sanctioning law.

David Bryden LL.B(Hons), Dip. LP, LL.M, studied for his LL.B and professional training qualifications at Edinburgh University, and completed a joint Masters in International Criminal Law at the University of Amsterdam and Columbia University. He undertook an internship with the Radovan Karadzic Defence team at the ICTY in 2010, and was admitted to the New York State Bar in 2011. He is currently practicing as a trainee solicitor with DLA Piper (Scotland) LLP.

Jocelyn Courtney graduated from Columbia Law School with a Juris Doctorate in 2011 with a focus on International Criminal Law. She also received a LLM in International Criminal Justice from the University of Amsterdam in 2011. She graduated magna cum laude from Yale University and completed a Masters in Military History also at Yale University. One of her more recent publications includes "Enforced Disappearances in Colombia: A Plea for Synergy Between the Courts" in the International Criminal Law Review. Ms. Courtney has also worked as an intern at the International Criminal Tribunal for Rwanda for the Office of the Prosecutor and with the Defence Team for Karadžić at the International Criminal Tribunal for the Former Yugoslavia. She currently practices law in the United Sates.

Masha Fedorova studied Dutch law at Utrecht University where she obtained her Master degree (LL.M.), *cum laude*, in 2004. She specialized in Dutch criminal law and international law, and wrote a combined Master thesis on international criminal law. Soon after the graduation, she began working at Utrecht University's Netherlands Institute of Human Rights (SIM) as a junior researcher/lecturer on a two-year project entitled 'International Criminal Tribunal for the Former Yugoslavia Database'. During that time she wrote a research proposal applying for a grant with the Netherlands Organisation for Scientific Research (NWO) Mozaic Programme. In 2006, she was awarded a four-year research grant and continued working at SIM in the capacity of a PhD candidate. From January 2012 she holds an assistant professor position in Criminal Law and Criminal Procedure at Radboud University Nijmegen, the Netherlands.

Anja Havedal-Ipp is an associate in the international litigation practice of Jones Day in New York. She holds a Juris Doctor from Columbia University (New York), an LLM in International Criminal Law from the University of Amsterdam, and a Bachelor's Degree in East and Central European Studies from Lund University (Sweden). She completed a summer internship with the Appeals Chamber of the International Criminal Tribunal for Rwanda in 2009. Prior to law school, Anja spent two years in Kabul as the senior editor at the Afghanistan Research and Evaluation Unit, and four years as an associate editor of the *Journal of Democracy* in Washington, D.C.

André Klip is Professor of criminal law, criminal procedure and international criminal law at Maastricht University. He is a Judge at the 's-Hertogenbosch Court of Appeal (2002). He is president of the Dutch section of the international association of penal law. He is also a member of the standing committee of experts on international immigration, refugee and criminal law, a member of the editorial board of 'Delikt en Delinkwent – Tijdschrift voor Strafrecht', as well as of the 'International Criminal Law Review' and co-editor of the 'Commentary on Dutch Law on International Cooperation in Criminal Matters'. He is the author of 'European Criminal Law. An integrative Approach', 2nd Edition, Intersentia Antwerp 2012.

Yvonne McDermott is a lecturer in Law at Bangor University, UK, where she is the School of Law's Director of Teaching and Learning and Deputy Director of the Bangor Centre for International Law. Yvonne joined Bangor Law School in November 2011 from the Irish Centre for Human Rights, National University of Ireland, Galway, where she recently submitted her Ph.D. thesis on the right to a fair trial in international criminal law. Yvonne's research interests are in international criminal law, international criminal procedure, human rights, and refugee law. She is the Managing Editor of the OUP 'Oxford Reports on International Criminal Law' database, an expert researcher on the project entitled, 'Model Code for the Investigation and Prosecution of International Crimes' and Associate Editor of the Criminal Law Forum journal. She was the winner of the inaugural Böhler Franken Koppe Wijngaarden Advocaten/Hague Academic Coalition Award for Young Professionals in June 2009, and has worked professionally with the Irish Department of Foreign Affairs and as a consultant to the United Nations High Commissioner for Refugees.

Chantal Meloni is an Italian criminal lawyer and academic at the University of Milan where she teaches International Criminal Law. She holds a PhD in comparative criminal law from the University of Pavia (Italy). She is currently working on a research project on "The protection of the right to life in asymmetrical conflicts" at the Humboldt University of Berlin for which she was awarded an Alexander von Humboldt fellowship. In the context of such project she was in Gaza (occupied Palestinian territory) in 2010, with the Palestinian Centre for Human Rights. In 2006/7 she worked at the International Criminal Court (The Hague) as Legal Assistant to the judges of Pre-Trial Chamber. Her research interests focus on International Criminal Law, especially on accountability mechanisms, individual responsibility for international crimes, and on the protection of victims of international crimes. She is the author of the volume "*Command Responsibility in International Criminal Law*" (T.M.C. Asser, 2010) and of several scientific articles published in international journals and collective volumes. She is also the co-editor of the book "*Is There a Court for Gaza? A Test Bench for International Justice*" (T.M.C. Asser/Springer, 2012), which documents the follow up to the UN Fact Finding Mission on the Gaza conflict (the "Goldstone Report").

Maria Nybondas is presently an independent researcher/lecturer in International Criminal Law/International Humanitarian Law. She holds a PhD from the University of Amsterdam, an LL M from Utrecht University and a Master of Political Science in Public International Law from Åbo Akademi University, Finland, her country of origin. Dr. Nybondas has worked as a Researcher at the T.M.C. Asser Institute in The Hague and as an Associate Public Affairs Officer at the ICC. In 2000 she was a law clerk at the ICTY. In 2010 her book 'Command Responsibility and Its Applicability to Civilian Superiors' was published by T.M.C. Asser Press (Springer).

Kelly Pitcher studied law at the University of Kent (1999–2002), the University of Aberdeen (2002–2003) and the University of Amsterdam (2007–2009). She has previously worked with counsel representing accused at the International Criminal Tribunal for the former Yugoslavia (2004–2007) and is currently working at the University of Amsterdam. In addition to undertaking PhD research in the field of international criminal procedure, she teaches subjects in Dutch and international criminal law.

Göran Sluiter is Professor of International Criminal Law at the University of Amsterdam (since 2006) and lawyer at Böhler Advocaten since (since 2010). He has been a judge at the Hague district court from 2004 to 2009. In the past, he has worked for the Department of International Law, the Netherlands Institute of Human Rights, and the Willem Pompe Institute of Criminal Law and Criminology at Utrecht University. His doctoral dissertation is entitled 'International Criminal Adjudication and the Collection of Evidence: Obligations of States' (Intersentia, 2002), for which he received the Max van der Stoel human rights award. He is a member of the editorial committees of the 'Journal of International Criminal Justice' and the 'International Criminal Law Review'.

David Turns graduated from the London School of Economics and Political Science with the degrees of LL.B. (Hons) and LL.M. (International Law) in 1990 and 1992, respectively. He studied for the Bar Vocational Course at the Inns of Court School of Law, and was Called to the Bar of England and Wales by the Honourable Society of the Inner Temple in 1992. From 1990 to 1994 he taught Public International Law at the LSE. In 1994 he was appointed Lecturer in Law at the University of Liverpool, before taking up a Senior Lectureship in Law of Armed Conflict and International Humanitarian Law at Cranfield University in 2007. He specialises in public international law, with particular emphasis on international humanitarian law and international criminal law, and has extensive experience of providing advanced instruction on the international laws of armed conflict for both military legal advisers and field operators, as well as for humanitarian aid workers.

Koen Vriend received an LLM In International Law and an MA in Holocaust and Genocide Studies at the University of Amsterdam. He specialized in international criminal law and works currently as a junior lecturer and PhD candidate in Dutch and international criminal law at the University of Amsterdam. His PhD research concerns the role and consequences of shortening mechanisms in the law of evidence of national and international criminal proceedings.

Alexander Zahar is Senior Lecturer at Macquarie Law School, Macquarie University, Sydney, Australia. He joined the United Nations in 2000 as a lawyer, first at the ICTR, and from 2003 to 2007 at the ICTY. Dr Zahar's research interests are split between international criminal law and climate change law. His most recent books are *The Legacy of the International Criminal Tribunal for the Former Yugoslavia* (Oxford University Press, 2011), edited with B. Swart and G. Sluiter, and *Australian Climate Law in Global Context* (Cambridge University Press, 2012), co-authored with J. Peel and L. Godden. Presently he is completing a monograph entitled *State Compliance in International Climate Change Law* (Routledge, forthcoming 2014).